AMERICA'S

Wonderful
LITTLE
HOTELS
& INNS
1990

U.S.A. and Canada

States, Territories, and Canadian Provinces Covered in This Edition

UNITED STATES

Alabama
Alaska
Arizona
Arkansas
California
Colorado
Connecticut
Delaware
District of Columbia
Florida
Georgia
Hawaii
Idaho
Illinois
Indiana
Iowa
Kansas
Kentucky
Louisiana
Maine
Maryland
Massachusetts
Michigan
Minnesota
Mississippi
Missouri
Montana
Nebraska
Nevada
New Hampshire
New Jersey
New Mexico
New York
North Carolina
Ohio
Oklahoma
Oregon
Pennsylvania
Rhode Island
South Carolina
South Dakota
Tennessee
Texas
Utah
Vermont
Virginia
Washington
West Virginia
Wisconsin
Wyoming

U.S. TERRITORY

Puerto Rico

CANADA

Alberta
British Columbia
New Brunswick
Northwest Territories
Nova Scotia
Ontario
Prince Edward Island
Quebec

Also in This Series

AMERICA'S
Wonderful
LITTLE
HOTELS
& INNS
1990

U.S.A. and Canada

Edited by Sandra W. Soule

Associate Editors:
Nancy P. Barker and Matthew Joyce

Contributing Editors:
Suzanne Carmichael and Susan Waller Schwemm

Editorial Assistants:
June C. Horn and Kirstin O'Rielly

St. Martin's Press
New York

Library of Congress Catalog Card Number: 89-63484

ISBN 0-312-03277-3

First Edition

10 9 8 7 6 5 4 3 2 1

Maps by David Lindroth, © 1990, 1989, 1988, 1987 by St. Martin's Press

This book is dedicated to the people who take the time and trouble to write about the hotels and inns they've visited, and to my children—Hilary and Jeffrey—my husband, and my parents.

Contents

CONTENTS

Canada

Acknowledgments

I would like again to thank all the people who wrote in such helpful detail about the inns and hotels they visited. To them belong both the dedication and the acknowledgments, for without their support, these guides would not exist. If I have inadvertently misspelled or omitted anyone's name, please accept my sincerest apologies.

I would also like to thank Hilary Rubinstein, who originated the concept for this series. Also thanks to my helpful and supportive editor Joshua Baskin; to my colleagues Nancy Barker and Matt Joyce; to Kirstin O'Rielly and June Horn, my invaluable assistants; to Judith Brannen, April Burwell, Marjorie Cohen, Dianne Crawford, Arlyne Craighead, Pat Fink, Kathryn and Bob Gearhead, Pam Harpootlian, Nancy Harrison and Nelson Ormsby, Debbie Joost, Keith Jurgens, Zita Knific, Pat and Glen Lush, Betty Norman, Carolyn Mathiasen, Carolyn and Bill Myles, Janet Payne, Mary Louise Rogers, Susan Waller Schwemm, Laura Scott, Jeanne Smith, Lee Todd, James and Janice Utt, Wendi Van Exan, and Diane Wolf, who went far beyond the call of duty in their assistance and support; and to Melania Lanni, for without her help, I'd never get anything done.

Key to Abbreviations

For complete information and explanations, please see the Introduction.

Rates: Range from least expensive room in low season to most expensive room in peak season.

Room only: No meals included; sometimes referred to as European Plan (EP).

B&B: Bed and breakfast; includes breakfast, sometimes afternoon/evening refreshment.

MAP: Modified American Plan; includes breakfast and dinner.

Full board: Three meals daily.

Alc lunch: À la carte lunch; average price of entrée plus nonalcoholic drink, tax, tip.

Alc dinner: Average price of three-course dinner, including half bottle of house wine, tax, tip.

Prix fixe dinner: Three- to five-course set dinner, excluding wine, tax, tip unless otherwise noted.

Extras: Noted if available. Always confirm in advance. Pets are not permitted unless specified.

Zip codes: If only one zip code applies, it is listed with the town name. If there is more than one, it is noted as part of the address.

We Want to Hear from You!

As you know, this book is only effective with your help. We really need to know about your experiences and discoveries.

If you stayed at an inn or hotel listed here, we want to know how it was. Did it live up to our description? Exceed it? Was it what you expected? Did you like it? Were you disappointed? Delighted?

Have you discovered new establishments that we should add to the next edition?

Tear out one of the report forms at the back of this book (or use your own stationery if you prefer) and write today. Even if you write only "Fully endorse existing entry" you will have been most helpful.

Thank You!

Introduction

Reading the Entries

Each entry generally has three parts: a description of the inn or hotel, quotes from guests who have stayed there, and relevant details about rooms, rates, location, and facilities. Occasionally you may find that no general description is given or that the factual data are incomplete. There are two reasons for this: Either the descriptions supplied by guests made this unnecessary, or the facility failed to supply us with adequate information because of time limitations or other problems.

Please remember that the length of an entry is in no way a reflection of that inn or hotel's quality. Rather, it is an indication of the type of feedback we've received both from guests and from the innkeepers themselves. Some hotel owners are totally unaware of this guide; others take an active role in encouraging their guests to write.

Wherever a location is of particular tourist interest, we've tried to include some information about its attractions. If we have only one listing for a town, you'll find this description within the body of the entry. If there is more than one inn or hotel listed for a town, the description of the town and information about its location precede the individual entries.

In some areas the magnet is not a particular town but rather a compact, distinct region. Travelers choose one place to stay and use it as a base from which to explore the area. But because this guide is organized by town, not by region, the entries are scattered throughout the chapter. When this applies, you will see the name of the region noted under the "Location" heading; check back to the introduction for a description of the region involved. For example, inns and hotels in Bucks County, Pennsylvania, start with Erwinna near the beginning of the chapter and extend to Upper Black Eddy at the end, but the description of the area itself is found at the beginning of the chapter.

The names at the end of the quotations are those who have recommended the hotel or inn. Some entries are entirely or largely quoted from one report; if several names follow the quotation, we have distinguished the writers of the quoted material by putting their names first. Some writers have requested that we not use their names; you will see initials noted instead. *We never print the names of those who have sent us adverse reports, although their contributions are invaluable indeed.*

Although we have tried to make the listings as accurate and complete as possible, mistakes and inaccuracies invariably creep in. The most significant area of inaccuracy applies to the rates charged by each establishment. In preparing this guide, we asked all the hotels and inns to give us their 1990 rates, ranging from the least expensive room in the off-season to the most expensive peak-season price. Some did so, while others just noted the 1989 rate.

Since the process of writing and publishing a book takes nearly a year, please don't rely solely on the figures printed. *You should always double-check the rates when you make your reservations; please don't blame the hotel or this guide if the prices are wrong.* On the other hand, given the current level of inflation, you should not encounter anything more than a 5% increase, unless there has been a substantial improvement in the amenities offered or a change of ownership. Please let us know immediately if you find anything more than that!

If you find any errors of omission or commission in any part of the entries, we urgently request your help in correcting them. We recognize that it takes extra time and effort for readers to write us letters or fill in report forms, but this feedback is essential in keeping this publication totally responsive to consumer needs.

Inngoers' Bill of Rights

We've read through a lot more brochures for inns and hotels than the average bear, and can attest to the fact that not one makes mention of a hotel's possible drawbacks, however slight. And rightly so. A brochure is paid advertising, no more obligated to provide the full picture—both pros and cons—than a TV ad for diet soda. Furthermore, unlike this guidebook, *which accepts no fee of any kind for an entry,* most inn guidebooks charge a listing or membership fee of some kind, making them basically paid advertisements. Despite brochure promises and glowing listings in other books, we all know that perfection isn't possible in this world, but we feel that (despite the irate reactions of some innkeepers) complete and honest reporting will give readers *reasonable* expectations, ones that are often surpassed in the best of hostelries.

On the other hand, although perfection may not be on the menu, as guests (and customers), travelers have the right to expect certain minimum standards. These rights are especially important in hotels and inns at the top end of the rate scale; we don't expect as much from more modestly priced places, although it certainly is often received.

So, please use this Bill of Rights as a kind of checklist in deciding how you think a place stacks up on your own personal rating scale. And, whether an establishment fails, reaches, or exceeds these levels, be sure to let us know. These rights are especially important because of the financial penalties levied by most establishments; with the exception of the larger hotels, nearly every establishment listed in this book requires a substantial advance deposit, yet travelers have little or no recourse if facilities prove to be substandard. We would also hope that innkeepers will use this list to help evaluate both the strong points and shortcomings of their own establishments.

The right to impeccable cleanliness. An establishment that looks, feels, and smells clean. Not just middle-of-the-room clean, but immaculate in all the nooks and crannies—under the radiators, in the dresser drawers, out on the balconies. Rooms should be immaculate prior to check-in, and kept as close as possible to that standard during your stay. You also have the right to prompt maid service, and should not have to wait until mid-afternoon for your room to be made up.

The right to suitable room furnishings. A comfortable bed with a firm mattress and soft pillows, fresh clean linens, and blankets is a minimum. On *each* side of a double or larger-size bed should be a reading lamp (ideal are three-way bulbs), along with a night table (or its equivalent) giving you a place to leave the bedtime necessities—a glass of water, a box of tissues, your eyeglasses and watch. Two comfortable chairs with good reading lights are a welcome addition, as is a well-lit mirror and readily accessible electric outlet in a room without a private bath. A well-equipped room also has adequate storage space for clothes, both in drawers and closets, along with extra pillows and blankets and a rack for your luggage.

The right to comfortable, attractive rooms. Guest rooms and common rooms that are not only attractive, but livable as well. Not just a visually handsome museum set piece, but a place where you'd like to spend some time reading, chatting, relaxing. You should be as comfortable as you are at home, without having to do any of the work to make yourself so.

The right to a decent bathroom. Of course, cleanliness heads the list here, followed by reliable plumbing, adequate supplies of hot water, decent lighting, an accessible electric outlet with wiring that can take a hair dryer, a fixed or hand-held shower added to old-fashioned tubs, a shelf or table for toiletries, and an ample supply of soft, absorbent towels.

The right to privacy and discretion. If you just "vahnt to be alone" like Garbo, then you're better off staying at motels or at home; on the other hand, even in the most familial of inns, you are entitled to conduct private conversations in common rooms, and even more private ones in your own room—and you have the right *not* to hear the equally private conversations of your neighbors. The right to discretion precludes prying hosts' questions about one's marital status or sexual preference. A truly offensive intrusion on a guest's privacy is the practice of displaying proselytizing religious brochures, tracts, and signs.

The right to good, healthful food. Fresh nutritious food, ample in quantity, high in quality, attractively presented, and graciously served in enjoyable smoke-free surroundings—whether the offering is a cup of coffee and a roll, a seven-course gourmet dinner, or anything in between. An end to dessert masquerading as breakfast and ample supplies of brewed decaffeinated coffee and herbal teas is applauded. Freedom from pretentious menus written in fractured French menuspeak would be a welcome companion.

The right to comfortable temperatures and noise levels. Rooms should be reasonably cool on the hottest of summer nights and warm on the coldest winter evenings. Windows that open, screens without holes, fans, air conditioners, and heating systems that run quietly are all key; although not always possible, individually controlled thermostats are ideal. In locations where traffic noise is a problem, double-glazed windows, drapes, and landscaping should all be in place.

The right to fair value. People don't stay in inns or small hotels because they are cheap, which is good, because very few of them are. What is expected, though, is a good value, with prices that are in reasonable relation to the facilities offered and to the cost of equivalent accommodation in the area. This right extends to the times when things go wrong. Even when the problem is beyond the innkeepers' control, guests have the right to an apology at the minimum, and restitution at the maximum, depending on the situation. Guests do not have the right to perfection, but they have the right to innkeepers who are concerned and solicitous when a problem arises.

The right to genuine hospitality. Owners and staff who are sincerely glad you've come, and who make it their business to make your stay pleasant and memorable without being intrusive. Innkeepers who help guests to get to know each other when appropriate and who leave the less sociable to their own thoughts. Resident owners are best, resident staff is often acceptable; someone should be readily available for emergencies around the clock.

The right to a caring environment and little luxuries. Seeing that the little extras have been attended to—asking about pet allergies and dietary restrictions, making dinner reservations, providing inside and accurate information on area activities and events. Offering afternoon or evening refreshments, and welcoming new arrivals with refreshments appropriate to the season. Leaving a personal note, fresh flowers, or candies to greet guests is another way of saying welcome. Being there to provide toothpaste or a toothbrush to guests who have forgotten theirs at home. A good hostelry is more than accommodation. It's an end in itself, not just a means to an end. Amenities are more than imported soaps; innkeepers who are attuned to guests' needs and wants, anticipating them before they're even expressed, are the most important amenity of all.

The right to personal safety. Facilities in large cities need to be located in reasonably safe neighborhoods, with adequate care given to security within the building. Where caution, especially at night, is advisable, innkeepers have an obligation to share this information with guests.

The right to professionalism. Running an inn or hotel is not a business for amateurs, and guests have the right to receive requested brochures promptly, after one request, and to have their room reservations handled efficiently and responsibly. Check-in and check-out should be smooth, with rooms available as confirmed.

The right to adequate common areas. One of the key distinctions between a motel and an inn is the existence of at least one common room where guests can gather to read, chat, or relax, free of any pressure (implied or otherwise) to buy anything.

The right of people traveling alone to have all the above rights. Those traveling alone usually pay just a few dollars less than a couple, yet the welcome, services, and rooms they receive are often less than equal.

The right to a reasonable cancellation policy. Before booking, get the details. Penalties levied for a cancellation made less than a week before arrival is a fair policy and is relatively standard at most Western inns; two to five days is even better. (We fail to understand why so many similar establishments in the East insist on a 14-day policy.) Most inns will refund deposits (minus a processing fee) even after the deadline if the room is rebooked. We feel that all should offer the chance to rebook within six months as an alternative to cancellation penalties. To be avoided are inns with policies such as this: "On cancellations received less than 45 days in advance, the deposit [approximately 50%] is not refundable, regardless if the room is re-rented or not."

Of course, there is no "perfect" inn or hotel, even when every provision of the bill of rights is met, since people's tastes and needs vary so greatly. But one key phrase does pop up in the hotel/inn reports over and over again, whether the writer is describing a small hotel in the city or a country inn: "I felt right at home." This is not written in the literal sense—a commercial lodging, no matter how cozy or charming, is never the same as one's home. What is really meant is that guests felt as welcome, as relaxed, as comfortable, as they would in their own home. One writer put it this way: "Where does one start in describing this inn? With mixed feelings. (It's a wonderful place, and I don't want the world to discover and spoil it.) But I'll tell you about this grand hideaway. It's clean, quiet, isolated, warm, and comfortable. The fireplaces work and the owners seem intent on making your stay happy. They describe dinner specials with smiles, remember you from trip to trip, and are willing to help in any way they can. The unique qualities of each room make you want to try them all. It's a wonderful place. Please don't take my room."

What makes for a wonderful stay?

We've tried our best to make sure that all the hotels and inns listed in this guide are as wonderful as our title promises. Inevitably, there will be some disappointments. Sometimes these will be caused by a change in ownership or management that has resulted in lowered standards. Other times unusual circumstances, which can arise in the best of establishments, will lead to problems. Quite often, though, problems will occur because there's not a good "fit" between the inn or hotel and the guest. Decide what you're looking for, then find the inn that suits your needs.

We've tried to give you as much information as possible on each hotel or inn listed, and have taken care to indicate the atmosphere each innkeeper is trying to create. After you've read the listing, write, if there is time, for a copy of the establishment's brochure, which will give you more information. Finally, feel free to call any inn or hotel where you're planning to stay, and ask as many questions as necessary.

A good guest is a good traveler

We travel because we want to see new places, meet new people, experience new sensations. When we travel we encounter many things that are different from the way they are at home. If we respond to these experiences in a positive way, our travels are enriching, entertaining, memorable. If we respond with endless adverse comparisons to "the way it is at home," our travels are doomed to disappointment before the key is out of the front-door lock.

Some people prefer to stay in an endless succession of almost identical motels and hotels to insulate themselves from the possible good and bad surprises of travel. They are rarely disappointed because their expectations are so modest. Readers of this guide have chosen a different path. Each hotel or inn listed here is very different from the next in a dozen different ways. Pick the ones that you'll enjoy visiting and then let them surprise you!

Hotels, inns . . . resorts and motels

As the title indicates, this is a guide to exceptional inns and hotels. Generally, the inns have 5 to 25 rooms, although a few have only 2 rooms and some have over 100. The hotels are more often found in the cities and range in size from about 50 to 200 rooms.

The line between an inn or hotel and a resort is often a fine one. There are times when we all want the extra facilities a resort provides, so we've added a number of reader-recommended facilities to this edition.

You'll also find that we've listed a handful of motels. Although they don't strictly fall within the context of this book, we've included them because we received letters strongly endorsing their positive qualities, particularly their concerned and involved owners and friendly atmosphere, two qualities usually lacking in even the best of motels. A number of these recommendations have come for properties in the Best Western chain. Please don't be put off by this; Best Western is a franchise operation, with no architectural unity from one property to the next. Those listed in this guide have substantial architectural or historical appeal, and concerned, professional management.

Rooms

All hotel and inn rooms are not created equal. Although the rooms at a typical chain motel or hotel may be identical, the owners of most of the establishments described in this book pride themselves on the individuality of each guest room. Some, although not all, of these differences are reflected in the rates charged.

More important, it means that travelers need to express their needs clearly to the innkeepers when making reservations and again when checking in. Some rooms may be quite spacious but may have extremely small private baths or limited closet space. Some antique double beds have rather high footboards—beautiful to look at but torturous for people over six feet tall! Many inns are trading their double beds in for queens and kings; if you prefer an oversize bed, say so. If you want twin beds, be sure to specify this when making reservations and again when you check in; many smaller inns have only one or two twin-bedded rooms.

Some rooms may have gorgeous old bathrooms, with tubs the size of small swimming pools, but if you are a hard-core shower person, that room won't be right for you. Many others have showers but no baths, which may be disappointing if you love a long, luxurious soak in the tub. If you are traveling on business and simply must have a working-size desk with good light, speak up. Some rooms look terrific inside but don't look out at anything much; others may have the view but not quite as special a decor. Sometimes the best rooms may look out onto a main road and can be quite noisy. Decide what's important to you. Although the owners and staff of the hotels and inns listed here are incredibly hard-working and dedicated people, they can't read your mind. Let your needs be known, and, within the limits of availability, they will try to accommodate you.

Our most frequent complaints center around beds that are too soft and inadequate reading lights. If these are priorities for you (as they are for us), don't be shy about requesting bedboards or additional lamps to remedy the situation. Similarly, if there are other amenities your room is lacking— extra pillows, blankets, or even an easy chair—speak up. Most innkeepers would rather put in an extra five minutes of work than have an unhappy guest.

If your reservation is contingent upon obtaining a particular room, make this very clear to the innkeeper. Some inns will not accept such reservations, feeling that they are too difficult to guarantee. Those that do accept them have an obligation to meet their guarantee; if circumstances prevent them from following through on the promised room, make it clear that you expect some sort of remuneration—either the return of your deposit or a reduction in the price of another room.

If you really don't like your room, ask for another; if you don't like the food, ask for something else—in other words, you're the guest, make sure you get treated like one. If things go terribly wrong, don't be shy about asking for your money back, and be *sure* to write us about any problems.

What is a single? A double? A suite? A cottage or cabin?

Unlike the proverbial rose, a single is not a single is not a single. Sometimes it is a room with one twin bed, which really can accommodate only one person. Quite often it is described as a room with a standard-size double bed, in contrast to a double, which has two twin beds. Other hotels call both of the preceding doubles, although doubles often have queen- or even king-size beds instead. Many times the only distinction is made by the number of guests occupying the room; a single will pay slightly less, but there's no difference in the room.

There's almost as much variation when it comes to suites. We would like to define a suite as a bedroom with a separate living room area and often a small kitchen, as well. Unfortunately, since suites are now a very popular concept in the hotel business, the word has been stretched to cover other setups, too. Some so-called suites are only one large room, accommodating a table and separate seating area in addition to the bed. If you require a suite that has two separate rooms with a door between them, specify this when you make reservations.

Quite a few of our entries have cabins or cottages in addition to rooms in the main building. In general, a cabin is understood to be a somewhat more rustic residence than a cottage, although there's no hard-and-fast rule. Be sure to inquire for details when making reservations.

Making reservations

Unless you are inquiring many months in advance of your visit, it's best to telephone when making reservations. This offers a number of advantages: You will know immediately if space is available on your requested dates; you can find out if that space is suitable to your specific needs. You will have a chance to discuss the pros and cons of the available rooms and will be able to find out about any changes made in recent months—new facilities, redecorated rooms, nonsmoking policies, possibly even a change of ownership. It's also a good time to ask the innkeeper about other concerns—Is the neighborhood safe at night? Is any renovation or construction in progress that might be disturbing? Will a wedding reception or other social function be in progress during your visit that might affect your use of the common areas or parking lot? If you're reserving a room at a plantation home that is available for public tours, get specifics about the check-in/out times; in many, rooms are not available before 5 P.M. and must be vacated by 9 A.M. sharp.

If you expect to be checking in late at night, *be sure to say so;* many inns give door keys to their guests, then lock up by 10 P.M.

Payment

Many innkeepers don't like plastic any better for payment than they do for decorating. Some accept credit cards for the initial deposit but prefer cash, traveler's checks, or personal checks for the balance; others offer the reverse policy. Still others have accepted credit cards as a part of modern living. When no credit cards are accepted at all, you can settle your bill with a personal check, traveler's check, or even (!) cash.

When using your credit card to guarantee a reservation, be aware that some inns and hotels will charge your card for the amount of the deposit only, while others will put a "hold" on your card for the full amount of your entire stay, plus the cost of meals and incidentals that you may (or may not) spend. If you're using your card to reserve a fairly extended trip, you may find that you're well over your credit limit without actually having spent a nickel. We'd suggest inquiring; if the latter is the procedure, either send a check for the deposit or go elsewhere.

Rates

All rates quoted are per room, unless otherwise noted as being per person. Rates quoted per person are usually based on double occupancy, unless otherwise stated.

"Room only" rates do not include any meals. In most cases two or three meals a day are served by the hotel restaurant, but are charged separately. Average meal prices are noted when available. In a very few cases no meals are served on the premises at all; rooms in these facilities are usually equipped with kitchenettes.

B&B rates include bed and breakfast. Breakfast, though, can vary from a simple continental breakfast to an expanded continental breakfast to a full breakfast. Afternoon tea and evening refreshments are sometimes included, as well.

MAP (Modified American Plan) rates are often listed per person and include breakfast and dinner. Only a few of the inns listed serve lunch, although many will prepare a picnic on request for an additional charge.

State and local sales taxes are not included in the rates; the percentage varies from state to state and is noted in the introduction to each state chapter or in the individual listing. *When inquiring about rates, always ask if any off-season or special package rates are available.* Sometimes discounted rates are available *only* on request. During the week, when making reservations at city hotels or country inns, it's important to ask if any corporate rates are available. Depending on the establishment, you may or may not be asked for some proof of corporate affiliation (a business card is usually all that's needed), but it's well worth inquiring, since the effort can result in a saving of 15 to 20%, plus an upgrade to a substantially better room.

If an establishment has a specific tipping policy, whether it is "no tipping" or the addition of a set service charge, it is noted under "Rates." When no notation is made, it's generally expected that guests will leave about 5 to 10% for the housekeeping staff and 15% for meal service. A number of inns have taken to leaving little cards or envelopes to remind guests to leave a tip for the housekeepers; some readers have found this objectionable, others don't seem to mind at all. Comments?

A few readers have indicated that they feel some innkeepers have taken advantage of the current popularity of B&Bs with a disproportionate increase in their rates: "I'm concerned about the pricing of some B&Bs. In England it's almost always less expensive to stay at a B&B than at even a middle-range hotel, so the lack of a private bathroom and hotel conveniences are easy to endure. But I've encountered a few American B&Bs without a private bath and serving only a barely adequate continental breakfast that charge two people as much or more than a good chain motel would. Granted, there's a more personal touch, but given the lack of motel amenities, I think the price should be somewhat lower. Even some B&Bs with private baths and considerable charm are, I fear, suffering delusions of grandeur when pricing themselves in the range of a grand hotel." *(AD)*

We agree. Comments, please?

Deposits and cancellations

Nearly all innkeepers print their deposit and cancellation policies clearly on their brochures. Deposits generally range from payment of the first night's stay to 50% of the cost of the entire stay. Some inns repeat the cancellation policy when confirming reservations. In general, guests canceling well in advance of the planned arrival (two to four weeks is typical) receive a full refund minus a cancellation fee. After that date, no refunds are offered unless the room is resold to someone else. A few will not refund *even if the room is resold,* so take careful note.

We would like to applaud many of the inns of the Northwest, where only two to seven days' notice of cancellation is required, and would love to see New England follow suit. We also feel that even if you cancel on short notice, you should be given the opportunity to rebook within a reasonable time period rather than losing your entire deposit.

Sometimes the shoe may be on the other foot. Even if you were told earlier that the inn at which you really wanted to stay was full, it may be worthwhile to make a call to see if cancellations have opened up any last-minute vacancies.

Minimum stays

Two- and three-night minimum weekend and holiday stays are the rule
at many inns during peak periods. We have noted these when possible,
although we suspect that the policy may be more common than is always
indicated in print. On the other hand, you may just be hitting a slow
period, so it never hurts to ask if a one-night reservation would be accepted. Again, cancellations are always a possibility; you can try calling on
a Friday or Saturday morning to see if something is available for that night.

Pets

Very few of the inns and hotels listed accept pets. When they do we've
noted it under "Extras." On the other hand, over one-half of the country
inns listed in this book have at least one dog or cat, sometimes more. If you
are highly allergic to animals, *we strongly urge that you inquire for details before
making reservations.*

Children

Some inns are family-style places and welcome children of all ages. Others
do not feel that they have facilities for the very young and only allow
children over a certain age. Still others cultivate an "adults only" atmosphere and don't even welcome children at dinner. When inns and hotels
do not encourage all children, we've noted the age requirement under the
heading "Restrictions." If special facilities are available to children, these
are noted under "Facilities" and "Extras." If an inn does not exclude children yet does not offer any special amenities or rate reductions for them,
we would suggest it only for the best-behaved youngsters.

Whatever the policy, you may want to remind your children to follow
the same rules of courtesy toward others that we expect of adults. Wall-to-
wall carpeting was not a Victorian specialty, and the pitter-patter of little
feet on an uncarpeted hardwood floor can sound like a herd of stampeding
buffalo to those trying to sleep in a bedroom on the floor below.

Children used to the indestructible plastics of contemporary homes will
need to be reminded (more than once) to be gentle with furniture that dates
back 100 years or more.

For some reason, Southerners seem to be more tolerant of children than
are New Englanders. Of the dozens of exquisitely decorated, antique-filled
inns in the South, there are very few that exclude kids. In the North, nearly
all do! And California innkeepers apparently would prefer it if children
never crossed the state borders at all! Most inns there won't take any
children under 12, and some are strictly for adults only.

State laws governing discrimination by age are affecting policies at some
inns. To our knowledge, both California and Michigan now have such laws
on the books, although this was rarely reflected in the brochures sent to
us by inns in those states. Some inns get around this by limiting room
occupancy to two adults. This discourages families by forcing them to pay
for two rooms instead of one. Our own children are very clear on their

preferences: although they've been to many inns that don't encourage guests under the age of 12, they find them "really boring"; on the other hand, they've loved every family-oriented place we've ever visited.

Porterage and packing

Only the largest of our listings will have personnel whose sole job is to assist guests with baggage. In the casual atmosphere associated with many inns, it is simply assumed that guests will carry their own bags. If you do need assistance with your luggage—because you have a bad back, because your bags are exceptionally heavy, or for any other reason at all—don't hesitate to say so; it should be gladly given. Ideally, innkeepers and their staff should ask you if you need help, but if they forget, don't suffer silently; just say "Could you give us a hand?"

If you're planning an extended trip to a number of small inns, we'd suggest packing as lightly as possible, using two small bags rather than one large suitcase. You'll know why if you've ever tried hauling a 50-pound oversize suitcase up a steep and narrow eighteenth-century staircase. On the other hand, don't forget about the local climate when assembling your wardrobe. In mountainous and desert regions, day- and nighttime temperatures can vary by as much as 40 degrees. Also, bear in mind that Easterners tend to dress more formally than Westerners; if you'll be traveling in New England or the South, men should pack a tie and jacket, women a skirt or dress.

Meals

If you have particular dietary restrictions or allergies—low-salt, vegetarian, or religious—be sure to mention these when making reservations and again at check-in. If you're allergic to caffeine or orange juice, an evening reminder will ensure that you'll be able to enjoy the breakfast that's been prepared for you: Most innkeepers will do their best to accommodate your special needs, within reason.

In preparing each listing, we asked the owners to give us the cost of prix fixe and à la carte meals when available. An "alc dinner" price at the end of the "Rates" section is the figure we were given when we requested the average cost, in 1989, of a three-course dinner with a half bottle of house wine, including tax and tip. Prices listed for prix fixe meals do not include wine and service. Lunch prices, where noted, do not include the cost of any alcoholic beverage.

Dinner and lunch reservations are always a courtesy and are often essential. Most B&B owners will offer to make reservations for you; this can be especially helpful in getting you a table at a popular restaurant in peak season and/or on weekends. Some of the establishments we list operate restaurants fully open to the public. Others serve dinner primarily to their overnight guests, but they also will serve meals to outsiders; reservations are essential at such inns, usually eight or more hours in advance.

Quite a number of restaurants require jackets and ties for men at dinner, even in rather isolated areas. Of course, this is more often the case in traditional New England and the Old South than in the West. Unless you're going only to a very casual country lodge, we recommend that men bring them along and that women have corresponding attire.

Breakfast: Breakfast is served at nearly every inn or hotel listed in this guide. Those that do not, should. No inn is truly "wonderful" if you have to get in your car and drive somewhere for a cup of coffee and a roll, and early-morning strolls should be the choice of the guest, not the host! Nor do we consider the availability of coffee and tea alone an appropriate substitute. The expense and effort involved in providing a minimal continental breakfast are more than compensated for by the civilizing influence it provides.

The vast majority of lodgings listed include breakfast in their rates. We haven't noted in the "Rates" section whether the breakfast is full or continental. The reason for this is that the definitions have become hopelessly blurred in current American usage.

Continental breakfast ranges from an inadequate offering of coffee and store-bought pastry to a lavish offering of fresh fruit and juices, yogurt and granola, cereals, even cheese and cold meats, homemade muffins and breads, and a choice of decaffeinated or regular coffee, herbal and regular tea. There's almost as much variety in the full breakfasts, which range from an uninspired offering of eggs, bacon, and toast, plus juice and coffee, to three-course gourmet extravaganzas. If the innkeeper or the guests feel that a breakfast is something special, you'll see it described in the write-up. If there's no particular mention of it, then either it's nothing special or we've missed it—so please let us know.

We've received occasional complaints about the lack of variety in the breakfasts served. No one likes to have pancakes three days in a row, and doctors now advise against having eggs every day. Sweet breads and muffins are the only breakfast offering at some establishments, yet many would prefer a roll or slice of toast. As one reader put it: "Bed and breakfast hosts seem to think that in order for a breakfast to be special, it has to be sweet. They should make plain toast or unsweetened rolls available to guests without the guest having to ask specially for them. People feel funny about making special requests—they don't want to cause trouble. What about diabetics? What about people like my husband who simply don't care much for sweets? There are plenty of good things for breakfast that don't have to be made with sugar." We agree. Do make your preferences known!

Lunch: Very few of the inns and hotels listed here serve lunch. Those that do generally operate a full-service restaurant, and you'll see some mention of it in the listing. Quite a number of B&B inns are happy to make up picnic lunches for an additional fee. We've noted this where we know about it; if we haven't, just ask if they can do one for you.

Dinner: Meals served at the inns listed here vary widely from simple home-style family cooking to gourmet cuisine. We are looking for food that is a good, honest example of the type of cooking involved. Ingredients should be fresh and homemade as far as is possible; service and presentation should be pleasant and straightforward. We are not interested in elaborate and pretentious restaurants where the descriptions found on the menu far exceed the chef's ability to prepare the dishes.

Here's how one of our readers put it, reporting on an inn in Virginia: "The inn had changed owners from our first to our second visit, a few years later. Although the rooms were much improved, the food was not. Dinner was of the type I describe as 'American pretentious,' the sort of ambitious would-be haute (and haughty) cuisine that a regional inn without a fine professional chef and kitchen staff is ill-advised to attempt. The innkeepers would have been much better off keeping the old cooks who were still in the kitchen the first time we visited, preparing the same delicious Southern home cooking they'd been doing for at least 30 years." *(Ann Delugach)*

Drinks

With very few exceptions (noted under "Restrictions" in each listing), alcoholic beverages may be enjoyed in moderation at all of the inns and hotels listed. Most establishments with a full-service restaurant serving the public as well as overnight guests are licensed to serve beer, wine, and liquor to their customers, although "brown-bagging" or BYOB (bring your own bottle) is occasionally encouraged. Bed & breakfasts, and inns serving meals primarily to overnight guests, do not typically have liquor licenses, although most will provide guests with setups, i.e., glasses, ice, and mixers, at what is often called a BYO (bring your own) bar.

Overseas visitors will be amazed at the hodgepodge of regulations around the country. Liquor laws are determined in general by each state, but individual counties, or even towns, can prohibit or restrict the sale of alcoholic beverages, even beer.

Smoking

Most of the larger inns and hotels do not have any smoking restrictions, except to prohibit cigars and pipes in dining rooms; restrictions at smaller establishments are becoming quite common. Where prohibitions apply we have noted this under "Restrictions." When smoking is prohibited in the guest rooms, this is usually for safety reasons; when it's not allowed in the common rooms, it's because your hosts don't care for the smell. A growing number of inns prohibit indoor smoking entirely. This has become quite common in California, Oregon, and Washington. We suggest that confirmed smokers be courteous or make reservations elsewhere.

When making reservations at larger hotels, nonsmokers should be sure to ask if nonsmoking rooms are available. Such rooms, which have been set aside and specially cleaned, are becoming more and more prevalent.

Physical limitations and wheelchair accessibility

We asked every innkeeper if the hotel or inn was suitable for the disabled, and if yes, what facilities were provided. Unfortunately, the answer was often no. A great many inns dating back 80 years or more have far too

13

many steps and narrow doorways to permit wheelchair access. If you do not need a wheelchair but have difficulty with stairs, we urge you to mention this when making reservations; many inns have one or two rooms on the ground floor. Similarly, if you are visually handicapped, do share this information so that you may be given a room with good lighting and no unexpected steps.

Where the answer was positive, we have noted under "Extras" the facilities offered. In some cases the response was not nearly as complete as we would have liked. Wheelchair access (via ramp) to inn and hotel restaurants tends to be better than guest room accessibility. City hotels often have street-level entrances and, of course, elevators. Some innkeepers noted that ground-floor guest rooms were wheelchair accessible but did not note whether that applied to the bathrooms, as well. Please do inquire for details when making reservations, and please share your findings with us.

Air-conditioning

Heat is a relative condition, and the perceived need for air-conditioning varies tremendously from one individual to the next. If an inn or hotel has air-conditioning, you'll see this listed under "Rooms." If it's important to you, be sure to ask when making reservations. If air-conditioning is not available, check to see if fans are provided. Remember that top-floor rooms in most inns (usually a converted attic) can be uncomfortably warm even in relatively cool climates.

Transportation

A car is more or less essential for visiting most of the inns and hotels listed here, as well as the surrounding sights of interest. Exceptions are those located in the major cities. In some historic towns, a car is the easiest way to get there, but once you've arrived, you'll want to find a place to park the car and forget about it.

If you are traveling by public transportation, check the "Extras" section at the end of each write-up. If the innkeepers are willing to pick you up from the nearest airport, bus, or train station, you'll see it noted here. This service is usually free or available at modest cost. If it's not listed, the innkeeper will direct you to a commercial facility providing this service.

Parking

Although not a concern in most cases, parking is a problem in many beach resorts and historic towns. If you'll be traveling by car, ask the innkeeper for advice when making reservations. If parking is not on-site, stop at the hotel first to drop off your bags, then go park the car. The compact size of these cities will allow you to forget about it until it's time to leave. In big cities, if "free parking" is included in the rates, this usually covers only one arrival and departure. Additional "ins and outs" incur substantial extra charges. Be sure to ask.

If on-site parking is available in areas where parking can be a problem, we've noted it under "Facilities." Since it's so rarely a problem in country inns, we haven't included that information in those listings.

Christmas travel

Many people love to travel to a country inn or hotel at Christmas. Quite a number of places do stay open through the holidays, but the extent to which the occasion is celebrated varies widely indeed. We know of many inns that decorate beautifully, serve a fabulous meal, and organize all kinds of traditional Christmas activities. But we also know of others, especially in ski areas, that do nothing more than throw a few token ornaments on a tree. Be sure to inquire.

Ranch vacations

Spending time on a ranch can give you a real feel for the West—far more than you could ever experience when driving from one tourist attraction to the next. Many families find a ranch they like and return year after year, usually for the same week, and eventually becoming close friends with other guests who do the same. When booking a ranch vacation, it's wise to ask about the percentage of return guests, and to get the names and telephone numbers of some in your area. If the return percentage is low, or the telephone numbers of recent guests are "unavailable," try another ranch. When reading a glossy brochure, make sure that the pictures shown *were taken on the ranch,* and clearly show its cabins, horses, and other facilities, rather than generic Western pictures available anywhere.

While wonderful, ranch vacations are expensive, especially when you're budgeting for a family. When totaling up the costs, remember to add on 10-15% for gratuities to the wranglers and staff—this is standard at almost every ranch but is not always mentioned in the rate information. Ranch vacations tend to be most expensive in Northern Colorado, but they're also most accessible, since you can fly into Denver, rent a car and be on the ranch within a two- to five-hour drive. Ranches in Idaho, Montana, and Wyoming tend to cost less for comparable facilities, but you may have to pay more to get there. When comparing prices, keep in mind that a ranch with a four-diamond AAA rating, gourmet cuisine, and resort facilities will not be in the same ball park as a working ranch with comfortable but more basic food, accommodation, and activities. Finally, make sure that you pay for the things you want. A ranch with a full-fledged children's program is likely to cost more than one with a more casual approach. The cost of a ranch which includes unlimited riding will inevitably be higher than one that charges for riding by the hour. If you live and breathe horses, unlimited riding is clearly a better value. If one or two rides is all you have in mind, then the a la carte approach makes better sense. Read the fine print to be sure of exactly what is included. By the way, if you or another member of your family is not too keen on horses, look for a ranch that offers other activities—tennis, water sports, and hiking—or for a ranch that near a major city or tourist center.

Is innkeeping for me?

Many of our readers fantasize about running their own inn; for some the fantasy may soon become a reality. Before taking the big plunge, it's vital to find out as much as you can about this very demanding business. Experienced innkeepers all over the country are offering seminars for those who'd like to get in the business. While these can be very helpful, they tend to be limited by the innkeepers' own experience with only one or two inns. (Some examples are the Chanticleer in Ashland, Oregon; the Wedgwood Inn in New Hope, Pennsylvania; and the Lords Proprietors Inn in Edenton, North Carolina; see entries for addresses.) For a broader perspective, we'd suggest you contact Bill Oates (P.O. Box 1162, Brattleboro, VT 05301; 802–254–5931) and find out when and where he'll be offering his next seminar entitled "How to Purchase and Operate a Country Inn." Bill is a highly respected pro in this field and has worked with innkeepers facing a wide range of needs and problems; his newsletter, *Innquest,* is written for prospective innkeepers looking to buy property. Another good source is Pat Hardy and Jo Ann Bell, publishers of *Innkeeping Newsletter,* as well as a number of books for would-be innkeepers. They also offer a biannual workshop in Santa Barbara, California, entitled "So, you think you want to be an innkeeper?" For details contact them at 1333 Bath Street, Santa Barbara, CA 93101; (805) 965–0707.

For more information

The best sources of travel information in this country and in Canada are absolutely free; in many cases, you don't even have to supply the cost of a stamp or telephone call. They are the state and provincial tourist offices.

For each state you'll be visiting, request a copy of the official state map, which will show you every little highway and byway and will make exploring much more fun; it will also have information on state parks and major attractions in concise form.

Ask also for a calendar of events and for information on topics of particular interest, such as fishing or antiquing, vineyards or crafts. If you're going to an area of particular tourist interest, you might also want to ask the state office to give you the name of the regional tourist board for more detailed information. You'll find the addresses and telephone numbers for all the states and provinces covered in this book in the Appendix, at the back of this book.

You may also want to contact the local chamber of commerce for information on local sights and events of interest or even an area map. You can get the necessary addresses and telephone numbers from the inn or hotel where you'll be staying or from the state tourist office.

If you are one of those people who never travel with less than three guidebooks (which includes us), you will find the AAA and Mobil regional guides to be helpful references. The Mobil guides can be found in any bookstore, while the AAA guides are distributed free on request to members. If you're not already an AAA member, we'd strongly urge you join before your next trip; in addition to their road service, they offer quality guidebooks and maps, and an excellent discount program at many hotels (including a number listed here). Membership is a particularly good buy if you join as a single person, rather than as a family.

We'd also like to tell you about a new guidebook that will make a delightful companion to our own. *The Traveler's Guide to American Crafts*, by contributing editor Suzanne Carmichael, will be published this May by E.P. Dutton. Divided into eastern and western editions, Suzanne leads readers to the workshops and galleries of outstanding craftspeople in every state.

Where is my favorite inn?

In reading through this book, you may find that your favorite inn is not listed, or that a well-known inn has been dropped from this edition. Why? Two reasons, basically:

—In several cases very well-known hotels and inns have been dropped from this edition because our readers had unsatisfactory experiences. We do not list places that do not measure up to our standards.

—Others have been dropped without prejudice, because we've had no reader feedback at all. This may mean that readers visiting these hotels and inns had satisfactory experiences but were not sufficiently impressed to write about them, or that readers were pleased but just assumed that someone else would take the trouble. If the latter applies, please, please, do write and let us know of your experiences. We try to visit as many inns as possible ourselves, but it is impossible to visit every place, every year. Nor is the way we are received a fair indication of the way another guest is treated. This system only works because of you. So please, keep those cards, letters, and telephone calls coming! As an added incentive, we will be sending free copies of the next edition of this book to our most helpful respondents.

Criteria for entries

If this guide to the inns and hotels of the U.S. and Canada had included all the entries appearing in the regional editions, plus the listings for the Midwest, Rocky Mountains, and Southwestern states (which don't yet have a regional guide to themselves), this publication would have totaled 500 pages. So how did we manage to condense the information to a mere 448 pages? With great difficulty. First of all, in areas of strong traveler appeal, where there are many inns, we included full write-ups on just a handful of those with broadest appeal, covering the others more briefly under the "**Also recommended**" heading. That part was relatively easy. Secondly, we did not include the inns in towns well off the beaten path. We felt that for a country-wide guide, attention must be focussed on key tourist and business centers, rather than the many remote rural villages covered on our regional editions. That required some really tough decisions, since it meant excluding so many really marvelous places from this guide. If you plan any in-depth exploring of a particular region, please consult the appropriate edition for optimal coverage, including appendices for inns with restaurants, places that welcome families, and resorts.

Unlike some other very well-known guidebooks, *we do not collect a membership or listing fee of any kind from the inns and hotels we include.* What matters to us is the feedback we get from you, our readers. This means we are free to write up the negative as well as the positive attributes of each inn listed, and if any given establishment does not measure up, there is no difficulty in dropping it.

Alabama

"Blue Shadows" Guest House, Greensboro

There's much to see and do in Alabama, from Huntsville's Alabama
Space and Rocket Center to historic Mobile, the gorgeous gardens at Bel-
lingrath, and the Gulf Coast beaches. Birmingham, of course, is a major
industrial city where many people go on business. Surely there must be
more small hotels and inns in this state to enjoy while en route. We've
received lots of mail from Alabamans, but nearly all of it is devoted to
the inns of New England! Business travelers heading for Montgomery
might want to check out the **Madison Hotel** (120 Madison Avenue 36104;
205–264–2231), a 190-room, recently renovated, atrium-style hotel. Comments please.

   Rates listed below do not include state sales tax of 7½%, unless otherwise noted.

BIRMINGHAM 35203   Map 6

The Tutwiler Hotel
Park Place at 21st Street North

Tel: (205) 322-2100
(800) 228-0808

With the recent opening of the Tutwiler Hotel, Birmingham can at last
boast of a luxury hotel of historic distinction. Built in 1914, the Tutwiler
was restored in elegant and luxurious style, with antique reproduction
furnishings created especially for the hotel. All amenities are provided, and
the hotel has earned a four diamond rating from the AAA. The restaurant
is equally plush, serving classic American cuisine in an environment meant
to simulate that of a private club. *(Lynn Fulman)*

19

Open All year.
Rooms 52 suites, 96 doubles, all with full private bath, telephone, radio, TV, desk, air-conditioning.
Facilities Lobby, restaurant, lounge with evening entertainment, terrace, patio. Free valet parking. Guest passes to health club with nautilus, swimming pool, tennis, racquetball.
Location Downtown.
Restrictions No smoking in guest bedrooms.
Credit cards Amex, CB, DC, MC, Visa.
Rates Room only, $135–500 suite, $115–135 double, $115–125 single. Extra adult in room, $12; children under 18 free in parents' room. Alc breakfast, $4–13; alc lunch, $12; alc dinner, $35.
Extras Wheelchair accessible; 6 rooms specially equipped for disabled. Airport/station pickups. Cribs, babysitting available. German, Spanish spoken.

MOBILE 36602   Map 6

Malaga Inn   *Tel:* (205) 438–4701
359 Church Street

The Malaga Inn, listed on the National Register of Historic Places, was originally two separate town houses built by two brothers-in-law in 1862, when the Civil War was going well for the South.

"This was a wonderful surprise because it is a lovely inn at a reasonable rate. It has a large reception area, with most of the rooms around a central courtyard with a fountain. Our spacious room had two big four-poster beds, a roomy armoire, marble fireplace, ceiling fan, and hardwood floors. The walls were a warm beige, trimmed with white. The room had a green and white Oriental rug and floral drapes with matching table covers. We had access to a balcony trimmed with wrought iron. The bath was fairly small, but clean. The restaurant is supposed to be very good; it was closed the night we were there, so they directed us to an excellent, popular neighborhood restaurant." *(MFD, also KJ)* More comments, please.

Open All year.
Rooms 3 suites, 37 doubles—all with full private bath, telephone, TV, desk, air-conditioning.
Facilities Restaurant, lounge, garden courtyard with fountain, swimming pool.
Location AL Gulf Coast. Church Street historic district.
Credit cards Amex, DC, Discover, MC, Visa.
Rates Room only, $125 suite, $48–56 double, $42–48 single, plus 8% tax. Alc lunch $7–12; alc dinner, $15–25.
Extras Elevator for wheelchair accessibility. Cribs available.

Alaska

Glacier Bay Country Inn, Gustavus

We wish we had more recommendations for places to stay in Alaska. It's one of our most extraordinary states and a fantastic place to visit. Its size and scope are difficult to imagine: It encompasses an area one-fifth the size of the continental United States and has 3,000 rivers, three million lakes, nineteen mountains higher than 14,000 feet, and more than 5,000 glaciers—one of which is larger than the state of Rhode Island.

Peak travel season to Alaska is during the summer months, when the weather is warmest and the days are the longest. Travelers are learning that the weather can be nearly as nice in the spring and fall, and the crowds far fewer.

Many people think that the only way to see Alaska is by cruise ship. That's certainly a wonderful way to travel, but for those who prefer independent travel, the state is accessible by air and road and, best of all, by ferry. Both the state of Alaska and the province of British Columbia maintain extensive schedules on their modern, well-equipped liners. For more information, get a copy of *Ferryliner Vacations in North America,* published by E. P. Dutton, and be sure to write to the Alaska State Division of Tourism, P.O. Box E-001, Juneau, AK 99811, for a copy of their very helpful "Alaska Official Vacation Planner."

Information please: We'd like to hear more about Skagway, a gold-rush boom town at the turn of the century; its historic district has been turned into a national park. Inns of interest include the **Golden North Hotel**, built in 1897 (Box 431, Skagway 99840; 907–983–2294) and the equally venerable **Irene's Inn** (Box 538, Skagway 99840; 907–983–2520). Another possibility is the **Skagway Inn**, built as a rooming house of similar vintage; today it has lots of gold-rush era furniture and a homey atmosphere (Box 3, Skagway 99840; 907–983–2289).

21

ANGOON 99820 Map 16

Favorite Bay Inn *Tel:* (907) 788–3123
Box 101

Along with bald eagles and brown bear, fishermen flock to this warm and sunny island in the Inside Passage in search of salmon (five species), trout, halibut, clams, crab, shrimp, and bottom fish. Overlooking the Angoon Boat Harbor at the entrance to Favorite Bay, this inn was built 50 years ago by the local Civilian Conservation Corps (CCC) foreman. Longtime owners Richard and Roberta Powers have decorated their home with teak, oak, brass, and leather furnishings; rates include a continental breakfast of muffins, cereal, fruit, yogurt, and beverages.

"The Powers have a corner on a little piece of heaven. Accommodations are warm, comfortable, and charming both inside and out. The atmosphere is convenient and relaxing, with lots of privacy if you want it." *(Elvia Torres-Cater)* "Incomparable natural beauty combined with genuine warmth and hospitality." *(CK)*

Open All year.
Rooms 4 doubles, with maximum of 4 sharing bath.
Facilities Dining room, living room, family room with TV. Waterfront property. Fishing, canoe and skiff rentals, boat charters.
Location SE AK, Inland Passage. 60 m S of Juneau, 60 m NE of Sitka. ¾ m from Angoon, on W side of Admiralty Island.
Restrictions No smoking. Angoon is a dry community; BYOB.
Credit cards None accepted.
Rates B&B, $59 double, $49 single.
Extras Free ferry pickups.

DENALI NATIONAL PARK 99755 Map 1

Denali National Park covers 5.7 million acres of land and is home to 3! kinds of mammals, from grizzly bears to caribou and moose, plus a variet of bird and plant life. Mosquitoes are probably the most populous specie in the park; fortunately they disappear by the latter part of the season Private cars are discouraged in the park; shuttle buses bring guests t campgrounds and transport visitors to places of interest throughout th park. Area activities include hiking, canoeing, natural history and photog raphy trips, rafting, bicycling, fishing, and panning for gold.

The park is 240 miles north of Anchorage, 120 miles southwest of Fair banks.

Camp Denali *Tel:* (907) 683–229
P.O. Box 67 (603) 675–224
Off-season: P.O. Box 216, Cornish, NH 03746

Your own wilderness cabin, with breathtaking views of Mt. McKinle (North America's highest mountain, at 20,320 feet), is one of the ke attractions of a stay in Denali National Park. While comfortable, the cabir are definitely rustic; each is equipped with spring water, propane lights, a hot plate, a wood stove, and a private path. (Yes, that's a *p,* not a *b.*) A hearty breakfast and dinner are served daily in the central dining room, but visitors "brown bag" their lunch. Long-time owners Wallace and Jerryne Cole work hard at providing a warm and welcoming atmosphere, with a guest/staff ratio of about two to one.

Those interested in a wee bit more luxury will want to ask about the Coles' latest venture, the North Face Lodge, with 15 guest rooms, all with full private bath. Per person double occupancy rate, including all meals, is $225. *(MB)* More comments, please.

Open Early June to early Sept.
Rooms 19 cabins with shared shower facility. All with desk.
Facilities Dining room, library/living room, natural history resource room, darkroom. Naturalist program in evenings. 60 acres with pond, hiking trails.
Location In center of park.
Restrictions No smoking. Alcoholic beverages not served; may BYOB to cabin.
Credit cards None accepted.
Rates Full board, $225 per person. Family, children's rates available. Alc lunch, $10; alc dinner, $20. 3–5 night minimum stay. 10% discount for weekly stays.
Extras Station pickup from Denali Park Rail Depot included in rates. Crib available. German, Swiss, some French spoken.

GUSTAVUS 99826   Map 16

Gustavus is a small and isolated community on southeast Alaska's famed Inside Passage about 50 miles west of Juneau. Located on a large sandy plain created by receding glaciers, the area contrasts with the typical rocky wooded shoreline of southeast Alaska. There are no roads or ferry service—the only way to get here is by plane.

The key attraction here is Glacier Bay National Park, a series of fjords and active tidewater glaciers extending over 65 miles. Activities include hiking in the rain forests of hemlock, spruce, and pine; cruising up the bay to watch for whales, bald eagles, black bear, deer, and 200 varieties of birds; or climbing into a kayak for a close-up look at the seals and porpoises that will accompany you. Fishermen will opt for deep-sea and river fishing for salmon, halibut, cutthroat and Dolly Varden trout, while winter visitors can add cross-country skiing to the recreation list. Another highlight is a bush plane flightseeing tour of the park, revealing the bay's deep crevasses, enormous ice fields, jagged peaks, and breathtaking beauty. Berry-picking and picnicking on the beach are a delight for children of all ages.

Although outdoor activities are limitless, one thing the town does not have is a liquor store; if you enjoy a glass of wine with dinner, bring your own. Remember that the weather can be cool and damp even in summer, so bring along warm and waterproof clothing, including hat and gloves.

Glacier Bay Country Inn   *Tel:* (907) 697–2288
Box 5

Al and Annie Unrein built Glacier Bay Country Inn in 1985, on their working farm, from trees cut and milled right on the property. Vegetables, fruits, and herbs are grown in their gardens, and guests enjoy the chance to observe haying, logging, sawmilling, and other Alaskan homesteading activities. Each room is decorated with a special theme, but the key ingredient is comfort. Although the cuisine will tempt the most stringent dieter, the chef can prepare menus to suit special dietary needs.

"As we drove up, we passed their large gardens. Entering, we saw rooms filled with flowers—lupine, fireweed, Livingston daisies, and poppies arranged in tiny vases. The inn is an eclectic assortment of old and new—white walls, wooden beams, and firm mattresses with flannel sheets, country-print comforters, antique furniture, and unusually shaped large windows overlooking pastures and snow-covered mountains. The owners and staff are like your favorite neighbors (or at least mine). Al and Annie were always available to organize a full range of activities.

"One cannot speak of this inn without raving about its excellent cuisine. Breakfast might feature blintzes, seafood crêpes, and lots of bacon and sausage. Lunches were packed for our daily excursion or were served about noon at the inn, including crab bisque, fresh garden salads, pasta, grilled meats, and more. After an afternoon nap, we returned to the table for fresh crab, prawns, tenderloin, and other delightful dishes decorated with nasturtiums." *(Kim & Ann Hutchinson)*

"The feeling of being 'at home' was increased by the hand-crocheted bedspread and the embroidered sampler on the wall of my room. The cleanliness is impressive and the service extremely well organized." *(Helen Majoros, also Bette Woodward)*

Open All year.
Rooms 6 doubles, 1 single—5 with private shower, 2 with maximum of 3 sharing bath. All with desk.
Facilities Dining room, living room with games, library. 160 acres with gardens, bicycles, hiking trails, creeks, ponds.
Location 4 miles from park headquarters. Take main road toward park, turn left at inn sign and follow to end.
Restrictions No smoking.
Credit cards None accepted.
Rates Room only, $104 double, $57 shared single, $87 single; B&B, $116 double, $63 shared single, $93 single; MAP, $152 double, $81 shared single, $111 single; Full board, $168 double, $89 shared single, $119 single. Extra adult in room, $37–69; extra child under 12 in room, $17–49.
Extras Airport/dock pickups. Crib, babysitting available. Limited German, Spanish spoken.

Gustavus Inn   *Tel:* (907) 697-2254
Box 60

In 1968 Jack and Sally Lesh bought this old Alaska homestead, built in 1928 for a family of 11, and started the inn. Ten years later, their son David and his wife JoAnn took over its management. In 1988 they completed a full remodeling of the inn, adding private baths to almost all the guest rooms. Over the years the Leshes have become known for their cuisine, featuring fresh seafood, and fruits and vegetables from their own garden. David presides over the kitchen. JoAnn reports that "our guests love planting their feet on the ground here to see the real Alaska. Days are spent touring, fishing, bicycling, beachcombing, mushroom- and berry-picking, swinging, and throwing horseshoes. Walks by the river under the midnight sun are always a pleasure."

"Newly remodeled, while retaining all its old charm. Cozy sitting room. We fished, visited Glacier Bay, picnicked and beachcombed, took long walks, nibbled wild strawberries, stopped at Park Headquarters for the films and lectures. Food is superb. Lunch is soup, garden-fresh salad, homemade jellies and sourdough bread, wonderful cake. Freshly caught salmon, crab, halibut and more for dinner. Incredible fishing. I caught a 70-lb. halibut and my wife caught another that weighed 170 lbs. The owners wrapped and froze them for us to take home." *(Joe Dwigans)*

Open All year.
Rooms 13 doubles—7 with private shower, 6 with maximum of 4 sharing bath. All with radio.
Facilities Dining room, bar, library, hearth room with fireplace, TV/VCR. 5 acres with gardens; bicycles, fishing poles.
Location 1 m from airport; at entrance to Glacier Bay National Park.
Restrictions "Smokers encouraged to go outside."
Credit cards MC, Visa.
Rates All rates per person. Full board, $100. Children's rates. Alc dinner, $25. Cooking seminars.
Extras Airport pickups; daily courtesy van to Park Service programs. Cribs available. French, Spanish spoken.

HAINES 99827   **Map 16**

The Summer Inn   *Tel:* (907) 766–2970
P.O. Box 1198

Named for owners Bob and Mary Ellen Summer, not the season, the Summer Inn was built at the turn of the century by Tim Vogel, a member of Skagway's infamous Soapy Smith gang. Situated in downtown Haines, the inn overlooks the Lynn Canal and provides a central location for enjoying the sites of the Chilkat Valley.

"Surrounded by steep mountains, glaciers, and the moody waters of the Inside Passage, Haines gives visitors a taste of southeast Alaska with the added convenience of road access to the interior. The town is rich in history, outdoor activities, and wildlife. Every November the world's largest concentration of bald eagles congregates on the Chilkat River only 15 miles from town. A week-long stay in Haines was not enough time to fully explore the area." *(M. Joyce)*

"The Summer Inn is a quaint house in a small town. Everything was clean and cozy with a country atmosphere; especially pleasing were the fluffy comforter and large, thirsty towels. Our breakfast of coffee, juice, fruit, walnut-banana pancakes, and sausage came in delicious he-man portions on china dishes. Hot blueberry muffins and tea really hit the spot after we returned from climbing nearby Mount Ripinsky." *(Charlotte Mansfield)*

Open All year.
Rooms 5 doubles—with a maximum of 5 persons sharing bath. All with fan.

Facilities Dining room, living room with library, games. Flower garden. Fishing, canoeing, kayaking nearby. 40 m to telemark skiing.
Location SE AK. Chilkat Valley. 60 m N of Juneau. 1½ blocks from Main St.
Credit cards MC, Visa.
Rates B&B, $50–55 double, $40–45 single. Extra person in room, $10. Family, weekly rates.
Extras Airport/ferry pickups. Crib available.

JUNEAU 99801   Map 16

Information please: The newly renovated **Alaskan Hotel**, the town's oldest, was built in 1913. Listed on the National Register of Historic Places, the hotel is decorated with antiques and highlighted by fifty stained glass windows (167 South Franklin 99801; 907–586–1000 or 800–327–9347).

Dawson's B&B   *Tel:* (907) 586–9708
1941 Glacier Highway

Dave and Velma Dawson "try our best to make our guests' stay pleasant" in their B&B, set on a wooded hillside. Always pleased to provide information, they are knowledgeable about sights and activities of interest. Rates include a full breakfast of fruit and juice, bacon, eggs, potatoes, toast, and coffee or tea.

"The Dawsons are very hospitable and caring people who really seem to enjoy the B&B business. They were extremely helpful, letting us park our car at their place when we flew to Glacier Bay, and even bringing us to and from the airport. Their home is clean and pleasant, the breakfasts delicious." *(Bette Woodward)*

Open All year.
Rooms 5 doubles—3 with private bath, 2 with a maximum of 4 people sharing 1 bath.
Facilities Breakfast room, sitting room, deck. Laundry facilities.
Location SE AK. 2 m to town; 9 m to airport.
Credit cards None accepted.
Rates B&B, $48–55 double, $40–50 single. Extra person in room, $10. No charge for children under 6.
Extras Airport/ferry pickups. Bus stops (on request) in front of house.

Arizona

Copper Queen Hotel, Bisbee

Arizona is a land of dazzling extremes. It will shake up your preconceptions about deserts with its varied plant and animal life; even the Grand Canyon won't look like the pictures you've seen (unless you have wide-angle eyeballs). Except for the greater Phoenix area, this is a state with little pollution and many wide open spaces and surprises.

Nature's many gifts to Arizona extend far beyond the Grand Canyon. Visit Organ Pipe Cactus National Monument in the southwest at the Mexican border and take the self-guiding Ajo Mountain Drive; see the huge weathered columnar lava cliffs at Chiricahua National Monument in the extreme southeast; also in the east, near the New Mexico border, is the scenic high-mountain drive on Route 666 between Clifton and Springerville. Be sure to include Sedona's fairyland Red Rocks on your itinerary. (It's a logical overnight en route from Phoenix to the Grand Canyon.)

A trip to Arizona isn't complete without an introduction to prehistoric and contemporary Indians. At Painted Rocks State Park (in the southwest, near Gila Bend), stands an isolated outcropping of petroglyphs that keeps its mysterious meaning to itself. In the Flagstaff area, the 500- to 700-year-old cliff dwellings at Tonto, Montezuma Castle, and Walnut Canyon national monuments seem still alive with their former occupants, while the striking tenth- to twelfth-century pueblo ruins at Wupatki give evidence of skilled craftsmanship in the decorative placement of lava, the carefully

27

formed door lintels, the curve of an outside patio. This same grace and craftsmanship can be found today at the Hopi Reservation in the northeast part of the state, where the casual visitor will feel he has stepped into another century, a foreign land.

Information please: Phoenix is one of the very few major cities where we've had little in the way recommendations; reports please! For B&B accommodation with genuine southwestern charm, the **Squaw Peak Inn** (4425 East Horseshoe Road, Phoenix 85028; 602–998–4049) is a classic adobe structure with massive ceiling logs and native stone fireplace, combined with such modern comforts as color TV, private baths, and cooking facilities. The inn is nestled near the solitude of the Squaw Peak Mountain Preserve, yet is just minutes from the airport, restaurants, and shops. For a B&B with laughs, call Bob Wolf for the brochure for the **Art Break Hotel** (1023 East Main Street, P.O. Box 10253, Scottsdale 85271). An easy stroll from Scottsdale's art and antique galleries and shops, Bob claims to offer clean comfortable rooms, a homey atmosphere, a "live-in manager who knows how to smile," and a professional artist-owner with "nearly 20 years experience with cruddy, overpriced, overnight accommodations." Business travelers may prefer the **Fifth Avenue Inn** (6935 Fifth Avenue, Scottsdale 85251; 602–994–9461 or 800–528–7396), with 92 balconied motel-style rooms overlooking the swimming pool or landscaped courtyard; peak season double rates are only $85, and there's no charge for children under 16.

Also in Phoenix but recommended too late for a full writeup is **Westways** (Valley of the Sun, P.O. Box 41624; 602–582–3868) located 25 minutes northwest of the airport, and offering seven casitas done in contemporary Spanish Mediterranean style. Rates include a full breakfast; the inn has its own swimming pool and hot tub, plus golf and tennis privileges at a nearby club. "Unbelievable service and privacy." *(Mrs. Thomas Poolun)*

If you're looking for a guest ranch close to Phoenix, your best bet is to head 60 miles northwest to Wickenburg. The **Rancho de los Caballeros** is a well-run, well-organized guest ranch, with a broad range of scheduled activities, including special programs for kids (P.O. Box 1148, 85358; 800–528–4227). The **Wickenburg Inn** has similar facilities but also provides tennis clinics on its 11 courts (P.O. Box P, 85358; 800–528–4227).

Another possibility if you're heading south from Phoenix toward Organ Pipe Cactus National Monument is The **Manager's House Inn**, in the town of Ajo. Developed by the New Cornelia Mining Company, the town developed because of the massive copper mine, now abandoned. Set on the town's highest hill this B&B was built for the mine manager and his family in 1919, and now has five guest rooms with private baths; rates of $60–90 include a full breakfast and evening brandy (1 Greenway Drive, Ajo 85321; 602–387–6505).

Rates do not include Arizona state tax of 6%, plus local taxes as shown. Guest ranch rates typically include all meals and activities in one comprehensive daily rate, sometimes referred to as "Arizona Plan"; a service charge of 15% is added to the total.

BISBEE 85603   Map 12

At the turn of the century, Bisbee was Arizona's largest town, known as the Queen of the Copper Camps. Although the mines are no longer active, visitors can tour them underground on the old mine train. The town is set along the sides of two narrow canyons at an elevation of 5,300 feet, which keeps summertime temperatures comfortable. Other area attractions include visits to the local historical museums, hiking in the nearby Chiricahua Mountains, and exploring Tombstone and area ghost towns; a visit to the Cochise stronghold in the Dragoon Mountains is also recommended.

Bisbee is in southeastern Arizona, 95 miles southeast of Tucson; from Tucson, take I-10 east to Benson, then take Route 80 south through Tombstone to Bisbee.

The Bisbee Inn   *Tel:* (602) 432–5131
45 OK Street, P.O. Box 1855

The view down Brewery Gulch is a lot quieter these days. When the Bisbee Inn was built in 1917 as the Lamore Hotel, it overlooked one of the Southwest's wildest boom-town streets. Joy and John Timbers bought the inn in 1982 and restored it themselves, including the oak furniture original to the hotel. Their all-you-can-eat breakfast will save you the price of lunch: fresh fruit salad, whole wheat and honey pancakes, bacon, eggs, hash browns, French toast made from homemade whole wheat bread, accompanied by juice, coffee, and tea.

"The rooms are bright, cheery, and always very clean." *(Pat Staeger)* "Relaxed atmosphere, beautiful restoration, excellent breakfast." *(GC)*

Open All year.
Rooms 18 doubles—all with sink in room, shared bath, desk, "evaporation cooling."
Facilities Dining room, TV room, porch.
Location In historic district. From Rte. 80, take "business exit" into Old Bisbee. Go straight up hill (OK St.) and follow signs to inn.
Restrictions No smoking.
Credit cards MC, Visa.
Rates B&B, $34–39 double, $29 single. Extra person in room, $5. Family rates; no charge for children under 5 in parents' room.
Extras Pets permitted in some rooms.

Copper Queen Hotel   *Tel:* (602) 432–2216
11 Howell Avenue, P.O. Drawer CQ   In AZ: (800) 247–5829

"A leftover from the days when Bisbee was a thriving mining town, the Copper Queen is built on the side of a hill—so much so that we climbed about 40 steps to reach the street in front of the hotel, then another 15 to the porch. The swimming pool is located in back of the hotel—on the third level! We had an enjoyable dinner and thought it a good value for the price. The dining room is pleasant, with hanging stained-glass panels and various antique and copper decorations. The lobby is compact, with a front desk and sitting area; there's also a parlor area near the stairway on each floor.

The halls are decorated with framed photos of Bisbee's heyday." *(Susan W. Schwemm)*

"This is a very spiffy hotel, built circa 1900 by the mining company that owned and dominated the town until the mine closed about 12 years ago. Set in hills that remind me of the Georgetown area of Colorado, the town is still worth seeing. I particularly recommend the corner room on the second floor—which is where John Wayne and Teddy Roosevelt both stayed; the baths have old-fashioned fixtures but are adequate." *(SC)*

Open All year.
Rooms 5 suites, 36 doubles—all with private bath. 40 with black-and-white or color TV, some with radio, desk.
Facilities Restaurant, sidewalk café, saloon with piano, guitar music 3 nights weekly. Swimming pool. Tennis, swimming, hiking, golf, rock collecting nearby.
Restrictions Light sleepers should request rooms away from the bar area.
Location Center of town.
Credit cards MC, Visa.
Rates Room only, $75 suite, $40–70 double, $35–65 single. Extra person in room, $5. Alc breakfast, $3–6; alc lunch, $5–9; alc dinner, $15–30.
Extras Airport/station pickups. Cribs available. Spanish spoken.

The Greenway House
401 Cole Avenue

Tel: (602) 432–7170

Although Joy O'Clock and George Knox had hoped to buy a small Victorian house, when they saw the 38-room Greenway Mansion they fell in love. Built in the Craftsman style by the Calumet and Arizona Mining Company it was first home to Rough Rider John C. Greenway, company manager. Joy and George, the mansion's third set of owners since 1906, turned the mansion into a bed & breakfast inn. All the baths and kitchens were redone. The original brass fixtures are balanced with brand-new tiling; 10,000 square feet of wall-to-wall carpeting, laid in 1938, were torn out to expose the original hardwood floors. Most rooms are decorated with Victorian antiques, although the living room effectively combines a beautiful Tiffany-style light fixture with comfortable contemporary sectional couches and Indian weavings. Rates include a continental breakfast and afternoon hors d'oeuvres. Joy notes that "we especially enjoy visitors who appreciate antiques and restoration and the historic character of our town."

"An outstanding example of what an inn should be, located in the small, quiet community of Warren. The owners have combined the ambience of early-twentieth-century mining company officialdom with present-day amenities. Especially noteworthy are the small kitchen facilities provided with each room, thoughtfully stocked with breakfast provisions." *(DC)*

"Lots of extras—exquisite imported toiletries, fruit plate at breakfast, chilled wine on arrival, basket of locally made chocolates. A wonderful experience." *(Lynne Proper)*

Open All year.
Rooms 3 suites, 5 doubles—all with private bath and/or shower, radio, fan.kitchenette. 1 with TV, 2 with desk, 2 with air-conditioning. 2 suites in carriage house.
Facilities Game room with pool table, TV, honor bar, juke box. 3 acres with patio.
Location Warren, 5 m from town. From I-80, drive past Old Bisbee and the Lavender

Pit mine; go around the traffic circle and turn right on Bisbee Rd. Turn left at Copper Queen Hospital (Cole Ave.) and go past school, up hill to 3rd house on left.
Restrictions No smoking. No children under 13.
Credit cards MC, Visa.
Rates B&B, $125 suite, $75 double. Extra person in room, $15. 2-day minimum stay.
Extras Wheelchair accessible; elevator to 2nd floor. Spanish spoken.

CAREFREE 85377   Map 12

The Boulders Resort   *Tel:* (602) 488–9009
34631 North Tom Darlington, P.O. Box 2090   (800) 223–7637

Set in the Sonora Desert foothills, the Boulders is an elegant resort, designed in pueblo style to effectively blend with its rocky desert environs. Each individual casita is positioned to disturb the natural setting as little as possible—the Rockresorts philosophy. The interiors continue the Southwestern theme, with Indian motifs, hand-hewn beams, and adobe walls. Set at an elevation of 2,500 feet, the days are generally warm and sunny, the nights cool and crisp.

"The casitas are very large, with a separate sitting area and fireplace, furnished in decorator Southwestern style. The bathrooms are sybaritic—positively huge—with a walk-in closet, dressing/makeup area, two sinks, tub, separate shower stall, and enclosed toilet closet. A phone call to the front desk brings an electric cart to transport you to the main building, a wonderful option for older guests. A luxurious lake (in this desert climate) is in front of the main entrance; the main building stands at the base of the largest tumble of boulders—a man-made waterfall cascades down one of them. There are two dining rooms, one featuring entrées with a Southwestern twist and the other with gourmet cuisine. The breakfasts are astounding, with several courses on the menu, supplemented with a fruit and bread buffet; dinners are equally excellent." *(Susan W. Schwemm)*

On the other hand, a well-traveled correspondent did have some complaints: Unless she had the "do not disturb" sign out, cleaning and maintenance personnel were constantly knocking at the door; the women's exercise facility lacks the sauna and steam room available in the men's facility. She also cautioned that this is really not a family-oriented resort.

Open Labor Day through Father's Day Weekend.
Rooms 120 casita doubles—all with full private bath, telephone, radio, TV, desk, air-conditioning, fireplaces.
Facilities 4 restaurants, lounge with pianist, living room, game room. 30 acres with 2 swimming pools, 6 tennis courts, 27-hole golf course, horseback riding, ballooning.
Location Central AZ. 30 m NE of Phoenix, 10 m N of Scottsdale. From airport, take 44 St. N (name changes to McDonald) 3 m to Scottsdale Rd. and turn left (N). Follow Scottsdale Rd. N 22 m to resort.
Credit cards All major credit cards accepted.
Rates MAP, $255–410 double, $185–325 single, plus 15% service. Extra person in room, $90–100. Nearby homes/condos also available. Minimum stay some holiday weekends. Alc lunch, $10–18; alc dinner, $50–60. Golf, tennis, family packages available.
Extras Several rooms equipped for handicapped. Airport/station pickups, $20. Cribs, babysitting available. French, Spanish spoken. Member, Rockresorts.

GRAND CANYON 86023 Map 12

Information please: People go to the Grand Canyon to see the Grand Canyon, and the quality of accommodations, beyond the basics, is relatively unimportant. Although obvious, this fact is fortunate, since reports on the majority of area accommodations are tepid at best. Some options we'd like to hear more about are **Bright Angel Lodge and Cabins**, especially the cabins right on the canyon rim; and **Thunderbird Lodge** with 50 motel units and cabins on the south rim of the canyon. For information and reservations on all accommodations in Grand Canyon contact: P.O. Box 699; 602–638–2631.

El Tovar Hotel   *Tel:* (602) 638–2631
P.O. Box 699   Advance Reservations: (602) 638–2401

The Grand Canyon was first discovered by the European world in 1540, but remained virtually unknown until it was rediscovered in 1869. It did not become a major tourist attraction until 1884, when the Santa Fe Railroad reached it at last. Construction of El Tovar was begun not long after. Completed in 1905, it was a luxury hotel built according to the highest standards of the day. Since its opening, it has been under the continuous management of the Fred Harvey Company, one of the earliest hotel and transportation companies in the West.

"Built at the south rim of the canyon at its most spectacular and colorful location, some of the rooms in the El Tovar and the nearby Kachina Lodge have canyon views, extraordinary at sunrise and sunset. The exterior of the original building, including the grand entrance, is in the 'log cabin' style, constructed of native boulders and Oregon pine. The interior spaces are large with the Southwestern Indian motif predominating. This grand old establishment has been carefully modernized and maintained and rooms are modern and comfortably furnished. The standards of service are extremely high, and wonderfully old-fashioned. The staff dresses and acts in a style long gone elsewhere. The maids still wear black uniforms with white aprons, and everyone is extremely polite, careful and courteous. From above the grand stairway looking down on the lobby is a great scowling portrait of Mr. Harvey, who appears ready to correct any fault or impropriety of the staff. The dining room serves the best food with the best service of any place on the canyon rim, with a nice selection of veal and beef entrées." *(Willis Frick)*

And another point of view: "The architecture is stunning, and everyone else raves about this hotel, but I didn't care for it. Our room was lovely, but I didn't feel that its dark, formal furnishings really fit with the environment; although we had a partial view of the canyon from our window, once the drapes were drawn, I could just have easily been in Washington, D.C., from the look of our room. I thought the dining room was expensive, the service pretentious; the food itself ranged from good to excellent. The second night we ate next door at the Arizona House, a typical steak house, in a comfortable setting for much less money."

Open All year.
Rooms 10 suites, 30 doubles—all with full private bath, telephone, TV, desk.
Facilities Restaurant, piano bar/lounge, mezzanine lounge for residents only.
Location N central AZ. 80 m N of Flagstaff, 230 m N of Phoenix.
Credit cards Amex, CB, DC, Discover, MC, Visa.
Rates Room only, $142–222 suite, $90–122 double. Extra person in room, $10. Children under 12 free in parents' room. Alc breakfast, $4–10; alc lunch, $8–12; alc dinner, $25–35.
Extras Some rooms wheelchair accessible. Cribs, babysitting available.

SEDONA 86336   **Map 12**

Some travelers feel that Sedona, one of the prettiest places on earth, has gotten much too touristy, especially in the summer months. Try to visit in spring or fall for a more relaxed stay. The 4,300-foot altitude here provides a climate that is mild year-round. Visitors come to see the striking red rock formations and the cool depths of Oak Creek Canyon. Other activities include golf, tennis, horseback riding, hiking, swimming, fishing, hunting, and visiting the many boutiques and art galleries of this popular resort. Sedona is in central Arizona's Red Rocks Country, 115 miles north of Phoenix, halfway between Phoenix and the Grand Canyon. For a spectacular drive with endless vistas, take the 12-mile back road east out of Sedona to I-17; it's a rough road, not suitable for motor homes or inexperienced drivers.

Also recommended: Received too late for a full writeup was an enthusiastic report on the **Arroyo Roble Hotel** (400 North Highway 89A, P.O. Box NN, Sedona 86336; 602–282–4001 or 800–528–1234), a 52-unit Best Western motel with heated swimming pool and hot tub, laundry room, and access to tennis and racquetball courts; rates range from $55–80. "All rooms have either balconies or patios overlooking the swimming pool and the beautiful red hills beyond. They're very spacious, immaculately clean, furnished with standard motel decor—but tasteful. It's a very comfortable place for families, and the kids we saw were all having a great time. A resident owner/manager was very much in evidence, and the staff was very helpful with sightseeing and restaurant recommendations. They referred us to a nearby restaurant called **Shugrue's** (282–2943) for a very relaxed and delicious meal. The motel's location is good, right in the old part of town, and there's a place for breakfast right across the street." *(AF)*

Garland's Oak Creek Lodge   *Tel:* (602) 282–3343
Highway 89-A, P.O. Box 152

If you're planning a last-minute trip, you should probably skip to the next listing, because Garland's Oak Creek Lodge is generally booked a year in advance (although there's always the hope of a cancellation). According to Gary and Mary Garland, owners since 1971, "the things that make this lodge special are the gorgeous setting, excellent food, and friendly staff." Rustic cabins, overlooking the creek or the gardens, are set against the beautiful red cliffs of Sedona. All the food is fresh—the home-baked muffins and breads, eggs from the Garlands' chickens, vegetables from the garden, and fruit and cider from the orchards. The icing on the cake here is in fact the food: the evening menu (no choice) changes daily, combining continental and Southwestern cuisine. A typical dinner might include carrot ginger soup, greens with balsamic vinaigrette, red chile bread, roast duck with pear jalapeño sauce, wild hazelnut rice, asparagus, and mocha walnut cake. Guests can accompany their meal with wine chosen from a short but select list, which favors California vintages. *(SHW)*

Open April 1–Nov. 15. Closed from Sun. noon to Mon. afternoon.
Rooms 15 cabins—all with private shower, desk. Some with fireplace.
Facilities Dining room, sitting room with fireplace. 9 acres with orchards, tennis, trout-stocked stream. Hiking, bicycling, golf nearby.
Location 8 m N of Sedona. Turn W at sign on Hwy. 89-A at Banjo Bill Campground, cross Oak Creek, and go ⅛ m to lodge.
Restrictions No smoking during dinner.
Credit cards MC, Visa.
Rates MAP, $130–150 double, $95–115 single. Extra person in room, $38. 15% service additional. 2-night minimum.
Extras Limited wheelchair access. Cribs, babysitting available. Spanish, German spoken.

Graham's Bed & Breakfast Inn

Tel: (602) 284–1425

150 Canyon Circle Drive, Oak Creek, P.O. Box 912

After searching the Southwest for the ideal location, Marni and Bill Graham selected this site in 1985 as the perfect spot to build their custom-designed bed & breakfast inn. Decorated with a contemporary Southwestern look, incorporating the work of local artisans, the inn offers excellent views of the nearby red rock formations. Breakfast, served at eight, is a leisurely affair and might include pears in plum sauce, homemade blueberry muffins, and a breakfast quiche.

"The downstairs public area includes a living/sitting area with cathedral ceiling and fireplace, and a dining area that overlooks the patio and pool area outside. The guest rooms are designer decorated, all different. Each has a lovely modern bath; the most spectacular room was the San Francisco Suite, with a custom-made king-size bed on a pedestal frame base and a mirror behind the bed. The Southwest Suite is more compact but is warm and cozy with a fireplace and earth-tone decor.

"The Grahams are warm and welcoming, intelligent and thoughtful folks who really want you to enjoy their area; they are helpful with restaurant and driving tour suggestions. Breakfast featured German pancakes one day and a soufflé another, accompanied by an assortment of fancy teas and juices, plus coffee, toast, and jams. I loved the breakfast; others in my party would have preferred slightly heartier fare." *(Susan W. Schwemm)* "Each room has oversize beds and a private balcony with spectacular views of the Red Rocks Country." *(Pat Hardy)*

Open Feb. through Dec.
Rooms 4 doubles with queen- or king-size bed, 1 double with 2 single beds—all with private bath, radio, air-conditioning, balcony. 2 with Jacuzzi tubs, desk. 1 with fireplace.
Facilities Dining room, living/game/TV room with double-sided fireplace. Patio/porch, heated swimming pool, spa. Fishing, golf nearby.

Location 5 m from center. From Rte. 179, turn W onto Bellrock Blvd., right onto Canyon Circle.
Restrictions No smoking. No children under 12.
Credit cards MC, Visa.
Rates B&B, $90–130 double, $80–120 single. Extra person in room, $15. 2-3 night minimum on weekends and holidays.

L'Auberge de Sedona Resort *Tel:* (602) 282–7131
301 Little Lane, P.O. Box B In AZ: (800) 331–2820
Outside AZ: (800) 272–6777

This resort offers a choice of luxury accommodations in a European-style lodge, individual cabins, or motel units, fitted out with fabrics and furnishings from southern France. The inn's two restaurants include L'Auberge, where a fixed price five-course dinner is served, and the Orchards Grill, specializing in light American cuisine. Reports on the food here are mixed, with positive reactions to the decor, and more critical ones regarding the actual food and service, especially considering the high prices.

"We stayed in the lodge, but next time would love to try the cottages or even the motel, set at the top of the hill with wonderful views of Oak Creek and the red rocks. Our room and bath were large, charmingly decorated, and exceedingly comfortable." *(Nicki Dresslar)*

"The log cabins are furnished in romantic floral fabrics and wallpapers, with canopy beds and fireplaces, and are connected by lushly landscaped paths." *(Virginia Richter, Ann E. Graham)*

Open All year.
Rooms 2 3-bedroom suites, 61 doubles, 32 cottages—all with full private bath, radio, desk, air-conditioning. 63 guest rooms with telephone, TV. Some with balcony, patio, fireplace, canopy beds. Suites have fully equipped kitchens.
Facilities 2 restaurants, lounge with fireplace. 11 acres with gardens, "hillevator," paths, picnic areas, 2 heated swimming pools, Jacuzzi. Tennis, golf, racquetball, fitness center nearby.
Location In center. Little Lane runs off 89A, 1 block N of intersection with 179.
Credit cards Amex, MC, Visa.
Rates Lodge: room only, $80–140 double. Extra person in room, $20. Cabins: MAP, $225–325 double. Extra person in room, $65. 10% senior discount. Minimum stay requirements during holidays. Weekday packages. Alc lunch, $10–15; alc dinner, $30–100.
Extras Some rooms equipped for the disabled. Airport pickups. Cribs, babysitting available. French, Spanish, Italian spoken.

TUSCON Map 12

Once known as the sleepy desert town of Old Pueblo, Tucson now has a population of over 600,000. Spanish, Mexican, American Indian, and pioneer influences, combined with a sunny, dry climate, draw increasing numbers of tourists from October to May.

Area attractions include the Sonora Desert Museum, an outstanding natural history facility and zoo; the Tucson Museum of Art; the Arizona Heritage Center; the Flandrau Planetarium; the Mission San Xavier del Bac; the Saguaro National Monument and Colossal Cave; Old Tucson, a combination western movie studio and theme park; the Kitt Peak National Observatory; and Tombstone, an infamous spot in the history of the Wild West.

Tucson is located in southeastern Arizona, 118 miles southeast of Phoenix and 63 miles north of Nogales, Mexico. Its status as a winter resort has resulted in a wide variety of attractive accommodations, quite unlike the situation 100 years ago, when a room in the town's best hotel was typically occupied by a dozen drunk or hung-over men and the washing facilities consisted of a ten-foot trough sink that emptied into the street!

Also recommended: Received too late for a full write-up was a report on **Peppertrees B&B** (724 East University Boulevard 85719; 602–622–7167), a turn-of-the-century Southwestern home two blocks from the university campus.

Information please: Several B&Bs have recently opened in Tucson and reports are needed. **El Presidio** in the historic district downtown offers elegant Victorian guest rooms highlighted with antiques and collectibles looking onto a flower-filled courtyard (297 North Main Avenue 85701; 602–623–6151). **La Posada Del Valle**, near the University of Arizona is a Santa Fe-style adobe with 1920s era decor (1640 North Campbell Avenue 85719; 602–795–3840).

In the cooler mountains altitudes (3000-5000 feet) about 60 miles south of Tucson, near the Mexican border, are several small appealing guest ranches we'd like to hear more about. The **Circle Z**, one of Arizona's oldest guest ranches, welcomes families and singles alike to its handsome rooms with Mexican decor, its hearty cuisine, and its twice daily rides (Patagonia 85624; 602–287–2091). **Rancho de la Osa** is over 200 years old, with many of its original buildings still in use; guest rooms are more modern but are built the traditional way of adobe, with walls as much as three feet thick. The ranch's pure-bred quarter horses are the key attraction, but the 200 species of birds seen here come in a close second for many guests (P.O. Box 1, Sasabe 85633; 602–823–4257). The **Grapevine Canyon Ranch** offers a taste of the Old West, with day and overnight pack trips into the mountains, but also offers riding as an optional extra, for guests unsure of their equestrian abilities (P.O. Box 302, Pearce 85625; 602–826–3185).

A note for those who like it hot: Tucson room rates drop as precipitously as the summer temperatures skyrocket!

Arizona Inn
2200 East Elm Street 85719

Tel: (602) 325–1541
(800) 421–1093

Mrs. Isabella Greenway, builder of the Arizona Inn, was a woman of no small ability or determination. Her wide-ranging projects covered everything from two terms in the Congress (as Arizona's only congresswoman) to providing a sheltered workshop for disabled World War I veterans. She also oversaw the construction of numerous homes around the country for her family, so when she decided to build the Arizona Inn in 1930, she had some very definite ideas in mind. One aim was to have it as homelike as possible, enabling guests to enjoy as much privacy as desired. One small construction oversight was noted during the grand opening dinner dance: She had forgotten to provide a men's room for her male guests! Although the inn was 2½ miles from town at the time, and the country sunk into depression, the establishment was an immediate success.

Today the inn is owned and managed by Mrs. Greenway's son John, who oversaw its modernization in the 1970s. The staff is nearly as stable as the ownership; many have worked at the inn for over 10 years, and several for over 30! The inn is no longer isolated in the desert; an attractive residential neighborhood and the University of Arizona have grown up around its well-planted site. Although the softly pink-stuccoed outside walls of the spreading one- and two-story structure convey its Southwestern character, the interiors have a more traditional look of homey elegance, with comfortable slipcovered couches highlighted by European antiques. The cuisine is as traditional as the decor—well prepared and served, but hardly adventurous.

"An ideal place to rest and relax in a traditional southwestern resort; not for the thrill-a-minute set." *(ST)* More comments please.

Open All year.
Rooms 10 suites, 70 doubles—all with full private bath, telephone, radio, TV, desk, air-conditioning. Many with patios.
Facilities Restaurant, lounge with pianist, library/living room. 14 acres with flower gardens, heated 60-foot swimming pool, 2 tennis courts. Golf nearby.
Location 3 m to downtown. ½ m N of Speedway and ¼ m E of Campbell.
Credit cards Amex, MC, Visa.
Rates Room only, $106–400 suite, $64–128 double, $52–118 single. Add (per person) $9.50 for B&B, $30 for MAP, $40 for full board. 16% service additional. Reduced rates for children under 9. Extra person in room, $10. Alc breakfast, $5–7; alc lunch, $7; alc dinner, $18. Prix fixe lunch, $9; dinner, $18.
Extras Wheelchair accessible. Airport/station pickups, $7.50. Cribs, babysitting available. Spanish, Portuguese, Taiwanese spoken.

Flying V Ranch
6800 North Flying V Ranch Road 85715

Tel: (602) 299–4900
(602) 299–4372

Set at the mouth of Ventana Canyon, bordering the Coronado National Forest, is the oldest guest ranch in the Tucson area, owned by the Shields family for three generations, and now run by Reed and Tilly Shields. For the past decade Reed and Tilly have been gradually restoring and updating the cabins. In 1988 they renovated the ranchhouse and have just reopened its kitchen and dining room. The Shieldses have a very low-key approach to vacationing and describe the Flying V as an "anti-resort."

"This ranch is the way an Arizona guest ranch should be operated: no glitzy trailblazer breakfasts, no ridiculous dude ranch ambience, no phony cowboy attitudes. Instead, guests find an atmosphere of quiet, unspoiled graciousness. Each of the well-maintained cabins has fully equipped kitchens, living/dining area, bedroom, and full bath. The quiet ambience of the ranch lends itself perfectly to reading, writing, hiking, or simply relaxing— no organized activities of any kind to interfere with guests' privacy. Unlike the gaudy and overdone guest ranches so common in this area, the Flying V is the only one that maintains the flavor and spirit of a classic guest ranch." *(George Kutlenios)* Rates include a continental breakfast.

Open All year.
Rooms 4 1- and 2-bedroom housekeeping cabins—all with full private bath, telephone, radio, TV, desk, air-conditioning, kitchenette. Some with screened porch.

Facilities Restaurant, living room, library, screened porch, recreation room with billiards, Ping-Pong. 90 acres with heated swimming pool, hiking, bird-watching. Golf, tennis, horseback riding nearby.
Location Sabino Canyon, 15 m NE of Tucson in Catalina foothills.
Restrictions "Children must be well-supervised as we are not child-proofed."
Credit cards None accepted.
Rates B&B, $110 2-bedroom cabin, $60–85 1-bedroom cabin. Extra adult in room, $7.50; child under 14, $5. 3-night minimum stay. Weekly, monthly rates.
Extras Airport/station pickups. Spanish spoken. Some pets permitted with prior approval, $5.

Hacienda del Sol

Tel: (602) 299–1501

5601 N. Hacienda del Sol Road 85718

From its construction in 1929 until 1941, the Hacienda del Sol was operated as an exclusive girls' school. With the onset of war, it became difficult to assemble a teaching staff, and the facility was converted into a guest ranch. The Hacienda reached its peak of celebrity in the early 1950s, when it played host to both well-known actors—Clark Gable and Spencer Tracy—and sports figures. By the 1970s the Hacienda had become a mostly private club, largely forgotten by all but its membership.

Now dwarfed by the adjacent Western La Paloma complex, the Hacienda still proclaims itself to be "The Best-Kept Secret in Tucson." Under the new management of longtime hotelier Frank Fine, the resort is awakening from a period of stagnation and now offers high-quality food and entertainment. The cuisine on most nights is elegant French, except on Thursdays, when nonresident guests reserve a week ahead to join the lively chuck wagon barbeque. The decor, although freshened up by the new owners, is still laden with mission-style charm—adobe walls, hand-hewn *vigas* (beams), and flowering patios. *(PHJ)*

"Very nice location, beautifully renovated room. High prices for average food though." *(DN)* More comments, please.

Open Oct. 1–May 31.
Rooms 3 1–2 bedroom casitas, 6 suites, 12 doubles, 6 singles—most with full private bath, telephone, TV, desk, air-conditioning. 4 singles with maximum of 2 people sharing 1 bath. Most suites with fireplace, patio, kitchenette and/or wet bar. Casitas with fireplace, kitchen, patio.
Facilities Restaurant with bar; lobby with fireplace, library, games; game building with entertainment, movies, dancing. 30 acres with heated swimming pool, hot tub, tennis court, stable with trail rides, naturalist lecture/tours, croquet, exercise room. Golf nearby.
Location 10 m NE of Tucson. From Sunrise Dr. turn S on Hacienda del Sol Rd.
Restrictions Smoking restricted in some areas.
Credit cards Amex, Discover, MC, Visa.
Rates Room only, $240–275 casita, $75–150 suite, $50–90 double, $40–80 single. Discount for 8-night stay. Continental breakfast, $5.25; prix fixe lunch, $9; prix fixe dinner, $16. Cowboy barbeque, Mexican fiesta nights.
Extras Wheelchair accessible. Airport/station pickups, $5. Cribs, babysitting available.

Lazy K Bar Guest Ranch

Tel: (602) 744–3050

8401 North Scenic Drive 85743

Nobody comes to the Lazy K for the decor—or for the food. But if you want gorgeous views down into the Santa Cruz valley and up into the

Saguaro National Monument and the Tucson and Catalina mountains, excellent trail rides for all abilities, gorgeous hiking trails, plus home-style cooking and comfortable accommodation at reasonable all-inclusive rates, this could well be the spot for you. Set at 2,300 feet, the ranch has been owned since 1975 by Rosemary Blowitz and William Scott and is managed by Carol Moore, who reports that "The ranch is noted for its relaxed, informal atmosphere—blue jeans, comfortable shirts, and sturdy shoes are the usual dress around here. Most of our guests are active people who enjoy the outdoors; children are very welcome and are included in all activities." Unlike some of the larger dude ranches, the Lazy K does not provide separate supervised children's programs; this is a plus for some and a drawback for others. *(CT)* More comments, please.

Open Sept. 1–June 15.
Rooms 20 suites and doubles—all with full private bath, desk, air-conditioning. Located in individual cottages.
Facilities Dining room, living room with fireplace, TV room, bar (bring your own liquor), library, Ping-Pong, billiards, patio. Square dancing 2–3 nights weekly. 160 acres with heated swimming pool, hot tub, 2 lighted tennis courts, horseback riding, shuffleboard, horseshoes. Golf nearby.
Location 16 m W of Tucson. Exit I-10 at Ina Rd.; go W to Silverbell. Turn right (N) on Silverbell Rd.; left (W) on Pima Farm Rd. to ranch at intersection with Scenic Dr.
Credit cards Amex, DC, MC, Visa.
Rates Full board, $160–200 suite, $150–190 double, $95–130 single. Extra adult in room, $60; child 12–17, $35; child under 12, $20. 15% service additional. 3-night minimum stay. 10% discount for 1-month or longer stays.
Extras Free airport/station pickups. Cribs available. Spanish spoken.

The Lodge on the Desert
306 North Alvernon Way, P.O. Box 42500 85733

Tel: (602) 325–3366
(800) 456–5634

The Lininger family has owned and operated the Lodge for more than 50 years. Most of the casita-style guest rooms are on the ground floor set among landscaped grounds.

"This place has been in operation for about 35 years and has retained its original flavor. While it is now in midtown Tucson, it is on ample ground with scattered cottages. The food is good and I think that almost everyone will find it charming." *(Paul H. Jones)*

"One leaves the drab world of Alvernon Way behind, traveling through sort of a time warp as one passes through the gates into the lodge grounds. The real world seems far away. The walkways are lined with tall cacti, citrus trees drooping with oranges and grapefruit, and other shrubbery unknown to this Hoosier. Towering palms mark the corners of the pool. The rooms have that magical Southwestern quality, spacious and serene, with high timbered ceilings, tiled floors and corner beehive fireplaces in which a mesquite fire will glow, flaring up intermittently through the night. We had a dressing room and a large bathroom with a mile of counter space, a wall of mirrors, bright lights and lots of thick white towels. The staff went out of its way to be friendly and helpful, and our breakfast, served overlooking a little patio where birds were clustering around a feeder, was very pleasant. At least one second floor room has a view of the mountains, a private deck, a small private pool and a fireplace—any room here is lovely and unforgettable, but that one would be doubly so." *(Cynthia Snowden)*

Open All year.
Rooms 6 suites, 31 doubles, 3 singles—38 with full private bath, 2 with shower only. All with telephone, TV, desk, air-conditioning; some with radio. 2–5 rooms share patios.
Facilities 3 dining rooms, cocktail lounge, lobby with library, TV. 6 acres with lawn games, heated swimming pool. 30 m from downhill skiing. 5-min. drive from 2 18-hole golf courses, 24 tennis courts, and 10 racquetball courts.
Location 4 m E of downtown Tucson, near the University of Arizona campus.
Credit cards Amex, CB, DC, MC, Visa.
Rates B&B, $70–159 suite, $52–131 double, $48–119 single. Extra person in room, $10. MAP, full board rates on request. Suggested service for housekeeping, $1.50 per day, double. Family rates in summer. Holiday package rates. Prix fixe lunch, $10; dinner, $15. Alc breakfast, $6; alc lunch, $8–11; alc dinner, $30.
Extras Some rooms equipped for the disabled. Airport/station pickups, $8–15. Small dogs permitted by prior arrangement. Cribs available. French, Spanish spoken.

Tanque Verde Ranch
14301 East Speedway 85748

Tel: (602) 296–6275

Rafael Carillo founded Tanque Verde Ranch in the 1880s, on a Spanish land grant; it became a guest ranch in the 1930s. Owned by the Cote family for 30 years, the facilities have gradually been expanded to provide *everything* one might expect in a Western ranch resort, combining luxurious surroundings and Western hospitality. One otherwise satisfied guest mentioned that their facilities (particularly the trail rides) are sometimes overtaxed during winter/spring school vacations, and recommended avoiding these periods.

"During the 20 years that we've been coming to TVR, it has changed radically from its origins as a fairly rustic place for adults interested in riding, but the Cote family has continued to maintain the hospitable atmosphere that brings many of us back year after year. Being adjacent to a million acres of wide-open public lands means that there is ample opportunity to find peace and solitude. The food is delicious, especially the home-baked bread and pastries." *(Mr. & Mrs. Paul Barnes)*

"Because it backs up onto Saguaro National Park, this old resort has not been gobbled up by urban sprawl. When you arrive, you sense that this ranch has not been polished, groomed, and soaked in water like so many newer desert resorts. Some plantings are labeled and look like they have been there forever. The whole place has a down-home, comfortable feel—rooms are done in Southwest comfortable, rather than Southwest decorator-style. The pool area is adequate, although the Jacuzzi/steam room is in a separate building, a bit dark and damp for my taste. Well cared for horses are the highlight here; the corral is built in 'old west' style of intertwined mesquite" *(SHW)*

Open All year.
Rooms 13 suites, 47 doubles, 2 cottages—all with private bath, telephones, desk, air-conditioning. Many with fireplaces, refrigerators, patios.
Facilities Dining room, living room, porch, health spa with indoor swimming pool, whirlpool, sauna, exercise room. 640 acres with 2 heated swimming pools, hot tub, 5 tennis courts, horseback riding, pack trips, nature walks, shuffleboard, square dancing, horseshoes, bingo, bridge, Ping-Pong. Supervised children's program.

Location 12 m E of Tucson. Take Speedway E, past Wilmot and Houghton Rds. to ranch.
Credit cards Amex, MC, Visa.
Rates Full board and use of all facilities, $210–285 suite (double occupancy), $175–265 double, $150–235 single. Extra person in room, $55. Cribs, $10 per week. 15% service additional.
Extras Airport/station pickups. Spanish, French, Japanese spoken.

White Stallion Ranch   *Tel:* (602) 297–0252
9251 West Twin Peaks Road 85743

The White Stallion is a casual, family-style ranch, owned and operated by the True family—Allen, Cynthia, Russell, and Michael—since 1965. Guests return year after year, often timing their trips to meet friends made on their last visit. The ranch offers a full range of activities—trail rides, swimming, and tennis, as well as weekly rodeos, desert cookouts, and Indian oven dinners.

"A stay here is a perfect vacation for the whole family. Whether looking out over the cactus garden or reading by the cactus lamps Cynthia has placed everywhere, it's relaxing and comfortable, yet offers lots to do. My son loves the Saturday night rodeo and steak barbeques, my mother enjoys the happy-hour hors d'oeuvres, while my favorite is the outdoor buffet lunch. All the guests fight over the ranch cookies. We debate about leaving the ranch, but we loved our visits to the Desert Museum, the San Xavier del Bac Mission, and shopping in Nogales." *(Carlene Bonner)*

"Although we ride only on our visits here, we love the challenge of Lookout Pass and Suicide Ridge but are comforted by the knowledge that our hosts place great importance on the safety of their guests (unlike some other spots we visited). The food is plentiful and excellently prepared. The staff is friendly and anxious to please. The happy hour is a relaxing way to greet old friends and make new ones. The Trues make a point of introducing all new arrivals at the family-style dinner hour, so no one feels isolated. Rooms are comfortable and clean, with lots of fresh towels, reading lights, and closet space." *(Chandler & Patricia Baldwin, also Al & Lucy Meade)*
More comments, please.

Open Oct. 1–April 30.
Rooms 8 suites, 12 doubles, 8 singles—26 with full private bath, 2 with shower only. All with desk, fan. Rooms in main house and casitas.
Facilities Dining room, bar, living room, family/game/TV room. Grounds cover 20 acres of 3,000-acre ranch. Petting zoo, exotic birds, shuffleboard, volleyball, heated swimming pool, hot tub, horseback riding, hayrides, 2 tennis courts.
Location 17 m NW of Tucson. Exit I-10 at Cortarto; N on Silverbell Rd. to Twin Peaks Rd.
Credit cards None accepted.
Rates Full board, per person, $99–110 suite, $86–102 double, $108–118 single. Extra person in room, $70–80. No charge for children under 2. Weekly rates.
Extras Free airport/station pickups for 4-night minimum stay. Cribs available.

Arkansas

The Heartstone Inn, Eureka Springs

Rugged mountain individualism is one of the first things that comes to mind when Arkansas is mentioned. Although the Ozarks are a very old mountain chain and not terribly high, the terrain is rugged and transportation was, until quite recently, very difficult. Distinctive crafts, cuisine, and culture developed as a result, much of which has been preserved through the Ozark Folk Center, located in Mountain View (see listing). Many famous springs dot this region of northwestern Arkansas as well, particularly Hot Springs National Park, 55 miles southwest of Little Rock, and Eureka Springs, in the north.

Information please: Little Rock, the state capital, is a clean and modern city; we appreciate any recommendations for hotels or inns of character here, other than the cloned facilities of the major chains. In fact, we would be pleased to receive more recommendations for this whole state. If you'd like to spend the night in jail on your way between Dallas and Little Rock—and pay for the privilege—try the **Old Washington Jail** just off I-30. Built as a jail in the late 1800s and converted into a B&B in 1982, historic convict graffiti has been combined with artful country Victorian decor here; rates are very reasonable (Old Washington State Park, Washington 71862; 501–983–2790). Another interesting possibility about 60 miles northwest of Little Rock is **Tanyard Springs**, a cluster of log cabins, rustically handsome yet with every modern convenience, in the woods atop Petit Jean Mountain; rates include all meals, most with a strong Cajun accent (Rte. 3, Box 335, Morrilton 72110; 501–727–5200 or 800–533–1450). Reports please!

Rates do not include 7% state sales tax.

EUREKA SPRINGS 72632 Map 6

Eureka Springs is the site of natural springs first discovered by the Indians, then lost for decades until rediscovered in the 1850s by a local doctor. The curative powers of the spring waters soon became renowned, and by the 1880s this hillside town boasted dozens of hotels. As the decades passed and medicine advanced, the town was forgotten and its Victorian charms thus preserved. The local Historic District Commission now stands guard to make sure that nothing is changed without its approval.

Local attractions include dozens of art galleries and mountain craft shops, the steam train ride through the Ozarks, the Passion Play, and the Pine Mountain Jamboree. Beaver Lake and the Buffalo and White rivers are nearby for swimming, boating, fishing, and canoeing.

Eureka Springs is located in northwest Arkansas, 50 miles northeast of Fayetteville, 200 miles northwest of Little Rock, and 100 miles south of Springfield, Missouri. It is best reached via Highways 62 or 23.

Information please: The **Old Homestead**, once a boarding house, even perhaps a bordello, is a century-old stone house across from the historical museum, restored as a four-guest-room B&B (82 Armstrong; 501–253–7501).

Dairy Hollow House
515 Spring Street

Tel: (501) 253–7444

When the doors of Dairy Hollow House opened in 1981, it was one of the first bed & breakfasts in the state. Since then Crescent Dragonwagon (she adopted the name after moving to Arkansas at age 18)and her husband Ned Shank have developed a nationwide reputation for their "nouveau Zarks" cuisine, combining classic French recipes with the Ozarks' best regional cooking. Given the number of both B&Bs and restored buildings now thriving in Eureka Springs, it's clear to see that Ned (a former president of the Eureka Springs Preservation Society) and Crescent have successfully demonstrated that tourism and historic preservation can be allies, not enemies.

The Dairy Hollow House now encompasses the Farmhouse in the Hollow, a fully renovated 1880s farmhouse decorated with handmade quilts and period antiques; Suites on Spring, housing two suites with fireplaces and private hot tub; and the Restaurant at Dairy Hollow, on the garden level of Suites on Spring. The central reception area is here also, next to the Restaurant.

In addition to her inn-keeping abilities, Crescent Dragonwagon is a children's book and cookbook author. Meals here are a highlight, and breakfast specialties (delivered to your room) include fresh fruit or juice, German baked pancakes with fresh berry sauce, or perhaps eggs Mornay and chicken-apple sausages, accompanied by homemade jams and jellies, gingerbread muffins, or blueberry coffee cake. Dinner can be a six-course repast or the more modest pre-theater supper; fresh fruits and vegetables (either wild or cultivated) are used whenever possible, and a typical menu might include mushrooms diablo in phyllo, mixed salad, and homemade bread, black-eyed pea soup, rainbow trout poached in white wine with zucchini and dill, fresh vegetables, and dark and white chocolate cream torte for dessert.

"If we were serious about world peace, we'd take a up a collection to send the head of nations, a few at a time, to the DHH. It's impossible to stay tense there. Exquisite food, unobtrusive and attentive staff, graceful surroundings, and fine quiet touches of comfort and convenience make it an extraordinary experience. Crescent and Ned are splendid innkeepers; we suggested a few minor improvements—a hook for robes in the bath, a tray for taking drinks to the porch or deck, and both are now in place." *(Judith Faust)*

Open Closed Jan. 3 through Mar. 15. Restaurant closed Mon.–Wed., also entire month of Oct.
Rooms 3 suites, 2 doubles—all with private bath and/or shower, telephone, air-conditioning, fireplace, kitchenette, coffee maker. 3 with desk. 1 suite with Jacuzzi.
Facilities Parlor with games, library; dining room; lobby. Suites have private living rooms. 2 acres with flower gardens, woods, hot tub.
Location 1 m from town.
Credit cards Amex, DC, Discover, MC, Visa.
Rates B&B, $115–145 suite, $95–105 double, $90–100 single, plus optional $2–5 daily for service. Extra person in room, $10. 2-3 night minimum weekends/holidays. Off-season discount for longer stays. Prix fixe dinner, $14 for Peasant's Feast, $34 for six-course meal, plus 15% service.
Extras Restaurant is wheelchair accessible. Crib, babysitting available.

The Heartstone Inn

Tel: (501) 253–8916

35 Kingshighway (Highway 62B)

Innkeepers Iris and Bill Simantel have owned this Victorian B&B inn since 1985 and have decorated the rooms with antique and reproduction furniture and decorative country touches, including plenty of hearts. In addition to the rooms at the main inn, the Simantels now offer accommodation at two neighboring cottages—one a pine-paneled country cottage, the other a small, more elegant Victorian home.

Quite a number of the Simantels' guests wrote to recommend this inn, all unanimous on the warmth of their hosts, the immaculate facilities, the high-quality service, the delicious breakfasts, and the convenient location.

"The Simantels have recently built a large dining wing at the rear of the inn. Each morning we entered to find our own private table complete with place cards and white linens. We loved the large assortment of teas and regular and decaffinated coffee. Fresh orange juice was served with a hot entrée accompanied by fresh baked muffins and sliced fruit, elegantly presented. The inn is very quiet with lots of birds singing and no traffic sounds; the parking is reserved with excellent lighting for security. Our room was spotless, and the bath had plenty of hot water." *(Carol Hawksley)*

"The exterior of the inn is inviting and colorful. Hanging pots of Boston ferns sway lazily above the long front porch, and huge crocks spill over with salmon-colored geraniums. Our room, the Bridal Suite, was decorated with an old lace wedding dress and dried bridal bouquet; a queen-size bed was covered with a red, white, and blue quilt in the double wedding-band pattern. I enjoyed a peek into the other guest rooms, which included a pink one with white wicker furniture, another in soothing shades of peach and pale blue, and still another decorated in a patriotic theme with lots of country crafts and a white iron bed.

"Breakfast, served at 8:30, included a soufflé of eggs, cheese, tomatoes, and sherried mushrooms; Ozark smoked ham; date bread; and fresh fruit, and was filling enough that we skipped lunch." *(Mr. & Mrs. J.D. Rolfe)* "Iris cooks and Bill serves; both wear Victorian-style clothes during the morning hours." *(Robin Diven)*

Open January–mid-December.
Rooms 1 2-bedroom cottage, 1 1-bedroom cottage, 1 suite, 9 doubles, all with full private bath, TV, radio, air-conditioning, ceiling fans. 4 rooms in annex.
Facilities Dining/breakfast rooms, guest lounge with piano, stereo, games, veranda, deck. Off-street parking.
Location Historic district, 4 blocks to downtown. City bus stop near house.
Restrictions No smoking. Children welcome in annex rooms.
Credit cards MC, Visa.
Rates Room only, $60–75 cottage. B&B, $60–70 suite, $50–60 double. Extra person in room, $12. Reduced charge for children under 5. 2-3 night minimum stay on holiday, special-event weekends.
Extras Crib available.

HELENA 72342   Map 6

Edwardian Inn   *Tel:* (501) 338–9155
317 South Biscoe

In 1904 cotton broker William A. Short built his family their dream house at the then-extraordinary cost of over $100,000. The Shorts were not the only prosperous family in town; Helena is known for its historic houses, both antebellum and postbellum. Most of the building's original beauty, such as the fine hardware and the beveled and leaded glass in the transoms, was uncovered in the restoration, along with its handsome oak paneling and intricate woodwork.

"Our room was furnished with period pieces and appointed with modern conveniences. The air conditioner was both effective and quiet; the bath was modern and in excellent condition. The restoration retained all of the original features, including the woodwork in the entrance hall and the inlaid wood 'carpets.' " *(Ronald C. Eastes)*

"All the rooms are beautiful, but ours had a bed with a headboard made from a church pew, an enormous bath, a glassed-in sitting area with a window seat, and access to the balcony porch. The delicious continental breakfast included homemade cinnamon rolls and carrot cake." *(Sally Garrison)* "Especially enjoyable is the sunny kitchen/dining room, complete with linen tablecloths and napkins, and fresh flowers." *(Margaret Holaway)*

"Just as you've described it. Try dinner at Evelyn's Southern Charm (922 Miller Street). Evelyn is a warm friendly hostess—we'd give it an 'A'." *(Yvonne Miller)*

Open All year.
Rooms 3 suites, 9 doubles, all with full private bath, telephone, radio, TV, air-conditioning, fan. Some with desk, fireplace.

Facilities Breakfast/sunroom. 5 m to lake for fishing, swimming.
Location SE AR, on Mississippi River, 70 m S of Memphis, TN.
Credit cards Amex, MC, Visa.
Rates B&B, $59 suite, $50 double, $44–50 single. Extra person in room, $10. Children under 12 free in parents' room. 10% senior discount.
Extras Wheelchair accessible. Small pets permitted. Crib, babysitting available.

HOT SPRINGS   Map 6

A visit to Hot Springs will allow you to take your place in a long line of tradition; records indicate that the Indians used this site 10,000 years ago. The springs reached their height of popularity in the 19th century, and the area became a national park in 1921. Although not as popular as they once were, the bath houses are still well worth a visit; the naturally hot water will soothe your aching muscles after a day of hiking or horseback riding in the surrounding Zig Zag Mountains. Several lakes—Catherine, Hamilton, and Ouachita—are nearby for all water sports.

Hot Springs is located in central Arkansas, 55 miles southwest of Little Rock.

Williams House   *Tel:* (501) 624–4275
420 Quapaw, Hot Springs National Park 71901

Listed on the National Register of Historic Places, this imposing 1890 brownstone-and-brick Victorian has been owned since 1980 by Mary and Gary Riley. Rooms are decorated with family antiques and lots of plants. Mary notes that "attention to detail and comfort are important to us, as is guest privacy." Rates include full breakfast; traditionalists will be relieved to know that eggs with ham, bacon, or sausage are always available; more adventurous palates will want to try the daily special, ranging from eggs Benedict to pecan waffles. *(BR)*

"Mary and Gary Riley are wonderful hosts. The house is filled with antiques the Rileys have gathered, and the food was excellent." *(Heather Fletcher)* "One of the highlights of a visit here is in the evening, when Mary tells us what the next day's breakfast special will be, and we choose our menu." *(Norman Garneau)* "Despite a late arrival, Mrs. Riley directed me to an excellent restaurant nearby. The Rileys have just the right touch, enough attention to be accommodating but not annoying." *(Gary Milam)*

Open All year. Sometimes closed in January.
Rooms 2 suites, 4 doubles—4 with private bath and/or shower, 2 with maximum of 4 people sharing bath. All with radio, most with air-conditioning. 2 rooms in carriage house.
Facilities Reception hall with fireplace, baby grand piano; reading room with games, TV; porches. ½ acre with patios, picnic table. Indoor heated pool at YMCA next door. Walking distance to Bath House Row. Several lakes nearby for fishing, swimming, boating.
Location 4 blocks from center, at corner of Orange and Quapaw. From Bath House Row, go S on Central Ave., right on Prospect, left on Orange.
Restrictions No smoking in common rooms. No children under 7.
Credit cards MC, Visa.
Rates B&B, $60–80 suite, $55–75 double, $45–55 single. Extra person in room, $10

$85 family rate. 10% senior discount midweek. 2-night minimum holiday/spring weekends.

Extras Pets permitted with advance notice in carriage house.

MOUNTAIN VIEW 72560   Map 6

The Commercial Hotel
Courthouse Square, P.O. Box 72

Tel: (501) 269–4383

It's hard to imagine how isolated Mountain View was until the beginning of the 1970s—no paved roads, no trains, no scheduled buses. Then, in 1973, the Ozark Folk Center opened, bringing with it improved transportation. Dedicated to preserving the local culture, the center offers daily demonstrations of indigenous crafts, music and dance, storytelling, and cooking. The perfect balance to a day spent absorbing cultural history is a good dose of natural history, exploring the fantastic formations in the Blanchard Springs Caverns, 15 miles northwest of town, in the Ozark National Forest.

Back in the old days a man traveling on business was a "commercial traveler"; an establishment that catered to such travelers was a commercial hotel. Today, of course, the warm and inviting Commercial Hotel, whose full name includes the subtitle, "A Vintage Guesthouse," doesn't seem very businesslike at all, with its relaxed and welcoming atmosphere, handmade curtains and dust ruffles, original iron beds and dressers, and immaculate baths. In 1982 Todd and Andrea Budy bought and fully renovated the hotel, now listed on the National Register of Historic Places. Sharing the hotel is the Hearthstone Bakery, "famous for four or five blocks around" for its freshly baked breads, pastries, cookies, and light lunches, all using fresh eggs, quality grains and flours, and real chocolate and nuts.

Mountain View is a mecca for local musicians, many of whom congregate on the hotel's front porch—even the local tax assessor is a lunch-time regular. Summer weekends, especially Saturday nights, see many outdoor concerts and dancing on the courthouse lawn.

"Nice clean rooms with pretty curtains and spreads, courteous and friendly staff. In the morning, wonderful smells arise from the bakery downstairs—you can't wait to get there for a Danish and coffee." *(Katherine Anderson)*

Open All year. Open November–April by advance reservation only.
Rooms 3 suites, 5 doubles—3 with private shower, 5 rooms share 2 baths. Some with desk, all with air-conditioning.
Facilities Lobby, bakery with dining area, gift shop, wraparound porch with frequent live music. 1 shaded acre. Pool, tennis, hiking, caves, rock-climbing nearby. Short drive to White River, Sylamore Creek, Greers Ferry Lake, for fishing, swimming, float trips.
Location N central AR, Stone Cty. 100 m N of Little Rock, 150 m W of Memphis, TN. Hwys. 66, 9, 5/14 all lead to Courthouse Sq.; Inn on sq. at corner of Washington and Peabody Sts. 1 m from Folk Center.
Restrictions No smoking. "Dry county."
Credit cards Amex.
Rates Room only, $41–46 suite, $29–34 double. Extra person in room, $4. No charge for children under 6 in parents' room.
Extras Limited wheelchair accessibility. Cribs available. Very limited French.

California

Babbling Brook Inn, Santa Cruz

California is the nation's third largest state and the most populous. Its terrain is incredibly diverse, offering virtually every possible land- and seascape, much of great interest to tourists. Though the clock puts them three hours behind the East Coast, Californians tend to think of themselves as being ahead of the rest of the country. Many of the country's dominant trends got their start here and spread eastward across the country—not the least of them being the popularity of the small hotels and inns described in this guide. Small wonder then that this is our longest chapter.

There is one category for which we'd really like to request more recommendations: inns that actually *welcome* children! We're all in favor of romantic adult getaways, but there are regions of California—the Wine Country, for example—where there is hardly a place that will tolerate children, let alone welcome them. Perhaps as a reaction to this, a law was recently passed in California making it illegal for hotels and inns to discriminate on the basis of age. As a result, when we note under Restrictions "No children under 12," this has no legal bearing whatsoever. It is rather an indication given to us by the inns involved that they feel their property is more appropriate for older children. We have mixed feelings on this whole subject; sometimes a kid-free atmosphere is valid, other times we feel its a cheap substitute for proper soundproofing on the innkeepers' part. Comments and reports, please!

In general, there's not too much seasonal variation in the rates of California's inns and hotels, although they do tend to be 10 to 20% higher on weekends in most areas. Exceptions are the North Coast region, where midweek rates are lower off-season (November to March), and the desert areas, where brutal summer heat cuts rates in half.

The California Office of Tourism divides the state into 12 distinct regions; we've noted them below, along with a few annotations and subdivisions of our own. At the end of each region, we list the towns with recommended inns and hotels, to help you in using this chapter. For more details, call the tourist office for their excellent free 200-page guide book, *Discover the Californias* (800–862–2543).

When reading the entries, you'll see these regional divisions noted in the "Location" heading for each entry. Check back to these thumbnail sketches if, like us, you are liable to get Monterey mixed up with Mendocino.

Finally, please note that most of the greater Los Angeles area (excluding Orange County) is listed under Los Angeles, so you don't need to look through the entire chapter to find out what's available in this most sprawling of cities.

Rates do not include state tax of 8% or additional local taxes.

Shasta-Cascade   This relatively undiscovered region in north-central and northeast California offers a dramatic introduction to California's wilderness and geologic past. Best known is the Whiskeytown-Shasta-Trinity National Recreation Area, near 14,000-foot Mt. Shasta, where you can backpack or rent a houseboat on Lake Shasta. At Lassen Volcanic National Park, see the strange formations and caves left by wide-ranging volcanic activity. Even more unusual is Lava Beds National Monument, near the Oregon border, where the Modoc Indians made their last stand, using volcanic rubble for protection. This area fronts on Tule Lake, where over one million waterfowl visit each fall and huge populations of bald eagles spend the winter. At the southern edge of this region, take Route 70 through Quincy and the spectacular Feather River Canyon.

North Coast   This region has three distinct subregions. The **Wine Country** is located northeast of San Francisco, along Routes 29 and 12. In addition to over 200 wineries with free tours and tastings, there are rolling green hills, mud baths in Calistoga, gliding, and ballooning. Not to be missed is Petaluma Adobe, a restored 1840s headquarters of the Vallejo agricultural empire.

Not surprisingly, food is taken as seriously here as wine, and the area is noted for its many outstanding restaurants. If you'll be visiting on a weekend, ask your host to make your dinner reservations when you book your room. Keep in mind that the Napa Valley, in particular, surpasses Disneyland in popularity with tourists; unless heavy traffic is your thing, avoid fall weekends when everyone goes wine-tasting!

The **Coast** area on Highway 1 north of San Francisco includes world-class scenery, shorelines, and accommodations. Near Jenner the road cuts through steep green slopes that sweep down to the sea. Close by is Fort Ross, an 1812 Russian trading post, complete with onion-domed Orthodox church. To the north are tiny towns and perfect beachcombing shores near Sea Ranch and Gualala, Elk, Little River, and trendy Mendocino. The area then becomes more remote and wild as it passes through Westport. One recommended side trip for the experienced driver is the back road to

Ferndale (from South Fork past Cape Mendocino), which winds up high bluffs with superb ocean views.

The Redwood Empire on Highway 101 stretches from Piercy to Crescent City. It's worth putting up with the cutesy tourist offerings to see the real scenery. Especially recommended are Avenue of the Giants near Pepperwood; Big Tree at Prairie City, north of Orick; and the Jedediah Smith area east of Crescent City.

San Francisco Bay Area   Here and elsewhere along the coast, fog often shrouds the area in spring and early summer. To some this means unwanted cool weather only miles away from a sunny, warm interior. To others this bespeaks the special romance and mystery of the area. Although few cities can surpass San Francisco for culture, shopping, and sightseeing (see description in listings), there is more to the Bay Area. Across the Golden Gate Bridge are Sausalito and Tiburon, both artists' colonies with unusual homes clinging to the cliffsides. Nearby Muir Woods provides an easy introduction to the giant redwoods. The East Bay includes Berkeley with its hillside residential area, lively university district, and excellent botanical garden. To the south, stroll the pretty seaside boardwalk at Santa Cruz, and visit Año Nuevo State Reserve to see lolling elephant seals and rocks covered with fossilized seashells.

Central Valley   Extremely hot during the summer, this region offers comparatively little of interest to tourists. Extending south from Chico through the central portion of California to Bakersfield, this area has over 11 million acres of rich farmland, and produces an astonishing variety of fruits, nuts, and vegetables. Worth seeing: the Chinese temple in Oroville; Old Sacramento (take the walking tour); and Route 160 from Sacramento to Isleton which winds along dikes, past almond and fruit groves, and through Locke, a bizarre, two-block, two-level town built in 1915 by Chinese workers. In the south, Bakersfield is near California's oil fields and is known as the state's country music center.

Gold Country   Gold mining brought thousands of people to this region in the 1850s, but these days the only thing that is mined are the tourists. Overcrowded with visitors in the summer, this area nevertheless has retained a genuine Old West flavor and should not be missed. Be sure to get off Route 49 to some of the smaller towns like Murphys and Volcano; see nearby Grinding Rocks State Park where the Mi-Wok Indians lived for centuries, and the restored town of Columbia, now a state historical park. Don't avoid the unnumbered back roads that wind up hills and through picturesque farms. To the north, visit Downieville, which is tucked into the northern Sierras, then take passable dirt roads to Malakoff Diggings to see how hydraulic placer mining washed away a mountainside.

We'd like reports on the **Coloma Country Inn,** beautifully decorated with country antiques, quilts, and collectibles (Box 502, Coloma 95613 916–622–6919).

High Sierras   For 400 miles, the Sierra Nevada mountain range defines eastern California, from north of Lake Tahoe to the northern terminus of the desert region. Yosemite, Kings Canyon, and Sequoia national parks provide unlimited outdoor opportunities for everyone from car window sightseers to rugged backpackers. See 14,495-foot Mt. Whitney, giant sequoias and torrential waterfalls, or ski at one of 20 areas. Lake Tahoe provides resort offerings, with famous casinos, gambling, and glitzy shows nearby at Stateline Nevada. The crowning jewel here is Emerald Bay. For a bizarre foray into history, visit Donner Memorial Park, two miles west of Truckee, where an 1846 pioneer group, stranded by heavy winter snows, resorted to cannibalism.

Central Coast   This photogenic region stretches from the Monterey Peninsula south to Santa Barbara. Inland, Pinnacles National Monument's volcanic spires, bluffs, and crags are worth a visit. On the coast, from Monterey (see description in listings), tour the peninsula via Seventeen-Mile Drive (a toll is charged) past Pebble Beach, wind-sculptured cypresses, cavorting otters, and on to Carmel. Highway 1 cuts through misty, ragged cliffs that rush into the sea. This is Big Sur—wild, beautiful, with almost no off-road access and too many crowds in the summer. To view the excesses of the rich, visit Hearst's San Simeon Castle (reservations required). To the south, Morro Bay marks the start of the renowned California beaches. Stop to see Solvang, a 1911 Danish settlement, and Santa Barbara, the heart of Spanish Mission country.

Greater Los Angeles   This city-region includes not only LA itself but the myriad surrounding cities, beaches, and islands. For relaxation, sail or fly to Santa Catalina Island, one of the top resort locations in the country. See listings for more information about the area.

Orange County   Welcome to the California of commercials and legend. Here you can experience the mythic and somewhat crazed California beach life at Newport, Laguna, and Balboa. It's all here: sun, sand, surfers, theme parks (Disneyland, Knott's Berry Farm), nouveau everything, Super Hype. Your children will love it, but you may need a week on a desert island to recover.

Inland Empire   From the San Gabriel Mountains in this region you can look down over Los Angeles. Route 2, east of Pasadena, twists through the mountains and past ski areas. East of San Bernardino, Route 18 is called the Rim of the World Drive. Although an overstatement, it is a pretty mountain road that leads to overdeveloped Lake Arrowhead and Big Bear Lake resort area. Southwest is Riverside, California's "citrus capital" and home of the famous Mission Inn, touted by Will Rogers.

San Diego County   Although San Diego (see description in listings) is the star of this region, there are several nearby areas in the county worth noting. La Jolla's natural caverns, formed by waves pounding against the sandstone cliffs, and the Mingei International Museum of prehistoric and contemporary crafts make for a special stop. I-8, which becomes Route 79, is a pretty drive to the old mining town of Julian. Farther on is the retirement community of Borrego Springs, with its superb Anza-Borrego Desert

State Park. Stop at the headquarters for an excellent introduction to the varied plant and animal life of California's desert country.

The Deserts From posh Palm Springs to Death Valley, from Mexico to Nevada, this region is unlike anything else on earth. Since the desert area covers almost one-sixth of the state, it is important to plan your itinerary carefully. Unless you are a dedicated desert aficionado, it can get repetitive. South of Palm Springs, don't miss the enormous date groves near Thermal and Mecca, or the restaurants offering date milkshakes and date pecan pies. Just to the south, senior citizen communities dot the shoreline of Salton Sea, created in 1905 by human error during the construction of the Colorado River aqueduct. To the east are the Chocolate Mountains and the sprawling Sand Hills. North is Joshua Tree National Monument, best in spring when the cacti blossom. Finally there is Death Valley, a bewitching place of startling contrasts in altitude, colors, vegetation, formations, and texture. A few reminders: Try not to visit this region in the summer, always heed the warning to stay on the highway, and carry extra water in your car.

Rates do not include local sales tax.

ANAHEIM 92802   Map 14

Anaheim Country Inn   *Tel:* (714) 778–0150
8516 South Walnut

While combining the words "Anaheim" and "Country" in the same name may seem like a contradiction in terms, Marilyn Watson and Lois Ramont, owners of this inn since 1984, describe it as "the only B&B located in a residential neighborhood, offering both easy accessibility to I-5 and the major tourist attractions, without all the confusion of the hotels, motels, RV areas, and concrete that surround Disneyland. Our ¾ acre gives a real country feel within the city and offers a sense of tranquility after being with crowds all day." Built in 1910 in the Princess Anne style by former Anaheim mayor John Cook, the inn is highlighted by beveled windows and turn-of-the-century country furnishings, with lace curtains and Oriental rugs. Rates include a full breakfast and predinner appetizers. "Great food and hospitality, soothing atmosphere, homey surroundings." *(Patricia Horton, also Becky Richardson)*

Open All year.
Rooms 7 doubles, 1 single—6 with private bath and/or shower, 2 with maximum of 4 sharing bath. All with desk, fans. 1 with air-conditioning.
Facilities Dining room, parlor, kitchen with guest refrigerator. ¾ acre with hot tub, croquet, horseshoes, garden. Off-street parking. 6 blocks to tennis; 1 m to golf.
Location Orange County. Take Disneyland exit off I-5; go W on Ball, N on Walnut to inn on right. 1 m to Disneyland.
Restrictions No smoking. No children under 12.
Credit cards Amex, Discover, MC, Visa.
Rates B&B, $50–75 double, $32 single, plus 10% bed tax. 20% senior, 10% weekly discount.
Extras Station pickups.

ARROYO GRANDE 93420   Map 14

Rose Victorian Inn   *Tel:* (805) 481–5566
789 Valley Road

Built in 1885 as the home of one of California's first walnut growers, the Rose Victorian has been owned by Diana and Ross Cox since 1982. After two years of restoration work, they describe their inn as "a paradise for incurable romantics." The decor is all Victorian, with hand-carved mahogany, rosewood, and oak furniture. The parlor has a working pump organ that is original to the house, while the living room features an 1875 grand piano. Vases of roses and other fresh flowers are everywhere. Each room is named after a different type of rose, with colors to suit—the Sterling Silver room is all mauves and silver, while the Summer Sunshine is done in pink, yellow, and green.

The inn maintains extensive flower, fruit, and vegetable gardens; the harvest from these gardens keeps the inn restaurant well supplied with fresh produce. Everything in the kitchen is prepared from scratch, and fresh fish is always featured among the entrées.

"Twenty wineries are within an easy drive of the Rose Victorian. The building is a four-story, century-old Victorian, painted four colors of rose. Dinner in the lovely garden restaurant is included, as is a breakfast of eggs Benedict, hot filled croissants, and champagne. The owners are very hospitable." *(Virginia Severs)*

Open All year. Restaurant closed Mon. to Wed.
Rooms 8 doubles—3 with private bath, 5 sharing 2 baths. Some rooms in 2 cottages.
Facilities Parlor with pump organ, living room with piano, dining room, bar. 6 acres with rose, fruit, vegetable gardens; gazebo; koi ponds.
Location Central Coast. 1 hr. S of Hearst Castle. 12 m S of San Luis Obispo. 1 m W of Hwy. 101. From Hwy. 101N take Traffic Way Exit. Turn left at stop sign (Fair Oaks). From Hwy. 101S take Fair Oaks Exit and turn right onto Fair Oaks. Go ¼ m and turn left onto Valley Road, ¼ m to inn.
Restrictions No children under 16. No smoking in inn; permitted in restaurant. No refunds for cancellations, although rooms may be rebooked within a 6 month period if 5 days advance notice received.
Credit cards MC, Visa.
Rates MAP, $125–145 cottage and double. 15% service additional. Extra person in room, $45. 2-night weekend minimum for "Cal Poly" graduation, "Poly Royal" and all holidays. Alc dinner, $30.

BIG SUR 93920   Map 14

Novelist Henry Miller, Big Sur resident for 20 years, noted that "There being nothing to improve on in the surroundings, the tendency is to set about improving oneself." Unfortunately, news of Big Sur's breathtaking beauty is now well-known, and summer traffic jams often clog the hairpin turns of Highway One. Our advice is to travel off-season, or to leave the crowds behind by hiking the beautiful trails of Pfeiffer–Big Sur State Park, Julia Pfeiffer Burns State Park, and the Ventana Wilderness. May and

October are probably the best times for minimum crowds and maximum good weather.

Information please: In addition to the very well-known Ventana Inn described below, we'd like to ask for reports on **Deetjen's Big Sur Inn** (Highway One; 408–667–2377), a 20-room rustic retreat built in the 1930s by Helmuth Deetjen, a Norwegian immigrant. While not fancy, rooms rent for a reasonable $30–80, and the restaurant has a very good reputation.

Ventana Inn   *Tel:* (408) 667–2331
Highway One   In CA: (800) 628–6500

Built in 1975, the Ventana has been expanded several times under the management of Robert Bussinger. The architecture is California-modern, with tall ceilings, large exposed beams, and natural woods. Twenty new rooms have recently been added, bringing the total count to 60, spread over 12 buildings on very ample grounds. Rooms have a modern, country look; 34 have ocean vistas. The restaurant, one-eighth of a mile from the inn, has spectacular views of the Pacific and specializes in California cuisine, with an emphasis on fresh seafood, vegetables, and fruits; advance reservations are essential. Rates include a continental breakfast, with fresh fruits and home-baked breads and pastries, brought to your room or available buffet-style, and an afternoon wine and cheese buffet.

"Positively sybaritic. At the end of our week-long stay we emerged feeling renewed and healthy, not jaded or sluggish." *(Marcia Layton)* "As the brochure says, Ventana really does provide a window outward to the most beautiful scenery in this country, and inward on your relationship with your partner. If you expect more, you might be disappointed, because there are no activities—it's all self generated. The environment is restful and peaceful, and the staff couldn't have been nicer, yet were unobtrusive and not chatty as in many smaller inns. The rooms are well done from the high vaulted redwood ceilings to the colorful quilts and matching headboards and window seat cushions. Extra amenities such as fresh flowers, fruit, extra wood for your fire delivered to your door all make you feel completely comfortable and cared for. The food is especially good, both in the restaurant and the wonderful baked goods with the freshest fruit for breakfast." *(Pamela Young)*

"Rooms are furnished with mostly king-size beds, fireplaces (it does get cool at night most of the year), comfortable furniture with lots of pillows, draped beds, large and clean bathrooms, a coffee maker plus a choice of regular and herbal teas. Breakfast is brought to your room with a newspaper between 8 and 10:30 A.M. Each room has a patio, where you can sit and feed the big blackbirds that wait for the remains of your breakfast goodies, and from which you can see deer peacefully grazing around the hills. The restaurant is excellent." *(Jerry Friedman)*

"A few minor irritations: avoid the lower-floor rooms in the new building—they're smaller, and noise from above comes through. We also had a hard time getting reservations at the restaurant." *(TD)*

Open All year.
Rooms 5 suites, 55 doubles, all with full private bath, telephone, TV/VCR, radio, desk, air-conditioning, fan, refrigerators. Many with fireplace, deck, wet bar, hot tubs. Rooms located in 12 buildings.

Facilities Breakfast room/lobby, restaurant. 243 acres with 2 heated swimming pools, sauna, Japanese hot baths, hiking trails. 3 m to ocean beaches for swimming, fishing.
Location Central Coast. On scenic Hwy. 1, 28 m S of Carmel, 152 m S of San Francisco, 311 m N of Los Angeles. 2½ m S of Pfeiffer-Big Sur State Park entrance.
Restrictions Children definitely not encouraged.
Credit cards All major cards.
Rates B&B, $285–400 suite, $155–285 double. Extra person in room, $50. 2-3 night minimum weekends, holidays. Alc lunch $19, alc dinner $43.
Extras Wheelchair accessible. Spanish, French, Italian spoken.

BODEGA BAY 94923   Map 14

The Inn at the Tides   *Tel:* (707) 875–2751
800 Coast Highway One, P.O. Box 640   In CA: (800) 541–7788

"Set on rising ground overlooking the bay, the inn is composed of weathered shingle lodges, each housing several units, most with a view. A relatively new operation, the inn is first-class in every respect." *(Robert J. White)* Rooms are decorated with contemporary decor and soft pastel colors, and each has a sitting area with queen sofa hide-a-bed. The inn's restaurant serves Sonoma-style country cuisine, with fruits and vegetables from local farms, wines from Sonoma's best vineyards, and fish from Bodega boats. A five-course prix fixe meal in the inn's Bayview Room might include oysters with cilantro-rice vinegar, smoked lamb and onion salad, fettucini Alfredo, salmon with saffron butter, and fresh blueberries and cream. Rates include a fresh-baked continental breakfast, morning paper, terry cloth robes, and bathroom amenities.

Open All year.
Rooms 88 suites, all with full private bath, telephone, radio, TV, air-conditioning, refrigerator. Most with fireplace, VCR.
Facilities 2 restaurants, bar/lounge, laundromat, board games. Heated indoor/outdoor pool, sauna, hot tub, massage. Golf, fishing, beaches nearby.
Location North Coast; Sonoma. 68 m N of San Francisco, 25 m W of Santa Rosa. Just N of Pt. Reyes National Seashore.
Credit cards Amex, MC, Visa.
Rates B&B, $110–185 suite. Extra adult in room, $10; no charge for children under 12. Prix fixe dinner $35; alc dinner, $20. Midweek, second night discounts. 2-night minimum holiday weekends.
Extras Cribs available.

CALISTOGA 94515   Map 14

Set in the North Coast's Wine Country, Calistoga is located at the northern end of the Napa Valley, about 75 miles north-northeast of San Francisco. Nestled in the foothills of Mt. St. Helena, it was founded in 1859 by Sam Brannan, a New Englander who moved west and started California's first newspaper. Brannan was familiar with New York State's Saratoga Springs, and his goal was to make the mineral springs of Calistoga equally well known. People still come for the spas—to sit and soak in tubs filled with volcanic-ash mud and naturally heated mineral water and in mineral-water whirlpools.

Other area attractions include the dozens of area wineries, many first-class restaurants and shops, a petrified forest, and a geyser, along with hot-air ballooning and gliding, bicycling, and outdoor summer concerts. The Sharpsteen Museum depicts Calistoga's early days. Summer and fall weekends are very busy; visit during the spring if possible.

Also recommended: The **Foothill House** (3037 Foothill Boulevard; 707–942–6933) is a luxurious B&B set in a turn-of-the-century farmhouse; rates include a continental breakfast of fresh fruit, homemade breads and muffins, juice, and an afternoon wine and cheese hour. The **Larkmead Country Inn** (1103 Larkmead Lane; 707–942–5360) is furnished with fine antiques, old paintings, and Persian carpets, all in the setting of a historic home. Rates include a continental breakfast of fruits, brioches and French rolls, preserves, and fresh-ground coffee. The **Silver Rose Inn** (351 Rosedale Road; 707–942–9581) is an airy contemporary structure with each guest room decorated in a different theme; it sits on an oak-studded knoll, landscaped with roses, a rock garden, and a waterfall. Guests enjoy a continental buffet breakfast, afternoon cheese and crackers, and a welcome bottle of the inn's private label Napa Valley Chardonnay. The **Wine Way Inn** (1019 Foothill Boulevard; 707–942–0680) was built as a private home in 1915 and is furnished with nineteenth-century American and English antiques; guest rooms are highlighted by heirloom Indiana patchwork quilts. Built with a redwood deck to take advantage of the view, the back of the inn looks out onto the Mayacamas Mountains, which form the western slope of the Napa Valley.

Information please: Listed on the National Register of Historic Places is the beautifully restored **Brannan Cottage Inn**, with six guest rooms done in country Victorian decor, with white wicker, primitive pine antiques, and hand-painted flower stencils (109 Wapoo Avenue; 707–942–4200).

To reach Calistoga, take Route 29 (St. Helena Highway) north from Napa.

Scarlett's Country Inn

Tel: (707) 942–6669

3918 Silverado Trail North

A turn-of-the-century farmhouse, Scarlett's Country Inn is built on the site of a Wappo Indian settlement; obsidian arrowheads are still to be found on the grounds. Guests are accommodated in one of two suites in the cottage or in a room in the nearby main house. Families should note that Scarlett's is one of the very few B&Bs in this area that *does* welcome children.

"Nestled off the main road, Scarlett's Country Inn is reached via a winding path. The first view we had was of an inviting porch tucked amid trees, with a tire swing hanging from a high branch. The main house is set behind the guest cottage. There was a beautiful deck around the swimming pool. Rooms are warmly decorated, with lots of small touches—scented soaps, plump pillows, and wine and cheese on the patio.

"The food was marvelous—fresh fruit, muffins, and pastries, with plenty of variety during our stay. Although there's no pressure if you prefer to stay to yourself, the best part was sitting around the table, deep in conversation with other guests, and getting to know Scarlett. Service was attentive but not fawning, and arranged for the convenience of guests." *(Dr. & Mrs. Joseph Drugay)*

"We loved the quiet and privacy. The country French decor is charming. We spent the cocktail hour in our cozy sitting room sipping wine and eating cheese, but my favorite part was our bathroom, with a great old tub for soaking after a day of shopping and wine tasting. Scarlett's suggestions for out-of-the-way wineries were excellent." *(Denise Whittington-Seger)*

"Our favorite is the Camellia Suite, with a mini-kitchen and a distinct living room, ideal when you're travelling with children. Scarlett made our daughters welcome with special placements and mugs, concern with special breakfast requests. The kids enjoyed the swing and all the animals to play with. We love the Laura Ashley decor, the fresh flowers everywhere— inside and out— the Crabtree and Evelyn toiletries, the thick towels, and the meals around the pool. Scarlett is terrific with referrals of everything from restaurants to babysitters, and has never steered us wrong." *(Bill & Cheryl Shonborn)*

Open All year.
Rooms 2 suites, 1 double—all with private shower and/or bath, telephone, radio, desk, air-conditioning, fan. Double in main house, suites in guest cottage.
Facilities Dining room, decks. 1 acre with flower gardens, swimming pool. Lake nearby for boating, fishing, swimming.
Location Midway between Calistoga and St. Helena. From St. Helena, go N on Hwy. 29 to Bale Lane. Turn right on Bale Lane, left on the Silverado Trail. Go ½ m and turn right on a dirt road with the sign "3918" on a fence under a tree. House is yellow 2-story farmhouse.
Credit cards MC, Visa.
Rates B&B, $95–125 suite, $85 double, $70–110 single. Extra person in room, $15. Tipping not expected. Children under 12 free in parents' room.
Extras Cribs, play equipment, games available. Spanish spoken.

CARMEL   Map 14

Carmel dates back to the early 1900s when it was an artists' colony and a popular summer resort for well-to-do San Franciscans. Opinion is divided on Carmel—most people think it's a charming seaside town filled with darling shops and beautiful art galleries; others find it a bit much. Whatever your opinion, there's no lack of suitable accommodations. Carmel probably has more attractive inns in its zip codes than any other town in the country except Cape May, New Jersey! A number of them were built in the 1950s as motels and have since been renovated as inns, making for an interesting hybrid—the mood, decor, and amenities of an inn, added to the convenience and independence found in a motel.

Location is important when booking an inn in Carmel. Parking in town is impossible, so be sure to book a place that's "within walking distance" of the places you want to see.

Other than shops and art galleries, Carmel's attractions include the historic Carmel Mission, golf and tennis, music festivals, and excursions to

Big Sur, Monterey, and the Seventeen-Mile Drive. Both Carmel Beach and Point Lobos State Reserve are nice for walking, but the water is generally too cold for swimming, and the undertow is treacherous.

Carmel, also known as Carmel-by-the-Sea, is located just south of the Monterey Peninsula, 120 miles south of San Francisco. Most of Carmel is laid out in a grid pattern, with numbered avenues running east/west, starting at First in the north end of town and ascending as you go south. The exception is Ocean, the town's main east/west thoroughfare. Streets are named and run north/south; Junipero is the main drag. The center of town is Carmel Plaza, where Junipero and Ocean avenues meet.

Also recommended: The **Happy Landing Inn** (Monte Verde Street, between Fifth and Sixth Avenues, 93921; 408–624–7917) was originally built as a Comstock-style family retreat in 1925 and the guest rooms, set in pink stucco cottages and furnished with period antiques, have cathedral ceilings and look out onto a central garden. The **Holiday House** (Camino Real at Seventh Avenue, P.O. Box 782, 93921; 408–624–6267), a 1905 Craftsman structure and a guest house for over 60 years, is convenient to downtown shopping and the beach. Rates include a full breakfast and afternoon sherry; rooms are highlighted with antiques, and look out onto the garden or the ocean. The **La Playa Hotel** (Camino Real and 8th Street, P.O. Box 900, 93921; 408–624–6476; 800–582–8900), fully restored in 1983, was originally built in 1904 as a private Spanish-style mansion. Guest rooms are decorated in soft colors, with good lighting and hand-carved Spanish mission–style furniture. The **Quail Lodge** (8205 Valley Greens Drive, 93923; 408–624–1581; in CA, 800–682–9303; outside CA, 800–538–9516), situated on the grounds of the Carmel Valley Golf and Country Club, is a luxurious resort which offers a full range of activities and amenities; its relatively small size permits emphasis on personal service. The **Sundial Lodge** (Seventh and Monte Verde, P.O. Box J, 93921; 408–624–8578), built in the 1920s, is a cozy European-style hostelry with courtyard gardens, located in the heart of Carmel. Rates include a continental breakfast and afternoon tea with sherry. The **Vagabond House** (Fourth and Dolores Streets, P.O. Box 2747; 408–624–7738) is a brick half-timbered English Tudor country inn with a comfortable, shaded courtyard. Rooms, furnished with antiques, follow themes ranging from nautical and early American to English hunt.

Recommended too late for a full entry is the **Tally Ho Inn**, an English-style country inn with flower gardens and ocean views, located close to the beach and shopping areas (Monte Verde St. at 6th Ave., P.O. Box 3726, 93921; 408–624–2232).

Information please: The reasonably priced **Cypress Inn** is a Carmel landmark built in 1929 in Spanish Mediterranean style and fully renovated in 1986 (Lincoln and 7th, P.O. Box Y, 93921; 408–624–3871). The **Sea View Inn is** a charming B&B Victorian that has been welcoming guests for over 60 years (Camino Real between 11th and 12th, P.O. Box 4138, 93921; 408–624–8778), and **Stonepine** is a 12-suite 330-acre estate offering every conceivable luxury and gourmet dining at suitably elevated prices (150 East Carmel Valley Road, Carmel Valley 93924; 408–659–2245).

Reader tip: Most Carmel inns define a two-night weekend minimum as being either Thursday and Friday nights *or* Saturday and Sunday nights, a definition we've encountered nowhere else. Call to double-check and plan accordingly.

The Cobblestone Inn
Junipero and Eighth Avenue, P.O. Box 3185, 93921

Tel: (408) 625–5222
(800) 222–4667

The Cobblestone is one of four California inns owned by Roger and Sally Post, all of them recommended by our readers—an admirable achievement indeed. The Cobblestone, built as a motel in 1950, is an example of traditional "Carmel architecture"—two stories with a balcony surrounding a courtyard with garden and patio. The inn was completely renovated and redecorated in 1984, and now includes an English garden with over 50 varieties of flowers. Rave reports continue to come in from all readers, and reservations should be made well in advance.

"Bedrooms and bathrooms are well appointed with bathrobes and sample cosmetics. The inn is quiet, and everything is new and well run. All the rooms, even the smallest, have sitting areas." *(MJF)*

"The inn is located on the outskirts of a busy shopping district of Carmel, yet it feels very private and removed. When you return at night you find the fire going, a teddy bear in your bed holding the remote control for the TV, and a single rose with a poem on your pillow. Tea is served every afternoon. Breakfasts are fabulous, with homemade muffins, omelets, and more. Staff only too anxious to please—will make dinner reservations, recommendations, and so on. Very romantic surroundings." *(Judy Margolin, also Laura Scott, Barbara Lekander)*

"Our room was rather small, but the appointments and accessories are so well done you feel instantly relaxed and ready to stay forever." *(Phil & Helen Schetky)*

Open All year.
Rooms 2 suites, 22 doubles, all with telephone, radio, TV, desk, fireplace, refrigerator. 2 with full private bath, 22 with shower only.
Facilities Living room/lounge/breakfast area; patio. Limited parking facilities.
Location In heart of town. From Monterey, follow Hwy. 1 into Carmel and turn right on Ocean Ave. Continue down Ocean to Junipero and turn left; go 2 blocks to inn at corner of 8th Ave.
Restrictions Street noise could disturb light sleepers in 3 rooms. No smoking in common rooms.
Credit cards Amex, MC, Visa.
Rates B&B, $155–170 suite, $95–140 double. Extra person in room, $15. Picnic baskets on request.
Extras Cribs, babysitting available. Member, Four Sisters Inns.

Mission Ranch
26270 Dolores Street 93923

Tel: (408) 624–6436

The Martin family was lured to California by the 1856 Gold Rush, but sensibly stayed to farm this ranch instead. Their large Carmel acreage encircled the old Spanish mission, and remained in the family as a dairy ranch until the 1920s. A resort since World War II, the century-old farmhouse now has guest rooms, the creamery is now the restaurant, and the original bunkhouse is a cottage.

"This ranch is supposedly owned by Clint Eastwood, but this was neither confirmed nor advertised. There are cottages, a main house for B&B, and individual motel-style rooms. The accommodations are not luxurious, but they are adequate. Best of all is the location. The beach is readily accessible, less than ½ mile away, but easily in view. There is a beautiful sheep meadow between the buildings and the beach; the sheepherder and his dog captivated all the guests when they did their stuff at sunset. The food is tasty meat-and-potatoes fare; the locals love to eat here too. It's served in a building overlooking the meadows and the beach. There is a piano bar where cheese and crackers are set out. A cold buffet breakfast is included in the room rate—muffins, breads, hot and cold cereals, juices, pastries and all sorts of coffee and tea. Tennis is very big here, with many courts and a pro for lessons, but you have to pay extra, so we opted to play for free on the local school courts. The ranch is situated behind the Mission, just out of town, but still very convenient to everything. The staff is pleasant and accommodating." *(Mary Aarons)*

Open All year.
Rooms 13 cottages with private shower and/or bath, kitchenettes, TV, telephone. 6 doubles in farmhouse with private bath, telephone. 6 motel rooms with private bath, TV, telephone.
Facilities Restaurant, piano bar. Parlor in farmhouse with fireplace, TV. 22 acres with 8 tennis courts, nature trails, swimming lagoon. 1 m to beach.
Location S end of Dolores St., behind Carmel Mission.
Restrictions No children in farmhouse except as part of family group rental.
Credit cards Most major credit cards accepted.
Rates B&B, $85–120 cottages, $50–80 double. Extra person in room, $10.
Extras Cribs available. Pets permitted in some cottages.

Sandpiper Inn   *Tel:* (408) 624–6433
2408 Bay View Avenue, 93921   In CA: (800) 633–6433

Longtime owner Graeme McKenzie believes that the Sandpiper has "the most unique ocean views in Carmel, looking along one mile of white sandy beach, attracting an adult clientele, with many honeymooners and international guests."

"As you approach, your first sight is of the multicolored flowers lining the walkway and entrance. Upon entering, you get the feeling of walking into a home. In an unobtrusive, small alcove you find Graeme McKenzie or one of the staff ready to make you feel welcome. You are shown to a comfortable room decorated with many antiques. Some of the rooms have wood-burning fireplaces; others have ocean views. All rooms have a sitting area and a supply of literature of local interest. Downstairs is a well-stocked, comfortable library, a good place to hide on a rainy day. Adjacent is a combination living/dining room: a large room with a beamed cathedral ceiling, big glowing fireplace, and comfortable furniture, a great place to read the daily paper, sip sherry, or talk with the other guests. Breakfast can be eaten at the dining table in the living room or carried to your room. Sherry is served after 5 P.M.; coffee is available all day, and a guest refrigerator is available for snacks and drinks. The staff is charming, with very little turnover, always a sign of a well-managed operation." *(Ted Goldfarb)*

Open All year.
Rooms 14 doubles, 2 cottages—all with private shower and/or bath, clock radio, desk. Some with ocean view, fireplace.

Facilities Living/dining room with fireplace, TV; library with game table, lobby with fireplace. ½ acre with rose garden, patio. 70 yards to beach. Off-street parking. Golf, swimming, tennis privileges. Bicycle rentals.
Location ½ block to center.
Restrictions No smoking in common rooms. No children under 13.
Credit cards Amex, MC, Visa.
Rates B&B, $90–145 double. Extra person in room, $15. Rollaway cot or futon, $15. 2-4 night weekend/holiday minimum.
Extras French, German spoken.

EUREKA 95501   Map 14

Visitors come to Eureka, still a major lumbering center and fishing port, to wander through its Old Town—once home to the area's many lumber barons—hike in the area's parks and forests, and fish in Humboldt Bay. Eureka is located on the North Coast (Redwood Country), 250 miles (6 hours) north of San Francisco. To reach Eureka from the north or south, take Highway 101; from the east, follow Route 299 to 101. The town is laid out in a grid, with the numbered streets running north/south, parallel to the water, and the lettered streets running east/west.

Reader tip: A reader-recommended restaurant is **Panama Jack's,** hospitably operated by Curt and Nancy Jones, offering a varied menu—Creole, California, Mexican, Italian—for all appetites in an art deco environment (421 Third Street; 707–445–8280). "This restaurant was even better on a return trip, when I savored an entrée of duck breast in a delicious sauce with all the trimmings, plus super desserts and local wine." *(Pat Fink)*

Also recommended: The **Eagle House** (Second and C Streets; 707–444–9207; in CA, 800–522–8686), a recently restored High Victorian stick-style hotel, is perfect for travelers who prefer a downtown location, an old-fashioned bar and grill, and lively theater for entertainment. Rates include a continental breakfast and a wine cocktail on arrival. The **Hotel Carter** (301 L Street; 707–444–8062) offers period atmosphere with all modern comforts— bright airy rooms, comfortable beds, and spacious baths. Seafood is the specialty at the hotel restaurant; rates include a continental breakfast of muffins and tarts, juice, and tea or coffee, and afternoon hors d'oeuvres.

Information please: We'd like to request comments on the **Old Town B&B,** a turn-of-the-century Victorian decorated with period pieces and featuring creative full breakfasts (1531 Third Street; 707–445–3951).

Carter House B&B   *Tel:* (707) 445–1390
1033 Third Street

Victorian reproduction furniture is fairly common in inns and hotels, but a reproduction of an entire Victorian home is what you'll find at Carter House. Mark and Christine Carter built their inn six years ago, following an original blueprint of an 1884 San Francisco mansion destroyed in the 1906 earthquake. Rooms are decorated with antiques, Oriental rugs, contemporary paintings and ceramics by local artists (which are for sale), and lots of flowers and plants.

"Mark and Christine make themselves accessible to guests and are an important part of the pleasure of one's stay. Both are gourmet cooks. You can expect a tasty breakfast—not to mention afternoon hors d'oeuvres and late-evening brandies, hot teas, and cookies. Rooms are well supplied with fresh towels and matching robes." *(M. A. Goodwin)*

"The full breakfast nearly defies description. All items are beautifully presented, and served with fresh, edible flowers. We had baked pineapple on banana mousse with toasted coconut; smoked salmon, cream cheese, and spinach crêpes with avocado cream sauce; potato leek pancakes with sour cream and chives; julienned carrots and red peppers; cherry plums in ginger; corn custard muffins; and fresh peach torte, along with fresh orange juice and, of course, coffee. We ate at 7:30 A.M., drove 350 miles, loaded and unloaded much luggage, ran several errands, and finally at 9 P.M. felt the first faint twinge of hunger." *(Pat Fink)*

Open All year. Restaurant closed Sun. through Wed.
Rooms 1 suite, 6 doubles—4 with private bath, 3 with maximum of 6 sharing bath. All with desk. Suite with Jacuzzi, fireplace.
Facilities 3 parlors with fireplaces, vegetable and herb garden. Deep-sea fishing, white-water rafting nearby.
Location Old Town Eureka. From the north, turn right off 4th St. (Hwy. 101) onto L St. for one block; from the south, turn off 5th St. (Hwy. 101) onto L St. for 2 blocks.
Restrictions Smoking in parlors only. No children under 8.
Credit cards Amex, MC, Visa.
Rates B&B, $125–250 suite, $69–109 double, $59–99 single. Extra person in room, $10. Senior, family discounts. Prix fixe dinner $28. Alc dinner $35.
Extras Airport/station pickups. Spanish spoken. Cribs available.

FERNDALE 95536   Map 14

Thought by many to be California's best-preserved Victorian village, the entire village of Ferndale is registered as a State Historic Landmark. The town has more than its share of pretty Victorian homes, originally called "butterfat palaces," since their owners made their money in the dairy industry. At the midpoint of Redwood Country, set off the tourist trail, Ferndale is a perfect town for an overnight stay. Although activities are planned year-round, a special effort is made for Christmas, highlighted (literally) by a 125-foot spruce, decorated with over 900 lights. Be sure to stop in at any shop for a free walking-tour brochure. Ferndale is located in the North Coast region (Redwood Country), 260 miles north of San Francisco, 15 miles south of Eureka, and five miles from Highway 101.

Also recommended: The **Shaw House Inn** (703 Main Street; 707–786–9958), a gabled Gothic carpenter house built in 1854 and restored by owners Norma and Ken Bessingpas, is listed on the National Register of Historic Places, and is furnished with the owners' collection of art, antiques, books and memorabilia.

Information please: Another possibility is the recently renovated **Victorian Village Inn**, with 18 suites and doubles decorated in period, on the second floor of what was built in 1890 as a commercial structure; downstairs is a restaurant and tavern (400 Ocean Avenue, P.O. Box 1028; 800–854–6111).

The Gingerbread Mansion
400 Berding Street

Tel: (707) 786–4000
Outside CA: (800) 441–0407

Within seconds of your first glimpse of the Gingerbread Mansion, you know why owner-innkeepers Wendy Hatfield and Ken Torbert chose that name and why this is the most photographed Victorian in northern California!

"From the moment we arrived on a chilly November day, we knew that this was a remarkable place. The ornate gingerbread—painted in soft yellow and peach colors—and beautiful English gardens beckoned us. The inn is located off the main street in a quiet, well-lit residential neighborhood only two blocks from the well-preserved downtown area of this historic town.

"Tea and coffee were brought to the landing early in the morning to whet our appetites for the delicious breakfast. The inn has several parlors, all nicely decorated and provided with adequate seating, lighting, and reading material." *(Patrick A. & Gloria J. Smith)* "Wendy and Ken are full of information on local history and current attractions, but sitting around the house doing jigsaw puzzles and wandering in the gardens are as much fun as any outing. Everything about the inn is first-rate, from good reading lights to bedtime chocolates." *(Caroline & John Blattner, and others)*

"Everything was immaculate and the setting was unhurried and relaxed. Our second-story room overlooked the blooming English garden below, where hummingbirds fed from the fuchsia blossoms. The lighting in bed was perfect, and the bath was an experience, with its mirrored ceiling and bubble-filled clawfoot tub. The superb breakfast included bran muffins, sour cream coffee cake, pumpkin bread, boiled eggs, fresh fruit compote, and fresh-squeezed orange juice. Tea and cake are served from four to six each afternoon, and a sweet is left on your turned-down covers at night." *(Deborah Morton)*

"We thought the Rose Suite was the nicest—the bathroom is huge (200 square feet), with an enormous clawfoot bathtub and a shower in the corner." *(Linda & Paul Duttenhaver)*

"The Gingerbread Suite has two clawfoot tubs facing each other in the room itself, with a complete bathroom attached. We enjoyed taking long luxurious baths together in our separate tubs! Guests are provided with bicycles, perfect for gadding about Ferndale. Since the town lies in a river floodplain, everything is flat and the riding is easy. You can even ride all the way to the ocean, five miles out of town." *(Mark Hall, and others)*

Open All year.
Rooms 4 suites, 5 doubles—all with private bath and/or shower. Some with desks, fireplaces, twin bathtubs.
Facilities 4 parlors with 2 fireplaces and library, dining room, porches. Formal English gardens, fountains. Bicycling; ocean, river nearby.
Location Take Ferndale exit off Hwy. 101, 5 m to Main St. Turn left at Bank of America; 1 block to inn.
Restrictions No smoking. No children under 10.
Credit cards MC, Visa.

Rates B&B, $145–160 suite, $100–115 double, $85–100 single. Extra person in room, $15. Tipping not necessary. 2-day weekend, holiday minimum.
Extras Portuguese, Spanish, French spoken. Member, Romantick Hotels.

FORT BRAGG 95437   Map 14

Also recommended: The **Avalon House** (561 Stewart Street; 707–964–5555), a restored 1905 Craftsman home with original woodwork and stained glass windows, has been completely updated with modern bathrooms, soundproofed guest rooms, firm mattresses, down comforters, and a full commercial kitchen. Rates include a full breakfast which might include sour cream pancakes with maple pecan syrup or eggs, ham, fried apples, and biscuits. **Information please:** We'd like to hear more from you about the **Pudding Creek Inn,** located in two Victorian homes, joined by an enclosed garden court filled with fuchsias, begonias, and ferns (700 North Main Street; 707–964–9529).

The Grey Whale Inn   *Tel:* (707) 964–0640
615 North Main Street   In CA: (800) 382–7244

A classic-style structure of old-growth redwood, the Grey Whale Inn was built in 1915 as a hospital. Innkeepers John and Colette Bailey converted the building into an inn in 1976 and have been fixing it up ever since. Accommodations are light and airy. The breakfast buffet changes daily and might include a selection of fresh fruit and juices, pineapple-pecan bread, raspberry yogurt, granola, and chocolate applesauce cake. In addition to the many attractions of the Mendocino coast, guests enjoy riding the scenic "Skunk Train" through the redwood forest to Willits.

"The rooms are well kept and clean. In keeping with the spirit of the Mendocino coast, the hallways and entrance are decorated with fine prints, paintings, and old photographs of logging days and of the great whales.

"The rooms are comfortable and roomy, and thanks to an efficient and caring staff, they're also spotless. The inn's location is one of its big pluses. A guest critique book of local eating places makes for interesting reading and is a big help in locating the best places to eat.

"There are two rooms on the third floor of the inn. One, facing west, with a view of the ocean, often offers picture-book sunsets. The other room faces east and provides an equally awe-inspiring view of the sunrise. Both have doors that open to balconies." *(Donald A. Hook, also Robin Azzalina)*

Open All year.
Rooms 6 suites, 8 doubles—9 with full private bath, 5 with shower only. All with radio; 3 with TV, fireplace; 1 with whirlpool tub. Some with balcony, patio, kitchenette.
Facilities Parlor, breakfast room, fireplace lounge, recreation room with billiard table, conference room, TV/VCR room. Garden, lawns. Health club, surfing, diving, fishing, whale watching (Dec.–March) nearby. 4 blocks to ocean.
Location North Coast, Mendocino County. 160 m NW of San Francisco. 12 m N of Mendocino.
Restrictions No smoking. Street noise in some rooms might disturb light sleepers. "Inn appropriate for children over 12."
Credit cards Amex, MC, Visa.

Rates B&B, $85–130 suite, $55–130 double, $50–95 single. Extra person in room, $30. Tipping encouraged. 2-3 night minimum holidays and weekends.
Extras 1 guest room/bath wheelchair accessible. Airport/station pickups. Spanish spoken.

GEYSERVILLE 95411   Map 14

People go to the Sonoma Valley to explore the area wineries, visit the Russian River resorts, and enjoy the area's inns and restaurants. In general, the pace here is quieter and slower than in the neighboring Napa Valley.

Geyserville is located in the North Coast region, in the Sonoma County Wine Country. It's seventy-five miles north of San Francisco and eight miles north of Healdsburg.

Also recommended: The **Hope-Merrill** and **Hope-Bosworth Houses** (P.O. Box 42; 707–857–3356), fully restored Victorian homes, face each other across Geyserville Avenue. The Hope-Bosworth House is in the Queen Anne style, built in 1904 entirely of redwood, while the Hope-Merrill is a nineteenth-century Eastlake Stick-style house. Both inns offer an unusual wine tour called "Stage a Picnic" from May through October.

Information please: The **Belle de Jour Inn** (16276 Healdsburg Avenue; 707–433–7892) was built in 1873 and is a single story Italianate farmhouse set on six acres overlooking rolling hills and vineyards; the Simi Winery is just across the road. Rates include a full breakfast, offered in the country kitchen or on the deck.

Campbell Ranch Inn   *Tel:* (707) 857–3476
1475 Canyon Road

"The ranch is set privately on a canyon hillside surrounded by gardens, terrace, and deck. Mary Jane and Jerry Campbell are congenial, helpful, and cordial hosts. The ranch-style house is large and comfortable, with many windows. The decor is pretty, with fresh, bright colors and whimsical touches. The rooms are immaculate, the beds comfortable, the linens clean and plentiful, and cut flowers, along with a bowl of fruit, are found in every room. There is often an inviting fire in the large fireplace and a jigsaw puzzle in progress on a well-lit table.

"Mary Jane is an excellent cook, and her full breakfast with choice of entrée and fruit is generous. In the evening she serves a fresh, delicious dessert—a pie, cake, or torte, depending on her inspiration that day. In addition, the Campbells provide information on wineries, restaurants, and current events in their area and occasionally play tennis with guests if a partner is needed on the court." *(Phyllis & Walt Reichle, also Joyce & Dick Asimus)*

"All bedrooms have unforgettable views of rolling hills covered with vineyards or a thickly wooded ravine. The second-story bedrooms have balconies, and the tree-shaded terrace is equally inviting." *(Stephen & Judy Gray)* "The thoroughness and efficiency of the Campbells' operation is impressive. I can't think of a way to improve the service or attention. It was just right. Business efficiency and friendship rarely coincide at the same moment. It did with the Campbells." *(KSB)*

"An innsitter was there when we visited; she was very nice and made fantastic omelets. We stayed in the bunkhouse, which was very comfortable with a terrific bed. The furnishings were pleasant but not distinctive in any way." *(JH)*

Open All year.
Rooms 1 suite, 4 doubles—all with private bath, desk, 1 with TV, 4 with air-conditioning.
Facilities Living room, family room with fireplace, TV; dining room, terrace. 35 acres with flower gardens, heated swimming pool, hot tub, tennis court. Ping-Pong, horseshoes, bicycles available. 4 m to Lake Sonoma for boating, swimming, fishing; 3 m to Russian River for fishing, canoeing.
Location 2 m from town. Take Canyon Rd. exit off Hwy. 101, go 1.6 m W to inn.
Restrictions No smoking. Teenagers preferred.
Credit cards MC, Visa.
Rates B&B, $80–100 double, $70–90 single. Extra person in room, $20. Tips not expected. 2-day weekend minimum March through Nov., 3-night holiday minimum.
Extras Airport/station pickups.

GLEN ELLEN 95442   Map 14

A quiet base for a tour of the Sonoma Valley, Glen Ellen's main claim to fame—other than its vineyards and wineries—is the Jack London State Historic Park, comprising the author's home and ranch, with a museum of his papers, personal belongings, and mementos. Its 800 acres also offer ample opportunities for walking, hiking, and riding. Glen Ellen is located in the Wine Country area of the North Coast, 55 miles north of San Francisco and 15 minutes north of Sonoma. From San Francisco, take Highway 101 north. Before Novato, take Highway 37 to Highway 121 toward Sonoma. Then take Highway 116 for a short distance and go right (north) on Arnold Drive to Glen Ellen.

Also recommended: The **Gaige House** (13540 Arnold Drive; 707–935–0237), an Italianate Queen Anne Victorian home built in 1890 and restored in 1980, combines Victorian antiques with Oriental rugs and the owners 20-year collection of art in a peaceful atmosphere where groups larger than four people are rarely booked. Rates include a full breakfast and afternoon wine and hors d'oeuvres.

Glenelly Inn   *Tel:* (707) 996–6720
5131 Warm Springs Road

This southern-style cottage, encircled by verandas on both the first and second floors, was built as an inn in 1916; in those days guests would arrive daily via the Southern Pacific Railroad. More recently, owners Addie and Gray Mattox, who restored the Glenelly Inn in 1985, report that "our guests enjoy the casual atmosphere and quiet country setting. We serve wine and cheese each evening, offer port in the common room, and help our guests select unique wineries to visit. Our library features books on wine and stories by Jack London." Rooms are decorated with Laura Ashley fabrics and brass and iron beds.

"The innkeepers made dinner reservations and provided us with extras for a picnic lunch. The rooms have lots of charm—comfortable beds, good lighting, nice soap, and fresh flowers. The resident dog, Bonnie, is friendly and adds a touch of homeyness to the inn. We enjoyed a wonderful breakfast of fresh berries, egg-cheese strata, and home-baked muffins; exceptional wines at cocktail hour are also served. The inn is clean, quiet, and parking is ample." *(Denny Lee, also Stanley Tick)*

Open All year. Closed Dec. 24, 25.
Rooms 6 doubles, all with full private bath. 2 with patio. All with private entrance.
Facilities Common room with fireplace, verandas. 1 acre with lawn, gardens. Creek nearby; 4 m to golf.
Location 2 blocks from center. Go N on Arnold Springs Rd., then turn left at Warm Springs Rd. (Hungry Wolf Deli on corner) to inn 1/3 m on right.
Restrictions No smoking. No children.
Credit cards MC, Visa.
Rates B&B, $75–110. 2-night holiday weekend minimum. Off-season discount, excluding holidays. 10% discount for 4-night stay.
Extras French spoken.

GRASS VALLEY 95945   Map 14

One of the richest gold-mining towns in California, Grass Valley's prosperity has lasted over the years, with lumbering, agriculture, and tourism now providing the gold. Don't miss a tour of the Empire Mine, now a state park with 367 miles of passageways.

Also recommended: The **Murphy's Inn** (318 Neal Street; 916–273–6873), built in 1866 as the private home of the gold-baron owner of several mines, was converted into an inn at the turn of the century, and is decorated with beautiful woods, period furniture, lace curtains, and brass beds. The **Swan-Levine House** (328 South Church Street; 916–272–1873) is a Queen Anne Victorian hospital converted into a B&B, with vibrant shades of color appearing throughout the eclectic decor. The inn is also a gallery for the owners' prints and paintings; the original carriage house is now a printmaking studio, where they both teach and work.

Grass Valley is located in Gold Country, 45 minutes northeast of Sacramento, three hours northeast of San Francisco.

Annie Horan's B&B   *Tel:* (916) 272–2418
415 West Main Street

Built in 1874, this Victorian was owned by the Horan family for 80 years and remained virtually unchanged until the '80s. In 1987 it was purchased by Pat and Tom Kiddy.

"From the wrought-iron fence and gate to the high ceilings and clawfoot bathtubs, Annie Horan's is charming. Rooms have eight-foot-high windows, allowing guests to enjoy as much natural light and fresh air as desired. The inn is located on the main street, but there's ample parking in the rear for guests. The furniture is all period; beds are very comfortable, and an armoire, luggage stand, and fan complete the furnishings. This house is warm in winter and naturally cool in summer. The breakfasts are delicious, and we especially like the homemade granola. Many fine restaurants and shops are within walking distance." *(Barbara Milliff)* "Homey yet elegant atmosphere, outstanding service, and efficient plumbing—a real find in an old house!" *(Joan Ragan)*

Open All year.
Rooms 4 doubles—2 with full private bath, 2 with shower. All with radio, air-conditioning.
Facilities Dining room, living room, deck. 6 lakes and rivers within 15 miles for rafting, fishing, boating, gold panning, and swimming. Golf, hiking nearby.
Location Gold Country. Northbound, take I-80 to Auburn (Rte. 49), then N on Rte. 49 to "Colfax 174" exit for Grass Valley. Left on S. Auburn, left on W. Main. 2 blocks from center.
Restrictions No smoking. No children. Some street noise in front room.
Credit cards MC, Visa.
Rates B&B, $65–85 double. Extra person in room, $10. 2-day holiday minimum. Discount for Silver Circle Club members.
Extras Airport/station pickups.

GUALALA   Map 14

Pronounced "wa-*la*-la" (in case you were wondering), the unusual name of this town is derived, some people think, from an Indian word meaning "water coming down place"; others think the name originated with the early German and Spanish settlers, who may have thought this area resembled heaven, or Valhalla.

Gualala is located in the Mendocino area of California's North Coast, three hours north of San Francisco and two hours west of the Napa Valley. To reach Gualala, take Highway 101 to Petaluma and proceed west through Two Rock and Valley Ford to Bodega Bay. Follow Highway 1 north to Gualala.

The "banana belt" climate here is mild and mostly free of coastal fog. Golf, tennis, hiking, fishing, swimming, and diving are all popular activities. For more information on area attractions, please see the chapter introduction.

Also recommended: The Old Milano Hotel 38300 Highway 1; 707–884–3256) is a Victorian landmark overlooking the Pacific and decorated in period; an intimate and private atmosphere prevails both in its restaurant and in its reservation—only hot tub with a 180-degree view of the ocean. The **St. Orres** (36601 Highway 1, P.O. Box 523; 707–884–3303), whose onion-domed main house reflects the influence of early Russian settlers, has cottages scattered throughout the property and hidden in the redwood forests. The key attraction is its superb restaurant, well known for its top chefs, who consistently turn out exquisite food.

Whale Watch Inn   *Tel:* (707) 884–3667
35100 Highway 1

Irene and Enoch Stewart started the Whale Watch in the mid-1970s, and have been expanding slowly ever since, adding small buildings with luxurious, contemporary-style furnishings and architecture. The Whale Watch rates superlatives from a number of contributors.

"Be forewarned that once you see the rooms here, you won't want to try anyplace else! Every room has a spectacular ocean view and is decorated in superb taste. Some rooms have a whirlpool tub, original art on the walls, and subdued, classy color schemes." *(Linda & Paul Duttenhaver)*

"This place deserves every superlative. The sound of the sea at night as one snuggles under a down comforter is unforgettable. There were several small bouquets of fresh flowers in our room, The Crystal Sea. On our balcony in the morning we had freshly baked currant scones, with slices of melon, grapes, strawberries, a large slice of brie, and a pot of coffee, and, of course, the sea always in view. We enjoyed a delicious dinner at St. Orres." *(Cynthia Snowden, also Kathryn Kincannon)*

"The most beautiful, restful inn we've ever visited. We stayed in Cliffside, perched on the cliff overlooking the Pacific. We were greeted with a glass of wine, offered menus to peruse from area restaurants, and in the morning were served a scrumptious full breakfast in the Whale Watch room." *(Susan & Clarence Ikerd)* "Everything—from the unique design of each room to the view of the ocean to the charming breakfast—breathes romance." *(Peggy Davis)*

Open All year.
Rooms 18 suites and doubles—all with full private bath, located in 5 buildings. Many rooms with desk, fan, Jacuzzi tubs, fireplaces, kitchens.
Facilities Living room with fireplace; library/game room. 2 acres with beach access.
Location 5 m N of Gualala on Hwy. 1.
Restrictions No smoking. Adults preferred.
Credit cards Amex, MC, Visa.
Rates B&B, $145–220 suites and doubles. Extra guest in room, $20. 2-3 night minimum weekends/holidays.
Extras Airport pickups.

HEALDSBURG 95448   Map 14

Aside from the serious business of wine tasting, visitors to Healdsburg enjoy swimming, fishing, boating, and canoeing in the Russian River and Lake Sonoma, plus hiking, bicycling, tennis, and golf.

Information please: Just across the road from the Simi Winery is **Belle de Jour**, with four shady cottages on a quiet hilltop. The owners bring a breakfast basket to your door, and will arrange a winery tour in their 1923 vintage automobile (16276 Healdsburg Avenue; 707–433–7892).

Also recommended: The **Camellia Inn** (211 North Street; 707–433–8182), an 1869 Italianate Victorian home,is decorated in period with antiques and Oriental rugs. In addition to a full breakfast, guests have the opportunity to taste the owners' award-winning homemade wine (which takes on new meaning in the Sonoma Valley). The **Haydon House** (321 Haydon Street; 707–433–5228) is a Queen Anne Victorian home built in 1912, with rooms decorated in pastel colors, Dhurrie rugs, French and American antiques, and Laura Ashley prints. A full breakfast is served family style; rates also include wine and cheese in the afternoon. The **Healdsburg Inn on the Plaza** (116 Matheson, P.O. Box 1196; 707–433–6991), originally housed a Wells Fargo office, and is now furnished with antique beds and lacy curtains framing the view of the plaza. Rates include a full breakfast, round-the-clock coffee and cookies, and evening wine and popcorn.

Located in the Sonoma Valley, along the Russian River Wine Road in California's North Coast region, Healdsburg is 70 miles north of San Francisco on Highway 101.

Madrona Manor *Tel:* (707) 433–4231
1001 Westside Road (707) 433–6831

Originally built as a summer home by a wealthy San Francisco businessman, Madrona Manor sits on a high knoll overlooking the town of Healdsburg and nearby vineyards. In 1983 it was bought by John and Carol Muir, who have turned it into a lovely country inn. Their son Todd acts as one of the chefs, and in the winter, a culinary exchange brings in chefs from France, Germany, and Austria. The inn maintains its own brick oven, smokehouse, orchard, and herb/vegetable garden to produce meals which might include wild mushrooms and spring vegetables with *beurre blanc;* seafood lasagna with salmon, shrimp, and scallops layered with saffron pasta, spinach, and sun-dried tomatoes; fresh garden greens; lamb with shallots and asparagus; and apricot soufflé baked in puff pastry with raspberry sauce. The Manor is a busy place in season, and reservations are essential for both the rooms and restaurant, especially on weekends.

"A gorgeous, secluded 1880s manor house offering the best in service, food, and surroundings, with a swimming pool and lovely grounds. The chef, Todd Muir, studied at the Culinary Academy in San Francisco under Alice Waters (of Chez Panisse fame). The best rooms are #203 and #204, but they are often booked months in advance. Otherwise, try #202, #303, or #304." *(Linda L. & Paul Duttenhaver)*

"We stayed in the Carriage House, in a very modern, comfortable room (without much of a view). The friendly staff was very helpful but unobtrusive; we never met the innkeepers themselves. This is obviously a large and busy but friendly place. We had an outstanding dinner here; the breakfast buffet of fruit, cheese, jams and eggs is fine but not up to the same standard. The vegetable and flower gardens are very appealing." *(Linda Bair)*

Open All year. Restaurant closed Mon., Tues. in Jan., Feb.
Rooms 2 suites, 18 doubles, all with full private bath. All with radio, desk, air-conditioning. 9 rooms in main house, 8 in Carriage House, 3 in 2 cottages.
Facilities 3 dining rooms, music room, lobby, billiard room, terrace. 8 acres with gardens, orchard, walking trails, swimming pool. Golf, tennis nearby.
Location ¾ m from town. Take 2nd Healdsburg exit off Hwy. 101, left on Westside Rd.
Restrictions No smoking.
Credit cards Amex, DC, MC, Visa.
Rates B&B, $123 suite, $88 double, $83 single. Extra person in room, $10–20. Jan.–April one night lodging free for each night purchased. 5-course prix fixe dinner, $43; alc dinner, $42. Sunday brunch, $14.
Extras Wheelchair accessible. Airport pickups. Pets permitted in some areas. Crib, babysitting available. Spanish spoken. Wine Makers dinners Jan.–March.

LAGUNA BEACH 92651 Map 14

Laguna became popular as a resort at the turn of the century and was established as an art colony in the 1930s. It provides both beautiful beaches and year-round sun, but life here isn't entirely without pressure—there are parking meters by the tennis courts to indicate remaining court time. Laguna offers theater and ballet as well as a number of arts and crafts festivals and plenty of shops. Of course, water sports, from surfing to scuba diving, are very popular.

Also recommended: The **Carriage House** (1322 Catalina Street; 714–494–8945) is within walking distance of town, yet in a quiet residential section. Each suite has a kitchen and separate living area, making this inn an ideal choice for families or those staying more than a night of two. The **Casa Laguna Inn** (2510 South Pacific Coast Highway; 714–494–2996; in CA, 800–233–0449), built in the 1930s in a combination of California mission and Spanish revival style, features gorgeous water views, a lovely swimming pool, and rooms decorated with both antique and contemporary furnishings. Access to an isolated section of the beach is available via steep steps from the courtyard. A short distance away, the **Aliso Creek Inn** (31106 Pacific Coast Highway, South Laguna 92677; 714–499–2271) offers a quiet resort setting, nestled in a narrow canyon. Rooms rest along either side of Aliso Creek, connected by a bridge. The nine-hole golf course pushes up against the steep hillsides, providing a pleasant challenge.

Eiler's Inn

Tel: (714) 494–3004

741 South Pacific Coast Highway

Located in the heart of Laguna Beach, Eiler's Inn, owned by Henk and Annette Wirtz, features a European atmosphere. Rates include a breakfast of fresh-baked breads, fresh fruit and juice, boiled eggs, and hand-ground Viennese coffee.

"The innkeepers set a friendly caring tone for each guest to enjoy in whatever degree he or she wishes. When asked they will always provide information about the nearby coastal access and excellent shopping." *(Lisa Simonetti)* "The half-block walk to the beach, the ocean view from the deck, the well-appointed rooms, and the sheltering atmosphere of the central courtyard define this inn for us. But the biggest plus is the personal attention. Wine and cheese in the evening, and wonderful pastries in the morning, both served in the courtyard, make for a real home away from home." *(M. DeWitt Daggett III)*

"The rooms all encircle a central courtyard, with a balcony providing access on the second floor. (Some might feel a bit dark when the door is closed and the curtains drawn.) Each is different, some with Victorian antiques, others with Laura Ashley comforters, but all are quite inviting. I'd recommend a room on the second floor because the in-room lighting is much brighter, and because fewer guests would pass your door. The plant-filled courtyard is lovely, with a large fountain and plenty of chairs and tables. Two rooms have ocean views—the suite has a stunning vista from the living room, and the other is a regular double—the ocean view is from the bathroom, not worth an extra charge.

"The location is outstanding—you can abandon your car and walk to everything—shops, galleries, the beach. Although on the main highway, the rooms are surprisingly quiet because of their courtyard focus, away from the street. The handsome living room has a fireplace, large sectional couch with lots of pillows, and ample reading material." *(SWS)*

Open All year.

Rooms 1 suite with kitchen, 11 doubles, all with private shower, fan.

Facilities Library with classical guitarist Saturday evenings, TV, games; lobby with fireplace; sun deck, garden courtyard with fountain. ½ block from ocean.
Location Downtown. Five lights south of the Main Beach at corner of Cleo and Pacific Coast Highway.
Restrictions No children on weekends. Parking "tight."
Credit cards Amex, MC, Visa.
Rates B&B, $150–170 suite, $85–110 double, $80–95 single. Extra person in room, $20. "Tipping appreciated." 2-3 day minimum weekends, holidays.
Extras Wheelchair accessible. German, Dutch, Danish, French spoken.

LA JOLLA 92037   Map 14

La Jolla (pronounced "La Hoya") is a suburb of San Diego, about a 20-minute drive north of downtown. Not just a bedroom community, this sophisticated village on the Pacific Ocean has a number of attractions, including the Museum of Contemporary Art, the Scripps Institute of Oceanography, and U.C. San Diego, along with over 30 restaurants and 120 shops, which range from trendy to traditional. Cove Beach, a marine-life preserve, is a favorite for snorkeling. The Torrey Pines Golf Course and the Del Mar Racetrack are a short drive away to the north.

Also recommended: La Valencia Hotel (1132 Prospect Street; 619–454–0771; 800–451–0772), built in 1925 of pink stucco and red tile, and recently restored, overlooks Cove Beach and is surrounded by some of La Jolla's finest boutiques. Rooms are traditionally decorated, most with ocean views; new bathrooms have been installed with all the expected amenities. Several restaurants, from the rooftop Sky View with its vista to Santa Catalina, to the old world charm of the Whaling Bar, provide a range of dining experiences.

Information please: Just a block from the beach, the **Colonial Inn** (910 Prospect Street; 619–454–2181 or 800–832–5525) dates back to the early 1900s, but was fully renovated in 1980. Rooms are large and comfortable, and the common areas charm guests with their Honduran mahogany, marble fireplaces, and ornate plaster wall moldings. In 1988 the inn was bought by a foreign investment group; we'd like to hear more from you before reinstating the Colonial for a full entry.

La Jolla is located 89 miles south of Los Angeles and 12 miles north of San Diego.

The Bed & Breakfast Inn at La Jolla   *Tel:* (619) 456–2066
7753 Draper Avenue

Built in 1913, this inn is one of the first examples of Irving Gill's "Cubist" architecture. When making reservations, please note that the three least expensive rooms are respectively described in the brochure as being "tiny," "small," and "little."

"The inn has a beige stucco exterior with tropical landscaping, and a foyer that opens into a beautifully decorated dining room. The decor varies from room to room: one is warm and cozy; another, simple and elegant; a third, romantic. Attention has been given to every detail, including high-quality linens and furnishings. The housekeeping is immaculate. Each room has a comfortable chair, current magazines, a carafe of sherry, and fruit; there's a cookie on each pillow at bedtime.

"The common sitting room always has a pot of coffee, and a jar of chocolates sits in the dining room. The breakfast consists of fresh-squeezed orange juice, croissants, and sweet rolls. The place settings are bone china. Breakfast in bed includes china specially selected to fit in with each room's decor. The tea is freshly brewed. There is well-lit off-street parking, reached through the inn's garden. The staff is friendly, cooperative, and always willing to assist. The best part is the location—you can hear the ocean waves and watch the sun set over the Pacific." *(Carol J. Klein)*

"The location is ideal, just a block from the ocean and the flower-filled cliffside cove path (two miles each way) is just perfect for walking or jogging. The inn is located in a quiet area, yet it's just a two-block walk from restaurants and shops; we never used our car. The rooms are quietly elegant—ours was spacious with a sitting area—with terrific beds, and the suite is spectacular. Only one minor complaint—there was no reading light on my side of the bed." *(Amy & Ernie Fleishman)*

"The fresh, bright rooms were thoughtfully supplied with a choice of bed pillows (from squashy to firm), electric blankets, fresh fruit, and flowers. The new baths, decorated in Laura Ashley fabrics to match each bedroom, had thick, fluffy towels, good lighting, and a delightful potpourri spray among the personal care amenities provided. The window design of this 1913 building is one worth copying—the small, horizontal windows above each of the large windows open out, like an awning, and provide not only ventilation but also the sound of ocean waves during a night of drizzling rain. The staff was most helpful in providing a breakfast for a very early morning departure." *(Nancy & Bruce Barker)*

Open All year.
Rooms 1 suite; 15 doubles—14 with private shower and/or bath, 1 shares bath with staff. 5 rooms in annex. Telephone on request, some rooms with desk, fireplace, ocean view.
Facilities Dining room, library/sitting room, garden, patio, sun deck. Tennis court across street. 1½ blocks to ocean, 4 blocks to beach for swimming, snorkeling.
Location Across the street from the Museum of Contemporary Art. Exit I-5 at La Jolla Village Dr. and go W to Torrey Pines Rd. Turn S (left) on Torrey Pines, right on Prospect Place, left on Draper. Inn is catty-corner from museum.
Restrictions No smoking in common areas. No children under 12.
Credit cards MC, Visa.
Rates B&B, $200 suite, $75–175 double. Extra person in room, $20. 2-day holiday minimum. Picnic lunches with advance notice.
Extras 1 guest room wheelchair accessible. Spanish spoken.

LAKE ARROWHEAD 92352   Map 14

Saddleback Inn   *Tel:* (714) 336–3571
State Route 173, P.O. Box 1890

In 1919 two middle-aged sisters moved from the Midwest to Lake Arrowhead to build Raven Hotel, their dream castle. The inn became a Hollywood favorite, and guests included Mae West, Howard Hughes, and Charles Lindbergh. In 1953 the inn's ownership passed to a local realtor and, in 1983, to the present owners.

Rooms are furnished with a blend of country, mountain, and Victorian styles, with Laura Ashley fabrics and wall coverings. The Saddleback makes a good base for enjoying the water sports available on Lake Arrowhead all summer long and for experiencing the Rim of the World Drive in the San Bernardino National Forest.

"A fully restored historic inn set in the trees along Lake Arrowhead, with rustic decor. Rooms are spacious and have all the necessities, and then some, i.e., heated brass towel racks, hair dryers, remote-control TV. The restaurant is very good and the staff efficient and pleasant." *(Arthur J. Faro & Eileen Cassidy)*

Open All year.
Rooms 34 cottages, suites, and doubles, all with full private bath, telephone, radio, TV, refrigerators. Many with desk, air-conditioning, fireplaces, double whirlpool tubs. 10 rooms in original inn, remainder scattered throughout grounds.
Facilities Restaurant, bar/lounge, lobby. 3½ acres with heated swimming pool, gazebo, patio.
Location SW CA, Inland Empire. 90 min. from Los Angeles. From I-10, go N on I-15E to Rte. 30 to State Hwy. 18. Follow Hwy. 18 to Rte. 173 (2 Mile Rd.). Go N to Rte. 189 to inn at entrance to Lake Arrowhead village.
Credit cards Amex, CB, DC, MC, Visa.
Rates B&B, $200–365 1- to 3-bedroom suites, $95–150 1-bedroom cottages and doubles. Extra person in room, $10. 2-night weekend minimum. Alc lunch $8, alc dinner $20.
Extras 1 room wheelchair equipped.

LITTLE RIVER 95456   Map 14

Little River is a tiny village located five miles south of the Victorian town of Mendocino. You can easily visit all of Mendocino's boutiques and restaurants during the day and then escape the evening noise and bustle by staying in Little River.

Located on the North Coast, it's 155 miles north of San Francisco. The town was originally settled in the 1850s as a major source of redwood lumber for San Francisco. (Redwood, being pitch-free, was found to be more fire-resistant than other woods.) Logs were floated down the river to the coast, then taken by schooner to San Francisco.

Also recommended: The **Heritage House** (5200 North Highway 1; 707–937–5885), whose original building was constructed in 1877 by the Dennen family, is an elegant inn perched on the cliffs above the ocean, with cottages overlooking the water, or tucked away in the trees.

Information please: Overlooking fruit orchards, the **Victorian Farmhouse**, built in 1877, has rooms highlighted by quilts and antique toys; guests enjoy a breakfast tray brought to their rooms each morning (7001 North Highway One, P.O. Box 357; 707–937–0697). Another possibility is the **Little River Inn** (707–937–5942) dating back to 1853; now as then, it's known for comfortable rooms and good food.

Glendeven   *Tel:* (707) 937–0083
8221 North Highway 1

A Maine-style farmhouse built in 1867, Glendeven has been owned by Jan and Janet deVries for over 10 years; the decor effectively combines antiques and country furnishings with contemporary arts and crafts. Rates include a continental breakfast of fresh juice and fruit, hard-boiled eggs, home-baked breads, and tea or locally roasted coffee, plus afternoon sherry.

"Glendeven is ideally situated for a romantic getaway. Just south of the village of Mendocino, it is a short walk to the ocean and to Van Damme State Park with its beautiful walking trails. A restored Victorian house, the inn also has a new building of several units, modeled after the original. Both are set back from the road and surrounded by beautiful gardens for privacy and quiet. We stayed in the original house, in a two-room suite with a fireplace, furnished entirely with antiques. The newer units have antiques and more modern baths, but we prefer the feel of an older house." (Irene Thomas, also Bill & Melissa Simpson)

Open All year.
Rooms 2 1-2 bedroom suites with private bath, 9 doubles—7 with private bath and/or shower, 2 with maximum of 4 people sharing bath. 6 with fireplace, deck or balcony. 4 rooms in Stevenscroft; 4 in Farmhouse.
Facilities Sitting room with fireplace and piano, gallery. 2½ acres with brick terrace, flower gardens. Fern Canyon nearby for walking, jogging. ¼ m to Van Damme State Park.
Location On Hwy. 1, just S of Mendocino, ¼ m N of Van Damme State Park.
Restrictions No smoking. Children by special arrangement only. Some traffic noise in a few rooms.
Credit cards MC, Visa by special arrangement, with 3% surcharge.
Rates B&B, $120–225 suite, $70–140 double, $50–120 single. Extra person in room, $20. Midweek discount. 2-3 night weekend/holiday minimum. Tipping encouraged.

LOS ANGELES   Map 14

From New Wave to ocean waves, you can find everything in Los Angeles. Larger than Rhode Island and Delaware combined, the city is both linked and separated by an amazing maze of freeways. In fact, if the people of Detroit could have dreamed up the perfect town, they would have invented Los Angeles, where it is impossible to get anywhere without a car.

Los Angeles is a hodgepodge of different ethnic groups—you can visit different restaurants and shops for a taste of countries from Hungary to Thailand, from Polynesia to Ethiopia. Large Mexican, Japanese, and Chinese neighborhoods have been intrinsic parts of Los Angeles for decades. There's really a lot to see in Los Angeles—not just the TV and movie industry tours but other kinds of cultural and historic sights as well, including a number of outstanding art museums. At the least, visit or write to the Los Angeles Visitors and Convention Center (505 South Flower Street 90071; 213–239–0204) for a copy of their "Visitor's Guide."

To make things a little easier, we've grouped all our listings for the Los Angeles area in this section, so you won't have to check through the whole chapter to find Beverly Hills or North Hollywood. Before you make reservations, it's a good idea to look at a map and identify the areas where you'll be spending most of your time; then book your room in that area of the city. Los Angeles is so spread out and the traffic so heavy (the afternoon rush hour starts at 3 P.M.) that you could easily spend your entire day in the car (and a car you must have). If you're traveling with the family and will mainly be doing the theme-park circuit, you'll be better off staying in Orange County (Anaheim, Buena Park) to the southeast.

Also recommended: The **Chateau Marmont** (8221 Sunset Boulevard, Hollywood 90046; 213–656–1010; 800–CHATEAU), built in 1927 in a French Normandy style, is a historic Los Angeles landmark surrounded by gardens and offering sweeping views of the city and Hollywood Hills. Every weekday evening the hotel prepares a complimentary buffet of wine, cheese, fruits, and vegetables, during which guests can get acquainted. The **Eastlake Inn** (1442 Kellam Avenue, Los Angeles 90026; 213–250–1620), built in 1887 in Los Angeles's oldest suburb, Angelino Heights, is located in a historic preservation zone that is lovely for walking and exploring. Restored and furnished with antiques, curiosities, and stained glass, the Eastlake is a good choice for business travelers, not only for its convenient location but also for the adaptability of the owners to the needs and schedules of their guests. The **L'Ermitage** (9291 Burton Way, Los Angeles 90210; 213–278–3344; 800–424–4443), an all-suite hotel that's received both the Mobil Four Star and the AAA's Five Diamond awards, provides guests with nearly every conceivable luxury: from fruit and wine on arrival to afternoon caviar and pâté in the bar; complimentary limousine service; state-of-the-art telephone service, and more. The hotel's restaurant, Café Russe, is open only to guests at the hotel and their invited friends. The **Terrace Manor** (1353 Alvarado Terrace, Los Angeles 90006; 213–381–1478) is tucked away in the middle of downtown Los Angeles in a small neighborhood of turn-of-the-century homes recently designated as a National Historic District. Renovated in 1984, this B&B not only provides a full breakfast but also, on occasion, magic tricks compliments of owner-magician Sandy Spillman.

Information please: For comfortable rooms under $100, try the **Beverly Crest Hotel**, a 54-room hotel with swimming pool near Wilshire Boulevard (125 South Spalding Drive, Beverly Hills 90212; 213–274–6801). A nearby alternative in the same size and price range is the **Beverly House** (140 South Lasky Drive 90212; 213–271–2145 or 800–432–5444). The **St. James's Club**, a former apartment house, has been restored to its original Art Deco flair in its 61 luxurious guest rooms, many with marvelous views over the city (8358 Sunset Boulevard, Los Angeles 90069; 213–654–7100 or 800–225–2637).

For beach lovers: If you'd rather fall asleep to the noise of pounding surf, the **Casa Malibu** is a 21-unit family-owned motel, recommended for its cheerful helpful employees and clean comfortable rooms literally on Malibu's white sandy beaches (22752 Pacific Coast Highway, Malibu 90265; 213–456–2219). The **Channel Road Inn** (219 West Channel Road, Santa Monica 90402; 213–459–1920) is just a block from the beach in Santa Monica Canyon. A Colonial Revival home built in 1910, it was restored as a B&B in 1988; guests enjoy the antique decor, continental breakfasts, afternoon wine and cheese, and hillside hot tub overlooking Santa Monica Bay. Another possibility for beach lovers is **Barnaby's**, long owned by the Post family, offering rooms elaborately decorated with European antiques and Viennese-style cuisine; it's a half-mile to the beach and boardwalk (Sepulveda at Rosecrans, Manhattan Beach 90266; 213–545–8466 or 800–421–0341). Comments?

Los Angeles is located in Southern California, about 400 miles south of San Francisco and 125 miles north of San Diego.

Hotel Bel-Air *Tel:* (213) 472–1211
701 Stone Canyon Road (800) 648–4097
Los Angeles 90077

Glowing superlatives seem to be the operative mode when it comes to describing the Bel-Air—it was recently named one of the top 10 hotels in the world by *Travel and Leisure* magazine. Bel Air natives had a few scary moments earlier in the decade when the hotel's longtime owner passed away and the hotel was nearly bought by former securities trader Ivan Boesky. Fortunately, Caroline Hunt Schoellkopf's Rosewood Corporation won the day; she's made a great old hotel even greater—albeit considerably more expensive.

"The Bel-Air is a classic pink stucco building in a spectacular setting—a wooded, secluded canyon close to the Bel-Air Country Club. The grounds are beautifully landscaped, and there's a fabulous swimming pool. You'd never know you are only minutes away from Beverly Hills, the beach, and most of the west part of Los Angeles.

"The Bel-Air has been completely remodeled, yet still retains its classic, sophisticated feeling. There's a bridge over a small pond (complete with swans) that you cross to enter the grounds. The lobby is cozy and well appointed, with a fireplace. The rooms are individually done in pastel colors and include nice little luxuries—down comforters, large vanities in the baths. Many of the rooms have small patios, and some even have Jacuzzis. The restaurant is excellent, and the bar is the former haunt of Humphrey Bogart and other movie stars of the 1940s." *(Linda L. & Paul Duttenhaver, also Truman Talley)*

"The Bel-Air is discreetly situated in a super-rich residential suburb, surrounded by the palaces of movie moguls. We had feared that the staff might be snooty, but they couldn't have been more considerate, amiable, and welcoming. We ate twice in the restaurant, where the atmosphere was *soigné* but the service was far from aloof; meals were excellent. The hotel does cater banquets, but these were discreetly handled without interfering with the prevailing atmosphere of tranquility." *(Hilary Rubinstein, also PL)*

Open All year.
Rooms 32 suites, 60 doubles, all with full private bath, telephone, radio, TV, desk, air-conditioning. Many with Jacuzzi, patio, fireplace, or balcony.
Facilities Restaurant, piano bar with fireplace, 24-hour room service, florist. 11½ acres with heated swimming pool. Ocean nearby. Valet parking.
Location Turn off Sunset Blvd. onto Stone Canyon Rd. to hotel.
Credit cards Amex, DC, MC, Visa.
Rates Room only, $450–1,300 suite, $230–385 double, $200–345 single. Extra person in room, $20. Alc breakfast, $12–15; alc lunch, $30–35; alc dinner, $55–60.
Extras Wheelchair accessible. Cribs, babysitting available. Spanish, French, Turkish, German, Russian spoken. Member, Preferred Hotels Worldwide; Relais & Chateaux.

La Maida House *Tel:* (818) 769–3857
11159 La Maida Street
North Hollywood 91601

La Maida House is an inn of distinction set in an otherwise undistinguished Los Angeles suburb. Antonio La Maida built this 7,000-square-foot old-world villa in the 1920s using lots of marble, oak, mahogany, tile, and stained glass. The house was restored and stunningly decorated by owner Megan Timothy, originally of Zimbabwe, who made many of the inn's paintings, sculptures, and stained glass. Rates include continental breakfast and afternoon aperitifs; four-course dinners are also available. Megan is also the chef, and culinary creativity is her signature. Dinner might be anything from a Middle Eastern couscous to a Caribbean pork roast or an Elizabethan banquet. Many of the fruits and vegetables served come from the inn's gardens.

"An all-time favorite—owner Megan Timothy hasn't missed a trick. Our room, Primavera, one of the less expensive bungalow rooms, was done in white wicker and shades of soft dusty pink with touches of apple green. The queen-size bed had a white iron and brass headboard and white eyelet comforter. Large bed tables, good reading lights (both sides!) large closet, well supplied with magazines and books, with a small refrigerator with a jug of drinking water completed the furnishings. The bathroom was equally lovely, with Jacuzzi tub, a color scheme coordinated (with the room), hand-stenciled tulips on wall, and a small stained glass window. Outside was a private grape arbor with table and chairs for our use, plus a gazebo in the backyard.

"The inn occupies a large mansion, and has overflowed to the surrounding bungalows. Originally modest private homes, typical of this residential neighborhood, Megan has completely redone each one in her inimitable style. The inn's common rooms are large and stunning, from the formal living room with marble fireplace and over-size, over-stuffed ivory-covered couches and chairs to the dining room, with its small round tables and crystal chandelier. To the back of the house is a plant filled atrium, its ceiling one of Megan's stained glass creations, as well as a cozy room perfect for relaxed conversation.

Open All year.
Rooms 5 suites, 7 doubles—all with private shower and/or bath. All with telephone, radio, TV, desk, air-conditioning. Some with whirlpool bath, fireplace. 7 rooms in annexes.
Facilities 2 dining rooms, living room, TV room, atrium, patio, conference room, gymnasium. Swan pond, gardens, fountains, gazebo, swimming pool, exercise room. Tennis nearby.
Location 20–30 min. from most attractions; 2 min. to Universal City. Near intersection of Hollywood and Ventura Fwys. Call for directions.
Restrictions No smoking.
Credit cards None accepted.
Rates B&B, $145–185 suite, $80–135 double. 2-day minimum stay. Discounts for extended stay (more than 1 week). Prix fixe dinner, $38, plus 20% service.

MENDOCINO   Map 14

Originally founded by Maine sea captains, Mendocino still looks very much like a New England fishing village—so much so that it has been used many times as a set for movies meant to be taking place on the East Coast.

The Angela Lansbury TV series *Murder, She Wrote,* which supposedly takes place in Maine, is filmed here; the cast stays at Hill House Inn, described below.

Aside from looking into the many craft shops and art galleries and discovering the area restaurants and vineyards, take the time to explore the shore and the redwood forests, accessible in the area's five state parks. Canoeing, trail rides along the beach, river and ocean fishing, and tennis and golf are all favorites. For more information on area attractions, please see the "North Coast" section of the chapter introduction, plus the listings for Fort Bragg and Little River.

Mendocino is located about 150 miles north of San Francisco, in the center of the Mendocino coast. From San Francisco, take Highway 101 through Santa Rosa to Cloverdale. Then take Route 128 to Highway 1 north to Mendocino. From Eureka, take Highway 101 south to Leggett, and follow Highway 1 through Fort Bragg to Mendocino.

Many Mendocino inns maintain the same rates year-round, while others offer reductions of about 20% in the (winter) off-season. A two-night weekend minimum is standard at almost all.

Also recommended: The **Hill House Inn** (10701 Palette Drive, P.O. Box 625; 707–937–0554) is a new country inn, built in 1978, that combines traditionally styled furniture, including brass beds and lace curtains, with modern baths and amenities. The restaurant specializes in continental cuisine and seafood dishes. The **Joshua Grindle Inn** (44800 Little Lake Road, Box 647; 707–937–4143) offers a view of the village, the bay, and the ocean; all Mendocino's attractions are a short walk away. In this restored Victorian farmhouse, rooms are light and airy, and furnished with antiques. The **MacCallum House Inn** (45020 Albion Street, P.O. Box 206; 707–937–0289, 707–937–5763), built in 1882 as a wedding present, contains many original furnishings, including carved beds, Tiffany lamps, and Persian rugs; some of the rooms are well suited to families, and children are welcome. Specialties at the inn restaurant include freshly caught salmon and veal and seafood dishes.

Recommended too late for a full write-up is the **John Dougherty House** (571 Ukiah Street, P.O. Box 817; 707–937–5266): "Beautifully furnished with early American antiques, most unusual in this Victorian town. Wonderful garden with a view of the coast. Good food and great hosts." *(Deidre Brillhart)*

Information please: For a quiet out-of-town setting, the evocatively named **Brewery Gulch Inn** offers comfortable accommodations, waterview rooms, and hearty breakfasts in a garden setting (9350 Highway One; 707–937–4752). We'd also like to hear more about the **Mendocino Hotel** (45080 Main Street, P.O. Box 587; 707–937–0511 or 800–548–0513), a small complex of nineteenth- and twentieth-century structures. Its 50 guest rooms are furnished with antiques and reproductions; the hotel offers California-style cuisine in its casual garden café and more formal dining room. Current reports are also needed for the **Mendocino Village Inn** (44860 Main Street, P.O. Box 626; 707–937–0246), a 1882 Queen Anne Victorian overlooking the dramatic Mendocino headlands, decorated with period decor and contemporary prints.

Headlands Inn   *Tel:* (707) 937–4431
Corner of Howard and Albion streets, P.O. Box 132

The Headlands Inn began life as a one-story barber shop in 1868. A second story was later added, and in 1893 the house was moved to its present location, transported by horses and using logs as rollers. The arduous trip was worth it just for the view: the front of the inn, including the front deck, two guest rooms and a parlor all overlook the ocean. Pat and Rod Stofle, owners since 1986, pride themselves on their breakfasts, complete with fruit dishes garnished with edible flowers and a different hot entrée with no repeats during a guest's stay; some favorites are bacon quiche, tomato shells with baked Gruyère-topped eggs, apples au gratin with sausages, and mushroom crêpes with bacon. Rates also include afternoon wine and mineral water, served with nuts. Holidays are also celebrated enthusiastically; at Christmas, each room has its own tree for guests to decorate with a basket of ornaments.

"Pat and Rod made us feel welcome from the start. The view from our room, the John Barry, was breathtaking. A delicious breakfast was delivered to our room, preceded by the newspaper. Mendocino's excellent walks and restaurants are to be highly recommended." *(Caroline & Jim Lloyd)*

"The setting of the inn is beautiful, with a flower garden in front and the Big River Bay to the south. The parlor and rooms are decorated with antique furniture and pictures. Pat and Rod keep a list of nearby restaurants with guests' comments in the upper sitting room, where wine is served in the late afternoon. Each breakfast tray is decorated with a small vase of fresh flowers form the garden. Rooms have views of the town, garden, or Big River Bay." *(David & Lanice Clark)*

Open All year.
Rooms 1 cottage, 4 doubles, all with queen/king beds, fireplace or parlor stove, clocks. 4 with full private bath, 1 with private shower, 1 with private deck.
Facilities 2 parlors, with piano, pump organ, games, books. Front porch, decks, gardens. 2 blocks to Big River Beach.
Location Historic District, 2 blocks from center. From Hwy. 1, turn left to business district; pass church, then right on Howard St. Inn is 1½ blocks on left.
Restrictions No smoking. No children under 16.
Credit cards None accepted.
Rates B&B, $89–125 double. Extra person in room, $20. 2- to 3-night weekend/holiday minimum. Reserve 1 to 3 months in advance for weekends and in summer.
Extras Free Skunk Train pickups. Limited Spanish spoken.

Stanford Inn by the Sea/Big River Lodge   *Tel:* (707) 937–5615
44850 Comptche-Ukiah Road and Highway 1

This modern inn provides spacious rooms, decorated with antiques and reproductions, quilts, fresh flowers, and works by Mendocino artists. Set atop a sloping meadow, the inn offers views of Mendocino and the ocean. Rates include a continental breakfast of fresh fruits and juices, champagne, coffee, tea, hot chocolate, and pastries. Afternoon wine and hors d'oeuvres are served in the common room, furnished with antiques and the Stanfords' collection of antique toys. Originally built as a motel, the building was bought in 1981 by Joan and Jeff Stanford, who have worked hard to upgrade the property into a quality bed & breakfast inn. Their other endeavors include raising their two children, operating a canoe livery service, raising llamas, and their organic gardens, which they're happy to show to guests.

"Nestled on a gentle hillside overlooking the ocean and the town, the inn's grounds are beautifully landscaped and were awash with wildflowers during our June visit. A staff member showed us to a our room, furnished in antiques and quality reproductions. A cozy sitting area, plants, and lovely artwork added to the room's charm and warmth. A decanter of red wine sat upon a silver tray on the coffee table. The king-sized four-poster bed was comfortable, the linens high-quality and luxurious, with lots of plump pillows and a down comforter. The bathroom was bright and clean, the towels over-sized and plush. The inn supplied a lovely selection of quality soaps and toiletries. Plumbing is modern, with good water pressure. Our private deck had a picture postcard view. In the early evening, white wine and banana bread was served in the lobby as we scanned the menus of local eateries; the staff assisted us with advice and reservations. We returned here in the morning for a generous well-presented breakfast. The inn is far enough from the main road so that it was very quiet, and sound-proofing is such that we were not disturbed by other guests." *(Timothy & Cynthia Egan)*

Open All year.

Rooms 3 suites, 22 doubles—all with private shower and/or bath. All with telephone, radio, TV, desk, wood-burning fireplace, deck.

Facilities Common room with fireplace. 10 acres with flower and vegetable gardens, horses, ducks, llamas. Free mountain bicycles; fishing; canoe rentals.

Location ¼ m S of village, at corner of Hwy. 1 and Comptche-Ukiah Rd.

Restrictions No smoking in common areas.

Credit cards All major cards.

Rates B&B, $185–250 suite, $129–160 double. Extra person in room, $20. Tips "not required or requested." 2-night weekend minimum.

Extras Wheelchair accessible. Cribs available. French, Spanish, spoken.

MONTEREY 93940   Map 14

Originally built up around the sardine fishing and canning business (which collapsed about 40 years ago), Monterey was first made famous by John Steinbeck's novel *Cannery Row*. The old cannery buildings have long been renovated and now house art galleries, antique shops, restaurants, and inns. Its newest attraction is the Monterey Bay Aquarium, home to over 100 species of ocean life. Unfortunately, only a few of the side streets retain any real character; the rest is all for "show."

For more information on the Monterey peninsula, see the Central Coast section of the introduction to this chapter.

On scenic Highway 1, Monterey is located about 120 miles south of San Francisco and 320 miles north of Los Angeles, on California's central coast. From Los Angeles, drive up Highway 101 to Salinas, then west on Route 56. If you have more time, exit 101 at San Luis Obispo and stay on Highway 1 to Monterey. From San Francisco, take Highway 101 to Route 156 to Highway 1, or stay on Highway 1 the whole way.

Also recommended: The **Old Monterey Inn** (500 Martin Street; 408-375-8284) is a half-timbered Tudor-style residence built in 1929 and decorated with stained-glass windows, period furniture, and family antiques. Rates include a full breakfast, hot and cold drinks available throughout the day, and sherry served at five. The **Spindrift Inn** (652 Cannery Row; 408-646-8900; in CA, 800-841-1879; outside CA, 800-225-2901), a luxurious oasis amid the bustle of Cannery Row, offers spacious rooms furnished with antiques, original art, wood-burning fireplaces, Oriental rugs, and marble baths. In addition, the inn welcomes families and does not charge for children under 13. Rates include a continental breakfast brought to your room with the morning paper and a rose; afternoon tea and cookies, wine, and cheese are also provided.

The Jabberwock

Tel: (408) 372-4777

598 Laine Street

Named after the Lewis Carroll poem, the Jabberwock carries its theme from the names of the rooms to the breakfast creations.

"The atmosphere is peaceful and full of warmth. The rooms are beautifully decorated. Our favorite is the Borogrove, with the Brillig a close second, and we're still trying to get a reservation for the Mome Rath, a unique room decorated in navy blue. The view from each room is either a full panorama of the bay or a delightful view of the gardens.

"Jim and Barbara were so down to earth that we felt that we were visiting a private home. We especially appreciated the homemade cookies and milk waiting in the living room when we returned after dinner. We felt free to pull out the Scrabble set and rearrange the chairs to get a good game going. Our rooms were very comfortable, with eyelet and goose-down comforters, cordials, books, mints, and big soft towels, the most delightful fragrance of orange pervaded the house. Parking is good and access to the town was convenient for both walkers and drivers. The Looking Glass theme was intriguing, especially with the custom-made 'backwards' clocks. The Allens helped us plan excursions around town, and they're glad to make dinner reservations. We were free to poke our heads into the kitchen and find our hosts if necessary, unlike the last B&B I visited, where guests were actually locked out of the kitchen! No one wanted to abuse the Allens' privacy, but their hospitality and trust of their guests is genuine." *(Janet Hardee)*

"Barbara and Jim recommended the perfect restaurant, then stuffed us with their ample breakfast the next morning. Their English bull 'Turkey,' the house mascot, is not to be missed." *(Caroline & Jim Lloyd)* "Our room had a clear view of the bay, with a sofa right in front of the fireplace. On the porch was a telescope that brought the water in so close it felt as if we could touch it. Thick terry robes hung in the closet and everything was spotless." *(Mary Lou & Albert Lautier)*

Open All year.
Rooms 1 suite, 6 doubles—1 room with full private bath, 2 with private shower, rooms with maximum of 4 people sharing bath.
Facilities Living room with fireplace, dining room, enclosed sun porch. ½ acre with waterfall, picnic table. 4 blocks to Monterey Bay. Off-street parking.

Location 4 blocks from Cannery Row and Aquarium. From Hwy. 1 turn N onto Hwy. 68 for 2½ m. Go right on Prescott, right on Pine, left on Hoffman 4 blocks, and turn right at Laine to inn.
Restrictions No smoking. No children under 12.
Credit cards None accepted.
Rates B&B, $160 suite, $85–130 double. 2-3 night minimum weekends, holidays.
Extras Spanish, French, Danish spoken.

MURPHYS 95247   Map 14

Murphys is in the heart of Gold Country's southern Mother Lode, one of the best preserved of the Calaveras County mining towns. The town has a community park, swimming pool, and tennis courts open to visitors. There are state parks nearby for hiking and fishing, and visitors enjoy gold panning and visiting caves and wineries as well as golf and skiing. While here, don't miss the enormous sequoias at Calaveras Big Trees State Park.

Also recommended: The **Murphys Hotel** (457 Main Street, P.O. Box 329; 209–728–3444), dates back to 1856; it was destroyed in the great fire of 1859 but was rebuilt all in masonry. Restored in 1978 but retaining its old-time atmosphere, the old register records such famous guests as Mark Twain, Horatio Alger, and John Jacob Astor. A two-story motel is also part of the facility, so be sure to specify which rooms you want.

Murphys is located in the foothills of the Sierras, 2½ hours east of San Francisco, just east of Angel's Camp on State Route 4.

Dunbar House, 1880   *Tel:* (209) 728–2897
271 Jones Street, P.O. Box 1375

The old TV series, "Seven Brides for Seven Brothers," used this Italianate Victorian home as its filming location. The inn was bought by Bob and Barbara Costa in April 1987. They offer guests a full country breakfast served in the dining room by the fire, in the garden, or in the privacy of one's room.

"The inn was built in 1880 and has been painstakingly restored and eclectically furnished with antiques from every era. The sitting room is comfortable for reading and listening to music, and there's a small library as well as parlor games to play." *(Jim & Sybilla Elrod)*

"The Costas are easy to talk to and go out of their way to make your stay worthwhile. The inn is situated just off the Main Street of Murphys, and the verandas and tree-shaded grounds are particularly inviting. Sleeping under a down quilt on a chilly spring night was a pleasure, and breakfast, served beside an open fire, was delicious, plentiful, and imaginative." *(L.L. Rowell)*

"Many small things made us feel special—the flowers, the lemon drops, bath amenities, potpourri, magazines. It was very quiet, even in the morning when other guests were moving around. For breakfast, we had a superb crab casserole, served with unlimited coffee and juice. The town of Murphys was very friendly; people here really do seem to move a whole lot slower." *(Elaine Rex)*

Open All year.
Rooms 1 suite, 4 doubles—all with private shower and/or bath, desk, air-condition-ing, fan, woodstoves.
Facilities Dining room, parlor. Veranda, gardens. Swimming pool, tennis courts, golf nearby. 35 min. to cross-country, downhill skiing.
Location Turn W off Main St. at Monument.
Restrictions No smoking. No children under 15.
Credit cards MC, Visa.
Rates B&B, $70–80 double, $65–75 single. Extra person in room, $10. No tipping.
Extras Airport pickup, $10.

NAPA 94559 Map 14

Although Napa's founding about 100 years ago was due to the gold rush, today's gold flows from the wine industry and the extensive tourism in-dustry that has developed along with it. The town is a popular base for wine touring—perhaps overly so during fall harvest weekends.

Napa is located in the North Coast region, in Napa Valley Wine Coun-try, just one hour north of San Francisco.

Coombs Residence Inn
720 Seminary Street

Tel: (707) 257–0789

Built in 1852, this B&B inn was for many years a private boarding school, then a public high school. In 1904 it became the private home of the ambassador to Japan, Frank Coombs. Purchased by Pearl and Dave Camp-bell in 1987, the house is decorated with European and American antiques in a homey and comfortable fashion. Rates include a continental breakfast, as well as afternoon wine, cheese, and fruit.

"Pearl welcomed us with a friendly smile and led us on a tour of this antique-filled home. Bed linens were crisp and fresh, the mattresses firm. Cold drinks were offered by the pool and Jacuzzi, and the living room offered plenty of menus to scan. Our evening ended with a pleasant talk with Dave, who had just come home from bagpiping practice. The next morning the smells of fresh-brewed coffee, warm croissants, and wonder-ful bran muffins awakened us." *(Debra Hendricks & Mary Wegner)* "The atmo-sphere is casual—I was free to watch TV, get my own soda, or just sit on the porch and read. Pearl's wonderful breakfast is served on white linen with silver." *(Cherri Galbiati, also Carine & Arnold Feist)*

Open All year.
Rooms 4 doubles—1 with private shower, 3 with maximum of 3 people sharing bath. All with air-conditioning.
Facilities Parlor with fireplace; living room with television. Patio, swimming pool, Jacuzzi, garden. 2 m to river for fishing. Bicycles.
Location Walking distance to town. Take Hwy. 29 to First St. E, go left on Second, right on Seminary. Inn is on middle of 2nd block on left.
Restrictions No smoking. No children.
Credit cards MC, Visa.
Rates B&B, $75–100 double. Extra person in room, $10. 2-night weekend minimum.

Founded in the heat of the Gold Rush, Nevada City remains one of the most picturesque towns along the Mother Lode. Victorian homes, white frame churches, and covered sidewalks still line the hilly streets, in spite of two fires that ravaged the town in the 1800s. Nevada City is located in the foothills of the Sierras, approximately 50 minutes northeast of Sacramento, and 3 hours northeast of San Francisco. Nearby are golf, tennis, swimming, hiking, fishing, downhill and cross-country skiing, river rafting, and horseback riding.

Ten miles north of Nevada City are the Malakoff Diggins, the site of the world's largest hydraulic gold mining operation where miners directed high-powered streams of water onto the hillsides. Effective as the practice was, entire mountainsides were washed away before some of the earliest environmental legislation stopped the practice.

Also recommended: Grandmere's Inn (449 Broad Street; 916–265–4660) was built in 1856 by A.A. Sargent, who was instrumental in the creation of the Transcontinental Railroad and, along with his wife, Ellen Clark Sargent, was a champion of women's suffrage. The inn is located in one of Nevada City's earliest residential areas and has been completely restored and redecorated with antique pine, wicker and country art.

Downey House Bed and Breakfast   *Tel:* (916) 265–2815
517 W. Broad Street

An Eastlake Victorian built in 1869, the Downey House offers common rooms restored to their original Victorian designs. Bright, cheerful soundproofed guest rooms are done in contemporary Southwestern decor in tones of blue, lavender, and pink. Innkeeper Miriam Wright explains, "Victorian antiques have been kind of overdone. It's comfortable, but the old is still there—the doors, wainscoting, and mirrors."

"Though I appreciate antiques, and most B&Bs are loaded with them, it's a refreshing change to stay in a place that has a significant historical background yet has been updated with beautiful modern decor. Soft lavender and peach colors highlight the bedding, towels, pottery and paintings, creating a fresh comfortable atmosphere. Everything is in excellent working order and the rooms are quite spacious. The sun room and garden are great places to relax. Innkeepers Miriam and Al Wright are just a delight and make you feel welcome from the first moment you arrive. She makes a great breakfast with all kinds of homemade baked goods, fresh fruits, egg dishes and fresh-squeezed orange juice." *(Connie English, also Martha Meredith)*

"Located at the top of the hill on Nevada City's main commercial street, this little place is within walking distance of everything." *(Jeanne & Steve Schmidt Herron)* "In warm weather you may take your breakfast out to the garden lily pond. Miriam will gladly help you with dinner reservations or any other request." *(WM, and others)* "The private parking garage in the back is a real plus in winter weather." *(Julie Denman)*

Open All year.
Rooms 6 doubles—all with full private bath, air-conditioning.
Facilities Parlor, library/sun room with TV. ¼ acre with lily pond, garden. Lake and rivers nearby for water sports. Off-street parking.
Location From I-80 at Auburn take Hwy 49 to Nevada City. Take Broad St. exit. Nabob Hill, 1 block from downtown historic district.
Restrictions No smoking.
Credit cards MC, Visa.
Rates B&B, $60–70 double. Extra person in room $10. Senior, mid-week discounts. 2-night weekend minimum May through Dec.

Red Castle Inn

Tel: (916) 265–5135

109 Prospect Street

On a steep hillside overlooking the center of Nevada City sits this dramatic red brick mansion, dripping white icicle trim with elaborately carved balconies. According to owners Conley and Mary Louise Weaver, the four-story Red Castle is one of only two genuine Gothic Revival houses on the West Coast. The Weavers have decorated the 1860 mansion with a mixture of antiques and period pieces; rates include a full buffet breakfast and afternoon tea. A special feature of a stay at the Red Castle is the horse-drawn carriage ride through the historic district into town every Saturday morning; in good weather, energetic guests also take the footpath leading from the inn to the town below.

"Beautiful and comfortable. Generous attractive culinary treats. Lush, yet restrained good taste in all categories. Service first class. The Red Castle Inn is a jeweled landmark easily noticeable from downtown." *(Anne & Joe Gray)* "Warm, friendly atmosphere, superb food, comfortable accommodation, fascinating decor." *(Donald Prout)*

Open All year.
Rooms 2 suites with private bath, 8 doubles—6 with private bath, 2 with a maximum of 4 people sharing 1 bath. 4 with air-conditioning, 3 with fan, 2 with radio. Some with private deck or balcony.
Facilities Parlor with pump organ, sitting room, foyer. 1½ acres with terraced gardens, fish pond with fountain, croquet, swing. Swimming, tennis nearby. Off-street parking.
Location Walking distance to historic district. From Hwy. 49, take Sacramento St. exit and turn right at Exxon station. Turn left on Prospect St.
Restrictions No smoking. "Well-behaved children over age 10 welcome."
Credit cards MC, Visa.
Rates B&B, $85–110 suite, $70–95 double, $65–105 single. Extra person in room, $20. 2-night holiday minimum. 2-night weekend minimum April–Dec.
Extras Vegetarian, diabetic meals available by prior arrangement. Spanish spoken.

ORLAND 95963   Map 14

The Inn at Shallow Creek Farm

Tel: (916) 865–4093

County Road DD, Route 3, Box 3176

"A quiet location, close enough to the freeway so as not to get lost, but far enough away not to hear it" *(Norma & Mike McClintock)* summarizes the initial appeal of this inn's location near Interstate 5, roughly a halfway point for those traveling the interstate between California and southern Oregon. Kurt and Mary Glaeseman have owned the farm since 1982, and in addition to the care and feeding of their guests, tend to citrus orchards of Mandarin and naval oranges, grapefruit trees, and a poultry flock. Local producers supplement the Glaesemans' harvests, so that breakfasts also feature fresh kiwi and a variety of berries, melons, and figs.

"The route to the inn leads down a country road, across a stream, along a tree-lined lane. When you come to the barn and vegetable garden, turn into the shade of the tree-lined front yard. Stepping out of the car, you are greeted by ducks, geese, guinea hens, and their chicks. Surrounding the inn are groves of citrus trees, which give the air a glorious scent when in bloom.

"The inn's entry leads to a cozy sitting room and fireplace. Our rooms included a large, comfortable bed and sitting area, decorated with antiques and an interesting selection of books. We were served a hearty and flavorful breakfast including eggs from the farmyard, served family-style around the big oak table." *(Geralynn Myrah, also Nina Moore, Nancy & Dan Santos)*

"Kurt is very knowledgeable about the area and was able to recommend historical sites, a quiet lakeside spot, and a nearby restaurant. It is very easy to get caught up in his enthusiasm for their citrus crop and poultry flock. Mary makes delicious preserves from their home-grown fruit." *(Collin Batey)*

Open All year.
Rooms 1 cottage, 1 suite, 2 doubles, all with air-conditioning. 2 with telephone, desk.
Facilities Dining room, living room with fireplace, sun porch with books, games. 3 acres with citrus orchards.
Location Central Valley. N. Sacramento Valley, Glenn County. 100 m N of Sacramento, 20 m W of Chico, 3 m W of I-5. Take Black Butte/Orland/Chico exit and go W 3 m on Newville Rd. Turn right at Rd. DD. Go ½ m, cross small concrete bridge, and turn right down the 1st country lane.
Restrictions No smoking. No children.
Credit cards None accepted.
Rates B&B, $75 cottage, $55 suite, $45 double. Extra person in room, $15. Includes tax and service.
Extras Airport/station pickups. French, German, Spanish spoken.

PACIFIC GROVE 93950   Map 14

Set on the Monterey Peninsula, bordering the town of Monterey, Pacific Grove begins at the Monterey Bay Aquarium on Cannery Row and extends along the bay to the beginning of the Seventeen-Mile Drive. Many think this is the peninsula's best town for bicycling and shore-walking. The town was founded by Methodists in 1875 as a "Christian seaside resort"; most of its Victorian inns were built during this period. Its rather stodgy character lingered on—until the late 60s, liquor could be bought in Pacific Grove only with a doctor's prescription.

The town is filled with flowers in the spring, but its most famous site is "Butterfly Park" (George Washington Park), where thousands of monarch butterflies winter from October to March.

Also recommended: The **Centrella** (612 Central Avenue, P.O. Box

51157; 408–372–3372), a Victorian inn, had deteriorated into a decaying flophouse when its current owners purchased it and spent over a million dollars to restore it to its original glory, while adding modern amenities. Rooms are light and airy, decorated with lots of wicker, some antiques, and Laura Ashley fabrics. The **Gosby House Inn** (643 Lighthouse Avenue; 408–375–1287; 800–342–4888), a Queen Anne Victorian mansion built in 1877, has a quiet in-town location and a friendly staff, happy to make dinner reservations or a picnic basket for a day of whale watching. The **Green Gables Inn** (104 Fifth Street; 408–375–2095; 800–841–5252), a half-timbered Queen Anne Victorian, offers the advantage of being right on the water, with ocean views from several of its guest rooms. Rooms are decorated with antiques, country fabrics, ruffled curtains, and wall-to-wall carpets.

Information please: We'd like to have reports on the **Pacific Gardens Inn,** a modern inn in a forest setting, with many rooms comfortable for families traveling with children (701 Asilomar Blvd.; 408–646–9414, 800–262–1566).

Pacific Grove is located about 120 miles south of San Francisco. For more information on the Monterey Peninsula, see listings for Monterey and Carmel (three miles away) as well as the Central Coast section of the introduction to this chapter.

The Martine Inn
255 Ocean View Boulevard

Tel: (408) 373–3388

Although built in 1899 as a Victorian cottage, the Martine Inn was remodeled over the years as a pink-stuccoed Mediterranean mansion. The inn was bought by the Martine family in 1972 and opened as an inn by Marion and Don Martine in 1984. It has been fully restored and decorated in period, from push-button light switches and authentic wall coverings to museum quality antique furnishings. The Martines are avid antiquers, and each bedroom is done in a different motif—one in Eastlake Victorian, another in art deco, a third in early American, and so on. Its location overlooking the bay provides dramatic views from many windows.

"Perfect location within walking distance of the aquarium, Cannery Row, and the Wharf. It is right on the ocean with a jogging trail that goes along the shore for miles." *(F. T. McQuilkin)* "There are no signs about checkout or rules in the rooms—like a friend's home. If you get in before 11 P.M., a friendly face awaits; after that you know the combination to the door lock." *(Mary Ellen Courtney)*

"During our December visit, the atmosphere was warm and cozy with lovely Christmas decorations throughout the inn. From the parlor, you get a magnificent view of the rocky coastline of Pacific Grove, while enjoying wine and hors d'oeuvres. Breakfast included fresh fruit, home made muffins, a hot entrée, piping hot coffee, and more beautiful views. Our room had a fireplace, draped for the holidays with a garland and tiny white lights." *(Mrs. Donald Hamilton)*

"Just as you described it in last year's book. We stayed in the Art Deco Room. The furniture was beautiful, the fireplace lovely, with a good supply of wood. Our bed was turned down with a Godiva chocolate left on the pillow. The atmosphere was gracious, but rather formal. The ocean view was breathtaking." *(Markita Whittingham)*

Open All year.
Rooms 2 suites, 17 doubles, all with private shower and/or bath, telephone, refrigerator. Many with fireplace.
Facilities Dining room, parlor, library, conference room, game room, sitting rooms. Courtyard with fountain, garden, gazebo, hot tub and steam room. Fishing, jogging, bicycling, tennis, golf nearby. Limited on-site parking.
Location 1 m from center, directly on Monterey Bay. 4 blocks to aquarium.
Restrictions Smoking permitted in guest rooms with fireplaces only. No children.
Credit cards MC, Visa.
Rates B&B, $210–240 suite, $99–165 double. Extra person in room, $35. 2-3 day minimun weekends, holidays. Picnic baskets on request.
Extras Wheelchair accessible; 1 room equipped for disabled. German spoken.

Seven Gables Inn
555 Ocean View Boulevard

Tel: (408) 372–4341

Built in 1886, Seven Gables is a grand Victorian home situated on a rocky point at the very edge of Monterey Bay. The inn features ocean views from all the guest rooms, and contains an extraordinary collection of Victorian antiques, including Tiffany stained-glass windows, crystal chandeliers, Oriental rugs, inlaid furniture, and canopy beds. The inn is owned and operated by the Flatley family, who've been in the B&B and antique collecting businesses since 1958.

"Just across the street from Monterey Bay. We stayed in the least expensive room yet still had a great view and very comfortable accommodations. The gardens are especially gorgeous, particularly the tremendous trumpet vine which climbs the back wall of the main house. A very tasty and generous continental breakfast of breads, fruits, juices, yogurt, and strawberry shortcake was served each morning. The inn's staff offers useful restaurant recommendations and makes reservations upon request. We particularly enjoyed Fred Flatley's suggestions of Andrea's Bayside Café, a tiny, informal eatery in nearby Monterey." *(James & Janice Utt)*

"Meticulously clean. Large rooms beautifully decorated, and a friendly efficient, hospitable staff." *(Adele & Paul Britton)*

Open All year.
Rooms 14 doubles, 3 cottages—all with private shower and/or bath, desk.
Facilities Parlor, dining room, breakfast area, porches. Gardens with patios.
Location Right on ocean, 2 blocks from beach. 1 block to downtown. From Hwy. 1, take Pacific Grove exit (Rte. 68W) to Pacific Grove. Continue on Forest Ave to Oceanview Blvd., then right 2 blocks to Fountain Ave. and inn.
Restrictions No smoking.
Credit cards MC, Visa.
Rates B&B, $95–165 double, $85–165 single. 2-night weekend minimum.
Extras Spanish, French spoken.

PALM SPRINGS
Map 14

Located in California's Desert Country, Palm Springs is 115 miles east of Los Angeles, 26 miles east of Joshua Tree National Monument. Palm

Springs is famous for its warm and dry winter climate and its championship golf courses. For instant air-conditioning, the tramway to the top of the San Jacinto Mountains is also a favorite; you can even cross-country ski there in winter. Hiking in nearby Palm Canyon, home to trees over a thousand years old, is also popular. Because summer is very definitely off-season here, rates drop considerably during the hottest months.

Reader tips: Although not quite right for a full entry, *Dianne Crawford* writes to recommend the **Palms at Palm Springs**, a spa located in a Mediterranean manor house within walking distance of the fashionable shops. Rooms are motel-style, but the atmosphere is relaxing and the rates very reasonable by spa standards (572 North Indian Avenue 92262; 619–325–1111). A well-known and highly regarded area resort is the **La Quinta** (P.O. Box 69, La Quinta 92253; 619–565–4111; 800–854–1271), located 19 miles southeast of Palm Springs. This resort has been a movie star favorite for over 60 years and was recommended by a well-traveled reader *(AB)* and is highly rated by Mobil and AAA. Although large for a listing here, its relatively small when compared to other resorts in the valley.

Also recommended: Le Petit Chateau (1491 Via Soledad, 92264; 619–325–2686) offers guests a blend of the owners' own travel experiences, coupled with a philosophy of complete relaxation. The inn and its property are enclosed by a fence and hedge, giving guests total privacy (and optional "au naturel" poolside sunbathing). **Maxim's De Paris** (285 North Palm Canyon Drive, 92262; 619–322–9000; in CA, 800–533–3556; outside CA, 800–5MAXIMS) is a new all-suite hotel with rooms decorated with contemporary furniture in soft and neutral tones. Located in the center of town, the hotel is attached to a mall that has some of the best shops Palm Springs has to offer.

Information please: Along with **La Quinta,** numerous other resorts ranging in size from 350 to 900 rooms have sprouted farther down the valley in Palm Desert and Indian Wells, overshadowing some of Palm Springs' lovely smaller properties. The following four properties have around 20 rooms or suites each: **Antares** has handsome one-story suites decorated in an Art Deco theme, surrounding a central courtyard with swimming pool (772 Prescott Drive 92262; 619–325–0229); **Casa Cody** is one of the city's oldest hotels, with rooms decorated in Southwestern motif, and very reasonable rates (175 South Cahuilla Road 92262; 619–320–9346); **L'Horizon** has spreading lawns for croquet, a large pool, and rooms decorated in soft pastels; views of the San Jacinto Mountains are excellent (1050 East Palm Canyon Drive 92264; 619–323–1858); **La Siesta Villas** have Spanish colonial-style architecture with private patios, set in a quiet residential district (247 West Stevens 92262; 619–325–2269).

Villa Royale
1620 Indian Trail 92264

Tel: (619) 327–2314

Co-owners Bob Lee and Chuck Murawski spent six years traveling through Europe and North Africa, buying furniture, woven hangings, and sculpture, then shipping it all back to Palm Springs.

Rates include a continental breakfast, morning newspaper, and a wine and cheese party on Saturday night. On special occasions Chuck also prepares international theme dinners—Greek, Spanish, or perhaps Cajun—for his guests.

"Privacy is emphasized at this small inn, comprised of several buildings connected by inviting paths and gardens. The staff is friendly, unhurried, and very competent—we soon felt like family. Service, food, and menus were all especially good." *(Mr. & Mrs. Len Dressler)* "Quiet, private, and serene is the best way to describe the surroundings, with ample parking within feet of the room of your choice." *(Al & Sara Levine)*

"The decor captures the flavor of different European countries, and everything reflects Chuck's talent as a TV art designer. We stayed in Switzerland, and all that was missing was a yodel! It has an airy, garden patio to one side and a fully equipped, immaculately maintained Pullman kitchen on the other. Ample bureau and closet space is provided in the changing area between the bedroom and the spotless, modern bathroom.

"Each of the rooms opens onto one of three swimming pools; a large Jacuzzi is located at the far end of the landscaped grounds, just beyond the musical fountain." *(Robin P. Hirst)*

Open All year, except Aug. 1-14. Restaurant closed Aug.
Rooms 32 units in 8 buildings—17 with full private bath, 15 with shower only. All with telephone, TV, desk, air-conditioning, kitchen. Some with radio, fan, fireplace, private patio.
Facilities Dining room, breakfast room, bar/lounge, living room, coin laundry. 3 acres with gazebo, 3 heated swimming pools, hot tub, rooftop sun deck, flower gardens. Bicycles. Tennis, golf nearby. 15 m to cross-country skiing.
Location South End, off E. Palm Canyon Dr.
Restrictions No children.
Credit cards Amex, BankAmericard, Visa.
Rates B&B, $150–325 suite, $120–195 double, $65–150. Extra person in room, $25. 2-3 night minimum weekends, holidays. Lunches available. Alc lunch, $4–10, alc dinner, $12–20
Extras Wheelchair accessible. Airport/station pickups. Spanish spoken.

PIERCY 95467   **Map 14**

Hartsook Inn   *Tel:* (707) 247–3305
900 Highway 101

For over 70 years, families have been coming to the Hartsook to enjoy a cabin in the woods. Not that these are your everyday woods: The inn is set in a giant redwood forest, and you can easily follow the hiking path from the Hartsook to Richardson Grove State Park, home to the Hartsook Giant, a giant redwood with a circumference of 59 feet! Other major points of interest along the Avenue of the Giants are within easy driving distance. Bordering the grounds is the Eel River, a favorite for swimming and floating gently downstream. Innkeeper/owners Robert and Lorraine Price note that "we do our best to see that everyone has a good time. We serve our own homemade bread and pies and make our own jam. Most evenings we have a campfire by the river." Lorraine notes that in 1989 "we remodeled many of the rooms, adding brand-new king-size beds."

"We returned to the Hartsook after many years to find that the blueberry pancakes are still worth a trip, as is the incredible location—each cabin plumb in the midst of the redwoods. In fact, everything produced by the kitchen was of excellent quality, and most reasonably priced. However, most of the accommodations are very rustic—some of the beds are really cots, and the curtains rudimentary, although the trees do filter the sunlight. We'd recommend it primarily for those who can pass on some of the creature comforts; the prices are very reasonable." *(Hilary Cohen)*

Open April 15 through Sept. 30.
Rooms 62 cottages accommodating couples, families. All with private bath and/or shower. Some with desk, kitchen.
Facilities Dining room with piano, lobby with large-screen TV, gift shop, library with games, sauna, patio. 30 acres with hiking trails, Eel River with sandy beach for swimming, fishing. Ping-Pong, shuffleboard, croquet, tetherball, badminton, horseshoes. 9-hole golf course nearby.
Location North Coast. 200 m N of San Francisco, 84 m S of Eureka, 7 m S of Garberville, 1 m N of Piercy bisected by Hwy. 101.
Restrictions No smoking in dining room. Light sleepers should request cabin away from hwy.
Credit cards Amex, MC, Visa.
Rates Room only, $36–85 cabin. Extra person in room, $8. Alc breakfast, $4–6; alc lunch, $6–9; alc dinner, $18. Discount for extended stays. 2nd night half-price April 15 to July 1 excluding weekends, holidays.
Extras Wheelchair accessible. Pets permitted, $5 daily fee. Cribs, play equipment available. Babysitting by prior arrangement.

RUTHERFORD 94573   Map 14

Auberge du Soleil   *Tel:* (707) 963–1211
180 Rutherford Hill Road

"Elegant yet rustic. New cottages added to a restaurant with a long-standing reputation. All the amenities of a European-style inn provided. Decorated with peach, beige, terra cotta and earth tones, leather furniture, skylights, gardens, quilts, rag rugs, plenty of reading lights, fridges full of champagne and juices, wet bar with coffeemaker. There are large baths, double sinks, lounging robes, fireplaces, and lovely views. Excellent service and hospitality. French doors and verandas. Truly a special inn of the finest quality." *(Trudy Reid, also Frederick Avery)*

"A series of chalets perched on the eastern rim of the Napa Valley, with stunning views from every room. In the morning, between 8 and 9 A.M., a van brings breakfast trays with hot breads and a copy of the *San Francisco Chronicle,* wrapped in pink paper and tied with a maroon ribbon. One must walk or drive up the hill to the main reception area and the bar and dining room. The famous cuisine is a happy blend of Franco-California-nouvelle cuisine. Our New Year's Eve dinner was a symphony of tastes and colors; it was priced like a New York opera, but we didn't begrudge it. Just off the main entrance is a small courtyard with a fountain, a favorite of hummingbirds in the summer. The staff is cordial and helpful, except for the maître d', who maintains his French accent and an appropriate hauteur." *(Cynthia Snowden)* "Chef Albert Tordjman's richly flavored cuisine has a mouthwatering accent of Southern France, with such luncheon dishes as linguine with fresh artichokes, mushrooms, olives, tomato and basil; and chicken sausages with pecans and lentil salad." *(WS)*

Although clearly a favorite of many, the Auberge is definitely not for all: "We were rather disappointed in the restaurant. They seemed to be trying too hard—just too many ingredients on the plate. We found the service effusive—and hard to take seriously. Breakfast was beautifully presented with fresh linen, flowers, and the morning paper, but actually consisted only of juice, coffee or tea, one croissant and one muffin. A minor quibble with our room was that the fridge and hot-water machine made irritating noises all night."

Open All year.
Rooms 19 suites, 29 doubles—all with full private bath (2 sinks, separate tub and shower enclosure), telephone, TV, radio, balcony, refrigerator, fireplace. 12 with whirlpool tubs.
Facilities Restaurant, bar with entertainment some nights; terrace. 33 acres with heated swimming pool, tennis courts, bicycling.
Location North Coast, Napa Valley. 13 m N of Napa.
Restrictions Smoking restricted to designated areas.
Credit cards MC, Visa.
Rates B&B, $240–350 suite, $215–250 double. 2-night weekend minimum. Prix fixe dinner, $50. Alc lunch $38, alc dinner $69.
Extras French, Spanish spoken. Cribs, babysitting available.

SACRAMENTO   Map 14

Sacramento was founded by John Sutter, who is best known as the man on whose property gold was discovered in 1848, precipitating the great California Gold Rush of 1849. The town grew into a key supply source for the northern Mother Lode country and was named the state capital in 1854. It remains a major transportation hub to this day. It has a few sights of interest—the State Capitol, Sutter's Fort, Old Sacramento, and the California State Railroad Museum—but most Sacramento visitors come for the business of government or the business of business. Those who want to get out of town enjoy swimming, fishing, and rafting in the nearby Sacramento and American rivers.

Also recommended: The **Driver Mansion** (2019 21st Street, 95818; 916–455–5243), built in 1899, is an elegant colonial revival home, with a corner tower, columned entrance porch, and leaded glass windows. Decorated with walnut and mahogany antique furnishings and handsome traditional fabrics, the inn offers a full breakfast.

Sacramento is located in Gold Country, 90 miles northeast of San Francisco and 90 miles southwest of Lake Tahoe. The center city is laid out in a grid pattern of numbered and lettered streets, with the former running east/west and the latter running north/south.

Briggs House   *Tel:* (916) 441–3214
2209 Capitol Avenue 95816

Briggs House is a handsome restored Victorian, owned and operated by Sue Garmston and her partners. Rates include a full breakfast of hot and cold beverages, homemade bread or muffins, and a breakfast entrée, such as a frittata or strata.

"The guest rooms are decorated with European and American period antiques. The service is impeccable and the rooms immaculate. I have never had a problem parking right out front, and there are several very good restaurants within walking distance." *(Stefanie Pleet)*

"The garden area offers a wonderful tree swing, sauna, hot tub and picnic area. The staff is very friendly, warm, and accommodating. The breakfast served on fine china, includes coffee made from fresh-ground beans, fresh fruit and juice, an egg dish or superb French toast and a wonderful assortment of homemade muffins. In the evening mulled wine is served by the fire in winter, or lemonade, fruit and nuts in summer. Complimentary sherry is available, as are robes, bathing suits and beach towels to enjoy the hot tub and sauna." *(Linda Wooden)*

Open All year.
Rooms 2 suites, 5 doubles—5 with private bath and/or shower, 2 rooms sharing 1 bath. All with radio, desk, air-conditioning. Telephone on request. Suites in carriage house.
Facilities Dining room, parlor with fireplace, games; library. Porch with swing; garden with brick patio, hammock, redwood deck, hot tub and sauna. Bicycles. 6 on-site parking spaces.
Location Downtown. 7 blocks E of Capitol Park, 1 block from Sutter's Fort.
Restrictions No smoking.
Credit cards Amex, MC, Visa.
Rates B&B, $95 suite, $60–85 double. Extra person in room, $10. Children under 3 free. Midweek corporate/government rates. Senior discount available.
Extras Crib available; babysitting by prior arrangement.

ST. HELENA 94574   Map 14

St. Helena is located 60 miles north of San Francisco, in the Napa Wine Valley region of the North Coast. Although there are many things to do in the area, the main activity is visiting wineries—there are nine in St. Helena alone. Keep in mind that this area is extremely popular from June through October, especially on weekends. Try November, April, and May for good weather and smaller crowds.

Also recommended: The **Wine Country Inn** (1152 Lodi Lane; 707–963–7077) was built in 1976, but designed to look as if it has been part of the Napa Valley for years. Each room in the main building and the barn annex has its own distinctive colors and furnishings, including handmade quilts.

Information please: Owned by the Sutter Home Winery, the **Sutter Home Inn** (225 St. Helena Highway, P.O. Box 248; 707–963–4423) offers accommodation in the tower, a replica of the original water tower, and in the converted carriage house. The inn features a classic Victorian garden, and rooms combine turn-of-the-century decor with modern amenities; rates include a continental breakfast.

For more information, see the North Coast section of the chapter introduction and the listings for Calistoga.

The Cinnamon Bear   *Tel:* (707) 963–4653
1407 Kearney Street

Genny Jenkins bought what is now the Cinnamon Bear in 1971; when her three children had all left for college, she turned it into an inn. The bear motif was inherited from her son, who couldn't take them all along when he left for school.

"This Victorian home was built at the turn of the century as a wedding present for the daughter of the president of Rexall Drug Stores. The guest rooms are furnished with antiques, brass beds with quilted bedspreads, and, of course, there are bears everywhere—stuffed bears, pictures of bears, bear clocks, bears on the dishes, and even candy cinnamon bears in the living room. The bathrooms have old-fashioned bathtubs and rubber duckies. It's clean, neat, quiet, and comfortable, and the owner, Genny Jenkins, takes very good care of guests." *(Mr. & Mrs. Jerry Friedman)*

"A comfortable bungalow in a residential area just a couple blocks from downtown, pleasant for taking a neighborhood walk. The rooms are attractive if not fancy; baths are standard and adequate. The front porch is large and is a good place to while away some extra time or have breakfast on nice mornings. Since the house is right across the street from the St. Helena elementary school, expect some early-morning weekday activity during the school year." *(Janice & James Utt)*

"A very warm and inviting B&B. We stayed in the downstairs suite and were graciously treated. We gathered with the other guests in the living room and on the front porch, and savored a breakfast of fresh fruit with cream, breads, and a hot egg dish, served with ample coffee and tea." *(Markita Whittingham)*

Open All year.
Rooms 1 suite, 3 doubles—all with private shower and/or bath, air-conditioning.
Facilities Living room, game room, dining room, porches, gift shop.
Location From Main St., go left 2 blocks on Adams to inn at corner of Adams and Kearney.
Restrictions Traffic noise might disturb light sleepers. No smoking. No children under 10.
Credit cards Amex, MC, Visa.
Rates B&B, $120 suite, $110 double. Extra person in room, $25. Midweek, monthly rates.

Meadowood Resort
900 Meadowood Lane

Tel: (707) 963–3646
In CA: (800) 458–8080
In USA: (800) 345–3457

Although reminiscent of an old-style Adirondack lodge or Newport cottage, Meadowood was originally built as a private country club in the 1960s and was recently expanded into a full-scale luxury resort. The restaurants and other common rooms are housed in the clubhouse, completely rebuilt after a 1984 fire; guest rooms are clustered in lodges scattered around the grounds.

Meadowood is home to the elegant Starmont Restaurant as well as the more casual Fairway Grill. The cuisine at both is creative and well regarded by local epicures; Chef Hervé Glin emphasizes fresh herbs and produce, combining his classical French training with the latest in California cooking. Of course, the wine list includes an extensive selection of California vintages. In fact, in addition to the usual facilities, Meadowood has its own wine school, offering everything from "Saturday Wine Workouts" to three-day seminars.

"Rooms are neat, clean, and well-planned, decorated in neutral colors and provided with fresh fruit and everything else that goes with a top-notch place. Unlike many other Wine Country lodgings, a family would feel comfortable here; there is a playground for kids and the setting is lovely, with lots of trees and green grass." *(Laura Scott, also Paul Lasley & Elizabeth Harryman)*

Open All year.
Rooms 46 suites, 24 doubles—all with private bath and/or shower, telephone, radio, TV, desk, refrigerator, coffee maker, porch. Most with air-conditioning, fireplace, bar.
Facilities Restaurant, bistro, bar/lounge with pianist; conference facilities, massage studio. 256 acres with heated swimming pool, 6 tennis courts, 9-hole golf course, playground, 2 croquet courts with teaching pro, hiking trails. Golf shop. Concierge, room service. Tennis, croquet equipment rentals.
Location 1 m E of town. From Rte. 29, go E on Pope St., across Silverado Trail (approx. 2 m) and veer left to Howell Mountain Rd. Turn left on Meadowood Lane.
Credit cards Amex, DC, MC, Visa.
Rates Room only, $205–565 suite, $165–265 double. Extra adult in room, $25; no charge for children under 12. 2-night weekend minimum. Alc lunch, $8–12; alc dinner, $25 (in grill); prix fixe dinner, $40.
Extras Wheelchair accessible; some rooms specially equipped for disabled. Cribs, babysitting available. Member, Relais et Chateaux, Small Luxury Hotels, Preferred Hotels.

SAN DIEGO   Map 14

San Diego is located in southernmost coastal California, 127 miles south of Los Angeles and about 20 miles north of Tijuana, Mexico. For many years a sleepy coastal town, San Diego didn't really start to grow until World War II, when the U.S. Navy moved its headquarters from Honolulu to San Diego. Since then, the city has grown to become California's second largest. San Diego's climate is arguably one of the best in America—very little rain, with an average winter temperature in the mid-60s and summer in the mid-70s. Major sights of interest include Balboa Park's many museums, the world-famous zoo, Old Town San Diego, Cabrillo National Monument, Sea World, the Maritime Museum, and trips on the Tijuana Trolley to Mexico.

Also recommended: The **Britt House** (406 Maple Street, 92103; 619–234–2926), a Queen Anne Victorian of impressive proportions, was built in 1887 as a family residence; highlights of the original decor include a beautifully carved stairway and magnificent stained glass. Furnished with period antiques, wicker, and an occasional stuffed animal, rates include a full breakfast, plus afternoon tea with such goodies as trifle, kuchen, Irish soda bread, and cucumber sandwiches.

For more information on San Diego area accommodations, see listings under La Jolla, 20 minutes north of the city.

Heritage Park Inn   *Tel:* (619) 295–7088
2470 Heritage Park Row 92110

Heritage Park is a seven-acre site, home to seven classic period structures from the 1800s, all saved from the wrecker's ball and moved to this location. The inn, an 1889 Queen Anne mansion owned by Lori Chandler, is adorned with a variety of chimneys, shingles, a corner tower, and encircling veranda. Rooms are furnished with nineteenth-century antiques that are for sale. Rates include a full breakfast, an afternoon social hour, and a classic film shown in the parlor evenings at seven. Catered, in-room candlelight dinners can be arranged by prior request. Readers will be sorry to hear that "Aunt B," a favorite staff member, has retired.

"The inn is situated high on a hill with a nice view of the city. Breakfast is brought to your room or served on the porch, and includes a tiny china vase of milk, delicious fruit cups, and various quiches and breads. Decorating touches included a pair of old gloves on the table, laces in a cabinet, and Victorian dresses hanging on a wall." *(Carla Lund)*

"Top marks for pleasant, personalized service, immaculate housekeeping, convenient up-to-date bathroom facilities, comfortable room furnishings and beds; quiet, well-lighted location ideal for dining and shopping, and easy parking." *(Helen Rudin, and others)*

Open All year.
Rooms 9 doubles—5 with private shower and/or bath, 4 with maximum of 4 people sharing bath. All with radio, desk, fan. Telephone on request.
Facilities Parlor, veranda. In 7-acre Victorian Park. 8 m to beach.
Location Old Town, 2 m from downtown. From Los Angeles: follow I-5 S to Old Town Ave. exit. Left on San Diego Ave., right on Harney to Heritage Park. From downtown San Diego and airport: take I-5 to Old Town Ave. exit. Left on San Diego Ave., right on Harney to Heritage Park.
Restrictions No smoking. No children under 14.
Credit cards MC, Visa.
Rates B&B, $75–115 double, $65–85 single. Extra person in room, $15. 2-night weekend minimum. 10% senior discount. Theme packages. Prix fixe dinners for two: $55 or $105.
Extras Ramp for wheelchair access; 1 bathroom equipped for disabled. Spanish, French spoken.

Horton Grand Hotel
311 Island Avenue 92101

Tel: (619) 544–1886
(800) 999–1886

One can safely say, without fear of contradiction, that there is no other hotel like the Horton Grand in the country. A Victorian re-creation, it's made up of a pair of century-old hotels—the Horton Grand and the Brooklyn— dismantled brick by brick and rebuilt on this site. The new complex opened in 1986, with the two hotels linked by a sunny atrium lobby filled with plants and white wicker. The staff dresses in Victorian costume, and the hotel restaurant, Ida Bailey's, is named for the madam of the famed Canary Cottage, a house of ill repute that first occupied this site. The cuisine combines American and continental fare with wild game specialties—venison, boar, even alligator. Rooms are decorated with antiques and reproductions, with Victorian-style fabrics and wallcoverings. The queen-size beds are modern, but the draped antique headboards lend a nostalgic air; the marble fireplaces are antique as well, but they frame gas-log fireplaces, and the mirror above each mantel hides a remote control TV. Many of the suites are named after historic figures of San Diego and are decorated accordingly—one in Chinese antiques, another in cowboy Victorian.

"Driving through the Gaslamp Quarter, between downtown and the new convention center is an experience in itself. At night, with a little fog, you can imagine London, New Orleans, or the Old West. When you step into the Horton, it's easy to continue the fantasy. Rooms have 12-foot high ceilings, canopied beds, gas fireplaces, and lots of wood and brass; despite the hotel's size, you feel as if you're in someone's elegant home. The Gaslamp area is being redeveloped; it used to be San Diego's skid row." *(Roy & Sari Martens)*

"In the part that was originally the Brooklyn Hotel, rooms are done in country Victorian, and one room has a resident ghost—Roger, a gambler who was 'done-in' while hiding in an armoire. The lower level of the old Brooklyn is a museum dedicated to the Chinese history of San Diego. Rooms on the 'Grand' side of the hotel are much more ornate and elegant, and those facing the courtyard are especially bright and cheerful. The main staircase on this side of the hotel took months to rebuild as pieces were missing and had to be painstakingly restored, supposedly at a total cost of $1,000,000. The Palace Bar has an 8½ foot gilt-edged mirror over the fireplace and marvelous carvings; jazz bands perform here and you can have a light supper. The food at Ida Bailey's is wonderful; at one lunch I enjoyed an outstanding hot salad of black and white pasta with smoked shrimp; at another Cobb salad dressed with red roquefort dressing.

Open All year.
Rooms 24 suites, 86 doubles—all with private bath and/or shower, telephone, radio, TV, desk, air-conditioning, fan, gas fireplace. Suites with kitchenette.
Facilities Restaurant, bar with piano entertainment Wed.–Sat., atrium lobby, Chinese museum, courtyard with fountain. Conference rooms. Concierge; valet parking, $5. Trolley service at front door. Carriage tours. 5 min to harbor tours.
Location Historic Gaslamp district. Between 3rd and 4th, 5 blocks S of Broadway. 3 blocks from Convention Center.
Credit cards Amex, DC, MC, Visa.
Rates Room only, $198–225 suite, $109–119 double, $94–105 single. Extra person in room, $10. 15% service additional. 10% senior discount. Alc breakfast, $6–9; alc lunch, $9; alc dinner, $28–35. Jazz, theater, midweek packages.
Extras Some rooms equipped for disabled. Airport/station pickups. Cribs, babysitting available. French, Spanish, German spoken.

SAN FRANCISCO   Map 14

Romanticized in song, hyped in commercials, featured in movies and sitcoms, San Francisco is everything promised and more. Compact, ethnically diverse, culturally rich, filled with wonderful stores, cable cars, and restaurants, it's what every city should aspire to be. The weather is best in late summer and early fall, but you don't come here to get a tan, so what does it matter? Bring your walking shoes and a sweater (even summer can be cool), and explore everything. Less well known but worth visiting are the exquisite Japanese Tea Garden and Asian Art Museum in Golden Gate Park and the museums and bookstores at North Beach. Watch the sea lions from Cliff House near Point Lobos Avenue.

Also recommended: The **Abigail Hotel** (246 McAllister Street, 94012; 415–861–9728; 800–243–6510), an English-style hotel, is decorated with Edwardian style furnishings and 18th- and 19th-century English prints. The clean and comfortable rooms and moderate prices have made the Abigail a favorite with both performers and audiences at the nearby opera and symphony. The **Archbishop's Mansion Inn** (1000 Fulton Street, 94117; 415–563–7872; 800–543–5820) was built for the archbishop of San Francisco in 1904 and fully restored as a small luxury hotel in 1984. Rooms are extravagantly decorated with European antiques, flower-painted ceilings, canopy beds, Oriental rugs, marble fireplaces, and crystal chandeliers. The **Bed & Breakfast Inn** (4 Charlton Court, 94123; 415–921–9784), located on a quiet mew just off bustling Union Street, is composed of two adjoining buildings. Owners Bob and Marily Kavanaugh note that "we feel we are particularly good for foreign visitors and women traveling alone, as we are located in a safe shopping district." The **Cartwright** (524 Sutter Street, 94102; 415–421–2865; in CA, 800–652–1858; in US, 800–227–3844) is a family-owned hotel; as they say in the real estate business, it has three key things going for it: location, location, and location. Although rooms are small, guests are delighted with its reasonable prices and the very friendly and helpful staff. The **Chancellor Hotel** (433 Powell Street, 94102; 415–362–2004; 800–428–4748), built in 1914, not long after the devastating San Francisco earthquake, was heavily reinforced with steel girders to ensure its stability to this day. In 1986 the hotel underwent a $2.5-million restoration, returning it to its original elegance while modernizing all facilities. The **Four Seasons Clift Hotel** (495 Geary Street (at Taylor), 94102; 415–775–4700; 800–332–3442), built right after the 1906 earthquake and fire, is a regular recipient of top honors from both Mobil and AAA, and recently underwent a $5.5 million restoration and redecoration program. Located at the bottom of Nob Hill, its convenience to Union Square and the attentiveness of its staff make it most appealing. The **Golden Gate Hotel** (775 Bush Street; 415–392–3702) has many repeat customers who come back for several basic reasons: the concerned and knowledgeable attention only resident owner/operators can provide; the reasonable rates and pleasant atmosphere; and the convenient location. The **Inn at the Opera** (333 Fulton Street, 94102; 415–863–8400; in CA, 800–423–9610; outside CA, 800–325–2708), built more than a half century ago to cater to opera stars, has recently been transformed into a luxury hotel for artists and fans alike. Rooms are handsomely decorated with quality reproductions; the lounge and restaurant, Act IV, is open from breakfast through 2 A.M. snacks. The **Inn San Francisco** (943 South Van Ness Avenue, 94110; 415–641–0188), an 1872 Italianate Victorian B&B, is convenient to both the MUNI and BART transportation systems. Its decor includes ornate woodwork, Oriental rugs, marble fireplaces, and fresh flowers. The **Monte Cristo** (600 Presidio Avenue (at Pine), 94115; 415–931–1875), built in 1875 as a saloon and hotel, has functioned as, among other things, a bordello, a refuge for 1906 earthquake victims, and a speakeasy. Renovated in 1980, rooms are furnished with period pieces; rates include a homemade continental breakfast. The **Monticello Inn** (80 Cyril Magnin Street, 94102; 415–392–8800; 800–669–7777) has patterned its decor after its namesake, with colonial reproduction furnishings and Williamsburg colors. In addition to valet parking, the inn offers a free morning limo to the financial district. The **Petite Auberge** (863 Bush Street, 94108; 415–928–6000), only 3½ blocks from Union Square, is decorated, as you might suspect, in the style of a French country inn, with soft colors, antiques, French-type wallpapers, fresh flowers, and fruit. Rates include a breakfast buffet and afternoon wine and hors d'oeuvres.

Recommended too late for a full write-up is the **Carlton Hotel** (1075 Sutter Street, 94109; 415–673–0242 or 800–227–4496): "The atmosphere is delightful, the rooms pleasant, and the proximity to Macy's basement, Chinatown, and the cable cars is just too good to pass up. The rates are reasonable, too." *(Mary Louise Rogers)*

Information please: The number of delightful small hotels in San Francisco is nothing short of incredible; some are luxury hotels, others are moderately priced "boutique" establishments, while still others are intimate Victorian bed & breakfast inns. It's too bad some of them can't be transplanted to other parts of the country! We've listed those recommended by our readers; our files are bulging with information on other establishments that might be suitable for the guide, but we await your opinions. Among those are the **Mansion Hotel,** a hilltop Queen Anne Victorian filled with luscious antiques and hosting a resident ghost (2220 Sacramento Street 94115; 415–929–9444); The **Huntington Hotel,** a Nob Hill luxury hotel (1075 California Street 94108; 415–474–5400); and two handsome Union Square "boutique" hotels, both with elegant rooms in the $100 range— the **Orchard** (562 Sutter Street 94102; 415–433–4434 or 800–433–4343) and the **Regis** (490 Geary Street 94102; 415–928–7900 or 800–345–4443). Yet another option is the **Washington Square Inn** (1660 Stockton Street 94133; 415–981–4220) recently opened in the Italian District of North Beach, almost midway between Fisherman's Wharf and Union Square. The 16 guest rooms are decorated with English and French antiques, and the reasonable rates include continental breakfast. Comments please!

Another possibility just 10 miles away is the **Mountain Home Inn**, on the slopes of Mt. Tamalpais overlooking the bay and city. Its restaurant serves lunch and dinner daily, while many rooms have private decks, fireplaces, and whirlpool baths; 41 miles of hiking trails start at the inn's door (810 Panoramic Highway, Mill Valley 94941; 415–381–9000).

A point to note: San Francisco may well be the only major U.S. city where only a minority of hotels offer weekend rates. Rates do not include 11% city room tax.

The Andrews Hotel	*Tel:* (415) 563–6877
624 Post Street 94109	In CA: (800) 622–0557
	Outside CA: (800) 227–4742

Location and price, combined with a friendly ambiance are key advantages of the Andrews. It's just a block or two away from the St. Francis and the Hyatt, yet the prices are about half. The hotel's Post Street Bar and Café is attractive, serving fresh, high-quality food.

"A pleasure indeed to find a well-located, clean, and cheerful hotel at a reasonable price. The Andrews is in a 'rehabbed' building two blocks from Union Square, in the heart of the shopping/restaurant/theater area. Parking is available next door. Our room and bath were small but immaculate and cheerful." *(Robin & Thomas Clarke)*

"We recommend dining in the Andrews' charming restaurant, the Post Street Bar and Café. It has received excellent reviews in the local press as well as a feature article in *Gourmet* magazine. The Andrews front office staff is kindly, friendly, and warm." *(Timothy F. Learny)*

"My room was on an airshaft, and I *still* liked it. Good breakfast, beautifully decorated rooms, reasonable prices." *(Ellen Cochran Hicks)* "Comfortable, clean, and wonderfully located. A delicious breakfast of croissants, muffins, and fruit was placed in the hallway each morning and guests wandered out in bathrobes to bring back breakfast in bed. The rooms are small, yes, but for those who will be spending the day sightseeing anyway, they're perfect." *(Barbara Mast James)*

Open All year. Closed Christmas, New Years.
Rooms 5 suites, 43 doubles—all with private bath and/or shower, telephone, clock radio, TV, desk.
Facilities Restaurant, bar.
Location On Post, between Jones and Taylor. 2 blocks W of Union Square and Powell/Mason Cable Car Line.
Restrictions No smoking in restaurant. City noises at night.
Credit cards Amex, MC, Visa.
Rates B&B, $90–99 suite, $76–82 double, $72 single. Extra person in room, $10. Alc lunch $15, alc dinner $30.
Extras Cribs, babysitting available. German, Spanish, French spoken.

Hermitage House
2224 Sacramento Street 94115

Tel: (415) 921–5515

Although built as an elegant redwood mansion at the turn of the century, Hermitage House was sadly neglected when it was bought by Marion and Ted Binkley in 1977. The living room had acquired seven coats of paint, and bunk beds were nailed to the walls. After a massive restoration, the original woods are again visible, and the rooms are now decorated with both antiques and a light country look. Rates include a varied breakfast of juice and fruit, cereals, homemade muffins, coffee cake, croissants and/or quiche, as well as afternoon wine.

"Great attention to detail—both in the rooms and for the guests. Breakfast is unhurried and gracious, with personal, courteous service. There is a private parking facility on the premises—in San Francisco!!!" *(Dr. & Mrs. Roger Sorg)*

"The inn evokes the warmth and style of San Francisco itself. I particularly like the down comforters, private phones, antiques, and Laura Ashley fabrics. Breakfast is served by the fire each morning." *(Robert Frisch)*

"Our room, with fireplace, was lovely. Breakfasts were sumptuous with a large buffet plus eggs to order. The location, in a lovely neighborhood, is close to buses, cable cars and is within walking distance to downtown." *(Caroline & Jim Lloyd)* "Lovely rooms, phenomenal service." *(Carine & Arnie Feist)*

Open All year. Closed Christmas through New Year's Day.
Rooms 3 suites, 2 doubles—4 with full private bath, 1 with shower only. All with radio, desk; telephone, TV on request. Most with fireplaces.
Facilities Living room with fireplace. Kitchen facilities. Patio garden, deck. Off-street parking.
Location Pacific Heights. On Sacramento, between Buchanan and Laguna, 5 blocks W of Hwy. 101.
Restrictions Smoking in living room only. No children under 7.
Credit cards Amex, MC, Visa.

Rates B&B, $125 suite, $85 double, $75 single. Extra person in room, $25. 2-night minimum stay. Long-term rates on request.
Extras Bus stop in front of house. Spanish, some French spoken.

Hotel Vintage Court
650 Bush Street 94108

Tel: (415) 392–4666
(800) 654–1100

"An appealing little hotel, located a few blocks from Union Square and just off the Powell St. cable car line. The bedrooms feature wainscoting, matching flowered chintz curtains and bedspreads, as well as all the basics. The mini bar includes a full bottle of Vintage Court wine for a reasonable price. Free breakfast coffee is available in the little lounge area on each floor." *(CM)*

"Our return here after a year found the hotel as attractive as ever, and the staff just as friendly and helpful. We had a spacious twin room on the seventh floor, decorated in an appealing dark flowered chintz and containing good reading light, a comfortable chair and ample closet space. The hotel is carefully maintained (some renovation was going on discreetly while we were there) and the amenities all remain—complimentary wine by the fire in the pretty lobby in the afternoon, and a very good reasonably priced buffet breakfast in the dining room. The hotel has a direct line for taxis, and someone is on duty at the front desk at all hours. The location can't be beat— it was less than a 15-minute walk to the financial district, and less than ten minutes walk to Chinatown or the shops of Union Square." *(Carolyn Mathiasen)*

One minor caveat: One very satisfied reader noted that in his experience, the single rooms were not as nice as the doubles, although they cost the same.

Manager Mark Allen reports that in 1989 the hotel completed a $500,000 redecoration that included the purchase of new beds for all rooms. He also notes that complimentary coffee and tea are available round-the-clock, and that Chardonnay is served in the lobby gratis each afternoon.

Open All year. Restaurant closed Sun., Mon., July 4, Christmas through New Years.
Rooms 106 doubles and singles—all with full private bath, telephone, radio, TV, desk, air-conditioning.
Facilities Lobby, restaurant.
Location Nob Hill/Union Square. 1½ blocks N of Union Sq., between Powell and Stockton.
Restrictions Smoking in designated areas only.
Credit cards All major cards.
Rates Room only, $229 suite, $79–107 double, $79–97 single. 10% AARP discount. Continental breakfast, $5.50. Prix fixe dinner, $65–150.
Extras Wheelchair accessible. Cribs, babysitting available. Spanish, German, Tagalog, Chinese spoken. Member, Kimco Co.

White Swan Inn
845 Bush Street 94108

Tel: (415) 775–1755

Built just after the famous 1906 earthquake, the White Swan is a Four Sisters Inn owned by Roger and Sally Post. The architecture is English, and the interior decor has been designed to match it with warm woods and English wallpapers. Rates include breakfast, and afternoon tea, wine, and hors d'oeuvres served in the library.

"Cozy and charming, filled with teddy bears, a carousel horse, and fresh flowers. The staff is very friendly and helpful. Wonderful breakfast with homemade muffins, an egg dish, and wonderful granola. In the afternoon they served finger sandwiches and vegetables with dip. Cookies or home-made sweet bread is available in the lobby, and tea, wine, sherry, and soft drinks are always available. Terry robes are provided in the large bath-room. The teddies have so much personality it's hard not to take one home (they are for sale)." *(Dianne Crawford, also Paul Lasley & Elizabeth Harryman)*

"The location was perfect. The food was good and plentiful, although we would have preferred more variety during our five-day stay. The rooms are decorated down to the last detail in country coziness: in short, a yuppie haven." *(MB)*

Open All year.
Rooms 1 suite, 25 doubles—21 with full private bath, 5 with shower only, all with telephone, radio, TV, fireplace, refrigerator.
Facilities Living room, dining room/solarium, conference room, library. Small gar-den with fountain, deck. Valet parking.
Location Union Square area. 2½ blocks NW of Union Square, 2 blocks from Nob Hill, 1½ blocks from Powell St. Cable Car.
Restrictions Street noise could disturb light sleepers. No smoking in common rooms.
Credit cards Amex, MC, Visa.
Rates B&B, $250 suite, $145–160 double. Extra person in room, $15.
Extras Cribs, babysitting available. French, Spanish spoken. Member, Four Sisters Inns.

SANTA BARBARA   Map 14

With its crystal-clear skies and steady 65-degree temperatures, Santa Bar-bara has been a popular winter seaside resort for over 50 years. The rest of the year has always been just as nice, with summer temperatures rarely exceeding the 70s, but people have only recently begun to discover Santa Barbara's year-round appeal. Most activities here are connected with the ocean—the beautiful beaches are ideal for swimming, surfing, diving, sail-ing, as well as whale and seal watching—but the city is also becoming known as an arts center, with several museums and galleries of interest. In addition to lots of lovely shops, Santa Barbara is the place to go for some of California's best food. Of course, this being California, there's no short-age of golf courses or tennis courts either.

The city's appearance is strikingly Spanish—adobe walls and red-tiled roofs abound. Part of this is because of the city's Spanish heritage—it was ruled by Spain for over 60 years—but a 1925 earthquake, which leveled much of the town, is also responsible. When rebuilding began, the local Architectural Board determined that Spanish, not Victorian, style would prevail.

Santa Barbara is located at the southern part of California's Central Coast, 91 miles north of Los Angeles, via Highway 101, and 335 miles south of San Francisco. Weekend traffic coming up from LA can be heavy.

If you'll be in Santa Barbara during the week on business, don't make a reservation without inquiring about corporate rates; nearly every establishment offers them! Rates also tend to be 10 to 20 percent lower from October to May.

Also recommended: The **Bath Street Inn** (1720 Bath Street, 93101; 805–682–9680), a Queen Anne Victorian built over 100 years ago, is decorated with period wallpapers and highlighted with handmade quilts and English antiques. Rates include a full breakfast with egg dishes, French toast, or pancakes, and afternoon refreshments. The **Glenborough Inn** (1327 Bath Street, 93101; 805–966–0589) has rooms in two buildings: the main house was built in 1906 and is a California Craftsman-style home; the second is an 1880s cottage located catty-corner across the street. Rates include full breakfasts, served in the parlor or in bed, and fresh cookies and hot beverages in the evening. The **Montecito Inn** (1295 Coast Village Road, 93108; 805–969–7854), built in 1928 by Charlie Chaplin and Fatty Arbuckle, was a favorite getaway for the movie stars of the day, with its wrought-iron balconies, white stucco walls, classic red Spanish tiles, and graceful arches. Rooms have recently been redecorated with French country furniture, overhead fans, and tiled baths. The **Simpson House Inn** (121 East Arrellega Street, 93101; 805–963–7067), restored to its original Victorian grandeur, is centrally located in town, yet close to the beach and museums. Breakfast can be taken on a large porch or on your own private balcony with fantastic views of the mountains.

Information please: Santa Barbara is full of delightful small hotels and inns, and many of them are listed here. We've heard good things about several more and would like to add them to our next edition, but we need more feedback from you. They are: the **Olive House,** a turn-of-the-century California Craftsman (1604 Olive Street 93101; 805–962–4902); the **Tiffany Inn,** built in 1898 and furnished with exceptional antiques, plus creative breakfasts (1323 De la Vina Street 93101; 805–963–2283), and the **Upham Hotel,** a recently renovated 40-room Victorian hotel dating back to 1870 (1404 de la Vina Street 93101; 805–962–0058).

Kids are not really welcome at most Santa Barbara B&Bs, so an attractive possibility for families is the **Circle Bar B Guest Ranch**, 20 miles to the north on Highway 101. The Brown family has been welcoming guests to their 1000-acre spread for over 50 years. The ranch offers comfortable rooms and cabins, horseback riding, swimming pool, hiking, barbecues, and comedy theater, and children are most welcome (1800 Refugio Road, Goleta 93117; 805–968–1113).

The Cheshire Cat Inn
Tel: (805) 569–1610
36 West Valerio Street 93101

In 1985 Christine Dunsman restored two of Santa Barbara's oldest homes, opening them as a B&B. Rooms are done Laura Ashley–style in country fabrics; most have sitting areas highlighted with English antiques. Rates include a continental breakfast and afternoon wine and cheese. Guests enjoy breakfast on the shaded patio, as well as soaking in the hot tub, which is discreetly tucked away in the gazebo set between the two buildings.

"Two adjoining homes, completely refurbished. Each room named after someone or something out of *Alice in Wonderland.*" *(William E. Simpson)* "We stayed in the Mock Turtle room, which has four huge windows overlooking the front garden. It was beautifully decorated, immaculate, and quiet. The grounds were glorious, with flowers everywhere. We particularly loved the Jacuzzi in the gazebo, with white lights twinkling in the trees and hanging potted plants and flowers. Fabulous food, friendly staff." *(Cynthia Grylov & Thomas Pinto, also CL)*

Open All year.
Rooms 4 suites, 7 doubles—all with private bath and/or shower, telephone, fan. Some with fireplace, Jacuzzi, patio, or balcony.
Facilities Dining room, parlor with fireplace, TV/game room. ½ acre with patio, swing, rose garden, gazebo with hot tub, bicycles. Off-street parking.
Location 3 blocks to theater, restaurants, shops. Take State St. to Valerio.
Restrictions No smoking. No children.
Credit cards None accepted.
Rates B&B, $139–189 suite, $89–129 double. 2-night weekend minimum. Midweek, off-season rates.
Extras Spanish spoken.

Old Yacht Club Inn

431 Corona Del Mar Drive 93103

Tel: (805) 962–1277

A California Craftsman-style home built in 1912, the Old Yacht Club owes its name to the fact that it served as headquarters for Santa Barbara's yacht club in the 1920s, when the first clubhouse was swept out to sea in a severe storm. Restored as Santa Barbara's first B&B in 1980 by Nancy Donaldson, Lucille Caruso, and Sandy Hunt, the inn continues to prosper under their decade of ownership. Rooms are decorated with period antiques and Oriental rugs, and the full breakfasts are highlighted by Nancy's signature omelets and home-baked breads. There's no choice at their Saturday night dinners, but that's no hardship with a sample menu like this one: marinated artichokes, cream of sorrel soup, spinach salad, swordfish with butter tarragon sauce, accompanied by orzo with zucchini and red peppers, concluded with Italian swirl cheesecake.

"Just a block to the wide beach on a quiet side street. A fun place to stay that smells of flowers in bloom as you walk up to the porch. The front room is a combination dining and social place with lots of antiques and knick-knacks and a piano for evening sing-alongs. The kitchen has a turn-of-the-century feel to it, with a big butcher block in the middle. In the evening, guests socialize over wine and hot beverages. A five-course gourmet dinner is served most Saturday nights, but be sure to make reservations well ahead—it's very popular." *(Roy & Sari Martens)*

Open All year.
Rooms 9 doubles, all with private bath and/or shower. Some with telephone, TV. 4 rooms in Hitchcock House, adjacent. 1 room with whirlpool tub.
Facilities Dining room, living room with fireplace, piano; deck, porch, off-street parking. Bicycles, beach chairs. Golf privileges at country club. 1 block to beach.
Location 1½ m to town. Exit Hwy. 101 at Cabrillo. Go W on Cabrillo past bird refuge to Corona del Mar, between Sheraton and Ming Tree hotels. Turn right to #431.
Restrictions Children over 12 permitted in Hitchcock House. No smoking.

Credit cards Amex, MC, Visa.
Rates B&B, $65–120 double. Extra person in room, $25. 2-night weekend minimum.

Villa Rosa
Tel: (805) 966–0851
15 Chapala Street 93101

Built in 1931, the Villa Rosa originally served as off-campus university apartments during the winter and as a modest hotel in the summer. In 1981 it was acquired by its current owners and underwent a total reconstruction, reopening a year later as an elegant small luxury inn.

"Nestled within a crowded enclave of apartments and homes, directly behind the beachfront hotels, is this simple stuccoed inn. Despite being only one block away from the ocean, the pier, and the beachfront drive, the Villa Rosa is superbly quiet. The atmosphere is tranquil and serene; the lobby and lounge are done in soft western colors of white, beige, mauve, and blue, with lots of greenery and handmade Indian baskets.

"Our room was small but nicely decorated, with a queen-size bed, plenty of closet space, and a clean modern bathroom. It had French doors leading out onto the deck, but we had no worries about security; someone is always on duty and the inn has a large wall around it, plus the doors are locked at 8 P.M., and only guests and staff have access." *(Gary & Julie Neiger)*

"The continental breakfast includes delicious cinnamon coffee, home-baked breads, jellies, fresh fruit, croissants. Wine and cheese is served in the afternoon. Very gracious staff; a relaxing, restful, intimate inn." *(Laura Bard)*

"I can add nothing to what has already been written, than to note that the *only* thing I could find in the entire hotel made of plastic was the telephone. Everything, including the attitude of the staff, was warm, genuine, and friendly. This inn has my unqualified recommendation." *(Willis Frick)*

Open All year.
Rooms 18 doubles, all with full private bath, telephone, radio. Some rooms with fireplace; 2 rooms with TV, desk.
Facilities Lobby/lounge. Courtyard with heated swimming pool, hot tub. 84 steps to the beach.
Location 2 min. from center. Off Hwy. 101 turn toward beach on Chapala St.
Restrictions Traffic noise in some rooms. No children under 14. Off-street parking limited; on-street parking can be difficult.
Credit cards Amex, MC, Visa.
Rates B&B, $165–185 double. Extra person in room, $10. 2-night weekend/holiday minimum. Senior discount. Midweek rates.
Extras Train station pickups. Spanish, French, Swedish, German, Flemish spoken.

SANTA CRUZ 95060
Map 14

Santa Cruz is a classic old beach resort, complete with a boardwalk and amusement park. The area's white sand beaches—fun for both swimming and fishing—have been a playground for San Franciscans for over 100 years. The municipal pier is filled with seafood restaurants and souvenir shops, while the local sea lion population frolics in the water below. Other nearby attractions include the redwood forests, golf, tennis, hiking, fishing, and, of course, shopping. Santa Cruz is also home to 20 wineries, seven with tasting rooms—and no tour buses.

"The drive to Santa Cruz (Spanish for holy cross) takes about 40 minutes from the San Jose Airport, a winding road over redwood-covered mountains. As you descend, you see the town nestled in the coastal plain with Monterey Bay as a backdrop. The best view is from the University of California Santa Cruz campus in the northwest part of town, and it's just as lovely at night as during the daytime. The campus itself is beautiful, especially the forest which the students call Elfland; you feel as though you've entered Tolkien's Middle Earth." *(Michael Salkind)*

Summer is peak season here; many, although not all, establishments lower their room rates from November through February. Located on Monterey Bay, on the Central Coast, Santa Cruz is 75 miles south of San Francisco, 35 miles south of San Jose, and 40 miles north of Carmel/ Monterey.

Also recommended: The **Chateau Victorian** (118 First Street; 408–458–9458), a restored turn-of-the-century building, caters mostly to couples wanting a relaxing, quiet atmosphere with all the comforts. Located one block from the beach, each guest room has a working fireplace, and antique and period furnishings. The **Darling House** (314 West Cliff Drive; 408–458–1958), built in 1910 by noted California architect William Weeks, is an imposing mission revival–style mansion with a most spectacular setting. The inn, with stunning beveled glass and rich hardwoods with intricate inlays, is furnished with quality antiques of the period, including a Spanish Mission Room and a Chinese Room to represent the two major cultures of 1910 California.

Although received too late for a full write-up, *Pat Fink* suggests the **Tyrolean Inn** (9600 Highway 9, Ben Lomond 95005; 408–336–5188), about ten miles north of Santa Cruz. "Several small cabins are nestled in the redwoods, and the restaurant serves hearty Bavarian fare, with a wild game specialty on Saturday nights. We enjoyed much that the Santa Cruz mountains have to offer, including the narrow gauge railroad at Roaring Camp, yet were just minutes from the boardwalk in Santa Cruz."

Babbling Brook Inn   *Tel:* (408) 427–2437
1025 Laurel Street

The site of the Babbling Brook Inn was a favorite fishing spot of the Ohlone Indians. Later it housed a gristmill, then a tannery, and was even used as a set for silent movies. It was converted into a B&B in 1981, and was bought by Tom and Helen King in 1986. Four of the guest rooms are in the original historic buildings, and the remainder in chalet-style buildings; the decor is French country.

"Although the inn is in the heart of Santa Cruz, the lovely garden gives it a tranquil feeling. It's on a busy street, but all the rooms face the garden, so we were not bothered by street noise. The guest rooms are charming and the common rooms are particularly inviting. Helen is happy to share her delicious breakfast recipes—after our last stay, she even called me up to make sure she had given me the right instructions!" *(Carla & Jim Farrell)*

"Our room had a large closet, queen-size bed, and wonderful antique pine furniture. Breakfast included fruit, granola, yogurt, homemade croissants, frittata, strawberry bread, and hot and cold beverages. Everything was laid out nicely on an antique sideboard, using pretty English china. The innkeepers were very friendly and helpful about suggesting restaurants and area activities and were glad to share the history of the inn." *(Deborah Nocero)*

"The garden, with many walks and nooks to rest in, is a profusion of calla lillies, pansies, poppies, phlox, hummingbirds, curios, and even Native American caves. The eight guest rooms which were added by the Kings are named for post-impressionist artists and are decorated with their works and colors. I stayed in the Pissaro Room, which was very bright and sunny, with a lemon tree outside my French doors. Tea and wonderful homemade cookies are available all day, and wine and cheese are served in the evening. Guests share their thoughts about the inn and area restaurants in guestbooks which make entertaining reading." *(Michael Salkind)*

Open All year.
Rooms 12 doubles, all with full private bath and/or shower, telephone, radio, TV, desk. 2 rooms with soaking tub. 8 rooms in annex with deck.
Facilities Living/dining room with fireplace, deck/patio. 1 acre with gardens, brook and waterfall, gazebo, hot tub. Off-street parking. Swimming, tennis, golf nearby.
Location In city. 1½ blocks off Pacific Coast Hwy. 1.
Restrictions Street noise in 2 rooms until 10:30 P.M. No smoking. No children under 12.
Credit cards Amex, Discover, MC, Visa.
Rates B&B, $85–125 double. Extra person in room, $15. No tipping. 2-night weekend minimum. Corporate rates midweek. Off-season packages.
Extras Common room, 3 guest rooms wheelchair accessible. Airport/station pickup, $25/person. Some Spanish, French spoken.

SANTA ROSA 95401   Map 14

Vintners Inn   *Tel:* (707) 575–7350
4350 Barnes Road   (800) 421–2584

As you would expect from its name, the Vintners Inn, built in 1983, is indeed surrounded by vineyards. Resident owners John and Francisca Duffy have decorated the spacious rooms in French country decor with antique European pine armoires and matching custom-made beds. Many rooms are quite spacious with exposed beams supporting cathedral ceilings.

The John Ash & Co. Restaurant, a leader in Sonoma regional cuisine, recently relocated in a new building adjacent to the inn; its architecture evokes both the mood of southern France and the mission-detailing of Sonoma County. Although menus change with the seasons to ensure the freshest local ingredients, a typical dinner might include bay mussels grilled with cilantro butter, duck breast with currant/port sauce, and sweet potato pie in pecan crust with homemade vanilla ice cream; the wine list is, of course, extensive.

"Our room was spacious, well-equipped and handsome with a dressing area and large bathroom. Everything was very clean and well cared for. The employees were friendly and courteous. A breakfast buffet consisted of various cereals, fruits, juices, made-to-order waffles, and coffee. *(Jack & Sue Lane)*

Open All year. Restaurant closed Mon. and Sat. lunch.
Rooms 5 suites, 39 doubles—all with full private bath, telephone, radio, TV, desk, air-conditioning, balconies or patios. Many with fireplaces, refrigerators, wet bars.
Facilities Breakfast room, library, restaurant, bar/lounge, hot tub, courtyard with fountain. 5 acres of gardens, 50 acres of vineyards. 2 min. to swimming pool, tennis courts; 1 m to golf.
Location North Coast, Wine Country. 60 m N of San Francisco. Take River Rd. exit off Hwy. 101; go W over freeway, left on Barnes Rd.
Credit cards Amex, CB, DC, MC, Visa.
Rates B&B, $125–165 suite, $98–138 double. Extra person in room, $10. Prix fixe lunch, $15; dinner, $43. Alc lunch, $20; dinner $50.
Extras Wheelchair accessible; rooms specially equipped for disabled. Pets permitted by prior arrangement, $6 charge. Cribs, babysitting available. French, Dutch, Spanish spoken.

SOLVANG 93463   Map 14

Solvang was founded in 1911 by midwesterners of Danish heritage, who wanted to start a traditional Danish folk school and ended up with an entire Danish-style town. Danish customs still prevail, and many come to Solvang for the European atmosphere, shops, bakeries, and outdoor theater. Even if you don't have time for an overnight stay, many travelers find it fun to stop to explore the town; others think it tacky and will "give it a miss."

Solvang is located in the Central Coast region, 135 miles north of Los Angeles in the Santa Ynez Valley Wine Country. It's 30 miles from Santa Barbara and about 15 minutes from the beach.

Alisal Guest Ranch   *Tel:* (805) 688–6411
1054 Alisal Road

Families who've despaired of ever finding a welcome for their children among California's inns will find an oasis at the Alisal, although it's enjoyed equally by adult travelers as well. Dating back to an 1803 land grant originally totaling 13,500 acres, the ranch is named after the Spanish word for sycamore. Despite many changes in ownership, the ranch was used primarily for raising cattle until 1946, when it was purchased by the Jackson family, who started taking in guests on the side. The Jacksons still own the ranch and cattle are still raised here, but the focus has now shifted from the four-legged to the two-legged inhabitants. Full resort facilities enable riders to spend their day on the trail, while golfers and tennis players need never depart from terra firma. Full western activities—trail rides, square dancing, cookouts, and hay rides—await the energetic, but one can just as easily spend the day reading in the library and dozing by the pool. The common rooms are decorated with western flair, highlighted by Indian rugs

109

and wall hangings, and the guest rooms are simply furnished with oak furniture and gingham fabrics. *(TW)*

Open All year.
Rooms 34 suites, 29 doubles, 3 3-bedroom cottages, all with full private bath, desk, fireplace.
Facilities Dining rooms, living room with fireplace, game/TV room, bar/lounge with pianist, library. 10,000 acres with heated swimming pool, hot tub, 7 tennis courts, 18-hole PGA golf course, horseback riding, 100-acre private lake for boating, fishing, windsurfing, sailing; hiking, bicycling, archery, lawn games; children's craft/activities program during summer months.
Location From Hwy. 101, take Solvang/Lompoc exit on Hwy. 246 and go E. Pass through Buellton and go 3 m to Solvang. Turn right on Alisal Rd. (past golf course) to entrance.
Credit cards Amex, MC, Visa.
Rates MAP, $450 (for 4) bungalow, $255 suite, $210 double. Extra person in room, $60 (excluding recreational activities). Service charge additional. 2-night minimum stay. Midweek, package rates.
Extras Wheelchair accessible; ramps, institutional bars. Cribs, babysitting available. Spanish, Italian, Portuguese spoken.

The Inn at Petersen Village
1576 Mission Drive

Tel: (805) 688–3121
(800) 321–8985

A modern facility constructed in the style of old Denmark, this inn shares its building with the 24 shops and cafés of Petersen Village. Rooms are luxuriously decorated with canopied beds and love seats, and TVs are discreetly hidden in armoires.

"Family-run place. Great shopping nearby. My homey room was large, with a canopy bed, couch, and table. Very quiet and clean. You are given a coupon for continental breakfast at a bakery nearby—Danish, juice, and coffee. Only negative was inadequate supply of towels." *(Dianne Crawford)*

Open All year.
Rooms 40 suites and doubles with private shower and/or bath, telephone, television, air-conditioning. Suites with whirlpool tub, wet bar, fireplace.
Facilities Restaurant, shops, lobby with pianist, parking garage.
Location In center. 1 block from theater.
Credit cards Amex, CB, Discover, MC, Visa.
Rates B&B, $195 suite, $70–145 double. Extra person in room, $10. Theater packages.

SONOMA 95476   Map 14

Sonoma is California's oldest mission, founded in 1823. Today people come to Sonoma primarily to visit the area wineries; California's first vineyard was planted here in 1855 by a Hungarian nobleman by the name of Haraszthy. Visitors also enjoy touring its historic buildings, playing golf and tennis, and going horseback riding or ballooning.

Sonoma is located in the North Coast region, in the Sonoma Wine Country, about 40 miles north of San Francisco. From San Francisco, take Highway 101 to 37 east, then 121 north to Highway 12, which runs right through the town.

Victorian Garden Inn *Tel:* (707) 996–5339
316 East Napa Street

A Greek Revival farmhouse built in 1870, the Victorian Garden Inn is furnished with period antiques, surrounded by authentic Victorian gardens, complete with mazes and secret corners. One guest room features Laura Ashley decor, while another has Marimekko blue and whites. Rates include a continental breakfast to be enjoyed in the dining room or taken on a bed tray to your room, and evening wine or sherry, served by the parlor fireplace or on the creek side patio. *(Susie & Rick Block)* More comments, please.

Open All year.
Rooms 1 cottage with fireplace, 3 doubles with private and shared baths. 2 with private entrance.
Facilities Dining room, living room with fireplace. Gardens, swimming pool.
Location Between E. 3rd and E. 4th St. 3 blocks E of Plaza.
Restrictions Smoking restricted. No children.
Credit cards Amex, MC, Visa.
Rates B&B, $125 cottage, $70–100 double. 2-3 night weekend/holiday minimum.

SONORA 95370 **Map 14**

The seat of Tuolumne County, Sonora was named by Mexican miners after their home state. Sonora's handsome Victorian homes date from gold rush days when it was the site of the richest gold mine in the Mother Lode. Today tourism, agriculture, and lumbering provide prosperity. For a look at gold rush mementos, visit the old County Jail, now a museum, and be sure to visit nearby Columbia (see entry). Drive over to neighboring Jamestown for lunch or dinner at the historic, reasonably priced **National Hotel** on Main Street; (209–984–3446). Summer activities include sightseeing and spelunking in the nearby caves. Winter offers skiing at Bear Valley and Dodge Ridge.

Also recommended: The **Lavender Hill Inn** (683 South Barretta Street; 209–532–9024) is described by its owner as being more in the European style of B&B—a private home that is open to welcome travelers. Built in 1900 and impeccably restored, it has antiques, reproductions, and contemporary furnishings.

Sonora is located 120 miles east of San Francisco, 70 miles west of Yosemite.

Jameson's *Tel:* (209) 532–1248
22157 Feather River Drive

In 1983 Jean and Virg Birdsall built this rustic lodge overlooking a waterfall, set among big boulders, shaded by pines, cedars, and a 200-year-old oak tree. Each guest room has a private entrance, three have private decks, and each has a different decor—Moroccan, French country, Mexican, and Irish.

"The hearty breakfast set us up well for a good day of skiing. Jean and Virg Birdsall, the owners, are most charming and hospitable, and we enjoyed a good cup of coffee in front of a blazing log fire before settling into a very comfortable bed." *(Mr. & Mrs. Donald Harvey)*

Open All year.
Rooms 4 doubles share 2 baths.
Facilities Common room with library, games, pool table, wood stove; deck. 4 shaded acres with waterfall. Swimming lake within walking distance. 30 min. to fishing, boating, downhill and cross-country skiing.
Location 10 m E of town off Rte. 108; map sent with confirmation.
Restrictions No smoking.
Credit cards None accepted.
Rates B&B, $45–60 double. No tipping. 2-night minimum on 3-day weekends.
Extras Spanish spoken.

SUTTER CREEK 95685 — Map 14

Sutter Creek is located in Gold Country, in Amador County, about 45 minutes west of Stockton and Sacramento and 2½ hours from San Francisco. In addition to gold panning, visitors look for gold of another sort in the liquid found at the many area wineries.

Information please: The **Gold Quartz Inn** (15 Bryson Drive; 209–267–9155) is a recently opened hostelry with 24 well-equipped guest rooms, combining spacious common areas, luxurious amenities, and Victorian decor and architecture; it was recommended to us by the owners of the Four Sisters Inns, whose properties in San Francisco and Monterey are long-time reader favorites.

The Foxes in Sutter Creek
77 Main Street

Tel: (209) 267–5882

This home dates back to 1857 when it was built by John Davis, a local gold-mining boss. Peter and Min Fox purchased the home 1980 and began inviting paying guests soon after. In 1986, the Foxes constructed a carriage house next to the original Victorian structure, adding three new rooms and a covered parking area in the process. The spacious rooms, some with fireplaces, are tastefully decorated and luxuriously furnished. Rates include afternoon refreshments and a full breakfast.

"Pete and Min Fox will treat you with privacy, respect, and courtesy in a lovely modernized Victorian home. Our large room was furnished with authentic antiques, and a delicious breakfast was brought to the room on a silver platter along with the morning paper." *(Dr. & Mrs. Howard Emery)*

Open All year.
Rooms 6 doubles—all with private bath, radio, air-conditioning. Some with fireplace, TV.
Facilities Dining room, living room. Gardens with gazebo, patio.
Location Gold Country. On Main St. (Hwy. 49) in town.
Restrictions No smoking. Inn not appropriate for children.
Credit cards Discover, MC, Visa.
Rates B&B, $85–125 double, $80–120 single. 2-night weekend minimum.

The Ahwahnee   *Tel:* (209) 252–4848
Yosemite National Park

Yosemite is one of America's most visited national parks, and the Ahwah-nee is one of the best-known hotels in the National Park System. Combine these two factors, and you won't be at all surprised to learn that reserva-tions one year in advance are recommended for weekends during the summer season. Built in 1926 and restored from 1976 to 1979, the Ahwah-nee is a massive six-story structure with three wings, faced with native granite and concrete stained to look like redwood. The rooms are decorated with an American Indian motif, including many original handcrafts and works of art. The landscaping was planned by Frederick Law Olmsted, the designer of New York City's Central Park.

"A classic. A landmark. It is a pleasure to luxuriate in its relative peace when the madding summer crowds are around. Those fortunate enough to be selected in the Christmas/New Year's lottery enjoy a truly special experience, with the majesty of Yosemite in the snow. The dining room is a joy and the staff remarkably helpful." *(Hilary Huebsch Cohen)*

"Everyone should stay here once, but try to book in the off-season, and be sure to see your room first (they vary in upkeep, restoration, size, and views). The Christmas Bracebridge dinner was a treat for everyone!" *(SC)*

Open All year.
Rooms 10 suites, 111 doubles—97 in main hotel, 24 in 7 cottages. All with private bath, telephone, radio, desk.
Facilities Restaurant, bar/lounge, lobby with 2 fireplaces, mural room, solarium, club room. Gift shop, game room, heated pool, 2 tennis courts. Horseback riding, bicycling, climbing, hiking, fishing, rafting, photography, nature programs, downhill and cross-country skiing, ice skating, snowshoeing nearby.
Location High Sierras.
Credit cards Amex, MC, Visa.
Rates Room only, $190 double, $185 single. Extra adult in room, $10; extra child, $5. Midweek rates off-season.
Extras Some rooms accessible for disabled. Cribs, babysitting available. Spanish spoken.

Colorado

The Stanley Hotel, Estes Park

Running from east to west, Colorado is divided into four distinct regions, each completely different from the others. The **eastern section** of the state is part of the Great Plains—flat, dusty, and sparsely settled. Next comes the **front range corridor,** where 70% of the population lives snuggled up against the Rocky Mountain foothills, running from Pueblo in the south, through Denver, to Fort Collins in the north. Natural attractions here include the Garden of the Gods and Cave of the Winds, located west of Colorado Springs; Elitch Gardens and Red Rocks State Park near Denver; and the Flatirons of Boulder. The **Rockies** make up the third region, dominating the state with their well-known ski areas, as well as remote ghost towns, invigorating hot springs, and hidden lakes. You can step back to the 1860s with a visit to Central City or Georgetown (best in spring or fall when the crowds have thinned out), sail on Lake Granby, or travel back roads for a rare glimpse of bighorn sheep and elk. Don't miss the incongruous Great Sand Dunes National Monument, located west of the Sangre de Cristo mountains in south-central Colorado. Standing in the midst of over 36,000 acres of dunes up to 700 feet high, it's easy to imagine Lawrence of Arabia and a host of camels heading over the next ridge. Moving west to the fourth region, are pine forests and wide plateaus, cut by deep canyons, that prevail on the **western slope** of the Rockies. Drive the spectacular rim road of the Colorado National Monument, peer into a 12-mile-long gorge at the Gunnison National Monument, or attend film and music festivals in Telluride. In nearby Durango ride a narrow-gauge Victorian passenger train through rugged mountains to Silverton. To visit Colorado's prehistoric past, stop by Mesa Verde Cliff Dwellings or the less

114

crowded Hovenweep National Monument, where you'll find a variety of pueblos, cliff dwellings, and towers over 600 years old.

Information please: In 1872 a Central City newspaper, describing the newly installed locks on the doors of the Teller House Hotel, reported that: "Guests may lie down to peaceful slumber, undisturbed by apprehensions of getting their heads blown off." Fortunately, this is no longer a major concern for Colorado travelers—a comfortable and welcoming atmosphere is a higher priority these days. You can stay at the **Teller House/Golden Rose Hotel** today—it was completely restored in 1983 and offers period rooms, an attractive restaurant and patio for dining, and a historic bar (102 Main Street 80427; 303–582–5060). More comments on this and any other favorite hideaways (whether the doors lock or not) would be most appreciated.

Another mining town-turned-resort is **Crested Butte,** a relatively unknown place we'd like to hear more about; a National Historic District, it offers uncrowded ski slopes in winter and beautiful Rocky Mountain weather in summer. Although it's only about 30 miles south of Aspen as the crow flies, the mileage for earthbound travelers is closer to 150; the distance from Denver is about 225 miles. One suggested place to stay, about 12 miles outside this attractive Victorian village, is the **Irwin Lodge** (P.O. Box 457, Crested Butte, 81224; 303–349–5140). Reports, please.

Colorado is filled with guest ranches—both working spreads and luxury resorts, and we'd really appreciate reports from riding fans on their favorites. Some possibilities: The **Drowsy Water Ranch** is a family-owned and family-oriented guest ranch offering reasonable rates, a variety of activities, and a strong riding program (P.O. Box 147, Granby 80446; 303–725–3456). Also in Granby (northwest of Denver) is the very luxurious **C Lazy U Ranch** with a full range of activities for children and adults; while it has an excellent reputation, it's rather on the large side for a Colorado ranch, accommodating 115 guests (P.O. Box 378, Granby 80446; 303–887–3344). In south central Colorado is the **Powderhorn Ranch**, a small, casual family-owned spread in the wilderness of south central Colorado 25 miles south of Gunnison; families enjoy rafting, cookouts, and old-time movies, although riding is the principal activity for all (Powderhorn 81243; 303–641–0220).

Rates do not include 7.1% state lodging and meals tax; some towns have additional local taxes.

ASPEN 81611   **Map 10**

Aspen has come a long way from its mining town heritage. Now a famous ski resort and artists' colony, the area offers mountain beauty and outdoor sports all year round. An Aspen summer offers a relaxed pace, an excellent music festival, fine trout fishing, and crisp mountain air, but skiing is still the premier tourist attraction, so winter hotel rates are nearly double those of summer.

Information please: Arguably the most popular hostelry in town is the

newly restored **Hotel Jerome,** its 94 rooms (27 original, 67 new) all beautifully decorated with Victorian antiques, period wallpapers, and modern
baths and amenities. The Jerome's three restaurants range from casual to
elegantly opulent, and its bars are longtime favorites (330 East Main Street;
800–331–7213). The **Molly Gibson Lodge** is known for a more casual
atmosphere (101 West Main Street; 303–925–2580 or 800–35 MOLLY).
The decor of its 54 guest rooms is contemporary and comfortable, and its
hot tubs and swimming pools are heated year-round. A far more rustic
alternative in nearby Maroon Creek Valley are the cabins of the moderately priced **T Lazy 7 Ranch** (Box 240, Aspen 81612; 303–925–7254). A
family-owned working horse ranch since 1938, the Deanes offer pond and
stream trout fishing, a heated swimming pool, sauna and Jacuzzi, and of
course, lots of riding for kids and adults alike in summer, skiing and
snowmobiling in winter.

Hearthstone House

Tel: (303) 925–7632

134 East Hyman Street

European ambience and service in a handsome, contemporary lodge are the
goal of owner-manager Irma Prodinger, whose family operates a similar
but smaller hotel in Lech am Arlberg, Austria. Rates include a buffet
breakfast of juice, fruit, croissants, coffee cake, cereal, granola, yogurt, and
eggs, plus afternoon tea and cookies, and an evening turndown service.
Guests gather in the oversize living room with views of Aspen Mountain,
to read and talk.

"Small, friendly, comfortable and nicely decorated. Irma and her staff
create a continental atmosphere of service and neatness; they are pleased
to make dinner reservations. After skiing there is a fire to warm you and
magazines to read. The herbal steam sauna is perfect for relaxing tired
muscles after a day on the slopes." *(Hamish Macaulay, also Peter Buck)*

Open Early Dec. to April 10; early June to Sept. 10.
Rooms 3 suites, 14 doubles—all will full private bath, telephone, radio, TV, desk.
3 with whirlpool, refrigerator. Some with fan.
Facilities Dining room, living room, library with fireplace, lobby, Austrian herbal
steam sauna.
Location 2 blocks from center. On-site parking.
Restrictions No smoking in dining room. No children under 5.
Credit cards Amex, MC, Visa.
Rates B&B, $136–198 suite, $96–168 double, $92–152 single. Extra person in room,
$30.
Extras Babysitting available. German, French spoken.

Hotel Lenado

Tel: (303) 925–6246

200 South Aspen Street

Rustic elegance is the theme at the Lenado, built in 1984, with all its guest
rooms opening up into a central space. Rates include a full breakfast.
"Lenado" means "wooded" in Spanish, and this theme is carried through
in its decor: "Written up in *Architectural Record,* the hotel and all of its
furniture were crafted of many woods. Each guest room is unique, and all
have carved applewood beds." *(Helen Magnusson)*

Open All year.
Rooms 2 1-2 bedroom suites, 17 double—all with private bath, telephone, TV, radio. Many with whirlpool bath, wet bar, wood-burning stove, vaulted ceiling, balcony or deck.
Facilities 2-story atrium/lounge with fireplace, breakfast room/piano bar, covered porch, library, conference and screening rooms. Rooftop deck with hot tub. Garden.
Location Near center. Overlooking Bass Park.
Restrictions Smoking in bar only. $45 cancellation fee.
Credit cards Amex, DC, MC, Visa.
Rates B&B, $250–400 suite, $100–260 double, plus service. Discount on weekly stays Jan. 3–Feb. 1. 2-3 night weekend and Christmas minimum.
Extras Cribs available. French, Spanish, Swedish, Polish spoken.

Independence Square Hotel
404 South Galena Street

Tel: (303) 920–2313

A 150-year-old building was gutted and completely rebuilt to create this hotel. Nearly all rooms have been outfitted with retractable custom-designed "Murphy" beds, as one correspondent describes below.

"The rooms are done in French country decor, and are very clean. One unusual feature compensated for the rather small size of our room—it came with a Murphy bed that we could pop out of the wall during the day, giving us plenty of extra space and changing the character of the room completely! Rates include a continental breakfast, and there's a hot tub on the roof with a great view.

"The location is very central—you can walk to everything, and the shuttle bus to all the other mountains is right across the street. The hotel staff is made up of a group of cheerful college-age kids; we didn't see any signs of the owner. Given the fact that prices in Aspen are high, we thought this hotel was an excellent value, compared to the others where we've stayed." *(CF)* More comments, please.

Open All year.
Rooms 28 doubles—all with private bath and/or shower, telephone, radio, TV, desk, air-conditioning, wet bar, refrigerator.
Facilities Atrium lounge, library, rooftop Jacuzzi and sundeck. Individual ski lockers.
Location In center. 1½ blocks to Rubey Park bus terminal.
Credit cards Amex, DC, MC, Visa.
Rates B&B, $95–275 double. Extra person in room, $10. No charge for children under 2.
Extras Cribs, babysitting available. French, German, Spanish spoken.

Sardy House
128 East Main Street

Tel: (303) 920–2525

A turreted Victorian, the Sardy House was built in 1893 by "Three-Fingered Jack" Atkinson and was one of the first houses in Colorado with central heating, indoor plumbing, and electric lights. The inn was renovated in 1985 by the same group that redid the Lenado (described above), in a decor combining period elegance with contemporary lightness. Many of the rooms have hand-rubbed cherry furnishings; some units have a view of the ski slopes. The red brick inn is composed of two buildings, the original mansion and the converted carriage house, connected by an enclosed gallery. Rates include a full breakfast of omelets or waffles, home-baked bread, and fresh juices; dinners are pricey but delicious, with Colorado specialties ranging from rack of lamb to filet mignon sauced with pink peppercorns and cream. *(MW)* More comments, please.

Open Late Nov.–mid-April; June 1–mid-Oct.
Rooms 2 suites, 13 doubles—all with full private bath, telephone, radio, TV, desk. Suites with whirlpool tub, stereo, VCR, bar. 11 doubles with whirlpool bath.
Facilities Dining room, bar, parlor, conference room, balcony, porch. Swimming pool, sauna, hot tub. Off-street parking for 6 cars.
Location 1 block from center.
Restrictions Smoking in bar only.
Credit cards Amex, DC, MC, Visa.
Rates B&B, $275–495 suite, $130–325 double, plus service. Weekend and holiday minimum stay. Alc dinner, $45–55.
Extras Cribs available. Spanish, French, Polish spoken.

BOULDER 80302   Map 10

Boulder is home to the University of Colorado and to outdoor sports of every kind. It is a friendly but sophisticated place, set against the backdrop of the Flatirons, a massive rock formation that juts 2000 feet up from the edge of town. Boulder is located in north central Colorado, 35 miles north-west of Denver via Highway 36.

Also recommended: Although there wasn't time to complete a full writeup, *Tatiana Maxwell* reports that the **Briar Rose B&B** (2151 Arapahoe Avenue 80302; 303–442–3007), in a quiet residential neighborhood, de-lights guests with "antique-filled rooms, down comforters, fireplaces, and real Boulder atmosphere. Rooms in the main house have a great deal of charm but share a bath, those in the annex have private baths but are not as cozy. My favorite room is a mini-suite added to the west wing of the house. It's a large bedroom with fireplace and private bath. Nothing is quite so romantic and inviting as a fire in the fireplace while the snow falls outside after a wonderful dinner for two at John's. Terrific breakfasts are served at a large communal table; guests come from all backgrounds and are often fascinating."

The Hotel Boulderado   *Tel:* (303) 442–4344
2115 Thirteenth Street   (800) 433–4344

By combining the words "Boulder" and "Colorado," the hotel's original owners came up with a name that guests could easily remember. The gesture proved unnecessary because few could forget the Victorian luxury this Boulder landmark provided. Built in 1909, the Boulderado Hotel expe-rienced prosperity through the 1920s and slow deterioration thereafter. Now returned to its former grandeur, the restored rooms are decorated with antique and reproduction furnishings; a modern wing was built in 1985 with larger rooms and more modern facilities, with an additional expansion planned for completion early in 1990.

"The hotel has a marvelous ambiance, a great old-fashioned bar, and a wonderful lobby with a restored stained glass skylight above the second floor and a cantilevered cherry staircase. My room had the amenities of a suite, at a rate many places would charge for a tiny room. The original man-operated elevator is a nice touch." *(Michael Crick)*

"Despite its frequent expansions, the Boulderado remains a wonderful little hotel. I prefer the rooms in the main hotel rather than the modern annex. Although the plumbing is not as good, each room is different and wonderful, full of antiques and comfortably furnished. A fifth-floor corner room provides views of the spectacular Flatirons. The lobby has two delightful bars and a pretty restaurant, Winston's. The location is good, just a block from Boulder's famous pedestrian mall, fun for all ages." *(Tatiana Maxwell)*

Open All year.
Rooms 103 suites and doubles with private bath. All with telephone, TV, radio, air-conditioning. 20 with refrigerator, wet bar. 48 rooms in annex.
Facilities Lobby, 3 restaurants, 3 bars. Complimentary health club passes. Off-street parking.
Location Downtown Boulder. Corner of 13th and Spruce Sts. 1 block from Boulder Mall.
Credit cards Amex, CB, Discover, MC, Visa.
Rates Room only, $135 suite, $77–88 double, $66–77 single. Extra person in room $11.

Pearl Street Inn
1820 Pearl Street

Tel: (303) 444–5584

In 1985 owner/manager Yossi Shem-Avi and his wife, Cathy Surratt, came to Boulder on vacation and, like many before them, decided to stay. The Pearl Street Inn is a turn-of-the-century Victorian, with a modern wing housing the guest rooms. The understated decor includes period antiques, soft colors, down comforters, wood shutters, and bleached oak floors. Rates include a full breakfast in winter, continental in summer, plus afternoon tea or wine, served in the garden courtyard in good weather.

"The inn is clean and pleasant, with working fireplaces in each room. The staff is very cheerful, polite, and helpful. Breakfast is delightful." *(Sylvia Kaye)* More comments, please.

Open All year.
Rooms 1 suite, 6 doubles–all with full private bath, telephone, radio, TV, air-conditioning. 4 with desk.
Facilities Dining room, living room with piano bar, garden courtyard. Off-street parking. 10 min. to cross-country skiing.
Location Take Hwy. 36 from Denver to Boulder; 28th St. to Pearl St. Go left on Pearl 10 blocks to inn on left. 3 blocks from Boulder Mall; 6 blocks from University of Colorado.
Credit cards Amex, CB, DC, MC, Visa.
Rates B&B, $68–98. Extra person in room, $10.
Extras Crib available. French, Spanish, Hebrew spoken.

Room with a View
545 Pearl Street

Tel: (303) 938–8813

A recently remodeled Victorian home within walking distance of the Boulder Mall and the university campus, a Room with a View is furnished with antiques, brass beds, and quilts, and has been owned by Heather Beadle since 1988. She notes that "I respect my guests' privacy while giving them a lot of personal attention."

"Gracious hostess, delicious breakfast. Rooms are immaculate, comfortable, and beautifully decorated." *(Julie Foster)* "Meticulous attention to detail, from the fine antiques to chocolates on the pillow." *(Robin Joseph, also Marilyn Kuntemeyer)*

Open All year.
Rooms 1 suite, 1 double—both with private bath, desk, fan. 1 with telephone, radio, TV.
Facilities Breakfast/living room with games, deck.
Location 3 blocks from center. Go N on Broadway to Canyon, turn W and continue to 6th St. Turn N on 6th, continue to Pearl St.
Restrictions No smoking in public rooms. No children under 5.
Credit cards Amex.
Rates B&B, $75 suite, $55 double, $45 single. Extra person in room, $10.
Extras Limited wheelchair access. Airport/station pickups, $10.

CLARK 80428   Map 10

Unless you're coming to Steamboat Springs for downhill skiing, plan to stay in Clark, which consists only of an old-fashioned general store/post office/library that sells *everything*.

If you don't have the time or money to stay at the Home Ranch (which has a weekly minimum in summer), the **Glen Eden Country Townhomes** (P.O. Box 822; 303–879–3907) is a very viable alternative just across the road. (It's owned by the same company as owns the Home Ranch) Although neither a ranch nor an inn it offers a "rustic western atmosphere, and comfortable units with handsome rock fireplaces. The Elk River runs right through the property, and we were thrilled to see a pair of golden eagles. There's also a restaurant and bar by the road where local cowboys gather for a drink." *(Truman Talley)* There are two units in each building, each with an ample living/dining area with fireplace, fully equipped kitchen, two bedrooms, and two baths; most have recently been spruced up with new curtains, bedspreads and carpeting; on the property is a heated swimming pool, hot tub, and tennis courts; rates start at $90 per day.

For additional area information, see also **Steamboat Springs.**

The Home Ranch   *Tel:* (303) 879–1780
54880 Routt County Road 129, P.O. Box 822

Managing partner Ken Jones built the Home Ranch in 1979 as a year-round guest ranch; he did an exceptionally good job of combining rustic, log-cabin qualities with the extra luxuries we all enjoy. In 1989 the main house was expanded to encompass six guest rooms, furnished with the same rustic elegance as the cabins. Extra thick insulation was added to soundproof one room from the next, and baths are tiled with enameled tubs—no fiberglass here.

"Bordered by mountains, the ranch contains broad meadows, thick aspen forests, a great deal of hilly terrain, and picturesque pine forests along the river. In the winter, snow is generally ample and the many groomed cross-country trails are kept in excellent condition. There is also adventurous back-country skiing on organized trips."

"The individual cabin accommodations are just what you would hope to find, with appointments and little extras that make them first-class. One of the clear pluses here is the food. Served family style, the meals are imaginative, portions are more than ample, and the quality is consistently high; breads and desserts are outstanding. Most important is the atmosphere of the ranch. It's a very friendly and open place, and new friends are quickly made. The management and staff have a knack for making you feel at home." *(Wood & Lillian Nordenholz)*

"The buildings are as handsome as the furnishings, with plenty of towels, comfortable beds, good reading lights, tiled bathrooms, and daily maid service. Horseback riding is the popular activity, but there is also fly fishing in the Elk River, hiking, and llama pack trips. We especially enjoy the four or five Forest Service trails within 10 miles. For quieter moments, the unusually attractive main lodge has a library of books." *(Maggie & Bill Scott)*

"The extra touches really set this place apart. Each room has a laundry bag (not plastic) for your grubbies—it's included in the price. Each room has coffee makers and mini-refrigerators, supplied with coffee, tea, milk, home-baked cookies, crackers and cheese. Baths have hair dryers, toiletries, and thick terry robes to keep you warm en route to the hot tub. Each room and cabin is individually decorated with rustic yet elegant decor—gently patterned or floral cottons, hand-woven bedspreads. Rooms have wonderful hangings and rugs—everything from Hmong appliques to antique crazy quilts to Native American carpets and weavings."

"Most ranches have a cook—the Home has a chef. Even a simple buffet lunch supplemented the traditional sandwich fixings with homemade breads and asparagus cream soup; a chicken/rice/nut salad; a green salad of bibb lettuce, radicchio and sprouts; and an eggplant chili bean casserole. Desserts included fresh fruit salad, homebaked nut cookies, and a selection of regular and decaf coffee, regular and herbal teas. Nor are the ranch dogs exactly run-of-the-pound—they're two delightful if funny-looking Sharpeis— André and Igor." *(SWS)*

Open May through Oct., Dec. through April.
Rooms 7 cabins, 6 doubles—all with private full bath, radio, desk, fan. Cabins with refrigerator, coffee maker, hair dryer, Jacuzzi on porch.
Facilities Main house with dining room; living room with fireplace, piano; library; rec room with TV/VCR, Ping-Pong. Evening entertainment weekly. Children's program (over age 2), play equipment. 700 acres with heated swimming pool (90° year-round), sauna, hiking, trail rides, weekly rodeo, fishing, tennis, cross-country skiing, sleigh rides, snowshoeing. Golf nearby. Shuttle bus to Steamboat for downhill skiing (30 min.).
Location NW CO. Elk River Valley, 18 m N of Steamboat Springs, at the edge of the Routt National Forest. From Denver, take I-70 to Dillon, Hwy. 9 to Kremmling, US 40 to Steamboat, County Rd. 129N to Clark. Alternative route (summer only), take Rte. 40 all the way to Steamboat.
Restrictions No smoking in dining room.
Credit cards Amex, MC, Visa.

Rates Full board, $325 suite, $285–325 double, $285 single, plus service. Extra person, $90; extra child age 3-5, $45. No charge for children under 2. 3-7 night minimum.

Extras Limited wheelchair access. Airport/station pickups. Cribs, babysitting available. French, Spanish spoken. Member, Relais et Chateau.

Vista Verde Guest Ranch

Seed House Road

Mailing address: Box 465, Steamboat Springs 80477

Tel: (303) 879–3858
Tel: (800) 526-RIDE

Frank and Winton Brophy left New York's Westchester County in 1975, headed for Colorado and the Vista Verde Ranch, and haven't looked back since. Set at an elevation of 7,800 feet, the ranch is surrounded by the Routt National Forest and the Mount Zirkel Wilderness and is bordered by the Elk River. The area is home to elk, deer, bear, fox, coyote, beaver, eagle, and crane.

Guests are accommodated in rustic but sturdy log cabins with rough spruce or pine walls and modern comforts—firm mattresses, warm carpeting, and well-equipped bathrooms. Food is wholesome and plentiful, with beef from the ranch pastures, eggs from the henhouse, and greens from the garden, all served family style, indoors and out.

In true guest ranch fashion, entertainment includes square dancing, barber shop quartets, and western music, with weekly rodeos and hayrides in summer. The Brophys raise quarterhorses, and the riding program is extensive, with instruction for all. Ranch work is also available to those who'd like to try their hand at riding herd, checking fences, or haying; guests are assigned their "own" horse for the week. The ranch is known for their friendly staff, and special activities are planned for children.

"The Brophys are warm and friendly hosts, and the ranch is a great place for a family vacation. The play fort alone would keep kids busy for hours, and that's only one of the possibilities. Furnishings are comfortably rustic, with handsome beds made from unpeeled logs, and plenty of comfortable seating in the cabins and the main house." *(SWS)*

"Most impressive was the staff—all extremely spirited and friendly. My daughter loved the children's counselor and happily went off with her to feed the farm animals and hunt for eggs, on scavenger hunts, and a trip to town on an antique fire engine. The food was delicious, and the chef, a sweet, slightly shy fellow named Jacques was wonderful about making special dishes for our vegetarian family." *(Marjorie Cohen)*

A few minor areas for improvement: Better bedside lighting for those who like to read at night; more flexible wranglers on the trail rides; a clearer advance policy on tipping. Another reader felt the rates were on the high side compared to other ranches with comparable facilities.

Open May through Oct.; Dec. through March.

Rooms 8 cabins, all with full private bath, kitchen, fireplaces, porches.

Facilities Dining/living room with fireplace, recreation room with TV/VCR, library. Children's program. Spa building with Jacuzzi, hot pool, cold plunge, sauna, exercise area. 600 acres with swimming hole, lake. Horseback riding, , fly fishing, bicycling, hunting, pack trips, float trips, 36 m of cross-country ski trails, ice-fishing, dog-sledding. Golf, tennis, hot-air ballooning nearby. 25 m to downhill skiing.

Location 25 m from town. From Steamboat, take Rte. 40W, then turn N to Clark; after Clark, bear right on Seedhouse Rd. to ranch.

Restrictions Smoking in cabins only.
Credit cards None accepted.
Rates All rates per person, double occupancy. Full board, $120–160. 15% service "suggested." Reduced rates for children under 12. Weekly rates. 3-night summer minimum.
Extras Free airport/station pickups. Cribs, babysitting available. French spoken.

COLORADO SPRINGS 80903   Map 10

Colorado's second largest city has two key attractions—the U.S. Air Force Academy and Pikes Peak. Other historic sights, both natural and man-made, include the Garden of the Gods, with unusual geologic formations, and a wide variety of museums and ranches, all commemorating various aspects of western history.

Information please: Not far away is Cripple Creek, once the site of incredible wealth after gold was discovered in 1891. At the turn of the century, the town's population exceeded 25,000; today it's less than 2,000. Now a National Historic Mining District, much of the town has been restored, including the **Imperial Hotel,** home to a reasonably priced restaurant, period rooms, and vintage melodrama summer theater (123 North Third Street 80813; 719–689–2713). We also would like reports on the recently sold **Outlook Lodge,** originally an 1889 parsonage, now a B&B, 15 minutes away from Colorado Springs on the flanks of Pikes Peak (Rte. 24, P.O. Box 5, Green Mountain Falls 80819; 719–684–2303).

Hearthstone Inn   *Tel:* (719) 473–4413
506 North Cascade Avenue

Two adjacent Victorian homes, connected by a converted carriage house, make up the Hearthstone Inn. The inn was started in 1978 by Dot and Ruth Williams after a massive renovation job involving no fewer than 792 rolls of wallpaper! Rooms are decorated with period antiques, and rates include a full breakfast with a menu that changes daily; a recent one included cheese soufflé with Dijon sauce, lemon raisin bread, and peaches and cream.

"Quiet homey atmosphere. Friendly innkeepers, always willing to bring you up-to-date on places to visit. Food is attractive and delicious." *(Mr. & Mrs. Bill Spafford)*

Open All year.
Rooms 1 suite, 24 doubles—23 with private bath and/or shower, 2 with maximum of 4 people sharing bath. Some with desk, air-conditioning; 3 with fireplace, 3 with private porch.
Facilities Dining room with fireplace. Carriage house with pump organ, couches; parlor with fireplace, piano; game area. Tree-shaded sitting area in garden, croquet. On-site parking. Tennis, swimming pool, jogging path nearby. 30 min. to fishing, cross-country skiing, white-water rafting.
Location Central CO, Pikes Peak region, 70 m S of Denver. 4 blocks from center. 3 blocks to Colorado College. From I-25, take exit 143 (Uintah St.) and travel E (away from mts.) to 3rd stoplight. Turn right (Cascade Ave.) and go 7 blocks. Inn is on right at corner of St. Vrain and Cascade.

Restrictions No smoking in dining room. Light sleepers should request rooms in back.
Credit cards Amex, MC, Visa.
Rates B&B, $89–99 suite, $68–99 double, $58–89 single. Extra person in room, $12. Summer picnic lunches on request.
Extras Cribs, babysitting available.

CREEDE 81130   Map 10

4UR Ranch   *Tel:* (303) 658–2202
P.O. Box 340

"Spread out amidst high mountains in a valley not far from the Rio Grande River is the 4UR. A pretty side creek of the Rio Grande flows right though the main part of the ranch property. The overall feel of the place is low-key, with no ostentatious incongruities or self-conscious attempts to be 'hip.' The buildings are wood, with three or four units in each. My room was comfortable, a place where you didn't mind trekking in the dirt you picked up exploring the ranch. The main building has a sitting area with a large fireplace and dining room. The food is hearty western—steaks, barbecue, corned beef hash for breakfast. Unexpectedly, the resident French pastry chef turns out wonderful desserts. It's a great place with plenty for families to do. Hiking is particularly good since there are several wilderness areas right near by. The nights here can be very cool even in summer, so the natural sulfur hot springs pool is perfect for loosening up all the muscles you over-exercised during the day." *(Don Carmichael)*

Open June through Sept.
Rooms 19 doubles, 1 cottage—all with private bath, desk.
Facilities Dining room, living room with fireplace. 3800 acres with trail rides, children's program, heated swimming pool, hot sulfur pool with Jacuzzi, sauna, exercise room, tennis court, stream and lake fishing, trap shooting, hiking, jeep tours, ranch store, laundry room.
Location SW CO. 20 m N of Rte. 160, approx. 80 m NE of Durango. 80 m NW of Alamosa.
Credit cards Amex, MC, Visa.
Rates Full board (price per person), $120 double, $130 single. Children 4-12 $95; under 4 free. 1 week minimum in July, Aug.
Extras Babysitting, cribs, play equipment.

DENVER   Map 10

The "mile-high" city sits on the high plains, as flat as a pancake, with the Rockies rising majestically in the near distance (when you can see them through the persistent smog). Settled in the middle of the nineteenth century, Denver has left behind its origins as a mining town to become the largest city in the Rockies. A major business and convention center, Denver also offers first-rate museums and theaters—the Natural History Museum and Planetarium, Museum of Western Art, the Denver Art Museum, and the Denver Center for the Performing Arts—as well as excellent shopping at Larimer Square and the Sixteenth Street Mall. And after watching all your cash disappear, you can stop by the U.S. Mint (several blocks from the capitol) to see more being made (no samples).

Most hotels reduce their rates substantially for the weekend; be sure to inquire about special rates. Rates do not include 11.8% rooms tax. For an additional Denver-area listing, see entry under **Golden.**

Information please: A new inn in Denver we'd like to hear about is the **Victoria Oaks Inn,** located near City Park and the Natural History Museum (1575 Race Street 80206; 303–355–1818).

The Brown Palace Hotel
321 Seventeenth Street 80202

Tel: (303) 297–3111
In CO: (800) 228–2917
Outside CO: (800) 321–2599

Arguably Denver's most famous hotel, the Brown Palace was built in 1892 by Henry Cordes Brown at a cost of $1.6 million, an incredible sum in those days. Built in the Victorian revival of Italian Renaissance architecture, the Brown Palace offers a lobby faced with Mexican onyx, highlighted by a six-story atrium, and topped by a stained-glass ceiling. Exceptional architectural features include central heating from the hotel's own steam plant, two 750-foot-deep artesian wells (still in use), and complete fireproofing. The hotel is listed on the National Register of Historic Places, and it has been updated carefully to include all expected modern amenities while preserving its original western Victorian feeling.

"If you ever saw the movie *Grand Hotel,* you will have a sense of déjà vu when you walk into the Brown Palace. Its public rooms and restaurants bespeak a slower, grander era, when elegance and taste dominated dining and lodging. While people now stay here on business or drop by for a 'power breakfast' (or lunch or dinner), the flavor of another era lingers and should be savored. One caution: Before you take a room, ask to see it. Most are well furnished, but more than a few are on the small side." *(MB)*

Open All year.
Rooms 25 suites, 205 doubles, all with full private bath, telephone, radio, TV, desk, air-conditioning. Some with VCR, wet bar.
Facilities 4 restaurants, lobby, shops. Afternoon tea, cocktail-hour entertainment in lobby, tavern. 1 block to health club. Concierge service. Valet parking.
Location In center.
Restrictions No smoking on some guest floors.
Credit cards All major cards.
Rates Room only, $210–625 suite, $144–184 double, $129–169 single. Extra person in room, $15. Children free in parents' room. Family suites. Weekend rates and packages.
Extras Airport pickups, for fee. Cribs, babysitting available. Spanish spoken. Member, Preferred Hotels Worldwide.

The Cambridge Club
1560 Sherman Street 80203

Tel: (303) 831–1252
(800) 752–1252

Rates at the Cambridge Club, a small luxury hotel with all the amenities, include continental breakfast (brought to your suite with the *Wall Street Journal*), bathrobes, shoeshines, steam pressing, and chocolates at bedtime.

"Located half a block from the state capitol in an unpretentious 1950s brick building, the Cambridge Club offers charm and luxury that take hold the moment you cross the threshold. From the time you check in, across a Chippendale desk, you are treated like a resident at a swanky private club. Each suite is individually decorated; decor ranges from French Provincial to English hunt decor to California wicker. I think the best rooms are #110, complete with a four-poster canopy bed, and #202, a larger, corner-room suite. Avoid the rooms in the back of the hotel—sometimes noise from the back alley can awaken you early. One particularly nice touch, especially for women traveling alone, is the hospitality suite, where you can pour yourself a drink, watch TV, or just relax." *(SC)*

"The Cambridge Club offers a home-away-from-home atmosphere ideal for someone who's often on the road, and the staff is happy to oblige with little extras as needed. I think the restaurant is second to none in Denver for service, food, and atmosphere." *(Marshall C. Watson)* "Profile, the hotel restaurant, is one of Denver's best. The food is excellent and served elegantly in a quiet atmosphere. Management and owners are always present and, in addition to the normal menu, will prepare other items on request." *(A.E. Naut)*

Open All year. Restaurant closed Sun., holidays.
Rooms 27 1- and 2-bedroom suites, all with full private bath and/or shower, telephone, radio, TV, desk, air-conditioning, refrigerator, wet bar.
Facilities Restaurant, lounge, hospitality suite, patio. Health club nearby. Valet parking. Concierge service. 24-hour room service.
Location Downtown. ½ block N of state capitol. 2 blocks from 16th St. Mall. Walking distance to financial district, shopping, theater.
Credit cards Amex, DC, MC, Visa.
Rates B&B, $110–265 suite. Extra person in room, $20. Weekend packages. No tipping. Alc lunch, $11; alc dinner, $35.
Extras Free bus/train station pickups; $15 from airport. Cribs available. Spanish, French, Farsi spoken.

The Oxford Alexis Hotel
1600 Seventeenth Street 80202

Tel: (303) 628–5400
Outside CO: (800) 228–5838

Described as Denver's oldest grand hotel, the Oxford was built in 1891. Colorado architect Frank E. Edbrooke designed it the year before he did the Brown Palace. Built to the highest standards of the day, the hotel featured a "vertical railway" (now more commonly referred to as an elevator) that guests rode to the fifth floor for an amazing view of the city. During the 1930s much of the hotel was remodeled, making it something of an Art Deco showcase, and it remained very popular until after World War II. With the decline of railroad travel, the Oxford's Union Station area location became a drawback, and the hotel became virtually derelict. Fortunately, the success of the Larimer Square renovation revived local interest in Denver's nineteenth-century architecture, and the Oxford was lavishly restored in 1982, at a cost of $12 million.

In 1986 the Oxford was purchased by the Alexis chain, which operates fine small hotels in Portland and Seattle (see Oregon and Washington chapters for listings). The in-house restaurant is now one of four McCormick's Fish Houses, specializing in a wide variety of fresh seafood, selected from a menu that changes daily.

"Lovely, small, restored hotel in downtown Denver. The rooms are beautifully furnished and the service excellent." *(Catherine Chester)* "A nice place to stay; the neighboring area has become very posh. Don't miss the bar, decorated in a Manhattan theme with neon and sculptured walls." *(MB)* More comments, please!

Open All year.
Rooms 2 suites, 79 doubles, all with full private bath, telephone, radio, TV, desk, air-conditioning.
Facilities Restaurant, bar/lounge with live jazz/piano. Adjacent health club. Valet parking. 24-hour room service.
Location Downtown, historic district. At corner of Wazee St., 1 block from Union Station.
Credit cards Amex, DC, MC, Visa.
Rates Room only, $160–300 suite, $110–300 double, $100–300 single. No tipping. Extra person in room, $10. No charge for children under 12 in parents' room. Corporate, weekend rates. Alc breakfast, $4–8; alc lunch, $11; alc dinner, $22; plus 15% service.
Extras All public areas, several guest rooms equipped for disabled. Station pickups. Cribs, babysitting available. Spanish spoken. Member, Alexis Hotels.

Queen Anne Inn   *Tel:* (303) 296–6666
2147 Tremont Place 80205

Once home to Denver's early leaders, the historic Clements district nearly fell to the wrecker's ball in the mid-1970s. Fortunately, Ann and Charles Hillestad were among the preservationists who helped save the area. Now owners of the Queen Anne Inn, they have meticulously restored this 1879 home, decorating it with period antiques, without abandoning more creative approaches—the Aspen Room, for example, is highlighted by a wrap-around hand-painted mural of a golden grove of trees, reaching to the very peak of the turret that caps this room. Guest comfort is also a key concern, and the Hillestads have provided working desks, easy chairs, and fresh flowers in nearly every room. In short, the Hillestads have done incredible things with a building that was a total mess when they bought it: "It just goes to show what a quart of paint, a dust mop, and a quarter million dollars of miscellaneous renovation supplies can do."

"The condition and furnishings of this restored home made us feel we were living in luxury, yet the ambience was never stuffy or uncomfortable. All the rooms are beautiful and spotless, the continental breakfast ample and delicious, and the owners are friendly and helpful. We thought the Fountain Room, with a luxurious sunken tub, to be the best, and also liked the Skyline, Aspen, Rooftop, and the Murphy rooms." *(CG)* "Updated plumbing and comfortable beds. You feel as though you're a guest in a friendly home." *(M. M. Wheeler)*

Open All year.
Rooms 9 doubles, 1 single—all with private bath and/or shower, telephone, radio. Most with desk, air-conditioning; 2 with fan.
Facilities Parlor, dining room, garden. Bicycle rentals, off-street parking. Benedict Fountain Park across street.
Location Clements Historic District, 4 blocks from business district. On Tremont, between 21st and 22nd Sts. 2.5 m to I-25; 3 m to I-70; 5 m to airport.
Restrictions No smoking. No children under 15.
Credit cards Amex, MC, Visa.
Rates B&B, $79–109 double, $54–99 single. Extra person in room, $15.

DURANGO   Map 10

At the base of the San Juan Mountains, Durango was once a tough and rowdy western town. Today summer visitors make it their base for a ride on the spectacularly scenic Durango & Silverton Narrow Gauge Railroad and for trips to the mysterious cliff dwellings of the Anasazi Indians at Mesa Verde National Park, about two hours away; winter travelers head for first-rate skiing at Purgatory, 25 miles north, on Route 550.

Durango is located in the southwestern corner of Colorado, at the intersection of Routes 160, running east/west, and 550, running north/south. The town is 174 miles south of Grand Junction and 349 miles southwest of Denver.

Information please: We need current reports on the **Blue Lake Ranch**, listed in previous editions. It's located in Hesperus, 16 miles west Durango, and now offers three rooms in a spacious log cabin overlooking a lake and the mountains beyond; rates include continental breakfast (16919 State Highway 140, Hesperus 81326; 303–385–4537 from 5/1–10/15; 505–983–1397 from 10/16–4/30).

Also recommended: Although most travelers visit the Anasazi ruins at Mesa Verde as a day trip from the Durango area, *Jack & Sue Lane* recommend overnighting at the **Far View Motor Lodge,** for a fuller experience. Located on Navajo Hill near the visitors' center, this 150-room motor lodge offers "spectacular views and comfortable accommodation" (Box 277, Mancos 81330; 303–529–4421). Rates range from $50–75, and children under 12 are free in their parents' room. When not admiring the view from your room's balcony, guests enjoy Southwestern dining in the lodge restaurant. Another possibility received too late for a full write-up is **Tucker's Mountain Meadow B&B** (37951 Highway 184, Mancos 81328; 303–533–7664), recommended with the greatest of enthusiasm by *Marjorie Cohen.* "The inn has a gorgeous setting on the road from Mancos to Dolores. We had an extraordinary breakfast of blueberry muffins, apple crisp, French toast, vegetable omelet, and scones. Our kids loved their cats, dogs, and horses—even a resident llama. Mesa Verde is just six miles away and the rates are a reasonable $40–65 a night."

General Palmer House	*Tel:* (303) 247–4747
567 Main Avenue 81301	In CO: (800) 824–2173
	Outside CO: (800) 523–3358

Built in 1898 and restored in 1982, the General Palmer is located next door to the historic station of the famous narrow-gauge Silverton train. Rooms are decorated in period, and the hotel's restaurant, the Palace, is a long-time Durango favorite.

"This is a small, elegant hotel, with a sedate quiet air to it. They set out a light breakfast each morning of coffee, juice, and bran muffins (the same every day), which gave us a quick easy start to the day. We had two different rooms during our stay. Both were very clean, attractively decorated with antiques and reproduction furnishings, with modern baths. Our first room was very spacious, but had no window—they accurately call it an 'inside' room. The next night we switched to a room with a window; also very nice, but much smaller than the first one." *(AF)*

Open All year. Restaurant closed Thanksgiving, Christmas.
Rooms 6 suites, 33 doubles—all with full private bath, telephone, radio, TV, desk, air-conditioning. 9 rooms in annex. 2 rooms with whirlpool tubs, 4 with refrigerator.
Facilities Restaurant, lobby.
Location At junction of U.S. 160 & U.S. 550. Adjacent to train station.
Credit cards Amex, CB, Discover, MC, Visa.
Rates B&B, $105–135 suite, $50–100 double. Extra person in room, $10.

Strater Hotel　　　　　　　　　　　　　　　*Tel:* (303) 247–4431
699 Main Street, P.O. Drawer E　　　　　　In CO: (800) 227–4431
　　　　　　　　　　　　　　　Outside CO: (800) 247–4431

Built in 1887, the Strater Hotel has been owned by the Barker family for over 60 years. About 25 years ago, the owners realized that their historic property could never be as modern as a new motel and decided to make the most of the Strater's history. They refurnished all the rooms with authentic Victorian antiques, while replacing the outdated heating, plumbing, and wiring systems. The hotel's Diamond Circle Theatre performs turn-of-the-century melodramas nightly during the summer; its saloon, the Diamond Belle, is a pleasant place to relax; and its restaurant, Harry's, is the scene of an outstanding prime rib buffet in summer.

"When you check into the Strater Hotel, you are also checking into the late 19th century. The Strater is a historic building with beautiful antique appointments and many authentic details. You can squint a bit and easily pretend that it is 1890, and you've come to town to do business with the local ranchers. While there are a lot of nice touches, there are also some things that just don't fit in, such as the Coke machines at the end of the halls and the imitation Tiffany lamps. Still, I'd be glad to go back, just not for an extended stay." *(FSC)*

"Stay at the Strater if you want to be where the action is. It's got a great bar, and a bustling lobby; the kind of place where something is always going on." *(AF)*

Open All year.
Rooms 1 suite, 92 doubles—all with private bath and/or shower, telephone, radio, TV, desk, air-conditioning.
Facilities Lobby, restaurant, saloon with ragtime piano. Jacuzzi. Theater 6 nights weekly in summer. Boating, golf, tennis, kayaking, hiking, skiing nearby.
Location Historic downtown. 1 block from narrow-gauge train station. On Main St., between 6th and 7th Sts.
Credit cards Amex, DC, MC, Visa.
Rates Room only, $105 suite, $59–105 double. Package rates. Alc lunch, $7; alc dinner, $15–20.
Extras Cribs, babysitting available.

Tall Timber　　　　　　　　　　　　　　*Tel:* (303) 259–4813
Silverton Star Route, Box 90 M

Five star/diamond luxury and rustic wilderness retreats rarely go hand in hand, as they do at Tall Timber, an intimate resort accessible only by helicopter or the Durango & Silverton Narrow Gauge Railroad. Built in

1974 and set at an altitude of 7,500 feet, Tall Timber offers guest rooms in several wood and stone lodges scattered about the property. Rates include all meals, using produce from the inn's gardens and homebaked goods. The food is hearty yet surprisingly creative, featuring everything from a lunch of potato leek soup, cucumber and sour-cream salad, crêpes saltimbocca, herb bread, and apple crisp, to a dinner of grapefruit avocado pinwheel, pork teriyaki, potato wheat rolls, and Amaretto torte.

Longtime owner Dennis Begrow notes that "If you depend upon telephones, television, radio, or for some reason enjoy noise, air, and water pollution, you may not find Tall Timber to your liking; we provide none of these." The goal here is "elegant accommodations and truly personalized service in the midst of nature's splendor." *(MC)* More comments, please.

Open Mid-May through Oct. 31; Thanksgiving through mid-Jan.
Rooms 2 2-bedroom suites, 8 1-bedroom suites, all with living room with fireplace, wet bar, full private bath, desk, fan.
Facilities Dining room, bar/lounge; recreation building with exercise room, game room, library. 200 acres with gardens, surrounded by San Juan National Forest. Heated swimming pool, 3 hot tubs, sauna, 1 tennis court, 9-hole golf course, trout fishing, jogging and hiking trails, horseback riding, cross-country skiing, snowshoeing, ice skating (equipment provided for most sports). Helicopter shuttle to downhill skiing.
Location 26 m N of Durango. Access by train or helicopter only.
Restrictions No smoking in public rooms.
Credit cards None accepted.
Rates All rates per person. Full board, $1,150–1,390 weekly, double occupancy, $1,800–2,300 single. 3-night stays, $775–990 double, $1,260–1,620 single. Discount for children ages 3–12. Rates include round-trip transfer by rail or helicopter from Durango.
Extras Cribs available.

EMPIRE 80438   Map 10

The Peck House   *Tel:* (303) 569–9870
83 Sunny Avenue

Despite the magnitude implied by its name, Empire is a tiny, one-horse town, about a mile from Interstate 70 and less than an hour's drive from Denver. Although popular with Denver and front-range residents for dinner or a weekend overnight, the Peck House is also perfect for anyone heading to or from Stapleton Airport, or at the beginning or the end of a trip through the Rockies.

Colorado's oldest operating hotel, built in 1860, the Peck House is decorated with antiques, many of them brought by Mrs. Peck from Chicago by oxcart; highlights include early mining memorabilia. The restaurant serves good food, attractively presented and reasonably priced; specialties include homemade pâtés, sausages, and smoked seafood: "We stopped for lunch on our way from the airport to Vail and couldn't have been more pleased." *(SWS)*

Owners Gary and Sally St. Clair added a hot tub to the back of the hotel; although one experiences a moment of "future shock" moving in one step from the 1880s to the 1980s, tired hikers and skiers will love it. Children will enjoy the farm animals, including the infamous "mountain donkey," and the numerous hummingbirds that visit the wildflower gardens in summer.

Open All year.
Rooms 1 suite, 10 doubles—9 with private bath and/or shower, 2 with maximum of 4 people sharing bath.
Facilities Restaurant, bar/lounge, parlor, hot tub. Gardens, farm animals. Fishing, cross-country skiing nearby. 15 min. to downhill skiing.
Location 40 m W of Denver. Take Empire exit off I-70; follow Rte. 40 N to hotel.
Credit cards Amex, CB, DC, MC, Visa.
Rates Room only, $85 suite, $35–65 double. Extra person in room, $8. Continental breakfast, $4. Alc lunch, $5–10; alc dinner, $25–30.
Extras Crib available.

ESTES PARK 80517   **Map 10**

Information please: We'd like to request reports on the **Longs Peak Guest Ranch** (6925 South St. Vrain Highway; 303–586–2110), a comfortable, reasonably priced place for families to enjoy riding, fishing, and hiking in the Rockies from June to September.

The Stanley Hotel   *Tel:* (303) 586–3371
333 Wonderview Avenue, P.O. Box 1767   (800) ROCKIES

F.O. Stanley, who invented the Stanley Steamer in 1897, moved to Colorado in 1903 at the recommendation of his doctor. An architect as well as an inventor, he completed the Stanley Hotel in 1909 and used specially built steam-powered mountain wagons to transport guests from the train to the hotel. Built to the highest standards of the day, the hotel prospered until 1929, when it passed out of the Stanleys' ownership. In 1974 Frank and Judith Normali purchased the hotel and began its restoration. Today it has been named to the National Register of Historic Places and, thanks to careful updating, offers all the amenities of a modern resort.

"This hotel has been a wonderful place to stay for a very long time. It has been tastefully restored and is a grand place for a family—enough for the children to do, restful for adults. The Sunday brunch is a culinary masterwork that satisfies your appetite for at least 24 hours (depending on how many times you return for seconds). One special offering is a dinner theater that even children enjoy. Sometimes the play is contemporary, sometimes an old-fashioned farce. The hotel is situated in a pretty setting, up on a hill just outside of the hubbub of downtown Estes Park. Try to visit in the spring or fall, when the streets aren't sardined with tourists." *(Suzanne Carmichael)* More comments, please.

Open All year.
Rooms 16 suites, 91 doubles—85 with full private bath, 15 with private tub, 7 with private shower. All with telephone, radio, TV. 15 rooms in annex.
Facilities Dining room, bar/lounge with live jazz, gift shop. Theater, classical concerts. 35 acres with heated swimming pool, Jacuzzi, health club, tennis court, croquet, skating, tobogganing. Golf, horseback riding, fishing, white-water rafting nearby. ½ m from Lake Estes, 4 m to cross-country skiing, 10 m to downhill skiing. 4 m to Rocky Mt. National Park.
Location N central CO. 65 m NW of Denver, at intersection of US 34 and US 36. ½ m from center of town.

Credit cards Amex, MC, Visa.
Rates Room only, $160 suite, $70–120 double, $65–115 single, plus tax and service. Extra person in room, $10. Crib or rollaway cot, $10. No charge for children in parents' room. 10% senior discount. 2-night minimum stay May 15–Oct. 15. Winter package rates. Alc lunch, $7; alc dinner, $25–30.
Extras Facilities for disabled. Airport/station pickups, $10. Cribs, babysitting, play equipment available. German spoken.

GEORGETOWN 80444   Map 10

A mining town dating back to the late 1800s, Georgetown is located just off I-70, 50 miles west of Denver. Summer attractions include hiking, fishing, swimming, and cycling, plus rides on the historic narrow-gauge railroad. Winter brings local cross-country skiing, plus downhill skiing at seven nearby ski areas.

Georgetown/Baehler Resort Service   *Tel:* (303) 569–2665
Box 247

Odette Baehler will arrange for you to stay in one of 15 unhosted Georgetown homes, from a simple miner's cabin to one of Georgetown's lovely Victorians. Each home is provided with a basket of information about the area—restaurants, antique shops, hiking, skiing, fishing, and places of historic interest.

"It was marvelously nostalgic to stay in one of Odette's private, secluded gingerbread houses last summer. It was our anniversary, and having the whole house to ourselves was grand . . . the all-alone leisure of enjoying the memorabilia and antiques, the hot tub and the fireplace. Odette had wine and gourmet cheese there when we arrived, along with provisions for our first breakfast. The kitchen was nicely stocked with staples, and the bath accessories were delightful." *(Evelyn & Edward Kendall)*

"We stayed in Serenity Cabin, a cozy and secluded log cabin, complete with huge stone fireplace, sauna, and oversize bathtub. Although our hideaway was convenient to town, it was hard to leave it." *(Debbie & Jim Wiley)*

Open All year.
Rooms 40 guest rooms in 12-16 separate homes. All homes have telephone, TV, air-conditioning, equipped kitchens.
Facilities Some homes have swimming pools, hot tubs, tennis courts.
Location Homes are in or close to town.
Credit cards MC, Visa.
Rates Accommodation and first day's breakfast supplies, $135–195, double occupancy. Extra person(s) in home, $10–25 each. 2-3 night minimum stay. Weekly rates.
Extras Some homes suitable for disabled. Cribs, babysitting, play equipment, games available.

The Hardy House   *Tel:* (303) 569–3388
605 Brownell Street, P.O. Box 156

Sarah Schmidt's breakfast of homemade granola, with yogurt and fresh fruit, hot eggs and meat dish of the day, plus muffins, coffee cakes, and rolls is sure to have you well fueled for a day of Rocky Mountain exploring!

"Because of Georgetown's location, history, and flavor, the Hardy House is a perfect introduction to the Rocky Mountains. Innkeeper Sarah Schmidt is a delight, and the food, atmosphere, and service are wonderful." *(Carolyn Miller)* "The location right in the village is convenient for exploring the shops. Sarah's cat added a very homey touch." *(Nancy & Richard Stuart)*

"The Hardy House was built in the late 1800s and is painted bright red with white trim. It has small but cozy rooms, a potbelly stove in the parlor for cool evenings, and down comforters on the beds. Georgetown is located in a deep valley cleansed by Clear Creek. The air is pure and crisp, the atmosphere relaxing and quiet, and the surrounding scenery spectacular." *(Patty Jo Taarp)*

Open All year.
Rooms 1 2-bedroom suite, 1 1-bedroom suite, 2 doubles—all with private bath and/or shower (some with hallway bath). 1 with desk, 1 with fan.
Facilities Dining room, library, parlor with TV, patio. Carriage rides.
Location ½ block from Main Street. From I-70, take Exit 228 and turn left under highway. Follow loop signs; take left fork to Guanella Pass. The inn is on right, across from The Place restaurant.
Restrictions No smoking. No children under 10.
Credit cards MC, Visa for reservations only.
Rates B&B, $65–80 suite (accommodates 4), $45–65 double, $35 single including service. Prix fixe dinner on request, $15–25 plus service. Anniversary/birthday special: Privately served dinner in suite with king-size bed, including cake and breakfast—$125 for two plus tax, gratuity.

GLEN HAVEN 80532   Map 10

The Inn of Glen Haven   *Tel:* (303) 586–3897
7468 Devils Gulch Road 43, P.O. Box 19

The Inn of Glen Haven has been known for good food and comfortable accommodation. After changing ownership three times in as many years, the inn is now owned by Tom Seller. We had planned to drop it from this edition until the report below arrived. Among other special events, Tom plans to continue the annual feast of the 12 days of Christmas, under the guidance of its originator, Mr. Wells. The feast begins December 25 and features such traditional dishes as roast suckling pig and flaming plum pudding.

"We felt renewed walking into this comfortable haven. Tom, the innkeeper, and his staff were most accommodating with a very warm and welcoming attitude. In order to provide us with the required bedding for our baby, they drove 30 miles to get a crib. We stayed in the spacious Gold Room, which comes complete with a comfortable window seat, small breakfast table, porcelain bath fixtures, live plants in brass pots, and baskets of potpourri. Everything was crisp and clean, with laces and ruffles abounding. The dining room served elegant dinners, and a breakfast of cinnamon rolls, fresh fruit cocktail, coffee and juice was brought to our room. In all, it has a convivial and delightful atmosphere." *(BCD)*

Open All year.
Rooms 2 suites, 4 doubles, 2 cabins, all with full private bath. All with desk.

COLORADO

Facilities Dining room, library, living room/lounge with fireplace, live music. English bowling green, trout stream, cross-country skiing, horseback riding. 16 m to downhill skiing. 12 m to Rocky Mt. National Park.
Location N central CO. 7 m NE of Estes Park, in "very quiet town of 101 people."
Restrictions Traffic noise in some rooms.
Credit cards Amex, DC, Discovery, MC, Visa.
Rates B&B, $50–90 suite, $50–80 double. Extra person in room, $10. 3-day minimum stay in cabins. Prix fixe lunch, $15; dinner, $25 plus service.
Extras Airport pickups. Dutch spoken. Cribs by prior arrangement.

GOLDEN 80401 Map 10

The Dove Inn *Tel:* (303) 278–2209
711 Fourteenth Street

The Dove Inn is a century-old Victorian, owned since 1985 by Jean and Ken Sims. Despite its proximity to Denver, Jean describes Golden as "a quiet, relaxing place to be," and suggests that travelers consider making Golden their home base both for sightseeing in the Denver area and for excursions into the mountains. Many guests stay at the Dove Inn when visiting Golden in connection with the Colorado School of Mines.

"The rooms are decorated to fit the style of the house. Ours was bright and cheery, and extremely clean, well ventilated, and comfortable. The Simses are helpful hosts—the information we received from them made planning our daily excursions easy. The meals (served at the guests' convenience) were delicious. We met people from our old hometown and people from places we had never been. Each morning the menu varied, so it was fun to come to the table and be surprised. Different mornings produced French toast, English muffins, biscuits, blueberry muffins, egg casseroles, cereals, fresh fruits, and juices." *(Hattie & Terry Fansler)*

"Our room had a bay window with an antique writing desk and a queen-size brass bed, plus decorator sheets and towels and a never-empty candy dish. The location is convenient and easy to find." *(Jack & Galene Sololik)*

"Our carpeted room was decorated in a mix of country and Victorian. The bed was comfortable, with reading lamps on both sides. The bath had a claw-foot tub with shower and big, soft bath towels." *(Jim & Geri Becknell and others)* "The inn is quiet, even when full, and parking is no problem." *(Ferol & Janyth Fell)*

Respondents differed in their opinion of the annex suite. One family found it to be "clean, convenient, well-decorated and comfortable," and made reservations to stay in the same room on a return visit. Another disappointed guest found it to be a "half-block away, in a non-Victorian building. Our room had one chair, no table, and poor lighting."

Open All year.
Rooms 6 doubles, all with full private bath and/or shower, telephone, TV, air-conditioning. 1 room in annex.
Facilities Dining room, decks. Swimming, fishing nearby.
Location Central CO. 12 m W of Denver. 1 block S of downtown; walking distance to Colo. School of Mines. From I-70W take Exit 265 to Golden. Turn left on Washington Ave., then turn left on 14th St.

Restrictions No smoking.
Credit cards Amex, DC, MC, Visa.
Rates B&B, $41–55 double, $36–44 single. Extra person in room, $5. Discount with Senior Saver card. Children under 6 free in parents' room.
Extras Airport/station pickups. Crib available. Spanish, Portuguese spoken.

LIMON 80828   Map 10

Midwest Motel & Country Inn   *Tel:* (719) 775–2373
795 Main Street

The Midwest Motel was built as a hotel in the 1950s; in 1981 it was bought by Harold and Vivian Lowe, who have given it the feel of a country inn. The lobby is decorated with Victorian lamps, old photographs, and Morris rockers, and the rooms are furnished with an individualized mixture of country quilts, wallpapers, collectibles, impressionist prints, antiques, and standard motel furnishings. Instead of offering the homogenized hospitality found at the motels along most interstates, the Lowes "try very hard to individualize our rooms and service to provide a memorable stay for our guests." Recent improvements include a flower garden complete with listening fountains, sculpture and a gazebo. Summer guests might also enjoy Limon's sunset excursions via a 1924 vintage diesel train.

"Stopped by this place on a trip from Kansas City to Boulder. A delightful experience in a small town with friendly restaurants nearby." *(AA)* More comments, please.

Open All year.
Rooms 1 suite, 31 doubles, all with full private bath, telephone, TV, desk, airconditioning.
Facilities Lobby/gift shop/sitting area with coffee, tea, books. Flower garden, gazebo, picnic table, fountains. Tennis nearby.
Location E Central CO. About 87 m SE of Denver, 75 m NE of Colorado Springs. 1 block from center. Exit 359 from I-70, go 1½ m on I-70 Business. 1 block from only stoplight.
Credit cards Amex, MC, Visa.
Rates Room only, $42–45 suite, $32–38 double, $26–32 single. Extra person in room, $3.
Extras Cribs available. Station pickups.

MINTURN 81645   Map 10

Eagle River Inn   *Tel:* (303) 827–5761
145 North Main Street, P.O. Box 100

Although Vail, located just 10 minutes away from Minturn, offers some of the best skiing in Colorado, not everyone is enamored of its Disney-style, instant-alpine architecture. For those with different tastes, the opening of the Eagle River Inn in Minturn comes as welcome news. An old railroad town located halfway between Vail and Beaver Creek, Minturn is also home to several restaurants, offering good food in a fun atmosphere, at very reasonable prices—especially in comparison to the tariffs in Vail Village: Chili Willy's for burgers and great fries, plus Mexican dishes; the

Minturn Country Club for grill-'em-yourself steaks, and salads; and the Saloon for Mexican food in a real Old West setting.

Originally built as the Eagle River Hotel in 1894, the building was gutted and completely rebuilt by owner Richard Galloway, reopening in February 1987 with a Southwestern adobe decor. Although this style seems a little out of place and shows the unmistakable look of a professional decorator, the overall effect is very attractive, with many soothing colors, brightly colored rugs, Indian pottery, and rustic furniture. Innkeeper Beverly Rude says that "we cater especially to couples seeking a quiet getaway, a chance to relax in front of the fireplace with a glass of wine, classical music playing in the background, away from the hustle and bustle of Vail."

"When I lived in Vail in 1968, this inn was a dump, on the verge of falling into the river. What a change! Our room was bright and immaculate; the bed was comfortable, the shower had good water pressure, the hand-painted tiling was pretty and well done. The many hand-painted touches on the walls, window shades, and in the halls showed both a loving touch and tremendous attention to detail. The continental breakfast included the best granola I've ever eaten—crisp and light—with juice, excellent coffee, and croissants. The staff is friendly and helpful." *(Patty Bareford)*

"Upon entering this delightful inn, one is immediately surrounded by a Southwestern atmosphere, a bright fire, and a cozy sitting room. The rooms are a good size and extremely comfortable. Warm flannel sheets on the beds are a godsend after an exhausting day on the slopes. Innkeeper Beverly Rude, as well as being a lovely hostess, is a super cook, and we relished the delicious breakfasts. From 5 to 7 P.M. there was also a convivial wine and cheese hour, when all the guests gathered about the downstairs beehive fireplace." *(Barbara Feldberg, also M.J. Krupp)*

Open June through Sept., Nov. through April.

Rooms 12 doubles, all with private shower, radio, TV, desk.

Facilities Breakfast room, parlor with fireplace. Hot tub. 10 min. to downhill, cross-country skiing. Golf, tennis, hiking, fishing, horseback riding, bicycling, white-water rafting nearby.

Location W Central CO. Approx. 100 m W of Denver. Midway between Vail and Beaver Creek (Avon). From Vail, take I-70 W to exit 171. Turn right at stop sign, go right 2 m. As you enter town, turn left and cross bridge; inn is clearly visible on left-hand side.

Restrictions Light sleepers should request a room on the river side. No smoking in common rooms. No children under 12.

Credit cards Amex, MC, Visa.

Rates B&B, $69–135 double, $59–125 single. 10% senior discount. Minimum stay requirement Dec. 21–Jan. 4.

Extras Shuttle bus to ski slopes.

OURAY 81427 Map 10

Named after a famous Ute chief, the town of Ouray (pronounced "you-RAY") experienced a population explosion when both gold and silver were discovered here in 1875. Now a historic district, the town's modern-day attractions include the many waterfalls in deep and narrow Box Canyon, dipping in the natural hot-springs swimming pool, gold mine tours, llama tours, plus horseback riding, hiking, trout fishing, and hunting in the surrounding San Juan Mountains.

Ouray is located on Route 550, the "Million Dollar Highway" blasted out of solid rock in southwestern Colorado, 98 miles south of Grand Junction, 75 miles north of Durango, and 45 miles east of Telluride.

Information please: Lots of other B&Bs have opened in Ouray recently and another possibility is the **Ouray 1898 House** built during the gold boom and now offering antique charm, wonderful views of the San Juans, and reasonable rates (Main Street, P.O. Box 641; 303–325–4871 or 816–665–0277). If a riding vacation is more your preference, the family-owned **MacTiernan's San Juan Guest Ranch**, just north of town, accommodates 20 guests in a comfortable lodge; rates are very affordable (2882 Highway 23, Ridgway 81432; 303–626–5360).

House of Yesteryear
516 Oak Street

Tel: (303) 325–4277

The House of Yesteryear is a rambling 15-room Victorian, built in 1898 and owned and run by Raymond and June O'Brien since 1975. Purchased on a hillside, most rooms and the inn's front porch offer beautiful mountain views. Rooms are decorated with a variety of Victorian antiques, including a massive oak table and buffet originally owned by Adolph Coors, a Russian walnut sleigh bed, and an antique brass bed. Rates include a continental breakfast with a variety of home-baked muffins, juice, and fresh fruit, plus coffee and tea.

"Service and cleanliness are perfect. Ray stays near the door at night to ensure that guests are not disturbed by those arriving late. You wake up to the smell of freshly baked sweet rolls each morning."*(James & Debra Jimenez)*

"Our favorite room is upstairs at the front of the house. There windows stay open and fresh air cools the room the old-fashioned way. About 100 feet below, the Uncompahgre River lulls you to sleep (under a blanket) on the antique brass bed." *(Bobby Fortenberry)*

Open Early June–late Sept.
Rooms 8 doubles—1 with full private bath, 2 with ½ bath, 5 with maximum of 5 people sharing bath, 2 rooms equipped with sink. 1 with desk.
Facilities Living room with piano and games, dining room with TV, balcony, porch. Swimming nearby.
Location SW CO, San Juan Mts. 30 m S of Montrose, 76 m N of Durango. Take Rte. 550 to Ouray; from Main Street, turn west on 7th Ave. and cross bridge. At Oak St. turn left up hill to inn. 4 blocks to Box Canyon.
Restrictions No smoking in guest rooms.
Credit cards MC, Visa.
Rates B&B, $32–55 double. Extra person in room, $5. 2-day minimum stay holidays/special events.
Extras Cribs available.

St. Elmo Hotel
426 Main Street

Tel: (303) 325–4951

In 1984 Dan and Sandy Lingenfelter restored the St. Elmo to its original 1898 glory days, furnishing it with period antiques, stained glass, polished brass, and hand-carved wood detailing. Rates include a breakfast buffet of fresh fruit and juice, cereals, hot entrée, and homemade breads and muffins. The hotel's restaurant, the Bon Ton, actually predates the original hotel and stood on the site of the hotel patio. Owner Kitty Heit moved the restaurant into the hotel when its construction was completed in 1898. Gold miners loved "Aunt Kitty" because she never turned away a miner who was down on his luck; today's prospectors can search for culinary gold in the Bon Ton's largely Italian menu, with veal and pasta dishes as particular favorites.

"The lovely rooms are always clean, done with antiques, yet avoid that phony Victorian look that touristy places aim for. After all, this was not a brothel but a respectable boarding house for miners and their families. It still is a good place to meet the locals if you're on your own. The Bon Ton restaurant is always agreeable, and many other pleasant eateries are within easy walking distance." *(Judith Trent, also Keith Jurgens)*

Open All year. Restaurant closed Tues., Weds. during winter months.
Rooms 2 suites, 9 doubles—7 with private shower and/or bath, 4 with maximum of 4 people sharing bath.
Facilities Restaurant with bar; breakfast room with games; parlor with TV, piano; lobby. Patio, sauna, hot tub.
Location Center of town.
Restrictions No smoking in guest rooms.
Credit cards MC, Visa.
Rates B&B, $55–70 suite, $45–60 double. Extra person in room, $7. Off-season packages; 2-night minimum some holiday weekends. Alc dinner, $23; children's menu.
Extras Cribs available.

PAGOSA SPRINGS 81147   Map 10

Echo Manor Inn   *Tel:* (303) 264–5646
3366 Highway 84

Known to many as the "Castle on 84," well-traveled contributor *Keith Jurgens* gives this B&B his highest praise and notes that many other Colorado guest houses pale by comparison. Owned and run by Sandy and Ginny Northcutt, this luxuriously decorated Victorian, complete with turrets and gables, sits just across the road from Echo Lake. Set in the San Juan Mountains, the area offers a full range of outdoor possibilities; plan to visit the natural hot springs for which the town is named to soothe aching muscles.

Open All year.
Rooms 1 2-bedroom apartment with fireplace, kitchen; 3 suites, 2 doubles, 1 single—5 with private bath and/or shower, 2 with maximum of 3 sharing bath.
Facilities Dining room, living room with woodstove, game room with TV, deck, hot tub. Echo Lake across road for fishing, water-skiing. 30 min. to downhill skiing at Wolf Creek. Hunting, hiking, snowmobiling nearby.
Location SW CO. 62 miles east of Durango. 3½ m S of town. Restrictions No children under 12. No smoking.
Credit cards None accepted.
Rates B&B, cabin, $130–150, $60–90 suite, $50–70 double, $40–60 single. Extra person in room, $20–30. Family rates, weekly discounts.
Extra Airport/station pickups. Some pets permitted with prior approval.

The town of Redstone was built as a showpiece at the turn of the century by iron and coal baron John Osgood, who felt that people who live in pleasant surroundings work better—a radical sentiment at the time. A company town, the homes of Redstone were originally occupied by those who worked in or serviced the mines. Today's visitors can select either the aristocratic or the proletarian lifestyle, by overnighting either at Osgood's residence, the Redstone Castle, or the home for bachelor miners, now the Historic Redstone Inn.

Area activities include cross-country skiing in winter and hiking, hunting, and fishing in the Crystal River.

Redstone is located in west-central Colorado, 50 miles west of Aspen, 30 miles south of Glenwood Springs. It's on Route 133, 18 miles south of Route 82, which connects Glenwood Springs and Aspen.

Redstone Castle   *Tel:* (303) 963–3463
58 Redstone Boulevard

John Cleveland Osgood and his wife, Alma Regina, a member of the Swedish nobility, built their imposing 45-room sandstone mansion around 1900 at a cost of millions, then traveled extensively throughout Europe to furnish it with the finest English silver, Tiffany lighting, Italian marble fireplaces, Oriental carpets, cherry sideboards, Belgian wall coverings, and French silks. Nearly all the original furnishings remain intact, so owners Ken and Rose Marie Johnson, along with manager Cyd Lange, have their hands full keeping everything in top shape.

"When at the Redstone, it's easy to imagine myself a member of the elite Rockefeller, Roosevelt, and Morgan set, all once guests at the Castle. The staff is warm and friendly and keep the Castle immaculately clean. Sharing a bathroom was never a problem, and the old plumbing works wonderfully. The claw-footed tubs are perfect for bubble baths, and the comfortable beds are all topped with eiderdown quilts." *(Bill & Janet Brunger)*

Open All year.
Rooms 3 suites, 13 doubles—8 with private bath, 8 rooms sharing 3 baths.
Facilities Grand room, loggia, dining room, library, music room, game room, sun parlor. 450 acres with courtyard, gazebo, gardens, fountain, woods.
Location Entrance 1 m from town, on the left side of Hwy. 133, opposite coke ovens. 1 m from entrance to castle.
Restrictions Smoking in game room only.
Credit cards Amex, MC, Visa.
Rates B&B, $125–150 suite, $65–95 double.
Extras Pets permitted with prior approval; damage deposit. Cribs available.

The Historic Redstone   *Tel:* (303) 963–2526
0082 Redstone Boulevard

Constructed in half-timbered Tudor style, the Redstone originally housed the bachelors who worked the nearby coke ovens. The mines closed in 1909 but, fortunately, the buildings were preserved and the area today is a designated historic site. The inn, listed on the National Register of Historic Places, was recently renovated and now combines antique furnishings and period wallpaper with modern conveniences.

"Glenwood Springs, one reason people travel out this way, is very touristy. The hot springs pool is overcrowded, and the vapor caves are interesting but old and run down. The Redstone, though, is fantastic. Our room, #207, was large. It looked out over a snowcapped mountain (in June), and you could hear the creek. When we ordered tea at dinner, a large mahogany box was brought out, and we had our choice of flavors. A side trip to Aspen is worthwhile, but without a four-wheel-drive vehicle, the trip to Marble and Crystal was disappointing. The drive to Redstone from Glenwood Springs is beautiful, relaxing, and truly enjoyable." *(Mark Goodman)* More comments, please.

Open All year.
Rooms 1 suite, 34 doubles—28 with private bath, 7 with a maximum of 4 people sharing bath. All with telephone, TV; some with desk.
Facilities Restaurant, reading room, game room, music room, bar. Hot tub, tennis court. Horseback riding, fishing, cross-country skiing.
Location In center, just off Rte. 133. From I-70, go S on Rte. 82 at Glenwood Springs to Rte. 133. Take Rte. 133 to the inn.
Credit cards Amex, MC, Visa.
Rates Room only, $70–75 suite, $45–70 double. Extra person in room, $5. No charge for children under 3. Alc breakfast, $3–5; alc lunch, $5–8; alc dinner, $15–25.
Extras Wheelchair accessible. Cribs available.

SALIDA 81201   Map 10

Poor Farm Country Inn   *Tel:* (719) 539–3818
8495 County Road 160

Listed on the National Register of Historic Places, the century-old Poor Farm is Salida's only B&B, owned since 1981 by Herb and Dottie Hostetler. The rates, which include a full country breakfast and afternoon wine, are sufficiently reasonable that you won't need a "poor farm" to recover.

"Herb and Dottie's warmth and friendliness are genuine. The breakfast is delicious, and rooms are comfortable and quiet. We sat with a glass of complimentary wine and made the acquaintance of the resident poodles, Cocoa and Charlie." *(Kathy Gumph)*

"The atmosphere, food, rooms, service, and cleanliness were all tops. The views are magnificent, and the location next to the Arkansas River is great. But best of all are Herb and Dottie." *(Gary Lacy)*

Open All year.
Rooms 5 doubles—2 with private shower or tub, 3 with maximum of 6 people sharing bath. All with radio.
Facilities Dining room, library. 11 acres. On Arkansas River for fishing. Hiking, rafting, hunting, swimming nearby. 18 m to downhill skiing.
Location S central CO. 108 m W of Colorado Springs, 3 hrs. SW of Denver. 2 m from center. Take Hwy. 50 to Salida Hot Springs Pool. Go N on Holman to Poncha Blvd. Go right to Grant, then left to Crestone, then left past golf course to Rte 160 (inn is past town on the right).

Restrictions No smoking in guest rooms.
Credit cards MC, Visa.
Rates B&B, $40–50 double. Extra person in room, $15.
Extras Airport/station pickups. Cribs, babysitting available.

SILVERTON 81433   Map 10

Fool's Gold Inn   *Tel:* (303) 387–5879
1069 Snowden

Nestled in the magnificent San Juan Mountains of southwest Colorado is the tiny mining town of Silverton, home to the Fool's Gold Inn. This B&B is a century-old Victorian with picture-postcard views from every window. "Host and superchef Ann Marie Wallace offers the most comfortable escape possible. It's not elegant—but it's charming; a place to curl up on the sofa with a great book. Here, orange juice comes out of the orange, not the can, and is served with a morning menu of homemade breads and elegant egg dishes." *(Karen A. Maas)*

Ann Marie reports that guests often enjoy riding the Durango Narrow Gauge Railroad to Silverton, spending a night or two, then returning to Durango. Ann is happy to meet the train and to arrange for the return trip; she'll also help you get to the trailheads, so that you can enjoy some of Silverton's mountain scenery.

Open April through Oct.
Rooms 3 doubles, 1 single—2 with private bath, 2 with maximum of 4 people sharing bath; 2 with sink in room. All with desk.
Facilities Living room with fireplace, games; dining room, patio with garden. Sunday afternoon concerts. Hiking, tennis, fishing, trail rides, jeep trips, mine tours, cross-country skiing nearby.
Location SW CO. 50 m N of Durango. Quality Hill area. From Hwy. 550, go 5 blocks E on Greene St., turn left at American Legion, and go 2 blocks to inn on left.
Restrictions No smoking in guest rooms.
Credit cards MC, Visa.
Rates B&B, $50–65 double, $25–35 single. Extra person in room, $10. Tipping unnecessary.
Extras Station pickup in stagecoach. Some pets permitted by prior arrangement. Crib available.

STEAMBOAT SPRINGS 80477   Map 10

Unlike Vail and Aspen to the south, Steamboat Springs is a "real" town, with a life apart from its role as a ski area and resort—it's surrounded by ranches, where sweet hay is grown to feed the massive herds of cattle raised here. Area activities include fishing, hiking, riding, bicycling, swimming in the hot springs (kids adore the steaming three-story high water slide), and downhill and cross-country skiing. Steamboat is known particularly as a family resort and offers families free skiing for kids 12 and under; most skiers stay in the masses of condominiums that encircle the ski area. "The only inn in Steamboat Springs when we visited was the

141

Clermont Inn (Lincoln Avenue, P.O. Box 774927; 303–879–3083), an old hotel spruced up with a hot tub and breakfast room. The location is within walking distance of the town's restaurants and shops; rates are reasonable but lacking are the personal touches which make an inn special." *(SWS)*

Steamboat Springs (the town) and Steamboat (the resort) are located in northwest Colorado, 160 miles northwest of Denver. From Denver, go west on Interstate 70 to exit 232, then north on Route 40 to Steamboat.

For two area entries, see listings for the **Home Ranch** and the **Vista Verde in Clark** the latter lists Steamboat as its mailing address but is not actually located in the town).

TELLURIDE 81435 Map 10

Originally a fairly wild mining town, then invaded by hippies in the '60s, Telluride today has mellowed into a small and isolated town, offering an authentic taste of western history (the town is a National Historic District), uncrowded yet challenging ski slopes, music festivals all summer long, and outstanding scenery. Telluride's new airport, with four daily flights from Denver, has made the town newly accessible to travelers with limited time. Several Victorian homes and hotels have recently been renovated for bed and breakfast accommodation; reports would be welcome.

Skyline Guest Ranch and Ski Lodge *Tel:* (303) 728–3757
Box 67

Set in the high meadows at 9,600 feet, the Skyline is surrounded by the 14,000-foot snowcapped peaks of the San Juan Mountains. With a maximum of 35 guests a week, longtime owners Sherry and Dave Farny really make an effort to share their mountain lifestyle and to accommodate their guests' wishes. Dave describes their attitude both modestly—"This area of Colorado is so spectacular that our job as hosts is made quite easy"—and less so—"We have great horses, wonderful hiking programs, and the best fishing in Colorado." Guests do agree; by March they are typically fully booked for the summer season.

New in 1989 was the ranch's winter season, handled by their daughter Cindy, a first-rate cook and cross-country skier. One of Cindy's typical dinners might include wild mushroom soup, mixed winter greens, free-range chicken with Ancho chili sauce on a bed of vegetables, and *profiteroles au chocolat.*

"Skyline Ranch is situated in some of Colorado's most outstanding mountain scenery—the San Juans. The Farnys are remarkably caring; finding a hostess warmer than Sherry would be difficult to do. Each year they have a staff of nice young people who help to make one's stay a delight. Breakfast and dinner are plentiful and good; the biweekly cookouts are also thoroughly enjoyable.

"Skyline is not luxurious. It was originally a logging camp, later a boys' mountaineering school run by the Farnys. Most of the guests live in the lodge, where the rooms and baths are small but comfortable. Everyone seems quite happy with the accommodations; the living room is a large, airy room where guests spend most of their indoor time. We have always stayed in one of the cabins but have eaten our meals in the lodge with the other guests.

"Dave and Sherry are skiers and mountaineers; they are always available for hiking, fishing (in stocked lakes), horseback riding (they have a good string of horses), and even camping in the mountains. This is a high-snowfall area, so in the spring, streams are full and the flowers are unusually lovely." *(Maggie & Bill Scott)*

Open Early June–early Oct.; mid Dec.–early April.

Rooms 2 suites, 7 doubles, 3 singles, 5 cabins—all with private bath and/or shower. 5 with radio, 7 with desk.

Facilities Living room with games, dining room, library, laundry. Classical music or square dancing 2 nights weekly. 160 acres with sauna, hot tub; horseback riding, hiking trails, rock climbing, raft trips, jeep trips, cross-country skiing; lake for fishing, swimming, ice skating. Daily shuttle van 3 m to downhill skiing.

Location SW CO. 8 m SW of Telluride. Going S on Hwy. 145, 3 m before town of Telluride, road takes right-hand turn to Ophir, Rico, Dolores, and Cortez. Take that turn; ranch driveway is exactly 5 m on left, just beyond lake. Coming from S (Cortez) the ranch sign and drive are on right, 7½ m from the top of Lizard Head Pass, 5½ m from Trout Lake.

Restrictions No smoking.

Credit cards Visa; checks preferred.

Rates Summer: full board, $700 per person weekly. 7-night minimum. Winter: B&B, $45 per person per night. Prix fixe lunch, $5; prix fixe dinner, $26.

Extras Airport pickups. Cribs, babysitting, play equipment available. German, French spoken.

We Want to Hear from You!

As you know, this book is only effective with your help. We really need to know about your experiences and discoveries.

If you stayed at an inn or hotel listed here, we want to know how it was. Did it live up to our description? Exceed it? Was it what you expected? Did you like it? Were you disappointed? Delighted?

Have you discovered new establishments that we should add to the next edition?

Tear out one of the report forms at the back of this book (or use your own stationery if you prefer) and write today. Even if you write only "Fully endorse existing entry" you will have been most helpful.

Thank You!

Connecticut

The Inn at Chapel West, New Haven

As small as Connecticut is, the state has several areas of particular interest to tourists, which are where the best inns tend to be found. Because the listings for each area are scattered throughout this chapter (listed alphabetically by town), here are a few notes on the different regions. (Check the "Location" heading for each entry.)

Connecticut River Valley Although the Connecticut River extends far past Connecticut all the way to northern Vermont, the area we're describing starts just below Middletown and extends south about 25 miles to the river's mouth at Old Lyme/Old Saybrook. Due to a happy accident of nature—a sandbar at the mouth of the river prevented deep-draft ships from entering—commercial traffic after the 1840s went to deep harbors such as New Haven. Consequently, these unspoiled river towns retain much of their early character.

Area attractions include the Goodspeed Opera House at East Haddam, Gillette Castle at Hadlyme, Florence Griswold Museum in Old Lyme, and the antique shops and train and riverboat rides starting in Essex. It's about a 2½-hour ride from New York and Boston, and only 45 minutes from Hartford.

Fairfield County Although it's better known for its high-priced real estate than for tourist attractions, this pretty part of New England is closest to New York City. We've listed a few inns in Fairfield County that might not have been included if they were located elsewhere. Although they are pleasant places to stay, these are simply not the equal of inns found in more remote corners of the state. The atmosphere is not as warm, and the prices are much higher in relation to the value received. We have listed them because of their location: Lodgings in Fairfield County are less than 1 to 1½ hours' drive from New York City and its airports. This makes them convenient for weekend getaways from the city, and good places for a first or last night's stay if you're touring New England.

Litchfield Hills Litchfield Hills occupies the northwest corner of the state and used to be known as the foothills of the Berkshires. It still is, of course, but tourist-board types felt that the name "Litchfield Hills" gave the area a more distinct identity. This area was a popular summer retreat 100 years ago; many of the places we list were built either as inns or as private mansions during that period. Today the area still offers beautiful lakes, mountains, and picturesque villages and is only 2 to 2½ hours from New York City. A full range of recreational pleasures is available, from tennis, golf, hiking, and canoeing to cross-country and downhill skiing, plus a number of art and antique shops, summer theater, and concert programs.

Mystic/Eastern Connecticut Shore From Madison up to the Rhode Island border at Westerly, the Connecticut shore offers many lovely towns and beaches. Areas of major interest are Mystic, with its seaport and aquarium; New London, with the USS *Nautilus* National Submarine Memorial and Connecticut Arboretum; Groton, for more submarines; and Stonington Borough, one of the prettiest coastal villages in Connecticut. This area is about 2 hours' drive from either New York or Boston, and 1 hour from Hartford.

Information please: We'd like to ask for comments on the **Lighthouse Inn** in New London, built in 1902 by a Pittsburgh steel magnate and now restored and expanded as a waterside inn and restaurant (6 Guthrie Place 06320; 203–443–8411); the spacious rooms combine Victorian period charm with all modern amenities. We'd also like to hear about **Randall's Ordinary** in North Stonington, an unusual eighteenth-century house offering overnight accommodations and early American recipes cooked over an open hearth (Route 2, P.O. Box 243 06359; 203–599–4540).

Peak-season rates along the shore generally run from May or June through October. Off-season rates are considerably lower and represent an especially good value during April and May, when the weather is usually just right for sightseeing.

Rates listed do not include Connecticut state sales tax of 8%.

DEEP RIVER 06417   **Map 2**

Riverwind   *Tel:* (203) 526–2014
209 Main Street

In 1983, Barbara Barlow left her native Smithfield, Virginia, for Connecticut. She discovered the abandoned 1850's farmhouse that is now Riverwind. She spent almost a year restoring it, doing nearly all the work herself—including the wiring and carpentry. The decor includes an exceptional collection of country antiques—quilts, jugs, baskets, and more—artfully displayed. Those planning a December getaway should note that Barbara decorates for Christmas "with a passion." Barbara has recently completed an addition to her house, meant to look older than the original house. The addition features a keeping room with a 12-foot cooking fireplace, and the new rooms have completely modern baths.

"Each room has a style of its own, yet the most modern of plumbing and bath facilities. It's clean, well lighted, and has ample parking facilities. The inn is centrally located for easy access to summer theaters in Ivoryton, Chester, and East Haddam. Several good restaurants are nearby, some of them among Connecticut's best. Breakfast is another outstanding feature, consisting of several fruit juices; fresh-baked, still-warm biscuits (some in the shape of pigs); assorted jellies, jams; pastry; coffee; and a substantial supply of genuine Virginia ham (Smithfield, of course, where Barbara grew up)." *(Mae & Henry Pauley, Jr.)*

"Upstairs is a game room with a variety of board games, cards, readable books, and coffee for early risers. Our room had the most comfortable mattress and quilt comforter we ever slept in away from home. We have always felt that the innkeeper can make a good inn better. In Riverwind's case, Barbara has made an excellent inn a memorable one." *(Merton & Kathleen Conley, also Louisa Ketron, Joe Wilcox)*

"A wonderfully restored inn—almost a museum. The town is nothing special but the location is very convenient. The absence of good reading lights are the only thing keeping it from perfection." *(AF)*

Open All year.
Rooms 2 suites, 6 doubles, all with private bath and/or shower. All rooms with desk, air-conditioning.
Facilities Living room with piano, keeping room with fireplace, library, 2 dining rooms, study with fireplace, game room, sun porch. 1-acre grounds with badminton, bocce, croquet.
Location CT River Valley, 35 m S of Hartford. On town green.
Restrictions No children under 12.
Credit cards MC, Visa.
Rates B&B, $125–135 suite, $75–100 double. Extra person in room, $20.
Extras Station pickups available.

GREENWICH 06830   Map 2

The Homestead Inn   *Tel:* (203) 869–7500
420 Field Point Road

The Homestead was built in 1799 by Augustus Mead; in 1859 it was sold and converted into an inn. Architecturally, it was transformed from a colonial farmhouse into a Victorian "carpenter gothic" house, complete with distinctive cupola and wraparound porches. In 1978, the Homestead was purchased by Lessie Davison and Nancy Smith, who, with the help of designer John Saladino, completely restored and transformed it into the elegant hostelry it is today. In the last few years, they have also converted the original out-buildings into additional guest rooms. The inn, set in the beautiful Belle Haven residential area of Greenwich, full of lovely old Victorian summer homes, is still very convenient to the interstate and to downtown Greenwich. The Homestead is also well known for its restaurant, rated three stars by the *New York Times*. Under the supervision of chef Jacques Thiebeult, excellent French cuisine is served at lunch on weekdays, and every night for dinner. The restaurant is set in what was once the barn of the original colonial farmhouse. It was incorporated into the main house during the 1859 rebuilding, and was discovered in the inn's restoration.

"The room was superior in every sense. Electric blanket, good reading lamps, terry bathrobes, huge towels, bidet, and all the shampoos and bath salts one could use. Dinner was excellent and the dining room atmosphere charming." *(MAA)* "The cleanest hotel we have ever visited. Fabulous food, delightful decor, charming staff." *(Ray & Linda Cooney)*

Open All year. Restaurant closed Labor Day, Christmas, New Year's Day.
Rooms 6 suites, 14 doubles, 3 singles, all with private bath and/or shower, telephone, radio, TV, desk, air-conditioning, electric blanket, extra pillows; 11 rooms in 2 separate cottages.
Facilities Bar, restaurant, backgammon room, porch. 3 acres. Large park, tennis, golf nearby.
Location Fairfield County, 29 m NE of NYC. 1 m from town center. From NY, take I-95 to Exit 3. Turn left at bottom of ramp. Go to 2nd light, turn left onto Horseneck Lane. At end of road, go left onto Field Pt. Rd.
Credit cards Amex, DC, MC, Visa.
Rates B&B, $135–165 suite, $105–150 double, $82 single. Full breakfast, $5–10 extra; alc lunch, $18–25; alc dinner, $45–55.
Extras French, Spanish spoken. Cribs available.

IVORYTON 06442   Map 2

Although not recommended for accommodation, the **Ivoryton Inn** (115 Main Street; 203–767–0422) is home to a new restaurant called **Daniel's Table**, where "fabulous nouvelle French cuisine is served." *(Rachel Gorlin)*

Copper Beech Inn   *Tel:* (203) 767–0330
46 Main Street

The Copper Beech Inn was built about 100 years ago by a wealthy ivory merchant. As the town's name suggests, ivory was once its principal product and source of income. The sprawling mansion derives its current name from the enormous copper beech tree that spreads over the front lawn.

The inn is most famous for its restaurant, which has a well-deserved reputation for its country French cuisine. The extensive list of entrées includes sautéed scallops and shrimp with a sauce of cream, mushrooms and tarragon; breast of duck served medium rare; and loin of lamb with garlic, lamb stock, butter, and brandy.

Eldon and Sally Senner bought the inn in 1988 and have rejuvenated the gracious terraced English gardens surrounding the inn. Thousands of bulbs add springtime color early in the season. Rates include a continental breakfast of fresh muffins, pastries, fruit, cold cereal, juices, and coffee.

"A gem in Ivoryton, a peaceful town featuring wonderful old homes and the Ivoryton Playhouse. A perfect base for exploring Connecticut's historic seaport towns, minutes away from Essex on the Connecticut River and close to Goodspeed Opera House and Gillette's Castle. You can do everything—or you can do nothing. The inn has beautifully carved oak doors and paneling. The guest rooms are spacious and artistically furnished with a blend of antiques and country flair. Although the plumbing is modern, the bathroom fixtures in the main house are splendidly authentic, featuring gargantuan footed bathtubs where one could soak blissfully for hours. The food is well prepared and graciously served in three charming dining rooms. Classical music plays unobtrusively in the background." *(Maria & Carl Schmidt)*

"We stayed in a beautiful, large room with a private bath, two triple bay windows, a cozy seating area with a fireplace and a romantic, antique king-sized canopy bed. Our dinner was delicious and the waiter and busboy were friendly." *(Cindy Lindemeyer)*

"We found the new owners to be professional and competent, helpful but unobtrusive. The dinners were exceptional, yet totally unpretentious." *(Lars Nilsson)*

Open All year. Closed Mondays; also Jan. 1, Dec. 25.
Rooms 13 doubles, all with private bath, air-conditioning; 9 rooms with Jacuzzi tubs, radio, TV, located in carriage house.
Facilities Restaurant, lounge, sitting room, parlor. 7 acres with gardens. Tennis, swimming, boating, fishing, antique shops nearby.
Location Eastern CT shore. 2 hrs. to NYC, Boston. 2 m from town. From I-95 take exit 69 to Rte 9. At exit 3, left off ramp, 1.5 m.
Restrictions No children under 9.
Credit cards Amex, DC, MC, Visa.
Rates B&B, $85–135 in main house, $105–145 in carriage house. Extra person in room, $20. 2-night weekend minimum May through Oct., also holiday weekends. Alc dinner, $50–60.
Extras Airport/station/marina pickups in the inn limousine.

LITCHFIELD 06759   Map 2

Tollgate Hill Inn and Restaurant   *Tel:* (203) 567–4545
Route 202 and Tollgate Road, Box 1399

Built in 1745 and listed on the National Register of Historic Places, the Tollgate was originally known as the Captain William Bull Tavern. The inn changed both its name and location in 1923, when it was renamed the Old Tollgate Tavern and was moved from the Old East Litchfield Road to its current spot on Tollgate Hill. Fifty years later, the Zivic family completed a total restoration, reopening the Tollgate in July 1983. In 1988 the number of guest rooms doubled, so more comments would be especially helpful.

The Tollgate is furnished with period reproductions, including Hinson wallpapers and fabrics, Hitchcock chairs and beds, and Shaker tables, and rates include a breakfast of juice, muffins, and coffee, served in the room. Lunch and dinner are served in the Tavern Room, which has exposed beams and wide pine paneling, and in the Formal Dining Room. On weekends, dinner is also served in the Ballroom, which boasts vaulted ceiling, a "fiddler's loft" used for piano music on Saturday nights, copper chandeliers, and an enormous fieldstone fireplace. The chef has a reputation for varied and creative American cuisine, with seafood a particular speciality.

"The Tollgate is far enough off Route 202 to be protected from traffic noise. The inn has no public rooms to speak of; you check in with the friendly young manager at the bar. But our room (#1) offered plenty of space to stretch out in. It was decorated with great style. The woodwork was painted sea green; the walls were covered with green and white fleur-de-lys wallpaper; the curtains, chair covers, and bedspread were in complementary green-and-white-striped fabric. The bath was in need of sprucing up, although it was clean and adequate. A delicious breakfast in a wicker basket was delivered to us in bed. It was served on pretty, strawberry-patterned china, and included fresh juice, lots of hot coffee, homemade spice bread, and muffins with sweet butter. We enjoyed a good dinner on the patio—smoked salmon tartare, saltimbocca, and roast duck with snow peas and saffron rice." *(Carolyn Mathiason)*

Open April through Feb. Restaurant closed Tues. from Nov. through June.
Rooms 6 suites, 14 doubles—18 with full private bath, 2 with private shower, 4 with fireplace. All with air-conditioning, radio; 14 with telephone, TV, desk. 14 rooms in 2 buildings.
Facilities Dining room, bar, lobby, small parlor with TV, ballroom with piano player during dinner Sat. nights. 5½ acres with woods. Tennis, golf, skiing, lakes nearby.
Location NW CT, Litchfield Hills. 2½ m to town. From I-84, take Exit 19, Rte. 8 N to Exit 42. Take Rte. 118 to Litchfield Center. Turn right onto Rte. 202. Go 2¼ m to Inn on left.
Restrictions Smoking restricted in some areas.
Credit cards Amex, DC, MC, Visa.
Rates B&B, $130 suite, $90–100 double. Extra person in room, $15. Alc lunch, $12–15; alc dinner, $40. 2–3 night weekend/holiday minimum.
Extras Airport/station pickups. Well-behaved pets allowed. Cribs, babysitting available. Finnish spoken.

MOODUS 06469   Map 2

The Fowler House   *Tel:* (203) 873–8906
Plains Road, P.O. Box 432

Barbara Ally and Paul Seals, owners of the Fowler House since 1984, describe their inn as an "exquisite example of 1890 Queen Anne Victorian architecture, complete with original stained glass windows, eight fireplaces, hand-carved woodwork, antique furnishings, and original ornate Lincrusta wallcoverings. Most of our guests are people anxious to escape the rigors of the city and relax in the quiet New England countryside." Fowler House was built in 1890 by Dr. Frank C. Fowler, who made his fortune as the "Medicine Man of Moodus." Dr. Fowler manufactured patent medicines and sold them by mail, keeping the tiny Moodus post office busy with 5,000 pieces of mail daily.

"Much has been done to restore this magnificent house to its Victorian splendor. From the light fixtures and fireplaces to the stained glass, carved woodwork, plants, and floral arrangements, everything reflects a genuine Victorian aura. The innkeepers put quite a bit of research and work into the house, making it authentic, charming, warm, and comfortable. They are also well informed about the house's original owner, Dr. Fowler, and all other past histories. Our hosts were gracious, helpful, humorous, and hospitable. Service was excellent and the inn was immaculate. The food served at the continental breakfast and at tea was simple yet distinctive. The location is excellent and parking is ample." *(Linda R. Biancalani, also Peggy Ann White)*

"We browsed through the sitting rooms enjoying the Victorian furniture and oddities of architecture and decor. When we returned from dinner in nearby Essex, a fire was crackling in the fireplace in our bedroom." *(Mr. & Mrs. Ernest Peters)*

Open All year.
Rooms 6 doubles—4 with private bath and/or shower, 2 with maximum of 4 sharing bath.
Facilities Library with games, books, fireplace; living and dining rooms with fireplaces. 2nd-floor sitting area, wraparound porch. Swimming, boating, fishing, canoeing, tennis, golf nearby.
Location CT River Valley, 40 min. from Hartford, New Haven. On the town green. Corner of Rtes. 149 and 151.
Restrictions No smoking in guest rooms. No children under 12.
Credit cards MC, Visa.
Rates B&B, $60–85. Picnic lunch in summer, $15–25 per couple; prix fixe dinner, $60 per couple. Extra person in room, $10. Weekly rates. 2-night minimum, weekend, holidays.
Extras Airport/station pickups.

MYSTIC 06355   Map 2

Information please: Overnighting in a 200-year-old gambrel-roofed home will certainly put you in the right frame of mind for touring Mystic. The **Adams House** is just five minutes from town, with a distinctly twentieth-century swimming pool (382 Cow Hill Road; 203–572–9551).

Red Brook Inn   *Tel:* (203) 572–0349
2800 Gold Star Highway, Box 237 06372

The inn is comprised of two neighboring center-chimney colonials. The Creary Homestead was built in 1770; the Haley Tavern, recently moved to this location, was built as a stagecoach stop in 1768 and is listed on the National Register of Historic Places. Three guest rooms are located in the former, and six in the latter. Innkeeper Ruth Keys has furnished the inn with an extensive collection of antiques, many of them eighteenth-century, and reports that she "has not remodeled the buildings into a hotel-like atmosphere." On selected dates, the inn offers "colonial weekends," which include a dinner cooked over the open hearth and in the beehive oven; breads, pies, and all entrées are homemade the day of the dinner. Rates include a full breakfast with pancakes or waffles and sausage.

"We enjoyed our stay at the Red Brook Inn. Our room was comfortable and charming, and the full breakfasts were superb—the waffles are my favorite. Ruth's hospitality was warm and friendly; good people make all the difference." *(JR, also Nancy & Nelson Ormsby)*

Open All year.
Rooms 11 doubles with private bath and/or shower, desk, fan; some with air-conditioning. 7 rooms with working fireplaces. In two historic buildings
Facilities Keeping room, 2 formal parlors, TV/game room, library, all with fireplaces. 7½ acre grounds with patio, hammock, woods, picnic areas. 3–5 m to beaches.
Location Coastal CT. 45 min. from Newport, RI; 1 hr. to Sturbridge. 2 m from Mystic Seaport. Take Exit 89 off I-95. Go N 1½ m to Rte. 184 (Gold Star Hwy.). Go E to inn at intersection of Rte. 184 and Welles Rd.
Restrictions No smoking. Not suitable for young children.
Credit cards MC, Visa.
Rates B&B, $80–150 double, $65–150 single. Extra person in room, $25. 2–3 night weekend/holiday minimum.
Extras Free station pickups available.

NEW HAVEN 06511   Map 2

The Inn at Chapel West   *Tel:* (203) 777-1201
1201 Chapel Street

"At last, an inn of distinction in New Haven! Forget about Yale graduation weekends—they were booked years ahead before the inn even opened in 1987—but for the rest of the year, a glorious treat awaits you." *(MS)*

Newly renovated by Steven Schneider, this 1847 Victorian home offers a parlor and dining room done in period antiques, plus luxuriously decorated bedrooms, each with a distinct decor. One room has a collection of Victorian masks; another has a canopy bed and antique star-patterned quilt; yet another highlights florals and lace. All have goosedown pillows, quality linens, and such special touches as padded hangers. Rates include a continental breakfast of juice, coffee, and pastries, plus afternoon refreshments; extra amenities include fresh flowers and bathrobes.

Open All year.
Rooms 10 doubles with full private bath, telephone, radio, TV, desk, air-conditioning, fan. Some with fireplace.
Facilities Dining room with 2 fireplaces, parlor with 2 fireplaces, art gallery. Courtyard with flower gardens. Off-street parking.
Location CT shore. 3 blocks to Yale campus, New Haven Green. From I-95 N, take Exit 47 to end of connector. Go right on York St., 3rd left onto Chapel. From I-91 S, take Trumbull St., Exit 3. Stay on Trumbull; go left at 4th light onto Prospect/College. Turn right at 3rd light to Chapel.
Restrictions No cigar or pipe smoking. Light sleepers should request rooms away from street.
Credit cards Amex, DC, MC, Visa.
Rates B&B, $125–175 double. Extra person in room, $15. 3-night minimum Yale commencement, 2-night Fall weekend minimum. Picnic lunches on request.
Extras Pets permitted by prior arrangement. Crib available.

Set in the Berkshire Hills, New Preston's key attraction is Lake Waramaug, an inviting spot for swimming, fishing, and boating in summer, and skating in winter. Other area activities include hiking to the top of Pinnacle Mountain for views reaching to Massachusetts and New York, canoeing, bicycling, golf, and horseback riding; in winter, there's sledding, plus cross-country and downhill skiing. Many plays and concerts are offered in the summer, along with craft fairs, and the supply of antique shops is plentiful year-round.

Also recommended: Also right on the lake is the **Hopkins Inn** (Hopkins Road; 203–868–7295) a Federal-style inn and restaurant set high on a hill offering delicious Austrian cuisine, with clean basic rooms at very reasonable prices.

Information please: We'd like to have current reports on the **Inn on Lake Waramaug** (North Shore Road; 203–868–0563 or 800 LAKE-INN), a mini-resort with a restaurant, and rooms both in the main house and scattered outbuildings. Colonial decor is combined with a casual atmosphere ideal for families. Although listed in earlier editions, two ownership changes in three years combined with a complaint about cleanliness and general maintenance prompted us to be on the alert for more feedback.

New Preston is located in northwestern Connecticut, 45 miles west of Hartford and 85 miles north of New York City. From NYC, take Hutchinson River Pkwy. to I-684 N, then I-84 E to Exit 7 onto Rte. 7. In New Milford take Rte. 202 (formerly Rte. 25) to New Preston. From Hartford, take I-84 W to Farmington to Rte. 4 to Rte. 118 to Litchfield. Take Rte. 202 to New Preston, then left on Rte. 45 to Lake Waramaug.

Rates are highest here in summer, and on weekends year-round, and are considerably lower midweek from November through May.

Boulders Inn   *Tel:* (203) 868–0541
Route 45

Nestled in the hills overlooking the lake, the Boulders was built in 1895 as a private home. Converted to an inn forty years ago, it had been owned and run by Jim Woollen for the last nine. Early in 1988, the inn was purchased by Kees and Ulla Adema. Under the Ademas' ownership, the menu has been expanded to include dishes with venison, rabbit, and quail, as well as other types of adventurous cuisine highlighting seafood and lamb, and standards in the dining room remain high. Rooms in the inn are handsomely furnished in country decor with antiques, while the cottages have a more modern look.

"Warm and comfortable inn on a quiet lakeside road—a wonderful place for an early morning jog or walk. One room is done all in blue; another, with a sleigh bed, is the best. Service is excellent, as is the cleanliness. The food is superior to most and is served beautifully. The living room with fireplace, books, and a full view of the lake is a super place to be on a winter afternoon." *(Dr. Hilda Templeton)*

"Our freshly redecorated room reflected the care and concern of the new

owners. The cuisine is first-rate, complemented by an excellent wine list."
(Thomas O'Connor)

"Our room had a large window facing this lake, with a comfortable window seat upholstered in floral fabric which matched the facing love-seat. Different kinds of soft and direct lighting from old, brass lighting fixtures make this a lovely corner at any hour. Our brass bed had an antique quilt and a firm comfortable mattress. The innkeepers and chef were particularly sensitive to our dietary needs." *(Shira Milgrom)*

Open All year. Restaurant closed Sun. to Tues. from Nov. 1 to June 1.
Rooms 2 suites, 4 doubles, 8 cottages with fireplaces. All with private bath and/or shower, telephone, fan. One with TV.
Facilities Restaurant, living room with fireplace, library/TV den, terrace, game room with Ping-Pong, darts. 30 acres with swimming, canoeing, sailing, tennis court, bicycling, hiking.
Location On Lake Waramaug, 5 m from town.
Restrictions Smoking permitted in certain public rooms; no cigars. No children under 12.
Credit cards Amex, MC, Visa.
Rates Room only, $90 suite or double, $75 single. Extra person in room, $25. MAP, $145–180 suite or double, $110–140 single. Extra person in room, $50. Also, 15% service added to all bills. 2-night weekend minimum. 4-night minimum for advance reservations for July, Aug. Alc lunch, $8; alc dinner, $35–40.
Extras Restaurant wheelchair accessible. Free station pickups. Dutch, German, French spoken.

NORFOLK 06058   Map 2

Norfolk is an interesting old town and the summer home of the Yale School of Music, which holds chamber music concerts from mid-June to mid-August. It's a good base from which to explore the wonderful old towns of Litchfield Hills, with their numerous art galleries, antique shops, artisans' workshops, and colonial mansions, not to mention the sheer beauty of the countryside.

Information please: We are pleased to note that the **Blackberry River Inn,** listed in an earlier edition of this guide, has re-opened under the ownership of Kim and Bob Zuckerman. Because the inn had been closed for several years previously, and may still need renovation and redecorating work, we have not prepared a full entry, but would like readers to keep us informed of its progress (Route 44, P.O. Box 326; 203–542–5100).

Also recommended: Just off the village green, the **Mountain View** is a turn-of-the-century Victorian with clean comfortable rooms and a restaurant called Maxfield's, specializing in seafood and pasta (Route 272; 203–542–5595).

Manor House   *Tel:* (203) 542–5690
Maple Avenue

The Manor House looks just the way you'd expect from its name: a large Victorian-era Tudor, with lots of chimneys, beautiful woodwork, and mullioned windows, surrounded by spreading lawns and large shade trees. The living room has an enormous fireplace, and both the living and dining rooms have Tiffany stained-glass windows. Antiques are everywhere, and several of the guest rooms have working fireplaces. A full breakfast is served on the sun porch or in the dining room, or may be enjoyed in bed; blueberry pancakes and orange waffles are favorites. Innkeepers Diane and Henry Tremblay have owned the Manor since 1985 and have established a reputation for providing a gracious, yet unpretentious, atmosphere.

"Clean, charming room, plentiful antiques; mansion and grounds are well kept." *(Ned Littlehales & Alice Botvin)*

"The hosts are warm, gracious, and always willing to assist. Breakfasts are varied and delicious. The town of Norfolk is a living picture postcard and is especially beautiful in the fall." *(Rick Littlehales, also Janet St. Clair)*

"Although we enjoyed our stay very much, stronger lights for reading would have been helpful." *(LB)*

Open All year.
Rooms 1 suite, 8 doubles—7 with private bath and/or shower, 2 with maximum of 4 people sharing bath. All with desk, fan. Some with fireplace and/or balcony.
Facilities Dining room, library, living room with piano, sun porch, gardens. Concerts by Norfolk Early Music Society. Trail, carriage, sleigh, hay wagon rides.
Location 5 min. walk to town. From NY, take I-84 to Danbury and take Rte. 7 N Exit. Take Rte. 7 N to Rte. 44. Go E to Norfolk.
Restrictions Smoking in living room only. No children under 12.
Credit cards Amex, MC, Visa.
Rates B&B, $90–110 suite, $65–150 double, $65–150 single. Extra person in room, $20. No tipping. 20% senior discount midweek. 2-night weekend minimum. Special B&B trail riding packages available.
Extras Elevator for disabled. French spoken. Station pickups.

OLD LYME 06371   Map 2

Information please: Just across the street from the Bee and Thistle is the **Old Lyme Inn** (85 Lyme Street; 203–434–2600), also known for fine cuisine elegantly served; the inn has thirteen guest rooms, highlighted with antiques; reports welcome.

Bee and Thistle Inn   *Tel:* (203) 434–1667
100 Lyme Street

Innkeepers Bob and Penny Nelson describe their inn as "a relaxing getaway, in a gracious warm setting, appealing to sophisticated couples." The inn, built in 1756, sits on the bank of the Lieutenant River. The Bee and Thistle serves breakfast, lunch, and dinner daily, and brunch and tea on weekends. Menus change with the seasons, but a recent one included such specialties as venison served with port and cranberries; sole cooked in parchment with julienne of vegetables, thyme, and an orange crème fraîche sauce; and rack of lamb with a ratatouille of white beans and tomato.

Old Lyme has a reputation as an art colony and is the home of the Florence Griswold Historical Museum, with an excellent collection of American Impressionist paintings, the Lyme Art Association Gallery, and many fine antique shops.

"There are fresh flowers everywhere, silk and dried arrangements in winter, fresh in summer. The menus are creative—I had an appetizer of sautéed Camembert, garnished with chives and served with French bread, noisettes of lamb sautéed with garlic and zinfandel, served with red Swiss chard. The guest rooms vary in size but are tastefully decorated and very inviting. If I were going to make a movie about the quintessential early American inn, this is the one I'd choose." *(Marjorie Cohen)*

"Although originally built in 1756, the building was moved several hundred feet away from the road about 65 years ago; various wings and porches were also added over the years. The house exudes an atmosphere of traditional elegance and charm, and is extremely clean and well kept. The location was quiet, and the inn is surrounded by lovely gardens." *(EL)*

"We stayed in one of the inn's less expensive rooms, but found it to be quite nice nonetheless. Our visit coincided with the annual Old Lyme Summer Festival, held during the first weekend of August, and many interesting events took place." *(James & Janice Utt)* "We appreciated the chairs and reading area, sufficient space and antique furnishings. Our dinner was most creative and nicely served." *(Jack & Sue Lane)*

Readers continue to rave about this inn, expressing only the desire that, given the rather high rates, guests be offered a continental breakfast and perhaps afternoon tea at no extra charge.

Open All year. Closed for 2 weeks in Jan. Restaurant closed Tues.
Rooms 11 doubles—9 with private shower and/or bath, 2 rooms with a maximum of 5 people sharing bath. All rooms with desk, air-conditioning, fan.
Facilities Restaurant with guitarist & harpist on weekends. 2 parlors with fireplace. 5 acres with gardens. Bicycles for guests. Swimming, boating, tennis, golf nearby.
Location E CT shore. Midway between NYC and Boston. In historic district. From I-95 N, take Exit 70. Go left off ramp to first traffic light, right to next light, then left. From I-95 S, take Exit 70, turn right off ramp.
Restrictions Cigars and pipes in parlors only. No children under 12.
Credit cards Amex, DC, MC, Visa.
Rates Room only, $62–105 double, $62–100 single. Extra person in room, $10. Alc breakfast, $5–7; alc lunch, $12; alc dinner, $41.
Extras Wheelchair accessible for dining only.

SALISBURY 06068   Map 2

Under Mountain Inn   *Tel:* (203) 435–0242
Route 41

"This inn is under Bear Mountain, one of Connecticut's loftiest peaks at 2,300 feet; after one of Peter and Marged Higginson's full English breakfasts, guests will want to follow the nearby Under Mountain Trail to its peak, to ensure that they'll have room for afternoon tea, plus the French and English dinners prepared nightly by chef Peter. The oldest parts of the inn date back to the early 1700s, with the wide boards and uneven floors you'd expect. The common rooms and the bedrooms are furnished with handsome antiques along with less interesting pieces of more recent vintage. Most appealing is the cozy pub with its 250-year-old paneling, found hidden in the attic when the inn was restored. Just across the road is a pretty lake and a country road that invites strollers and joggers. The Higginsons have owned the inn since 1984 and are friendly and relaxed innkeepers." *(SWS)*

Open Dec. 24 to March 15; April 15 to Dec. 10.
Rooms 7 doubles, all with private bath and/or shower, fan.
Facilities Living room with games; library, pub, 3 dining rooms with fireplaces. 3 acres with croquet; lake nearby. 15–20 min. to downhill and cross-country skiing.
Location NW CT. 4 m N of village center on Rte. 41.
Restrictions No smoking in some guest rooms; cigarette smoking only in public rooms. No children under 6.
Credit cards Amex, MC, Visa.
Rates MAP, $120–150 double, $80–115 single, plus 10% service. Senior discount midweek. 2–3 night weekend/holiday minimum. Midweek/weekend packages.
Extras Restaurant wheelchair accessible.

TOLLAND 06084   Map 2

Set halfway between Hartford and Sturbridge, Tolland remains a traditional New England town, with many buildings clustered around the central town green. Founded in 1715, Tolland has long served as a resting point for travelers on the old post road from New York and Boston.

Area activities include bicycling, golf, swimming, fishing, and boating, plus cross-country skiing and ice skating.

Tolland is located in northeastern Connecticut, just a mile or so from Interstate 84, 25 minutes southwest of Sturbridge Village, 25 minutes northeast of Hartford, and 15 minutes northeast of the University of Connecticut at Storrs.

Also recommended: For a truly colonial experience, visit the **Old Babcock Tavern** (484 Mile Hill Road; 203–875–1239), dating back to 1720. Rooms are decorated with early-American antiques, and rates include a full breakfast of fruit or juice, eggs and bacon or sausage, herb-seasoned homefries, and home-baked muffins, plus a welcoming tray of tea and cookies.

The Tolland Inn   *Tel:* (203) 872–0800
63 Tolland Green

Recommendations from well-traveled readers combined with a convenient location make this historic B&B well worth a stopover. "Spotlessly clean with a well-lighted driveway and friendly young owners, Susan and Stephen Beeching. Even though the inn is close to the road, our room was quiet and restful. Our mattresses were firm, and we awoke to a very tasty, hearty breakfast of a baked apple filled with raisins and nuts, zucchini bread, peach coffee cake, juice, and coffee. The inn is filled with lovely period furniture, much of it restored by Stephen, a talented artist and carpenter." *(Arlyne & Colette Craighead)*

"Comfortable beds, lovely antiques, ample reading lamps and books, along with a small sofa and two chairs completed the decor of our impeccably clean room. We also enjoyed the enclosed porch which overlooks the garden for reading and relaxing. There is a small restaurant in town, full of local color, which serves good and inexpensive Italian food. It might not suit everyone, but we found it fine." *(Gillian Austin)*

Open All year.
Rooms 4 doubles, 1 single—3 with private shower, 2 with maximum of 4 people sharing bath. All with desk.
Facilities Living room, dining room, sun porch. 1 acre with gardens, hammock. Lakes, fishing streams nearby.
Location From I-84, take Exit 68 to Rte. 195 N into Tolland; inn is on town green on left after stop sign.
Restrictions No smoking. No children under 10.
Credit cards MC, Visa.
Rates B&B, $45–55 double, $35–50 single. Extra person in room, $10.
Extras Airport/station pickups if prearranged.

WESTBROOK 06498   Map 2

Information please: Newly opened in Westbrook is the **Water's Edge Inn,** a restaurant, inn, and condo-complex, originally dating back to the forties, when it was a popular summer retreat. The elegant restaurant overlooks the water and specializes (as might be expected) in seafood, while the hotel rooms are done in period decor. Full resort facilities are available: tennis, health club, swimming pool and hot tub, private beach for swimming and sailing (1525 Boston Post Road; 203–399–5901 or 800–222–5901).

Also recommended: Built in 1890, **Talcott House** (161 Seaside Avenue, P.O. Box 1016; 203–399–5020) is a spacious Victorian beach cottage; four guest rooms have private baths and water views.

Captain Stannard House   *Tel:* (203) 399-7565
138 South Main Street

A gracious home with gracious hosts is the best way to describe this 1860s sea captain's house, today restored to its original appearance, with appropriate concessions to modern amenities. Captain Elbert Stannard sailed widely, to San Francisco, China, and Japan, carrying freight and passengers for the Hudson Bay Company, but Westbrook was his home. Clearly a man of vision; today, Westbrook is a boater's mecca, home to more boats than any other place in Connecticut except Stamford. "Slightly removed from it all, just one block away from the town beach, sits the Capt. Stannard House, which combines a small inn with an interesting antique store. The guestrooms are comfortable and clean, each furnished with a mixture of antiques and not-so-antiques, with hand-stencilling on the walls. A continental breakfast of fruit, cold cereal, and homemade breads and muffins is served on tables scattered through the antique shop or by the fire. Guests often eat breakfast outside in the pleasant yard." *(MS)*

"The owners were unpretentious and obliging, the price was right, and our room was gracefully proportioned and pleasantly furnished. We especially liked the tray with three pairs of different-sized glasses to accommodate our beverage of choice. The basket of fruit, candy, and cheese was also a nice touch." *(Sally Sieracki)*

Open All year.
Rooms 9 doubles, all with private bath and/or shower, radio, air-conditioning.
Facilities Parlor with wood burning stove, lounge with TV, library, piano, organ, antique shop. 1 acre with tables, lounges, lawn games; bicycles, beach chairs. 8 min. walk to beach.
Location E CT shore. 15 m W of New London. ½ m from center of town.
Restrictions Smoking restricted in some rooms. No children under 6.
Credit Cards Amex, CB, DC, MC, Visa.
Rates B&B, $60–80 double, $55–75 single. Extra person in room, $20. Senior, AAA, Mobil discounts.

Key to Abbreviations

For complete information and explanations, please see the Introduction.

Rates: Range from least expensive room in low season to most expensive room in peak season.
Room only: No meals included; sometimes referred to as European Plan (EP).
B&B: Bed and breakfast; includes breakfast, sometimes afternoon/evening refreshment.
MAP: Modified American Plan; includes breakfast and dinner.
Full board: Three meals daily.
Alc lunch: À la carte lunch; average price of entrée plus nonalcoholic drink, tax, tip.
Alc dinner: Average price of three-course dinner, including half bottle of house wine, tax, tip.
Prix fixe dinner: Three- to five-course set dinner, excluding wine, tax, tip unless otherwise noted.
Extras: Noted if available. Always confirm in advance. Pets are not permitted unless specified.
Zip codes: If only one zip code applies, it is listed with the town name. If there is more than one, it is noted as part of the address.

Delaware

The Lord and Hamilton Seaside Inn, Rehoboth Beach

Delaware is a small but historic state. The Brandywine Valley, overlapping both Delaware and Pennsylvania, is particularly rich in sites of cultural interest such as Winterthur, the Hagley Museum, and the Nemours Mansion. Wilmington, Delaware's major city, has restored many of its historic areas in recent years and is small and very manageable in size. If you're traveling through on I-95, be sure to stop in historic New Castle for at least an hour or preferably overnight.

The beaches Rehoboth and Lewes are favorite escapes from the heat and humidity of summertime Washington. They are 120 miles (approximately 3 hours) from Washington, Baltimore, and Philadelphia. If you're coming from New York or New Jersey, take the New Jersey Turnpike over the Delaware Memorial Bridge, then take Route 13 to Route 1 to Lewes and Rehoboth. An alternate route (recommended for the trip home) is to take the 70-minute ferry ride from Lewes to Cape May to the Garden State Parkway (call 302–645–6313 or 609–886–2718 for details); it's about a 5-hour drive to New York City.

Peak rates generally run from June 15 to September 15; off-season rates are considerably less. Rehoboth is a favorite family resort, combining all the boardwalk stuff kids love with chic shops and gourmet restaurants; Lewes is a bit more sedate.

Rates do not include 6% room rental tax.

NEW CASTLE 19720   Map 4

New Castle is a delightful town, an ideal spot to stop for lunch or for the night if you're traveling along I-95 between Washington and New York.

In the few minutes it takes to drive from the highway to the historic section, you can travel back 250 years to a living colonial village.

The town was founded in 1651 by Peter Stuyvesant. It was claimed alternately by both the Dutch and the Swedish governments, until the Duke of York took it for the British in 1664 and renamed it New Castle. The town served as Delaware's first capital until the early eighteenth century, when the capital shifted to Wilmington. Development stopped, and a lovely piece of history was preserved. The town is built right along the Delaware River, nearly under the Delaware Memorial Bridge. In the colonial-era Battery Park, along the river, the modern bridge looms almost overhead—a strange but beautiful juxtaposition.

"Within easy walking distance in the historic area are a magnificent 1732 Court House, Delaware's colonial capitol, with informative and amusing free guided tours; the home of George Read II, built between 1797 and 1804; a lovely and inspiring Presbyterian Church built in 1707. Be sure to see how the Dutch settlers lived by visiting the Amstel House and the Old Dutch House museums." *(Nancy Harrison & Nelson Ormsby)*

While in New Castle, be sure to stop for a leisurely meal at the **Newcastle Inn,** built as an arsenal in 1809—crab cakes and walnut rum pie are specialties (1 Market Street; 302–328–1798).

Information please: We'd also like to hear more about the **Terry House,** a B&B with four guest rooms overlooking the Delaware, located in an 1860 townhouse just a few doors away from the David Finney Inn.

Also recommended: Two well-equipped suites await guests at the **Janvier-Black House**, a Federal townhouse built in 1825, with private decks overlooking the Delaware (17 The Strand; 302–328–1339).

The David Finney Inn
216 Delaware Street at Third

Tel: (302) 322–6367

There was an inn on the site of the David Finney as early as 1685. The present-day inn was originally two buildings, connected in 1757 and expanded in 1804. In 1903, the mansard roof and third floor were added, and the inn was renamed the Hotel Louise. It was completely renovated and re-opened in 1985 by Tom and Louise Hagy. Rates include continental breakfast weekdays, and a full breakfast on weekends. The inn's tavern serves lunch and light meals, while the dining room offers excellent meals, from chicken with leeks and pears to rack of lamb with Madeira and Boursin. Light meals are served in the courtyard in good weather.

"The inn faces onto the town green and is a short walk from the park that borders the river. The citizens here enjoy late-evening strolls with family and friends through the streets and parks. They have tremendous pride in their community and enjoy sharing its history with you. The guest rooms are simply furnished with antiques and period reproductions. The off-white walls are complemented by coordinating draperies and woodwork painted in colonial blue, mauve, and brown. The modern baths have everything from a shelf to hold your toiletries to overhead exhausts and heat lamp. Rooms are clean, neat, and well maintained. The food is exceptional. The main dining area is pleasantly congenial, and service is prompt but not hurried. The tavern serves excellent cocktails in a nautical atmosphere." *(E.P. Joyce, also Mark L. Goodman)*

"This inn has been nicely restored and decorated, and the welcome basket of wine, snacks, and sweets was a nice touch. The bed was comfortable, and the bath facilities modern. Dinner is served both in the inn's tavern and in its dining room; the ambience is more formal in the latter, but the menu is the same. We especially enjoyed the subdued atmosphere in the tavern, and the service was good. From soup through dessert, we found the food to be very tasty, the portions generous, and the presentation attractive. A special bonus was the good music and excellent Eckstine-style vocals of the tavern's regular musician. Seating is limited and we'd advise advance reservations. The continental breakfast was good and offered a variety of selections." *(James & Janice Utt)*

And a less positive report: "At the time of our mid-summer visit, our room in the annex was not air-conditioned, yet we couldn't get the windows opened. Nor were the furnishings or housekeeping up to par."

Open All year. Restaurant closed Dec. 25.
Rooms 4 suites, 16 doubles, all with private bath and/or shower, air-conditioning, fan. Telephone, TV on request. 3 rooms in annex, one with kitchenette.
Facilities Living room with games, tavern with pianist weekends, restaurant. Courtyard and garden. Tennis nearby. Off-street parking.
Location Historic district. 15 m S of Wilmington, 108 m NE of Washington, DC. From I-95, take Exit 5A (Hwy. 141 South). Continue to end and turn left (E) on Hwy. 273. Continue 0.6 m to fork and bear right. Proceed 4 blocks to inn.
Restrictions No children under 10.
Credit cards Amex, CB, DC, Discover, MC, Visa.
Rates B&B, $110–120 suite (sleeps 4), $66–100 double, $60 single. Alc lunch, $8; alc dinner, $34. Weekend packages. Long term rates available for annex.
Extras Station pickups.

REHOBOTH BEACH 19971   Map 4

Rehoboth is located on the Delaware's Atlantic shore, 125 miles east of Washington D.C., and has been a mecca for Washingtonians escaping the oppressive summer heat and humidity ever since the Chesapeake Bay Bridge was completed in 1952. Rehoboth's beautiful white sands are bordered in most areas by shady pine forests, offering a welcome respite from the summer sun. Children love the mile-long boardwalk, complete with snack bars of all persuasions alternating with miniature golf courses and video games and capped with the rides at Funland. Those in search of more sedate entertainment will prefer the weekend evening concerts at the bandstand nearby on Rehoboth Avenue. Area activities center on the water, and include swimming, surf-casting, sailing, windsurfing, clamming, and fishing.

As is the case in most beach towns, parking is a hassle in season, when Rehoboth's population zooms from 3,000 to 90,000. Once you've found an unmetered parking space, just leave your car where it is, and walk or bicycle to in-town destinations. To avoid congestion, visit mid-week.

The Corner Cupboard Inn
50 Park Avenue

Tel: (302) 227–8553

The Corner Cupboard Inn was built as a private home for Alice and Jess Gundry, aunt and uncle of the present innkeeper, Elizabeth Gundry Hooper. Today, the inn's eighteen guest rooms are spread among several buildings and cottages. Mrs. Hooper describes her inn as a place where people are encouraged to gather for conversation and refreshments in front of the fire in the winter and on the patios in summer. "We try to provide a relaxed, homelike atmosphere which will attract congenial guests." Only breakfast is included in the off-season rates; summer rates include both full breakfast and dinner. Dinners feature good home-style cooking, with lots of seafood dishes, plus a beef and chicken entrée, and home-baked desserts.

"Located in a beautiful, quiet residential section of Rehoboth, the inn is about [a] fifteen minutes' walk away from the hubbub on Rehoboth Avenue. Rooms vary considerably in decor; the Blue Room, with a four-poster bed, is quite nice, while others are more basically furnished." *(Mike Spring)*

"A truly small inn, graciously kept, homelike and comfortable. Mrs. Hooper carries on the traditional hospitality of her late uncle and aunt. It offers fine food, a convenient location near the uncrowded beach, and reasonable rates. Guests are treated as friends." *(Paul Podgus)*

Open All year, except Christmas, New Year's. Restaurant open Memorial Day weekend to mid-Sept.
Rooms 18 doubles, all with private bath and/or shower, air-conditioning; several with desk, TV. 9 rooms in inn, 4 in annex, 5 in cottages.
Facilities Restaurant, living room with fireplace, breakfast room, Ping-Pong, patios. 1½ blocks to beach for swimming, fishing. Tennis, golf nearby.
Location 8 blocks from town center. Between 1st and 2nd sts.
Credit cards Amex, MC, Visa.
Rates B&B, $75 double, $70 single; extra person in room, $25 (Sept. 15–late May). MAP, $225 double, $185 single; extra person in room, $75 (Memorial Day—Sept. 15). Alc dinner, $35.
Extras Pets permitted in some rooms, $7.50 daily. Cribs, babysitting available. Airport/station pickups.

The Lord and Hamilton Seaside Inn
20 Brooklyn Avenue

Tel: (302) 227–6960

The Lord and Hamilton was opened in 1982 by Marge and Dick Hamilton after considerable restoration work. Marge says, "We named the inn the Lord and Hamilton because we need all the help we can get."

"We were greeted warmly by the Hamiltons, and their friendly shepherd Bianca, proudly outfitted in her purple neck bandana. Marge and Dick are extremely witty and fun; their gregarious personalities invite guests to lounge around the cozy sitting room or sunny, sprawling veranda for convivial breakfasts or lazy afternoon conversations. There's plenty of sturdy, comfortable wicker furniture on the wraparound veranda, and the hammock for two is always in demand. All the rooms are beautifully decorated with family antiques, comfortable beds—most of them canopies—showcased by charming quilts and spreads, with overstuffed chairs and lounges. Plenty of sunlight streams through the windows, and Laura

Ashley curtains lend delicacy to the decor. Marge's special touches include antique lamps, candles, baskets of potpourri, antique dolls and collectibles, and plenty of reading material.

"Our room had a huge canopy bed high off the floor, with an antique wardrobe with its own latchkey. Right around the corner was the community fridge, convenient for the late-night munchies. Another fun thing about the inn is the spacious outside shower and dressing room, which really puts you in touch with nature. Nobody thinks twice about meeting a fellow guest wrapped only in a towel on their way up the back stairs. Less adventuresome B&Bers will prefer the rooms with indoor plumbing, one with a shower, the other housing an old-fashioned tub, perfect for a relaxing bubble bath. The location is very quiet, yet is just a half-block from the beach, and two from the town center, so you can forget about your car. Marge gladly made recommendations for local outings and dinner reservations!" *(Victoria Berman)*

"Immaculately clean, lighting and plumbing above average and perfect location. I stayed in a large room on the top floor, with ocean views. It had an antique white iron bed and two twins with wicker headboards, Victorian lamps and furnishings; linens and towels were all a Laura-Ashley type lavender print. I had a chance to see all the rooms and my favorite was #1, with a canopy bed, porch entrance, beautiful wood, and special decor. The breakfast buffet is served in the front parlor and includes lots of fresh fruit, juice, coffee, pastry, bagels, cheese, toast and muffins. The front parlor is filled with antiques, yet is still homey and cozy." *(Mrs. John Wooley)*

Open April 15 to Oct. 15.
Rooms 7 doubles—1 with private bath and/or shower, 2 with private half-bath room, 4 with a maximum of 4 people sharing bath. All rooms with desk, fan; 2 with air-conditioning.
Facilities Dining/living room, wrap-around porch, grill, picnic tables, guest refrigerator. Beach, fishing ½ block away. Tennis nearby. Unmetered parking 1 block away.
Location 3 blocks to center of town.
Restrictions No smoking. No children.
Credit Cards None accepted.
Rates B&B, $30–80 double. Extra person in room, $10. 2–3 night weekend/holiday minimum. 7th night free.
Extras Bus station pickup.

WILMINGTON 19807 Map 4

Christina House *Tel:* (302) 656-9300
707 King Street (800) 543–9106

Wilmington, long a sleepy small city dominated by the DuPonts, has started to grow. Christina House is its first all-suite luxury small hotel, specializing in personal service. Furnishings are contemporary, and the spacious rooms are supplied with all modern amenities, including a television in both the living room and bedroom, three telephones (one in the bath, of course), plus built-in hair dryers and makeup mirrors. Rates include a continental breakfast; a full breakfast is available for an additional charge.

"A welcome addition to the Wilmington hotel scene. The hotel is built in what was originally a clothing department store, which was gutted and rebuilt with the brick walls exposed. The three-story-high lobby gives [the hotel] a spacious feeling, although the restaurant sounds at lunchtime can make it a bit noisy. Once your door is closed though, you don't hear [them]. The location, right across from the Radisson, is very convenient, and the bistro-style restaurant has quite an innovative menu for Wilmington. For a taste of old Wilmington, do go back to the Hotel DuPont for an Old World dinner in the Green Room." *(Diane Wolf)* More comments, please.

Open All year.

Rooms 39 suites, all with private bath and/or shower, telephone, radio, TV, desk, air-conditioning, wet bar, refrigerator, hair dryer.

Facilities Restaurant, bar, atrium lobby/lounge with fireplace, banquet, meeting rooms. Guest privileges at local health club. Valet parking, $5.

Location Central business district. Take Exit 7A off I-95. Go N on Delaware Ave. to 11th St. Turn right on King St.; hotel is between 7th and 8th on King.

Credit cards Amex, DC, MC, Visa.

Rates B&B, $130–140 suite, $115 single. $95 weekend rate. Extra person in room, $10. Corporate, long-term rates available. Alc lunch, $10; alc dinner, $25. Weekend packages.

Extras Free airport/station pickups and downtown limo service. 1 suite designed for disabled. Cribs available.

We Want to Hear from You!

As you know, this book is only effective with your help. We really need to know about your experiences and discoveries.

If you stayed at an inn or hotel listed here, we want to know how it was. Did it live up to our description? Exceed it? Was it what you expected? Did you like it? Were you disappointed? Delighted?

Have you discovered new establishments that we should add to the next edition?

Tear out one of the report forms at the back of this book (or use your own stationery if you prefer) and write today. Even if you write only "Fully endorse existing entry" you will have been most helpful.

Thank You!

District of Columbia

Kalorama Guest House

Washington is one of the many cities where weekend rates drop dramatically at most hotels. Spring and fall are peak periods; weekday rates also drop considerably from December through February and during the summer, when Congress adjourns and many Washingtonians escape the city's infamous heat and humidity. When making reservations always ask if any special rates are in effect. If cost is a concern, and you will be in Washington during the week, then one of the smaller guest houses will offer you a better value than a hotel.

Also recommended: The **Canterbury Hotel** (1733 N Street, NW 20036; 800–424–2950 or 202–393–3000) is a modern all-suite hotel with spacious rooms, ideally located on a quiet street near Dupont Circle. Rates include continental breakfast and morning paper, evening cocktail, bathrobes, and chocolates. Another possibility in the Dupont Circle area is the **Windsor Inn**, with Art Deco style rooms and very reasonable rates (1842 16th Street 20009; 202–667–0300 or 800–432–9111). Within an easy walk of the Kennedy Center is the **Inn at Foggy Bottom** with spacious comfortable suites, decorated in soft tones, and reasonably priced (824 New Hampshire

Avenue, N.W. 20037; 202–337–6620 or 800–426–4455). The **River Inn** (924 Twenty-Fifth Street NW 20037; 202–337–7600 or 800–424–2741) is a small, all-suite hotel of recent construction, also in the Foggy Bottom district. The **Jefferson Hotel**, just four blocks north of the White House, is decorated with Scalamandre fabrics, canopy beds, and original paintings; the hotel has long been a favorite with the political, literary, and theatrical worlds (1200 16th Street 20036; 202–347–2200 or 800–368–5966). The **Morrison Clark Inn** (Massachusetts Avenue and Eleventh Street NW 20001; 202–898–1200 or 800–332–7898) combines two historic townhouses dating to 1864 with a complementary modern structure. Rooms are furnished in period, while the restaurant serves American cuisine with a southern accent.

Rates do not include 10% sales tax and $1 daily occupancy tax.

Bristol Hotel
2430 Pennsylvania Avenue, NW 20037

Tel: (202) 955–6400
(800) 822–4200

Originally built as an apartment house, the Bristol was converted into a hotel in 1985. Rooms are furnished with reproductions of classic English furniture and art and have kitchenettes, including a coffee maker and mini-bar. Terry robes are available with the bath, and rates include the *Washington Post* and overnight shoe shine service. Although the Bristol advertises itself as an "all-suite" hotel, many of the rooms are actually doubles with the extras noted above. "Executive" suites have dining alcoves, and only the one-bedroom suites have a living room separate from the bedroom. The Bristol Grill serves breakfast, lunch, and dinner, and has gained a reputation for good food, especially their mesquite grilling; the Grill was recently chosen by the *Washington Post* as one of the city's top new restaurants.

"The Bristol is a beautiful place, warm and friendly with an elegant ambience. The suites are very spacious and comfortable, and they're all organized for the guests' convenience, from multiple telephones and remote-controlled television to large, comfortable, and well-lit working areas for business travelers. The rooms are very quiet, an unusual pleasure in a city with many parties and emergency vehicles with loud sirens. The location is excellent, just a short walk from the Kennedy Center, Georgetown, and the Metro. Room service and maintenance are excellent; should a problem arise, it's fixed immediately. Best of all is the staff, who are well trained and exhibit a real commitment to serve their guests." *(Charles Head)*

Open All year.
Rooms 37 suites, 203 doubles and singles—all with full private bath, telephone, radio, TV, desk, air-conditioning, kitchenette.
Facilities Restaurant, bar/lounge, lobby, gift shop.
Location West end of DC. 1 m to downtown.
Credit cards Amex, CB, DC, MC, Visa.
Rates Room only, $190–395 suite, $160–180 double, $140–160 single. No charge for children under 17 in parents' room. Extra person in room, $20. Alc breakfast, $6–10; alc lunch, $15; alc dinner, $45. Weekend packages. 50% senior discount, subject to availability.
Extras Spanish, Italian, French, Chinese, Vietnamese, Farsi spoken. Cribs, babysitting available. Member, Wyndham Hotels.

The Hampshire Hotel
1310 New Hampshire Avenue, NW 20036

Tel: (202) 296–7600
(800) 368–5691

The Hampshire is a small, modern hotel that has developed a good reputation since its opening in 1983. Most rooms have king-size beds or two doubles, sitting and dressing areas, and kitchenettes; guest rooms are decorated with traditional furniture and coordinating flowered drapes, valances, and bedspreads. Ample storage space is provided, and although the baths are small, they're well equipped with amenities and big, thirsty towels. Lafitte, the hotel's French-Creole restaurant, has been well reviewed by the Washington food critics. The Hampshire is owned by Taj International Hotels, the same company that owns the Canterbury.

"The Hampshire is a delightful small hotel. The rooms are large and have small kitchenettes with complimentary coffee and tea, which is a real convenience, and the newspaper at the door each morning is a great help. Valet parking is convenient, quick, and appropriately priced. But nothing is as important as the staff, which is genuinely concerned with your comfort and well-being. Bellmen, front-desk people, and housekeeping staff all make clear that they are there to help you and do so efficiently and cheerfully." *(Walter N. Lambert, also Sidney & Mary Flynn, DV)*

"Only minor problems are small lobby and bar area for meeting friends, occasional fluctuations in water temperature, and the typical big-city noises of fire engines and police sirens." *(AN)*

Open All year. Restaurant closed Christmas and New Year's Day.
Rooms 61 suites, 21 doubles, all with full private bath, telephone, radio, TV, desk, air-conditioning, wet bar, balcony.
Facilities Lounge, restaurant with live music nightly, meeting rooms. Swimming pool. Room service; valet parking, $6 nightly. Health club privileges.
Location 1 block SW of Dupont Circle.
Credit cards Amex, CB, DC, Discover, MC, Visa.
Rates Room only, $134–184 doubles and suites, $119–169 single. No charge for children under 12 in parents' room. Extra person in room, $15. Lower rates Dec.–Feb. Weekend, long-term rates. Alc breakfast, $5–10; alc lunch, $20; alc dinner, $40.
Extras Cribs available. French, German, Spanish, Italian spoken.

Kalorama Guest House
1854 Mintwood Place N.W. 20009

Tel: (202) 667–6369

The Kalorama is made up of two connecting townhouses, renovated in 1982 by Roberta Piecznik; also under the same ownership is the Kalorama at Woodley Park (202–328–0860), near the Washington Zoo.

"Guests are accommodated in one of the two beautiful Victorian houses, lavishly furnished with antiques and old-world memorabilia. On the wall of both the hallways and individual bedrooms you can peruse old cartoons, magazine covers and family photographs from the last century. The bedrooms are elegantly furnished with Liberty-style prints; you can relax in the sitting room and watch a little television. Breakfast is taken downstairs in the main house, at pretty French-style tables; there's always an interesting conversation to join over continental breakfast of juice, fruit, coffee, muffins and the morning papers." *(Tessa Lamb, also Gregory Roberts)* "Large variety of ethnic restaurants within a short walk. Easy access to city by bus and metro." *(Gregory Roberts)*

"Breakfast included a selection of croissants and bagels, and variety of juices, coffee and tea. The innkeeper was very helpful, giving guests instructions to the subway, sightseeing information, and directions to the many nearby ethnic restaurants. I felt she really cared about the place and wanted guests to like it too. The decor is largely Victorian antiques; my room was quiet, medium in size, with a king-size bed and a small bathroom. Overall, an excellent value." *(Robert G. Schwemm)*

Open All year.
Rooms 3 suites with private bath, 28 doubles—9 with private bath and/or shower, 19 with a maximum of 6 people sharing bath. All with clock/radio, desk, air-conditioning.
Facilities Parlors with library, games; breakfast room, courtyard. Limited parking.
Location Residential area, 10 min. by Metro from Smithsonian and White House. Between Columbia Rd. and 19th St. N.W.
Restrictions No children under 6.
Credit cards Amex, DC, MC, Visa.
Rates B&B, $65–95 suite, $40–85 double, $35–80 single. Extra person in room, $10. 10% AARP discount. 2–night weekend minimum Mar.–Nov.

Normandy Inn
2118 Wyoming Avenue, NW 20008

Tel: (202) 483–1350
(800) 424–3729

Like many of Washington's small hotels, the Normandy was built as an apartment building, then converted to a hotel in 1981. Complimentary tea and coffee are available in the tea room from 11 A.M. to midnight; cookies are added at 3 P.M.

"The Normandy has very clean, comfortable rooms, on the small side but well appointed with the amenities one expects. It is the atmosphere here that really makes it stand out—in some ways it resembles a European pensione. The location is ideal, right off Connecticut Avenue, in the Embassy District. It's within easy walking distance of the Metro and bus routes, yet its side street location ensures quiet. It is truly an international hotel; this is apparent any morning in the breakfast room, when one normally hears five or six languages being spoken. But the truly remarkable thing about this hotel is the management and staff, who treat guests with great courtesy, going out of their way to make each guest's stay pleasant. I received many telephone messages with no problems; if I was in the lobby or breakfast room, the call was forwarded to me; if I was out, an accurate message was relayed upon my return." *(Robert A. O'Connell, also Bob Schwemm)*

"Tuesday wine and cheese gatherings offer guests the opportunity to meet one another. There is a wonderful variety of restaurants nearby, both north and south on Connecticut Avenue, and in Adams Morgan—all within easy walking distance, reasonably priced, and inviting dinners with a whole world of ethnic variety." *(Gerald E. Hillier)*

Open All year.
Rooms 4 suites, 35 doubles, 35 singles—all with full private bath, telephone, radio, TV, desk, air-conditioning. Some rooms with refrigerator.
Facilities Lobby, breakfast room, patio with plants. Underground parking.
Location Adjacent to French Embassy, Dupont Circle (Metro); 20-min. walk to center. 8 m S of I-495. Just off Connecticut Ave.
Credit cards Amex, MC, Visa.
Rates B&B, $180 suite, $90 double, $80 single. Extra person in room, $10. Weekend, group rates. No charge for children under 12 sharing room with parents.
Extras Cribs, babysitting available. Arabic, French, German, Spanish spoken. 2 rooms equipped for disabled.

Florida

Chalet Suzanne, Lake Wales

There *is* a real Florida apart from giant theme parks, condo developments, and endless chains of cloned hotels and motels. It's just not that easy to find, so please be sure to share the good news whenever you discover something special. There are B&B inns in many areas, as well as older hotels of character that are being restored; we've added many of them to this edition, and would like to hear of more.

Rates do not include 6% Florida sales tax, plus additional local taxes where applicable. Peak season rates in most of Florida generally extend from December 1–15 through May 1–15; off-season rates are considerably lower. Do remember that August and September are the height of the tropical storm/hurricane season, so it might be best to avoid these months when planning a trip.

Also recommended: Although at 200-plus rooms plus full conference facilities, rather big for a full write-up but enthusiastically recommended by several readers (and avid fishermen) is the **Cheeca Lodge** (Mile Marker 82, P.O. Box 527, Islamorada 33036; 800–327–2888). Recently spiffed up by a multi-million dollar restoration, the rooms and food are first rate, the service excellent, and the fishing superb. Those who prefer to stay on terra firma will enjoy the three swimming pools, private beach, six lighted Laykold tennis courts, and Jack Nicklaus-designed par 3 nine-hole golf course. Don't go if you're on a budget—double room rates start at $250 in season, nothing included.

CAPTIVA 33924   **Map 6**

Information please: About 80 miles north of Captiva, in Sarasota, is the **Crescent House** (459 Beach Road, Siesta Key, Sarasota 34242; 813–346–

0857), a pleasant, reasonably priced B&B near Crescent Beach, with some of the whitest sand in the world.

'Tween Waters Inn	*Tel:* (813) 472–5161
Captiva Drive, P.O. Box 249	In FL: (800) 282–7560
	In U.S.: (800) 223–5865

Set on a narrow strip of land between the Gulf of Mexico and Pine Island Sound, the 'Tween Waters Inn was started as a one-cabin operation in 1926. A variety of cottages were added over the years, but the whole inn was nearly bulldozed in the 1970s to make way for a condominium complex. Instead, the inn was bought in 1976 by Rochester Resorts, which has attempted to preserve the best features of the old while adding all the facilities most travelers expect in a luxury resort. While far from perfect, readers are consistently delighted with their stay and ever ready to return.

"The setting is less commercial than I thought possible in Florida. You can rent a canoe at the inn to go on a canoe trail through a nearby nature preserve, and you can walk a long way down the Gulf beach without seeing any buildings. The shelling is wonderful, as is the birdwatching. We thought the breakfasts were exceptionally good, and the dinners rather unexciting for the price." *(Pamela Mack)*

"The 'find' of our trip. This old resort consists of many cottages and two large motel-type buildings overlooking either the Gulf of Mexico or Pine Island Sound. We chose a room on the gulf side; the view was magnificent, but there was a good deal of traffic noise. Next time we'll request the bay side. The cottages are quite nice, but the only ones that really have a water view face the highway. The dining room was outstanding, the musical review delightful. Our room was clean and comfortable, the bed good; it would have been nice to have it made up a little earlier. Parking is barely adequate." *(SN)*

"Gorgeous place overlooking the Gulf of Mexico, with outstanding food, served in a light and airy dining room." *(MH)* "Good service, very clean, lots of attention paid to our kids." *(Steve Shipps)*

Open All year.
Rooms 10 suites, 83 doubles, 51 cottages—all with private bath and/or shower, telephone, TV, air-conditioning. Many with kitchenette, screened porch, balcony.
Facilities Dining room, lounge with live entertainment, game room, laundry facilities. 13 acres with marina, heated swimming pool, 3 tennis courts, shuffleboard, private beach on Gulf, fishing; boat, canoe, bicycle rentals.
Location SW FL. 25 m W of Ft. Myers.
Credit cards MC, Visa.
Rates Room only, $140–185 suite or cottage, $100–140 double, $75–85 single. Extra person in room, $12. 3–night holiday and/or winter minimum. No charge for children under 12. 7–night packages, midweek specials. Alc breakfast, $4–7; alc lunch, $6–9; alc dinner, $25.
Extras Public areas wheelchair accessible; some cottages specially equipped for disabled. Pets permitted by prior arrangement in some cottages. Cribs available.

CORAL GABLES 33134   Map 6

Information please: The Colonnade Hotel, a 1920s Mediterranean masterpiece, has recently been restored to new heights of elegance; its 157 guest rooms have dark mahogany furniture, softly lit with brass lamps, and all the amenities one expects of a deluxe hotel. The hotel's art deco restaurant, the Cafe Aragon, has been winning raves from the local press for its French nouvelle cuisine (180 Aragon Avenue; 305–441–2600 or 800–533–1337).

Hotel Place St. Michel

162 Alcazar Avenue

Tel: (305) 444–1666
(800) 247–8526

Built as the Sevilla Hotel in 1926, the Hotel St. Michel has been restored to its original character by owner Stuart Bornstein.

"The hotel is close enough to the airport to avoid most of the traffic, and it has an outstanding restaurant. The menu is French with creative Florida touches, and the service and presentation were faultless. The reasonable rates include a continental breakfast, the morning paper, and a basket of fresh fruit. The hotel was built in 1929 with a Moorish tiled entry hall and has been restored faithfully to the period. It's decorated in turn-of-the-century furnishing with parquet floors, new plumbing, room-darkening drapes, and silver ice buckets. Most of the rooms are on a side street but even on the main street the air-conditioning drones out the noises. Shoppers will love the fact it's a quick walk to the shop-laden Miracle Mile. Our only problem came in the morning when management forgot that both the dining room and bar had been booked for a breakfast meeting. We were relegated to the deli where there was no juice, milk, butter, or jam—just self-service coffee and croissants with styrofoam cups and plates. Hopefully, this was a one-time glitch since we really liked this place." *(MAA)* More comments, please.

Open All year.
Rooms 30 suites & doubles—all with full private bath, telephone, TV, air-conditioning, ceiling fan.
Facilities Restaurant, piano bar, deli, room service, roof-top garden, concierge, free parking.
Location From U.S. 1, go N on Ponce de Leon Ave. to inn at corner of Alcazar. 7 min. from Miami Int'l Airport; 10 min. to downtown. 3 blocks to Miracle Mile.
Credit cards Amex, MC, Visa.
Rates B&B, $130 suite, $110 double, $95 single. Extra person in room, $10. Alc dinner, $30.

FERNANDINA BEACH 32034   Map 6

For another area listing, see entry for St. Mary's, Georgia.

Also recommended: The nearby **1735 House** (584 South Fletcher Avenue 32034; 904–261–5878) Built in the 1920s, the inn sits on a narrow strip of land the beach and the road—it's just 100 yards from the water at high tide (good) but even closer to a busy road (not so good). Rooms are comfortable, casually decorated with a nautical theme, and breakfast is brought to your door in a wicker basket; rates are very reasonable.

The Bailey House

28 South 7th Street, P.O. Box 805

Tel: (904) 261–5390

The Bailey House is an 1895 Queen Anne Victorian, listed on the National Register of Historic Places. The house was built by Effingham W. Bailey for his bride. She was given a choice of a modest home with fine furnishings, or an elaborate one with the furnishings to come. She very clearly chose the latter—the Bailey House is a profusion of turrets, gables, bays, fish-scale decoration, and many stained glass windows. It took three years to complete at the then-outrageous price of $10,000.

Diane and Tom Hay have owned the Bailey House since 1982 and have decorated it with period antiques; Ken Nolan is the manager.

Everybody's tastes are different, which may account for the two very different reports received this year: "A delightful light airy home with ceiling fans and beautiful stained glass windows. Our room, the Victorian, had marble-topped furniture and a small sitting area. It was comfortably furnished, supplied with magazines, with good bedside lamps by which to read them. The bathrooms had antique fixtures which functioned as well as modern ones. We relaxed on the porch and in the parlor, and enjoyed a breakfast of home-baked bran muffins, good coffee, juice, and fresh fruit salad in the dining room. Our host offered interesting insights about the area along with good tips about restaurants and shops. Both he and his wife seemed genuinely concerned with our comfort. We were a bit surprised by the heavy industry in the area; there are two paper mills just outside of town. There were some distant rumbles from one of the plants, but with the central air-conditioning it was not disturbing." *(Amy Peritsky)*

Another reader (who visited during the same month) was less positive: "Our bedroom was not comfortable. It needed a painting, new linens, and overall freshening up."

Open All year. Closed Christmas.
Rooms 1 suite, 5 doubles—all with private bath and/or shower, TV, air-conditioning, ceiling fans.
Facilities Dining room, reception hall, parlor with organ, Victrola, books, games; veranda with porch swing. Bicycles. 2 blocks to lighted tennis courts. Swimming, fishing, surfing, marina, horseback riding, golf nearby.
Location NE FL, Amelia Island. 35 m NE of Jacksonville. In center of historic district. From I-95, go E on A1A to Centre St. Turn left on Centre St., then left onto 7th St. to inn on left.
Restrictions No smoking. No children under 10.
Credit cards Amex.
Rates B&B, $95–105 suite, $65–95 double. Extra person in room, $10. Weekly rates. 2-day holiday weekend minimum.
Extras Local airport pickups.

KEY LARGO 33037   Map 6

Also recommended: For a truly unusual inn experience, **Jules' Undersea Lodge** is the "world's only underwater hotel," with two suites beneath the water's surface in Bora Bora Lagoon (P.O. Box 3330, 51 Shoreland Drive; 305–451–2353).

Largo Lodge   *Tel:* (305) 4510424
101740 Overseas Highway, Route 1, Box 302   (800) IN–THE–SUN

"Just across the highway from John Pennekamp Underwater Park, Largo Lodge is made up of a half-dozen duplex cottages, each with a kitchen/ dining and living room area, a separate bedroom with two double beds, and a screened porch. The units were spotlessly clean, and the grounds are lushly landscaped. The dock has many comfortable lounge chairs, and is romantically lit at night. One can bring a picnic dinner and watch the sun go down, or feed the resident ducks. The manager is very friendly and warm, and has lots of brochures and a lending library of paperbacks. Although the furnishings are basic, they are comfortable, and our unit had such unexpected extras as a full-length mirror on the bathroom door and very thick towels. The atmosphere is very peaceful and relaxing, although you can hear the highway noise (as you can almost everywhere in Key Largo). Nearby are restaurants, grocery stores, and a seafood retailer." (Linda Bambu)

Open All year.
Rooms 6 suites—all with telephone, TV, air-conditioning, ceiling fan, kitchenette, screened porch.
Facilities Dock and ramp for ocean, backwater fishing; swimming, diving swimming nearby.
Location On Rte. 1, 1 m from Pennecamp Coral Reef Park.
Restrictions No children.
Credit cards MC, Visa.
Rates Room only, $75–85 double. Extra person in room, $10.

KEY WEST 33040   Map 6

One hundred sixty-one miles south of Miami, Key West is the southern-most city in the continental United States. Since the completion of the Overseas Highway in 1938 there have been major changes to Key West, particularly in recent years. No longer a sleepy fishing village, the town is often filled with tourists, hustlers, and assorted weirdos. It's not a place people are neutral about. One of our readers wrote that "Key West is lovely—unlike any other place I've been in America. Sophisticated and funky. There is something for everyone. Even the tacky is interesting." (Elaine Malsin) Another reported that: "Key West is a tourist trap, over-crowded and crawling with escapees from the north, but that's what's so endearing about it. The Key West Aquarium and Audubon House are well worth visiting, but the fabled sunset festival at Mallory Dock is over-rated. It's a faded re-make of San Francisco in the sixties, with lots of unem-ployed actors but without the spontaneity and freshness to make it work, especially if you remember what the real thing was like. Good food here though, which was hard to find elsewhere in the Keys." (Wayne Braffman)

If the sun and water overwhelm, some other Key West sights of interest include Ernest Hemingway's Home, Key West Lighthouse Museum, Wrecker's Museum, and Mel Fisher's exhibit of sunken treasure. Those who feel their stay will be incomplete without a taste of key lime pie (or two or three), may want to sample the offerings at the Deli Restaurant, the Buttery, Pier House, or Sloppy Joes; remember the real thing is *never* green or thickened with gelatin—it's yellow, creamy, and sweet.

A word of advice about navigating in the Keys—the Florida Keys' Over-seas Highway (U.S. 1) is studded with 126 mile markers starting at the corner of Fleming and Whitehead streets in Key West and ending near Florida City. Watch for the small green signs with white writing, found on the right shoulder of the road, since they're often used as reference points when directions are given.

Also recommended: The **Popular House** (415 William Street; 305–296–7274) is a turn-of the century Victorian B&B offering casual Caribbean decor and a knowledgeable Key West innkeeper; the **Island City House** (411 William Street; 800–634–8230 or 305–294–5702) is three guest houses with well-equipped suites sharing a private tropical garden.

Eaton Lodge
511 Eaton Street

Tel: (305) 294–3800

The Eaton Lodge was built as a private residence over 100 years ago and was purchased in 1980 by transplanted Englishmen Denison Tempel and Sam Maxwell. They have decorated in a traditional English style, with many Victorian pieces, yet have managed to give the rooms a light, airy, tropical feeling. Lots of windows, French doors, and paddle fans further enhance the Key West breeze.

"The location is ideal, just a few steps from Duval Street near Mallory Square. Eaton Street itself is quiet and shaded; the lodge is surrounded by foliage which assures privacy and even more quiet. The exterior and grounds are most appealing, kept in exquisite condition, and the inside of the lodge is charming. Every room is different, with its own unique decor and balcony or terrace. The sitting room at the front of the house is lovely and full of books and magazines, but what really sold us was the back garden. Here continental breakfast is served, and it's a great chance to talk to other guests, read *The New York Times,* and soak up the early morning sun. The area is so pretty, with brick paths and overhanging tropical foliage, that we always have to force ourselves away at lunch time. At night it is equally nice, with tiny lights in the trees, ideal for pre-dinner cocktails.

"Sam and Denison are the perfect innkeepers. They are always there when you have a question or to provide advice on restaurants, but are completely unobtrusive." *(Judith K. Brannen)* "We were welcomed with a fruit basket and a bottle of seltzer. Breakfast includes fruit, juices, coffee and an assortment of nice (but commercial) pastries. There is also evening turndown service with chocolate. The beautiful living room is filled with books and magazines that patrons can borrow." *(Linda Bamber)*

Open All year.
Rooms 2 suites, 8 doubles—all with private bath and/or shower, radio, desk, refrigerator, air-conditioning, fan, and balcony or terrace. Some rooms in carriage house.
Facilities Drawing room with TV, games, and library; telephone room. Tropical gardens with terrace, hot tub. Off-street parking. Fishing, swimming nearby.
Location Half a block from Main Street.
Restrictions Well-behaved children accepted. 2 front rooms affected by street noise.
Credit cards Personal checks preferred but Amex, MC, Visa accepted.
Rates B&B, $130–200 suite, $70–130 double, $60–120 single. Extra person in room, $20. Family rates available. 3–6-night holiday/winter minimum. 2–night summer weekend minimum.
Extras Airport/station/marina pickups. Cribs available. French spoken.

The Watson House
525 Simonton Street

Tel: (305) 294–6712

Dating back to 1860, the Watson House was purchased by an Ohio family named Baron during the middle of the Civil War. Key West was then a

Union stronghold, and the Barons must have been quite confident of the eventual outcome of the war to make the purchase.

"The Watson House is a beautifully done guest house, newly restored by owners Ed Czaplicki and Joe Beres. From the street you see a lovely old Bahamas-style home, surrounded by a wrought-iron fence. Entering through the backyard gate, you discover a swimming pool, Jacuzzi, and patio. There is one complete apartment for rent on the second floor, plus the cabana suite off the pool. Each has its own distinct style, but both are done with the finest materials and the best in furniture. We stayed in the apartment and slept in pine four-poster beds and cooked our meals in the all-white new kitchen, and spent our evenings in the living room with the two French doors open to the back porch and pool area. Privacy prevails. We felt as though we had slipped away to our own little resort in the heart of Key West. Cat lovers will enjoy the resident cat, Princess." *(Kathleen Novak & Michael Niedenfuehr)*

Open All year.
Rooms 2 suites, 1 double—all with private shower and/or bath, telephone, radio, TV, air-conditioning, fan. Suites have full kitchens.
Facilities Patio, swimming pool, hot tub.
Location Center of Historic Preservation District. At corner of Simonton and Southard sts. 1 block E of Duval.
Restrictions No children.
Credit cards MC, Visa.
Rates Room only, $100–225 suite, $75–105 double, $75–95 single. Extra person in room, $15. 2-night minimum stay.
Extras Ground-floor cabana wheelchair accessible.

LAKE WALES 33859   Map 6

Chalet Suzanne   *Tel:* (813) 676–6011
U.S. Highway 27 and 17A North   (800) 288–6011

In the most unlikely setting, amid the orange groves and alligators of central Florida, yet not far from "Theme Park USA"—a.k.a. Orlando—is the Chalet Suzanne. Set on beautiful green lawns and bordering a lake, it is about as far as you can get from Florida's standard motel accommodations.

Over fifty years ago Bertha Hinshaw turned her home into an inn and restaurant, to support the family after her husband died and the stock market crashed. The inn soon gained a reputation for good food and lodging and was included in Duncan Hines's first *Guide to Good Eating*. During World War II, the main building, including the kitchen and many dining rooms, burned down completely. No building materials were available because of the war, so the stables, rabbit hutches, and chicken coops were added to existing structures. Additional rooms have been built since then, and the result is an unlikely hodgepodge of munchkin-size towers, turrets, and gables that ramble in all directions on fourteen levels. You might think that the Good Witch of the North had it specially delivered from the Land of Oz.

Bertha Hinshaw made eighteen trips around the world; the chalet's Swiss, Scandinavian, French, Oriental, Spanish, and Turkish architecture was inspired by what she saw. She brought back tiles and stained glass windows from around the globe. In the dining room, no two tables are set alike. Not surprisingly, rooms vary dramatically in size and decor, although most are spacious, with cozy seating areas and inviting thirties-era decor; bathrooms are dated but functional, many decorated with stunning hand-painted tiles. Extra touches include fresh flowers, sherry, and fruit and hard candy.

After Carl Hinshaw, Bertha's son, returned from World War II, he and his wife Vita gradually took over the management of the inn and continue to operate it today, with the help of their children Tina and Eric. Carl also developed the Chalet Suzanne line of gourmet canned soups, based on his mother's original recipes.

Although expensive, the restaurant is one of the best in Florida: "Service is excellent—attentive but totally unobtrusive, professional yet completely relaxed and friendly. The menu never changes: you start with their signature broiled grapefruit with chicken liver—you have to eat it to believe how good it tastes—followed by the peppery romaine soup—the ingredients are secret but lettuce is not among them—a seasonal salad—ours included zucchini and artichoke, seasoned with dill, served with their tiny but addictive potato rolls. The choice and originality of the main courses is limited, but they are prepared to perfection, and portions are extremely generous—the Chicken Suzanne is probably the best I've ever eaten. Although I may have been too full to do them justice, I thought the desserts were very good, but not superlative. In sum, it's well worth splurging for a meal or an overnight stay; if you are in the Orlando area for any reason, you must add it to your itinerary." (SWS)

"The appearance is exactly what Bertha Hinshaw had in mind when she started to build the Chalet—her first instruction to the men she hired was to throw away their plumb bobs and measuring tapes. The results are delightful. The inn's interior is compatible with the exterior, which is to say that the floors are not always level and you may find a step or two between bedrooms, bath, and sitting areas.

"The restaurant is composed of several dining rooms, adjoining at odd levels and angles, of course, with no uniformity in furniture or place settings, which are, for the most part, put together from many old sets of fine china and flatware collected by the Hinshaws during years of European travel." (Jim & Marty Marsden)

"The atmosphere is gentle, leisurely, and serene. Visitors are treated like honored guests by every staff member, and Carl and Vita Hinshaw pay attention to the smallest details." (Jan Gregory Frazer)

Open All year. Restaurant closed Mon. May through Dec.
Rooms 4 suites, 26 doubles, 1 single—all with private bath and/or shower, telephone, TV, air-conditioning. Some with radio, desk, fan.
Facilities Restaurant, bar, lounge, living room, wine dungeon, library, patio, gift shop, antique shop. Pianist, organist in restaurant and lounge weekends. 70 acres with swimming pool, lake, badminton, croquet. Private airstrip. Tennis, golf nearby.
Location Central FL; Polk County. 1 hr. S of Orlando, 40 min. S of Disney World, 4 m N of Lake Wales. From I-4, take Rte. 27 S to Rte. 17A. Go E on Rte. 17A to inn.
Credit cards Amex, CB, Discover, MC, Visa.
Rates Room only, $95–155 suite, $75–155 double, $65–145 single; extra person in room, $10. MAP, $225 suite or double, $215 single. Alc breakfast, $7–15; alc lunch,

$25–36; alc dinner, $49–65. 6% sales tax and 18% restaurant food service charge additional. Mini-vacation package May–Nov.; honeymoon packages available.
Extras Two rooms wheelchair accessible. Airport/station pickups. Pets permitted by prior arrangement. Cribs, babysitters available. German, Spanish, Yugoslavian spoken.

LITTLE TORCH KEY 33042   Map 6

Also recommended: Travelers who prefer a resort with a full range of family activities will enjoy **Hawk's Cay** (Mile Marker 61, Duck Key 33050; 305–743–7000 or 800–327–7775) with everything from 8 tennis courts and resident pro to a dolphin and sea lion training facility.

Little Palm Island   *Tel:* (305) 872–2524
Mile Marker 28.5, Route 4, Box 1036   (800) GET–LOST

If you'd like to escape to a private tropical island, complete with hand-thatched bungalows, luxurious South Seas style decor, and gourmet French cuisine—just 120 miles from Miami—read on. Occupying the whole of a five-acre island, Little Palm Key is located at the western end of the Newfound Harbor Keys, where the Newfound Harbor meets the Atlantic. This advantageous location gives it a sand and coral base, not mangrove like most other islands. Originally known as Little Munson Island and long used as a private family retreat and fishing camp, the island was a favorite vacation spot of President Truman. John Kennedy came to watch the filming of *PT 109* in 1962, and because of his visit, the state of Florida supplied the island with telephone and electric service.

In 1988, the island was converted into a resort. The original fishing lodge is now the Great House, home to the restaurant and two suites. Most guests are accommodated in bungalows holding two suites each.

"The spacious suites are decorated with wicker furnishings, vivid prints, and Mexican tile accents. The atmosphere is very quiet and relaxed. Although the island was nearly fully booked during our visit, we often felt as if we were the only ones there. The location is good, isolated yet near to Key West for its airport and activities. The entire island is beautifully landscaped, and the pool area is lovely, with comfortable lounge chairs and big plush towels." *(Ken & Karen Gruska, also Mrs. L.B. Callicott)*

"The refrigerator and bar in each room was always kept fully stocked, often replenished twice daily. The mosquito netting over our king-sized bed, while not functionally necessary, was a very lovely touch. The food is creatively prepared and attractively presented at a consistently high standard. LPI is not for everyone, though. Although we found its small size most appealing, it might be a deterrent to others; there are no tennis courts or golf courses on the island." *(J. Hatcher Graham, also Dr. S.T. Canale)*

"Managing partner Ben Woodson does more than go the extra mile to make sure his guests are taken care of—along with partner Jack Rice and the staff, they work hard to make everyone feel welcome and cared for. The food is good by any standard, but its quality is even more impressive when you realize that everything has to be shipped down to the Keys, transported to the island by boat. " *(Bob Blitz)*

Amid the flurry of kudos, a few areas noted by guests for improvement: "We had some minor problems using the sporting equipment; at times there wasn't enough fishing equipment or bait, and finding someone to get us set up to use a canoe was inconvenient. More importantly, improvement is needed in the area of lighting, pathways need to be better lit, and the stairs up to our suite were completely dark. Parking (off the island) is shared with a marina and is very tight; the lot itself is not very well marked." These may well have been first-season problems, sorted out by now.

Open All year.
Rooms 30 suites—all with full private bath with whirlpool tub, double sinks, and outside shower; desk, air-conditioning, fan, deck with hammock, coffee maker, wet bar.
Facilities Restaurant. 5 acres with swimming pool, beaches, bicycling, fishing, snorkeling, sailing; all equipment provided. Dive shop, fishing; scuba certification.
Location FL Keys. At Mile Marker 28.5 (Little Torch Key), turn into Dolphin Marina and park at shore station (pink building on R) for Little Palm Island.
Restrictions No smoking on launch boat. No children under 9.
Credit cards Amex, MC, Visa.
Rates Full board, $350–395 suite for 2 persons. Extra person in room, $100. No tipping. 2–3 night holiday/weekend minimum.
Extras Wheelchair accessible. Pickup from Key West airport, $25 per couple. French, Chinese, Spanish spoken.

ST. AUGUSTINE 32084   Map 6

St. Augustine, founded in 1565, is the oldest city in North America. With a few interruptions, it was under Spanish rule until 1821, and many of its restored Spanish colonial homes were built in the 1700s. The city's architecture also has a strong Victorian component, dating back to the 1880s, when Henry Flagler did much to popularize St. Augustine as a fashionable resort.

St. Augustine is on the northeast Florida coast, 30 miles north of Daytona and south of Jacksonville, and 100 miles northeast of Orlando.

Kenwood Inn   *Tel:* (904) 824–2116
38 Marine Street

The Kenwood was built as an inn between 1865 and 1885 and was renovated in 1984; Mark, Kerriane, and Caitlin Constant bought the inn in 1988. Rooms are decorated in a wide variety of New England styles, from Shaker to country Victorian. The inn is described as having the "charm and informality of a New England country inn, providing an escape from the modern environment for young and old."

"The rooms are furnished with functional antiques, from iron beds to canopied four-posters. The owners make you feel that you are a most welcome family friend. The self-service continental breakfast includes fresh orange juice, freshly baked coffee cakes, muffins, sweet rolls, and coffee. You can eat at the large dining room table, in front of the living room fireplace, in the light and airy wicker-furnished sun room, or outside in the courtyard. The innkeepers have menus from the better restaurants in town and will advise you and make your reservations.

"The common areas are comfortable, homey, and inviting. The whole inn is spotless, the guest rooms have many touches one would only expect in a private home." *(Ted & Laura Phelps, also SB)*

"One of my favorite pastimes is simply sitting on the upper porch, with book, pipe, and libation, watching the horse-drawn carriages pass. Meanwhile, my wife is ensconced in a chair by the pool enjoying the sun and conversation with other guests." *(Mr. & Mrs. Earl Cranston)*

Open All year.
Rooms 2 suites, 11 doubles—all with private bath and/or shower, air-conditioning, fan; some with radio, desk.
Facilities Foyer, living room with fireplace, dining room, TV/game room. Courtyard, swimming pool. Tennis, golf nearby. 5 m to beaches.
Location Historic district. 3 blocks S of Bridge of Lions.
Restrictions No smoking in guest rooms. No children under 9. Some street noise in two rooms. On-street parking only; very limited due to narrow streets. Guests can leave bags at inn, then park 1 block away at Avenida Mendez or at private parking lot also 1 block away.
Credit cards MC, Visa.
Rates B&B, $75–100 suite, $55–75 double, $45 single. Extra person in room, $10. 2-night weekend minimum.

St. Francis Inn
279 St. George Street

Tel: (904) 824–6068

The St. Francis Inn was built in 1791 of *coquina*, a limestone formed of broken shells and corals cemented together. The inn was used as a private residence until 1845, when it became a boardinghouse; a guide to St. Augustine published in 1869 describes it as one of the city's best. Numerous modernizations were made over the years, including all modern conveniences. The inn has been owned by Joseph Finnegan, Jr., since 1985 and is managed by Marie Register.

"The inn is centrally located, within walking distance of many of the old homes, the oldest store, wax museum, the Spanish Fort, and much more. Every morning Marie greeted us with fresh rolls, doughnuts, and coffee. The morning paper awaited us in the sunlit sitting room, where you could sit down and eat, or pick up a tray to take to your room." *(June Harrah)*

"Marie greets all her guests with warmth, always eager and ready to help and [accommodate] all possible requests. The atmosphere is very friendly, especially during the winter season, with guests returning year after year." *(Carlo Borrelli)*

"We stayed here on Christmas Eve, and the Registers really helped to make it special. They held a small cocktail party with a singer and guitarist and had plenty of food. Everyone made us feel so welcome. We stayed in a suite with a private balcony running along two sides, where we sat sipping cocktails at sunset, listening to the sounds of horse hoofs pulling carriages along the cobblestone streets. The inn was cozy, very clean, with an eclectic but very comfortable decor." *(Diane Schuyler & Jim Storm, also Mrs. Marc Fleishel)*

"The St. Francis Inn is decorated throughout with an eclectic assortment of antiques and Persian rugs. Rooms and baths are clean to a Swiss standard, and the entire inn has a lovely freshness despite its age. A tremendous collection of old and new books is available to guests. There is a nice (but small) pool in the back courtyard, and a small fountain in the front garden." *(Janet Lay)*

"My room was very comfortable; breakfast and afternoon refreshments were plentiful and delicious. The innkeepers went out of their way to explain local folklore, make restaurant suggestions, and provide many ideas for local sights to see." *(Christine Woolard)*

Open All year.
Rooms 4 suites, 6 doubles—all with private bath and/or shower, TV, air-conditioning; some with desk, fireplace, kitchenette. Separate 2-bedroom cottage with kitchen, fireplace, sleeps 4.
Facilities Living/family room, sitting room with TV, books; balcony. Bicycles. Patio, courtyard, swimming pool. Ocean swimming and fishing nearby. On-site parking.
Location Historic district; 3 blocks from restored town.
Restrictions No smoking on 3rd floor.
Credit cards MC, Visa.
Rates B&B, $50–68 suite, $40–57 double. Extra person in room, $8. Weekly, monthly rates available.
Extras Spanish spoken. Cribs available.

Key to Abbreviations

For complete information and explanations, please see the Introduction.

Rates: Range from least expensive room in low season to most expensive room in peak season.
Room only: No meals included; sometimes referred to as European Plan (EP).
B&B: Bed and breakfast; includes breakfast, sometimes afternoon/evening refreshment.
MAP: Modified American Plan; includes breakfast and dinner.
Full board: Three meals daily.
Alc lunch: À la carte lunch; average price of entrée plus nonalcoholic drink, tax, tip.
Alc dinner: Average price of three-course dinner, including half bottle of house wine, tax, tip.
Prix fixe dinner: Three- to five-course set dinner, excluding wine, tax, tip unless otherwise noted.
Extras: Noted if available. Always confirm in advance. Pets are not permitted unless specified.
Zip codes: If only one zip code applies, it is listed with the town name. If there is more than one, it is noted as part of the address.

Georgia

Ballastone Inn, Savannah

We're pleased to note that we have quite a good selection of hotels and inns to recommend in the areas of Atlanta, the North Georgia Mountains, and Savannah. We're less pleased to note that we have had no recommendations for any hotels or inns anywhere in the entire southwest corner of the state, and would love to have your suggestions for this area and elsewhere.

Also recommended: A major resort complex too large (800 units) for a full writeup here is the **Callaway Gardens** (Pine Mountain 31822-9800; 800–282–8181), "about 70 miles south of Atlanta. Built around beautiful gardens, the resort has a golf course and large lake with a full complement of water sports. There are five restaurants altogether, but we ate amazingly well from the Plantation Room buffets. A variety of accommodation is available, but we stayed in the very comfortable Mountain Creek Villas." *(Susan Waller Schwemm)*

Information please: One northeast Georgia B&B we'd like to hear more about is the very reasonably priced **Hartwell Inn,** a southern mansion in the lakeside town of Hartwell, near the South Carolina border (504 W. Howell Street 30643; 404–376–3967).

Farther north, closer to the North Carolina border, are a few more where inn-vestigation work would be appreciated: The **Fieldstone Inn,** a small resort hotel on the shores of Lake Chatuge in Georgia's Little Switzerland, is a handsome stone and wood contemporary 40-room structure (P.O. Box 670, Hiawassee 30546; 404–446–1550). The **Lake Rabun Hotel** is a rustic

181

and reasonably priced lodge, dating back to 1922 and furnished with hand-made rhododendron and mountain laurel furniture (Lake Rabun Road, Route 1, Box 2090, Lakemont 30552; 404–782–4946). And the **Moon Valley Resort** is a handful of isolated lakeside cabins, but people come from all over for the gourmet meals (Route 1, Box 680, Rabun Gap 30568; 404–746–2466).

If business brings you to the little town of Swainsboro, in the east-central part of the state, about halfway between Savannah and Macon, stop by the **Edenfield House Inn,** a recently renovated turn-of-the-century mansion with nine guest rooms (358 Church Street; 404–554–3232).

Rates listed do not include 7% Georgia sales tax, plus additional local taxes where applicable.

ATLANTA   Map 6

Virtually leveled by General Sherman during the Civil War, Atlanta recovered fairly quickly, becoming a major rail hub by the end of the century. Today, Atlanta is a modern city whose population has exploded in the past two decades; its airport is one of the busiest in the country; the traffic jams on its highway rival those of Los Angeles. If you're visiting in the summer, and have a couple of extra hours, drive to the Wren's Nest, home of Joel Chandler Harris—of Uncle Remus fame—where you'll find a storyteller at work three times a day (404–753–8535).

Also recommended: When you're in the mood for the best in a big city hotel (551 rooms), the **Ritz-Carlton Buckhead** (3434 Peachtree Road NE, 30326; 404–237–2700) "is well worth the money for an all-around luxurious yet friendly atmosphere. Wonderful rooms done in antique reproductions, and baths with all the extras—thick fluffy towels and robes, full length mirrors, nightly turn-down service. No noise from the street, hall, or other rooms. Two of Atlanta's most exclusive malls are nearby; ask for a room with the Phipps Plaza view—you can see to the horizon. Good food and service in both restaurants, too." *(Susan Waller Schwemm).*

Another possibility in nearby Marietta is the **Marlow House** (192 Church Street, Marietta 30060; 404–426–1887) a century-old B&B in a neighborhood of Victorian and antebellum homes. Rooms are furnished with antiques, and rates include a full southern breakfast.

Information please: The **Stone Mountain Inn** (P.O. Box 771; 404–469–3311) is located in Stone Mountain Park, Atlanta's favorite escape, sixteen miles east of the city, which offers just about every possible outdoor activity except skiing. The inn has 92 guest rooms decorated with Queen Anne reproduction furniture and a full-service restaurant. Comments please.

Shellmont Bed & Breakfast Lodge   *Tel:* (404) 872–9290
821 Piedmont Avenue, NE 30308

Built in 1891, and listed on the National Register of Historic Places, Shellmont is an excellent example of Victorian design. Stained, leaded, and beveled glass abounds, as do intricately carved interior and exterior wood-

work, elaborate mantels, mosaic-tiled fireplaces, and accurately repro-
duced original stenciling. Ed and Debbie McCord, owners since 1984, cater
to individuals who appreciate fine craftsmanship, architecture, and turn-
of-the-century design.

The Shellmont is located in midtown; some of the city's best restaurants,
live theaters, art cinemas, museums, and shopping are within walking
distance. Rates include a breakfast of fresh fruit and juice, cereal, dried
fruit, and pastries.

"The McCords are exceptional hosts, and did far more to assist us than
any other innkeepers we've ever met. We were amazed at the authenticity
they have worked so hard to make evident in this beautifully restored
home." *(Ilona Jill Meza)*

"Conveniently located not far from a MARTA stop and trendy Virginia
Highland, this Victorian house filled with antique furniture and complete
with a front porch and rockers has been lovingly restored. The McCords
are a gold mine of information on old houses, architecture, and interior
design. The inn provides a delicate balance between big-city hotel privacy
and the casual friendly hospitality of a private home. Except for in-room
telephones, all the amenities were there—plenty of towels and soap and
hot water, comfortable beds, terry robes, a clock radio, reading materials,
fruit, chocolates, and a carafe of wine. Directions to points of interest with
maps and suggestions for restaurants were cheerfully provided." *(JS)*

"Our family stayed in the carriage house; it was perfect—we enjoyed
privacy, plenty of room, a kitchen (ideal when traveling with kids), and a
very relaxing atmosphere. With the huge bathtubs, common in older
homes, you have a fear of running out of hot water, but there was always
more than enough to enjoy a relaxing bath." *(Jimmy & Kimberly Fike)*

Open All year.
Rooms 1 suite (in separate carriage house), 4 doubles—all with private bath and/or
shower, air-conditioning, radio, TV. Full kitchen in carriage house.
Facilities 3 parlors, library, all with books, magazines, games, fireplaces. Shady
garden with fish pond. Free off-street parking. ¼ m to Piedmont Park.
Location Midtown; 1¼ m from city center. Exit I-75/85 N Peachtree to Piedmont;
Exit I-75/85 S at North Ave. to Piedmont.
Restrictions City street noises might disturb light sleepers. Children under 12 in
carriage house only.
Credit cards Amex, MC, Visa.
Rates B&B, $80–120 suite, $75–90 double, $65–80 single. Extra person in room, $15.
No tipping. Discount for AARP members. Children under 6 free. $5 firewood charge.
2-night minimum weekend stay.
Extras Electric elevator available for disabled. Cribs available.

AUGUSTA 30901   **Map 6**

Telfair Inns   *Tel:* (404) 724–3315
326 Greene Street   In GA: (800) 282–2405
                                     In SE: (800) 241–2407

Well-traveled contributor *Keith Jurgens* found the service and rooms in this
a collection of 14 beautifully restored Victorian homes to be most satisfac-

tory, and its restaurant, excellent. The menu is surprisingly sophisticated, given the location—a recent meal began with spinach salad with duck confit and shallots, then an entree of salmon with saffron cream sauce, concluding with an apple tart for dessert. Rates include a full southern breakfast, and guests can arrange to cruise the Savannah River aboard the inn's boat.

Open All year.
Rooms 14 homes with 22 suites, 44 doubles and singles. All with private bath and/or shower, telephone, TV, and desk. Some with fireplaces, whirlpool bath. Suites with desk, kitchenette, parlor.
Facilities Breakfast and living rooms, conference rooms, pool, hot tub. River boat.
Location 150 m E of Atlanta. From I-20 take Washington Rd. to Calhoun Expressway. Cross Rte. 78, straight on Greene St. to inn on right. In "old town" Augusta. 3 blocks to Savannah River for boating, fishing, waterskiing.
Credit cards All major credit cards accepted.
Rates B&B $100 suite, $90 double, $80 single. Extra person in room $10. Children under 12 free. 10% senior discount. Alc lunch $7, alc dinner $30.
Extras Handicap accessible room. Free airport/station pickups. Cribs, babysitting, games available. French, Spanish spoken.

DAHLONEGA 30533   Map 6

Nestled in the foothills of the Blue Ridge Mountains, Dahlonega was the site of the first gold rush in the United States The old saying "There's gold in them thar hills" refers not to California but to Dahlonega! The name of the town is Cherokee for precious yellow metal. Area activities include hiking, rafting, canoeing, fishing, and panning for gold. Dahlonega is located in the North Georgia mountains, 65 miles north of Atlanta; from Atlanta, take Route 19/400 from I-285.

Also recommended: The **Worley Homestead** (410 West Main Street; 404–864–7002) dates back to 1845, with rooms decorated in antiques, and a staff dressed in period costume; rates include a full Southern breakfast.

Information please: A historic country hotel in Dahlonega is the **Smith House**, with 16 basic guest rooms and a dining room serving traditional southern cooking; rates are very reasonable (202 South Chestatee; 404–864–3566).

Mountain Top Lodge at Dahlonega   *Tel:* (404) 864–5257
Route 3, Box 173

Built in 1986 by innkeeper David Middleton, the Mountain Top offers 360° views of the North Georgia mountains. Guest rooms are decorated with pine furniture, mountain crafts, antiques, and flea market treasures. Readers continue to report nothing but delight with the Mountain Top: "On a return visit, we found everything just as wonderful as when we first reported on this inn, except that Dave has now added a dining room serving delicious dinners. The lower level has been renovated for both morning and evening dining, opening up more sitting areas for guests. Of all the inns we've visited, this one has the best, most pampering breakfast." *(Leslie Ellis)*

"When you walk in, you find yourself in a cozy den complete with fireplace. Also on the first floor are four bedrooms. Upstairs are four more bedrooms, a game room, and a reading room. A veranda surrounds the inn, and provides a great place to sit, sip a glass of tea, relax, and enjoy the scenery. In the morning, you wake to a scrumptious country breakfast of grits, sausage, biscuits, eggs, and bacon." *(Betty C. Hilburn)*

"The innkeepers make every effort to suit your stay to your taste and requirements. Located in beautiful quiet country, it's convenient to the lovely parks and historic towns of northern Georgia. The rooms are charmingly furnished, with thoughtful touches everywhere." *(EM, also John & Cheryl Stohler)*

Open All year.
Rooms 2 suites, 6 doubles—all with private bath and/or shower, desk, air-conditioning. Radio on request.
Facilities Dining room, common room with TV, stereo, books; game room, deck, covered porch. 40 acres with pool, trails, picnic areas. Rafting, trout fishing, hiking, horseback riding nearby.
Location 5 m from town.
Restrictions No children under 12.
Credit cards Amex, MC, Visa.
Rates B&B, $75 suite, $65 double, $50–60 single. 20% discount for 5-day stays. Extra person in room, $10.
Extras Ground-level rooms wheelchair accessible; 1 small step to porch.

MOUNTAIN CITY 30562   Map 6

The York House   *Tel:* (404) 746–2068
2210 Old Orchard Drive, P.O. Box 126

Listed on the National Register of Historic Places, the York House has been in operation for almost 100 years and is the oldest inn in the North Georgia mountains, located in the coolest spot in Rabun County.

"York House is just far enough off the main road to be rural, yet still accessible to several ski areas and numerous other attractions in the forests of northeast Georgia. Owners James and Phyllis Smith have lovingly restored each room with period antiques and have created an atmosphere of calmness." *(Carl R. Brown)*

"Rooms are spotless, with great attention to detail. The hosts were friendly and helpful with suggestions for nearby dining and doing. Breakfast arrived in our room just when we ordered it, and consisted of homemade breads, sweet buns, and the best coffee ever, brought on a huge silver tray." *(Brent Blake)*

"This beautiful inn is set right up against the Georgia mountains, with two stories of wrap-around porches. Our room was clean and comfortable, although the little TV seemed out-of-place, and the walls are very thin—not surprising in an old place. Hiking in the nearby state parks was wonderful; we followed a trail leading from Lake Burton into the mountains, past gorgeous waterfalls." *(BK)*

Open All year.
Rooms 1 suite with full private bath, fireplace; 12 doubles—all with private bath, TV, ceiling fans. Some with balcony, air-conditioning, radio, desk, fireplace.
Facilities Double parlor with fireplaces, games, and piano. 5 acres with tree swing,

picnic area, spring house. White-water rafting on Chatooga River, trout fishing in nearby creeks, boating on Lake Burton. Hiking in nearby state parks; horseback riding nearby. 10 m to downhill skiing at Sky Valley and Scaly Mt.

Location NE GA; Rabun County. 100 m to Atlanta; 3 m to NC border, 7 m to SC border. Inn located between Mt. City and Dillard, ¼ m off Hwy. 441.

Restrictions Smoking in lobby and on porches only.

Credit cards MC, Visa.

Rates B&B, $65–70 suite, $55–60 double, $50–55 single. Extra person in room, $10. Children under 6 stay free.

Extras Ramp from driveway for disabled. Bus station pickups. Cribs available.

ST. SIMONS ISLAND 31522   Map 6

Little St. Simons Island   *Tel:* (912) 638–7472
P.O. Box 1078

To get to Little St. Simons, you leave your car at the locked parking lot on St. Simons Island and take a 20-minute boat ride to this private retreat. Since the maximum capacity of the lodges on this 10,000-acre island is twenty-four people, you'll find as much solitude as you desire. With the variety of habitats on the island, and its location in the path of a number of migratory patterns, the opportunities for bird-watching are outstanding. You can hear the alligators bellowing in late spring, and see the loggerhead sea turtles coming ashore in the summer to lay their eggs. Three resident naturalists are available to answer questions, and readers report that their presence really adds to the experience.

Rates include three meals a day, evening hors d'oeuvres, wine with dinner, snacks and hot and cold beverages on request, picnic lunches, and use of all facilities and equipment. All food is home-cooked, including southern and creole specialties, such as shrimp creole, smoked ham, cornbread, and pecan pie. Guest rooms are located in several cottages, with the main lodge dating back to 1917; the Honeymoon Cottage was built in 1920 and refurbished in 1986, while the remaining two were constructed in the eighties.

"Not a place for everyone, but for those who like peace and quiet, pleasant surroundings, superb service, hiking, shelling, [bird-watching,] and fishing, along with eating good solid meals in a family setting, and just plain doing nothing. This place is closest to owning one's own secluded camp . . . without having to do any of the work. We found that the naturalists in residence were knowledgeable and went out of their way to see to your needs. This is not a place for someone who sweats out the arrival of his *New York Times* until late in the day . . ." *(Percy H. Ballantine)*

"One of the country's best-kept secrets. LSSI is a privately owned island, very irregular but roughly five by two miles. The attraction is the island itself. Great for bird-watchers (the number and variety of birds are incredible), animal-watchers ([for the] armadillos, alligators, deer, occasional snakes), swimmers (six miles of beach for twenty-four guests), horseback riders, surf-fishers, boaters, loafers, honeymooners, and anyone who doesn't want an 18-hole golf course and disco at their resort. Best times are spring and fall. Summer may be hot and, in some parts of the island, a bit buggy. Winter is for the owners and deer-hunters, mostly. We were there in May, which was great." *(Robert Saxon)*

"Swimming in a pool fed with artesian well water was heavenly, and all equipment, including the riding horses, were in good condition. The island itself is a beautiful place, although we felt a bit like a movable feast for the mosquitoes during our late April/early May visit." *(EB)*

Open Feb. to mid-Nov.
Rooms 2 bedrooms in main lodge. 2 cabins with 2 bedrooms, 1 cabin with 4 bedrooms—all with private bath and/or shower, fan, screened porches, living rooms.
Facilities Dining room, living rooms with library/bar, family room. Swimming pool, hot tub. Slide shows, games, crafts, stargazing. 8 acres for lodge complex; barrier island is 10,000 undeveloped acres, with 6 m of ocean beach. Swimming, surf-casting, shelling, boating, bird-watching, windsurfing, hiking, horseback riding, canoeing.
Location SE GA, Glynn County. 70 m S of Savannah, 70 m N of Jacksonville, FL. Northernmost of the Golden Isles. Nearest mainland town, Brunswick, GA.
Restrictions No smoking at meals. No children under 5. Children must have good table manners.
Credit cards MC, Visa.
Rates Full board, $235–375 double, $150–275 single, plus 15% service. Extra person in room, $100. Children's rates. 2-night minimum. Extended-stay discounts. Rates available for meals only, or for day trips.
Extras Airport/station pickups; varying fee. No charge for boat transportation from St. Simons to Little St. Simons. Cribs available.

SAVANNAH 31401   Map 6

Savannah was founded in the eighteenth century by the English general James Oglethorpe and has been a major port ever since. Today, elegant yachts have replaced the pirate ships and China clippers of the early days, but a surprising number of Savannah's original buildings have survived. Over the last ten years a number of them have been restored, some as museums and many more as inns and restaurants. In fact, it seems to us that Savannah has more B&Bs these days than you can shake a croissant at!

Also recommended: Built in 1847, the **Eliza Thompson House** (5 West Jones Street; 912–236–3620 or 800–348–9378) is in the heart of Savannah's historic district, and combines nineteenth-century ambience with modern conveniences. The **Foley House Inn** (14 West Hull Street; 912–232–6622 or 800–647–3708) was built in 1896 and restored in 1982. Among the more interesting finds of the renovation was a skeleton lying behind a wall—a knife still stuck in its breastbone! Rooms are furnished with four-poster Charleston rice beds, antiques, and Oriental rugs, and rates include a continental breakfast and afternoon tea.

Two possibilities for families or others who would prefer the convenience of an apartment for their Savannah stay are **417 The Haslam/Fort House** (417 East Charlton Street; 912–233–6380) and the **Liberty Inn** (128 West Liberty Street; 912–233–1007 or 800–637–1007) the former has one two-bedroom suite with kitchen and garden, along with the knowledgeable assistance of owner Alan Fort, while the latter, built in 1834, has five one and two-bedroom suites, fully equipped with kitchens and washer/dryers.

Ballastone Inn
14 East Oglethorpe Avenue

Tel: (912) 236–1484
In GA: (800) 822–4553

Originally known as the old Anderson House, the Ballastone Inn dates back to 1853. When the inn was restored, the original owners renamed it the Ballastone in recognition of the ballast stones of which much of the city had been built. In the early nineteenth century, English sailing ships dumped their ballast stones at nearby Yamacraw Bluff, to make room for the bales of cotton to be taken to England.

Rates at the Ballastone include a welcoming glass of sherry and bowl of fruit, continental breakfast with fresh flowers and a morning paper, brandy and chocolates at bedtime, overnight polishing of shoes, and terry robes in the bath. Rooms are individually decorated in a variety of styles, with quality reproduction furniture, queen- and king-size beds, and modern baths. Authentic Savannah colors are used throughout, coordinated with Scalamandre fabrics. Late-afternoon tea and cocktails are served in the garden or in the antique-filled parlor.

In 1987, the inn was purchased by Richard Carlson, but readers continue to be delighted with this inn. "Located next to the Juliette Low House, the inn was surprisingly warm in feeling, due in large part to the friendly reception we received from the manager and desk clerk. Meal suggestions were wonderful, and menus were available to help in the decision." *(Caroline & Jim Lloyd)*

"The gracious hosting of this inn extends from the very top to the most junior staff member; each one seems to feel proprietary about the house and responsible for the comfort of its guests. Best of all is the considerate care of strangers—I was watched going to and from my car, given dining suggestions, and even assisted in meeting locals who could help with my research." *(Joan Severa)*

"The inn feels more like a gracious home than a hotel. There are only five or six rooms on each floor, with spacious halls and sitting rooms on each floor. The doors of unoccupied rooms are left open for guest to sneak a peek; all we saw were spacious and beautifully decorated, with canopy or Charleston rice beds. A bowl of fresh fruit and magazines awaited us. The terry robes were a nice touch, as was the brandy and chocolate, and fresh towels at bedtime. Best was a breakfast of fresh orange juice, fresh strawberries and pineapple, and two different types of muffins, delivered to our room on a silver tray at the appointed hour with the Sunday paper." *(Linda Bambu)*

"Our bed had an excellent mattress and reading lamps on each side of the canopied bed. The bathroom was pristine white and sparkled. We enjoyed the small garden off the parlor—a lovely place to sit with a glass of complimentary sherry. All parking is on the street. We were assured that we would have no problems despite signs forbidding overnight parking. When we found a ticket the next morning, the host graciously took care of it." *(Amy Peritksy)*

Open All year.
Rooms 3 suites, 15 doubles with private bath and/or shower, telephone, radio, TV/VCR, air-conditioning. Some with whirlpool bath, fireplace.
Facilities Parlor with fireplace, videotape library, breakfast room, bar/lounge, patio. Small garden. Off- and on-street parking.
Location Historic district. 6 blocks from riverfront.
Restrictions No children under 17.
Credit cards Amex, MC, Visa.
Rates B&B, $175 suite, $95–135 double, $85–125 single. Extra person in room, $10. Corporate rates Sun.–Thurs.
Extras Small pets allowed. Limited accessibility for disabled, elevator.

The Gastonian

Tel: (912) 232–2869

220 East Gaston Street

From California modern to Savannah historical was quite a change in location and life-style for Hugh and Roberta Lineberger. But they were sure enough of their innkeeping plans to invest $2 million in the 1986 restoration of two connecting Savannah mansions, built in 1868 in the Regency Italianate style. The interiors are highlighted with fine woods and hearty pine floors, decorative moldings and brass, and wallpapers in the original Scalamandre Savannah pattern. Depending on the room, the decor ranges from French, Italianate, English, Victorian, or colonial, but all have authentic antiques, Persian rugs, and rice poster or Charleston canopied beds. Rates include a full breakfast and the morning paper; wine, fresh fruit and flowers to greet your arrival; and afternoon tea and evening sweets and cordials.

"Beautiful decor without being cute or precious. The whirlpool baths are relaxing and a big change from home. Wine and fruit awaits when you check in, and peach liqueur and a praline is placed in your room every night. The Caswell-Massey toiletries are a nice extra, as are the warm terry cloth robes. The Linebergers are very knowledgeable about Savannah, and made terrific restaurant recommendations. Breakfast is served family style in either the kitchen or the lush dining room, depending on the number of guests; the food is good, especially the bacon quiche. "*(Rachel Gorlin, also Robert Berrey, and others)* "Southern hospitality with California efficiency." *(Bill Jordon)*

"Our large room was beautifully appointed, the bath spotlessly clean. The Linebergers are gracious hosts, and pay careful attention to detail. Off-street parking is provided behind the inn and although it looks small, we had no problems. Two blocks away is Forsyth Park, a real treat when the azaleas are in bloom." *(Lynda Oswald)*

Open All year.
Rooms 3 suites, 10 doubles—all with whirlpool bath, telephone, TV, air-conditioning, fireplace. Some with desk, fan. 1 in carriage house with kitchenette.
Facilities Kitchen/breakfast room, parlor, dining room, courtyard with hot tub, off-street parking.
Location Historic district.
Restrictions No children under 12. Smoking discouraged.
Credit cards All major credit cards accepted.
Rates B&B, $185–200 suite, $95–150 double. Corporate rates.
Extras Hotel equipped for disabled.

Hawaii

Poipu Bed & Breakfast Inn, Koloa, Kauai

Hawaii is one of our most beautiful states. Until recently, for most visitors Hawaii meant only Honolulu and the beaches of Waikiki, because that's where all mainland flights arrived. Lately, though, the combination of overcrowding in Honolulu and the expansion of direct air service to several other islands has changed the picture substantially. Whatever your schedule, we strongly recommend that you make the time to explore Oahu away from Honolulu and to visit one or more of Hawaii's other islands: Hawaii (the Big Island), Maui, Kauai, Molokai, and Lanai.

Information please: Diehard get-away-from-the-crowd types now head directly for Molokai, once known as the Forgotten Isle, for empty beaches, hidden coves, and dramatic sea cliffs and waterfalls. Accommodations are limited here (that's the idea), but one possibility is the newly renovated **Pau Hana Inn,** a 39-unit oceanfront hotel, landscaped with tropical trees and plants, with very reasonable rates (Box 546, Kaunakakai, Molokai 96748; 800–423–MOLO).

Although hardly undiscovered (it's third among total visitors), Kauai has maintained the relaxed island pace now lost on some of the other islands. Hotel possibilities include the picturesque **Coco Palms**, the island's first luxury resort, where the "ancient rituals" of blowing the conch shell at sundown and the torch-lighting ceremony were invented in the early fifties (Box 631, Lihue 96766; 808–822–4921); its 139 rooms have Polynesian decor, set among peaceful lagoons and towering palms.

Entries are listed alphabetically by island, then town. Rates do not include 9.43% state lodging tax.

KAUPULEHU-KONA, HAWAII 96745   Map 15

Information please: Also on the Big Island is the **Manago Hotel** (Box 145, Captain Cook-Kona 96704; 808–323–2642), 1,400 feet above the Kona Coast, on the slopes of Mauna Loa. This 42-room hotel, owned by the Manago family since its founding in 1917, offers spectacular views from the clean new rooms in the back, with balconies and private baths, and rates of only $30. Japanese and American food is available three times daily, at equally reasonable prices, in the hotel restaurant. Reports, please.

Kona Village Resort	*Tel:* (808) 325–5555
P.O. Box 1299	In HI: (800) 432–5450
	Outside HI: (800) 367–5290

Kona Village is built on the site of the ancient Hawaiian village of Kaupulehu. In 1801, when Mt. Hualalai erupted, this cove was the only one spared the massive lava flows that devastated the area. The village's thatched *hales* (Polynesian-style bungalows) have been built in and among the actual stone platforms of the ancient Hawaiians. Although a wide variety of activities are available, nothing is programmed, and guests are free to do as much or as little as they choose.

Recent improvements here include the addition of a second, more formal dining area and the construction of a second swimming pool, designed especially for children.

"To arrive at Kona Village, one drives through several miles of lava fields, surely one of the most barren sights this side of the moon. The *hales* here are done in the style of different South Pacific cultures and are widely spaced for nice views. They are in three separate areas within the resort—surrounding the lagoon, along the beach, and in a lava field along the ocean. We were in the lava field, which was very interesting, and not at all barren here, due to extensive plantings of brilliant exotic flowers. Our designer-decorated *hale* was quiet and large, with separate dressing and bath areas.

"This is a beautiful, private, and peaceful haven from some of the crowds and overbuilding on the more popular beaches of Waikiki, Kaanapali, and Kona.

"One really doesn't need to leave this self-contained resort for any reason. We visited the volcano and toured the Kona area as well as Mauna Kea, and decided that Kona Village was the prettiest spot on the island. If we are fortunate enough to visit again, we won't even leave for a morning. The meals have a continental flair. Lunch is an open-air buffet, different every day, with wonderful variety. Service is competent.

"The beach is a lovely little crescent, although the sand is grayish. Snorkeling is good, with brightly colored large fish everywhere. The water is dark blue and quite swimmable, even in January. We enjoyed the catamaran ride and saw humpback whales from a safe distance." *(Susan W. Schwemm, also Paul Lasley & Elizabeth Harryman)*

Open All year (closed early Dec. for refurbishing).
Rooms 38 suites, 87 doubles, all in individual thatched *hales*. 83 with full private bath, 42 with shower only. All with desk, fan.
Facilities Dining room, bar/lounge, nightly entertainment. 82 acres with 2 swimming pools, 3 lighted tennis courts, 15-acre petroglyph field. Located on the beach; snorkeling, sailing, canoeing, boat excursions included in rates. Golf nearby.
Location W side of the Big Island, 15 m N of Kailua-Kona on Hwy. 19.
Credit cards Amex, CB, DC, Discover, MC, Visa.
Rates Full board, $400–540 suite, $330–540 double, $255–465 single, plus 15% service. Extra person in room, $117 adult, $90 children 6–12, $45 children 2–5; crib, $20. Family, honeymoon packages. Senior discount available. 7-night minimum during Christmas season.
Extras Dining room, pool, some guest rooms wheelchair accessible. Kona Airport pickups, $18 per car. Cribs, babysitting available. German, French, Japanese spoken.

HANA, MAUI 96713   Map 15

Information please: If you've always dreamed of Hana's remote beauty but found the prices at the **Hana-Maui** (below) beyond your grasp, the **Hana Kai Maui Resort** (1533 Uakea Road, Box 38; 800–346–2772) offers studio and one-bedroom apartments for under $100. Most have balconies, and the decor combines bamboo furnishings with tropical prints.

Hotel Hana-Maui   *Tel:* (808) 248–8211
P.O. Box 8 (I)   (808) 536–7522
                              (800) 321–HANA

One of Hawaii's oldest luxury hotels, the Hotel Hana-Maui was purchased several years ago by Rosewood Hotels, Inc., a small group of first-rate hotels that includes the highly acclaimed Bel-Air in Los Angeles. Rosewood has spent over $25 million improving the property, upgrading the food, and refurbishing the rooms, which now feature oversize rattan furniture, Hawaiian quilts, and lots of wood and plants. The Hawaiian-American cuisine, served in the poolside pavilion or the restaurant, is supplemented by cookouts, clambakes, and luaus. Although rates are very high, the overwhelming consensus is that its very much worth it. Although many guests choose to relax and do nothing, others prefer to sign up for daily activities ranging from beachside cookouts to tours of the working Hana Ranch to jeep tours. With the exception of drinks, souvenirs, horseback riding, taxes, and service are included—eliminating unpleasant surprises at check-out time.

"The Hana-Maui, part of a 4,500-acre ranch, offers total rest and relaxation. Getting there means taking either a beautiful but nerve-shattering three-hour drive over narrow curving mountain roads or a breathtaking small-plan or helicopter ride. Our room was filled with flowers and plants, and had a coffee maker for us to brew our own Kona Gold coffee. The food was delicious, with creative use made of Hawaii's tropical fruits and fishes; only meat is flown in from California—everything else is locally grown. An unforgettable getaway at unforgettable prices." *(MW)* "Everything you said in last year's book . . . and more."*(Toni & Lee Marteney)*

Open All year.
Rooms 19 suites, 76 doubles, all with private bath and/or shower, telephone, desk. Almost all with ceiling fans, refrigerators, private patios. Some with Jacuzzis.
Facilities Restaurants, bar/lounge, club room with TV, games, library. Nightly entertainment. 23-acre grounds, with heated swimming pool, tennis courts, 3-hole practice golf course, croquet, bicycling, horseback riding, scuba diving, snorkeling, fishing. Executive meeting center. Free shuttle bus to nearby beach.
Location E coast of Maui. Take Hwy. 36 to Hana. Hotel is close to intersection of Uakea Rd. and Hana Hwy.
Restrictions No smoking in dining room.
Credit cards Amex, JCB, MC, Visa.
Rates Full board, $555–855 suite, $360–755 double, $278–673 single. Extra adult in room, $140; child 7–17, $90; child 2–7, $40. Extra rollaway and crib charge, $20. No charge for children under 2. Special honeymoon/anniversary, family plans. Rates higher at Christmas.
Extras Some rooms equipped for disabled. Hana Airport pickups. Cribs, babysitting, play equipment available. Member, Rosewood Hotels.

LAHAINA, MAUI 96761   Map 16

Information please: We've had good reports on the **Manoa Valley Inn** in Honolulu (see entry) and hope for similar ones on the newly opened **Lahaina Hotel**, under the same ownership (127 Lahainaluna Street; 808–661–0577). Originally built in the 1860s, the inn just underwent a year-long restoration, resulting in 12 air-conditioned guest rooms with balconies; furnishings include turn-of-the-century antique beds and armoires and Laura Ashley and Ralph Lauren fabrics. Rates range from $110–175. Farther up the west coast of Maui from Lahaina, near Kapalua, is the **Coconut Inn,** a modern 41-room hotel, with rooms clustered around the swimming pool and lush tropical garden. All rooms have a private bath and fully equipped kitchen, and continental breakfast is included in the very reasonable $60–80 rates (P.O. Box 10517, Napili 96761; 800–367–8006). Comments, please.

The Plantation Inn
174 Lahainaluna Road

Tel: (808) 667–9225
(800) 433–6815

Although the inn looks as if it dates from 1890, it was actually completed in 1987, combining period charm with air-conditioning, soundproofing, plumbing, and electronics. The Victorian theme is carried throughout with stained-glass windows, brass and four-poster beds, country pine, wicker, and bamboo furnishings, flowered fabrics and wallpapers, and oak flooring; even the baths have Victorian pedestal sinks and chain-pull toilets. The inn's restaurant, Gerard's, is well established and reputed to be one of Maui's best, specializing in French cuisine. Rates include an expanded continental breakfast of fresh fruit, French toast, Kona coffee, and hot chocolate. Guests receive a discount for dinner at Gerard's.

The Plantation is partly owned by Central Pacific Divers, a Maui-based operation. The inn pool was intentionally dug to a depth of 12 feet to facilitate diving certification courses, and many guests spend their days on CPD dive charters.

"Perfect location right in Lahaina. Large comfortable rooms, delicious tropical breakfast buffet, excellent dinners, great dive packages. Families or groups will enjoy the poolside cottage." *(Dianne Crawford)*

Open All year.
Rooms 1 suite, 8 doubles, 1 3-bedroom cottage, all with private bath and/or shower, telephone, radio, TV/VCR, air-conditioning. Most with desk.
Facilities Dining room, bar, verandas. Deck, gardens, gazebo, heated pool, hot tub, on-site parking. Tennis, golf nearby. 1½ blocks from beach, harbor. Free scuba lessons, diving certification.
Location Historic Lahaina town. From airport, take Rte. 30 (Honoapilani Hwy.) into Lahaina. Turn right at Texaco/Union 76 gas stations onto Lahainaluna Rd. to inn 1½ blocks down on left.
Restrictions No children under 10 in main building.
Credit cards Amex, Discover, MC, Visa.
Rates B&B, $129 suite, $95–109 double, $78 single. Extra person in room, $10–25. 40% meal discount. Alc breakfast, $6; alc lunch, $7.50; alc dinner, $40. Dive packages, $579 weekly per person.
Extras French spoken.

HONOLULU, OAHU   Map 15

Manoa Valley Inn   *Tel:* (808) 947–6019
2001 Vancouver Drive 96822   (800) 634–5115

Those who think that Honolulu is all high-rise hotels will be amazed by their first sight of the Manoa Valley Inn, a Victorian-style cottage dating back to 1919. Listed on the National Register of Historic Places, this marvelously ornamented brown-and-white structure has numerous gables and elaborately buttressed eaves and was renovated in 1978 by Rick Ralston.

Rooms are decorated with iron and four-poster beds, marble-topped dressers, and flowered wallpapers. Rates include continental breakfast; coffee, tea, and soft drinks on request throughout the day; afternoon fruit and cheese; and extra room amenities, such as terry robes and fresh flowers.

"Very clean with an accommodating and friendly manager. A quiet and relaxing escape from the hustle and bustle of Waikiki; a pleasant envirnment for the business traveler." *(KBG)*

Open All year.
Rooms 1 cottage, 1 suite, 6 doubles—5 with private bath, 3 with shared bath. All with telephone, 2 with desk.
Facilities Parlor with piano, game room with pool table, porches. Gardens with croquet.
Location 2 miles from Waikiki, downtown Honolulu. Manoa Valley, 1 block from U. of Hawaii. From the airport, take H-1 Fwy. to University Ave. exit toward the mountains. At Vancouver Dr. turn left and continue to 2001.
Restrictions No children under 14. No smoking in common rooms.
Credit cards MC, Visa.
Rates B&B, $145 suite, $125 cottage, $80–115 double.

New Otani Kaimana Beach Hotel
2863 Kalakaua Avenue 96815

Tel: (808) 923–1555
In CA: (800) 252–0197
In US, Canada: (800) 421–8795
In NYC: (212) 308–7491

The New Otani is a 25-year-old hotel, with recently renovated rooms and lobby. Ideally located in the center of Kapiolani Park, the hotel is adjacent to Waikiki's central hotel and shopping area. It is also set right on San Souci beach, one of the best swimming beaches on Oahu, according to general manager Stephen Boyle. The New Otani's relatively small size enables the staff to provide personal and efficient service.

"This spot was a favorite haunt of Robert Louis Stevenson, who passed the time relaxing under the large Hau trees. Today the area includes the hotel, the beach and ocean, 277-acre Kapiolani Park, and Diamond Head. The hotel has one of the few outdoor restaurants in Waikiki, the Hua Tree Lanai, and also has one of the finest Japanese restaurants, Miyako. With 125 rooms, it is much smaller, quieter, and more personal than its Waikiki competitors, and has the only garden apartments in the Diamond Head area. It's a 10-minute walk past the beach to the main Waikiki strip. Less than five minutes away are 13 tennis courts, a golfing range, archery, and jogging paths with exercise stations. A short walk away are the Honolulu Zoo, Honolulu Aquarium, the Waikiki Shell, and bus and trolley stops." *(Michael Virgintino)*

"The hotel sits in the shadow of Diamond Head, yet feels light years away from Waikiki. Newly done in restful pastels, it's a typical nine-story high-rise on the outside, but inside the decor, airy lobby and friendly staff lend it charm. We breakfasted each morning at the beachside Hau Tree Lanai restaurant. The San Souci Beach in front of the hotel is populated by hotel guests and Oahu locals who favor its tranquility. My son played for hours on the beach with another child he met. We enjoyed the city trolley tour, especially the stops at the Maritime Center and the Palace. An easy bus ride away, is the Bishop Museum where we learned about the Polynesian islands and cultures." *(Debbie Joost)*

Open All year.
Rooms 23 suites, 102 doubles, all with full private bath, TV, telephone, radio, desk, air-conditioning, balcony, mini-bar. Some with kitchenette.
Facilities 2 restaurants, room service, beach. Concierge service. Swimming, windsurfing, golf, tennis, hiking, jogging, bicycling nearby.
Location 1 m S of Waikiki, at Diamond Head.
Credit cards Amex, CB, DC, JCB, MC, Visa.
Rates Room only, $140–325 suite, $78–180 double. Extra person in room, $10. No charge for children under 12. 5-night minimum stay, Dec. 20–Jan. 5.
Extras Cribs, babysitting available. Cantonese, Japanese, Korean, Spanish, German, Tagalog, Ilokano spoken.

Idaho

Busterback Ranch, Ketchum

Idaho was the only western state settled by an eastward flow of settlers—waves of prospectors swarmed here from California and other western regions when gold was discovered in 1860. Now prospectors have largely been replaced by tourists, but Idaho's rugged terrain still provides the allure. With 200 mountain peaks over 8,000 feet in height, Idaho also boasts North America's largest gorge (Hell's Canyon), rivers turbulent with white-water rapids, remote forests, numerous large lakes, and Craters of the Moon National Monument—83 acres of twisted globules, rivers, and cones of lava.

Idaho is ideal for the outdoor enthusiast: rafting, fishing, hunting, hiking, mountain climbing, cross-country and downhill skiing. The list is endless. The less energetic can take comfort in the fact that many tempting spots can be seen along the state's two north-south highways.

North of Magic City, State Route 75 winds through farmland, past Hailey (where Ezra Pound was born), then climbs to Ketchum/Sun Valley (a ski resort since 1936) and on into the magnificent Sawtooth Mountains. From here north to Salmon, every bend in the road looks like a picture postcard. In June, the road is bordered by a profusion of delicate wildflowers. For a different view, take U.S. 95 north from Weiser to the Canadian border. Broad valleys, steep mountains, and rolling fields of alfalfa lead to the forests and famous lake country of northern Idaho.

Cutting across Idaho? Take U.S. 12, which follows Lewis and Clark's 1805 trail from Lolo Pass on the Montana border through lush forest along the Lochsa River, one of Idaho's prettiest. Staying in Boise? You'll find it one of the friendliest capitol cities in the country. While here, don't miss the capitol rotunda, where huge, beautiful faux marble columns blend in spectacularly with the real thing from Vermont and Italy. One warning:

Southern Idaho (including Boise) can be very hot in summer; when you reserve a room, make sure it is air conditioned.

Information please: River Birch Farm is set on the banks of the Pend Oreille River 15 minutes from Sandpoint in the Idaho panhandle. Most rooms of this turn-of-the-century house have river views, and use of the canoes and rowboats is included in the reasonable rates (Highway 2, P.O. Box 608, Laclede 83841; 208–263–3705).

Rates do not include 7% state tax.

BOISE 83702   Map 13

Notwithstanding the fact that it is the capitol and largest city in Idaho, Boise is a pleasant small city in southwest Idaho and serves as a gateway for those en route to Sun Valley.

Idaho Heritage Inn   *Tel:* (208) 342–8066
109 West Idaho

Listed on the National Register of Historic Places, the Idaho Heritage Inn was built in 1904 by Henry Falk, and remained in the Falk family until 1943, when it was purchased by Governor Chase Clark. The governor passed along the house to his daughter Bethine and son-in-law, Senator Frank Church, who owned it until Tom and Phyllis Lupher restored the home as a bed & breakfast inn in 1987.

The Luphers note that "we may be new to the B&B business, but we are proud of our house and its past, we offer the best personal service to our guests. Our inn is within walking distance of several great restaurants, the city zoo, art museum, historical museum, Boise State, and the Greenbelt, a paved path following the Boise River for several miles."

"The inn is located on a tree-lined street just off the main boulevard yet seems a million miles removed from the hustle and bustle of major motels. Owner/innkeepers Tom and Phyllis Lupher greeted us with a wonderful glass of Idaho's own blush wine. Our sunny room, the Governor's Suite, was done in soothing green and rose colors, with antique linens. Our dresser was topped with a vase of fresh flowers, the bath had thick, fluffy towels, and the bed a firm, comfortable mattress. Our bathroom had a deep tub with ample hot water, plus a separate art deco–tiled shower. The ample breakfast consisted of fresh orange juice, fresh-brewed decaffeinated coffee, juicy melon, and homemade breads and muffins that were moist and satisfying.

"Boise is a small, clean city, with quaint brick buildings housing everything from small restaurants, delis, and antique shops, to stores full of mountaineering equipment or handmade woolens. The Luphers love to discuss antiques in general and the history of their inn in particular. At the end of our stay, they drove us back to the airport in their red 1940s-era convertible." *(Susan & Darrell Engler, also Carolyn O'Dell)*

Open All year.
Rooms 1 suite, 4 doubles—all with private bath and/or shower, desk, air-conditioning.

Facilities Dining room, living room, TV room, sun room, veranda, courtyard. Bicycles. Fishing nearby. 16 m to downhill, cross-country skiing.

Location Warm Springs district. Walking distance to downtown, 8th St. Marketplace, Old Boise. 1 block to St. Luke's. From I-84, follow Broadway onto Idaho to inn on left, between 1st and 2nd.

Restrictions No smoking in guest rooms. No children under 16.

Credit cards Amex, MC, Visa.

Rates B&B, $65 suite, $45–65 double. Extra person in room, $10. Ski, day trips.

Extras Airport/station pickups.

Idanha Hotel
928 Main Street

Tel: (208) 342–3611

We are delighted to welcome back this Idaho landmark into the pages of our guide. Resembling a medieval donjon, with four corner turrets and a crenellated rooftop, the Idanha was the grandest hotel and most expensive building in Boise when it opened in 1901. It has remained in continuous operation since then, and a recent renovation has done much to reinstate it to a position of prominence.

"This wonderful old hotel has been completely refurbished and offers a very pleasant place to stay. The lobby and dining room are comfortable and inviting, and the guest rooms have lots of brass and pretty fabrics. But the highlight is the lounge where Gene Harris plays regularly. A nationally known jazz pianist, Gene Harris does frequent gigs in New York City and Los Angeles, but calls Boise home 'because the people are so friendly.' One area for improvement; we were there during a heat wave and the air-conditioning wasn't up to snuff." *(SC)*

Open All year.

Rooms 2 suites, 38 doubles—all with full private bath, telephone, radio, TV. Some with desk.

Facilities Restaurants, bar, lounge, lobby.

Location Downtown Boise. At corner of 10th and Main sts.

Credit cards Amex, CB, DC, Discover, MC, Visa.

Rates B&B, $90 suite, $40–55 double, $35–50 single. Extra adult in room, $5. Children stay free in parent's room. Senior discounts. Weekend packages. Full breakfast $5, alc lunch $7, alc dinner $18.

Extras Cribs available. Airport pickups.

Owyhee Plaza
1109 Main Street at Eleventh

Tel: (208) 343–4611
In ID: (800) 821–7500
Outside ID: (800) 233–4611

The Owyhee Plaza, which first opened its doors in 1910, has been updated to accommodate business travelers and expanded many times over the years.

"I'd recommend the motel section of the hotel for families and others who prefer easy access to their car and the swimming pool. For anyone else, the best rooms are on the third floor. They're quieter and more spacious than the lower floors, with king-size beds, electrically operated drapes, and electric blankets. Street-side rooms can be noisy on weekend nights." *(LS, also Keith Jurgens)*

Open All year.

Rooms 100 doubles and suites—all with full private bath, telephone, TV, air-conditioning; some with desk, coffee maker, mini-refrigerator. 2-bedroom suite with jacuzzi, wet bar.

Facilities Restaurant, coffee shop, bar/lounge, swimming pool, hairdresser, gift shop, health club, room service, off-street parking.

Location Downtown. Short walk to state capitol.

Credit cards Amex, MC, Visa.

Rates Room only, $50–75 double, $40–65 single.

Extras Airport pickups.

COEUR D'ALENE 83814   Map 13

Coeur d'Alene is a lovely resort town set on the banks of the lake of the same name. Located in Idaho's northern panhandle, it's only 30 miles east of Spokane, Washington, and is a very popular getaway with the inhabitants of that city. Activities include lake cruises, canoeing, paddleboating, plus hiking, picnicking, and, in winter, cross-country skiing, and snowmobiling. About 30 minutes away is downhill skiing.

Information please: We'd like to have reports on the turn-of-the-century **Gregory's McFarland House** (601 Foster Avenue; 208–667–1232), a beautifully restored home with birds-eye maple flooring, leaded glass windows, and period decor. Ample common areas for guests include a living room with piano, a family room with TV and pool table, a wraparound porch with swing, and a redwood deck overlooking the garden. B&B rates for the four guest rooms range from $55–65.

The Blackwell House   *Tel:* (208) 664–0656
820 Sherman Avenue

The Blackwell House was run down and vacant when Kathleen Sims bought this 1904 Victorian in 1983 and restored it for use as a B&B. The handsome woodwork has been returned to its original glow, and the rooms have been decorated with lace curtains, velvet-covered wing chairs, stenciling, and antiques.

"An elegant white house with columns supporting a wraparound porch. On entering, you feel as if you have just been admitted to an exclusive private club—lots of warm rich wood, thick dark-green carpets, gracious rooms with antiques and lots of nice sitting areas. Every room has something special to offer. The breakfast room, light and airy, has small tables with bright cloths, and overlooks the gardens and gazebo. Every room is decorated with real antiques (not just old furniture trying to pass), and special touches you'd love to try out at home. Even the smaller rooms are bright, cheerful, and cozy. My favorite was the Blackwell Suite, a huge room with a large sitting area, including a white wicker loveseat sporting two gigantic white bears, a male and female, wearing appropriate bows and holding hands. Two of the rooms on the second floor share a huge bath. One on the top floor is called the Playroom and is reminiscent of Grandmother's attic. On this floor is also a superb bath with every amenity, even a bathroom book which guests are encouraged to write in; one guest wrote, 'Princess Di, eat your heart out.' "*(SC)*

"Our room was spacious, spotless, and beautifully furnished. The old

199

clawfoot tub was great for relaxing bubble baths. The owners are delight-ful, and the service was excellent." *(David Studur)*

Open All year.
Rooms 5 suites, 3 doubles—6 with private tub or shower, 2 with maximum of 4 people sharing bath. All with radio; 3 with air-conditioning, 5 with fan.
Facilities Dining room, living room with fireplace, breakfast room with fireplace, TV room with games, piano. Patio, garden with gazebo. 5 blocks from lake.
Location 2 blocks from center.
Restrictions Street noise in front rooms might disturb light sleepers. No children under 12.
Credit cards Amex, MC, Visa.
Rates B&B, $65–85 suite, $45–85 double, $45 single. Extra person in room, $10. 2-night minimum holiday weekends.
Extras Airport pickups, $10.

KELLOGG 83837   Map 13

Montgomery House   *Tel:* (208) 786–2311
305 South Division Street

Kellogg is a turn-of-the-century gold and silver mining town; this inn was originally built as a boardinghouse for miners. Joan and Wayne Dorsett bought the house in 1967 and converted it to a bed & breakfast in 1982; Terry and Robert Montgomery took over in 1988. The first floor of the inn is a casual, family-style restaurant, serving three square meals a day— steaks are a specialty—with the modestly furnished upstairs rooms avail-able for overnight guests. Nearby sights of interest include the silver mine tours, Old Mission State Park, and downhill skiing at Silverhorn.

"The food was excellent, rooms clean, and hospitality fine." *(Evelyn Thompson)* "Liked the personal service and friendliness of the owners." *(Carol Armitage)* More comments, please.

Open All year.
Rooms 10 doubles and singles, sharing 3 baths. Some with radio, 1 with TV, all with desk.
Facilities Restaurant, TV/VCR room, library, porch. River and lake fishing, hunting, rafting, downhill skiing nearby.
Location N ID panhandle, Shoshone County. I-90 to exit 51; turn S on Division, 3 blocks to inn, in center of town.
Credit cards MC, Visa.
Rates B&B, $30 double, $25 single. Alc lunch, $4; alc dinner, $12.

KETCHUM   Map 13

Busterback Ranch   *Tel:* (208) 774–2217
Highway 75/93, Star Route

A 2,800-acre working cattle ranch with rustic country accommodations, the Busterback offers a full range of summer activities from pack trips and hayrides to canoeing and windsurfing on the Salmon River. In winter, cross-country skiing is the order of the day, with miles of groomed trails and plenty of professional instruction.

Busterback is the result of a lifelong vision of L.L. Breckenridge, a miller from Twin Falls, who made his first land purchase of 160 acres in 1929 and completed his acquisitions in 1946. After clearing the land with horse-drawn equipment, the acreage was hand seeded, and from that effort received its name: as L.L.'s wife, Florence, described it, "We used to come to the mountains for fun. Now you just bust your backs working."

In 1972, the Sawtooth National Recreation Area was established in this part of the alpine meadows, rolling hills, and the Sawtooth mountain range by an act of Congress; L.L.'s son, John, and wife, Miriam, had spent 15 years negotiating with the government so that the area could continue to be a productive part of Idaho's economy while maintaining its fragile environment. In 1976, L.L.'s granddaughter, Katie, established the cross-country skiing program that is now a well-known feature of central Idaho. Owned since 1983 by Lee and Nancy Enright, the ranch manager is Jim Root.

In addition to all the glorious outdoor scenery, the indoor views are pretty impressive as well. The White Cloud Lodge is constructed of peeled logs, with a cathedral ceiling and a Palladian window; the wood's golden color casts a warm glow over the simple furnishings. The Busterback must be the inspiration for the Ralph Lauren school of country decor—peeled log beds are layered with lumberjack plaid blankets, quilts, and lace dust ruffles.

Not forgetting the comforts of good food and good wine, a typical dinner menu might include boneless breast of duck with orange shallot sauce, carrots with dill, baby Red Bliss potatoes, and Roaring Meg's chocolate cake with fresh raspberries; another night's selection could be a salad of snow peas, yellow peppers and mushrooms, baked Idaho trout with sweet onions and herbs, sautéed cucumbers, Roman cheese bread, and Patsy's pear cream tart. A wide selection of Idaho and California wines is available to complement each meal.

"The 7,000-foot elevation of the ranch gives the air a special crisp and clear quality. In the warmth of the summer, a profusion of wildflowers carpet the meadows and the streams provide the loudest noise in the landscape. The main lodge of massive pine logs is the center of activity. Everyone gathers here for meals, to sip a drink from the honor bar and to enjoy the huge stone fireplace. Guests really are expected to treat the place as if it were their own; this policy seems to attract guests who are quiet, fun-loving people who come for the scenery and the opportunity to enjoy the outdoors."*(Paul Lasley & Elizabeth Harryman)*

Open All year.
Rooms 3 cabins with woodstove, 5 doubles—5 with private bath and/or shower, 3 rooms sharing 2 baths. All with desk.
Facilities Living room with fireplace, dining room, bar/lounge, gift shop, sauna, hot tub, laundry room, heated swimming pool. 2,800-acre working cattle ranch. Volleyball, kite flying, horseback riding, guided hiking and backpacking trips, whitewater rafting, hayrides. Mountain bike, canoe, sailboard rentals. 30 m of groomed cross-country ski trails with instruction, equipment rentals.

Location Stanley Basin, Sawtooth National Recreation Area. 40 N of Sun Valley and Ketchum, 25 m S of Stanley. On Hwy. 75/93.
Restrictions No smoking.
Credit cards MC, Visa.
Rates Full board, $120–135 per person. Children under 5 free in parents' room. Children's rates. Ski, ranch packages. Winter prix fixe lunch, $12; prix fixe dinner, $29.
Extras Crib, babysitting available by prior arrangement. Member, Special Places.

River Street Inn   *Tel:* (208) 726–3611
100 River Street West
Mailing address: P.O. Box 182, Sun Valley 83353

The River Street Inn is a new bed & breakfast inn, combining neo-Victorian architecture with Palladian windows, brass beds, and bleached oak furnishings in a relaxed, comfortable atmosphere, with beautiful views of Bald Mountain. The living room is done in shades of dusty rose, sage green, and ivory, while the guest room decor is softer, with pastels and soft prints. Ginny Van Doren, owner since 1985, notes that "guests are always delighted with our round Japanese-style bath tubs, and the separate stall showers in each room." Rates include a full breakfast of fresh fruit and juices, omelets, homemade Danish, and fresh-ground coffee, prepared by innkeeper Ginny Van Doren.

"Although the inn is fairly new, it has a homey warmth and all the amenities you could want. Even better is the genuine warmth of inn-keeeper Ginny Van Doren." *(Robert Baughan)* "Spacious, well-furnished, sunlit rooms; the Japanesse soaking tubs are a real revitalizer. Everything is spotless. Ginny makes each guest feel special, from food-to-order to lending out her skis or extra gloves. Great in-town location just above the river. The free bus stops outside the door, and ski lifts and town are just a few blocks away. The fireplace is always going in winter, and snacks and drinks are served après-ski. " *(Anita McCann)*

Open Late May through April.
Rooms 8 doubles—all with stall shower and Japanese soaking tub, telephone, radio, TV, refrigerator.
Facilities Living/dining room with fireplace, deck. 3 blocks to downhill, 1 m to cross-country skiing. Free ski bus across street. Golf, tennis, hiking, horseback riding, bicycling, white-water rafting nearby.
Location S central ID. 150 m E of Boise. 1 m to Sun Valley. 2 blocks to center. From Rte. 75N, turn left at River St., just after Trail Creek Bridge. 2 blocks to inn.
Restrictions Smoking in common area only.
Credit cards Amex, Discover, MC, Visa.
Rates B&B, $95–140 suite, $85–130 double. Extra person in room, $15. $10 per night discount for 3-night stays in summer, 7-night stays in winter. 15% senior discount.
Extras Pets permitted.

NORTHFORK 83466   Map 13

Indian Creek Ranch   *Tel:* (208) O (Salmon operator) ask for 24F-211
Rte. 2, Box 105

"If you're vacationing at Indian Creek, you can leave your fancy duds and antacids at home. Jack and Lois Briggs, the owners, are wonderful hosts, very warm and hospitable. Through their stories we learned much about the history of the area's ghost towns and the town of Salmon. Lois always does her best to accommodate guests' schedules when it comes to meals—early breakfasts for hunters, later ones for those sleeping in—and she'll pack a picnic lunch for all. Although there's no electricity, the bathrooms are fully equipped, but don't forget to bring a flashlight for nighttime trips to the john—propane lamps don't have switches on the walls. At the end of a busy day, we often sat and watched while the bears came up to the apple tree in the yard to eat their evening meal!" *(Rethia McGuire)*

"Our rustic cabin was very clean and well equipped. Lois is a superb cook, and our meals were delicious and ample. The cuisine was traditional western, but Lois caters whenever possible to individual dietary preferences. Her meals are guaranteed to be fresh, wholesome, and usually homemade!

"Jack is an excellent guide on horseback or in jeeps. He can set up float trips down the Salmon River or point out likely fishing holes in the nearby stream. Their horses are a cut above the average dude ranch stock." *(Mike & Rethia McGuire, Linda Paul)* More comments, please.

Open April 1–Nov. 1.
Rooms 4 cabins—all with private shower; one with desk.
Facilities Dining room, living room, study. 130 acres. Fishing in Indian Creek and Salmon River, hiking, hunting, trail rides, riverboat rides.
Location N central ID, 11 m from MT border. 35 m N of Salmon, 100 m S of Missoula, MT. Take I-93 to North Fork and ask for directions.
Credit cards None accepted.
Rates B&B, $60 double. Reduced rates for children. Prix fixe breakfast, $6.50; lunch, $6.50; dinner, $12.
Extras Airport/station pickups. Pets permitted. Crib available.

PRIEST LAKE 83856   Map 13

Hill's Resort   *Tel:* (208) 443–2551
Route 5, Box 162A

Owned by the Hill family for over 40 years, this family resort offers condo and townhouse-type accommodation in a relaxed and casual setting. A relatively undeveloped wilderness, Priest Lake is likely to retain its pristine beauty because nearly 80% of the shoreline is controlled by state and federal governments.

"This resort is set apart from others by the Hill family. One of them solves the needs of every guest, and each guest is treated as a personal friend." *(Mr. & Mrs. Byron Stephan)* "The Hill family attracts an eclectic crowd, from the BMW and cashmere sweater crowd to those in flannel shirts, jeans, and work boots; both the monied and the influential and young families returning with parents and grandparents. Likewise, accommodations range from rustic cabins to luxury chalets with picture windows, plush carpets, and king-size beds. Wild huckleberries and morel mushrooms, native to the area, are featured in Hill's award-winning restaurant, along with fresh fish, chicken, or beef. Every table has a view of the lake, trees, and mountains." *(Janice Adams, also Ritch Fenrich)*

Open All year. Restaurant open daily May through Oct., Dec. 26–Jan. 1; open weekends rest of year.

Rooms 124 1- to 3-bedroom housekeeping units with kitchens. All with telephone, radio, desk. Most with fireplace, dishwasher, balcony. TV available upon request.

Facilities Restaurant, lounge with dance floor, live music; game room, laundry, gift/sport shop, grocery store, guest laundry. 12 acres with sandy sloping beach for swimming, fishing, waterskiing, sailing, canoeing, wind-surfing. 2 tennis courts, pickleball court, golf, cross-country skiing, snowmobiling, hiking, and mushroom and berry picking. Children's games and play area director.

Location N ID, Bonner County, 85 m N of Spokane, WA. In Luby Bay, at SW end of Priest Lake.

Credit cards MC, Visa.

Rates Room only, $78–122 suite, $46–122 double, $40–70 single. Extra person in room, $8. Weekly minimum stay in summer. Weekend packages. Alc breakfast, $3–6; alc lunch, $5; alc dinner, $24.

Extras Some guest rooms wheelchair accessible. Pets permitted in some units, $5 daily; must be kept on leash. Cribs, babysitting, play equipment available. Spanish, Italian spoken.

STANLEY 83278   Map 13

Information please: The **Idaho Rocky Mountain Ranch** offers rustic but comfortable log cabin accommodation, outstanding food—salmon and steak are specialties—and a natural hot springs pool, all on the banks for the Salmon River in the beautiful Stanley Basin, in the White Cloud and Sawtooth Mountains of central Idaho (HC64, Box 9934; 208–774–3544). Another possibility for in-town accommodation is the historic Sawtooth Hotel, with a restaurant, B&B, and very reasonable rates (Box 52; 208–774–9947).

Redfish Lake Lodge   *Tel:* (208) 774–3536
Highway 75, Box 9   During winter: (208) 774–3326

"The lodge is surrounded by pine trees and overshadowed by the rugged peaks of the Sawtooth Mountains. The lodge itself, run by a National Park concessionaire, includes the main building with restaurant, cabins and suites scattered through the woods, a small store, and a sizable dock. Our suite was nice and modern, with a separate living room with comfortable chairs and sofa, a refrigerator and a Murphy bed. Decorated in subdued colors, we looked out into the forest and woke up to birds singing. We also had our own front porch with chairs and tables and a glimpse of the lake through the trees. There's a sandy beach and the lake is cold but a refresh-ing alternative on hot summer days. It was a little buggy during our June visit, but I was told that the mosquitoes are gone by July. At the dock you can rent canoes, rowboats and pedal boats.

"In sum, it's a pretty but busy place, ideal for a family vacation. The only area for improvement is the food, which was adequate but uninspired." *(SC)*

Open Memorial Day weekend through early Oct.
Rooms 6 suites, 16 doubles, 14 cabins—most with private bath and/or shower. 12

rooms in lodge with community men's, women's baths; private sink in room. Suites, cabins with fireplace or Franklin stove.

Facilities Restaurants, bar, guest laundry, general store. 11 acres with beach, boat rentals, fishing, raft trips, hiking, hunting, horseback riding, volleyball, horse shoes. Guides available.

Location Central ID, 135 m NE of Boise, 60 m N of Sun Valley. From Boise, take Hwy. 21 to Stanley. In Stanley, turn S on Hwy. 75 and continue 5 m to bridge at junction of Redfish Lake Creek and the main Salmon River. Turn right at bridge and go 2 m to lodge.

Credit cards MC, Visa.

Rates Room only, $65–170 cabin, $83–91 suite, $38–55 double. Extra child in room, $4. Children under 3 free in parents' room; cribs, $4. No rollaways available. 2–3 night weekend/holiday minimum. Off-season midweek specials. Alc lunch, $5; alc dinner, $15.

Extras Airport pickup from Stanley airstrip. Pets permitted in cabins, $4 daily. Spanish spoken.

WALLACE 83873   **Map 13**

The Historic Jameson   *Tel:* (208) 556–1554
304 Sixth Street

Once known at the "Richest Little City in the World," Wallace was founded in 1884 and grew wealthy because of its gold and silver deposits, made accessible after a narrow gauge railroad was built. Jameson's was built as a hotel in 1908. The restaurant provides comfortable dining in a turn-of-the-century atmosphere, with original woodwork and Oriental rugs. The saloon features a handsome mirrored back bar, complete with ceiling fans and brass trim. Irish coffee made with Jameson's Irish Whiskey is a specialty.

"Very good food at both lunch and dinner; the recently redone B&B rooms on the third floor are small but cozy and filled with antiques. Baths are down the hall but very clean. We spent the evening visiting with Dolly, the B&B manager. She gave us a delightful description of the history of Wallace and the surrounding towns. Across the street is a charming old railroad museum in the old depot." *(Marguerite Papenfus)*

Open All year.
Rooms 6 doubles with a maximum of 6 people sharing a bath.
Facilities Restaurant, saloon.
Location N Idaho, 13 W of MT border. Approx. halfway between Missoula, MT, and Spokane, WA, on I-90. Center of town.
Credit cards MC, Visa.
Rates B&B, $37 double, $36 single. Full breakfast $4; alc lunch $6; alc dinner $15.

Illinois

Aldrich Guest House, Galena

Chicago, with its dynamic business and convention activities, outstanding museums, and cultural offerings, is the key attraction of Illinois. Southern Illinois is rural and agricultural, home to Springfield, the state capital and hometown of Abraham Lincoln. Other areas of interest lie along the Mississippi, from Galena in the north, to St. Louis, on the Missouri side, in the south.

We'd love to have some more Illinois recommendations, especially for the central part of the state—Springfield, Decatur, Champaign/Urbana!

CHICAGO   Map 8

Set along the banks of Lake Michigan, Chicago has much to offer business traveler and tourist alike. The list of must-see attractions is a long one, but the following rank high on any list: the Art Institute, the Field Museum of Natural History, and the Museum of Science and Industry. And a trip to the top of the Sears Tower or the John Hancock Center for wide-ranging views is a must. Those with more time to spare will enjoy the city's many ethnic and special-interest attractions, ranging from institutions devoted to Lithuanian culture to free tours of the world's largest post office facility. For all the details, contact the Chicago Convention & Visitor Bureau, McCormick Place-on-the-Lake, 60616; 312–225–5000.

As is the case in most major cities, weekend rates at Chicago's hotels offer substantial savings over midweek rates. Always inquire if any promotional rates are in effect when making reservations.

Also recommended: Although hardly "little" at 255 rooms, *Dorothy A. Otting* wrote to recommend the **Park Hyatt,** "a fine hotel, beautifully furnished, with an elegant and excellent restaurant, La Tour." The Park Hyatt is located on Water Tower Square, at 800 North Michigan Avenue 60611; 302–280–2220 or 800–228–9000.

Information please: Another good-sized hotel we'd like to hear more about is the newly built **Hotel 21 East.** Its 247 rooms are equipped with state-of-the-art technology, and a sleek contemporary look; its Cafe 21 is a must for creative cuisine (21 East Bellevue Place; 312–266–2100 or 800–443–2100).

The Barclay Chicago
166 East Superior Street 60611

Tel: (312) 787–6000
(800) 621–8004

Located in the heart of Chicago's Magnificent Mile, the Barclay is an intimate all-suite hotel, with only six suites per floor. Rooms are furnished in an elegant style and equipped with the amenities you'd expect to find in a small luxury hotel. As in many all-suite hotels, only the "one-bedroom suites" have two separate rooms; the smaller suites combine the sitting and sleeping areas in the same room. "*The* place to stay in Chicago." *(Laura Scott)*

Open All year.
Rooms 120 suites—all with telephone, radio, TV, desk, refrigerator, wet bar. Most with kitchen.
Facilities Restaurant, lounge, swimming pool. 2 blocks to Lake Michigan. Valet parking.
Location Downtown. Magnificent Mile. 1 block E of Michigan Ave., at corner of St. Clair Ave.
Credit cards Amex, CB, DC, Discover, MC, Visa.
Rates Room only, $175–215 suite (double occupancy), $155–195 suite (single occupancy). 18% service additional. No charge for children under 12 in parents' room. Free continental breakfast, weekdays. Alc breakfast, $5–10; alc lunch, $30; alc dinner, $60. Weekend rates and packages from $117.
Extras Cribs, babysitting available. Spanish spoken. Member, Preferred Hotels Worldwide.

Claridge Hotel
1244 North Dearborn Parkway 60610

Tel: (312) 787–4980
(800) 245–1258

Built over 60 years ago, the Claridge (formerly the Tuscany) was completely gutted in 1986, reopening $10 million later, in the spring of 1987. The hotel is described by the manager as "quietly elegant and modestly priced, with European-style concierge service." The lobby is done in wood and brass, and rooms have a largely traditional decor. Rates include a continental breakfast and morning paper.

One reader complained that his small plain room was overpriced at $115 per day (midweek) plus $14 for parking, while another enjoyed the bargain weekend rate and the continental breakfast, served casually on white butcher paper. More comments, please.

Open All year.
Rooms 3 suites, 170 doubles—all with full private bath, telephone, radio, TV, desk, air-conditioning, refrigerator.

Facilities Restaurant, café, bar/lounge with entertainment. Guest privileges at health club. 2 blocks to Lake Michigan, Dearborn beach. Valet parking.
Location Gold Coast, 1 m to Loop, 3 blocks to Magnificent Mile. From I-90/94 (Kennedy Expressway), exit at North Ave. E to Dearborn, then S 3½ blocks.
Restrictions Designated non-smoking guest rooms. Traffic noise might disturb light sleepers.
Credit cards Amex, AirPlus, CB, DC, MC, Visa.
Rates B&B, $176–280 suite, $88–140 double, $75–140 single. Extra person in room, $15. No charge for children under 17 in parents' room. $68–80 weekend packages. Inquire about special packages. Alc lunch, $10; alc dinner, $30.
Extras Wheelchair accessible. Small pets permitted. Cribs, babysitting available. Spanish, French, Danish spoken.

Richmont Hotel
162 East Ontario Street 60611

Tel: (312) 787–3580
(800) 621–8055

The Richmont continues to maintain its reputation as a pleasant hotel with a friendly staff, relatively small and fairly priced by big-city standards. Rates include a continental breakfast and are a particularly good value on weekends. The Richmont's restaurant, the Rue St. Clair, has an eclectic menu of American, French, and Italian dishes and a good reputation, and an attractive little café.

"The Richmont is right off Michigan Avenue in the heart of the shopping district and is very accessible to everything you'd ever need in Chicago." *(EH)* One reader noted that the rooms on the air shaft are "tiny." More comments, please.

Open All year.
Rooms 13 suites, 180 doubles and singles—all with full private bath, telephone, radio, TV, desk, air-conditioning, refrigerator.
Facilities Restaurant, piano bar. Valet parking. Parking garage 1 block away. Guest discount at Grand Ohio health club ½ block away. 2 blocks to McClurg Court sports facility. 5 blocks to Oak St. Beach.
Restrictions Traffic noise in front rooms might disturb light sleepers.
Location Downtown. N of Loop, 1 block E of Michigan Ave.
Credit cards Amex, CB, DC, Discover, MC, Visa.
Rates B&B, $160 suite, $118–140 double, $116–136 single, plus 12.4% tax. Extra person in room, $12; children free in parents' room. Alc lunch, $8–13; alc dinner, $25–30. Weekend B&B rates, $95–100 suite, $85–90 double. Senior discount.
Extras Wheelchair accessible; some rooms specially equipped for disabled. Airport pickups, $9–13. Cribs, babysitting available. French, Spanish spoken.

Ritz-Carlton
East Pearson Street at Water Tower Place 60611

Tel: (312) 266–1000
(800) 621–6906
(800) 828–1188

Although the Ritz-Carlton is in no way a small hotel, with a recommendation like the one below, we felt we had to include it. Our respondent felt that although the rates are high, the value is excellent, in contrast to equally expensive hotels where the accommodations are merely adequate.

"Chicago's only hotel, as far as I'm concerned. Far and away the best in town. The dining room serves the best food of any hotel in the U.S." *(Zacharias Rosner)*

Open All year.
Rooms 326 suites and doubles—all with full private bath, telephone, radio, TV, desk, refrigerator.
Facilities Restaurant, café, bar/lounge with entertainment, heated indoor swimming pool, sauna. Shopping arcade. Health club, tennis, racquetball privileges.
Location Water Tower.
Credit cards All major cards.
Rates Room only, $500–700 suite, $210–250 double, $185–225 single. Children free in parents' room. Weekend packages.
Extras Cribs available.

The Tremont Hotel
100 East Chestnut Street 60611

Tel: (312) 751–1900
(800) 621–8133

Guests come to the Tremont for its clubby English atmosphere, its decor of dark polished woods, gleaming brass, leather wingback chairs, and reproduction furnishings, and antiques. Originally built as an apartment house in 1923, The Tremont was converted into a luxury hotel in 1976 by John Coleman and further restored in 1982. Crickets, the hotel restaurant, perpetuates the clublike atmosphere and is known for its high-society clientele as much as for its fine cuisine—top-quality meat and fish, with continental touches. Under the same management, with similar atmosphere is the **Whitehall Hotel**, just a block away (105 East Delaware Street 60611; 312–944–6300 or 800–621–8295). *(MG)* More comments, please.

Open All year.
Rooms 9 suites, 130 doubles—all with full private bath, telephone, radio, TV, air-conditioning. Half with desks. 12 rooms in annex.
Facilities Restaurant, bar/lounge with pianist. Lobby with fireplace. Valet parking.
Location Gold Coast, ½ block W of John Hancock Center.
Credit cards Amex, DC, MC, Visa.
Rates Room only, $375–950 suite, $155–205 double, $145–175 single. Children under 18 free in parents' room. Weekend packages. Alc breakfast, $6–10; alc lunch, $30; alc dinner, $50.
Extras Wheelchair accessible; several rooms equipped for disabled. French, Spanish, German spoken.

ELSAH 62028   Map 8

Green Tree Inn
15 Mill Street, P.O. Box 96

Tel: (618) 374–2821

For a welcome break from the big-city bustle of St. Louis, head upriver to Elsah for a relaxing return to the nineteenth century. This entire village, little changed since its founding in 1853, is listed on the National Register of Historic Places and is known for its New England–style architecture. The village is right on the Mississippi River, surrounded by towering limestone bluffs. Antiquers will head for the dozens of shops in nearby Alton, while cyclists will pedal straight for the 14-mile Vadalabene Bike Trail, which goes right through Elsah, following along the base of the limestone bluffs that line the river.

The Green Tree, opened in 1984 by Mary Ann and Michael Pitchford, combines spacious guest rooms (on the second floor) furnished in either

Victorian, Federal, or country styles, with a general store featuring nine-teenth-century merchandise on the lower level. The store stocks every-thing from spices, herbs, and fruit syrups to hand-crafted pottery, glass, baskets, and wreaths. Also available are river tours aboard their antique yacht, and nineteenth-century garden workshops.

Rates include a continental breakfast of cinnamon rolls, freshly baked by the Elsah Landing restaurant; special breakfast arrangements can be made for guests on sugar-restricted diets. *(GR)* More comments, please.

Open All year.
Rooms 6 doubles—all with full private bath, clock radio, TV, desk.
Facilities Gathering room with fireplace, TV, games; balconies. Herb gardens. Gardening workshops, winter eagle sighting tours, fishing, swimming, boating, ice-fishing, cross-country skiing, bicycling, horseback riding nearby. 20 min. to golf. 10 min. to Pere Marquette State Park.
Location SW IL. Great River Road, 40 m N of St. Louis, 8 m W of Alton. 5½ hrs. SW of Chicago. Walking distance to town.
Restrictions No smoking in guest rooms. No children under 12.
Credit cards MC, Visa.
Rates B&B, $65 double. Extra person in room, $15. No tipping. Special packages available.
Extras Wheelchair accessible. Airport/station pickups.

FREEBURG 62243   **Map 8**

Westerfield House   *Tel:* (618) 539–5643
RR 2, Box 34

The drive to Westerfield House is a trip back in time. The inn is shielded by evergreen trees planted from seed; adjacent is an herb garden home to 120 varieties, including 30 species of mint. When you arrive, Jim and Marilyn Westerfield will show you through the three-level log cabin, furnished with antiques, some dating back to colonial times. But the high point here is the food. Promptly at seven, guests are seated on antique Windsor chairs, at candlelit tables, and are served a leisurely seven-course meal by their hosts, clad in colonial garb. The no-choice menu changes monthly, but a sample menu might include hot buttered cider, Parmesan rounds, salad with house dressing, chicken with basil stuffing and tomato-zucchini sauce, celery soufflé, and pear cobbler with vanilla crust.

"The Westerfields provide lodgings, furnished with beautiful antiques for two couples. Outstanding meals, and a well-kept secret in the St. Louis area." *(Chris & Linda Erkmann)*

Open All year. Restaurant Open Fri., Sat., Sun. by reservation only.
Rooms 2 doubles with private bath.
Facilities Restaurant, gardens.
Location SW IL. 25 min. SE of St. Louis. From St. Louis, take Poplar St. bridge to I-64 E to I-255 S to Rte. 15 E. When you come to only stoplight on Rte. 15, you are 1 m from Jefferson Rd. (Jefferson Rd. is 12 m from I-255 exit). Turn left on Jefferson Rd. (watch for "Save" sign on right, American Legion sign on left). Go 2 m to sign for Westerfield House on left.
Restrictions Guest rooms not available before 6:30 P.M.; guests should come dressed for dinner.

Credit cards None accepted.
Rates MAP, $155 double. Prix fixe lunch, $12; dinner, $35.

GALENA 61036   Map 8

A handsome river town, Galena boasts such sights as Grant's Home, Grant Park, and the Belvedere Mansion, plus many craft and antique shops. The town's original fortune (and even its name) came from the local lead mines and later from the steamboat business on the river. When the mines were depleted and the railroads came through in the 1850s, prosperity ended and construction stopped. As a result, nearly 85 percent of the town's buildings are listed in the National Register of Historic Places.

In addition to seeing the sights and shops of the town, area activities include canoeing, fishing, boating, and steamboat rides on the Mississippi and Galena rivers, along with swimming, tennis, golf, horseback riding, and downhill and cross-country skiing in season.

Galena is located in the northwest corner of Illinois, 150 miles west of Chicago and 15 miles south of Dubuque, Iowa. For another area entry, see listing for the **Wisconsin House Inn** in Hazel Green, nine miles to the north.

Information please: The town's ample supply of Victorian buildings may account for the fact that Galena and the surrounding area is now home to over 25 B&Bs and country inns. We'd love to have more feedback on the following: The **Hellman House** is a Victorian home, set high above downtown on Quality Hill, decorated with both Victorian and contemporary furnishings (318 Hill Street; 815–777–3638). Equally historic is the **Farmers' Home Hotel,** built in 1867 as a bakery and in-town residence for farmers and now restored in period with all modern conveniences (334 Spring Street; 815–777–3456). **DeSoto House** (230 South Main Street; 815–777–0090) was called the best and largest hotel west of New York when it opened in 1857. It was restored at a cost of nearly $8 million in 1986; both rooms and restaurant soon merited plaudits from our readers, and the hotel was added to our earlier editions. Although a recent report noted that the guest rooms were elegant and comfortable, financial difficulties has plagued the inn, and more feedback is needed before they can be reinstated for a full entry.

Aldrich Guest House   *Tel:* (815) 777–3323
900 Third Street

Aldrich House was built in 1845 as a one-room house. A major Greek Revival–style addition was constructed in 1853, and in the 1880s the house was further enlarged with Italianate ornamentation. The house was restored in 1984 and is owned by Judy Green, who left the publishing world to become a B&B innkeeper.

"Judy Green has a good sense of humor, and is very informative. The delicious breakfast consisted of fresh fruit, homemade coffee cake, great coffee, and sour cream and cottage cheese pancakes. The house is clean, the plumbing good, and the location convenient, within walking distance of

Galena's antique shops and art galleries." *(Paula & Doug Rogers, also Susan Jacques)*

"This house is decorated in greens, mauves, and ivory, with marvelous antiques. The rooms, especially the bathrooms, are meticulously clean; towels are changed daily." *(Joan & Denis Bohm, also Michael & Sheila Campbell, Ron Essig)*

"All rooms here are open to enjoy, unlike some other B&Bs. The grounds are well maintained and have a lovely array of seasonal flowers. During nice weather, guests congregate on the side porch to get acquainted, enjoy complimentary wine and soft drinks, and peruse the menus of area restaurants; the living room serves the same function in the cooler months. The dining room is beautifully set each morning with lace cloths, china and crystal. Since guests have already become acquainted the evening before, breakfast is most enjoyable as each reports on dinners and activities, and plans for the day ahead. Guests linger long after the meal simply to visit with each other." *(Mr. & Mrs. CarlCarli)*

Open All year.
Rooms 5 doubles—3 with private bath and/or shower, 2 with a maximum of 4 people sharing bath. 2 rooms with adjoining bath may be booked as suite. All with air-conditioning.
Facilities Dining room; living room with grand piano, fireplace, stereo; library; screened porch. Yard games. 8 m to downhill, cross-country skiing.
Location Just off Rte. 20. 5–10-min. walk to center.
Restrictions Smoking in living room, screened porch only. No children under 6.
Credit cards Discover, MC, Visa.
Rates B&B, $120–140 suite (for 4), $55–80 double, $50–75 single, plus 9% tax. Senior rate same as single rate. Extra person in room, $15. 2-night minimum most weekends.
Extras Airport/station pickups.

Log Cabin Guest House
11661 West Chetlain Lane

Tel: (815) 777–2845

If you've always wanted to stay in one of those primitive, *Little House on the Prairie*–type cabins without forfeiting those modern conveniences we've all come to depend on, then one of Scott and Linda Ettleman's four country cabins may be just the thing. The Ettlemans live in a farmhouse dating back to 1826 and have converted the original servants' quarters into a guest house. They have also brought three cabins, dating from the 1860s, to their property, and have decorated them with rustic antiques. There's plenty of room in the cabins for kids, and one even has an antique iron crib; children also enjoy the farm atmosphere, complete with chickens, ducks, and cows in the nearby fields. Rates include a light breakfast of rolls, juice, and coffee.

"Comfortable clean cabins in the peaceful countryside. Friendly owners." *(Philip Wolf, also Joseph Oakes)*

Open All year.
Rooms 4 cabins—all with private shower and/or bath, radio, TV, desk, air-conditioning, fan. 2 with whirlpool tubs, fireplaces; 1 with kitchenette.
Facilities 40 acres with farm animals. ½ m to golf.
Location 1 m from town. From Hwy. 20, go S on Chetlain Lane ¼ m to driveway for inn.

Credit cards None accepted.
Rates B&B, $45–85 cabin. Extra person in room, $10. 2-night weekend minimum. Family rates.
Extras 1 cabin wheelchair accessible. Station pickups. Cribs, babysitting available.

Victorian Mansion
Tel: (815) 777–0675
301 South High Street

Civil war buffs who overnight in Galena should head directly for the Victorian Mansion, furnished entirely in authentic period antiques. Built in 1861 of red brick walls twelve inches thick, the mansion has been owned since 1984 by Brigadier General (Ret.) Robert G. McClellan. A descendant of Civil War General George McClellan, Bob McClellan started collecting military memorabilia 25 years ago, and today part of the inn is operated as a museum, filled with rare antiques and heirlooms.

"We enjoyed the feeling of returning to another era and our hosts' stories about President Grant's frequent visits to the mansion. Our room had a handsome brass bed and marble fireplace, although better reading lights would have been welcome." *(MW)* More comments, please.

Open All year.
Rooms 11 doubles—1 with private bath, 10 with maximum of 3 people sharing bath. All with desk, air-conditioning.
Facilities Common room, porch. 2½ acres with lawns.
Location In town. At corner of High and Green Sts.
Restrictions No smoking. No children under 9.
Credit cards MC, Visa.
Rates B&B, $50–70 double or single. 9% tax not included. Extra person in room, $10. 2-night minimum May–Nov.

GENEVA 60134
Map 8

The Oscar Swan Country Inn
Tel: (312) 232–0173
1800 West State Street (Route 38)

Jessie and Oscar Swan built this colonial revival home in 1902 and owned it until the 1950s, when it was sold to Frank and Mary Jo Harding. Mrs. Harding, an interior designer, added many unusual touches, which remain part of the decor today. Hans and Nina Heymann bought the estate in 1985, thus beginning its new life as a bed & breakfast inn. The decor is eclectic but features some fine 1920s art deco pieces as well as collectibles ranging from carved swans to American Indian artifacts.

"Owner Nina Heymann greeted us on arrival, showed to us to our room, and went out of her way to make us feel welcome. We woke up to a lovely view of the gardens and the sound of birds singing. Breakfast consisted of an assortment of breads and muffins, fresh fruit, coffee, tea, and juice." *(Karen Graef)*

Open All year.
Rooms 2 suites, 6 doubles—5 with private shower and/or bath, 3 with maximum of 4 people sharing bath. 1 with kitchen, sauna, 1 with fireplace, 1 with waterbed.
Facilities Breakfast room, parlor with fireplace, conservatory. 7 acres with terrace,

gardens, heated swimming pool, cross-country skiing. Tennis, fishing, bicycling nearby.

Location NE IL. Approx. 35 m W of Chicago. From Chicago, follow Rte. 38 W to Geneva; becomes State St. in Geneva. Inn on W side of Fox River.

Restrictions No smoking in guest rooms.

Credit cards MC, Visa.

Rates B&B, $75–125 suite, $60–95 double. Extra person in room, $15. Midweek, extended stay discounts.

Extras German spoken.

LAKE FOREST 60045   Map 8

The Deer Path Inn   *Tel:* (708) 234–2280
255 East Illinois Road

Although there has been a Deer Path Inn for almost 100 years, the inn as it exists today was constructed about 1930, in a traditional English Tudor style, with period detailing and accessories. The decorating theme is definitely English, from the furniture to the artwork. The inn has three separate eating areas, popular with locals as well as visitors: the English Room, serving three meals a day; the Hunt Room with blazing hearth; and the Garden Room and Patio, for lunches and light dinners in season. *(Keith Jurgens)*

Open All year.

Rooms 60 suites and doubles—all with full private bath, telephone, TV. Most with desk.

Facilities Lobby with fireplace, 3 dining rooms with piano entertainment, parlors, patio. Flower gardens with fountains.

Location NE IL. Approx. 1 hr. N of Chicago, 30 min. from O'Hare.

Credit cards All major cards accepted.

Rates Room only, $115–125 suite, $99–125 double, $85–125 single. Extra person in room, $10.

Extras Cribs available.

OAKLAND 61943   Map 8

Inn on the Square   *Tel:* (217) 346–2289
3 Montgomery Square

Innkeepers Max and Caroline Coon invite travelers to relax and enjoy the country pleasures of the area—historic homes, outdoor recreation, and visits to a nearby Amish settlement. Their inn, set right in the heart of this little town, is an imposing white building with a two-story portico running along the front. Rooms are decorated with some antiques, and rates include a full breakfast.

"Our room was large, cheerful, and homey. The bathroom was very clean, with plenty of hot water, towels, and extras. The food was delicious and plentiful; the tea room is quaint, with lots of country charm. The location is quiet and parking is abundant." *(Jackie Karle)*

"Rooms are immaculate and comfortable for sleeping; a three-way bulb is an unexpected bonus. Well-appointed shops in the inn are fun for browsing and buying. Max and Carolyn always offer an after-dinner snack or beverage." *(Mrs. George Rutkoskie, also EJS)*

Open All year. Inn, restaurant closed major holidays.
Rooms 4 doubles—3 with private bath and/or shower, 1 with a maximum of 4 sharing bath "only when booked to capacity and if sharing with family members". All with radio, air-conditioning, fan.
Facilities Tea room, TV/game room, library; gift, antique, apparel shops. Tennis, swimming pool, golf, boating, fishing nearby.
Location E central IL. 45 m S of Champaign/Urbana, 20 m N of Lincoln Log Cabin State Park. On Rte. 133, 15 m E of I-57.
Restrictions No smoking in guest rooms. No children under 4.
Credit cards MC, Visa.
Rates B&B, $49 double, $43 single. Extra person in room, $10. Alc lunch, $6–8.

STOCKTON 61085   Map 8

Maple Lane Country Inn   *Tel:* (815) 947–3773
3114 South Rush Creek Road

After 23 years of farming, Carson and Elizabeth Herring are making this inn their retirement career. The Maple Lane is run as a B&B on weekends, while during the week a "New Start" weight- and stress-reduction program is offered. This program runs from Sunday to Friday, and includes the individual attention of a fitness instructor, nutritionist, medical doctor, and nurse.

"This inn is on a working farm on the eastern edge of beautiful hilly northwest Illinois. I stayed in the Rose Suite, which was very cheerful and clean, with a comfortable bed. I had my choice of full breakfasts, including delicious buttermilk pancakes. The countryside is inviting for quiet, peaceful walks." *(Susan Jacques, also Len & Gerry Persino)*

"The inn is neat, clean, and comfortable, the grounds well maintained. Clean linens and towels are provided daily; lighting and plumbing is in good order. The area is beautiful and quiet—well off the beaten path—not at all touristy or gimmicky. The breakfast was delicious, generous, and the menu varied each day. The Herrings give tips on local points of interest and restaurants, and provide brochures and a large map of the area." *(Janet Brendel, also Virginia Sanders)*

Open April 15–Nov. 15.
Rooms 3 suites with private bath and/or shower, 2 doubles with shared bath; radio, TV, desk. 1 suite in annex.
Facilities Dining room, living room with grand piano, family room with TV, books. 6 acres with lawn games, heated swimming pool, whirlpool/sauna, exercise room, creek fishing, bicycles.
Location NW IL, 50 m W of Stockton, 136 m W of Chicago. 5 m to town. Approx. 25 m E of Galena.
Restrictions Smoking restricted.
Credit cards None accepted.
Rates B&B, $50 suite, $40–45 double. Full board, "New Start" program, $350–425 double occupancy for 5 days, plus 9% tax. Third person in room, $10.

Indiana

Creekwood Inn, Michigan City

While few travelers plan a trip just to see Indiana, many come on business, or to visit friends, relatives, or kids at college; plenty of others pass through on cross-country trips. Those who like to explore will discover that the state has much more to offer than most people realize. From the Lake Michigan beaches in the north to Brown County in the south-central part of the state to the wooded hill country along the Ohio River at the Kentucky border, there are a surprising number of places worth visiting. You've told us about some exceptional places to stay, but we could certainly make room for some more!

Information please: We'd like to hear about the **Story Inn**, built in 1850 as a general store, now a well-known country restaurant with rooms available for B&B (State Road 135 South, P.O. Box #64, Nashville 47488; 812–988–2273). Further south is the **Queen Anne Inn**, a 1893 Victorian home just three blocks from the Convention Center; its five guest rooms are furnished with antiques and reproductions (420 West Washington Street; South Bend 46601; 219–234–5959).

Rates do not include 5% state sales tax.

COLUMBUS 47201 Map 8

The Columbus Inn *Tel:* (812) 378–4289
445 Fifth Street at Franklin

In what surely must be one of the most creative architectural recycling jobs in the country, the old Columbus City Hall, built in 1895, was converted in 1985 into a luxurious bed & breakfast inn. Of course, architectural innovation is no stranger to this small city of 30,000. For the past thirty years, the Cummins Foundation has maintained a program sponsoring internationally known architects, from Eero Saarinen to I.M. Pei to Henry Moore, to design major public buildings in Columbus. Rooms are elegantly decorated with American Empire reproductions, many with sleigh beds or handmade log cabin quilts, and rates include a full buffet breakfast, with everything from fresh fruit and juice to egg casseroles, bagels, and quick breads. Business travelers will find all required amenities, and just about any traveler is bound to enjoy the helpful and enthusiastic personality of innkeeper Paul Staublin. Correspondents have praised both the beauty of the inn and the efficient service here. Vacationers may choose to make Columbus their headquarters for explorations of nearby Brown County, known as the "Bucks County of the Midwest," and for visits to the area's innumerable antique shops. *(MW)* More comments, please.

Open All year.
Rooms 5 suites, 20 doubles, 9 singles—32 with full private bath, 2 with private shower only. All with telephone, radio, TV, desk, air-conditioning.
Facilities Dining room, lobby/library, game room/lounge area. 1 acre with flower gardens. Tennis, golf, fishing, swimming, playground, skiing, skating nearby.
Location S central IN. 85 m N of Louisville, KY, 35 m S of Indianapolis, 80 m W of Cincinnati, OH. On 5th St., in between Washington and Franklin sts.
Restrictions Smoking not encouraged.
Credit cards All major cards accepted.
Rates B&B, $95–215 suite, $72–80 double. Extra adult in room, $7; no charge for children under 13. Senior discount; weekend packages.
Extras Wheelchair accessible; baths equipped for disabled. Spanish spoken. Crib, babysitting available. Airport/station pickups.

CORYDON 47112   **Map 8**

The Kintner House Inn   *Tel:* (812) 738–2020
101 South Capitol Street

Indiana's first state capital, Corydon is so close to the Kentucky border that Confederate General John Hunt Morgan made the original Kintner House his headquarters during the Civil War, after he had captured the town on July 9, 1863. After an 1871 fire destroyed an entire block of buildings, a new Kintner House was constructed as a three-story brick hotel, with elaborate Victorian furnishings. Restored in 1986, each lavishly decorated guest room is named after a significant person from Corydon's past (President William Henry Harrison is remembered, along with the "infamous" General Morgan). The decor includes flowered wallpapers, period lighting fixtures, coordinating bedspreads and draperies, and plentiful Victorian antiques. Rates include a breakfast of homemade bread, an egg casserole, fresh fruit, coffee and juice.

"Mary Jane Bridgwater is a warm and outgoing innkeeper. One can easily tell it is 'not just a job' to her, but that she too seems to be wrapped up in the beauty of this inn.

"Room furnishings are true to the period and are remarkably authentic. I would wish only for a slightly lesser degree of authenticity on to the subject of bedside lighting." *(GR)*

Open All year.
Rooms 14 doubles—all with private bath and/or shower, telephone, air-conditioning. Some with desk.
Facilities Dining room, parlor with TV, library, games; porch. Guest privileges at nearby club for swimming, tennis, golf. Fishing, boating, cave exploring nearby.
Location S IN, 18 m E of Louisville, KY. Center of town. From I-64, take Exit 105 (S.R. 135) to Rte. 62 (2 m). Go E on Rte. 62 to inn.
Restrictions No smoking.
Credit cards Amex, DC, MC, Visa.
Rates B&B, $70–90 double. Extra person in room, $5.
Extras Crib available.

GOSHEN 46526   Map 8

Checkerberry Inn   *Tel:* (219) 642–4445
62644 County Route 37

If you'd like to combine a visit to Indiana's Amish Country with unusually elegant accommodations for this area, then the Checkerberry Inn will be of interest. Owned and managed by John, Susan, and Chris Graff, this new inn, opened in 1987, offers comfortable contemporary decor and is set amid 100 acres of rolling farmland. Under the supervision of chef Rob Davis, guests can select from a small but carefully chosen menu, with such dishes as breast of duck served on a bed of puréed pine nuts and mushrooms; veal roasted with peppercorns and dill sauce; or salmon sautéed with lobster citrus sauce. The Checkerberry also boasts the distinction of having Indiana's only professional-quality croquet court.

"Impeccably clean and well managed. Service is courteous and efficient. The innkeeper went out of his way to make us feel comfortable, and the food was excellent." *(Donald Risser)*

Open Feb. through Dec. Restaurant closed Sun., Mon.
Rooms 2 suites (1 with whirlpool tub), 10 doubles—all with private shower and/or bath, telephone, radio, TV, desk, air-conditioning.
Facilities Dining room, library with fireplace, porch. 100 acres with swimming pool, tennis, croquet green, bicycling, hiking. Golf nearby.
Location N central IN. Amish country. 120 m E of Chicago, 150 m N of Indianapolis, 30 m E of South Bend. 5 m from Goshen, 16 m S of I-80/90. From I-80/90, take Exit 107 (Middlebury); go S (left) on S.R. 13, W (right) on Rte. 4, S (left) on C.R. 37 to inn on right.
Restrictions No smoking in dining room, guest rooms.
Credit cards Amex, MC, Visa.
Rates B&B, $132–165 suite, $92–115 double, $68–85 single. Extra person in room, $25. Alc lunch, $8–10; alc dinner, $20–30.
Extras Some areas wheelchair accessible.

GREENCASTLE 46135   Map 8

Walden Inn   *Tel:* (317) 653–2761
2 Seminary Square, P.O. Box 490

Built in 1986 on land leased from DePauw University, and owned by local businessmen, the Walden Inn serves the needs of visitors to the university and to the area. Guests have access to all of DePauw's athletic facilities and cultural events.

Reservations for parents' weekend and other special university events must be made long in advance; at other times, there's usually no problem. Rooms are furnished with hand-crafted local and Amish furniture; public rooms are decorated in a "country look" with antiques and original art. The inn's restaurant, the Different Drummer, serves three meals a day. Dinners include daily and seasonal specials; a typically creative dinner might include a salad of avocado, smoked salmon, and melon; lamb grilled with olive oil, garlic, and rosemary, sliced on a bed of panfried red potatoes and onions, and raspberry cheesecake for dessert.

"One of the best chefs in the Midwest, Matthew O'Neill, an Irishman, was lured to Greencastle (population 8,000) to be chef and general manager. The inn is small and full of archival material from DePauw and central Indiana. Worth the nine-mile side trip from I-70. On a return trip, I wasn't in the room five minutes before the manager called to welcome me back. He later showed me a marvelous routing past lovely covered bridges." *(Norval Stephens)*

"Brand-new, beautifully done, long needed in the town of Greencastle; just on the edge of campus. Staff are more than willing to please." *(T.E. Aschenbrener)*

Open All year. Restaurant closed Dec. 25.
Rooms 5 suites, 50 doubles—all with private bath and/or shower, telephone, radio, TV, desk, air-conditioning, fan.
Facilities Restaurant, bar with entertainment, library with fireplace, books, games, cards; veranda with rockers. Indoor swimming pool at DPU, tennis court. Fishing, boating, swimming at 3 nearby state parks. Golf nearby.
Location Central IN. 45 m WSW of Indianapolis. 40 min. from Indianapolis airport. 3 blocks to Courthouse Square. Take U.S. 231 to Greencastle. Turn W on Seminary St. and go 3 blocks.
Restrictions Smoking restricted.
Credit cards Amex, DC, Discover, MC, Visa.
Rates Room only, $110–125 suite, $66–93 double, $61–88 single. Extra person in room, $8. Alc lunch, $7; alc dinner, $25. Weekend packages.
Extras Ramp, elevator, 1 room equipped for disabled. Airport/station pickups, $50–75. Cribs available.

INDIANAPOLIS   Map 8

For many years maligned as "India-no-place," Indianapolis is in fact an attractive city that dates back to 1820, when it was selected as the site for the state's capital because of its location at the geographical center of the state. Streets were laid out in a wheel pattern similar to Washington, D.C.

Sights of interest include, of course, the Indianapolis Speedway and Hall of Fame. Hotel rates skyrocket on Memorial Day Weekend, when the famous "Indy 500" is held. Cultural attractions include the Museum of Art, with collections of Medieval, Renaissance, and 19th-century arts; the Children's Museum, with carousel, Egyptian mummies, and limestone cave; and the Museum of Indian Heritage.

The Canterbury Hotel
123 South Illinois Street 46225

Tel: (317) 634–3000
(800) 538–8186

A small, full-service establishment, the Canterbury caters to business travelers during the week, and is arguably the state's most luxurious hotel. Guest rooms, furnished with Chippendale four-poster beds and Queen Anne furniture, include such amenities as refrigerators, televisions, telephones in the bedroom and bath, bathrobes, and the morning paper. Rates include a continental breakfast, served in the parlor; airport transfers are provided in a stretch limo previously owned by Frank Sinatra.

"The Canterbury Hotel is a remodeling of an old faded downtown hotel. The lobby has a subdued, expensive-but-tasteful look, sort of British, with thick deep green carpeting, lots of shining brass, and hunting prints. The dining room is also clubby looking, with fine wood paneling and more hunt prints—very low-key. The food certainly ranks among the city's best, if not the best. The service is slow but attentive; the idea, I guess, is to make the meal your entire evening. Not a bad approach, since dinner for two with wine will total over $100." *(Cynthia Snowden, AH)*

Open All year.
Rooms 15 suites with whirlpool tubs, wet bars; 87 doubles with queen- or king-size bed—all with full private bath, telephone, radio, TV, desk, air-conditioning.
Facilities Restaurant, 3 parlors, bar/lounge, atrium with pianist. Concierge service. Valet parking. 5 min. to swimming pool.
Location Downtown. On Illinois between Maryland and Georgia sts.
Credit cards Amex, DC, MC, Visa.
Rates B&B, $205–300 suite, $145–195 double, plus 10% tax. Extra person in room, $20. Corporate rate, $125. Weekend packages, $110–250. Alc lunch, $12–20; alc dinner, $55.
Extras Wheelchair accessible; some rooms specially equipped for disabled. Cribs, babysitting available. Airport/station pickups. Spanish, French, Norwegian, Japanese, Chinese spoken. Member, Preferred Hotels.

Le Chateau Delaware
1456 North Delaware Street 46202

Tel: (317) 636–9156

Built in 1906, Le Chateau Delaware was known for years as "The Castle," because of its appearance—an imposing red brick mansion topped at every opportunity with crenalated white trim. Inside, the neo-Gothic look continues with vaulted ceilings and Romanesque-style windows in many of the common rooms. Inside the decor is eclectic, combining Oriental rugs and antiques with more modern furnishings and fabrics. Rates include a breakfast of home-baked rolls and muffins, fresh fruits and juices. *(IV)* More comments, please.

Open March 16 through Dec. 31.
Rooms 2 suites, 6 doubles—1 with private shower, 7 rooms sharing 3 baths. All with radio, air-conditioning, fan. Telephone on request.
Facilities Living room with library, dining room. Off-street parking.
Location Downtown. Historic northside. 20 min. walk to center. From 11th St. go N on Delaware to inn at corner of 16th St.
Restrictions Smoking in common areas only. Children over 12 preferred.
Credit cards MC, Visa.
Rates B&B, $120–300 suite, $60–65 double. Extra person in room $15. 2-night minimum Indy 500 weekend; rates higher.
Extras Airport/station pickups.

Hollingsworth House Inn
6054 Hollingsworth Road 46254

Tel: (317) 299–6700

George Hollingsworth built a one-room log cabin on this site in the 1820s; in 1854, he constructed the existing two-story structure. It stayed in the Hollingsworth family until 1941; the farm was eventually sold to the city parks department for use as a park. Although efforts were made to have the house torn down, a descendant of George Hollingsworth and a local historical society managed to save the house by placing it on the local and national historic registers. Susan Muller and Ann Irvine bought the house in 1984 and, after major renovation, opened their inn in June of 1985.

"This old Indiana farmhouse has been painstakingly restored with impeccable taste and no expense or detail spared. The ambience is that of an elegant and modern home decorated with good Indiana antiques, suffused with light and the gleam everywhere of silver, polished brass, and lovely china. Not everything is authentically Victorian; some pieces of furniture—couches, easy chairs—are comfortable reproductions, combining the best of both worlds. Our room had, as they all do, down comforters, and a beautiful modern bath.

"Breakfast was served in what was the original one-room house, with a door that opens onto a deck. The coffee was abundant and good. We had scrambled eggs flavored with cheddar, half a grapefruit adorned with grapes, a croissant and bun—we couldn't eat it all. To the rear and sides of the house is just-mown grass, a cornfield, a little creek with trees. Across from the house at the front, however, is an apartment development. Although it's reasonably attractive, it sort of breaks the spell. In sum, though, a delightful place to spend a night or two." *(Cynthia Snowden)*

"The innkeepers definitely know fine hospitality and are on top with service and cleanliness." *(Terry Tatsch)*

Open All year.
Rooms 2 suites, 3 doubles—all with private bath and/or shower. 1 with desk.
Facilities Dining room, kitchen, parlor, common room. 4 acres with creek.
Location Within city limits. 5 min. from Lafayette Square. 12 m from downtown. 1 block W of 62nd St. and Georgetown Rd.
Restrictions No children.
Credit cards Amex, MC, Visa.
Rates B&B, $95–120 suite, $75 double, plus 10% tax. 2-night weekend minimum.

MADISON 47250 Map 8

Set on the Ohio River, Madison reached its zenith in the 1850s with the rapid growth of river traffic. Much of its downtown area, now listed on the National Register of Historic Places, dates from this period. Architecture buffs will enjoy the variety of styles of its restored buildings, including Gothic Revival, Classic Revival, Federal, and Italianate.

Madison is located in southeast Indiana, near the Kentucky and Ohio borders, about a 1½-hour drive from Louisville, Cincinnati, and Indianapolis.

Cliff House
Tel: (812) 265–5272
122 Fairmont Drive

The Cliff House is a century-old Victorian built on a cliff overlooking Madison and the Ohio River. Jae and Thomas Breitweiser have spent years restoring it. Four guest rooms have river views. A doll museum occupies the third floor of the house. Rates include a breakfast of fruit, homemade breakfast cake, and croissants, served on 100-year-old Haviland china, and an evening snack of fruit and homemade cookies.

"In an area markedly short of pleasant places, the Cliff House is indeed a find. All the rooms are filled with antiques, some of them massive pieces in keeping with the size and style of the house.

"Our favorite place was the widow's walk, with a panoramic view of the river and Kentucky on the river side—*the* place to be on the Fourth of July. Our reception was very warm, the rooms comfortable and the breakfast, served in the dining room, was pleasant." *(Cynthia Snowden)*

Open All year.
Rooms 1 suite, 5 doubles—all with private bath and/or shower, air-conditioning. Some with canopy bed.
Facilities Dining room, parlor, music room, porches, widow's walk.
Location Near center. From Main St., turn N on West St., then left on Michigan St. Turn right on Fairmont St., 1st driveway on right.
Restrictions Smoking not encouraged, permitted in parlor only.
Credit cards MC, Visa.
Rates B&B, $75–150 suite, $75 double, $50 single. Extra adult in room, $25; extra child, $15; baby, $10. Family rates for suite.
Extras First floor guest room has walk-in shower. Crib, babysitting available.

Clifty Inn
Tel: (812) 265–4135
Clifty Falls State Park, Box 387

"A stay at Clifty Falls makes a nice balance with a tour of historic Madison. After a rainy day spent visiting the town's many historic buildings, the next morning was clear and sunny, perfect for hiking the park's beautiful trails. We hiked past deep gorges and saw the beautiful waterfalls for which the park is named. Our motel-style room was basic, but clean and well equipped, and had a balcony with a view of the Ohio. The food is nothing fancy, but neither are the prices. Our kids adored the curving, bumpy waterslide which feeds into their huge pool, and must have zoomed down a dozen times." *(MW)* More comments please.

Open All year.
Rooms 62 doubles, 10 singles—all with private shower and/or bath, telephone, radio, TV, desk, air-conditioning.
Facilities Restaurant. 100 acres with 2 swimming pools, hiking trails, tennis, nature center. Golf nearby. Guided hikes, nature talks in summer.
Location 1 m to town.
Credit cards Amex, MC, Visa.
Rates Room only, $39–42 double. Crib, $3; rollaway, $5. State park daily entry fee, $2 per car. Alc breakfast, $2.50–5; alc lunch, $3–6; alc dinner, $5–9.
Extras Wheelchair accessible; 4 rooms equipped for disabled. Cribs available.

MICHIGAN CITY 46360   Map 8

Creekwood Inn   *Tel:* (219) 872–8357
Route 20-35 at I-94

The Creekwood was built in the 1930s by Dr. Lawrence Robrock, as an English Cotswold-style manor house. Mary Lou Linnen and Peggie Wall refurbished the house and built a guest wing five years ago. Rooms are individually decorated in a variety of styles, with coordinated fabrics, wall coverings, and window treatments, and quality reproduction furniture. Rates include a continental breakfast of homemade breads, fresh fruit, and coffee.

"The Creekwood has a casual but elegant atmosphere. The lounge and dining area are in the original house, with some marvelous hand-hewn beams and leaded windows, looking out on the woods. The guest rooms are in a new wing that is architecturally compatible with the original home but also modern in every sense." *(Jackson Sloan)*

"Aptly named, the Creekwood Inn is nestled in a lovely wooded area with a creek running through the property. There are winding trails through the woods as well as a patio, screened porch, and large lawn area for enjoying the outdoors. Although the Creekwood is only two blocks off the expressway, it seems much removed from the hustle and bustle. Mary Lou, Peggie, and their staff are pleasant and helpful and go out of their way to accommodate their guests.

"The rooms are large and appointed with attention to detail—from the ice-maker refrigerator to the fresh fruit in every room. Housekeeping throughout the inn is first-rate.

"The continental breakfast includes fruit, juice, coffee, and delicious homemade croissants, breads, and muffins. Our Saturday night dinner had a real home-cooked freshness." *(Patricia M. Snyder)*

"The Creekwood is attractive and comfortable, welcoming but not cutesy. Our room was large, with sliding doors onto a patio. The grounds are wooded; nice for short walks. The only drawback here is the inn's proximity to the highway; during our August visit, we could hear the noise of traffic whenever we were outside. Readers should also be warned to bring along a bottle of wine to enjoy with dinner; finding a liquor store in Indiana is no easy task." *(CS)*

Open All year. Closed 2nd week of March.
Rooms 1 suite, 12 doubles—all with private bath and/or shower, 2 queen- or 1 king-size bed, telephone, radio, TV, desk or table, air-conditioning, refrigerator/ice maker. Some have fireplaces, private terraces.
Facilities Parlor, dining room, sun porch, game/library area, piano, meeting room, screened porch, patio. 33 acres with woods, creeks, small fishing pond, trails for cross-country skiing, walking. Lawn games, bicycles. Golf, tennis, horseback riding, charter boat fishing nearby.
Location NW IN, near Lake Michigan. 35 m W of South Bend; 50 m SE of Chicago, IL. Willow Creek; 3 m from town. From I-94, take Exit 40 B. Take first street on left, then turn left to inn.
Credit cards Amex, MC, Visa.
Rates B&B, $135–145 suite, $85–100 double, $80–95 single, plus 10% tax. Extra

person in room, $15. 20% service on meals. 5% senior discount. Continental breakfast included; full breakfast, $4. Afternoon tea, $6. Prix fixe dinner, $25. 2–3 night holiday weekend minimum. Weekend packages.

Extras Wheelchair accessible; wide halls, specially equipped shower. Airport/station pickups. Cribs available. German spoken.

MIDDLEBURY 46540   Map 8

Essenhaus Country Inn   *Tel:* (219) 825–9447
240 U.S. Highway 20

"Opened in 1986, the inn is beautifully decorated and situated in a lovely quiet country setting. The Das Dutchman Essenhaus restaurant on the grounds has been an Indiana institution for years. The food is superb and the prices are unbelievably low. After you eat, visit the inn's gift shop, furniture store, and bakery. Since it is in Amish country, there are no bars or liquor stores and the restaurant is closed on Sunday.

"Our room was done in deep green and light mauve. The furniture was bleached pine and very plain, yet classy. There was a handsome armoire in lieu of a closet and another, smaller cupboard housing the TV. We also had a small couch, a desk, and several comfortable chairs. We paid a small extra fee for a room with a whirlpool tub which was really great. The towels were luxurious, and the bath was supplied with attractive soaps and other amenities. We would also recommend the Patchwork Inn in Middlebury for a delicious meal." *(Virginia Reidy)* More comments, please.

Open All year. Restaurant, shops closed Sundays and major holidays.
Rooms 5 suites, 27 doubles— all with telephone, radio, TV, desk, air-conditioning. Some suites with whirlpool.
Facilities Restaurant, atrium, bakery, gift shops, game room, sun porch. 40 acres with small lake, landscaping, playground. Swimming, fishing nearby. 10 m to cross-country skiing.
Location NE IN. 15 m E of Elkhart. 10 m W of Shipshewana. 1 m E of Middlebury. 4 m S of I-80/90. On U.S. Hwy. 20, 1 m W of intersection with Indiana State Rd. 13.
Restrictions No smoking in dining room. No alcohol.
Credit cards Amex, MC, Visa.
Rates Room only, $75–105 suite, $65 double, $52 single. Extra person in room, $6. No charge for children under 12 in parents' room. Rollaway, $5; crib, $2. Restaurant open from 6 A.M. to 9 P.M. daily. Alc breakfast, $3–5; alc lunch, $5; family style dinner, $10. Continental breakfast included on Sunday only. "Amish Country Tours" available May 29– Oct. 27.
Extras Wheelchair accessible; 1 room equipped for disabled. Cribs, playground available.

NEW HARMONY 47631   Map 8

The New Harmony Inn   *Tel:* (812) 682–4491
North Street, P.O. Box 581

The town of New Harmony was founded in 1814 by a group of Harmonists, who were persecuted in their native Germany and came to the fertile Wabash valley to start anew. After eleven years of hard work they moved to Pennsylvania, leaving many sturdy and ingeniously constructed buildings behind. They sold the town to the British social reformer Robert Owen, who arrived in 1825 with many distinguished scholars to start an experiment in communal living. Although the experiment failed, much of its intellectual heritage lives on. Many of the historic buildings have been restored, contrasting modern ones have been built, and a variety of music, art, and drama programs are offered.

The inn is a simply designed contemporary structure, spare, yet very handsome in decor, blending well with the clear lines of the original Harmonist structures. Two restaurants are connected with the inn, the Red Geranium and the Bayou Grill.

"Just as you described it. Food at the Red Geranium was excellent as was the service and wine selection. The Shaker lemon pie was good and properly tart; the buffet breakfast at the Bayou Grill included very good bread pudding, plentiful fruit and juice, tasty corned beef hash and bacon. As often happens in a buffet, the scrambled eggs and sausage didn't look too appetizing, but they happily fixed eggs to order." *(Al & Jeanine Muller)*

"The New Harmony Inn is a quaint, down-to-earth inn. Each room is original and some have their own fireplace—very cozy, especially in the fall. The whole town is historically significant, so a two- or three-day stay is rewarding." *(Stephen Tucker)*

"Grounds were lovely. Our room faced the river. The lobby was peaceful, with rocking chairs, a fireplace, books."*(KLH)*

"Very nice, but 'stark,' as it should be, considering the background of New Harmony. Our room had bare wooden floors, although some of the others have small scatter rugs. The bath was very clean but merely functional. Although the inn has expanded in recent years, and has added a conference center, this did not detract from the wonderful atmosphere. We enjoyed good service, food, and accommodations in a peaceful, historic setting." *(Carolyn Snyder)*

Open All year.
Rooms 5 suites, 85 doubles—all with full private bath, telephone, radio, TV, desk. Some with kitchenettes, balconies, fireplaces.
Facilities Family room, lobby, bar, restaurant, TV/game room. Rose garden and pond, indoor/outdoor heated swimming pool, hot tub, sauna, health club, tennis court, chapel.
Location SE corner of IN. 25 m W of Evansville.
Credit cards Amex, CB, DC, MC, Visa.
Rates Room only, $50–60 double, $40–50 single. Extra person in room $10. No charge for children under 12. Corporate rates. 10% AARP discount. Alc lunch, $6; alc dinner, $15–20. 15% winter discount.
Extras Wheelchair accessible. Airport/station pickups.

ROCKPORT 47635   Map 8

The Rockport Inn   *Tel:* (812) 649–2664
Third at Walnut

Built around 1855, the Rockport Inn was one of the first buildings in the area to have glass windows; a number of the original panes are still in place. Although the inn has been renovated several times over the years, much of the 1855 structure is still intact, including the hand-hewn logs and beams, held together with square-shaped iron nails. One otherwise pleased respondent noted that the "hall carpets are a disgrace."

"I was astonished that you overlooked a little treasure-box not more than 60 miles from New Harmony. In the small town of Rockport, set on the beautiful Ohio River bluffs, is the Rockport Inn, just across from the courthouse. For some years, it has been operated by a college professor from Owensboro, KY. An old boardinghouse, it has six bedrooms with new baths and very, very good food served to the general public. Spencer County is where Abraham Lincoln spent his boyhood years." *(Edith Wells)*

"The place is great. The food is wonderful. The people are friendly." *(Paul & Mona Pierce)*

Open All year. Restaurant closed Mondays, major holidays.
Rooms 6 doubles— all with private bath and/or shower, telephone, TV, desk, air-conditioning.
Facilities Restaurant, lobby.
Location SE IN. 30 m E of Evansville. In center, by courthouse.
Credit cards None accepted.
Rates B&B, $32–45 double, $25–35 single. Inquire about family discount. Alc lunch, 6; alc dinner, $15–23.
Extras German, Swedish spoken. Cribs, babysitting available.

Key to Abbreviations

For complete information and explanations, please see the Introduction.

Rates: Range from least expensive room in low season to most expensive room in peak season.
Room only: No meals included; sometimes referred to as European Plan (EP).
B&B: Bed and breakfast; includes breakfast, sometimes afternoon/evening refreshment.
MAP: Modified American Plan; includes breakfast and dinner.
Full board: Three meals daily.
Alc lunch: À la carte lunch; average price of entrée plus nonalcoholic drink, tax, tip.
Alc dinner: Average price of three-course dinner, including half bottle of house wine, tax, tip.
Prix fixe dinner: Three- to five-course set dinner, excluding wine, tax, tip unless otherwise noted.
Extras: Noted if available. Always confirm in advance. Pets are not permitted unless specified.
Zip codes: If only one zip code applies, it is listed with the town name. If there is more than one, it is noted as part of the address.

Iowa

Die Heimat Country Inn, Homestead

Since you've turned to this chapter, we assume you know better than to think of Iowa as an endless cornfield. There's a lot to do here. Many of the historic towns along the Mississippi and Missouri rivers sponsor summertime events and river excursions, while other towns proudly display their ethnic heritage—Dutch, German, Czech, and Native American. The Amana Colonies, in eastern Iowa, offer a fascinating glimpse into a religious communal society dating back to the mid-1800s. Several historic reconstructions will appeal to visitors, from the Living History Farms and the Boone & Scenic Valley Railroad near Des Moines, to the Fort Museum at Fort Dodge. Iowans love fairs, and you'll find them sponsored by towns around the state from April through October. Highlights include the Iowa State Fair in Des Moines and the National Hot Air Balloon Championships at Indianola.

Information please: A Davenport B&B we'd like to have reports on is the **River Oaks Inn,** an 1850s Italianate Victorian overlooking the Mississippi, owned by Mary Jo Pohl (1234 East River Drive 52803; 319–326–2629). Also on the Mississippi is the **Klaytonian B&B Inn** (that's how they spell it), with riverview suites a mile off the Great River Road in northeastern Iowa (RR 2, Box 125A, Clayton 52049; 319–964–2776). Those looking for a small B&B in the Omaha, Nebraska, area might do well to check out the **Robin's Nest Inn,** a three–guest room B&B, built in 1881 (327 Ninth Avenue, Council Bluffs 51501; 712–323–1649). And, if business or family brings you to northwest Iowa, the **Hannah Marie Country Inn** (Highway 71 S, RR #1. Spencer 51301; 712–262–1286) is a restored farm home with three guest rooms with Iowa-made quilts and teddy bears, a hearty country breakfast, and lots of extras; Spencer is about 100 miles northeast of Sioux City.

Rates do not include 4% sales tax.

ADEL 50003   Map 10

Walden Acres B&B   *Tel:* (515) 987–1338
RR 1, Box 30   (515) 987–1567

Legendary Cleveland Indians pitcher Bob Feller built this home for his parents in 1940; true baseball history fans will want to see the 100-year-old barn where he practiced pitching with his father. Phyllis and Dale Briley have lived here for a dozen years; as their children grew up and left home, they made two rooms available for B&B. Dale is a semiretired veterinarian, and the Brileys offer B&B for your horse in their barn.

"Beautiful home, peaceful setting. The Brileys went out of their way to help me, providing me with every comfort." *(Susan MacWilliams)* "The house is very clean; our room had ample closet space and a comfortable bed. Both a fan and extra blankets were available if needed. The bathroom had everything we could possibly need in the way of toiletries. Dale and Phyllis Briley are gracious people who seem to have thought of everything." *(Karen Burkhart)*

"We had a great hike through the wooded pastures by the lake. Deer were in the woods and a herd of horses were playfully running in the pasture. The grounds are immaculately kept and the brick porch with white wicker furniture and lots of flowers was a nostalgic place to sit. The family has lots of pets, kept near or far at guests' request. We stayed in the bright Sunrise room, with its homey quilts. Phyllis is a friendly and gracious hostess, very helpful with all requests and directions to local attractions. We had a wonderful breakfast of scrambled eggs, ham, juice, toast with homemade jelly, and apricot/lemon bread." *(Bonnie & Ken Ellis)*

Open All year.
Rooms 2 doubles sharing 1 bath. Both with radio, TV, desk, air-conditioning, ceiling fan.
Facilities Dining room, living room with fireplace, country kitchen, game room with piano, TV, books, games; solarium, patio, antique shop. Yard with trampoline, volleyball, badminton. 40 acres with hiking, fishing, cross-country skiing.
Location Central IA. 15 min. W of Des Moines. Take exit 117, Waukee/Booneville, off I-80. Go S 1 m; turn right (W) 1 m to farm.
Restrictions Smoking in game room or kitchen only.
Credit cards None accepted.
Rates B&B, $55 double, $45 single. Extra person in room, $10. Children under 13, $5.
Extras Airport/station pickups. Pets permitted (in veterinary kennel on property); horses boarded. Crib, babysitting available.

AVOCA 51521   Map 10

Victorian B&B Inn   *Tel:* (712) 343–6336
425 Walnut Street, Box 249

This 1904 Queen Anne Victorian is covered in fish-scale shingles on the outside, finished with restored southern golden pine on the inside. Rates include a full breakfast of eggs, meat, breads, fruit, juice, and beverages; lunch and dinner are available by advance reservation. The inn was bought in fall of 1987 by Gene and Jan Kuehn.

"Well-kept grounds and home. Interior and furnishings are handsome antiques yet comfortable and all usable. Appointments were quite elegant and everything was very clean and well kept. The meals were marvelous, excellent in quality and more than ample in quantity. Our hosts were most gracious—never stuffy or pompous, very pleasant and accommodating." *(Michael & Judith Brisso)* "It really made a difference when the owners sat and visited with us at meals and during the evening." *(Bon & Becky Blazek)*

"Our room had a handmade quilt and eyelet dust ruffle, an antique wardrobe, and a little ice-cream-parlor table with two chairs in the alcove. The colors are sunny, and there are plants and romantic touches everywhere. The plumbing is modern and the parking convenient, with an unloading area in front of the inn. There's good access from the interstate and nice antique shopping five miles away in Walnut. There is some regular traffic on Walnut Street, but it wasn't bothersome." *(Barbara Durbin)*

Open All year. Closed Christmas.
Rooms 4 doubles sharing 2 full baths. All with desk, air-conditioning.
Facilities Dining room, parlor, wraparound porch. Swimming pool, tennis, fishing nearby.
Location SW IA, 45 m E of Omaha, 90 m W of Des Moines. From I-80, take exit 40 to Rte. 59 S to Avoca. Inn is 2 blocks from center.
Restrictions No smoking. No children under 12.
Credit cards MC, Visa.
Rates B&B, $44 double or single. Prix fixe dinner, $15–20.

DUBUQUE 52001   Map 10

Redstone Inn   *Tel:* (319) 582–1894
504 Bluff Street   (800) 331–5454

The Redstone was built in 1894 by A. A. Cooper as a wedding present for his daughter. Mr. Cooper owned the Cooper Wagon Works, the company that manufactured many of the prairie schooners that made their way to the West. When Henry Ford proposed converting one of Cooper's factories for the building of horseless carriages, Cooper turned him down, saying it was a fad that would never last.

In 1984 a group of local businessmen purchased the Redstone and, at considerable expense, converted it into an elegant small hotel. Now listed on the National Register of Historic Places, it combines Victorian furnishings and styles with modern baths, air-conditioning, private telephones, and television.

Also under the same ownership is the nearby **Stout House,** a red sandstone mansion built in 1890 in the Richardson Romanesque style. Its interior, carefully preserved during 75 years of ownership by the Archdiocese of Dubuque, displays an exceptionally lavish decor, with elaborate wood carvings using four kinds of wood, marble fireplaces, mosaics, and stained glass in nearly every room. Doubles there start at $55, and reservations should be made through the Redstone Inn.

"Beautiful decor, gourmet treats, delicious breakfasts. The staff was cheerful and very accommodating." *(GR)* More comments please.

Open All year.
Rooms 6 suites, 9 doubles—all with private bath and/or shower (6 with whirlpool tub). All with telephone, radio, TV, air-conditioning; 3 with desk, 2 with fireplace.
Facilities Dining room, parlor, bar/lounge with games. Fishing, riverboat cruises, greyhound racing, skiing nearby.
Location E central IA, 186 m NW of Chicago. In center of town, 1 block from Civic Center and cable car.
Restrictions Traffic noise could disturb light sleepers.
Credit cards Amex, DC, MC, Visa.
Rates B&B, $115–160 suite only. Room only, $55–85 double, $46–68 single, plus 9% tax. Extra person in room, $10. Children under 12 free in parents' room. 2-night weekend minimum for some rooms. Alc breakfast, $2–6. Lunches, dinners for groups by advance request.
Extras Cribs, rollaway available; $5 daily.

HOMESTEAD 52236   Map 10

To escape religious persecution in Germany, the ancestors of the Amana colonists came to the U.S. in 1844. They pooled their money and resources and established a communal religious society that built seven villages and acquired 26,000 acres of farm and timberland. The colonies prospered and became well known for their delicious food and wine and their quality craft and industrial products. In 1932 the membership voted to end communal ownership, and all property reverted to private hands. The colonists purchased the town of Homestead because it was on the railroad line to Iowa City.

One common point of confusion among visitors: There is no connection between the Amana colonists and the Amish, except for a coincidental similarity in their names and the fact that both sects originated in Germany. Although both are devout peoples, the Amana colonists are not opposed to 20th-century innovation, as evidenced by the Amana Refrigeration company, manufacturers of refrigerators, stoves, and microwave ovens, once owned by the Amana's communal society.

For an additional listing in the Amana Colonies, see the entry for the **Rettig House** in Middle Amana.

Die Heimat Country Inn   *Tel:* (319) 622–3937
Main Street, Amana Colonies

"Amid 25,000 acres of rolling Iowa landscape is the Amana complex of seven colonies and Homestead. These pleasant, kindly people make this an ideal place to enjoy pure relaxation in a serene atmosphere. The Jandas prepare an incredible selection of foods, mostly grown or raised here in the colonies, all served family style." *(Alfred G. Chione, M.D.)*

"The feeling of welcome and of coming home is the first thing you notice as you enter the lobby of Die Heimat. Soft zither music is playing, and the lobby is furnished with Amana furniture and an antique chiming clock. Don and Sheila Janda are very friendly, guest rooms are spotless and so cozy. Breakfast in the lobby includes fresh-baked Amana breakfast rolls, coffee, orange juice, or hot chocolate. It doesn't seem at all unusual that you soon find yourself deep in conversation with all of the other guests. As for the noise level, all we heard were the comfortable sounds of cattle in some of the nearby fields and the sound of a train once a day. The large, well-kept lawn surrounding Die Heimat has lawn chairs and old-fashioned wooden lawn swings. The well-lit parking lot is immediately behind the home." *(Elizabeth Young)*

"The personal service is remarkable, and the rates very reasonable. The staff helped to arrange our weekend of visiting the colonies—sights, attractions, and restaurant reservations." *(Terri & Jeff Patwell)*

"Die Heimat is a quaint older building, left untouched by previous managers, but the Jandas have upgraded much of the inn and are making good progress on the rest. Requests for services such as extra pillows are cheerfully handled. Several excellent restaurants are within walking distance or a short drive for lunch or dinner." *(Boots & Howie Kreger)* More comments, please.

Open All year.
Rooms 19 double- and twin-bedded rooms—all with full private bath, TV, desk, air-conditioning; 5 with radio.
Facilities Lobby. 1-acre grounds with lawn swings and benches.
Location E central IA. 18 m SSW of Cedar Rapids, 18 m NW of Iowa City. Take exit 225 off I-80, N on Rte. 149/151 to Rte. 6 E to Homestead. Inn is at end of Main St.
Credit cards MC, Visa.
Rates B&B, $34–47 double, $27 single. Extra person in room, $4; children under 6, $1. Cribs, rollaway cot, $2. 4% cash discount. Winter weekend specials.
Extras Cribs, babysitting, games available. German spoken.

MCGREGOR 52157   Map 10

We'd also like to have reports on the **Alexander Hotel,** a turn-of-the-century hotel renovated in 1988; its café serves three meals daily, with seafood and homemade pies as specialties. Rates are reasonable and all rooms have TV and air-conditioning (213 Main Street; 319–873–3454).

Little Switzerland Inn   *Tel:* (319) 873–3670
126 Main Street, Box 195

Once a busy river town with a population of 5,000, McGregor moves at a slower pace these days, with all of 900 inhabitants, not counting the tourists who come to enjoy the cliff-lined beauty of the upper Mississippi and explore its antique and craft shops. The Little Switzerland Inn was built in 1862 as the home for Iowa's oldest weekly newspaper, the *North Iowa Times*. Today the building houses a bakery downstairs and the B&B upstairs; a balcony, original to the building, provides a handsome view of the Mississippi, less than a block away. Just next door is a log cabin, built in 1848 and moved to this location by owners Bud and Chris Jameson.

Rooms in the B&B are decorated with turn-of-the-century furnishings, while the cabin decor mixes contemporary and primitive pieces.

"Great cabin, large and delicious breakfast. Enjoyed the shops of McGregor and local hiking trails." *(Tiri & Steve Larson)* "The owners were at our disposal day or night, and brought us a delicious breakfast of fresh fruit, homemade pastries, coffee, and tea. The location is convenient, and parking is ample." *(MS)* "Owners are very friendly, helpful, and outgoing." *(Connie & Don Albaugh)*

"After a good night's sleep and fresh-baked muffins, we drove to the top of Pikes Peak State Park for a perfect view of the juncture of the Wisconsin and Mississippi rivers." *(TL)*

Open All year.
Rooms 1 cabin (sleeping 6) with private bath; 2 suites (sleeping 4 to 6) with private bath, 3 doubles—2 with private half-bath, 1 sharing hall bath with maximum of 6 people. All with radio, desk, air-conditioning; some with telephone, TV. Whirlpool bath, fireplace in cabin.
Facilities Swimming pool across street; tennis, golf, fishing, cross-country skiing nearby. State park, historic sites nearby.
Location NE IA. On Mississippi River, 60 m N of Dubuque, 60 m S of LaCrosse, WI.
Restrictions No smoking.
Credit cards MC, Visa.
Rates B&B, $100–140 cabin or suite, $55 double, $45 single. Extra person in room, $10.
Extras Limited wheelchair accessibility. Pets permitted by prior arrangement. Free airport pickups. Crib available.

MIDDLE AMANA 52307   Map 10

For more information about the Amana Colonies, see entry for **Homestead** above.

The Rettig House   *Tel:* (319) 622–3386
Box 5

The Rettig House was built in 1893 from bricks made of native clay, fired in the Middle Amana brickyard. As one of the original community-kitchen houses of old Amana, the Rettig House's kitchen was used to prepare meals for 40 people three times a day. After the "Great Change" in 1932, its ownership passed to Lina Rettig and eventually to the current owners, Ray and Marge Rettig. Rooms are furnished with family heirlooms and authentic Amana antiques. The Rettigs note that they "like visitors who appreciate the history of the Amanas. Our yard is beautifully landscaped and offers a quiet and relaxing atmosphere."

"Mrs. Rettig, a charming, wholesome lady, welcomed us to her immaculate home, located in the center of the block, away from the street, with convenient, private parking. Middle Amana is about two miles from Main Amana, where most of the shops are located. (Shops are closed in the evening anyway.) Our bedroom was cozy, comfortable, and well ventilated; the bathroom had new fixtures and fresh wallpaper. A small sitting room nestled between three bedrooms had magazines and inspirational reading material available. Breakfast consisted of juice, garden-fresh strawberries, homemade coffee cake, and plenty of coffee. A freshly picked rose adorned the table, which was set with old-fashioned dishes. The large yard was meticulously kept with vegetables and beautiful flower gardens, large trees, and a marvelous four-person glider swing. A lovely evening was spent in the yard with Mr. and Mrs. Rettig, the other guests, and seemingly hundreds of singing birds." *(Janet Jessup)* "Absolutely spotless. Not a speck of dirt or chip of paint missing." *(Darrell & Betty Frohrib)* "Our gracious hosts gave us the chance to learn firsthand the history of the Amana Colonies." *(Neil Schroeder, also Tom & Lorrie Ludwig)*

Open All year.
Rooms 5 doubles—3 with private shower, 2 with maximum of 4 people sharing bath. 2 with TV, all with air-conditioning. Telephone, radio on request.
Facilities Dining room, living room. 1 acre with gardens, swing. Fishing, indoor swimming pool nearby.
Location E central IA. 20 m SW of Cedar Rapids, 20 m NW of Iowa City. From Des Moines or Iowa City, take exit 225 off of I-80. Go N on Rte. 151 to Rte. 220. Go W on Rte. 220 to Middle Amana. Inn is behind print shop and old school.
Restrictions No smoking, no alcohol. No children under 12.
Credit cards None accepted.
Rates B&B, $40 double or single, plus 9% tax.
Extras Airport pickups. German spoken.

We Want to Hear from You!

As you know, this book is only effective with your help. We really need to know about your experiences and discoveries.

If you stayed at an inn or hotel listed here, we want to know how it was. Did it live up to our description? Exceed it? Was it what you expected? Did you like it? Were you disappointed? Delighted?

Have you discovered new establishments that we should add to the next edition?

Tear out one of the report forms at the back of this book (or use your own stationery if you prefer) and write today. Even if you write only "Fully endorse existing entry" you will have been most helpful.

Thank You!

Kansas

Heritage House, Topeka

Set right at the center of the continental U.S., Kansas has a history far more complex than most people realize. From 1492 to 1845 six nations claimed all or part of what is now Kansas. Although included as part of the U.S. with the Louisiana Purchase, it became part of the Republic of Texas until that state was admitted to the Union in 1845. Kansas's own admission to the Union was delayed until 1861 by intense and bloody feuding between the territory's pro- and anti-slavery factions.

Although Kansas is known as one of the country's leading wheat producers, its farmers have never had it easy, from the hardships faced by the first settlers of the early 1800s, through the "dust bowl" period of the 1930s, to the present day. Industry now plays an important role in the state's economy, with meat packing and aviation among the leading fields.

While it is by no means a tourist mecca, Kansas does have many towns of interest, including Wichita, center of the state's aircraft industry; Lawrence, home of the University of Kansas; and Dodge City, once known as the Wickedest City in America, with a saloon for every 50 citizens. Many towns sponsor fairs and festivals during the warmer months; ask the tourist office for a calendar of events.

Information please: We'd like to have reports on the **Halcyon House**, in the lovely college town of Lawrence, about 40 miles west of Kansas City. A century-old Victorian home, this eight–guest room B&B has been totally restored with such contemporary touches as floor-to-ceiling glass windows in the vaulted kitchen (1000 Ohio, Lawrence 66044; 913–841–0314).

Rates do not include 5% state tax plus local taxes.

More recommendations for this state would be appreciated!

CIMARRON 67835 Map 10

Cimarron Hotel *Tel:* (316) 855–2244
203 North Main Street, P.O. Box 633

One of the town's first brick structures, the Cimarron is now listed on the National Register of Historic Places. It was built in 1887 as the New West Hotel; innkeeper Kathleen Holt restored and reopened it as the Cimarron in 1977.

"Housed in a lovely old brick building, the Cimarron's rooms are decorated with antiques and period wallpaper; guests share clean and spacious baths at the end of the hall. The downstairs restaurant features wonderful pan-fried chicken and mashed potatoes, and the innkeeper, Kathi Holt, cooks breakfast for guests each morning, at guests' convenience.

"The atmosphere is a cross between going back 100 years in time and staying with the family next door. Kathi's sons are friendly and personable; her cat wanders around greeting guests. If you like, you can become part of the family, sit out on the balcony and talk philosophy or grain prices, or watch TV with the boys in the family den. On the other hand, if you want to get away from it all, the third floor, where the guest rooms are located, is quiet and off-limits to the family. The choice is yours." *(Lynne Wagner)* More comments, please.

Open All year. Restaurant open Sat., Sun. only.
Rooms 9 doubles, 1 single—most with sink in room and a maximum of 5 people sharing baths. Radio, air-conditioning. 2 rooms with desk. TV on request.
Facilities Dining/breakfast room, family room with fireplace, games. Gazebo. Swimming pool, tennis courts, playground, golf nearby.
Location SW KS. 20 m W of Dodge City, on Hwy. 50.
Credit cards None accepted.
Rates B&B, $30 double. Reduced rates for families, seniors. Prix fixe dinner ($10) served Sat. night, Sun. noon; other days on request for groups. Mystery weekends.
Extras Airport/station pickups available at moderate cost. Pets permitted. Babysitting available.

LINDSBORG 67456 Map 10

Swedish Country Inn *Tel:* (913) 227–2985
112 West Lincoln

The Smoky River Valley was homesteaded in the 1860s by Swedish immigrants, and its Swedish heritage has been well preserved. Lindsborg, known as Little Sweden, is the area's hub and offers a number of Swedish-style restaurants and shops selling Scandinavian imports. The Swedish Country Inn, built in the early 1900s as a feed store, was later used as a Studebaker showroom and was converted into a hotel in 1929. In 1985 Quintin and Florence Applequist remodeled it into a country inn; Virginia Brunsell is the innkeeper.

Rooms are decorated with natural hard-pine furniture and lamps imported from Sweden or made by local craftsmen, handmade American quilts, and lace curtains from Holland. Most rooms are done in blue or rose and white, and the effect is light, airy, and very inviting. The Swedish buffet breakfast includes fruit, juice, cereal, specialty breads, pastries, cheeses, two kinds of eggs, meat, and herring.

"Our room was clean, spacious, and comfortable, with the added charm of pleated cloth bonnet-type lampshades and shuttered windows. The restaurant has a similar decor; at breakfast, the tables were set with flowers, and cloth placemats and napkins. The rooms are color-coordinated and very relaxing. Especially interesting are all the handmade quilts. This inn is as clean as soap and water can make it." *(Mr. & Mrs. William Harford)*

"The ladies who greeted us were very kind and made our dinner reservations before we even unpacked. They were also very helpful with suggestions on shops and museums we might want to visit." *(Doug & Linda Kirmer)*

"Our room had colorful wallpaper and a modern but modest bathroom. We borrowed the tandem bike and explored Lindsborg's many shops, eateries, and sites of interest." *(James Doyle)*

"Downtown, with its shops featuring Swedish crafts and furniture, is just around the corner. The Swedish Crown Restaurant, well known for its Swedish and American menu, is also nearby. Residents of Lindsborg also pride themselves on the Old Mill Museum and the Messiah Festival, sponsored by Bethany College and held annually during Easter Week." *(Carolyn Ward)*

Open All year. Restaurant closed Sundays.
Rooms 1 suite, 18 doubles—all with private shower and/or bath, TV, air-conditioning.
Facilities Dining room, lobby with TV, game table; gift shop; sauna; bicycles. Fishing, swimming pool nearby.
Location Central KS. 60 m N of Wichita. Approx. 20 m S of Salina, 12 m N of McPherson. From I-135S take exit 78, from I-135N take exit 72. ½ block W of Main St.
Restrictions No smoking.
Credit cards MC, Visa.
Rates B&B, $60–70 suite, $50–60 double, $40 single, plus 7% tax. Buffet breakfast, $4.50 (outside guests).
Extras Wheelchair accessible; 1 guest room suitable for wheelchairs. Station pickups. Cribs available. Some German, Swedish spoken.

TOPEKA 66606   **Map 10**

Heritage House   *Tel:* (913) 233–3800
3535 Southwest Sixth Street

Once home of the famous Menninger Clinic, Heritage House was transformed into a B&B by a 1988 designer showcase. Now listed on the National Register of Historic Places, its individually decorated guest rooms are equipped for business and pleasure travelers alike; because each room was done by a different designer, the furnishings run the gamut from contemporary to period, formal to country casual. Rates include a continental breakfast.

"Beautifully and thoughtfully decorated, pristinely maintained and helpfully staffed with eager-to-serve cleancut students, it works extremely well as either a simple overnight business stop or as a romantic destination. Although we've found some other midwestern B&Bs which rivaled Heritage House for looks, what sets it a country mile apart from the others is its incredible restaurant. To our view, it offers the finest dining in Kansas." *(Charles Hillestad)*

Open All year.
Rooms 15 doubles—11 with private shower and/or bath, 4 with maximum of 4 people sharing bath. All with telephone, radio, TV, air-conditioning. Some with desk, 1 with whirlpool tub.
Facilities Restaurant, 2 living rooms, sun room, patio. Gage Park (home of Topeka Zoo) across street.
Location E KS. 60 m W of Kansas City. ½ m from I-70. From Rte. 40 W, take Exit 357B. Go S on Gage St., E on 6th St. to inn on right. From I-70 E, take Rte. 4/40 to Exit 357A. Go E on 6th St. to inn on right.
Credit cards Amex, MC, Visa.
Rates B&B, $45–105 double.

VALLEY FALLS 66088   Map 10

The Barn   *Tel:* (913) 945–3303
Rte. 2, Box 87

The Ryan family took what was a 100-year-old barn of sturdy post-and-beam construction and converted it into a family-style country inn. Despite the addition of seven new guest rooms in 1989, the Ryans report that "we work hard to keep a family atmosphere and make everyone feel at home. Our guests come for R&R, but love to go through the stores in Valley Falls, population 1200."

"The Ryan family was friendly with down-on-the-farm hospitality, making us feel right at home." *(Mr. & Mrs. Robert Dayton)* "The rooms are spacious, very clean, and comfortable. The whole Ryan family cooked and served the farm breakfasts then visited with us. After the meal we felt so much at home that we were tempted to help with the dishes. They provided everything we needed, including daughters to entertain the little ones while their parents ate. There is a beautiful balcony area filled with plants that overlooks wooded, rolling farmland and a pond where you can fish. Being in the country, it is very quiet, but you are within a few miles of a delightful small town and not too far from a large reservoir for sailing, waterskiing, picnicking, and fishing." *(Don & Janet Burton)* More comments, please.

Open All year.
Rooms 16 doubles—all with private shower, telephone, TV, air-conditioning. Most with king-size beds.
Facilities Living room with fireplace, piano; dining room, enclosed sundeck, year-round heated swimming pool, exercise room. 80 acres with fishing pond, games, play

equipment, tennis. Golf nearby. Perry Lake for swimming, fishing, boating; hunting nearby.
Location NE KS, 23 m NE of Topeka. Turn N at milepost 354 off Hwy. 4, E of Valley Falls. 2 m from town.
Restrictions No smoking.
Credit cards MC, Visa.
Rates MAP, $54 double. Extra person in room, $10. No tipping. Senior discount.
Extras Limited wheelchair accessibility. Airport/station pickups, $20. Cribs, baby-sitting available.

WICHITA 67218   Map 10

The Max Paul Inn   *Tel:* (316) 689–8101
3910 East Kellogg

Opened in 1984, the Max Paul is a luxury B&B inn, housed in three side-by-side, 50-year-old English Tudor cottages. It caters to business travelers on weekdays and to couples on weekends. Rooms are lavishly and imaginatively decorated in a country Victorian mood, with European antiques, English chintzes, and memorable featherbeds. Rates include a continental breakfast of fresh-squeezed juice, fresh fruit, and home-baked muffins, croissants, bagels, or turnovers stuffed with ham and cheese, served in the breakfast room on weekdays and brought to your room on weekends. Conscientious innkeepers Roberta and Jill Eaton have added extra insulation, storm doors and windows, a fence and plantings to further insulate the front rooms from possible traffic noises.

"Although all that is claimed in the inn's brochure is accurate, what doesn't show up are the warm, friendly, almost bubbly personalities of innkeepers Jill and Roberta Eaton. In my business-travel world of Holiday Inns, this place is a true oasis of warmth and friendship." *(Jeff Lee)* "Wonderfully quiet and gracious, with unexcelled service and the warmth of home. Enjoyed the Jacuzzi and well-stocked kitchen." *(Sheila Hochhauser, also Dr. Sei-Jong Chung)* "My room had a small crystal chandelier with a well lit working area." *(Louis Barr)* The Rob Roy Suite was perfect with a fireplace, king-size feather bed, and cozy sitting area." *(Dr. Ted Delhotal)*

"Our favorite for anniversaries and birthdays, with its European antiques, fireplaces, and 'tubs for two.' The light breakfast is always superb and fresh, served on antique dishes and trays coordinated to the rooms' decor. Private balconies overlooking the beautiful gardens add to the feeling of privacy." *(Rob & Debbie Robbins, also Sandy Broadland)*

Open All year. Closed Dec. 24, 25.
Rooms 8 suites, 6 doubles, in 3 adjacent cottages. All with full private bath and/or shower, telephone, radio, TV, desk, air-conditioning. Some with working fireplaces, balconies, kitchenettes.
Facilities Breakfast room, library, gallery, conference room, exercise room and deck with Jacuzzi. ½ acre with garden, pond. College Hill Park several blocks away for tennis, swimming, jogging, picnicking.
Location S central KS. On the edge of College Hill. From U.S. 54 (Kellogg): westbound, turn right into inn just west of Bluff; eastbound, turn right off Kellogg just after exit 135 onto Roosevelt; continue left on Lakeview and turn left at Bluff; turn left onto Kellogg westbound as above.

Restrictions Traffic noise might disturb light sleepers. Children "discouraged, but please inquire." Those allergic to cats should ask for a room not in the main cottage.
Credit cards Amex, DC, MC, Visa.
Rates B&B, $85–105 suite, $60–70 double, $50–95 single. Extra person in room, $10.

Key to Abbreviations

For complete information and explanations, please see the Introduction.

Rates: Range from least expensive room in low season to most expensive room in peak season.

Room only: No meals included; sometimes referred to as European Plan (EP).

B&B: Bed and breakfast; includes breakfast, sometimes afternoon/evening refreshment.

MAP: Modified American Plan; includes breakfast and dinner.

Full board: Three meals daily.

Alc lunch: À la carte lunch; average price of entrée plus nonalcoholic drink, tax, tip.

Alc dinner: Average price of three-course dinner, including half bottle of house wine, tax, tip.

Prix fixe dinner: Three- to five-course set dinner, excluding wine, tax, tip unless otherwise noted.

Extras: Noted if available. Always confirm in advance. Pets are not permitted unless specified.

Zip codes: If only one zip code applies, it is listed with the town name. If there is more than one, it is noted as part of the address.

Kentucky

Doe Run Inn, Brandenburg

Kentucky's history is a rich and complex one—Daniel Boone explored and hunted here, Abraham Lincoln was born here, and Stephen Foster and Harriet Beecher Stowe wrote about Kentucky. In the development of the U.S., Kentucky has served as a bridge state: Linking the north and south, it was a slave state but fought for the Union in the Civil War; from Virginia to Missouri, settlers passed through on their way west.

And there is far more to present-day Kentucky than Churchill Downs, the Derby, and horses. A key common denominator is the dominant limestone strata responsible for the state's bourbon (the water), bluegrass (the color), and dramatic scenery (cliffs, canyons, and caves). At Cumberland Falls State Park visitors can walk out on flat limestone slabs to watch a 125-foot-wide, 68-foot-high swathe of water plunge dramatically to the boulders below. During a full moon, the resulting pervasive mist forms a rare "moonbow" visible only here and at Victoria Falls in Zimbabwe, Africa. If you're not claustrophobic, explore some of the 300 miles of charted limestone passages in Mammoth Cave, including some areas used for human habitation over 4,000 years ago.

Other spots to explore: Shaker Village at Pleasant Hill, with its architecturally distinctive buildings where superb design emphasizes stately simplicity; nearby Harrodsburg's Old Fort Harrod—site of the first permanent English settlement west of the Alleghenies; Hodgenville, where visitors can see Abe Lincoln's birthplace and an enormous sinkhole; and the many TVA lakes scattered throughout the state, which offer limitless recreational opportunities.

Information please: We'd like to request recommendations for Louisville, known best for the Kentucky Derby, and the state's cultural center year-round, with great jazz clubs, superb live theater, and several truly gracious residential areas where homes date from the 1870s. Probably the two best places to stay in Louisville are the **Brown** (4th & Broadway 40202; 502–583–1234 or 800–HILTONS) and the **Seelbach** (500 4th Avenue 40202; 502–585–3200 or 800–626–2032), two historic hotels that have been lavishly restored to their original turn-of-the-century splendor. Both have excellent restaurants, rooms furnished in period, and an elegant atmosphere, but at 300 rooms each, they may be a bit beyond the scope of this guide; reader reports and additional recommendations are invited!

Reader tip: If you're traveling on I-64 between Louisville and Frankfort or Lexington, stop in Shelbyville for lunch at the **Science Hill Inn,** a beautifully restored historic complex including some attractive shops, a gallery of English antique furniture and silver, and a restaurant specializing in Kentucky rainbow trout, corn bread, and lemon chess pie (502–633–2825). *(GM)*

Rates do not include 5% state sales tax and 3% lodging tax.

BARDSTOWN 40004   Map 5

Bardstown is one of Kentucky's oldest towns, with many historic buildings, and is a center for the growing of tobacco and the distilling of bourbon. Sights of interest include the local historical museum, the Getz Museum of Whiskey History—from colonial days to Prohibition—and My Old Kentucky Home State Park. This park is home to Federal Hill, a mansion that probably inspired Stephen Foster to write "My Old Kentucky Home." From June to early September the "Stephen Foster Story," a musical pageant featuring the composer's melodies, is sung in the park's amphitheater. Bourbon aficionados will want to take the tours of the nearby Jim Beam and Maker's Mark distilleries. Here also is a Trappist abbey that sells a very distinctive (and strong) cheese.

Bardstown is in central Kentucky's Bourbon County, 35 miles south of Louisville.

The Old Talbott Tavern   *Tel:* (502) 348–3494
107 West Stephen Foster Avenue

The Talbott is one of Kentucky's most historic inns. Built of stone in 1779, it was the first permanent structure erected in Bardstown, then America's western frontier. Patrick Henry, governor of Virginia (of which Kentucky was then a part), granted the tavern its operating license in 1785. In 1797 the exiled King Louis Philippe of France stayed at the Talbott on a trip to the New World; a member of his party painted the murals, which can still be seen on the walls of one of the upstairs rooms. The bullet holes in the murals are said to have been put there by Jesse James, who supposedly used them for target practice. Other famous guests at the tavern included Abraham Lincoln, Daniel Boone, Stephen Foster, and James Audubon.

Rooms at the Talbott are simply furnished with antiques, and meals include both typical American cuisine—steak, shrimp, chicken—and old Kentucky favorites—rabbit, quail, fried chicken with cream gravy, and catfish with hush puppies. Rates include a continental breakfast. The tavern has been owned and operated for the last eight years by the Kelley family.

Although one respondent indicated that some of the rooms could do with some sprucing up, the consensus is still that it's worth a visit: "Bardstown is known for 'My Old Kentucky Home,' but the place to be is Talbott Tavern." *(Virginia M. Slimmer)* "Definitely great for antique lovers. Dinner good and unusual. Parking is not always close to the entrance, because of the inn's location in the center of town." *(Mr. & Mrs. A.D. Moscrip)* "Slow service, but the best fried chicken ever." *(SHW)*

Open All year. Closed Christmas Day.
Rooms 1 suite, 5 doubles—all with private full bath and/or shower, air-conditioning. 1 with desk.
Facilities Restaurant, pub. Country and other music weekends. Limited parking; municipal lot nearby. Fishing, golf nearby.
Location Center of town, Courthouse Square.
Credit cards Amex, DC, MC, Visa.
Rates B&B, $62 suite, $50–56 double, $41–50 single. Alc lunch, $4.50–7; alc dinner, $20.

COVINGTON 41011 Map 5

Amos Shinkle Townhouse
215 Garrard Street

Tel: (606) 431–2118

Former Covington mayor Bernie Moorman and his partner, Don Nash, bought this 1850s brick riverboat house in 1983 and began its renovation, uncovering some of the original wall murals in the process. Many of the original plaster ceiling medallions and cornices were preserved, and several of the public rooms retain their Rococo Revival chandeliers. Much of the decorating was completed by a group of Cincinnati-area design firms when the house was showcased as a local fund-raiser. In 1987 four additional bedrooms were added to the inn when the carriage house was converted into guest rooms.

"Our rooms were lovely, and the delicious full breakfast included a crisp-fried German sausage that is a local specialty. Our gracious host was a great source of restaurant suggestions." *(MW, also A. Kessler)*

"Rooms are decorated with gorgeous antiques—my favorite includes a carved four-poster bed; the baths are well supplied with big fluffy towels. Bernie and Don are the most delightful hosts. The Riverfront, home to some excellent restaurants, is a short walk away." *(Jean Alexander Hayes)*

Open All year.
Rooms 7 doubles, all with full private bath, radio, TV, air conditioning. 3 in main house, 4 in coach house. 1 with whirlpool tub; 2 with desk.
Facilities Dining room, parlor with grand piano, pump organ; porches.
Location N central KY. On Ohio River, 2 m S of Cincinnati, OH; 90 m N of Lexington. 1½ blocks from river, in Riverside Historic District; across the Roebling Suspension Bridge from Riverfront Stadium.
Credit cards DC, MC, Visa.
Rates B&B, $55–90. Extra adult in room, $10. No charge for children under 15. No tipping. Senior discount.
Extras Airport/station pickups, $5. French, German spoken.

HARRODSBURG 40330   Map 5

The Harrodsburg area is home to two of Kentucky's finest inns. If your time in the state is limited, this town, oldest in the state, is probably the one to visit. Sights of interest include Old Fort Harrod State Park, with its historic buildings and amphitheater, featuring dramatizations of the stories of Daniel Boone and Abraham Lincoln; Morgan Row; and Shakertown at Pleasant Hill (see page 139).

Harrodsburg is located in central Kentucky's Bluegrass Region, 32 miles southwest of Lexington.

Beaumont Inn   *Tel:* (606) 734–3381
638 Beaumont Drive

Listed on the National Register of Historic Places, the Beaumont dates back to 1845. Formerly a school for girls, it was first known as the Greenville Institute, then Daughter's College, and finally as Beaumont College. Annie Bell Goddard, a graduate of Daughter's College and a teacher at Beaumont, bought the property with her husband in 1917 and converted it into an inn. Ownership and management passed to her daughter, Mrs. Pauline Dedman; four generations later, Chuck and Helen Dedman continue the family tradition. The inn's rooms are spread out over a number of buildings, including the original main building of the school, a brick building with Greek Revival–style Doric columns, as well as several other buildings and cottages of varying sizes. Restaurant specialties include the inn's own Kentucky cured ham, fried chicken, corn pudding, and orange-lemon cake. The Dedmans note that Mercer County is "dry"; bring your own if you'd like a glass of wine or Kentucky bourbon.

"The Beaumont Inn is situated well off the main highway (but clearly marked) on a peaceful knoll. The main structure is exquisitely Victorian. The sitting room is extremely gracious—large mirrors, lace curtains, floral wallpapers, and velvet-covered furniture. In spite of the apparent formality, we received a warm welcome. Our room, at the end of the hall on the second floor, had two big double beds and a single. The furniture in this cheerful, high-ceilinged room was also Victorian—antique dressers, tables, chandeliers, patterned rugs, and rose-patterned wallpaper. Not neglecting modern demands, it also has a TV and private bath—rather small and plain, but clean. The inn serves wonderful huge country-style meals at a very reasonable price." *(MFD, also Al Meade)*

"Renowned for its food—diners come from miles away. Mr. Dedman is a very interesting Southern gentleman who arranged for us to visit a nearby horse-breeding farm." *(Pat & Sherwood Cuyler)*

Open Mid-March–mid-Dec.
Rooms 1 cottage, 29 doubles—all with private bath and/or shower, telephone, TV, air-conditioning. Rooms in total of 4 buildings—main building, Bell Cottage, Goddard Hall, Greystone House.
Facilities Restaurant, parlors, lounge, library. 30 acres with 2 tennis courts, swimming pool, gift shop. Fishing, boating, golf nearby.
Location Central KY, Bluegrass Region. 32 m SW of Lexington.
Credit cards MC, Visa.

Rates Room only, $60–90 double, $45–80 single. Extra child in room, $4; adult, $20. Full breakfast, $5.50; alc lunch, $6–10; alc dinner, $11–16.
Extras Airport/station pickups for additional fee. Cribs available.

Shaker Village of Pleasant Hill
3500 Lexington Road

Tel: (606) 734–5411

Shaker Village preserves 27 original nineteenth-century buildings, accurately restored and adapted. Visitors (day and overnight) take self-guided tours of the buildings where interpreters and craftsmen explain the Shaker approach to life and religion. Shaker music programs are also offered on many weekends.

Shakertown at Pleasant Hill is a nonprofit educational corporation; it is listed on the National Register of Historic Places and has been declared a National Landmark. It is the only such restoration with all services in original buildings, and the only historic village offering all overnight accommodation in original buildings.

Don't be confused by references to both the Shaker Village of Pleasant Hill and to Shakertown at Pleasant Hill; both are mentioned in their literature and both names refer to the same place. It's also helpful to note that although their mailing address is in Harrodsburg, Pleasant Hill is actually seven miles away. Advance reservations are strongly recommended.

"This place is unique in every aspect and is worth the trip for the day, overnight, or to linger for a week. In anybody's rating, Shaker Village is four stars." *(Jim Lyle, also Kathy & Mike Still)*

"Our room in the Trustees' House was large, clean, comfortable with twin beds, rockers, desk, and chair. Some noise drifted upstairs from the dining rooms. We preferred our smaller room above the broom maker on our last visit because it was more quiet and remote. The grounds are lovely—serene and inviting. Food is top quality, simple and more than ample. Undoubtedly one of the best values anywhere." *(KLH)*

"An educational and relaxing treat. I stayed in an authentic Shaker room—with chairs up on pegs—over the Wash House; the bathroom was new and modern. The food was wonderful, with freshly picked vegetables right from the garden outside the back door. After dinner, drive ten minutes to see the outdoor dramatization of the life of Daniel Boone or take a ride on a river ferry boat." *(Susie Preston)*

Open All year. Closed Christmas Eve and Day.
Rooms 72 doubles with private bath and shower, telephone, TV, desk, air-conditioning. Accommodations in 14 restored buildings.
Facilities Sitting rooms, restaurant. 2,200 acres. Paddlewheel riverboat rides on Kentucky River. Craft shops and demonstrations.
Location Central KY, Bluegrass Region. 80 m SE of Louisville, 25 m SW of Lexington, 7 m NE of Harrodsburg, on US Rte. 68.
Restrictions No alcoholic beverages in dining room (dry county).
Credit cards None accepted.
Rates Room only, $40–75 double, $30–55 single, plus 8% tax. No charge for children under 18 in parents' room. Extra adults, $5. Country buffet breakfast, $5.25; alc lunch, $6–9; prix fixe dinner, $11–16. Children's menu. No tipping. Winter package rates, excluding holidays, $85–115 per person, including 2 nights' lodging, 5 meals, tours, and programs. Summer harvest weekend events.
Extras Cribs available.

LEXINGTON   Map 5

A city wealthy from the tobacco industry, Lexington is home to the University of Kentucky, Transylvania University, and many beautiful antebellum and Victorian buildings, a number of which are now open to the public as museums. But the real attraction here is Thoroughbred horses. Head for the Kentucky Horse Park, for 1,000 acres of bluegrass, where you can learn everything you ever wanted to know (and more) about equines, then sign up for a tour of the area's best horse farms.

Lexington is located in central Kentucky, 101 miles south of Cincinnati, Ohio, and 78 miles east of Louisville.

Gratz Park Inn   *Tel:* (606) 231–6666
120 West Second Street   Outside KY: (800) 227–4362
Corner of Second and North Upper
   Streets 40507

Although Lexington is well supplied with chain hotels and motels, there was no small hotel here until the Gratz Park Inn opened in July of 1987. Located downtown in the historic Gratz Park area, it is a small luxury hotel with a comfortable but elegant atmosphere. Housed in a 1916 Georgian Revival–style building; the interior was gutted as part of the renovation process.

"Over $9 million was spent to renovate the building, and it shows. Each room is decorated differently, but all have antique reproduction furniture, four-poster beds, and armoires that conceal TVs. The baths are huge, with marble sinks and vanities, plenty of shelf space, and good lighting.

"Our dinner was exquisite: salads came beautifully prepared; entrées were very elegantly presented on huge warm plates; dessert was homemade ice cream—coconut amaretto and raspberry/blueberry bourbon. The service was remarkable; our waiter was attentive without being obtrusive. Classical music plays softly in all public areas. The ambiance is wonderful—quiet and elegant in a well-partitioned room with overstuffed semicircular banquettes and French doors to a brick patio." *(Susan W. Schwemm)* Another reader may have hit an off night—he reported that service at dinner was very slow, even though the restaurant was not crowded.

Open All year.
Rooms 6 suites, 38 doubles, all with full private bath, telephone, radio, TV, desk, air conditioning.
Facilities Lobby, restaurant, bar/lounge with entertainment Wed.–Sat., conference rooms. Concierge service; 24-hour room service. Off-street parking.
Location Downtown. Historic Gratz Park area.
Credit cards Amex, CB, DC, MC, Visa.
Rates Room only, $155–185 suite, $99–140 double. Extra person in room, $10. Senior discount. Alc lunch, $10; alc dinner, $36.
Extras Equipped for the disabled. Airport/station pickups. Cribs, babysitting available.

Louisiana

A Hotel—The Frenchmen, New Orleans

Everybody goes to New Orleans sooner or later, and although it's a big city, you can get a good taste of its delicious food and famous jazz in just a few days' visit. Try to rent a car and travel outside the city. Visit Louisiana's many restored antebellum plantations and learn something about the state's Acadian heritage—the French settlers of Nova Scotia, who were expelled by the British in the 1750s and settled in what was then French territory. (The word *Cajun* is derived from the word *Acadian.*)

Information please: Less than 30 minutes from the French Quarter is **Seven Oaks**, a new home built in the style of an antebellum cottage. Much of the building material came from the original Seven Oaks, a Greek Revival Mansion demolished in the 1970s. The decor combines antiques, collectibles, and contemporary furnishings in just the right balance and the surrounding gardens invite guests for a relaxing stroll (2600 Gay Lynn Drive, Kenner 70065; 504–888–8649). If you're heading up the River Road from New Orleans, consider overnighting at **Oak Alley,** a columned Greek Revival mansion prefaced by a magnificent double row of 250-year-old live oaks (Route 2, Box 10, Vacherie 70090; 504–265–2151).

Natchitoches, the oldest permanent settlement in the Louisiana Purchase, is worth exploring. Those wishing to overnight in this pretty, lakeside town may enjoy the **Fleur-de-Lis Inn,** an inviting B&B in the historic district (336 Second Street 71457; 318–352–6621).

246

Rates listed do not include Louisiana sales tax of 7½%, plus local taxes where applicable.

NAPOLEONVILLE 70390   Map 6

Madewood Plantation House   Tel: (504) 369–7151
Route 2, Box 478

A 21-room Greek Revival mansion, Madewood was designed in 1846 by Henry Howard and is a National Historic Landmark. The white-painted mansion has six imposing Doric columns and was built from bricks produced in the plantation's kiln and from cypress grown on its lands. Madewood was purchased in 1964 by Mr. and Mrs. Harold Marshall and is now owned by their son Keith and his wife Millie. Keith and Millie work in New Orleans during the week, spending weekends at Madewood. Redecorated in 1988, the rooms are furnished with an extensive collection of period antiques, including canopy or half-tester beds, marble fireplace mantels, hand-carved woodwork, and fanned windows.

The double rooms are located in the mansion (hence the higher price); the two suites are located in an 1820s Greek Revival cottage, and the three-room renovated cabin has a kitchen, working fireplace, and more casual country furnishings. MAP rates include wine and cheese before dinner, candlelit dinner, and full breakfast in the dining room. Guests staying in the suites or cabin can stay on a B&B basis, with continental breakfast brought to the room, or MAP. Unless otherwise requested, meals are served family style, with everyone sharing the same table.

"Daily operations are taken care of by head cook Thelma Parker, who has been there over 20 years. It is evident that the Marshalls think a great deal of her, as there is a portrait of her in the library. Thelma gave us a tour of the plantation. Room are fairly authentic to the period, but have been adapted to current needs. The four-poster and test beds are especially inviting. Our favorite bedroom was on the first floor. Individual thermostats let guests adjust the temperature to their liking. Red wine, Brie, crackers, and grapes were set out in the library at 6 P.M., and at 7 we sat down to a candle-light dinner at an oval mahogany table that could seat at least 20 people. Clem served us turkey and sausage soup, salad, creamy shrimp enclosed in puff pastry, sweet potatoes with raisins, fresh green beans, cornbread, white wine, and spice cake pudding dessert. I thought Thelma's cooking better than Galatoire's in New Orleans. A bell had been placed at the head of the table to ring for Clem to clear away each course. The tinkling of a music box behind massive wooden doors was our cue to move into the adjoining parlor to sip brandy and coffee. We spent the evening looking through scrap books with pictures of the plantation as the setting of various movies and festivals, and in books about neighboring plantations. We returned to our rooms to find a praline on the pillow. A silver pot of chicory coffee was brought to our room in the morning, and breakfast of scrambled eggs, sausage, grits, and orange juice was served in the dining room at 9 A.M. The most notable landmark on the grounds is the family cemetery complete with an ancient oak tree draped with moss creating an appropriately spooky atmosphere." *(Diane Camp)*

One minor drawback typical of many plantation homes: because rooms are kept open for tours during the day, a 5 P.M. check-in and a 10 A.M. check-out is requested for rooms in the main house.

Open All year. Closed 2 days at Thanksgiving, Christmas, New Year's.
Rooms 1 cottage, 2 suites, 6 doubles with private bath and/or shower, air-conditioning. 4 rooms in annex; 1 2-bedroom cottage. 4 with desk. TV on request.
Facilities Double parlors, dining room, library, music room, verandas. 20 acres with patio, spreading live oaks, bayou. Swamp tours available nearby.
Location SE LA. Sugarcane country. 75 m W of New Orleans, 45 m S of Baton Rouge. On Bayou Laforche, facing LA Hwy. 308. 4 m from town.
Restrictions No smoking.
Credit cards Amex, MC, Visa.
Rates B&B, $85 double; extra person in room, $10. MAP, $135 suite, $150 double including tax and service. Reduced rates for children. Extra person in suite, $30–50. Prix fixe dinner, $25.
Extras Cribs available; advance notice required. French spoken.

NEW ORLEANS   Map 6

Cognoscenti inform us that the city under discussion here is called *Nu-Awluns,* never *New Orleens*.

Rates here are generally lowest from mid-June to Labor Day and highest during Mardi Gras, Sugar Bowl, Super Bowl, and other peak festival times. (Mardi Gras rates are not listed here.) Advance reservations are also recommended during the city's famous Jazz and Heritage Festival, usually held during late April and early May. State and local sales tax is 11% and is not included in the rates. Parking can be a problem; if traveling by car, be sure to ask for information when reserving your room. A few hotels provide on-site parking; most have arrangements with nearby garages. One reader complained that the garage she used closed very early, making it difficult to get the car in or out at night.

Hotel rooms in the French Quarter tend to be small, with a bed and not much in the way of easy chairs or usable desk space. If you plan to do anything other than sleep in your room, ask about the availability of larger doubles; if finances permit, book a suite. Although most bed & breakfast inns have attractive balconies and courtyards, very few offer parlors or even dining rooms for guests to gather inside. If you'll be visiting when it's either too hot or too chilly to enjoy being outdoors for long, make an effort to book a room in one of the establishments that does provide interior common space.

People come to New Orleans for many reasons, but peace and quiet are not usually among them. It is a noisy city, and light sleepers should request the quietest possible rooms, or bring along some ear plugs! Visitors should also be alert to the problem of street crime, especially at night in the residential area of the French Quarter and in the Garden District. If the streets are crowded, there's generally no problem; if they're empty, get a cab right away.

Also recommended: The **French Quarter Maisonnettes** (1130 Chartres Street, 70116; 504–524–9918), built in 1825 by the Soniat-Duffossat family, has maintained much of its original architecture, including the flagstone carriage drive and inner courtyard. Rates include the morning paper and a copy of the owner's very helpful folder on restaurants and sights of interest. Although clearly not as luxurious as the other French Quarter hotels we've listed, the Maisonnettes represent an excellent value. The **Grenoble House** (329 Dauphine Street, 70112; 504–522–1331) is an all-suite inn, in a restored nineteenth-century home right in the French Quarter. Rooms combine antiques and contemporary furnishings with kitchens fully equipped with everything from dishes to microwave ovens and ice-makers. The rates, especially reasonable for a week's stay, include a continental breakfast; maid service is provided twice weekly. The **Le Richelieu Hotel** (1234 Chartres Street, 70116; 504–529–2492, 800–535–9653) is made up of several restored buildings, including five nineteenth-century Greek Revival row houses and a macaroni factory. Longtime owner Frank Rochefort lives on the hotel property and tries to make sure his staff "do their best for guests," which is probably why the hotel has such a high rate of both occupancy and returning guests. The **Park View Guest House** (7004 Saint Charles Avenue; 504–861–7564), with stained-glass windows, and unusual architectural detailing, began accepting paying visitors when New Orleans hosted the World Cotton Exchange Exposition in 1885. Located next to Audubon Park in the Garden District, the reasonably priced B&B is just a trolley ride away from the French Quarter and downtown. The **St. Louis Hotel** (730 Bienville Street, 70130; 504–581–7300, 800–535–9706) is a relatively new hotel, built around a central courtyard and fountain. The elegant decor is French, as is the cuisine in its restaurants, the Louis XVI and the Savoir Faire Bistro. The **Soniat House** (1133 Chartres Street, 70116; 504–522–0570, 800–544–8808), centrally located yet quiet even during the busiest hours, was created from two adjoining townhouses that date back to 1829 and 1840, and is furnished luxuriously with antiques as well as paintings and sculptures by contemporary New Orleans artists.

A Hotel—The Frenchmen
417 Frenchmen Street 70116

Tel: (504) 948–2166
(800) 831–1781

Located on the border of the French Quarter in an area that is showing signs of a renaissance, the Frenchmen is a hotel created from three 1850s buildings. Rooms are individually furnished with period antiques and reproduction furniture; rates include a full breakfast, served in your room or on the patio.

"Its location, one block from Decatur, makes it very convenient for walking in the Quarter. Our room, while small, overlooked the tropical courtyard where the swimming pool is, and had a comfortable double bed, an antique armoire concealing the color TV, and a very effective air-conditioning unit. Upon check-in, you are given a front-door key, as the hotel is kept locked for security reasons. Every morning, at a time of our choosing, we enjoyed a breakfast brought to our room on a silver tray with linen napkins, fresh flowers, and good china. One morning we had quiche, toast, fresh fruit, and juice; another produced pecan waffles; and the third day we had French toast with ham and blueberry muffins. At night our bed was turned down and a mint left on the pillow. The hotel is very clean and our room was made up promptly every morning. The entire staff, especially John Harty, the concierge, and his assistant, Oscar, went out of their way to make certain our visit was very pleasant, including recommending places to eat and tips on getting around town. The hotel is very quiet; we thought we were the only guests the first two days we were there. Three doors down is a restaurant called Ruby Red's; it doesn't look like much, but it serves the best hamburgers I've ever had." *(EL)*

Open All year.
Rooms 4 suites, 21 doubles, all with private bath and/or shower, telephone, radio, TV, desk, air-conditioning, ceiling fan. Rooms in two separate townhouses.
Facilities Dining room, sitting room. Courtyard patio, swimming pool, hot tub. Off-street parking, $5.50 daily. 24-hour concierge and beverage service.
Location Just behind the Esplanade border of French Quarter (eastern side); across from the Old US Mint at Esplanade and Decatur.
Restrictions No children between the ages of 3 and 14.
Credit cards Amex, MC, Visa.
Rates B&B, $99 suite, $64–79 double or single. Additional person in room, $17. 10% senior discount. Prix fixe lunch, $6.50. Alc dinner, $16. Packages available.
Extras Ramps, large bath available for wheelchair accessibility. Small, well-behaved pets permitted. Cribs available. French spoken.

Lamothe House
621 Esplanade Avenue 70116

Tel: (504) 947–1161
(800) 367–5858

Lamothe House was built in 1830 by Jean Lamothe, a wealthy sugar planter from the West Indies. The hotel's courtyard still has the original flagstones, which were imported as ships' ballast. The original double townhouse had a porte cochere leading to the courtyard, but in 1860 this was converted to twin stairways, and the hand-carved Corinthian columns were added. The inn has been owned since 1986 by Susan and Bill Prentiss, and a number of the rooms have been redecorated and updated under their management.

Rates include a breakfast of croissants, juice, tea and coffee, evening port, and coffee, morning newspaper, bathroom toiletries, and nightly pralines.

"Manager of the Maison de Ville before buying the Lamothe House, Bill Prentiss really loves this place, and has an extraordinary eye for detail. The entire inn is done in genuine Victorian furnishings, authentic to the period and of very good quality. First-floor suites are huge and gorgeous. The third-floor suites are somewhat smaller, but are lovely. Plans are underway to remodel the carriage house suites. The patio has lots of greenery, and the free on-site parking is a real plus. The inn sits on a pretty, quiet, boulevard, at the eastern edge of the French Quarter. If you really like Victorian furniture and antiques, it's the best place to stay in New Orleans." *(SHW)*

"The suites in the main house are spectacular and comfortable double parlors. The sitting areas have authentic Victorian furniture that is actually comfortable to sit on! There are no reproductions; all furniture is authentic antique." *(Caroline Weintz)* "The inn is near the Mint Museum and the

French Market. Breakfast was good, the service attentive, and the innkeepers were very nice." *(Laurie & Bruce Ford)* A few minor negatives: "Our lovely suite was over the garage, and the noise of the garage door opening was bothersome." And: "The regular doubles here are very tight, with small baths. Although the three-way bulbs are a help, some rooms have rather dark furnishings and wall treatments—accentuated, perhaps, by the dark rainy weather during our visit."

Open All year.
Rooms 9 suites, 11 doubles, all with private bath and/or shower, telephone, radio, TV, air-conditioning. All suites with desk. 2 suites, 4 doubles in annex.
Facilities Dining room, small courtyard, free on-site parking.
Location Eastern boundary of French Quarter, between Royal and Chartres sts. 7 blocks from Jackson Square. Take I-10 to Esplanade exit.
Restrictions No smoking in common rooms.
Credit cards Amex, MC, Visa.
Rates B&B, $165–225 suite, $85–105 double or single. Extra person in room, $15.
Extras Cribs, babysitting available. French, Spanish spoken.

Pontchartrain Hotel *Tel:* (504) 524–0581
2031 St. Charles Avenue 70140 (800) 777–1700

Small and elegant, the Pontchartrain was built in 1927, and was *the* place to stay in New Orleans for many years. The hotel was becoming shabby when new owner David Burrus treated it to a million dollar plus restoration, with first rate results, according to our readers.

"One of the nicest small hotels I have ever visited. Each room is different and delightful. Each floor has nine rooms, and the suites are unusually large with living room, dining area, study, large bathroom and dressing area, and bedroom. The decor in the suites varies from library paneling and English antiques, to chintz and wall-to-wall carpeting, to a bathroom of brown marble, with a copper sink and a bidet. Most of the regular rooms have tole flower paintings on the doors, with dressers and headboards to match. The small doubles face the rear for an unattractive view; suites overlook St. Charles Avenue and the streetcar. Our room had such luxuries as triple-sheeted king-size beds, Neutrogena bathroom amenities, overnight shoe shines, turndown service with petit fours left on the pillow, and three morning papers. Our room was very quiet, even though it was right next to the elevator. The personnel were friendly and attentive—most knew our names and the elevator men knew our floor immediately. Everyone was so accommodating and caring. The hotel was both luxurious yet comfortable and homey. We hated to leave." *(Susan Waller Schwemm)*

Open All year.
Rooms 36 suites, 64 doubles—all with private bath and/or shower, telephone, radio, TV, desk, air-conditioning.
Facilities Restaurants, bar, courtyard.
Location Garden District. 5 min. from French Quarter, business district.
Credit cards Amex, DC, MC, Visa.
Rates Room only, $175–375 suite, $105–135 double, $75–105 single. Extra person in room, $17.50. Summer family rates. Alc breakfast $6, alc lunch $12; alc dinner $15–40.
Extras Spanish, French, German spoken. Cribs, babysitting available. Airport pick-ups; complimentary limo service to downtown, university, and medical center areas.

SAINT FRANCISVILLE 70775   Map 6

St. Francisville is in the heart of Plantation Country, an area much favored by Audubon when he worked in this area during the 1820s, living at Oakley Plantation. With one of the inns below as your base, you can explore the area's historic plantations, wandering slowly through air scented by magnolia and cypress. For those who'd rather focus on the present, there's excellent hunting and fishing in season on the rivers off the Mississippi.

Reader tip: "St. Francisville is worth a two-day visit. The historic section is sparkling clean, with pretty gardens and many renovated homes and shops. Nearby are two outstanding plantations open to visitors: Rosedown and Greenwood" *(Norman & Catherine Ronneberg)*

St. Francisville is set on the Mississippi River, 25 miles north of Baton Rouge and 60 miles south of Natchez, MS, via Highway 61. **Also recommended:** The **Cottage Plantation** (Route 5, Box 425, on U.S. Highway 61; 504–635–3674), built from 1795 to the 1850s and furnished with antiques, is like a step back in time. A restaurant has recently opened in the restored house that originally belonged to the plantation cook, Mattie; specialities include crawfish and a variety of shrimp and chicken dishes. The **St. Francisville Inn** (118 North Commerce Street, P.O. Box 1369; 504–635–6502), originally the Wolf-Schlesinger House and restored in 1984, has a spectacular parlor ceiling medallion decorated with Mardi Gras masks. The owners, Florence and Dick Fillet, pride themselves on their warm hospitality, good food, and reasonable prices.

Barrow House   *Tel:* (504) 635–4791
524 Royal Street, P.O. Box 1461

Built in the saltbox style in 1809 with a Greek Revival wing added in the 1850s, Barrow House is listed on the National Register of Historic Places and is furnished in 1860s antiques. Rates include a continental breakfast; a choice of four New Orleans' breakfasts are available for $5 extra.

"Our delightful stay started with iced tea (or wine) on the screened porch, while we watched the cardinals, finches, and sparrows feeding outside. Dinner was served in the formal dining room at a table beautifully set with crystal, silver, candles, and fresh flowers. Shirley is a gourmet cook; we enjoyed phyllo pastries stuffed with crabmeat, shrimp and crayfish salad, chicken with rice, and strawberry crêpes and praline parfaits. Thoroughly stuffed and satisfied, we enjoyed visiting with owners Shirley and Lyle Dittloff. In the morning, after a delicious continental breakfast of juice, fresh fruit compote, homemade muffins, and coffee, we set out to tour this little town. Shirley armed us with a map and cassette player and walking tour tape, and we spent a wonderful morning seeing (and hearing about) the sights—from the historic bank with its stained-glass windows to the fascinating graveyard of the Grace Episcopal Church." *(Beverly Simmons, also Janet Turnbull)*

Open All year. Closed Dec. 22–25.
Rooms 1 suite, 4 doubles—3 with private bath and/or shower, 2 with maximum of 4 people sharing bath. All with TV, air-conditioning; 2 with desk.

Facilities Dining room, living room, screened porch. 1 acre with camellia collection. Golf nearby.
Location In town, behind the courthouse.
Restrictions "Well-behaved children welcome."
Credit cards None accepted.
Rates B&B, $80 suite, $55 double, $40 single. Extra person in room, $8. Full breakfast, $5 extra. Prix fixe lunch, $10; prix fixe dinner, $15. "Special Occasions" package.
Extras Port-a-crib available.

We Want to Hear from You!

As you know, this book is only effective with your help. We really need to know about your experiences and discoveries.

If you stayed at an inn or hotel listed here, we want to know how it was. Did it live up to our description? Exceed it? Was it what you expected? Did you like it? Were you disappointed? Delighted?

Have you discovered new establishments that we should add to the next edition?

Tear out one of the report forms at the back of this book (or use your own stationery if you prefer) and write today. Even if you write only "Fully endorse existing entry" you will have been most helpful.

Thank You!

Key to Abbreviations

For complete information and explanations, please see the Introduction.

Rates: Range from least expensive room in low season to most expensive room in peak season.
Room only: No meals included; sometimes referred to as European Plan (EP).
B&B: Bed and breakfast; includes breakfast, sometimes afternoon/evening refreshment.
MAP: Modified American Plan; includes breakfast and dinner.
Full board: Three meals daily.
Alc lunch: À la carte lunch; average price of entrée plus nonalcoholic drink, tax, tip.
Alc dinner: Average price of three-course dinner, including half bottle of house wine, tax, tip.
Prix fixe dinner: Three- to five-course set dinner, excluding wine, tax, tip unless otherwise noted.
Extras: Noted if available. Always confirm in advance. Pets are not permitted unless specified.
Zip codes: If only one zip code applies, it is listed with the town name. If there is more than one, it is noted as part of the address.

Maine

Captain Jefferds Inn, Kennebunkport

Coastal Maine has long been one of the foremost tourist areas in the Northeast, with its striking rock cliffs and innumerable coves and sheltered inlets. The coastline is so curving, in fact, that it supposedly twists through 3,000 miles to cover a distance of 240 miles as the crow flies. Inland Maine brings other, quieter pleasures of wooded mountains and peaceful lakes. The Lakes Region, about 100 miles northwest of Portland, in the White Mountains along the New Hampshire border, combines relatively easy accessibility with inviting small towns and villages. North of Route 2, the (human) population density diminishes rapidly, with the exception of winter visitors tackling the challenging ski slopes at Sugarloaf, or those making the pilgrimage to Baxter State Park and Mt. Katahdin, northern terminus of the Appalachian Trail.

By the way, if you've ever wondered why the natives (Maine-iacs?) refer to going "Down East" when the rest of the world thinks of it as "up north," we're glad to report that it dates to sailing days, when coastal winds made the trip from Boston to Bar Harbor an easy trip "Down East."

Peak season in Maine is very short—late June through Labor Day weekend—and rates are significantly higher during these months. Two-night to three-night minimum stays on weekends and holidays are the rule. Many coastal inns are open only from May through October, although a few stay in operation year-round. If you can get away in September, the chances are you'll have great weather and fewer crowds. Rates at most coastal inns are lower in May, June, September, and October, and are lowest during the winter months. Maine's 5% sales tax is not included in the rates quoted.

BAR HARBOR 04609 — Map 1

Bar Harbor is Mt. Desert Island's main town. It's where you'll find most of the island's shops and restaurants; in season (mid-May to mid-October), it's the center for a wide variety of shows, lectures, festivals, and theater. From the center of town, it's a short drive to the Blue Nose Ferry to Nova Scotia, and to Acadia National Park. The Bangor Airport is 45 miles to the northwest, and Boston is about a 5-hour drive.

Most of the island is occupied by Acadia National Park, a Rockefeller legacy of breathtaking beauty. From the top of Cadillac Mountain, to the road along the shore, you'll find extraordinary vistas at every turn. The park is honeycombed with innumerable trails for hiking and wide carriage paths for jogging, strolling, horseback riding, bicycling, and cross-country skiing. Unfortunately, it's hardly a secret: Acadia is the second-most-visited national park, after the Smokies. August is the busiest month; if you can visit the area in June, or better yet, in September, you'll avoid most of the crowds and still have good weather. Aside from the park, area activities include golf, tennis, swimming, as well as whale watching and kayaking.

"Especially recommended is eating at one of the lobster pounds on the island. You pick out a lobster and it is cooked right in front of you. You then proceed with your plate out to picnic tables on the pier, piled high with lobster traps, and surrounded by lobster boats. A real New England experience. We also suggest getting up very early to see the sunrise at the top of Cadillac Mountain—they say it's the first place in the U.S. from which to view the dawn—and returning at night with a bottle of wine and a hunk of cheese to enjoy the sunset." *(SP)*

Also recommended: The **Black Friar Inn** (10 Summer Street; 207–288–5091) is a three-story house built in 1910, set back a short block from one of Bar Harbor's main streets. Restored with all new plumbing and wiring, the inn combines the best of old and new, and is owned by delightful and accommodating Jim and Barbara Kelly. The **Graycote Inn** (40 Holland Avenue; 207–288–3044) combines a light fresh country decor with a location that's both central and quiet.

For additional area listings, see the entries under **Southwest Harbor**.

The Bayview *Tel:* (207) 288–5861
111 Eden Street Outside ME: (800) 356–3585

Owned by John E. Davis, Jr., for nearly 25 years, The Bayview is made up of a 6-room inn, a 26-room hotel, and six 2- and 3-bedroom town houses.

"This is the former vacation home of well-to-do Houstonians, and its atmosphere is much like that of a private home. It's a Georgian mansion on the rugged coast near the ferry terminal (but without a view of it), surrounded by trees, and far enough off the road to be quiet. When we were there a fire was lit and the guests were playing the piano—a very relaxed atmosphere in an elegant setting. Our room was originally a child's room, small but completely refurbished, with all the amenities. Our friends had what must have been the master suite—huge, with an old-fashioned, deep bathtub. Good lighting and electric blankets.

"Our room in the hotel was well appointed and had a great view of the water and of the *Blue Nose Ferry*, sounding its horn each morning on its way to Nova Scotia. The inn portion of The Bayview looks very nice as well; we toured all the rooms and learned its history from the innkeepers. Several intimate dining rooms—the college-age waiters were pleasant and fun, and the food was very good." *(Susie Preston)*

Open May through Oct.
Rooms 38 doubles, suites—all with full private bath, telephone, radio, desk. Hotel rooms with TV. 6 rooms in inn, 26 doubles in hotel. 6 2–3 bedroom townhouses with whirlpool tub, laundry, TV.
Facilities Dining rooms, parlor with Steinway piano, bar/lounge with weekend entertainment, exercise room. 8 acres with croquet, heated pool; on ocean. Island tours.
Location Near ferry terminal. ½ m to town. Coming into Bar Harbor on Rte. 3, the Bayview is on left approx. 200 yds. after ferry terminal.
Restrictions No children under 12 in inn.
Credit cards All major credit cards accepted.
Rates Room only, $200–425 townhouse (sleeps 4–6 people), $55–200 double. Extra person in room, $20. Crib, $10. Alc breakfast, $4–8; alc lunch, $9; alc dinner, $25. Weekly rates. 2-night minimum stay, inn and townhouses. Package, special event rates.
Extras Airport/station pickups. Wheelchair accessible; some bathrooms specially equipped for the handicapped. Cribs, babysitting available.

Hearthside Inn
7 High Street

Tel: (207) 288–4533

Barry and Susan Schwartz bought the Hearthside, originally built as a doctor's home and office at the turn of the century, in 1987. After months of painting, wallpapering, and redecorating, plus building several brand-new private baths, they reopened the inn as a very clean and inviting place, decorated with both antiques and contemporary pieces. Three years later, Susan and Barry report that they still love being innkeepers.

Well located on a quiet side street, yet still near the center of town, it's just a few doors down from the Ridgeway Cottage Inn. In summer, Susan's homemade breakfast includes hot and cold cereals, juice, fruit, muffins and breads, jams and jellies; in the winter, she adds eggs, omelets, French toast, or waffles to fortify cross-country skiers. Afternoon tea and cookies and evening wine and cheese are also provided.

"Barry and Susan are great hosts and great people. It's clear that they enjoy what they're doing from their attention to every detail. Susan's breakfasts are delicious, and the quiet but central location is ideal." *(Louis & Jill Vales, also Hannah & Mort Cooper)*

Open All year.
Rooms 9 doubles—7 with private bath and/or shower, 2 with maximum of 4 people sharing bath. All with fan. 2 with fireplace.
Facilities Living room with fireplace, books, games. Dining room, porch, patio.
Location From Rte. 3, go left on Mt. Desert St., left again on High St. to inn on left.
Restrictions No smoking. No children under 10.
Credit cards MC, Visa.
Rates B&B, $50–95 double. Extra person in room, $15. 2-night minimum July, Aug.
Extras Airport/station/ferry pickups.

The Inn at Canoe Point
Hull's Cove, Box 216

Tel: (207) 288–9511

"At first, all you see of the inn is a tasteful sign on a road flanked only by woodsy scenery—no building of any kind, just the beginning of an inviting little road beyond which you can see glimpses of water. Turning in, you come to the inn at the end of the road, a century-old house set in the pines and rocks just above the water. Proprietor Don Johnson is a very able and cordial innkeeper. Despite the fact that he does nearly all the cooking, cleaning, and handy work, he always seemed to have time to visit with his guests and make suggestions when asked, never seeming hurried or harried. Each room is different, but all are lovely. Each has a wine decanter and two glasses on a tray, fresh flowers, and comforters on the beds. Bathrooms are equipped with thick, thirsty towels. Guests tend to congregate in the Ocean Room where Don serves the most delectable full breakfasts imaginable. A sectional sofa with lots of pillows faces the roaring fire. There are books to browse, chocolates in little bowls, and the water side deck for sunning. We walked on the beach and through the woods, yet were still close to Acadia National Park and the bustle of town." *(Mrs. James Todd)*

Open All year.
Rooms 3 suites, 3 doubles—all with private shower and/or bath. 1 with fireplace.
Facilities Living room with fireplace, ocean room with fireplace, library, deck. 2 acres on waterfront.
Location 2 m from Bar Harbor, 1 m from Bluenose Ferry. From Ellsworth, take Rte. 3 approx. 15 m to Bar Harbor. Just beyond the village of Hulls Cove, watch for entrance to Acadia National Park on right. ¼ m past entrance, watch for inn driveway on left.
Restrictions No children under 12.
Credit cards None accepted.
Rates B&B, $75–160 suite, $55–100 double. Extra person in room, $10.

The Ledgelawn Inn
66 Mount Desert Street

Tel: (207) 288–4596

The Ledgelawn was built in 1904 in the colonial Revival style as a summer "cottage" for a wealthy Bostonian. The interior proportions are gracious, and most of the furnishings are original. (Longtime owners Nancy and Michael Miles have added lots of comfortable chairs and couches.)

Rates include a breakfast buffet of sliced meats, hard-boiled eggs, yogurt, cereal, fruit, breads, jams, coffee; tea in season; and a smaller continental breakfast off season. Most rooms are quite luxurious, but some of the rooms in the original inn are smaller or are more simply furnished; these are less expensive and are often favored by families and budget travelers. The carriage house, although built to complement the architecture of the inn, is actually a new building, with all modern amenities. Rooms have queen-size beds, quality reproduction furnishings, and "country" decor, and baths have either Jacuzzi tubs or steam showers.

"We felt we had stepped back in time to the days when very wealthy people summered in Bar Harbor. The inn is impressive, with its beautiful, old-fashioned decor. It's centrally located, within walking distance of the town. The back of the inn is wooded, with a swimming pool, and the front faces a beautiful tree-lined street." *(Rebecca E. Corey, also SWS)*

Open April through Nov.
Rooms 3 suites, 36 doubles—all with private bath and/or shower. Most with telephone, TV, desk, air-conditioning. Rooms in 3 buildings: inn, carriage house, mansion. 18 rooms with working fireplaces; many with whirlpool tub, sauna, or steam shower, screened porches.
Facilities Living room, bar with fireplace, porches, veranda, widow's walk, gift shop. Hot tub, swimming pool. Tennis privileges at Bar Harbor Club.
Location On Rte. 3, 3 blocks from town.
Restrictions Smoking discouraged.
Credit cards MC, Visa.
Rates B&B, $175 suite, $90–155 double. Extra adult in room, $15; children 4–12, $8; no charge for children under 4. Off-season rates.
Extras Airport/ferry pickups. Minimal Italian, Portuguese, French, German spoken. Cribs available.

BELFAST 04915   Map 1

Settled in 1773, Belfast prospered through much of the nineteenth century from the fishing and shipbuilding industries. Well-to-do captains (of both sea and industry) built handsome houses for their families, and their legacy of historic homes in all styles from Greek Revival to Italianate to Queen Anne makes a walking tour of town a real pleasure.

Located in mid-coastal Maine, Belfast is set on Penobscot Bay, and provides a good base for touring many area attractions. It's approximately 55 miles east of Augusta and west of Bangor, and 100 miles northeast of Portland. There's a park nearby with a swimming pool, tennis courts, playground, and a rocky beach for swimming; other outdoor activities include fishing, horseback riding, and cross-country skiing.

Also recommended: The **Jeweled Turret Inn** (16 Pearl Street; 207–338–2304) is a restored Victorian home with many unusual architectural details, warm and gracious hosts, and hearty yet creative breakfasts, and very reasonable rates.

Penobscot Meadows Inn   *Tel:* (207) 338–5320
Route 1

Dini and Bernie Chapnick renovated this turn-of-the-century Victorian in 1984, adding modern baths and decorating with antiques. Dini notes that while they want families to be comfortable, the inn is not a "kid's place." Weather permitting, dinner is served on the deck overlooking Penobscot Bay. Under the supervision of chef Kate Hanbury, the food is "worth a detour" according to most guests. Menus change with the seasons— winter entrées might include pork stuffed with sage sausage, or lasagna with seafood and red and white sauces; homemade ice cream and six-layer cakes are the featured desserts. Rates include a continental breakfast; brunch is served on Sunday.

"This inn was refurbished with guests' comfort in mind, including such details as the clean private baths and the excellent fire alarm system. Dini and Bernie (retired after twenty years in the Foreign Service) are very comfortable, casual, intelligent people; Dini has a great dry sense of humor. Rooms are simply decorated with shuttered windows, rag rugs, and handmade quilts. The wine list and menu are superb; try the veal or scallops and don't pass up the homemade chocolate ice cream with walnuts. The coffee and conversation can't be beaten." *(Pat Lewis)*

Open All year. Restaurant closed Tues., after Labor Day until July 1.
Rooms 1 efficiency apt., 6 doubles—all with private bath and/or shower, radio. 2 with desk.
Facilities Restaurant, parlor with TV, fireplace, board games; deck. 5½ acres.
Location Mid-coastal ME. Penobscot Bay. 100 m NE of Portland. On Rte. 1, just S of town.
Credit cards Discover, MC, Visa.
Rates B&B, $89 efficiency, $39–$79 double. Alc dinner, $25. Extra person in room, $5. 20% discount for weekly stays.
Extras Pets permitted with advance notice. Airport/station pickups. Wheelchair accessibility in restaurant only. Cribs available.

BLUE HILL 04614   Map 1

Blue Hill is an old shipping town on the east coast of the Penobscot peninsula, bordering magnificent Blue Hill Bay, on the other side of which is Acadia National Park. It's 40 miles south of Bangor and an easy drive to Bar Harbor, Camden, and Rockport. Blue Hill is popular with hikers, bikers, and sailors. Summertime brings first-rate concerts to Kneisel Hall.

Also recommended: The **Blue Hill Farm Inn** (Route 15, P.O. Box 437; 207–374–5126) is comprised of a century-old house and renovated barn, furnished with antiques, and highlighted with flowers and patchwork quilts. Rates include continental breakfast and afternoon tea and cookies. The **John Peters Inn** (Peters Point, P.O. Box 916; 207–374–2116) is an elegant 1815 brick mansion listed on the National Register of Historic Places; the decor is antique, the breakfast, elaborate six-course affairs.

The Blue Hill Inn   *Tel:* (207) 374–2844
Route 177, P.O. Box 403

A visit to the Blue Hill Inn in 1990 will give you a chance to share in the inn's sesquicentennial celebration—it's been an inn since 1840. Owned by Don and Mary Hartley since 1987, this brick and clapboard structure is decorated with antiques and period reproductions. Guests all remark on the inn's dinners, finding both the quality of the food and the atmosphere to be exceptional. Lobster is almost always available as an alternative to the evening entrée in season (May to October) and a typical menu might include hazelnut and morel soup finished with Marsala, Maine crabmeat with lemon and capers, Cointreau sorbet, rack of lamb with garlic and rosemary, sweet potato squash purée, watercress and tomato salad vinaigrette, and flourless chocolate torte with coffee cream.

"This building's long history as an inn somehow gives it a feeling that you don't often get in a conversion, no matter how well done. The differing levels of the floors and ceilings are a great part of its charm. At 6 P.M. guests gather in the sitting room to have cocktails in front of the fire, (or in the garden in summer) and nibble on cheese and crackers. It is so warm and friendly that there are introductions all around and the weekend soon seems like a country house party of old friends. At 7 P.M. Mary called us into the dining room, and after seating us, welcomed us and gave us a detailed description of the six-course set menu. Though there are tables for two and four, the most fun is sitting at the table for eight. The guests came from all over, a very stimulating and compatible group. An authentic touch—the chandelier in the dining room is lit with real candles." *(Judith Brannon & Larry Machum)*

Open All year. Restaurant closed mid-week Mar., April.
Rooms 3 suites, 8 doubles—all with private bath and/or shower, desk, fan. 5 with fireplace, 1 with air-conditioning.
Facilities Restaurant, parlor with fireplace, games. 1 acre with perennial gardens. Concert tickets, bike tours, sleigh rides, picnic day sails arranged. Cross-country skiing nearby.
Location Coastal ME. 40 m S of Bangor, 150 m N of Portland. 1 block from town center. At intersection of Rte. 15 and Rte. 177.
Restrictions No smoking. No children under 13.
Credit cards Amex, MC, Visa.
Rates B&B, $75–120 suite or double, $60–120 single. MAP, $120–160 suite or double, $80–140 single. Extra person in room, $20–40. 15% service. 2-night minimum July 1–Oct. 15. Prix fixe dinner (guest) $20, (public) $25. Box lunch by pre-arrangement.
Extras Airport/station pickups, nominal fee. Limited wheelchair access.

BOOTHBAY HARBOR 04538

The Howard House　　　　　　　　　　　　　*Tel:* (207) 633–3933
Route 27

The Howard House is a contemporary barn-shaped structure, with natural wood siding, sliding glass doors, skylights, and balconies, set on a large lawn with lots of trees. Many of the spacious rooms have wood paneling and high beamed ceilings. The furnishings are mostly comfortable colonial maple reproductions.

"Howard House is located in a rural setting about halfway between Boothbay and Boothbay Harbor, free of all traffic noises. It is quiet, yet provides easy access to the many picturesque villages in the area. Ginny and Jim Farrin are warm and friendly hosts, providing spacious, clean rooms at modest prices." *(Henry Hubbard, Jr.)* "Plumbing is A1, with all modern sparkling bathrooms." *(Mr. & Mrs. R. Butler)*

"Ginny Farrin even took the time to give us elaborate directions to a special playground in the next town for our three-year-old." *(Kirsten Miller)*

"Our spacious room was simply decorated, but had a great king-sized bed. Ginny Farrin couldn't have been more accommodating, helping out with sightseeing maps and restaurant menus. Her hot muffins and breads were delicious." *(Mrs. James Todd)*

Open Mid.-Feb.to Dec. 1.
Rooms 15 double rooms—all with full private bath, balcony, TV, desk. 10 with radio.
Facilities Breakfast room. Set on 20 wooded acres. 1 m from ocean. Tennis, golf nearby.
Location 60 m from Portland. 1 m from center of village. About halfway between Boothbay and Boothbay Harbor, on Rte. 27.
Restrictions No smoking in breakfast room.
Credit cards None accepted.
Rates B&B, $39–70 double, $33–69 single. Extra person in room, $7.
Extras 5 rooms equipped for disabled with ramps and wide entrance doors. Cribs, babysitting available.

Spruce Point Inn   *Tel:* (207) 633–4152

The Spruce Point is an old-time Maine family resort, with lots of activities for all, from swimming, fishing, tennis, sailing, and golf during the day, to dancing and movies at night. There's even the "exclusive" Penguin Club, whose membership is limited to those brave (crazy?) enough to swim in the ocean on three different days during their stay. Spruce Point is made up of a spreading old inn, surrounded by smaller lodges.

"The glorious setting—on a wooded pine peninsula overlooking the beautiful entrance to Boothbay Harbor, with lobster boats coming in and out, along with the pleasure craft coming and going from the inn's private dock—is just part of the charm and beauty of this peaceful spot. There are lovely trails to walk, along with a wide variety of other activities. Thursday night features the chef's gourmet buffet, an unforgettable dining experience. The inn with its adjacent lodges is superbly run, the cuisine is excellent, and the service near perfect. The lodges have units with a living room with fireplace, bedroom, small TV, refrigerator, and a lovely porch. The rooms in the main inn all have decks so one can enjoy the air and the view to the fullest. The owners, Charlotte and John Druce, are perfect hosts, offering warm and gracious hospitality we've not found duplicated anywhere." *(Anne L. Hogan)*

Open Mid-June to mid-Sept.
Rooms 13 suites, 57 doubles, 2 cabins—all with full private bath. Many with fireplaces, refrigerators or kitchenettes, porches. 12 with telephones, 18 with TV. 12 rooms in main inn, remainder in lodges, cabins. Several 1–3 bedroom condominiums with living room, kitchen, fireplace, porch, balcony, telephone, TV available also.
Facilities Dining rooms, bar/lounge with dancing, entertainment. 100 acres with 1 freshwater and 1 saltwater swimming pools, 3 tennis courts, 3 shuffleboard courts, putting green, croquet, horseshoes, badminton, boat rides, sailing, fishing, children's playground, rainy day children's programs, hiking trails. Golf nearby.
Location 2 m from town. At entrance to Boothbay Harbor.
Credit cards Amex, MC, Visa.
Rates MAP (all rates per person, late June through Labor Day), $94–119 double occupancy. MAP (mid-June to Sept.) $72–87 double occupancy. Extra adult in room, $30; child 5–16, $20; child under 4, free if no crib or cot required. Crib, $5; cot, $10. Room only, (sleeps 2–8) condominium, $185–395 in season. MAP available at $30 per person daily. 15% service additional. 3-night, weekly, package rates. Prix fixe breakfast, $6; prix fixe dinner, $20. Alc lunch, $9. Picnic lunch, $7.50.
Extras Babysitting available. French, German, Polish spoken. 1 suite accessible for disabled.

CAMDEN 04843   Map 1

Camden is one of Maine's most popular summer coastal resorts. It's about halfway up the coast, between Portland and Bar Harbor—40 miles east of Augusta, 185 miles northeast of Boston, and 414 miles northeast of New York City; take I-95 to Route 1, and follow it into the town.

A large village by Maine standards, Camden offers lots of shops and restaurants to explore (but don't expect to explore them alone, at least in summer). Summer activities include tennis, hiking, swimming, sailing, waterskiing, and picnicking. There are chamber music concerts and a resident theater. The Farnsworth Collection in nearby Rockport has a fine Andrew Wyeth collection. The harbor is filled with yachts and with the two-masted schooners of the windjammer fleet. In winter, there's ice-skating and cross-country and downhill skiing within 5 miles. The tops of the two mountains that rise over the town, Mt. Battie and Mt. Megunticook, offer beautiful views of Penobscot Bay.

Also recommended: The **Maine Stay** (22 High Street; 207–236–9636) is an old New England house, furnished with antiques; guests especially enjoy the hearty breakfast, served on the deck with views of Mt. Battie. **Mansard Manor** (15 High Street; 207– 236–3291) has the roof you'd expect from its name, and Victorian decor to match. Full breakfast is included in the reasonable rates.

Information please: If you'd like a century-old stone castle to call home—at least for the weekend—**Norumbega** may be just right. Elaborately towered and turreted, this luxurious inn offers views of the harbor and bay from rooms beautifully decorated in period; rates of $130–190 include a full breakfast and afternoon refreshments (61 High Street; 207–236–4646).

Edgecombe-Coles House   *Tel:* (207) 236–2336
64 High Street, P.O. Box 3010

Originally built as a private summer home in 1891, the Edgecombe-Coles House sits on a hillside overlooking Penobscot Bay, just a short walk to the Camden Harbor. The inn sits far back from the omnipresent noise of traffic behind an old stone wall and a wide expanse of lawn. Owners Terry and Louise Price renovated the inn several years ago, furnishing it with country antiques, original art, and Oriental rugs, with coordinating fabrics and wallpapers. Rates include a full breakfast of fruit and juice, eggs and home-baked goods served in the dining room, or a continental breakfast brought to your room or out onto the deck.

"The inn is charmingly furnished and immaculately kept. The Prices are the most charming and cordial of hosts. The other guests are always interesting and the inn has a real family feeling to it. The view from our window, of the bay and the autumn foliage was just perfect. Fabulous breakfasts." *(Sharon & Jack Timmer)*

Open All year.
Rooms 6 doubles—all with private bath, fan, 1 with fireplace, 4 with TV.

Facilities Dining room, living room with piano, library—all with fireplaces; wrap-around porch, deck. Lawn overlooks Penobscot Bay.

Location 1 m N of town center, on Rte. 1 (High St.).

Restrictions No children under 8. No smoking in common rooms.

Credit cards Amex, DC, MC, Visa.

Rates B&B, $70–145 double, $65–140 single. Extra person in room, $30. Off-season rates. 2-night minimum in high season and all holiday weekends. Tipping encouraged.

CENTER LOVELL 04016   Map 1

This remote hamlet is set in the foothills of the White Mountains of southwestern Maine, near the New Hampshire border. It's about 60 miles west of Portland, and 25 miles east of North Conway, New Hampshire.

In addition to all the outdoor pleasures of this area, bargain hunters will enjoy the factory outlets along routes 302 and 16 in nearby New Hampshire. Others will prefer to avoid this stretch at all costs!

Also recommended: Music buffs will love **Quisisana** (Pleasant Point Road, off Route 5; 207–925–3500 or in winter, 914–833–0293); its rustic cottages are set beside Lake Kezar, and the staff are all top music students, who perform for guests nightly.

Westways on Kezar Lake   *Tel:* (207) 928–2663
Route 5, Box 175

A rustic, well-weathered shingled lodge, Westways was built over sixty years ago as a corporate retreat for the owners and employees of the Diamond Match Company. It has been owned by a group of Boston investors since 1970, and is managed by Nancy Tripp. The living room decor contains down-stuffed furniture, hand-carved oak tables, California red pine paneling, and a large fieldstone fireplace. Bedrooms are spacious, supplied with books guests have been reading since the lodge was built in the twenties. In addition to all the activities available on the lake, Westways offers a variety of indoor options for those inevitable rainy summer days. Dinner menus change daily; a possible meal might include sautéed mushrooms, chilled blueberry soup, salad, fresh Maine seafood of the day, and Aunt Effa's sour cream raisin pie.

"Westways has all the niceties of a first-class inn: beautifully appointed, diverse, and carefully maintained premises, superb food (including an out-of-this-world cheesebread), meticulous attention to service and cleanliness." *(Steven B. Singer)*

"Rustic but idyllic. Not luxurious but carefully kept. Our room was large and comfortable, but had a limited view and was noisy because of the kitchen nearby. I'll request a lake view room next time. Stronger lights for reading would also be a helpful improvement. Cocktails in the boat house, watching the sun set over Kezar Lake gives a sense of beauty and peace that's hard to find elsewhere. The lake is lovely because it is very residential and not built up like some of the bigger lakes, and the inn's activities are great fun." *(YP)*

Open May through Oct.; Dec. through March. Restaurant closed Mon., Tues., in winter.

Rooms 7 doubles—3 with private bath, 4 with maximum of 2 people sharing hall baths. 6 3- to 7-bedroom cottages, most with fireplace or woodstove, porch; 3 with laundry. All with desk.

Facilities Restaurant, living room, library, recreation room with games, bowling alley, billiards, Ping-Pong; boathouse. 120 acres on Kezar Lake. Swimming, tennis, fishing, canoes, sailboats, hiking, handball, baseball, cross-country skiing. Golf, downhill skiing nearby.

Location 7 m N of Lovell village; 3 m N of Center Lovell. Take 302 W into Lovell village, turn left at stop sign, then turn right at the Yield sign (Rte. 5). Proceed 7 m N to Westways sign and turn left.

Restrictions No smoking in some cottages.

Credit cards Amex, MC, Visa.

Rates Room only, $80–125 double, $70–95 single. MAP, $130–175 double, $95–120 single, plus 15% service. Extra adult in room, $30–50 (MAP); child under 12 in parents' room, $20–30. Weekly rates. 2-night minimum in some rooms. Cottage, room only, $750–1,500 weekly; security deposit, $300–600. Box lunches with advance notice. Alc dinner, $32.

Extras Pets permitted in some cottages only. Cribs, babysitting available.

DEER ISLE 04683   Map 1

Deer Isle is an unspoiled island in Penobscot Bay with 100 miles of road leading to the villages of Deer Isle, Sunset, Sunshine, and Stonington Harbor. There are many antique and craft shops; activities include hiking, swimming, boating, bird-watching, deep-sea fishing, golf, tennis, and musical and theatrical events. For a look at some first-rate craftspeople at work, visit the Haystack Mountain School of Crafts, where master craftsmen conduct workshops in blacksmithing, weaving, pottery, and glass.

Information please: We'd like to request reports on the **Inn at Ferry Landing,** an antique-filled inn recently restored by Stephen and Donna Ghormley. Before the suspension bridge to the mainland was built, this 1850s farmhouse served as the general store and docking facility for the ferry, and offers beautiful water views (108 Old Ferry Road, RR 1, Box 163; 207–348–7760).

Deer Isle is located in mid-coastal Maine, 60 miles south of Bangor and 280 miles northeast of Boston, and is accessible by bridge. To get there, take I-95 to Bangor, then go south on Route 15 through Blue Hill to Deer Isle.

Pilgrim's Inn   *Tel:* (207) 348–6615

The Pilgrim's Inn is a 200-year-old inn listed on the National Register of Historic Places. We continue to receive a number of unusually enthusiastic, articulate, and detailed reports about this establishment—its longtime owners, Jean and Dud Hendrick, its rooms, and especially the food. All raved about the delicious hors d'oeuvres, fabulously fresh fruits and vegetables, original recipes, attractive presentation, and good service (dinner nightly at seven). Breakfasts come in for similar plaudits, especially the homemade granola and yogurt, and fresh Maine blueberries.

"I have been searching for the Ventana East and found it here. While the

Ventana (in Big Sur) is true California, the Pilgrim's is real old New England. Part of the genius of the place is the famous hors d'oeuvres and cocktail hour. Not only are they fabulous—much of the atmosphere generated carries through your stay. Dud is so friendly and such a good host that the spirit is catching. The dinner service in the lovely rustic dining room is very well engineered. Everyone is seated at the same time, but service is so efficient that you never feel neglected. Our room was light and airy with country furniture, Laura Ashley fabrics and *good lamps*. Why do other country inns think they need to use 40-watt bulbs to maintain a gaslight atmosphere? Our bathroom was modern, comfortable and cheery." *(Pamela Young)*

"Fresh breads (whole wheat and orange), wonderful soups, great salads with interesting dressing, beef Wellington Saturday nights, lobster bake once a week, wonderful salmon recipe . . . and what desserts! Tarts, mousses, different every night." Also: "The soups are divine. In spring, when the fiddleheads are growing, we are treated to Jean's special way of preparing them. If you haven't had Queen Mother's Cake, you haven't lived." Yet: "Even after four or five courses, you don't feel 'overstuffed.' "

"If it's 'New England' you want, this is the inn. Small and cozy in a most spectacular setting—out one window is the mill pond, out another is an inlet leading to the sea. It's a short drive to Stonington, where you can catch the mail boat to Isle au Haut. This island has miles of gentle hiking trails. From the top of the hill you can look out over Penobscot Bay. Ask Jean the night before, and she'll pack you a box lunch the likes of which you've never had before!" *(Annie & Andy Stickney)*

"The atmosphere is very quiet and understated. You immediately feel welcome and at home. Everything is run very efficiently, and any member of the staff will be glad to help you with any request. The rooms are large, furnished comfortably in period, and despite the age of the building, fairly quiet." *(Linda Moran)*

Open Mid-May to mid-Oct.
Rooms 1 cottage with 1½ baths, 12 doubles—7 with private bath and/or shower, 5 with maximum of 4–5 people sharing bath. All with air-conditioning.
Facilities Dining room, parlor, library, 2 common rooms with fireplaces, tap room, games, books; bicycles. Patio with barbecue. 2 acres, leading to water. Sailing, swimming beach, 2½ m.
Location In Deer Isle village.
Restrictions Smoking in common rooms only. No children under 10.
Credit cards None accepted.
Rates All rates per person. MAP, $65–75 double. Extra person in room, $40. $20 deducted for those not eating dinner, $5 deducted for those not eating breakfast. 12% service additional. 10% senior discount. Prix fixe dinner, $20. Picnic lunches on request. Cottage, $125 daily without meals, $175 with meals; extra person in cottage, $20. 3-night minimum stay in August. Weekly rates.
Extras 1st-floor rooms wheelchair accessible by ramp. Airport pickups from Bangor, $50 one way.

FREEPORT 04032 Map 1

Many travelers feel that a visit to Maine is incomplete without a stop at L.L. Bean, the famous supplier of clothing and gear for outdoorsmen and, more recently, preppies. Over the past few years other retailers have noticed the number of shoppers passing through Freeport, and the result has been a transformation of this quiet town into a shopper's mecca. Dansk, Anne Klein, Ralph Lauren, White Stag, Stanley Roberts, Cole Hahn, Frye Boot, Post Horn, and Sawyer Sheepskin are just a few of the companies that have opened factory outlet stores within walking distance of L.L. Bean. To rephrase a well-known saying: "When the going gets tough, the tough go shopping—in Freeport." Or so it will seem if you ever attempt a summer weekend stroll on Main Street's people-packed sidewalks.

Freeport is close to Wolf's Neck State Park for fishing, boating, and swimming; in winter, cross-country skiing is nearby as well. The town is in mid-coastal Maine, 16 miles north of Portland, 125 miles northeast of Boston, and 3 hours southwest of Bar Harbor.

Also recommended: If you're more in the mood for a small hotel than a B&B, the **Harraseeket Inn** (162 Main Street; 207–865–9377) combines country inn ambience with such extras as Jacuzzi tubs and steam showers, with fine dining in a full service restaurant. The **Isaac Randall House** (Independence Drive; 207–865–9295) is a Federal–style farmhouse, built over 160 years ago, and at one time was a stop on the Underground Railway, for slaves escaping to freedom in Canada. Guests gather in the kitchen for blueberry pancakes and lively discussions, and most rooms have antique decor.

Information please: The **Bagley House** (R.R. 3, Box 269C; 207–865–6566) is a fairly new B&B in a house dating back to 1772. Possibly the area's oldest home in the area, it served as an inn and schoolhouse; today its five guest rooms are furnished with antiques or custom-crafted reproductions, handmade quilts and stencilled rugs. Sig Knudson, the owner/innkeeper, a Freeport native, recently returned home after ten years working with the Inuit in Alaska. Rates are reasonable and Sig's breakfast are very filling.

181 Main Street
181 Main Street

Tel: (207) 865–1226

The Creech brothers, master mariners, built this Greek Revival-style home in the 1840s. When Ed Hasset and David Cates renovated it as a B&B in 1986, they selected 181 Main Street as the name—"Creech House" just did not strike the right note, they felt. After a hot summer's day of bargain hunting, travelers will enjoy the swimming pool in the inn's large and private backyard.

"Ed and David have done extensive renovations and restoration on this old cape-style home, just a few blocks north of the busy shopping area. The guest rooms are small but adequate and are decorated with either Victorian or colonial motifs; the private bath facilities are very nice. The common areas are all comfortable and inviting, well stocked with games, books, and magazines. A very generous and tasty full breakfast is served (with seconds offered), and special orders accommodated. The owners are very congenial and enthusiastically demonstrate the extra effort required to make their inn an especially good one." *(Janice & James Utt, also Mary Johnston, Wayne Vaundell)*

Open All year.
Rooms 7 doubles—all with private shower.
Facilities 2 dining rooms, library, parlor with TV, games. 1 acre with swimming pool. Off-street parking.
Location 2 min. walk to downtown. Take Exit 20 off I-95, go W to Main St. Go left (N) on Main St. to inn on left at corner of Maple.
Restrictions No smoking in guest rooms. No children under 10.
Credit cards MC, Visa.
Rates B&B, $89 double. Extra person in room, $15. 5% senior discount. Off-season rates.
Extras Airport/station pickups. French, some Spanish spoken.

KENNEBUNK BEACH 04043   **Map 1**

The Ocean View   *Tel:* (207) 967–2750
72 Beach Avenue

Bob and Carole Arena describe their B&B as being "the closest you'll find to a bed on the beach in the Kennebunks. Our beach cottage is not a New England mansion; it's light and airy, casual but not rustic." During the winter of 1988–1989, the Arenas added several new apartment suites and gave their home a "face lift." A typical breakfast might include strawberries with cream and a brioche with cheese, or broiled grapefruit with brown sugar and fruit pancakes.

"A terrific location, with cool ocean breezes on the hottest night. An early-morning walk along the beach is invigorating and tunes you up for the great breakfast, served in the glassed-in breakfast room. Service is excellent, rooms spotless. There's a good choice of books plus a large color TV, and an interesting boutique with unusual handmade items. Carole is very helpful about making dinner recommendations and reservations." *(Roy & Ruth Baltozer)*

"Our suite had a sitting room with a southern exposure while the bedroom had windows on three sides with a view from each. The Arenas have great personalities and really enjoy their guests. Breakfasts were different each morning of our seven-day stay. Plenty of quiet and privacy, and the beach across the street is perfect." *(Susan Prizio)* "Guests gather on the front porch to talk and watch the tide come in." *(Diane Phillips)*

Open April through Oct.
Rooms 5 suites, 4 doubles—7 with private bath and/or shower, 2 with maximum of 4 people sharing bath, sink in room. 4 suites in annex; with wet bar, TV, private porch.
Facilities Breakfast room, living room with fireplace, TV room, front porch, gift shop. Ocean frontage, sandy beaches.
Location SE ME, 85 m NE of Boston, 30 m SW of Portland. 1 m from Kennebunkport village.
Restrictions No smoking in guest rooms. No children under 12.
Credit cards MC, Visa.
Rates B&B, $90–125 suite, $65–95 double. 2-night weekend minimum. Extra person in room, $25. Weekly rates.
Extras Airport/station pickups.

KENNEBUNKPORT 04046   Map 1

Kennebunkport is one of Maine's most popular resort towns, located along the coast in the southwest corner of the state; it's also one of the most crowded during July and August. It has many sea captains' homes from the seventeenth and eighteenth centuries, as well as "cottages" built later by wealthy summer visitors. In addition to many fine gift and antique shops, art galleries, and restaurants, sights of interest include the Seashore Trolley Museum, the Brick Store Museum, and the Rachel Carson Wildlife Refuge. Visitors head to the beach for swimming, fishing, and boating; there are plenty of tennis courts in the area, and golf at the Cape Arundel course (also available for cross-country skiing in winter). Bicyclists can bring bikes along or rent them on arrival.

As much of America knows, Kennebunkport is the traditional summer home of President George Bush. Most of the townspeople are very proud of Bush, yet were relieved and grateful when he met with them to discuss his summer vacation plans. He was sensitive to the congestion which a peak-season presidential visit would cause—with squadrons of secret service agents and reporters—and basically promised not to do anything which would detract from the town's summer charms.

Also recommended: In nearby Kennebunk is the The **Kennebunk Inn** (45 Main Street, Kennebunk 04043; 207–985-3351), close to the turnpike, and recommended especially for its food; rooms vary greatly in size and decor. In Kennebunkport is **The Inn on South Street** (South Street, P.O. Box 478A; 207–967–5151) an intimate B&B in a early 1800s Greek Revival home, owned by long-time Kennebunkport residents; an elaborate breakfast is served, and rates include lots of extras.

Recommended too late for us to complete a full writeup is the **Green Heron Inn** (Ocean Avenue, P.O. Box 2578; 207–967–3315), a simple but homey guest house located near the mouth of the Kennebunk River, with a small beach for sunbathing. Rates are a reasonable $55–75 in season, including a cottage ideal for families. *(KJ)*

Kennebunkport is 264 miles northeast of New York City, 75 miles northeast of Boston, and 30 miles south of Portland. From I-95 (Maine Turnpike), take Exit 3 to Kennebunk, and turn south (left) on Route 35 into Kennebunkport.

Captain Jefferds Inn   *Tel:* (207) 967–2311
Pearl Street, Box 691

The Captain Jefferds is a 180-year-old Federal mansion; its longtime owner, Warren Fitzsimmons, has decorated the inn with a variety of fascinating pieces, from Italian terra-cotta wall plaques to pottery, antique quilts, art deco wicker, Oriental rugs, and shell tables, along with Laura Ashley wallcoverings and coordinated fabrics and linens—eclectic but very original and effective. Most of the collectibles are displayed in the common areas, leaving the bedrooms clean and uncluttered. You won't find at the inn any plastics or synthetics, which Warren can't abide. Blankets are wool, tubs and showers porcelain, and bathroom floors tiled in ceramic.

Rates include a full breakfast, served around the enormous dining room table; blueberry crêpes, Grand Marnier French toast, and eggs Benedict are all specialties. *(SWS)*

Open April through Oct.; Dec.
Rooms 3 suites, 12 doubles—all with private shower and/or bath, desk. Suites in separate carriage house; with living room, kitchen.
Facilities Dining room, living room with fireplace, grand piano; sun-room, terrace. 1 acre with gardens, croquet. ½ m to beach.
Location Historic district. In Kennebunkport, go left at traffic light, then over draw-bridge. Take right at monument to Ocean Ave. Travel on Ocean Ave. 5 short blocks and go left on one-way street. Go left at corner to Pearl St. and look for white fence.
Restrictions No arrivals after 8 p.m. No smoking in dining room. No children under 12.
Credit cards None accepted.
Rates B&B, $110–125 suite, $75–110 double. Extra person in room, $20. 2-night minimum, July–Oct.
Extras 2 bedrooms wheelchair accessible. Station pickups. French spoken. Pets permitted with prior approval.

Captain Lord Mansion
Tel: (207) 967–3141
Pleasant and Main streets, P.O. Box 800

Bev Davis and her husband Rick Litchfield escaped to Kennebunkport from the advertising world in 1978. They've devoted incredible amounts of time and energy to bringing the Captain Lord Mansion back to its nineteenth-century elegance, while adding the modern conveniences expected by today's travelers. This Federal mansion, which dates back to 1812 and is listed on the National Register of Historic Places, is truly spectacular both inside and out. Many of the house's original architectural features have been preserved; guest rooms are spacious, immaculately clean, and individually decorated with antiques and quality reproductions. Guests enjoy a breakfast of eggs, vanilla yogurt with fruit toppings, whipped butter, cream cheese, preserves, hot breads and muffins, juice, and coffee and tea, "served punctually at set times" in the large country kitchen, along with afternoon tea and sweets.

"A beautiful inn set on landscaped grounds. The rooms are big, with high ceilings and large windows—it must have seemed a veritable palace when it was built. The decor suits the house perfectly, without being tied to any particular period. One of the rooms is done largely in Oriental pieces, commemorating the good captain's many trips to the Far East. There are, of course, many antiques, along with (hallelujah) good reading lights, night tables, and comfortable chairs." *(SWS)*

"Thought you would like to know that we are in total agreement with previous reports on the Captain Lord. The bedrooms are 'the thing,' and are truly wonderful with quality antiques, four-poster beds, and a great number of working fireplaces. The bathrooms are not great—mostly small and very few with bathtubs, but one tends to overlook this. Eating breakfast at long tables in the big kitchen is a great way to meet people; the food is very informally served and it all is quite fun. The innkeeper is full of suggestions on places to go for dinner, the best being the White Barn." *(Judith Brannon)*

Open All year.

Rooms 24 rooms—22 double rooms—all with private bath and/or showers (3 baths are *very* small). Many with desk, radio, fireplace, fan. 2 luxury rooms in separate cottage with TV, telephone, whirlpool tubs.

Facilities Spacious gathering room with fireplace, games, puzzles; dining room; gift shop. 1 acre of lawns and gardens with outdoor furniture. Walking distance to ocean, short drive to beach. Golf nearby.

Location Walking distance to village shops and restaurants. In Kennebunkport, go left at light at Sunoco station, over drawbridge. Take 1st right on Ocean Ave., 5th left off Ocean Ave. to inn on left.

Restrictions No children. Smoking in guest rooms only. No cigars.

Credit cards Checks required for deposits; Discover, MC, Visa accepted for balance payment.

Rates B&B, $175–249 suite, $69–159 double. $3 additional daily charge for firewood. 10% discount for weekly stays; off-season midweek discounts. 2–3 night weekend/holiday minimum.

Extras Airport/station pickups. French spoken.

The Old Fort Inn
Old Fort Avenue, P.O. Box M

Tel: (207) 967–5353

In 1980, David and Sheila Aldrich took an old barn and carriage house and converted the two into the Old Fort Inn. The barn, built in 1880, became the lodge, where guests gather for breakfast and conversation, while the guest rooms are found in the carriage house, built at the turn of the century.

"All the rooms are furnished with antiques and each is color coordinated. The rooms have kitchenettes, adequately equipped for preparing a meal. The small refrigerator is handy for keeping cold drinks and fruit. Our room was large, immaculately kept, and decorated in Laura Ashley yellows, greens, and white. The bath is furnished with lots of extra-thick towels.

"Conversations begin and friendships form around the delicious continental breakfast buffet served each morning in the lodge—a large and beautifully furnished room with a magnificent fireplace. These early-morning associations are resumed later in the afternoon around the pool." *(Carole & Bud Spiro)*

Open Mid-April to mid-Dec.

Rooms 2 suites, 14 doubles—all with private bath and/or shower, telephone, radio, TV, desk, fan, kitchenette; 1 room in annex.

Facilities Lodge room with fireplace and piano. 3 acres with heated swimming pool, tennis court, shuffleboard, bicycles, antique shop. 1 block from beach.

Location 1 m from town. From Rte. 35 in Kennebunkport, go left at traffic light at Sunoco station. Go over drawbridge and take first right onto Ocean Ave. Take Ocean to Colony Hotel, turn left in front of Colony. Go to the "T" in the road, go right ¼ m to inn on left.

Restrictions No children under 12. No smoking cigars or pipes in rooms.

Credit cards Amex, Discover, MC, Visa.

Rates B&B, $125–200 suite, $79–150 double. Extra person in room, $15. Midweek spring, fall package rates. 3-day minimum stay, July through Labor Day, Memorial and Columbus Day weekends.

The White Barn Inn
Beach Street, RR #3, Box 387

Tel: (207) 967–2321

Long known as one of Kennebunkport's best restaurants, the White Barn has recently upgraded its overnight guest accommodations under the ownership of Laurie Bongiorno, who purchased the inn in 1987. Guest rooms have been redecorated with color-coordinated fabrics of floral prints, crewels, tweeds, and period reproductions. The newly renovated carriage house now houses luxurious suites with working fireplace, marbled baths with whirlpool tubs, and four-poster beds. The inn's living rooms have also been refurbished with antique furnishings, new fabrics, wallcoverings and drapes.

Dating from the days when New England travelers frequently stopped at the closest farmhouse for a meal, the inn's restaurant is set in a restored three-story barn with picture windows at each end. Under the watchful eye of long-time chef Richard Lemoine, menus are changed seasonally, although certain customer favorites—like bacon wrapped sea scallops with maple mustard cream—remain on the menu year-round. "Beautiful place, outstanding food." *(John Linnell, also CA, JB)*

Open All year. Restaurant closed Jan. 2 through Feb. 15.
Rooms 7 suites, 17 doubles, 1 cottage—all with private bath and/or shower, fan. 20 with desk. Suites with telephone, TV, whirlpool tub, fireplace.
Facilities Restaurant with piano bar, breakfast room, living room, lounge with games, TV; sun-room, porches. 3.8 acres with lawns, bicycles. Swimming beach, hiking, golf nearby.
Location 7 min. walk from town. Take Rte. 35 through town, Beach St. is continuation of Rte. 35.
Restrictions No smoking in restaurant or guest rooms. No children under 13.
Credit cards Amex, MC, Visa.
Rates B&B, $150–170 suite, $65–120 double. Extra person in room, $25. 2–3 night weekend/holiday minimum. Seasonal "getaway" packages. 10% discount for 7-night stay. Alc dinner, $35. Theme packages.
Extras Airport/station pickups, $25. French, Italian spoken.

NAPLES 04055   Map 1

Inn at Long Lake   *Tel:* (207) 693–6226
Lake House Road, P.O. Box 806

In pre-railroad days, the Cumberland and Oxford Canal bridged the gaps between Maine's lakes and Portland's Casco Bay. The Inn at Long Lake lies along this route, and in honor of this history, guest rooms are named after the canal boats which transported wood in one direction, molasses and rum in the other, among other products. Built in 1906 as part of a larger resort, the four-story inn was completely restored in 1987 by Stephen and Leslie Vlachos. They tripled the number of bathrooms, while reducing the room count to 16. Rooms are individually decorated in period, some with cheerful florals, others in more masculine tones, and rates include a continental breakfast.

"Service is impeccable. Managers Terry and Bob Denner are friendly and courteous. They clearly love their job and do it well."*(Paula Kapulka, also Kristina Savage)* "Guests gather in the spacious parlor for breakfast, or to read by the stone fireplace. All water sports are available at Long Lake, and antique shops and restaurants are just a short drive away." *(Joanna Aamodt)*

Open All year.
Rooms 2 suites, 14 doubles—all with private shower and/or bath, TV, air-conditioning.

Facilities Living/dining area with fireplace, library, porches. 2 min. walk from lake. 20 min. to downhill skiing, 5 min. to cross-country.
Location Lakes region. 45 min. NW of Portland, 45 min. E of Conway, NH. From I-95, take Exit 8 to Route 302W to Naples. Go left on Lake House Rd.
Credit cards Amex, MC, Visa.
Rates B&B, $70–80 double. 2-night holiday weekend minimum. Special event packages.

PORTLAND 04101   Map 1

The Inn at Park Spring   *Tel:* (207) 774–1059
135 Spring Street

The Inn at Park Spring is a three-story townhouse, built in 1835 and located in Portland's West End, within walking distance of the restored Old Port district, the Civic Center, the Portland Museum of Art (don't miss its collection of Winslow Homers), and the Portland Performing Arts Center. Rooms on the first floor are done in traditional period decor; third-floor accommodations are more contemporary, and the second floor falls somewhere in between.

Rates include a continental breakfast of fresh-squeezed juice, coffee, and Danish, and afternoon brandy and tea. *(DB)*

Open All year.
Rooms 7 doubles—5 with private shower and/or bath, 2 with maximum of 4 people sharing bath. All with radio, 4 with telephone on request, 1 with balcony, 1 with fireplace.
Facilities Living room, kitchen, library with TV.
Location S coast ME. Center city. From I-295, take Exit 6A, Forest Ave. S. Bear right and turn right at the traffic light. Follow signs for Rte. 77 S through Deering Oaks Park. Stay in left lane, turn left at 3rd light onto Congress St. (at Longfellow Monument). Go 1 block and turn right on Park St. Go 1 block to inn at corner of Spring and Park.
Restrictions No children under 5.
Credit cards Amex, MC, Visa.
Rates B&B, $60–90 double. Extra person in room, $10.

PROUTS NECK 04074   Map 1

Black Point Inn   *Tel:* (207) 883–4126
510 Black Point Road

Built over a century ago, the Black Point offers an elegant resort atmosphere—guests are still encouraged to dress for dinner. But it's by no means behind the times; new facilities and renovations are constantly in progress, under the supervision of owner Normand Dugas. Rooms are traditional, with colonial-style maple furnishings and wallpapers; most have ocean views.

"The inn is set at the end of a quiet peninsula where Winslow Homer had his artist's studio. A private residential enclave of elegant old summer cottages occupies the remainder of the peninsula. Views are marvelous, with beaches below the inn on each side. The main building of the inn features a lovely spacious lobby, with comfortable decor, a sun porch, a screened porch, an open porch, and a reading room. We had a one-bedroom suite with ocean view. The furnishings are all antique reproduction, of fine quality and in good repair. Down pillows were available, and the plush carpet seemed new. The bathroom had an elegant old hotel bath, fully tiled, with thick, white hotel towels and high-quality toiletries. The staff was very helpful; when we told the front desk of a loose toilet seat, it was repaired by the time we returned to the room." *(Susan W. Schwemm)*

"Prouts Neck is a delightful, unspoilt place, and this inn is just right for it. We breakfasted very well in the dining room—a proper breakfast at last—including marmalade. Our well-furnished bedroom was large, with lovely views, although the small bathroom was a disappointment. The staff was welcoming and helpful; a squad of young men dealt with our bags." *(David Felce)*

Open Early May through late Oct.

Rooms 4 suites, 71 doubles, 5 singles—all with private bath and/or shower, telephone, desk, air-conditioning.

Facilities Dining room, living room, music room with grand piano, lounge, porches. 10 acres with beaches, rose garden, heated indoor swimming pool and heated outdoor saltwater pool, hot tub, sauna, walking path, putting green. Tennis, golf, fishing, sailing nearby.

Location S coastal ME. 20 min. S of Portland. Take Rte. 1 to Oak Hill, then turn right on Black Point Rd. Go S 5 m to Prouts Neck.

Restrictions No smoking in dining room. No children under 8 in July, Aug.

Credit cards Amex, MC, Visa.

Rates Full board (July 1–Sept. 6), $300–350 suite, $230–300 double, $170–180 single. MAP (May–June; Sept.–Oct.) $250–300 suite, $220–240 double, $160–180. Extra person in room, $60–70. 15% service additional. No tipping. 2-3 night minimum stay. Prix fixe lunch $15, prix fixe dinner $30.

Extras Handicap accessible. Free airport/station pickups. French spoken.

SOUTH BROOKSVILLE 04617   Map 1

Also recommended: Buck's Harbor Inn (P.O. Box 268, Route 176; 207–326–8660) is a comfortable country inn located in the small coastal town of South Brooksville, a favorite East Coast yachting center. The inn is just a few steps from the harbor, the yacht club, and all possible yachting/boating activities and supplies. The atmosphere is homey and dinners stress fresh local produce. South Brooksville is far enough away from the well-trodden tourist paths to be quiet and peaceful, but close enough for day trips to Bar Harbor, Castine, and Stonington.

Breezemere Farm   *Tel:* (207) 326–8628
Route 176, Breezemere Farm Road, Box 290

If you're looking to combine the pleasures of a farm vacation with an exploration of the beauty of Penobscot Bay, Breezemere Farm is a good choice. Long-time owners Joan and Jim Lippke report that people "who love nature, star-gazing, hiking, shore exploring, sailing, rowing, clamming, organic vegetables, watching ponies, pigs, sheep, our beagle Packy, Maine coon cats, and privacy, will like it here." The inn is set on the water in a sheltered cove, with an 1850s farmhouse and several secluded cottages that are ideal for families. Rooms in the inn are decorated with some antiques; cottages have more basic furnishings. Rates include a hearty breakfast with granola, farm fresh eggs, blueberry pancakes with maple syrup, and a five-course dinner with plenty of fresh seafood (or chicken or beef), garden-fresh vegetables, and homemade bread and desserts.

Open May 15 to Oct. 15.
Rooms 7 cottages, 7 doubles—all cottages with private bath and/or shower, 7 rooms with a maximum of 4 people sharing a bath. all cottages with fireplace. Some rooms with desk.
Facilities Dining room, living room, library, game lodge with fireplace, TV; veranda. 60 acres with beach, gazebo, boat house and dock. Swimming, biking, boating, clamming, hiking, fishing. Evening entertainment.
Location ME coast. 50 miles from Bar Harbor. Call for directions.
Restrictions Smoking in cottages, and inn screened porch. Families with children under 12 must stay in cottages.
Credit cards MC, Visa.
Rates Room only, $100 cottage, $85 double, $75 single. Extra person in room, $15. Rates per person—B&B, $55 cottage, $45 double, $80 single. Extra person, $20. MAP, $75 cottage, $60 double, $95 single. Extra person, $35. 12% service charge. Reduced rates for children, families. 3 day minimum in July, Aug. Prix fixe dinner $20.
Extras Airport/station pickups for additional charge. Cribs, babysitting, games available. Pet accepted.

SOUTHWEST HARBOR 04679   Map 1

Southwest Harbor is located on Somes Sound, almost on the opposite side of Mt. Desert Island from Bar Harbor (about a 15-minute drive). Many peak season visitors prefer its fishing village atmosphere to Bar Harbor's more hectic pace. It's best reached by taking Route 3 onto the island, then bearing right onto Route 102, then right again when 102 and 198 split.

"An absolute don't miss in Southwest is the Oceanarium (207–244–7330), found in an unprepossessing old house on the docks that's been converted into a marine museum. Although we went there 'just for the kids,' the whole family was fascinated. The kids got to touch the sea cucumbers and the adults were riveted by a fascinating lecture on our favorite crustacean—the lobster." *(SWS)*

Also recommended: The Inn at Southwest (Route 102, Box 593; 207–244–3835) is a welcoming B&B offering pleasant accommodation at the edge of the village. The **Kingsleigh Inn** (100 Main Street, P.O. Box 1426; 207–244–5302) is a turn-of-the-century turreted Victorian home. Many rooms have water views and rates include a full breakfast and afternoon tea served on the flower-filled porch overlooking the harbor.

The Claremont Hotel   *Tel:* (207) 244–5036
Claremont Road, Box 137

Another of Mt. Desert Island's classic old inns, the Claremont was built in 1884 and is listed on the National Register of Historic Places. Gorgeous views of the Northeast Harbor and Cadillac Mountain can be had from various points throughout the complex—including the green rockers on the porch, the strategically placed dining room tables, and many of the guest rooms. Guests visiting in August will want to get involved in the hotel's annual Croquet Classic, either as participants or as spectators; for the rest of the season, water sports, tennis, lawn games, and explorations of Mt. Desert Island keep everyone occupied.

The decor in most of the rooms follows the tradition of the Maine summer resort—white chenille spreads, plain curtains, old (not antique) but clean and comfy furnishings—although some of the cottages are more contemporary in feeling. The food is best at simpler dishes; there's lots of fresh fish, and boiled Maine lobster is always on the menu.

"The Claremont is a famous old place. The food is not 'gourmet,' but it is good. The service is excellent, polite, unobtrusive, and the view is possibly the best on Mt. Desert Island. We stayed at the Phillips House, the beautiful old guest house right next to the main hotel. It was just like having an old family home in Maine, minus the cooking and cleaning! There was a lovely rustic living room with fireplace (stocked with wood daily), a sofa, chair, and bookcases. It has a lovely porch with a great view of Somes Sound. Phillips House is very nice if you are there with friends, since you have the living room and porch for getting together." *(Linda Lee Moran)*

"We followed your recommendation and loved the feel of having our own home in the Phillips House. Our spacious room, P4, was decorated with antiques and had wonderful views from its five windows." *(Betty Norman)*

Open May 20 to Oct. 15.
Rooms 5 suites, 19 doubles, 2 singles in hotel, 6 guest houses, 11 cottages. All with private bath and/or shower, desk.
Facilities Dining room and bar, living room with piano, TV; library with games, fireplace, lobby with fireplace, boat house lounge. Evening lecture series, card games. 5 acres with croquet, mooring dock, beach, tennis court. Golf nearby.
Location ½ m to village.
Restrictions Smoking in lobby only.
Credit cards None accepted.
Rates Room only, $70–90 suite, $55 double, $45 single. MAP, $125–155 suite, $105–140 double, $70–80 single, plus 15% service. Extra person in room, $30–55. 3-night minimum preferred for cottages, 2-night minimum for hotel. Weekly rates. Alc lunch, $7; alc dinner, $25.
Extras Some areas wheelchair accessible. French and German spoken. Airport/station pickups.

The Moorings
Shore Road, P.O. Box 744

Tel: (207) 244–5523
244–3210

"Whereas the plunging cliffs and seaward vistas of Acadia National Park draw us back to Mt. Desert Island each year, my wife and I are not enamored of the cutesy tourist malls and expensive resorts in Bar Harbor. The Moorings Inn, located in the quiet lobstering community of Southwest Harbor, offers a superb alternative.

"A large, two-story white frame house, the Moorings has been in operation as an inn since 1916. Neither fancy nor precious, it is one of the homiest, least fussy places we have ever stayed in, thanks to the attentions of longtime owners Betty and Leslie King. They have furnished the rooms with country antiques, and added balconies to a couple of suites upstairs. The fireplace in the living room is lit in the evening, and doughnuts, coffee, and orange juice are left for guests in the morning.

"The great attraction for us, however, is the inn's uncommon setting. The broad lawn in back slopes down to the waters off Somes Sound, providing a panoramic view of low mountains, pine-covered islands, and the Great Bay. Sleek yachts built at the Hinckley boatyard next door rest at anchor in the harbor, and lobstermen ply the sound at dawn. Last year while we were there a seal swam up to play.

"A favorite ritual of ours is to paddle one of the inn's canoes across the harbor to the town lobster pound, where we feast on the day's catch at outdoor picnic tables. A seafood restaurant next door to the inn offers fancier preparations and a bar with the same waterfront views.

"Though we prefer either of the balconied upstairs suites in the main house, also available are cottages with and without kitchenettes and motel units." *(Tony & Donna Gentry)*

"Sitting up in the bed in our great big suite, we could almost convince ourselves we were on a boat: Our huge picture window showed us nothing but the sound and the neighboring yachts. We've been thinking about the Moorings since the day we left, and we can't wait to go back again." *(Janet & Michael Pietsch)*

"We found the Moorings to be exactly as your readers had described it." *(Barb & Dan Bickel)*

Open April through Dec.
Rooms 4 suites, 9 doubles and singles in main house; 6 cottages with 8 bedrooms; motel with 5 units. All with private bath and/or shower, telephone, desk. Some (in cottages) with kitchenette, fireplaces, radios, TV.
Facilities Living room with TV, library, games. Restaurant. Bicycles, canoes, sailboats, rowboats, clamming equipment, gas grills. Sailing lessons in season.
Location Take Rte. 102 to Southwest Harbor, then 102A on left 1 m to inn. Adjacent to Hinckley Yacht Yard.
Restrictions No smoking in some cottages.
Credit cards None accepted.
Rates B&B, $70–80 cottages, $65–70 suites, $50–65 doubles, $45 single. (Breakfast is juice, coffee, doughnuts.) Extra person in room, $10. Alc dinner $25–45.
Extras Wheelchair accessible. German spoken. Cribs available.

Maryland

The Inn at Buckeystown, Buckeystown

In addition to Baltimore, historic Annapolis, and the gracious countryside of western Maryland, the Eastern Shore is the state's main area for attractive inns and hotels. This area is actually part of a large peninsula, extending south from Pennsylvania and Delaware like a fist with one long pointing finger. Delaware is on the western side of this peninsula; Maryland is on the east; the "finger" itself is part of Virginia. The entire area is very flat, ideal for bicycling, and, of course, fishing and other water sports are always options. It's also rich in history, with many well-preserved eighteenth- and early nineteenth-century houses to be found in Chestertown, Easton, St. Michaels, Oxford, and Cambridge. For a change of pace, stop in Crisfield, self-proclaimed "Crab Capital of the World," and a departure point for ferries to Smith and Tangier Islands, both pleasant afternoon excursions.

Rates do not include 5% sales tax; some areas have additional lodging taxes.

ANNAPOLIS 21401 Map 4

Annapolis is an historic city with restored buildings spanning three centuries—a large section has been named a National Historic District. It's full of interesting shops and galleries; there's the Maryland State House and several eighteenth-century mansions, along with the harbor to tour, and, of course, the U.S. Naval Academy. Streets in the historic district are narrow, and on-street parking is limited to two hours during the week.

Unload your luggage at your inn, then park at the Navy Stadium and ride a trolley shuttle back. Forget your car—it's a compact area and everything's in easy walking distance.

Information please: We'd like to request reports on some additional Annapolis possibilities, ranging from intimate B&Bs to full-service inns: A small but historic B&B is the **Jonah William's House,** dating back to 1830, owned and run by Dorothy Robbins (101 Severn Avenue 21403; 301–269–6020). Another B&B is **Gibson's Landing,** two neighboring eighteenth- and nineteenth-century homes in the historic district, both filled with antiques; rates include a breakfast of home-baked goodies and free on-site parking (110 Prince George Street; 301–268–5555). We'd also like comments on the **Historic Inns of Annapolis,** a group of restored inns and private homes, ranging in size from 9 to 44 rooms. We'd also like to hear about the **Maryland Inn,** a 44-room inn dating to 1776, with an equally venerable restaurant, the Treaty of Paris (Church Circle and Main Street; 301–263–2641 or 800–847–8882).

Prince George Inn
Tel: (301) 263–6418
232 Prince George Street

The Prince George, a 100-year-old Victorian, is located in the heart of the historic area and is handsomely decorated in a mix of antiques and comfortable contemporary pieces. The very reasonable rates include a breakfast of juice, fruit, cereal, cheese, croissants, and muffins.

Innkeepers Bill and Norma Grovermann are very knowledgeable about their city, and can suggest things to see and do. Norma says that her "favorite type of guests are those who enjoy seeing restoration in progress, and make themselves at home."

"A jewel of a B&B. All four guest rooms are nicely furnished, and the two shared baths are quite comfortable. The parlor is filled with an interesting selection of current and vintage reading material. A large self-service continental breakfast is provided. All the sights of historic Annapolis are within walking distance." *(James & Janice Utt, also John Marsh, Susan Leopold)*

Open All year.
Rooms 4 doubles sharing 2 full baths. All rooms with radio, air-conditioning, fan.
Facilities Parlor with TV, fireplace; breakfast porches, bricked courtyard area. 4 blocks from city dock for cruising and dining.
Location 45 min. S of Baltimore, E of Washington, D.C. In historic district, 1½ blocks from State Circle. From Rtes. 2/50/301 (John Hanson Hwy.) take Rte. 70/Rowe Blvd. exit. Follow Rowe Blvd. (name changes to Bladen St.) to College St. Go left on College, right on King George, right on Maryland Ave., right on Prince George to inn on right.
Restrictions Smoking on 1st floor only. No children under 12. Parking limited.
Credit cards MC.
Rates B&B, $75 double, $60 single (midweek only). Extra person in room, $10.

BALTIMORE   Map 4

Baltimore has changed considerably in recent years. Once a city tourists deliberately bypassed on their way to Washington, it has now actually become a tourist attraction, thanks in part to the opening of the National Aquarium and of Harborplace, and to the renovation of many of its historic areas. Other attractions include the Revolutionary War frigate U.S.S. *Constellation,* the Maryland Science Center, the Power Plant indoor amusement park, the Baltimore Museum of Art, the Walters Art Gallery, and the Edgar Allan Poe House. Of no less importance is Baltimore's remarkably varied cuisine, with seafood houses and the restaurants of Little Italy among the leading contenders. Although cabs are not expensive, another good way to get around is the old-fashioned trolleys; rides cost around a quarter.

Baltimore is located 37 miles northeast of Washington, D.C., 67 miles southwest of Wilmington, Delaware, and 96 miles southwest of Philadelphia, Pennsylvania. Rates do not include 11% sales tax.

Reader tip: Baltimore enjoys an active night life, and from time to time, readers visiting on a weekend have reported being awakened by the street noise of rowdies at 2 P.M. when the bars close. If you're a light sleeper, be sure to request a room away from the street.

Also recommended: Society Hill Hotels have three properties in Baltimore, all individually decorated with traditional wood furnishings and Victorian antiques, brass beds, brass fixtures in the bathroom, and fresh flowers; rates include a continental breakfast. One property is located across the street from Symphony Hall, the other in the Mt. Vernon district, the third near Johns Hopkins University (301–837–3630). About 20 minutes north of Baltimore is the **Twin Gates B&B** (308 Morris Avenue, Lutherville 21093; 301–252–3131 or 800–635–0370), a Second Empire mansard-roofed Victorian, built in 1857, with eclectic decor, full breakfast and afternoon wine and cheese.

Admiral Fell Inn	*Tel:* (301) 522–7377
888 South Broadway 21231	(800) BXB–INNS

The Admiral Fell Inn ("don't ask how, the staff has heard it before") is a good example of the kinds of changes Baltimore has undergone in recent years. The inn is located on the waterfront in Fell's Point, among Market Square's historic town houses. The town of Fell's Point was Baltimore's original seaport on Chesapeake Bay, and dates back to the 1730s. Some of the earliest wharves, taverns, and shops are still in operation, and the area remains a working seaport today.

The inn consists of seven contiguous buildings, the oldest of which dates back to 1770. The interiors have been renovated to combine historical accuracy with modern comfort. Rooms are individually decorated with antiques and reproductions. The inn also houses a pub serving drinks and casual food, and a restaurant providing more elaborate meals.

"It's within walking distance of the National Aquarium and Harborplace (if you're hearty and like to walk). Our room had a canopied bed, a large armoire, and a color TV, and included the morning paper; continental breakfast was served in the library. The staff is one of the friendliest of any place we've ever stayed. In a city once known only for grime and crime, the Admiral Fell Inn is like a breath of fresh air. It is also near Baltimore's Little Italy, where you'll find some of the best Italian restaurants anywhere." *(Mark L. Goodman, also BP, Diane Wolf)*

279

Open All year.
Rooms 1 suite, 39 doubles—all with full private bath, telephone, TV, desk, air-conditioning. 2 nonsmoking rooms. 4 rooms with Jacuzzi baths.
Facilities Restaurant, drawing room, library with games, atrium, pub, reception areas on each floor, courtyard garden. On the water.
Location Downtown, in Fell's Point. 1 m from Harborplace. From I-95 S, go N (downtown) on Russell St. to Pratt St. Turn right and go E 1 m around Inner Harbor on President St. (I-83) and Fleet St. to Broadway. Go right on Broadway to end at Thames St.
Restrictions Occasional late Saturday night street noise in some rooms.
Credit cards Amex, MC, Visa.
Rates B&B, $135 suite, $90–115 double. Extra person in room, $10. Alc lunch, $9; alc dinner, $25–35. Weekend packages available.
Extras Entrance accessible to handicapped; bathroom. 4 guest rooms equipped for disabled. Free station pickups; free van transportation within city. Cribs, babysitting available.

The Shirley Madison Inn
205 West Madison Street 21201

Tel: (301) 728–6550

This beautifully restored hotel offers a warm and friendly atmosphere; it has been owned by Roberta Pieczenik since 1986, and is managed by Ellen Roberts. Trees, shrubs, and lots of flowers brighten the front of the building; interior highlights include stained glass windows, mirrored fireplaces, and a polished oak staircase. If you'd rather skip the stairs, you can ride the 100-year-old lift, original to the building. The rooms are furnished with Victorian and Edwardian antiques and collectibles; most have kitchenettes. Continental breakfast is served in the sitting room, and complimentary cocktails are offered in the parlor.

The Shirley House is part of the historic Mt. Vernon neighborhood, within walking distance of nearly all of downtown Baltimore, including the Inner Harbor, as well as numerous art galleries, antique shops, concert halls, and some of the city's best restaurants.

"The atmosphere lends itself to relaxation and a warm friendly feeling. The staff goes out of their way to assure you of a pleasant stay. Friendly conversation over a good continental breakfast or an evening glass of sherry or lemonade was always enjoyed and appreciated." *(Nina James)*

"A charming dining room for breakfast. Our suite had a bed, night stands, desk and chairs, reading chair, armoire with TV, and decorative fireplace, all facing a colonial-era church. Adjoining was a large room with a dining room table, four chairs, kitchenette, and modern bath. Rooms are decorated in beautiful colors—mint green, rose, mauve, soft teal. The inn is two blocks from Antique Row, the Maryland Historical Society, and Mount Vernon park." *(MM, also Alvin Safran)* "The inn lived up to the writeup you gave it in last year's edition." *(Sally Sieracki)*

Open All year.
Rooms 8 suites, 17 doubles—all with full private bath, radio, desk, air-conditioning. Most with kitchenettes. Many with telephone and TV. 9 rooms in courtyard house.
Facilities Breakfast room, 2 parlors with TV, living room with library, fireplace. Landscaped courtyard. Garage, $3.
Location Mt. Vernon district. 10-min. walk to center, Inner Harbor. From I-95 S, take I-695 W, Exit 23 (I-83 S/Baltimore). Take St. Paul St. exit, go S on St. Paul, right onto Madison.

Restrictions Occasional late Saturday night street noise in rooms facing Park St.
Credit cards Amex, DC, MC, Visa.
Rates B&B, $105 suite, $55–80 double, $65–95 single. Extra person in room, $10. Children under 12 stay free. Weekend, weekly, monthly discounts. 10% senior discount. No tipping.
Extras French, German, Polish spoken. Cribs available.

CHESTERTOWN 21620   Map 4

A quiet colonial town on the Eastern Shore, Chestertown's area attractions include the Eastern Neck Island Wildlife Refuge and the Chesapeake Bay Maritime Museum, while boating, fishing, crabbing, bicycling, hiking, hunting, golf, tennis, and swimming are among the favorite activities.

Chestertown is 90 miles east of Washington, DC; take the Chesapeake Bay Bridge to Route 301 north to Route 213 north.

Also recommended: The Country Inn at Rolph's Wharf (P.O. Box 609; 301–778–INNS or 800–662–INNS) dates back to 1830 is both a B&B and a family restaurant. Another possibility is the **The White Swan Tavern** (231 High Street; 301–778–2300) a B&B dating back over 200 years for a truly historic atmosphere.

The Inn at Mitchell House   *Tel:* (301) 778–6500
Tolchester Estates, RD2 Box 329

This imposing manor house was built in 1743, with an addition in 1825, and was bought by Tracy and Jim Stone in 1987. It's set on a sweeping lawn, next to a pond, and Tracy notes that "the inn is right for people who wish to get away from the fast pace of the city. We are away from every-thing, so guests should be looking for a bit of seclusion. Plenty of restaurants are within a short drive for dinner, though." The inviting rooms are furnished in a colonial motif with antiques and period reproductions. Rates include a full breakfast. Waffles, French toast, and eggs Bearnaise are all specialties.

"Set well back from the road, down a long, long driveway is this delight-ful retreat. The Stones are gracious hosts, the food is excellent, and the decor—a mixture of antique and traditional furnishings—is lovely. Each guest room has a special touch; I especially liked the flapper dresses from the 20s hung on the walls. Our room had a four-poster bed with an extremely comfortable mattress, good reading lights and was immaculately clean." *(Madeleine Hart)*

Open All year.
Rooms 6 doubles—4 with private bath and/or shower, 2 with maximum of 4 people sharing bath. All with air-conditioning.
Facilities Dining room, 2 parlors with TV/VCR, games, 1956 jukebox. 10 acres with pond, stream, woods. ½ m to Chesapeake Bay for swimming, fishing, boating, crabbing. Tennis, golf nearby.
Location 10 m from Chestertown. From the Delaware Memorial Bridge, take Rte. 13 S to Rte. 301; connect with Rte. 291 W to Chestertown. Turn right on Rte. 20 S, right again on Rte. 21 (3 m on right).
Restrictions Children of all ages welcome by special arrangement.

Credit cards MC, Visa.
Rates B&B, $75–90 double, $75–85 single. Extra person in room, $15. 2-night minimum stay, holiday weekends.
Extras Free marina pickups.

FREDERICK 21701   Map 4

Frederick is a historic town, located just 46 miles west of Baltimore. A prosperous agricultural center, it boasts a number of restored eighteenth-century buildings, many now open as museums. It was also a center of fighting during the Civil War and changed hands between the Union and Confederate forces several times. According to local legend, it was here that Barbara Fritchie dared the forces of Stonewall Jackson to shoot her "old gray head" before she would take down her Union flag. Plan ahead if you want to visit the third weekend in May, when the craft fair is in full swing, or in late September, during the county fair. Stop at the Visitor Center (19 East Church Street; 301–663–8703) for information on walking tours and other activities. The town of New Market, billed as the antiques capital of Maryland, is nearby.

Also recommended: The **Turning Point Inn** (3406 Urbana Pike; 301–874–2421 is a Victorian mansion with Georgian colonial features, built in 1910. Food is just as important as decor here, and guests enjoy full breakfasts with specialties ranging from eggs Benedict to sautéed apples. Lunches include everything from original salad creations to Maryland crab, and the four-course dinners offer a choice of such entrées as veal with mushrooms and sherry, and swordfish with herb butter and sun-dried tomatoes.

Spring Bank   *Tel:* (301) 694–0440
Harmony Grove, 7945 Worman's Mill Road

The Spring Bank Farm is home to an 1880 mansion listed on the National Register of Historic Places. It is owned by Beverly and Ray Compton. Rates include a continental breakfast, served in your room, and afternoon sherry.

Beverly describes the quiet, relaxing atmosphere of Spring Bank as being particularly appealing to guests. "Paths to walk, expansive lawns, a grand house of spacious proportions and architecturally significant features—such as plaster ceiling medallions and moldings, marbled fireplaces, and grained woodwork. We've tried to achieve an 1880s touch in the 1980s, which our guests seem to appreciate."

"The outstanding thing about Spring Bank (besides the architecture) is the owners, Beverly and Ray Compton. Both are very knowledgeable about the region and have shelves full of books on the area.

Beverly describes the house as a restoration, not a reproduction. What that means is that the antique beds are double size, and that our hexagonal white tile bathroom had a charming old upright sink but little shelf space for hair dryers or toilet articles. More importantly, it means enormous bedrooms, homey antique furniture, stenciled ceilings, interior room shutters that disappear into casements, hardwood floors, Oriental carpets, floor moldings, and bay windows.

"Breakfast was home-baked muffins, fresh fruit, and coffee served on china and cut glass with linen napkins. It was delivered on an antique stand tray. Exquisite presentation and ample quantities.

"A particularly pleasant moment of our stay came around 5 P.M. when we plopped down on the back porch and opened a cold beer. Beverly and Ray came out to chat and we were soon joined by other guests returning from their jaunts. One guest entertained us with his description of Antietam Battlefield; a National Geographic photographer pulled up to ask about the house, and a neighboring farmer stopped by on his tractor to say hello." *(Diane Camp)*

Open All year.
Rooms 6 doubles—1 with private bath, 5 with maximum of 3 people sharing bath. All with air-conditioning.
Facilities Double parlors, 10 acres with gardens, walking paths. Swimming, fishing, hiking nearby.
Location Take I-70 or I-270 to Rte. 15 to Frederick (near Mile Marker #16), then Rte. 355 S for ¼ m; inn on left. 2½ m to center.
Restrictions No smoking. No children under 12.
Credit cards Amex, Visa.
Rates B&B, $75–120 double. 2-night weekend minimum in spring and fall.

NEW MARKET 21774   Map 4

Strawberry Inn   *Tel:* (301) 865–3318
17 Main Street, P.O. Box 237

Innkeepers Jane and Ed Rossig describe their B&B as the oldest in Maryland, established well before the "trend," in 1972. Rooms are decorated with Victorian antiques and reproduction wallcoverings, but baths and plumbing is modern. Rates include a breakfast of fruit, coffee or tea, and homemade muffins delivered to your bedroom door at the hour requested.

The town of New Market dates back nearly two hundred years and is listed as an Historic District on the National Register of Historic Places—all the houses are over one hundred years old. It's also known as the antiques capital of Maryland, and makes a convenient base from which to explore the Civil War battle sites of Antietam, South Mountain, and Monocacy.

"We had a spacious room upstairs in the rear, with large bath and sitting room. The Rossigs were friendly and interesting people. Mrs. Rossig was on hand to greet us when we arrived, and both were there when we left. They directed us to the town tea room for a tasty lunch, and to Mealey's Inn for an outstanding meal." *(WW)* "The downstairs bedroom is our favorite, with its own back porch, just right for a summer breakfast. Be sure to visit Ed's framing and print shop in the log cabin he has restored behind the inn." *(Pat & Cramer Riblett)*

Open All year.
Rooms 5 doubles with private bath and/or shower, air-conditioning. Telephone on request.
Facilities Common room with fireplace, books, magazines. Back porch. Fully equipped restored 1840 log cabin available for meetings. ¾ acre of shade and quiet. Tennis 2 blocks away, golf ¼ m.
Location Halfway between Baltimore and Frederick. 35 m W of Baltimore on I-70, Exit 62. Center of town.

Restrictions Smoking in first-floor rooms only. No children under 8.
Credit cards None accepted.
Rates B&B, $85 double. Extra person in room $15.
Extras First-floor guest room wheelchair accessible.

OXFORD 21654   Map 4

We'd like to hear more about the **1876 House,** a restored Queen Anne
Victorian B&B, furnished in period and owned by Eleanor and Jerry Clark
(110 North Morris Street, P.O. Box 658; 301–226–5496).

Robert Morris Inn   *Tel:* (301) 226–5111
Morris Street, P.O. Box 70

The Robert Morris Inn is one of the oldest buildings in one of Maryland's
oldest towns. The earliest part of the inn was built prior to 1710 by ships'
carpenters using wooden pegged paneling, ships' nails, and hand-hewn
beams. Several fireplaces were made from English bricks used as ballast in
the early sailing ships. Robert Morris, Sr., moved into the house in 1738
and became prominent in the shipping business. His son, Robert Morris,
Jr., achieved fame as the financier of the Continental Army during the
Revolutionary War and was a close friend of George Washington. Oxford
is also the home of one of the oldest ferries in the U.S. The line, which
connects Oxford with Bellevue, was started in 1760 by Elizabeth Skinner,
who collected her fares in tobacco, the currency of the time.

Wendy and Ken Gibson, who have owned the Robert Morris for seventeen years, describe Oxford as "one of the most relaxed places on the
Eastern Shore. We offer quiet walks along the beach, peaceful spots to read,
and breathtaking sunsets. The inn is couple-oriented, providing good food
in a charming colonial atmosphere." The Gibsons also own the **Sandaway,**
located one block away from the inn, which offers somewhat more luxurious accommodation at correspondingly higher rates.

One reader noted it with pleasure, while another was disturbed by the
strong smoky smell. Similarly, the baths vary considerably in comfort, so
mention this as well if it's a priority for you.

"The inn offers clean, comfortable rooms with wonderful views of the
bay and village. The drawing rooms are old and attractive, filled with
antiques. The menu in the dining room is typical of this area—crab cakes,
fresh fish, and wild duck. The food is outstanding, especially the seafood
and is served in an old tavern atmosphere." *(Mrs. John M. Schmunk)*

"My parents had a lovely, large, ground-floor room in the annex, with
a screened porch and view of the river. Breakfast was good but quite
expensive." *(SHW)* More comments, please.

Open Mid-March to mid-Jan.; closed Christmas Day.
Rooms 33 rooms—21 doubles with full private bath, 9 with private shower, 3
doubles with maximum of 6 people sharing bath. All rooms with air-conditioning,
4 with desk. 15 rooms in annex.
Facilities Sitting room. ¾ acre by Tred Avon River, tennis, golf nearby.
Location Eastern Shore. 80 m SE of Baltimore, E of Washington, DC.
Restrictions Smoking restricted. No children under 10.

Credit cards Amex, MC, Visa.
Rates Room only, $50–150 double, plus 8% tax. Extra person in room, $20. Alc breakfast, $5–10; alc lunch, $5–14; alc dinner, $40–60. Children's menu available.
Extras Dining room, some guest rooms wheelchair accessible.

ST. MICHAELS 21663   Map 4

Also recommended: The **Kemp House Inn** (412 Talbot Street, Box 638; 301–745–2243) was built in 1805, and has rooms decorated with period antiques, many with four-poster rope beds with trundle beds underneath, patchwork quilts and down pillows. Old-fashioned night shirts are also provided. Continental breakfast is brought to the room in a wicker basket at whatever hour you request between eight and ten A.M., or you may eat on one of the porches.

The Inn at Perry Cabin   *Tel:* (301) 745–5178
308 Watkins Lane

Dating back to the early eighteenth century, the Inn at Perry Cabin has been restored with its historic value in mind and has been owned since 1986 by Walt and Sandy Johnson. The three dining rooms all have river views; lunch is served in the restored carriage house, now decorated with thoroughbred racing memorabilia. Nearby is the Chesapeake Bay Maritime Museum, and the historic ferry across the Tred Avon River to Oxford (see preceding). Those without a yacht of their own will enjoy a Miles River cruise on the excursion boat *Patriot*.

"St. Michaels has many things to offer, not the least of which is Perry Cabin Inn. It is noted for its food, location, and friendliness. Sail and motor boats anchor offshore, or dock at the inn's pier." *(John C. Ferrara)* More comments, please.

Open All year.
Rooms 6 doubles—all with full private bath, telephone, air-conditioning.
Facilities Restaurant; bar/lounge with entertainment weekends. 27 acres, docking facilities, bicycles. Golf, tennis, hunting, sailing nearby.
Location Eastern Shore, 50 m E of Baltimore, Washington, DC. ¼ m from town. On Miles River.
Restrictions Music on weekends might disturb light sleepers.
Credit cards Amex, MC, Visa.
Rates B&B, $90–135 double. Alc dinner, $40. Extra person in room, $10.
Extras Wheelchair accessible. Limo service.

SHARPSBURG 21782   Map 4

Inn at Antietam   *Tel:* (301) 432–6601
220 East Main Street, P.O. Box 119

This turn-of-the-century Victorian has been owned and run by the Fairbourns since 1984, and has been recommended with exceptional enthusiasm by our readers:

"The inn is set at the edge of the picturesque town of Sharpsburg in the Potomac Valley, overlooking the Antietam battlefield. This rambling Victorian farmhouse is spotless and beautifully decorated. Particularly handsome is the suite created from the old summer kitchen/smokehouse with a huge fireplace and bedroom loft.

"The Fairbourns are delightful—he's a retired GM regional manager. They serve a good hearty breakfast of blueberry pancakes, with fresh-squeezed orange juice; in the afternoon they offer tea, coffee, cider, or lemonade with homemade cookies. A fine restaurant nearby gave us free wine when they learned we were 'from the inn.' A high point of our weekend was our tour of the battlefield, arranged by the Fairbourns; a local Civil War historian, John Powell, arrived in a Union army uniform and gave us a fascinating tour for a very reasonable price." *(David Fogle, also Dr. & Mrs. Marvin Sears)*

"The hospitality of the owners can hardly be surpassed. Rooms are furnished with carefully selected antiques, and the home-cooked breakfast is served in elegance on beautiful china. Nearby is the battlefield tour route, including Burnside's Bridge and Bloody Lane. The Visitor Center displays and films explain the events as they took place nearly 125 years ago. Outdoor enthusiasts will also find the inn an ideal location for hiking and bicycling excursions along the C & O Canal, just a few miles away, where they will pass deserted locks and quiet natural areas along the Potomac." *(Esther M. Bittinger)*

Open All year. Closed Dec. 20 through New Year's Day.
Rooms 3 suites, 2 doubles—4 with full private bath, 1 with tub only. All with air-conditioning, 1 with TV, 2 with desk.
Facilities Sitting room, sun-room, dining room, porches. 8½ acres with patio, gardens. Fishing, swimming, hiking, bicycling, cross-country skiing nearby.
Location W MD. 4 m E of Shepherdstown, WV. 13 m from intersection of I-70 and I-81. Take I-70 to Braddock Heights, Exit 49 and turn left to Alt Rte. 40 W. Go W through Middletown and Boonsboro to Rte. 34. Turn left onto Rte. 34, 6 m to Sharpsburg. Approaching Sharpsburg is the Antietam Battlefield Cemetery on left; inn is just past it.
Restrictions No children under 6. Smoking in common rooms only.
Credit cards Amex.
Rates B&B, $90 suite, $65 double, $55 single. Extra person in room, $20. No tipping. Senior discount, mid-week.
Extras Airport/station pickups, $25.

Massachusetts

The Charlotte Inn, Edgartown, Martha's Vineyard

Although there's plenty of beautiful country in between, most of our listings cluster around the East Coast—Cape Cod, Martha's Vineyard, and Nantucket—and the Berkshires, in western Massachusetts.

Information please: We'd especially like to hear more about inns and hotels along the coast north of Boston: Gloucester and Rockport, and the restored historic town of Newburyport. Some inns in Newburyport we'd particularly like to have reports on are the **Essex Street Inn,** a 16-room inn furnished with antiques (7 Essex Street, Newburyport 01950; 508–465–3148); the **Windsor House** (38 Federal Street 01950; 508–462–3778), a two-century old home with six guest rooms and hearty breakfasts served in a kitchen designed after a ship's chandlery; the **Morrill Place Inn** (209 High Street 01950; 508–462–2808), one of Newburyport's imposing mansions; and the **Garrison Inn,** dating back to 1809 (11 Brown Square; 508–465–0910).

The Berkshires: About a 2½-hour drive from New York and slightly less than that from Boston, this region of gentle mountains is known for Tanglewood—the summer home of the Boston Symphony Orchestra, Jacob's Pillow Modern Dance Theater, the Berkshire Theater Festival, the Norman Rockwell Museum, Chesterwood, the Hancock Shaker Village, and many recreational facilities—and its summer festival. The area also features trails for hiking and lakes for fishing and swimming in summer, plenty of golf courses and tennis courts, foliage in October, and downhill and cross-country skiing in winter.

Peak season rates in the Berkshires generally apply in July, August, and October; rates are usually lower the rest of the year. Expect two- and three-night minimum-stay requirements on weekends and holidays in peak season, and book well in advance.

Cape Cod: The Cape officially starts at the Cape Cod Canal, about 50 miles south of Boston, and extends out into the Atlantic like an arm, bent at the elbow at a 90° angle. Buzzards Bay is formed by the shoulder, to the south, and Cape Cod Bay by the bend of the arm, to the north.

Peak season rates on the Cape generally extend from mid-June through Labor Day, and on weekends through October. Two- and three-night minimum stays are the rule in peak season.

Rates do not include 5.7% Massachusetts room tax, and 5% meals tax.

BARNSTABLE 02630   Map 2

Dating back to 1637, Barnstable is a quiet and attractive village, with none of the honky-tonk found in some Cape towns. It is located on Cape Cod's north shore, 77 miles southwest of Boston, and 4 miles from Hyannis.

Also recommended: The **Charles Hinckley House** (Route 6A, Old King's Highway, P.O. Box 723; 508–362–9924) is a small jewel of an inn, perfect for special occasion escapes. Built around 1809 in the Federal colonial style, rooms are furnished with antiques providing a truly colonial ambiance. Guests are greeted with fresh fruit and flowers, and wished good night with bedside chocolates, and fortified in the morning with an English breakfast.

Ashley Manor   *Tel:* (508) 362–8044
3660 Old King's Highway, Box 856

Ashley Manor dates back to 1699, and evidence of its age can be seen in its wide-board flooring, open-hearth fireplace with beehive ovens, and a secret passageway connecting the upstairs and downstairs. Fay and Donald Bain, who bought the inn in 1986, have done an excellent job of redecorating the inn with an elegant yet comfortable flair. The inviting living room, for example, has antique sidepieces, richly colored Oriental rugs, a baby grand piano, and dark blue velvet couches that were just made for curling up with a book. A delicious, multicourse breakfast is served on the backyard patio in good weather; in cooler months, guests are seated on the Chippendale chairs in the formal dining room, complete with candlelight, fine china, and linens, before a blazing fire. Candies, wine, sherry, and port are also included in the rates.

"The inn is lovely, and the Bains couldn't have been nicer or more helpful—we'd go back any time. Most guest rooms are done in an elegant version of the 'country look,' with some lovely antiques. The cottage is set partially into the hillside, with big sliding glass doors to let in the sun and a dehumidifier to ward off the damp; its spacious and private, but I'd take a room in the main house first." *(SWS)*

"The grounds are spacious and beautifully landscaped. The white gazebo and Adirondack chairs in the back are perfect for meditation or romance. Our room was very large, with a fireplace, comfortable chairs, and separate dressing room. We enjoyed the full breakfast. We followed one of the owners' dining suggestions and had one of the best meals of our trip. The atmosphere is serene and homey." *(Julia Hapsch & Thomas R. Wilson)*

Open All year.
Rooms 4 suites, 2 doubles—all with private bath and/or shower. 5 with fireplaces; 1 suite in cottage with kitchenette.
Facilities Dining room, living room, keeping room, all with working fireplaces. 2 acres with terrace, gardens, gazebo. Town beaches for swimming, fishing, whale watching. Golf, tennis, nearby.
Location 6/10 m from village. Walking distance to historic district.
Restrictions Restricted smoking. No children under 14.
Credit cards Amex, MC, Visa.
Rates B&B, $135–145 suite, $100–115 double. Extra person in suite, 25%. 2-night weekend minimum.
Extras French spoken. Airport/station pickups. Bicycles.

BOSTON   Map 2

Founded in 1630, Boston is one of America's oldest cities, yet its historic area is compact and easy to explore on foot. This is fortunate, considering that it is nearly impossible for the uninitiated to navigate the center city by car; the town plan was "laid out by the cows," according to legend. Boston is rich in sights and museums of all periods, from the historic Freedom Trail to the John Hancock Observatory, from the Boston Tea Party Museum to the Computer Museum. Be sure to write or call the Greater Boston Convention and Vistors Bureau, Prudential Plaza, Box 490, (617–536–4100) for details.

Information please: For a small but elegant B&B, try the **Townhouse Terrace,** a newly restored 1870 home, with handsome English-style furnishings, a creative full breakfast, and an inviting garden (60 Chandler Street 02116; 617–350–6520), and tell us what you think; rates from $105–$125.

Also recommended: The Federal House (Back Bay Annex, P.O. Box 915 02117; 617–350–6657) is a small informal B&B in an 1836 townhouse, just five blocks from the Commons, with owners who really know the city.

Boston Harbor Hotel   *Tel:* (617) 439–7000
70 Rowes Wharf 02110   (800) 752–7077

Anyone who has sat stewing in the stop-and-go (mostly stop) traffic in the Callahan Sumner tunnel on the way to or from Logan Airport will immediately appreciate one key advantage of the Boston Harbor Hotel: to get there, you simply take the airport courtesy shuttle to Logan Dock, then hop the 7-minute water shuttle right to the hotel at Rowes Wharf.

The hotel, opened in the summer of 1987, is part of a mixed-use project of the Beacon Companies and Equitable Insurance, combining hotel, residential, office, and marine uses, although Rowes Wharf itself dates back over two hundred years. This luxury facility is appointed with traditional furnishings and all the requisite amenities; of particular note is its art collection, with many historic maps and paintings. The hotel prides itself on the high level of guest service provided. Managing Director Dennis Mills comes to the Boston Harbor after long service in the Four Seasons chain, an excellent proving ground. The restaurant offers sweeping water views and specializes in seafood and American regional cuisine. *(Paul Lasley & Elizabeth Harryman)*

Open All year.
Rooms 28 suites, 202 doubles—all with telephone, radio, TV, desk, air-conditioning.
Facilities 2 restaurants, bar/lounge. Health club with heated indoor lap pool. On harbor. Parking garage, docking facilities.
Location Straddles waterfront and downtown area. 2 blocks to Faneuil Hall, NE Aquarium.
Credit cards All major cards accepted.
Rates Room only, $350–450 suite, $220–270 double, $190–240 single. Extra person in room, $20. Alc breakfast $9–12; alc lunch, $10–25; alc dinner, $35.
Extras Station pickups. Water shuttle to airport, $5. Wheelchair accessible; some guest rooms specially equipped for the handicapped. French, Japanese, Spanish spoken. Cribs, babysitters, games available.

Lenox Hotel
710 Boylston Street 02116

Tel: (617) 536–5300
(800) 225–7676

A traditional turn-of-the-century hotel, the Lenox is known for its fine service and convenient location, and has been owned by the Saunders family for over 25 years. Despite the length of ownership, management is not resting on its corporate laurels, but has been involved in a substantial improvement program. The Lenox has been undergoing major renovation and restoration work over the past few years; completed in 1989 was a new air-conditioning/heating plant. Guest rooms are appointed in either Oriental, colonial, or French provincial decors, and nearly all have recently been redone; most have walk-in closets. The public rooms have a fine traditional air, with a grandfather clock and lots of working fireplaces. The hotel is home to two restaurants, an English-style pub and a grill.

"An older building, well decorated and maintained, with a special charm of its own. Front desk staff very pleasant, efficient, and accommodating, helpful with both large and small requests and questions. The bellmen and housekeepers were friendly; the latter don't stint on towels or soap. Our room was quiet and was cleaned nicely each day, and the corridors and common rooms were neat and clean. Ice and drink machines are located on alternate floors, which is a bit inconvenient. Decor is American colonial, with good carpets, lots of lamps, and separate closets. Our bath was rather small, but it was supplied with a hair dryer and magnifying mirror." *(Noland Fields)*

"An older hotel, immaculately clean and beautifully maintained. Our top-floor room had a king-size bed, a dresser, couch and chair, coffee table, television table, and desk with windows overlooking the city. The closet was huge with full-length mirrors, the bath was old-fashioned but neat and clean. The hotel's location in the Back Bay area is a plus—wonderful to explore, with several great restaurants just down the street." *(Wendi Van Exan)*

Although readers remain very pleased overall with the hotel, a few areas for improvement were noted: "The staff was nice but could be more efficient—I had to call three times for an extra blanket." And: "The door to our bathroom did not close all the way."

Open All year.
Rooms 3 suites, 216 doubles—all with private bath and/or shower, telephone, radio, TV, desk, air-conditioning. 14 rooms with fireplace.
Facilities Restaurant, pub and grill, piano bar. Parking garage next door, $10 daily. Near river for jogging trails.
Location Back Bay. Subway stops across street.
Restrictions Light sleepers should request rooms on higher floors or toward back. Smoking in designated areas only.
Credit cards Amex, CB, DC, Discover, MC, Visa.
Rates Room only, $250–350 suite, $104–210 double, $104–190 single. Extra person in room, $20. No charge for children under 18 in parents' room. Alc breakfast, $5–8; alc lunch, $18, alc dinner, $25–40.
Extras Wheelchair accessible. Spanish, Italian, French spoken. Airport pickups, $5.

BREWSTER 02631   Map 2

Brewster is located on the bay side of Cape Cod, north of the "elbow." It's about a 20-minute drive northeast of Hyannis and is 90 miles southeast of Boston. In addition to the usual activities—swimming at nine public beaches, fishing, golf, tennis, hiking, bicycling, horseback riding, and antiquing—nearby attractions include the Brewster Historical Society Museum, the Drummer Boy Museum, and the Cape Cod Museum of Natural History.

Old Sea Pines Inn   *Tel:* (508) 896–6114
553 Main Street

Though it was founded in 1907 as the Sea Pines School of Charm and Personality for Young Women, the Sea Pines now welcomes people of *all* ages and sexes to partake of its charm. Michele and Steve Rowan bought the abandoned school in 1977 and opened it as an inn in 1981, after doing virtually all the renovation work themselves. Michele reports that "we pride ourselves on our old-fashioned atmosphere, reminiscent of a more unhurried age, and on our attention to our guests. Our food, in keeping, is home-style New England—fresh seafood and vegetables, home-baked breads and desserts." Rates include a full breakfast of fresh fruit and juice, cereal, eggs, homemade breads and muffins.

"Michele and Steve Rowan have done a beautiful job of restoration. All the rooms are furnished in comfortable Cape Cod style with beautiful hardwood floors. The atmosphere is quiet and 1930s-ish; there's a great living room with fireplace and a front porch with old-fashioned rockers. The Rowans are excellent hosts and everything is meticulously clean. As a bonus, the dining room serves truly outstanding meals. We have eaten at many of the most highly rated restaurants on the Cape and none are better." *(Marshall E. Armand)*

"The Rowans set a standard of friendliness, service, cleanliness, and attention to detail that any inn would do well to imitate. Their Sunday brunch is the best I've ever had—lobster salad, eggs Benedict, Portuguese sweet bread." *(John Bullis)*

Open All year.
Rooms 1 suite, 19 doubles—15 with private shower and/or bath, 5 with maximum of 4 people sharing bath. Many with air-conditioning, desk, TV; some with fan.
Facilities 2 living rooms with fireplaces, dining room, bar, wraparound porch. 3½ shaded acres.
Location Take Exit 10 off Mid-Cape Hwy. (Rte. 6). Follow Brewster signs to Rte. 6A (Main St.) and go right. Inn 1 m on left.
Restrictions Smoking in first-floor common rooms only. No children under 8.
Credit cards Amex, CB, DC, MC, Visa
Rates B&B, $65–85 suite, $38–90 double, single. Extra person in room, $15. 2-night minimum, holidays, weekends June to Oct. Alc brunch, $12, alc lunch $5–7.
Extras Restaurant and room wheelchair accessible. Italian, German, Spanish spoken. Airport/station pickups.

CENTERVILLE 02632   Map 1

Inn at Fernbrook   *Tel:* (508) 775–4334
481 Main Street

Built in 1881 by Howard Marston, owner of Boston's Parker House, the inn's grounds were originally landscaped by Frederick Law Olmstead, designer of New York's Central Park and the Boston Public Garden. During the 1930s it was used as a summer house for Hollywood glitterati; in the 50s and 60s it became a retreat for Cardinal Francis Spellman. In 1986 hoteliers Brian Gallo and Sal DiFlorio bought the mansion and restored it as a B&B. Although in many respects a typical Victorian summer home, the Inn at Fernbrook boasts an unusual feature. According to the owners, "no two rooms share the same wall, thus assuring guest privacy." Although the full breakfast is served at a set time, continental breakfast is thoughtfully provided to early and late risers alike. Rates also include afternoon tea or lemonade.

"Elegant, charming B&B with congenial helpful hosts. Nice touches are the fresh flowers and crystal decanter of sherry in your room—no plastic-covered water glasses here. We stayed in the Kalmus Suite, decorated with antiques and Oriental rugs, and a turret-shaped sitting room. A delicious breakfast of freshly squeezed orange juice, fresh fruits, eggs, and Dutch baby pancakes, and home-made breads was cooked by Brian and served by Sal. The grounds are lovely, the heart-shaped rose garden is very romantic. " *(Ellen Goren)*

"What a contrast to the T-shirt shops and sweaty crowds of Hyannis. Centerville is a quiet residential town, and the inn is a graceful Victorian mansion with etched-glass windows and inviting porches. Brian and Sal combine warmth and friendliness with a professionalism rarely found in a B&B. We loved the Spellman Room, originally the Cardinal's chapel and now decorated with a white canopied bed, pyramid ceiling, tiled fireplace and stained-glass window."*(Paul & Elizabeth Lasley)*

Open All year.
Rooms 1 cottage, 2 suites, 3 doubles—all with private bath and/or shower. 1 suite with fireplace, deck. Cottage with wraparound porch.
Facilities Dining room, sitting room, porch. Lawn with rose garden, ponds. ½ m to beach.
Location SE MA, Cape Cod. Historic district. From Rte. 6 take Exit 6 (Rte. 132) S to 1st stop light. Turn right on Phinney's Ln. (which becomes Main St.) and continue to center of town. Inn is on the left.
Restrictions No children under 14.
Credit cards None accepted.
Rates B&B, $115 cottage, $115–225 suite, $95–125 double. Midweek corporate rates. Weekly rates.

CHATHAM 02633 — Map 2

Chatham is located at Cape Cod's "elbow," on the south shore, about two hours' drive (100 miles) from Boston.

Also recommended: The Captain's House Inn of Chatham (371 Old Harbor Road; 508–945–0127) was built in the Greek Revival style in 1839. Random-width pumpkin-pine floors, lots of fireplaces, and antiques complement guest rooms furnished with four-poster and fishnet-canopied beds; rates include a continental breakfast. The **Cyrus Kent House** (63 Cross Street at Kent Place; 508–945–9104) is a beatifully restored sea captain's house, with large, light airy rooms furnished with antiques and highlighted by fresh flowers. If you prefer the atmosphere of an old-time beach resort the **Chatham Bars Inn** (Shore Road; 508–945–0096) was recently redone, combining old-fashioned elegance with a comfortable family atmosphere, attractive rooms and good food.

Chatham Village Inn
207 Main Street

Tel: (508) 945–0792

Ellen and Walter Ripley bought the Chatham Village Inn in 1986, and have decorated it in comfortable country style, with some antiques and period reproductions. A typical Cape Cod home with a small tavern attached, the structure dates back to the early 1900s. Ellen notes that "our goal is to make our guests feel like they are friends being entertained in a home. We want them to experience a quiet and serene environment, different from their everyday lives. Soft classical music plays throughout the day." The inn's tavern is under separate management, and specializes in seafood, including local scallops and scrod. Rates include a continental breakfast; full breakfast is served at the tavern.

"We passed by the inn en route to the Chatham Light, just a block away, and were immediately charmed by its warmth and the friendliness of owner Ellen, and the casual greeting of the resident cat. The parlor, with its inviting fire, comfortable wicker rocker and warm wood paneling created a wonderful memory for us. Fresh-from-the-oven cranberry muffins served by an early morning fire were a highlight." *(Pam & Bob Hamilton)*

Open All year. Restaurant closed Oct. through March.
Rooms 14 doubles—8 with private bath and/or shower; 6 rooms share 2 baths. All with fan; some with desk. 3 rooms in annex with parlor.

Facilities Living room with fireplace, piano. Restaurant, tavern. ½ acre with patio, gardens. 200 yards from beach. Fishing, golf, nearby.

Location From Rte. 6, take Exit 11. Turn left on Rte. 137. Go 3 m to Rte. 28 (Main St.). Turn left. Go through town to stop sign at Main and Shore Sts. Turn right, then right again onto Hallet Ln. Inn parking lot on right. Short walk to village center, harbor.

Restrictions Smoking on patio in summer, parlor in winter. No children under 10.

Credit cards Amex, MC, Visa.

Rates B&B, $80–110 double, single. Extra person in room, $20. 2-3 night weekend/holiday minimum in season. Full alc breakfast $4, alc dinner $25.

Extras Airport/station pickups.

DEERFIELD 01342   Map 1

Also recommended: Another possibility about ten miles north of Deerfield is the **Parson Hubbard House** (Shelburne 01370; 413–625–9730), built in 1774, a small B&B offering "traditional decor, lovely hosts, peaceful setting, and good breakfasts." *(Mel Cohen)*

Deerfield Inn   *Tel:* (413) 774–5587
The Street

Historic Deerfield consists of a mile-long street of buildings dating back to the early nineteenth century that, since 1952, have been restored by the Historic Deerfield Foundation. Most of the buildings are lived in by staff members of the Foundation, and by faculty members at Deerfield Academy. Twelve of the buildings are open to the public as museums.

The Deerfield Inn was built in 1884. In 1979 it was seriously damaged by fire. Fortunately, students, staff and townspeople arrived with the firefighters and saved virtually all the inn's valuable antiques. The rebuilt inn opened in 1981, with most of its nineteenth-century atmosphere intact, and with modern heating, cooling, and fire safety systems.

We are delighted to welcome this inn back to the pages of our guide, after a two-year absence caused by deficiencies both in the kitchen and overall management. Several readers have written again to report that the restaurant, which serves more formal lunches and elegant dinners, is back on track with traditional New England cooking, using fresh, first-quality ingredients, although the basement coffee shop, which serves breakfast and casual lunch, continues to combine overwhelming crowds with underwhelming food at peak periods. The parlors and dining rooms are filled with eighteenth- and nineteenth-century antiques. Rooms are simply decorated with antique furniture and quality reproductions.

"Our room combined modern comforts with period charm, and our candle-lit dinner was romantic and delicious." *(AF, also Nancy Harrison & Nelson Ormsby, SHW)*

Open All year. Closed Christmas Eve and Day.

Rooms 23 doubles—all with private bath, telephone, air-conditioning. 12 rooms in annex.

Facilities Restaurant, coffee shop, tavern, lobby with fireplace, parlor with TV. Downhill, cross-country skiing 10–20 m.

Location Central MA; 100 m W of Boston, 40 m N of Springfield. Historic Old Deerfield.
Credit Cards Amex, DC, MC, Visa.
Rates MAP, $170 double, $125 single. Extra person in room, $59. B&B, $115 double, $100 single. Extra person in room, $31. Crib or cot, $25. 10–15% service additional. Alc dinner, $25–40.
Extras Ramp for wheelchairs; 2 rooms equipped for disabled. Small pets permitted by prior arrangement.

DENNIS 02638   Map 2

Isaiah Hall B&B Inn   *Tel:* (508) 385–9928
152 Whig Street

Marie and Richard Brophy have owned the Isaiah Hall since 1984 and have furnished it with antiques, quilts, and Oriental rugs. "It's everything you could want in a relaxed country B&B—a comfortable place for families, with rooms that are both casual and inviting. The Brophys really listen to what their guests say and continually work hard to improve their inn— adding and upgrading baths, converting double beds to queen size while maintaining their antique character, putting in all new mattresses, providing ample nightstands and reading lights. There is a light and airy common room, filled with white wicker, for games and casual conversation, and a cozy parlor with a fireplace for chilly fall and winter evenings. Ask Marie to show you the hand-painted doors and wall trim, done forty years ago." *(SWS)*

"This Greek Revival farmhouse was built in 1857 as the private home of Isaiah B. Hall, a builder and cooper. It is on a street off the main thoroughfare, and is quiet and peaceful, with its own convenient parking. The beach, a good restaurant, the Cape Playhouse, and some antique shops are a pleasant walk away. The rooms are well heated. Hot water is ample in the well-lighted, clean bathrooms. The continental breakfast is served in the dining room at a wonderful long antique table. There's a choice of juice, fruit, homemade muffins and breads, dry cereals, English muffins, jams, marmalade, coffee, herbal and regular tea. Everyone comes together for breakfast, and you soon feel that you have made new friends. The owners are very friendly, warm, and extremely helpful, making you feel at home." *(Margaret & Tom McAlone)*

Marie notes that the Cape Museum of Fine Arts, on the grounds of the Cape Playhouse, features the works of Cape artists and antique restoration projects: "A fabulous facility."

Open Mid-March to mid-Nov.
Rooms 11 doubles—10 with private bath and/or shower, 1 with maximum of 3 people sharing bath. All with radio, fan; some with desk, balcony; one with fireplace.
Facilities Dining room, parlor with TV, games, library; great room, porch. 1 acre with gardens, lawn games. ½ m from ocean beach, ¾ m from lake. Bicycle trails, golf, tennis nearby.
Location N shore Cape Cod. 73 m SW of Boston, 12 m NE of Hyannis. ⅓ m from village. Take Rte. 6 to Exit 8, go left ½ m to Rte. 6A, turn right and go ¾ m to Hope Lane (opposite cemetery & church). Turn left on Hope, to end; go right on Whig St. to inn on left.

Restrictions No smoking in dining room, certain guest rooms. No children under 7.
Credit cards Amex, MC, Visa.
Rates B&B, $44–85 double, $38–75 single. Extra person in room, $10. 10% discount for weekly stays. 2-night weekend minimum in season. Mystery weekends in fall.
Extras Some rooms wheelchair accessible. Various European languages spoken.

EAST ORLEANS 02643   Map 2

Nauset House Inn   *Tel:* (508) 255–2195
143 Beach Road, Box 774

Diane and Albert Johnson, owners of the Nauset House since 1982, describe their 1800s farmhouse as a "quiet, old-fashioned country inn, located in a residential zone. It's intimate and quaint, and the rooms do not have TVs, radios, refrigerators, or air-conditioning. Fresh flowers in each room, edible flowers garnishing breakfast plates, patchwork cats sitting on the beds, and whimsical painted furniture are a few of the details which make Nauset House special. We also have a one-of-a-kind conservatory, with Cape Cod flowers and greenery and wicker furniture, attached to our brick-floored pub/dining room." Breakfasts feature a different kind of home-baked muffin each day, as well as fresh fruit or juice, and a variety of specialties such as Portuguese omelets or blueberry pancakes; afternoon refreshments include wine or cranberry juice and hors d'oeuvres.

"The inn provided a quiet, serene, comforting atmosphere; Diane and Al Johnson were extremely warm, helpful, and oh-so-interested innkeepers. They provided valuable hints on exploring not only the Cape, but Boston as well. My room, 'Johnny-Jump-Ups,' was warm and cozy, with a lovely homemade quilt on the bed. The walls were bordered with a stencil design hand-painted by Diane and her daughter Cindi." *(Susan Tirone)*

"Every breakfast starts with fresh-baked muffins followed by your choice from among several entrées. Each night at 5:30 you can have wine or cranberry juice with a light hors d'oeuvre, while chatting with the other guests about the day's activities and dinner plans." *(Mary Francis & Howard Small)* "The inn sits on a little hill, in a beautiful residential neighborhood." *(BK)* "Diane's breakfasts are irresistible. Although we had vowed to dislike the Cape, the Johnsons changed our views." *(Judith Strull)*

"Our room was beautifully appointed, with a comfortable king-sized bed and a small bath. The hosts were friendly without being intrusive, and the other guests were an especially congenial group of people who also enjoy the beach and a peaceful environment. The breakfasts were good and the mood so convivial that guests were reluctant to leave the table. Nauset Beach is one of the most glorious in the world." *(Ernie & Amy Fleishman)*

Open April 1 to Oct. 31.
Rooms 12 doubles, 1 single, 1 cottage—8 with private shower and/or bath, 6 with maximum of 6 people sharing bath; 5 rooms in carriage house and cottage.
Facilities Living room with fireplace, dining room with fireplace, conservatory, bar, terrace. 2½ acres with picnic tables, gardens. ½ m to Nauset Beach, 3 m to bay, 2 m to lake.
Location N shore Cape Cod, at the "bend of the elbow," 28 m NW of Hyannis, 100 m SW of Boston. 3 m from Orleans. Take Rte. 6 to Exit 12. Go right to 1st light; go

right on Eldredge Parkway and straight to light. Straight across Rte. 28 (Tonset Rd.) to next light. Right on Main St. to fork in road at Barley Neck Inn. Bear left on Beach Rd. to inn 8/10 m on right.

Restrictions No children under 12. No smoking in dining room.

Credit cards MC, Visa.

Rates Room only, $80–90 suite, $55–70 double, $40 single. Full breakfast, $4; continental, $2.50. 2-night weekend minimum.

Extras Bus station pickups.

FALMOUTH 02540   Map 2

Falmouth is 72 miles south of Boston and east of Providence, on the south shore of Cape Cod's "shoulder." It's three miles north of Wood's Hole, departure point for the Martha's Vineyard and Nantucket ferries.

Also recommended: The **Elm Arch Inn** (Elm Arch Way; 508–548–0133) bears the scars of a cannonball fired by the British in 1812, and has been owned by the same family since 1926. The location is quiet yet very convenient, the atmosphere genuinely historic (except in the annex rooms). Children will love the antique toys and swimming pool and their parents will be equally delighted with the very reasonable rates. The **Wyndemere House at Sippewissett** (718 Palmer Avenue and 718 Goodings Way; 508–540–7069), a B&B with English country decor, offers full breakfast and afternoon tea.

Mostly Hall B&B   *Tel:* (508) 548–3786
27 Main Street

Captain Albert Nye built Mostly Hall in 1849 as a wedding present for his New Orleans bride. It has 13-foot ceilings; grand, shuttered windows; an enclosed widow's walk; a spacious wraparound porch; and hallways that dominate three floors—the source of the inn's name.

Caroline and Jim Lloyd, who bought the inn in 1986, combine Yankee hospitality with a southern ambience in this plantation-style home. Set well back from the road, Mostly Hall is located on the village green. Breakfast, served on the veranda in warm weather, features such specialties as stuffed French toast, plantation eggs, or cheese blintzes with blueberry sauce, accompanied by fresh fruit and juice, breads and muffins.

"Caroline and Jim Lloyd make staying in their home like staying with family. They are so helpful with information about the area; they have restaurant menus for all over and seem to know most places firsthand. They love what they are doing and it shows. They are there if you need them but don't intrude. We had one of the smaller rooms, a front one on the main floor. It had a queen-size reproduction canopy bed, two wingback chairs, and ample storage and closet space. The bath was small but all one needed and we received loads of fresh towels each day. The ceilings are 13 feet high and the windows at least 10. The enclosed widow's walk has been turned into a little lounge with lovely views and the inn's only TV. We enjoyed sitting on the back porch with a beer, cheese and crackers, then went into the backyard to try out the swing in the gazebo. Falmouth is a very casual town; no need to dress for dinner." *(Wendi Van Exan)*

"The large living/dining room has a mixture of Victorian antiques and contemporary furnishings. All the guest rooms have reproduction queen-size beds, antique dressers, and Oriental rugs; two of the larger rooms have a single-size antique sleigh bed to accommodate an extra guest. The rooms are decorated in soft colors, with dusty pink and soft blues special favorites. Bedside tables and lights would be a welcome addition in a few rooms. Exceptional owners; location very convenient for touring the Cape and the Vineyard." (SWS)

Open Mid-Feb. through Dec.
Rooms 6 doubles—1 with full private bath, 5 with private shower. All with radio; some with desk, ceiling fan.
Facilities Dining room, living room, widow's walk with TV, porch, gazebo with swing. 1½ acre with badminton, croquet, bicycles. 10-minute bike ride to beach. 3⅓ m bikeway, island ferries nearby.
Location Walking distance to center. Take Rte. 28 over the Bourne Bridge South into Falmouth.
Restrictions No smoking. No children under 16.
Credit cards None accepted.
Rates B&B, $75–100 double, $55–85 single. Extra person in room, $15. 10% discount on 6-night stays. 2-night minimum weekends and in season. Honeymoon packages.
Extras German spoken. Airport/station pickups.

GREAT BARRINGTON 01230   Map 2

Windflower Inn   *Tel:* (413) 528–2720
South Egremont Road, Route 23
Mailing address: Egremont Star Route, Box 25

The Liebert and Ryan families have owned the Windflower since 1980. All the cooking is done by Barbara Liebert and her daughter Claudia. The dinner menu changes daily, and one of three entrées—seafood, poultry, or meat—is selected in advance by guests. Rooms are furnished with antiques and comfortable country furniture.

"Every aspect of this inn is delightful. The attitude of the owners is especially friendly and courteous and this reflects also on their staff. The food is carefully prepared and served well. There is always a minimum of three choices of appetizer, entrée, and dessert. The taste is excellent, the quality outstanding. The atmosphere at the inn is relaxed, comfortable, and friendly. The owners are always willing to extend themselves to the utmost for their guests." (Carol & Barry Beyer)

"This 200-year-old building looks like a classic country inn, both inside and out. The public rooms are inviting and spacious—the living room has a large stone fireplace, while the common room has a piano and lots of games. Dinner is served to outside guests with advance reservations only, which means the inn's atmosphere is not disrupted by restaurant hubbub. The guest rooms are unusually spacious, with some nice antiques and Victorian beds. (A few have high footboards, so six-footers might want to avoid these rooms). Even the least expensive room is perfectly acceptable, with Laura Ashley–type sheets and comforters, good reading lights (but no night tables), and full bath. One area for improvement: The carpeting in some rooms could stand updating, and, in one enormous room, was very stretched out, with an easy-to-trip-over ripple. Dinner is served in the casual dining room by the friendly young staff; the food is original and delicious, with vegetables from the inn's gardens." *(SWS, also Rob Lennick)*

Open All year. Closed Thanksgiving Day.
Rooms 13 doubles with private bath and/or shower. All with TV, some with fireplaces.
Facilities Living room, game/library/piano room. 10 acres with vegetable and flower gardens, swimming pool. Tennis, golf across street; cross-country, downhill skiing nearby.
Location SW MA, Berkshires. 3 m W of Great Barrington on Rte. 23.
Restrictions No smoking in dining room or guest rooms.
Credit cards None accepted.
Rates MAP, $140–180 double, plus 15% service on food cost. Half price for children under 10 sharing parents' room; ¾ for 10 and older. Prix fixe dinner, $30 by advance reservation only.
Extras Crib available.

LEE 01238   **Map 2**

Haus Andreas   *Tel:* (413) 243–3298
Stockbridge Road, RR 1, Box 605-B

The Haus Andreas was originally built by a Revolutionary War soldier. The original structure was razed, then rebuilt in 1928 by John Bross Lloyd. During the summer of 1942 it was the residence of Queen Wilhelmina of the Netherlands, her daughter, Princess Juliana, and her granddaughters. The inn has been owned by Lilliane and Gerhard Schmid since 1980.

Rooms at the Haus Andreas are immaculate and are well furnished with some antiques. A continental breakfast of fresh fruit and juice, coffee, bagels and cream cheese, bran and blueberry muffins, and croissants is served in the sunny dining room.

"We used this inn as our home base for sightseeing in western Massachusetts, but we could easily have holed up here for four days. The living room and grounds of the house are spacious and comfortable—inside there are lots of books, games, and magazines, plus a stereo and TV; outside there are a heated pool and plenty of lawn chairs. The owners provide a pantry for guests, with refrigerator, sink, dishes, and more. The rooms are nice— ours was small but very comfortable. Some of the larger rooms are lovely, with four-poster beds and a sitting area." *(Ellen C. Hicks)*

"The beauty of the decor and the inn's setting is surpassed only by the warmth and professionalism of its owners." *(SWS, also Paula and Kenneth Marks)*

Open All year.
Rooms 2 suites, 6 doubles—all with full private bath. All with air-conditioning; some with fireplace, TV, desk.
Facilities Dining room, living room with working fireplace, books, stereo, baby grand piano, games, puzzles; TV room, guest pantry with refrigerator, hot plate. 5½ acres with patio, lawn games, heated swimming pool, tennis court, bicycles. Golf across the road. Downhill, cross-country skiing nearby.

Location W MA, Berkshires. 1 m from town. From Mass. Pike, take Exit 2. Bear right on Rte. 20 to Lee. At stop sign go straight on Stockbridge Rd. ⁹/₁₀ m to inn.
Restrictions No smoking in common rooms. No children under 10.
Credit cards MC, Visa.
Rates B&B, $65–205 double, plus 5% daily service charge. Extra person in room, $14–25. Weekly rates. 2- to 4-night weekend minimums May–Oct.
Extras French, German spoken. Station pickups.

LENOX 01240   Map 2

Lenox is most famous for Tanglewood, the summer home of the Boston Symphony, in residence from mid-June through August. Call (617) 266–1492 for schedules and ticket information. Also in Lenox is The Mount, a restoration of Edith Wharton's house; Shakespeare is presented at The Mount's outdoor amphitheater from July to October. Rates are highest from late June through October, and weekend minimum stays are the rule.

When you need a break from all that culture, you'll find that there are lakes nearby for fishing, swimming, and boating, along with tennis courts and golf courses. In winter, there's plenty of cross-country and downhill skiing nearby.

Lenox is in the Berkshires, 7 miles south of Pittsfield, approximately 10 miles west of the New York border, and 150 miles north of New York City.

Information please: A handsome "painted" lady, the **Rookwood Inn** was totally renovated and furnished with English and American antiques, Oriental rugs, and period wallpapers. Owners Tom and Betsy Sherman note that the inn, dating from 1830, is located on a quiet side street, just a ½ block from the town center (19 Old Stockbridge Road, P.O. Box 1717; 413–637–9750). The **Candlelight Inn** (53 Walker Street; 413–637–1555) has eight guest rooms, some with Shaker-style furnishings, and a sizable restaurant. The **Underledge** (76 Cliffwood Street; 413–637–0236) is a turn-of-the century mansion; many of its spacious rooms have fireplaces and sunset views of the mountains. Reports?

Also recommended: The Gables Inn (103 Walker Street, Route 183; 413–637–3416) was built in the 1880s as an elaborate summer "cottage." Rooms are furnished with authentic period furnishings, enhanced by the owners' extensive art collection and library. **Whistler's Inn** (5 Greenwood Street; 413–637–0975) a French/English Tudor–style mansion dating back to 1820, Whistler's Inn features most of its original chandeliers, oak panel-ing, and leaded-glass windows, supplemented by European and American antiques and Persian rugs. Rates include a continental breakfast and after-noon sherry. If Lenox is sold out, the **Tuckered Turkey** (Old Cheshire Road, Lanesboro 01237; 413–442–0260) is a clean pleasant B&B recom-mended for its lovely views, comfortable beds, and delicious breakfast; its quiet location is 12 miles north of Lenox.

Blantyre   *Tel:* (413) 637–3556 (May–Oct.)
Route 20   298–3806 (Nov.–April)

Blantyre is a dark-brick castle built at the turn of the century, now lavishly restored. Rates include a continental breakfast of coffee, muffins, and croissants; full breakfast is available at an additional charge. Five-course prix fixe dinners are served in the paneled dining room, with a selection of several appetizers, entrées, and desserts. Standards at Blantyre are very high, as are the prices and reader expectations.

"Resident manager Roderick Anderson and his staff provided us with privacy and pampering, without intrusion. Our spotless room in the Carriage House was very comfortable—beds with duvets and plump pillows, traditional furnishings, cozy chairs, table, several lamps, color TV, and terrace. Waiting for us were a complimentary bottle of wine, a fresh fruit basket, and a tray of assorted cheeses. Two luscious terry robes hung in the closet. The well-equipped bathroom was stocked with the usual amenities—shampoo, bath gel, body lotion, etc. Breakfast, which can be taken in your room or in the beautiful conservatory in the main house, includes fresh-squeezed juices and seasonal fruit, hot cereal, warm croissants and muffins, imported jams. All are presented in a dignified and efficient manner. The interior of the property abounds with exquisite antiques and fresh flower arrangements. Reservations a must!" *(Mrs. Eileen Yudelson)*

"Absolutely gorgeous, and worth the considerable expense. They've restored this magnificent mansion beautifully. Not a single detail has been overlooked—even the drawers are lined to match the wallpaper! Rates in the Carriage House are more reasonable than the main house. There's also a special croquet court, where championship games are played." *(Patti Barrett, also Lynn Blau)*

Open May to mid-November.
Rooms 4 suites, 19 doubles—all with private bath and/or shower, telephone, radio, TV, desk, air-conditioning; most with fireplace. 8 rooms in main house, rest in Carriage House and cottages.
Facilities Dining rooms; parlors; music room with pianist, harpist weekends; conservatory. 85 acres with flower gardens, heated swimming pool, 4 tennis courts, hot tub, exercise room, sauna, 2 croquet courts, walking paths.
Location 2–3 miles from town, Tanglewood. ½ m from Rte. 20. From Stockbridge, go N on Rte. 7 to 2nd light (5 m), turn right on Rte. 20, ½ m to Blantyre. From Lee, take Exit 2 off Mass. Pike, go N on Rte. 20 to inn on right.
Restrictions No children.
Credit cards All major cards.
Rates Room only, $250–500 suite, $190–300 double, plus 10–17½% service. Extra person in room, $40. Continental breakfast, $8–20. Alc lunch, $45; prix fixe dinner, $65, plus 20% service. 2-night weekend minimum.
Extras French, German, Spanish, Portuguese, Russian, Japanese spoken. Airport/station pickups, $65.

Brook Farm Inn   *Tel:* (413) 637–3013
15 Hawthorne Street

Given the motto of the Brook Farm Inn: "There is poetry here," this entry should perhaps be written in iambic pentameter, or at least rhyming couplets, but straightforward text will have to suffice unless we receive a more creative response from our readers.

Brook Farm is a 100-year-old Victorian, bought by Bob and Betty Jacob in 1985. Rooms are furnished with period antiques, and rates include a full breakfast, ranging from bacon and eggs to pancakes. What makes the inn special is the Jacobs' love of poetry and the way in which this is shared with guests. Their 1,200-book library contains 650 volumes of poetry, with another 70 poets recorded on tape. There are occasional poetry readings, and some poets stay on as guests. Bob says: "A person doesn't have to like poetry to enjoy Brook Farm Inn, but if they have ever had even a small brush with the muse, their stay will be memorable."

"The inn enjoys an enviable location on a quiet tree-lined street just at the bottom of the hill below the Lenox monument. It is a large comfortable house in very good repair and charmingly decorated with antiques. Especially cozy is the living room, furnished with hundreds of poetry books, usually filled with the sound of classical music, and with people reading or talking quietly. Our room was very large, airy, impeccably clean, furnished with a big four-poster bed, divan, chairs, and well-placed lighting. It was comfortable to lounge and read in, and was supplied with a welcoming decanter of sherry. Breakfast included blueberry pancakes, fresh-squeezed orange juice, strong coffee served in the airy comfortable dining room. Late afternoon tea is also served, and on weekends, poetry readings often occur. Bob and Betty manage to be warm and hospitable without being intrusive. We felt we were the guests of gracious hosts, cultured and intelligent, who were quite happy to share with us their good fortune." *(Kirtland Snyder, also Gary Tabor and others)*

Open All year.
Rooms 8 doubles, 4 singles—all with private bath and/or shower. Some with desk, air-conditioning; all with fan.
Facilities Library with fireplace, stereo, piano; breakfast room with guest refrigerator. 1¼ shaded acres with heated swimming pool. Tennis, boating, fishing, skiing nearby.
Location 3/10 m from town. From Stockbridge, take Rte. 7 N through Stockbridge, bear left on Rte. 7A to Lenox. From Mass. Pike, take Exit 2. Go W on Rte. 20 to Rte. 183 W to Lenox.
Restrictions No smoking in summer; in guest rooms only in winter. No children under 15.
Credit cards MC, Visa.
Rates B&B, $55–135 double. Extra person in room, $20. 2- to 3-night weekend minimum in season.
Extras Free station pickups.

MARTHA'S VINEYARD   Map 2

Martha's Vineyard is a 20-mile-long island, located 5 miles south of Woods Hole in Cape Cod, and 80 miles south of Boston. It is easily reached by air from LaGuardia or White Plains, NY; Bridgeport, CT; Bedford and Boston, MA; or by a 45-minute ferry ride from Woods Hole or a longer one from Hyannis. Its beautiful beaches—many of them free—offer full surf on the south side of the island, and gentle waves along the state beach between Edgartown and Oak Bluffs. Swimming, fishing and sailing are always popular, as are horseback riding and bicycling. A 15-mile bicycle path leads along the water and through the woods.

The Vineyard is a very popular (and very crowded) place in the summer, and you should make car reservations for the ferry three to six months in advance. You can also rent a car after you arrive, but again, advance reservations are essential. If you're staying at an inn in Edgartown or Vineyard Haven, you can manage quite well without a car at all; in the up-island towns, such as Menemsha or West Tisbury, a car is essential. Rates are highest in July and August, and two- and three-day minimum stays are the rule; a number of inns charge peak season rates from early June through mid-October. If you can get away in September or October, you'll find sunny weather minus the crowds.

All the towns on the island, except for Edgartown and Oak Bluffs, are dry; when you're going out to dinner, bring your own wine, and the staff will be happy to chill and serve it for you.

Beach Plum Inn
North Road, Menemsha 02552

Tel: (617) 645–9454

Overlooking the sea, the Beach Plum has been owned by Janie and Paul Darrow since 1983. The comfortably furnished guest rooms are scattered among the weathered main house, private cottages, and old farmhouse, all surrounded by marvelous flowerbeds. The restaurant combines a rustic atmosphere with superlative cuisine, both continental and native New England seafood.

"Menemsha is an old fishing village; there's not too much to do but relax and watch the trawlers going in and out of the harbor, or stroll down to the bay beach for a swim. Its location is quite remote—ideal for a honeymoon or a romantic getaway. If you can't stay overnight, do make a reservation for dinner. Have a drink at one of the tables on the sloping lawns, watch the bunnies come out to eat, and take in the spectacular sunset. The limited-choice menu offers generally excellent food, beautifully presented on hand-painted china." *(Judy Margolin)*

"The inn is composed of a small group of weathered cottages surrounded by flowers, in an isolated and quiet location. The dining room and living room are elegantly furnished, while the guest rooms are done in country Victorian decor, with flowered fabrics and reproduction furnishings. The rooms are lovely but not luxurious for the price—remember that this is the Vineyard and the rates reflect the high cost of real estate and everything else." *(SWS)*

Open Mid-May to mid-Oct.
Rooms 3 cottages, 1 suite, 9 doubles—11 with private shower and/or bath, 2 with maximum of 4 people sharing bath. All with radio, desk; some with air-conditioning.
Facilities Restaurant with pianist, living room with library, TV. 7 acres with English gardens, tennis court. Stocked fishing pond. Golf nearby. Boat charters.
Location W side of island ("up island"); 20 min. from Edgartown.
Restrictions No children under 12.
Credit cards MC, Visa for rooms only.
Rates B&B, $200–250 suite, $100–200 double. MAP, $36 per person additional, including tax, tip. 4-night minimum in season. Prix fixe dinner, $40–45.

The Charlotte Inn
South Summer Street
Edgartown 02539

Tel: (508) 627–4751

The Charlotte has a well-deserved reputation as the most elegant inn on Martha's Vineyard. Each guest room is decorated differently, but all have

303

beautiful European antiques, original paintings and engravings, and brass lamps. Rich, dark-colored wallpapers contrast handsomely with the light-colored carpets and window trim in the main inn, while the Garden House is done in a French country decor in mauve, plum, and white.

Gery and Paula Conover bought The Charlotte Inn in 1980, and have gradually expanded it from the original Captain's House, built in 1860, adding suites in the Carriage House and guest rooms in the 200-year-old Garden House, the Summer House, and the Coach House. Rates include a continental breakfast of coffee, juice, and homemade muffins; full breakfast is available for an additional charge. The inn's restaurant, L'Etoile, serves excellent French cuisine in a beautiful setting. A recent meal included shellfish soup with leeks, scallions, and saffron; veal with basil and cheese ravioli in pignoli sauce; chocolate nut mousse cake with coffee sauce for dessert.

"Beautiful rooms, each different. Ours had a four-poster bed with an eyelet coverlet and a goose-down comforter, and nice antiques. L'Etoile is a first-class gourmet restaurant." (Susie Preston)

"Excellent location on a quiet lane, just off one of Edgartown's main shopping streets. The grounds are a lovely expanse of well-tended greenery, and the antique-filled rooms are exceptionally handsome. The restaurant feels much like a greenhouse—it's light and airy with lots of glass, plants, and even a little waterfall." (SWS)

Open All year. Restaurant closed Jan. 1 to Feb. 14.

Rooms 2 suites, 23 doubles—23 with full private bath, 2 sharing 1 bath. All with radio, fan; some with fireplace, TV, telephone, and desk. Guest rooms in the Main House, Garden House, Carriage House, Summer House, Coach House.

Facilities Restaurant, bar, art gallery, gift shop. Living room in Garden House with fireplace, TV; sitting room in Main House, game room in Summer House. Outside sitting areas, decks, porches, gardens. Walking distance to tennis, beaches, charter fishing.

Location 15-minute ride from the ferry. ½ block to Main Street. Follow signs to Edgartown. Turn right onto S. Summer St. Inn ½ block down on left.

Restrictions No cigars or pipes. No children under 14.

Credit cards Amex, MC, Visa.

Rates B&B, $275–335 suite, $65–295 double. Full breakfast $7 extra; prix fixe brunch, $25, dinner, $50. 2-night minimum stay.

Lambert's Cove Country Inn

Tel: (508) 693–2298

Lambert's Cove Road, Box 422
West Tisbury 02568

Driving down the narrow winding road to Lambert's Cove Country Inn, you might fantasize that you were coming home to Grandma's house. Entering the inn, with its country comfortable antiques and furnishings, will not disturb your reverie. Built as a farmhouse in 1790, the inn was substantially expanded in the 1920s, and additional guest rooms were added in the restored barn and carriage house.

Rooms are individually furnished and have attractive accessories; beds have firm mattresses. Rates include a continental breakfast of juice, coffee, and homemade breads; dinners feature fresh island seafood, vegetables from the inn's garden, and homemade soups, breads, and desserts. The

Sunday brunch is very popular, and picnic lunches are available on request. Some think it's the island's best restaurant. Marie Burnett is the innkeeper here; the inn has been owned by Banning and Elizabeth Repplier since 1980.

"Run by friendly, hospitable, delightful people. Delicious food, attractive decor, inviting guest rooms." *(Jennifer Josephy, Judy Margolin)*

"A lovely 'up island' pastoral setting, secluded grounds. The inn still looks like the farmhouse it once was, beautifully kept but not fancy. The common rooms are filled with Victorian antiques—one is a more formal, the other a more homey one with plenty of books, board games, and a TV. The guest room I saw was simply decorated, done mostly in ivory tones, very clean with adequate lighting. An adjacent room with canopy bed had more character. Prices are very fair by island standards." *(SWS)*

Open Feb. through Dec.
Rooms 15 doubles—all with private bath and/or shower. 8 rooms in annex. Some rooms with private decks; 1 with greenhouse sitting room, 1 with working fireplace.
Facilities Restaurant, sitting room with fireplace, TV; library with fireplace, books, games; decks. 7½ acres with tennis court. Lambert's Cove private beach available to inn guests. Cross-country skiing, skating.
Location Near W side of island. 4 m from Vineyard Haven. Take left after driving off ferry. Right at next stop-sign intersection. Stay on this road for 1½ m to Lambert's Cove Rd. on right. 3 m from this point look for inn sign, on left. Inn is at end of rd., ½ m in.
Restrictions Smoking discouraged. No children under 6 in season.
Credit cards Amex, DC, MC, Visa.
Rates B&B, $70–130 double, plus 4.3% service. Additional person in room, $15. Minimum stay requirements. Alc dinner, $30 (BYOB).
Extras French spoken.

NANTUCKET 02554   Map 2

Nantucket is a relatively small island, about 7 by 15 miles, set 25 to 30 miles south of Cape Cod in the Atlantic Ocean. Peak season runs from Memorial Day through Labor Day weekend, although spring, fall, and Christmas are becoming increasingly popular. During July and August, expect crowds, high rates, and minimum-stay requirements at all inns. If you're making last-minute plans and aren't having any luck at the inns recommended here, call the Nantucket Information Bureau (25 Federal Street; 508–228–0925); they can tell you where rooms are available.

You can fly to Nantucket from New York, Boston, or Hyannis, or take the ferry from Woods Hole, Hyannis, or Oak Bluffs (Martha's Vineyard). Reservations are essential in peak season, and should be made several months in advance for cars. Most innkeepers recommend leaving your car on the mainland, if possible.

Brant Point Inn   *Tel:* (508) 228–5442
6 North Beach Street

Peter and Thea Kaizer built this new house as a B&B inn in 1986. The living room has wide pine flooring, exposed oak beams, and a Belgian block fireplace, while the guest rooms are decorated with an attractive country look. Rates include a light continental breakfast of juice, coffee, and muffins.

"Nantucket in the autumn is like no other place in the world. The Brant Point Inn is a beautiful post-and-beam structure located five minutes from Nantucket town, harborside beaches, and the ferry boat dock. Each guest room has a small refrigerator and sitting area. There is a garden patio and a large front porch for relaxing." *(Meg Ruley)*

Open All year.
Rooms 1 apartment suite with full kitchen; 7 doubles—all with private shower, telephone, radio, TV, sitting area, guest refrigerator.
Facilities Living room with fireplace, porch, terraces. 2-min. walk to beaches. Fishing charters.
Location 5-min. walk to town. At corner of Easton and N. Beach sts.
Credit cards Amex, MC, Visa.
Rates B&B, $150 suite, $40–120 double.

Jared Coffin House   *Tel:* (508) 228–2400
29 Broad Street

The inn comprises the Jared Coffin House (1845), two attached wings built in the 1700s and in 1857, and two other nineteenth-century buildings less than 50 feet away. One building, the Daniel Webster House, is of recent construction, built in 1968. Margaret and Philip Read, innkeepers at the Jared Coffin House for over twenty years, describe their inn as a good place for "country inn travelers, honeymooners, people who don't need a lot of artificial entertainment, conservationists, students of colonial architecture, and beachcombers (classy ones)."

"Breakfasts and dinners are served daily from May through October in the inn's restaurant—Jared's—and on weekends and holidays in November and December. The Tap Room serves casual lunches, snacks, and dinners year-round.

"The Jared Coffin House is one of our fondest inns in the world, especially at Christmas, when I feel like I'm coming home. The Reads and their excellent staff add to this quality. All facilities and departments of the inn and its annexes work perfectly. If, for any reason, there is a problem, their good man, Mike Bedell, who has been there for a number of years, takes care of it immediately. The ambience of the inn is strictly Nantucket/New England, and the cuisine is excellent." *(Bob Tucker)*

"The Jared dining room is extremely good but expensive. The staff is friendly, accommodating, and helpful. This is not a place for everyone: The main house has creaky floors, no TV, and erratic hot water. It is also on the large size and the public rooms are filled with people. I would recommend the rooms in either the Henry Coffin House or the Harrison Gray House. The location is great, right next to the village. Be sure to have breakfast at the Downyflake on Water Street. I found everyone on the island to be very helpful." *(Dianne Crawford)*

Open All year.
Rooms 52 doubles, 8 singles—all with private bath and/or shower, telephone. 50 rooms with TV, 36 with desk. 30 rooms in 3 additional buildings.

Facilities Restaurant, tap room with evening entertainment, several sitting rooms, patio, garden. ½ m to beach.
Location Center of historic district.
Restrictions Street noise could disturb light sleepers in summer.
Credit cards Amex, DC, MC, Visa. Payments for advance deposits by check.
Rates Room only, $100–175 double, $50–70 single. Extra person in room, $10. Alc lunch, $15; alc dinner, $50.
Extras Cribs available; babysitters on call. Well-behaved pets welcome. Ramps, elevator for limited wheelchair access. Some French, Spanish, Russian spoken.

Seven Sea Street Inn
7 Sea Street

Tel: (508) 228–3577
(800) 228–4886

Matthew Parker and Mary Parker welcome guests to their recently constructed red oak post-and-beam guest house. Built in the style of old Nantucket, complete with rooftop widow's walk and colonial-style furnishings, the inn offers such modern comforts as up-to-date plumbing and in-room amenities.

"The owners are friendly and hospitable, good about making dinner reservations and offering sightseeing and beachgoing advice. The inn is done all in natural woods and is spotlessly clean. We enjoyed a breakfast of fresh fruit salad, juices, and our fill of home-baked cranberry, corn, and bran muffins. The Parker family also owns several other inns on the island." *(Dottie & Frank Scarfone)*

Open All year
Rooms 2 suites, 6 doubles—all with private shower, queen-size beds, telephone, TV, desk, fan, refrigerator.
Facilities Breakfast room with fireplace, 2 common rooms with woodstove, books; Jacuzzi room, patio. Limited parking. Beaches for swimming, surf casting nearby.
Location Historic district. On Sea St. between N. Water and S. Beach Sts.
Restrictions No smoking. No children under 7.
Credit cards Amex, MC, Visa
Rates B&B, $100–200 suite, $75–155 double, $65–145 single. Extra person in room, $15. 2- to 3-night weekend/holiday minimum.
Extras French spoken.

The Summer House
Ocean Avenue, Siasconset 02564

Tel: (508) 257–9976

'Sconset, as it is always pronounced and often written, is set at the southeastern edge of Nantucket, with ocean views broken only by the horizon. Its location, seven miles via road or bike path from Nantucket town, gives it a more peaceful air, even in the height of the summer season. A famous escape in the 1920s, The Summer House was recently restored and redecorated. High on a bluff, the inn is composed of a main building, with big pillars and a wide front porch, housing the restaurant and bar, filled with white wicker and lots of plants. It's surrounded by small rose-trellised cottages, furnished with English antiques and Laura Ashley wallpapers. At the base of the bluff is the swimming pool, with the beach just a short walk beyond. Even if you're not staying overnight, the inn restaurant is well worth a visit. Under the supervision of chefs Everett and Stuart Reid, entrées include such creative efforts as lobster and crayfish sausage, tuna grilled with dried cherries, and roast chicken with honey-lemon sauce and chile cornbread stuffing, all served with a variety of fresh vegetables. Dinner is made even more pleasant by the nostalgic tunes of Sal Gioe, longtime island institution, on the grand piano.

"A stay at The Summer House is lovely at any time, but a weekend in the fall, while the water is still warm, but the island is empty, is a perfect way to extend the sense of summer. Although small, the rooms are charmingly furnished and retain a character and privacy heightened by the profusion of flowers spilling over the rooftops, framing the windows and straying across the path to the bluff overlooking the ocean. A perfect balance is struck by the truly excellent restaurant on the one hand, and by the broad stretch of beach bordering the Atlantic on the other. The management knows its clientele and does an admirable job of providing courteous service, attentive to detail. The welcoming niceties include sprays of native flowers, scented soaps, constantly replenished firewood, thick towels, and fresh linens, yet the staff is very aware that tranquility is what they offer on this now sometimes hectic island. The only sounds remain sea birds, surf, and the faint stream of a Cole Porter tune from the restaurant's grandly played grand piano." *(Patricia Ross)*

Open May 15 to Oct. 15.
Rooms 10 cottages with full private bath, radio, desk. Some with kitchenette, fireplace.
Facilities Dining room, lounge with fireplace, pianist, porch. 1 acre with flower gardens, heated swimming pool. Tennis, golf nearby.
Location SE corner of island. Walking distance to Siasconset; 7 m E of Nantucket town. Take Siasconset Rd. to Siasconset rotary; turn right, take the high road to inn sign.
Restrictions Traffic noise in some cottages.
Credit cards Amex, MC, Visa.
Rates B&B, $160–335 double, plus 10% service. 3-night minimum preferred. Alc lunch, $15–20; alc dinner, $50. Approx. 50% discount May 15–June 15; after Labor Day–Oct. 15. Weekly discounts.
Extras Wheelchair accessible; some rooms equipped for disabled. Pets permitted with prior permission. French, Italian spoken. Cribs, babysitting available.

ROCKPORT 01966   Map 2

Rockport is on Massachusetts's "other" cape—Cape Ann, with a coastline more like that of Maine than Massachusetts, yet located only 40 miles northeast of Boston. To get there, take Route 128 north until it ends at a set of traffic lights, then pick up Route 127 to the center of Rockport. Rockport has one of the country's oldest artist colonies, along with dozens of craft and antique shops, although recent reports indicate a tacky "honky tonk" atmosphere. Other activities include hiking and bicycling, and of course swimming, fishing, boating, and whale-watching in season—from April through October. Rockport is a "dry" town, so bring your wine from Gloucester; restaurants will gladly chill and serve it for you.

Seacrest Manor   *Tel:* (508) 546–2211
131 Marmion Way

Leighton Saville and Dwight MacCormack offer bed & breakfast accommodation in their beautiful 1911 manor house, set in a quiet residential area. Rooms are decorated in a sensible way, with chenille bedspreads, writing desks with pierced lampshades, and utilitarian carpets. A full breakfast of blueberry pancakes, corn fritters with hot syrup, or ham and eggs is beautifully served on Wedgwood china in the lovely breakfast room. Other amenities include nightly turndown, shoeshine service, and the morning newspaper delivered to your door.

"Being innkeepers ourselves, we are very critical of comfort and cleanliness especially. This inn passes muster easily on these two counts. The view is spectacular, the common rooms are magnificent, the breakfast superb, the innkeepers gracious and very attentive." *(Bob Jewett)*

"Pleasant place with a slightly formal atmosphere, good breakfast, attractive room. The innkeepers suggested a great little restaurant, the Hungry Wolf, about four blocks away. The staff was courteous and helpful. Although we had relatively little contact with the owners, we would be delighted to return." *(Mrs. James Todd)*

Open All year.
Rooms 8 doubles—6 with private full bath, 2 with maximum of 4 people sharing bath.
Facilities Breakfast room, parlor, library, rooftop-deck gardens.
Location 1 m from downtown. Just off Rte. 127A.
Restrictions No children under 16.
Credit cards None accepted.
Rates B&B, $62–90 double, $58–86 single. 10% service. 2- to 3-night holiday/weekend minimum in season.

SALEM 01970   Map 2

Founded in 1628, Salem has many historic attractions. It's infamous for the Witch Trials of the late seventeenth century, but it is also the home of Hawthorne's House of the Seven Gables. Two major museums, the Peabody Museum and the Essex Institute, are fascinating reminders of the town's importance as a port in the late 1700s. The former started with the trinkets sea captains brought back from their voyages, while the latter encompasses the reconstruction of houses dating back to the seventeenth century.

Salem is located on the North Shore, 18 miles northeast of Boston, and about a 45-minute drive from Boston's Logan Airport. Boston and the North Shore are easily accessible from Salem via commuter rail. Marblehead, a yachting center and the birthplace of the American Navy, is just five minutes' drive away.

Stephen Daniels House   *Tel:* (508) 744–5709
1 Daniels Street

Catherine Gill, who has owned the Stephen Daniels House for 27 years, describes her inn as "a favorite with history buffs and antique collectors, because it is completely furnished with authentic period furniture and accessories."

When Catherine B. Gill welcomes you through the front door, you step back in time. If you turn to the right, you enter the 1667 portion of the house. If you turn to the left, you enter the "new addition," built in 1756. In either case, you will have your lodging in rooms—and have the run of a house—that you would generally only be able to glimpse from behind velvet ropes in a museum. The house is one of the oldest in Salem. Fortunately for today's guest, after the 1756 addition, the owners were not able to modernize, so, aside from electricity and indoor plumbing, no changes were made. The bedrooms, several with original working fireplaces, are on the second floor and have canopied beds, many antiques, old books, original colonial paint colors, antique Oriental carpets, and wide-board floors.

"This place has it all! Mrs. Gill's years of experience really shine through here. She did everything right—when we arrived she took us on a house tour which included the bedrooms, and we oohed and aahed at every turn. Later, she spent time talking with us and making suggestions. In the morning, she presided over breakfast in a chair by the fireplace, and a great time was had by all." *(Shirley & Lyle Dittloff)*

Open All year.
Rooms 2 suites, 3 doubles, with private or shared baths and/or shower.
Facilities 3 common rooms with wood-burning fireplaces. Shaded lawn with tables and chairs. 1 block to ocean.
Location 3–4 blocks to center.
Credit cards Amex.
Rates B&B, $65–85 suite, $60–75 double, $50–75 single. Reduced rates for children, families, seniors, 3-day stays.
Extras Babysitting sometimes available. Well-behaved pets permitted.

The Stepping Stone Inn
19 Washington Square North

Tel: (508) 741–8900
(800) 338–3022

Built in 1846 for naval officer Benjamin True, The Stepping Stone Inn was bought by the Stone family in 1987. The renovation and redecoration of the inn were recently completed; rooms are furnished simply, with reproduction period furniture.

"Very pleasant, friendly, hospitable atmosphere. Staff is personable, attentive, and willing to answer questions. The common rooms have handsome Oriental rugs and lots of fresh flowers. My room was clean and spacious, with lovely polished wood furniture. The lighting, plumbing, cleanliness and service are all fine. The continental breakfast included cereal, croissants, bagels, fruit, tea, and coffee, and was served in the hotel barroom." *(Katherine Crowley)*

"Central location across from the Witch Museum, within walking distance of everything. We enjoyed it all, from the four-poster bed turned down and with a chocolate left on the pillow, to the expertly prepared eggs Benedict served with homemade muffins. There's even a potpourri spice bag, matched to the bed linens, tied to the headboard." *(Mrs. Erin Schembri)*

Open March through Dec. 23.
Rooms 8 doubles—all with private shower, TV, air-conditioning.
Facilities Dining room, parlor with TV, games. Salem Commons are across street with jogging paths, basketball court, playground. Fishing, swimming nearby.
Location In town center. Hotel is next to Witch Museum.
Restrictions Light sleepers should request back rooms.
Credit cards Amex, CB, DC, MC, Visa; 4% service fee additional.

Rates B&B, $75–125 double. Extra person in room, $10. 2-night weekend/holiday minimum. Weekly rates.
Extras Airport pickups by prior arrangement. Cribs, babysitter available. Small, well-behaved pets permitted. French, Spanish spoken.

STOCKBRIDGE 01262   Map 2

Information please: The **Inn at Stockbridge** offers seven guest clean rooms decorated with antiques, and delicious full breakfasts served in a friendly atmosphere; work off the waffles in the forty-foot swimming pool (Route 7; 413–298–3337).

The Red Lion Inn   *Tel:* (413) 298–5545
Main Street

The Red Lion Inn is probably the best-known inn in the Berkshires. Founded in 1761, it burned to the ground in 1896. Soon rebuilt, it has since been enlarged and renovated many times and now accommodates two hundred guests. Furnishings combine antiques and period reproductions.

Although the Red Lion is undoubtedly a wonderful institution and the granddaddy of many a country inn, it may well be too big for some readers; its in-town location too noisy for others. But, we've had very positive reports from readers about the pleasant staff and good food served in its several restaurants for breakfast, lunch, dinner, and brunch. Long-time manager Betsy Holtzinger reports that many rooms have recently been redecorated, and are most handsome.

"Located in the lovely village of Stockbridge, where Norman Rockwell lived and worked, the Red Lion is an exceedingly well operated and managed inn. Its antique-filled lobby is a delight, and the rooms are spacious and quiet. The food is good and we especially enjoy sitting on the inn's long veranda (where refreshments are served), watching the Main Street traffic go by. In addition to Tanglewood, other Stockbridge attractions are the Berkshire Theater Festival and the Norman Rockwell Museum." *(Irving Litvag, also Mrs. Kirk Fisher)* "Exceeded our expectations in every regard." *(SWS)*

Open All year.
Rooms 12 suites, 93 doubles, most with private bath and/or shower, 22 with shared bath. All with air-conditioning, telephone, TV, and desk. 13 rooms in annex. Some rooms accessible by elevator.
Facilities Restaurant, bars, tavern, TV rooms, living rooms, meeting rooms. Live music in bars, restaurant. Courtyard, gardens, swimming pool, tennis court.
Location S central MA, Berkshires. Center of town.
Restrictions Traffic noise in some rooms. Limited parking.
Credit cards Amex, CB, DC, MC, Visa.
Rates Room only, $105–217 suite, $50–135 double, $43–88 single, plus $2 daily housekeeping charge. Extra person in room, $17–25. Full breakfast $4–12. Alc lunch $8–15, alc dinner, $25–40. Children's menu. Off-season midweek packages available Nov. to mid-May. Special holiday menus and programs.
Extras Wheelchair equipped room and bath. Japanese, Spanish, German. Cribs, babysitting available.

STURBRIDGE 01566   Map 2

Old Sturbridge Village Motor Lodge   *Tel:* (508) 347–3327
Route 20 West

"The Old Sturbridge Village Motor Lodge is composed of eight single-story buildings of six rooms apiece. Each building represents a different New England style and is painted in appropriate colors. We stayed in the cottage, done in antique reproduction decor, Oriental and rag rugs, broad-plank hardwood floors, and hand-stenciled walls with bedspreads and shower curtains to match. Despite its setting near a busy road, the ample soundproofing and landscaping made for a handsome setting and eliminated any traffic noise. The entrance to Old Sturbridge Village is only 200 yards away.

"I also saw rooms in the Oliver Wight House, which was equally lovely, although the rooms were not quite as large as those in the cottage. Rooms in the motel section were quite nice, of average size, with country-style decor. The lodge provides a free daily newspaper and coffee. There is no dining facility, but Friendly's is right next door for breakfast." *(Susan W. Schwemm)*

Open All year.
Rooms 2 suites, 57 doubles—all with private bath, telephone, TV, desk, air-conditioning, fan. 12 rooms in 2 separate historic buildings.
Facilities No common facilities. 5 landscaped acres. ½ m to cross-country skiing.
Location S central MA. 50 m W of Boston, 45 m NE of Hartford, CT. 1 m from center. From I-84/86 take Exit 3. From Mass. Tpke. take Exit 9. Follow signs to Rte. 20 W.
Restrictions Smoking in designated areas only.
Credit cards Amex, MC, Visa.
Rates Room only, $75–95 suite or double. Extra person in room, $5.
Extras Wheelchair accessible rooms. Cribs available.

WELLFLEET 02667   Map 2

The Inn at Duck Creeke   *Tel:* (508) 349–9333
East Main Street, Box 634

"The delectable little town of Wellfleet, with its many art galleries and craft shops, is as charming as Provincetown, ten minutes up the road, is gaudy and honky-tonk. Wellfleet is well served by its chief inn, the Inn at Duck Creeke, a fine early-eighteenth-century building. Formerly a sea captain's house, it overlooks a duck pond on one side and a tidal creek and salt marsh on the other. The inn lies just off Route 6, a few minutes' walk from the center and the harbor.

"Rooms are furnished with sympathetic period pieces—Boston rockers, spool beds, and the like. The rooms are comfortable without being plush—shabby/friendly. Most have private baths; some have only showers or shared showers. Towels could be larger, and bathroom fittings upgraded, but most visitors will be willing to overlook minor austerities in the fur-

nishings and fittings for the agreeableness of the ambience and the modest
tariff. Only continental breakfast is served—coffee, fruit juices, and muffins. For a richer breakfast, drop in at the Lighthouse in the town center—a
highly popular venue, famous for its blueberry pancakes and other delica-
cies. For lunch, try the Lunch Box (also in the center) with its amazing
sandwich options. For dinner, the inn's restaurant, Sweet Seasons, is as
good as you will find in Wellfleet, according to locals. We can vouch for
an exemplary poached lobster.

"The inn isn't grand. It isn't one of those places where the owners keep
a high profile. The front desk is often unattended. But everyone, staff or
owners (we never discovered which were which), were unfailingly cheerful
and helpful. We thoroughly enjoyed our three-day stay." *(Hilary Rubinstein)*
More comments please.

Open Mid-May to mid-Oct. Restaurant open weekends only May, June, Sept., Oct.
Rooms 3 suites, 22 doubles—17 with private bath and/or shower, 8 with a maxi-
mum of 4 people sharing a bath. Some with air-conditioning; all with fan. 7 rooms
in annex.
Facilities Restaurant, tavern, breakfast room, common room, screened porch. Swim-
ming, boating, fishing, hiking, bicycling nearby.
Location Cape Cod, 17 m S of Provincetown, 100 m SE of Boston. Take Rte. 6 to
Wellfleet; turn left at Wellfleet Center sign at traffic lights. Go 500 yds. to inn on
right. ½ m to village.
Credit cards Amex, MC, Visa.
Rates B&B, $70–90 suite, $45–85 double, $40–80 single. Extra person in room, $12.
Children under 5 in parents' room, $5. 2–3-night weekend minimum in season. Alc
dinner $15–23.
Extras Limited handicap access. Cribs available.

WILLIAMSTOWN 01267   Map 2

Williamstown is a beautiful country town, the home of small but prestigi-
ous Williams College, and of two fine art museums—the Clark Institute,
particularly famous for its Impressionist collection, and the Williams College Art Museum, with some impressive nineteenth- and twentieth-
century paintings.

Williamstown is located in the northern Berkshires of northwest Massachusetts, 40 miles east of Albany, and 130 miles west of Boston.

Also recommended: Field Farm Guest House (554 Sloan Road; 413–
458–3135) is an isolated country home, whose key appeal is the surrounding 250 acres of rural beauty.

The Orchards   *Tel:* (413) 458–9611
222 Adams Road (Route 2)   In MA: (800) 231–2344
    Outside MA: (800) 225–1517

There are no longer any fruit trees at The Orchards—in fact, its location
on a busy road in a commercial zone is far from rural. To compensate, the
inn's architects focused on a central courtyard, highlighting the luxury of
the rooms and appointments. The inn is relatively new, built only in 1985,
ambitiously designed to be an "elegant country hotel in the English tradi-

tion." "Once you step inside, you enter another world. The owners have brought all of the charm of a top English hotel to New England. The rooms are large and gorgeous, each one decorated differently, following an English country theme. Other amenities included: fresh fruit and ice brought to the room in late afternoon; tea and goodies served between 4 and 5 P.M. in the main living room; terry-cloth robes, nightlights, telephones, and lots of big fluffy towels in the luxurious bathroom; three types of pillows, and our comfortable king-size bed turned down at night with a chocolate-chip cookie on the pillow. There is a lovely and elegant dining room, and a nice lounge with a huge fieldstone fireplace. You can take your dessert and cordials in the living room, a nice English tradition." *(Jo Carol & George Wood)*

"The Orchards's outstanding feature is the service it offers. Nothing was too much to ask of the staff—my husband asked about getting the *Wall St. Journal,* and the next morning it appeared at our door. We asked about getting a blanket to take to Tanglewood, and immediately, a woolen one was produced. The rooms are immaculately clean, with many extra touches—ours had a bottle of Perrier and a basket of apples. We had a superb dinner—the seafood was especially good—nicely served in the restaurant." *(SR)*

"Our room was so gorgeous I could have lived there permanently. Just as you've described it—beautiful decor, delicious food, excellent service, and mediocre location." *(Eileen Yudelson)*

Open All year.
Rooms 2 suites, 47 doubles—all with full private bath, telephone, radio, TV, desk, air-conditioning. Some rooms with refrigerators, fireplaces.
Facilities Restaurant, living room, lounge with weekend pianist, breakfast room, courtyard with pond, heated swimming pool, exercise room with sauna, Jacuzzi. Ice-skating, cross-country/downhill skiing, tennis, golf, fishing, hiking nearby.
Location 1 m from town, on Rte. 2E.
Credit cards Amex, DC, MC, Visa.
Rates B&B, $160–180 suites, $125–170 double, $120–175 single. MAP, $47 additional per person. Rates include service. 10% AARP discount. Additional person in room, $20. Full breakfast, $5–7; alc lunch, $10; alc dinner, $35. Package rates available. 2-night weekend minimum, June to Nov. $20 surcharge in winter for fireplace rooms.
Extras Cribs available. Wheelchair accessible; 3 rooms equipped for disabled. Spanish, French, Italian spoken. Station pickups available by prior arrangement.

Michigan

Wickwood Inn, Saugatuck

Michigan has many lovely resort towns and fishing villages, on the western (Lake Michigan) side of the state, and on the eastern (Lake Huron) side, on both the Lower and Upper Peninsulas. The peninsulas are connected at the Straits of Mackinac by the Mackinac Bridge, a twentieth-century achievement that forms a pleasant contrast with the nineteenth-century charms of Mackinac Island. Michigan's industrial strength, centered on the automobile industry, is found in the south, in the Detroit area. Although hardly a tourist mecca, Motor City is also home to the Detroit Institute of Arts, one of America's finest art museums. In nearby Dearborn, the Henry Ford Museum and Greenfield Village are home to outstanding collections highlighting the history of transportation and technology in the U.S. We'd love to have more recommendations for this area, and would particularly like to request comments on the **Dearborn Inn,** Henry Ford's vision of the ideal inn, set on 23 acres with 94 rooms in the Georgian style, with additional accommodations in five colonial-reproduction homes and a motor lodge (20301 Oakwood Boulevard 48124; 800–221–7237).

Rates do not include 4% state sales tax.

Information please: We'd like reports on the **Atchison House**, an Italianate Victorian B&B, built in 1882. It's located in Northville's historic district, 20 miles northwest of Detroit (501 West Dunlap Street, Northville 48167; 313–349–3340).

ALDEN 49612   Map 7

Torch Lake B&B   *Tel:* (616) 331–6424
10601 Coy Street

A compact pink "painted lady," the Torch Lake is highlighted by its
original gingerbread trim and stained glass windows.

"We toured this beautiful inn, and what a gem it is. Its owner, Patti
Findlay, is equally charming. Clean and welcoming, with a view of Torch
Lake (one of the world's loveliest, according to *National Geographic*). Alden
is within an easy drive of Harbor Springs, Traverse City, Petosky, and
Charlevoix." *(Sue Gradel)*

Open Late May to Oct. 19.
Rooms 3 doubles—1 with private bath, 2 sharing 1 bath.
Facilities Living room, dining room, garden. Golf, bicycling, walking, skiing nearby.
Location NW MI. Approx. 22 m NE of Traverse City. Take M-72 E to Rapid City
turnoff (Cty. Road 597); turn N to Alden. Inn is on NE corner of Coy and Alden
Street, just S of downtown.
Restrictions No children. No smoking.
Credit cards None accepted.
Rates B&B, $50–60. 2-night weekend minimum.

BATTLE CREEK 49017   Map 7

The Old Lamplighter's Homestay   *Tel:* (616) 963–2603
276 Capital Avenue NE

Roberta Stewart, a retired schoolteacher, opened her B&B in 1987; it's the
kind of place that can make all the difference in an otherwise routine
business trip. Listed on the National Register of Historic Places, it is always
fairly well maintained and boasts many original features, including hand-
painted murals, mahogany beams and trim, and beveled and stained glass
windows. Rooms are decorated with period antiques; Oriental carpets
highlight the restored hardwood floors.

"The Old Lamplighter's Inn is a very big old brick mansion, built in the
Arts and Crafts style in 1912, in a prosperous, early Battle Creek neighborhood. Many of the fine old homes lining Capital Avenue have been put
to commercial use, and some restored to their original elegance. This house
is fun to explore, with all its many nooks and crannies, from the 'drying
room' in the basement to the butler's pantry and library on the first floor,
the elegant bathrooms on the second, and the servants' sitting room on the
third. My favorite room has a four-poster bed with a beautiful handmade
quilt, a velvet Victorian love seat in the window alcove, a marble-topped
table on little wheels, and an old-fashioned rocker. The whole house is
scrupulously clean and very nicely appointed. Towels are trimmed with
lace borders, and each room has fresh flowers. Breakfast includes juice and
a selection of cereals, plus delicious muffins, eggs, sometimes a pan-baked
cake, fresh fruit, good jams and jellies, plenty of fresh coffee, and some
cheese spreads.

"The inn is in walking distance of downtown, and there is ample parking. Capital is a busy street, and traffic is constant, but the back bedrooms are pretty quiet." *(L. Carolyn Sorensen)*

"Roberta and Evelyn Stewart are friendly without being pushy. Guests may join in as family members if they wish, or will be left alone if preferred. Fine service, adequate lighting and parking, convenient location. All the plumbing is okay, with the main bathroom being almost decadent—with a large marble shower, long and deep antique tub, two sinks, and beveled glass windows." *(Frederick F. Fellers)*

Open All year.
Rooms 7 doubles, 5 with private shower and/or bath, 2 sharing 1 bath. All with TV. Four with air-conditioning. Phone on each floor.
Facilities Dining room, library with fireplace, parlor, music room, pantry with guest refrigerator, microwave, porch. Lakes, cross-country skiing nearby.
Location Walking distance to downtown.
Restrictions No smoking.
Credit cards Amex, MC, Visa.
Rates B&B, $55 double, $49 single. Weekly and corporate rates. Golfing, skiing packages available.
Extras Cribs available.

BAY VIEW 49770 Map 7

Bay View was founded as a Chautauqua summer campground and has hosted, among other notables, Helen Keller and William Jennings Bryan. Because of its four hundred Victorian summer homes, Bay View is listed on the National Register of Historic Places. The town offers a wide variety of recreational activities, as well as chamber music concerts, drama, and musical theater productions. Little Traverse Bay and Lake Michigan are available for all water sports, and nearby Boyne Mountain offers excellent golf in summer and downhill skiing in winter. Cross-country skiing is available right in town.

Technically a part of the town of Petoskey (1 mile away), Bay View is located on Little Traverse Bay, near the northeastern end of Lake Michigan, about 30 miles southwest of the Straits of Mackinac. To get there from I-75, take Rte. 31 south from Mackinac, or take Route 68 west from Indian River to Rte. 31.

Also recommended: On the very day of our press deadline, we received *Zita Knific's* report on the **Main Street B&B** (403 East Main Street, Harbor Springs 49740; 616–526–7782) just a few miles north of Petoskey. "Donna and Jerry Karson are the new owners of this 180-year-old transplanted hotel, brought to its current location across the frozen bay about 80 years ago. Their enthusiasm and delight in meeting people is contagious. Our room was lovely in wicker, with peach and ivory colors, and the shared bath was immaculate. Breakfast was served on the wraparound screened-in porch decorated in wicker with blue accents. Breakfast was decaf coffee (by request), bacon and eggs, homemade muffins with honey butter and fresh sliced strawberries and bananas. The pier, restaurants and shops are just a ten-minute walk away."

Information please: The **Perry Hotel** (Bay and Lewis streets, Petoskey 49770; 616–347–2516 or in MI 800–654–2608) was built as a resort hotel in 1899. Several years ago, under new ownership, it underwent a multi-million-dollar renovation and expansion, which increased the hotels size by 54 rooms. The views remained as lovely as ever, and readers noted that the food improved dramatically. In 1989 the hotel changed hands again, and more reports are in order before the Perry can be reinstated with a full entry.

Stafford's Bay View Inn   *Tel:* (616) 347–2771
613 Woodland Avenue (Route 31), P.O. Box 3

When it was built in 1886, the Bay View Inn had fifty tiny rooms, many large enough to hold only a single twin bed, and none had a private bath. One hundred years later, longtime owner Stafford "Duff" Smith renovated all the rooms, adding private baths and increasing the guest rooms in size by decreasing the total to thirty. Rooms are decorated with period antiques and lots of wicker. Rates include an extensive breakfast buffet.

"Set in a quiet part of town, just a block from the bay, the inn offers lovely rooms, friendly service, and wonderful food. We dined on spicy pumpkin bread, a creamy vegetable soup, mixed salad with cherry-vinaigrette dressing, whitefish with almonds, fresh squash and tiny round potatoes. For dessert we had real strawberry shortcake and a cream puff with rich fudge sauce. We consider the meals at Bay View to be among the best in northern Michigan." *(Paul & Elizabeth Lasley)*

"My room came with a large dressing and bath area that was surprisingly spacious for such a historic building. Dinner was very good as was the service. The ample breakfast was equally tasty and featured cherry muffins and cherry sauces—apparently a local speciality. The public rooms are homey, and Mr. Smith was there to chat with the guests." *(Constance Trowbridge)* "Pleasant ambience, relaxed pace; excellent food and attentive service." *(Robert & Barbara Van Ess)* "Charming and classic, just as described. A bit overpriced for off season, though." *(MS)*

"We were delighted with our large and extravagantly decorated room, with its wild floral paper above the chair rail and its coordinating striped design below. All unoccupied rooms were open-top-view; all had dried flower wreaths on the doors, and a complimentary bottle of wine, handsome glasses, and an ice bucket, matching, of course. Staff was helpful about making reservations and such extras as bringing you coffee on the porch. The breakfast was solid and satisfying, elegantly served." *(Zita Knific)*

Reader tip: "Ask for a room on the second floor; ventilation on the third floor didn't seem so good, and I thought the air-conditioners were noisy."

Open All year. Restaurant closed mid-March through mid-May, Nov. and Dec.
Rooms 6 suites, 24 doubles, all with full private bath, radio, desk, air-conditioning.
Facilities Lobby, restaurant, parlor, sun-room with TV, games. 100 feet from Bay. Off-street parking. Tennis, golf, beach, cross-country and downhill skiing nearby.
Location 1 m from Petoskey.
Credit cards Amex, MC, Visa.
Rates B&B, $88–160 suite, $50–122 double, $40–88 single. Extra person in room, $10–30. No charge for children under 3. Family rates. Packages available. Alc lunch, $7; alc dinner, $18.

Extras Free airport/station pickups with prior notice. Wheelchair accessible. Cribs, games available.

The Terrace Inn
216 Fairview, P.O. Box 266

Tel: (616) 347–2410

The Terrace Inn was restored in 1985, and was bought by Patrick Barbour in 1987. The lobby and dining room are paneled in pine, and many of the original oak furnishings are in use in the bedrooms. Readers have noted some of the pros and cons of this establishment; we think that more careful management could easily turn things around.

"The rooms, all spotlessly clean, have been restored to their original 1910 style and decor. Dinner was a delightful experience. The food is well-balanced traditional American fare, prepared and served with care and style. The waitresses and maids all dress in 1910-style walking skirts, aprons, and blouses; all were so thoughtful and courteous. The continental breakfast of freshly homemade muffins, rolls, breads, assorted juices, and homemade granola was very nice. Although the inn does not have a liquor license, guests are provided with appropriate setups should they want to bring their own." *(Pati Kane)*

"The newly decorated rooms are fairly small and sparsely decorated, but have pretty wallpaper, new mattresses and box springs, and new bathrooms, most with stall showers. The dining room is pleasant in appearance, but can be noisy when full." *(ELC)*

"The inn is tucked in among Bay View's beautiful Victorian homes and offers easy access to the attractive beach, which has plenty of Petoskey stones—the coral-filled state rock. *(BS)* "The large pine-paneled lobby is reminiscent of a hunting lodge, with an open view of the country Victorian-style dining room and the long porch. We caught the early bird special ($7.95) and were delighted with both the service, quality, and apprearance of our meal." *(Zita Knific)*

Some areas for improvement: "Although the oak and marble lobby is impressive, we found it to be too brightly lit—in need of more nooks and crannies. A better library, with local restaurant menus and area guidebooks, would also help; only 'tourist trap' pamphlets were available." And: "It seemed that the receptionists at the front desk were more in tune with their own conversations than our needs; we never felt welcomed to the inn. Our room was small but comfortable, but was papered in drab brown. They may have been having maintenance or housekeeping problems when we visited, because the inside of the original bathroom door had been sanded but appeared unstained; the shade was ripped; the shower had loose tile and mildew." More comments please.

Open All year. Restaurant closed April.
Rooms 44 doubles—all with private bath and/or shower, fan.
Facilities Restaurant, ice cream parlor, sitting room with fireplace, TV room, games; veranda. Next to Fairview Park; 2 blocks to private beach on Little Traverse Bay. Hiking, tennis, bicycling, sailing, fishing, horseback riding, golf nearby.
Location N Lower Peninsula, on Lake Michigan. 60 m NE of Traverse City, 250 m NW of Detroit. 2 m N of Petoskey on Rte. 31.
Credit cards Amex, MC, Visa.
Rates Room only, $62–82 double. Extra person in room, $10. Family discounts.

2-night weekend minimum in high season. Alc breakfast, $4; alc lunch, $6–9; alc dinner, $17, plus 20% service.

Extras Cribs, play equipment available. Dining room, one guest room wheelchair accessible.

BIG BAY 49808   Map 7

The Big Bay Point Lighthouse   *Tel:* 906) 345–9957
3 Lighthouse Road

Lighthouses and islands, either separately or in combination, are probably our most favorite places for an inn. At Big Bay, all the guest rooms are in the lighthouse, set on a wooded point 120 feet above Lake Superior with magnificent views of the water and the Huron mountains beyond. Keeper of both the lighthouse and inn is Buck Gotschall, whose interests include sports of all kinds, and whose travels have taken him nearly around the globe. He reports that "we are near the end of the world, so bring your compass, your camera and film, and a pair of warm slippers." He also notes that Big Bay is a small, quaint village composed of many spirited individualists and craftsmen. Its citizens do not necessary go along with accepted modes and are ingenious in their substitutions (be careful—it's catching). The lighthouse is surrounded by miles of forest, and is ideal for hiking and cross-country skiing. Rates include a continental breakfast, and dinner is available by prior arrangement. *(MW)* More comments, please.

Open All year.
Rooms 6 doubles—4 with full bath, 2 sharing 1 bath.
Facilities Dining and breakfast rooms, living room with fireplace, game room with potbelly stove, lighthouse tower. 100 acres, lawns, 1 m of shoreline. ½ million acre forest for public use. Hiking, swimming, fishing, cross-country skiing. Downhill skiing, marina nearby.
Location Upper peninsula. 30 m N of Marquette, MI. From Marquette take Rte. 550 to Big Bay. Go right on Rte. 352, then left on Lighthouse Rd. to Big Bay Point. On Lake Superior.
Restrictions No smoking. No children.
Credit cards None accepted.
Rates B&B $80–110 double, $55–65 single. Discounts for second day. 2-night minimum on holidays. Prix fixe dinner, $15.

ESCANABA 49829   Map 7

The House of Ludington   *Tel:* (906) 786–4000
223 Ludington Street

Although the original hotel dates back to 1865, the current House of Luddington was built in 1883, with a wing added in 1910. Unusual and impressive in appearance, it's a white stucco building, with medieval turrets and green window awnings. Pat Hynes bought the hotel in 1939 and did much to establish its reputation with his eccentric personality and such innovations as a glass-walled elevator, installed in 1959. Gerald and Vernice Lancour bought the Ludington in 1982; they restored and expanded the rooms, decorating them simply but comfortably with period antiques and reproductions. Meals are hearty and portions generous; the menus feature a selection of both steaks and such German-style dishes as schnitzel and smoked pork tenderloin with sauerkraut. *(MH)*

"Rooms were quiet, well-furnished, and comfortable—like a bedroom in a home. The bar area was quite relaxing and featured good quality live music on Saturday night." *(Pat & Glen Lush)*

Open All year. Restaurant closed Sun. evening.
Rooms 4 suites, 17 doubles—all with private shower and/or bath, telephone, TV, air-conditioning. Some with desk.
Facilities Dining rooms, bar/lounge with entertainment, gift shop, garden. Lake nearby for swimming, fishing, boating.
Location Upper Peninsula, near WI border. 100 m N of Green Bay, WI. On Little Bay de Noc near Yacht Harbor; across from Luddington Park.
Credit cards Amex, CB, DC, Discover, MC, Visa.
Rates Room only, $55–64 suite, $54–58 double, $48–52 single. Extra person in room, $5. Alc breakfast, $3–8; alc lunch, $5–8; alc dinner, $20–30.
Extras Wheelchair accessible. Pets permitted. Cribs available.

FENNVILLE 49408   Map 7

The Fenn Inn   *Tel:* (616) 561–2836
2254 South 58th Street

Located in the countryside near Fennville, the Fenn Inn is a stately house with white pillars that was built in 1900. Rates include a full breakfast.

"A lovely home with several newly decorated guest rooms. Fully stocked medicine chest in bathroom. Tasteful decorations. Extremely clean. Breakfast was good and plentiful. Located across from cornfield at the end of town." *(Karen Hughes)*

Open All year.
Rooms 1 suite, 5 doubles—3 with private bath, 3 with a maximum of 6 people sharing a bath. 1 with waterbed. Suite with kitchen, living room, eating area.
Facilities Breakfast room with fireplace, sitting room with TV, sundeck. Lake nearby for swimming, fishing.
Location 15 min S of Saugatuck. From I-196 take exit 34 to M-89 E to Fennville. Go 6 m, then go right on South 58th St. go 7/10 of a m to Lake Land Dr. Inn on right.
Restrictions No smoking. No "small children."
Credit cards MC, Visa.
Rates B&B, $45–65 double. Extra person in room $25. 15% senior discount. 15% discount for stays over 3 days.
Extras 1 room and bath with handicap facilities.

GRAND HAVEN 49417   Map 7

Harbor House Inn   *Tel:* (616) 846–0610
Corner of Harbor and Clinton

"Innkeeper Carolyn Gray showed me five rooms and all the common areas of this beautiful inn. Each bedroom is different and lovely. The harbor view from most rooms is wonderful. Grand Haven is a busy resort town on Lake Michigan, but this must be the nicest place in town. The atmosphere is light, airy, comfortable, and clean, clean, clean." *(Elizabeth L. Church, also MN)*

Open All year.
Rooms 15 doubles, all with full private bath, radio, air-conditioning. 9 rooms with desk, whirlpool tub, fireplace.
Facilities Living room, den with TV and library, wraparound porch. Lake beaches, cross-country skiing nearby.
Location SW MI, on Lake Michigan. From US Rte. 31 N go left on Washington St., then left again on Harbor. Go 1 block to Clinton St. Inn on corner.
Restrictions No smoking in bedrooms. No children under 12.
Credit cards MC, Visa.
Rates B&B, $115 deluxe, $95 standard, all doubles. Extra person in room, $25. Second night half price from Labor Day to Memorial Day. Corporate rates, weekend packages in off-season.
Extras Wheelchair accessible.

Highland Park Hotel
1414 Lake Street

Tel: (616) 842–6483

The original Highland Park Hotel, dating back to 1899 was destroyed by fire about twenty years ago. Only the annex, built in 1923 escaped the blaze, and this building has been restored as a B&B by Terry Postmus. Set on a bluff overlooking the lake, rooms are furnished with period antiques and rates include a continental breakfast and afternoon refreshments.

"Our room was beautifully decorated, clean, quiet, comfortable. Our hosts were warm and friendly—Terry has a great sense of humor. The food was fabulous. The guests have their own small dining porch, where a buffet-style breakfast is attractively displayed. We were never rushed; the peace and quiet made us want to watch the lake, drinking coffee and chatting all day. The ambiance is relaxed, the decor antique." *(Dr. & Mrs. Lemmer)*

Open All year.
Rooms 6 doubles—all with private bath, telephone, desk, fan. TV on request.
Facilities Lounge with TV, guest refrigerator and microwave; porch, conference room. Patio, flower gardens.
Location SW MI, on Lake Michigan. Take U.S. 31 to Grand Haven, go W on Franklin to Harbor Drive, then S on Harbor Drive to past state park to Lake Michigan. 10 min. walk to center of town.
Restrictions No children under 12.
Credit cards Amex, MC, Visa.
Rates B&B, $60–85 double. 2-night minimum on weekends in season. Corporate rates.
Extras Airport/station/dock pickups. Japanese spoken.

HARRISVILLE 48740
Map 7

Big Paw Resort
818 North Lake Huron Shore, P.O. Box 187

Tel: (517) 724–6326

Big Paw is a small but complete family resort set on the Lake Huron side of the northern Lower Peninsula, with a four-diamond AAA rating. It was started by Chuck and Emily Yokom in 1938, when they bought the property and built a cabin for their own use. Over the next ten years, they constructed all the remaining buildings, cutting the trees from their own forests to make the log structures. The resort is now run by son Ron and daughter-in-law Nancy, with help from their children.

The Yokoms' spring newsletter to former guests is filled with chatter about their children's baseball teams and girlfriends/boyfriends—Big Paw is a homey kind of place. One somewhat unusual feature: Both the four motel units and the secluded cabins are connected to the main lodge and to the beach by a series of smooth paths, a real boon to those with limited vision or mobility. The Yokoms note that they "try not to change the atmosphere at Big Paw. It seems much of the world has been changing so fast, and not always for the better. We want to keep Big Paw as quiet, serene, and restful as it has been for the past 46 years."

"Big Paw is utter relaxation, peace, quiet—a place to read, commune with nature, walk, and, for those inclined, tour Michigan and play golf. Cabins are spotlessly clean; food is simple but good and homemade." *(Lola Rothman, also Mark Slen)*

"Flowers abound around every unit, especially the main lodge/dining room, where we all gather twice a day for meals. Ron and Nancy Yokom are what all visitors hope to find in their innkeepers, but seldom do. They are warm and friendly, always available, helpful, and never too busy to stop for a chat.

"The Yokoms share the cooking chores, with Ron doing the steaks on 'steak night,' and the delicious fish for the outdoor cookout on Wednesday. The Sunday hot dog roast on the beach is always a high point—huge fire, hand-cut green branches shaved to a point, homemade hot dog rolls, with lemonade and brownies for dessert. Although lunch is not served, fresh homemade cookies are always left out around noontime. While you are at breakfast, your cabin is cleaned and beds made." *(Betty & Harry Morley)*

"I went to Big Paw as a child with my family. When I returned many years later with my own family, I was startled to find that it was just as good as I had remembered it." *(Mark E. Morley)*

Open May 26 to Nov. 1.
Rooms 3 cottages with 1- to 3-bedrooms, 6 suites, all with full private bath, radio, TV, desk, working fireplaces.
Facilities Dining room, rec room with library, Ping-Pong, pool, puzzles, magazines, games. 60 acres with 1,300-foot sandy beach, swimming, motor & row boats, Sunfish sailboats, shuffleboard, hiking trails, flower gardens, tennis court. Charter fishing for lake trout, salmon. Golf, horseback riding nearby.
Location NE Lower Peninsula. 100 m N of Saginaw, 200 m N of Detroit. Turn right off Rte. 23, 1¼ m N of town at sign.
Credit cards Discover, MC, Visa.
Rates MAP, $140–175 double, plus 10% service. Reduced rate for children and families.
Extras Paved walks to 2 cottages for wheelchair access. Airport/station pickups. Cribs, babysitting available.

LAWRENCE 49064   **Map 7**

Oak Cove Resort   *Tel:* (616) 674–8228
58881 46th Street   (312) 983–8025

One of Michigan's oldest and smallest resorts, Oak Cove dates back to the turn of the century, and has been owned by Susan and Bob Wojcik since

1973. Over the past few years, the Wojciks have redecorated rooms in turn-of-the-century style. During the summer months, families return year after year for week-long stays; off-season, the lodge has just recently opened for B&B getaways.

"The comfortable cabins and lodge rooms are clean and well lit, with good plumbing. The food surpasses the quality of most area restaurants; in fact, many locals come just for lunch or dinner. Be prepared for fresh fruit and vegetables, delicious main dishes, and superb desserts—all in large quantities. Any special food needs are easily accommodated. The grounds are beautiful, quiet, and exceptionally peaceful. The lake and pool are as clean as can be. The most wonderful part about Oak Cove is the people who operate it: Susan and Bob, along with their adult children, and the high school girls who work there, spread warmth and cheer and comfort. They always make a special effort to know everyone's name, and spend time visiting with guests. This family-type warmth and caring cannot be matched." *(R. Paul)*

"A rustic family resort, nestled in the trees. We come to sail, swim and snorkle, and walk the country trails. Our room in the lodge was clean and refurbished with new curtains and linens. The owners are always warm and friendly, and we have formed lasting friendships with the other returning guests." *(John & Margo Rannells)*

Open May to mid-Sept.
Rooms 7 doubles in main lodge share 4 baths. 7 2-bedroom cottages with shower and porch.
Facilities Living room with TV/VCR; "Fun House" with pinball, jukebox, pool table, books, games, bar. 10 acres with heated swimming pool, lake with beach, boats, canoes, fishing. Golf, bicycling, hiking, snowmobiling, cross-country skiing nearby.
Location SE MI. 3 hrs. W of Detroit, 2 hrs. E of Chicago. Take Exit 56 off I-94. Go N ½ m on Rte. 51 to Red Arrow Hwy. Go W 1 m to fork; bear left and follow signs.
Restrictions No smoking in lodge guest rooms.
Credit cards None accepted.
Rates Weekly, full board, $480 lodge double, $500 cottage. Daily, full board, $100 double, $55 single. Children, $60–215 weekly; $20–45 daily, depending on age. 15% service additional. Prix fixe lunch, $6; prix fixe dinner, $13. Theme weeks: women only, French camp. Packages available.
Extras Airport/station pickups. Cribs, babysitting, games, play equipment available.

LELAND 49654   Map 7

Leland Lodge   *Tel:* (616) 256–9848
565 Pearl Street, P.O. Box 344

Leland (originally Leeland) received its name because of its lee position on the shore of a lake, a hard place for sailors to reach. The French added their word *eau,* for "water," giving Lake Leelanau its name. The town is situated between Lake Leelanau and Lake Michigan and abounds in recreational activities. In addition to a full range of sports (see below), Leland offers numerous antique and craft shops and five vineyards to tour.

Rooms at Leland Lodge are furnished with reproductions and some antiques; the bar has an interesting collection of photographs of Leland and Fishtown at the turn of the century. The lodge serves breakfast, lunch, dinner, and Sunday brunch. Food is fresh and locally produced, desserts are homemade.

"A most charming hotel/motel . . . warm and clean, with delightful decor both in the lobby and guest rooms." *(Eve Berland, also Keith Jurgens, Elizabeth L. Church)*

Open Late May through Oct.
Rooms 4 suites, 18 doubles and singles, all with full private bath, telephone, radio, TV, desk, air-conditioning.
Facilities Restaurant, bar/lounge, living room with fireplace, books, TV/game room, bar, deck. 2.5 acres with gardens. Bicycling, tennis, beaches, sailing, windsurfing, canoeing, horseback riding, fishing charters, Manitou Island cruises, golf nearby.
Location NW Lower Peninsula, Leelanau Peninsula. 20 m N of Traverse City. 3 blocks from main street.
Credit cards Amex, MC, Visa.
Rates B&B, $90–150 suite, $70–115 double. Additional person in room, $10. No charge for children under 10. Weekly rates. Alc lunch, $7–10; alc dinner, $27–30. Suites in annexes do not include breakfast.
Extras Barrier-free room/ramp entrance for wheelchair access. Cribs available. Airport/station pickups.

LEXINGTON 48450   Map 7

Vickie Van's B&B   *Tel:* (313) 359–5533
5076 South Lakeshore Drive (Route 25)

"The inn is a majestic 100-year-old farmhouse overlooking Lake Huron. Vickie Van, the owner, is what makes a stay here so memorable; as she takes you through the house, she tells wonderful stories about each room and its contents. In the summer, her busiest time, breakfast consists of freshly baked muffins and croissants, fresh-squeezed orange juice, and fresh handpicked berries from the nearby fields. Tea and lemonade are always available." *(Anne Kralik)* "Homey atmosphere, beautiful antiques, very clean, nice location." *(Mr. & Mrs. Brian Ewald)*

Open All year.
Rooms 1 suite, 3 doubles—2 with private tub or shower, 2 sharing 1 bathroom.
Facilities Living room, TV/game room, kitchen, dining room, tea room, porches. 5 acres with swing, walking paths, berry picking, tennis in walking distance. Lake Huron across street. ¾ m to beach and marina. Cross-country skiing on property in adjacent woods. Golf nearby.
Location E MI, Sanilac Cty., on Lake Huron. 20 m N of Lake Huron, 80 m N of Detroit. ¾ m from town. Take I-94 N to Rte. 25. ¾ m N of Lexington traffic light, on left side of road.
Restrictions No smoking. Light sleepers should request rooms at back of house. Children over 12 preferred.
Credit cards None accepted.
Rates B&B, $45–50 double, $40–45 single. Extra person in room, $10. 10% discount Sun.–Thurs.

LUDINGTON 49431   Map 7

White Rose Country Inn   *Tel:* (616) 843–8193
6036 Barnhart Road   (800) 545–2264

Originally built as the "Sportman's Haven," the inn was a total wreck when Dave and Terry Rose first encountered during their search for an inn of their own. Many months of renovation later, they opened the White Rose Country Inn, its guest rooms individually decorated in a variety of styles—one with a canopied bed, another with formal Victorian decor, a third with heirloom quilts, white wicker, and a white, iron bed. The Rose's new venture is a restaurant, located in another restored house across the street.

"An absolutely charming, delightful inn. I stayed in the Calico Room, overlooking Hamlin Lake, decorated country-style with blue and red calico curtains, a denim ruffled coverlet, and lots of white eyelet. The facilities are clean, the parking adequate. The bathroom fixtures, plumbing, and electricity are all new; the owners totally rehabilitated the inn after purchasing it in 1984. Breakfasts are delicious, with fresh fruit, hard boiled eggs, croissants, yogurt, cereal, and muffins (zucchini, pecan, and rosemary raisin on the days we were there). The owners are lovely, cheerful people who have worked hard to establish themselves." *(Susan Jacques)*

Open May 1–Oct. 31.
Rooms 1 suite, 6 doubles—3 with shared bath, 4 with private bath and/or shower. Most with fan. Some with desk, air-conditioning.
Facilities Dining room, living room, game room. Lakefront with dock for swimming, boating. Fishing, wind-surfing, fruit-picking, canoeing, rafting, hiking, golf nearby.
Location SW MI, on Lake Michigan. 8½ m N of Ludington. Take Rte. 31 or Rte. 10 towards Ludington. Just E of town, go N on Jebavy Dr. 8½ m to Hamlin Lake. Pass Barnhart Marina and watch for inn. Ludington is port city for Wisconsin ferry.
Restrictions No smoking. No children under 12. Alcohol in guest rooms only.
Credit cards MC, Visa.
Rates B&B, $85–100 suite, $65–75 double. Extra person in room, $10. Weekly rates, 10% discount. 2-night weekend/holiday minimum. Prix fixe lunch $4–6; prix fixe dinner $9–12.
Extras Airport pickups, $1 per person.

MACKINAC ISLAND 49757   Map 7

A trip to Mackinac (pronounced *Mackinaw*) Island is a trip back to another era. Cars were banned from the island in the thirties; you drive to either Mackinaw City (Lower Peninsula) or St. Ignace (Upper Peninsula) and park at the ferry. The dock porters meet all boats as they arrive at Mackinac, and help transfer luggage to the hotels. You can get around the island on foot, hire a horse-drawn carriage, or rent a bike from one of the many rental shops.

"It's not difficult to see why Mackinac Island has become such a popular summer resort. As you approach by ferry or hydroplane, you see high cliffs rising from the shoreline change to wooded bluffs dotted with some remarkable houses. Then, rounding a bend, you see a charming village nestled around the harbor. The sheer number of tourists milling about the village, along with the inevitable fudge and T-shirt "shoppes," may cause you momentary panic, but don't let it deter you from exploring the island's natural beauty. About 3 miles long and 2 miles wide (four-fifths of the island is a state park), Mackinac is basically a limestone outcrop with ravines, natural bridges, caves, and interesting rock formations. Rent a bicycle and explore the beach road and the cliffs—it doesn't take long to get away from the crowd. Be sure to spend some time at Old Fort Mackinac, built in 1780, and now preserved as a museum, with interpretive exhibits. The tearoom offers nice lunches and views of the bustling town below and the Straits of Mackinac." *(Maria & Carl Schmidt)*

Although with 275 rooms and plenty of convention business, the **Grand Hotel** is not right for this guide, it is a splendid century-old establishment, and well worth seeing. You can pay $3 to tour the grounds, or dress up in your finest and come for dinner (call 906–847–3331 for reservations).

An inveterate inngoer told us of her stay at **Stonecliffe**, a huge mansion high on a bluff overlooking the straits and the bridge. Although she felt the rooms were unsatisfactory (and overpriced), our correspondent found the food to be quite good, and more reasonably priced than at the Iroquois. The restaurant is open both for dinner and for Sunday brunch; telephone (906) 844–3355.

Information please: The **Inn on Mackinac** (Main St. and Bogan Ln., P.O. Box 476; 906–847–3361) is decorated with 12 colors of paint on the exterior; this 44-room establishment may qualify as the most colorful on Mackinac. Rates range from $69 to $150 and include a continental breakfast. Reports please.

Haan's 1830 Inn   *Tel:* (906) 847–6244
P.O. Box 123, Huron Street   Off-season: (312) 234–5682

Among Mackinac's oldest buildings, Haan's Inn sits on the foundations of a log cabin built in the late 1700s. The present structure, a pillared Greek Revival cottage, dates back to 1830. In the early 1900's, the house served as the residence of Colonel William Preston, an officer at Fort Mackinac and the mayor of the island. The Haan family bought the inn in 1976, and restored it as a bed and breakfast, furnishing it with period antiques. Breakfast includes fruit, juice, and fresh-baked breads, muffins, and coffee cakes.

"Our room was fairly small, but beautifully decorated and furnished with antiques. We enjoyed a tasty breakfast while talking with the other guests at one big table. The innkeepers, Joyce and Vernon Haan, are very congenial and went out of their way to make our stay pleasant." *(Pat & Glen Lush)*

Open Late May to mid-Oct.
Rooms 1 suite, 6 doubles—5 with private bath and/or shower, 2 share sharing 1 bathroom. All with fan. Some with desk.
Facilities Dining room, living room. 2 open porches, 1 screened porch. Large yard adjacent to garden of church. Four blocks from historic fort and village. Near ferry dock and charter fishing. Bike, horse, carriage rentals nearby.

Location Four blocks E of ferry docks on Huron Street.
Restrictions No smoking.
Credit cards None accepted.
Rates B&B $100 suite, $65–95 double. Extra person in room, $10. Child's discount. No tipping.
Extras Cribs, babysitting, games available.

Hotel Iroquois on the Beach
298 Main Street

Tel: (906) 847–3321

The Hotel Iroquois is a rambling Victorian structure, with plenty of turrets and gables. It's been owned and operated by Sam and Margaret McIntire for the last thirty years. Rooms overlook the beautiful Straits of Mackinac. Rates vary with room size, location, and view. Continental breakfast is served in the rooms, and lunch, dinner, and drinks are available in the hotel's Carriage House restaurant.

"We first visited Mackinac and the Iroquois in 1978 as starry-eyed newlyweds and loved it. Now we visit with three children, who are always made welcome. The hotel staff is well trained and personable. We've sampled much of Mackinac over the years and have found the food and service at the Iroquois to be far superior to that at any other establishment on the Island. The dining room is glass-enclosed, and it is truly relaxing to watch the freighter traffic pass through the Straits of Mackinac right before your eyes. Mackinac is a great place for a family vacation. The island is filled with sports activities and history; it was a major Great Lakes center of the fur industry until the 1830s." *(Rebecca M. Barnwell, also Arlyne & Collette Craighead, Mark Slen)*

Open Mid-May to mid-Oct. Restaurant opens in June.
Rooms 6 suites, 41 doubles—all with private bath and/or shower, desk, fan. All suites with TV.
Facilities Lounge, veranda, patio by water, family room, TV room. Right on beach. Golf and tennis nearby.
Location N Michigan, 290 m from Detroit. Island in Lake Huron, at Straits of Mackinac, between Upper and Lower Peninsula. 1 block from center of town; short walk from ferry dock. SW end of Main Street on Windemere Point.
Credit cards MC, Visa at checkout; check required for deposit.
Rates Room only, $195–250 suite, $58–185 double and single. Extra person in room, $10. Reduced rates for 2-night stays in fall. No charge for children in off-season. $1.50 baggage charge. Alc lunch, $7–12; alc dinner, $30–50. 2-night weekend minimum, July, Aug.
Extras French, Spanish, German spoken. Cribs, babysitting available.

Island House
Main Street

Tel: (906) 847–3347
Off-season: (313) 759–5530

A registered historic site and the oldest hotel on Mackinac, the Island House dates back to 1852. Rooms are decorated with traditional furnishings as well as some Victorian-style fabrics and decorative touches.

"Despite the hotel's size, the staff really tries to personalize the Island House; they are more than willing to assist guests in making dinner reservations anywhere on the island. One can relax on the huge porch, watching the boats coming in and the horse-drawn carriages rolling past. The restaurant has a fine selection of entrées, and the rooms are nicely decorated." *(Jeff & Terri Patwell)*

Open May 1 to Oct. 31.
Rooms 95 doubles with private bath, radio.
Facilities Restaurant, lounge, lobby with fireplace, porches.
Location Across from State Yacht Marina. 2 blocks from Ft. Mackinac.
Credit cards None accepted.
Rates Room only, $100–115 double. MAP, $150–175 double. Extra adult in room, $15–35; children under 13 free.
Extras Ferry pickups.

Metivier Inn   *Tel:* (906) 847–6234
Market Street, P.O. Box 285   Off season: (616) 847–6234

Built by Louis Metivier in 1877, this turreted Victorian home stayed in the Metivier family until 1984, when it was bought by Mike and Jane Bacon and Ken and Diane Neyer, who restored it as a bed & breakfast inn. Rooms are decorated with antiques and reproductions, some with four poster or brass beds. Rates include a buffet breakfast of fresh fruit and juice, coffee cake and croissants. *(TL)*

"Everything at the Metivier Inn appears clean, efficient, and new, yet it has the pleasant aura of a much older establishment. Two rooms are done with antique decor, while the rest feature white wicker or brass furnishings. The porch is a great spot for sitting and watching the parade of carriages, bicycles, and pedestrians. The stable across the street takes a bit of getting used to, but don't let it deter you from a wonderful stay." *(Pat & Glen Lush)*

Open May through October.
Rooms 2 suites, 15 doubles—all with private bath and/or shower, fan.
Facilities Living room with fireplace, porch.
Location 1 block from ferry dock.
Restrictions No smoking in common rooms.
Credit cards MC, Visa.
Rates B&B, $145–160 suite, $88–130 double. Extra person in room $15.
Extras Cribs, babysitting available.

MARSHALL 49068   **Map 7**

Marshall was founded in 1830 by northeastern settlers who fully expected the town to become the state capital. They built beautiful Victorian homes of many different styles; the houses have all been restored recently. Marshall is located in south central Michigan, halfway between Detroit and Chicago, at the juncture of interstates 94 and 69. In addition to historic home visits, area activities include lakes for swimming and fishing, golf, and cross-country skiing. Sunday night specials are available at inns and restaurants. Inquire for details.

McCarthy's Bear Creek Inn   *Tel:* (616) 781–8383
15230 "C" Drive North

Bear Creek Inn, built in the 1940s, is a cream-painted brick home, set on a knoll overlooking Bear Creek; it's encircled with fieldstone fences built by the original owners. After managing The National House (see below) for several years, Mike and Beth McCarthy purchased the inn in 1985, and say that they "welcome all kinds of travelers, but those looking to slow down the pace and relax are particularly well served by what we offer." First-floor highlights include an intricate fieldstone floor, wide bay windows, and oak staircases, while the country-style guest rooms feature brass or four-poster beds and flowered wallpapers. During 1988, the McCarthys completed reconstruction of the original barn, now called the Creek House. Decorated with furniture built by Mike, it's highlighted by antiques and balconies overlooking the creek. Beth serves a tasty breakfast of fresh fruit, eggs, baked goods, cheese, cereals, and juice, coffee, and tea.

"The atmosphere is so relaxing, and the inn beautiful. The McCarthys and their staff treated us like part of the family during our entire stay." *(Janice Stafford)*

Open All year. Closed Dec. 23–25.
Rooms 14 doubles, all with private bath and/or shower, radio, desk, and air-conditioning. 7 rooms in Creek House with balcony.
Facilities Dining room; living rooms with books, games; porch. 14 acres cross-country skiing, stream for trout fishing.
Location 1 m from town. From I-69/I-94 juncture, take I-69 S 1 exit to Michigan Ave. Go W on Michigan Ave., left on 15-mile Rd., right on "C" Dr. N to inn on left.
Credit cards Amex, MC, Visa.
Rates B&B, $49–76 double. Extra person in room, $5. Children under 5 free. No tipping.
Extras Free airport/station pickups. Cribs, play equipment, games available.

The National House Inn
102 South Parkview

Tel: (616) 781–7374

Built in 1835 as a stagecoach stop, this Greek Revival structure is the oldest operating inn in Michigan, and is listed on the National Register of Historic Places.

"This building felt truly historic. The whole town loves its history. The innkeeper was extremely accommodating. Our room was delightfully done in wicker and looked out onto a little garden with a lighted fountain." *(Dr. & Mrs. Kurt Neumann)*

"The bedrooms and public rooms are tastefully and authentically furnished in the style and ambience of the inn's era. The inn has been extensively renovated with a modern heating and air-conditioning system, using designs and fixtures in keeping with the early American decor. Of special interest is the very personal and friendly atmosphere maintained by Barbara Bradley." *(Walter Willey, also Keith Jurgens)*

One otherwise pleased guest noted that the bed was too soft, and the breakfast treats too sweet for her taste.

Open All year. Closed Christmas.
Rooms 1 suite, 15 doubles—14 with private bath and/or shower, 2 with maximum of 5 people sharing bath. All with TV, air-conditioning. 2 with desk.
Facilities Dining room, sitting rooms with fireplaces, games, family room. Gift shop. Garden. Racquet club privileges. Lake, swimming pools, fishing, cross-country skiing, golf nearby.
Location On the village circle.
Credit cards Amex, MC, Visa.

Rates B&B, $93 suite, $61–82 double, $53–87 single. Extra person in room, $6. Senior discount.
Extras Cribs, babysitting available.

MENDON 49072   Map 7

Mendon Country Inn   *Tel:* (616) 496–8132
440 West Main Street

Dating back to the 1840s, the Mendon was rebuilt in 1873 by Adams Wakeman, who added the 8-foot windows, the high ceilings, and the winding walnut spiral staircase. Dick and Dolly Buerkle bought the inn in 1987 and have added two fireplaces, private baths for all rooms, and picnic facilities down by the creek. The inn is a collector's paradise—the rooms are decorated with wonderful old quilts, decoys, signs, gameboards, and native American art. Guests enjoy antiquing, visiting the Amish settlement, and exploring the river.

"Dick greeted us warmly, and Dolly always had delicious smells wafting from the kitchen, which emerged as homemade soups, apple crisp, brownies, cookies, and more. She also invited us to make use of the kitchen at our convenience. The rooms are lovely, with Amish themes, and with fresh fruit always in the nightstand." *(Patricia Vodry)*

"The rooms are clean, cozy and comfortable, each with individual charm." *(Judy Thompson)*

"We found we could be as busy or relaxed as we wanted. The inn offers bicycles for a spin around quiet little Mendon, and a canoe livery for paddling down the calm and picturesque St. Joe River. I think the romance of the inn is definitely contagious—after watching a peaceful sunset from the rooftop terrace, we ended our weekend by deciding to get married!" *(Kim Sanwald-Reimanis)*.

"The handsome quilts, grandmothers' trunks, high-button shoes and dried flower arrangements all transport you to a more gentle time, yet there is modern plumbing, lots of hot water, good reading lights, and ample parking spaces." *(Jack & Betty Fitzpatrick)*

Open All year.
Rooms 3 suites, 10 doubles, all with private bath and/or shower. Some with radio, air-conditioning, whirlpool tub. 2 rooms in annex.
Facilities Breakfast room, common room with fireplace, TV, games, cards, books, self-serve coffee/tea. Rooftop garden for sunbathing. 4½ acres, picnic area. Badminton, croquet, horseshoes, bicycles, canoe rentals. Fishing and canoeing on St. Joseph River. Golf, tennis, downhill, cross-country skiing nearby.
Location SW Michigan. Halfway between Chicago and Detroit; 22 m S of Kalamazoo. 3 blks. from center of town.
Restrictions Smoking in common rooms only.
Credit cards Amex, MC, Visa.
Rates B&B, $72–115 suite, $56–72 double, $40–62 single. Extra person in room, $6. 10% senior discount on request. 2-night weekend minimum. Quilting, skiing, mystery packages.
Extras Wheelchair accessible. Airport/station pickups, $10 per person. Spanish spoken.

ONEKAMA 49675   Map 7

Portage Point Inn   *Tel:* (616) 889–4222
P.O. Box 248

Originally separate from Lake Michigan, Portage Lake was connected by a 500-foot channel hand-dug by settlers in 1876. Several years later, the U.S. government constructed a permanent channel to provide one of the best protected harbors on the Great Lakes. In 1902, the Portage Point Inn was built as a health resort, with natural mineral springs that drew visitors by rail and steamship from hundreds of miles away. Expanded and modernized over the years, it remains a favorite lakeside resort. *(Mary Jane Clark)* More comments please.

Open May through Oct.
Rooms 94 suites and doubles, most with private full bath; 10 cottages.
Facilities Restaurant with dinner dancing, bar with entertainment, lobby, recreation room, sun deck. Heated swimming pool with lifeguard, playground with children's program, tennis, bicycles, badminton, shuffleboard, softball, driving range, private beachfront on Portage Lake, Lake Michigan. Boating, sailing, windsurfing, fishing, canoeing. Golf nearby.
Location NW MI, on Lake Michigan. Approx. 10 m N of Manistee, 50 m SW of Traverse City. Take U.S. 31 to M-22. At Onekama, drive 4 m along western shore of Portage Lake to inn.
Credit cards All major cards.
Rates Full board, per person, $75–100 suites and cottages, $75 double, $90 single. Reduced rates for children. Weekly rates. No charge for children under 3, except $25 crib fee. Box lunches available.
Extras Free airport pickups from Traverse City, Manistee. Cribs, babysitting available.

PORT HURON 48060   Map 7

The Victorian Inn   *Tel:* (313) 984–1437
1229 Seventh Street

J. H. Davidson, owner of a prominent home furnishings store in Port Huron, built this Queen Anne Victorian in 1896. When Ed and Vicki Peterson and Lew and Lynne Secory purchased the Davidson home in 1983, they were lucky enough to receive the original plans, drawings, and specification sheets, which helped them to make the restoration as accurate as possible. Fortunately, the house had never been divided into apartments, and the original woodwork and leaded glass were still intact. After six months of intensive work, the inn opened, decorated in period with reproduction wallcoverings and window treatments. A dinner at the inn's popular restaurant might include crab and mushroom bisque; pecan chicken, done with a honey-mustard glaze and served with rice and salad; and chocolate nut pie for dessert. *(IK)* More comments please.

Open All year. Restaurant closed Sun., Mon.
Rooms 1 suite, 3 doubles—2 with private bath and/or shower, 2 with maximum of 4 people sharing bath. All rooms with air-conditioning.
Facilities Restaurant, bar/lounge with entertainment Fri. night, patio. Lake Huron, St. Clair River nearby for boating.

Location SE MI. 55 m N of Detroit. 4 blocks N of Bus. I-69. On Seventh St., between Union and Court Sts.
Credit cards Amex, Discover, MC, Visa.
Rates B&B, $85 suite, $45–60 double. Alc lunch, $10; prix fixe dinner, $20. Alc dinner, $25–30.
Extras Airport/station pickups.

PORT SANILAC 48469   Map 7

Raymond House Inn   *Tel:* (313) 622–8800
111 South Ridge Street (M-25)

The Raymond House is a red brick Victorian, complete with gingerbread façade, steep, sloping roofs, and white icicle trim dripping from the eaves. Inside, the rooms are furnished with antiques; one bedroom features a "Lincoln" bed, the same kind as the one on display in the White House. A recent development in Port Sanilac is the discovery of the *Regina,* a ship that went down in a terrible storm in 1913; charter boats are available for scuba divers wishing to explore the wreck.

"The moment you walk in the door you feel calm and comfortable. The rooms are large and very clean. In the morning you can help yourself to a continental breakfast of coffee, juice, fresh fruit, and datenut bread, and the morning paper. If the weather is nice, we take ours outside to the patio. Shirley Denison, the innkeeper, goes out of her way to make everyone's stay pleasant. We make it a point to stop in the kitchen just to visit with her. She is a potter and has quite a collection of local art and antiques that can be purchased or just admired. The inn is located within walking distance of Lake Huron, and during the summer the Arts Council sponsors an arts and crafts fair and a Renaissance fair. We enjoy the fishing, swimming, boating, shopping, and the good restaurants for perch dinners." *(Raymond & Patricia Harkey, also Mr. & Mrs. Thomas Muer, Gerald & Pam Maloney)*

Open May through Oct.
Rooms 7 double rooms, all with private bath and/or shower, fan.
Facilities Parlor with TV/VCR, card games; dining room, library. Pottery studio. 1½ acres with shade trees, patio, bicycles. 1 block from Lake Huron and marina. Beaches, charter boats, golf, horseback riding nearby.
Location "Thumb" area of E MI. 90 m N of Detroit; 30 m N of Port Huron. 2 blocks from center of village.
Restrictions Smoking only in parlor and dining room. No alcoholic beverages. No children under 12.
Credit cards None accepted.
Rates B&B, $50–65 double. $45–65 single. Extra person in room, $15. 10% senior discount.

SAGINAW 48601   Map 7

The Montague Inn   *Tel:* (517) 752–3939
1581 South Washington Avenue

"The Montague, opened in 1986, is a renovated Georgian mansion named after the family that built it in the early 1900s. The main house has been completely restored and decorated with period furnishings and pictures. There are many examples of superior, old-fashioned craftsmanship, including the hidden panels in the library. Coffee is served there, among the many volumes of books, all available to guests on a 'return when you visit again' basis." *(Sally Williams)*

"The dining room offers lunch and dinner to the public, along with a continental breakfast for guests. The food is well prepared and served, and the creative menu is changed regularly. The hospitality of the staff, the elegant decor and furnishings, and the beautiful and spacious grounds all create a delightful atmosphere." *(Donald T. Gibbons)*

"We stayed at the Montague just after Christmas, and the inn was very pretty with its seasonal decorations. One really great feature is the old carriage house, with five guest rooms that are as pretty as those in the main house. Since we were there with two other families, we were able to take over the carriage house, which made for a very homey atmosphere." *(Bob & Sandy Dekema)*

"An extremely young but very professional and enthusiastic staff made the visit more than enjoyable. In fact, the college senior night receptionist/accountant regaled us with the history of this magnificent inn and gave us a tour from the hidden prohibition library panel to the kitchen and boiler rooms. Breakfast was elegantly served in fine china, and the tiny touches (genuine cream in a pitcher and precisely softened sculptured butter) separates the Montague from ordinary inn. Additionally, the cooling color schemes of ice green and forest green and seemingly endless cantilevered circular staircases provided an aura of comforting sophistication." *(Zita Knific)*

Open All year. Restaurant closed Sun., Mon. Closed Christmas, New Year's.
Rooms 1 suite, 17 doubles—16 with private shower and/or bath, 2 with maximum of 4 people sharing bath. All with telephone, TV, air-conditioning; some with desk. 5 in Carriage House.
Facilities Dining room, library with fireplace, reception room, lounge. 8 acres with river for fishing nearby. Health club nearby.
Location Central MI. Take I-75 100 m NW of Detroit. Exit I-75 at Holland M-46, bear right on Remington, left on S. Washington.
Restrictions Smoking in library, reception room, lounge only.
Credit cards Amex, MC, Visa.
Rates B&B, $125 suite, $55–90. Extra person in room, $5. Alc lunch, $15; alc dinner, $35–40.
Extras Wheelchair accessible; 1 guest room equipped for disabled. Cribs available.

SAINT CLAIR 48079 Map 7

Murphy Inn *Tel:* (313) 329–7118
505 Clinton Street

The St. Clair River, a historic waterway connecting Lake Huron with Lake St. Clair and Lake Erie, was the scene of busy riverboat traffic through the nineteenth century. What is now the Murphy Inn was built in 1836 as the Farmer's Hotel, a white clapboard structure surrounded by porches; horses were brought here for auction by riverboat from Detroit. The inn was restored in 1985 by Ron and Cindy Sabotka, who have decorated the rooms simply, with a few antiques. The dining room serves light meals throughout the day at very reasonable prices.

"Our impeccably clean room was well appointed with a country inn atmosphere. The owners went out of their way to make us feel at home, even delivering the continental breakfast of juice, rolls, and coffee to our door." *(Shelby Fox)* "As you would expect from its name, the Murphy Inn combines an Irish atmosphere with a warm and hospitable staff." *(Vince & Revea Mecallef)*

Open All year. Restaurant closed Christmas.
Rooms 1 suite, 6 doubles, all with private bath and/or shower, telephone, radio, TV, desk, ceiling fans, air-conditioning. 1 room with balcony.
Facilities Dining room, bar/lounge. St. Clair river, golf nearby.
Location 2 blocks from center of town.
Credit cards Amex, MC, Visa.
Rates B&B, $55–75 suite, $47–65 double. Extra person in room, $10. Children stay free. Alc lunch/supper, $4–6.

SAUGATUCK 49453   Map 7

A well-known art colony on the shores of Lake Michigan, Saugatuck is an attractive resort town. It's most popular in the summer months, for swimming and windsurfing on Lake Michigan, plus hiking in the dunes and canoeing on the Kalamazoo River. Cross-country skiing in the winter is becoming very popular as well. Most visitors enjoy browsing through the town's lovely shops and art galleries.

The town is located in southeastern Michigan, 35 miles southwest of Grand Rapids and 10 miles south of Holland. Rates are generally highest on weekends, May through October, and a two-night minimum stay on weekends is usually required for advance reservations.

One Saugatuck inn we'd like to hear more about is the **Maplewood Hotel**, a 125-year-old Greek Revival building with thirteen recently remodeled guest rooms and a restaurant serving continental cuisine (428 Butler Street, P.O. Box 1059; 616–857–2788).

Kemah Guest House   *Tel:* (616) 857–2919
633 Pleasant Street

Built at the turn of the century, the Kemah features elaborate stained glass windows, hand-carved wooden landscapes, and beamed ceilings, all added in 1926. An unusual addition is the airy solarium, built by a contemporary of Frank Lloyd Wright. Guest rooms are furnished with Victorian antiques, and rates include a continental breakfast, and in summer, a pre-dinner drink in the Bavarian-style rathskellar.

"Fluffy white towels, eyelet-trimmed sheets, mints at night, and the morning paper were all nice touches. Downstairs, we especially enjoyed the sun porch, a homey, white-wicker oasis." *(Virginia Britton)*

"Owners Cindi and Terry Tatsch were more than willing to share the history of the house and its contents with us. The inn is very clean, comfortable, and well kept." *(Mr. & Mrs. Brian Pace)*

"Not a stodgy museum, Kemah House is an active and dynamic place that happens to be a historic home. It has an indoor waterfall, two player pianos, a beer cellar, and a man-made grotto. *Kemah* means "in the teeth of the wind," an appropriate name, given the inn's location on the crest of a hill overlooking this small resort town. I enjoyed discussions about bicycling with Terry, and reading a few of his books on sailing. My wife and I enjoyed the Saturday night pre-dinner party, which gave us a chance to meet the other guests." *(David & Carole Marzke)*

Open All year.
Rooms 1 suite, 6 doubles—all with maximum of 6 people sharing bath. 2 rooms with air-conditioning, 4 with fan.
Facilities Living room, dining room, study with fireplace, sun porch, solarium with waterfall, rathskellar, game room with pool table. 2 acres with patios, wooded trails.
Location 3 blocks from downtown, at the corner of Allegan St.
Restrictions No smoking. No children.
Credit cards MC, Visa.
Rates B&B, $85–95 suite, $75–85 double. Extra person in room, $15. Senior discount. 2 night weekend minimum May– Oct.
Extras Spanish spoken. Bus station pickups.

The Park House   *Tel:* (616) 857–4535
888 Holland Street

The oldest home in Saugatuck, the Park House is listed on the National Register of Historic Places; its most famous guest was Susan B. Anthony. Rooms have wide-plank pine floors and are decorated with lots of craftwork; furnishings include Victorian antiques and brass beds. Rates include a continental breakfast of fruit, juices, granola, and muffins. Guests are welcome to relax in the parlor with an afternoon cup of coffee or tea.

"The atmosphere was very relaxing and enjoyable. All the facilities—plumbing, parking, cleanliness—were fine." *(Mr. & Mrs. C.B. Davis)* More comments please.

Open All year.
Rooms 1 2-bedroom suite, 7 doubles, all with full private bath; some with desk.
Facilities Common room with fireplace, parlor. Fountain, wraparound porch, picnic table.
Location 4 blocks from center.
Restrictions Smoking in common rooms only.
Credit cards Discover, MC, Visa.
Rates $100–120 suite, $55–85 double. No tipping. 2-night weekend minimum May– Oct. Package rates.
Extras Airport/station pickups at moderate cost. Wheelchair accessible; 1 guest room equipped for disabled.

Wickwood Inn   *Tel:* (616) 857–1097
510 Butler Street

Warren and Sue Louis fulfilled a longtime dream when they opened the Wickwood in 1982. The rooms are individually decorated, the baths are modern and comfortable, and the entire inn is air-conditioned. Continental breakfast is served at the guest's convenience, and a special brunch is prepared on Sundays.

Summer is peak season in Saugatuck, when Lake Michigan and the Kalamazoo River attract boaters, bathers, and fishermen in abundance. Although rates are lower in winter, the Wickwood goes in for Christmas in a big way: from mid-November until mid-January, there's a tree in every bedroom, one in the living room, and one in the garden room. Many tree ornaments are handmade and coordinate with each room's decor. Evergreen garlands, tiny white lights, and unusual displays are everywhere.

"All the rooms are extremely comfortable, visually pleasing, and the facilities are first-class. Hot coffee, fresh juice, fresh-baked goodies, and the morning paper start each wonderful day. The common rooms make Wickwood a wonderful place for relaxing alone, or for having (BYO) cocktails and hot hors d'oeuvres with the other guests." *(Dr. & Mrs. Birmingham)*

"You could eat off the hardwood floors; the bathrooms are meticulously clean, with plenty of hot water for bathing. If you have been cross-country skiing and are chilled when you come in, they will make hot coffee or tea for you. This place is marvelous!" *(Maureen Schell)*

"Saugatuck is small enough to be friendly and intimate, but it offers interesting shops and art galleries, good restaurants, great beaches, and live theater in summer. The Wickwood's location, right on the edge of the main business district, puts all the shops and restaurants within a few blocks' walk, so parking is never a problem." *(Ben & Connie Forcey)*

"The air in the inn is scented by potpourri, just one of the delicate touches. The furniture is exquisite—country English style. Our only regret is that we weren't able to meet the owners." *(Steven Braddon & Kathi Best)*

"Manager Dottie Berghuis is bright, bubbly, efficient and an instant friend to all guests. We spent two very rainy days at the inn and were not bored for a moment. Every imaginable table game is available along with a well-stocked library." *(Sara Walters)*

Open All year except Dec. 24 and 25.
Rooms 2 suites, 9 double rooms, all with full private bath, desk, air-conditioning.
Facilities Living room with fireplace, library/bar, large garden room for conversation and games, puzzles, cards; screened gazebo with hand-carved redwood furniture. Large garden with patio, chairs. Fishing 1 block away in lake or river. Cross-country skiing nearby.
Location SW Michigan. 135 m from Chicago. 2 blocks from town center, 1 sand dune from Lake Michigan.
Credit cards Amex, MC, Visa.
Rates MAP, $70–120 suites, $70–120 double. Conference rates available weekdays off-season. 2-night minimum on weekends.
Extras Ramp; one bedroom and bath equipped for disabled. Free airport/station pickups.

SOUTH HAVEN 49090   Map 7

South Haven is located on Lake Michigan, in the southwestern part of the state, about 2 hours northeast of Chicago, and 3½ hours west of Detroit. Area activities include all the water sports Lake Michigan makes possible, plus golf, cross-country skiing, winery tours, and fruit-picking in season.

A Country Place B&B
Tel: (616) 637–5523

North Shore Drive, Route 5, Box 43

The Niffeneggers invite you to share the slow-paced, relaxing atmosphere of their B&B, opened in 1986. "We encourage guests to sleep in—our full breakfast with lots of home-baked goodies is served leisurely on the deck during the summer and by the fireside in winter. Our quiet location and no-smoking policy work well, bringing us well-educated, well-traveled guests, open to new experiences."

"This restored old farmhouse is very comfortably decorated. The owners, Art and Lee Niffenegger, are very friendly, thoughtful, and accommodating. The house is immaculate, and the parking, plumbing, and lighting were all fine. Just one block away is a large Lake Michigan beach—a perfect place to watch the sunset!" *(Susan Jacques)*

Open All year.
Rooms 1 cottage, 5 doubles—1 with private bath, 2 with private ½ bath and shared shower, 2 sharing 1 full bath. Ceiling fans.
Facilities Living/dining area with fireplace. Enclosed porch with guest refrigerator, games; deck. 6 acres. 1 block to beach.
Location 2 m N of town. From I-196, take Exit 22. Go W on N. Shore Dr. 1 m to inn on left.
Restrictions No smoking. Children discouraged.
Credit cards None accepted.
Rates B&B, $45–55 double, $40–45 single. Extra person in room, $5. Inquire for weekly cottage rates.
Extras Free station pickups. Limited wheelchair access.

The Last Resort
Tel: (616) 637–8943

86 North Shore Drive

The Last Resort may well have been the first of South Haven's Lake Michigan resorts; it was built in 1883 by Civil War captain Barney Dyckman and his wife. The Babcocks bought the building in 1979 and spent three years renovating it before opening it as a B&B inn. Rooms feature handsomely restored wood detailing, and are named after the ships built in South Haven's shipbuilding days of the late nineteenth century.

"The inn is a very charming, very old-fashioned resort. The rooms are small but clean, and each is decorated differently, with nice little country touches throughout. Innkeepers Wayne and Mary Babcock are outgoing, friendly, artistic, and very enthusiastic about the town and their inn. Overall, the inn is nice and clean, including the shared baths; plumbing, both old and new, works fine. There's a lovely large veranda in front where guests assemble to watch the sun set into Lake Michigan." *(Victoria Nelson)*

"A short walk (500 feet) takes you to North Beach, one of sandy Lake Michigan's finest beaches; stroll 200 feet in the other direction to admire the harbor's sailboats." *(Daniel R. Williamson, Jr.)*

"Whether the weather is great or not, there's lots to see and do in and around South Haven. There's a good selection of restaurants, a marina, a park, a beautiful beach, antique and apparel shops, all within walking distance. The Babcocks are gracious, caring innkeepers who respect your privacy while seeing to your needs. The smell of freshly ground coffee and the taste of bakery-fresh pastries start the morning off just right." *(Sandra L. Feuerstein, also John T. Halen)*

Open Mid-April through Oct.
Rooms 3 suites, 8 doubles—2 with private bath, 9 rooms with sink and a maximum of 8 people sharing a bath. All rooms with air-conditioning. 2 suites with fireplace, whirlpool tub. 1 guest house (sleeps 8–10).
Facilities Dining room, living room/library with games, deck, art/jewelry gallery. ½ block from Lake Michigan beach; ½ block from city marina on Black River. Fishing, swimming, sailing, golf nearby.
Location SW MI. 2 hrs. 15 min. NE of Chicago, W of Ann Arbor. 35 m W of Kalamazoo. Take Exit 20 or 22 off I-196. Follow North Shore Dr. to inn. 10-min. walk to center.
Restrictions Smoking allowed in some guest rooms only. Light sleepers should request room on harbor side. No children under 9.
Credit cards None accepted.
Rates B&B, $100–135 suite (sleeps 4), $44–55 double, $42–52 single. Extra person in room $6. 10% discount over 65. 5 nights for price of 4, Sun.–Thurs. 2-night weekend minimum. Weekly rates.
Extras Station pickups.

UNION CITY 49094   Map 7

The Victorian Villa   *Tel:* (517) 741–7383
601 North Broadway Street

The Villa dates back to 1876, and has kept much of the ambience of that period, with the addition of some modern conveniences. But, as innkeepers Ron and Sue Gibson say, "our air isn't 'conditioned' and our guest chambers aren't wired for either phones or TV."

Each room at the Villa is furnished in a style of the 1800s, from Empire to Edwardian; the Tower Suite is a favorite with newlyweds. Rates include an afternoon beverage and a breakfast of home-baked Amish pastries, muffins, and seasonal fruit.

"The unique condition of this restored home, with its antique furniture and finishings makes it outstanding. The afternoon refreshments are delightful, and the morning breakfast is superb." *(Claude Saum, also Brian Pauley)*

"An inn of immense charm and indescribably excellent Victorian furnishings. Mr. Gibson has an eye for tiny details such as handsome glassware and for great details such as the best pillows and mattresses I have experienced anywhere. Mr. Gibson himself is a most charming and kind host in an understated way." *(M. Landon Spencer)*

Open All year.
Rooms 2 suites, 6 doubles—6 with full private bath, 2 with maximum of 4 sharing bath. A few with air-conditioning. All with fan.
Facilities 2 parlors with fireplaces, piano, games. 2-acre grounds with Victorian landscaping.
Location S Central Michigan. 2½ hrs. W of Detroit; 3½ hrs. E of Chicago. 2 blocks from downtown. From I-94 take I-69 S to Rte. M-60, Exit 25. Take Rte. M-60 W to Union City. Broadway is main street.
Restrictions No smoking.
Credit cards MC, Visa.
Rates B&B, $85 suite, $75 double, $70–80 single. Extra person in room, $5. Set

dinner available Friday and Saturday, $20 additional. Special rates for "theme" weekends: Old-fashioned Christmas, Summer Daze, Sherlock Holmes, Valentine's Day. Prix fixe meals available.

Extras Free pickup from train/bus. Cribs available.

UNION PIER 49129   Map 7

Gordon Beach Inn   *Tel:* (616) 469–3344
9708 Berrien Road, P.O. Box 222

"Just north of the Indiana border, along the Lake Michigan shore, lies the harbor of New Buffalo, Michigan. The Gordon Beach Inn is to the north along the Lakeshore Drive not far from town. The inn was once a getaway resort for Chicagoans, and has been restored by William Kirksey to that purpose. The rooms are simple and slightly small, but quaint and peaceful. The parlor is huge, with a fireplace and filled with antique furniture. New Buffalo is a sailor's port with a large marina and excellent restaurants; Skip's Other Place and the Miller House are within walking distance. The inn shares beach access with the Gordon Beach homeowners and is well worth the half-mile walk. The sandy beach is not as spacious as nearby Warren Dunes State Park, but it's usually sparsely populated and you can stake out a large section all to yourself. Our other favorite pastime is riding our bikes to visit the nearby wineries—it's ten miles to Tabor Hill Winery. The dunes in Warren Dunes State Park make scenic and relaxing hiking terrain. If you're there on a weekday, drive to the north end of Lakeshore Drive to the Swedish Bakery; people drive the 50 miles from Chicago every weekend to stock up." *(Dave Marzke)*

Open All year.
Rooms 4 suites, 14 doubles—all with private bath and/or shower, air-conditioning, fan. Suites with TV.
Facilities Breakfast room, living room. ½ with private beach access.
Location 80 E of Chicago. Take I-94 to exit 6. Go N 1 m to Lakeshore Rd. (thru stoplight). Turn left to inn.
Restrictions Smoking in living room only. No children under 10.
Credit cards MC, Visa.
Rates B&B, $100–150 suite, $55–75 double, $50–65 single. Extra person in room $10. 2-night minimum.
Extras Station pickups.

The Inn at Union Pier   *Tel:* (616) 469–4700
9708 Berrien Road, P.O. Box 222

Chicagoans are thrilled to have found a relaxing retreat less than two hours' drive around the lake—the Inn at Union Pier, opened in 1985 by Madeleine and Bill Reinke. The inn features a open and sunny great room, inviting decks for summer breakfasts or a soak in the hot tub, and elegantly decorated guest rooms. Lake Michigan's beaches are "just two hundred steps from the front door."

"Madeleine greets you with a special treat of homemade soup in winter, and fresh fruit in summer. She really cares about her guests and goes out of her way to make you feel at home. Best of all are the rooms, which are lavishly furnished—comfortable without stuffiness." *(Kathryn M. Havlish)*

"Winter weekends are particularly nice because almost every room has its own Swedish fireplace. If you've forgotten to bring reading matter, each room has an assortment of books and magazines. Plenty of hot water, thick towels, and truly comfy beds make the individually decorated rooms most relaxing. Breakfasts are served for two hours and you need that amount of time to eat the multiple courses and savor the homemade muffins. They encourage you to drown in coffee (or tea). The Reinkes manage to make you feel as though you are guests in their home, yet they aren't hovering about. The location is superb as well—beautiful surroundings close to home yet far away from sounds of traffic or jet planes." *(Ann Scher)*

Open All year.

Rooms 15 doubles—all with full private bath, radio, desk, air-conditioning. Some with balcony, fireplace. 10 rooms in 2 adjoining buildings.

Facilities Dining room, great room with piano, meeting room, rec. room, library, decks. 1 acre with hot tub, sauna, hammock, croquet, bicycles. ½ block to Lake Michigan for swimming, fishing, windsurfing. 8 m to cross-country skiing.

Location SW MI. 80 m E of Chicago. 5 m N of New Buffalo. Take Exit 6 off I-94 N onto Townline Rd. Go .7 m to Red Arrow Highway. Go right .6 m, then turn left on Berrien. Go 1½ blocks to inn on left.

Restrictions No children under 12.

Credit cards MC, Visa.

Rates B&B, $78–125 double. Extra person in room, $10. 2-3 night minimum weekends, holidays.

Extras Station pickups. Wheelchair accessible; baths equipped for disabled.

We Want to Hear from You!

As you know, this book is only effective with your help. We really need to know about your experiences and discoveries.

If you stayed at an inn or hotel listed here, we want to know how it was. Did it live up to our description? Exceed it? Was it what you expected? Did you like it? Were you disappointed? Delighted?

Have you discovered new establishments that we should add to the next edition?

Tear out one of the report forms at the back of this book (or use your own stationery if you prefer) and write today. Even if you write only "Fully endorse existing entry" you will have been most helpful.

Thank You!

Minnesota

Pratt Taber Inn, Red Wing

Minnesota is best known for being a nice place to live. The Twin Cities, Minneapolis/St. Paul, have outstanding theaters, museums, and cultural attractions; the countryside has more lakes than you can count, as well as numerous historic river valleys to explore by boat, foot, or bicycle. Travelers driving up Route 61 to Minneapolis would do well to stop and explore the historic Mississippi River bluff towns of Hastings, Red Wing, Frontenac, Lake City, Winona, and Wabasha.

Also recommended: Although there wasn't time to complete a full writeup, **Schmacher's New Prague Hotel** (212 West Main Street, New Prague 56071; 612–758–2133), about 35 miles southwest of Minneapolis, is a well-known German-style inn with 11 guest rooms and delicious German and Czechoslovakian cuisine. *(JH)*

Information please: One classic hotel we'd like reports on is the **Archer House,** an imposing French Second Empire hotel with 28 suites and doubles, recently renovated in turn-of-the-century country decor. It's located in Northfield, home to Carleton College (212 Division Street, 55057; 507–645–5661).

Rates do not include 6% state sales tax, plus additional local taxes, where applicable.

ANNANDALE 55302 Map 7

Thayer Hotel *Tel:* (612) 274–3371
Highway 55

Listed on the National Register of Historic Places, this 1895 hotel was restored by owners Wally and Steve Houle. The pressed-tin walls and ceilings, and much of the woodwork, have been retained, and some of the furniture is original to the building. Period antiques, including brass and canopied beds, and handmade quilts complete the decor. The restaurant features specially aged meats and fresh vegetables, along with homemade ice cream and baked goods. Afternoon tea is served each day from 2–4 P.M. *(MW)* More comments, please.

Open All year.
Rooms 4 suites, 10 doubles—all with full private bath, air-conditioning. Telephone, TV, radio on request.
Facilities Restaurant, bar/lounge, sauna. 25 lakes within 5 miles. Off-street parking.
Location Downtown. Lakes Region, approx. 45 m NW of Minneapolis.
Credit cards MC, Visa.
Rates B&B, $55–85 suite, $25–65 double. Alc lunch, $4–6; alc dinner, $14–18.
Extras Station pickups. Pets permitted with prior approval. French spoken.

BLUE EARTH 56013 Map 7

Super Eight Motel *Tel:* (507) 526–7376
1120 North Grove Street, P.O. Box 394 (800) 843–1991

If you're driving through Minnesota on I-90 and need a welcoming place to stay overnight, this motel may be just the thing. Although we're not particularly eager to add motels to this guide, particularly large economy chains like Super Eight, this one's a bit different. It's owned by Ernie and Mickey Wingen, and all the furniture "with the exception of the chairs" was built by Ernie. The decor includes Mickey's hand-painted murals over each bed and her hand-sewn drapes, bedspreads, and blankets. "Although our decor was originally intended to be early American, it has taken an international flavor, due to friends from near and far who have sent us gifts." The continental breakfast features juice and coffee with home-baked caramel cinnamon rolls.

"Don't bother stopping here for big-city sophistication; what you will get is a taste of real country hospitality." *(RS)*

Open All year.
Rooms 1 suite, 39 doubles, all with full private bath, telephone, TV, desk, air-conditioning. 10 rooms in annex.
Facilities Lobby with fireplace, TV, exercise room with hot tub, bicycle. Courtyard with garden, fountain. Cross-country skiing, snowmobiling, golf, tennis, swimming nearby.
Location S central MN. 130 m SW of Minneapolis. 1 m from downtown, ¼ m from I-90. At the jct. of I-90 and US Hwy. 169.

Credit cards Amex, CB, DC, Discover, MC, Visa.
Rates B&B, $30 suite, $34 double. Extra person in room, $4. No charge for children under 12. 10% senior discount.
Extras 2 rooms fully equipped for disabled. Station pickups. Pets allowed, $10. Cribs available.

CHASKA 55318 Map 7

Bluff Creek Inn *Tel:* (612) 445–2735
1161 Bluff Creek Drive

A Victorian farmhouse, built in 1864, the Bluff Creek Inn was restored as a B&B in 1984, and was bought by Anne Karels in 1989. Rooms are decorated with family antiques, quilts made by the innkeeper, and designer linens. A full breakfast is served on English china with Bavarian crystal, and an evening snack is left at the bedside.

"An Appalachian carved canopy bed waited in our bedroom, which was furnished with antiques, lace linens, handmade quilts, and baskets. The lavish bathroom had baskets of lotions, talcs, and soaps; beautiful cotton linens hung along with the other towels. Drinking glasses from England were on the shelf with other mementoes and a grouping of flowers." *(Evelyn Carey)* More comments please.

Open All year.
Rooms 4 doubles—1 with private shower, 3 with private sink/toilet share 1 bath. All with radio, air-conditioning, fan. 1 with balcony.
Facilities Dining room with fireplace, parlor with fireplace, porches. 1 acre. Cross-country skiing, bicycling nearby.
Location SE MN. 30 min. SW of Minneapolis. From I-494, go W on Rte. 169/212; turn right on Bluff Creek Dr. 2 m from Shakopee.
Restrictions No smoking. No children under 12.
Credit cards MC, Visa.
Rates B&B, $65–85 double, $60–80 single. Extra person in room, $25. Prix fix dinner $25.

COOK 55723 Map 7

Ludlow's Island Lodge *Tel:* (218) 666–5407
(800) 537–5308
Box 1146, Lake Vermilion

The Ludlow family has owned and run this rustic family resort for over 50 years. Mark and Sally Ludlow, the second-generation owners, welcome back a fair share of second-generation guests each year. Sally notes that "our staff caters to families with such activities as pontoon rides, hot dog roasts, marshmallow campfires, nature hikes and fishing contests. The cabins are well spaced out over their small private island, with several more on the nearby south and north shore of the lake. To facilitate your travels between your cabin, the main lodge, and the recreation center, rates include both shuttle service and your personal fishing boat for the week (in addition to free use of their many canoes, kayaks, sailboats, and more).

Lake Vermilion is 40 miles long, with 365 islands and 1,200 miles of shoreline, and offers fishing for walleye, northern pike, large and small-mouth bass, plus crappies and panfish.

"Our family loves the outdoors, and Ludlow's was the perfect place to enjoy it. Service was very helpful and friendly." *(BH)* More comments, please.

Open Mid May–Oct. 1
Rooms 19 cabins, with 1–5 bedrooms, full bath, kitchen with microwave and dishwasher, fireplace, decks or screened porches, barbeque grills; whirlpool tub.
Facilities Lodge with fireplace, TV/VCR, library, game room; grocery store, laundry. Recreation center with 2 tennis courts, racquetball. Children's program, playground, water slide, camping island. 4 acres with lake for swimming, fishing, boating; hiking trails. 5 m to golf; horseback riding nearby.
Location NE MN. 8 m from Cook, 80 m N of Duluth, 225 m N of Minneapolis. From Minneapolis, take Rte. 35 W to Cloquet. Then take Rte. 33 to 53 north to Cook. From Cook, take Rte. 1 E, to 78 N to 540 E to lodge.
Credit cards MC.
Rates Room only, $130 double, $600–1,200 weekly; includes 16-foot aluminum boat. Extra person in room, $20 daily, $50 weekly. Children under 2 free. Weekly maid service $60 additional. 2-night minimum stay. Fishing, honeymoon packages.
Extras Airport pickup, $40; station pickup, free. Cribs, babysitting available.

DULUTH 55802   Map 7

Fitger's Inn   *Tel:* (218) 722–8826
600 East Superior Street   (800) 548–1077

In this creative preservation, a 100-year-old, historic brewery was converted into an inn, restaurant, and group of specialty shops, called Fitger's On The Lake, listed on the National Register of Historic Places. The lobby has many features of the original building, including a leaded glass skylight, an iron cashier's cage, and hand-crafted oak woodwork. The guest rooms have more of a country decor, with some featuring floor-to-ceiling windows overlooking Lake Superior and original stone walls. The restaurant serves classic American cuisine, with walleye pike a particular favorite. "A fairly expensive place for the area, but rooms have lots of personality, and some have terrific views." *(JH)*

Open All year. Restaurant closed Christmas, New Year's Day.
Rooms 6 suites, 42 doubles—all with full private bath, telephone, TV, desk, air-conditioning. Some with whirlpool bath. 22 rooms in annex.
Facilities Restaurant, bar/lounge with dancing, game room. Room service. Off-street parking. 30 specialty shops in complex. Overlooking Lake Superior for fishing, boating. Downhill and cross-country skiing nearby.
Location E central MN. 165 N of Minneapolis, via I-35, on Lake Superior. 3 blocks from center, 6 blocks E of downtown.
Credit cards Amex, DC, MC, Visa.
Rates Room only, $135–270 suite, $85–105 double, $80–100 single. Extra person in room, $10. No charge for children under 17. Alc breakfast, $3–6; alc lunch, $6; alc dinner, $15–20.
Extras Wheelchair accessible; 2 guest rooms equipped for disabled. Cribs, babysitting available.

EXCELSIOR 55331 Map 17

Christopher Inn *Tel:* (612) 474–6816
201 Mill Street

You may have been to many Howard Johnson's in your travels, but we can guarantee that you've never stayed at one like this inn owned by the Howard Johnson family. Built in 1887 and listed on the National Register of Historic Places, the Christopher Inn is a classic Victorian mansion, traditionally known as the Wyer-Pierce House, with lots of gables and porches. Its restoration in 1985 by Joan and Howard Johnson included the addition of new plumbing, central air-conditioning, and a handsome decor combining Laura Ashley fabrics with late Victorian furnishings. A Wimbledon grass tennis court is original to the house and is kept in top shape by Howard, a tennis pro. "We are a Christian family and attempt to promote a Christian atmosphere with peaceful serenity, accompanied by literature that our guests can take," say the Johnsons.

Full breakfasts include fresh fruit and juice, served with such specialties as eggs Benedict on croissants, peaches and cream, French toast, seafood strata, or Swedish pancakes with apples. *(MW)* Reports, please.

Open All year.
Rooms 8 doubles—6 with private bath and/or shower, 2 with maximum of 4 people sharing bath. All with radio, desk, air-conditioning; telephone on request. 2 with fireplace.
Facilities Breakfast room, porch. 1½ acres with gardens, croquet, tennis court. Bicycles, horse-drawn carriage, cross-country skiing. Across the street from Lake Minnetonka for fishing, boating, swimming.
Location 15 m E of Minneapolis. 2 blocks from center. From I-694, take I-494 to Hwy. 7. Go W on Hwy. 7 to Excelsior.
Restrictions No smoking. No unmarried couples. Children permitted by prior arrangement.
Credit cards Amex, CB, DC, MC, Visa.
Rates B&B, $60–110 double. Extra adult in room, $20. Midweek, off-season rates available Sept. 15–May 15.
Extras Wheelchair accessible; 1 room equipped for disabled. Crib available.

FARIBAULT 55021 Map 7

Hutchinson House *Tel:* (507) 332–7519
305 Second Street Northeast

When prosperous mill owner John Hutchinson built a home in 1892, he spared no expense in the construction of this three-story Queen Anne Victorian, now listed on the National Register of Historic Places. When Marilyn Coughlin bought the house in 1987 for use as a B&B, it had already been restored, its handsome woodwork and fretwork gleaming once again. She furnished the house with her 25-year collection of Victoriana, and has added such distinctive touches to the decor as a wall mural fancifully painted with cherubs in delightful "neo-Rococo" style. Rates include a three-course breakfast and afternoon hors d'oeuvres; breakfast entrees, all made from scratch, might be a seafood asparagus quiche or a sausage, eggs, and cheese casserole with homemade scones. Guests especially enjoy relaxing on the wraparound porch in fine weather.

"The inn is set on a quiet residential street lined with old elms which shade large, turn-of-the-century Victorian homes typical of southern Minnesota. Occasional sounds are those of children's voices, singing birds, and Sunday-morning church bells. The common areas are ample, and Marilyn urges guests to mingle over afternoon tea, wine, and hors d'oeuvres. Breakfast during our stay included home-baked breads, fresh fruit, quiche, and coffee. The decor is Victorian, with period wallpaper and lots of individual detail. On the dresser, tucked into a crocheted cup and saucer, we found two little chocolates. The rooms were spotless, the sheets crisp and clean. In the Crystal and Lace Room were we stayed, the large bed is covered with a thick, cozy down-filled comforter and lots of pillows. Soap and towels are plentiful. Marilyn senses when you need quiet time to browse through the bookshelves, visit with your spouse, or play the piano. Restaurant menus are available for inspection, but Marilyn will be glad to recommend a favorite." *(Janna Hang)*

"It's an easy walk to downtown where I toured the historic Faribault House. Marilyn really knows how to make your stay special. She is lots of fun and is very knowledgeable about the area and local events." *(Stephanie Blohm)*

Open Feb. through Nov.
Rooms 1 suite, 4 doubles—all with private bath or shower, air-conditioning, fan. 1 with telephone, desk; 2 with radio.
Facilities Parlor with fireplace, living room with piano, lounge with TV, porch with swing. Golf, indoor and outdoor swimming pools, cross-country skiing nearby. Lakes, state parks with water sports, picnic areas, hiking trails nearby.
Location SE MN. 45 m S of Minneapolis, 50 m N of Rochester.
Restrictions No smoking. No children under 12.
Credit cards None accepted.
Rates B&B, $105–110 suite, $75–85 double, $50–60 single. 5% senior discount. 10% midweek discount. 2-night weekend minimum.
Extras Airport pickup from private airstrip.

GRAND MARAIS 55604 Map 7

Cascade Lodge *Tel:* (218) 387–1112
Highway 61, East Star Route, Box 693 In MN: (800) 322–9543

"We reached our romantically decorated, rustic cabin by crossing a private bridge over a small brook. The cabin had a fireplace and a modern bath. The lodge has a restaurant offering good food at reasonable prices; it's decorated with numerous wildlife heads and skins. Also available are comfortable common rooms and a game room in the basement. We discovered during our vacation around Lake Superior that it can be difficult to find nice accommodations and were very happy with Cascade Lodge. One note of caution—the facility is, at times, entirely booked by bus tours. *(Jeff & Terri Patwell)*

Open All year. Restaurant closed Christmas Day.
Rooms 1 suite, 16 doubles, 9 cabins, all with private shower and/or bath, desk. 5 with TV. Rooms in Main Lodge, motel, and cabins.
Facilities Restaurant, gift shop, TV lounge, fireplace lounge, game room with pool table, Ping-Pong, games. 14 acres; surrounded by Cascade River State Park. Badminton, horseshoes, hiking, fishing, berry picking, 40 m of cross-country ski trails. Bicycle, canoe, fishing gear rentals. Evening lectures, slide shows, movies. 9 m to downhill skiing. Golf, tennis, heated swimming pool nearby.
Location NE MN. 9 m S of Grand Marais, on Hwy. 61.
Credit cards Amex, MC, Visa.
Rates Room only, $70–80 suite, $40–85 double, $40–60 single. Extra adult in room, $8; extra child, $4. Senior discount midweek. Alc breakfast, $3–6; alc lunch, $3–6; alc dinner, $8–15.
Extras Airport pickups. Pets permitted in cabins. Cribs, babysitting available. German, Finnish spoken.

Gunflint Motel
Gunflint Trail, P.O. Box 1028

Tel: (218) 387–1454

David Peterson has owned the Gunflint since 1983 and notes that "our units have cathedral ceilings, ash paneling, and lots of flowers—even a sod-roofed entryway."

"Our unit had a living room with fully equipped eat-in kitchen and separate bedroom with lots of closet space. The rooms are clean and well stocked with cooking necessities. It is near the lake, only a few blocks from downtown in a quiet and restful area. Owners Dave and Andrea Peterson are just great, and many guests come back year after year, forming lasting friendships. The area is blissfully pollen-free and has beautiful hiking trails and scenery, along with a summer theater and art colony." *(Howard Kreger)*

Open All year.
Rooms 5 suites (sleeping 2-4 people)—all with full private bath, TV, desk. 4 with kitchenette.
Facilities Municipal swimming pool nearby. 1 block from Lake Superior.
Location On the Gunflint Trail, 1 block from Hwy. 61.
Credit cards None accepted.
Rates Room only, $32–45 suite. Extra person in room, $2. Senior discount. Off-season rates.
Extras Pets "invited." Cribs, babysitting available. Norwegian, Korean spoken.

Naniboujou Lodge
Highway 61, North Shore Drive Star Route 1, Box 505

Tel: (218) 387–2688

Naniboujou was planned in the 1920s as a private club; Babe Ruth, Jack Dempsey, and Ring Lardner were among its charter members. This log cabin lodge's most striking feature is its dining room, with the largest native rock fireplace in Minnesota and walls and windows painted brightly with Cree Indian designs. The club couldn't survive the Crash and went bankrupt shortly thereafter. In 1981 Tim and Nancy Ramey bought Naniboujou, now listed on the National Register of Historic Places, and restored it as a comfortable family resort.

"We discovered this beautiful lodge by accident several years ago and have returned every year since then. It's located on the north shore of Lake

Superior, where there are many hiking trails and waterfalls, including a spectacular one right across the road. The Brule River, with its great trout fishing, is a few steps from the door. The food is excellent; they even serve a great afternoon tea. It's in the midst of state and national forests, and one can experience the pleasure of the north woods without the discomforts of primitive camping." *(Marilyn & Arthur Hanson, also Pam Little)*

Open May 15 through Oct. 15; weekends only late Dec. through mid-March.
Rooms 29 doubles—15 with full private bath, 14 with maximum of 8 people sharing bath. Some rooms with fireplace.
Facilities Dining room, solarium, tea room, games, play equipment. 15 acres on Lake Superior and Brule River for swimming, fishing. Cross-country skiing nearby.
Location NE MN. 125 m NE of Duluth, 275 m NE of Minneapolis. 15 m NE of Grand Marais, on Hwy. 61. Approx. 45 m SW of Canadian border.
Restrictions No alcohol in public rooms. Minimal soundproofing between rooms.
Credit cards Amex, CB, DC, MC, Visa.
Rates Room only (summer) $59–72 suite, $37–64 double, $30–42 single. Winter weekend packages. Alc breakfast, $2–7; lunch, $5; alc dinner, $12–17. Picnic lunches available.
Extras Cribs, babysitting available.

LANESBORO 55949   Map 7

Mrs. B's Historic Lanesboro Inn   *Tel:* (507) 467–2154
101 Parkway

Lanesboro is a historic town, most of whose buildings date back to the 19th century. Walled in by wooded bluffs, the village is set on the Middle Fork of the Root River, surrounded by farmland and hardwood forests. By some fortuitous fluke of nature, the area is virtually free of mosquitoes.

The Lanesboro Inn was a furniture shop and undertaker's parlor for about 110 years before Nancy and Jack Bratrud and their children converted it into an inn and restaurant in 1982. Rooms are furnished with antiques, comfortable chairs, and good lamps. Full breakfasts are served at the hour of your choice. Mrs. B and her son do most of the cooking, offering fresh American-style (no-choice) meals at lunch and dinner, with occasional Scandinavian specialties.

Here's how Mrs. B describes their inn: "We are quiet, rural, historic, picturesque, nurturing, sensually enriching, small, unexpected. We are not slick, stylish, imposing, exciting, fast-paced, elegant, or exclusive. We are devoted to comfort, peace, beauty, plumbing, thick towels, fresh food, and, in season, bikes and air-conditioning!"

"Superb in all respects: very clean, well appointed, quiet, relaxing, with excellent food and service." *(Michael A. Lange)*

"It has been our good fortune to visit inns throughout much of the western world. Those that we value most have several things in common— an appealing setting (both house and terrain), grand guests, gratifying food and drink, and gracious innkeepers. This combination of virtues makes for a most enjoyable ambience—one so attractive that coming back seems the most natural thing to do. So it is with Mrs. B's." *(Richard and Helga Van Iten)*

"My wife made me change our schedule and routing across three states so that we could stay here again." *(GBR)*

Open All year. Restaurant open Thurs.–Sat.
Rooms 10 doubles–all with queen-size beds, private bath and/or shower, telephone, radio, TV, desk, air-conditioning, access to balcony.
Facilities Lobby with library and piano, bar, dining rooms, decks, porches, garden. Cross-country skiing from door. Tennis, canoeing, tubing, hiking, trout fishing, golf, spelunking nearby.
Location SE MN. 120 m SE of Minneapolis, 120 MN of Cedar Rapids, IA, 300 m NW of Chicago, IL. In center of village.
Restrictions Smoking restricted.
Credit cards None accepted.
Rates B&B, $40–85 double. Extra person in room, $8. Prix fixe lunch, $6, dinner, $16, plus tax, tip, drinks by advance reservation. ½ price dinners under 8. 2-night (Thurs., Fri.) packages available. Midweek group meeting rates.
Extras Dining room, 1 bedroom wheelchair accessible. Norwegian, Hebrew, German, Arabic, Spanish spoken.

LITTLE FALLS 56345 Map 7

Pine Edge Inn *Tel:* (612) 632–6681

An old hotel with a separate (more recent) motel wing, the Pine Edge has hosted such luminaries as Charles Lindbergh, Sinclair Lewis, Jack Benny and General George Marshall. Then called the Elks Hotel, Lindbergh was honored by a banquet here after his historic flight. It's slowly being updated and refurbished, with new carpets and curtains being added each year. "A quaintly restored 50-year-old hotel. The old rooms have huge windows and radiators; the service is good and the food in both the restaurant and coffee shop is tasty. Charles Lindbergh's home is nearby, as are many lakes and state parks." *(M. Voigt)*

Open All year.
Rooms 2 suites, 22 doubles in hotel; 30 doubles in motel wing across street. All with private bath, telephone, TV, desk, air-conditioning.
Facilities Restaurant, coffee shop, lounge, conference room.
Location 90 m NW of Minneapolis. On Mississippi River.
Restrictions No smoking in some guest rooms.
Credit cards Amex, DC, Discover, MC, Visa.
Rates Room only, $56 suite, $32–46 double, $28 single. No charge for children under 13 in parents' room. 10% senior discount. Alc breakfast, $2–5; alc lunch, $6–8; alc dinner, $15–25.
Extras Limited wheelchair accessibility. Pets permitted in motel units only, $25 deposit. Cribs, babysitting, play equipment available.

MINNEAPOLIS Map 7

Minneapolis is a very inviting city, as is its sister city, St. Paul. Known for its exceptional cultural and educational facilities, it offers outstanding restaurants, theaters, and museums and the largest single college campus in the U.S., the University of Minnesota, with about 65,000 students.

Information please: For rooms filled with beautiful Art Deco furnishings and stained glass, **Evelo's B&B** offers a friendly atmosphere, filling and healthy breakfasts and modest prices for shared bath accommodation (2301 Bryant Avenue South 55405; 612–374–9656). Another possibility across the river in St. Paul is the **St. Paul Hotel**, handsomely refurbished with a lovely setting across from Rice Park (350 Market Street, St. Paul 55102; 612–292–9292 or outside MN, 800–457–9292).

Our entries for **Chaska** and **Excelsior** are less than a half-hour drive to the west of the city, for visitors who prefer a rural environment.

Nicollet Island Inn
95 Merriam Street 55401

Tel: (612) 331–1800

Built in 1893, this building on Nicollet Island began life as a company making wooden window sashes and doors. After a stint as a Salvation Army headquarters, the inn was virtually gutted and restored. Rooms are decorated with period antiques and reproductions, and many have beautiful views. Rates include morning coffee and the paper, and turndown service.

"The River Café offers good food in a superb setting, overlooking river travel in all directions. We understand the rooms are equally pleasing." *(JH)* More comments, please.

Open All year.
Rooms 2 suites, 22 doubles, all with private full bath, telephone, radio, TV, desk, air-conditioning.
Facilities Restaurant, pub with live music, lobby, patio, garden, off-street parking.
Location On island in middle of Mississippi River. Between downtown and Riverplace. Heading NE on Hennepin Ave., cross river at Henn. bridge. Go right on Main St. at light. E. Henn. is at next light; go straight onto Cobblestone Rd. (ignore sign saying rd. is closed). ½ block on right is Merriam St. bridge; go right, then straight through stop sign to inn on right. Heading SW on Hennepin, go left on Main St. before crossing river; then as above.
Restrictions No smoking in guest rooms.
Credit cards Amex, CB, DC, Discover, MC, Visa.
Rates Room only, $95–130 suite, $90–100 double. Extra person in room, $10. Alc breakfast, $3–7; alc lunch, $4–10; alc dinner, $10–30. Packages available. Corporate rates.
Extras Wheelchair accessible; 2 rooms equipped for handicapped. Cribs available. Airport/station pickups. French, Swedish, Italian, Greek, Spanish spoken.

The Whitney Hotel
150 Portland Avenue

Tel: (612) 339–9300
(800) 248–1879

For a memorable stay in Minneapolis, try the Whitney, a recently opened luxury hotel located in a fully rebuilt riverfront warehouse. Decorated in rich, dark, slightly masculine tones of deep brown, moss green, and ivory, the hotel claims to have more than one staff member for each of its 97 rooms. The traditional decor includes burnished mahogany and cherry woods; brass chandeliers, door handles, and bath fixtures; marble floors and vanities; four-poster beds and wingback chairs. The extensive free amenities list runs from the morning paper to in-room hairdryers, bathrobes, and toiletries, evening turndown service with chocolates and cognac, and free limousine service to the business district. The Whitney Grille offers classic American cuisine in elegant surroundings, while the Garden Plaza awaits for casual outdoor meals (weather permitting).

"Very European and top-of-the-line in furnishings, service, and food. Truly exquisite, and the weekend packages are very reasonable." *(Kathleen Novak)*

A minor note of caution: "As in many large cities, the commercial district in which this beautiful hotel is located is fairly deserted at night. As a woman, I wouldn't feel comfortable walking alone after dark."

Open All year.
Rooms 97 suites and doubles, all with full private bath, 2 telephones, radio, TV, air-conditioning, wet bar. Penthouse suite with 2 living rooms, fireplace, grand piano, circular bar; 3 bedrooms, each with Jacuzzi; balconies.
Facilities Lobby, restaurants with entertainment, bar/lounge, 24-hour room service. Courtyard with fountain, benches, walking paths, gardens. Free parking; valet service.
Location Historic Mill District. On Portland Ave., between 1st and 2nd sts. From I-94 E take 5th Ave. exit. Follow 5th Ave. 8 blocks to Washington Ave. and go right, then left on Portland Ave. to hotel. From I-94 W take 4th Ave. exit. Turn right on 10th St. S and go 1 block to 5th Ave. From Rte. 35 W, take 5th Ave. exit.
Restrictions No smoking in some guest rooms.
Credit cards Amex, MC, Visa.
Rates Room only, $1,600 penthouse suite, $175–190 suite, $135–150 double. Extra person in room, $20. Weekend rates, packages. Alc lunch, $13; alc dinner, $25.
Extras 4 rooms equipped for disabled. Pets in cages permitted, by prior arrangement. Free limousine service to business district. Cribs available. Spanish, French, German spoken. Member, Small Luxury Hotels, Preferred Hotels.

PIPESTONE 56164   **Map 7**

The Calumet Inn   *Tel:* (507) 825–5871
Corner of Main and Hiawatha Streets

Pipestone was known as "Tall Grass Prairie" by the Dakota Indian nation who held the local soft red stone sacred; they welcomed other tribes in peace who came to quarry the stone for ceremonial pipes. Logically named Pipestone by early white settlers, by 1888 this prairie town with railroad links in all directions welcomed 200 train passengers daily. A hundred years later, the entire town is listed in the National Register of Historic Places and takes pride in its homespun atmosphere.

The Calumet Inn opened its doors on Thanksgiving Day of 1888, complete with quartzite trimwork accenting its stone structure. Still welcoming guests a century later, the inn has been completely restored with Victorian and period furnishings, from fainting couches to clawfooted sideboards. Rooms are furnished with some antiques; its restaurant, furnished casually with classic oak chairs and Victorian floral wallpaper, serves food that claims to "rivals Granny's home cooking" at reasonable prices.

"Our room was spacious and comfortable, filled with antique oak furniture and with its own modern bathroom; other rooms have more contemporary decor. The inn is a lovely restored building with a good restaurant. The town itself has an interesting museum, and the Pipestone National Monument, well worth a visit. We bicycled the environs, enjoying the clear skies, immaculate farms, and pleasant streets." *(Howard Zar)*

Open All year.
Rooms 42 doubles—most with private bath and/or shower.
Facilities Restaurant, lounge, pub with entertainment. Pipestone National Monument, Split Rock Creek State Park nearby.
Location SW MN. 50 m NE of Sioux Falls, IA; 175 m SW of Minneapolis. Downtown.
Credit cards Most major credit cards accepted.
Rates Room only, $55 double, $45 single. Extra person in room, $6. Children under 12 free in parents' room.

RED WING 55066   Map 7

A historic river town, Red Wing was named for a famous Dakota Indian chief. Although known particularly for its pottery, the town is still home to many prosperous industries as well as several beautiful riverfront parks, ideal for hiking and swimming. Climb to the top of Barn Bluff and Sovin's Bluff for dramatic river views and stop by the colorful harbor, Boathouse Village.

Located in southeastern Minnesota, Red Wing is set among the limestone bluffs lining the Mississippi River Valley, 55 miles southeast of Minneapolis/St. Paul via Route 61, and about the same distance from Rochester, via Route 58Y.

Pratt Taber Inn   *Tel:* (612) 388–5945
706 West 4th Street

A. W. Pratt built this 13-room Italianate-style home in 1876 and sold it to his son-in-law, Robert Taber, in 1905, which is why it's listed on the National Register of Historic Places as the Pratt-Taber House. Innkeepers Darrel and Jan Molander converted it into a B&B inn in 1985 and have furnished it with a wonderful collection of Renaissance revival and country Victorian pieces. The woodwork is typical of the period, from the gingerbread trim with a star motif (celebrating the 1876 centennial) on the outside of the house to the elaborate walnut and butternut interior carvings.

"Charmingly refurbished, truly Victorian Italianate mansion. Beautiful period antiques throughout, with much attention to detail. Reproduction period wallpapers, lovely central hall staircase, many fireplaces. We had a wonderful, comfortable visit." *(Kay E. Chapman)*

"My favorite is Aunt Polly's Room, with a slate fireplace—painted to look like marble—crystal chandelier, antique dressers, and a brass bed that words can't describe. The continental breakfast of muffins, pastries, fruit platter, juice, and tea or coffee is served to you in bed, in the dining room, or on the porch in season. The china is lovely Red Wing Pottery and the food is delicious. The aroma of breakfast cooking makes one want to rise early and enjoy the hostess, good food, and good conversation with the other guests." *(Mrs. Marie Hassler)* More comments, please.

Open All year.
Rooms 7 doubles, with radio, desk—1 with private bath, 1 with private ½ bath, 5 with a maximum of 4 people sharing 1 bath.
Facilities Dining room, sitting room, parlor, conservatory with Jacuzzi, screened

porch, library, Victorian garden, gazebo, bicycles. 2 blocks from Mississippi River; golf, cross-country and downhill skiing nearby.
Location In historic district, 3 blocks from downtown. 2 blocks off Hwy. 61 on 4th and Dakota sts.
Restrictions No smoking in guest rooms. No children under 7.
Credit cards MC, Visa.
Rates B&B, $69–89 double. Extra person in room, $10. Group rate for entire house, $399–499.
Extras Minneapolis airport pickup, $15. Pets permitted.

St. James Hotel
406 Main Street (Route 61)

Tel: (612) 388–2846

Red Wing's initial prosperity arose from its key role as a port for the shipping of wheat. The St. James was built in 1875 as a symbol of this early success. Owned for 72 years by the Lillyblad family, the hotel became famous for fine food. It is said that the trains used to stop in Red Wing "just so the passengers could eat at Clara Lillyblad's restaurant." In 1975 the Red Wing Shoe Company bought the hotel, restoring it completely and combining it with a shopping, parking, and office complex, without disturbing the hotel's historic charms. Each of the 60 guest rooms is named for a Mississippi riverboat, and half have views of the river and the bluffs; all the rooms have been individually decorated with period antiques and reproductions and lovely handcrafted quilts. Still known for good food, the hotel is home to three restaurants: the Port of Red Wing Restaurant, serving American food; the Victorian Dining Room, offering French cuisine in elegant surroundings; and the Veranda Café, providing three casual meals daily, overlooking the Mississippi. *(Tom & Liba Stillman)*

"Good food, gorgeous decor, great setting. Climb to the top of the nearby bluffs for great river views." *(Jeanne Hanson)*

Open All year.
Rooms 60 doubles, all with private bath and/or shower, telephone, TV, air-conditioning. 6 with single or double Jacuzzi. Some with desk.
Facilities 3 restaurants, pub, lounge with weekend pianist. ½ block to YMCA with full athletic facilities.
Location Downtown.
Restrictions No smoking in some guest rooms.
Credit cards Amex, CB, DC, Discover, MC, Visa.
Rates Room only, $61–115 double. Extra person in room, $5. No charge for children under 18. Theater, "Winterlude" packages. Alc breakfast, $3–6; alc lunch, $5–10; alc dinner, $10–35.
Extras Wheelchair accessible; 2 rooms equipped for disabled. Cribs, babysitting available.

ROCHESTER 55902   Map 7

Canterbury Inn
723 Second Street, S.W.

Tel: (507) 289–5553

Guests at the Canterbury Inn tend to be an unusual mix—about a third are tourists, a third are IBM executives visiting their Rochester plant, and a third are patients at the Mayo Clinic.

"The two delightful women innkeepers at the Canterbury are Mary Martin and Jeffrey Van Sant (her maternal grandmother's maiden name was Jeffrey). The inn was built in 1890 and has been lovingly restored. Although each room has a modern private bath, guests may also use the original deep, oak-rimmed bathtub on the first floor. Each of the rooms has its own personality, from the butterfly room in the rear to the antique-furnished master bedroom in the front. The rooms are bright, quiet, cheerful, and exceedingly clean, with good bedside lighting for reading in bed.

"The full breakfasts are very special. Eggs Benedict, wild rice and gingerbread waffles, Swedish pancakes with lingonberries, fruit soup, omelets, and homemade breads are among the possibilities, served at the time guests request it. The rates also include late-afternoon tea, including coffee, and wine, plus a variety of hot and cold hors d'oeuvres that may tempt you to skip dinner. It's a wonderful time to get to know Mary and Jeffrey and meet the other guests.

"The owners manage to make each visitor feel like a welcomed guest and friend. They willingly try to meet each guest's individual needs whether this be a special diet, a ride in bad weather, or taking messages." (*Jean Mohrig, also J.C. Bradley*) "The inn is professionally run, yet its owners offered the warmth and security we needed at a time of great stress." (*Judy Herron*)

Open All year.
Rooms 4 doubles with private bath, telephone, radio, air conditioning.
Facilities Breakfast room, parlor, living room with fireplace, TV, books, games, music, porch. Cross-country skiing nearby. Off-street parking.
Location SE MN. 88 m SE of Minneapolis/St. Paul. Center of town, 3 blocks from Mayo Clinic.
Restrictions No smoking in bedrooms. Children over 10 sometimes accepted.
Credit cards MC, Visa.
Rates B&B, $65 double, $55 single, plus 10% tax.
Extras Italian spoken. "Courtesy car (ancient Volvo) almost always available for free airport and clinic trips."

Lowell Inn   *Tel:* (612) 439–1100
102 North Second Street

A Williamsburg-style hotel, the Lowell was built in 1927. Its first managers, Nelle and Arthur Palmer, had traveled through the Midwest—she as an actress, he as a piano player—and had stayed in so many poor hotels that they decided to run a truly superior one. Beginning in 1930, they started collecting antiques, fine linens, china, and glassware, and eventually purchased the inn in 1945. Although both senior Palmers have passed away, the inn has continued to prosper under the ownership of their son and daughter-in-law, Arthur Jr. and his wife Maureen.

The inn has several different dining rooms, each with a different character and menu—the elegant George Washington Room, the Garden Room with indoor trout pond, and the Matterhorn Room, filled with antique Swiss wood carvings. Many of the inn's specialties have been served for decades—by guest demand. Rooms are decorated traditionally, highlighted with antiques; some have elaborate draped or gilt beds and marble sinks.

"Very southern atmosphere and delicious dinners. The Palmer family runs this inn with impeccable taste." *(Liba & Tom Stillman)* "The best inn we've ever visited, hence the constant returns. Rooms have many extra touches, the food outstanding, service tops." *(Stephen Shipps)*

"Your current listing does not do this wonderful institution justice. I've been going there for half a century and it not only stays uniform but get better. Food and service in the George Washington and Matterhorn Rooms is incomparable. In the Garden Room one can net a trout from the spring-fed pond and have it cooked and served right away. The prices are high but worth it. I wish they had an elevator to make an overnight stay easier for older folks (the guest rooms are on the second floor). The rooms have small bottles of wine, special embroidered towels, soaps, and a comfortable quiet setting. The hall carpets are the thickest I've found anywhere." *(David Fesler)*

Another guest had a slightly different viewpoint: "Stillwater is a delight-fully quaint river town, with interesting buildings and neat shops, al-though the inn is not right in the historic section. I have friends who became engaged at Lowell's 25 years ago, and still love to return on their anniversaries; others visiting recently for the first time found it overrated."

Open All year. Closed Thanksgiving, Christmas.
Rooms 4 suites with Jacuzzi baths, 17 doubles—all with private bath and/or shower, telephone, radio, desk, air-conditioning.
Facilities Restaurant, lounge, lobby with fireplace. Fishing nearby.
Location SE MN, 19 m E of Twin Cities. Take Rte. 35 W north to Rte. 36 E. One block off of Main St., on corner of Myrtle and 2nd Sts.
Restrictions Light sleepers might be disturbed by street noise on east side of building.
Credit cards Amex, DC, MC, Visa.
Rates Room only, $139 suite, $89–129 double. MAP rates, add $100. 15% service additional. Alc breakfast, $6–9; alc lunch, $12; alc dinner, $30. Prix fixe fondue dinner for 2 (Matterhorn Room), $90.
Extras Restaurant wheelchair accessible. Cribs, babysitting available. German spoken.

WABASHA 55981   Map 7

Anderson House   *Tel:* (612) 565–4524
333 West Main Street   In MN: (800) 862–9702
                                                  In Midwest: (800) 325–2270

In Anne Tyler's book *The Accidental Tourist,* the protagonist says that hotel rooms should come with a pet, to keep you company. The Anderson House does just that: You can pick, or even reserve, one of the inn's 10 cats to keep your toes warm for the night.

It's the oldest operating hotel in Minnesota, dating back to 1856, and is owned and managed by the fourth generation of the Anderson family. Grandma Ida Anderson, who started running the inn at the turn of the century, learned how to cook in the Pennsylvania Dutch country, and many of her favorite recipes are still being served—cinnamon rolls, red flannel hash, scrapple, *fastnachts* for breakfast; chicken with dumplings, smoked pork chops with red cabbage for lunch or dinner; plus a dozen different breads and an equal number of desserts ensure that no one goes to bed hungry. Rooms are furnished with period antiques, many of them original to the building.

"Anderson House is a homey inn with over 130 years' worth of character. It's a clean establishment with great food, reasonably priced. The inn is a block from downtown Wabasha, a quaint southern Minnesota town on the Mississippi River; Nelson, Wisconsin, is on the other side." *(Lanie Paymar, also Mark Slen)*

Open All year.
Rooms 52 suites and doubles—suites with private bath, doubles with shared or private baths.
Facilities Restaurants, bar/lounge, lobby, ice cream parlor, patio, greenhouse, picnic lunch caterer. Mississippi River for swimming, boating, fishing. Cross-country skiing nearby.
Location SE MN, Mississippi River Valley, off Rte. 61.
Credit cards None accepted.
Rates Room only, $80–95 suite, $37–75 double. Midweek family, B&B rates. Special event, seasonal, weekend packages.
Extras Children's menu.

WINONA 55987   Map 7

The Hotel   *Tel:* (507) 452–5460
Johnson and Third Streets

Winona was one of the busiest lumbering towns on the Mississippi at the turn of the century, and the Hotel was built by the Schlitz brewing family of Milwaukee to provide good food and first-rate lodging for local and visiting businessmen. Restored in 1981, the rooms are decorated with Victorian furniture and have modern amenities and plumbing. Lunch and dinner are served in the Hotel's period restaurant; steaks and seafood are specialities. Winona offers attractions both natural and historic: hunting and fishing, watersports, hiking or cross-country skiing; visits to historic buildings and museums, including the Julius Wilkie Riverboat Museum.

"We stopped to see Winona's restored steamboat and for the great views from the bluffs at Garvin Heights, and had a very tasty lunch at the Hotel." *(Ralph Miller)* Reports, please.

Open All year.
Rooms 6 suites, 18 doubles—all with private bath and/or shower, telephone, TV, air-conditioning, fan.
Facilities Restaurant, bar/lounge, conference room. On-street parking, some spaces in nearby parking lot. Mississippi River area for fishing, hunting, water sports, hiking, horseback riding, skiing.
Location SE MN, Mississippi River Valley, off Rte. 61. At corner of 3rd and Johnson. From Hwy. 61, take Huff St. exit to 3rd St. Turn right on 3rd St. and go 3 blocks to inn.
Credit cards All major credit cards accepted.
Rates Room only, $84 suite, $46–63 double, $37–54 single. Extra person in room, $5. No charge for children under 12. 1-2 night B&B packages. Alc breakfast, $3–4; alc lunch, $5–6; alc dinner, $15–20.
Extras Restaurant wheelchair accessible. Crib available. Spanish spoken.

Mississippi

The Burn, Natchez

Andrew Jackson was one of Mississippi's first heroes. After he defeated the Creek Indian nation and won the Battle of New Orleans, the state's capital was named for him. The Civil War played a major role in Mississippi's history; in addition to the famous siege of Vicksburg, innumerable battles took place across the state, leaving tremendous destruction in their wake.

Today history buffs visit Natchez and Vicksburg in search of antebellum ambience, while beach buffs head south to the Gulf Coast. Plan to spend some time (spring and fall are best) exploring the Natchez Trace Parkway, a 400-mile parkway administered by the National Parks Service. Extending from Natchez nearly to Nashville, Tennessee, it follows the historic trail (or trace) that was one of the region's most frequented roads at the beginning of the 1800s. We'd love to have more recommendations on places to stay while traveling in Mississippi, either on business or for pleasure!

If you're booking a room in an antebellum mansion that can also be visited by the public, remember that rooms on a tour will rarely be available for occupancy before 5 P.M., and must typically be vacated by 9 A.M. Rooms in adjacent buildings may not be quite as fancy, but have more liberal check-out policies.

JACKSON 39202   Map 6

Millsaps Buie House   *Tel:* (601) 352–0221
628 North State Street

Jackson is the capital of Mississippi and its largest city, with a population of 400,000. Back in the 1880s, the city's social elite built mansions along

State Street and gathered in each other's homes for dinner parties, tea dances, and croquet. The Millsaps Buie House dates from this period and is listed on the National Register of Historic Places. Its renovation as a bed & breakfast inn began in 1985; the house survived a near disastrous fire and opened fully restored and decorated with beautiful period antiques late in 1987. Rates include a breakfast of fresh fruit and juice, grits, home-baked pastries, sausages and biscuits, and predinner refreshments and hors d'oeuvres.

"Jackson's only bed & breakfast inn offers beautiful decor and gracious southern hospitality, combined with spotless housekeeping and professional service. Rooms on the first and second floors are furnished with period antiques; those on the third floor have a more contemporary decor but are still lovely. Baths are very modern. TVs are discreetly tucked into cabinets. The touch-tone phones have a special plug for your computer modem!" *(Jean Rawitt, also Gary Milam)*

Open All year.
Rooms 1 suite, 10 doubles with private bath, telephone with computer dataport, radio, TV, air-conditioning. Some with desk.
Facilities Breakfast room, dining room, parlor with grand piano. 1½ acres with patio, off-street parking.
Location Central MS. 5 blocks from Capitol. From Hwy. 80, go N on State St. to inn at corner of High St.
Restrictions No smoking in public rooms. No children under 12.
Credit cards Amex, DC, MC, Visa.
Rates B&B, $125 suite, $75–110 double. Extra person in room, $10.

NATCHEZ 39120   **Map 6**

Natchez was founded in 1716. Since then the flags of six nations have flown over the city—France, England, Spain, the sovereign state of Mississippi, the Confederacy, and the U.S. Natchez's greatest wealth and prosperity came in the early 1800s with the introduction of cotton and the coming of the steamboat. Extraordinary mansions were built during this period, which ended with the Civil War. Unlike Vicksburg to the north, Natchez was not of military importance, so although little property was destroyed during the war, further development ceased. As a result, over 500 antebellum mansions survive.

About a dozen mansions, including some of the most important, such as the palatial Stanton Hall, are open to visitors year-round. Most, however, are open only during festivals, called Pilgrimages, which are held for two weeks from early to mid-October and for a month in the spring, from early March to early April. If you plan to visit during one of the Pilgrimages, make your reservations six weeks to three months in advance. Alternative bed & breakfast lodging, as well as tickets for the house tours, can be arranged by calling Pilgrimage Tours at (800) 647–6742.

Natchez is in southwest Mississippi, on the Mississippi River, 114 miles southwest of Jackson. Try to travel here via the Natchez Trace, once an Indian footpath, now a two-lane parkway run by the National Park Service between Natchez and Nashville, passing centuries of American history enroute. Call the Natchez Trace Parkway Visitors Center for more information (601–842–1572).

"Natchez may not have Vicksburg's Civil War history, but it is small and manageable. The people are friendly and there are lots of antique shops to explore. The Pilgrimage attracts crowds, but it is well-established and organized, with two evening entertainments: *Southern Exposure*, a comedy play, and the *Confederate Pageant*." (SHW)

The Burn
712 North Union Street

Tel: (601) 442–1344
(800) 654–8859

The Burn was built in 1835 in the Greek Revival style, with a front portico supported by large Doric columns. It survived the Civil War first as the headquarters for Union troops and later as a Union hospital. It was restored in 1978 and is owned by Tony and Loveta Byrne. Mr. Byrne was mayor of Natchez for twenty years. The interior features a beautiful semispiral flying staircase and rooms decorated with elaborately carved beds and handsome Belgian fabrics. Most of the guest rooms are in the original attached dependency or Garçonniere (so called because it served as bachelor quarters for the young men of the family). Rates include a full southern breakfast and house tour.

"The Burn's location is good; although its acreage is limited, the gardens are lovely. The owners live on the third floor full time, and a fun part of staying here is visiting with them. Breakfast is served in a dining room on the ground floor. The music room has an operating Regina music box. Overlooking the rear garden is a porch with ornate blue and cream wicker furniture. Two guest rooms are rented in the main house: The Pink Room on the main floor is very large with a four-poster tester bed swagged in pink satin, while the blue room is cool and spacious. Most rooms in the Garçonniere have four-poster beds, although the staircase leading up to them might be a bit tricky for older folks." (SHW)

"This is perhaps my favorite B&B, full of beautiful antiques, with several spacious rooms and a great plantation breakfast, with plenty of variety, served on fantastic china with beautiful silver." (Ann Delugach)

"We stayed in the Garçonnierre, in a lovely room with private bath and tester beds. Later we enjoyed wine and boiled peanuts by the fire with the Byrnes. In the morning we had a wonderful plantation breakfast with cheese grits, then a tour of the beautifully maintained yet comfortable main house. The grounds are gorgeous." (Caroline & Jim Lloyd)

"We had bedroom #1—blue and beautiful, with a fascinating carved tester bed. The Byrne family was a joy, newly discovered dear old friends." (Yvonne Miller)

Open All year.
Rooms 2 suites, 8 doubles, all with private bath and/or shower, TV, air-conditioning. 8 rooms in annex.
Facilities Dining room with fireplace, living room. 4 acres with swimming pool, patio, camellia gardens, off-street parking.
Location N. Union, between Oak and Bee sts.
Restrictions No smoking in common rooms. No children under 6.
Credit cards Amex, DC, Discover, MC, Visa.

Rates B&B, $80–125 suite, $70–100 double, $60–115 single. Extra person in room, $15–20.

Weymouth Hall
One Cemetery Road

Tel: (601) 445–2304

"This Greek Revival mansion, built in 1855, is set high on a bluff above the Mississippi River with a fine view. When it was bought by Gene Weber and Durrell Armstrong in 1975, the house had deteriorated to a shell and was on the verge of sliding down the hill into the river. An engineer was hired to assist in reconstructing the bluff and the building was saved. The inn is a total restoration; the ground floor was originally made of concrete finished to look like marble; before rebuilding, it had crumbled back to dirt. Gene Weber has a scrapbook of photos and articles chronicling the restoration. He lives on the third floor and is always available to guests.

"Rooms are furnished with the owners' collection of Victoriana of the rococo period, 1840s to 1860s—ornate with carving. European and Chinese porcelains abound. The public rooms upstairs include a center entry hall, with the ladies' parlor at the rear and the gentlemen's parlor at the front, both available to guests at any time. The airy guest rooms are average in size with plenty of room for a couple of chairs and a reading table. They have tester, four-poster or canopied beds, and one room has a river view. Baths are modern with fiberglass tubs and linoleum floors, with full-size bars of quality soaps." *(Susan W. Schwemm)*

"Breathtaking view and sunset over the river. Very comfortable room with dazzling early Victorian antiques. Gene Weber was most hospitable, and the tasty southern breakfast kept us full for the day. Across the street is an interesting old cemetery where many Confederate soldiers are buried." *(Victor Thorne)*

Open Feb. through Dec.
Rooms 5 doubles, all with full private bath, radio, air-conditioning. 4 with desk.
Facilities Dining room, sitting room with TV, 2 parlors. 13 acres with gardens.
Location ½ m from town. From post office, go N on Broadway or Canal to Linton Ave. to Old Cemetery Rd. Inn on left, overlooking river.
Restrictions No smoking. No children under 14.
Credit cards MC, Visa.
Rates B&B, $70 double, $60 single. 10% AAA discount.

VICKSBURG 39180   **Map 6**

When folks talk about "The War" in Vicksburg, it's the Civil War they're referring to, not any of more recent vintage. Because of the town's controlling position, high on the Mississippi River bluffs, Union forces felt Vicksburg's surrender was essential to victory. Repulsed in repeated attempts both from land and water, the town surrendered to General U. S. Grant only after a 47-day siege of continuous mortar and cannon bombardment.

Must-see sights in Vicksburg include the National Military Park and Cemetery and the nearby Cairo Museum, with numerous exhibits and audiovisual programs that bring the history of the battle and the period to life. Amazingly enough, many of Vicksburg's antebellum mansions survived the siege and can be visited today. Check with the Vicksburg Tourist Commission for Pilgrimage dates: (800) 221–3536. For a lighter taste of history, stop at the Biedenharn Candy Company Museum to see where Coca-Cola was first bottled in 1894.

Vicksburg is located in southwest Mississippi, 44 miles east of Jackson, via I-20.

Although a great many antebellum mansions are open for B&B in Vicksburg, relatively few are owner-operated; most have a resident manager and the owners live elsewhere. In some instances, this has created problems, and we have received complaints about well-known plantation homes whose standards have slipped considerably. As always, reports are welcome!

Reader tips: *Janet Howe* recommends the **Martha Vick House** as "the most delightful place to dine at any hour of the day. Created by two gentlemen of great artistic bent, it is a visual joy in its decor. The food is special . . . and to die for. Bill and David exude southern charm and humor like you've never heard and seen it." Another well-traveled reader notes that although Vicksburg is well worth visiting, much of the town is depressing and poverty-stricken.

The Corners   *Tel:* (601) 636–7421
601 Klein Street   (800) 444–7421

Resident owners Cliff and Bettye Whitney will greet you on arrival at the Corners with a complimentary beverage, and you may well want to sit right down and enjoy it in a lazy rocking chair on the wide gallery as you watch the sun set over the Mississippi River. Built in 1873, The Corners is listed on the National Register of Historic Places and built in a style combining Greek Revival and Victorian features. John A. Klein, of Cedar Grove, had the Corners constructed as a wedding present for his daughter Susan. The floors are original heart-of-pine boards 20 feet long and the support walls are three bricks thick. Rooms are elegantly furnished with period antiques, while baths are modern.

"In my experience, the Corners provides the most consistently warm, comfortable experience of all the B&Bs in Vicksburg, perhaps because the Whitneys actually live there full-time and because they treat their guests like family. The Corners has rooms that are beautifully and (more important) comfortably appointed, with magnificent views of the river, and hosts who leave no stone unturned to please and entertain you. It's charmingly restored, and filled with personal treasures. Arriving feels like a homecoming; departing is heart-wrenching." *(Janet Howe)*

"Bettye made dinner reservations for us at the Delta Point, and ordered them to take good care of us. We had a window table with a fine view of the Mississippi Bridge in the lovely dining room, and returned there again the next night. Breakfast is served in the formal dining room. The first morning we had ham, scrambled eggs, cheese grits, tomato with dill mayonnaise, fresh-squeezed orange juice, and the best biscuits of our Mississippi trip. The Whitneys waited until everyone had gathered in the parlor for coffee before inviting us all to the table. The food was served piping hot, and the breakfast conversation was very pleasant.

"We stayed in the Master Bedroom suite, with two 12-foot windows facing the Mississippi River. The rug in this room took two ladies 2½ years to hand hook. The bed is a massive half tester, and there is plenty of room for an armoire, straight and overstuffed chairs, a tea table and a dresser. The bath was supplied with very thick towels, and imported toiletries; the bathtub was heavily draped with lace and curtains, which made using it a bit tricky." *(Susan W. Schwemm)*

Open All year.
Rooms 1 2-bedroom suite, 8 doubles, all with private shower and/or bath, air-conditioning. 2 with telephone, 8 with TV, 3 with desk. 2 rooms in former slave quarters.
Facilities Dining room; parlor with 2 fireplaces, piano, library; veranda. 1½ acres with parterre gardens, croquet.
Location 1 m from center. From I-20, take exit 1A. Go N on Washington, left on Klein to inn at corner of Klein and Oak.
Restrictions No smoking.
Credit cards MC, Visa.
Rates B&B, $120 2-bedroom suite, $65–95 double, $55–85 single. Extra adult in room, $20; child under age 6, $15. House tours, $4.
Extras Wheelchair accessible. Pets allowed.

Duff Green Mansion
1114 First East Street

Tel: (601) 636–6968
(601) 638–6662

Duff Green, a prosperous Vicksburg merchant, built this 12,000-square-foot Paladian mansion in 1856 as a wedding gift for his bride, Mary Lake Green; her parents had provided the land, also as a wedding gift. Once the scene of many parties, the mansion was converted into a hospital during the Civil War (Union soldiers on the third floor, Confederates on the second). Mary Green gave birth to a son during the siege of Vicksburg while taking shelter in a nearby cave and named him Siege Green. The recent restoration of the mansion combines antiques and period reproductions with exceptionally luxurious appointments; rates include a welcoming drink and a full southern breakfast.

"Probably the most luxurious B&B in Vicksburg, the Duff Green has more the feel of an elegant hotel than a cozy homestay. It is not a museum, and the whole house is open to guests. The pine floors are original, as are the 14½ foot ceilings and 12-foot windows. The house's relatively high elevation protects it from the noise and less attractive elements of the street below. The French chandelier in the ballroom dates from 1860, while the one in the dining room is of Waterford crystal. The location is quiet, and although the grounds are limited, they are well designed and private, with brick terraces everywhere. Likable owner Harry Sharp lives elsewhere in Vicksburg, but loves the house, and is very enthusiastic about its virtues. Lynn Foley is the pleasant daytime manager; another innkeeper stays on the first floor overnight. All guest rooms are individually furnished and good sized; the Duff Green suite is massive, covering one-half the third floor." *(SHW)*

Open All year.

Rooms 3 suites, 4 doubles, all with full private bath, air-conditioning, fireplace. 5 with desk, 1 with kitchenette.

Facilities Dining room, parlor, library, porches, rooftop sundeck. 1 acre with swimming pool, brick patio with fountain.

Location Historic District. From Hwy. 61, go E on First East St. to inn between Adams and Locust.

Credit cards MC, Visa.

Rates B&B, $95–140 suite, $75–95 double, $50–85 single. Extra adult in room, $10; kids 6-12, $5; under 6, free.

Extras Ground floor rooms wheelchair accessible. Airport/station pickups, $65. Spanish spoken. Cribs available.

Key to Abbreviations

For complete information and explanations, please see the Introduction.

Rates: Range from least expensive room in low season to most expensive room in peak season.

Room only: No meals included; sometimes referred to as European Plan (EP).

B&B: Bed and breakfast; includes breakfast, sometimes afternoon/evening refreshment.

MAP: Modified American Plan; includes breakfast and dinner.

Full board: Three meals daily.

Alc lunch: À la carte lunch; average price of entrée plus nonalcoholic drink, tax, tip.

Alc dinner: Average price of three-course dinner, including half bottle of house wine, tax, tip.

Prix fixe dinner: Three- to five-course set dinner, excluding wine, tax, tip unless otherwise noted.

Extras: Noted if available. Always confirm in advance. Pets are not permitted unless specified.

Zip codes: If only one zip code applies, it is listed with the town name. If there is more than one, it is noted as part of the address.

Missouri

Garth Woodside Mansion, Hannibal

Missouri's two major cities, Kansas City and St. Louis, developed on the state's two major rivers—the Missouri and the Mississippi, which form its eastern and part of its western borders. The central part of the state is more rural, with the Lake of the Ozarks and the Ozark Mountains regions as major tourist attractions; recommendations for this area would be especially welcome.

Also recommended: Ste. Genevieve is the oldest town west of the Mississippi; it sits on the river, about an hour's drive south of St. Louis. Although we didn't have time to complete a full entry, frequent contributors *James & Janice Utt* reported that the **Inn St. Gemme Beauvais** (78 North Main Street, 63670; 314–883–5744) "is a pleasantly furnished inn and restaurant. The rooms are large with comfortable beds. Thick, soft towels were appreciated at bath time. A delicious full breakfast was served in the lovely dining room. Our children were welcome and well taken care of. Several good restaurants are within walking distance and this pretty little town is well worth a few hours of exploration."

Information please: We've listed some other St. Genevieve possibilities we'd like to hear more about. If you were traveling the Mississippi back in the mid-1800s, you might well have spent a comfortable night there at **The Southern Hotel.** This opportunity still exists today, thanks to the restoration job recently completed by owners Barbara and Mike Hanley.

Rooms are individually decorated with period antiques, and rates include a creatively home-cooked breakfast (146 South Third Street 63670; 314–883–3493). Another possibility in Ste. Genevieve is the **Steiger House**, a B&B offering reasonably priced suites and cottages and use of the inn's indoor swimming pool (1021 Market Street 63670; 314–883–5881).

In the southwestern part of the state, the city of Springfield is home to the **Walnut Street Inn** (900 East Walnut, Springfield 65806; 417–864–6346), a Queen Anne Victorian home built in 1894. The seven guest rooms are furnished with antiques, and rates include a full breakfast with such Ozark specialities as persimmon muffins, walnut bread, sparkling juice, plus afternoon cheese and wine.

For additional entries in neighboring Illinois, see our entry for the **Westerfield House,** in Freeburg, about 20 miles southeast of St. Louis, known especially for its outstanding dinners; and our entry for the **Green Tree Inn,** in Elsah, about 40 miles upriver from St. Louis, for a pleasant B&B in a 19th-century village.

Rates do not include 10% state sales tax and room tax.

ARROW ROCK 65320 — Map 10

Borgman's Bed & Breakfast *Tel:* (816) 837–3350
706 Van Buren

Founded in 1829, Arrow Rock is a Historic Landmark town, noted as the beginning point of the Santa Fe Trail. Its most prosperous period was when it served as a Missouri River steamboat port; its decline started with the Civil War, and by the turn of the century the town was largely forgotten. In the 1920s local groups began restoring its historic buildings, and today people come to visit those buildings as well as the local antique shops and Arrow Rock's well-regarded summer repertory theater, the Lyceum.

"Kathy and Helen Borgman have personally restored and decorated this two-story white frame house. The clean, well-lighted rooms (with ample bathroom facilities) are decorated with antiques they've collected. The food is home-cooked, and the smell of homemade cinnamon rolls makes you aware that Helen is preparing breakfast especially for you. Parking is ample and the house is within walking distance of the historical area and the Lyceum Theater." *(Darleen F. Mueller)*

Open All year.
Rooms 4 doubles with maximum of 3 people sharing bath; air-conditioning.
Facilities Kitchen/breakfast room, 2 sitting/TV rooms with games, porches. Missouri River nearby for fishing.
Location Central MO. 2 hrs. E of Kansas City, 3 hrs. W of St. Louis. 50 min. W of Columbia. From I-70 W, take exit 98 to Hwy. 41 to Arrow Rock. From I-70 E, take exit 89 to Hwy. K to Hwy. 41. B&B is 1 block E of Hwy. 41.
Restrictions No smoking.
Credit cards None accepted.
Rates B&B, $35–40 double, $30 single, including tax. Extra person in room, $5. 10% discount on 3-night stays.
Extras Crib available.

BRANSON 65616   Map 10

The Branson House   *Tel:* (417) 334–0959
120 Fourth Street

"The Ozarks are a wonderful place for a vacation, even for Missourians. Rooms in this area are expensive and often full. To our delight we found space in this turn-of-century home. This B&B is very quiet, with nicely decorated rooms and a delicious breakfast. We had a chance to visit with innkeeper Opal Kelly and the other guests, but also had lots of privacy—a perfect combination. All this for a price less than the average area motel." *(Kathy & Helen Borgman)*

Open March through Dec.
Rooms 1 suite, 6 doubles—all with private bath and/or shower, air-conditioning.
Facilities Parlor with books, games; dining room, porch. Tree-shaded yard. Walking distance to Lake Taneycomo, shops, restaurants.
Location SW MO. 45 m S of Springfield, 250 m SW of St. Louis, 100 m NE of Fayetteville, AR. Center of town.
Credit cards None accepted.
Rates B&B, $50–65 double.

HANNIBAL 63401   Map 10

Information please: Another Hannibal B&B, also once owned by the Garth family is the **Fifth Street Mansion**, an Italianate mansion on "Millionaire's Row," beautifully decorated in period and highlighted by Tiffany stained-glass windows (213 South Fifth Street; 314–221–0445)

Garth Woodside Mansion   *Tel:* (314) 221–2789
New London Gravel Road, R.R. #1

Mark Twain lived in Hannibal as a boy and as a young man, when the prosperity of the river and of steamboating were at their height. Twain remains Hannibal's main claim to fame to this day, and while there are many worthwhile historic sights to see, others, such as the "Huck Finn Shopping Center," fall into a rather different category.

John W. Garth built Woodside, an imposing Victorian mansion, in 1871. A longtime friend of Mr. Garth's, Twain is believed to have stayed in the mansion in 1882 and again in 1902.

"This B&B is located on a parklike hillside shaded by stately oak and maple trees. While we enjoyed tea on the veranda, a young doe grazed in the nearby meadow. Our third-floor room had a lovely view, the hospitality was friendly and relaxed, and the delicious breakfast was elegantly served by Dianne and her daughter Carrie." *(Doris & R.B. Thomas)*

"Prior to its present ownership, the mansion was open only as a museum, and it is listed on the National Register of Historic Places. It has almost all the original furniture in each of the rooms, with 12-foot high headboards, tables, and even knickknacks. Our room had a claw-foot tub and a European hand-carved armoire with mirror. Even 19th-century-style nightshirts are provided for guests to wear! The fresh homemade breakfasts are served on a different china pattern every day." *(Cristina Goodman)*

"The outstanding features include a magnificent flying staircase that floats to the third floor with no visible means of support and seven hand-crafted Italian marble mantels." *(Duane & Clare Baylor)*

"Coffee is served at 8 A.M., with breakfast following at 8:30. Irv took time to answer our questions and fill us in on the history of the Garth family. The Garths had a tradition of hospitality which the Feinbergs are clearly upholding." *(Diann Lutz)* "Our delicious breakfast included fresh pineapple and watermelon with yogurt sauce, still-warm lemon sponge cake, and outstanding peach French toast." *(Pat DeLaney)*

"The busy innkeepers gladly stopped to answer our frequent questions about the fascinating history of the mansion, gave complete information about local points of interest, teased our children, and in every way developed at homey atmosphere during our stay." *(J. Regis O'Connor)*

"We felt totally at home yet transported back in the Victorian era. The Garth family history, illustrated by many photographs, was especially interesting." *(Marilen Pitler, and others)*

Open All year.
Rooms 8 doubles—4 with private bath and/or shower, 4 with maximum of 4 people sharing bath. All with air-conditioning; some with desk, telephone on request.
Facilities Dining room, living room, parlor, library, verandas, porches. 39 acres with gardens, fish pond, croquet. Swimming, boating nearby.
Location NE MO. 2 m S of town. From town go S on Hwy. 61, go E on Warren Barrett Dr. (1st rd. S of Holiday Inn); at 2nd bridge follow signs to S to inn.
Restrictions Smoking in living room only. No children under 12.
Credit cards MC, Visa.
Rates B&B, $53–66 double. Extra person in room, $10. Tipping encouraged. 2-night holiday minimum. Midweek specials.

HERMANN 65041   Map 10

A Missouri River town founded by German immigrants over 150 years ago, Hermann has maintained a strong sense of its heritage, celebrated vigorously in May, August, and of course in the fall, with Octoberfest. Hermann boasts over 100 buildings and two districts listed on the National Register of Historic Places. The community's winemaking roots reach back to its founding, and two local wineries welcome visitors.

Information please: We'd like reports on **Birk's Goethe Street Gasthaus**, a century-old brick Victorian mansion furnished in period with oversize claw-foot tubs (700 Goethe Street; 314–486–2911); **Das Brownhaus**, of similar vintage but with a more eclectic decor (125 East Second Street; 314–486–3372).

William Klinger Inn   *Tel:* (314) 486–5930
108 East Second Street

Local miller William Klinger built this sturdy red brick house in 1878; it was converted into an inn a little more than a century later, with a great deal of its hand-crafted woodwork, stained glass, and ceiling medallions still intact. Owned by John and Nancy Bartel since 1986, and managed by LaVerne Rickher, it is decorated with antique and reproduction furnishings, including stained-glass windows and period lighting. Rates include a full "gourmet" breakfast.

"Capable, friendly innkeeper, immaculate common rooms; elegant guest room with canopy bed and large private bath; delicious breakfast served on lace tablecloth." *(Amy Sleeter, also Dr. & Mrs. Leroy Ortmeyer)*

Open All year.
Rooms 2 suites, 5 doubles, all with private shower and/or bath, TV, desk, air-conditioning, fan.
Facilities Dining room with fireplace, parlor, conference room. Patio.
Location E central MO. 90 m W of St. Louis, 30 m E of Jefferson City. Wine Country, on Rte. 100 (Lewis and Clark Hwy.)
Restrictions No smoking. No children.
Credit cards MC, Visa.
Rates B&B, $90–110 suite, $70–95 double. Extra person in room, $20. 2-night minimum festival weekends. Midweek, winter discounts.

KANSAS CITY 64112 Map 10

Located close to the geographic center of the continental U.S., Kansas City has long been a favorite of convention planners. Lesser known is the fact that it is a pleasant city, with lots of parks and open spaces, several museums of note, including the Nelson Gallery of Art, with world-class collections, and the Liberty Memorial, with museums dedicated to World War I artifacts. Although KC has several major shopping and restaurant plazas of note, serious shoppers will want to pay homage (and probably more) at the many fine shops of Country Club Plaza, with its Spanish towers and Moorish tiled fountains—probably the country's first suburban-style shopping mall, built in the 1920s.

Kansas City is located in western Missouri, straddling the Kansas border.

Doanleigh Wallagh Inn   *Tel:* (816) 753–2667
217 East 37th Street   (800) 232–2632

Ed and Carolyn Litchfield were so sure that they wanted to run an inn that they spent their honeymoon looking at properties in Key West, Florida. They didn't find their dream house there but have done considerably better here in Kansas City. Doanleigh Wallagh is a Georgian mansion, built in 1904 and handsomely restored and decorated with American and European antiques and quality reproductions.

"A lovely inn in a quiet section, walking distance to the art museum and Country Club Plaza. Our room was beautifully restored with modern amenities; breakfasts varied and tasty, and innkeepers most accommodating." *(Adam Platt)*

Open All year.
Rooms 12 rooms in 2 adjacent homes, all with private bath or shower, telephone, radio, TV, air-conditioning. 2 rooms with fireplace. Fully equipped kitchen for guest use in 1 home.

Facilities 3 Dining rooms, 2 living rooms with grand piano, pump organ, fireplace, library; solarium with TV/VCR, video library; porch. Park with tennis across street.
Location 5 min. to Crown Center, Country Club Plaza, and Westport; 10 min. to downtown. 3 blocks E of Main.
Restrictions Smoking on first floor only. No children under 12 except infants.
Credit cards Amex, MC, Visa.
Rates B&B, $60–90 double. Extra person in room, $7.50. 2-night holiday weekend minimum. Extended stay discount.
Extras Airport/station pickups.

The Raphael   *Tel:* (816) 756–3800
325 Ward Parkway   (800) 821–5343

Originally built as an apartment house, the Raphael was converted to a hotel about a dozen years ago. The lobby is paneled in beautiful woods, with traditional furnishings; guest rooms are warm and comfortable, and most have been updated with classic reproduction decor. The atmosphere is warm and friendly, and good food is served at the hotel restaurant. The suites are an excellent value in comparison to the newer hotels in the area; ask about their "Suite Deal" package for $98. *(Virginia Slimmer)* More comments, please.

Open All year. Restaurant closed Sunday.
Rooms 90 suites, 33 doubles, all with full private bath, telephone, radio, TV, desk, air-conditioning, refrigerator, mini-bar.
Facilities Restaurant, lounge with nightly piano bar. Swimming pool across street. Free parking. Tennis courts, jogging course nearby.
Location Country Club Plaza, 10 min. from downtown.
Credit cards Amex, DC, MC, Visa.
Rates B&B, $98–120 suites, $96–110 double. Extra adult in room, $12; no charge for children under 12. Weekend packages.
Extras Cribs, babysitting available. Spanish, German, French spoken.

ST. LOUIS   Map 10

Long known as the Gateway to the West, St. Louis is located in eastern Missouri, at the Illinois border. Although the Gateway Arch remains its premier tourist attraction, there's lots else to keep you busy. The once-decaying downtown area has been transformed in recent years by several major restoration projects. The once-proud Union Station has restored to its original glory and now functions as a shopping, entertainment, and hotel complex. The *U.S.S. Admiral* is now permanently moored on the Mississippi as an entertainment complex, and Laclede's Landing has been transformed from an abandoned warehouse district into a 19th-century river town. The St. Louis Science Center offers lots of hands-on exhibits, while the free tours (and samples) available at the Anheuser-Busch plant provide hands-on experiences of a totally different kind.

Also recommended in St. Louis is the **Coral Court Motel,** "an institution in St. Louis and one of the last remaining Route 66 motels, complete with rounded glass brick windows and garages." *(Jeff Lee)* Contact them at 7755 Watson Boulevard/Rte. 66, 63119; (314) 962–3000.

Lafayette House   *Tel:* (314) 772–4429
2156 Lafayette Avenue 63104

Overlooking Lafayette Park, this 1876 brick Queen Anne house has been owned by Sarah and Jack Milligan since 1984 and is decorated with many Victorian antiques. Sarah serves a full breakfast of casseroles, quiches, waffles, pancakes, or eggs, with bacon or sausage, and fruits, juices, and homemade breads; "I love to cook, so there is something different every day."

"Excellent service with very gracious and helpful hosts. Wine, cheese, and crackers always available. This Victorian mansion has been elegantly restored and is very comfortable." *(Dr. William Mania)*

"The Lafayette Square area has been extensively and attractively restored and is very convenient to many attractions in St. Louis. We stayed in the third-floor suite with our kids and had room to spare. The Milligans were gracious and helpful hosts who were eager to provide whatever advice or assistance we needed. The full breakfast was very good and included Sarah's excellent homebaked speciality breads. The Millilgans have several resident cats so allergic persons should take note." *(James & Janice Utt)*

Open All year.
Rooms 1 suite, 3 doubles—2 with full private bath, 2 with maximum of 4 people sharing bath. All rooms with air-conditioning. Suite with kitchenette.
Facilities Dining room, living room, lounge, library. Park across street.
Location 2 m from center. Exit I-44 at Jefferson; go N 1 block and turn right on Lafayette; or exit Rte. 40 at Jefferson and go S 7 blocks to Lafayette and turn left.
Restrictions Smoking in lounge area only.
Credit cards None accepted.
Rates B&B, $65 suite, $45–55 double, $40–50 single. Extra adult in room, $10; extra child, $7. 2-night minimum stay in suite.
Extras Airport/station pickups, $5 per person. Pets allowed with prior approval. Crib available.

Seven Gables Inn   *Tel:* (314) 863–8400
26 North Meramec, Clayton 63105   (800) 433–6590

Inspired by Nathaniel Hawthorne's *House of the Seven Gables* and its illustrations, a St. Louis architect designed the Seven Gables as an apartment building in the early 1900s. In 1985 it was completely renovated and converted to a hotel and restaurant. Rooms are traditionally furnished, and its two French restaurants have excellent reputations: Chez Louis, the fancier one, was named as one of the country's top hotel restaurants by *The New York Times.*

"The Seven Gables is just 10 minutes from the St. Louis airport and is very much like one of the Relais de Campagne in France. The service was faultless and the food exquisite." *(Ethel Aaron Hauser)*

"This lovely little European-style hotel provides quiet and tasteful accommodation in a historic building in the middle of a bustling office and shopping area. The furnishings and service are impeccable, worthy of a large, luxury establishment. The crowning glory of the Seven Gables is its food. Chez Louis is a marvelous French restaurant, and Bernard's is a bistro with a lighter menu. Both are very popular with St. Louisans as well as

with the inn's guests. The restaurants share an outstanding wine cellar."
(Irving Litvag)

One well-traveled writer noted that light sleepers should request the third-floor rooms to eliminate overhead noise, and felt that rooms in this price range should come with a proper closet, not just an open rod. Comments?

Open All year.
Rooms 4 suites, 28 doubles—all with full private bath, TV, telephone, radio, desk, air-conditioning.
Facilities Restaurant, bistro, bar, garden courtyard. Shaw Park nearby for jogging, swimming, tennis, ice skating.
Location E central MO. Clayton is at the intersection of Hwys. 40 and I-70. 7 m from downtown. ½ block from St. Louis County Government Center.
Credit cards Amex, DC, Discover, MC, Visa.
Rates Room only, $150–220 suite, $120–150 double, $105–130 single. Extra person in room, $30–45. Weekend rates, $80–90 including continental breakfast. Alc breakfast, $6–10; alc lunch, $15–20; alc dinner, $20–50 (lower prices in bistro, higher in restaurant).
Extras Wheelchair accessible; some guest rooms equipped for disabled. French, Italian, Spanish, German spoken.

WASHINGTON 63090   Map 10

Washington House, a newly opened B&B, offers antique-filled rooms in the historic home of Mr. and Mrs. Charles Davis (3 Lafayette Street; 314–239–2417). Reports, please.

The Schwegmann House   *Tel:* (314) 239–5025
438 West Front Street

With a population of 10,000, Washington is the largest town of the Missouri Rhineland, so named by the many Germans who settled here in the early 1800s. Schwegmann House was built over a century ago by a prosperous miller who needed a house large enough to provide overnight accommodation for his customers. It has been run as a B&B since 1983 and is furnished with antiques and handmade quilts. Innkeeper Norma Lause provides a continental breakfast of juice and fruit, croissants, jam, and cheese. *(Ralph Miller)* More comments, please.

Open All year.
Rooms 9 doubles—7 with private bath and/or shower, 2 with maximum of 4 people sharing bath. All rooms with air-conditioning, fan; some with desk.
Facilities Living/dining room, parlor with fireplace. Grape arbor, patio, gardens. River for fishing across street.
Location E central MO. Wine country, 1 hr. W of St. Louis. 1 block to center. From Hwy. 44, drive W 10 m to Hwy. 100. Turn right on Jefferson, left on Front St. to inn.
Credit cards MC, Visa.
Rates B&B, $60 double, $50 single. Extra person in room, $10. Reduced family rates.
Extras Limited wheelchair access. Babysitting available.

Montana

Lone Mountain Ranch, Big Sky

Montana is the perfect antidote to urban angst. Fourth-largest state in the country and 44th in population, its majestic landscapes put people in their place. With 10 national forests, a national park, and innumerable state parks, Montana appeals to the hardy who can backpack into spectacular country. Don't miss Glacier National Park with its accessible glaciers and glacier-carved valleys, sparkling lakes, and boundless variety of mammals, birds, and wildflowers.

Other high points include Route 93, which passes through a spectacular valley south of Missoula to the Idaho border; Virginia City, a well-restored mining town best visited in spring or fall; Bannock State Park, a haunting ghost town 17 miles west of Dillon; and Helena, a friendly little capital city. For curiosity's sake, visit the site of a major 1959 earthquake, which moved streams and mountains—a visitor's interpretive center is located on Route 287, 22 miles north of West Yellowstone.

Perfectly flat eastern Montana offers little to interest visitors, except for Pompey's Pillar on I-94, 23 miles northeast of Billings. Named after Pomp, the son of Lewis and Clark's guide Sakajawea, travelers can see where Clark carved his name on this sandstone monolith in 1806.

One reader added this observation on most Montana restaurants: "You have your choice of either family restaurants or supper clubs. The food is basic but delicious in both, with wonderful steaks—they don't believe in cholesterol here. As far as we could tell, the only differences between the two are that the latter don't have windows, they serve shrimp as well as steak, and the men take off their hats." *(Truman Talley)*

Also recommended: Received too late for a full write-up is a new entry to the B&B business, the **Copper King Mansion** (219 West Granite, Butte 59701; 406–782–7580), a 1884 Victorian mansion with a restaurant and three guest rooms, furnished in period. "We toured this historic mansion and returned for an excellent dinner. Service was great and the atmosphere was exceptionally warm and friendly." *(Roger & Wanda Acton)*

Information please: In Billings, in the south central part of the state, is the **Northern Hotel**. It's a big hotel for a small city, but a well-built one that retains a sense of its western heritage (Broadway at First Avenue North 59103; 406–245–5121); about 40 miles south of Billings, the **Cottonwood Ranch Retreat,** a pleasant B&B on a 500-acre working ranch (Star Route, Box 1044, Roberts 59070; 406–445–2415 or (800) 342–2345, ext. 999). In Helena, to the northwest of Billings, is the **Sanders B&B,** a beautifully restored Victorian home, built in 1875 and still housing many of the original furnishings (328 North Ewing; 406–442–3309); and for those who'd like a taste of the old West, the **Fairweather Inn** and the **Nevada City Hotel,** both under the same management in Virginia City in southwestern Montana. Rooms at both century-old establishments are simple but clean, and rates are modest (P.O. Box 338; 406–843–5377). In the northwest corner of the state, skiers at Big Mountain might rest up from all that powder at the **Garden Wall B&B,** a restored home built in 1920 and decorated with English florals and antiques (504 Spokane Avenue, Whitefish 59937; 406–862–3440).

BIGFORK 59911 — Map 13

On the northeast shores of Flathead Lake, in northwestern Montana, Bigfork has a reputation as an artists colony, in addition to offering a full range of water sports and other types of outdoor recreation.

Information please: The **O'Duach'Ain Inn** is a rustic B&B offering comfortable rooms and very reasonable rates (675 Ferndale Drive, Bigfork 59911; 406–837–6851).

Bigfork Inn
Box 967

Tel: (406) 837–6680

A rambling, half-timbered rustic Tudor-style structure, the Bigfork Inn has a restaurant serving an eclectic menu and a lounge which features jazz. "A class place in a class area. Terrific dining room." *(Keith Jurgens)* More comments please.

Open All year.
Rooms 7 doubles with private and shared baths.
Facilities Restaurant, lounge with music, dancing; theater. On NE shore of Flathead Lake.
Location NW MT. 100 m N of Missoula.
Credit cards None accepted.
Rates Room only, $25–30.

Flathead Lake Lodge
Route 35, Box 248

Tel: (406) 837–4391

An ideal spot for an all-inclusive week-long family ranch vacation, Flathead Lake Lodge has been owned by the Averill family since 1945. The main season here is during July and August, when returning guests from all over the country come to enjoy the lodge's unusual combination of both ranch activities and a full, water sports program—from breakfast rides to windsurfing, from children's rodeos to lake cruises. Accommodations are in both the main lodge and in rustic but comfortable, well-equipped cabins. Meals feature fresh cuts of meat, home-baked breads, fresh vegetables and homemade desserts. The entrées include baked salmon, tips of sirloin, crown roast, and Cornish game hen. *(TL)* More comments please.

Open May 1–Oct. 1
Rooms 18 2–3 bedroom cabins, 20 doubles—all with private bath and/or shower. Each cabin shares 1 bath. All with desk.
Facilities Main lodge with dining room, lounge with fireplace, bar; south lodge with large lobby, fireplace. Recreation hall with games; laundry facilities. 2,000 acres with heated swimming pool, 4 tennis courts, volleyball, hiking, horseback riding. On lake for all water sports. Children's program. Scheduled activity program with rodeos, cookouts, breakfast rides. Optional activities include river tubing, white water river float, wilderness fishing expedition, pack trip, tour of Glacier Park; $10–70 per person. Golf nearby.
Location NW MT. 100 m N of Missoula.
Credit cards MC, Visa.
Rates All rates per person. Full board, $1040 weekly (adult), $825 (13–17), $700 (4–12), $110 (under 4). Rates include all sports and activities (except those noted above). Daily rates off-season. 1-week minimum July and Aug.
Extras Limited wheelchair accessibility. Airport/station pickups, $20 per family. Cribs, babysitting available.

BIG SKY 59716   **Map 13**

Lone Mountain Ranch   *Tel:* (406) 995–4644
P.O. Box 69

Homesteaded in 1915, the Lone Mountain Ranch started out as a working cattle ranch. Ownership passed to the Butler family, who constructed most of the outbuildings as showcases for Mrs. Butler's collection of Indian artifacts. The ranch started taking in paying guests during the '40s and was bought by Viv and Bob Schaap in 1977. The Schaaps see a stay at their ranch as a family experience and offer programs to interest every age group; an effort is made to keep activities flexible "so that guests can enjoy the ranch in their own way." Horseback trips, trout fishing, and wilderness hikes (accompanied by the ranch naturalist) occupy the warm-weather days; cross-country skiing highlights the winter. The Schaaps have upgraded the trails to such an extent that the U.S. Biathlon Team trains here early each winter. With all this activity, it's no wonder that guests work up a healthy appetite for the ranch's hearty home-cooked meals, with breads and desserts baked "from scratch"; there's even fresh seafood, here in the heart of meat-and-potatoes country.

"The maximum number of guests is 60, and the ratio of staff to guests remains low. All families live in modern, fully equipped log cabins with wood-burning fireplaces. Meals are served family-style in the dining hall. The chef, lured from a Minneapolis area country club serves both gourmet meals and western barbecue. One does not have to be a riding 'nut' to enjoy Lone Mountain; the list of alternative activities provides many choices, geared to the abilities and interests of the guests—from a two-hour bird walk to a 16-mile hike over mountainous terrain." *(Howard & Susan Levine)*

"After many trips to Lone Mountain I have seen that underneath the surface of warm, cordial, inviting western hospitality is more warm, cordial, inviting western hospitality—with a slight Minnesota flair. Bob and Vivian are the soul and heart of Lone Mountain Ranch. Along with the outstanding crew they assemble each season, it's no wonder that so many guests return each year. As one of many guests who does not eat red meat, I can attest to the kitchen staff going out of their way to insure that everyone's diet receives the highest degree of attention." *(Patrick McGownd)*

Open June 1–Oct. 1; Dec. 1–April 1.
Rooms 20 cabins with full private bath, fireplace.
Facilities Dining room, bar, living/family room, hot tub, laundry. Ski rental/repair shop. 10 acres with access to 45 m of cross-country ski trails, fly-fishing, horseback riding, horseshoes, rock-climbing, hiking, birding, whitewater rafting. Evening programs, ski instruction, children's programs, sleigh rides, guided tours, cookouts, and compass workshops. 7 m to downhill skiing, golf, tennis at Big Sky resort.
Location 30 m S of Bozeman; 120 m W of Billings. 20 m N of Yellowstone. From Hwy. 191, take Big Sky exit. Go 4½ m and turn right at sign. Go 1 m to ranch.
Restrictions Smoking in bar only.
Credit cards Amex, MC, Visa.
Rates Full board, $570–930 per person per week. Reduced rates for children. Skiing, fishing packages. Prix fixe lunch, $5; prix fixe dinner, $13.
Extras Cribs, babysitting available.

BOZEMAN 59715   **Map 13**

Voss Inn   *Tel:* (406) 587–0982
319 South Willson

The elegantly decorated rooms of this century-old Victorian mansion are highlighted by white bedspreads, curtains, and trim, contrasting with handsome dark flowered wallpapers. The parlor combines Victorian furnishings with a gleaming hardwood floor, Oriental rug, and lots of plants. Restored by Ken and Ruthmary Tonn in 1984, the inn was sold to Bruce and Franklee Muller in 1989. The Mullers could certainly win the "traveled the farthest to run this B&B" award; Ruthmary reports that they are a fascinating couple, having managed a photographic safari camp in Botswana, Africa.

"The guest rooms feature antique brass and iron beds, intricately carved armoires, Duncan Phyfe table/chair sets, Oriental rugs strewn on beautifully waxed hardwood floors—and always such marvelous fragrances. The rooms are large, airy, and papered in a multitude of complementary wallpapers. The baths have ball and claw-foot tubs, updated with showers. Even with all the water those old-fashioned tubs hold, I never ran out of hot, hot water. Fragrant bath salts are always on the shelf near the tubs; they're replenished daily, as are the bedside evening chocolates. Robert's Roost, my favorite room, is done in forest greens with white wood trim, white eyelet bedspread and window flounces, and antique white wicker table and chairs, with a brass bed. It's a short walk to downtown where there are some superb restaurants and fun shops." *(Patricia Newton)*

"The inn is located in a residential neighborhood, on a tree-lined street with many other lovely old homes. The Muellers are cordial, efficient, and accommodating. The baths have been modernized, yet retain a Victorian ambience." *(Patrick & Rebecca Torrans)* "The parlor was inviting with plenty of reading materials. Room lighting was adequate for reading." *(Sherry Smith)*

"My room was spacious and immaculately clean, very quiet, with a comfortable bed. I breakfasted on the deck adjacent to my room, and had fresh juice and muffins, good coffee and a baked egg dish, all served at the time I requested. Bruce was friendly and helpful in directing us to restaurants and local attractions; after we left, he even drove to the airport to return a pair of forgotten sunglasses." *(Anne Hart)*

Open All year.
Rooms 6 doubles, 4 with full bath, 2 with tub only. All with telephone, radio, breakfast table. Some with desk, air-conditioning.
Facilities Parlor with TV, piano, books, games; porch. 10 m to trout streams, 5 m to cross-country skiing, 15 m to downhill.
Location SW MT, 90 m N of Yellowstone National Park. 12 blocks from MSU; 4 blocks from downtown. Bozeman exit off I-90 to Main St.; S on Willson Ave.
Restrictions Smoking in guest parlor only. Limited early morning weekday traffic in front rooms.
Credit cards MC, Visa.
Rates B&B, $55–65 double, $45–55 single. Extra person in room, $10.

CHOTEAU 59422 Map 13

Pine Butte Guest Ranch *Tel:* (406) 466–2158
HC 58, Box 34C

From 1930 to 1978, the Pine Butte was owned by the Gleason family, who worked it as the Circle 8 Ranch. It was then purchased by the Nature Conservancy, an international nonprofit agency whose "mission is to find, protect, and maintain the best examples of communities, ecosystems, and endangered species in the natural world." The ranch is managed by Genny and Lee Barhaugh.

Guests are housed in rustic log cabins with fieldstone fireplaces and gather in the main lodge for plentiful meals prepared from fresh produce and homemade breads, soups, and pastries. Pine Butte combines traditional guest ranch activities—wrangler-led high country rides in the morning and afternoon—with daily treks led by a full-time naturalist, focusing on the plants, animals, geology, and paleontology of the East Front. During the spring and fall, regional experts lead week-long natural history workshops and tours for real enthusiasts.

"At the end of our week here, we felt like we'd been away a month. My husband liked the trail rides, I enjoyed the beauty, peace, and quiet, and our kids actually had fun learning new things. The naturalist took our kids in tow and introduced them to birdwatching and the intricate ecosystems of Pine Butte Swamp. We all became fascinated by dinosaurs—nearby is the site where the first baby dinosaurs in nests were discovered anywhere in the world. Be sure to bring along a powerful pair of binoculars to see the birds, bighorn sheep, and an occasional grizzly. Our cabin was comfortable and homey, the food hearty with very generous servings, and the swimming pool a refreshing indulgence after a day of hiking." *(Donna Michaels)*

Open May–Sept. 30.
Rooms 10 cabins with full private bath, fireplace.
Facilities Central lodge with living room with fireplace, dining room. Natural history center with exhibits, reading material, fossils, gift shop. 2 acres with horeshoes, volleyball, basketball, heated swimming pool, riding. Guided riding tours, workshops, weekly square dance, evening slide shows.
Location NW MT. 60 m NW of Great Falls, 80 m SE of Glacier Park.
Restrictions Smoking permitted in cabins or lodge living room only. Children over 8 preferred.
Credit cards None accepted.
Rates Full board, $550–650 per person weekly. 7% suggested service. Reduced rates for children. 1-week minimum in summer; 2-night minimum off-season.
Extras Airport pickup. Cribs, babysitting available.

Seven Lazy P Ranch
Box 178

Tel: (406) 466–2044

Thirty years of experience as owners of the Seven Lazy P Ranch have made Chuck and Sharon Blixrud experts on the kind of pacing needed to get harried guests to slow down and really enjoy the Montana countryside. The ranch is set in Teton Canyon, with the Teton River flowing along the property.

"We had a terrific time at this working ranch, owned by the very knowledgeable Blixrud family. There's all the horseback riding you could want, and many guests use the ranch as a base for pack trips into the Bob Marshall Wilderness or fishing trips into the north fork of the Tetons. There's no minimum stay, a rarity among guest ranches and a terrific boon to those en route to or from Glacier National Park. The ranch house is full of wonderful mountain memorabilia. Nearby is the home of A. B. Guthries, author of several best-selling western novels some 30 years ago." *(Truman Talley)*

Open Mid. June–early Nov.
Rooms 6 cabins—5 with private bath, 2 with fireplace.
Facilities Lodge with dining room, living room with stone fireplace, porch, laundry room. Central bath house, hot tub. Trail rides, pack trips, fishing, nature hikes.
Location NW MT. 80 NW of Great Falls, 25 m W of Choteau. On the edge of the Bob Marshall Wilderness; 80 m south of Glacier National Park.
Restrictions Not recommended for children under 8.
Credit cards None accepted.
Rates All rates per person. Full board, $75 daily, $500 weekly.

DARBY   Map 13

Triple Creek Mountain Hideaway
West Fork Stage Route

Tel: (406) 821–4664

Homer Tolliver, a successful Detroit industrialist was planning only a private getaway when he purchased what is now Triple Creek. By 1987, he decided to share his dream with others, and Triple Creek Ranch now combines a western atmosphere with an eastern dedication to luxury. Managed by Wayne and Judy Kilpatrick, the ranch features cabins built of either knotty pine or whole logs, and furnished with contemporary western decor. Rates are all-inclusive, covering all meals and activities on the ranch, as well as the open bar and laundry service.

"We were totally exhausted upon arrival, yet despite the fact that we stayed only a night, we were surrounded by such luxurious accommodations and such pampering hosts that we left the next day feeling rested, relaxed, and renewed. Upon arrival, the reservations manager, Becky, explained to us that we were to be treated as though we were the owners of the ranch; anything we would like, anything at all we could think of, they would try to provide. If we didn't care for the daily special at mealtime, the chef would be glad to prepare an alternative. Although roast beef sandwiches were offered at lunch, greens were what we wanted (there are no fresh vegetables or salads worth talking about served in Montana restaurants). No sooner said than done. The chef whipped up a lovely fresh vegetable-en-croute salad with roast beef. Dessert, a beautiful white chocolate mousse cake with raspberry sauce, was delivered to our cabin and left in our refrigerator to be devoured after an afternoon nap. If we wished to go horseback riding, all we had to do was give them an hour or so notice and they would saddle up the horses and arrange for a guide. When an unexpected June snow blanketed the woods, we awakened to find that our considerate hosts had silently left high, furry, lace-up boots on our porch to keep our toes toasty. Our ride was magical; we wandered through the woods and past their small buffalo herd, and our guide was relaxed and fun to talk to.

"Our cabin was extraordinary. Complete with private Jacuzzi built into the deck overlooking the woods, a refrigerator stocked with wine, beer, and those scrumptious desserts (all included in the rates), and a living-room fireplace prepared with wood and needing only a match to get it going. Our bedroom had a gorgeous massive log four-poster bed drowning in pillows and down comforters, and the mattress was legendary. There were two color televisions, one above the fireplace in the living room along with a VCR, and the other in the bedroom. Best of all was the bathroom. We each had our own toilet and dressing area (mine complete with makeup mirror), divided by a huge double shower which also functioned as a steam room. The toilet area even had overhead spotlights built into the rough-hewn wood to facilitate reading.

"Guests are encouraged to congregate before dinner in the bar area of the main lodge where before-dinner drinks and hors d'oeuvres were served. A talented local musician played a guitar quietly in the background. I only wish they gave you a choice of entrée at dinner; I felt uncomfortable asking the chef for a special dish." *(Peggy King)*

Open May–Oct.; Dec.–Feb.
Rooms 11 1–2 bedroom cabins, all with private bath and/or shower, telephone, radio, TV, desk, fireplace, air-conditioning, fan, wet bar/refrigerator, deck. Some with dining area, double steam shower, private Jacuzzi.
Facilities Main lodge with dining room, library with games, bar, decks, fireplaces. 400 acres with heated swimming pool, hot tub, tennis court, trout ponds, putting

green, hiking trails, horseback riding, cross country skiing (and equipment), snow-mobiling. Fishing, river rafting nearby. 28 m to Lost Trail ski area.

Location W MT. 74 miles S of Missoula, 12 m S of Darby. Take Hwy. 93 through Darby. Go 5 m to Hwy 473 (West Fork Rd.) and turn W. Go 7½ m to lodge, sign on right.

Restrictions No smoking in dining room. No children under 16.

Credit cards Amex, MC, Visa.

Rates Full board, $275–450 double. Extra person in room, $100. 2-night minimum preferred.

Extras Airport pickups.

ESSEX 59916   Map 13
(GLACIER NATIONAL PARK)

Izaak Walton Inn   *Tel:* (406) 888–5700
P.O. Box 653

Essex is so isolated that, until the mid-eighties, to phone the Izaak Walton you called the Montana operator and asked for "Essex #1"! Listed on the National Register of Historic Places, the inn was built in 1939 to house the Great Northern Railway workers and has been owned since 1982 by Larry and Lynda Vielleux. A virtual museum of railroad memorabilia, Essex is appropriately now served by Amtrak via an on-demand flag stop, and the inn is a must-see for train buffs.

Although outdoorsmen are attracted to the Glacier National Park Area year-round for hiking, fishing, river rafting, and skiing, the fall brings a unique treat for nature lovers. In past years, over 80,000 salmon flooded nearby McDonald Creek to reproduce and die. This tremendous amount of accessible food draws record numbers of bald eagles to the spawning site as well as grizzly bears, coyotes, and other wildlife. Unfortunately, manager Paul Wick notes that in recent years "the salmon population has decreased substantially, and thus the number of eagles has also dropped." On a more cheery note, he goes on to report that "the inn makes a comfortable base camp from which to explore the beauty of Glacier Park and the surrounding wilderness; in the winter, the Izaak Walton Inn becomes the coziest cross-country ski area in the Rockies."

The dining room overlooks the rail yard, and meals are hearty and basic, with eggs, pancakes, and French toast at breakfast; sandwiches and burgers at lunch; and steak, chicken, and fish at dinner. Rooms are simple and clean, with basic furnishings and wood-paneled walls and ceilings.

"It was a real treat to stay in at an inn with such a colorful railroad past, and a friendly staff eager to tell me about it. Twice a day, the Amtrak Empire builder passed by the inn about 50 feet in front of my bedroom window. At other times, helper engines idled out front like contented cats, adding to the special flavor of the inn. It's also a great place for a woman traveling solo; I felt perfectly comfortable from the moment of my arrival. A third delightful component of my stay were the cross-country skiing trips though Glacier National Park, guided by the inn's Dave Streeter. After his fact-filled overview of all the history, wildlife and spectacular scenery the park has to offer, we enjoyed a delicious dinner in the homey, informal dining room. The food was well-prepared and filling, especially the honey-basted chicken." *(Elizabeth Bradburn)*

"Pleasant atmosphere, accommodating staff, modern plumbing." *(George & Jane Cleary, also Mr. & Mrs. Gary Houser)*

Other readers added a few minor caveats: Rooms can be warm and stuffy in hot weather; some beds have soft mattresses; and guests should not expect gourmet cuisine. Readers should also be aware that the noise of train engines idling at night is a lullaby to some guests, disturbing to others.

Open All year.
Rooms 29 doubles—10 with full private bath, 20 with sinks in rooms and 5–8 people sharing bath. All with desk.
Facilities Restaurant, bar, pool table, movie room, games, Ping-Pong, sauna. 2 acres of lawn, surrounded by "1,000,000 acres of wilderness." Bike, ski rentals. Lake and stream fishing nearby, 18 m of cross-country skiing from door.
Location NW MT. Flathead County, on southern border of Glacier National Park. 60 m E of Kalispell. Essex is on Hwy. 2, midway between East and West Glacier.
Restrictions Smoking in lounge only. Train noise will disturb light sleepers.
Credit cards MC, Visa.
Rates Room only, $45–74 double, $40–69 single. Extra person in room, $5; children under 2 stay free. 2-3 night minimum stay winter and holiday weekends. Alc breakfast, $2–5; alc lunch, $6; alc dinner, $17.
Extras Free station pickups. Cribs, play equipment available.

GALLATIN GATEWAY 59730　　　　　　　　　　　　Map 13

Gallatin Gateway Inn　　　　　　　　　　*Tel:* (406) 763–4672
Hwy. 191, P.O. Box 376

If you need a good dose of luxury after a week "on the range," head directly for the Gallatin Gateway Inn, a newly restored hotel, lavishly built in neo-Spanish Colonial style in 1927 by the Chicago, Milwaukee, and St. Paul Railway. The railroad sold the inn in the 1950s and by the time Bill Keshishian and his mother, Catherine Wrather, bought it in 1985, the building was a shambles. Under their supervision, as well as that of manager Bill Webster, the inn was scrubbed, painted, plastered, and rewired back into shape. It's now listed on the National Register of Historic Places.

Guest rooms are individually decorated in light pastels—such as yellow, melon, and moss—with simple contemporary furnishings. The spectacular common rooms are home to an enormous fireplace, a grand piano, rose-colored carpets and upholstered chairs, and handsome wood floors and mahogany ceiling beams. Although expensive by Montana standards, the restaurant has quickly garnered an excellent reputation for creative cuisine. The menu changes seasonally, with numerous daily specials, but typical entrées include duck breast and sausage with strawberry-rhubarb confit, grilled quail with mushrooms and artichoke hearts in Madeira cream sauce, double lamb chops broiled with pesto and Parmesan, and salmon in puff pastry with white wine sauce. The inn maintains an extensive wine list to accompany your meal. "Wonderful place, superb restaurant, beautiful decor."*(Sheila Smyth)*

Open All year.

Rooms 3 suites, 23 doubles—16 with full private bath, 8 with maximum of 4 people sharing bath. All with telephone, TV. Radio on request.

Facilities Dining room, lounge with fireplace, bar, piano. 15 acres with heated and covered swimming pool, hot tub, tennis court, flycasting pond. Golf, hiking, hunting, fishing, horseback riding, cross-country skiing nearby; 30 min. to downhill.

Location SW MT. 90 m N of Yellowstone Park. From Bozeman and I-90, go S 12 m on Hwy. 191 to inn.

Credit cards Amex, MC, Visa.

Rates Room only, $70–90 suite, $60–75 double. Extra person in room, $10. Children under 12 free in parents' room. Alc breakfast, $5–6; alc dinner, $25–27. Fly fishing package available.

Extras Restaurant wheelchair accessible. Airport/station pickups. Cribs, babysitting available.

GLACIER PARK   Map 13

Containing some of the most beautiful mountain scenery in the country, Glacier Park in northwestern Montana is a largely untamed wilderness, crossed by only one stretch of pavement, the Going-to-the-Sun Road. The fourth largest park in the continental U.S., it is bisected by the Continental Divide, and has 50 glaciers, 200 lakes, and 700 miles of horse and hiking trails. The season here runs from June to mid-September, with the largest crowds in July and August, when advance reservations (several months ahead) are essential. The Izaak Walton Inn in Essex borders the park to the south (see entry).

Glacier Park Lodge   *Tel:* (406) 226–5551
State Route 49, East Glacier 59434   Off-season: (602) 248–6000
Mailing address: Glacier Park, Greyhound Tower, Station 5510,
Phoenix, AZ 85077; May 15–Sept. 15, East Glacier MT 59434-0147

"Built about 75 years ago, the Glacier Park Lodge is constructed of huge fir and cedar logs, each so large that it required a separate railroad car for transport from the Pacific coast. About 50 years before the atrium hotel was 'invented' in Atlanta, the lodge's builders designed a grand, four-story atrium with rooms facing inward to an immense lobby. Although part of the lobby has been defaced by a modern snack bar and gift shop, the overall effect is stunning. Huge pillars made of complete tree trunks stretch four floors to the ceiling, creating a great open space to match the "Big Sky" country outside.

"Accommodations are modest but comfortable and modernized. The lodge is clean and well maintained; some rooms are on the small side. The staff is carefully trained, courteous and ready to help or answer any questions. The dining room, the Goat Lick, offers hearty meals (barbecued chicken and ribs, steak and trout) in an Old West atmosphere. There is a vast array of hiking, camping and riding facilities in the park and a number of interesting day trips by car or by antique bus can easily be arranged. Amtrak's 'Empire Builder' still stops daily at the East Glacier Station, a short walk away, and a considerable number of patrons still arrive and depart by train." *(Willis O. Frick)*

Open Early-June to mid-Sept.
Rooms 155 suites and doubles, all with private shower and/or bath, telephone.
Facilities Restaurant, bar/lounge with entertainment, coffee shop, lobby. Heated swimming pool, playground, 9-hole golf course, horseback riding, hayrides, hiking, white water rafting.
Location NW MT. SE border of Glacier National Park. ¼ m N of U.S. Rte. 2. 40 m S of Going-to-the-Sun Road.
Credit cards MC, Visa.
Rates Room only, $94–116 suite, $64–75 double. Extra person in room, $4. No charge for children under 12. Alc dinner, $14–20.
Extras Pets permitted.

Lake McDonald Lodge
Going-to-the-Sun Road
Mailing address: Glacier Park, Greyhound Tower, Station 5510, Phoenix, AZ 85077; May 15–Sept. 15, East Glacier MT 59434-0147

Tel: (406) 226–5551
Off-season: (602) 248–6000

Originally built in 1913 as a private lodge, Lake McDonald Lodge has a newly refurbished lobby sporting numerous hunting trophies and a massive stone fireplace. *Truman Talley* noted that although you have to make reservations six months ahead, it's well worth it: "This lodge is the only one that is really *in* the mountains, and is convenient to everything you'd want to see and do in the park."

Open Early June to mid-Sept.
Rooms 100 cabins and doubles in main lodge, motel annex. All with private shower and/or bath, telephone.
Facilities Restaurant, coffee shop, lounge, lobby. On lake for all water sports. Trail rides, white water rafting.
Location 12 m NE of West Glacier.
Credit cards MC, Visa.
Rates Room only, $72–80 double (lodge), $50–60 double (motel and cabins), $45–68 single. Extra person in room, $4. Alc dinner, $13–25.
Extras Pets permitted.

GREAT FALLS 59401   Map 13

The Chalet B&B
Fourth Avenue North

Tel: (406) 452–9001

Owner Margie Matthews says that she is currently doing the research needed to put the Chalet, a stick-style Victorian house built in 1909, on the National Register of Historic Places. Once the home of a former Montana governor, the inn features the original wood paneling, leaded glass, and high-beamed ceilings. Common rooms are furnished with traditional decor, while the guest rooms have more of a simple country Victorian look. Rates include a breakfast of eggs Benedict, baked French toast, or perhaps a Spanish omelet. Dinners are available by advance reservation, ranging from linguine with clam sauce to cheese-topped enchiladas.

"Margie was very helpful, prompt, and reliable. The atmosphere is warm and friendly. The delicious breakfasts were different each day, served at a time convenient to our schedule." *(Melissa & Steve Mehring)* "Good location, close to the Charles Russell Museum." *(PT)*

Open All year.
Rooms 1 suite, 6 doubles—3 with private bath, 4 with maximum of 4 people sharing bath. 1 with balcony, all with window fans, radio. Some with telephone.
Facilities Dining room, living room with TV, fireplace, reading materials; guest pantry. Garden, picnic area. Missouri River for fishing, boating, swimming.
Location W MT. Across st. from CM Russell Museum. Walking distance to town.
Restrictions Smoking "not encouraged." Children by prior arrangement.
Credit cards MC, Visa.
Rates B&B, $75–95 suite, $28–65 double, $24–60 single. Extra person in room, $5–15. Senior citizen discount, weekly rates. Prix fixe lunch, $6; prix fixe dinner, $12.
Extras Airport/station pickups, $5. Spanish, Czech spoken.

POLSON 59860   Map 13

Borchers of Finley Point   *Tel:* (406) 887–2500
225 Borchers Lane

Visit Polson in May or June to see water pouring through the Flathead River Gorge into the lake at half-million gallons per second; return at the end of July for the Montana State Fiddler's contest.

Surrounded by evergreens, this rustic B&B overlooks the calm waters of Flathead Lake, the largest natural freshwater lake west of the Mississippi. The focal point of the cedar and stone lodge, constructed in 1937, is the ten-foot-long fieldstone fireplace. Other highlights include beamed ceilings with hand-hewn timbers, while guest rooms combine pine paneling with soft floral wallpapers and draped beds. Lou and Alice Borchers bought the lodge in 1954 and opened their B&B in 1986. Rates include a continental breakfast that features homemade breads and jams. *(KJ)*

Open All year.
Rooms 4 doubles—1 with private bath, 3 rooms share 1 bath. TV, fan available.
Facilities Living room with fireplace, kitchen, dining room, porches, deck. 7/10 acre with gardens, lake front access. Marina facilities, lake tours, king, fishing, hunting, watersports nearby.
Location NW MT. 20 min. N of Polson, 30 min. S of Bigfork. Near the 6 m marker N of Polson on Hwy 35 (East Shore Rd.), turn W onto Finley Pt. Rd. Follow signs until you see Timbershor sign, go right. Lodge is straight ahead, across from marina.
Restrictions No children under 16.
Credit cards MC, Visa.
Rates B&B, $85–105 double. $75–95 single. 7 nights for price of 6. Full breakfast $5.

PRAY 59065   Map 13

Chico Hot Springs Lodge   *Tel:* (406) 333–4933
P.O. Box 127

Michael and Eve Art left New York City 16 years ago to start a new career as the owners of the then-rundown old hotel at Chico Hot Springs. Since then they've remodeled and renovated much of the hotel without destroying its casual, rustic western flavor. Guest rooms are furnished simply, with Victorian bedsteads and bunkhouse chairs; soundproofing hasn't changed much since the hotel was built. Reserve space in one of the modern cabins if you prefer more luxurious surroundings. The food at the lodge's restaurant, the Chico Inn, has won raves from reviewers throughout the country. Here, in the heart of steak and potatoes country, you can enjoy dinner dishes ranging from lamb Wellington—baked in puff pastry with fresh spinach and served with Madeira wine sauce—to fresh swordfish garnished with capers, lemon, and butter. Not that steak lovers are neglected; they have a choice of nine beef dishes on the menu, including Beef Bones—extra-large beef ribs in barbeque sauce.

Chico Hot Springs is set in Paradise Valley, beneath the nearly 11,000-foot-high Emigrant Peak, with the Absaroka Range to the east, the Gallatin Range to the west, and the Yellowstone River running down through the valley to Yellowstone National Park in the south.

Guests come to Chico to enjoy the natural mineral hot water pools year-round, plus hiking, trout fishing, horseback riding, and river rafting in the warmer months, and cross-country skiing in winter. *(SC)* More comments please.

Open All year.

Rooms 71 rooms, in hotel and adjacent motel units. 28 rooms, including 3 suites, with full private bath, 43 with shared bath—some with sink in room. 8 rooms in annex. Approx. 8 cabins and chalets also available.

Facilities Restaurant open for breakfast and dinner, snack bar, game room, lounge and saloon, lobby, family room with games. Live entertainment in saloon on weekends. 150 acres with 2 naturally heated swimming pools (94°F and 104°F), 4 hot tubs, private trout pond, BBQ pit, horseback riding, cross-country skiing. 3 m to Yellowstone River for blue-ribbon trout fishing

Location SW MT. 128 m W of Billings, 25 m S of Livingstone, approx. 25 m N of Yellowstone National Park at WY border. Take Hwy. 89 to Emigrant; lodge is approx. ¼ m E of river.

Credit cards MC, Visa.

Rates Room only, (lodge and motel) $35–52 double. Extra person in room, $5; children under 7 free in parents' room. Cabins and chalets, $50–275. Alc dinner, $20–30, plus service. Weekly rates.

Extras Saloon, pool area, ground-floor rooms wheelchair accessible. Pets permitted by prior arrangement. Cribs, babysitting available.

STEVENSVILLE 59870   **Map 13**

Although really not big enough to merit a full entry, we couldn't resist including **The Country Caboose,** a 1923 CB & Q wooden caboose, recently visited by *Arlyne Craighead:* "It's all fixed up cozy with coordinating blues and soft tones. There is a shower and private toilet, nice closet, extra ¾ bed for a guest, double bed, full-length mirror. A full breakfast is served at the wooden table or inside the owner's home. A hammock awaits in a perfect shaded spot nearby. Absolutely splendid views of the mountains and valley area. Lisa Thompson was very friendly and helpful; her husband Kirk is a retired railroad worker; the rates are a modest $37." (852 Willoughby 6 Road; 406–777–3145).

Bass House Inn   *Tel:* (406) 777–5675
100 College Street

The Bass House Mansion, built in 1908 and listed on the National Register of Historic Places, has been home to the Siphers family for over two decades. In 1985, Mrs. Siphers decided that Stevensville needed a bed & breakfast inn, and now travelers can share in the history of this Georgian-style mansion, complete with massive white pillars and gracious portico. Readers are advised to inquire about ownership of the inn; Mrs. Siphers is getting on in years and would like to sell the inn and retire.

"Charline Siphers greeted me at the door; she is a charming, warm, and gracious hostess. The rooms are attractive, clean, and airy—one of my favorites has a wonderful high-backed antique wooden bed. On sunny mornings she serves a full hot breakfast on the porch, with a beautiful view of the mountains." *(Arlyne Craighead)*

Open May 1–Oct. 1.
Rooms 4 doubles with maximum of 6 people sharing bath. 3 rooms with desk.
Facilities Dining room, living room, billiard room, wraparound porch. Golf, hiking, lakes, and rivers for fishing nearby; hot springs for swimming nearby.
Location W MT, 30 m S of Missoula via Rte. 93. Inn is on corner of 1st and College Sts. 2 blocks off Maine St. at N edge of town.
Restrictions No smoking. No children under 12.
Credit cards None accepted.
Rates B&B, $40 double, $35 single plus 20% service.

We Want to Hear from You!

As you know, this book is only effective with your help. We really need to know about your experiences and discoveries.

If you stayed at an inn or hotel listed here, we want to know how it was. Did it live up to our description? Exceed it? Was it what you expected? Did you like it? Were you disappointed? Delighted?

Have you discovered new establishments that we should add to the next edition?

Tear out one of the report forms at the back of this book (or use your own stationery if you prefer) and write today. Even if you write only "Fully endorse existing entry" you will have been most helpful.

Thank You!

Nebraska

The Offutt House, Omaha

Although Nebraska is the fifteenth-largest state, this chapter is one of the shortest in our guide. We've tracked down a number of inns which might make interesting additions to future editions, and have described them briefly below. We would love to hear more about these or any other bed & breakfasts, country inns, guest ranches, or city hotels of character and distinction. So, if you're doing business in Omaha, visiting the university in Lincoln, or stopping in North Platte while traveling on Interstate 80, please do join our corps of inn-vestigators!

Also recommended: Although an unyielding deadline made a full writeup impossible, *Jeannie Swoboda* wrote to recommend the **Rogers House,** a brick Jacobean Revival house built in 1914 and furnished in period antiques (2145 "B" Street, Lincoln 68502; 402–476–6961). "A lovely house with eight comfortable guest rooms and a gracious hostess."

Information please: Located in southeastern Nebraska, in a historic town on the Missouri River, the **Thompson House** is a fully restored home dating back to 1869, with such modern amenities as private baths and air-conditioning (Fifth and College Sts., Brownville; 402–825–6551). In Red Cloud, in south central Nebraska, once home to Willa Cather, is **The Meadowlark,** built in 1915 and highlighted by beveled and leaded windows, period decor, and original stenciling (241 West 9th Avenue, Red Cloud 68970; 402–746–3550). In southwestern Nebraska is the town of North Platte, once the home of Buffalo Bill Cody. It's now the home of **Watson Manor Inn,** a B&B moved here from Wallace in 1897. Rebuilt after a fire in 1985, owners Ron and Patty Watson invite guests to share their hospitality and guest rooms furnished with antiques and hand-sewn quilts (410 South Sycamore, P.O. Box 458, North Platte 69103; 308–532–1005).

If you're driving west through Nebraska on I-80, think about breaking up the interstate monotony with a few days of family fun. About 30 miles north of North Platte is the **Cedar Lane Ranch** (HC 2, Box 9C, Stapleton 59163; 308–587–2233), a family-owned working ranch, which invites guests to join in trail rides, canoeing on the Dismal River (whose appearance is quite the opposite), hunting for Indian artifacts, or joining the boss to check stock or bring salt to the livestock. Kids love to cool off in the indoor pool complete with slide and hot tub. Accommodation in the ranch house or bunk house is basic, but clean and comfortable; meals are hearty, homemade, and filling.

OMAHA 68131   Map 10

The Offutt House   *Tel:* (402) 553–0951
140 North 39th Street

Even if you're not familiar with 'Chateauesque-style" architecture, you'll still recognize it immediately when you see the Offutt House. An imposing yellow brick 14-room mansion, with a red-tile roof, it sports the massive chimneys and gables that you would expect. Built in 1894 in a section developed by Omaha's wealthiest residents, the area is known today as Omaha's Historic Gold Coast. The house was one of the only ones to survive the Easter Sunday Tornado of 1913; according to a local source, "an open decanter of sherry was carried 35 feet from the dining-room sideboard to the living room without spilling a drop." Jeanne Swoboda has owned the inn since 1978.

"The house, simply but elegantly furnished with many antiques, is clean and exceptionally comfortable. Jeanne Swoboda is a gracious and charming hostess who was very helpful in providing all the information I needed." *(Dr. William Mania)* "If you are willing to deal with a bathroom down the hall, it is a first-class place to stay. The breakfast is terrific." *(Stephen Shipps)*

"Great atmosphere; furniture and linens delightfully in tune with the building; friendly and helpful owner; peaceful setting in a cul-de-sac; ample and easy parking, with quick access to all points of interest and downtown. Three minutes' walk to public transport." *(Barbara Edna Kaye)*

Open All year.
Rooms 1 suite, 6 doubles—2 with private bath, 5 with maximum of 4 people sharing bath. All with desk, air-conditioning, fan. Telephone, TV on request. Some with fireplaces.
Facilities Living room with library, stereo, piano; dining room, lounge, porch. Golf nearby.
Location 2 miles from center; Historic Gold Coast. "1 block N of main thorough-fare."
Restrictions No children under 12.
Credit cards Amex, MC, Visa.
Rates B&B, $70 suite, $50–60 double, $40–50 single. Extra person in room, $15. Prix fixe lunch, $8–10; prix fixe dinner, $15–35 (meals only by advance arrangement).
Extras Airport/station pickups, $5. Pets "possibly" allowed.

Nevada

Walley's Hot Springs Resort, Genoa

Nevada's richness extends far beyond the glittering casinos of Las Vegas. Over a century ago enormous gold and silver strikes created wealthy boom towns overnight—and left a fascinating legacy of historic ghost towns for today's visitor. Within a day's drive of Las Vegas lies Death Valley to the northwest and the incredible rock formations of the Valley of Fire to the northeast. While there's no shortage of giant casino hotels in Las Vegas, some recommendations for the southern part of the state are hereby requested!

At the California border, Lake Tahoe beckons with over a dozen major downhill ski areas, including Heavenly Valley and Squaw Valley, while Reno sponsors a major Basque festival in addition to its gambling attractions. Just east of Tahoe are the historic mining towns of the Comstock Lode and Carson City, the state capital.

Information please: Just 20 minutes from Reno, Lake Tahoe, and Carson City is the **Winters Creek Ranch**, offering private bath accommodations with hearty breakfast and evening hors d'oeuvres, plus beautiful views of the Sierra Nevada (1201 U.S. Route 395 North, Carson City 89701; 702–849–1020). In northeastern Nevada is the **Breitenstein House**, nestled at the foot of the Ruby Mountains. Part of a working cattle ranch, activities include fishing and horseback riding; three hearty meals are served in the antique-filled dining room (Lamoille 89828; 702–753–6356). If you need some European *gemütlichkeit* after the glitz of Reno, head south 30 miles to the **Haus Bavaria** (593 North Dyer Circle, Incline Village 89405, P.O. Box 3308; 702–831–6122), a chalet-style B&B with five guest rooms, each with private bath. Reports on these and any other discoveries would be most helpful.

Rates do not include 7% state sales tax.

GENOA 89411 Map 12

Walley's Hot Springs Resort
2001 Foothill Road, Box 26

Tel: (702) 782–8155
883–6556

In 1862 David and Harriet Walley built a spa and hotel on the site of these newly discovered hot springs, adjacent to the Pony Express route and the Emigrant Trail. A luxury resort in its day, the spa drew wealthy locals who'd struck it rich in the Comstock Lode, as well as such well-known names as Ulysses S. Grant and Mark Twain. Although Walley's passed through some difficult times after the mines closed later in the century, it was supposedly a favorite of Al Capone's during Prohibition and, later on, of screen idols Clark Gable and Ida Lupino.

With the exception of a few stone buildings, the entire complex was destroyed by fire in 1935. In 1981 the complex was rebuilt, and although all facilities are modern, an attempt has been made to preserve the 19th-century atmosphere. Cottages are furnished with reproduction period pieces, including oak furniture and brass beds. Rates include a continental breakfast of fresh fruit and juice, croissants, and coffee or tea, plus full use of all spa and sports facilities. The inn's Zephyr Restaurant serves American food, with choices ranging from beef to fresh seafood.

"We like to ski at Lake Tahoe, then go over the mountain to these wonderful hot springs. The new all-stone restaurant looks out over the springs; the food is good. Accommodations are clean and adequate, with updated bathrooms and new carpeting, but the hot springs are the real attraction here." *(Cathy Kaufman)*

Open All year.
Rooms 1 suite, 4 cottages, all with full private bath, radio, TV, refrigerator.
Facilities Restaurant, bar, weight-training room with exercise classes, massage and herbal wraps, sauna, steam room, locker room. 6 flow-through hot mineral spring pools; heated freshwater swimming pool, 2 tennis courts, par course. 30 min. to downhill skiing.
Location W NV. 40 m S of Reno, 12 m E of Lake Tahoe. From Reno, Carson City, take Hwy. 395S, then Rte. 206S to Genoa. Going N on Hwy. 395, take Rte. 57E to Genoa. Resort is 2 m from town; watch for signs.
Restrictions No smoking in spa area. No children under 12 in spa area (state law).
Credit cards Amex, DC, MC, Visa.
Rates B&B, $118 suite, $81–102 cabin. 2-night weekend minimum. Alc lunch, $7; alc dinner, $21. Nonguest fee for spa use, $5–7.
Extras Ramps, elevator for wheelchair access. Airport pickups. Spanish spoken.

IMLAY 89418 Map 12

Old Pioneer Garden & Guest Ranch
Unionville #79

Tel: (702) 538–7585

Unionville was settled during the 1860s as an early Nevada mining camp and had a population of 2,000 at its peak. Now the quiet, tree-shaded canyon is home to about 20 people, including Lew and Mitzi Jones, owners of the Pioneer Garden since 1983. Guests enjoy hiking in the Humboldt range or fishing in the nearby river and streams. The Old Pioneer Garden consists of the Hadley House, built in 1861, the Ross House, a 1868 rustic cabin, and the Talcott House, dating to 1865. The decor is country casual, with iron, oak, and brass beds and bouquets of dried flowers. In their gardens, the Joneses raise almost all of the produce served at meals; apple pancakes and sausages make up a typical breakfast, while dinner might be biscuits and stew or pasta, salad, and fruit cake, served at the eight-foot-long kitchen table.

"Delightful B&B in a country atmosphere. Perfect place for peace and quiet, set in a picturesque, off-the-road canyon, surrounded with trees, a bubbling stream, farm animals, and even some deer. Food is excellent farm cooking. The owners are charming and warm, making all feel welcome and comfortable." *(Nedra Bazhaw)* More comments, please.

Open All year.
Rooms 10 doubles, 1 single, 1 cabin—4 with full private bath or shower, 8 with maximum of 3 people sharing bath.
Facilities Living room with VCR and old movie library; game room with Ping-Pong, pool; library. 114 acres with gazebo, fishing, hiking, hot springs. Rye Patch reservoir for fishing, swimming, water sports.
Location NW NV. 160 m NE of Reno, 50 m SW of Winnemucca. Exit I-80 at Mill City, go S on Hwy. 400 16 m, then W 3 m to Unionville.
Restrictions No smoking.
Credit cards None accepted.
Rates B&B, $45 double, $35 single. Prix fixe dinner, $7.50.
Extras Station pickups, $10. Well-behaved pets permitted.

MINDEN 89423   Map 12

Carson Valley Inn   *Tel:* (702) 782–9711
1627 Highway 395, P.O. Box 2560   (800) 321–6983

"For travelers taking the long north–south drive along Highway 395 (stretching from Mexico to Canada), or those seeking a respite from the gambling halls of Reno, a modestly priced inn is a blessing. The Carson Valley Inn is located in the hamlet of Minden (pop. 2,000 at most), at the foot of the eastern slopes of the Sierra Nevadas. It's a new building, constructed with quality workmanship, and one feels that the management has an eye toward long-term success, not short-term profits.

"The rooms on the south side of the building have a breathtaking view of Job's Peak, Job's Sister, and Freel Peak, three 10,000-foot granite spires topped with snow year-round. Rooms facing north overlook the Carson Valley and the dusty Pine Nut Mountains, with the Great Basin desert beyond.

"The inn's rooms are large and the bathrooms positively huge. Original photographs grace the walls, depicting the beauty and variety of the desert. Our room had a king-size bed that was firm without being rock-hard. The personnel are very friendly, from the maid to the desk clerk; I got the feeling that the staff tries extra hard.

"As is the case with any public place in Nevada, gambling is available in the inn's casino. We met the local ranch hands, truckers, cattlemen, as well as fellow visitors, sharing jokes and friendly insults.

"The food is excellent and prices very modest. This is beef country and the prime ribs are especially good. There are also many Basque shepherds in this area, and fresh lamb is in ample supply from their herds.

"Being so close to the Sierras, the inn organizes many different packages for skiers, with trips to Kirk, Heavenly Valley, Squaw Valley, and others. Guided hunts are arranged during pheasant season. Fishermen can cast their lines in the Carson River or try the many alpine lakes nearby." *(Mark Hall)*

A recent expansion of the hotel to 160 rooms may move it beyond the range of this guide; comments please.

Open All year.
Rooms 7 suites, 153 doubles—all with full private bath, telephone, radio, TV, desk.
Facilities 3 restaurants (24-hour restaurant, deli lunch, fine dining), cabaret lounge with live entertainment, dancing, quiet bar, wedding chapel (!), game room, spa deck. 10 acres. 30 min. E of Lake Tahoe, downhill, cross-country skiing.
Location W NV. 12 m S of Carson City, 16 m E of Lake Tahoe, 45 m S of Reno.
Restrictions "Children OK but not encouraged due to casino entertainment."
Credit cards Amex, Discover, DC, MC, Visa.
Rates Room only, $79–139 suite, $39–59 double. Alc breakfast, $3–7; alc lunch, $4–7; alc dinner, $7–11. Skiing, golf, pheasant hunting packages.
Extras Wheelchair accessible; 2 guest rooms specially equipped. Airport pickups. Cribs available. Spanish spoken.

VIRGINIA CITY 89440   Map 12

Virginia City was the site of the world's largest gold and silver strike—the Comstock Lode. At the city's peak in the 1870s, it was the richest in the world, with a population exceeding 30,000. Today it is a national landmark and the permanent residents number about 750. Some travelers find the town an enjoyable re-creation of the Old West, with restored mansions, mine and railroad tours, while others consider it an overpriced tourist trap and head for Nevada's lesser known historic towns.

Information please: The **Gold Hill Hotel**, established in 1859, is the state's oldest, and is furnished with light floral fabrics, brass, sleigh and canopy beds, many original to the hotel; its rubble stone and wood-beamed tavern and elegant restaurant are equally historic. Menu favorites include shrimp with black pepper fettucini and rack of lamb with mint dijon butter. Mark Twain found the tavern a convivial place for writing stories (Gold Hill, P.O. Box 304; 702–847–0111). Another possibility is the **House on the Hill**, a new Victorian with three guest rooms furnished with antiques. Rates include a continental breakfast and afternoon wine and cheese; guests enjoy relaxing in the sun room hot tub (Sky Lane, P.O. Box 625; 702–847–0193).

Edith Palmer's Country Inn   *Tel:* (702) 847–0707
South B Street, Box 756

Edith Palmer's Country Inn was built in 1862, during the silver boom, for a local wine merchant. It became famous among Hollywood stars of the

'60s for its four-star restaurant. The Browns bought the inn in 1984, and serve a full country breakfast of fresh orange juice and fruit, egg and meat dishes, plus homemade rolls or sourdough biscuits.

"The hospitality shown to guests always makes me feel welcome and right at home. I like to stay several days to be able to relax and enjoy this fine old country home. The gardens are quite unusual; they are carved out of the mountain behind the inn, with handsome rock walls and an abundance of flowers and fruit trees.

"The food is always delicious. Norman and Erlene Brown enjoy preparing specially tasty dishes and often surprise you with unexpected treats. There is no pressure to hurry when eating and there is always pleasant and interesting conversation." *(Bernice Gordon)* More comments please.

Open All year.
Rooms 5 doubles—3 with private bath and/or shower, 2 with maximum of 4 people sharing bath. All with fan.
Facilities Dining room, living room, library; landscaped gardens with patios.
Location W elbow of NV. Approx. 30–45 min. from Reno, Carson City, Tahoe. From Reno, take Hwy. 395S to Rte. 341S to Virginia City.
Restrictions No smoking. No children under 12.
Credit cards MC, Visa.
Rates B&B, $65–80 double. Extra person in room, $10.
Extras Airport/station pickups, $15.

Key to Abbreviations

For complete information and explanations, please see the Introduction.

Rates: Range from least expensive room in low season to most expensive room in peak season.

Room only: No meals included; sometimes referred to as European Plan (EP).

B&B: Bed and breakfast; includes breakfast, sometimes afternoon/evening refreshment.

MAP: Modified American Plan; includes breakfast and dinner.

Full board: Three meals daily.

Alc lunch: À la carte lunch; average price of entrée plus nonalcoholic drink, tax, tip.

Alc dinner: Average price of three-course dinner, including half bottle of house wine, tax, tip.

Prix fixe dinner: Three- to five-course set dinner, excluding wine, tax, tip unless otherwise noted.

Extras: Noted if available. Always confirm in advance. Pets are not permitted unless specified.

Zip codes: If only one zip code applies, it is listed with the town name. If there is more than one, it is noted as part of the address.

New Hampshire

Loch Lyme Lodge, Lyme

First settled in 1623, New Hampshire was originally part of the Massachusetts colony. Showing early the autonomy of spirit it maintains to this day, the colony broke away and declared its independence in January 1776, half a year before the country's Declaration of Independence was signed; today, its presidential primary officially launches the national campaign.

Although people outside New England tend to lump New Hampshire and Vermont together, the two states have very different personalities. Tourism is now vital to the economic well-being of both states, but New Hampshire has a significant industrial base, while Vermont is primarily agricultural; politically, New Hampshire is much more conservative, with far less in the way of zoning and environmental control.

There are several areas of particular tourist interest in New Hampshire. The southwest corner, also called the **Monadnock Region**, has low mountains and lovely small lakes, as well as the "world's most climbed mountain," Mt. Monadnock. Attractive inns are found as far north as Littleton, close to St. Johnsbury, Vermont. Two major roads run north/south through New Hampshire—Interstate 93, through the center of the state, and Route 16 in the east. Both intersect the White Mountains National Forest, I-93 at Franconia Notch, and Route 16 through the Mt. Washington Valley. These two areas are home to New Hampshire's best skiing, and to many wonderful inns as well. Just south of the White Mountains is New Hampshire's Lake Region, centering around the beautiful, if built up, Lake Winnipesaukee.

New Hampshire is popular with tourist in all season but "mud" (late November and April), although the demand for rooms is highest during the period of peak foliage in October, and the Christmas/New Year's holidays. Many inns either close or scale back operations during mud season.

Rates do not include 7% state room and meals tax.

BRADFORD 03221   Map 1

Mountain Lake Inn   *Tel:* (603) 938–2136
Route 114   (800) 662–6005

The Mountain Lake Inn dates back to the late 1700s, and is furnished with antiques and comfortable traditional furniture; Carol and Phil Fullerton bought the inn in 1986, and have recently redecorated a number of the rooms. "We found the major pluses to be the really delightful hosts (Carol and Phil were very friendly, helpful, and hospitable; and Carol is a superb cook) and the lovely setting, with views of the lake and mountains. The inn is nicely furnished, with a spacious living room. Our corner room on the second floor or the addition was airy and pleasant, just big enough for a king-size bed, small dresser, a rocking chair, and a luggage rack. The bathroom had a claw-foot tub with a circular shower attachment and modern fixtures. Everything was very clean." *(Marcia G. Doty)*

"My favorite place was the screened-in veranda along the front of the inn. It was comfortable, private, and for a confirmed bookworm, it was heaven. Plenty of books are available on all subjects, and I had a glorious time browsing. Information regarding nearby craft centers, theaters, concerts, and hiking trails was readily offered, and if not sufficient, no effort was spared to accommodate individual needs and preferences."*(Susan Jane Taylor)*

Open All year, except 2 weeks in Nov.
Rooms 1 2-bedroom cottage, 9 doubles—all with private bath and/or shower, fan. Some with desk.
Facilities Dining room, 2 sitting rooms, and game room with library, fireplaces, TV, games, pool table. 167 acres with waterfalls, streams, woods, trails, bicycles, 1500-foot lakefront and private beach for swimming, boating, canoeing, fishing. Golf, tennis, cross-country, downhill skiing nearby.
Location S central NH; Lake Sunapee region. 35 m W of Concord; 35 m SE of Hanover; 75 NW of Boston/Logan Airport. 2½ m S of town on Rte. 114.
Restrictions No smoking in guest rooms.
Credit cards Discover, MC, Visa.
Rates B&B, $150 cottage (sleeps 4), $70–80 double, $45–50 single. Extra person in room, $18.50. MAP, $60–75 per person. 10% senior discount. 2-night minimum some weekends. Prix fixe dinner, $15–20; half-price for children. Ski and snowshoe packages available.
Extras Cribs, babysitters, play equipment available.

CONWAY 03818   Map 1

The Darby Field Inn   *Tel:* (603) 447–2181
Bald Hill, P.O. Box D   (800) 426–4147

Over 150 years ago, the Littlefield family settled on the land that now belongs to the Darby Field Inn. By the late 1800s, the Littlefields were taking in guests. In the 1940s a Boston florist moved north and expanded the farmhouse into a full-fledged inn. After meeting in Venezuela, Marc and Marily Donaldson purchased the inn in 1979, naming it after Darby Field, the first white man to ascend Mt. Washington.

Rooms are furnished with a pleasant mix of genuine antiques and casual country pieces, while the cuisine is enhanced by the views of twelve mountains from the dining room. There's ample choice of both menu and seating time at breakfast and dinner; a typical dinner might include smoked trout with Dijon mustard sauce, duck glazed with blackberry Chambord, and Darby cream pie for dessert.

"All of the rooms are cheerful and clean, with a real country atmosphere. The spacious living room, with its divided areas, has ample comfortable seating with plenty of lights for reading or playing games. The Tavern is a cozy place to relax with newfound friends or to sit by the woodstove in winter. From the window of the dining room the views of the White Mountains are spectacular. At night, with the curtains drawn, it becomes a place to linger over the excellent food. Special attention is paid to fresh vegetables, meats, and seafood. Dishes are well prepared without being pretentious or overly sauced. The inn lies up a quiet (but well-cleared) country road." *(Lucille & Ben Bond)*

"But, all of the above could be enjoyed at any good inn. The real reason we return to The Darby Field is the warm family atmosphere created by the Donaldsons and their staff. From the cooks who come to your table at breakfast (upon request) to share recipes, to the serving and cleaning people, all who are involved are nice, friendly, helpful folks." *(Lynn & Theo Blue)*

Open Late Nov. to late March; late April to late Oct. Restaurant closed Labor Day weekend.
Rooms 1 2-bedroom suite, 15 doubles—14 with private shower and/or bath; 2 with maximum of 5 people sharing bath. Some with desk, fan.
Facilities Dining room, living room with fireplace; lounge with piano. 6 acres with cross-country skiing, swimming pool. Fishing, hiking, bicycling, canoeing, downhill skiing (6 areas within 8–30 m) nearby.
Location E central NH. White Mts., 60 m W of Portland, ME. 3 m from Conway. ½ m S of Conway on Rte. 16, turn onto Bald Hill Rd. Follow signs 1 m, then go right 1 m to inn.
Restrictions Smoking in common areas only.
Credit cards Amex, MC, Visa.
Rates B&B, $140–160 suite, $120–140 double, $80–90 single. MAP, $160–180 suite, $140–160 double, $90–100 single. Extra person in room, $40–60. 15% service additional. Foliage surcharge. Discount for 3- to 6-night stays. 2–3 night holiday/weekend minimum. Children's rates. Alc dinner, $30.
Extras Station pickups. Spanish spoken.

FRANCESTOWN 03043   Map 1

The Inn at Crotched Mountain   *Tel:* (603) 588–6840
Mountain Road

John and Rose Perry have owned The Inn at Crotched Mountain since 1976 and offer a relaxing escape only 75 miles from Boston. The original inn was built in 1822 and was later a stop on the Underground Railroad, with a secret tunnel built to help slaves escape. Destroyed by a fire in 1929, the inn was rebuilt in its present form.

"Although the view from the inn is spectacular, overlooking the rolling hillsides, it is owners John and Rose Perry who make this a special place. They are always willing to put forth an extra effort for their guests, be it fresh flowers in the rooms or a phone call to a local merchant. If you need directions, John will draw you a map. In addition to being an excellent chef, Rose always makes sure that the meals are visually pleasing. Besides the appetizing entrées, with many of the vegetables and garnishes grown in the inn's garden, several desserts are prepared daily by John. His chocolate mousse cake is not to be believed. Before or after dinner, drinks are available in the pub. The pub fireplace takes away the evening chill; it's one of many in the inn that are often in use. Guest rooms are clean and comfortable, individually decorated country-style, and supplied with extra pillows and blankets. The inn is very quiet, far from major roadways. The staff is always gracious and happy to help or answer questions." *(Mary Little & Ronald Perri)*

Open Mid-May through end of Oct.; Thanksgiving to end of ski season.
Rooms 13 doubles—5 with full private bath, 3 with private shower, 5 with maximum of 6 people sharing bath. 4 with desk; several with fireplace.
Facilities Dining rooms, sitting rooms, pub. 60 acres with walking paths, gardens, swimming pool, 2 tennis courts, cross-country skiing. ¼ m to downhill skiing. Golf, fishing, hiking nearby.
Location S central NH. 75 m NW of Boston. From Francestown, follow Rte. 47 2½ m; turn left onto Mt. Rd., 1 m to inn.
Credit cards None accepted.
Rates B&B, $60–90 double, $50–60 single. MAP, $100–120 double, $75–95 single. Extra person in room, $25–40. 15% service additional. Some 2–3 night minimum weekend stays. Alc dinner, $25.
Extras Wheelchair accessible. Chinese spoken. Babysitting available. Pets permitted.

FRANCONIA 03580   Map 1

Franconia, one of New Hampshire's oldest mountain resort areas, is full of activities in both summer and winter. Mt. Washington and the surrounding mountains are as beautiful as ever, but unfortunately some of the tourist "attractions" are pretty tacky. We advise getting out of the car and walking the lovely trails of Franconia Notch State Park and the White Mountains National Forest.

Also recommended: The **Franconia Inn** (Easton Road; 603–823–5542) combines the atmosphere of a country inn with the facilities of a small resort, with activities from tennis to cross-country skiing. The inn dates from the mid-1800s, and rooms are simply furnished; the menu is continental yet surprisingly creative.

Franconia is located in the White Mountains, 150 miles northeast of Boston; it's about 10 miles southeast of the Vermont border, and about 20 miles from St. Johnsbury. Cannon Mountain is the closest major ski area.

Sugar Hill Inn   *Tel:* (603) 823–5621
Route 117

Constructed as a farmhouse in 1789 by one of the original settlers of Sugar Hill, this building was converted into an inn in 1929. Jim and Barbara

Quinn purchased the inn in 1986; she had worked for Sears, he in the supermarket business, and both understand the value of good customer relations. "I'm in this business to make friends," says Barbara.

Rooms in the main inn are bright and cheerful, decorated with antiques, hand-stenciled walls, and country wallpapers and fabrics. Cottage rooms, originally motel clones when the Quinns bought the inn, have been transformed into country cottages, with pitched roofs, porches, flower boxes, and country decor; these rooms are best for families.

"Our bedroom had lighthearted pink and green floral-strawberry chintzes, and its graceful windows gave us a view of the adjacent farm and meadows. Service in the downstairs dining room is gracious and friendly. Chef Jim's specialties included a basket of delicious homemade miniature rolls, blueberry/cranberry muffins, and cheese pancakes to die for." *(Mr. & Mrs. H. Butler McCauley)*

"The inn has a peaceful country setting on a low hill, surrounded by trees, mountains, and rolling estates, with glorious sunsets. Everything is immaculate." *(Sue & Urban Gradel)*

"Plenty of reading material, and good lighting, both in our room and the sitting room, by which to read it." *(Martha & Ed Trask)*

Open May to Oct., Dec. to March.
Rooms 7 doubles, 3 singles, 6 cottages, all with private bath and/or shower, radio. Some with TV, desk. 10 rooms in inn; 6 cottages.
Facilities Dining room, 2 common rooms with games, TV, books, fireplace, player piano. 3 lakes nearby for swimming, fishing, canoeing. Downhill, cross-country skiing nearby.
Location ½ m to village. On Rte. 117, ½ m W of Rte. 18, 2 m E of Rte. 302.
Restrictions Smoking in cottages only. No children in inn.
Credit cards MC, Visa.
Rates B&B (spring/summer), $80–100 double, $65–85 single; MAP (fall/winter), $130–170 double, $80–135 single, plus 15% service. Each additional person, $25–50. Prix fixe dinner, $25. Midweek rates. 2-night minimum during foliage season.
Extras Cribs available. Station pickups.

HANOVER 03755   Map 1

Also recommended: The Trumbull House (Etna Road, Box C-29; 603–643–1400) is an elegant B&B in a turn-of-the century farmhouse, decorated with soft floral wallpapers, antiques, and plenty of comfortable couches. The setting is peaceful and quiet, just three miles from town. For an even more rustic setting, the **Moose Mountain Lodge** (Etna 03750; 603–643–3529) overlooks the Connecticut River Valley and the Green Mountains of Vermont beyond. Although isolated on a dirt road, this log lodge is just seven miles east of Hanover.

Hanover Inn   *Tel:* (603) 643–4300
East Wheelock and Main streets, P.O. Box 151   (800) 443–7024

The Hanover Inn dates back to the early nineteenth century. It was completely rebuilt after a fire in 1887, and has been redone many times since then, including a multi-million dollar renovation in 1988/89, which increased the size of rooms and baths, added elegant furniture and appointments, and even hookups to the Dartmouth computer center. It is owned by Dartmouth College, and guests are welcome to use the college's athletic facilities. The inn is a favorite of Dartmouth alumni, so reservations are imperative during football season, parents' weekend, graduation, and reunions.

"Summer or winter, there are always people occupying the row of white rocking chairs on the wide porch of the Hanover Inn—reading newspapers, meeting friends, or just watching the world go by. That's the kind of place it is. This lovely rambling inn faces the elm-lined green of Dartmouth College, ringed with the original white brick buildings, the spectacular Baker Library and Hopkins Center for the Arts, and, rising above them all, the surrounding mountains.

"The inn itself combines the warmth and charm of old New England with modern amenities. Guest rooms are comfortable and well-furnished with reproduction pieces. Service is excellent. A large sitting room off the lobby is a great place to meet people. The Ledyard Boatyard, with canoes and windsurfers for rent, is a couple of blocks away; you can get trail maps of wonderful hiking trails from the Dartmouth Outing Club. The Hopkins Center has a full schedule of shows and exhibits year-round." *(Maria & Carl Schmidt)* More comments, please.

Open All year.
Rooms 23 suites, 69 doubles, all with full private bath, telephone, radio, TV, desk, air-conditioning.
Facilities Restaurant, living room, coffee shop, bar/lounge, terrace. Dartmouth College facilities include heated pool, squash/tennis courts, golf course, ski slopes, boats. Downhill, cross-country skiing nearby.
Location SW NH; 130 m NW of Boston. 8 min. from intersection of I-89 and I-91 at White River Junction, VT. In town on Dartmouth campus.
Credit cards Amex, DC, MC, Visa.
Rates B&B, $159–179 suite, $119–139 double, single. Extra person in room, $30. No charge for children under 12 sharing parents' room. 10% senior discount. Special seasonal packages. Alc lunch, $10; dinner, $32.
Extras Pets permitted. Cribs, babysitting available. Ramp at entrance, elevators, wide door in some bathrooms for wheelchair accessibility. French, Spanish, Cambodian spoken. Airport/station pickups.

HOLDERNESS 03245 Map 1

Holderness is best known for the lake it borders, Squam Lake, made famous in *On Golden Pond*. And yes, the lake really is as beautiful as it looks in the movie. Squam Lake is perfect for swimming, fishing, and boating in summer, skating and ice fishing in winter. Holderness is near the White Mountains National Forest, offering splendid hiking in summer and fall, and excellent cross-country and downhill skiing in winter. Plenty of tennis courts and two golf courses are also nearby.

Also recommended: The Inn on Golden Pond (Route 3, Box 680; 603–968–7269) is a 110-year-old farmhouse set in the woods, with a homey atmosphere and serving hearty breakfasts.

Holderness is located in the central New Hampshire lakes region, about a two-hour drive from Boston, and 4 to 5 miles from Exit 24 of Interstate 93.

The Manor
Route 3, Box T

Tel: (603) 968–3348

The Manor was built during 1903–1907 by a wealthy Englishman, Isaac Van Horn, who spared no expense in making his new home a work of art. Mr. Van Horn lost the property in 1920 for nonpayment of taxes, and the estate went through many owners until it was purchased in 1983 by Jan and Pierre Havre. The Havres have restored and renovated extensively, preserving the carved moldings, rich wood paneling, leaded glass windows, and grand fireplaces. Jan Havre reports that The Manor is the only inn directly on Squam Lake.

"The Manor sits on a hill above Squam Lake, and offers fine water views. Our room was very large and lovely, with a narrow balcony and an angle view of the lake. It was very light, with two sliding glass doors opening onto the balcony. Overhead lights supplemented the table lamps. Furniture included a king-size brass bed, large functional armoire, loveseat, coffee table, two wing chairs, and a desk and chair. The room was decorated in dark green and beige, with matching wallpaper in bedroom and bath. The thick plush carpet was very clean. The bath was also large, with a huge clawfoot tub and separate shower stall. The pedestal sink was lovely, and complimentary toiletries included shampoo and large soaps. The huge bath sheets were thick and exceedingly soft. Meals were excellent; breakfast included fantastic Belgian waffles, covered with blueberry butter, fresh blueberries, and whipped cream.

"The outdoor swimming pool is surrounded by flower tubs and has lovely mountain views. The tennis courts are surrounded by huge pine trees and are shady—what a rarity! Several rooms are in newer wings and separate buildings; some of these do not have lake views. The highlight of our stay was a boat tour of Squam Lake in a wooden Chris Craft boat, exactly like the one used in *On Golden Pond.*" *(Susan W. Schwemm)*

A few minor niggles: "Feels more like a small hotel than a country inn. We received a friendly greeting from Mrs. Jan Havre, but no one offered to help with the bags or show us to our room. Our bathroom overlooked a path to the lake, but had no shade or curtain for its clear glass window, which was somewhat embarrassing." Also: "Surprised to find Duraflame logs in our fireplace, although we could understand their advantages."

Open All year. Restaurant closed Mon., Tues. in winter; also some off-season months.
Rooms 2 suites, 18 doubles, 3 singles, 4 cabins—all with private bath and/or shower, radio, TV. Some with desk, fireplaces, balconies, air-conditioning, fan. 17 rooms in main inn; other rooms in carriage house and 1- and 2-bedroom cottages.
Facilities Living room/lobby, library with TV, piano bar/lounge, restaurant. Verandas, 13 acres with swimming pool, clay tennis court, private sandy beach, free canoes, sailboats, swimming, fishing.
Location NH Lakes Region; 1 hr. 45 min. from Boston; 4.5 m from Exit 24, I-93 on Rte. 3.
Restrictions No cigars or pipes in public room.
Credit cards Amex, DC, Discover, MC, Visa.

Rates Room only, $155 suite, $59–155 double, $44–140 singles. Children 10 and under free in parents' room; extra person over 10 in room, $15. 2-night minimum, weekends in season. Breakfast, $6; alc dinner, $35.
Extras Free station pickups. Some French spoken. Cribs, babysitting.

JACKSON 03846   Map 1

Jackson, in the White Mountains of northeast New Hampshire, lies in the Mt. Washington Valley, 8 miles north of North Conway (use the Jackson covered bridge). It's 3 hours (150 miles) north of Boston, and 1½ hours (65 miles) west of Portland, Maine. There's ample opportunity for fishing, hiking, canoeing, golf, and tennis in summer; in winter there are five downhill ski areas and several cross-country ski centers within a short drive, making up an extensive trail system.

Also recommended: The **Christmas Farm Inn** (Route 16B, Box 176; 603–383–4313) is a year-round family resort, spread out over a collection of old and new buildings and cottages. The food is hearty, the Christmas theme a big hit with kids, and the atmosphere relaxed and friendly. The **Ellis River House** (Route 16, P.O. Box 656; 603–383–9339) is a restored colonial farmhouse, decorated with antiques, comforters, and fresh flowers. It's a working farm, complete with animals, vegetable gardens, and a vineyard. Set well back from the road, its location is ideal for cross-country skiing.

Whitney's Village Inn   *Tel:* (603) 383–6886
Route 16B, P.O. Box W   Outside NH: (800) 252–5622

Founded as a country inn more than fifty years ago, Whitney's has been owned by the Tannehills since 1982. When they bought the inn, their plan was to "provide the best in family vacations for a good value," and they have apparently been quite successful in meeting that goal. There's a wide range of year-round activities both at the inn and in the surrounding area, and the staff makes a special effort to accommodate families with young children. Children have the option of eating early, under the supervision of the staff, then watching a movie, giving their parents time to enjoy dinner in peace

Rooms in the main inn vary greatly in size and are decorated in a comfortable country style, with floral wallpapers and white chenille bedspreads. They have adequate lighting and clean, modernized baths; the cabins were all redecorated in 1988. There are a few antiques, but this is not the kind of place you come to for the decor. The food is both good and ample—there's a separate menu for the kids, with pizza, burgers, and fried chicken, and a more adventurous one for adults.

"What a relief to leave the dreadful strip called Route 16 and find this quiet country inn. We enjoyed having the extra space our cabin's two bedrooms, sitting room, and porch provided—and the kids loved it. It was quiet and peaceful, surrounded by flowers, looking out over the inn's own beginner ski slope. The staff couldn't have been nicer or more friendly, and we were pleasantly surprised by the food. We were expecting very basic cooking, but in fact had some delicious dinners—everything from gazpacho to mussels with sautéed vegetables in wine sauce to duck with a thankfully not sweet pepper sauce. The homemade desserts are sinfully good—blueberry pie, brownies topped with ice cream and fudge sauce." *(Diane Wolf)*

Open All year. Restaurant closed in April.
Rooms 10 suites, 23 doubles, 2 cabins. 31 with private bath, 4 with maximum of 5 people sharing bath. All with desk, fan. Some with fireplace, sink in room. Refrigerators in cabins.
Facilities Dining room; library; living room; teen room; family activities room with TV/VCR, games, nightly movie; bar/lounge with music. 200 acres with pond for fishing, swimming, boating; badminton, volleyball, shuffleboard, croquet, tennis, hiking; downhill and cross-county skiing, sledding, sleigh rides, ice-skating, paddleboats. Canoeing, kayaking, golf, major downhill and cross-country ski areas nearby.
Location 12 m N of N. Conway, about 2 m from Jackson. From Rte. 16, take Rte. 16A in Jackson through the covered bridge to 16B.
Restrictions No children under 2.
Credit cards Amex, MC, Visa.
Rates MAP, $118–154, $118–144 double, $69–84 single. Extra person in room, $45. 15% service additional. Reduced rates for children; special family rates. Package rates. Alc dinner, $22.
Extras Cribs, babysitting, play equipment available. Free bus pickups.

JAFFREY 03452   Map 1

Also recommended: The nearby **Monadnock Inn** (444 Main Street, Box B, Jaffrey Center 03454; 603–532–7001) is set in a classic little New England village, complete with steepled church and white clapboard houses circling the common. The Monadnock Inn was built in 1830 and has been an inn for over 100 years. Although rooms are comfortable, the inn is known for its neighborhood bar and its popular restaurant.

The Benjamin Prescott Inn   *Tel:* (603) 532–6637
Route 124 East

In 1853, Benjamin Prescott built a two-story frame house on the Old Turnpike Road. Soon after, the Prescotts built an inn adjoining the homestead; the family's ownership extended for over 100 years, during which time the property became one of the largest and most up-to-date farms in the area.

Barry and Janice Miller bought the Benjamin Prescott in 1988. Rates include a breakfast of fresh fruit and juice, homebaked breads, cereal, and a hot entrée and rooms are furnished with antiques and traditional decor.

"The Millers spare nothing in their efforts to make guests welcome. From their puffed apple pancakes to the delicious chocolate truffles placed at your bedside each night, nothing is overlooked. The inn itself is a beautifully restored old farmhouse filled with wonderful antiques. Breakfasts are served at small tables set for two or three or at the larger dining room table. Fresh flowers and plants abound. The living room is comfortable and cozy with an excellent variety of magazines and other reading materials. The bedrooms have super quilts, lots of pillows, good reading lights and an abundance of thick towels. We stayed in John Adams's Attic, a third-floor suite well worth the climb, with a sitting room overlooking the endless field of the neighboring dairy farm." *(Patricia Aarons, also Judy McKnight)*

Open All year.
Rooms 3 suites, 5 doubles, 2 singles—3 with full private bath, 6 with private shower. All rooms with fan; some with radio, TV, desk. 1 suite with kitchenette.
Facilities Living room with fireplace, TV, 2 dining rooms, screened porch. Lake swimming, trout and bass fishing, hiking, downhill and cross-country skiing, golf nearby.
Location S NH, Monadnock region. 1½ hrs. to Boston and Springfield, MA, 2 hrs. to Hartford, CT, 3½ hrs. to NYC. 2 m to town on Rte. 124.
Restrictions Smoking in living room only. No children under 6.
Credit cards MC, Visa.
Rates B&B, $130 suite, $60–80 double, single. Extra person in room, $10. 2-night weekend minimum.
Extras Airport pickups.

LYME 03768   **Map 1**

Information please: We'd like to hear more about the **Lyme Inn**, right on the common opposite the church. Dating back to the early 1800s, its 14 guest rooms are filled with antiques, its tavern and restaurant favorites with locals and visitors alike (One the Common; 603–795–2222 or 4404).

Loch Lyme Lodge   *Tel:* (603) 795–2141
Route 10, RFD 278

Loch Lyme has been taking guests since 1924. It overlooks Post Pond, a spring-fed lake about three quarters of a mile wide, and about the same distance in length. Paul and Judy Barker, former schoolteachers, have been running the inn since 1977.

"A very special place, whose charm is its rustic simplicity and its clientele; there is nothing formal or pretentious about either the accommodations or the people. Meals are simple but substantial—good home-baked food with good desserts and breakfasts that our kids love.

"Post Pond is especially delightful for youngsters; it's clean and peaceful, rarely disturbed by motorboats. The owners make Loch Lyme a full-time occupation, and devote special attention to making the vacation experience a special one for young families.

"Loch Lyme offers a chance to get away from the phone and schedules, yet with proximity to Hanover, with its films, plays, concerts, and all the resources of Dartmouth College. Our children learned canoeing, hiking, rowing, and croquet at Loch Lyme, and computer programming during the evening in Hanover. Loch Lyme attracts families who prize its informality, location, and stability. Most are professionals, with many academics, financial analysts, etc., who are quiet but friendly; there's no organized activity, and those who want such should stay away." *(Elizabeth & Sydney Nathans)*

"One of the nicest features for parents is the assortment of children's toys on the lodge lawn. Parents can linger over coffee and the morning paper while the kids play. I enjoy antiquing and my husband golfs, while the sitters watch the kids by the lake. The sitters are good at night, too, when we go to the summer playhouse at Dartmouth.

"Our cabin had a brand-new bathroom with ample supplies of hot water, but was otherwise very rustic. Our double bed was very uncomfortable, and the kitchen was minimally equipped—4 plates, 5 glasses, 1 sharp knife, etc." (DMK)

Open All year except Thanksgiving and Christmas. Dinner served late June to Labor Day.

Rooms 4 doubles sharing 2 baths. 24 summer cabins with private bath. Most with kitchen, fireplace, screened porch.

Facilities Dining rooms, living room with fireplace, piano room, library, game room. 125 acres with tennis, lawn games, fields, woods, cross-country skiing. Lakefront with dock, canoes, boats, fishing, beach. 3½ m to downhill skiing.

Location W NH, CT River valley. 2¾ hrs. NW of Boston. 11 m N of Hanover. On Rte. 10, 1 m N of town.

Restrictions No smoking in dining rooms.

Credit cards None accepted.

Rates B&B, $50–75 double, $25–38 single. Extra person in room, $21. MAP, $80–110 double, $40–55 single. Extra person in room, $34. Picnic lunch, $5. Prix fixe dinner, $13. Reduced rates for children under 16. Weekly rates. 2-night weekend minimum in foliage season.

Extras Pets in cabins only. Some cabins wheelchair accessible. Spanish, limited French spoken. Airport/station pickups, $14. Cribs, babysitting, play equipment available.

NORTH CONWAY 03860   Map 1

North Conway is an old mountain resort town, home of Mt. Cranmore, one of the country's first downhill ski areas. Located in the White Mountains, in the Mt. Washington Valley, it's about 2½ hours north of Boston, and 1¼ hours' drive west of Portland. North Conway is right at the edge of the White Mountains National Forest; the area offers many opportunities for hiking, fishing, swimming, golf, bicycling, and tennis in summer, along with concerts and summer stock theater, with a wide choice of cross-country and downhill ski areas in winter, plus outdoor ice-skating. The area has also become a mecca for serious shoppers, with dozens of stores offering name-brand goods and apparel at tax-free discount prices. Even L. L. Bean has an outlet.

Also recommended: The 1785 Inn (Scenic Vista at Route 16, P.O. Box 1785; 603–356–9025) is a historic country inn with beautiful views of Mt. Washington, delicious food and hospitable owners; children are welcome and will enjoy the heated swimming pool. **The Merrill Farm Resort** (Route 16, RFD Box 151; 603–447–3866 or 800–445–1017) combines the appeal of a two-hundred-year-old farmhouse with modern rooms in a family atmosphere. For those who'd prefer a more elegant adult atmosphere, **Stonehurst Manor** (Route 16, P.O. Box 1937; 603–356–3113 or 800–525–9100) is an impressive English Tudor country manor house complete with hand-carved oak woodwork, a huge fireplace, and cut glass windows, along with beautifully landscaped grounds. Food is a highlight here, with a menu of many classic European dishes.

Old Red Inn & Cottages
Route 16, P.O. Box 467/302

Tel: (603) 356-2642

The Old Red Inn dates back to 1810, although a Victorian remodeling job gives its exterior a slightly schizophrenic (but still pleasant) appearance. Don and Winnie White have owned the inn since 1980. Although the inn is on quite busy Route 16, guests do not seem to mind, feeling that its convenient location and quiet atmosphere more than compensate.

"Winnie's prize-winning herb and flower gardens greatly enhance the natural attractiveness of the inn's setting." *(Chuck & Rachel Sherrill)* "A delightful inn, with nice firm beds and clean rooms. The continental breakfast—served in the living room or on the porch—is a great start to the day—with Winnie's homemade jams and jellies, a variety of excellent muffins, and maple butter made from their own trees." *(John R. Allen)*

"The blazing living room fire and the camaraderie among the guests help to make the atmosphere homey. But the real attraction here is the Whites. Their friendliness and outgoing personalities set this inn apart. They are both knowledgeable about the area and are more than willing to share with you all the little tidbits that will help make your stay memorable." *(Stanley Sullivan)*

"Don't miss the homemade sticky buns. The fragrance of Winnie's potpourri permeates the house. Each room is appealing, done in old (not necessarily antique) furniture. The efficiency apartment on the second floor has a spectacular view of Mt. Washington from the kitchen table window (glorious in the fall). We love the lemon soap and the quiet atmosphere. North Conway is a hub of activity and the inn is so convenient. *(Lora Jane Anderson)*

Open All year, except April 1 to 25 and Nov. 1 to 15.
Rooms 1 suite, 16 doubles—15 with private shower and/or bath; 2 with maximum of 4 people sharing bath. All rooms with TV; some with air-conditioning or fan. 7 rooms in inn, 10 cottages, some with kitchenettes, screened porches.
Facilities Living room with woodstove, dining room, porches. 1¼ acres with herb & flower gardens. Lake, river, downhill and cross-country skiing nearby.
Location 5-minute walk to town. On Rte. 16, S of town.
Restrictions Smoking in cottages only.
Credit cards Amex, Discover, MC, Visa.
Rates B&B, $78–96 suite, $48–80 double, $42–65 single. Cottages $58–88, for 2–5 people. Extra person in room, $10. 2-day minimum in foliage season. Weekly rates; ski packages.
Extras Cottages wheelchair accessible. French spoken. Station pickups. Cribs, games available; play equipment nearby.

PORTSMOUTH 03801   Map 1

In the pell-mell rush to Maine, many travelers zoom through New Hampshire's "don't blink or you'll miss it" seventeen-mile coastline with nary a second glance. Although it's just an hour north of Boston, those in the know will plan an overnight in Portsmouth, a historic town founded in 1623. Made wealthy in the nineteenth century as a shipbuilding seaport, the town has much to offer, including Strawbery Banke (the town's original name), a restoration of the original waterfront buildings (open May 1 to October 31); several historic buildings turned museum; and Prescott Park, home to lovely gardens, various festivals, and a folk art museum. To placate fidgety children, we'd suggest a steamship cruise of the harbor, and a visit to the local children's museum. For ocean swimming, beaches can be found at two nearby state parks. For details, contact the Chamber of Commerce (500 Market Street; 603–436–1118).

Information please: We'd like to have reports on the **Bow Street Inn** (125 Bow Street; 603–431–7760), which claims to be Portsmouth's only waterfront inn, with 12 riverview rooms. The decor is country Victorian, and each room has a telephone and TV; rates include a continental breakfast.

Leighton Inn
69 Richards Avenue

Tel: (603) 433–2188

Built in 1809, this high-style Federal home has been restored with great care and authenticity. Plaster samples from the third-floor bedrooms were sent for analysis, so that the rooms could be repainted in exactly the same tones. Nearly all the fireplace mantels, window ornaments, and mahogany-railed stairs are original to the house. Period antiques, reproduction Federal wallpapers, and Oriental carpets have been used throughout. The inn has been owned since 1986 by Catherine Stone.

"Lovely restored mansion, in a quiet residential area, within walking distance of town. Immaculate housekeeping. Fresh flowers in tiny vases throughout the house. Large rooms, with nice touches—herbal soaps and shampoos, magazines, plush towels and robes, heavy quilts, and feather-soft pillows—no paper bath mats here! Our room was on the top floor and had maple twin beds, desk, drop-leaf table, night stand, rush-seat chair, and a rocking chair perfect for reading. A large mirror and wrought iron clothes stand were nice touches. Our room had plenty of cross ventilation, but fans are available if necessary. We had a nice deep claw-foot tub for baths; a shower was also available. If all the baths were in use you did lose hot water for a bit. Halls were well lit. Plenty of parking.

"Breakfast is served with china and linen napkins, on an enclosed porch. Delicious home-baked muffins, fresh fruit and juice, eggs blended with cheese and basil, wonderful potatoes with fresh parsley. The breakfast porch overlooks lovely gardens in the back of the house, where Catherine grows all her own herbs, raspberries, grapes, and flowers in all colors.

"The house is a wonderful Federal residence, not quite a mansion but very gracious, with a gorgeous mahogany railing leading up the impressive staircase. An exceptional Empire chaise longue in a striped silk moire made us feel like royalty when we sat on it. The owner's former life in the music world is immediately apparent from the Steinway baby grand in one parlor, and an amazing early-nineteenth-century clavichord in the yellow parlor across the hall. Our favorite room is the one on the second floor with a smart bathroom en suite, an inviting four-poster mahogany bed, and a tremendous Oriental rug spanning the room." *(Seth & Joan Koven, also Patricia Martin-Shaw, Doris Walsh)*

Open All year.
Rooms 5 doubles—1 with full private bath, 2 with private shower, 2 with maximum of 4 people sharing bath. All with desk, fans. Telephone on request.
Facilities 2 parlors, country kitchen, library with grand piano, wicker porch, breakfast porch. Garden with Victorian lawn furniture. 2 m to beach. Playground nearby.
Location SE NH. 50 m N of Boston. 5-min. walk to town, and Strawbery Banke.
Credit cards MC, Visa.
Rates B&B, $65–75 double, $55–65 single. Extra person in room, $15. Tipping not necessary. Reduced rates for children under 4.
Extras Station pickups. Some French spoken.

Sise Inn *Tel:* (603) 433–1200
40 Court Street

While corporate ownership of multiple inn properties rarely makes for a winning combination—at least as far as this guidebook is concerned—we're always delighted to report exceptions. Someplace(s) Different is a Canadian company whose speciality is restoring architecturally distinctive buildings as inns. Their goal in all their properties is to combine turn-of-the-century decor with inn-keeping warmth and the full business facilities not usually found in B&Bs. Besides the Sise Inn, the company owns several Canadian inns, most listed in our Ontario chapter.

The Sise Inn, which dates back to 1881, connects the original Queen Anne Victorian structure with a modern addition that houses the majority of the inn's guest rooms. Rooms are decorated in period with antiques and reproductions, and rates include a buffet breakfast of yogurt, cereal, fruit and juices, and a variety of baked goods—croissants, bagels, English muffins, and coffee cakes. The inn has been managed by Carl and Giselle Jensen since its opening in 1986.

"Everywhere you look—the hallway, front parlor, breakfast room, stairway—is extravagantly paneled in butternut wood (similar to golden oak). Both the parlor and breakfast rooms have built-in sideboards and bookcases that match the paneling (all the way to the 12-foot ceilings).

"The new owners have not missed a thing in the renovation of this classic building. Oriental rugs lay on gleaming floors, brass chandeliers and sconces sparkle, and comfortable wing chairs welcome you to sit down and play chess in front of the fire. The breakfast room and adjoining sunroom have Victorian oak tables and chairs, and a lavish buffet arranged on a massive oak cupboard. In the new wing, oak doors and trim match the antique butternut woodwork—even the elevator is oak paneled, with brass trim. A clever touch is a public phone hidden in an old, red, British phone booth.

"Each guest room has a brand-new bathroom with fluffy towels, herbal bath amenities, and excellent lighting. Hidden away in an antique armoire is a remote control TV/VCR, extra blankets, and pillows. Every bed has a table and lamp on both sides, and some rooms have an ample seating area with sofa, chairs, and coffee table. Large windows are elegantly draped to coordinate with the floral wallpapers.

"If you're splurging, I'd recommend the third-floor suite or the ground-floor suite as being especially luxurious. The Jensens were eager to make sure that everything was just right during my visit. They succeeded." *(NB)*

Open All year.
Rooms 9 suites, 21 doubles, 4 singles—all with full private bath, telephone, clock/radio, TV/VCR, desk, air-conditioning, fan. Some rooms with whirlpool tub, stereo, fireplace, skylight. 2 rooms in annex.
Facilities Dining room, 3 meeting rooms, private bar, sun porch. Hiking, cross-country skiing, golf, ocean nearby.
Location From I-95 take Exit 7. At end of ramp turn right (left if going south). Go through blinking light. At fork go right on Russell St. At stop sign turn right. At first light, turn left on Maplewood Ave. Go through 3 lights. Pass Gulf gas station on right, then turn left on Court St. Inn on right.
Credit cards Amex, MC, Visa.
Rates $160 suite, $65–102 double, $65–92 single. Extra person in room, $10. Children under 3 stay free. 10% senior discount. Special weekend packages, corporate, weekly rates available.
Extras One room equipped for disabled. Cribs available. Office equipment, secretarial services on 24-hr. notice. Fax machine.

SHELBURNE 03581   Map 1

Philbrook Farm Inn   *Tel:* (603) 466–3831
North Road

Philbrook Farm Inn is located in the foothills of the White Mountains. Innkeepers Connie Philbrook Leger and Nancy Philbrook are the fourth generation of Philbrooks to operate the inn since 1853. Guests return year after year, generation after generation, to find the inn operates much as it did a century ago. The warm, friendly innkeepers receive their guests in an atmosphere that makes them feel that it is their second home.

"The aroma of home-cooked food greets you as you enter the front door. Nancy prepares the meals on a 75-year-old black woodstove. Only one entrée is prepared each night, generally a roast. The homemade soup, fresh vegetables from the garden, fresh home-grown herbs, and fresh-baked desserts complete the dinner. The full breakfast includes homemade doughnuts and breads. The innkeepers gather fruits from their yard in the summer to make jams and jellies. Guests celebrating birthdays and anniversaries are made a special cake.

"Several guest living rooms abound with comfortable chairs and adequate lighting for reading the many books provided, some of which were contributed by authors who visited the farm. Puzzles and a vast collection of White Mountain memorabilia are on display for guests to enjoy. The inn is spotlessly clean, with old but adequate plumbing and early American–style bedrooms furnished in lovely antiques. The atmosphere is relaxed and quiet. Cross-country skiing and casual walks can be enjoyed on the property's trails and old logging roads." *(Judith Carroll)*

"A great place to go with kids—mine loved everything about it, from the inner tubes in the swimming pool to the antique pool table in the basement. No planned activities, but lots to do on the farm and in the area.

Combines a very relaxed ambience with a great sense of history. Terrific location and setting, on an isolated back country road. Be sure to ask for the map which shows all the inn's own hiking trails. Would have preferred a firmer mattress and a bathroom with shower." *(SWS)*

Open May through Oct.; Dec 26 through March.
Rooms 18 doubles, 1 single—10 with private shower and/or bath; 9 with maximum of 4 people sharing bath. All rooms with desk, fan. Also 2 1-room, 4 4-bedroom summer cottages.
Facilities Dining room; 3 living rooms with fireplace, puzzles, games; playroom with pool table, Ping-Pong, TV. 950 acres with swimming pool, horseback riding/lessons, lawn games, climbing, hiking, fishing, cross-country skiing. Golf, tennis nearby. Downhill skiing 15–20 miles away.
Location NE NH; 90 m W of Portland, ME; 115 m N of Portsmouth, NH. 7 m E of Gorham; 1½ m off U.S. Rte. 2—take Meadows Rd. 1 m, E on North Rd., or call for directions.
Credit cards None accepted.
Rates MAP, $90–100 suite, $85–90 double, $65–70 single, plus 15% service. Weekly rates. Children's rates. Housekeeping cottage, $250 weekly; sleeps 8.
Extras Limited wheelchair access. Pets permitted in cottages. Cribs, play equipment available.

SNOWVILLE 03849   Map 1

Snowvillage Inn   *Tel:* (603) 447–2818
Foss Mountain Road, Box 50

The Snowvillage Inn was built as a summer estate in 1916 and offers spectacular views of the White Mountains from its quiet country setting. Owned since 1986 by Frank, Trudy, and Peter Cutrone, they have been working hard to improve the inn, putting in more gardens and restoring the tennis courts outside, and painting, papering, and soundproofing rooms on the inside. The most recent addition is the Chimney House, with four fireplaced guest rooms. Trudy reports that "people remember our inn for three reasons: one is the welcoming basket of fresh chocolate chip cookies in their room; the second is my collection of 200-year-old portraits of my Austrian ancestors; and third is our guests' delight in Boris, our Samoyed, a really friendly inn dog. Guests also love the inn's end-of-the-road location, an island of serenity far from the sounds of any traffic."

Guests are very appreciative of Trudy's cooking, which blends American cuisine with Austrian specialties. One evening's dinner might feature a minted spinach soup, Viennese beef tenderloin (stuffed with herbed mushrooms and topped with a creamy Madeira sauce) and finished with a delicate French silk pie. A single entrée is served at dinner each night, although vegetarians and others with special dietary needs are accommodated with advance notice.

The living room has plenty of comfortable couches, often occupied by guests reading one of the inn's hundreds of books. Guest rooms, each named after a writer, are comfortable and pleasantly decorated; bathrooms are basic but functional and clean.

"Stunning location—the sun porch and dining room look onto the Presidential range. The grounds have lovely perennial gardens and woods with hiking paths. We were accompanied by Boris, a 'people' dog who delighted in escorting us around the grounds. Frank is always concerned that guests are comfortable and have their needs met. He even offered to shut off the outside lights so that we could stargaze. Our room was very clean and the king-size bed was very comfortable. The food was delicious with home-made breads and soups. Breakfast offered a choice of entrées along with homemade muffins, juice and coffee. Rose, our waitress, took a motherly interest in seeing that everyone was well pampered." *(Bob & Amy Peritsky)*

Open May through March.
Rooms 19 doubles with private bath and/or shower, desk, fan. 6 rooms in inn, 13 in converted barn and Chimney House.
Facilities Dining room, living room with fireplace, games, family/TV rooms, bar, library, screened porch, sauna, indoor and outdoor games, sleds. 30 acres with gardens, clay tennis court, cross-country ski touring center with rentals, trails. 1 m to lake swimming, ice-skating. 6 m to downhill skiing.
Location NE NH, White Mts. 60 m W of Portland, 120 m N of Boston, 315 m N of NYC. 7 m from town. Take Rte. 16 or 25 to Rte. 153. Turn at Snowville sign. Turn right in village onto Foss Mt. Rd.
Restrictions No smoking in dining room. No children under 7.
Credit cards Amex, MC, Visa.
Rates All rates per person. MAP, $55–75 double, $65–85 single. B&B rates, deduct $15 per person. Extra person in room, $25–45. Weekly discounts, midweek packages. 15% service additional. 2-3 night weekend minimum. Alc dinner, $40.
Extras Airport/station pickups. Polish, French, German spoken.

SUNAPEE 03782 Map 1

The Inn at Sunapee *Tel:* (603) 763–4444
Burkehaven Hill Road, P.O. Box 336

The Inn at Sunapee is a rambling 1880s farmhouse, with a classic wrap-around porch. Adjacent is the original barn, now transformed into a lounge, with a fieldstone fireplace, perfect for a game of darts or Monopoly. The dining room has beautiful views of the mountains and lakes, and innkeeper Kate Crawford is "particularly proud of our food. We use produce grown by an organic farmer nearby, and we get our fish directly from the Boston docks. Cider and cookies are offered to guests after skiing in the winter; in the summer, we give ice cream makers and the needed ingredients to guests so that they can make their own by the pool. Our breakfasts include fresh fruit, orange juice, homebaked muffins, and a choice of pancakes or omelets with sausage or bacon."

"I always knew that the way a business is run starts at the top. This is clearly evident here—the owner treats you warmly and graciously, the cook and housekeeper make you feel welcome, and so on down the line— even the dog and cats greet you pleasantly. Our room was bright, airy, and charming; we returned late at night to find a welcoming note on the kitchen door, a full ice bucket, and a fireplace needing only a match for the kindling." *(Paul Shirk, also Karen Carr)*

"Rooms are exceptionally pleasant, with marvelous views. Considering the swimming pool and tennis court, the rates are very reasonable. The chef is outstanding and produces truly memorable meals. Sunapee Harbor is a pleasant village, a short walk away, and Lake Sunapee is a delightful area to explore." *(Carla Cohen)*

Open May through Oct.; Thanksgiving through March. Restaurant closed Mon., Tues. nights.
Rooms 4 family suites, 18 doubles, all with private shower and/or bath, fan. 8 rooms in annex.
Facilities Dining rooms, lounge/bar with fireplace, games, living room, TV room, porch. 10 acres with swimming pool, tennis court, volleyball, shuffleboard. Near Lake Sunapee for boating, fishing, swimming, scuba diving. 10 min. from downhill, cross-country skiing.
Location SW NH. 2 hrs. NW of Boston, 3 hrs N of Hartford. ½ m from Sunapee Harbor. From Sunapee, turn at blinking light to Sunapee Harbor. Take 1st right after Osborne's Marina; go ½ m up hill to inn.
Credit cards MC, Visa.
Rates B&B, $110–140 suite (up to 4 people), $55–79 double, $50–55 single. MAP, $110–130 suite, $130 double, $65–85 single. 15% service. Extra person in room, $10–40. Alc dinner, $32. 2- to 3-night weekend/holiday minimum. Weekend ski packages. Discount for 3-night stay midweek. 10% midweek senior discount.
Extras Airport pickups, $10. Babysitting (with advance notice), play equipment, games available. Children's menu.

WEST CHESTERFIELD 03466   **Map 1**

Chesterfield Inn   *Tel:* (603) 256–3211
Route 9

The Chesterfield Inn stands on property granted in 1762 to Joanna Wetherby—one of the few women to be granted land by the King of England. Although built as a farmhouse, it was operated as a tavern from 1798 to 1811. It went through many uses over the years, but was restored as an inn in 1984, and was bought by Judy and Phil Hueber in 1987. Phil notes that "our inn appeals to travelers looking for luxurious and romantic accommodations with all the modern conveniences, yet with the style of a traditional grand country inn." Guest rooms are spacious and luxuriously furnished with antiques. Four rooms have fireplaces, two have Jacuzzis, and all have stocked refrigerators. Chef Carl Warner receives accolades from all, and dinners include such specialties as duck with mango chutney, veal stuffed with St. André cheese and walnuts, and rabbit with Pommery Mustard sauce.

"This inn has style born of the grace and charm of a welcoming New England homestead. Phil and Judy Hueber imbue the romantic surroundings with a rare enthusiasm for what they do. Each of the nine rooms is individually decorated in rich colors, old barn beam woods, plants, quilts, and wall stencils. Our fireplace was laid with wood and replenished from the hearth bin. A skating pond awaits outside, and local hiking, skiing, and sights kept us busy. Just as well to work off the generous homemade breakfast in the cozy glassed-in dining room, with its view of the pond and mountains. New Year's Eve was a special treat, as we took a sleigh ride through the woods, then lingered three hours over a seven-course dinner prepared by chef Carl Warner." *(Diane Wyzga)*

Open All year.
Rooms 2 suites, 7 doubles, all with full private bath, dressing room, telephone, radio, TV, desk, air-conditioning. Some rooms with fireplace.
Facilities Restaurant, living room with fireplace, sun porch. 10 acres with herb and flower gardens, skating pond. ¼ m from CT River for canoeing; 2 m from Lake Spofford for swimming, boating. Cross-country, some downhill skiing nearby.
Location SE NH, CT River. 13 m W of Keene, 2 m E of Brattleboro, VT, 1 m E of Exit 3, I-91; 1½ hrs. W of Boston, 3½ hrs. N of NYC.
Restrictions No children under 10.
Credit cards Amex, DC, MC, Visa.
Rates B&B, $145–155 suite, $95–105 double. Extra person in room, $15. Corporate rates. Alc dinner, $35.
Extras Wheelchair accessible.

WEST SPRINGFIELD 03284   Map 1

Wonderwell   *Tel:* (603) 763–5065
Philbrick Hill Road

Susan and Sam Alexander decided to convert their home, built in 1911 as a summer residence, and owned by the Alexander family since 1935, into an inn in 1983. They describe Wonderwell as a place "for peaceful people with pampered palates who prefer romantic vistas, panoramic sunsets, woodland seclusion, civilized plumbing in rustic surroundings, luxurious privacy, and unobtrusive hospitality." A spacious country "cottage" in the grand manner, Wonderwell is unusual in that it provides a welcoming environment for both couples and families. Especially handsome is the Great Room, a two-story living room with twin fieldstone fireplaces, encircled by a second-floor balcony. Rough-hewn support beams contrast effectively with the polished hardwood floors and trim and the English chintzes of the couches, window seats, and window treatments. The spacious guest rooms have all been renovated, fitted out with reproduction furnishings and up-to-date plumbing. Breakfast includes fresh fruit and juice, hot and cold cereals, fresh rolls, croissants, muffins, or bagels, and the daily special, ranging from walnut waffles with strawberry cream to baked buttermilk pancakes with sliced peaches, topped with sour cream and cinnamon sugar; eggs any style with bacon, ham, or sausage are always available for traditionalists.

"This mountaintop inn has sweeping vistas—sit on the back porch and soak it all in. Or go over acres and acres of rolling landscape. Spacious beds and reading lights abound here, along with many chairs beneath huge skylights; for readers the common room on the third floor with triple skylights is heaven. Attention to renovation detail was typified by the installation of soundproofing in walls between all bedrooms. Dining here is delightful, with breakfast the culinary high point." *(Ed Okie)*

Open May to Nov. 23; Dec. 26 to March 31.
Rooms 2 suites, 6 doubles, all with private shower and/or bath, radio, ceiling fans. 7 with air-conditioning; TV on request.

Facilities Breakfast room, dining room with fireplace, parlor with TV, Great Room with Caesar's balcony, 2 fireplaces, grand piano; 2 sitting rooms, screen porch, game porch. 15 acres with flower gardens, croquet, badminton, gazebo with fireplace. 5–10 m to swimming, fishing, boating, hiking, golf, tennis, cross-country & downhill skiing.

Location SW NH; Dartmouth/Lake Sunapee area. Approx. 10 min NW of Lake Sunapee, 20 min. SE of Hanover. 6 m from I-89, Exit 12A.

Restrictions Smoking on first floor only. No children under 3.

Credit cards None accepted.

Rates B&B, $180–210 suite, $95–125 double, $85 single. MAP, $220–250 suite, $150 double, $105 single. Child in room, $30–50. 10% service. Off-season rates lower. Family rates in suites. 2-night minimum holiday weekends. Prix fixe lunch, $12.50; prix fixe dinner, $25 (beverages included).

Extras Airport/station pickups $15 (free with 3-day stay). Babysitting available.

We Want to Hear from You!

As you know, this book is only effective with your help. We really need to know about your experiences and discoveries.

If you stayed at an inn or hotel listed here, we want to know how it was. Did it live up to our description? Exceed it? Was it what you expected? Did you like it? Were you disappointed? Delighted?

Have you discovered new establishments that we should add to the next edition?

Tear out one of the report forms at the back of this book (or use your own stationery if you prefer) and write today. Even if you write only "Fully endorse existing entry" you will have been most helpful.

Thank You!

The Queen Victoria, Cape May

Those who have seen New Jersey only from the turnpike have given the state a bad reputation. Others, familiar with Atlantic City and the more raucous beach towns, assume that it simply is not their sort of place. In truth, the state has quite a lot more to offer. Gracious beach resorts are found from Bay Head to Spring Lake to Cape May; many pleasant country towns along the Delaware River invite you to relax and explore.

The rates listed here do not include the 6% state sales tax. Most inns at beach resorts provide beach badges or passes to guests, which eliminates the need for guests to buy expensive nonresident passes. Two- and three-night minimums are the rule in most beach towns and resorts.

BAY HEAD 08742   **Map 3**

Information please: Another possibility in Bay Head is the **Bay Head Gables**, an elaborate Newport-style cedar-shake "cottage" with Art Deco furnishings and ocean views (200 Main Avenue; 201–892–9844). Reports?

Conover's Bay Head Inn   *Tel:* (201) 892–4664
646 Main Avenue

Only an hour away from New York City, Bay Head offers a quick trip back to the turn of the century. The town was developed in 1879 by a group of wealthy Princeton men as a summer retreat for their families; many homes are still owned by these families. Bay Head has no neon signs, no

414

supermarkets, no movie theaters, no parking meters, and no fast-food restaurants. It does have beautiful, uncrowded beaches and Victorian summer "cottages" and gardens.

Carl and Beverly Conover, who have operated the Bay Head Inn for many years, describe it as "a small place where we can pay attention to detail. We try to equip rooms as you would the guest room in your own home. Everything is home-baked for breakfast every day. Our continental summer breakfast includes local fruits in season; winter breakfast is full and hearty, and afternoon tea is also served."

"Everything is tidy and beautifully kept up. Rooms are decorated with a mixture of reproduction wicker, English chintz, and Victorian furniture. Beverly Conover hand-quilted the bedspreads and color-coordinated the sheets and towels. Carpeted hallways keep noise at a minimum. Breakfasts are luscious. Altogether a charming place to stay." *(Michael Spring)*

"The beach is one of the nicest in New Jersey, and the well-kept yard offers shade on hot sunny days; shopping is nearby for rainy ones. Beverly and Carl made us feel very welcome." *(Susan Klimley)*

Open All year, weekends only in winter.
Rooms 1 suite, 11 doubles—6 with private bath and/or shower, 6 with maximum of 6 people sharing bath. All air-conditioned.
Facilities Living, sitting rooms with fireplace, books, porches. Shaded yard with flower gardens, lounge chairs, picnic tables, grill, croquet. 1 block to swimming, fishing, water skiing. Beach passes. Horseback riding nearby.
Location 3 blocks from town. 60 m S of NYC; 65 m E of Philadelphia. 1½ blocks past the 3rd traffic light on Rte. 35 S out of town.
Restrictions No children under 13. No smoking.
Credit cards Amex, MC, Visa.
Rates B&B, $75–125 suite, $50–115 double; $5–10 less for single occupancy. Extra person in room, $30. 2-3 night minimum weekends and holidays. Sunday to Friday stay, 1 night free.
Extras Train station pickups.

CAPE MAY 08204   Map 3

Cape May has so many Victorian gingerbread houses that the town has been designated as a National Historic Landmark. Cape May's heyday as a beach resort stretched from 1850 to 1900, when thousands of visitors arrived by train or steamer each summer from Philadelphia and points farther south. Many of today's guest houses date from a disastrous fire in 1878. From the ashes rose this extraordinary collection of elaborate beach "cottages" designed by Philadelphia's best architects, built by the town's master carpenters, and paid for by the millionaires of the day. These "cottages" actually come in three sizes: cottage, villa, and mansion, or big, bigger, biggest.

Cape May has an unusually large number of high-quality owner-operated inns. When calling for reservations you may find that your first choice is full; inn owners are very good about referring you to a nearby establishment of equal appeal, and you'll do well to follow their suggestions. Almost none of Cape May's inns serves dinner; there are so many good restaurants within an easy walk that there's no need. People usually name the Chalfonte, Maureen's, and the Mad Batter among their favorites. One respondent did note that "many of Cape May's best restaurants do not have liquor licenses, a fact which we were dismayed to learn after we'd been seated for dinner." We suggest you ask when making reservations, and, if necessary, stop by a liquor store on your way to dinner.

Activities in Cape May include swimming, fishing, birding and bike riding on the town's flat roads, and, of course, touring the Victorian mansions. The Mid-Atlantic Center for the Arts sponsors walking tours, summer theater, and special Victorian programs. The walking tours are a special treat; many are guided by the innkeepers of the establishments listed below. A number of the most famous inns serve afternoon tea along with an afternoon tour; we recommend that you give it a try. Many special events are sponsored at Christmas time; call the Chamber of Commerce (609–884–5404), or ask your favorite inn for details.

Most guest houses require a two- to three-night minimum stay on weekends and holidays during the spring, summer, and fall. Quite a few inns restrict smoking; this number has risen in recent years because of strict state fire regulations. Be prepared for parking problems during the summer; once you find a spot, leave the car and forget it until it's time to go home. Peak season crowds also create noise, as people walk around at night from place to place; if you want a more peaceful visit, we urge you to visit before Memorial Day or after Labor Day. Keep in mind that few of these inns are air-conditioned. Although ceiling fans and the ocean breezes are normally cool enough for comfort, if you hit a real August heat wave, you will be hot. Most inns in Cape May provide an outside shower, and refrigerators for guest use.

Also recommended: The Abbey (Columbia Avenue and Gurney Street; 609–884–4506), a striking Victorian was built in 1869, and has been authentically restored and decorated in period. The **Abigail Adams B&B** (12 Jackson Street; 609–884–1371) is a casual, comfortable B&B, just 100 yards from the beach. **The Brass Bed** (719 Columbia Avenue; 609–884–8075) is a Carpenter Gothic cottage. Rooms are decorated in period, with you-know-what-kind of beds; rates include a full breakfast and afternoon tea. The **Chalfonte** (301 Howard Street; 609–884–8409) is the oldest hotel in Cape May, and is the kind of old-fashioned resort that families return to generation after generation. The rooms are very basic, but the atmosphere and food are exceptional. **Columns by the Sea** (1513 Beach Drive; 609–884–2228) is a brick mansion with fluted columns, colonial revival accents, and a touch of Italian palazzo, just across the road from the ocean in East Cape May; rates include a full breakfast and afternoon tea. **The Duke of Windsor Inn** (817 Washington Street; 609–884–1366) is a Queen Anne Victorian mansion, with hand-crafted woodwork, tiled fireplaces, Tiffany stained glass, and elaborate plaster ceiling medallions. The **Gingerbread House** (28 Gurney Street; 609–884–0211), built in 1869, is decorated with period furnishings and lace curtains, highlighted by the owners' photography and shell collections. The **Manor House** (612 Hughes Street; 609–884–4710) was built in the classic colonial revival/American shingle style, and is decorated with late Victorian pieces and period wallpapers. A filling, creative breakfast and afternoon tea are included in the rates, along with lots of extras. **The Seventh Sister** (10 Jackson Street; 609–884–2280) offers very reasonable rates, Victorian summer decor, and many rooms with a view of the nearby ocean. The **White Dove Cottage** (619 Hughes Street; 609–884–0613) was built in the Second Empire style, with a mansard roof faced with original hand-cut octagonal slate tiles; breakfasts are lavish, the decor light and airy.

Cape May is at the southernmost tip of New Jersey, 3½ hours from New York and Washington, 2 hours (90 miles) from Philadelphia, and 38 miles south of Atlantic City. To get there, follow the Garden State Parkway to the very end, when it becomes Lafayette Street. From the south, take the ferry from Lewes, Delaware; call (302) 645–6313 for information.

The Mainstay   *Tel:* (609) 884–8690
635 Columbia Avenue

There are wonderful inns in Cape May, and then there is The Mainstay, which really is in a class by itself. It's one of those "velvet rope" inns—the kind with furnishings you'd normally only see, and not touch, in a museum. Although the environment is a bit intimidating at first, the owners' goal is to offer a relaxing, fun vacation experience. Innkeepers Tom and Sue Carroll were pioneers in Cape May's redevelopment, having opened The Mainstay in 1971.

The Mainstay was built in 1872 as a private club for wealthy gentlemen gamblers. They spared no expense; the villa was complete with 14-foot ceilings, ornate plaster moldings, and lavish furnishings, many of which are still in place today. Some, such as the 14-foot-high hall mirror, would be virtually impossible to move. Last year, in one of the Carrolls' latest projects to improve the inn, all rooms were provided with a private bath en suite.

Advance reservations are imperative at The Mainstay, at least several months ahead for summer weekends. Rates include a full breakfast in spring and fall (continental in summer), and afternoon refreshments. If you're staying elsewhere in Cape May, stop at The Mainstay at 4 P.M. on Tuesdays, Thursdays, Saturdays, or Sundays for a tour of the downstairs rooms, and afternoon tea.

"Our travels have taken us around the world, and rarely do we return to the same place, with the exception of The Mainstay. Sue and Tom Carroll are superb innkeepers. Their knowledge of and commitment to Victoriana is infectious and they welcome guests as friends, but balance that with a perfectly run hostelry. Sue's home-baked goodies at breakfast and afternoon tea are real treats. Tom brews the frosty iced tea.

"On each visit we have chosen a different room and enjoyed its individual decor. It would be hard to name our favorite. The elegance of The Mainstay is matched by the charm of The Cottage, next door. They are connected by a lovely garden, and guests may use the common areas of both houses. The large rooms are authentically decorated, beautifully furnished with choice Victorian pieces yet very comfortable for relaxing." *(Dr. & Mrs. Robert E. Dunn)*

"Breakfast on the veranda is the key event of the day. During the hour or so of serious munching, Tom and Sue make sure that no inquiries relative to what's going on around town, or who is serving the best soft-shell crabs, go unanswered. Everyone compares notes on last night's dining or carousing and plans their day accordingly—browning at the beach, napping on the oversize veranda swings, or sauntering downtown for a book." *(John & Linda Kelleher)*

Open Mid-March to mid-Dec.
Rooms 3 suites, 9 doubles, all with private shower and/or bath. 10 with desk, all with fans. 6 rooms in Cottage.
Facilities Dining room, library, music room, parlor, veranda. Flower garden with fountain, croquet, swings. Beach passes; 2 blocks to ocean.
Location Historic district, 3 blocks to center, 2 blocks to beach. Turn left at first light after Canal Bridge, then right 3 blocks later onto Columbia.
Restrictions No smoking. No children under 12. On-street parking tight in summer. Occasional street noise in summer.
Credit cards None accepted.
Rates B&B, $95–130 suite, $80–120 double, $70–110 single. Extra person in room, $20. 3-night minimum stay, June–Sept.

The Queen Victoria
102 Ocean Street

Tel: (609) 884–8702

The Queen Victoria was built in 1881 and was restored 100 years later as a B&B inn by Dane and Joan Wells, innkeepers. They have decorated the rooms with authentic Victorian furnishings, attractive wallpapers and quilts, and antique iron, brass, and four-poster beds. The Wellses take their innkeeping seriously; they are very involved in the operation of their inn and most knowledgeable about the town's activities.

"Joan and Dane were attentive without being cloying; they are pleasant and informative conversationalists and excellent sources of knowledge and lore about both the area in particular and Victoriana in general. Breakfast is an exceptionally pleasant time, with the guests and innkeepers gathered around the dining room table exchanging views and eating . . . and eating. Breakfast includes one egg dish, one fruit dish, several breads, homemade granola, juices, and plenty of coffee and tea. Tea, with little sandwiches, is served in the afternoon. Two wonderful cats mingle among the guests and add to the atmosphere. The inn is within walking distance of most of Cape May's attractions; you can park your car and not use it for your entire stay." *(Sharon & Michael Henry)*

"Among the little but influential niceties that we have particularly enjoyed is the fact that we always returned to a freshened room, regardless of what time of day or evening we left it. Also, the turndown treat of semisweet chocolate was one of the best around." *(Laura & Thomas McMillan)*
"Especially appealing were the free bicycles, beach tags, and equipment." *(Sandra S. Grant)* "The whole inn is spotlessly clean. Even under the tub in the bathroom not a drop of dirt was to be found." *(Judith Jacobs.)*

We've had extremely positive feedback on the Queen Vic; only the plumbing was rated by a guest as being just "adequate," hardly a fault in a building of this vintage; another would have liked just one TV somewhere in the house to watch a key game or political event, while a third pointed out that the street can be a bit noisy at night, especially Thursdays; all of these guests were otherwise totally delighted and plan to return.

Open All year.
Rooms 7 suites, 17 doubles—20 with private bath and/or shower. 4 rooms have sink

in room with maximum of 4 sharing bath; some rooms have desk, refrigerator, air-conditioning, fan. Suites in adjacent carriage house & cottage with telephone, TV, air-conditioning, kitchenette.

Facilities Dining rooms, parlor with fireplace, parlor with TV, library of books on Victoriana. Victorian flower garden, beach passes, chairs, towels; beach shower with changing room, bicycles. Limited on-site parking for extra fee; free parking 5 blocks away.

Location Historic district, 1 block to beach, 2 blocks to shops. Turn left at second stoplight off of Lafayette St. onto Ocean St. The inn is 3 blocks down on the right.

Restrictions No smoking except in library in inclement weather only. No toddlers; infants or older children in suites only.

Credit cards MC, Visa.

Rates B&B, $130–180 suite, $75–125 double, $10 single discount. Extra person in room, $10. Winter packages. 2- to 4-night weekend minimum.

Extras 1 room equipped for disabled. 1 block to bus. Cribs, babysitting, beach toys available. French, some Spanish spoken.

The Wooden Rabbit
Tel: (609) 884–7293
609 Hughes Street

Although a few other Cape May inns tolerate children, The Wooden Rabbit is the only B&B in Cape May (to our knowledge) that actually welcomes children of all ages. Owners Greg and Debby Burow explain: "We have a comfortable (unbreakable) country decor that is practical for children but is still very special for adults. We have two young sons of our own who enjoy being playmates, but we try to keep them out of the way of adult guests." In a high Victorian town, The Wooden Rabbit is also unusual in that it was built by a sea captain in 1838; Robert E. Lee spent summers here, and the house was also used by the Underground Railroad.

"The Wooden Rabbit is a cozy inn, decorated in countrylike cheeriness with Peter Rabbit collectibles throughout. Just 1½ blocks from the beach and close to the shopping mall and antiquestores, this inn is very convenient to all attractions—park your car on arrival, and your feet can do the rest. Our room was spacious and spotless, decorated in small country prints with coordinating borders. Lovely handmade accents—quilts, pillows, and wall hangings—highlight the decor; the furnishings are mainly wicker, except for the beds and bureaus. Our suite had a sitting room, which accommodated our children nicely.

"A buffet-style breakfast is served from 8:00 to 9:30 A.M. and consisted of homemade blueberry muffins, quiche (a different variety daily), fresh fruit salad or apple crisp, orange juice, and a delicious granola cereal blend. Coffee and an assortment of herbal teas topped off the meal. While the children recall the piece of fudge left on their pillows in the evening, I remember fondly the clip-clop of the horses going past the inn and the aroma of fresh-baked breakfast goodies emerging from the kitchen." *(Beverly Lang)*

Open All year.

Rooms 1 suite, 2 doubles, all with private bath and/or shower, TV, air-conditioning, fan.

Facilities Dining room with fireplace, living room with fireplace, enclosed sun porch. Flower garden with sandbox, outside shower. Beach passes, off-street parking.

Location In historic district, 2 blocks from beach. From Lafayette St., turn left on Franklin St., then right onto Hughes St.

Restrictions No smoking.

Credit cards MC, Visa (for deposits only).
Rates B&B, $80–125 suite, $65–105 double. Extra person in room, $15. Thanksgiving, Christmas packages available. Minimum stay requirements.

LAMBERTVILLE 08530   Map 3

Information please: We'd like reports on **York Street House**, a turn-of-the-century home built by a local coal baron that offers six elegantly furnished bedrooms (42 York Street 08530; 609–397–3007); those who'd like a larger establishment might prefer the **Inn at Lambertville Station**, a country hotel and restaurant (11 Bridge Street 08530; 609–397–4400).

Chimney Hill Farm   *Tel:* (609) 397–1516
Goat Hill Road

A quiet river town just across the Delaware from New Hope, Lambertville has much of the same bucolic scenery, with a fraction of Bucks County's summer hustle and bustle. Chimney Hill Farm began as a small farmhouse in 1820, but was greatly expanded in 1927, giving it the imposing presence of a stone manor house. In 1988 it was bought by Frederick Root, Kenneth Turi, and Dorothy McGinley, and owes much of its distinctive furnishings—highlighted by chintz florals and antiques—to the fact that it was decorated as a designer showcase prior to opening as a B&B. Rates include a breakfast of freshly squeezed orange juice, homemade muffins, and jam made from the farm's own raspberries, as well as extras like fresh flowers, all-cotton sheets, robes, and a continual supply of coffee, tea, soda, snacks and ice.

"Beautiful place; the innkeepers are delightful and attentive yet not overbearing." *(Rochelle Mason)*

Open All year.
Rooms 5 doubles, all with private bath and/or shower. 2 with fireplaces, 1 with porch.
Facilities Dining room with fireplace, sun room with fireplace, guest pantry. 10 acres with gardens, terraces, greenhouse.
Location 1½ hours W of NYC, 45 min. N of Philadelphia. ½ m to town. From town, go S on River Rd. to Swan St. Turn left on Swan St. to Studdiford–Goat Hill Rd., inn on left.
Restrictions No smoking. No children under 13.
Credit cards Amex, MC, Visa.
Rates B&B, $75–135 double. 2–night weekend minimum. Corporate, long-term rates.

SPRING LAKE 07762   Map 3

Spring Lake is one of New Jersey's most pleasant shore towns. It offers a 2-mile-long boardwalk (with no commercial facilities) for strolling along the ocean; wide, tree-lined streets, with many turn-of-the-century houses; and, in the center of town, a lovely lake, surrounded by a park. Outdoor activities include golf, tennis, horseback riding, and canoeing. Joggers will enjoy the path around the lake or the boardwalk. Peak season in Spring Lake extends from Memorial Day through mid- to late September. The town is located in Monmouth County, 1½ hours south of New York City, 1½ hours north of Philadelphia and Atlantic City. Take Exit 98 off Garden State Parkway to Route 34. Go 1½ miles to traffic circle and go left on Route 524 (Allaire Rd.). Go east on Route 524 for 3 miles into town.

Also recommended: The **Ashling Cottage** (106 Sussex Avenue; 201–449–3553) is a mansard-roofed Victorian built in 1877, and offers sunken bathrooms, private porches, scrumptious breakfasts, lace curtains, cool ocean breezes, and friendly, helpful hosts. **The Chateau** (500 Warren Avenue at Fifth; 201–974–2000) combines turn-of-the-century atmosphere with modern amenities. Nestled between two parks and overlooking the lake, rooms are done in colorful contemporary florals and wicker.

Information please: We like reports on **Hollycroft** (506 North Boulevard, South Belmar, 07719; 201–681–2254). Located in nearby South Belmar, the Hollycroft's log beams and columns, knotty pine walls, and massive stone fireplace will remind you of a mountain lodge.

The Normandy Inn
21 Tuttle Avenue

Tel: (201) 449–7172

The Normandy Inn was built as a private home in 1888, and was moved to its present site in the early 1900s. Michael and Susan Ingino have owned the inn since 1982, and have decorated it with period wallpaper and furniture. White wicker tables and chairs furnish the wraparound porch; antique clocks, stained glass lamps, and gilded mirrors grace the parlor; and brass, walnut, and mahogany beds can be found in most of the bedrooms. The Inginos also restored the outside of the house, painting it with accurate Victorian colors—shades of green, burgundy, and terra-cotta. Breakfast items are featured on a menu, with guests choosing their favorite style of eggs, omelets, or pancakes—blueberry, chocolate chip, or pecan.

"Anytime you go 60 miles out of your way to stay at an inn for one or two nights, that says something about the inn—its innkeepers, location, food, and calm and beautiful surroundings—only a block from the Spring Lake boardwalk. Where else can you get porridge to go along with an outstanding full breakfast—served in a fine dining room with classical music—extremely courteous waitresses, and a fine presentation by the chef-owner? Others enjoy the two large TV's in the living room and family room, the VCR and library. The inn is extremely clean, from its antiques to its six-foot towels." *(Bill Wagner)*

"Susan and Mike are friendly and most gracious in meeting your every need. The inn is clean and comfortable, pleasant and homey. Mike's breakfast will hold you till dinner if you let it. The pancakes are the size of the plate and the freshly baked muffins are a perfect way to start the day." *(Bob & Bonnie Larson)*

Open All year.
Rooms 15 doubles, 2 singles, all with private bath and/or shower, radio, air-conditioning. 2-bedroom apartment in separate building.
Facilities 2 parlor areas, with TV. Dining room, open and enclosed porches, flower gardens, bicycles. Beach is 4 houses away. Golf, tennis, horseback riding, fishing, and thoroughbred racing nearby. Parking for ½ of guests on property, remainder at beach.
Location 1½ hrs. from NYC, Atlantic City, and Philadelphia. 4 blocks from town. Take Rte. 524 E to Ocean Ave. Go right 1 block and right again on Tuttle.

Restrictions No smoking in dining room. Limited parking.
Credit cards Amex, MC, Visa. 5% discount for checks, cash.
Rates B&B, $75–127 double. $18 per additional adult in room. Child under 12 in room, $1 per year of age additional; family of four needs 2 rooms. 2- to 4-night weekend minimum stays. 15% discount for 7-day stays. Full breakfast for outside guests, $6.50.
Extras Station pickups available. Cribs available.

We Want to Hear from You!

As you know, this book is only effective with your help. We really need to know about your experiences and discoveries.

If you stayed at an inn or hotel listed here, we want to know how it was. Did it live up to our description? Exceed it? Was it what you expected? Did you like it? Were you disappointed? Delighted?

Have you discovered new establishments that we should add to the next edition?

Tear out one of the report forms at the back of this book (or use your own stationery if you prefer) and write today. Even if you write only "Fully endorse existing entry" you will have been most helpful.

Thank You!

Key to Abbreviations

For complete information and explanations, please see the Introduction.

Rates: Range from least expensive room in low season to most expensive room in peak season.
Room only: No meals included; sometimes referred to as European Plan (EP).
B&B: Bed and breakfast; includes breakfast, sometimes afternoon/evening refreshment.
MAP: Modified American Plan; includes breakfast and dinner.
Full board: Three meals daily.
Alc lunch: À la carte lunch; average price of entrée plus nonalcoholic drink, tax, tip.
Alc dinner: Average price of three-course dinner, including half bottle of house wine, tax, tip.
Prix fixe dinner: Three- to five-course set dinner, excluding wine, tax, tip unless otherwise noted.
Extras: Noted if available. Always confirm in advance. Pets are not permitted unless specified.
Zip codes: If only one zip code applies, it is listed with the town name. If there is more than one, it is noted as part of the address.

New Mexico

Casa del Galvilan, Cimarron

New Mexico is a land of contrast and contradiction. Prehistoric Indians lived here 12,000 years ago; the first atomic bomb was detonated near Alamogordo 45 years ago. Flat desert plains are broken by high mountains and ski areas. Most intriguing are the Indian, Spanish, and Anglo cultures that have coexisted for centuries but have retained their unique heritages, art, and architecture.

Sample different parts of the state to fully experience these contradictions. In southern New Mexico, explore Carlsbad Caverns; climb the 40-foot dunes at White Sands National Monument; ski the Sacramento Mountains; drive through the largest pecan grove in the world, past fields of cotton and hot red peppers. To retrace the state's Indian heritage, visit the modern Mescalero Reservation, examine the thousand-year-old Three Rivers petroglyphs, and inspect the Gila Cliff Dwellings dating from A.D. 400. In fall or winter, stop at Bosque del Apache National Wildlife Refuge to see sandhill cranes, snow geese, and, if you're lucky, whooping cranes.

Seventeenth-century Spanish influence begins in the central part of the state; take Route 14 north from Mountainair through Albuquerque to Santa Fe. This winding, scenic back road goes through still-occupied old Spanish settlements of crumbling adobe and past nineteenth-century mining towns. Stop in Albuquerque to see Old Town and the Indian Pueblo Cultural Center.

Northern New Mexico, best known for Santa Fe and Taos, is the crossroads for diverse cultures and arresting scenery. The spectacular "High Road" from Santa Fe to Taos (Routes 4, 76, and 3) reaches over 9,000 feet in altitude and passes through small Spanish villages (Chimayo, Cordova, Truchas) noted since the sixteenth century for their weaving and woodcarving. For an intriguing sample of prehistoric pueblo ruins, visit Chaco Canyon National Historic Park in northwest New Mexico. Closer to the

423

Rio Grande see the cliff dwellings of Bandelier National Monument and the numerous valley pueblos still occupied by descendants of ancient Indians. Farther north, ski and backpack in the Sangre de Cristo Mountains, or visit the beautiful Rio Grande Gorge National Recreation Area.

Information please: Although you've told us about some delightful resort towns to enjoy on vacation, we'd like to have some recommendations for **Albuquerque.** Considering its current population of over 500,000 we're sure there must be some! We've heard that the **Sheraton Old Town** (800–325–3535) is both well located and distinctive architecturally; reports? **La Posada de Albuquerque** (800–621–7231), a 114-room hotel listed on the National Register of Historic Places, is another possibility—it was built by Conrad Hilton in 1939, and has been restored in Spanish/New Mexico style.

On a more intimate scale, two appealing Albuquerque B&Bs include the **Mauger Estate,** a Queen Anne Victorian built in 1902 and listed on the National Register of Historic Places; rooms are decorated in period, with private baths. The inn is located halfway between the downtown area and historic Old Town (701 Roma Ave. NW 87102; 505–242–8755). For a more rural experience try the **Casita Chamisa** (850 Chamisal Rd. NW; 505–897–4644), a restored 19th-century adobe home with Mexican furnishings, homemade jellies and sourdough bread, along with an indoor pool and Jacuzzi; the home is built over an Indian archaeological site. For an additional area listing, see the entry for the **Corrales Inn,** in Corrales, 14 miles north of Albuquerque.

One reader couldn't resist mentioning a favorite Albuquerque restaurant, Stephen's, on Central Avenue: "Soothing decor, delicious food, relaxed service—even the ladies' room is elegant." *(SW)*

Reader tip: "If you're driving south from Albuquerque on I-25, stop at Gil's Café in Belen for coffee and home-baked goodies. A great place."

Rates do not include state and local taxes of approximately 5 to 8.6%.

ALTO 88312   Map 12

Sierra Mesa Lodge   *Tel:* (505) 336–4515
Fort Stanton Road, P.O. Box 463

Quite a few guests at the Sierra Mesa Lodge wrote in to express their pleasure with this B&B, opened in 1987, giving it the highest marks for outstanding cleanliness, good-to-excellent lighting in both the guest rooms and baths, and first-rate plumbing, along with plaudits for good food and gracious hospitality:

"Owners Larry and Lila Goodman are genuinely interested in their guests. They receive you as if you're part of the family, offering cake and coffee in the afternoon, wine and cheese in the evening. The lodge is spotless, and each of the five guest rooms has been individually decorated with top-of-the-line furnishings, down comforters, and linens, according to a different theme: Victorian, country western, Oriental, French country, and Queen Anne. All are beautifully done, with art, wall hangings, and pillows that complete the theme. The living room is a large comfortable area where all the guests can sit and visit." *(Orm & Karen Ellis, and others)*

"Extra-nice light fixtures (plenty of them and in the right places), ample hot water, no parking problems, great location, and peaceful view of mountains." *(Mary R. Clark)*

"The outstanding breakfasts are different every day; one started with warm fruit compote, orange juice, and coffee, and then the largest, most delicious popover, cut and filled with savory scrambled eggs served with sausages, sliced tomatoes, and more popovers with strawberry butter." *(Joy & William Maxwell)* "We stayed in the Queen Anne room, which had a high poster bed with a crocheted canopy, fresh white lace sheets and pillow cases, flowered wallpaper, and a window seat overlooking the woods. For breakfast, Lila served Belgian waffles with strawberries and whipped cream." *(Susan Banta)* "My husband is a diabetic, and they insisted on making something special for his breakfast." *(DB)*

"Extra touches include the robes and toiletries provided for guest use and the little loaf of homemade bread to take with you when you leave." *(Virginia & Alan Burke)* "Along with a supply of menus, the Goodmans keep a book of comments by other guests on the area restaurants." *(Mrs. Joseph Peters)* "We went to La Lorraine for dinner, and found the service and food to be very good. The atmosphere is very homey, especially with their dog Magnum." *(NP)*

"The lodge is two miles from the main road, well away from the noise and traffic of skiers in winter and horseracing fans in summer. The short courtesy ride to the airport makes it an ideal get away for private pilots." *(Elsie & Karen McCague)* "Paradise is what came to mind as I soaked in the Jacuzzi, overlooking the towering snowclad pine trees topped by a clear blue sky." *(Arlene & Allen Smith)*

Open All year.

Rooms 5 doubles—1 with full private bath, 4 with private shower.

Facilities Dining room, living room with fireplace, game room, spa room, deck. 2½ acres with walking trails. Fishing, golf, hunting, tennis, hiking, horseracing and riding nearby. 14 miles to downhill skiing (Ski Apache).

Location S central NM. 180 m SE of Albuquerque, 125 m NNE of El Paso. Take I-70 to Ruidoso, then go N on Rte. 37 6 m to Alto. Turn right (E) on Ft. Stanton Rd. 2 m to inn on left.

Restrictions No smoking. No children under 14.

Credit cards MC, Visa.

Rates B&B, $75 double, $65 single. 2–3 night holiday minimum.

Extras Airport/station pickups.

BRAZOS   Map 12

Casa de Martinez   *Tel:* (505) 588–7858
Old U.S. Rte. 84
Mailing address: P.O Box 96, Los Ojos 87551

A double adobe dwelling dating back to 1869, the Casa de Martinez is located in the village of Brazos (where the rivers fork), with a view of the El Chorro waterfall. The B&B is run by a great-granddaughter of the

Martinez family, early settlers in this area. Rates include a breakfast of coffee, cereal, eggs and sausage, fruit, juice, and pastry.

"A 'must stop' for anyone who cares to be at total peace. Situated between the rivers Chama and Los Brazos, the most northern port of New Mexico, Señora Sanchez has opened her home and created a marvelous B&B." *(Deborah Rahal)*

Open Feb. through Oct.
Rooms 1 suite, 6 doubles—3 with private bath, 4 with maximum of 4 people sharing 1 bath. 1 with balcony, 1 with fireplace.
Facilities Dining room, 2 sitting rooms, den with TV, courtyard with waterwell, flowerbeds. Fishing, hunting, cross-country skiing nearby.
Location N central NM, near Colorado border.
Restrictions Smoking permitted in one guest room only.
Credit cards None accepted.
Rates B&B, $55–65. Extra person in room, $6.
Extras Wheelchair accessible.

Corkins Lodge   *Tel:* (505) 588-7261
Highway 512
Mailing address: P.O. Box 396 Chama 87520

High in the mountains of northern New Mexico, Corkins Lodge is surrounded by pine, fir, and aspen trees. Rugged gray cliffs rise more than 2,000 feet, while a waterfall plunges into the valley below. In operation since 1929, the lodge has been run by John and Nino Trujillo since 1981.

"Corkins Lodge is not for everyone, but if you have ever imagined yourself in a log cabin with a river roaring nearby and tame deer eating apples from your hand—then this place is for you. The cabins come equipped with basic provisions, but you supply your own groceries. Our cabin had three tiny bedrooms, a kitchen, and one bath. Everything was spotlessly clean. The river and lake are well stocked with fish. My husband caught several trout, which we cooked according to John and his father Nino's advice. The Trujillos are excellent hosts, who were most accommodating about any needs we had." *(Yvonne Miller)*

Open All year.
Rooms 15 cabins with bath, full kitchen, charcoal grill. 1 cabin with 2 baths. 7 cabins open in winter.
Facilities Main lodge, game room, heated pool. 738 acres with hiking, cross-country skiing, and snowmobiling trails, river and lake for trout fishing.
Location N central New Mexico. 100 m NE of Santa Fe. From Hwy 84 in Brazos, turn E on Hwy 512. Go 7 m until rd. ends at lodge.
Credit cards MC, Visa.
Rates Room only, $80–140 cabin (sleeps 4-10). Extra person $8.
Extras Airport pickups.

CHIMAYO 87522   **Map 12**

La Posada de Chimayo   *Tel:* (505) 351–4605
P.O. Box 463

"This lovely adobe guest house is located way up a dirt road dotted with small adobe houses, horses, cacti, and even wild bunnies. Although it has only two suites in a separate house, it is a very special place indeed. It's been owned by Sue Farrington since 1981. Each suite has a living room with a traditional corner fireplace, viga (hand-hewn ceiling beams) ceilings, tile floors, leather table and chairs; there's a separate cozy bedroom and bath, and a shared front porch with swings. Mexican art is everywhere, along with books about New Mexico and Indian artists.

"In between the two units is a kitchen where Sue prepares breakfast and brings it to your room. Ours consisted of fresh juice, coffee/tea, huge fluffy omelets stuffed with potatoes and chiles and garnished with sour cream, plus sausage, rolls, jam.

"Chimayo is a wonderful little Spanish mountain town with three weaving shops—Ortega's has been here since the early 1700s, and Trujillo's has been here for about four generations; Centinela is also an excellent shop." (SC)

"While in Chimayo, be sure to visit the Sanctuario, an old church filled with folk art and religious icons, then have lunch or dinner at the Rancho de Chimayo. They serve some of New Mexico's best sopapillas." (Gail Gottleib)

Open All year.
Rooms 2 suites in guest house, each with living room, private shower, desk.
Facilities Sunny and shaded decks, porch. Hiking, skiing nearby.
Location N central NM. 30 m N of Santa Fe on the High Road (Rte. 76) to Taos. 1 m from Rte. 76 to inn. Turn N off 76 onto Gravel Rd. opposite Manzana Center. Bear right at fork, past El Chimayo weavers, and continue bearing right to La Posada.
Restrictions "Children over 12 preferred."
Credit cards MC, Visa accepted for deposits only.
Rates B&B, $75 suite. Extra person in room, $20. Weekly rate in winter. Minimum stay during holidays, fiestas.
Extras Pets accepted with prior approval. Spanish spoken.

CIMARRON 87714   Map 12

We don't know if Cimarron, Spanish for "wild" and "unbroken," refers to the untamed stream which ran through town, or to the inhabitants, but it's clear that Cimarron typified the "Wild Wild West" of the late 1800s. A local paper once reported that "Things are quiet in Cimarron. Nobody has been killed in three days." A mecca for the infamous outlaws of the day (Billy the Kid and Blackjack Ketchum both lived here for a time before things settled down towards the end of the century), Cimarron is set on the Santa Fe trail, 3½ hours northeast of Albuquerque, 2½ hours northeast of Santa Fe, and 1 hour west of Taos.

Casa del Galvilan   *Tel:* (505) 376–2246
Route 21, P.O. Box 518

Imagine a white adobe dwelling, nestled in the foothills of the Sangre de Cristo Mountains, surrounded by seemingly endless land and sky, and you will have a good idea of the Casa del Galvilan, House of the Hawk. Harriet Faudree opened her home as a B&B in 1988; it had been a working ranch for the previous 20 years. The house was built in the early 1900s in traditional adobe style, with vigas, twelve-foot ceilings, and eighteen-inch walls. Rooms are furnished with southwestern antiques and handmade furniture; rates include a breakfast of fruit and juice, eggs and breakfast meats, as well as afternoon refreshments. Guests enjoy hiking, bird watching, and exploring the historic sights of the Santa Fe trail. *(MW)*

"Warm atmosphere, prompt service, excellent accommodations, and good food. The manager and staff made us feel special." *(Mrs. Lloyd Pool)* "Quiet, peaceful, restful and relaxing. Rooms are large, comfortable, clean, and well lit. Decorated with handsome Western art." *(Mary Wilson)* "Breathtaking views. Betty Knox knows how to please, and keeps trying all the time." *(DD)* "A perfect contrast to the bustle of Santa Fe." *(JJ)* "Spectacular setting. Noteworthy attention to detail." *(David Van Hulsteyn)*

Open All year.
Rooms 1 suite, 6 doubles—5 with private bath and/or shower, 2 with a maximum of 4 people sharing bath. 3 with fan.
Facilities Dining room, living room with fireplace, TV, library; porches. 250 acres with hiking, bird watching. 6 m to Cimarron River, 28 m to skiing.
Location From Cimarron, turn S on Rte. 21 and continue 6 m to inn on right.
Restrictions No smoking. "Well behaved, older children are welcome."
Credit cards Amex, MC, Visa.
Rates B&B, $95 suite, $70 double, $55 single. Extra person in room, $10. Family rates.
Extras Airport/station pickups, for fee. Crib, babysitting available.

St. James Hotel   *Tel:* (505) 376–2664
Corner of Routes 58 & 21, RR 1, Box 2

They say that ghostly happenings are not unknown at the St. James Hotel; perhaps it's connected to the fact that 26 men were killed within its two-foot thick adobe walls. Ed and Pat Sitzberger restored and reopened the long-shuttered hotel in 1985, but left intact the original tin ceiling in the dining room, complete with bullet holes. Cimarron was a key stop on the Santa Fe Trail, and other famous (and infamous) guests at this hotel included Jesse James and Wyatt Earp; here Buffalo Bill Cody met Annie Oakley to plan his Wild West Shows. Today, rooms in the original hotel (dating to 1880) are furnished with Victorian antiques; a modern motel annex is also available. The hotel has both a full service restaurant serving continental cuisine and a coffee shop.

"Wonderful rooms both in hotel and motel sections. Great food, reasonably priced, with exciting events in the evening as well. The staff and owners are very nice and informative about local history. The setting in the Sangre de Cristos Mountains is beautiful. The ambience is romantic, even with an occasional guest ghost." *(Jenny Frizzle)*

Open All year.
Rooms 4 suites, 24 doubles—22 with full private bath, 2 with a maximum of 4 people sharing bath. All with fan. 12 annex rooms with telephone, TV, desk.
Facilities Restaurant, coffee shop, parlor, bar/lounge with billiard table. Patio, unheated swimming pool. Trout fishing, hunting nearby. 35 m to skiing.
Location NE NM. Center of town.
Credit cards MC, Visa.
Rates Room only: in hotel, $75 suite, $65 double; in annex, $35–37 double. Extra person in room, $3. 10% senior discount. "Murder Mystery" weekend packages. Alc breakfast, $3–5; alc lunch, $5; alc dinner, $25.
Extras Pets permitted in annex only. Spanish spoken.

CLOUDCROFT 88317   Map 12

The Lodge   *Tel:* (505) 682–2566
P.O. Box 497

Originally constructed in 1899 by the Alamogordo and Sacramento Mountain Railway to help house those involved in the railroad's search for timber to make railway ties, Cloudcroft quickly became a successful mountain retreat for thousands of overheated Texans. It remains one today; although the resident population is about 500, summer and winter visitors number in the thousands.

Although the lodge was destroyed in a disastrous fire in 1909, it was rebuilt in 1911 on its current site. Since then it has undergone many renovations—most recently those undertaken by partners Jerry and Carole Sanders, who purchased the inn in 1983—but its basic appearance remains almost unchanged. One of the inn's most prominent features is a five-story copper-clad tower with views stretching from the snow-covered pines to snow-white White Sands. The lodge's restaurant, Rebecca's, is named after the resident ghost: A beautiful young woman with blue eyes and red hair, she disappeared when her lumberjack lover found her in the arms of another.

"Friendly and efficient service. The owners' pride is conveyed by the keen interest they've taken in restoring this historic property. The inn is very well kept, with no lighting or plumbing problems. Even when surprise snowstorms occur, the staff is out at the crack of dawn making sure that parking areas are well plowed. The half-hour drive from Alamagordo is scenic in four seasons." *(William Hauprich)* More comments please.

Open All year.
Rooms 7 suites, 26 doubles, 14 singles—27 with full private bath, 20 with shower only; all with telephone, radio, TV. 3 townhouses, with 1 to 3 bedrooms.
Facilities Dining rooms, saloon with music and dancing, lounge. 50 acres with 9-hole golf course, heated pool, hot tub, cross-country skiing. Tennis, downhill skiing, fishing nearby.
Location S central NM, in Sacramento Mts. 19 m E of Alamogordo, 107 m NNE of El Paso, TX. Take Hwy. 82 to Cloudcroft, turn at US Forest Office. ¼ m from town.
Credit cards Amex, MC, Visa.
Rates Room only, $100–150 suite, $65–85 double. Extra person in room, $7.50. No charge for children under 12. Alc breakfast, $3–6; alc lunch, $8; alc dinner, $32. Golf, ski packages.
Extras Airport/station pickups available at extra charge. Cribs, babysitting, play equipment available. Spanish spoken.

CORRALES 87048   Map 12

Corrales Inn   *Tel:* (505) 897–4422
Plaza San Ysidro, P.O. Box 1361

The pueblo village of Corrales stands sleepily in the desert sun, much as it did when the conquistadors passed through several hundred years ago.

The Corrales Inn has been owned by Mary Briault and Laura Warren since 1986. They note that "we most enjoy guests who like to talk about books and their travels." The inn is a traditional adobe structure, with an enclosed courtyard and fountain. A highlight is its 2,000-volume library, with books on the Southwest, European and American literature, Eastern and Western philosophy, mystery, poetry, and more. The inn's restaurant serves French country cuisine from a menu that changes daily. Seafood is always fresh, and a typical dinner might include the house pâté, Normandy-style chicken, and a raspberry cream tart. A Corrales breakfast of eggs, bacon, potatoes, fruit, and croissant will fuel you for a day of sightseeing; nearby attractions include Bosque, a bird sanctuary; the reconstructed Indian settlement at Coronado State Park to the north; Albuquerque to the south; and the volcanic hills to the west.

"Co-owners Laura Warren and Mary Briault together possess high levels of culture, good taste, warm hospitality, erudition, and culinary expertise. The heart of the inn is the library, with comfortable seating and walls of loanable books on a wide variety of subjects. A selection from an impressive collection of classical music can usually be heard at any civilized hour. The decor includes antique furniture, painting, sculpture, primitive masks, Renaissance medals, and more, all collected by the owners. Each guest room has a different theme; I stayed in the Japanese room, but also had a look at a very attractive Southwestern room. My accommodations were spotless, the bed extremely comfortable, large fluffy towels were provided fresh each day, and one could control the air-conditioning and ventilation levels. The lighting and plumbing are both modern and of high quality. The well water is slightly sulfurous, and guests may prefer bottled water for drinking.

"The atmosphere of the inn is cordial but laissez faire—at registration you are given a key to your own room and front door. If you want to be alone, the adobe walls ensure a quiet which may fool you into thinking there are no other guests. On the other hand, should you wish, information on day trips, local events and shopping, or simply fascinating and wide-ranging conversation are all available.

"Parking is provided in an adjacent lot, and all meals are taken in a separate building 200 yards away. Breakfast is a meal to be reckoned with. Ramon, the breakfast chef, takes pride in preparing ample, imaginative, and well-cooked meals that will hold most people until evening. Mary Briault is the dinner chef. There is a short menu of essentially French/continental cuisine; the ingredients are all fresh and everything is superbly cooked. Lastly, the inn has the great advantage of being in an unspoiled and delightful community just ten miles from Albuquerque." (Susan Ritter)

"The physical facilities could hardly be better—it's elegant, well designed, comfortable. The art is both real and good. The public spaces are highly inviting. Service is right on the mark. The owners are refreshingly informal but highly professional." (Eugene & Linda Mihaly)

Open All year. Restaurant closed Mon., Tues.
Rooms 6 doubles, all with full private bath, TV, desk, air conditioning.

Facilities Dining room with fireplace, common room with fireplace, books, games. 1 acre with courtyard, fountain, hot tub. 1 m to Rio Grande for fishing. Skiing, horseback riding, hiking trails nearby.
Location 14 m N of Albuquerque, 40 m S of Santa Fe. Take I-25 N to Alameda exit, #233. Go W 4.1 m to Coors Rd., then N 2.7 m to school on right. Go left and inn will be on right.
Restrictions Smoking in common room only.
Credit cards MC, Visa.
Rates B&B, $60–75 double, $50–65 single. Extra person in room, $20. 10% discount beginning 3rd day. Weekly, monthly rates. Alc dinner, $12–18.
Extras Wheelchair access. Cribs, babysitting available. French spoken.

GALISTEO 87540   Map 12

The Galisteo Inn   *Tel:* (505) 982–1506
Box 4

The Galisteo is a 200-year-old adobe house surrounded by huge cotton-wood trees. Horses graze in the nearby fields. Guests concur on the atmosphere here—serene, extremely peaceful, low key, and relaxed are all adjectives that are used over and again. The classic New Mexican decor offers beamed viga ceilings, gleaming wood floors and trim, white walls, Indian rugs, kiva fireplaces, and simple, sturdy furnishings. Rates include a continental breakfast of fruit, juice, and muffins, while the creative dinners might include phyllo stuffed with spinach and boursin; shrimp with garlic, pesto, and tomatoes over pasta; broccoli with lemon butter; home-baked bread; and chocolate roulade with whipped cream, strawberries, and Grand Marnier.

"The location is remote but that is clearly one of its assets. The inn fits in harmoniously with its desert surroundings and provides enough amenities to make guests comfortable." *(Robert A. Ravitz)*

"Charming ambience and decor. Service excellent and unobtrusive. Very clean. Food is good and often outstanding. Close to fantastic petroglyphs, horse farms, ghost towns, and pueblos; also the Light Institute." *(Isabel Taylor, also Roberta Glasser)*

"Small, digestible, and run by persons of taste, consideration, and lively curiosities. Smiles all around—an atmosphere as warm as an old-fashioned kitchen." *(Virginia Mahone)* "Exceptionally quiet restful atmosphere." *(GG)*

Open All year.
Rooms 1 suite, 6 doubles, 2 singles—3 with full private bath, 6 with maximum of 4 people sharing bath. 6 rooms with desk.
Facilities Dining room, living room with fireplace, meeting room, exercise room, sauna, massage. 8½ acres with pond, herb garden, heated swimming pool, sauna, hot tub, horseback riding, mountain bikes.
Location N central NM. 23 m SE of Santa Fe. From Santa Fe take I-25N to 285S, to 41S to Galisteo.
Restrictions No children under 12. No smoking.
Credit cards MC, Visa.
Rates B&B, $150 suite, $85–115 double, $60 single. Extra person in room, $15. Prix fixe lunch, $12; prix fixe dinner, $20.
Extras Restaurant wheelchair accessible. Spanish spoken.

LAS CRUCES 88005   Map 12

Lundeen, Inn of the Arts   *Tel:* (505) 526–3327
618 South Alameda Boulevard

Jerry and Linda Lundeen's longtime home also serves as an architect's office, art gallery, and now a B&B. Although parts of the original adobe house are over 100 years old, the Lundeens have quadrupled its size of the house in the years they've been there. Furnishings combine English and American antiques with traditional Mexican white walls and polished wood plank and tiled floors; each room is named for a southwestern artist.

"Atmosphere is delightful; one is surrounded by lovely pictures, objets d'art, and well-chosen furniture in attractive, well-planned rooms. Although it is close to the center of the city, it has a delightful and quiet location. The inn is extremely clean and well kept." *(Mrs. Howard Katzenberg)*

"The Lundeens and their staff go out of their way to visit with the guests and make them feel at home." *(Col. & Mrs. George Patterson)*

"The food was excellent. We stayed in the Georgia O'Keeffe room, which was clean and cheerful with a sunny balcony. Lovely artwork was on the walls, and we had comfortable beds and soft pillows." *(Diane & Anita Wheeler)*

"As an architect, Jerry has designed the B&B addition to their charming Victorian adobe with comfort in mind." *(Dorothy Tuma)*

Open All year.
Rooms 2 suites, 12 doubles—all with private bath and/or shower, desk, air-conditioning. Some with telephone, radio, TV, fan.
Facilities Great room with fireplace, dining area, library, gallery; game/TV room, patio garden. 1 acre with lawns, fountain. Tennis, golf nearby.
Location S central NM, 45 m N of El Paso, TX. On Alameda, just S of Hwy. 70/80, 1 block W of Main St.
Restrictions Smoking permitted only in upstairs bedroom. "Well-behaved children welcome."
Credit cards Amex, MC, Visa.
Rates B&B, $70 suite, $50 double, $40–45 single. 10% senior discount.
Extras Spanish spoken. Airport shuttle service, $25.

LAS VEGAS 87701   Map 12

Once the toughest town in New Mexico, Las Vegas is now quite the opposite of its namesake in Nevada. A stopover on the Santa Fe Trail and site of a government fort, the town dates back to 1835. Las Vegas boomed in 1879 when the railroad came to town, but lapsed into decades of somnolence when the track routing was changed. With the renewed interest in historic preservation in the 1980s, over 900 buildings were listed on the National Register, ranging in style from early adobe to late Victorian. "Las Vegas is very 'eastern' in appearance, with many houses built of brick and stone, with large front porches; adobes are rare inside of town." *(MLR)*

Information please: We'd like reports on the **Carriage House,** an antique-filled B&B inn with seven guest rooms (925 Sixth Street; 505–454–1784).

Las Vegas is about 50 miles east of Santa Fe, via I-25.

The Plaza Hotel
230 On the Old Town Plaza

Tel: (505) 425–3591

"Constructed in Italianate bracketed style in 1882, the Plaza Hotel was built to accommodate travelers headed west on the Santa Fe Railroad. For years it was considered the finest hotel in the territory. Restored in 1983, rooms are decorated in period and have 10- to 12-foot ceilings and lace curtains that make you feel like you've stepped back in time. On each side of the lobby rises a grand staircase that I'm sure I've seen in some western movie. I had an excellent piñon chicken dish with cream sauce for dinner, and breakfast was equally good. The dining room is small, but waiting is no problem as you can sit in the bar and listen to live music while looking at old pictures of the hotel and town. The entire staff is friendly and pleasant. A marvelous little hotel." *(Mary Louise Rogers)*

Open All year.
Rooms 4 suites, 33 doubles—all with full private bath, telephone, TV, air-conditioning, fan.
Facilities Dining room, bar/lounge with live weekend entertainment. Activity and tour services.
Location N New Mexico. 59 m E of Santa Fe. In historic district. From I-25 take 2nd Las Vegas Exit (Exit 345-University) and follow signs.
Credit cards All major cards accepted.
Rates Room only, $70–80 suite, $47–52 double. Extra person in room $5. Children under 12 free. 10% AARP discount. Alc breakfast $5, alc lunch $8, alc dinner $25.
Extras 1 handicap equipped room. Spanish spoken. Cribs, babysitting available. Member, Best Western.

LINCOLN 88338   Map 12

Case de Patrón
Highway 380, P.O. Box 27

Tel: (505) 653–4676

Lincoln was once home to such legendary figures as Billy the Kid and Pat Garrett. Listed on the National Register of Historic Places, the Casa de Patrón is an adobe home with prominent vigas, high ceilings, Mexican tiled baths, and a quiet courtyard. Rates include a breakfast of fresh fruit and homemade breads.

"The house is done in beautifully appointed Spanish style with exceptionally comfortable rooms. Cleis and Jeremy Jordan are charming hosts with many talents. Cleis is an accomplished organist, who graciously entertained us with Bach during a superbly prepared breakfast." *(Bernice Talmatch)*

Open March through Dec.
Rooms 3 doubles, 1 casita—2 with private bath, 1 with half bath, 2 with a maximum of 4 people sharing a shower. Casita with kitchenette.
Facilities Dining room, parlor, courtyard with patio, garden.

Location S central NM. 60 m NE of Alamogordo. 50 m W of Roswell. East side of town on south side of US Hwy. 380.
Restrictions No smoking. No children under 12.
Credit cards MC, Visa.
Rates B&B, $95 casita, $50–65 double, $42–57 single.

MESILLA 88046   Map 12

Meson de Mesilla   *Tel:* (505) 525–9212
1803 Avenida de Mesilla, P.O. Box 1212

Chuck and Merci Walker invite guests to their southwestern-style inn and restaurant, in a quiet setting with beautiful mountain views. Chef Bob Herrera prepares continental cuisine for a menu that changes weekly. The guest rooms, located primarily on the second floor, lead onto a balcony with tables and chairs for enjoying the peaceful surroundings.

"Mesilla is removed from traffic noise—very relaxing. Rooms are nicely furnished with antiques; some have fireplaces. The popular restaurant is very good; breakfast is huge and wonderful. The atmosphere is friendly and cozy and we enjoyed our stay. The inn is very close to Old Mesilla Plaza, where you can spend an interesting morning admiring the restored Territorial architecture and exploring the shops." *(Nicki Dresslar, also JE)*

Open All year.
Rooms 3 suites, 8 doubles, 2 singles, all with private bath and/or shower, air-conditioning. 2 rooms with fireplace. Telephone, TV on request.
Facilities Dining room, living room with fireplace, TV/VCR, game table, balcony. 1 acre with swimming pool, putting green, horseshoes, bicycles.
Location S NM. 210 m S of Albuquerque. 10 min. drive to Las Cruces. From El Paso, take I-10 N to Hwy. 28 exit. Turn left off ramp and go ¾ m on Hwy. 28 (Avenida de Mesilla) to inn, on left. From Albuquerque, take I-25 S to University Ave. exit. Turn right (W) off ramp and go 3.1 m to Hwy. 28. Turn right onto Hwy. 28. Go ¾ m on Hwy. 28 to inn, on right.
Credit cards Amex, MC, Visa.
Rates B&B, $65–75 suite, $50–55 double, $45 single. 10% weekly discount.
Extras Airport pickups.

SANTA FE   Map 12

Founded in 1610, Santa Fe is the state capital and the center of New Mexico's lively arts scene, highlighted each summer by performances of the renowned Santa Fe opera. The colorful old plaza area, encircled by Paseo de Peralta, contains historic homes, adobe churches, the Palace of Governors, Indian traders, and art galleries. Also worth visiting is Canyon Road, lined with art galleries. Prices in general are higher and restaurants more crowded June through mid-October. A good time to visit is during Christmas, when the roofs of the old buildings are outlined with lights. Downhill skiing is just 18 miles away at the Santa Fe Basin.

Santa Fe is in north-central New Mexico, 60 miles north of Albuquerque and 70 miles south of Taos.

Although nearly everyone is delighted with their visit to Santa Fe, one reader did point out that the "city different" becomes the "city noisy" in the downtown area; during the middle of the night, workers are out very thoroughly washing the streets and compacting the garbage.

One correspondent noted that she especially enjoyed dining at **El Nido,** a restaurant not far from the Rancho Encantado: "Although big and quite busy, it was divided into small rooms, decorated with charming baskets, brightly painted windows, and white adobe walls; the food was good and the prices reasonable." *(SW)*

Also recommended: Although there wasn't time to complete a full writeup, *Mildred Herndon* wrote to report on **Alexander's Inn** (529 East Palace Avenue, 87501; 505–986–1431). "A large and attractive old house; our room was spacious and clean. The owner is friendly and warm, and we enjoyed a breakfast of grapefruit and fresh-baked apple muffins." Another last-minute report was received for the **Water Street Inn** (427 West Water Street, 87501; 505–984–1193), a three guest room B&B in an award-winning adobe restoration, just four blocks from the Plaza. Rates include continental breakfast and complimentary wine. "Perfect service, incredibly clean, handsome decor, very quiet. Each morning we sat on our private patio for a breakfast of homemade muffins, croissants, and fresh fruit salad." *(Lisa Sweeney)* Yet another possibility, recommended for families wanting an in-town location is the **Inn at Loretto** (211 Old Santa Fe Trail 87501; 505–988–5531), a 140-unit Best Western built in the adobe style with an excellent location across from the park, a heated pool, and a laundry room. *(YM, also AF)*

Information please: We'd like to hear more about the 200-year-old **El Paradero,** a reasonably priced B&B with rooms surrounding a central courtyard; local crafts and colorful rugs highlight the decor, and guests get a hearty start to the day in the breakfast room (220 West Manhattan 87501; 505–988–1177).

The Bishop's Lodge   *Tel:* (505) 983–6377
Bishop's Lodge Road, P.O. Box 2367
(State Route 22) Tesuque 87504

The Archbishop Lamy, immortalized in Willa Cather's book *Death Comes for the Archbishop,* came to this area about 100 years ago. Reminded of his native France, he purchased this ranch as a retreat. Later the ranch was bought by Joseph Pulitzer, who added two elaborate summer homes to the original adobe house and the chapel built by the archbishop. In 1918 the ranch was bought by the Thorpe family, who expanded it into a full-service resort. They still own and run the ranch today.

Bishop's Lodge is very much a family-oriented resort, offering a full range of special programs for children during the summer months. Food is basically hearty American cooking, with a few continental and Mexican dishes. Rooms vary in style; those in the older buildings have a more authentic southwestern flavor, while the newer ones have a typical motel-style decor, with a few regional touches. *(AF)* More comments, please.

Open Apr. 1 to Jan. 2.
Rooms 19 suites, 45 doubles, all with full private bath, telephone, TV, desk, air-conditioning. Some with fireplace.
Facilities Lobby, dining room, bar. 40 acres with heated swimming pool, hot tub,

5 tennis courts. Children's play area; summer children's program, children's dining room. 1,000 acres with hiking trails, fishing streams, stocked trout pond, flower gardens, trap and skeet range, horseback riding, pack trips. 2 golf courses nearby.
Location 3 m N of Santa Fe Plaza, on State Rte. 22 (Bishop's Lodge Rd.).
Credit cards None accepted.
Rates Room only, $96–225 suite, $80–175 double. MAP, $194–300 suite, $150–230 double. Extra person in room, $10–39. Buffet breakfast, $7.50; alc lunch, $9; alc dinner, $20.
Extras Airport/station pickups. Cribs, babysitting available. Spanish, German, French spoken.

Grant Corner Inn   *Tel:* (505) 983–6678
122 Grant Avenue 87501

In 1983 Louise Stewart and her husband, Pat Walter, renovated this Victorian manor home, built 80 years ago by a wealthy New Mexican ranching family. Louise ("Wiggy") grew up at Scottsdale's Camelback Inn, founded by her father in 1936. Although Pat used his background in spatial design to oversee the inn's renovation, he has since changed hats, and dons a chef's toque when preparing the inn's breakfasts. Daily specials may include banana waffles, eggs Florentine, or New Mexican soufflé, accompanied by fresh juice and fruit, homemade rolls and jellies. Louise has used her training as an interior designer to decorate the rooms elegantly with Victorian antiques, Oriental rugs, handmade quilts, and Indian weavings.

"This inn is really charming, and the food is out of this world. Its style and decor are not typical of Santa Fe, but it's a nice change from the adobe/southwestern feeling." *(M. Jones, also Gail Gottlieb)*

"Location a big plus—just one block from the famous plaza, so that a great deal of shopping and museum-hopping can be done without a car. A rabbit motif carries through the decor, with a terrific collection of stuffed and ceramic bunnies. A quaint, three-story gabled dwelling, the house is something of an oddity in this city of low adobe buildings. Picket fences and arches set it off from the surrounding businesses and the wonderful Presbyterian Church. Breakfast on the veranda is a delight in summer. A great plus of the desert is the ability to dine outside without fighting off hordes of flying things." *(Jody Adams)*

"Our corner room with private bath and porch was clean and decorated with a brass and iron bed, handworked quilt, armoire, and ceiling fan. We enjoyed exchanging ideas with other guests over complimentary afternoon wine. The staff was most helpful with ideas about restaurants, shopping, and area attractions. Anything in the historic Plaza area is within easy walking distance." *(Jack & Sue Lane)*

"The rooms vary considerably, with the differences reflected in the rates charged. Louise is a very gifted decorator. Our room had a comfortable queen-sized bed and a fabulous hand-painted armoire. It had only one window, so it was a little warm. The deluxe doubles are fabulous, with great balconies. The breakfasts are excellent and very creative, although one morning's experiment didn't come off as well as the others. The staff is extremely helpful with dinner reservations." *(AF)*

Amid this flurry of kudos, one reader did complain that the inn made a small mistake in tabulating his bill. When it was brought to the owner's attention, this reader felt their response was less than gracious.

Open Feb. through Dec.
Rooms 12 doubles, 1 single—4 with full private bath, 2 with private shower, 7 with maximum of 4 people sharing bath. All with telephone, radio, TV; some with desk. 2-bedroom townhouse also available.
Facilities Breakfast/living room, porch, veranda, small garden. Tennis, swimming nearby. Off-street parking.
Location Downtown Santa Fe. 2 blocks from plaza. From plaza, take Palace Ave. 2 blocks W to Grant. Inn is at corner of Grant and Johnson.
Restrictions No children under 6.
Credit cards MC, Visa.
Rates B&B, $50–110 double, $45 single, plus service. Extra person in room, $15.
Extras Room 2 equipped for wheelchair access with ramp, wide doorways, bars in shower. Spanish spoken.

Hotel El Dorado

309 West San Francisco Avenue 87501

Tel: (505) 988–4455
(800) CLARION

This new, full-service luxury hotel—with all the amenities you'd expect—was built with careful attention to Santa Fe's heritage, incorporating traditional materials in the building's design, including vigas and kiva fireplaces.

"The El Dorado is the best. Its pueblo architecture enhances the historic scenery of Santa Fe—no mean trick, that. We still can't figure out how the huge public rooms manage to be so enfolding and cozy, but they are and that's what counts. In the best of Santa Fe style, the rooms are understated (no cute Indian kitsch), elegant, and homey.

"The key element here is the staff. We have never encountered such a happy, unobtrusively friendly, warm gang as the multitudes that look after us there. The very first time you pick up the phone, the operator knows your name. When you walk down the hall, maids you never saw before in your life greet you by name and with a smile. If a mistake is made, they actually run to correct it. There is nothing servile about their attitude. It's more like being surrounded by old friends eager to make your visit a happy one. Even if Santa Fe wasn't one of the most interesting places in the world, it would be worth the trip to stay at the El Dorado." *(Ted Flicker)*

"Santa Fe done Los Angeles style, with lots of glitz. Many people love it." More comments, please.

Open All year.
Rooms 18 suites, 112 doubles, 88 singles, all with full private bath, telephone, radio, TV, desk, air-conditioning. Most rooms with balcony, fireplace; some with wet bar, whirlpool.
Facilities 3 restaurants, lounge with music nightly, courtyard. Heated rooftop pool, whirlpool, sauna. Underground parking.
Location 2 blocks from the plaza. Take exit 282 off I-25. Right on St. Francis Dr.; right on Cerrillos Rd.; left on Guadalupe; right on St. Francis Ave.
Credit cards Amex, CB, DC, MC, Visa.
Rates Room only, $170–295 suite, $105–155 double, $95–145 single. Extra person in room, $20. No charge for children under 18 in parents' room. 10% AARP discount. Alc breakfast, $4–7; alc lunch, $5–12; alc dinner, $20–35. Ski packages.
Extras 3 rooms equipped for disabled with wheelchair access and telephone for hearing impaired. Shuttle bus from Albuquerque airport stops across street. Small pets allowed. Cribs, babysitting available. Spanish, French, Portuguese, Italian spoken.

Hotel St. Francis   *Tel:* (505) 983–5700
210 Don Gaspar Avenue 87501   (800) 666–5700

Built in 1924 and originally called the De Vargas Hotel, the St. Francis was fully reopened in 1986 after a $6 million restoration. Rooms have high ceilings and big casement windows; furnishings are pleasantly eclectic, with brass and iron Victorian-style beds, cherrywood armoires, and comfortable contemporary couches. Three meals a day plus afternoon tea are served; dinner cuisine is northern Italian with many seafood and veal specialities.

Guest feedback was extremely positive, with all ready to return; singled out by many for exceptional praise was the concierge, Inger Boudouris, who "always manages to secure the perfect table in the most popular eating establishment with the friendliest of help. She produces opera tickets with this same ease." *(Dr. & Mrs. John Ashley)* In response to comments in last year's guide, manager Jacqueline Thompson notes that "lighting improvements are under way, and that the dining and kitchen staff are now functioning smoothly. Some respondents noted that the rooms and baths are on the small side, typical for a hotel of this period.

"The St. Francis has all the amenities of a big-city hotel. The 1920s restoration is careful but restrained. The rooms are light and airy, with great windows that actually open, period furniture, modern heating and cooling, extra soaps and shampoos. The bright and spacious dining room provides a convenient breakfast. We also had one of our best dinners here, in a city that has many fine restaurants. The hotel is situated on a quiet narrow back street, just a block from the plaza. Service is prompt, attentive but not obtrusive." *(David Hyslop & Chip Bailey)* "The best showers of any hotel on our ten-day trip through Arizona and New Mexico." *(Anita Mardikan)*

"The hotel has an ambience both European and southwestern, and the art underlines the fact that Santa Fe is an American art capital. The smallest rooms are decorated with the same care as a more expensive room." *(Laura Nadworny)* "Nothing is more refreshing than to take tea and biscuits in the afternoon in front of the massive fireplace, with piñon logs burning and a gentle guitar playing soft music in the background."*(JRA)*

"With its tall ceilings, marbled bathrooms with gold fixtures, comfortable and attractive furniture, including a large armoire with hidden remote-control television and small refrigerator, the St. Francis is perfect for a romantic getaway. I enjoyed the inviting veranda complete with chamber music, quality art throughout the hotel, the sociable bar, and the restaurant, Francisco's, featuring fine northern Italian cuisine." *(Randall Jones)*

"We were delighted to find that despite the renovation, all the original square-paned windows still opened! At dinner, we enjoyed the high ceilings, large windows, candles, flowers, soft lighting, crisp napery and excellent soup and salads of the hotel restaurant. Desserts were delicious, and we relaxed over coffee and liqueurs in the comfortable panelled bar." *(Dorothy Wallnut)* "Location is ideal, in the center of everything the visitor wants to see and do." *(Bernice & Morgan Lawrence)*

Open All year.
Rooms 2 suites, 80 doubles—all with private bath and/or shower. All with telephone, radio, TV, air-conditioning, refrigerator; some with desk.

Facilities Dining room, bar/lounge, veranda. Off-street parking.
Location 1 block from plaza.
Restrictions No smoking in some guest rooms.
Credit cards Amex, CB, DC, MC, Visa.
Rates Room only, $200–275 suite, $65–135 double, $55–120 single. Extra person in room, $15. Children under 12 stay free. Alc breakfast, $5–10; alc lunch, $6–12; alc dinner, $20–30.
Extras Wheelchair access. Cribs, babysitting available. Spanish, German, Swedish, French, Japanese spoken.

Preston House
106 Faithway Street 87501

Tel: (505) 982–3465

Restored in 1981 by owner Signe Bergman, the Preston House is a century-old Victorian, decorated with period furnishings and the paintings of its artist/designer/owner. The Queen Anne architecture is combined with an atypical red-tile roof. Unusual for Santa Fe, the decor is mostly country Victorian, with hand-carved fireplaces, stained-glass windows, lacy curtains and floral wallpapers, and brass and iron beds. Rates include a breakfast of fresh orange juice and fruit, cereal, breads and muffins, yogurt and granola.

"Preston House is known for its turn-of-the century architecture, its authentic decor, its central location, and the quality of its breakfasts—freshly squeezed orange juice, fresh fruit, homebaked muffins and nut breads, bread pudding, and local jams and jellies. Other assets include the high caliber of the personnel, from the owner to the young men and women who thoroughly clean your room. At breakfast, taken either in the dining room or outside under the apricot trees, guests share reactions to the previous night's performance or other events. Another advantage—Preston House is on a dead-end street, quiet even during Indian Market week when tourists swell the town nearly beyond its capacity. Other perks include the large bowl of fresh fruit in the front hall, the honor system phone, teatime with hot tea, cold juice, and snacks from baklava to popcorn. There's sherry in your room, rocking chairs on the front porch, and flowers all over the place. And would you believe a fresh pot of coffee on the stairway landing every morning before breakfast?" *(Priscilla Chave)*

"The living room is an inviting place to visit with the other guests and read the various pamphlets on Santa Fe attractions. On the landing of the wide stairway is a long window seat where we enjoyed curling up with a book, afternoon tea, sherry or juice and cookies. Our room was very relaxing and comfortable with refreshing breezes through the two big windows." *(John & Spotswood Shotton)*

Open All year.
Rooms 3 cottages, 9 doubles—7 with private bath and/or shower, 2 with maximum of 4 people sharing bath. All with radio, desk; some with telephone, TV.
Facilities Dining room, living room. Patio, garden, off-street parking.
Location 3 blocks from plaza. From plaza, go E on Palace Ave., and go left on Faithway to inn on right. (Faithway is street right after Paseo de Peralta, opposite La Posada Hotel.)
Restrictions No smoking. No children under 12.
Credit cards Amex, MC, Visa.
Rates B&B, $110–125 cottage, $50–110 double. Extra person in room, $7.
Extras Pets allowed.

Pueblo Bonito Bed & Breakfast Inn   *Tel:* (505) 984–8001
138 West Manhattan at Galisteo 87501

Pueblo Bonito lives up to its name; it is pretty both inside and out, exemplifying authentic Santa Fe architecture. Owned and run by Herb and Amy Behm since 1987, this turn-of-the-century compound is surrounded by high adobe walls with graceful archways. Flagstone paths lead through flower gardens to individual casitas with wood-beam ceilings, kiva fireplaces, and Native American rugs and pottery.

"Pueblo Bonito is the essence of Santa Fe with its wooden floors, antique lace curtains, Navaho rugs, and Pueblo pottery. Every room is unique, but all are private and cozy. (Numbers 11 and 12 are my favorites.) Most rooms overlook trees and old buildings. The common breakfast room and porch encourages mingling among guests, but privacy is still the main attraction. There is always a place to park in the gravel courtyard, and the inn is within walking distance of the plaza and Canyon Road. The friendly owners are always around in the morning, and are professional and unobtrusive." *(Robin Lynn Hell)*

"Herb and Amy provide thoughtful care and gracious hospitality. Breakfast includes a selection of cereal, muffins, and rolls with a choice of fruit and beverages. The architecture is beautiful, the landscaping scenic, and the rooms comfortable." " *(Karen and Kent James)*

One otherwise pleased guest noted a few areas for improvement: "The chairs in the visiting area could be improved upon. Typical of this kind of renovation, the bath facilities were small and cramped, but livable."

Open All year.
Rooms 4 suites, 11 doubles—all with full private bath, radio, TV, fan, fireplace.
Facilities Dining room, patio, deck, guest laundry and kitchen. On-site parking. Golf nearby. 1 block to river.
Location 3 blocks to plaza. From E or S via I-25, take the Old Pecos Trail exit and go into town. Turn L on Paseo de Peralta, turn R on Galisteo. From N via I-25, take St. Francis Drive exit and follow it to Hickox. Turn L (it becomes Paseo de Peralta), cross Cerrillos Rd. and turn L at Galisteo. Inn on R at corner of 1st cross st. (W. Manhattan).
Restrictions No smoking in dining room.
Credit cards MC, Visa.
Rates B&B, $100–150 suite, $65–95 double, $55–85 single. Extra person in room, $10. 2 night holiday minimum.
Extras Crib available.

Rancho Encantado   *Tel:* (505) 982–3537
Route 4, Box 57C, Tesuque 87501

Betty Egan and her son John have been running the Rancho Encantado since 1968. Betty has taken what was a deserted ranch house and carefully developed and expanded it into a first-class resort.

"The tiled first-floor area is filled with antique furniture, Mexican and Indian art, photos of famous people who have stayed here (royalty and movie stars). Generally places that display such photos turn us off, but here you understand that the rich and famous also find this a very special getaway. The first floor has a variety of little sitting areas, a huge corner bar area, and the dining area, which is built on three levels, looking out toward the high desert and the mountains, with elegant New Mexican decorations.

"The food is first rate, like everything else. I had duck in some sort of berry sauce, and all the accompaniments were done to perfection. Breakfast was similar—I felt so full, satisfied, and happy that I would have been content to curl up in a lobby chair for a long, self-indulgent morning nap.

"Our room, #8, was large and luxurious, with two balconies, a king-size bed, Indian and Spanish antiques, a large bath, and a bright cerise rug." *(Suzanne Carmichael)*

"Our room turned out to be the master bedroom and bath of one of the condos on the property. It had southwestern decor and was very quiet— you couldn't tell you had a neighbor. They offer buffet and table service at breakfast; we preferred the latter. The public rooms are lovely, and the food very good. We were there in August for the opera and found Santa Fe to be a bit crowded; staying out at the Rancho proved a peaceful alternative." *(Sally & Webb Williams)*

And another viewpoint: "We loved the Rancho, but would prefer an in-town location for our next visit to Santa Fe." *(AF)*

Open All year.
Rooms 10 suites, 12 doubles—all with full private bath, telephone. Many with TV, desk, air-conditioning, fireplace. 7 rooms in main lodge, rest in nearby cottages and casitas. Pueblo Encantado, 27 2-bedroom pueblo-style condominiums located across the road, also available for rental.
Facilities Dining room, lounge with fireplace, family room, library. 168 acres with heated swimming pool, hot tub, 2 tennis courts, tennis instruction, shuffleboard, trail rides, play equipment. Fishing nearby. 26 m to downhill skiing.
Location 8 m N of Santa Fe. From I-25, take Santa Fe exit 282, marked St. Francis Dr. (Rte. 285), N to Tesuque exit (*not* Tesuque Pueblo exit). Go 3 m to State Rte. 592. Turn right, go 2 m to Rancho Encantado.
Credit cards Amex, CB, DC, MC, Visa.
Rates Room only, $150–300 suite or condo, $100–195 double. Extra person in room, $10. Crib or rollaway, $15. Alc breakfast, $6; alc lunch, $6–8; alc dinner, $40.
Extras Ramps to 1st floor rooms. Cribs, babysitting available. Spanish spoken.

TAOS 87571   Map 12

Taos is a delightful, small artists' colony, a compact town centered around a lovely old plaza. In the Taos area you can visit over 80 galleries, ski at one of five nearby downhill areas, fish for trout, or go white-water rafting. North of town, and not to be missed, are the magnificent Millicent Rodgers Museum and the still-occupied 1,000-year-old Pueblo de Taos. In summer, and sometimes during the height of ski season, the hordes of tourists can obscure Taos's charm. It's best to visit in spring or fall to capture the real Taos and avoid high season rates.

"Don't miss El Rincon, Taos's original trading post, selling and trading Indian jewelry. Located on Kit Carson Street, it has been there since the last century and is the best one we've ever been to—and we've been to a lot! They also have two pleasant rooms available for B&B." *(SC)*

Taos is located in north-central New Mexico, 70 miles north of Santa Fe and 129 miles north of Albuquerque.

Suggestions for hotels and inns at Taos Ski Valley, 19 miles away, would be most helpful.

American Artists Gallery House
132 Frontier Road, P.O. Box 584

Tel: (505) 758–4446

This combination B&B and art gallery offers magnificent views of the Taos Mountains from every room. Myra and Benjamin Carp, the owners since 1984, share their knowledge of area history, art, culture, and geology. Rates include a full breakfast of fresh fruit, coffee and tea, and a hot entrée such as French toast stuffed with nuts and soft cheese. Those who prefer to stay closer to town may be interested in the Carp's second B&B, the **Gallery House West,** just four blocks from the Plaza.

"Very comfortable and inviting, with fantastic mountain views. Owners are extremely accommodating, interested in having their guest know as much as possible of what to do in Taos. Rooms are super clean, each highlighted by the work of a different local artist. High point of any stay is Ben and Myra's breakfast!" *(Freddy Allison)*

Open All year.
Rooms 1 cottage, 5 doubles—all with private bath and/or shower. All with radio, desk, kiva fireplace. 4 with private entrance.
Facilities Dining room, living room with fireplace, TV; sun-room, deck with hot tub. 1/3 acre with courtyard gardens. Off-street parking. Rio Grande River for swimming, fishing, rafting.
Location 1 m to Plaza. From main road into Taos, turn E on Frontier Rd. to inn, last house on right.
Restrictions No smoking. "No teething babies."
Credit cards None accepted.
Rates B&B, $80–85 cottage, $55–70 double. Extra person in room, $15.
Extras Limited wheelchair accessibility. Airport/station pickups. Some Spanish, Hebrew.

The Brooks Street Inn
207 Brooks Street, P.O. Box 4954

Tel: (505) 758–1489

To look at it, you'd never guess that the Brooks Street Inn was built in 1956. Constructed in the traditional adobe manner, with mud and hay bricks, wood-beamed viga ceilings, and kiva fireplaces, the inn conveys an ageless charm. Sue Stevens and John Testore left the high-pressure world of a Chicago advertising agency to try their hand at running a bed & breakfast inn here in 1987; judging from the reactions of their guests, they made a good choice. Czech coffee cakes and Lithuanian bacon buns are among the breakfast specialties.

"The inn sits on a large, heavily wooded lot, with ample parking available. The main house has three large suites decorated in traditional Taos style. The living room, dining room, and kitchen have been opened up to allow easy circulation and a feeling of spaciousness. Susan prepares a light breakfast and provides wine, fruit, and cheese at night. Her wine selections included the better California, Washington, and New Mexico vineyards. Opposite the rear patio, set among evergreens about 50 feet behind the main house, are the most interesting rooms. These brand-new rooms feature southwestern antiques, kiva fireplaces, and traditional architectural details. Each is individually heated, and even in August no air-conditioning is needed.

"Susan and John are familiar with Taos and the nearby ski areas. Their restaurant recommendations were excellent, and they were able to get us tickets for a local theater production. The house, outbuildings, and grounds are secluded, beautifully kept, and very charming, all enhanced the owners' enthusiasm and graceful skill in handling a full house in a seemingly effortless manner." *(Peter Gleszer)*

"On a quiet street off the main thoroughfare is the Brooks Street Inn. Our guest house room had a large skylight over the bed. A small bouquet of fresh-cut flowers was arranged in a vase on an antique table. Lots of throw pillows lay along the wall, so you could lounge beside a glowing fire. The room was immaculate, and the bath clean and modern. The white walls and sunlight made the room bright and airy. The main house has a comfortable and spacious family room where guests could read or visit in front of the fireplace. Every evening a small snack of wine and finger food was provided." *(Debra Gander, also Evelyn & Gil Hegmier, Howard & Ingrid Nudelman)*

"The purpose of our trip was to ski the incomparable slopes of Taos mountain, but the inn made our experience even more delightful. John's wit and sense of humor is topped only by Sue's abilities with the pan and oven." *(Kyle Lombardo)*

Open All year.
Rooms 7 doubles—5 with private bath and/or shower, 2 with maximum of 4 people sharing bath. All with desk. 3 rooms in separate guest house.
Facilities Common room with fireplace, books; patio. Fishing, white-water rafting, downhill and cross-country skiing nearby.
Location Take Hwy. 68 to Brooks St. (opposite post office). Inn is on left.
Restrictions No smoking. No children under 5.
Credit cards MC, Visa.
Rates B&B, $45–80 double, $40–75 single. Extra person in room, $10. 4-night minimum during Christmas week.
Extras Wheelchair accessible. Airport/station pickups. Spanish spoken.

Hacienda del Sol   *Tel:* (505) 758–0287
109 Mabel Dodge Lane, Box 177

Only in America . . . would you find a 180-year-old hacienda by turning right at the "Lotaburger" stand. Fortunately, the Hacienda del Sol is well screened from this neon-lit charmer by dense foliage and fences, and guests can focus on the more appealing views of Taos Mountain and the adjoining 95,000-acre Taos pueblo. Purchased in 1988 by Los Angeles escapees Carol and Randy Pelton, the inn was originally built as a hideaway by art patron Mabel Dodge Luhan, who hosted such literary and art world luminaries as Georgia O'Keeffe, Aldous Huxley, Thomas Wolfe, Willa Cather, and D. H. Lawrence. The inn is unusually well shaded by huge cottonwoods, blue spruce, ponderosa pine, and willow trees. The guest rooms offer kiva fireplaces and mountain views. All are furnished with antiques, hand-crafted southwestern furniture, and local art, along with down quilts and comfortable beds. Rates include a breakfast of homebaked bread and muffins, fresh-squeezed juice, and just-ground coffee.

"Fine accommodations, exquisite service, and knowledgeable innkeepers. We especially enjoyed Carol and Randy's suggestions as they helped us plan our day trips and surprised us with little extras that made our stay a joy." *(Phillip Wolford, also Bernice Talmatch)*

Open All year.
Rooms 1 suite, 6 doubles—6 with private bath and/or shower, 2 with a maximum of 4 people sharing bath. 3 with fireplace, 1 with double whirlpool bath. 2 rooms in adobe casita, both with fireplace, 1 with kitchenette.
Facilities Dining room, living room with TV/VCR. 1.2 acres with lawn furniture, garden, hot tub. Swimming nearby.
Location 1 m N of Taos Plaza. From plaza, go ½ m N of post office on Hwy. 3 to sign for inn S of "Lotaburger," on E (right) side of st. (just past "Laughing Horse Inn" sign). From Hwy. 150, go S on Hwy. 3/64 to inn on left.
Restrictions No smoking.
Credit cards MC, Visa.
Rates B&B, $98 suite, $45–95 double, $35–75 single. Extra adult in room, $20; child, $10. 3-night Christmas minimum.
Extras Crib available, $10. Spanish, some French spoken.

La Posada de Taos
309 Juanita Lane, P.O. Box 1118

Tel: (505) 758–8164

In 1984 Sue Smoot sold her New York City co-op and used the proceeds to buy and restore an old adobe house not far from the Old Plaza. Sue notes that honeymooners especially enjoy the cottage, with its double loft bed complete with a skylight for stargazing, while nearly everyone enjoys the camaraderie, good conversation, and funny stories that abound at her breakfast table.

"Owner Sue Smoot is thoroughly delightful, charming, and a wonderful cook. For breakfast (served at 8 A.M.) we had fresh grapefruit, coffee, and a flour tortilla filled with eggs, bacon, beans, and cheese, and topped with an excellent salsa. We stayed in the Beautler Suite and I highly recommend it. Very large and well decorated, it is heated by a huge wood stove and has a bathroom complete with Jacuzzi. The Lino Room, also in the main house, is smaller but nice, with a beautiful Persian rug and small wood-burning stove." *(SC)*

"A perfect introduction to Taos, with its blend of cheerful serenity, irrepressible vitality, and a beauty that borders on the spiritual. Our room was lovely and breakfast was super—both the food and the conversations with other guests. Best of all is Sue Smoot. If it every becomes possible to pick family members the way the Dallas Cowboys pick linebackers, she's our first draft choice." *(Mark Myers)*

"Sue provides lots of extra touches—bookmarks with our names written on them was a favorite. Breakfast included delicious quiche and fruit. Our room was clean and cozy, the common area colorful with local decor." *(Carol Moritz)*

One otherwise delighted guest noted an area for improvement: "Although we had understood that our room would have twin beds, in fact it had a bed with a trundle underneath. We found the trundle difficult to maneuver to create a separate space for each of us in the small room."

Open All year.
Rooms 1 cottage with kitchenette, fireplace. 7 doubles with private bath and/or shower. 4 rooms with wood-burning stove or fireplace; 2 rooms with desk.
Facilities Dining room, living room with fireplace, library; courtyard, Japanese garden.
Location 2½ blocks to plaza. From plaza, go W on Don Fernando, S (left) on Manzanares, right on Juanita.
Credit cards None accepted.
Rates B&B, $46–80 double, $42–76 single. Extra person in room, $10. Rollaway, $12.50. 2-night weekend minimum, Memorial Day through Oct. 15.
Extras Wheelchair accessible. Airport/station pickups. Pets permitted with prior notice. Spanish spoken.

The Taos Inn　　　　　　　　　　　　　　　　*Tel:* (505) 758–2233
125 Paseo del Pueblo Norte　　　　　　　　　　　(800) TAOS–INN

The Taos Inn is composed of several adobe buildings, some of which date back to the 1600s. For many years it was the home and office of Doc Martin, the county's first doctor. After closing in 1981 for a one-year, nearly $1 million restoration, the inn reopened as one of Taos's most appealing accommodations, retaining a strong southwestern flavor. Rooms are decorated with warm colors and antiques or locally made furniture. The many Indian and Mexican touches include the handwoven Zapotec bedspreads and tiled baths. The lobby, restaurant, bar, and nearly all the guest room fireplaces were individually designed by Carmen Velarde, a skilled adobe artisan. Doc Martin's, the inn's restaurant, is open for breakfast, lunch, and dinner. It specializes in made-from-scratch dishes featuring New American cuisine, fresh seafood, and pasta, and is known for its outstanding wine list. The Adobe Bar is a favorite of locals and visitors alike, with good margaritas and inexpensive New Mexican food.

"The two-story lobby is a stunning example of New Mexican decor, and the staff is friendly and helpful. Rooms are handsome and comfortable, and the location is ideal, right in the center of town—just a quick walk to all the galleries." *(SC, also VF)*

Open All year. Restaurant closed 3 days in early April, Nov.
Rooms 1 suite, 39 doubles, all with full private bath, telephone, TV. Some with desk, air-conditioning, fan, fireplace.
Facilities Lobby with fountain, fireplace, games, entertainment; restaurant with 3 fireplaces, library, bar with fireplace; greenhouse Jacuzzi. Courtyard with heated swimming pool, hammock. Tennis nearby. On-site parking.
Location Just off plaza. Next door to Stables Art Center.
Restrictions No smoking in some rooms. Light sleepers should request courtyard rooms.
Credit cards Amex, CB, DC, MC, Visa.
Rates Room only, $95 suite, $50–95 double. Children under 12 stay free. Roll-a-way, $10; crib, $7. 10% senior discount. Alc breakfast, $2–5; alc lunch, $5–9; alc dinner, $48.
Extras 1 room equipped for disabled. Cribs, babysitting available. Spanish spoken.

New York

The Sedgwick Inn, Berlin

Although to some people, New York is synonymous with New York City, the state is an exceptionally diverse one. In fact, the New York State Tourism Council divides the state up into the following distinct regions (not counting the Big Apple, which most consider a region unto itself): Long Island, the Hudson Valley, the Catskills, the Capital (Albany)/Saratoga, the Adirondacks, Thousand Islands Seaway, Central/Leather-stocking, the Finger Lakes, the Niagara Frontier, and Chautauqua/Allegheny. The New York State Tourism Division publishes first-rate materials on all these regions; see the appendix for the address and telephone.

Information please: On the east side of the Hudson River, just 50 miles north of New York City, are the little towns of Garrison and Cold Spring, both amply supplied with charming restaurants, antique shops, and several inns. One possibility is the **Hudson House** (2 Main Street, Cold Spring 10516; 914–265–9355) popular for both food and lodging, while another is the **Pig Hill Inn** (73 Main Street, Cold Spring 10516; 914–265–9247), a B&B with antique-filled rooms and hearty breakfasts.

New York State sales tax is 7%, plus additional local taxes applicable in most counties.

ALBANY 12202   **Map 3**

Mansion Hill Inn   *Tel:* (518) 465–2038
115 Philip Street

Built in 1861 for brush-maker Daniel Brown, the Mansion Hill Inn was used as a tavern for many years. In 1984, Maryellen and Steve Stofelano restored it as a restaurant and inn. They note that "our inn is especially convenient for the business traveler, due to our downtown location; our suite accommodations are ideal for families." The inn restaurant offers Italian cuisine and New York state wines; veal, shrimp, and pasta dishes are specialties.

"The inn is small with a homey atmosphere; very friendly owners and staff. The food is excellent—fresh, well prepared and attractively presented; rooms are completely renovated, sparkling clean, and large." *(Jim Goacher)* "Ample parking, welcoming atmosphere." *(Diane Fleming)*

Open All year. Restaurant closed Sun. evening, Mon., Tues.
Rooms 2 suites, 5 doubles, all with full private bath, telephone, radio, TV, desk, air-conditioning; suites with kitchen, deck.
Facilities Dining/breakfast rooms with fireplace. Room service. Off-street parking. Hiking, boating, fishing nearby.
Location South End; "Mansion Neighborhood," around the corner from the Governor's Mansion. From NYS Thruway or I-787, exit at Madison Avenue; follow Rte. 20 (Madison Ave.) through 4 traffic lights; turn left onto Philip St.; continue to 2nd blinking light and inn on right at corner of Park Ave.
Credit cards Amex, DC, MC.
Rates B&B, $85–125 suite, double or single. Extra person in room, $10. Alc lunch, $7; alc dinner, $23.
Extras Wheelchair accessible. Airport/station pickups. Cribs, babysitting available.

BLUE MOUNTAIN LAKE 12812   Map 3

Information please: Similar to Hemlock Hall, described below, is **The Hedges**, once a private estate turned a summer lodge with cottages in a beautiful lakeside setting (518–352–7325). Reports?

Hemlock Hall   *Tel:* (518) 352–7706
Route 28N   Winter: (518) 359–9065

"The Hall is owned and operated by Paul and Susan Provost. Paul had been a regular visitor since the 1950s, before he bought it for himself just a couple of years ago. The cottages are equipped with range and refrigerator, should you decide to cook for yourself . . . but who would want to? Breakfast and dinner are served in a sunny room at the lodge. Every morning we were called to breakfast by the large bell on the porch of the lodge (usually rung by one of the visiting kids). We had bacon, eggs made to order, pancakes, and hot cereal both days. Homemade bread is served with dinner each evening. They seated us at a different table at each meal so that we could meet other guests. We also considered it a real bonus that children are welcome here. Their mealtime conversations were often humorous and added much to the charm. Each evening Paul would place a snack of fresh fruit or homemade cookies out for us to serve ourselves. There was no shortage of activities to keep us occupied—they provide free use of their canoes, sailboats, paddleboats, and rowboats. Children and adults enjoyed relaxing on the private beach complete with lounge chairs. There are numerous hiking trails in the area, including Blue Mountain. If the weather isn't favorable to outdoor activities, you can curl up in a chair by the fireplace in the lodge and read one of the books from their library, or go shopping in any of the many art and craft stores in the region. The Adirondack Museum is also just five minutes away.

"Hemlock Hall is definitely a jewel in the rough, tucked away in the Adirondack wilderness and combining companionable comfort far from the tourist crowds." *(Tim & Susan McDaniel)*

Open May 15 to Oct. 15.
Rooms 23 rooms in motel units, lodge rooms, and 1- and 2-bedroom cabins, with private or shared bath. Some with kitchen, porch, fireplace.
Facilities Restaurant, living room, game room, library. Lakefront with beach, canoeing, boating, sailing, fishing, hiking.
Location N NY, Adirondacks. From S & W: take I-90 to Exit 31 at Utica; take Rte. 12 N 20 m to Alder Creek; go N on Rte. 28 to Blue Mt. Lake. From E, take I-90 to Exit 24 at Albany. Go N on I-87 to Exit 23 at Warrensburg. Follow sign to Rte. 28 & go N. At intersection of Rtes. 28, 30, & 28N, go N on 28N ¾ m and look for sign. Lodge is 1 m off road on N shore of lake.
Credit cards None accepted.
Rates MAP, $101–113 cottages, $70–97 doubles. For single rate deduct $15. Extra person in room, $27; child 2–8, $18. 3-night minimum for advance reservations. Alc breakfast $5, alc lunch $5, alc dinner $10.

CAZENOVIA 13035   Map 3

Founded in 1793, lakeside Cazenovia became a summer retreat for wealthy big-city families after the Civil War, and many of its finest mansions date from this period. The lake remains a focus of activity to this day, with fishing, swimming, and sailing leading in popularity, along with golf, hiking, tennis, and horseback riding. Winter favorites include ice-skating, hockey, ice-fishing, sleigh rides, downhill and cross-country skiing.

Information please: We'd appreciate more feedback on the **Brewster Inn** (6 Ledyard Avenue; 315–655–9232), an elaborate mansion-turned-inn with antique-filled rooms and a well-regarded lakeside restaurant.

Cazenovia is in central New York state, 20 miles southeast of Syracuse.

Brae Loch Inn   *Tel:* (315) 655–3431
5 Albany Street, Rte. 20

With so many innkeepers falling victim to burnout, and uncounted inns changing hands every few years, we have a special fondness for long-time family-owned inns. The Brae Loch was opened in 1946 by Scottish-born Adam Barr; 44 years later, the inn is still run with a Scottish theme by Adam's son Grey and his grandson Jim. Dinner specialities change nightly but might include Cornish game hen with apricot sauce or salmon grilled with fresh vegetables and sauced with bearnaise.

"We arrived on a hot, humid day and were shown to our air-conditioned suite, with a king canopy bed in a huge room, decorated in antiques. I had a chance to see the other rooms and even the least expensive, with two antique sleigh beds, is delightful." *(Wendi Van Exan)*

"The old country Scottish theme, the delicious meals, the warmth of owner Grey Barr and his staff take you back to a quieter time. Everything, from parking to plumbing to the peaceful lakeside location, makes for a delightful stay." *(Richard Streeter)*

Open All year. Restaurant closed Dec. 24, 25.
Rooms 12 doubles, all with private bath and/or shower, telephone, radio, TV, desk, air-conditioning.
Facilities Parlor with fireplace, restaurant, lounge, bar, banquet room, gift shop. Golf nearby, 1 block to Lake Cazenovia for water sports.
Location 3 blocks from town center.
Credit cards Amex, DC, MC, Visa.
Rates Room only, $80–125 suite, $69–80 double. Extra person in room, $7. Cot, $5. 10% senior discount. Alc dinner $25–35.
Extras Crib available.

CHESTERTOWN 12817   Map 3

The Balsam House   *Tel:* (518) 494–2828
Friends Lake Road   (518) 494–4431

The Balsam House was built as the Valentine Hotel in 1891, a typical Adirondack hotel of the period, with 39 rooms and four baths. Frank Ellis bought the building in 1981 and gutted it, leaving mainly doors, woodwork, and hardwood floors from which eleven layers of paint were scraped. The interior is furnished eclectically, with Victorian pieces, comfortable couches, and Oriental rugs. During the winter, Saturday-night sleigh rides are offered to guests (at an extra charge). Summer attractions include the inn's private beach, with lunches served at the beach house. Chef Paul C. Mullins prepares "country French" cuisine, including such entrées as shrimp in cream sauce with Pernod, garlic, and white wine; braised sweetbreads with bordelaise sauce; and veal cordon rouge. The inn is managed by Michael and Kathy Aspland.

"The inn and its setting are quite lovely. We had a comfortable room up under the eaves, with windows on the fall foliage we had come to see, and skylights to let in the morning sun. The inn provides bicycles, rowboats, picnic baskets, and all sorts of other amenities, along with menus of local restaurants. We chose to eat at the inn, and we chose well. Every part of our dinner, from the cold smoked fish plate and hot shrimp appetizers, through fine continental main dishes, to peach melba and *poire Hélène,* was well prepared. The wine list contains a good selection of California wines, fairly priced. The service was terrific, careful but not smothering." *(Hillary Huebsch Cohen)* Please, more reports.

Open All year.
Rooms 1 suite, 19 doubles, all with private bath and/or shower.
Facilities Restaurant; living room; breakfast room; TV room with movies, games; lounge with guitar music weekends in winter, nightly in summer. 22 acres on Friends Lake, with croquet, shuffleboard, beach, swimming, boating, fishing, cross-country skiing, and skating. 15 m to downhill skiing at Gore Mt. Horseback, carriage riding nearby.
Location Adirondack region, NE NY. 70 m N of Albany, 18 m NW of Lake George.

5 m S of town. Off I-87, take Rte. 9 to Rte. 28. Turn right off of Rte. 28 onto Potter Brook Rd. 4 m down on left is The Balsam House.

Credit cards Amex, DC, MC, Visa.

Rates All rates based on double occupancy. B&B, $95–145 suite, $75–95 double, $60–80 single. MAP, $145–185 suite, $125–145 double, $75–95 single, plus 7% tax and 18% service. Extra person in room, $10. 2-night minimum on weekends. Alc lunch, $8; alc dinner, $33.

Extras Cribs, babysitting, games available.

CLARENCE 14031 {: .clearfix} Map 3

Asa Ransom House
10529 Main Street (Route 5)

Tel: (716) 759–2315

A country inn that combines good food and comfortable lodging in a pleasant and welcoming atmosphere is the kind of inn we are most pleased to list in this guide, and the Asa Ransom House fits the bill to a "T." Longtime owners Robert and Judith Lenz have decorated the inviting rooms with antiques and period reproductions, country wallpapers and colonial motifs. The inn is popular with visitors and locals alike for its good country cooking. Prices are extremely reasonable, and among the many house specialties are a variety of tempting deep-dish pot pies—chicken and leek, steak and kidney, and salmon and vegetable topped with cheese pastry. As might be expected from an inn located in a wine-growing region, the cellar features an excellent selection of New York's finest labels at very fair prices.

"Bob and Judy Lenz are a charming couple who obviously care deeply about high-quality inn service. Beds are excellent, lighting is good for reading in bed, the bathrooms are modern—spotlessly clean without a hint of wear. The food is consistently well prepared and delicious, with interesting menu innovations. Particularly outstanding are the dessert selections, including homemade ice creams; the special breads; and the beautiful presentation." *(Mr. & Mrs. David McConnell)*

"Our room had just been refurbished, and the bathroom had new plumbing. Parking is ample and the inn's location well back from the highway was quiet. The sitting room invites guests with its blazing fire, jigsaw puzzles, and comfortable chairs for reading." *(Ronald & Shirley Martin).*

Open Closed Fri., Sat. Also closed Feb. through Dec.

Rooms 4 doubles, all with private bath and/or shower, telephone, radio, air-conditioning. 1 with desk.

Facilities Restaurant, tap room, library with games, gift shop. 2 acres with herb & flower gardens, pond. Swimming pool, tennis nearby; 2 m to golf.

Location W NY. 16 m NE of Buffalo, 28 m SE of Niagara Falls. Take Exit 49 from I-90. Go N on Rte. 78 (Transit Rd.) to Rte. 5. Go E 5 m to inn at corner of Main and Ransom Rd.

Restrictions No smoking. "Well-supervised children welcome."

Credit cards Discover, MC, Visa.

Rates B&B, $70–115 double, $68–78 single. 10% tax additional. Extra person in room, $10. Alc lunch, $7-8; alc dinner, $22. Children's menu.

Extras Station pickups. Crib available.

COOPERSTOWN 13326   Map 3

Cooperstown was founded in 1786 by William Cooper. His son, James Fenimore Cooper, became world famous as the author of a series of books known as the Leatherstocking Tales. Cooperstown is also the place where Abner Doubleday invented the game of baseball in 1839, and the home of the National Baseball Hall of Fame. The Glimmerglass Opera Theater, noted for its original productions of operas, has a new opera house, right on the lake. Other attractions include the Farmer's Museum, a working museum depicting eighteenth- and nineteenth-century life; Fenimore House, with a collection of American folk art and Cooper memorabilia; and Otsego Lake, with three areas for public swimming, boating, and good fishing. There's plenty of hiking, bicycling, golf, and tennis in summer, and cross-country skiing, skating, and snow-tubing in the winter.

Also recommended: The Inn at Cooperstown (16 Chestnut Street; 607–547–5756) is a mansard-roofed structure designed by the architect of the Waldorf-Astoria. The downtown location is very convenient, and rates include a continental breakfast. **Lake View Motel** (RD 2, P.O. Box 932; 607–547–9740) is a small country motel owned and operated by the Muehl family, who pride themselves in "knowing our guests have had more than a place to sleep—someone's guest bedroom, not an impersonal motel room." **The Phoenix on River Road** (RR 33, RD 3, P.O. Box 150; 607–547–8250) is a century-old hotel. Its tavern, which once served mill workers, has been restored as a cheery Williamsburg blue and white breakfast room.

Cooperstown is in New York's Central/Leatherstocking district, 30 miles south of the NY State Thruway (I-90), 20 miles north of Oneonta, and 70 miles west of Albany. From the west, use Thruway Exit 30 at Herkimer (Route 28); from the east, Thruway Exit 25A at Route I-88.

The Inn at Brook Willow   *Tel:* (607) 547–9700
RD 2, Box 514

Brook Willow is a Victorian "cottage" house, owned by Jack and Joan Grimes since 1976. Guest rooms are airy and spacious, furnished with antiques, collectibles, and ceiling fans. It's located in a part of Cooperstown known as Lentsville, whose population peaked in 1878 at 36 inhabitants.

"A wonderful country getaway that is tended to in every detail. With a lovely main house and a cozy, comfortable restored barn for most of the guest rooms, this site is picturesque and natural in atmosphere. Antiques and carefully chosen combinations of wallpapers, fabrics, and colors abound, right down to the changes in china to match the breakfast tablecloth. Our hosts greeted us each morning with sunny smiles, warm coffee, rich muffins, and eggs of our choosing. Plan to enjoy relaxed conversation with the other guests, and with Joan and Jack." *(Jo-Ann & Lloyd Jaeger)*

"I was little dubious when told that our room was in the barn, but it turned out to be perfect, furnished with beautiful antiques. Joan and Jack Grimes are the quintessential hosts, making you feel warm and welcome and introducing you to your fellow baseball fans (after all, that's why most of us were there). Breakfast-time is filled with funny anecdotes about the town and tips on how to get a great buy at an antiques auction." *(Mary & Roger Bow)*

Open All year.
Rooms 1 double in main house with private bath. 3 doubles in restored barn with private bath and/or shower, desk, ceiling fans.
Facilities Dining area, living room, family room with TV, games; fireplaces; wicker garden room, porch, barbecue. 14 acres with pond, brook, gardens, meadows, cross-country skiing.
Location 6 m to town. Turn E on Rte. 33 and follow to inn.
Restrictions No smoking.
Credit cards None accepted.
Rates B&B, $55–85 double, $40–50 single. Extra person in room, $10. No charge for children under 2. No tipping. 2-night minimum stay on weekends.
Extras Station pickups. Cribs, babysitting, games available.

The J.P. Sill House
63 Chestnut Street
Tel: (607) 547–2633

The J.P. Sill House is a late-nineteenth-century Italianate Victorian built of brick and cut stone, listed on both the National and New York State historic registers. Joyce Bohlman and co-owner Robert Lake have restored the original handcrafted woodwork, marble fireplaces, and etched glass. They have wallpapered the house with magnificent Bradbury & Bradbury period reproduction papers, with striking results.

"The beds are comfortable, the atmosphere romantic, and the rooms private. The two bathrooms (both with showers) have good lighting and modern plumbing, but one has the added charm of an old tin tub for a leisurely soak; bubble bath is provided. The living room is inviting, with its tables of reading material and decanter of sherry on the side table."

"The inn is within walking distance of the town and the street is quiet at night. The large yard provides ample off-street parking.

"The condition of the rooms shows Joyce Bohlman's love of this old home; she has made the quilts and most of the draperies herself. Her breakfasts are out of this world. Juice in crystal goblets, oven-baked French toast, sausages, and sautéed apples one morning; fresh fruit, baked eggs with salsa, and crispy croissants the next. Plus light, tasty muffins in baskets.

"My only minor suggestion for improvement might be to add brighter lighting for the bedroom mirrors." *(Margaret R. Riefe)*

Open All year.
Rooms 5 doubles (queen-size beds) all with shared bath.
Facilities Dining room, parlor with games, books, fireplace, porches. 1 acre with lawns, carriage house.
Location State Rte. 28 becomes Chestnut St. historic district, 2 blocks from center of town and Otsego Lake.
Restrictions No smoking in house. No children.
Credit cards MC, Visa.
Rates B&B, $50–80 double. 2-night minimum stay weekends, June–Oct.
Extras Station pickups.

CORNING 14830 Map 3

Rosewood Inn *Tel:* (607) 962–3253
134 East First Street

Built in 1855 as a Greek Revival home, and then redone as an English Tudor style in 1917, the Rosewood is furnished in Victorian antiques and handmade quilts. Each guest room has a special theme, from railroading to whaling to antique glass. Owners Winnie and Dick Peer are knowledgeable about Corning and will gladly assist with dining, shopping, or sightseeing plans.

"Best part was the intellectual milieu at the elaborate breakfast table, from our affable host to the other guests who included a tin smith, a violinist turned engineer, and a stock broker. A two-hour stimulating conversation carried us through baked apples with cinnamon, maple syrup, walnuts, and raisins; scrambled eggs with jalapeño cheese, fresh baking powder biscuits, pumpkin bread, brandied sweet butter, and orange scented coffee. Breakfast was accompanied by Dick's own morning paper with weather forecast, headlines of the day and local sights. Dick greeted us on arrival with a basket of fresh fruit and candy and welcomed us with tea and cookies in the lovely fire lit sitting room." *(Zita Knific)*

Open All year.
Rooms 2 suites with private bath; 4 doubles—2 with private bath and/or shower, 2 with a maximum of 4 people sharing bath. Some with telephone, TV, fireplace. 2 with air-conditioning; 4 with fan. 1 suite with kitchen and private entrance.
Facilities Dining room, sitting room with TV. Off-street parking.
Location C NY, Finger Lakes Region. Town center. Follow Rt. 17 to downtown Corning. Turn S on Chemung St., go 1 block, turn right on First St. to inn.
Restrictions No smoking in guest rooms.
Credit cards Amex, DC, MC, Visa.
Rates B&B, $90–95 suite, $68–78 double, $60–65 single, plus 7% tax. Extra person in room, $15. 2–night weekend minimum June through Oct.
Extras Station pickups. Crib available.

EAST HAMPTON 11937 Map 3

Although known best for its beaches and fashionable restaurants and shops, East Hampton actually has many historic homes dating back to the eighteenth century. If you're visiting on a rainy day, stop by to see the Mulford House, dating back to 1680, now a museum of architectural history. East Hampton is on the South Fork of eastern Long Island, reached via the Long Island Expressway or the Southern State Parkway to Route 27.

"The Hamptons are best enjoyed off season, either in the late spring or early autumn. My favorite time is September, when the weather is usually good and the ocean temperature is still relatively high. July and August can be a nightmare on weekends, with unbelievable traffic jams and mobs of trendy people everywhere, although things are much quieter during the week." (SWS)

Typical for a resort town, two- and three-night weekend minimums are the rule in season, with four or five nights required for July 4th and Labor Day weekend. Be very sure of your plans before booking; most East Hampton inns give no refunds on canceled space (which we find to be a really repugnant policy).

Also recommended: The **Bassett House Inn** (128 Montauk Highway; 516–324–6127), an 1830's house that has been restored and furnished with antiques and curios, is amply supplied with a pleasant atmosphere of camaraderie by its owner. The **Centennial House** (13 Woods Lane; 516–324–9414), an 1876 summer cottage, has marble bathrooms adjoining bedrooms and a formal parlor which boasts two crystal chandeliers and an Italian marble hearth. Breakfast is served buffet-style in an equally elegant setting. The **Hedges Inn** (74 James Lane; 516–324–7100) is named for William Hedges, who held the original land grant in 1652. The property remained in the Hedges family for over 270 years, until 1923. The inn is now home to the Palm Restaurant and fourteen guest rooms. The **1770 House** (143 Main Street; 516–324–1770), dating back to the 18th century, has served such diverse functions as a general store, private home, and even a boarding school dining hall, until its restoration in 1977. Guest rooms are furnished with antiques—four with canopy beds—and rates include a continental breakfast.

Maidstone Arms Tel: (516) 324–5006
207 Main Street

The Maidstone is set across from the town pond and village green in East Hampton's National Historic District. It was originally built as a private home, then converted to a hotel in the 1870s. Rates include a continental breakfast, served on the wicker sun porch. The inn's deservedly popular restaurant, run by Morris Weintraub, serves French cuisine, emphasizing fresh fish and local produce. Innkeepers Rita and Gary Reiswig have owned the Maidstone since 1979; Donna Cullum is the manager.

One of our English readers reports: "Thoroughly in the style of what this book is after—homey and comfortable, with sound, unobtrusive hospitality by the management. This New England–style inn has a clapboard exterior, kept warm with double glazed windows and no drafts. Interior doors never quite fit, but that's all part of the charm. Our room had pleasantly crisp if slightly frilly furnishings (the late Laura Ashley would undoubtedly have approved), old-style but thoroughly serviceable bathroom fittings, a large comfortable bed, and no shortage of hot water.

"The public rooms are very pleasant, and include a considerable library. There is a front sitting/breakfast room, mainly glass on one side, with a large woodstove. The dining room is well frequented, and dinner conducted with style, close attention, and gently self-confident humor." (Jeremy Larken)

"Excellent dinners, beautiful glassware. Mrs. Reiswig was warm and gracious. A minor annoyance—the bed sheets were too small for the mattress, and came off without much encouragement; a thoughtless neighbor played his radio or TV too loudly for comfort late one night. Overall a fine choice; we wish we could have stayed longer." *(DF)*

Open April to mid-Jan.
Rooms 5 suites, 11 doubles, all with full private bath, telephone, air-conditioning. Some with radio, TV, desk. 3 cottages available for weekly rental.
Facilities Restaurant, bar, sun porch, library. 2 acres with lawn furniture.
Location 15-min. walk to beaches, shops, entertainment. Take Rte. 495 E from NYC to Exit 70. Continue E on Rte. 27 to East Hampton. ½ m from town.
Restrictions Some traffic noise in front rooms. No children in season; no children under 6.
Credit cards Amex, MC, Visa.
Rates B&B, $150–190 suite, $95–135 double, $85–125 single, plus 7½ % tax and 3% service. Extra person in room, $10. Senior discount midweek, off season. Alc dinner, $35.
Extras Airport/station pickups.

GENEVA 14456   Map 3

The Inn at Belhurst Castle   *Tel:* (315) 781–0201
Lochland Road, P.O. Box 609

Over a century ago, fifty craftsmen labored for four years to construct a mansion of red Medina stone at a cost of $475,000—in 1885 dollars. The result, a castle built in the Richardson Romanesque style, was the private home of Mrs. Carrie Collins until 1926. Red Dwyer, her nephew, was the next owner, and turned the place into a restaurant, speakeasy, and gambling casino. In 1975, Robert and Nancy Golden bought Belhurst and set about transforming it into a gracious inn. Fortunately, all the original leaded glass, marble fireplaces, and hand-carved woodwork were well preserved, and needed only a thorough cleaning—to remove layers of tobacco smoke—to restore them to their original beauty. Rooms are decorated with period antiques, including canopied four-poster beds and leather wingback chairs.

The popular restaurant serves hearty portions of prime rib, a variety of Italian-style veal dishes, and a nice choice of fresh seafood entrées; we'd suggest a bottle of wine from one of the nearby Finger Lakes wineries as an appropriate accompaniment.

"We splurged on the sumptuous Tower Suite. Sparkling clean, Oriental rugs, and not one damn goose, grapevine, or crocheted toilet paper holder in sight. The decor defies description. Good service too. The only thing lacking was a make-up mirror. The restaurant was over-extended when we were there, but the maitre d' was accommodating about providing us with a romantic dinner in our room. The food was just average, but by candlelight, who cared?" *(KZ)*

Open All year.
Rooms 3 suites, 9 doubles, all with private bath and/or shower, telephone, radio, TV, desk, air-conditioning. Most rooms with fireplace. 1 room in annex.
Facilities Dining room, bar/lounge. 23 acres on lake for fishing, swimming, boating. Golf nearby.
Location W NY, Finger Lakes. 50 m W of Syracuse, 35 m SE of Rochester. On Rte. 14, 2 m S of center of town.

Credit cards Amex, DC, MC, Visa.
Rates Room only, $160–200 suite, $80–115 double. Prix fixe lunch, $7; alc dinner, $28. Early bird, children's dinners, $11.
Extras Airport/station pickups. Cribs, babysitting available. French, Spanish spoken.

GROTON 13073   Map 3

Benn Conger Inn   *Tel:* (607) 898–5817
206 West Cortland Street

Since Pat and Mark Bloom bought the Benn Conger Inn in 1985, they've built up an excellent reputation for fine lodging and outstanding French and Italian food. The limited-choice menus change with the seasons, but are mouth watering year-round.

Pat Bloom reports that "we really concentrate on food and wine, modeling our inn on the classic chef-owned European auberge, with the guest rooms being large and comfortable but not decorated with museum-quality furnishings. We're an inn for people who love to eat and love wine. Our wine list is extensive and growing, with many treasures and surprising values—it's our passion. We've received the *Wine Spectators* 'Award of Excellence' for the past two years."

"The exterior of the inn is impressive: a well-maintained Greek Revival structure with several large and unusual arched windows. The grounds are attractively planted. We particularly enjoyed conversing with the other guests by the fireplace in the comfortable library. The dining rooms are spacious and attractively furnished. A handsome center hall staircase leads to the guest rooms. Each of the oversized rooms is well appointed and offers its own distinctive charm—an old-fashioned fireplace, a reading porch, or Empire antique furnishings. Care is taken to anticipate any guest's needs, seen in the surfeit of fluffy towels and the fine bed linens. Our visit was truly made memorable by the hospitality of our hosts, Pat and Mark Bloom. We especially enjoyed one of their special dinners, wine and food of the Rhône. The five-course meal featured fall vegetables, venison from fallow deer, special chèvre, all prepared to perfection. Each course was accompanied by a thoughtfully chosen Rhône wine." *(Jane & Tom Jacobs)*

Open April through Feb.; restaurant closed Sun., Mon.
Rooms 3 suites, 1 double, all with private bath and/or shower, desk, fan. 1 suite with fireplace.
Facilities Restaurant, bar/library with fireplace, upstairs common room with TV. 18 acres with hiking, cross-country skiing. Tennis, golf, water sports nearby.
Location Central NY, Finger Lakes. Approx. halfway between Ithaca and Cortland, 45 min. S of Syracuse. From Cortland, take Rte. 222 to Groton. Cross Rte. 38, making no turns; inn is up hill on right. From Ithaca, take Rte. 13 N to Rte. 366E to Rte. 38. Turn left on Rte. 38; go N about 4 m to Groton. Stay on Rte. 38 to Rte. 222. Turn left to inn up hill on right.
Restrictions No smoking in guest rooms. No young children.
Credit cards Amex, DC, MC, Visa.
Rates B&B, $80–100 suite, $65 double. Extra person in room, $15–35. 2-night weekend minimum stay, May–Nov., holidays. Alc dinner, $35–40.
Extras Spanish, Russian, some French spoken.

HADLEY 12835 Map 3

Saratoga Rose B&B Inn *Tel:* (518) 696–2861
4870 Rockwell Street

Built in the late 1800's, the Saratoga Rose was restored as an inn by Tony and Nancy Merlino in 1988, and has been decorated in Victorian country decor. Grand Marnier French toast and eggs Anthony are breakfast favorites, while dinner entrees have an Italian accent, with homemade pastas a speciality.

"The Saratoga Rose is built on top of hill overlooking the little town of Hadley, just a short drive from Saratoga Springs. The interior furnishings of the inn look like they had just been photographed for *Country Living* magazine. Our bedroom had a big, cozy four-poster bed covered with an old-fashioned quilt and strewn with fluffy, ruffled throw pillows. The fireplace was well-supplied with logs for chilly nights. We awoke to the smell of freshly brewed coffee and Tony's full breakfast. He and Nancy were invaluable assistants in planning our daily activities and excursions. The inn also serves delicious dinners, prepared by an expert chef. *(Ligaya & Ronald Duncan)*

"Charming building, in a quiet setting just across the bridge from Lake Luzerne, with equally charming owners. We were in the Blue Room, which was lovingly appointed and spotlessly clean, as was the bathroom. The pleasant library is well supplied with reading materials, and dinners in the attractive dining room were delicious." *(Vreni Ness)* "The Merlinos really make an extra effort for their guests. They are flexible about mealtimes, not clock watchers like some other innkeepers we've encountered." *(Eileen & Jorge Yajure)*

Open All year.
Rooms 5 doubles, all with private bath, fan.
Facilities Library with TV, restaurant with fireplace, foyer, veranda. 1 acre with woods. Tennis, golf, cross-country skiing nearby. 5 min. to Lake Sacandaga for water sports. 5 m to downhill skiing.
Location NE NY, in Adirondack Park. 45 m N of Albany, 15 m N of Saratoga, 10 m S of Lake George. From Saratoga, take Rte. 9N N through Corinth to Lake Luzerne. Left on Bay Rd. to Main St. Turn left on Rockwell St. Inn is 500 yards on left, past Rockwell Falls Bridge.
Restrictions No smoking in guest rooms. No children under age 12.
Credit cards MC, Visa.
Rates B&B, $60–110, double. Extra person in room, $6–11. 2-night summer weekend minimum. Picnic lunch by prior arrangement, $10. Alc dinner, $25.

HAGUE 12836 Map

Trout House Village Resort *Tel:* (518) 543–6088
Lake Shore Drive (Route 9 N)

Those underwhelmed by the overdeveloped town of Lake George should head directly north to Hague, where the natural beauty of the lake is not obscured by dozens of tacky T-shirt shops. Trout House is an old-fashioned family resort, owned by Lynn and Bob Patchett since 1971, and managed by son Scott and daughter Alice Patchett. Rooms are furnished with comfortable "colonial-style" upholstered furniture, although some guest rooms in the main lodge have four-poster and brass beds. Although no organized children's programs are offered, kids will keep busy for days with all the lake has to offer; be sure to save a day for visiting nearby Fort Ticonderoga.

"Spread out along the lake front, the resort consists of the comfortable old lodge, basic motel rooms and handsome new log cabins. We stayed in the Library Room with a spectacular view of the lake, shelves of great books, and good lighting. We spent a pleasant summer evening in rocking chairs on the big veranda." *(Gladys & Jim Gilliland)*

Open All year.
Rooms 13 suites, 10 doubles, 16 cabins—most with private bath. 3 rooms share 1 bath. All with TV, fan. Some with telephone, radio, desk, porch. 2 with whirlpool bath, fireplace.
Facilities Dining room, living room, TV/game room, lounge. 5 acres with putting green, lawn games, bicycles. 400-foot beach/lake front for swimming, canoeing, kayaking, sailing, fishing. Cross-country skiing, snowmobiling, hiking. Golf, tennis nearby.
Location NE NY. N end of Lake George. 8 m S of Ticonderoga. From I-87 take exit 25 and follow Rte 8 to Hague. Turn left onto Rte. 9. Resort on right.
Credit cards Amex, MC, Visa.
Rates Room only, $79–204 suites and cabins, $41–83 double, $35–75 single. Full breakfast, $5. Extra person in room $5. 5% senior discount. Weekly rates. 2-night minimum summer holiday weekends.
Extras Airport pickups. Cribs, babysitting available.

ITHACA 14851   Map 3

Information please: Some Ithaca B&Bs we'd like to hear more about are **The Peregrine House** (140 College Avenue 14850; 607–272–0919), an eight guest room B&B built in 1874 in the French Mansard style. It's three blocks from the Cornell campus, and rooms are furnished in period and rates include a full breakfast. The **Buttermilk Falls B&B** (110 East Buttermilk Falls Road; 607–273–3947), a sturdy brick house built in 1825, and owned by the Rumsey family for five generations. Located just across the street from the falls, convenient for a summertime dip, the B&B rates of $50–100 include a full breakfast.

Rose Inn   *Tel:* (607) 533–7905
Route 34 North, P.O. Box 6576

There's little we need to add to the highly enthusiastic reports we've received on the Rose Inn, except to note that the Rosemanns reopened the mansion in 1983, after renovating and redecorating it. In 1986, they completed an addition to the inn—two luxurious honeymoon suites and several new guest rooms. More recently, they began serving dinners to the public. Charles, who was born in Berlin, is delighted to help guests plan tours of the Finger Lakes wineries; Sherry is an interior designer specializing in pre-Victorian nineteenth-century furniture.

"The inn is situated in beautiful farm country north of Ithaca, overlooking Lake Cayuga. The house was built by a wealthy farmer during the 1800s; a remarkable spiral mahogany staircase (completed in 1924) runs through the core of the building. Throughout, Rose Inn is furnished in antiques. More important is the feeling of gracious comfort found in each of the inn's rooms.

"Both Charles and Sherry Rosemann contribute to the absolutely superb food served at the inn. Charles's breakfast features French toast, eggs Benedict, and German apple pancakes, accentuated by Sherry's homemade preserves, and accompanied by cider from the inn's orchard. Their personal blend of coffee has a subtle hint of almonds. Sherry's dinners are a joy. Creatively designed menus and superb food beautifully presented are the norm—from sweetbreads with black butter to chateaubriand." *(William Bennett)*

"Sherry and Charles Rosemann advised us on restaurants, skiing, bookstores, and other interests; their suggestions eliminated the usual trial-and-error approach of visitors to a strange town. By the end of the week we felt as warm and comfortable as we do in our own home. The house was well heated, the bathrooms spotless, and stocked with amenities to comfort sore, cold, wet legs after a day of skiing." *(Marie D. Osborne)*

Open All year. Restaurant closed Sun. and Mon. from Dec. through March
Rooms 3 suites, 12 doubles—all with full private bath, radio, fan. Some rooms with desk, whirlpool tub.
Facilities Dining room, 3 public rooms with TV, stereo, library, games. 20 acres with lawns, fishing pond. 4 m to sailing, fishing, swimming on Lake Cayuga. 15–20 m to cross-country, downhill skiing.
Location Central NY, Finger Lakes region. 55 m S of Syracuse. 9 m from town. 9 m to Cornell University. 12 m to Ithaca College. From Ithaca, take Rte. 34 N 5.7 m to a "T," turn right, go ½ m to fork, stay left 3.5 m to inn.
Restrictions No smoking. No children under 11.
Credit cards Not accepted for deposit. Amex, MC, Visa.
Rates B&B, $175–250 suite, $100–150 double, plus 9% tax, 15% service. Extra person in room, $25. 2- to 3-night weekend/holiday minimum. Prix fixe dinner, $45. Sunday brunch ($12.50) can be arranged for minimum of 12 persons.
Extras Airport pickup. German, Spanish spoken.

LAKE LUZERNE 12846   Map 3

The Lamplight Inn   *Tel:* (518) 696–5294
2129 Lake Avenue (Route 9N), P.O. Box 70

In 1984, Gene and Linda Merlino left jobs in the textile printing business to renovate The Lamplight, a Victorian summer cottage built in 1890 by Howard Conkling, a wealthy lumberman and summer resident. Conkling was a very eligible bachelor, and his home was designed for entertaining. Five doors off the parlor lead out to the wraparound porch. The first floor has 12-foot beamed ceilings, with chestnut wainscotting, moldings, and a keyhole staircase all crafted in England. Linda reports that "we have tried to make our inn as comfortable as we can, with good mattresses, reading lights on both sides of the beds, individual thermostats, and modern baths. Flannel sheets and fluffy comforters are provided for winter warmth." An addition completed in 1988 expanded both the common areas and number of guest rooms, without detracting from the integrity of the original structure.

"The atmosphere is very friendly, comfortable, and warm—a perfect place for couples to get away and relax. The downstairs consists of a huge sitting room with fireplace and TV, library, and sun porch. Parking is adequate, less than 100 feet from the house. Gene and Linda have all the activities of the town and surrounding areas posted and are happy to set up dinner reservations." *(MB)* "Location is optimum. Off the beaten path yet accessible to all the things the Adirondack region has to offer." *(Joseph DiRocco)*

"A fire was usually roaring in the fireplace in the large parlor area; the TV is discreetly tucked away in an antique cabinet. The hardwood floors are beautiful, covered with Oriental rugs. Gene cooks breakfast, a really sumptuous meal, served on the sun porch or in the dining room. The weekend specials were waffles and strawberries, peach crepes, and raisin French toast, but you could also order any style of eggs. Along with this Linda serves homemade breads, muffins, and cakes." *(Nancy Sosinski)* "The inn is as clean as a hospital operating room with the charm of a Victorian manor house." *(Howard & Arlene Williamson)*

Open All year. Closed Christmas.
Rooms 10 doubles—all with private shower, ceiling fan. 5 with fireplaces. 1 with full bath, 2 with double showers.
Facilities Breakfast room; living room with fireplace, TV; library with fireplace, chess table; wraparound veranda. 4 acres with perennial garden. 1 block to Lake Luzerne for swimming, fishing. White-water rafting, cross-country skiing nearby.
Location E central NY. S Adirondack Region. 45 min. N of Albany, 17 m NNW of Saratoga Springs, 9 m SW of Lake George village. Take the Northway I-87 to Exit 21; go left & follow Rte. 9N W 10 m to inn on right. 1 block from town.
Restrictions Smoking in living room only (no cigars or pipes). No children under 12.
Credit cards Amex.
Rates B&B, $65–125 double. Extra person in room, $25. 2-night weekend minimum, summer. Except Aug., 10% discount for 5-night stay; 1 night free with 7-day stay.

NEW YORK CITY   Map 3

There are many very wonderful things to be found in New York City, but little hotels are unfortunately not at the top of the list. An unusually high number of hotels can't even be bothered to return questionnaires, and although some readers have been very helpful, others are less likely to report on big-city establishments.

What to do? We sent contributing editor Lisa Davis onto the streets to check out some of the more likely prospects. Based on her inspections, we've included some of the best, and intentionally omitted some small hotels with big names and reputations, but shabby rooms and unfriendly staffs. Please do write and let us know what you think of these entries, and if you've any suggested additions.

In making our selections, we considered anything under 300 rooms was small by Big Apple standards; more important was the attentiveness of the staff and the quality of the rooms and public areas. You may want to think of a visit to New York City as a lesson in assertiveness training. Particularly in the older hotels, the quality of the rooms is uneven, and you may be shown to a room that appears dirty or stained, or has sagging beds, or is in otherwise poor repair. Reject it immediately on one of these grounds, and ask to be shown one that has been more recently redecorated. Another decision in selecting a room is the choice of light or quiet. Ideally, a room on a top floor will provide both; if one is not available, front rooms will usually be noisier, back rooms darker. Don't be shy about making your preferences known.

When booking a room, expect to pay a bare minimum of $100–150 for a double on weekdays; weekend, summer, and Christmas week rates offer considerable savings, so always ask about any promotional rates when booking. Budget-conscious travelers will want to plan their NYC visits to spend the weekend in the city, when rates are lowest, and weekdays exploring the countryside, when country rates are lower. If the hotel rates quoted here are beyond your means (not at all difficult considering the midweek rates), we'd advise booking a room in a B&B through one of the half-dozen agencies available. One frequent contributor stayed in a pleasant unhosted apartment that she found through **City Lights, Bed & Breakfast Ltd.** (P.O. Box 20355 Cherokee Station, 10028; 212–737–7049). Drop us a line if you'd like more names and addresses.

Rates do not include city, state, and local hotel taxes, which total 13–25%, plus a $2 room fee.

Also recommended: The **Hotel Beverly** (125 East 50th Street at Lexington Avenue, 10022; 212–753–2700, 800–223–0945), family owned for over twenty years, has an inviting wood-paneled lobby with old-fashioned furniture and crystal chandeliers, and traditionally styled guest rooms with large, comfortable couches for relaxing. Long before the concept became so popular, the Beverly was virtually an all-suite hotel. The **Hotel Empire** (44 West 63rd Street at Broadway, 10023; 212–265–7400, 800–545–7400) is included mainly because of its superb location just across the street from Lincoln Center. The hotel was fully renovated as of April 1987, and once drab and dingy rooms have been attractively redone. Midweek rates are extremely reasonable by New York City standards. The **Hotel Plaza Athénée** (37 East 64th Street, 10021; 212–734–9100, 800–CALL–THF), once the site of a rundown old hotel, was reopened in 1984 with hardly an inch of floor space unrestored. A definite five-star luxury hotel, it's European in style, clientele, and ownership. **The Lowell** (28 East 63rd Street, 10021; 212–838–1400) is exceptionally small for New York, with 60 suites and doubles, so it is able to offer truly personalized service to guests. Built in 1928, the building was overhauled in 1984 in a no-expense-spared renovation. Rooms are individually and distinctively furnished, with an eclectic mixture of French and Oriental pieces, eighteenth- and nineteenth-century prints, and Art Deco light fixtures. **Morgans** (237 Madison Avenue, 10011; 212–686–0300), opened in 1984, has rooms and baths which are small and low-ceilinged but their elegant, contemporary design helps to compensate for these drawbacks. The owners' goal, to create bedrooms that did not look like those in conventional hotels, has been effectively achieved. The **Park Avenue Sheraton** (45 Park Avenue at 37th Street, 10016; 212–685–7676, 800–325–3535), formerly the Sheraton Russell, is a small hotel whose quiet, elegant accommodation is its hallmark. The entire building was completely redone in 1987—and it shows. **The Pierre** (5th Avenue and 61st Street; 212–838–8000, 800–268–6282) —when many New York City hotels have become newly elegant after multi-million-dollar renovations—has *always* been that way. From the frescoed charm of the Rotunda for drinks or tea to the handsome guest rooms traditionally decorated with muted fabrics, formal draperies, Chippendale and Chinoiserie furnishings, the Pierre offers all the luxuries and extra amenities you'd expect from a hotel of this caliber. **The Stanhope** (995 Fifth Avenue, 10028; 212–288–5800, 800–828–1123) is located across the street from the Metropolitan Museum of Art and from Central Park. In November 1986, the Stanhope opened under new ownership, sporting a $26 million restoration. A 250-member staff provides the ultimate in service for the 117 guest rooms.

Doral Tuscany   *Tel:* (212) 686–1600
120 East 39th Street 10016   (800) 847–4078

Very much a small hotel by New York City standards, the Doral's location on a relatively quiet residential street is convenient to most city activities. Rooms are decorated with traditional furnishings, and vary considerably in size—but not in price. A nearby hotel under the same management and similarly recommended is the **Doral Court,** (130 East 39th Street; 212–889–0287 or 800–624–0607) with oversize rooms and a pleasant courtyard cafe.

"The doorman, desk folks, and elevator man were so friendly and helpful that we felt very much at home. They are older professionals who take their work seriously. We had a pleasant room, fairly large by New York City standards, with a decorative fireplace. The housekeeping staff were very responsive. There's a lovely little lobby with brass and wood paneling and fresh flowers, and the midtown location is great." *(Kathleen Novak, also Ethel Aaron Hauser)*

Open All year.
Rooms 7 1–2 bedroom suites, 112 doubles, all with full private bath, telephone, radio, TV, desk, air-conditioning, refrigerator. Some with exercise bikes.
Facilities Restaurant, bar/lounge, valet parking, health club.
Location Midtown Manhattan, Murray Hill, just E of Park Ave.
Credit cards Amex, DC, MC, Visa.
Rates Room only, $350–700 suite, $220 double, $195 single. Alc breakfast, $6–10; alc lunch, $45; alc dinner, $70. Lower weekend rates.
Extras Wheelchair accessible. French, Spanish spoken. Cribs, babysitting available.

Dumont Plaza   *Tel:* (212) 481–7600
150 East 34th Street 10016–4601   (800) ME–SUITE

Nine family-owned hotels throughout midtown make up the chain of Manhattan East Suite Hotels. The Dumont is the newest, having been completed in 1987. Suites at the Dumont are spacious and adequately decorated, the kitchenettes well-equipped. Staff members were hospitable, proud of the new quarters, and eager to address particular guest requests. The 2-bedroom suites are particularly recommended for families or for two couples traveling together; the extra space and the weekend rates make this a very good option. If the location of the Dumont isn't convenient, call their reservations number for the addresses of their other properties.

Open All year.
Rooms 252 suites, all with full private bath, telephone, radio, TV, desk/table. Some with kitchenettes.
Facilities Restaurant, lounge, health club, garden terrace. Concierge service.
Location Midtown, East Side.
Restrictions Light sleepers should request back rooms.
Credit cards All major cards.
Rates Room only, $185–340 suite. Extra person in room, $20. Weekend rates, $89–220. Summer packages, $95–230.
Extras Limited wheelchair access. French, Spanish spoken. Cribs, babysitting available.

Grand Bay Hotel at Equitable Center
152 West 51st Street, 10019

Tel: (212) 765–1900
(800) 239–0990

Imagine leaving the hubbub of midtown Manhattan, lined with faceless glass towers, for a totally calm and elegant marble-floored lobby, done in soft salmon and taupe, lined with plush Oriental carpets. To the side is a quiet lounge, with conversational groupings of period furniture and soft couches, eighteenth- and nineteenth-century art, and a discreet service bar, should you care for a drink or afternoon tea. The attentive staff awaits you at the thankfully small registration area—the intimate (by Big Apple standards) size of the hotel eliminates check-in lines. The hotel is built inside the gutted shell of the old Taft Hotel; virtually the only thing left of the old hotel are the carved bronze panels in the lobby.

Guest rooms are spacious by New York City standards, and supplied with every conceivable luxury—two-line telephones, one TV discreetly concealed in the armoire, another on a swivel base in the bathroom; the bathrooms also have a make-up mirror, hair dryer, Crabtree and Evelyn toiletries, and robes. Mineral water and a bucket of ice are left when the beds are turned down at night. Room decor varies from country French to Art Deco to modern; all are very handsome and supplied with oversize beds and comfortable reading chairs.

Another advantage here is the location, an easy walk from the theater district, yet far enough removed from the 42nd Street sleaze. Fifth Avenue and Rockefeller Center are also close by, and it's a reasonable walk to Carnegie Hall, Central Park, Lincoln Center, and many of the city's museums. *(SWS)*

Open All year.
Rooms 52 suites, 126 doubles, all with full private bath, telephone, TV, radio, desk, air-conditioning.
Facilities Restaurant, lobby/lounge with piano music, beauty salon, gift shop. Concierge services. Valet parking. Health club nearby with heated swimming pool, hot tub, exercise equipment.
Location Midtown Manhattan. At corner of 7th Ave.
Credit cards Amex, DC, Encore, MC, Visa.
Rates Room only, $345–900 suite, $255–285 double, $235–265 single. Extra person in room, $20. Holiday packages. Alc breakfast, $15.

Extras Wheelchair accessible. Morning limousine service to Wall St. Cribs, babysitting available. Spanish, French, Portuguese, Italian, German, Arabic, Chinese spoken. Small pets allowed. Member, Preferred Hotels.

Manhattan Viscount Hotel
127 East 55th Street 10022

Tel: (212) 826–1100
(800) 221–1074

This 36-floor hotel was originally built as a condominium, and was converted into a hotel at the end of 1985. It still has something of that feeling—resembling an exclusive private apartment house, rather than a hotel. The lobby, bar, and restaurant are all small but elegant, and the rooms are done in handsome contemporary styles, with custom-made Italian furniture, French carpeting in an unusual but attractive plaid; there are no more than three or four rooms to a floor.

"This is a great hotel in a superb location. With so few rooms to a floor, a woman traveling alone can feel quite secure. The lobby is posh with mirrors everywhere, light woods, and a comfortable seating area—understated elegance. My room had a separate sitting area with sofa, coffee table, and two chairs at a small round table. There was also a separate desk and chair. The walls were a light medium yellow, the curtain, bedspread and sofa a strong blue with wide yellow borders. A separate dressing room had a built-in chest and dressing table, even a lighted makeup mirror. The bath was all beige marble, with a huge tub and a bidet. The towels included a fluffy bath sheet as well as the usual sizes. There were phones everywhere, along with tasteful modern prints and a subtle gray plaid rug with narrows strips of yellow, blue, black and white. Rates include a continental breakfast of coffee and rolls; room service was very fast, the servings generous. The staff was very friendly and generally accommodating.

"The minor drawbacks—one day my bed was made up with a torn sheet; the next, there was no problem with the sheets but obtaining a clean washcloth and bath sheet required several calls to housekeeping. At $195 a day, one would hope such minor annoyances could be ironed out." *(SC)*

Open All year.
Rooms 106 suites and doubles, all with full private bath, telephone, radio, TV, desk.
Facilities Restaurant, bar.
Location Midtown, East Side. On a (relatively) quiet street.
Credit cards All major cards.
Rates B&B, $195 suite, $175 double, $155 single. Weekend rate, $120. Extra person in room, $20. No charge for children under 12 in parents' room.
Extras Several foreign languages spoken. Wheelchair accessible. Airport/station pickups. Cribs available.

Wyndham
42 West 58th Street, 10019

Tel: (212) 753–3500

In a city of hype, the Wyndham's profile is so low as to be almost invisible. The management is not interested in publicity of any kind, and does not even publish a brochure or rate card. But their individually decorated rooms and reasonable rates make the hotel very popular with those in the know, including more than a few celebrities from California and England. Its location is ideal—a relatively short walk (5–20 minutes) to Carnegie Hall, City Center, Lincoln Center, and the Broadway theaters.

"The Wyndham is small and European in character and traditional in decor. The service is good and personal." *(Elizabeth Ring)*

"A wonderful hotel. Women traveling alone like the security. My suite had a living room, bedroom, bathroom, and little eating area with a refrigerator. I found it quiet, compared to other New York City hotels; the staff was very friendly, more like staying in an apartment." *(Dianne Crawford)*

Open All year.
Rooms 148 suites, doubles, and singles, all with full private bath, telephone, TV.
Location Midtown Manhattan.
Credit cards Amex, CB, DC, MC, Visa.
Rates Room only, $160–190 suite, $115–125 double, $100–110 single.

ONEIDA 13421   Map 3

The Pollyanna Bed & Breakfast   *Tel:* (315) 363–0524
302 Main Street

If you're looking for a pleasant overnight to break up the long haul up the New York State Thruway, consider the Pollyanna. It's a good example of what B&Bs are all about—well-traveled, multi-faceted hosts with a large and architecturally distinctive house to share with guests. Ken Chapin is a business consultant who also collects canes and makes English baskets, while Doloria is a textile artist and craftswoman who plays the dulcimer and tends their beautiful gardens of roses, lilies, and 100 kinds of iris. Their home is a turn-of-the-century brick Italian mansion with the original woodwork, crystal chandeliers, and eclectic detailing. Rates include a full breakfast.

"Lovely home, very clean and comfortable. Very gracious hosts—Ken is always open to a game of chess and Doloria will gladly show you her loom or play her dulcimer for you." *(Trudy Staples)*

Open Closed Jan. 15–Feb. 15.
Rooms 6 doubles—with shared baths. All with fan. TV on request.
Facilities Parlor, dining room, common room with library, games, organ. Perennial, rose, Japanese gardens. Laundry facilities available.
Location N NY. 25 m E of Syracuse, 23 m W of Utica. Historic district. From Utica, take I-90 to Exit 33. Go W on Rte. 5 to town.
Restrictions No smoking. Some traffic noise on summer Fri. evenings. "Well mannered children welcome."
Credit cards MC, Visa; 5% surcharge.
Rates B&B, $50–65 double, $30–40 single. Extra person in room, $10. 10% discount for 4 day visit. 2-night college and holiday weekend minimum.
Extras Airport/station pickups for fee. Crib, babysitting available.

PITTSFORD 14534   Map 3

Oliver Loud's Inn   *Tel:* (716) 248–5200
1474 Marsh Road

In its first life, Oliver Loud's Inn was located in the village of Egypt, which was on a busy stagecoach route in days past. When the Erie Canal was completed, the stagecoach business died out, and the once busy tavern lost much of its trade. In 1985, the inn was scheduled for demolition, but the owners of Richardson's Canal House decided to move it next to their four-star restaurant, to provide luxury lodgings in a historic setting.

"A restored nineteenth-century building, the inn has been decorated with reproduction furniture and colors documented from the period. The owners have done much research into the history of the building. The Erie Canal, a beautiful backdrop in any season, is close to Rochester and many activities." *(Bonnie Gibson)*

"Freshly painted in an appealing yellow color, the inn has an extremely inviting appearance. The hostess warmly welcomed us into a beautifully furnished sitting room, decorated with historic mementos relating to the history of the inn. Our second-floor room was furnished with a four-poster canopy king-size bed, with appropriate lamps, tables, and desk completing the decor. It was evident that much skilled planning had gone into the furnishing of the inn. Immaculate linens, floors, and baths were also a plus. Our dinner at Richardson's Canal House was superb. The wonderful breakfast served in our room included fresh fruit and juice, coffee, home-made rolls and muffins, cheese, and jam." *(George & Myra Trautman)*

Open All year. Restaurant closed most Sundays, Christmas, New Year's Day.
Rooms 8 doubles, all with full private bath, telephone, radio, TV, desk, air-conditioning.
Facilities Common room with fireplace, books, games; porch, restaurant adjacent with weekend musical entertainment. 5 acres. On Erie Canal, with towpath for walking, bicycling, cross-country skiing, fishing.
Location NW NY. Finger Lakes region. 12 m SE of Rochester, 3½ m from Pittsford. From I-90, take I-490 W to Bushnell's Basin exit. Turn right and go 400 yds to Richardson's Canal House Village, where inn is located. From downtown Rochester, take I-490 E to Bushnell's Basin; proceed as above.
Restrictions No children under 12.
Credit cards Amex, CB, DC, MC, Visa.
Rates B&B, $125 double. Alc lunch, $8; alc dinner, $25.
Extras Wheelchair accessible; 1 room equipped for disabled. French, Spanish spoken.

RHINEBECK 12572   Map 3

Rhinebeck combines the charms of a beautifully preserved historic village with the modern-day appeal of first-class craft shops and galleries and innovative restaurants. The village recently celebrated its 300th birthday, and dozens of its buildings, ranging in style from Dutch colonial to Federal to Gothic and Greek Revival, are listed on the National Register of Historic Places. A key annual event in Rhinebeck is the Dutchess County Fair, held since 1919 during the third week of August; it's a real old-fashioned country fair, with ox-pulling contests and flower and vegetable displays (expect rate surcharges). From May through October, there's some kind of festival on the calendar nearly every month—crafts, antiques, and others. Be sure to catch an air show at the Old Rhinebeck Aerodrome, highlighting aircraft from World War I and earlier.

Also recommended: The **Beekman Arms** (4 Mill Street; 914–876–7077), founded in 1766, is one of the oldest inns in America and remains a delightful place to go for a drink or dinner. Although we've had mixed feedback about noise problems with guest rooms in the main building, the adjacent Delamater House, dating back to 1844, is now enthusiastically endorsed for its lovely and quiet accommodations. *(JB)*

Information please: The **Montgomery Inn** is a turn-of-the-century Victorian B&B with wraparound porch and flower gardens (67 Montgomery Street; 914–876–3311); the **Village Inn**, a small motel with country inn charm (Route 9, P.O. Box 941; 914–876–7000). For a more rural feeling, drive down a winding dirt road to reach **Whistle Wood Farm**, a horse breeding farm with four guest rooms and a friendly, informal atmosphere (11 Pells Road; 914–876–6838).

Rhinebeck is about 100 miles north of New York City, and is easily accessible by train from Grand Central Station. By car, take the NY State Thruway (I-87) to Exit 19 (Kingston-Rhinecliff Bridge). Continue to light. Right onto Rte. 9G to light. Right onto Route 9 to Rhinebeck. Another route is the Saw Mill Parkway to the Taconic to Route 199 west to Route 308 west into Rhinebeck.

Village Victorian Inn   *Tel:* (914) 876–8345
31 Center Street

Judy and Rich Kohler bought the Village Victorian in 1987. With the help of innkeeper Julie Kirsh they have done, by all reports, a fine job of converting this 1860s home into a bed & breakfast inn.

"The inn is set on a quiet street in the middle of town, within walking distance of the Fairground, the revival movie theater, and two charming restaurants. We had the downstairs bedroom, a Victorian suite with a king-size reproduction canopy bed, a huge, fascinating armoire, and a small bath—pretty wallpapers, nice colors, all spotlessly clean. There's a nice dining room and a small but pleasant parlor with a sofa, several upholstered chairs, and a card table, all antiques of various vintages and value. The owners live in Stanfordville, about twenty minutes away." *(JR)* "Julie, the innkeeper, never intruded on our privacy, but was always there to take care of our needs. Our room had an Oriental mauve rug, a gorgeous and comfortable brass bed with Victorian-style sheets trimmed with ruffles and lace. The pillows, with satin shams, were artfully arranged on the bed, and the quilt, a slightly different print than the sheets, was beautiful, as was the matching dust ruffle and coordinating wallpaper. The potpourri gave the room a lovely clean aroma. The bath was handsomely done with dusty rose towels and white wicker, and the closet was even supplied with peach-colored satin hangers."*(Debra Segal)* "The decanter of sherry and glasses in the sitting room to sip as you please is a delightful touch." *(Don & Rachel Shive)*

"This yellow house with wraparound veranda is surrounded by a white picket fence. Inside are the original hardwood floors, moldings, and paneling, all polished and shining. Every corner of the inn shone and sparkled, starting with the crystal drops that hung from the lamp next to the guest book. Judy Kohler greeted us warmly at the door, whisked us inside, and showed us around. The house is furnished with meticulously cared for antiques. The gorgeous bed linens—sheets, dust ruffle, comforter, pillow shams—all complemented one another, and were crisp, clean, and new. On the dresser, covered with an antique crocheted doily, was a basket with lovely soap, shampoo, and a travel toothbrush, along with a vase of fresh flowers. We awoke in the morning to the aroma of fresh coffee and all kinds of wonderful baking smells wafting through the house. We entered the dining room to find a sideboard overflowing with a variety of fruits, fresh croissants and fresh-baked muffins. We were then served French bread toast, accompanied by fresh strawberries and whipped cream, followed by any style of eggs, potatoes, and bacon (for those who could find room). Along with all of this came homemade jellies, preserves, and jams, tasty coffee, and a choice of fine teas. Afternoon tea was equally delightful, with a snifter of brandy to ward off the autumn chill. Breakfast our second day was just as good, with a mouthwatering soufflé as the special entrée."

And less favorably: "The yard was unkempt, and the porch needed sweeping." *(Olivia & Carl Johnsen)*

Open All year.
Rooms 5 doubles, 2 with private tub, 3 with private shower. All with ceiling fans, air-conditioning.
Facilities Dining room with fireplace; parlor with games, TV; porch. 2 m from Hudson River for swimming, fishing, sailing. 3 m to cross-country skiing; 25 min. to downhill.
Location 18 m N of Poughkeepsie, 4 m E of Kingston, 15 m SW of Berkshires. 1 block from center of town. From Rte. 308 in Rhinebeck, turn right on Center St. Inn is on corner on right. From Rte. 9, turn left on Livingston St. to inn on right at corner.
Restrictions Smoking on veranda only. No children under 16.
Credit cards Amex, MC, Visa.
Rates B&B, $85–120 double. Extra person in room, $40. 2-3 night minimum weekends, holidays.
Extras Airport/station pickups.

SARATOGA SPRINGS 12866　　　　　　　　　　　　　Map 3

"Queen of the Spas," and one of the most popular and fashionable resorts of late Victorian America, the heritage of Saratoga Springs was nearly destroyed by the wrecker's ball in the 1960s. Fortunately, the voice of the preservationists was heard before all was lost, and the town has not only restored much of its past glory, but has added some important new attractions as well. In August, horse lovers head early in the morning for the 127-year-old track to watch the horses work out, return in the afternoon for the races, then move on to the polo fields at 6 P.M. for world-class matches. (If you can't make it in August, the Saratoga Harness Track has races nearly year-round.) Culture buffs are equally delighted with the summer program at the Saratoga Performing Arts Center, with the Philadelphia Orchestra and the New York City Ballet in residence during much of July and August. Open most of the year are the town's museums, including the country's first dance museum, the National Museum of Racing, and the Casino in Congress Park, with exhibits depicting the town's heyday. Last but certainly not least are the famous waters—sample them in town at Hathorn Spring No. 1, or head to Saratoga Spa State Park for a soak or a swim in the baths or swimming pools. Contact the Chamber of Commerce, 494 Broadway (518–584–3255) for a calendar of events.

The good news on the spa front is that TW/Recreation Services, competent operators of the parks and lodges in many national parks, is investing $5.2 million in renovating the historic **Gideon Putnam Hotel** and adjacent spa buildings. Reports?

For an especially good meal in Saratoga, a reader suggests **Eartha's Kitchen,** a tiny place serving exceptional food.

August is *the season* in Saratoga Springs, when room rates triple. Unless you expect to make up the difference at the track, consider staying in a neighboring town, where prices are more reasonable (see suggestions below). Another alternative, if you are something of a gambler, is to not make reservations and just see which hotels still have rooms available after six o'clock; we have heard that the Adelphi drops rates on unbooked rooms in the evening.

Information please: The **Six Sisters** (149 Union Avenue; 518–583–1173) is named in honor of the innkeeper's siblings—but if they come to visit all at once, they'll have to share the three guest rooms in this century-old Victorian home. Seven miles west of Saratoga is the **Mansion Inn,** an elegantly restored and decorated Victorian home, built in 1866 in the style of a Venetian villa by a man who had made a fortune from his invention—the folded paper bag (Route 29, P.O. Box 77, Rock City Falls 12863; 518–885–1607).

Saratoga is in eastern New York, about 35 miles north of Albany and about 30 south of Lake George via I-87. Take Exit 13 to South Broadway.

For additional Saratoga area listings, see the entry for the **Saratoga Rose Inn**, in Hadley.

Adelphi Hotel   *Tel:* (518) 587–4688
365 Broadway

When Gregg Siefker and Sheila Parkert bought the Adelphi in 1979, this century-old hotel was badly run down and neglected. Since then, little by little, these two energetic innkeepers have restored the hotel, starting with the piazza overlooking Broadway, to the three-story columns supporting a maze of Victorian fretwork and airy verandas, to the grand lobby and spacious guest rooms. The Adelphi's two restaurants, the Saratoga Club and the Cafe Adelphi, specialize in imaginative entrées and home-baked French desserts.

"Since the 1960s, the town of Saratoga has undergone a rebirth, resurfacing with much of the glamour, elegance, and pure fun that characterized it in the 1870s. Perhaps the most marvelous reincarnation is the Adelphi—the only remaining grand hotel. You approach its Italianate villa–style veranda and enter a small-scale Victorian world. After checking in at the antique desk, amid palms and fascinating decor, we quickly mounted the high Victorian staircase and were shown to our luxurious rooms, with 15-foot ceilings, very tall doors, and French doors opening onto the second-story veranda overlooking Broadway. Gregg and Sheila have carried out a detailed restoration effort—their goal is to return the hotel to its original grace and elegance. They have been undeniably successful. Elegant fabric bed hangings and draperies (along with a very firm and comfortable bed) set the mood in our airy bedroom and sitting room. The furnishings are an eclectic collection of attic and auction finds rather than expensive antiques, and it all works very well. The updated 1920s bathroom had a good shower and Caswell Massey soaps and treats (not renewed the second day), while our modernized sink was in our room.

"A continental breakfast of fresh muffins and breads is served in the fabulous second-floor parlor, but we took ours outside to the veranda in front of our room. We also enjoyed the veranda for late afternoon drinks brought up from the bar. I'd suggest asking for a front or courtyard room. We didn't try their restaurant, but other Saratoga favorites include Hattie's Chicken Shack, Mrs. Long's Bake Shop, the Ash Grove Inn, Charles, and, for a splurge, Chez Sophie, a 45-minute drive away." *(Deborah Reese)*

Another reader, visiting during the height of the season, in August, felt her room was overpriced and noisy, with an uncomfortable bed. Comments?

Open May to Oct. Restaurant open July, Aug.
Rooms 17 suites, 17 doubles, all with private bath and/or shower. All with telephone, TV, desk, air-conditioning.
Facilities Restaurants, bar, lobby, breakfast room, veranda, courtyard.
Location 35 m N of Albany. Downtown Saratoga Springs.
Restrictions Light sleepers should request back rooms. "Older children preferred."
Credit cards Amex, MC, Visa.
Rates B&B, $80–280 suite, $55–190 double or single. Extra person in room, $15. 2–3 night weekend minimum. Alc lunch, $12; alc dinner, $25.
Extras Cribs, babysitting available. French spoken.

WARRENSBURG 12885 Map 3

The Merrill Magee House　　　　　　　　　　*Tel:* (518) 623–2449
2 Hudson Street

It's hard to believe that a classic Greek Revival country inn like The Merrill Magee House, set on the village green, is only five miles away from the tee-shirted commotion at Lake George village. Longtime owners Ken and Florence Carrington offer elegant, English-style innkeeping in their antique-filled establishment, which dates back to the early 1800s. Rates include a full breakfast and afternoon tea. Warrensburg is known for its antique shops, and 25 are within walking distance of the inn.

"The Merrill Magee House is a romantic and cozy country inn. The antique floorboards give a friendly creak as you go up the stairs to the old-fashioned bedrooms in the main house. The shared bath is equipped with a huge claw-foot tub, where you can soak up to your neck. The handmade coverlet on the four-poster bed, antique settee, and fireplace gave us a feeling of having stepped back in time. On a return visit, we stayed in one of the new rooms in the addition, and were delighted to find that our room had just as much charm and atmosphere. The owners are most attentive, making us feel very much at home. Whenever they have a free moment, they are happy to spend time chatting with guests by the fire. The food at the inn is a delight, and there is always something new to try. Caution goes out the window in the face of all the homemade breads and desserts. The atmosphere at dinner is casually elegant; we thought it nice that people like to dress up a bit." *(Mr. & Mrs. Dean Holbrook)* More comments, please.

Open All year.
Rooms 13 doubles—10 with full private bath, 3 sharing 1 bath. Some with whirlpool bath, desk; all with radio, air-conditioning. 10 rooms in annex. Most rooms with king- or queen-size beds, fireplaces, sitting areas.
Facilities Restaurant; parlor with TV, fireplace; tavern with fireplace, games; porch. 5 acres with hot tub in greenhouse, swimming pool. Cross-country ski rentals. Tennis, hiking, golf, fishing, sailing nearby. 1 m to cross-country skiing, 15 min. to downhill.
Location E central NY. Adirondack Region, 5 m W of Lake George, 60 m N of Albany. Take I-87 (Northway) to Exit 23 and follow signs to Warrensburg. Inn is adjacent to bandstand in center of town.
Restrictions No smoking in dining room. No children under 12.
Credit cards Amex, MC, Visa.
Rates B&B, $70–95 double, $50–80 single. 2-night weekend minimum. Midweek, special tour, ski packages. Alc dinner, $30–35. 15% service added to meals.
Extras Wheelchair accessible; 1 guest room equipped for disabled.

WESTFIELD 14787 {Map 3}

Westfield is home to a number of excellent antique shops, and is 10 miles from the Chautauqua Institution, offering a full summer program of concerts, theater, opera, and lectures. The self-proclaimed grapejuice capital of the world, it is also home to seven wineries and many antique shops.

Also recommended: The **Westfield House** (7375 East Main Road; 716–326–6262) is an 1840s-era brick home with a later Gothic Revival addition, framed by old maple trees and overlooking the local vineyards. Rates include a full breakfast and evening drinks and snacks.

The William Seward Inn
South Portage Road, RD 2

Tel: (716) 326-4151

The original section of the William Seward Inn was built in 1821, and was bought by William Henry Seward soon afterward. Seward, at that time the agent for the Holland Land Company in Westfield, later became famous as the secretary of state under Abraham Lincoln and Andrew Johnson when he arranged the purchase of Alaska from Russia—known at the time as Seward's Folly. Seward made several additions to the house, including the two-story Greek pillars that give the inn the look of a mansion. In the 1840s the house was sold to George Patterson, then lieutenant governor of New York, and remained in that family for 100 years. It was moved from town to its present location about 25 years ago, and was bought by Peter and Joyce Wood in 1986.

"Our room looked out on Lake Erie and was furnished with a four-poster bed and period antiques. Two comfortable chairs at one end provided a small sitting area. The sink was in the bedroom, while the commode and shower were in a closet-size room off the sitting area. There was plenty of space to put things away in the dressers and closet. The bed was very comfortable, with an abundance of blankets and numerous fluffy pillows to lounge on.

"The atmosphere of the inn is quiet and relaxing. Several delicious breakfast courses were served at a leisurely pace, and both the presentation and the conversation were excellent. Another opportunity for socializing with other guests was provided early each evening, when wine and cheese, hot buttered rum, and appetizers were served in the living room. Best of all is the level of service provided by the owners. There were chocolate hearts on the bedside table, and fresh flowers in our room when we arrived; the selection of magazines in our room was changed daily; every morning while we were at breakfast, the snow was brushed off our car." *(Jim & Cathy Sirianni)* "We are particularly finicky about cleanliness, and this inn certainly passed with flying colors. Menus are available from nearby restaurants, and Peter is only too happy to call for reservations." *(Carolyn & Bill Myles)*

Open All year.
Rooms 10 doubles, all with private bath and/or shower, radio, fan. Some with desk, air-conditioning. Telephone, TV available on request.
Facilities Parlor with fireplace, library, dining room, gift shop. 1½ acres. 4 m to Lake Erie, Chautauqua Lake for swimming, fishing. 20 min. to cross-country skiing, 35 to downhill.
Location W NY, 2½ hours. NE of Cleveland, OH. 1 hr. SW of Buffalo, 45 min. NE of Erie, PA. 3 m to town. 4 m S of I-90, on Rte. 394.
Restrictions No children under 12. No smoking. Check-in before 9 P.M. is requested.
Credit Cards MC, Visa.
Rates B&B, $58–84 double, $48–74 single. Extra person in room, $15. 2-night summer/special weekend minimum. No tipping. 10% senior discount, midweek. Theme weekends, special packages. Prix fixe dinner, $16–24.

WINDHAM 12496   Map 3

Albergo Allegria   *Tel:* (518) 734–5560
Route 296

Leonore and Vito Radelich, originally from Veneto Province (once part of Italy, but now in Yugoslavia), ran a restaurant for many years on Long Island. They moved to Windham and, ten years ago, opened La Griglia, a restaurant specializing in northern Italian cooking, with two Italian Renaissance dishes offered nightly. Pork Michelangelo, scalopini of pork with fruit juices, grilled apples, tomatoes, and garlic, is a favorite.

In 1985, the Radelichs completed the total renovation of the Albergo, created from two of the original cottages of the former Osborn House, a summer boardinghouse complex built in 1876. Interior spaces were redesigned to create roomy accommodations, while preserving the original Victorian woodwork, trim, and moldings. Rooms are decorated with period wallpapers and Victorian furnishings. Rates include a full breakfast on weekdays, and a buffet breakfast on weekends.

Michael Willis reports that although the Radelichs recently sold their restaurant, La Griglia, "the food remains as excellent as ever." Meanwhile, the Radelichs, never ones to rest on their laurels, have built an addition onto the Albergo, which "combines period decor and country inn warmth with luxurious new baths with heat lamps and Jacuzzi tubs."

"Most charming. The common rooms were quite nice, and I had a wonderful, clean, comfortable room and bath. The location is convenient to good restaurants, quiet, and very low-key." *(Richard A. Gerweck, Jr., also Steve Koenig)*

Open All year. Restaurant closed Monday.
Rooms 4 suites, 12 doubles, all with full private bath, telephone, TV. 4 in annex. 1 suite with double Jacuzzi.
Facilities Restaurant, 2 large living rooms with fireplaces, games, library, TV. 3 acres with herb gardens, creek with swimming hole, waterfall, trout fishing. ½ m to Ski Windham, 7 m to Hunter Mt. 2 m to cross-country skiing. Golf across street; tennis nearby.
Location SE NY, Northern Catskills, Greene City. 1 hr. S of Albany, 2½ hrs. N of NYC. 1 m to town off Rte. 23.
Credit cards Amex, DC, MC, Visa.
Rates B&B, $85–175 suite, $55–105 double, $45–95 singles. Extra person in room, $10–15. 2-night weekend minimum. Alc dinner, $30.
Extras Entrance ramp; some baths specially equipped for disabled. Italian spoken. Cribs available. Station pickups.

Key to Abbreviations

For complete information and explanations, please see the Introduction.

Rates: Range from least expensive room in low season to most expensive room in peak season.
Room only: No meals included; sometimes referred to as European Plan (EP).
B&B: Bed and breakfast; includes breakfast, sometimes afternoon/evening refreshment.
MAP: Modified American Plan; includes breakfast and dinner.
Full board: Three meals daily.
Alc lunch: À la carte lunch; average price of entrée plus nonalcoholic drink, tax, tip.
Alc dinner: Average price of three-course dinner, including half bottle of house wine, tax, tip.
Prix fixe dinner: Three- to five-course set dinner, excluding wine, tax, tip unless otherwise noted.
Extras: Noted if available. Always confirm in advance. Pets are not permitted unless specified.
Zip codes: If only one zip code applies, it is listed with the town name. If there is more than one, it is noted as part of the address.

North Carolina

Mast Farm Inn, Valle Crucis

Few states offer as much to the traveler as North Carolina—beautiful beaches and historic towns in the east, and breathtaking mountain scenery in the west. Mt. Mitchell, at 6,684 feet the highest point east of the Mississippi, lies in the High Country, in the northwestern part of the state. The center of the state, called the Piedmont, is rich in industry, agriculture, and has some of the state's most beautiful golf courses.

In North Carolina, liquor is sold only through state-owned "A.B.C." stores, although beer and wine are sold in grocery stores in most counties. Some inns provide setups if you bring your own beverage; others prefer that drinks not be consumed in public. Some counties are completely dry, so be prepared! State law prohibits pets in commercial accommodations. Rates do not include 5% state sales tax; some areas charge additional local tax.

ASHEVILLE   Map 5

Asheville is in western North Carolina, at the juncture of interstates 26 and 40, 106 miles southeast of Knoxville, Tennessee; it's just an hour's drive to the Great Smoky Mountains National Park. Asheville is surrounded by more than a million acres of national forest, and is known for its cool mountain summers. Golf, rafting, horseback riding, and hiking are all available nearby. It's also the home of the Biltmore House and Gardens, the

Vance Birthplace, the Thomas Wolfe Memorial, and many craft shops and galleries. The Biltmore House is probably its best-known attraction; George W. Vanderbilt (of the railroad/steamship Vanderbilts) was so enamored of the area that he bought 125,000 acres and built this 255-room castle, completed in 1895. Several inns sell reduced-rate tickets to the castle.

Also recommended: The **Cornerstone Inn** (230 Pearson Drive 28801: 704–253–5644) is a Dutch Tudor-style home built in 1924 and furnished with European antiques, offering quick access to the downtown area. The **Flint Street Inns** (116 Flint Street 28801; 704–253–6723) are a pair of restored 1915-era homes whose decor reminds the age of gracious living— of horse-drawn carriages, fans, and silk hats. Both B&Bs serve a full breakfast, and are only short walk from downtown.

The **Old Reynolds Mansion** (100 Reynolds Heights 28804; 704–254–0496) offers guests comfortable rooms and unlimited supplies of fresh fruit, coffee cake, and beverages. A Colonial Revival–style home built at the turn of the century, the **Ray House** (83 Hillside Street 28801; 704–252–0106) features antique-filled rooms that are named for famous people who lived in Asheville. Located in a quiet residential neighborhood, the inn is a short way from the Biltmore Mansion.

Information please: The newly-opened **Richmond Hill Inn** overlooks the French Broad River from its hilltop location. The 30-room Queen Anne-style mansion has been renovated at great expense after years of decline. Now restored to its original splendor, both B&B accommodation and dinners are offered (87 Richmond Hill Drive 28806; 919–273–9409).

Applewood Manor
62 Cumberland Circle 28801

Tel: (704) 254–2244

"A lovely turn-of-the-century Colonial Revival set at the top of a wooded hill, the Applewood makes you feel as if you are in the country. The house itself is in mint condition. The front door opens onto a large foyer with a large parlor and living room to the left and dining room to the right. All rooms are divided by pocket doors and are furnished with handsome period antiques and Oriental carpets. Breakfast is served on the wicker-filled porch. Jim and Linda both do the cooking and caretaking, and they are the icing on this already lovely cake of a place. A young couple, the LoPrestis bought the inn after relocating from the New York City area. Their concern for your comfort is always present and they are always more than eager to chat with you about your day or help with dinner plans. Jim is an aspiring writer with a dry sense of humor. The inn is very clean, very quiet, convenient to everything, and with excellent plumbing—hot water in abundance." *(Susan McMullen)*

The LoPrestis really enjoy cooking. Their ever-changing breakfast menu might include cream cheese French toast with fresh raspberries one day, and Havarti omelets with lemon poppyseed bread and peach jam the next. Favorite afternoon refreshments are peach spice tea with chocolate almond cookies or hot apple cider with spinach-cheese squares.

Open All year.
Rooms 4 doubles, all with private bath and/or shower, radio, air-conditioning, fan. 3 with fireplace.

Facilities Dining room with fireplace, parlor with fireplace, library, porches. 2 acres with flower gardens, swings, croquet, volleyball, badminton, bikes. Tennis nearby.
Location 1 m from downtown. Off-street parking. From Rte. 240 W take Asheville Business District Exit. Go right on Haywood. Turn right on Montford Ave. Right again on Soco. Go to stop sign at Cumberland Ave. Cross to Cumberland Circle.
Restrictions No smoking. No children under 12.
Credit cards MC, Visa.
Rates B&B, $60–90 double, $55–75 single. Extra person in room $12. 20% senior discount in Sept. 2-night minimum holiday weekends.
Extras Italian, American Sign Language spoken.

Cedar Crest Victorian Inn
674 Biltmore Avenue 28803

Tel: (704) 252–1389

Cedar Crest was built in 1891 by William E. Breese, one of Asheville's leading citizens. Listed on the National Register of Historic Places, this Queen Anne–style Victorian has a captain's walk, projecting turrets, and verandas at different levels. The interior features original oak woodwork, with stained and beveled glass windows. Innkeepers Jack and Barbara McEwan have owned the Cedar Crest since 1984, and the rates include a very ample breakfast, afternoon iced tea or lemonade on the veranda in the summer, wassail in the parlor in the winter, and evening tea or hot chocolate.

"Not only is the building and its interior beautiful, it is fantastic . . . rich, ornate Victorian decor. Linens were crisp, and the oak floors shone. Nearby, the old Weaversville Mill is a very good, quaint dinner restaurant on Reems Creek." *(Leneta Appleby)*

"The McEwans are really knowledgeable about the history of the area and have lots of books on the subject. The house is as handsome as described; the woodwork was done by the same artisans who worked on the Vanderbilt estate. The entrance to the Biltmore House is within walking distance, as is Vanderbilt Village, which has several good restaurants." *(Maria Schmidt)*

"Our room was large, comfortable and beautifully decorated. The McEwans are charming hosts and offered an excellent breakfast—cereal, breads, sweet breads, and wonderful ripe strawberries with real whipped cream. We found the house very quiet, even though we had a front room overlooking the road." *(Lynda Oswald)*

An oft-heard refrain—one correspondent requested better lighting in his bedroom.

Open All year.
Rooms 2 suites, 10 doubles—8 with private bath and/or shower, 4 with maximum of 4 people sharing bath. All rooms with telephone, desk, air-conditioning. 3 rooms in separate cottage with parlor, fireplace, sitting room.
Facilities Parlor, dining room, study, grand foyer, large veranda, sitting areas with TV, fireplaces, table games. 4 acres with sitting areas, gardens, croquet. Swimming, fishing, white-water rafting, 10 to 30 min. Cross-country and downhill skiing, 35 min.
Location 1½ m from downtown, ¼ m N of Biltmore House. Take Exit 50 or 50B off I-40; stay right to Biltmore Ave.
Restrictions Smoking in study only. No children under 12. Traffic/train noise in some rooms.

Credit cards Amex, Discover, MC, Visa.
Rates B&B, $80–140 suite, $70–100 double, $64–90 single. Extra person in room, $15. 2-night minimum, weekends and holidays.

BEAUFORT 28516   Map 5

Also recommended: Recommended too late for a full entry is the 36-room **Inlet Motor Inn** (601 Front Street; 919–728–3600), with porches overlooking the waterfront. Rates are reasonable, and include afternoon wine and cheese. "Comfortably furnished and immaculately clean. There is a good seafood restaurant close by and another nearby restaurant with barbecued ribs to die for." *(Jeanne Smith)*

Langdon House   *Tel:* (919) 728–5499
135 Craven Street

In 1983 Jimm Prest restored and opened the Langdon House, a relatively new B&B in one of Beaufort's oldest homes. He prides himself on meeting the individual needs of his guests, and will be pleased to arrange anything from a home-baked birthday cake to a sailboat charter.

"Langdon House was built in 1732, and has been beautifully restored. We were so pleased with the accommodations that we made it our headquarters for four days for sightseeing within a 75-mile radius." *(William A. Toombs, Jr.)*

"The Langdon House itself is a beautiful example of the kind of careful restoration that's currently going on in Beaufort. It's at once period-authentic and modern-convenient. The proprietor, Jimm Prest, did the work himself, and showed me the original attic frame, the addition line of the floorboards, the eighteenth-century stone chimney, and the many knickknacks that make the ambience genuine." *(Jonathan Mudd)*

"A weekend spent at Langdon House was one of the finest of the year. Brandy on the mantel, beds turned down, hot coffee in the morning, followed by fresh OJ, gingerbread waffles, and country ham. When I wanted a rowboat to get to Carrot Island, there it was. Enough said, the service was first-rate.

"It's just a short walk to the working waterfront . . . the restoration of old sailboats, salty dogs living upon the water, and many shops are fun to watch and visit. Guests are served breakfast at the requested time. A beautiful display of fruit breads, fresh fruits, pastries, cheeses, and coffee is served in the sunny parlor." *(Sally Thomas Kutz)*

"Jimm Prest is absolutely charming and gracious, but we found the rooms a bit noisy because of all the wooden floors, and thought the price was slightly high relative to the size of the rooms." *(BG)*

Open All year.
Rooms 4 doubles with queen-size beds, private bath and/or shower, radio, air-conditioning.
Facilities Dining room; parlor for reading, games, breakfast; porch; gardens. Bicycles, fishing rods, beach baskets. 1 block to boardwalk, shops, restaurants. Cape Lookout National Seashore nearby. 5 m to ocean.

Location S coastal NC. 45 m S of New Bern, 100 m N of Wilmington, 150 m SE of Raleigh. Historic district, corner Craven & Ann sts. From Hwy. 70, turn at light onto Turner St., then left on Ann St. 1 block to inn at corner.

Restrictions No smoking. No children under 12.

Credit cards None accepted.

Rates Room only, $69–79 double. B&B, $79–115 double, $73–83 single. Extra person in room, $15. 10% discount for 6-day stays or equivalent, e.g., 2 rooms, 3 days; 3 rooms, 2 days. 2-night weekend minimum. Packages available.

Extras Airport/station pickups.

BLOWING ROCK 28605   Map 5

Blowing Rock is a resort town along the Blue Ridge Parkway, named for a unique rock formation, where air currents from the Johns River Gorge return light objects thrown toward the rock. The town has many attractive craft shops. It's located in northwestern North Carolina's High Country, approximately 7 miles south of Boone, and 110 miles northwest of Charlotte. Blowing Rock is known as the "ski capital of the south." With an elevation of almost 4,000 feet, it also offers cool summers and beautiful fall foliage.

Gideon Ridge Inn   *Tel:* (704) 295–3644
6148 Gideon Ridge Road, P.O. Box 1929

The Gideon Ridge Inn was built in 1939 as an elegant yet rustic stone mansion, and offers beautiful views of the Blue Ridge Mountains. In 1983 Cobb and Jane Milner converted this house to an inn, and have furnished the rooms with many antiques. Jane says that "most of our guests are couples who come to enjoy a break from their routines, or to celebrate special occasions. They do not come to be entertained, but to enjoy our beautiful, restful atmosphere. They leaf through our art books and listen to Mozart and Bach at breakfast; they hike, play bridge, shop for crafts and antiques."

Rates include a full breakfast; dinners are served on weekends to guests and others by reservation only. A recent menu included scallion and mushroom soup, salad, choice of roast tenderloin of beef or baked mountain trout, and chocolate pâté.

"Guests' needs are always well provided for, with big thick towels, cozy comforters, and quiet advice and assistance with dinner reservations given when requested. There are opportunities to mingle with other guests if you like, or complete privacy if preferred. The stone terrace that wraps around the inn is a perfect place to watch the moon rise over the mountains, serenaded by the frogs, crickets, and owls. Breakfast is prepared and served by the Milners; Jane ideally balances the textures, colors, and tastes in her presentation of the meal." *(Jane & Luther Manners)*

"The whole area of Blowing Rock is stunning, even in winter. We were told that it gets quite crowded in summer; in January it was deserted and charming. Since the inn does not serve dinner in winter, the owners sent us to the Speckled Trout, where we enjoyed the best trout and oysters I've ever had. The inn's grounds are perfect for strolling and the view is outstanding. A very classy place." *(BLK)*

Open All year. Closed a few weeks in March. Dinner served June 15 to Oct. 31 only.
Rooms 8 doubles—all with private bath and/or shower, desk; some with fireplaces.
Facilities Dining room, living room/library with TV, fireplace, terrace. 5 acres with herb garden, wooded paths. 3–6 m to downhill and cross-country skiing.
Location 2 m to town, ¼ m W of Rte. 321.
Restrictions No smoking in guest rooms or dining room. No children under 12.
Credit cards Amex, MC, Visa.
Rates B&B, $80–120 double. Extra person in room, $10. 20% discount for 3 or more days midweek. 2-night weekend minimum in season. Prix fixe lunch, $10–16; prix fixe dinner, $25–30, plus 15% service.

CHAPEL HILL 27515   Map 5

The Inn at Bingham School   *Tel:* (919) 563–5583
P.O. Box 267

A combination of Greek Revival and Federalist styles, The Inn at Bingham School provides elegant accommodation in rooms in the main house, as well as in a log cabin dating back to 1791.

"Although the Bingham School, operating between 1845 and 1865 as a preparatory school for the University of North Carolina, no longer stands, Jane and Bob Kelly did a truly first-class restoration of the headmaster's home. They have created a warm inn, rich in architectural detail and southern hospitality, set in the rolling farmland of central North Carolina. The southern breakfast is a treat of the highest order, with homemade heart-shaped biscuits, grits, fresh country eggs, baked apples, sausage or bacon, and a variety of fruit. Jane Kelly's fresh muffins with strawberry butter are not to be missed. During football season, she prepares an egg casserole second to none, to prepare her guests for the afternoon at Keenan Stadium, home of the Tarheels. Gracious proprietors, outstanding architecture, period antique furnishings in comfortable settings, the Carolina countryside, and Jane Kelly's cooking and baking all combine to make our stays memorable." *(Nancy Harrison & Nelson Ormsby)*

Open All year. Closed Dec. 15 to Jan. 1.
Rooms 1 suite, 5 doubles—all with private bath and/or shower, radio, TV, desk, air-conditioning. 2 with whirlpool tubs, fan. 1 with fireplace.
Facilities Common room with fireplace, game table; dining room, sun-room. 10 acres with croquet. Golf, tennis nearby.
Location Central NC. 11 m W of Carrboro/Chapel Hill, about 10 m S of I-85.
Restrictions No children under 12.
Credit cards None accepted.
Rates B&B, $110 suite, $85 double, $75 single. Extra person in room, $15. 2-night minimum peak weekends.
Extras Airport pickups.

CHARLOTTE   Map 5

Located in the southwestern part of the state, Charlotte is one of North Carolina's largest cities, and is a major textile producing center, with hundreds of factories in the surrounding area. The city is home to a number of museums and parks of interest, as well as the University of North Carolina at Charlotte.

Also recommended: The Inn on Providence (6700 Providence Road 28226; 704–366–6700), a Federal-style brick colonial with white trim and black shutters, and a collection of nineteenth-century furniture, antique quilts, and family heirlooms. **The Morehead** (1122 East Morehead Street 28204; 704–376–3356) was built as a private home in 1917, and was renovated and opened as a country inn in 1984. Located in a tree-lined residential neighborhood, the inn's proximity to downtown Charlotte makes it popular with business travelers.

The Homeplace   *Tel:* (704) 365–1936
5901 Sardis Road 28226

Peggy and Frank Dearien had never stayed in a B&B, let alone run one, when they decided to buy The Homeplace in 1984. A turn-of-the-century Victorian, the inn has been completely renovated, from the foundation to the widow's walk. Windows, insulation, wiring, plumbing, heating and air-conditioning—even the roof was redone, while the house's original hand-crafted staircase, ten-foot-high ceilings, and heart-of-pine floors were preserved. Peggy Dearien has decorated the house with Victorian and country-style furnishings; the guest rooms are done in shades of blue and rose, and many are highlighted by the primitive paintings done by Peggy's father.

"The Homeplace has airy porches, plenty of rocking chairs, and cross-stitchings everywhere. Combine that with the fact that I was greeted at the door with a pitcher of lemonade, and I felt like I was visiting Grandma. The Deariens pay attention to the little details that make their guests feel truly comfortable and welcome in their home. The full breakfast was indeed wonderful. I especially recommend The Homeplace to business travelers who are tired of the coldness of hotel chains." *(John A. Hill)*

"My room was spotless, as was the entire home. Hospitality was the next best thing to going home to see your folks after a long time away. Food was superb, graciously served with an option of serving times which made it convenient to schedule personal plans. A bonus was a plate of cheese, crackers, and fresh fruit in the evening, along with homemade cookies. The grounds were lovely, the front porch inviting, the bath immaculate, the warmth pervasive." *(Lynn Grisard Fullman, also Lynn Edge)*

Open All year.
Room 4 doubles—2 with full private bath, 2 with maximum of 4 people sharing bath. All with radio, desk, air-conditioning.
Facilities Dining room, living room, study with TV, wraparound porch. 2½ acres with gazebo, hammock, gardens.
Location 2 m from Rte. 74. 15 min. from center. SE Charlotte at corner of Sardis and Rama rds. 15 min from I-77 and I-85.
Restrictions No children under 10. No smoking.
Credit cards Amex, MC, Visa.
Rates B&B, $63–68 double, $55–60 single. 2-3 night holiday weekend minimum.

Map 5

Squire Watkins Inn   *Tel:* (704) 586–5244
Haywood Road, P.O. Box 430

J.C. and Flora Watkins were among Dillsboro's first settlers when they built their home in the 1880s. Unfortunately, J.C. died quite young, leaving Flora with a heavily mortgaged house and business, and a large family to raise. The sheriff arrived with foreclosure papers and the house was to be sold at auction. Flora and her son wrote letters to 150 Masonic Lodges, explaining the situation, and enough money arrived to hold off the sale and save the family home. Flora opened the house to boarders, but when she found some of them drinking and gambling up on the widow's walk, she had the railing (and the boarders) removed. The inn stayed in the Watkins family until it was purchased and restored (including the railing) in 1983 by the Wertenberger family.

"I've stayed at many B&Bs and inns, and the Squire Watkins is a top favorite. The location is very convenient, just off the highway leading to Cherokee; the national park is less than an hour away. Dillsboro itself is crammed with good-quality arts and crafts shops, and is much nicer than the over-commercialized town of Cherokee. The inn is a gracious home that makes one feel like a visitor, not just a customer. Tom and Emma Wertenberger provide super service: attentive yet unobtrusive. They're easy people to talk with, and adept at including everyone in the conversation. My room was a delight—quiet, sunny, lovely furnishings, and sparkling clean, just like the rest of the inn. The continental breakfast was a taste of heaven. Emma is up at an early hour daily, to make the fresh breads—the raspberry coffee cake was sheer bliss!" *(Patricia Harrington)* More comments please.

Open April through Dec. Open on a limited basis Jan. through March.
Rooms 2 suites, 3 doubles with private bath and/or shower, desk. 2 efficiency cottages; 1 family cottage with kitchen.
Facilities Parlor; game room; sun porch with books, magazines, games; gift shop. 3½ acres with gardens, pond. Stream, lake fishing, horseback riding, white-water rafting, canoeing nearby.
Location W NC, 50 m W of Asheville. 2 blocks from town. At intersection of U.S. 441 and Haywood Rd.
Restrictions No children under 12 in inn; any age welcome in cottages.
Credit cards None accepted.
Rates Room only (cottages), $50–65 double, $45–60 single. B&B (inn), $65–70 double, $55–60 single. No tipping. Extra person in room, $10 (inn), $5 (cottages). Weekly rates in cottages.
Extras Cribs available for cottages. Airport/station pickups.

 Map 5

Information please: In neighboring Kill Devil Hills is **Ye Olde Cherokee Inn**, with six reasonably priced guest rooms just 600 feet from the beach

(500 North Virgina Dare Trail, Kill Devil Hills 27948; 919–441–6127). Not far to the south, in the Nag's Head area, is the **Tranquil House Inn**, a new building designed to evoke a turn-of-the-century inn. Guest rooms overlook Shallowbag Bay, and are decorated with scrubbed pine furniture (Queen Elizabeth Street, Box 1411, Manteo 27954; 919–473–1404). Another area possibility is the **Scarborough Inn** (Highway 64/264, P.O. Box 1310, Manteo 27954; 919–473–39979), a comfortable family inn with period decor and reasonable rates.

Sanderling Inn
SR Box 319 Y

Tel: (919) 261–4111

As much as we love historic old inns, we are equally delighted when readers recommend newly constructed facilities built with style and distinction. The Sanderling is just such a place. Traditional beachfront architecture is combined with a modern sense of space, and the decor combines natural oak with wicker, soft pastel fabrics, and Audubon prints. In an adjacent building is the inn's restaurant, housed in a restored turn-of-the-century lifesaving station; shrimp is a particular specialty, but other local favorites include pan-fried chicken with apple fritters, and Carolina duckling.

"The Sanderling is located on the Outer Banks of North Carolina, north of the shopping strip and tourist area. Built on the beach, the inn is a modern 28-unit hotel that is probably one of the best places to stay in the area. It is very near the town of Duck, which has good shops for browsing. Each room is equipped with a small kitchenette, sitting area, and large bathroom. Guests receive a generous wine and fruit basket, compliments of the management. The restaurant adjacent to the inn serves extensive breakfasts, lunches, and gourmet dinners." *(Carolyn & Bill Myles)*

"Fully endorse existing entry. Hotel is beautifully decorated with bird models and prints. Fortunately, the restaurant is very good, since there are few alternatives nearby." *(Michael Crick)*

Open All year.
Rooms 5 suites, 56 doubles, all with full private bath, telephone, TV, radio, desk, air-conditioning, kitchenette, porch. 28 rooms in main inn; all others in 2 separate buildings.
Facilities Restaurant; bar with rooftop deck; library; living room with TV/VCR, games; meeting facilities; gallery. Health club, hot tub, private beach, swimming pool, tennis courts. Golf, jogging trails nearby.
Location NE NC, Outer Banks. Take Rte. 158 or 64 onto Outer Banks. From Kitty Hawk, go N approx. 12 m to Sanderling.
Credit cards Amex, MC, Visa.
Rates Room only, $100–200 suite, $70–185 double. MAP rates add $64 to room rate. Extra person in room, $20–40. 15% service additional. 10% discount 5-night stays; 4 nights Sun. to Thurs. Room-only rates include continental breakfast in summer. Alc breakfast $4–8; alc lunch, $8; alc dinner, $25.
Extras Wheelchair accessible. French, German, Italian, Spanish spoken. Cribs, baby-sitting available.

DURHAM 27712   Map 5

Arrowhead Inn   *Tel:* (919) 477–8430
106 Mason Road

The Arrowhead dates from 1775, when it was a large slave-holding property. Owners Jerry and Barbara Ryan have preserved the inn's colonial architecture, and have decorated the rooms in a homey and comfortable style, ranging from colonial through Victorian. A five-foot stone arrowhead stands by the door; erected sixty years ago, it once marked the Great Trading Path to the Smokies, which carried Indians, and then white settlers, to the West. Rates include afternoon refreshments and a full country breakfast. Jerry notes that the year's highest scorer in Scrabble wins a free overnight, while the teen scoring highest in Labyrinth gets the same.

"Our room had a complimentary bowl of fruit and a clean, quiet room with a fireplace and a door onto the back patio. This home has been carefully restored and charmingly furnished in period. The bathrooms that have been added are modern and kept spotlessly clean. The Ryans provided us with maps, brochures, and discount coupons for area attractions. Although our hours were irregular they took it all in stride, providing us with breakfast when we got up and coffee when we got home." *(John & Kris Driessen)*

"We stayed in one of the new rooms in the carriage house, with beautiful country-style antique furnishings and primitive quilts hung over the bed. The Ryans are great people and gave us a tour of the inn. They keep menus of local restaurants and provided good recommendations." *(Rachel Gorlin)*

"Barb and Jerry Ryan now top our list of favorite innkeepers!" *(Nancy Harrison & Nelson Ormsby)*

Open All year.
Rooms 1 suite, 7 doubles—4 with full private bath, 4 with maximum of 4 people sharing bath. All with air-conditioning. Some with telephone, radio, TV, desk, fireplace. 2 rooms in carriage house.
Facilities Living room, dining room, keeping room, sitting room, game/TV room. 4 acres with gardens, picnic area, swings, fish pond. Tennis, golf nearby.
Location Central NC. 7 m N of I-85. Take Rte. 501 (Roxboro Rd.) N; inn is at intersection of 501 and Mason/Snow Hill Rd., on left. Watch for arrowhead.
Restrictions Smoking in keeping room only.
Credit cards Amex, MC, Visa.
Rates B&B, $95 suite, $45–80 double. Extra person in room, $10. Family discount for extended stays. Winter & summer historic house tour weekend packages.
Extras Cribs, babysitting, play equipment, games available. French spoken.

EDENTON 27932   Map 5

Edenton is filled with tree-lined streets of eighteenth- and nineteenth-century houses. It's located in northern coastal North Carolina, on the Albemarle Sound, 90 miles south of Norfolk, 125 miles south of Richmond, VA, and 150 miles east of Raleigh.

The Lords Proprietors' Inn
300 North Broad Street

Tel: (919) 482–3641

Since they first opened The Lords Proprietors' Inn in 1981, Arch and Jane Edwards have renovated three adjacent Victorian buildings: the White-Bond House, the Satterfield House, and the Pack House. Rooms are furnished with antiques, and beds have been specially constructed by local cabinetmakers. Rates include an expanded continental breakfast.

"We had a beautifully decorated suite in one of the three Victorian homes the inn owns. Everything was spotless, and we had access to a small kitchen; modern conveniences such as TV and VCR did not affect the period atmosphere. Jane and Arch Edwards do everything to get to know their guests and make them feel special, without intruding. Breakfast consists of juice, fresh fruit, homemade breads, coffee, tea, and warm smiles. Edenton is a beautiful little town near Albemarle Sound. The people are very open and friendly, and we count it as one of our favorite getaway places." *(Denley & Ann Coughman, also Mr. & Mrs. James Rinehart)*

"The inn is a charming southern home with gracious southern hospitality to match. Many of the antiques in the rooms are for sale. Our room, No. 4, had an antique bed that stood high off the floor. Rooms are very spacious. In the afternoon, after a hard day's sightseeing, we were treated to tea in the living room." *(Carolyn & Bill Myles)*

"Edenton is a lovely town off the beaten track. The oldest courthouse in the nation is there, and I would particularly recommend a visit to the charming St. Paul's Episcopal Church (1736), within walking distance of the inn. We found our hosts very gracious; breakfast was delicious." *(Harrison Gardner, also Nancy Harrison & Nelson Ormsby)*

Open All year.
Rooms 20 doubles—all with full private bath, telephone, TV/VCR, desk, air-conditioning. Inn occupies 3 adjacent restored homes.
Facilities 4 parlors, 1 dining/meeting room, patios. 1.5 acres with swimming pool. Docks, marinas, tennis, river for fishing; swimming nearby. 1 hr. to Outer Banks beaches.
Location Center of historic district. Follow Hwy. 17 until it becomes Broad St.
Restrictions No smoking in dining room.
Credit cards None accepted.
Rates B&B, $70 double, $48 single. Extra person in room, $10. Winter weekend program Nov. through March includes Saturday-afternoon historic home tour, 2 nights B&B, candlelight dinner: $235 for 2.
Extras Handicap accessible room and bath. Station pickups. Cribs, babysitting available.

GLENDALE SPRING 28629   Map 5

Glendale Springs Inn

Tel: (919) 982–2102

"An extremely attractive Victorian wayside inn, built in the 1890s. Owner Gayle Winston grew up within two miles of Glendale Spring, and remembers thinking, as a child, that the inn was the most beautiful building she'd ever seen. It has five antique-furnished guest rooms, each with its own private bath, hooked rugs, quilts, and period furnishings, along with modern conveniences such as electric heat and electric blankets. The bed was the first inn bed we've yet found that was firm enough to suit. Our room was reputed to have its own ghost, whom we were not privileged to meet.

"Breakfast included a choice of fresh-squeezed juice or fruit platter, croissant and pastries, and a choice of a cream cheese omelet with bacon or sherried eggs with ham. Coffee was hot, good, and plentiful. The dinner menu offers a very unusual choice of appetizers, entrées, and desserts for this diminutive community. One might begin with coquilles St. Jacques, continuing on to chicken stuffed with artichokes, black olives, and Béarnaise. A pecan cheesecake and coffee will complete the picture.

"The inn is listed on the National Register of Historic Places, and served as the headquarters for the WPA when the Blue Ridge Parkway was constructed in the mid-thirties. Gardner David Bare has done an intriguing job with flowers, herbs and shrubs. Glendale Spring also has a most attractive gift and antiques center, and is home to the Holy Trinity Church of Frescoes." *(David & Cheri Kendall)*

"All the guest rooms are lovingly furnished and have amazingly beautiful country quilts on the beds. But even better is the food, some of the greatest in the country—quite a shock in this little town. There are three dining rooms and a new menu nightly. Gayle also owns two restaurants in Winston-Salem: the Salem Tavern, and Stars, in the Stevens Center Concert Hall." *(Stephen Shipps)*

Open April through December.
Rooms 2 suites, 7 doubles, all with private bath. 2 in guest house with fireplace, whirlpool bath.
Facilities Restaurant, sitting room, library, porches. Hiking, bicycling, golf, canoeing, fishing, swimming nearby.
Location NW NC, Blue Ridge Mts. Just off Blue Ridge Pkwy., at mile marker 259, near junction with Rte. 16.
Restrictions No children under 10.
Credit cards Amex, MC, Visa.
Rates B&B, $95 suite, $75 double, $65 single. Extra person in room, $15. Alc lunch, $3.50–8; alc dinner, $29.
Extras Wheelchair accessible.

HIGHLANDS 28741   Map 5

Highlands is in western North Carolina, 125 miles north of Atlanta, and 60 miles southwest of Asheville. The town has auction galleries, antique shops, and summer theater, along with hiking, tennis, swimming, horseback riding, fishing, white-water rafting, and skiing. Surrounded by national forest lands, it has little of the commercialism found in other tourist areas.

"One of the prettiest towns of the Blue Ridge Mountains. Highlands is a marvelous place in summer—cool, fresh, and with lots of charming little shops. There are many hiking trails nearby, and the people in the hiking store will advise you on the level of difficulty." *(SN)* "This is waterfall country, and Smoky Mountains National Park is just a one-hour drive away." *(ML)* "We were surprised at the high quality of Highlands' restaurants—for such a small town, they were very good and surprisingly sophisticated." *(MS)*

Also recommended: The **Long House** (Route 2, Box 638; 704–526–4394) is a completely renovated 100-year-old log cabin with natural wood walls, oak floors, antiques, and handmade quilts. This B&B offers a full breakfast and great views of the surrounding woods.

Information please: The **Old Edwards Inn** (Main Street, Box 1778; 704–526–5036 or in winter 912–638–8892) is a Victorian inn and restaurant, recommended in past editions for its clean comfortable rooms, good service and superb food. Reports please, on whether the inn should be reinstated for a full entry.

Colonial Pines Inn   *Tel:* (704) 526–2060
Corner Hickory and 4½ streets, Route 1, Box 22B

Chris and Donna Alley moved from Atlanta in 1984 and renovated this old farmhouse with modern baths and antique and modern country furnishings. Readers continue to rave about Donna and her inn, making advance reservations imperative. (If the Colonial Pines is full, she's very helpful about referring you elsewhere.)

"A really restful place, with a porch swing which overlooks the mountains. The breakfast was by far the best we have been served anywhere. Donna Alley has done a tremendous job decorating the inn and making it comfortable for guests; her attention to detail makes the difference between adequate and special." *(Sibyl Nestor)*

"The inn is set back from the road on a hillside, offering beautiful mountain views from a three-sided porch. Donna's little extras made our stay delightful—things like an explanation of the specialty breads served at breakfast, the constant aroma of cinnamon and fresh-baked bread, and local directions and advice. The beds are comfortable and the breakfasts—which include fresh fruits, homemade breads, delicious sausage or ham, eggs, and excellent coffee—are great." *(Mark Lampe, also Dorothy C. Hill)*

"Donna Alley is a very thoughtful hostess, and the inn is spotless." *(Mrs. Mary S. Decicco)* "There is a nice library of books of local interest, and a grand piano for those inclined." *(Nance Pettit)*

Open All year.
Rooms 1 suite, 2 doubles, 1 single, 1 cottage—all with private bath and/or shower. 1 with TV. 2 bedrooms in cottage.
Facilities Dining room, living room with TV, grand piano; porches. 2 acres with picnic table, berry picking. Trout fishing, hiking, waterfalls, skiing, skating, canoeing nearby.
Location ½ m from town. 6 blocks from Main St. at corner of Hickory & 4½.
Restrictions No smoking. "Small children preferred in cottage."
Credit cards MC, Visa.
Rates B&B, $60–70 suite, $50–60 double, $45–55 single. Extra person in room, $10. 2-night minimum peak weekends.

NEW BERN 28560   Map 5

New Bern is located in mid-coastal North Carolina, 2 hours east of Raleigh, at the confluence of the Trent and Neuse rivers. It's a 45-minute drive to the Atlantic Ocean beaches. The town was founded in 1710 by German and Swiss colonists searching for political and religious freedom. New Bern prospered from the production of tar, pitch, and turpentine. When the royal governor of the Carolinas, William Tryon, saw the need for a permanent capital, New Bern was selected as the site. Tryon Palace, completed in 1770, was the colonial capitol and the first state capitol of North Carolina. New Bern's prosperity continued through much of the nineteenth century, and many of its finest buildings date from the early 1800s. A number of historic buildings have been restored and are open to the public as museums. On a more commercial note, Pepsi-Cola (known originally as "Brad's Drink") was invented here in the 1890s by a local pharmacist, C.D. Bradham.

Also recommended: The **Aerie** (509 Pollock Street; 919–636–5553) was built in 1870 and remained in the same family for over 100 years. Renovated as an inn in 1985, it's rooms are decorated with reproduction and antique furnishings; rates include a full breakfast. A classic brick colonial, the **New Berne House** (709 Broad Street; 919–636–2250; 800–842–7688) was also owned for generations by a single family. In 1987 it changed hands and began providing bed and breakfast. Rooms come furnished with antiques, including many accent pieces original to the house. New Bern's historic sights are all within walking distance of both establishments.

Harmony House Inn
215 Pollock Street

Tel: (919) 636–3810

Harmony House was built for Benjamin Ellis in the 1850s as a four-room, two-story home with Greek Revival styling. As the Ellis family grew, additions were made, porches were built and then enclosed. Around 1900, two sons of the builder sawed the house in half and separated it enough to add another hallway, front door, staircase and four more rooms; they each lived in their own half for the next twenty years.

Buzz and Diane Hansen opened the Harmony House in May 1985. They are "delighted that people seem to feel 'at home' in our home!" The inn is furnished with antiques and reproductions, many made by local craftsmen. The Hansens are pleased to offer advice on walking tours and local restaurants, and complimentary soft drinks and juices.

"The warmest, most gracious home away from home you can imagine. Breakfast includes egg/sausage casserole, spiced fruit compote, Diane's own coffee cake, and world-class coffee." *(Lois Cummings)* "Everything about the inn is first-rate, especially the innkeepers. The guest refrigerator, packed with assorted drinks was an expecially thoughtful touch." *(Elizabeth McPhelan)*

"Diane and Buzz Hansen are very proud of their home; it's obvious from Buzz's description and tour when you first register. Rooms are airy and spacious, with high ceilings; our bathroom was large and very clean, with a terrific shower, a rarity in renovated inns. Harmony House is well situated on a street with other inns and within walking distance of many of New Bern's restaurants and historic sites." *(Carolyn & Bill Myles)*

Open All year.
Rooms 9 doubles with full private bath, TV, air-conditioning. Many with ceiling fans.

Facilities Dining room, guest parlor with game table. Porch with swings, rockers. Landscaped ½ acre with gardens, lawn furniture. 1 block from 2 rivers, public park, boat ramp, fishing.
Location Center of town, historic district.
Restrictions Smoking in bedrooms only.
Credit cards Amex, MC, Visa.
Rates B&B, $70 double, $49 single. Extra person in room, $10. No tipping.
Extras Airport/station pickups. Crib available. Some Spanish spoken.

OCRACOKE 27960   Map 5

Ocracoke is on the Outer Banks of coastal North Carolina, about 1½ hours south of Nags Head, and 40 minutes by ferry from Hatteras village.

"Come to Ocracoke to heighten your awareness of the incredible forces of nature. Violent summer storms sweep through in minutes, and the pounding of ocean waves never ceases. The island is mercifully undeveloped, since most of it is part of the Cape Hatteras National Seashore. There's not a great deal to do but relax and enjoy the beautiful uncrowded beaches, fish and swim, rent a bicycle, and explore. The seafood is delicious; some of it familiar, some unusual to Yankee tastebuds." *(MS)*

Berkley Center Inn   *Tel:* (919) 928–5911
On the Harbor, P.O. Box 220

The Egan family has restored the Berkley Center, originally built as a center for employees of the Berkeley Machine Tool Company, as an inn, refurbishing its hand-carved fireplace mantels and the beautiful fir, cypress, and cedar-paneled walls and ceilings. Rooms are highlighted with quilts, baskets, and the work of local artists.

"Our spacious suite was beautiful, with a nice bath and a large sitting area. The inn is roomy and the grounds are well kept, with chairs for sitting and reading in the yard. The innkeepers, Ruth and Wes Egan, were helpful and really seem to love the building and its history. They had a book of menus from the island's restaurants—we thought the Back Porch was excellent." *(Ellen Olbrys)*

Open April–Nov.
Rooms 21 suites and doubles, with private and shared baths, air-conditioning.
Facilities Living room, dining room. 3½ acres.
Location On the harbor.
Credit cards None accepted.
Rates B&B, $60–80 double.

PINEHURST 28374   Map 5

Pinehurst is home to 34 golf courses and the Golf Hall of Fame. Beginning in 1895, the area was developed as a warm-weather refuge by a wealthy Boston industrialist, who hired the famed Frederick Law Olmsted, landscape architect of New York's Central Park and Asheville's Biltmore Estate. Pinehurst soon developed into a golfer's paradise, with the Pinehurst Hotel and Country Club its headquarters. With 310 rooms, the hotel is too big for this guide, but readers are pleased with the smaller establishment described below. Less-than-fanatic golfers will be happy to note that the area offers other recreational opportunities, including tennis, swimming, horseback riding, skeet and sport shooting, bicycling, hiking, and sailing.

Pinehurst is in the Piedmont Sandhills region of south central North Carolina, 70 miles southwest of Raleigh, and 45 miles northwest of Fayetteville.

Pine Crest Inn (919) 295–6121
Dogwood Road, P.O. Box 879

Owned by the Barrett family for over 25 years, the Pine Crest was founded in 1913 and was previously owned by Donald Ross, architect of more than 600 American golf courses. Although rooms are clean and comfortable, the inn is especially known for its bar and restaurant. The former, a local gathering place called Mr. B's Old South Lounge, is the domain of bartender and local golf columnist Bill Jones, CBS golf funnyman Bob Drum, and pianist Bob Israel. The inn's fine southern cooking is just as popular; Bob Barrett notes that the chef has been with the inn for over half a century, and "he surely knows what's cookin' in the kitchen." Barrett also describes the Pine Crest's business as being "80 percent repeat, with March, April, May, October, and November being the busiest times," and further suggests that "you leave your stuffed shirt at home." *(MW)* More comments, please.

Open All year.
Rooms 4 suites, 34 doubles, 2 singles—36 with private shower and/or bath, 4 with maximum of 4 people sharing bath. All with telephone, TV, desk, air-conditioning.
Facilities Dining rooms, bar/lounge, piano bar, lobby/game room. 5 acres with patio, terrace, porch. Use of Pinehurst Country Club for heated swimming pool, health club, tennis courts, access to lake for fishing, swimming, boating. 5 Pinehurst Country Club golf courses in walking distance; 12 more nearby.
Location Sandhills, "Golf Capital of the World." 1 block from village.
Credit cards Amex, DC, MC, Visa.
Rates All rates per person, based on double occupancy. MAP, $50–65 suite, $44–60 double, $58–75 single. 15% service. Reduced rates for children sharing parents' room. Senior discount. Alc dinner, $20. Golf packages.
Extras Wheelchair accessible. Cribs, babysitting available. Airport/station pickups.

RALEIGH 27604 Map 5

The Oakwood Inn *Tel:* (919) 832–9712
411 North Bloodworth Street

Pressured business travelers with appointments in North Carolina's capital city will find a welcome respite at The Oakwood Inn, opened in 1984. Built in 1871 as the Raynor Stronach House, the inn is listed on the National Register of Historic Places, and is located in the historic Oakwood District, home to twenty blocks of Victorian buildings, ranging in style from Greek Revival to Steamboat Gothic. Rooms are furnished entirely in period, and innkeeper Diana Newton describes her inn as an "exquisite example of careful historic restoration and vintage Victorian decor—an antique lover's delight." Guests are greeted with refreshments on arrival, and are served a full breakfast, including fruit, juice, home-baked breads or muffins, breakfast meat, and a changing menu of hot dishes, ranging from quiche to pancakes, from asparagus and almond strudel to cheese-stuffed French toast with apricot glaze.

"The attention to detail is carried through to every aspect of your stay. Home-baked breads or cakes await your arrival. Fresh fruit fills the silver bowl in the hallway. The dining room was complete with a lace tablecloth and fresh linen napkins, beautiful china, and silver service. Breakfasts are unsurpassed, with no repetition of dishes during a three- or four-day stay. The meal includes fresh fruit, homemade muffins or bread, and entrées varying from French toast stuffed with three cheeses and topped with homemade sauce to a light cheese, egg, and sausage casserole. Even better is to coax Diana to join you for a cup of coffee and good conversation." *(Leigh Farver)*

"I curled up with a book on the front porch swing. The decor is a perfect blend of colors and collectibles; private baths and air-conditioning were artfully included without spoiling the period ambiance." *(Jeanie Goodridge)*

"Our room had a comfortable bed, sofa, and rocking chair, with ample storage space in the closet and dresser. Our bright and cheerful bathroom was well supplied with fresh soap, shampoo, and conditioner. Our room was kept clean, as was the rest of the inn. Parking is provided behind the inn as well as on the street in front. We had a key to the front door, so we could come and go and we chose." *(Penelope Elliott)*

Open All year. Closed Christmas.
Rooms 5 doubles, 1 single, all with private bath and/or shower, air-conditioning. Many with fireplaces. TV on request.
Facilities Dining room, parlor with fireplace, porches. ½ acre with rose gardens.
Location In historic district.
Restrictions No children under 12. Smoking in designated guest rooms only.
Credit cards Amex, MC, Visa.
Rates B&B, $70–80 double, $60–70 single.
Extras Limited wheelchair access. Some French spoken.

VALLE CRUCIS 28691   Map 5

Also recommended: Enthusiastically recommended too late to complete a full writeup is the **Inn at the Taylor House** (Highway 194, Box 713; 704–963–5581), built in 1911 as a farmhouse, now restored as a European-style B&B with Oriental rugs and imported duvets. "Lovely decor, caring, gracious innkeepers, outstanding breakfasts." *(Valerie Vogler Stips)*

Mast Farm Inn   *Tel:* (704) 963–5857
P.O. Box 704

The Mast Farm began as a log cabin in 1812, and grew to include a blacksmith shop, meat house, spring house, wash house, apple house, and barn. The main house was completed in 1885 and served as a thirteen-bedroom, one-bath (!) country inn through the first half of this century, but it fell into disrepair and was sold by the Mast family. Francis and Sibyl Pressly, who left very different careers in Washington, DC, bought the inn late in 1984; they spent nearly a year restoring it and all the outbuildings.

Reporting after a return visit, *Sibyl Nestor* wrote: "This is our very favorite inn—a very friendly place. The Presslys make an effort to seat guests in compatible groups at meals. The food is something special—much of it is grown on the grounds, and after a big meal you can walk alongside the immense garden. We especially enjoyed staying in the blacksmith shop, which was restored as a room for the Presslys' son."

"Staying here is like visiting good friends in their well-restored, but not fancy, old country farmhouse. The principal activity, aside from eating, is rocking on the porch and watching the cars go by, and making the acquaintance of fellow guests. The rooms are airy, large, and clean, with comfortable beds and appropriate decorative touches; unpretentious yet most attractive. Service is mostly provided by the Presslys themselves (except at meals), and is unfailingly gracious. A housekeeper cleans the guest rooms and the rest of the house daily, changing towels and making beds. Rooms are adequately lighted, and include at least one easy chair by a window, for rainy days. Sibyl Pressly oversees the kitchen, house, and cutting garden (lovely dried flowers are for sale). Her recipes form the basis of memorable meals, served family-style in two dining rooms. Breakfast is simple—juice and coffee, fresh fruit and home-baked muffins, breads, honey-pecan rolls, pancakes, homemade apple butter, and locally made preserves. Dinner is a major event, with a set menu for every day of the week. Thursday is chicken and dumplings, Friday is sautéed trout with vegetable strudel, and Sunday brings outstanding fried chicken and country ham with biscuits and gravy. All the superb entrées are accompanied by home-style vegetables (corn, beans, potatoes, black-eyed peas, carrots, and more, many fresh from the inn's garden) and fresh salad and savories. No alcoholic beverages are served, but the staff is happy to chill your wine and serve it at dinner." *(Beth & Vaughn Morrison)*

While truly wonderful, the Mast Farm is not perfect; some minor complaints noted in otherwise glowing reports: Parking is tight at dinnertime; the third floor can be hot in summer, despite plenty of fans; and there is some road traffic noise, mostly caused by "motorists whizzing past the inn much too fast on their way to the Mast General Store, a wonderful place."

Open May through Oct., Jan. through Feb.
Rooms 11 doubles, 1 cottage—10 with private bath and/or shower, 2 with maximum of 4 people sharing bath. 5 rooms with desk; all with radio, fan. 3 rooms in out-buildings.
Facilities Restaurant, parlor with fireplace, sun porch, library/game room. 18 acres with river for trout fishing; pond for fishing, swimming. 5–12 m to golf, lake, downhill, cross-country skiing.
Location NW NC, High Country. 7 m W of Boone, 100 m N of Charlotte, 93 m W of Winston-Salem. On SR 1112, 3 m from NC 105.
Restrictions No smoking. No children under 12.
Credit cards MC, Visa.
Rates MAP, $120 cottage, $72–125 double. Children under 12, $15. Extra person in room $28. Sunday prix fixe lunch, $12; dinner, $12. 2-night weekend minimum.
Extras First-floor bedroom equipped for disabled. Portuguese spoken. Airport/station pickups.

WILMINGTON 28401   Map 5

Located in southeastern North Carolina, on the Cape Fear River, Wilmington is the state's largest port and a major trading center. Its historic district has been restored in recent years, and is now home to several B&Bs. The city has plenty of charm and several museums of interest, including the U.S.S. *North Carolina* Battleship Memorial; it's just a short drive to the ocean beaches and to several restored plantation homes.

Information please: The **Murchison House** is an imposing 1876 mansion in the historic district, now refurbished with period antiques, and offering a beautiful walled garden for relaxing (305 South Third Street; 919–343–8580). The **Graystone Guest House**, an imposing gray limestone mansion, was listed favorably in our earlier editions. It is now under new ownership, and has reopened after remodeling (100 South Third Street; 919–763–2000). Comments?

Also recommended: The **Five Star Guest House** (14 North Seventh Street; 919–763–7581) is turn-of-the-century Victorian highlighted by rich woods and handsome stained glass windows. Rooms are furnished with antiques, plants, and ceiling fans. A full breakfast is served each morning. **The Guest House at St. Thomas Court** (101 South 2nd Street; 919–763–4933) was designed to provide the privacy and business facilities of a hotel with the ambience of an inn. Rooms combine turn-of-the-century decor and polished hardwood floors with skylights and lofts. Rates include a welcome basket, bottle of wine, breakfast fixings, and choice of newspaper.

The Inn on Orange   *Tel:* (919) 251–0863
North 410 Orange Street

Whether traveling for pleasure or business, a small inn like this one can really make a difference in the quality of your trip. One of Wilmington's newer B&Bs, owner Catherine Ackiss offers guests a full breakfast, afternoon refreshments, and a bedtime liqueur. Summertime visitors will enjoy a cooling dip in the backyard swimming pool.

"The inn is conveniently located in the historic, restored area, a short and walkable distance to waterfront restaurants, shops and museums. The inn is charming, decorated with a variety of antiques. Our room had a king-sized bed with a firm mattress, abundant towels and bathrobes laundered daily, and a fabulous breakfast served on fine china, silver, and crystal. The service, cleanliness, and hospitality were impeccable." *(Diane Mrva, also Pearl & George Tippin)*

Open All year.
Rooms 3 doubles with private bath and/or shower, fireplace.
Facilities Dining room, living room, library. Swimming pool in yard.
Location Historic area. From highways 74, 76, 17 take 2nd St. to right on Front St. Go 6 blocks and turn right on Orange St.
Restrictions Street noise in front rooms. No children under 10.
Credit cards MC, Visa.
Rates B&B, $55 double. AARP discount.
Extras Airport/station pickups.

WINSTON-SALEM 27101   Map 5

Winston-Salem is known for its attention to the arts, and is the home of Old Salem, a restored eighteenth-century Moravian village. Other sites of interest include Reynolds House, the estate of the late R. J. Reynolds, founder of the tobacco firm that bears his name. The residence and gardens are open to the public; the house has an excellent collection of American art. If all that culture makes you thirsty, we suggest a free tour of the Joseph Schlitz Brewing Company; their Winston-Salem facility produces 4 million barrels of beer annually.

While in Winston-Salem, *Judy Lamberti* suggests dining at **Michael's** (858 West Fifth Street; 919–777–0000), a restored Victorian mansion, "where we had a lovely dinner accompanied by live piano music."

Winston-Salem is in central North Carolina, 144 miles east of Asheville, 80 miles north of Charlotte, and 104 miles west of Raleigh.

Brookstown Inn   *Tel:* (919) 725–1120
200 Brookstown Avenue

The Brookstown Inn is based in an old cotton mill complex dating back to 1836. After a century of industrial operation, the mill had become obsolete, and was scheduled for demolition in the 1970s, when historians identified it as the city's first factory. The mill was placed on the National Register of Historic Places, and was restored as an inn, surrounded by shops and a restaurant.

Many rooms at the Brookstown have loft ceilings, exposed, handmade brick walls, and rough-hewn beams. The decor is an eclectic mixture of Appalachian handmade quilts, traditional pieces, antiques, and twentieth-century industrial chic. Rates include a continental breakfast of coffee, orange juice, and Moravian buns. Wine and cheese are served in the parlor in the early evening. The Brookstown is located between Winston's commercial center and the restored colonial village of Old Salem. The inn has been open for only two years; it is managed by Ms. Pat S. Bryan, and is owned by a local hotel management firm.

"Large rooms, beautifully decorated. Staff is friendly and helpful. Plenty of parking right at the front door. Evening wine and cheese and continental breakfast were delicious. Old Salem is conveniently located right at the back door of the inn." *(Ernest & Catherine Long)* "Our room was quite large with wonderful wooden beams. Even the bathroom was huge. It is easy to see that this inn is a converted mill. Next door is a great fudge shop." *(BLK)*

A few minor niggles: "I only wish the windows opened." And, "The people running the inn—at the front desk and elsewhere—are a little impersonal, not surprising, I guess, given the inn's size."

Open All year.
Rooms 11 suites, 15 doubles, 14 singles. 12 additional rooms in annex. All with telephone, TV, air-conditioning. Some with whirlpool bath, fireplaces.
Facilities Parlor, dining area.
Location Central NC. 4 blocks to downtown. From I-70, take Cherry St. Exit to Marshall Ave. Follow signs to Brookstone Ave.

Credit cards Amex, CB, DC, MC, Visa.
Rates B&B, $95 suite, $79–89 double, $69–85 single. Extra person in room, $10. Children under 12 free.
Extras Disabled accessible; baths specially equipped. Cribs available.

We Want to Hear from You!

As you know, this book is only effective with your help. We really need to know about your experiences and discoveries.

If you stayed at an inn or hotel listed here, we want to know how it was. Did it live up to our description? Exceed it? Was it what you expected? Did you like it? Were you disappointed? Delighted?

Have you discovered new establishments that we should add to the next edition?

Tear out one of the report forms at the back of this book (or use your own stationery if you prefer) and write today. Even if you write only "Fully endorse existing entry" you will have been most helpful.

Thank You!

Key to Abbreviations

For complete information and explanations, please see the Introduction.

Rates: Range from least expensive room in low season to most expensive room in peak season.
Room only: No meals included; sometimes referred to as European Plan (EP).
B&B: Bed and breakfast; includes breakfast, sometimes afternoon/evening refreshment.
MAP: Modified American Plan; includes breakfast and dinner.
Full board: Three meals daily.
Alc lunch: À la carte lunch; average price of entrée plus nonalcoholic drink, tax, tip.
Alc dinner: Average price of three-course dinner, including half bottle of house wine, tax, tip.
Prix fixe dinner: Three- to five-course set dinner, excluding wine, tax, tip unless otherwise noted.
Extras: Noted if available. Always confirm in advance. Pets are not permitted unless specified.
Zip codes: If only one zip code applies, it is listed with the town name. If there is more than one, it is noted as part of the address.

Ohio

The Buxton Inn, Granville

Ohio, with an economy based on manufacturing and agriculture, has both major industrial cities and rich farmland. It is not a state one associates with small hotels or inns, but with the help of some knowledgeable Ohioans, we've managed to discover several quite wonderful ones in urban as well as rural locations. One particularly appealing area is Holmes County, in the northeastern part of the state, home to a large Amish community. (See entries for Danville, Loudonville, and Millersburg.)

Information please: We'd like to learn more about the **Pleasant Valley Inn**, an Italianate Victorian under new ownership (4247 Roswell Road SW, Dellroy 44620; 216–735–2987). Furnished in period, the Pleasant Valley is near Atwood Lake, about 20 miles southeast of Zoar (see entry). Also we'd like to hear about the **Centennial House**, in the little town of Peninsula, about halfway between Cleveland and Akron. Ideal for a convenient rural retreat, it's set in the Cuyahoga Valley National Recreation Area, perfect for hiking and bicycling. The inn was built in 1876 (hence the name) and is decorated with period antiques and memorabilia from around the world (5995 Center Street, Peninsula 44264; 216–657–2506). In east central Ohio is Roscoe Village, just outside of Coshocton. Now restored to its mid-19th century glory days as a major port on the Ohio & Erie Canal, the **Roscoe Village Inn** offers comfortable accommodation in antique-studded rooms, and good food in King Charley's Tavern (Roscoe Village, Coshocton 43812; 614–622–2222).

Also recommended: If you'll be travelling in east central Ohio, *Martha Long* suggests the **Versailles Hotel,** (21 West Main Street, Versailles 45380; 523–526–5252), located about 10 miles northeast of Greenville. "The hotel takes up the second floor of a building in the center of this friendly small town. The rooms are large, remodeled beautifully in contemporary style and comfort."

Although we don't have any reader recommendations for Cincinnati (but would be delighted to receive some), we can suggest the **Amos Shinkle House** just across the Roebling Suspension Bridge from Riverfront Stadium (home of the Cincinnati Reds), in Covington, Kentucky (see entry for full details).

Rates do not include 5.5% sales tax.

CLEVELAND 44106 — Map 8

Also recommended: Although a tight deadline forestalled a full entry, *Zita Knific* wrote to recommend Cleveland's newest B&B, the **Glidden House.** "The house is lovely, and within walking distance of Severance Hall, major museums, and Little Italy, as well as the Baricelli Inn, which you already list." This French gothic-style mansion was built in 1909; a new addition houses most of the 52 guest rooms, which combine period charm with hotel-type conveniences (1901 Ford Avenue 44106; 216–231–8900).

The Baricelli Inn   *Tel:* (216) 791–6500
2203 Cornell Street

The Baricelli Inn, with its hand-carved stone exterior, was built in 1908 and is located in the cultural center of the city. Rates include a continental breakfast of coffee, juice, fresh fruit, muffins and pastry. The Baricelli is famed for its restaurant, serving creative cuisine with an Italian accent. Menus change seasonally, and entrée possibilities include saffron and black linguine with shrimp and Little Neck clams in Italian Fontina sauce or lamb in a veal and spinach mousseline with a rosemary and tarragon wine sauce. Paul and John Minnillo also own several other popular area restaurants.

"The Baricelli Inn opened on New Year's Day, 1986. It's located near University Circle, an elegant neighborhood close to the huge Cleveland Clinic complex, adjacent to the University Hospitals and Case Western Reserve, and just up the street from Severance Hall, winter home of the Cleveland Orchestra. The Minnillos redid this large old house, saving the beautiful woodwork and stair rails, and obviously took great pains to make the new blend with the old. The front entrance is porticoed and faces the brightly lit parking lot.

"The rooms are big, with four-poster beds—king-size in the three largest and queen-size in the other four bedrooms. The bathrooms are sizable; they saved the old porcelain basins, but the rest is new. I was pleased with the fact that the inn is run by the owner, John Minnillo, and that the chef is his brother Paul. Dinner was wonderful, but expensive; I'm told, by East Siders that the restaurant is considered to be the equal of any around. There are four dining rooms, with about five tables in each." *(Pete Blake)*

"Rooms are elegantly furnished with antiques. The food is superb and presented as a visual feast as well as a culinary one. Within walking distance of the Symphony Hall, Art Museum, Garden Center, Natural History Museum, Western Reserve Historical Society, and the Auto Museum." *(Mrs. S. Busch)*

And another opinion: "While highly praised, I found the atmosphere snooty, and my garlic-smothered fish unappealing."

Open All year. Restaurant closed Sundays. Inn/restaurant closed holidays.
Rooms 7 doubles, all with full private bath, telephone, color TV, radio, desk, air-conditioning, fireplaces.
Facilities Restaurant, lobby, patio, garden. Near Lake Erie for fishing, boating.
Location NE Ohio. 5 m from downtown, in "Little Italy," on the East Side. At corner of Cornell & Murray Hill. 2 blocks from Severance Hall.
Restrictions No children under 12.
Credit cards Amex, MC, Visa.
Rates B&B, $90–125 double. Alc dinner, $50.
Extras Spanish, French spoken.

COLUMBUS   Map 8

Information please: If you would like to visit a larger hotel (196 rooms) with a true taste of the past, *Susie Preston* suggests the restored **Great Southern Hotel,** with two restaurants and a beautiful ballroom (310 South High Street 43215; 614–228–3800 or 800–328–2073). More reports please.

Built in 1860, the **Central House** is a totally restored country hotel, newly opened as a B&B in historic Pickerington, a suburb southeast of Columbus (27 West Columbus Street, Old Village Area Pickerington 43147; 614–837–0932).

See also entry for **The Worthington Inn** in Worthington.

Fifty Lincoln   *Tel:* (614) 291–5056
50 East Lincoln Street 43215

We're delighted to add a new entry for Columbus. Owned by Jack and Zoe Johnstone, Fifty Lincoln is a 19th-century brick manor, situated between the downtown area and Ohio State University, in a neighborhood of restored homes, unique shops, and restaurants. Known as the Short North District, Jack describes it as lively mix of "art galleries, furniture and antique shops, clothing stores, and restaurants." Originally a large two-family home, the building was converted to a rooming house in the 1950's. The Johnstones renovated it in 1986, decorating the eight guest rooms with eclectic furnishings. Zoe is a musician, interior designer, business consultant and devotee of international cooking; Jack has worked with businesses world-wide, and has a doctorate in music—he's also a self-described itinerant gardener and "master of the American breakfast." Both have traveled and lived extensively in Europe. Rates include a full breakfast and early evening refreshments. *(NB)* Comments, please.

Open All year.
Rooms 8 doubles with private bath, telephone, TV, desk, air-conditioning.
Facilities Dining room, parlor, garden, off-street parking.
Location Central Ohio. 1 m from downtown, 1 m S of Ohio State Univ., in "Short North" gallery district.
Credit cards Amex, MC, Visa.
Rates B&B, $89 double, $79 single.

DANVILLE 43014 Map 8

The White Oak Inn *Tel:* (614) 599–6107
29683 Walhonding Road (Route 715)

Set deep in the countryside of the Walhonding Valley, The White Oak is decorated with nineteenth-century antiques and handmade quilts. Rates include a full breakfast with meat, eggs, juice, coffee, and fresh baked goods.

"A beautifully restored old farmhouse, with all new plumbing, wiring, and so on. The food and service at breakfast and dinner were excellent. Both the inn and its owners are very gracious. One outstanding feature of The White Oak is its quiet country setting on a little-used back road." *(Philip Eramo)*

"Wide, welcoming porches; gleaming woodwork; spotlessly clean; comfortable bed with fresh, crisp, sweet-scented linens; spacious, light, airy rooms; peaceful, quiet, rolling countryside. The Actons are warm hospitable people who make you feel like you're going home for the weekend." *(Lee Siegrist)*

Open All year.
Rooms 1 suite, 6 doubles, all with private bath. Some with radio, TV, ceiling fans. Telephones on request.
Facilities Dining room, common room, porch. 14 acres. ½ m to river. Hiking, fishing, biking, golfing, canoeing nearby.
Location N central OH. 1 hr. NE of Columbus. 4 m E of junction of rtes. 36 & 62 at Millwood. On SR 715.
Restrictions No smoking. No children under 12.
Credit cards MC, Visa.
Rates B&B, $85 suite, $70 double. Extra person in room, $15. Prix fixe dinner (by prior arrangement only), $15–20. 2-night weekend minimum, May, Sept., Oct., holidays.

GRANVILLE 43023 Map 8

The Buxton Inn *Tel:* (614) 587–0001
313 East Broadway

Granville was settled by New Englanders from Granville, MA, and Granby, CT, at the beginning of the nineteenth century. The town was laid out to look like a New England village; it is still a small town today, and the home of Denison University.

The Buxton Inn was one of the town's first buildings, constructed in 1812, and now listed on the National Register of Historic Places. It changed hands a number of times before 1865, when it was purchased by Major and Mrs. Buxton, who ran it for 43 years. Over that time, the inn was expanded often; additions included a two-story wing with a Victorian dining room and guest rooms. Orville and Audrey Orr bought and restored the inn in 1972; according to local sources, inhabitants at the inn include not only the paying guests, but two (friendly) ghosts, both innkeepers here at different stages of the inn's history.

"This is truly a restored, not reconstructed, inn; the floors are uneven and sagging, the rooms are furnished with genuine antiques and quilts. The food is continental and some of the best anywhere, with excellent wine choices. We ate in a lush courtyard." *(EJS, also DB, Virginia Mahone)*

"While staying at the Buxton Inn, be sure to go to the Bryn Mawr restaurant for dinner. It's a beautifully restored, white, columned mansion with wonderful dinners and brunches, located a couple miles south of Granville on Route 37." *(Susie Preston)*

Open All year. Closed Christmas, New Years.
Rooms 7 suites, 12 doubles—all with private bath and/or shower, telephone, radio, TV, desk, air-conditioning. 15 rooms in annex.
Facilities Restaurant, tavern, courtyard.
Location Central OH. Approx. 30 m E of Columbus. In center.
Credit cards Amex, DC, CB, MC, Visa.
Rates Room only, $80 suite, $70 double, $60 single. Children under 5 free. Full breakfast, $3–7; alc lunch, $6; alc dinner, $24. Children's menu.
Extras Wheelchair accessible. Cribs available.

LEBANON 45036   Map 8

The Golden Lamb Inn   *Tel:* (513) 932–5065
27 South Broadway

Lebanon was founded in 1796, and The Golden Lamb just seven years later, making it Ohio's oldest hotel. A two-story brick Federal-style building replaced the original log structure in 1815; this building now houses the lobby, but it has been added to many times over the years. The Golden Lamb had many famous visitors in the 19th century, including seven U.S. presidents, Charles Dickens, and Mark Twain. The inn's 18 guest rooms are individually furnished with antiques and reproduction furniture. Rates include a continental breakfast.

"We visited just before Christmas and thoroughly enjoyed two meals at the inn, including their traditional 'Mount Vernon' dinner, featuring smoked ham and turkey. Carollers dressed in 19th-century costumes visited each of the dining rooms. The eggnog, served from a large polished pewter punch bowl during our brief wait in the lobby, was an extra treat. Christmas is an excellent time to visit here; the inn is decorated with hand-stitched Christmas samplers from all over Ohio, and the tree beside the fireplace is hung with handmade ornaments. *(Kathy Still, also SHW)*

While reports are unanimously positive on the inn's food, readers felt that the plumbing and air conditioners could stand updating. One noted the noise of guests touring the Shaker Rooms can be disturbing if one is trying to get to sleep. Comments?

Open All year. Restaurant closed Christmas Day.
Rooms 1 suite, 17 doubles with private bath and/or shower, telephone, TV, air-conditioning. Some with radio, desk.
Facilities Restaurant, tavern, lobby/parlors, gift shop, Shaker museum. Hiking, canoeing, boating, tennis, golf nearby.

Location 45 min. NE of Cincinnati, 15 m S of Dayton. Just off I-75 and I-71, on Rte. 42.
Credit cards All major cards.
Rates B&B, $85 suite, $60–70 double, $48 single, plus 9½% tax. Extra person in room, $6. Alc lunch, $6–8; alc dinner, $20.
Extras German spoken.

LEXINGTON 44904   Map 8

White Fence Inn   *Tel:* (419) 884–2356
8842 Denman Road

Situated almost halfway between Columbus and Cleveland, the White Fence Inn is a 98-year-old farmhouse owned by Bill and Ellen Hiser. This B&B offers a country retreat among apple trees, grape vines, gardens, and fields. Rates include a full country breakfast with homemade jams, juices, and cider.

"This immaculately clean farmhouse has owners who went out of their way to make us comfortable. Each guest room has a different decorating theme, from Amish to Victorian to Southwestern. Breakfast was delicious, and our young son loved the farm animals and the tire swing." *(RMN)*

"The Hisers have completely renovated this old farmhouse—ask to see the before and after pictures. It's surrounded by farmland, woods, and with its own fishing pond. When traveling under the stress of business, it's incredibly relaxing to see a full moon in a night sky and hear only the sound of crickets. When sitting on the front porch or back deck, be sure to have some of Ellen's iced tea—there's always a pitcher in the fridge. You literally wake up to birds singing and if it's a nice morning you can have breakfast on the deck. Don't miss Ellen's blueberry muffins." *(Bob Fletcher)*

"What makes the White Fence Inn a great place to stay is the hosts, Bill and Ellen—they made us feel like family. Their attention to detail covers everything from the decor of the rooms to the outstanding breakfasts and desserts. The fresh strawberry pie was so irresistible that I ate three pieces." *(Scott Daley)* "An unexpected breakfast treat was homemade grape juice." *(Walter Wittich)*

Open All year.
Rooms 4 doubles—2 with private bath, 2 with a maximum of 4 people sharing a bath. All with fan. Suite with TV.
Facilities Dining room, parlor with fireplace, piano, games; TV room with stereo; library, porch. 73 acres with orchard, chicken yard, pond and brooks for fishing, hay and sleigh rides, tennis, walking and cross-country skiing trails.
Location N central OH. From I-71 take exit 165 to Rte 97. Go through Lexington and follow signs to Mid-Ohio Racetrack. Go left on Lex-Steam Corners Rd. Go 2 m then turn left onto Denman Rd. Inn is 1st farm on right. 2.5 m from town.
Restrictions No smoking.
Credit cards None accepted.
Rates B&B, $70–82 suite, $42–72 double, $32–55 single. Extra person in room, $10. Children under 5 free. 2 night minimum on race weekends. Discount for 5 night stay.
Extras 1 room wheelchair equipped, station pickups, babysitting, cribs, play equipment available.

LOUDONVILLE 44842   Map 8

The Blackfork Inn   *Tel:* (419) 994–3252
303 North Water Street

Built in 1865, The Blackfork is listed on the National Register of Historic Places. Albin and Suzanne Gorisek have owned the inn since 1983, and have furnished it with a collection of antiques ranging from the colonial to the Victorian. Recent reports confirm last year's entry: "Immaculate; interesting hosts; friendly guests; outstanding breakfast. Could only ask that the town had a restaurant in the same league." *(KLH)*

"The Blackfork Inn is a lovely, graceful Victorian mansion in a quiet town in the heart of Amish country. Every room is beautifully done with Victorian antiques and memorabilia. Sue and Al Gorisek strike that rare balance that allows one to feel like a privileged guest in their home, with the freedom to enjoy as much privacy or interaction as desired.

"Morning begins with leisurely breakfasts around the dining room table, chatting with other guests or simply concentrating on the delicious Amish pastry and apple butter, fresh croissants, cheese, fruit, and more. Guests are given keys to come and go as they please, in order to enjoy the area attractions—canoeing, antiquing, visiting craft and specialty shops, or simply exploring the winding backcountry roads. (We did just that and happened on an Amish farm auction!) Sue and Al are full of ideas and have maps for newcomers. The inn has several cozy nooks for conversation or reading, in addition to the spacious bedrooms. Each is decorated differently, and all have updated baths. Our favorite room is the Josephine—the only room without a brass bed; it connects to another room, if one travels with children or another couple. The inn is located at the end of a quiet street; parking is plentiful and the atmosphere restful." *(Marion Carroll & Bill Brink)*

Open All year.
Rooms 6 doubles with full, private bath.
Facilities Dining room, 2 parlors, library. ¾ acre. Hiking, swimming, fishing, canoeing, cross-country skiing nearby.
Location N central Ohio, halfway between Columbus and Cleveland. Holmes County, 20 m NW of Millersburg. In village, 2 blocks from Main St.
Restrictions Children only by prior arrangement. Trains on nearby tracks might disturb light sleepers.
Credit cards MC, Visa.
Rates B&B, $75 double, $65 single.
Extras Pets allowed by prior arrangement. Airport/station pickups.

MILLERSBURG 44654   Map 8

The Inn at Honey Run   *Tel:* (216) 674–0011
6920 County Road 203   In OH: (800) 468–6639

Built in 1983, this inn is a handsome contemporary structure of glass, wood, and stone, surrounded by trees. Rates include continental breakfast, and the cuisine at lunch and dinner is straightforward American cooking—beef, pork, turkey, chicken, locally caught rainbow trout, fresh vegetables, and homemade breads and desserts—all prepared "from scratch." The inn attracts many executive seminars during the week; weekends bring professional couples looking for rest and relaxation. Added in 1988 were the "Honeycomb" rooms; set on a hillside above the inn, overlooking a pasture of wildflowers and grazing sheep, these luxury rooms have a private patio, wood-burning fireplace and a whirlpool bath.

Among Ohio's inns, this one is clearly a reader favorite: "The decor is a lovely blend of Amish pieces, e.g., rockers, quilts, handmade furniture (much of it made in Holmes County), and contemporary work. Holmes County is the heart of one of the biggest Amish settlements in Ohio, and the small town of Millersburg is its center. Our room was furnished with twin beds, a small table with two chairs, and two wing chairs. A floor-to-ceiling window looked out onto a bank of ivy and a bird feeder. The inn has a small library for its guests; you can take home unfinished books and return them by mail when done. Meals are served in a dining room whose only decoration is baby-size Amish quilts hung between the large windows. The food was delicious, very generous in portions, and well presented. The grounds are wooded and hiking trails are marked, the longest being a mile and a quarter." *(Shirley & Perry Noe)*

"Our second-floor corner room overlooked a heavily wooded area. No curtains were needed, and we felt as though we were in the forest, with all the comforts of a first-class hotel. The inn is immaculate. We had a king-size bed, a table with lounge chairs, and a desk and chair; books on inns and birds were in the room. Sunday night supper is called 'Raid the Kitchen,' and included fresh roast turkey, ham, salads, soups, and rolls, all set in up in the kitchen. Six or seven desserts were on a table in the dining room." *(KLH, also Mary Wabeke)*

"I enjoyed sitting in my room in a cozy chair, feet propped up, while reading and enjoying the birds feasting at the bird feeder outside my window. A bird book is in each room, and is a great aid in identifying many species I'd never seen before. Truly down-home cooking. During the summer, I would highly recommend the 20-mile drive to Wooster to see the Gilbert & Sullivan productions." *(Susie Preston)*

Open All year. Closed Jan. 1–15. Restaurant closed to public Sun.
Rooms 1 suite, 36 doubles, all with private bath and/or shower, telephone, radio, desk, air-conditioning. Extra charge for TV. Some rooms with whirlpool tub. 12 rooms in annex.
Facilities Restaurant, lobby with fireplace, family/game room with fireplace, meeting rooms, Ping-Pong, movies. 60 acres with hiking trails, farm animals.
Location N central Ohio; 85 m S of Cleveland, 85 m NE of Columbus. Holmes County; 3½ m from Millersburg. Take E Jackson St. in town to Rte. 241, to County Rd. 203.
Restrictions No alcohol in public rooms; no smoking in dining room. Children discouraged.
Credit cards Amex, MC, Visa.
Rates B&B, $95–120 suite, $50–150 double. Extra person in room, $20. 2-night weekend minimum. Alc lunch, $8; alc dinner, $18.
Extras Wheelchair access—elevators, ramps, no stairs. Airport pickups. Cribs available. German spoken.

OBERLIN 44074 Map 8

Oberlin College Inn *Tel:* (216) 775–1111
State Route 58, On Tappan Square

Both the town of Oberlin and the school, an outstanding college in the liberal arts tradition, date back to 1833. A key campus attraction is the college art museum, one of the country's best.

The Oberlin Inn predates the Civil War; unfortunately, little of its history is evident in the pleasant if undistinguished decor, although we hope the renovation now in progress will change that. The food served in its restaurant is another story. The cuisine is excellent and imaginative: A recent dinner included chilled pear soup, pan-roasted duck seasoned with tomatoes, oranges, and wine, and chocolate walnut cake for dessert. *(RC)* More comments, please.

Open All year. Closed Christmas.
Rooms 2 suites, 72 doubles, 1 single—all with full private bath, telephone, TV, desk, air-conditioning.
Facilities Restaurant, lounge with entertainment, lobby, gardens. Use of all sports facilities on campus. Beaches, fishing, golf nearby.
Location N OH. 35 m SW of Cleveland, 15 m S of Lake Erie.
Restrictions No smoking in some guest rooms.
Credit cards Amex, DC, Discover, MC, Visa.
Rates Room only, $78–85 suite, $65–75 double, $52–60 single. Extra person in room, $10. No charge for children under 12. Alc breakfast, $3–6; alc lunch, $11; alc dinner, $18–25.
Extras Wheelchair accessible. Cribs available.

TIPP CITY 45371 Map 8

The Willowtree Inn *Tel:* (513) 667–2957
1900 West Route 571

The Willowtree was built in 1830, and restored in 1974 by owner/innkeeper Martha DeBold.

"The Willowtree, with its willow tree, pond, ducks, antique shop, huge lawns, beautiful, airy, spacious rooms, and, most of all, owner Martha DeBold, is a must whenever we want a lovely, relaxing weekend. Breakfasts are delicious too; we had fresh strawberries and bananas, eggs Benedict, and coffee." *(William C. Burr)*

"The decor is beautiful, and Martha is so gracious with a wonderful sense of humor. The lovely grounds are a haven for those who love animals. The inn is well located between two quaint towns, Tipp City and Milton." *(Vickie Van)*

Open All year.
Rooms 4 suites and doubles, all sharing bath.
Facilities Living room, TV room. 5 acres, lawn games, antique shop.
Location SW OH. 5 m N of Dayton. 2½ m W of Exit 68, I-75, on State Rte. 571. 4 m N of Dayton Airport.

Restrictions Smoking in public rooms only. No children under 12.
Credit cards Amex, MC, Visa.
Rates B&B, $65 suite, $50–55 double. Extra person in room, $10. No tipping. 10% senior discount, weekly rate, business rates.

WOOSTER 44691   Map 8

The Wooster Inn   *Tel:* (216) 264–2341
1 East Wayne Avenue

Built in 1959 and owned by the College of Wooster, the Wooster Inn offers both the friendly atmosphere of a country inn and convenient access to all the college's facilities. Rooms are done in colonial decor, and the lobby is well supplied with comfortable couches and chairs. The restaurant has an excellent reputation, serving tried and true favorites, expertly prepared, at very reasonable prices—filet mignon, rainbow trout, veal Marsala, and lamb chops are among the entrées. The homemade soups are inventive, salads are fresh, and the desserts are all baked on the premises, with mocha mousse and apple pie among the favorites. *(Ann Almy)*

"Great home-cooked food. Guest rooms are very clean and nice, but lack the character of a true country inn. If you visit in the summer be sure to go to the Light Opera series—they do a different Gilbert & Sullivan production every evening." *(SP)*

Open All year. Closed Christmas.
Rooms 2 suites, 15 doubles—all with private bath and/or shower, telephone, TV, desk, air-conditioning.
Facilities Restaurant, terrace. Golf course, cross-country skiing adjacent, tennis courts nearby.
Location NE OH. 60 m S of Cleveland, 90 m NE of Columbus. From US Rte. 250, exit to Rte. 585. Go N onto Wayne Ave. Follow Wayne Ave. to inn on the left.
Credit cards Amex, CB, DC, MC, Visa.
Rates B&B, $100 suite, $59–64 double, $45–50 single. Extra adult in room, $14; child 3–12, $5; child under 3, free. Alc lunch, $6–10; alc dinner, $15.
Extras Wheelchair accessible. Pets allowed. Cribs, babysitting available. German, Spanish spoken.

WORTHINGTON 43085   Map 8

The Worthington Inn   *Tel:* (614) 885–2600
649 High Street (Route 23)

The Worthington Inn was built in 1831 as a stagecoach stop. It was expanded many times over the years, most notably in 1901, when the mansard roof, front porches, and exterior spiral staircase were added. After many changes of ownership, the inn was a decaying white elephant when it was bought and totally renovated in 1983 by Hugh Showe. Some guest rooms have hand-stenciled walls and are furnished with early American reproductions, while others have a Victorian decor. Rates include a breakfast of fresh fruit and juice, coffee, and pastry—and the inn's restaurant serves an ambitious menu of French and continental specialties.

"We watched the renovation in progress—one of the most well done I've seen. They've restored the old-time flavor with elaborate attention to detail. Meals are elegantly served, with rich desserts, in a very charming atmosphere. The inn is on a street with lots of quaint shops with crafts and quilts." *(ES)* "Be sure to ask to see the Van Loon ballroom, with its elegant Czechoslovakian chandelier." *(Nancy Brightman)*

"A beautifully restored landmark in an excellent location. The staff is extremely accommodating, making you feel comfortable and pampered. The inn is clean, quiet, and very romantic." *(Rebecca M. Ward)* "Each room is different, beautifully done in antiques." *(Susie Preston)*

"Worthington is a well-to-do northern suburb of Columbus. Fairly good wine list; attractive bar. Everything done in good taste." *(Virginia Mahone)*

Open All year. Restaurant closed Christmas, New Year, Memorial Day.
Rooms 3 suites, 23 doubles—all with full private bath, telephone, radio, TV, desk, air-conditioning. 4 rooms in annex.
Facilities Restaurant, pub and wine bar, meeting rooms. 2 acres with picnic area.
Location Central OH. 15 m N of downtown Columbus, 5 m N of Ohio State University. 1 block S of Rte. 161. 2 m S of I-270 N.
Credit cards All major cards.
Rates B&B, $125–135 suite, $95–105 double, $85–95 single. Extra person in room $10. Children under 12 free in parents' room. Alc lunch, $7; alc dinner, $30. Holiday and weekend rates.
Extras Airport pickups, $25. Korean spoken. Cribs available.

YELLOW SPRINGS 45387   Map 8

Morgan House   *Tel:* (513) 767–7509
120 West Limestone

Built in 1921 as the home of Antioch College president Arthur Morgan, Morgan House became a dormitory, then a food co-op and office, before Marianne Britten renovated it as a B&B, opening in November 1986.

"Marianne Britten, an enterprising woman from California, cooks the wonderful breakfast herself, and has found lovely antiques at local auctions to decorate the rooms. Yellow Springs is a town of about 4,500 people transplanted from East and West. John Bryan State Park is a mile away, and Glen Helen, a 1,000-acre nature preserve, is adjacent to the town. Small but diverse shops and restaurants abound." *(Sue Parker)*

"Yellow Springs is one of our favorite places, an old, progressive, cultured town in rural Ohio. The Morgan House fits right in. Rooms are small but comfortable. The parlor and screened-in porch are great places to sit with a good book. Plenty of nice walks, interesting shops, and fine places to eat. Marianne is a terrific innkeeper." *(Jack Johnstone)*

Open All year.
Rooms 4 doubles with maximum of 4 people sharing bath. All rooms with air-conditioning.
Facilities Living room, TV/sitting room, dining room, screened porch. ½ acre with flower garden. Swimming, hiking nearby.

Location SW OH. 15 min. NE of Dayton, 45 min. NE of Cincinnati, 1 hr. W of Columbus. 9 m S of I-70. In historic district, ½ block from downtown.
Restrictions No smoking.
Credit cards None accepted.
Rates B&B, $40–50 double, $35 single. Extra person in room, $10. Weekly rates. Saturday afternoon tea every other Sat.
Extras Crib available. Chinese spoken.

ZOAR 44697 Map 8

Cider Mill Bed & Breakfast *Tel:* (216) 874–3133
Second Street, P.O. Box 441

During the 1860s, Zoar was the nation's most successful communal religious village; later, because of its charm and serenity, President McKinley picked it for his summer retreat. Today, the entire village is listed on the National Register of Historic Places. The cider mill was built in 1863, and was used as a cabinetmaker's shop in the off-season. In 1972 Judy and Ralph Kraus renovated the mill and have opened it up to B&B guests. "The mill is located on a side street of the tiny artist colony and Separatist community of Zoar. It is very quiet and secluded, though only about a 5-mile drive from the interstate. The ground floor of the inn is an antique shop, the main floor has lots of space and high ceilings and is decorated with antiques, featuring the owners' favorite motifs of violets and geese (but not together). Up a spiral staircase, the top floor has two guest rooms and a shared bath. The guest rooms are relatively small, but beautifully decorated, also with antiques. We asked for an extra lamp for reading, which the innkeeper gladly provided. Judy Kraus was wonderful. She loves animals and has several different kinds. She was very friendly, and we had interesting conversations while she was preparing our breakfast in the lovely country kitchen. One morning we had bread and butter pudding, grapes, watermelon, and apple juice, and the second, we had sliced cantaloupe, sausage and omelet, homemade pear jam, and grapes. Among the best B&B breakfasts we've ever had." *(Susan W. Schwemm)*

Open All year.
Rooms 2 doubles with air-conditioning, sharing 1 bath.
Facilities Living/family room with TV, fireplace; antique shop. Fishing, canoeing, swimming, sailing, golf, bicycling, hiking nearby.
Location NE OH. 75 m S of Cleveland; 15 m S of Canton. On Rte. 212, 3 m SE of I-77. In town center.
Restrictions Smoking in family room only. No children under 6.
Credit cards Amex, MC, Visa.
Rates B&B, $60 double, $50 single. Extra person in room, $15. Canoeing packages.
Extras Pets allowed. Airport/station pickups.

Oklahoma

Harrison House Inn, Guthrie

Despite Oklahoma's "Sooner State" moniker, it's definitely a later addition to this guide; as of the present edition, it's running neck and neck with Nebraska for last place as the guide's shortest chapter! (It could be worse—North Dakota has yet to make an appearance at all.) We know that Oklahomans love to travel, because they write to us all the time recommending their favorite inns and hotels—in *other* states. That's great, of course, but we'd really like to hear about some home-state favorites too.

Information please: We'd like to know what you think of the **Skirvin Plaza Hotel,** a century-old National Historic Landmark in Oklahoma City. At 202 rooms, it's about half the size of the city's biggest hotels, and was recently renovated to combine its original elegance with up-to-date luxuries (One Park Avenue 73102; 800–654–4500).

Oklahoma City celebrated its centennial last year, and, as proud residents know, it has far more to offer travelers than its claims to being the birthplace of both the parking meter and the shopping cart. The Cowboy Hall of Fame is devoted to western history and art, while the Kirkpatrick Museum Complex is an outstanding attraction, with museums devoted to the American Indian, a hands-on Science and Art Museum, an Air and Space Museum, and more.

In Tulsa, a B&B we'd like to hear more about is **The Holloway House,** a New England-style clapboard house built in 1924 by the city's most famous retail businesswoman, Nellie Shields Jackson (P.O. Box 52432, Tulsa 74152; 918–582–8607). Its three elegant guest rooms are decorated in eighteenth- and nineteenth-century antiques and reproductions, at rates ranging from $55–70; each bath has a whirlpool tub. Guests enjoy breakfast in the dining room or on the garden patio; in the evening, relax before the living room fireplace or play a favorite tune on the baby grand piano. Your reports please!

GUTHRIE 73044   Map 11

Guthrie was born over 100 years ago, when the Oklahoma territory was opened to settlement and the land rush was on. The territorial, and later state, capital until 1910, Guthrie was a prosperous town, with lots of substantial Victorian commercial and residential buildings and such prominent inhabitants as O. Henry, Lon Chaney, Carrie Nation, and Tom Mix. When the capital was transferred to Oklahoma City, development here tapered off. As has often been noted before, poverty is the preservationists' friend, and by 1980, many citizens realized that (after years of neglect) Guthrie had something unique in the state. After a several-million-dollar restoration effort, Guthrie is well worth a visit to see its historic downtown, enjoy its theater and concerts, and participate in its month-long Victorian Christmas celebration. Guthrie's historic district lists over 2,000 buildings on the National Register of Historic Places; the chamber of commerce proudly claims Guthrie to the B&B capital of Oklahoma, which we find something of a giggle, all things considered.

To get to Guthrie, take I-35 north from Oklahoma City. It's about a 30 minute drive to Exit 153.

Harrison House Inn   *Tel:* (405) 282–1000
124 West Harrison, P.O. Box 1555

Harrison House is very much a part of the town-wide restoration of Guthrie. It occupies what was originally the Guthrie Savings Bank, as well as two adjacent once-commercial structures. The buildings were renovated in 1983 and are owned by a group of local investors; Phyllis Murray is the innkeeper. Rooms are decorated in period with dark woodwork, brass fixtures, mirrored armoires, velvet-covered chairs or settees, iron beds, lace curtains, reproduction wallpapers, and colorful new patchwork quilts.

"Our room was charming and spacious. We were impressed by how much thought went into the renovation of the building. The inn is full of marvelous antiques and collectibles. Each room has a theme or atmosphere characteristic of the famous Oklahoman it was named after. Breakfast was delicious, and included cereal, waffles, banana nut bread, and other goodies; we helped ourselves to as much as we wanted. Phyllis, the innkeeper, was very gracious as she poured coffee and visited with the guests, greeting each one by name. Most of the staff were young college-age kids. They were all very polite and helpful. The inn is right in the heart of town, with a fine restaurant and saloon across the street and a live theater next door. We parked next to the inn and walked everywhere." *(AP)*

"The parlor has an intimate atmosphere, providing a space for guests to relax during the day, exchanging ideas and conversation." *(John & Donna Clements)* "We were greeted warmly and made to feel at home. The inn is very quiet, slow-paced, and restful." *(Ray Trammell & Eileen Lieberz)*

Open All year.
Rooms 23 doubles, all with private bath and/or shower, telephone, air-conditioning.
Facilities Parlor.
Location In center of town.
Credit cards Amex, MC, Visa.
Rates B&B, $60–80 double, $50 single. Extra adult in room, $10; children under 12, free. 10% senior discount. Lower weekend rates. Dinner/theater packages.
Extras Airport/station pickups. Pets allowed. Cribs available.

Stone Lion Inn   *Tel:* (405) 282–0012
1016 West Warner

Named for the two stone lions that guard the front door, the Stone Lion Inn was built by Guthrie pioneer F. E. Houghton in 1907. After its sale by the Houghtons, it served as an apartment house, then was used as a funeral home, and was eventually abandoned. In 1986 it was restored as a B&B by Santa Fe, New Mexico, native Becky Luker. Becky had restored two other B&Bs in Santa Fe, and turned her experience to good use in refurbishing the Stone Lion. The leaded glass windows sparkle again, and the original oak woodwork of the floors, common rooms and main stairway have been returned to their original luster. Oriental rugs, fine art and antiques complete the decor—and all are (discreetly) for sale. Rooms are named after women important in Oklahoma's early history. Rates include a breakfast of Amaretto coffee, fresh fruit and juice, cereal and milk, homemade muffins and jam, and waffles, omelets, or quiche. Afternoon refreshments might include a bowl of strawberries and cream to be enjoyed on the porch swing in summer, or a glass of wine and slice of cheese to be savored by the fire in winter.

"Romantic Victorian atmosphere, comfortable rooms, and good food." *(Christine Mickels)*

Open All year.
Rooms 1 suite, 7 doubles, 1 single with private or shared bath.
Facilities 2 parlors with fireplaces, library with piano, dining room, porches.
Location In center.
Restrictions Smoking in smoking parlor only. No children.
Credit cards MC, Visa.
Rates B&B, $40–80.

Oregon

Cowslip's Belle Bed & Breakfast, Ashland

Oregon has incorporated the best of the late 1960s, making it the most mellow and relaxing state in the country. Along with a less hurried pace and spectacular scenery, you will find a variety of cottage industries, aging hippies, and a legislature that takes social concern and the environment seriously.

Coastal Oregon: Rich coastal diversity can be sampled by visiting some of the 66 state parks that provide virtually unlimited access to the shore. The southern coast, from the California border to Bandon, has few visitors. It features quiet beaches and cranberry fields and the wild Rogue River. The midcoast area, from Coos Bay to Lincoln City, can get crowded, especially in summer, but there is good reason—here there are beaches up to 500 feet wide and 10 miles long, 300-foot sand dunes, sea lion caves, high bluffs with exquisite views (Otter Crest), and inviting rocky shores. Don't miss Devil's Punchbowl, north of Newport, where the ocean bursts through the rock in "spouting horns." The northern coast, from Lincoln City to the Columbia River, boasts summer sand castle contests, Tillamook's renowned cheddar cheese factory, forested headlands, and Cannon Beach's famous monolith, Haystack Rock. A visit to the coast during winter can be particularly romantic with its misty fog, huge storms, totally isolated beaches, and migrating whales.

Central Oregon: Leaving the coast, you'll find the gentle Coast Range mountains and the fertile southwestern area, with its famous wineries and Shakespeare festival at Ashland. More centrally, the lush Willamette River Valley holds most of the state's population from Eugene to Portland, while still retaining large expanses of rich farmland and forest. East of the Willamette are the Cascades, with 10,000-foot-high mountains. A recommended introduction to this part of the state is Route 126, east of Eugene up the rambling McKenzie River Valley, then Route 242 through one of the most bleak, unusual, and unvisited lava areas in the country. Nearby Bend provides excellent skiing and more unusual sites: Lava River Caves, Lava Coast Forest, and, 90 miles south, Crater Lake National Park.

Eastern Oregon: Sparsely populated, the southeastern part is dominated by the dramatic Steen Mountains, wide expanses of desert and dry lakes that still display the wheel ruts of the pioneer wagons. By contrast, the northwestern corner has the heavily forested Blue and Wallowa mountains, a destination for gold miners in the 1860s and for backpackers today. The Columbia River divides the states of Oregon and Washington, descending past dry, striped cliffs, the narrow Columbia River Gorge, Portland, and Astoria, to the Pacific. While the trip down I-84 along the Columbia is attractive, we recommend driving on the Washington side for better views and a more leisurely pace.

A word on the weather: It doesn't rain as much as you have heard. The winters are mild and although west of the Cascades it does often rain from November to mid-April, there are few downpours—just a goodly amount of the (in)famous "Oregon mist."

Rates are generally lowest midweek, from October to May. Oregon has no state sales tax, although many towns have lodging taxes of 5 to 10%.

Information please: Oregon has a number of first-class resorts, all of them recommended by readers: **The Inn at Otter Crest** at Otter Rock; and the **Inn at Spanish Head** in Lincoln City on the coast; as well as the **Lodge at Black Butte Ranch** near Bend, in central Oregon. All three offer all comfortable facilities for family enjoyment, but since they range in size from 150 to 400 units (including condominiums) we felt they were too big for this guide, especially given the number of more intimate alternatives. Comments?

Reader tips: If you're traveling in southwestern Oregon, *Pat Fink* recommends the **Windmill Inns,** with locations in Ashland, Medford, and Roseburg as particularly well-run motels, with clean rooms, friendly staff, reasonable rates, and such extras as coffee and doughnuts delivered to the room with the morning paper, free bicycles, a bestseller library, an indoor sauna and whirlpool, a swimming pool, and an unending supply of hot and cold beverages, apples, and newspapers available free in the lobby (800–452–5315 in OR; 800–547–4747 outside OR). Another trustworthy northwestern motel chain is **Nendels:** "Clean, comfortable, convenient and well kept, with a restaurant and heated pool." *(LS)*

ASHLAND 97520 Map 13

Ashland is a small mountain town, set in the foothills of the Siskiyou Mountains near the Oregon/California border. It is particularly well known as the home of the 50-year-old Oregon Shakespearean Festival, held annually from late February through October. Over 300,000 people come from all over the Northwest every year to watch first-class professional repertory performances of Shakespeare and other classic and contemporary playwrights, performed in three different indoor and outdoor theaters. (Call 800–547–8052 or 503–488–1011 for ticket information; performances for July and August sell out soon after the tickets go on sale in the winter.)

To accommodate and entertain all these theatergoers, Ashland offers a wide variety of boutiques and galleries, concerts and ballets, restaurants for every taste, and over two dozen B&Bs, yet it remains an attractive small town. It's full of visitors in July and August, so make your reservations early, or visit during June or September. Rates tend to be highest on summer weekends and lowest midweek in winter, and do not include 6% city tax.

Outdoor activities include hiking in Lithia Park or along the Pacific Crest Trail, rafting, windsurfing, waterskiing, and sailing on nearby rivers and lakes; and skiing ½ hour away at Mt. Ashland. Crater Lake is a reasonable drive, and the area also has several wineries worth visiting.

Reader tip: *Pat Fink* suggests **Tommy's** on the Plaza, "with good sandwiches, all fresh fruits, homemade soups and excellent breakfasts."

Also recommended: The **Chanticleer Inn** (120 Gresham Street; 503–482–1919), open since 1981, is built in the Craftsman style, and guest rooms are furnished with antiques, queen-size beds, flowered wallpapers, and fluffy quilts. Breakfast includes a creative variety of fruits, eggs or pancakes, ham or bacon, and home-baked bread. The **Mt. Ashland Inn** (550 Mt. Ashland Road, P.O. Box 944; 503–482–8707) combines the cozy comfort of a rustic mountain lodge with conveniences like a private bath and in-room thermostats. Built by Elaine and Jerry Shanafelt in 1987, the Mt. Ashland Inn has such distinctive touches as log arched doorways, a log slab circular staircase, and beds made from black oak and madronae. The **Romeo Inn** (295 Idaho Street; 503–488–0884), built in the 1930s, is a Cape Cod house surrounded by 300-year-old Ponderosa pines and furnished with both antique and traditional furnishings, highlighted with Amish quilts or Oriental rugs. Breakfast might include Belgian waffles with fresh fruit and whipped cream one day, and a baked chili rellenos casserole the next. The **Winchester Inn** (35 South Second Street; 503–488–1113), a Queen Anne Victorian now listed on the National Register of Historic Places, is known for having one of the best restaurants in Ashland as well as for its attractive rooms. Rates include a full breakfast and afternoon sherry in the parlor.

Ashland is in southwestern Oregon, in the Rogue Valley, 350 miles north of San Francisco and 290 miles south of Portland. From the north, take I-5 to Ashland; from San Francisco, take I-80 east to I-505, then north on I-5.

Cowslip's Belle Bed & Breakfast
159 North Main Street

Tel: (503) 488–2901

Carmen and Jon Reinhardt describe their B&B as "a 1913 Craftsman home, with down comforters, fresh flowers, antiques, chocolate truffles, stained glass, Maxfield Parrish antique quilts, Italian roast coffee, espresso, rose garden, willow swing—a special treat." New treats such as cheese blintze soufflé with cinnamon blueberry sauce, frittata, peach pandowdy, sour cream Belgian waffles with maple pecan cream, raspberry oozies, and fresh fruit fluffs, or ham and cheese strata, make up the very filling breakfast. Guests also enjoy the chocolate delights made in the inn's kitchen—chocolate mocha pastilles, chocolate truffles, and chocolate mousse truffle tortes—one is left on the pillow every night.

"Carmen and Jon run probably the most welcoming inn we have visited. They are relaxed and interested in you, yet everything runs very smoothly. The living room is a comfortable gathering place, but guests are always welcome in the kitchen to chat while Jon works on one of his chocolate masterpiece desserts he sells about town. The rooms are filled with quilts and charming objects to please the eye, and the place is spotless. Park right at the end of the garden, walk only a short distance to enjoy the charming town and its plays. Breakfast starts with some kind of fruit delight (lime mousse or sliced fruit) and just baked brioches or biscuits. Soon you think of Carmen as a favorite sister and before leaving you will reserve your next stay." *(Kathryn & Bob Gearheard)*

Open All year.
Rooms 4 doubles—all with full private bath, radio, air-conditioning. 2 rooms in main house, 2 in carriage house.
Facilities Dining room, living room with library, fireplace; porch. Rose garden, patio, deck, willow swing. Paved off-street parking.
Location 3 blocks to theater and plaza. On North Main St. between Laurel and Bush.
Restrictions No smoking in house. No children under 10.
Credit cards MC, Visa.
Rates B&B, $48–78 double, $43–73 single. Extra person in room, $20. 2-day minimum stay June–Sept.
Extras Free airport/station pickups.

The Morical House
668 North Main Street

Tel: (503) 482–2254

The Morical House was built in the 1880s and was restored 100 years later with particular care given to its stained-glass windows and detailed woodwork. Guest rooms are decorated with antiques and homemade comforters, and all have mountain views. Rates include a full breakfast and afternoon refreshments, served in the parlor or garden.

New owners Pat and Peter Dahl report that "our commitment is to make our guests' stay as comfortable, relaxing and enjoyable as possible, so that our guests will feel that they are staying with friends."

"Morical House is a beautifully restored Victorian home on the outskirts of Ashland. The owners' warmth and hospitality made us feel pampered. Our room was comfortable, the plumbing modern. Our beautifully served breakfast included fresh fruit, muffins, an egg dish and sausage. All our needs were accommodated by the owners in a loving way; their joy in being B&B owners is demonstrated by their hospitality." *(Sandra Fowler-Hill)*

Open All year.
Rooms 5 doubles with full private bath, air-conditioning.
Facilities Dining room, lobby, parlor with library, lounge, porch. 1½ acres with gardens, putting green, croquet, off-street parking.

513

Location About .7 m from downtown Ashland.
Restrictions No smoking. Traffic noise in front rooms. No children under 12.
Credit cards MC, Visa.
Rates B&B, $55–80 double, $45–60 single. Extra person in room, $15.

BEND 97701

On the eastern edge of the Oregon Cascade Mountains in central Oregon, Bend is host to many sporting and cultural events throughout the year. Visitors enjoy strolling through the downtown area and visiting the many ducks, geese, and swans in Drake Park. The Deschutes River runs through town and is noted for its fly-fishing and white-water rafting. Golf courses, picnic and boating areas, and hiking trails can all be found nearby; downhill skiing is only 20 minutes away at Mt. Bachelor.

Reader tip: Families visiting Bend or skiing at Mt. Bachelor, 17 miles away, will enjoy the **Entrada Lodge** (19221 Century Drive 97702; 503–382–4080 or 800–528–1234), "a family-operated Best Western motel. The owners constantly make improvements and it is a very friendly place to stay. With a pool, sauna, and whirlpool, I don't think you can find a better value for families to stay this close to the mountain." *(Laura Scott)*

Also recommended: The **Mirror Pond House** (1054 Northwest Harmon Boulevard, 97701; 503–389–1680), a small Cape Cod–style house, overlooks Mirror Pond, a tranquil part of the Deschutes River. Opened in 1986, it features rooms decorated with both traditional and contemporary furnishings; the living room is light and airy, accented with chintz fabrics.

House at Water's Edge
36 N.W. Pinecrest Court

Tel: (503) 382–1266

Sally Anderson and Samuel Plaut fulfilled their dream of running an inn in late 1988 when they finished construction on their new home and opened their doors as a B&B. The House at Water's Edge sits at the end of a quiet lane overlooking the Deschutes River. The contemporary cedar-shake house has spacious common areas with light wood panelling, field-stone fireplace, skylights, cathedral ceiling, and large windows. Rooms come with queen-size beds and down comforters. Rates include a full breakfast and afternoon refreshments.

"A serene location in a quiet residential area, overlooking Mirror Pond and the Deschutes River that flows through it. All the facilities are new and well-kept; the food is excellent, with service to match. Hosts Sam and Sally welcome guests to their home with openness and sincerity. Their attention to your comfort is complete but never intrusive." *(Charlie Hopkins, also Nora Guzewicz)*

Open All year.
Rooms 2 doubles with private shower, telephone, TV. 1 with radio.
Facilities Great room with living and dining areas. Flower garden, pond. Hot tub, canoe.
Location Central OR, Deschutes County. From Hwy. 97 go left on Greenwood/Hwy. 20 to Newport St. Cross river and go left on Drake, then left again at Pinecrest. 2 blocks to downtown.

Restrictions No smoking. No children.
Credit cards None accepted.
Rates B&B, $60 double.
Extras Airport/station pickups $10–20.

CANNON BEACH 97110   Map 13

Cannon Beach is a very popular Oregon beach resort, named for the cannon that washed ashore here in 1846. It's also known for Haystack Rock, which sits just offshore at 235 feet, and is the world's third largest monolith. With seven miles of beach, ideal for beachcombing, swimming, surfing, and surfcasting, and a location just a 1½-hour drive west of Portland, finding a room here in peak season can be very difficult; early bookings are strongly advised.

    Also recommended: The **Land's End Motel** (Second Street at Ocean Front, P.O. Box 475; 503–436–2264), owned by Bonny Blanchard and Geoff Steenberg, is just a few feet from Ecola Creek, the end of the Lewis and Clark Trail and a favorite play area for children and seagulls. The **Surfview** (1400 South Hemlock, P.O. Box 547; 503–436–1566; 800–345–5676), although furnished in standard motel decor, has large and well equipped rooms; sliding glass doors open onto ample balconies with marvelous views. Its many facilities make it ideal for a family vacation.

The Waves   *Tel:* (503) 436–2205
224 North Larch Street, P.O. Box 3

Right on the Seawall, The Waves includes both modern condo-style units with enormous windows, and old-fashioned beach cottages. The shops, restaurants, and galleries of Cannon Beach are an easy walk away.

    "A terrific beachfront motel, one of the most placid places we've ever stayed. The word 'motel' is sort of misleading, because that conjures up images of something tacky and garish, but The Waves has no common lobby and one parks right outside the room, so I guess that will have to do. Our room was beautifully decorated, with blond wood, handsome contemporary prints, skylights, and stone fireplace, with a deck overlooking the fabulous beach. There was even a handwoven throw on the bed. Our room had a full kitchen and a supply of firewood. The building is shingled with cedar, nicely weathered. Cannon Beach is artsy and fun, with lots of good restaurants." *(Rachel Gorlin)*

Open All year.
Rooms 11 cottages (some in duplex or triplex arrangement), 2 townhouses, 13 doubles—all with private bath. Most with kitchen, fireplace, deck. Some cottages sleep 4–6 people.
Facilities Ocean front spa, beach.
Location Center of town, on beach. Take Second St. toward beach, entrance to motel just before Larch St.
Restrictions No smoking in some guest rooms.
Credit cards MC, Visa.

Rates Room only, $46–115 cottage, $95–105 townhouse, $59–101 double. 3-7 night minimum July, Aug. 2–3 night weekend/holiday minimum Sept.–June.
Extras Wheelchair accessible; 2 rooms equipped for disabled. Cribs available.

CORVALLIS 97330   Map 13

Huntington Manor   *Tel:* (503) 753–3735
3555 N.W. Harrison Boulevard

Ann Sink welcomes guests to her Williamsburg Colonial, built in the 1920s, set beneath towering trees and surrounded by flowering gardens. Rooms are decorated with French, English, and American antiques, and guest rooms feature down comforters and lace-trimmed linens. Ann was an interior designer for 22 years and is justly proud of the restful atmosphere and elegant decor of her home. One guest room, done in sage green and taupe with coral highlights, has an impressive canopy bed, while the other has a white iron and brass bed with a lovely salmon-color comforter. The sunny common rooms have lots of plants and elegant furnishings. A full breakfast is served at the round table under the brass dining-room chandelier.

"Ann combines an interest in her guests, a love of her home, and a mother-like feistiness. Her immaculately clean home is beautifully decorated with antiques, fine wood furnishings, and a variety of plants. A high level of comfort, warmth, and relaxation is maintained without pretention. The location on a tree-lined street offers easy access to the downtown area and Oregon State, and yet is only minutes from the surrounding wilderness. The brick patio and latticed sitting area are delightful on warm summer evenings. Ann's breakfasts combine delicious new recipes with handsome presentation. Another treat is the port or sherry, fresh fruit and chocolate chip cookies Ann leaves in the rooms." *(Mark Mahady)*

Open All year.
Rooms 3 doubles with private bath and/or shower, telephone, radio, TV, fan.
Facilities Dining room, living room with fireplace, sun-room, patio, gazebo.
Location W OR. 84 m S of Portland. 4 blocks from OSU. From I-5, take Corvallis exit (Hwy. 34) to Corvallis, where name changes to Harrison Blvd. Stay on Harrison about 1.7 m to inn.
Restrictions Smoking in sun-room only. No children between ages 1-12.
Credit cards None accepted.
Rates B&B, $50 double. Extra person in room, $5. 10% weekly discount.
Extras Station pickups, fee. Crib available.

DEPOE BAY 97341   Map 13

Channel House   *Tel:* (503) 765–2140
Foot of Ellingson Street, P.O. Box 56

Owned since 1978 by Paul Schwabe and managed by Vi Stivahtis, the Channel House has been remodeled and expanded several times in recent years.

"Depoe Bay is a small town with the usual main street shops selling caramel corn, salt-water taffy, and T-shirts. The lure here is the narrow channel, maybe 40 feet wide, which leads from the ocean through cliffs of volcanic rock to a tiny peaceful harbor. From here leave fishing boats and whale cruises. Best of all is the Channel House, perched up on the rocks right at the edge of the Channel, where it opens to the ocean. I especially recommend room #11, called the Foredeck. An appealing, irregularly shaped room, it is furnished in a very classy modern style with white cast-iron and brass bedstead, huge blue comforter, very pretty brass fixtures, a comfortable sofa, and fireplace (regrettably with gas jets and fake logs). The pièce de résistance is the view. On the west, sliding glass doors lead to a deck with your private hot tub, views of tidepools below and the ocean beyond. We saw whales spouting and even one tail in the morning. An enormous hexagonal window faces north and provides views of boats navigating the narrow channel. Rooms 9 and 10 look to the west and the ocean, not the channel; the Channel Watch and Cuckoo's Nest suites were also nice, but the most fun was looking right into the channel.

"The breakfasts here were perfect—large, tasty, and not too elaborate. Orange juice, coffee and tea, followed by corned beef hash, crisp fried potatoes, fried eggs, and cinnamon buns one day; the next we ate on the porch and had bacon, scrambled eggs, and muffins. Hearty and just right for a serious day of exploring the many beach parks nearby." *(SC)*

"We requested Room #11 as suggested and had a wonderful time relaxing in the hot tub, watching the boats returning to the harbor. Breakfast was excellent—juice, coffee, and quiche." *(Caroline Miller)*

Open All year.
Rooms 4 suites, 7 doubles—all with full private bath, radio, TV. Some with desk, kitchen, private deck, fireplace and/or whirlpool bath.
Facilities Breakfast room, library, deck, oceanfront garden. Fishing off rocks in front of inn.
Location Central OR Coast. 100 m W of Portland. 1 block off Hwy. 101, at foot of Ellingson St. At S end of bridge turn W.
Restrictions Smoking allowed but not encouraged.
Credit cards MC, Visa.
Rates B&B, $130–150 suite, $48–120 double. Extra person in room, $25. 2- to 3-night weekend/holiday minimum.
Extras Wheelchair accessible. Airport/station pickups. Pets permitted with prior approval. Cribs, babysitting available.

GLENEDEN BEACH 97388 Map 13

Salishan Lodge *Tel:* (503) 764–2371
Highway 101 (800) 452–2300

Owned by John Gray for almost 25 years, the Salishan Lodge has developed an excellent reputation as a first-class, full-service resort, holding five-star/diamond awards from both Mobil and AAA.

Set on a bluff overlooking Siletz Bay, Salishan is a spread-out complex of two-story contemporary buildings, finished in natural wood and connected by covered bridges and walkways. The guest rooms and public rooms are decorated with original art by northwestern artists. The lodge's five restaurants offer everything from casual to elegant dining, and its wine cellar houses over 21,000 bottles. Although many guests find it hard to tear themselves away from this resort's very complete facilities, nearby attractions include the coastal state parks, whale watching in winter, and Oregon's wine country.

"We stayed in one of the newly opened rooms, and it was superb. Service was good—I asked for an iron and it arrived within minutes. The lodge is separated from the beach by U.S. Hwy. 101, but it is a pleasant walk. We watched a heron fishing on the way, and at the nearly deserted beach we were followed by a sea lion playing in the surf." *(P. Bottomley)*

"Great food, marvelous accommodation and service, beautiful scenery, outstanding wine cellar. Expensive but worth every dollar." *(Dorothy & Jeré Helfat)*

Some readers indicated that the growing size of the Salishan was affecting the quality of their experience there: "The recommended walk to the main building must have been three times as far as walking along the road. The lodge is getting too big for the original concept of being linked by walkways."

Open All year.
Rooms 3 suites, 197 doubles—all with full private bath, telephone, radio, TV, desk, carport, balcony, fireplace. 8 rooms in annex.
Facilities 5 restaurants, library, 2 lounges—1 with piano bar, dancing, art gallery, game room. 700 acres with fitness center, nature paths, heated and covered swimming pool, hot tub, beaches, indoor and outdoor tennis courts, playground, gift shops, 18-hole golf course. Charter deep-sea fishing, crabbing, clamming.
Location Central coastal OR. 90 m SW of Portland, 675 m N of San Francisco, CA. On Hwy. 101 between Newport and Lincoln City.
Credit cards Amex, CB, DC, Discover, MC, Visa.
Rates Room only, $85–175 double. Extra person in room, $15; crib, $6; child under 6, no charge. 3-day summer minimum. Midweek, winter holiday packages. Alc lunch, $8; alc dinner in the lodge's most expensive restaurant, $44.
Extras Rooms wheelchair accessible. Pets allowed. Cribs, babysitting, play equipment available. French, Spanish spoken.

GOLD BEACH 97444   Map 13

Set on the southern coast, Gold Beach was named for the deposits obtained by placer mining, which lasted until the 1860s, when a flood washed all the remaining gold out to sea. It's a popular resort area, and visitors enjoy exploring the beaches and hiking trails as well as the jet boat trips up the Rogue River. Fishing, golf, and horseback riding are other favorite diversions.

Also recommended: The **Ireland's Rustic Lodges** (1120 South Ellensburg, P.O. Box 774; 503–247–7718), offering both rustic lodges and more modern motel rooms, is right on the beach. The cottages are in a park-like setting near the water; most rooms have fireplaces and balconies.

If your first choices in Gold Beach are fully booked, *Laura Scott* reports that the **Inn of the Beachcomber** (1250 South 101 Highway; 503–247–6691 or 800–524–1234), a 50-unit Best Western, has spacious rooms, ocean views, and a convenient location.

Gold Beach is on Highway 101 in southeastern Oregon, 35 miles from the California border.

Tu Tu' Tun Lodge
96550 North Bank Road, Route 1, Box 365

Tel: (503) 247–6664

This lodge takes its name from the Tu Tu' Tun Indians, whose name means the "people close to the river." Designed by owner Dirk Van Zante's architect parents, the Tu Tu' Tun Lodge is built in a rustic but contemporary style; guest rooms are highlighted by views of the Rogue River and lots of fresh flowers. All is sufficiently well done to have earned the inn a four-diamond rating from AAA and four stars from Mobil.

"The physical aspect of the inn is perfection; furnishings are simply comfortable, but all are secondary to the glorious setting provided by the Rogue River. Dirk and Laurie Van Zante make their guests feel very special but never self-conscious. Small amenities are everywhere—fresh flowers, good soaps, wonderful reading material.

"As to the food—Laurie should do a cookbook. The hors d'oeuvres served before dinner would fill more than a chapter. Everything is fresh and delicious and graciously presented. The service is equally outstanding; we've noticed that the staff remains the same, visit after visit, so that when we arrive we are welcomed by people we know. Plumbing, lighting, and other necessaries are all adequate—but one really doesn't notice that much because life flows so evenly here. Everything works. In addition to everything else, there is the Rogue—you can ride on it up to the wilderness, or just sit on your private porch and watch it flow." *(Jack & Harriet Oppenheimer; also Jack & Sue Lane)*

Open May 1–Oct. 31.
Rooms 2 suites, 16 doubles—all with private bath, balconies, or patios.
Facilities Restaurant, lounge, bar, library. Heated swimming pool, boat dock and ramp, fishing, horseshoes, pitch and putt. Hiking, golf, horseback riding nearby.
Location 7 m E of town on N bank of Rogue River. From Hwy. 101, at N end of bridge, follow North Bank Rd. to inn. 7 m from ocean.
Restrictions Smoking in guest rooms only.
Credit cards MC, Visa.
Rates Room only, $120–130 suite, $93 double, $90 single. MAP, $170 suite, $144 double, $115 single. Extra person in room, $10 (room only). Prix fixe breakfast, $7; lunch, $8; dinner, $19. Alc dinner, $20.
Extras Wheelchair accessible. Airport, excursion boat pickups. Some pets allowed. Cribs, babysitting, play equipment available. Spanish spoken. Jet boat rides.

HOOD RIVER 97031   Map 13

Columbia Gorge Hotel
4000 West Cliff Drive

Tel: (503) 386–5566
In OR: (800) 826–4027
Outside OR: (800) 345–1921

A hotel was first built on this site in 1903 by Bobby Rand. Guests arrived from Portland via steamers traveling the Hood River. In 1920 Oregon

519

lumber magnate Simon Benson was instrumental in having the dirt road to Portland paved and developed into a scenic highway. He purchased the old hotel, tore it down, and completed the Columbia Gorge Hotel in 1921. Dubbed the "Waldorf of the West," it boasted indoor plumbing for every room, manicured grounds, and excellent cuisine. Unfortunately, management problems plagued the hotel, and it was converted into a retirement home. In 1977 its renovation began, and the hotel is now listed on the National Register of Historic Places. These days the Columbia Gorge is extremely popular as a romantic getaway, and all the guest rooms are gradually being redone. Its dining room has a good reputation and features food of the Pacific Northwest—salmon and sturgeon, venison and pheasant, with Hood River apple torte a favorite for dessert.

"The location is very pretty, and the waterfalls that descend precipitously from the grounds down to the Columbia are gorgeous. The dining room is nice in an old-fashioned way." (SC)

"When we were there in late October, the leaves in the gorge were gold, orange, and red, making for a spectacular sight. The six-course 'World Famous Farm Breakfast' is included in the rates and is more than anybody we know can eat." (Linda & Paul Duttenhaver) "The best breakfast we've ever had. Our table had a beautiful view, and with harp music playing softly in the background, we lingered for four hours. The food was excellent and the presentation superb—starting with our choice of 15 different fruits." (FSC)

"Beautiful grand old hotel, refurbished in a very comfortable manner, and set in the most beautiful terrain on the West Coast. Across the river is the state of Washington. Views from the window are spectacular." (MJF) "Several have wood-burning fireplaces and canopy beds. The Valentino Lounge, named for Rudolph Valentino, a frequent guest in the hotel's early days, has been redecorated with lovely 1921 era furniture." (John McGary) "A few super rooms—the corner room near the waterfall is the best in the house." (Laura Scott)

Another guest was less pleased: "We thought $120 was a lot to pay for a room that had no view and no window screens, but did have noise from the interstate. Brunch (included) was fine but not spectacular, and dinner was disappointing. Only the gorge views were truly special."

Open All year.
Rooms 4 suites, 42 doubles—all with full private bath, telephone, TV, desk, fan.
Facilities Restaurant, lounge with piano music nightly in season, ballroom. 5 acres with formal gardens, waterfall. Hiking, fishing, river rafting, tennis, golf nearby. 35 m to downhill, cross-country skiing.
Location N central OR, at the WA border. 60 m E of Portland. 1 m from Hood River. From Portland, take I-84E to exit 62, Hood River.
Restrictions Traffic noise in some rooms.
Credit cards Amex, DC, Discover, MC, Visa.
Rates B&B, $210–265 suite, $125–185 double, $98–118 single. Extra person in room, $35. Alc lunch, $15; alc dinner, $45. Full breakfast (for nonresident guests), $17.
Extras Public areas wheelchair accessible. Airport/station pickups, fee. Cribs, babysitting available. Spanish spoken.

Newport, on the central Oregon coast about 120 miles southwest of Portland, has been a popular resort and fishing town for over 100 years. Visitor attractions include the Devil's Punchbowl, a rock formation that fills with a roar at high tide; the OSU Science Center and Aquarium, and the restored Yaquina Bay lighthouse.

Reader tip: Although not quite right for a full entry, *Laura Scott* wrote to recommend the **Embarcadero Resort Hotel** (1000 SE Bay Blvd.; 503–265–8521) as an attractive family resort, with 110 suites, most with fireplaces and balconies overlooking Yaquina Bay. "Heated indoor pool, saunas, whirlpool, rental boats, marina, fishing and crabbing equipment, seafood restaurant—the whole family can relax and enjoy." *(Laura Scott)*

Sylvia Beach Hotel   *Tel:* (503) 265–5428
267 Northwest Cliff

Newport has many beaches, but you will search in vain for one called Sylvia. This beachfront hotel, aptly described as a cliffhanger by its literary owners, is named for Sylvia Beach, owner of the legendary Paris bookstore Shakespeare and Company and first publisher of James Joyce's *Ulysses.* Now owned by Goody Cable and Sally Ford, and managed by Ken Peyton, the inn was built between 1910 and 1913 as the New Cliff House and was recently granted National Landmark status. "All of our rooms are named after a different author and are decorated differently, either in period or based on the author's books—from Agatha Christie to Jane Austen; from Mark Twain to F. Scott Fitzgerald. Our library on the third floor with a fireplace and large overstuffed chairs, is always full. We serve hot spiced wine in the library at 10 P.M." The full breakfast includes a variety of juice and fruit, cereal, fresh-baked cinnamon rolls, and a hot entrée—eggs to order, quiche, *huevos rancheros,* German or poppy seed pancakes, or French toast. Dinners are served family style at tables of eight, and include appetizer, salad, fresh bread, vegetables, rice, pasta or potato, usually a fish entrée, and dessert and beverage.

"This inn is an adult literary fantasy, with a bookish ambience extending to every corner. You can talk books at the family-size tables in the inn's Tables of Content restaurant, outwits other guests at games in the lobby, or read quietly in the third floor library. Forget to bring a book? Curl up on the floor of the attic loft after selecting a volume from the stacks; be sure to comment in the fat notebook of ideas left by previous guests. Good conversation floats about constantly, usually cerebral, but you can always ask Sally or Goody what it's like to be interviewed by *People* magazine. If you get there early you can tour the rooms; if not, friendly fellow guests will probably trade you a tour of their 'Oscar Wilde' for your 'Agatha Christie.' " *(Kathryn & Bob Gearhead)*

"Wonderfully situated old beach front hotel. Our room, done in the style of F. Scott Fitzgerald, contained copies of his books and was furnished in slightly dilapidated 1920s style. The sink was in the room, but there was a private shower and toilet in what looked to be a converted closet." *(Rachel Gorlin)*

Open All year.
Rooms 3 suites, 17 doubles—all with private bath and/or shower, desk. 3 with fireplace, balcony.
Facilities Dining room, library, gift shop, lobby with puzzles, deck. ½ acre on 4 m of beach for fishing, hiking, whale watching, bicycling.
Location ½ m from center. From Hwy. 101, turn W on NW 3rd and follow it down to beach where it meets Cliff St.
Restrictions No smoking. "Children are not encouraged."
Credit cards MC, Visa.
Rates B&B, $90–110 suite, $60–80 double, $40–60 single. Extra person in room, $10. 2-night weekend minimum. Prix fixe dinner, $15–16.
Extras 1 room wheelchair accessible. Cribs available.

PORTLAND   Map 13

Oregon's largest city, Portland straddles both sides of the Willamette River near its confluence with the Columbia. A friendly, manageable city, Portland is known for its parks and its lively arts scene. Over 160 parks and public gardens dot the area, including the 5,000-acre Forest Park, the largest wilderness preserve located within the limits of any U.S. city. Portland's vigorous public arts program includes the Saturday market that brings over 300 quality craftsmen and performers together every weekend from April through Christmas. In September you can visit "Artquake," when downtown streets are closed for lively displays by artists and entertainers. Don't miss the March kite-flying contest, the antique shops lining N.E. 13th Avenue in Old Sellwood, or the Skidmore/Old Town Historical District with its mix of people, ethnic restaurants, and funky shops. Also of note is the controversial Portland Building designed by Michael Graves. This city office complex boasts a most unusual façade and a functionally disastrous interior.

Although city regulations limit Portland's B&B inns to three guest rooms, the ones listed here are in fact much more spacious than the room count would normally suggest. Room tax in Portland is 9%. From Portland, it's about a 1½-hour drive west to the ocean and a 1-hour drive to the east for skiing. The Columbia and Willamette River recreation areas are about 15 minutes away.

Reader Tip: For a taste of old Portland, try **Jake's** for dinner. A Portland institution since 1862, this downtown restaurant is a favorite with locals and visitors alike for its old-fashioned atmosphere, delicious seafood, and berry cobblers (402 S.W. Twelfth Street; 503–266–1419).

Also recommended: The **Allenhouse Bed & Breakfast** (2606 N.W. Lovejoy, 97210; 503–227–6841), built in 1914 and a B&B since 1985, is furnished with family heirlooms and antique shop "finds." Located on a quiet residential street, the inn sits at the edge of a charming, trendy Northwest Portland neighborhood, filled with charming shops, good restaurants. The **Eastmoreland B&B** (6702 Southeast 29th Avenue, 97202; 503–775–7023), a grand-style Colonial built over 75 years ago, and close to Reed College, is decorated with tiger maple furnishings and other unusual antiques. Delightful breakfasts are prepared from the bounty of Oregon's rivers and coast; some specialties are salmon soufflé, halibut in herbed cream, and Dungeness crab cakes, along with home-baked English muffins or scones and jams, and the state's freshest fruits and vegetables. The **Portland's White House** (1914 Northeast 22nd Avenue, 97212; 503–287–7131) is an impressive historic landmark which did not get its name solely by virtue of its paint job—it really does look like *the* White House! This B&B, built at the turn of the century and fully restored, features hand-painted murals, stained-glass windows, brass fixtures and hardware, and strikingly handsome mahogany woodwork throughout. Full breakfasts are served to guests in their room or in the dining room.

The Heathman Hotel
S.W. Broadway at Salmon Street 97205

Tel: (503) 241–4100
(800) 551–0011

Built in the late 1920s, the Heathman is listed on the National Register of Historic Places. It was almost completely gutted and rebuilt in 1983. Now a full-service luxury hotel, its amenities include down comforters, terry bathrobes, and twice-daily maid service; rooms are furnished with quality reproductions. The hotel restaurant serves three meals daily, specializing in northwestern cuisine, and overlooks the Willamette River.

"This is the type of hotel where it would be fun (and appropriate) to drive up in a limousine. When you enter the lobby you are enveloped in a luxurious room of exciting colors and textures. The guest rooms have wonderful color schemes, quality furniture, many nice touches. Don't forget to make reservations for high tea—a special treat at this hotel. Every city should have a hotel like this, where you can be totally self-indulged. They also have a very charming and competent concierge." *(SC, also Laura Scott)*

Open All year.
Rooms 16 suites, 136 doubles—all with full private bath, telephone, radio, TV. Some with desk. Movie library for in-room use.
Facilities Restaurant, bar, lobby lounge with piano/guitar music nightly, conference rooms. Valet parking. Nearby athletic club facilities.
Location Downtown. Exit I-405 at SW 6th, left on SW Salmon to hotel or left on SW Main, right on SW Broadway to hotel. Adjacent to the Portland Center for the Performing Arts. From I-5N, take the Oregon City/City Center exit; cross the Morrison Bridge and end up on Washington St. Go left on Broadway to Salmon. From I-5S, take I-405 to 6th Ave. exit. Go up 6th Ave to Taylor and go left. Go 1 block and left again on Broadway 1 block to hotel, at corner of Broadway and Salmon.
Restrictions Some street noise in front rooms. Some guest rooms nonsmoking.
Credit cards All major cards.
Rates Room only, $185–260 suite, $135–150 double, $110–130 single. Extra person in room, $15. Alc breakfast, $4–8; alc lunch, $15; alc dinner, $35. Weekend rates. No charge for children under 6.
Extras All public rooms, some guest rooms equipped for the disabled. Cribs, baby-sitting available. French, Spanish, German, Japanese, Tagalog spoken. Member, Preferred Hotels.

Mumford Manor
1130 S.W. King Street 97205

Tel: (503) 243–2443

A Queen Anne Victorian built in 1895, Mumford Manor was restored as a B&B in 1988, with great attention to luxury and detail: beds have 100%

cotton sheets, feather pillows, and goosedown comforters. Rates include a full breakfast with fresh fruit and whole-grain breads and cereals, afternoon Oregon wine and hors d'oeuvres, and nightly turndown service with sherry and a cookie.

"On a pleasant residential street of Northwest Portland is one of the city's newer B&Bs. Owned by Janice and Courtland Mumford, this beautifully restored house has antique-filled rooms done with an old-fashioned air, some with flowered wallpapers and English chintzes. Third-floor rooms are smaller and less expensive than those on the second floor, but we didn't see one that wasn't inviting. Most appealing is the cozy library, decorated in unusual shades of red and green—sort of a Ralph Lauren look. We were there on a damp dark December afternoon with a fire roaring in the marble fireplace—it couldn't have been more inviting. The location is very good, near all the restaurants and shops of the 23rd Street Nob Hill district; it's a about a 10-minute walk to the rose garden in Washington Park, and to downtown." *(SWS)*

Open All year.
Rooms 1 suite, 3 doubles—2 with private bath, 2 with a maximum of 4 people sharing a bath. All with radio, desk, fan. 1 with fireplace. ½ acre with croquet, gazebo.
Facilities Dining room, living room with fireplace, piano; library with fireplace, porch. English garden with gazebo, croquet. Zoo, rose and Japanese gardens nearby.
Location NW Portland. King's Hill, Portland Heights. From I-405, exit at 12th St. and turn left on Jefferson St. Continue to 18th St. and turn right. Continue to Main St. and turn left. Inn is at the corner of Main and King Sts.
Restrictions No smoking. No children under 14.
Credit cards Amex, MC, Visa.
Rates B&B, $125 suite, $70–90 double, $70 single. 2-night weekend minimum.

Riverplace Alexis
1510 S.W. Harbor Way 97201

Tel: (503) 228–3233
(800) 227–1333

An elegantly furnished, new luxury hotel, the Alexis is part of Portland's recently built Riverplace Esplanade. Hotel amenities include continental breakfast, afternoon sherry, terry bathrobes, jogging suits, overnight shoe shine, morning newspapers, and more. The hotel restaurant, the Esplanade, enjoys a good reputation.

"The Riverplace has a view of the marina to the east and the city of Portland to the west. The city center, downtown financial district, and theaters are all within walking distance." *(LS)* "Wonderful views, cheerful service, large clean rooms, free continental breakfast with some of the best muffins and scones ever. We had very small children with us, and the staff never wavered." *(Candace Cutrone & Steven C. Littlewood)*

"Despite the no-tipping policy, the staff was only to eager to help in every way. Our suite was lovely; it looked just like the one pictured in their brochure with a Jacuzzi, working fireplace, and river views. The walls were a pale yellow, the furniture and trim, Williamsburg blue. Firm comfy bed, fluffy pillows, excellent lighting and ample night stands. The almost isolated location on the river, set back from the main drag makes it exceptionally quiet for a big city hotel." *(SWS)*

Open All year.
Rooms 34 suites, 50 doubles—all with full private bath, telephone, radio, TV, desk, air-conditioning. Many with fireplaces, wet bar, whirlpool baths. 1- and 2-bedroom fully equipped condos also available for 1-week minimum stays.
Facilities Restaurant, bar with jazz band weekends, patio, hot tub. On the water with marina, fishing, waterskiing, boating. Valet parking. Adjacent to health club.
Location Part of Riverplace Esplanade, adjacent to Tom McCall Park, walking distance to downtown area.
Credit cards Amex, CB, DC, MC, Visa.
Rates B&B, $160–500 suite, $150–160 double, $130–140 single. $105 weekend B&B package. Extra person in room, $20. No tipping. Alc lunch, $9–12; alc dinner, $50.
Extras Several guest rooms equipped for the disabled. Pets permitted. Cribs, baby-sitting available. German, Spanish, French, Japanese spoken. Member, The Grand Collection.

SEASIDE 97138   Map 13

Oregon's largest and oldest ocean resort, Seaside offers numerous activities, including beachcombing; deep-sea, stream, and lake fishing; clamming and crabbing; plus tennis, golf, bicycling, and horseback riding. Seaside is on Oregon's north coast about 90 miles northwest of Portland (via Route 26) and 17 miles south of the Columbia River. Seattle lies 170 miles to the northeast.

The Gilbert House   *Tel:* (503) 738–9770
341 Beach Drive

Alexander Gilbert, one of Seaside's founding fathers, built the first South Promenade as well as several buildings on Broadway. Owners Carole and Dick Rees have put in a lot of work on the house, redoing the dining room and adding private baths to all rooms; in 1989 they built on four new guest rooms.

"The house is a beautiful 1880s Victorian with the original tongue-and-groove paneling and period light fixtures. The inn has a wood-paneled library; an airy sunporch filled with white wicker and plants; a living room complete with full-length lace curtains, leather furniture, and a fireplace; and a dining room. The bathrooms are large, newly remodeled, and stocked with designer linens. Evening brings a warm fire and chilled wine in the parlor." *(Mary Robinson)* "Carole and Dick welcomed us to their beautiful inn. We breakfasted on juice, coffee, and wonderful homemade sticky buns." *(Caroline Miller)*

Open All year.
Rooms 2 suites, 8 doubles—all with full private bath, TV.
Facilities Dining room, living room with fireplace, conference/TV room. 1 block from beach.
Location 1 block from ocean. ½ block S of Broadway, at corner of Beach Dr. and Ave. A. From Hwy. 101 N turn right on "B" to Beach.
Restrictions No smoking.
Credit cards MC, Visa.
Rates B&B, $75 suite, $55–60 double. Extra person in room, $5. 2-night weekend/holiday minimum in summer. Winter special, 3 nights for price of 2.
Extras Airport/station pickups. Crib available.

SISTERS 97759   Map 13

Lake Creek Lodge   *Tel:* (503) 595–6331

Lake Creek Lodge is a quiet, family-style resort, with comfortable cabins and relaxed, buffet-style meals. Set in the midst of the Willamette National Forest, it offers a full range of activities for outdoor enjoyment. Children are made especially welcome with their own "kids only" stocked fishing pond, plus weekly hayrides and hot dog roasts.

"Tucked away in the forests of north-central Oregon, with spacious cabins set around a small lake. Our cabin was enormous, with a living room, large bath, and kitchen, decorated with knotty pine paneling and comfortable furniture. We visited in the fall, and it was exceptionally peaceful, perfect for long walks during the day and a good rest at night." *(SC)*

Open All year. Restaurant open May 30–Oct. 1.
Rooms 15 1- to 3-bedroom cabins with private bath and/or shower. Most with kitchen, screened porch or deck, fireplace.
Facilities Dining room, living room, recreation room. 60 acres with tennis courts, shuffleboard, horseshoes, volleyball, heated swimming pool, bicycling, hiking, horseback riding, children's stocked trout pond. Fly, bait, and spin fishing; golf; cross-country and downhill skiing nearby.
Location Central OR. 35 m NW of Bend. Take Rte. 126NW out of Sisters. At Metolius Junction (past Black Butte), bear right, then left at fork, toward Camp Sherman.
Restrictions No smoking in dining room.
Credit cards None accepted.
Rates Summer: MAP, $95–125 double, $60–90 single. Extra adult in cabin, $42; extra child under 7, $32. Rest of year: Room only, $55–150. Extra person in room, $6. Weekly rates. Prix fixe breakfast, $5; dinner, $15. No charge for children under 2. 2-night minimum stay.
Extras Airport/station pickups. Pets permitted off-season only, by prior arrangement.

WOLF CREEK 97497   Map 13

Wolf Creek Tavern   *Tel:* (503) 866–2474
P.O. Box 97

Listed on the National Register of Historic Places, Wolf Creek Tavern is owned by the Oregon State Parks Department. Today's Interstate 5 roughly parallels the old Oregon/California stage road, and this inn was built to provide accommodation for genteel travelers along that route—the original owner served no alcohol. In 1975 the building was acquired by the state and was restored to its original appearance, with the addition of modern conveniences such as heating and air-conditioning.

"To stay at Wolf Creek Tavern is to experience what it was like to stay at a stagecoach inn about 1870. The halls are narrow and plain, the rooms are small, spartan, and tidy. The beds are obviously better than what was available then, but that is about the only updating that has been done, other than adding indoor plumbing. The downstairs parlors are fancy and filled with memorabilia. The food is quite good. While you may not get your life's most comfortable sleep here, everyone should sample what it was like to travel in the 19th-century American West. And you'll be joining famous people who have stayed here: Jack London, Sinclair Lewis, Rutherford B. Hayes, Clark Gable, and Mary Pickford." (SC)

"We loved it. It was really fun to feel oneself transported back to an earlier era. The room was fine, the ambience fun, and our dinner and breakfast excellent." (Joanie & John Payton)

Open All year. Closed Christmas, 1st 2 weeks in Jan.
Rooms 5 doubles, 3 singles—all with private bath.
Facilities Dining room, parlor. 3 acres with horseshoe pit. 12 m from Rogue River for fishing, rafting.
Location SE OR. 20 m N of Grants Pass. At exit 76 off I-5.
Restrictions Smoking restricted.
Credit cards MC, Visa.
Rates Room only, $36–52 double, $34 single. Extra person in room, $6. Alc breakfast, $2–4; alc lunch, $3–6; alc dinner, $8–14.
Extras 1 room equipped for disabled.

YACHATS 97498   **Map 13**

Pronounced "YAH-hots," this central Oregon coast resort village (140 miles southwest of Portland and halfway between Newport and Florence) offers miles of rocky shoreline and dense forest. Its uncrowded beaches are a favorite with rockhounds (looking for agates, jasper, and petrified wood), beachcombers, fishermen, and clamdiggers. Perhaps best of all is watching the surf pound against the rocky cliffs, especially dramatic during winter storms. South of town, walk to the stone lookout on Cape Perpetua, highest point on the Oregon coast, or follow the hiking trails into the rain forest or along the coast to the sea lion caves, 13 miles to the south.

Also recommended: The **Fireside Motel** (1881 Highway 101 North, P.O. Box 313; 503–547–3636), a smallish motel situated in a geologically spectacular area, has two wings: Oceanview rooms face out to the ocean, with direct views of the surf crashing on the basalt ledge; second-floor Northview rooms look up the coastline, while the downstairs units have little or no view. Rooms are spacious and attractive, and set well away from the highway so there is no traffic noise; a friendly staff and easy access to several restaurants earns this motel high marks from respondents. The **Shamrock Lodgettes** (P.O. Box 97498; 503–547–3312) is recommended for its rustic log cabins well-spaced on landcaped grounds, with the beach at your doorstep.

Adobe Resort Motel   *Tel:* (503) 547–3141
1555 Highway 101 North, P.O. Box 219   (800) 522–3623

Owned by Ed Pfannmuller since 1975, the Adobe offers rooms done in the original adobe as well as more modern ones and a handsome restaurant of adobe brick and rough-hewn cedar beams. All rooms have large picture windows to take in the gorgeous ocean views, perfect for whale and storm watching. The dining room is known for its romantic setting and excellent seafood. Some entrée possibilities: grilled or baked oysters; razor clams dipped in eggs and sautéed; Dungeness crab with mushrooms and cheddar cheese; fettucine in garlic cream sauce with shrimp, scallops, and crab; and Oregon shrimp Sonora style in a corn tortilla with onion, chiles, sour cream, and melted cheeses.

"A motel but all of adobe, with wonderful fireplaces, on a cliff overlooking the beach. The waves sometimes crash and break and splatter onto the dining room windows. You can pick agates out of the cliff along the beach. In the dining room, the less complicated meals tend to be the best prepared, especially the fresh fish dishes." *(SC)*

"The guest rooms range from original adobe to modern, and are large, attractive, and comfortable. The bar and restaurant are most inviting and preparation of local seafood is superb, especially the oysters and the salmon. Spend your day exploring the beach, rocks, and tidal pools or just admiring the breathtaking ocean views." *(Jack & Sue Lane)*

Open All year.
Rooms 2 suites, 56 doubles, most with private bath and/or shower, 2 with maximum of 6 people sharing bath. All with telephone, TV, desk. Some with fireplace, porch, kitchen or wet bar.
Facilities Dining room, lounge, gift shop, meeting rooms, sauna, Jacuzzi. Parking for recreational vehicles available. 4 acres on ocean for fishing, crabbing.
Location 1 m from center.
Credit cards Amex, DC, Discover, MC, Visa.
Rates Room only, $83–93 suite, $44–63 double. Extra person in room, $4. 2-night holiday minimum. Alc breakfast, $2–7; alc lunch, $5; alc dinner, $25.
Extras Limited wheelchair access. Station pickups. Pets allowed in some rooms. Cribs, babysitting available.

We Want to Hear from You!

As you know, this book is only effective with your help. We really need to know about your experiences and discoveries.

If you stayed at an inn or hotel listed here, we want to know how it was. Did it live up to our description? Exceed it? Was it what you expected? Did you like it? Were you disappointed? Delighted?

Have you discovered new establishments that we should add to the next edition?

Tear out one of the report forms at the back of this book (or use your own stationery if you prefer) and write today. Even if you write only "Fully endorse existing entry" you will have been most helpful.

Thank You!

Pennsylvania

Tattersall Inn, Point Pleasant

Eastern Pennsylvania alone has several different geographic areas, all of them with varied cultural and natural attractions and history. These include Bucks County, Chester County, Lancaster County, and the Poconos. (Look under the "Location" heading for each listing if your sense of geography is fuzzy.) Because the listings for each area are scattered throughout this chapter (we list them alphabetically by town), here are a few background notes on the different regions:

Bucks County: Although only 1½ hours from New York, and 45 minutes from Philadelphia, Bucks County is a peaceful rural retreat of rolling green meadows dotted with cows and deep forests, with the beautiful Delaware River running through. New Hope, its best-known town, was founded in 1681. Many of its inns and hotels date back to the 1850s, when the Delaware Canal was in full operation. After the railroad made the canal's mule-drawn barges obsolete, nothing much changed until the end of the century, when some New York artists discovered its charms. Its reputation as an artists' colony really grew during the 1930s, when it was rediscovered by some of New York's most well-known artists and writers.

Although it has its overtouristed side (Main Street in New Hope being the leading example), Bucks County offers fine-quality food and lodging, excellent antique and craft shops, a wide river for canoeing and rafting, lovely walking and hiking trails, and numerous historical sites relating to the Revolutionary War. Rates in Bucks County do not vary with the seasons, but are generally lower midweek and higher on weekends.

For additional area listings, see the New Jersey chapter, where you'll find descriptions of inns just on the other side of the Delaware.

Chester County/Brandywine Valley: Only 30 miles southwest of Philadelphia, this area of rolling hills and pastures is known for the 350-acre Longwood Gardens, the Wyeth Collection at the Brandywine River Museum, and the collection of American decorative arts and furniture at the Winterthur Museum.

Lancaster County: Also called Pennsylvania Dutch country, this area of rich rolling farmland is known for the Amish people, a religious group that eschews much of the twentieth-century world, including most modern conveniences we take for granted. We are able to learn much about their way of life through the Mennonites, who follow many of the same religious precepts, but feel that it is all right to have contact with the outside world, and are willing to adopt some modern ways.

Although Lancaster County has some tacky tourist traps, the area offers many attractions of genuine historic and cultural interest; if you saw the movie *Witness* you know how beautiful the region is. Accommodations in this area range from historic and elegant inns to working farms with guest rooms—nothing fancy, but they're clean and inexpensive.

Reader tip: "A highlight of my trip was having dinner and spending an evening with Jack and Dee Dee Meyer. These are wonderful plain folk with six children who open up their home to share their life with others. It is an evening not to be missed. Jack can be found at Abe's Buggy Rides near Bird-in-Hand, or write them at 869 West Sunhill, Manheim 17545." *(Dianne Crawford)*

The Poconos: Although some may know the area only by the heart-shaped beds featured in ads for the "honeymoon capital of the East," there is a great deal of natural beauty to be found in the Poconos, from the Delaware Water Gap, at the entrance to the Poconos, to the areas further north, around Canadensis.

BLOOMSBURG 17815   Map 3

The Inn at Turkey Hill   *Tel:* (717) 387–1500
991 Central Road

Located just off Exit 35 of Interstate 80, the Inn at Turkey Hill provides good food and lodging to travelers on this major east-west route. The main part of the inn is a farmhouse dating back to 1839; most of the guest rooms are in a modern wing, built onto the back of the original structure. The dinner menu is quite adventurous; one of their specialties is rolled duck glazed with orange and ginger and stuffed with wild rice, walnuts, and raisins. The guest rooms face a landscaped courtyard with a gazebo and pond.

"Owner Babs Pruden was so friendly and helpful that we really felt like special guests in her home. She and her father shared the dream of turning their home into an inn, and shortly she will see her son running the inn. Our room was huge, one of only several in the original home. We had a lovely queen-size bed, lots of closets, windows, wing chairs, and a very large private bathroom with a single Jacuzzi.

"Dinner was served in the Stencil Room, one of three dining rooms. The food was beautifully prepared and presented. The inn is very popular with locals, and the Greenhouse room fills up first. Babs, while not hovering, was around the whole time and well aware of how her staff treats her guests. Fresh fruit, pastries, muffins, and toast, along with coffee and every kind of tea imaginable, were spread out along with the morning papers. The sun poured in through the Greenhouse windows and the local geese paraded outside by the pond." *(Wendi Van Exan)*

Open All year.
Rooms 2 suites, 16 doubles—all with full private bath, telephone, TV, desk, air-conditioning. Both suites with fireplace and Jacuzzi.
Facilities Restaurant; living room; library with fireplace, TV, games; lounge. 2 acres with patio, gardens, pond, gazebo. Tennis, golf, fishing, swimming nearby.
Location 3 hrs. NW of Philadelphia and W of NYC. 2 m from center of Bloomsburg, at Exit 35 off I-80.
Restrictions No pipe or cigar smoking in dining room.
Credit cards Amex, Discover, MC, Visa.
Rates B&B, $110–130 suite, $68–90 double, $60–80 single. Corporate rates. Extra person in room, $15. Children under 12 free. Alc lunch, $6; alc dinner, $19.
Extras Wheelchair accessible. Cribs, babysitting available. Airport/station pickups. Pets permitted.

CANADENSIS 18325   Map 3

The Pine Knob   *Tel:* (717) 595–2532
Route 447, Box 275

The Pine Knob dates back to 1847, when Dr. Gilbert Palen built himself a home and started a tannery. In the process he renamed the town (originally called Frogtown—anything would have been an improvement) Canadensis, after the botanical name of the hemlock, whose bark was used in the tanning of leather. The building was turned into a guest house in 1886, and was purchased by Dick and Charlotte Dornich in 1987. Rates include full breakfast and dinner; favorite entrées include trout steamed with fresh vegetables and herb butter, rack of lamb with apricot cream sauce, and Cornish game hen with cranberry-walnut sauce. From May through October, the Pine Knob sponsors five-day art workshops (additional fee).

"The inn is nicely situated on a fairly quiet road, surrounded by land-scaped grounds, with a large swimming pool just across the road. The inn has a light and spacious parlor, hung with lovely watercolors by local artists, an airy dining room, and a cozy Victorian-style bar. The guest rooms are most inviting, comfortably decorated with brass or carved oak beds, cheery wallpaper, and period antiques; nearly all the baths have recently been redone, and are clean and fresh. Ample porches run along the side of the inn, facing the flower gardens, and are well supplied with rocking chairs for sitting and chatting. Innkeeper Dick Dornich really enjoys his work—he and his wife used to run a motel and 'love the kind of people who stay at inns.' The only minor drawback to this very lovely inn is the rather rundown if historic house next door, which the Dorniches would dearly like to buy and renovate." *(SWS)*

Open All year.
Rooms 25 doubles, 2 singles—20 with private bath and/or shower, 7 with sink in room and shared bath. 9 rooms in 3 cottages.
Facilities Bar, restaurant, living room with piano, books, games. 6 acres with gardens, woods, swimming pool, tennis court, lawn games, trout fishing, art gallery. Golf, downhill and cross-country skiing nearby.
Location Poconos, Monroe County. ½ m S of center of town. From I-80 W, take Rte. 447 N to inn.
Restrictions No pipe or cigar smoking. No children under 5.
Credit cards MC, Visa.
Rates All rates per person. MAP, $74 suite, $53–69 double, $63–74 single, plus 10% service. $40 for children 12 and under sharing room. 2-3 night minimum, weekends and holidays. Weekly rates. 3–5 day art workshop packages. Alc dinner, $27.
Extras Bus station pickups, $3.

CHURCHTOWN 17555   Map 3

Churchtown Inn   *Tel:* (215) 445-7794
Route 23
Mailing address: Box 135, Narvon 17555

A handsome fieldstone house dating back to 1735 and enlarged in 1810, the Churchtown Inn offers a winning combination—cozy rooms furnished with antiques and handmade quilts plus hospitable innkeepers: Stuart and Hermine Smith, and Jim Kent.

"Our room was furnished with two beautiful canopy beds. Stuart Smith is a retired choral director who has a great voice and is master at making everyone feel at home and comfortable. Each breakfast was different—cereal, sausages, and a delightful apple custard pancake. Great coffee and juices. The countryside is delightful, and you can sit on the front patio and watch the Amish ride by in their buggies." *(Stuart Barrett, also Donald S. Tamutus, and others)*

"The friendly ambience is due to Stuart Smith's graciousness; he encourages guests to interact and is an excellent pianist." *(Marily R. Watson)* "Our room and bath could not have been cleaner, and hot water and parking were plentiful. The Smiths arranged for us to have dinner with an Amish family, which was a fantastic experience." *(Steve and Betsy Noal)* "Beautiful and spotlessly clean." *(Joel Abrams)* "White baseboards and windowsills that gleamed. A big plus was the very comfortable beds." *(Pat Dusa)*

Open All year. Closed Christmas.
Rooms 8 doubles—6 with private shower and/or bath, 2 with maximum of 4 people sharing bath. Some with TV, desk, fireplaces; all with air-conditioning.
Facilities Dining room; 2 parlors, with library, game corner, piano; TV/den room; enclosed porch. Swimming pool, lake, cross-country skiing, tennis, golf nearby.
Location SE PA, Pennsylvania Dutch Country. 16 m NE of Lancaster. Take Exit 22 (Morgantown) off I-76 (PA Tpke.). Go S on Rte. 10, then W on Rte. 23 to inn.
Restrictions Some traffic noise in 2 guest rooms. Smoking on enclosed porch only. No children under 12.
Credit cards MC, Visa.

Rates B&B, $50–85 double, $45–80 single. Extra person in room, $20. 10% senior discount. 2-3 night minimum weekends, holidays. Prix fixe dinner, $13 (by prior arrangement). Weekly rates.
Extras Limited German, Italian spoken.

COOKSBURG 16217   Map 3

Clarion River Lodge   *Tel:* (814) 744–8171
River Road, P.O. Box 220

Owner/manager Skip Williams describes the lodge as having a "spectacular natural setting along the gentle Clarion River, adjacent to Cook Forest Park, the oldest and largest stand of virgin pine and hemlock in the East." Built as a private estate, the original house is now the dining area and is highlighted by a massive fieldstone fireplace, log beams, and cherry paneling. A breezeway connects the newly built guest rooms that are decorated with modern Scandinavian decor. Favorite activities include hiking or skiing through the Cook Forest and canoeing on the river. The dinner menu includes a good selection of steaks, seafood, and pasta dishes.

"Highlights were a leisurely stroll on a river road with picture perfect scenery; carefully selected wines served in front of the fire; deer just outside the windows; a tour of local interest spots—virgin timber, quaint little towns, museums, and craft shops. The food was wonderful; great fish dishes and delicious peanut butter pie. Complimentary breakfast includes juice, cereal, rolls, and endless cups of good coffee. Our room had a balcony overlooking the river, a comfortable king-size bed, and a bathroom with all the latest features—no roughing it here." *(Kathryn Powell)*

"Rooms are comfortable and extremely clean, the staff friendly and helpful. Peaceful relaxing atmosphere." *(Susan Grady)*

Open All year.
Rooms 20 doubles with full private bath, telephone, TV, desk, air-conditioning, fan, refrigerator.
Facilities Dining room, enclosed breezeway with books, magazines, fireplace, bar/lounge, meeting room. 30 acres with river for canoeing, fishing, swimming.
Location Great forest of NW PA. 2 hr N of Pittsburgh. From I-80 take Exit 13. Go N 15 m on Rte. 36. Turn right on River Rd. Go 5 m.
Restrictions No infants.
Credit cards Amex, MC, Visa.
Rates B&B, $57–99 double. Extra person in room, $15. 2-night holiday minimum. Prix fixe lunch $6, prix fixe dinner $20. Alc lunch $5–7, alc dinner $12–35.

EPHRATA 17522   Map 3

Ephrata's key attraction is the Cloister, a Protestant monastery for men and women founded in 1732 by Conrad Beissel. An early experiment in communal living, the Ephrata Cloister became renowned for its German medieval-style architecture. Known for its prose, poetry, and music, it was a famous colonial printing and publishing center. Tours and craft demonstrations are offered year-round; a musical drama depicting eighteenth-century cloister life is offered summer weekends.

Ephrata is located in the Pennsylvania Dutch Country of southeastern Pennsylvania, 5 miles south of Pennsylvania Turnpike Exit 21, 12 miles northeast of Lancaster, and 15 miles southwest of Reading. It's 1½ hours northeast of Baltimore, and 1 hour west of Philadelphia.

Also recommended: The Guesthouse at Doneckers (318–324 North State Street; 717–733–8696) was created by connecting and restoring two turn-of-the-century brick houses; an addition was completed in 1988. The breakfast buffet includes croissants, breads, cheese, fruit, cereals, sausage, juice, tea, and coffee. **Hackman's Country Inn** (140 Hackman Road; 717–733–3498) fits just about anyone's vision of the ideal country B&B—a sturdy farmhouse, painted white, with green shutters and trim, encircled by big old shade trees, in a quiet, rural location surrounded by fields. Inside, the spell is not broken; the central keeping room has a walk-in fireplace, handsome country antiques and braided rugs.

Smithton Inn
900 West Main Street

Tel: (717) 733–6094

The Smithton Inn was built as an inn and tavern in 1763 by Henry and Susana Miller, married members of the Ephrata Cloister. It continued in use as an inn through the Civil War, and stayed in the Miller family for over 200 years. It's been owned by Dorothy Graybill and her partner since 1983; be sure to request a copy of their helpful booklet, *Smithton Suggestions.* Recent improvements include the triple glazing of windows on the street side to eliminate traffic noises, and an upgrading of the quantity and quality of the towels; improved but not quite there is the need for better in-room lighting.

"The peaceful, gracious atmosphere of the home itself, its comfortable furniture and wonderful rooms, reflects the attitude of innkeeper Dorothy Graybill. Wonderful Amish and Mennonite history was at the tip of Dorothy's tongue whenever asked, and her help in visiting the area around the inn was priceless. To top it off, we were invited to share an evening meal with an Old Order family. We shall always remember the lovely meal, and the experience of talking with and learning about the Plain People." *(Jean Cashen)*

"Our room was spotlessly clean, furnished with antiques and a good, firm, king-size bed, with a fire laid in the fireplace. Upon our return from a delicious dinner at nearby Lincoln House, we found the candles lighted in our room." *(Stuart Rider, Jr.)* "Our beautiful room had a canopied bed, handmade quilts, hurricane lamps, and fresh flowers and fruit, with FM music to mask any traffic noise. The breakfasts are wonderful and cookies and lemonade were offered each evening along with teas and coffee. Dorothy Graybill is a walking information/visitor's center." *(Dianne Crawford)*

Open All year.
Rooms 1 suite, 7 doubles, with private bath, desk, canopy beds, working fireplaces. Kitchenette, dining area, whirlpool tub in suite.
Facilities Tavern with games, library, common room. Garden with fountain, patio furniture.
Location 5 m S of PA Tpke., From Exit 21 take Rte. 222 to Ephrata Exit. Go W on Rte. 322 for 2½ m to inn.
Restrictions Traffic noise in some rooms.

Credit cards Amex, MC, Visa.
Rates B&B, $130–160 suite (4 rooms), $55–105 double. Children, $15; no charge under 18 mos. 2-night weekend minimum. Tipping encouraged.
Extras Pets permitted. 1 bedroom/bath wheelchair equipped. Airport/station pick-ups. Low trundle beds available.

GETTYSBURG 17325   Map 3

The Brafferton Inn   *Tel:* (717) 337–3423
44 York Street (Route 30)

Built of stone in 1786, The Brafferton Inn is one of the oldest homes in Gettysburg and is listed on the National Register of Historic Places. A "new" brick wing was added before the Civil War and now houses most of the guest rooms. Rooms are decorated with eighteenth-century stencils, primitive antiques, samplers, and quilts.

Mimi and Jim Agard bought the inn in 1986 and have done an imaginative job of restoring it. A full breakfast is served in the dining room each morning; peaches and cream, French toast, or strawberry pancakes with whipped cream are specialties. The dining room is highlighted by a hand-painted mural of eighteenth-century Gettysburg.

"A very pleasant inn in the heart of Gettysburg, within easy walking distance of plentiful shopping and dining. A hearty walk takes you to the National Cemetery, site of Lincoln's address, and several historic attractions. Our room was spacious and quiet with an extremely comfortable bed. Our bath was small but charming, with a thrown pottery sink. The dining room was welcoming and warm, and the Agards and their staff are especially hospitable. The tiered decks and herb and flower gardens in back are great places to sit with a book or a glass of wine." *(Judy Lamberti)*

Open All year.
Rooms 10 doubles—6 with full private bath, 4 with maximum of 4 sharing bath. All with telephone, desk, air-conditioning. 6 rooms in annex.
Facilities Dining room, library, living room with player piano, atrium, back garden/deck. Skiing, golf, swimming, hiking nearby.
Location S central PA. 50 m NW of Baltimore. Just off square.
Restrictions No smoking. Children over 7 preferred. Traffic noise in some rooms.
Credit cards MC, Visa.
Rates B&B, $80–90 double, $50–65 single. Extra person in room, $15. 2-night minimum.
Extras Wheelchair accessible. Babysitting available.

GREENSBURG 15601   Map 3

Mountain View Inn   *Tel:* (412) 834–5300
1001 Village Drive (Route 30 East)

While originally built in 1924, with a more recent guest wing, the Mountain View has the appearance and feel of a much older building, partly due to the good taste of the owners, who have furnished it almost entirely with antiques and good reproductions, and partly due to the frame construction, which has resulted in floors that squeak just enough to make it sound much older. Many rooms have lovely views of the Laurel Mountains.

"Our room oozed charm in wallpaper and furnishings, and was large enough to hold our king-size bed with plenty of room around it. Private baths, closets, and excellent maid service made our stay a delightful experience. The inn is a local favorite for dining, justified by the varied menu and excellent food. The staff, from busboys to managers, are exceedingly pleasant and helpful, and can take criticism and complaints in the manner in which they are intended, truly making every effort to make your stay a happy one." *(Jim & Marty Marsden)*

"Our room had a four-poster cannonball pine bed, complete with step-up stool, covered with a white chenile George Washington bedspread. A beautiful pine table spanned the large wall of windows. The colorful floral wallpaper, soft colored wing chairs, and a stunning floral basket completed the room. The bath was spotless and well equipped with toiletries, even a telephone. The inn's dining room is large with one wall of windows, a fireplace, china cupboards and shelves full of antique glassware and china. We enjoyed barbecued shrimp and medallions of veal accompanied with soup, salad, and homemade bread. Service was prompt and efficient. The breakfast menu included several low-cholesterol choices, as well as light fluffy blueberry pancakes." *(Donna & Peter Christensen, also George Gunn)*

Open All year. Closed 3 days over Christmas.
Rooms 16 suites, 40 doubles—all with full private bath, telephone, TV, desk, air-conditioning, fan. 22 with radio.
Facilities Dining room with pianist, living room, tavern with evening entertainment. 15 acres with grounds for strolling, fish pond. Tennis, golf, cross-country skiing nearby. 15 min. to swimming, trout fishing, white-water rafting.
Location 35 m E of Pittsburgh, via Rte. 30.
Credit cards Amex, CB, DC, MC, Visa.
Rates Room only, $75–80 suite, $55–80 double, $50–75 single. Extra person in room, $5; children, $3. 10% senior discount with Senior Club card. Alc breakfast, $3–7; alc lunch, $6–8; alc dinner, $27.
Extras Wheelchair accessible. Airport/station pickups. Cribs, babysitting available.

HOLICONG 18928   Map 3

Barley Sheaf Farm   *Tel:* (215) 794–5104
Route 202, Box 10

If you had spent the weekend at Barley Sheaf Farm in the 1930s, Harpo Marx, Dorothy Parker, and Lillian Hellman might have been among your fellow guests; the farm was then owned by playwright George Kaufman, who often invited his many theater and literary friends. The farm dates back to the mid-1700s, although the buildings have been expanded and renovated many times over the years. Don and Ann Mills bought the farm in 1974, and opened it in 1978 as Bucks County's first B&B. The rooms are decorated with exceptional charm, from the somewhat formal colonial parlor to the warm, inviting guest rooms.

"The atmosphere is warm and welcoming, and all the rooms are furnished with lovely antiques. Our room on the third floor was charming and our bathroom was fun—very large, with an old-fashioned tub in the center of the floor with shiny brass shower ring and faucets, and a shower curtain completely surrounding the tub. We enjoyed the main house, but the cottage is also delightful, with three charming bedrooms and a lovely small living room. Breakfast is a standout—fresh fruit, hot breads, perhaps an omelet or French toast with hot apricot syrup and the best ham ever. The innkeeper welcomed us, cooked breakfast, and made our stay extra special. A scrapbook of menus helps one decide where to go for dinner." *(Jack & Billie Schloerb)*

Open All year. Closed Dec. 25 through Jan. 1.
Rooms 1 suite, 9 doubles—all with private bath and/or shower, air-conditioning; 3 with desk. 3 rooms in separate cottage.
Facilities Living/family room with fireplace, TV room with fireplace, sun porch. 30 acres with swimming pool, farm animals. Near Delaware River for canoeing, fishing, tubing.
Location Bucks County. 90 m S of NYC, 50 m N of Philadelphia, 10 min. SW of New Hope. Follow Rte. 413 to Buckingham. At Buckingham, go left (E) on Rte. 202 to Holicong and inn.
Restrictions No children under 8.
Credit cards Amex.
Rates B&B, $122–159 suite, $86–133 double. Extra person in room, $15. 2-3 night minimum, weekends and holidays. 15% senior discount. 15% midweek off-season discount.
Extras Station pickups. Limited wheelchair access. French spoken.

LITITZ 17543 Map 3

Reader tip: "While in Lititz, be sure to visit the Wilbur Chocolate Company and the Sturgis Pretzel factory. Sundae Best is an ice cream parlor to die for." *(Dianne Crawford)*

The General Sutter Inn
14 East Main Street (Route 501) *Tel:* (717) 626–2115

Lititz was founded in 1756 as a Moravian community. To ensure the high moral caliber of the town, all inhabitants were required to abide by strict regulations, which prohibited, among other things, all "dancing, taverning, feasting, common sports, and the playing of children in the streets." The inn was built in 1764, and named Zum Anker. The name was changed in 1930 to honor John Sutter, the California gold rush pioneer who lived his last seven years in Lititz. The inn was renovated in 1981 by owners Richard and Joan Vetter; rooms are furnished with Victorian and country antiques. Breakfast and lunch are served in the coffee shop, while American cuisine is served at dinner in the Zum Anker room.

"The General Sutter is a well-maintained old inn with friendly management, on the main street of Lititz. We had a big, comfortable room on the second floor in front. It was freshly painted, spotless, not noisy, and very reasonably priced. The room was furnished with a nice mixture of heavy

Victorian pieces and wicker and lots of character. The ceiling was decorated with lovely plasterwork and a striking hanging lamp. The only niggle I have relates to an excess of knickknacks and fake flowers.

"The public rooms are comfortable, and there is a pretty little library on the second floor. We did not eat in the restaurant. The inn is perfectly placed for walking to the beautiful public buildings that remain from the original Moravian settlement, as well as for wandering about the rest of the lovely and remarkably clean old town. Rather than appearing gentrified, Lititz seems never to have gone downhill. There is splendid public park, which was full of fireflies and happy middle-aged square dancers on a summer Friday night." *(Carolyn Mathiason)* More comments please.

Open All year. Closed Christmas and New Year's.
Rooms 2 suites, 10 doubles—all with private bath and/or shower, telephone, TV, radio, desk, air-conditioning.
Facilities Restaurant, coffee shop, lobby with fireplace, library with table games. Patio with fountain, porch swing, tables, and chairs.
Location SE PA, Pennsylvania Dutch country. 6 m N of Lancaster. Center of town.
Restrictions Traffic noise could disturb light sleepers.
Credit cards Amex, MC, Visa.
Rates Room only, $115–130 suite, $65–85 double, $50–60 single. Extra person in room $4. Alc lunch, $5; alc dinner, $25.
Extras Cribs, available. Airport pickups.

MERCER 16137   Map 3

Magoffin Guest House   *Tel:* (412) 662–4611
129 South Pitt Street

A Queen Anne Victorian, the Magoffin House was built in the late 1800s, and was occupied by the Magoffin family for over fifty years. Next door is the Magoffin House Museum, and the Mercer County Courthouse is just across the street. Janet and Rod McClelland renovated the house, and opened it as a B&B in November 1985; Gene and Gala Slagle bought the inn in 1988. The area is a favorite of antiquers, with shops in all directions. The Magoffin House is furnished with antiques, supplied by local dealers, which are available for purchase.

"This large brick home has been beautifully restored and furnished with period antiques. Our room had a mahogany four-poster (with a good, firm mattress), a dresser, a wardrobe with a beveled-glass mirrored door, a comfortable chair, and a fireplace. Some rooms are air-conditioned, and the others equipped with a fan. The McClellands are friendly and made us feel welcome. The breakfast room is opened to the public for lunch and dinner, served Monday through Saturday. The menu is interesting—well prepared and nicely presented; herbs are used to season many of the dishes." *(Shirley Noe)*

"Impressive rooms with beautiful antiques. Quaint dining area with floor-to-ceiling bay windows. The tables are close together in order to encourage conversation, and the decor includes Victorian print tablecloths and high-backed chairs, some grouped in front of a fireplace. The covered front porch with chintz-covered wicker rockers is a great reading spot.

Small town atmosphere—great area for antiquing." *(Karen Hughes)* "The perfect overnight between New York and Chicago." *(Dave Nelson)*

Open All year. Restaurant closed Christmas, Easter, Thanksgiving.
Rooms 2 suites, 8 doubles, 8 with private bath and/or shower, 2 with a maximum of 4 sharing a bath. All with clock/radio, desk, air-conditioning, fireplace. Some with telephone, TV.
Facilities Parlor with windup Victrola, fireplace, books, TV, games; breakfast room; gift shop; veranda. Swimming pool, tennis, waterskiing, boating, fishing, hiking nearby. 20 min. to cross-country skiing.
Location W PA, approx. 50 m N of Pittsburgh. 5 min. N of I-80 & W of I-79, one block from intersection of rtes. 19, 58, & 62. 1/3 block from county courthouse.
Restrictions No smoking.
Credit Cards Amex, MC, Visa.
Rates B&B, $75 suite, $65 double, $60–70 single. Extra person in room, $10. Children under 8 free. Alc lunch, $6; alc dinner, $13. 15% discount for week stays.
Extras Crib available. Babysitting with advance notice. Airport/station pickups.

NEW HOPE 18938　　　　　　　　　　　　　　　　　　　　**Map 3**

See chapter introduction for information on New Hope and Bucks County, as well as additional accommodation suggestions in the general area.

Also recommended: The **Centre Bridge Inn** (Star Route, Box 74; 215–862–9139, 215–862–2048) offers comfortably furnished rooms, some with canopy beds and river views. The restaurant has an excellent reputation for its French continental cuisine. The **Pineapple Hill** (1324 River Road; 215–862–9608) is a 1780 farmhouse with walls 18 inches thick, fireplaces, and traditional woodwork, furnished with country antiques and American folk art. A breakfast of fruit or berries, yogurt, homemade jams, croissants, coffee and tea is served. **The Whitehall Inn** (Pineville Road, RD 2, Box 250; 215–598–7945) is an elegant country manor house, with high ceilings, wide pine flooring, and wavy-glass windows. Rooms are furnished with antiques, and rates include a multi-course breakfast, afternoon tea, and evening sherry.

Information please: Established in 1727, the recently renovated **Logan Inn** is now equipped with the latest in modern conveniences (10 West Ferry Street, New Hope 18938; 215–862–2300).

The Wedgwood Inn　　　　　　　　　　　　　*Tel:* (215) 862–2570
111 West Bridge Street

Carl and Nadine (Dinie) opened the Wedgwood in 1982; guest rooms are located in two adjacent buildings, one built in 1833, the other in 1870. Carl points out that "our land was the bivouac site of George Washington's army in 1776, before the famous Christmas Eve crossing of the Delaware; four times a year the Wedgwood hosts New Hope's own Revolutionary War reenactment group, of which I'm a member. Memorabilia of the era are on display at the inn."

"The Wedgwood is run with all the comfort and efficiency of a highly professional operation, yet with all the warmth and hospitality that personal friends would extend. Four-posters, canopied beds, and antique furnishings set the standard of taste. The innkeepers are inexhaustible sources of advice on all area restaurants and activities." *(David & Joanna Sachar)*

"Beautiful and comfortable, with nice attention to detail in rooms, parlors. Location on main road was the only drawback because of traffic noise. However, it also meant that the Wedgwood was only a convenient two blocks from the center of New Hope. Cleanliness, plumbing, parking, lighting were excellent." *(Teresa Grazia)*

"My well-appointed room included a king-size mahogany four-poster pineapple bed with reading lights on both sides and Amish quilts. Breakfast in the gazebo is a great way to start the day; and afternoon tea is a welcome treat." *(Ronald Jay Leff)*

Open All year.

Rooms 2 suites, 10 doubles—10 with private bath and/or shower, 2 with maximum of 4 people sharing bath. All with radio, desk, air-conditioning, fan. 2 with telephone, TV.

Facilities 2 parlors with fireplaces, 2 sun porches. 2 acres with gazebo, croquet, badminton, paths, gardens, cross-country skiing. Club privileges for swimming, tennis. Downhill skiing nearby.

Location Bucks County. Historic district, near town center. From NY, take NJ Turnpike S to Exit 10; take Route 287 N for 15 miles; Rte. 202 S for 30 m over Delaware River Bridge. Take first New Hope exit; follow Rte. 32 S 1 m to traffic light. Turn right on Bridge St. to inn at top of hill on left.

Restrictions No smoking. No children. Possible traffic noise in 2 rooms.

Credit cards None accepted.

Rates B&B, $100–140 suite, $70–110 double, $65–105 single. Extra persons in room, $15. 2-3 night weekend minimum.

Extras First-floor rooms with wide doors for wheelchair access. French, Dutch, Spanish, Hebrew spoken. Station pickups.

NORTH EAST 16428   Map 3

Brown's Village Inn   *Tel:* (814) 725–5522
51 East Main Street

In the heart of Lake Erie's wine country is North East, a town ideal for enjoying the lake, the four local wineries, and a handful of local festivals. A visit to the Chautauqua Institution, just a half-hour away, is also recommended.

Dating back to 1832, the Federal-style inn once served as a stagecoach tavern and as a stop on the Underground Railway. In 1987 it was converted into a restaurant and inn by the Brown family. Guest rooms have brass and iron beds with down quilts and antique armoires. Rates include such breakfast specials as French toast with blueberry conserve or peaches and cream pancakes. Several dining rooms make up the restaurant (although there is still a private sitting room for overnight guests). Veal, flamed with brandy and oranges or sauced with Dijon mustard, cream, and mushrooms is the house specialty.

"The rooms are homey, clean and bright. All facilities worked well; the parking is more than ample; the overall ambience and atmosphere delightful." *(Richard Barber)* "Our room was appointed with comfortable antiques with a modern private bath. Breakfast was delicious, exquisitely arranged and laid out, with beautiful linens and tableware. The Browns are warm and delightful hosts." *(Richard Streeter)*

Open All year. Restaurant closed Christmas, New Year's.
Rooms 3 doubles—all with private bath and/or shower, radio, desk, air-conditioning, fan.
Facilities Restaurant, sitting room with TV.
Location 10 m E of Erie on Lake Erie. Downtown location with off-street parking.
Restrictions Smoking in common areas only. BYO alcohol policy.
Credit cards MC, Visa.
Rates B&B, $65 double, $50 single. Extra person in room $10. Reduced rates for week long stay. Alc lunch $6, alc dinner $14.
Extras Airport/station pickups. Cribs, babysitting, play equipment, games available. Pets accepted.

PHILADELPHIA   Map 3

Philadelphia has come a long way since W.C. Fields issued his less than complimentary opinions of the city. In addition to fine museums and historical sights, the city now offers many restored neighborhoods, fine shops, and quality restaurants. History buffs will head straight for Independence National Historical Park, a collection of historic buildings including Independence Hall and Congress Hall, then to the Betsy Ross House and Elfreth's Alley, the oldest continuously inhabited street in the country. For more information, call or write the Visitors Center at 1525 Kennedy Blvd. 19102; 215–636–1666.

Also recommended: The Earl Grey B&B (2121 Delancey Place, 19103; 215–732–8356) is located in a registered landmark house dating back to the 1860s. Little details are not overlooked—fresh flowers, fruit, sherry, special soaps, designer linens, and bedtime treats of chocolates, cookies, or fresh strawberries. The **Independence Park Inn** (235 Chestnut Street, 19147; 215–922–4443, 800–624–2988), built in 1856 as a dry goods store, was restored as a small, luxury inn in 1988. Listed on the National Register of Historic Places, its location and amenities (afternoon tea and sherry) appeal to both business and pleasure travelers alike. **The Thomas Bond House** (129 South Second Street; 215–923–8523), a 1769 brick home inside Independence National Historic Park, was purchased and renovated by the Department of the Interior as part of the park. In addition to a full complement of modern amenities for both business and pleasure travelers alike, extra soundproofing was installed to prevent street noise from disturbing the guests. A full breakfast is served on weekends while a continental breakfast is provided midweek.

Society Hill Hotel   *Tel:* (215) 925–1394
301 Chestnut Street 19106

The Society Hill Hotel was built in 1832 to provide temporary accommodation for longshoremen, and later served as a recruiting station during the Civil War. It became Philadelphia's first B&B hotel in 1981, and is under the same ownership as the Society Hill hotels in Baltimore, MD (see listing). Their popular bar/restaurant is ideal for light suppers with a menu ranging from Philadelphia steak sandwiches and burgers to Buffalo wings and nachos.

"If the Liberty Bell and Independence Hall were not so close, you would think you were in Europe. Granted, the rooms are tiny, large enough for only a brass double bed, and desk or small bureau. There is no elevator for this three-story hotel and the stairs are steep. The bathrooms are even smaller, with only stall showers, but come equipped with hair dryers, fancy soaps, and shampoos. Fresh flowers and chocolates are placed in every room, and the housekeeping is impeccable. Hotel guests have their continental breakfast of freshly squeezed citrus juices, and croissant and muffin, and newspaper delivered to the door. Children are warmly welcomed.

"While the hotel is located on a busy and noisy corner, the security is excellent. Guests receive keys, but the public, although they frequent the bar/restaurant, are denied access to the hotel. Live jazz is featured in the bar, and in summer, the crowd spills out onto a sidewalk café. Parking is one block away in a municipal lot, so leave your car and get around the historic area and center city Philadelphia by taxi or public transportation." *(Wendy Robbins)*

"Even though we were on the second floor it was very quiet, despite the bar. The staff was friendly and helpful. Our corner room had a lovely brass antique bed, brass lamps, an antique dresser with local sightseeing information, a round table and two comfortable chairs, and a color TV. What the room lacked in size was more than made up for with little extras. Heavy curtains blocked out noise and light when closed. The best part is the hotel's location—all the historic sites are within a five-minute walk. The hotel is across the street from a park on one corner and the Visitors' Center on the other. Ben Franklin lived next door. The wonderful old homes and the redone streets of Society Hill make for a terrific walk while you work your way down to South Street's shops and restaurants. Downtown is only a short ride away." *(Wendi Van Exan, also Mr. & Mrs. S.L. Herndon)*

Open All year. Restaurant closed Thanksgiving, Christmas.
Rooms 6 suites, 6 doubles—all with private shower, telephone, clock-radio, TV, desk, air-conditioning, hair dryer.
Facilities Bar/restaurant with jazz piano Tues.–Sat. Parking in municipal garage, 1½ blocks away.
Location Historic district at 3rd & Chestnut. Across from Federal Visitors' Center, 2 blocks from Independence Hall. 10 blocks from center.
Restrictions Traffic noise in some rooms.
Credit cards Amex, DC, MC, Visa.
Rates B&B, $98–125 suite, $90 double, plus 11% tax. Light lunches and suppers, $6–10; Sunday brunch. 2-night weekend minimum. Dinner/theater packages.

PITTSBURGH 15212   Map 3

Information please: If you want to stay near the city but not in it, then the **Sewickley B&B** may suit. A century-old Queen Anne mansion owned by Clark and Diane Race, rooms are filled with antiques but are named after pop singers—friends from Race's years in radio and TV (222 Broad Street, Sewickley 15143; 412–741–0107). If you've always wanted to curl up by the fire in an authentic log cabin, then **Cole's Log Cabin B&B** (RD#1, Box 98, Pine Bank 15354; 412–451–8521) may be just the right thing. It's nestled in the country hills and hollows, yet is just 55 miles southwest of Pittsburgh.

The Priory—A City Inn
614 Pressley Street

Tel: (412) 231–3338

For 93 years The Priory housed the Bavarian and Benedictine priests and brothers of neighboring St. Mary's Church. In 1986, Ed and Mary Ann Graf restored the building as an inn, decorating the rooms with nineteenth-century antiques.

"A beautifully restored building with a warm, friendly staff. Given the bad weather during our visit, the limo service provided in their vintage Chrysler was very enjoyable. The tasty continental breakfast (fresh fruit, juice, bagels, pastry, muffins, and hot beverages) was served in a lovely large room adjacent to the courtyard. The neighborhood, while still in transition, was not unsafe." *(Anthony & Susan Smith, also MM)*

Open All year.
Rooms 3 suites, 21 doubles, 2 singles—all with private bath and/or shower, telephone, radio, TV, air-conditioning. Some with desk.
Facilities Dining and breakfast rooms, sitting room with fireplace, library. Courtyard with fountain, outdoor seating. Off-street parking.
Location East Allegheny/Deutschtown. Across 9th St. Bridge, ½ m from center.
Restrictions Children under 7 discouraged.
Credit cards Amex, DC, Discover, MC, Visa.
Rates B&B, $125 suite, $75–90 double, $65 single. Extra person in room, $7. Weekend rates. 10% AARP discounts.
Extras Free limo service to city. Crib, babysitting available. Wheelchair accessible; 1 suite equipped for disabled.

POINT PLEASANT 18950   **Map 3**

Tattersall Inn
Cafferty and River Road, Box 569

Tel: (215) 297–8233

Built in 1740, the Tattersall Inn is a plastered stone mansion painted pale lilac with cream trim and deep green shutters. Innkeepers Herb and Gerry Moss have owned the inn since 1985. Rooms are furnished with antiques and decorated with Gerry's paintings and needlework, while the dining room is highlighted by Herb's collection of vintage phonographs, including a 1903 Edison cylinder talking machine.

The Tattersall is only a short walk from a tiny country store where you can buy sandwiches and other picnic supplies, and just a bit farther to Point Pleasant Canoes, where you can rent canoes, rafts, and inner tubes; you travel upstream by bus, then you can float lazily back down to your starting point.

"The Tattersall is an exquisite eighteenth-century home with four large pillars supporting a balcony that runs the entire length of the second story. We stayed in the Lavender Room, with a four-poster queen-size bed, silk

moiré walls, lavender and wood furnishings, and a small foyer and bath."
(PBB, Louise Weiss)

"Herb and Gerry are warm and welcoming hosts and are excellent sources of information on local highlights and tourist attractions. Cider and cheese is served nightly in the common room, where menus from many local restaurants are available for review." *(Kathleen Walther)*

Open All year.
Rooms 2 suites, 4 doubles—all with private bath and/or shower. Some with desk.
Facilities Dining room, library, common room with fireplace, guest refrigerator, porches. 1½ acres with flower gardens, lawns. Swimming pool, boating, fishing, playground, hiking, cross-country skiing nearby.
Location Bucks County. 7 m NW of New Hope. 2 blocks from village center. Take Rte. 32 to Cafferty Rd. 150 yds. to inn on right.
Credit cards Amex, MC, Visa.
Rates B&B, $83–93 suite, $68–83 double, $58–73 single. Extra person in room, $15. Senior discounts. 2-night weekend miminum.

STARLIGHT 18461   Map 3

The Inn at Starlight Lake   *Tel:* (717) 798–2519
Route 370

An inn since 1909, and owned by Judy and Jack McMahon since 1974, the Inn at Starlight Lake is a longstanding favorite of many travelers. Judy says that "the turn-of-the-century atmosphere of the inn's interior and the natural appeal of the lake, rolling hills, and fields are key attractions here. With its warm, informal, congenial atmosphere and the excellent food and spirits, the inn appeals to a wide variety of families and couples." New chef Michael O'Neill has introduced a continental menu with such highlights as beef en brioche with bordelaise sauce; stuffed pheasant with two sauces; homemade pastas; and venison.

"The best thing about this inn is not the food, although it is delicious; not the ambience, although is charming; not the rooms, although they are clean, eclectically furnished, and very comfortable; not the setting, although the lake and wooded hills are beautiful in all seasons. The best part is Judy and Jack McMahon—always a smile, always the right word at the right time, always charming and friendly." *(Vernon Lubs)*

"You can sit in a deep, cozy chair and read a book while warming your toes at a fire that has chestnuts roasting in a pan on its grate. You can exercise moderately, strenuously, or not at all. You can be solitary or social. You can change for dinner or come down in ski knickers . . . to sip a marvelous hot 'schnocolate' (peppermint schnapps and hot chocolate) after skiing for hours. Families are welcome, yet couples can dine romantically on the glassed-in porch where there are only tables for two.

Open All year.
Rooms 27 rooms in main house and separate cottages—20 with private bath, 7 with maximum of 4 people sharing bath. 3-bedroom house also available.
Facilities Restaurant, bar, reading room with fireplace, game room, TV room. 400 acres with shuffleboard, tennis, biking, hiking, children's play area; 20 m of cross-

country ski trails with lessons and rentals. On Starlight Lake for swimming, canoeing, boating, sailing, fishing. Riding, golf, downhill skiing nearby.

Location NE PA, Wayne County. Approx. 35 m SE of Binghamton NY, 35 m NE of Scranton. From NY, take Rte. 17 W to Exit 87 (Hancock NY). Take PA Rte. 191 S to Rte. 370 W to Starlight.

Credit cards MC, Visa.

Rates MAP, $110–140 double, $64–85 single. Extra person in room, $49; children 7–12, $37; children under 7 free (food extra). Weekly rates. Alc lunch, $5–7; alc dinner, $12–29.

Extras Cribs, babysitting available. Station pickups.

TYLER HILL 18469	**Map 3**

Tyler Hill Bed & Breakfast   *Tel:* (717) 224–6418
Route 371, P.O. Box 62

Wayne Braffman and Roberta Crane opened the Tyler Hill B&B in 1986, and have worked hard to make it a warm and inviting place to stay.

"Despite our midnight arrival, we were greeted warmly with a glass of sherry. Roberta and Wayne are perfectly charming hosts who treat their guest to the best—naturally and effortlessly, it seems. Wayne is a gourmet breakfast chef—fresh fruit; light, fluffy pancakes; bread like my mother never made; and good, strong coffee." *(Laura McKenna)*

"Wayne and Roberta know the area well, including restaurants and activities. They also encourage guests to enjoy movies from the large videocassette collection." *(Sally Barhydt)*

"The Ephemera Room is an area devoted to vintage newspaper clippings, magazines, and posters. Browsing through the room (items are for sale) and noting the variety of art objects that grace the rooms ensures much discussion with former gallery curator Roberta." *(Sue Bartholomew)*

"The gleaming hardwood floors covered with Oriental rugs and the white walls adorned with paintings by local artists make this a truly charming renovated turn-of-the-century home. The upstairs rooms are furnished with antiques, and beds are piled high with pillows and down comforters. Sunday morning, I met Roberta as I started up the quiet main street for a walk. She had already been to the General Store for papers to be shared by all the guests—another thoughtful touch." *(Suzanne Zivic, and others)*

"Our room was spacious, comfortable, and had lots of reading material. The bathroom was spotlessly clean, with plenty of hot water, and big soft towels in abundance.

"There's a big front porch where you can sit and relax and watch the coming and going of the Tyler Hill community. The personal touch was evident throughout, down to the parting photograph taken of us by our hosts." *(Laurie Leslie)*

"The rooms have well-chosen antique furniture, prints, paintings, and extra touches such as *Life* magazines from 1940–1960 on the nightstand. There was a beautiful view of the snow-covered Poconos from our rooms. One scrumptious breakfast included homemade sour cream coffee cake, pears with raspberry sauce, and eggs Benedict. After a day of cross-country

skiing, I curled up in a rocker, while Roberta fixed us hot fudge sundaes."
(Eric Schmitt)

Open April through Feb.
Rooms 4 doubles share two full baths; air-conditioning.
Facilities Dining room, living room/library, TV/VCR room, gift shop. 1¼ acres with hammock, gardens, lawn chairs. 2½ m to Delaware River for swimming, rafting, tubing, canoeing, fishing; 8 m to lake with beach; 10 downhill/cross-country ski areas within 25 m.
Location NE PA. N Poconos, Wayne County. 16 m NE of Honesdale, 25 m W of Monticello, NY. 110 m NW of NYC. 2 houses away from general store.
Restrictions Smoking downstairs only. No children under 8.
Credit cards MC, Visa.
Rates B&B, $75 double, $65 single. Extra person in room, $25. 2-night minimum holiday weekends.

Key to Abbreviations

For complete information and explanations, please see the Introduction.

Rates: Range from least expensive room in low season to most expensive room in peak season.
Room only: No meals included; sometimes referred to as European Plan (EP).
B&B: Bed and breakfast; includes breakfast, sometimes afternoon/evening refreshment.
MAP: Modified American Plan; includes breakfast and dinner.
Full board: Three meals daily.
Alc lunch: À la carte lunch; average price of entrée plus nonalcoholic drink, tax, tip.
Alc dinner: Average price of three-course dinner, including half bottle of house wine, tax, tip.
Prix fixe dinner: Three- to five-course set dinner, excluding wine, tax, tip unless otherwise noted.
Extras: Noted if available. Always confirm in advance. Pets are not permitted unless specified.
Zip codes: If only one zip code applies, it is listed with the town name. If there is more than one, it is noted as part of the address.

Rhode Island

The Melville House, Newport

Rhode Island is the country's smallest state, squeezed in by Connecticut to the west and Massachusetts to the north and east. It does, however, offer many attractive shore resorts, and two well-known islands, Newport and Block Island—the former accessible by a bridge, the latter by ferry or airplane. Providence, Rhode Island's capital, is home to many colleges and universities, most notably Brown.

Rates do not include state and local taxes of 6% to 10%.

BLOCK ISLAND 02807   Map 2

Only 3 miles wide and 7 miles long, Block Island is 140 miles northeast of New York City, and 120 miles southwest of Boston. It's 14 miles east of Montauk Point, NY, and just about the same distance from Point Judith, RI. Ferries run frequently from Point Judith, and take about an hour. June through September, ferries also run from New London, CT (about 2½ hrs.), and from Montauk, NY. When making reservations ask the innkeeper for information, or call Nelsco/Interstate Navigation at (203) 422–7891 (New London) or (401) 783–4613/789–3502 (Point Judith).

Most innkeepers recommend leaving your car on the mainland, but if you must bring your car on the ferry, make reservations months ahead for peak-season crossings. Many innkeepers will pick you up and return you to the ferry for free; taxis are also available, and most people rent bicycles or mopeds. You can also fly to Block Island via Watch Hill Air Charter from Westerly, RI, in about 15 minutes, or take Action Airlines from Groton, CT.

High season runs from around Memorial Day through Columbus Day or the end of October. Expect two- to four-day weekend minimums in season; rates drop substantially off season, and the general atmosphere is calmer and more relaxed.

Although Block Island was first settled in 1661, most development took place in the late nineteenth century, giving the island its characteristic Victorian appearance. Points of interest include "The Maze" on the bluffs overlooking Clay Head, and the Southeast Lighthouse at Mohegan Bluffs. Visitors spend most of their time exploring the many beaches and ponds; there are few tennis courts and no golf courses.

Reader tip: "Typical of most summer resorts, college students make up most of the island's supply of waiters, waitresses, and maids; cheerful but inept service is par for the course."

Also recommended: The **Atlantic Inn** (High Street; P.O. Box 188; 401–466–2005), built as a hotel in 1880, was renovated a century later. Its small but comfortable rooms are furnished with Victorian antiques, most of them original to the hotel and purchased in the early 1900s when Sears, Roebuck offered free freight to the island. Children are welcome and child care can be arranged to enable adults to have a brief "vacation" from parenting. The **Sea Breeze** (Spring Street, Box 141; 401–466–2275, off-season: 212–724–4453) is a weathered shingle house, renovated in 1979, whose guest rooms are furnished with old island pieces, including some nineteenth-century painted furniture and lovely English chintz fabrics. Rates include a breakfast of Viennese coffee or tea, juice, fresh fruit, croissants or muffins. The **Spring House Hotel** (Spring Street; 401–466–2633) sits on a hill overlooking the village and the Atlantic, within an easy walk to town, and with water views from most of the rooms and the veranda. A continental breakfast buffet is included in the rates.

Information please: Probably the best known inns on the island are the **1661 Inn** and **Hotel Manisses**, long owned by the Abrams family (Spring Street; P.O. 1; 401–466–2421). Although we received a bitter complaint from a reader who resented paying the $145 peak-season rate for a small, very noisy room with a tiny poorly restored bath in the 1661 Inn, another correspondent expressed great pleasure at her lovely room and the excellent food at the Hotel Manisses. Reports please!

Blue Dory Inn
Dodge Street

Tel: (401) 466–2254

The Blue Dory was built at the turn of the century, and was renovated in 1983 by innkeepers Bob and Sandy Sherman. The inn is decorated with period antiques and has modern conveniences.

"The location is convenient, right in town and on the beach; the inn was extremely comfortable. My room had a large window facing the ocean, and was furnished with antiques, along with fresh fruit and flowers and many personal touches. Bob and Sandy Sherman are very nice people, and very knowledgeable about restaurants, places to see, etc." *(Alberto Isoni)*

"The atmosphere was cozy and quaint. Our room was clean and lovely. The staff was helpful and efficient. The continental breakfast consisted of fresh fruit, breads, juice, and good coffee—very important! We definitely preferred it to a larger place, because of the ambience created by the help and owners." *(Julia Hapsch & Thomas Wilson)*

Open All year.
Rooms 13 doubles—all with private bath and desk. 1 cottage, sleeping 2 to 4.
Facilities Living room, with TV, games; breakfast room, kitchen. "Virtually on the beach"; fishing, boating, swimming. Bike rentals.
Location Crescent Beach, historic district. 2 blocks from ferry, 1 m from airport.
Restrictions No children under 10.
Credit cards Amex, Discover, DC, MC, Visa.
Rates B&B, $190–245 cottage, $85–160 double, $85–120 single, plus 14% tax and service. 3-night minimum stay, Memorial Day through Columbus Day. Extra person in room, $20.
Extras German, Spanish spoken. Airport/ferry pickups.

White House   *Tel:* (401) 466–2653
Spring Street, Box 447

"A rambling seaside mansion dating back 200 years, loaded with rare French Provincial antiques" is how the Connollys describe the inn they've owned since 1985. Joe Connolly is also proud of his collection of presidential autographs and other twentieth-century notables. All guest rooms have water views and rates include a "hearty Block Island breakfast."

"Our lovely room had French doors opening onto a balcony overlooking the Old Harbor and the ocean. We were greeted at the door by Joe Connolly who told us that 'everything in the house is antique and I'm getting there.' Joe and Violette are superb hosts, who shared their home and lives with us. Theirs was also the only Block Island inn to reply to our letter of inquiry with a personal note." *(Eileen Connell)*

Open All year.
Rooms 1 suite, 2 doubles, 2 singles—1 with private bath, 4 with a maximum of 4 people sharing 1 bath. All with telephone, radio, TV. 2 with desk. 4 with balcony.
Facilities Dining room, living room with TV, library. Lawns, Japanese garden. Village, beaches nearby.
Location 5-min. walk from town.
Restrictions No children.
Credit cards Amex, MC, Visa.
Rates B&B, $60–120 suite, $50–100 double, $40–75 single. 10% discount for 1 week stay. 3-night weekend minimum May–Oct. 15.
Extras Airport/ferry pickups.

NEWPORT 02840   Map 2

Newport is a well-known town, often mobbed with tourists during the height of the season—July through Labor Day weekend. People come to see the extraordinary mansions built in the late nineteenth century by the Astors, Vanderbilts, and others of the superrich: thirty-room "cottages" that are now museums open to the public. Newport offers a fascinating collection of colonial-era buildings as well, plus quality shops, restaurants, theater, music, beaches, sailing, and fishing. The America's Cup Races and the Tennis Hall of Fame also add to its appeal.

"Newport is difficult in season. Summer traffic is thick, streets are poorly marked, restaurants and lodging are costly, and merchants are not always friendly. The mansions, however, are wonderful, and if you want to see any number of them, it is best to stay in Newport, as driving in and out of town is not pleasant." *(SHW)*

Newport is 35 miles south of Providence, 90 miles south of Boston, and 115 miles northeast of New Haven, CT. Rates are highest from June through September, and two- to three-night minimums are often required. Rates drop substantially off season.

Also recommended: The **Brinley Victorian Inn** (23 Brinley Street; 401–849–7645), although not decorated elaborately, is furnished with authentic period elegance and modern comfort. Rates include a light breakfast of muffins, juice, fruit and tea or coffee; toast and cereal are available on request. The **Cliff Walk Manor** (82 Memorial Boulevard; 401–847–1300), built in 1855 by Margaret Astor Ward, is one of the first "great houses" on the Cliffs. It is Newport's only hotel located right above a beach. Rooms are decorated in Victorian antiques, many of them original to the mansion. The **Merritt House** (57 Second Street; 401–847–4289), with only two bedrooms, really is not an inn. But when one of our most reliable correspondents sends us such an enthusiastic report, we can't resist. Because of its layout, the Merritt House is recommended especially for families, or two couples traveling together. The **Mill Street Inn** (75 Mill Street; 401–849–9500) is located in a nineteenth-century mill, and its renovation was completed in 1985. Families will welcome a stay here as children under age 18 stay free in their parents' room; the rooms are also air-conditioned.

Information please: Some Newport inns we'd like to hear more about are the **Cliffside Inn**, built in 1880 as a Newport cottage by the Governor of Maryland, and now furnished with antiques. It is a five-minute walk to the Cliff Walk, at 2 Seaview Avenue (401–847–1811). The **Spring Street Inn** is an Empire Victorian home, built in 1858 and opened as a B&B in 1987 after extensive renovations (353 Spring Street; 401–847–4767). Located in the heart of Newport, the **Inntowne** offers antique-filled rooms, only a few minutes' walk from the harbor and wharf areas (6 Mary St.; 401–846–9200). A brand-new and rather different place is the **Jailhouse Inn**, built in 1772 and used as a house of detention for over 200 years; these days, however, they give you a set of keys when you check in, along with a modern comfortable room and continental breakfast (13 Marlborough Street; 401–847–4638).

The Admirals

Admiral Benbow, 93 Pelham Street	*Tel:* (401) 846–4256
Admiral Farragut, 31 Clarke Street	(401) 849–0006
Admiral Fitzroy, 398 Thames Street	(401) 847–4459
Mailing address for all: 8 Fair Street	

Beginning in 1981 with the Admiral Benbow, Jane and Bruce Berriman have built up a fleet of fine inns in several eighteenth- and nineteenth-century buildings of historic Newport. The first, the Admiral Benbow Inn, was built in 1855 by a sea captain and has rooms decorated with brass beds and antiques; the inn is listed on the National Register of Historic Places and many rooms have large Palladian-style windows. The Admiral Fitzroy dates to 1890 and also appears on the National Register; it has particularly attractive hand-painted wall designs and reproduction and antique furnishings. The Admiral Farragut is a colonial inn, with reproduction Shaker four-poster beds, stenciled armoires, and colonial cove moldings. Rates at the Fitzroy include a full breakfast, while continental fare is offered at the other two. Each inn has its own manager.

"We had a fabulous early spring visit in Newport—no crowds, no stress—and *very* reasonable off-season rates. Our room at the Admiral Benbow had floor-to-ceiling windows and a lace-topped canopy bed; a light breakfast was served in the lower level breakfast room, kept cozy by a big cast iron stove. We bundled up for an invigorating stroll down the Cliff Walk, and later navigated the infamous Newport bridge with no delays!" *(DG)*

Open Admiral Benbow, Admiral Fitzroy closed Jan., Admiral Farragut closed Feb.
Rooms Admiral Benbow: 1 suite with kitchen, 14 doubles—all with private bath and/or shower, telephone, air-conditioning, brass beds; 10 with desk. Admiral Farragut: 10 doubles—all with private bath and/or shower, telephone, air-conditioning; 5 with desk. Admiral Fitzroy: 3 suites, 15 doubles—all with full private bath, telephone, radio, TV, desk, air-conditioning, refrigerator, coffee maker.
Facilities Each inn has breakfast room, lobby. On-site parking.
Location Historic waterfront district. From N take Rte. 138 into Newport, follow Farewell St. (becomes Thames St.) into historic district. Inns are on cross streets which intersect Thames St.
Restrictions No children between ages 1 and 11. Credit cards Amex, MC, Visa.
Rates B&B, $65–125 suite, $45–145 double. Extra person in room available at Admiral Fitzroy, $15. 2-night weekend minimum.
Extras Admiral Fitzroy: 1 room equipped for the disabled; wheelchair accessibility via elevator, ramp.

The Inn at Castle Hill
Ocean Drive

Tel: (401) 849–3800

To say that this fine inn is popular is equivalent to noting that the French enjoy wine. Regulars make reservations for their subsequent visits before leaving, so the inn is often fully booked months ahead. Weekends in season are virtually impossible to book.

Built in 1874 as a private home, the inn sits on a headland overlooking the water. The inn's decor is as lovely as the views are spectacular. Rooms in the main house are handsomely furnished, with fine paneling and Oriental rugs. Rooms in the original servants' quarters are less luxurious and less expensive; they are not booked quite as far ahead. Meals are excellent, with a wide variety of well-prepared dishes; jackets are required and jeans are *verboten*. If you're staying in Newport, you'll want to make dinner reservations to see what all the fuss is about.

"Even though we made reservations months in advance, the best we could get for our October visit was one of the Harbour House rooms. This is a low six-room structure, situated behind the kitchen area of the inn. Our room resembled a rustic cabin—knotty pine, high-beamed ceilings, maple furniture, stuffed rattan chairs. Unless you are in an end room, the walls are rather thin. The best aspect of our room was the fantastic view of Newport, especially at night.

"The staff was extremely helpful and pleasant—even though they were busy, they took the time to offer recommendations and advice. The continental buffet breakfast was excellent, and the dining room offers a great view. Dinner was superb—very gracious atmosphere and excellent food. The grounds are extensive, and you can watch the fishermen on the rocks below the inn." *(MFD)*

"Castle Hill is our favorite inn. Every time we go, we make a reservation for our next visit six months hence. Our favorite room is #7, with a high ceiling, beautiful mahogany paneling, and lovely antiques. The bathroom has big, fluffy towels and bathmats; all details have been attended to perfectly. Both the restaurant and piano bar are excellent, and the atmosphere is extremely friendly." *(Katherine McGavern, also JE)*

Open All year. Restaurant closed Nov. through mid-April.
Rooms 1 suite, 17 doubles—13 with private bath and/or shower, 3 with maximum of 6 people sharing bath. 6 rooms in Harbour House; available March–Oct. only. 18 beach cottage efficiencies also available.
Facilities Restaurant (4 dining rooms), piano bar, tavern, deck. 32 acres with private beach, lighthouse. Sailing, swimming, fishing.
Location 5 m S of town. From N take Rte. 138 into Newport, follow Thames St. 4½ m to Ocean Dr. From W come across Newport Bridge, take scenic Newport Exit into Thames St.
Restrictions No children under 12.
Credit cards Amex, MC, Visa.
Rates B&B, $120–225 suite, $85–175 double. Extra person in room, $20. 2-night weekend minimum. Alc lunch, $15–20; alc dinner, $40.

The Melville House
39 Clarke Street

Tel: (401) 847–0640

The Melville House, built in 1750, was bought by Sam and Rita Rogers in 1985; rooms are furnished in traditional colonial style.

"The inn's authentic furnishings, wall coverings, rugs, bric-a-brac, charming nooks and cornices, and wide-board floors make it easy to imagine what a house was like back in the Revolutionary period. Along with all this we enjoyed the convenience of a spotlessly clean bathroom with ample lighting, hot water, and an ample supply of soft towels. Another special touch was the fresh flowers and fruit in our room. The delicious healthy breakfast included granola with cream or yogurt, home-baked muffins, and freshly squeezed orange juice. You could find good conversation and a glass of sherry in the late afternoon with Sam and Rita and the other guests, and learn about the best in sights and restaurants. The Rogers are very accommodating, warm, and friendly." *(Mrs. & Mr. Ted Proehl)*

"Our bathroom was tiny but fresh and new. Lighting was fine. The inn is on a quiet street right next to the action, with beautiful gardens alongside. At breakfast, little tables encourage visiting among guests. The location is good, just a few blocks from Trinity Church, Touro Synagogue, the Meeting House, and the harbor and its restaurants and shops. We walked everywhere from Melville House and yet when in it we were secluded and relaxed." *(Margaret Gordon)*

Open March through December.
Rooms 7 doubles—5 with private shower, 2 with maximum of 4 people sharing bath.

Facilities Breakfast room, sitting room. Garden, picnic table, parking area. 1 m to beach; charter boats nearby.
Location Historic Hill section. 1 block from center. From Newport Bridge, take Farewell St. S, bear left to Thames St., left at Washington Square, then right on Clarke.
Restrictions No children under 12.
Credit cards Amex, MC, Visa.
Rates B&B, $40–85 double. 2- and 3-night holiday/weekend minimums.
Extras 3 blocks to bus stop.

PROVIDENCE 02903   Map 2

The Old Court Bed & Breakfast
144 Benefit Street

Tel: (401) 751–2002
(401) 351–0747

Built in 1863 as a rectory, The Old Court was renovated in 1986 as a luxury B&B. Rooms are decorated in a variety of Victorian styles, from rococo Revival to Eastlake, and feature the original marble fireplaces, plaster moldings, and 12-foot ceilings. To ensure twentieth-century comfort the antique beds have been modified to accommodate queen-size mattresses. Rates include a continental breakfast of fruit, croissants, and muffins, with espresso and cappuccino.

"Comfortable room; delicious breakfast." *(Dr. E. Colemen)* "Old-world elegance, with brass beds and antique appointments, and homey atmosphere. The modernized bathroom was immaculate, as was the entire hotel." *(Linda Simon)*

Open All year.
Rooms 10 doubles—all with full private bath, telephone, desk, air-conditioning. Some rooms with fireplace, wet bar.
Facilities Breakfast room with TV. Off-street parking.
Location 3-min. walk from downtown Providence, Brown, or RISD. From Rte. 95, take Rte. 195 E to Exit 2. Go left at first light, then left again onto Benefit St. Inn is 2 m down Benefit St.
Restrictions No children under 12.
Credit cards Amex, MC, Visa.
Rates B&B, $105–115 double. Extra person in room, $15.
Extras French, German spoken.

WEEKAPAUG 02891   Map 2

Weekapaug Inn
1 Spring Avenue

Tel: (401) 322–0301

The Weekapaug Inn has been owned by the Buffum family for four generations, and is managed by Darryl Forrester. The inn was originally built on the neighboring private crescent-shaped barrier beach, but was destroyed in the fall of 1938 by a massive hurricane (which caused major destruction along the whole Rhode Island and Connecticut shore). The inn was completely rebuilt, in time for the 1939 summer season, on a slightly more protected spit of land just behind the beach. In addition to the beach, guests have the use of an adjacent salt pond, ideal for protected windsurfing and sailing.

"The Weekapaug is an old-time family inn, with many older guests who return each year for the whole summer. The atmosphere is very Yankee, with a two-to-one ratio of college-age staff to guests. Guest rooms are kept immaculately clean, and are simply furnished with twin beds and 1950s-era maple furniture. The public rooms are very spacious and comfortable but are also furnished with maple everything—comfort, not decor, is the key concept at Weekapaug. The food is prepared from scratch using fresh, local ingredients, and the facilities are terrific. There's a children's program for the three- to twelve-year-olds, and there's plenty for the teenagers as well. No liquor is sold here; guests bring their own and setups are provided." *(SB)*

Open Late June through Labor Day weekend.
Rooms 6 suites, 25 doubles, 25 singles—all with full private bath, desk.
Facilities Lobby, sitting rooms, TV room, game room, play room, deck. Movies, bingo, bridge, speakers, travelogues. 2 Omni tennis courts, 1½ m private beach, bocce, shuffleboard. Children's program (extra charge), play equipment. Windsurfers, Sunfish, canoes, rowboats. Golf nearby.
Location SW RI coast; close to CT border. 2 hrs. S of Boston, 40 min. W of Newport. 20 min. to Mystic Seaport. 5 m from town. Take I-95 to Rte. 2 to Westerly, then Rte. 1 to Dunns Corners, then right to the shore.
Restrictions No children under 3.
Credit cards None accepted.
Rates Full board, $270 suite, $260 double, $140 single, plus 12–15% service. Children's rates, $30–70. Box lunches available. Prix fixe meals: $12–14 lunch; $27–30 dinner, plus 20% service. 2-night minimum stay.
Extras Cribs, babysitting available. Airport/station pickups. French, Spanish spoken.

WESTERLY 02891   Map 2

The Shelter Harbor Inn   *Tel:* (401) 322–8883
Route 1

The Shelter Harbor Inn occupies a much restored and expanded eighteenth-century farmhouse. Innkeepers James and Deborah Dey have recently redecorated nearly all the guest rooms with reproduction period furniture and modern baths; the look is light, bright, and cheery. Rates include a full breakfast, and the lunch and dinner menus feature fresh seafood, with smoked bluefish and seafood pot pie among the specialties.

"Shelter Harbor is a delightful place for a family getaway. The atmosphere is friendly, the rooms pleasant, the food good, and the location convenient for exploring the Rhode Island and Connecticut shore. The dining room has a handsome fieldstone fireplace and a low-beamed ceiling, which does make it a bit noisy at times. My favorite spot is the rooftop deck and hot tub, with gorgeous views all the way to Block Island on clear days." *(Maureen Wolf, also NE)* More comments, please.

Open All year.
Rooms 24 doubles with twin- or queen-size beds, private bath and/or shower, tele-

phone, TV, desk, air-conditioning. 10 rooms in barn, 4 in carriage house. Some rooms with fireplaces, private decks.
Facilities Restaurant, lounge, library, living room, sun porch, screened porch, roof-top deck with hot tub, barbecue. 3 acres with flower gardens, 2 paddle tennis courts, swing set. 2 m to private beach (shuttle bus), fishing. Golf, charter fishing boats nearby.
Location SW RI coast, at CT border. 2 hrs. S of Boston, SE of Hartford. 2½ hrs. NE of NYC. 5 m E of town. 5 m to Watch Hill; 16 m to Mystic. From I-95, take Exit 92 to Rte. 2 S to Rte. 78 to Rte. 1. Go N 4 m to inn.
Credit cards Amex, DC, MC, Visa.
Rates B&B, $78–98 double, $58–88 single. Extra child under 12, $10; extra adult, $15. Weekend/holiday minimums. Alc lunch, $9; dinner, $24. Box lunches available.
Extras Cribs, babysitting, play equipment available.

We Want to Hear from You!

As you know, this book is only effective with your help. We really need to know about your experiences and discoveries.

If you stayed at an inn or hotel listed here, we want to know how it was. Did it live up to our description? Exceed it? Was it what you expected? Did you like it? Were you disappointed? Delighted?

Have you discovered new establishments that we should add to the next edition?

Tear out one of the report forms at the back of this book (or use your own stationery if you prefer) and write today. Even if you write only "Fully endorse existing entry" you will have been most helpful.

Thank You!

South Carolina

The Rhett House Inn, Beaufort

South Carolina's major area of tourist interest is the Low Country, extending from Charleston down along the coast from Beaufort and Hilton Head to Savannah. This area's original wealth came from shipping and rice plantations, and later from cotton. With your help we have been able to provide information on inns and hotels of quality in several other areas of the state as well, so please keep those reports coming.

Although wine is sold by the bottle in South Carolina restaurants, liquor can be sold only in mini-bottles (outside of package stores), tending to produce skimpy libations at relatively high prices and leading one reader to campaign for reform: "The state of South Carolina should change its laws so you can buy a reasonable drink at a reasonable price!" *(WB)*

Rates do not include 7% state sales and accommodation tax.

ABBEVILLE 29620   **Map 6**

The Belmont Inn   *Tel:* (803) 459–9625
106 East Pickens Street, Court Square

A major transportation hub through much of the nineteenth and early twentieth century, Abbeville was once a very prosperous town—"where the Confederacy began and ended." Bypassed when the interstate highways were built in the fifties and sixties, its once handsome structures were neglected and even abandoned. Restoration began in the late sixties with the Abbeville Opera House, and has since spread to historic structures throughout the downtown area.

Listed on the National Register of Historic Places, The Belmont Inn was built in 1903 and fully restored in 1984 by owners Allyson and Joe Harden. The inn is managed by former golf pro Bill Robinson; Bill's brother Bruce is the chef at the inn's Heritage Room.

"Big, bright, high-ceilinged rooms, an attentive staff, convenient off-street parking, all in the heart of a delightful piece of the small-town South. We had a lovely corner room overlooking the town square. We started the day with a fine southern breakfast, served buffet-style. In the evening, the chef distinguished both himself and this outstanding inn. The food was uniformly outstanding—a unique and highly successful blend of cuisines resulting in French food with a southern accent. Only the freshest local ingredients were used. The excellent she-crab soup reminded us of Charleston, while the chicken was given a spicy, blackened Cajun treatment. Visitors and natives alike know a good thing when they see and taste it—the lovely dining room was filled both nights we were there. Clemson University is nearby, and the weekend football package is a real value. On game day be sure to walk up the hill from 'Death Valley' stadium and visit 'Fort Hill,' the home of antebellum South Carolina Senator John C. Calhoun. The home and grounds are authentically restored and the Duncan-Phyfe Empire furnishings are original to the house." *(Nancy Harrison & Nelson Ormsby)*

Open All year. Restaurant closed Sun. evening.
Rooms 1 suite, 16 doubles, 7 singles—all with private bath, telephone, TV, air-conditioning. Some with desk, fireplace.
Facilities Restaurant, lounge, parlors, meeting rooms, theater, courtyard garden. Hickory Knob State Park nearby for golf. 12 m to Lake Russell for swimming, fishing, boating.
Location NW SC. 50 m S of Greenville; 137 m E of Atlanta, GA. In historic district, on Court Square.
Credit cards Amex, MC, Visa.
Rates B&B, $65 suite, $50–60 double. Commercial rates midweek, $40–60. Theater package rates, $175. 10% AARP discount. Extra adult in room, $6; child under 12 free. Alc lunch, $5; alc dinner, $25.
Extras Cribs, babysitting available. Small pets permitted. Wheelchair accessible.

BEAUFORT 29902   Map 6

The Rhett House Inn   *Tel:* (803) 524–9030
1009 Craven Street

Innkeepers/owners Steve and Marianne Harrison moved to Beaufort from Wilton, Connecticut, and opened the Rhett House in January 1987, after a complete renovation. Their background in the New York textile and fashion business helped them plan the decoration of this antebellum house, done in period antiques. Rates include a full breakfast of eggs or French toast, homemade breads and muffins served with preserves and fresh fruit, plus afternoon tea and evening sherry.

"The Rhett House is a very imposing, two-story white home that features a wraparound piazza. Each bedroom is provided with a welcoming decanter of sherry as a delightful extra touch. Our immaculate corner room opened onto the upstairs porch, complete with rocking chairs and rope hammock. The inn is located one block from Main Street in a beautiful historic section; the area is delightfully quiet and private parking is provided. The garden is lovely and the inn is filled with fresh flowers arranged by Marianne. A family-style breakfast is served at a long pine table in the dining room. After breakfast, guests relax in the parlor, furnished with comfortable antiques, including a pool table." *(Dr. & Mrs. Henry Price)*

"The inn is polished to the nth degree. Marianne Harrison has a real eye for color. Each room is attractively turned out, and most are larger than in a typical B&B; I looked hard to find some fault, but failed—it's all so well done. The staff is knowledgeable and courteous. Although the area is primarily residential, there's a small business across the street from the inn, so the rooms with the best views are those that face the garden and courtyard." *(Jeanne Smith)*

"Silent paddle fans, quiet heating and air-conditioning systems, fine linens, extensive reading material, and other amenities contributed to a relaxing stay." *(Nancy & Joe Lipton)*

"Live oaks, gracefully draped with Spanish moss, rocking chairs on the porch, designer bedrooms with plumped-up pillows, and delicious morning wake-ups to the smell of baking bread and fresh coffee make The Rhett House a place you never want to leave. Innkeepers Marianne and Steve, both well-polished New Yorkers, warm the inn with their sense of humor and meticulous care of both guests and inn. This southern inn, freshened by lighthearted northern spirits, will melt your heart." *(Claudia & Gerry Venable)*

"Breakfast is served in an elegant but understated style. The veranda was a wonderful place to sit and sip sherry; the gardens, bursting with azaleas, Spanish moss, flowers, and herbs, were a visual and aromatic delight." *(Bob Kolton)*

Open All year.

Rooms 8 doubles—all with full private bath, radio, desk, air-conditioning. 2 with fireplace.

Facilities Dining room, living room with pool table, fireplace, library, gift shop, veranda, gardens, patio with fountain. Club privileges for tennis, golf, and swimming. 15 m to ocean for fishing, boating.

Location S coastal SC, Low Country. 50 m NE of Savannah, GA, 62 m SW of Charleston. 1 block from Beaufort marina on Intracoastal Waterway. Take Exit 33 off I-95 to Beaufort. Inn is 1 block N of Bay St. (on waterfront), at corner of New Castle and Craven sts.

Restrictions No children under 5. No smoking.

Credit cards MC, Visa.

Rates B&B, $175 suite, $70–100 double, $60–90 single. Extra person in room, $15. 2-3 day minimum holiday minimum.

Extras Station pickups. Some Spanish spoken.

CHARLESTON 29401   Map 6

Charleston, founded in 1670, was at one point the wealthiest city in colonial America. Many think that it is still the most beautiful. The Civil War brought major devastation and poverty to the city and halted development.

Efforts to preserve the city's priceless heritage began in the 1920s. Restoration work progressed slowly until around 1975, when the American Bicentennial, followed by the founding of Spoleto Festival U.S.A., sparked the restoration and conversion of numerous homes and commercial properties into bed & breakfast inns and restaurants.

Sights of interest in Charleston and the surrounding area include the many restored houses and museums, antique shops, the city market, tours of the river and harbor, the public beaches and resorts (with full golf and tennis facilities) at Folly Beach, Seabrook Island, and Kiawah Island, and last but far from least, the beautiful gardens of Middleton Place, Magnolia Gardens, and Cypress Gardens. Although all three gardens bloom year-round, many think that they are at their most magnificent from late March to early April, when the azaleas are in full bloom.

The peak season in Charleston runs from March to mid-June, and from September through October. The times of highest demand are in late March and early April for the azaleas, and in late May and early June for the Spoleto Festival. Charleston is located midway along the South Carolina coast, at the confluence of the Ashley, Cooper, and Wando rivers and Intracoastal Waterway. It's 106 miles northeast of Savannah, GA, 113 miles southeast of Columbia, SC, and 94 miles southwest of Myrtle Beach.

Also recommended: The **Barksdale House Inn** (27 George Street; 803–577–4800), built in 1778, was restored in 1985 and decorated with antiques and luxurious fabrics from Scalamandre and other top-quality firms. Rates include a continental breakfast, afternoon tea and sherry, and evening wine and chocolates. The **Church Street Inn** (177 Church Street; 803–722–3420) combines the intimate mood of an inn with the longterm comfort of a fully equipped suite. Amenities include champagne on arrival, continental breakfast and morning paper, and evening wine in your room. **The Elliott House Inn** (78 Queen Street; 803–723–1855, 800–729–1855), newly renovated, was originally a private residence built in the mid-1700's. The structure was expanded over the years and now encircles a central courtyard where guests can enjoy breakfast and afternoon refreshments. The Battery and Charleston's shops are an easy walk away. The **Indigo Inn** (1 Maiden Lane; 803–577–5900, 800–845–7639), which resembles a windowless warehouse from the outside, has guest rooms which all face a lush central courtyard. Rates include an extensive breakfast buffet. The **Kings Courtyard Inn** (198 King Street; 803–723–7000, 800–845–6119), constructed in 1853 and restored in 1983, incorporates unusual Egyptian design elements into the Greek Revival style of the building. Rates include wine or sherry on arrival, brandy and chocolate at bedtime, and a continental breakfast of juice, croissant, home-baked muffin, and coffee or tea. The **Lodge Alley Inn** (195 East Bay Street; 803–722–1611, 800–845–1004), originally built as a series of warehouses, offers the amenities of a small luxury hotel, combined with the feeling of a historic inn. Rooms have the exposed brick walls and pine flooring of the original warehouses, but have been decorated with Oriental rugs and elegant period reproduction furniture. The **Maison Du Pré** (317 East Bay Street; 803–723–8691) is one of Charleston's newest "old" inns. It's composed of five adjacent buildings, dating as far back as 1804; two of the buildings had been slated for demolition, and were brought to this site as part of the renovation process. Rates include the morning paper, continental breakfast and afternoon refreshments.

Information please: We'd like to hear more about the **Rice Hope Plantation**, 39 miles north of Charleston. A meeting place since Revolutionary War days, it has been open for B&B accommodation and afternoon tea since 1987. It's right on the Cooper River for fishing and river tours, and even has a tennis court (River Road, P.O. Box 355; 803–761–4832).

Sword Gate Inn
111 Tradd Street

Tel: (803) 723–8518

The Sword Gate is located in an eighteenth-century building, in a wing of the Sword Gate House. Rooms are simply furnished with antiques, and rates include a full Charleston breakfast, coffee and tea at all hours, and evening wine and cheese.

Innkeeper Walter Barton reports that "the Sword Gate's ballroom is the last one in Charleston in its original condition, with beautiful gilt work and floor-to-ceiling rococo mirrors. The house itself has been both a Prussian and a British consulate, and a girls' seminary. Of course, as all old inns do, we have a resident ghost on the property as well."

"The innkeeper was full of great ideas for sightseeing and eating, and he arranged a delightful inside look at the city with one of the local ladies as our guide. The evening wine and cheese hour was a great time to meet the other guests and make dinner plans; we joined another couple for dinner the first night we were there. The full breakfast included delicious cheese grits and cinnamon breakfast apples. We stayed in one of the upstairs guest rooms, where a carefully laid fire awaited us each evening." *(Caroline & Jim Lloyd)* "The dining room, sitting room, and third-floor rooms are elegant. The innkeeper was friendly, helpful, hardworking." *(A.M. Hannan)*

Open All year. Closed Dec. 24–26.
Rooms 6 doubles with full private bath, telephone, radio, TV, desk, air-conditioning.
Facilities Dining room, ballroom with comfortable seating, courtyard. Bicycles. 1 block from harbor for fishing.
Location Historic district. Private off-street parking. On Tradd St., between Legare and King sts.
Restrictions No children under 5.
Credit cards Amex, MC, Visa.
Rates B&B, $89–125 double. Extra person in room, $15. 2-3 night weekend minimum in peak season.
Extras Limited wheelchair access.

Two Meeting Street Inn
2 Meeting Street

Tel: (803) 723–7322

Two Meeting Street is Charleston's only Victorian inn, built in 1890 as a father's wedding present to his daughter. The corner house at the Battery, it's been a guest house for over half a century; innkeeper David Spell took it over in 1981 from his aunt, who had owned it for the previous 35 years. The building has been recently refurbished and is filled with antique furniture, china, and silver. Particularly handsome are the stained glass windows, including two by Tiffany. Larger rooms with private baths are on the first and second floors; rooms on the third floor are smaller, have shared baths, and are less expensive. Rates include a continental breakfast.

"An excellent location with beautiful views; staying among the historic houses gives you a real Charleston feel. The main floor of the house has a huge entry hall, fireplace, and staircase, all with the most beautiful English oak paneling. The living room and dining room are equally fine, with Victorian furnishings, more paneling, built-in cabinets, and at least seven stained glass windows. It is my understanding that Louis Comfort Tiffany himself installed the windows in the living room. Family silver, crystal, and mementos are displayed everywhere, but the display is tasteful, not cluttered. A fine continental breakfast of home-baked pastries, different each morning, is served in the dining room. Although all guests share the table, they come and go at will and are served individually on china and silver. Guests share restaurant and tourist experiences, and we've found many excellent restaurants by talking with the other guests. Mr. Spell is always congenial and happy to see us.

"We recently returned here for another visit, and found the inn to be as fine as ever. A new downstairs bedroom has been added, with a stately queen-size bed with half-canopy. This room is richly decorated and has a modern bathroom. Although I didn't see them, I was told several other rooms have also been redone.

"Mr. Spell is quite generous and trusting to allow his guests to be 'at home' with his wonderful antiques, but this is not an inn for children, or for people who aren't at ease with antiques." *(Susan Waller Schwemm)*

"My favorite in Charleston; worth every penny for a true Charleston feel." *(Betty Norman)*

Open All year.
Rooms 8 doubles—6 with private bath and/or shower, 2 with maximum of 5 people sharing bath. All with radio, desk, air-conditioning. 4 with TV.
Facilities Dining room, lobby, parlor, guest refreshment bar, piazzas, formal garden. Bicycles.
Location Historic district, opposite Battery Park. Exit I-26 or Rte. 17 onto Meeting St. Inn is at end of Meeting St., near Battery Park.
Restrictions No children under 8.
Credit cards None accepted.
Rates B&B, $55–125 double. Extra person in room, $15. 2-night weekend minimum. 10% discount with "Seniority" card.
Extras German spoken.

Vendue Inn/Vendue West   *Tel:* (803) 577–7970
19 Vendue Range   Inside SC: (800) 922–7900
                                   Outside SC: (800) 845–7900

Evelyn and Morton Needle purchased the Vendue Inn in 1977, when it was an abandoned and dilapidated nineteenth-century warehouse. They renovated it and furnished the rooms with Oriental rugs and Charleston reproduction furniture, wallcoverings, and fabrics. Rooms are individually decorated, some with rice beds, others with canopy, brass, or cannonball beds. Updated in 1989 was the carriage house, which a reader had enjoyed but recommended for some spiffing up.

The inn's popular restaurant, Morton's, has an excellent reputation for French and continental cuisine, with a relatively small but interesting selection of appetizers and entrées. Entrées include a puff pastry filled with shrimp, scallops and lobster with soubise sauce, and a rib-eye steak sauteed in butter and bacon and simmered with onions, carrots, and capers. Although very popular with locals, one reader liked the food very much, but found the service pretentious and unpleasant: "The staff tried to force us into the meal they thought we should have, rather than the meal we wanted." Other readers felt differently: "Morton's Restaurant is excellent. We had fresh fish, *al dente* vegetables, and wonderful she-crab soup. Delightful service." *(Flora Blumenthal, also Margaret Katzenberg)*

"The location is within walking distance of anything I want to do, so I park my car in their convenient parking lot and leave it." *(Laura Myers)*

"Mrs. Needle showed me through the inn. Although she has a resident manager, she feels the need to be present most of the time. Her love for the inn and attention to detail shine through. The inn has grown in stages since it opened in 1977. There is a small sunken library at the front of the inn; the receptionist is located in an alcove off a lovely entrance hall. At the rear of the building is a small parlor/lobby that features a wrought iron spiral staircase. Rooms in the main building were quite formal; those in the connecting inn had beamed ceilings and were just as beautiful. All were average to above average in size and most had sitting areas. Vendue West has four of the most fabulous suites I have ever seen in a country inn, with large living rooms, elegant bedrooms and stocked wet bars. Mrs. Needle was specific in saying that there was no extra charge for any service that the inn provided, including beverages, ironing, and so on. The modern bath was huge, with a Jacuzzi tub, separate shower stall, and bidet. So that you will not have to walk from Vendue West to the main inn for breakfast, a full meal is delivered to your room at the appointed time. In sum, the Vendue has the personal touch of an inn, with the amenities of a small hotel." *(Susan Waller Schwemm, also Marilyn Van Raalte)*

"Front desk staff are friendly and helpful with suggestions for sightseeing and restaurants, suggesting special events as well as the standard tourist fare. Our room was small but nicely decorated. The library was filled with books and antiques, and a breakfast of muffins, pastries, biscuits, melon and juice is served in the dining room. Afternoon wine and cheese is offered in the sitting room, and is available for a reasonable length of time. Turndown service (done between 6:30 and 8 P.M.) includes a small decanter of coffee liqueur and chocolates." *(LB)*

Open All year.
Rooms 8 suites, 26 doubles—all with full private bath, telephone, radio, TV, air-conditioning. Some with desk, Jacuzzi, fireplace, wet bar. 2 rooms in carriage house.
Facilities Indoor courtyard, restaurant, library with fireplace, roof terrace. Chamber music. Bicycles. Inside parking. Tennis nearby.
Location Historic district, off East Bay & Queen sts. 1 block from waterfront.
Restrictions Traffic noise in some rooms fronting on East Bay Street. "Children over 1 year old preferred."
Credit cards Amex, MC, Visa.
Rates B&B, $120–185 suite, $79–110 double, $75–95 single. $5 for child sharing parents' room. Extra adult in room, $10. Alc dinner, $38.
Extras Cribs, babysitting available. Dutch, German, French spoken.

COLUMBIA 29205   Map 6

Also recommended: The Whitney (700 Woodrow Street at Devine; 803–252–0845) looks more like an apartment building than a hotel; it offers handsome spacious rooms, furnished traditionally with American and English antique reproductions, in a quiet residential neighborhood.

Claussen's Inn at Five Points
2003 Greene Street

Tel: (803) 765–0440
Outside SC: (800) 622–3382

Originally constructed in 1928 as Claussen's Bakery, the structure was rebuilt in 1986 as a small luxury inn, owned by Richard T. Widman (owner of the Kings Courtyard in Charleston) and managed by Dan Vance. While the bakery's aromas once tempted passersby, now only guests are greeted with the good smells of the inn's breakfast of coffee, juice, homemade blueberry muffins, and croissants from a neighborhood bakery. Rates also include evening wine and sherry, and turndown service with chocolates. Many of the building's original architectural features were preserved in the renovation, while skylights and terra-cotta tiling were added. Rooms are decorated with lots of plants, overstuffed furniture, four-poster or iron and brass beds, and traditional furnishings, along with all modern amenities.

"Quiet, elegant atmosphere. Staff is eager to serve guests' needs from ironing boards, dry cleaning services, and Xeroxing, to restaurant recommendations." *(David Ransdell)*

"Spotlessly clean, with friendly, helpful staff. The inn is interesting architecturally and ideally located within easy walking distance of the Unversity of South Carolina. The Five Points area is a mixture of sidewalk cafes, small shops and good restaurants." *(Pam Harpootlian)*

Open All year.
Rooms 8 suites, 21 doubles—all with full private bath, telephone, radio, TV, desk. Some with lofts.
Facilities Lobby with breakfast area, bar. Hot tub.
Location Central SC. Five Points section, near intersection of Saluda, Greene, and Harden sts., in SE section of city. 4 blocks to center.
Credit cards Amex, MC, Visa.
Rates B&B, $78–88 suite, $75–88 double, $65–78 single. Extra person in room, $10. Corporate rates.
Extras Wheelchair accessible. Cribs available.

MYRTLE BEACH 29577   Map 6

Information please: About 30 minutes south of Myrtle Beach and an hour north of Charleston is the port city of Georgetown, with beautiful beaches at Huntington State Park and Pawley's Island. Today, rice plantations, the area's original source of prosperity, have largely been replaced with golf courses. Two reasonably priced B&B possibilities include the **1790 House**, a two-century old raised cottage surrounded by verandas, combining historic ambience and modern amenities (630 Highmarket Street, Georgetown

29440; 803–546–4861), and the **Shaw House**, overlooking the Willowbank Marsh, offering rooms decorated with antiques and a full southern breakfast (8 Cyprus Court, Georgetown 29440; 803–546–9663).

Serendipity, An Inn
407 71st Avenue North

Tel: (803) 449–5268

Cos and Ellen Ficarra built this Spanish mission–style inn in 1985; they offer comfortable motel-style accommodation at reasonable prices. Their continental breakfast includes juice, fruit, cereal, hard-boiled eggs, and home-baked breads and muffins.

"Very much a family-type inn—quiet and relaxed atmosphere, very, very clean and neat. Each room is decorated differently. Good parking and lighting. The owners say they offer a continental breakfast, but it's much more, with different items each day. The beach is nearby and the pool and spa are lovely." *(Arthur Beck, also Mrs. Vincent D'Esposito)*

"Staying here is like a home away from home. The morning breakfast brings a lot of fun with the people who stay here. Best of all are the host and hostess, Cos and Ellen." *(Elizabeth Subock & William L. Evans)* More comments, please.

Open March through Nov.
Rooms 9 suites, 6 doubles—all with private bath and/or shower, radio, TV, desk, refrigerator, air-conditioning. Most with kitchenettes. 8 rooms in annex.
Facilities Living room, garden room, TV room, patio with fountain. Heated swimming pool, Jacuzzi, gas grill, shuffleboard, garden, Ping-Pong, bicycles. 300 yds. to ocean beaches, fishing. Tennis, 40 golf courses nearby.
Location N coastal SC, Norry County. 90 m NE of Charleston, SC; 40 m NE of Georgetown, SC; 60 m SW of Wilmington, NC. Center of town. Take Hwy. 17 to 71st Ave. N. Turn E toward ocean; inn is just off Hwy. 17.
Restrictions No smoking in common rooms.
Credit cards Amex, MC, Visa.
Rates B&B, $60–82 suites, $45–58 doubles. Extra person in room, $10. Tipping encouraged.
Extras Spanish, Italian spoken. Cribs available.

PENDLETON 29670   Map 6

Liberty Hall Inn
Business Route 28

Tel: (803) 646–7500

Pendleton was founded in 1790, and grew to some prominence in the nineteenth century as a local center of commerce, and an attractive place for Low Country planters and politicians to build their summer homes. The town is now one of the largest historic districts on the National Register of Historic Places, extending to Lake Hartwell. There are several plantations and historic homes worth seeing, plus craft and antique shops; a Spring Jubilee Festival is held each year during the first weekend in April.

Liberty Hall was built in 1840 by Thomas Sloan, and was totally rebuilt as an inn in 1984, with all new bathrooms, period antiques, and quality bed and bath linens. Tom and Susan Jonas bought the inn in 1987, and have decorated it with period antiques, Susan's collection of antique glass lamps, and the work of a local potter, quilter, and basketmaker. Along with their two sons, they have adjusted well to the country life after many years in St. Louis. Limited-choice dinners are served: a sample menu might include hot soup, marinated beef tenderloin, salad with poppyseed dressing, and apple crisp with vanilla ice cream.

"Pendleton is near Clemson and the university there. The inn is charming—a very lovely, restful, and pleasant place to stay. It has been beautifully and appropriately decorated to suit its 1840s origin. The breakfast of fruits, cereals, and homemade quick breads is a treat. The dinners are very tasty and attractively served, and the dining rooms and patio are pleasant and comfortable." *(Katherine Dunham)*

"Each guest room has its own personality and style, beautifully coordinated down to the small details. Bathrooms are modern, towels thick and plush. All facilities were very clean, the neighborhood quiet. The Jonases suggested places to visit and explore in the area. Food was delicious, especially the cinnamon rolls and bath buns. " *(Angela Anderson)*

Open All year. Restaurant closed Sundays and holidays.
Rooms 10 doubles with private full bath or shower, ceiling fans, air-conditioning, TV. Radio on request.
Facilities Dining room, upstairs lounge, deck, porches with hammock, verandas. 4 acres with gardens, walking paths. Lake swimming, hiking, fishing, golf, tennis, white-water canoeing and rafting nearby.
Location NW SC, Up Country. 30 m SW of Greenville, 130 m NW of Columbia, 88 m S of Asheville, NC. ½ m from town on Business Rte. 28, just off U.S. Route 76/28. 7 m from I-85.
Restrictions Smoking in public rooms only.
Credit cards Amex, DC, MC, Visa.
Rates B&B, $57–67 double, $52–62 single. Extra person in room, $15. Prix fixe dinner, $17, plus 15% service.
Extras Station pickups. Babysitting available.

We Want to Hear from You!

As you know, this book is only effective with your help. We really need to know about your experiences and discoveries.

If you stayed at an inn or hotel listed here, we want to know how it was. Did it live up to our description? Exceed it? Was it what you expected? Did you like it? Were you disappointed? Delighted?

Have you discovered new establishments that we should add to the next edition?

Tear out one of the report forms at the back of this book (or use your own stationery if you prefer) and write today. Even if you write only "Fully endorse existing entry" you will have been most helpful.
Thank You!

South Dakota

Hotel Alex Johnson, Rapid City

Visitors come to South Dakota to enjoy its outdoor pleasures—hiking, fishing, swimming, cross-country and downhill skiing—and to see the natural and man-made wonders found in the southwestern part of the state. Must-see sights in the Black Hills include Mt. Rushmore, Custer State Park, Jewel and Wind caves, and the gold rush towns of Deadwood and Lead; many are fascinated by the Mammoth Site in Hot Springs. Just to the east of the Black Hills is Badlands National Park, an extraordinary landscape of sharply eroded spires, ridges, and buttes.

Longtime correspondent *Mark L. Goodman* suggests that although "most people see Mt. Rushmore at night, it was made to be seen by natural light. A drive along the scenic Needles Highway and Iron Mountain road is a must."

Rates listed do not include 4 to 7% state and local sales taxes.

CUSTER 57730   **Map 10**

State Game Lodge   *Tel:* (605) 255–4541
Route 3, HCR 83-Box 74, Custer State Park

Located near the center of Custer State Park, the State Game Lodge complex is composed of the original lodge, listed on the National Register of Historic Places, forty modern motel units, and a variety of cabins of different sizes. The lodge rooms, decorated with period furnishings, once hosted

Presidents Coolidge and Eisenhower. The motel rooms are furnished in Danish modern, so be sure to specify your preference.

The lodge restaurant specializes in buffalo, pheasant, pike, and trout. If you've never had buffalo, here's your chance—you can try the steaks, burgers, or stew. *(Ralph Miller)* More comments, please.

Open May through Sept.
Rooms 47 doubles and suites in lodge and motel units, 20 cabins. All with full private bath, telephone, desk. Some cabins with kitchenettes.
Facilities Dining room, cafeteria, lounge, lobby, grocery store, gift shop. Heated swimming pool. Fishing, hiking, jeep rides to buffalo herds, horseback riding, ranger programs nearby.
Location SW SD, in Black Hills. Approx. 14 m E of Custer. Lodge is on Alt. 16, approx. 7 m E of Rte. 87 (Needles Hwy.) and 13 m W of Rte. 79.
Credit cards None accepted.
Rates Room only, $40–70 double. Cabins (accommodate 2–8), $35–125. 4-night minimum stay in cabins with kitchens. State park entrance fee additional. Alc breakfast, $2.50; alc lunch, $5–8; alc dinner, $12–20. Children's portions.
Extras Dining room, some guest rooms wheelchair accessible. Pets permitted. Cribs, play equipment available.

DEADWOOD 57732 Map 10

Information please: Other possibilities in Deadwood include the **Dove Cottage**, built in 1896 and listed on the National Register of Historic Places. Three attractively decorated guest rooms are available and rates include a full breakfast (8 Van Buren Street; 605–578–1825). The **Adams House** (22 Van Buren; 605–578–3877) is a century-old Queen Anne B&B decorated in period with wallcoverings, linens, and china original to the house.

Franklin Hotel   *Tel:* (605) 578-2241
700 Main Street   In SD: (800) 742-7713

"Deadwood is a picturesque mining town filled with the spirit of the gold rush days and wild-west history as well as a fair share of tourist traps. Entering the Franklin Hotel, a big brick building in the center of town, is like stepping back to the turn of the century in an honest, comfortable, non-glitzy way. Built in 1903, the Franklin was a premier hotel of its day.

"The friendliness of the owners and staff and its great location for exploring Deadwood's famous saloons, graveyard, shops, and museums, make this a delightful place to stay. Deadwood is within easy driving distance of Mt. Rushmore, downhill skiing, the Passion Play in Spearfish, the Homestake Opera House and Gold Mine in Lead, buffalo herds, the Badlands, and the Black Hills.

"Many famous people have stayed at the Franklin, including Pearl Buck, Teddy Roosevelt, and John Wayne. Their presence can still be felt in the spacious lobby, with its dark wood, Doric columns, molded ceilings, huge fireplace, and grand staircase. In the early days the hotel's large dining room was the scene of some fine meals, and that tradition is being revived. The menu is impressive and imaginative, but not overpriced.

"The owners are putting a lot of effort into restoring the hotel. Drab carpeting and heavy drapes in the dining room have been removed to expose a lovely wood floor and huge beveled glass windows. Early American-style chairs and wagon-wheel lighting fixtures have been replaced with bentwood chairs and chandeliers. The effect is open, airy, and elegant.

"Our room was large, clean, and comfortable, with iron beds, rocking chairs, and a dresser that probably dated back to when the hotel was new. Our bath had a big claw-foot tub but no shower, although one was available down the hall." *(Linda Meyer)*

While in Deadwood, take time to tour the Chinese Museums and tunnels, and to poke through the Public Library (right behind the hotel), with a fascinating collection of books and papers covering western history; visit the Chamber of Commerce on Main Street for more suggestions.

Open All year.
Rooms 2 suites, 45 doubles, 11 singles—all with private bath and/or shower, telephone, TV, desk, air-conditioning, fan. 13 rooms in motel annex.
Facilities Dining room, pub with band on weekends, dances in lobby for special occasions, gift shop, veranda. Swimming pool, tennis nearby. 3 lakes within 20 m; 15 m to snowmobiling, cross-country/downhill skiing.
Location SW SD, Black Hills. 50 m NW of Rapid City. Take I-90 NW from Rapid City, E 12 on Alt. 14 to Deadwood. In center of town, at the end of Main St.
Restrictions Light sleepers should request rooms away from street.
Credit cards Amex, DC, Discover, MC, Visa.
Rates Room only, $55–75 suite, $29–41 double, $27–37 single. Extra person in room, $2. Pets, $6. Children under 12 free in parents' room. 10% senior discount. Alc breakfast, $3–5; alc lunch, $5; alc dinner, $12.
Extras Wheelchair accessible. Pets permitted. Cribs available.

HILL CITY 57745   Map 10

Sylvan Lake Resort   *Tel:* (605) 574–2561 (May–Sept.)
Needles Highway, Custer State Park,   (605) 255–4521 (Oct.–April)
P.O. Box 1000

This resort is located at the northwest tip of Custer State Park, a 72,000-acre home to elk, mountain goats, deer, buffalo, bighorn sheep, antelope, and eagles. The lodge was built in 1936 as a WPA project and has undergone a complete face-lifting in recent years, under the longtime management of Art and Mary Janklow.

"Probably the nicest place to stay in the Mt. Rushmore area. Our room, #210, was very large and looked out over the lake. The buffalo steak at dinner was gamy but very good, and there was a fire in the lodge fireplace, even in June! All in all, a comfortable, quiet, relaxing place." *(Mark L. Goodman)* More comments, please.

Open All year.
Rooms 24 lodge rooms—5 suites, 19 doubles; 31 cabins. All rooms with private bath and/or shower, telephone, TV, desk. Some cabins with fireplaces, kitchenettes.
Facilities Dining room, lounge, lobby/living room, terrace, game room, café, gift/food shops, coin-operated laundry, meeting rooms. 50 acres with sandy beach on

lake, canoeing, paddle boating, trout fishing, cross-country skiing, snowmobiling. Rock climbing, hiking nearby.

Location SW SD, Black Hills. 28 m SW of Rapid City. From Rapid City, take Hwy. 16 (Rushmore Rd.); left onto Rte. 385 S; left on Rte. 87 S (Needles Hwy.) to lodge. 7 m N of Custer.

Credit cards CB, DC, Discover, MC, Visa.

Rates B&B, $66–94 suite/cabin, $50–69 double, 2- to 3-bedroom cabins, $89–140. Extra person in room, $5. State park entrance fee additional. Alc breakfast, $2–5; alc lunch, $3–7; alc dinner, $17.

Extras Some guest rooms and baths wheelchair accessible. Cribs, babysitting, play equipment available.

RAPID CITY 57701   Map 10

Hotel Alex Johnson   *Tel:* (605) 342–1210
523 Sixth Street   (800) 843–8800, Ext. 25

Construction on the Alex Johnson began in 1927, about the same year as Gutzon Borglum started work on Mt. Rushmore. Intended to be "the Showplace of the West," the hotel's lobby is highlighted by a massive fieldstone fireplace, handcarved Sioux Indian busts, and a chandelier of warrior lances. The rooms were fully remodeled in the early 1980s and are decorated with contemporary furnishings. The hotel restaurant, the Landmark, serves South Dakota specialty items such as buffalo, pheasant, walleye pike, and beef.

"The atmosphere is wonderful throughout. Paddy O'Neill's Pub is designed for fun and the lounge for quiet discussion. The rooms are tastefully decorated, and the staff is friendly and willing to accommodate." *(Pat Kurtenbach)*

"Although clean and comfortable, my room was somewhat small and dark, decorated in standard hotel/motel furnishings with none of the period or Western feel of the common areas." More comments, please.

Open All year.

Rooms 35 suites, 85 doubles, all with full private bath, telephone, radio, TV, desk. Suites with Jacuzzis and/or wet bars.

Facilities Lobby, restaurant, pub with weekend entertainment, lounge, sauna, health club.

Location SE SD. 35 m NE of Custer, 42 m S of Deadwood. On Sixth St., between Main and St. Joseph Sts.

Credit cards Amex, CB, DC, MC, Visa.

Rates Room only, $90–250 suite, $72–88 double, $55–75 single. Extra person in room, $5. No charge for children under 18 in parents' room. Weekend packages. 10% senior discount. Alc breakfast, $3–6; alc lunch, $5–10; alc dinner, $20.

Extras Wheelchair accessible. French, Spanish spoken.

Tennessee

Hale Springs Inn, Rogersville

We're delighted to note that we now can list fine inns and hotels from the mountains of east Tennessee to Memphis, at the state's western border. We'd love to have some more entries though, and would especially like to have more recommendations for Nashville and Memphis.

Rates do not include Tennessee sales tax of 7¾%.

GATLINBURG 37738   **Map 5**

People come to Gatlinburg because it is a convenient starting point for explorations of the Great Smoky Mountains National Park. Unfortunately, the road from Knoxville to Gatlinburg is littered with one tourist trap after the next. Gatlinburg itself is even worse, with dozens of tacky souvenir shops. Leave the town and then your car behind as soon as possible, and spend your time exploring the beauty and peace of the park.

Also recommended: The **Best Western Fabulous Chalet Inn** (Sunset Drive, P.O. Box 11; 615–436–5151, 800–528–1234) is set high on a quiet hillside above the hustle and bustle of narrow downtown Gatlinburg. You may wonder "Will she be listing the Dew Drop Inn next?" but this accommodation is highly recommended by a most trusted respondent; the rates are also extremely reasonable ($35–75 double). The rooms are large, with floor-to-ceiling windows with a view of the Smokies. The large bathrooms have high-pressure showers, built-in hair dryers, and heated-tile floors. The **LeConte Lodge** (Atop Mt. LeConte in the Great Smoky Moun-

tains National Park, P.O. Box 350; 615–436–4473) is not going to be a
"wonderful" choice for everyone. There's no electricity, no indoor plumbing, and no way to get there by motorized vehicle of any kind! Advance
reservations and a five mile hike will get you there. The lodge was built
four years before the Great Smoky Mountains National Park was created
in 1930. The LeConte is self-sufficient, with propane gas for cooking, and
kerosene for heating and lighting. **The Wonderland Hotel** (RFD 2, Box
205; 615–436–5490), constructed in 1912 when the only access was on
logging roads, continues to maintain a rustic environment in the midst of
the Great Smoky Mountains National Park. Old-fashioned rocking chairs
on the veranda provide evening relaxation after a day hiking in the mountains.

Gatlinburg is located in southeastern Tennessee, 50 miles southeast of
Knoxville.

BUCKHORN   Map 2

Buckhorn Inn   *Tel:* (615) 436–4668
Route 3, Box 384

The Buckhorn's white-columned porch overlooks a panorama of green
hills and blue-gray mountains. Enter the inn to find a spacious living room
and dining area furnished with antiques and country-comfortable sofas.
Guest rooms in the inn are furnished simply, with spindle beds and some
antiques; the nearby rustic cottages all have a fireplace and porch. Rates
include a full breakfast and a dinner of soup or salad, choice of entrée, fresh
vegetables, home-baked bread, and dessert. The Buckhorn has been owned
by the Young family since 1979, and is managed by John and Connie
Burns.

"The inn overlooks the Greenbriar section of the Great Smoky Mountains National Park. The food is very good and the portions are just right—
not overwhelming. The atmosphere is homey, relaxed, and friendly,
reflecting the hosts' nature." *(Betty & Ed Sternberg)* "The Buckhorn is located
in a secluded spot; the accommodations are excellent, with a magnificent
view from all the rooms." *(Mrs. Creed Reagan)* More comments, please.

Open All year. Closed Dec. 24, 25.
Rooms 6 doubles, 4 cottages—all with full private bath and/or shower, desk, air-
conditioning. TV in cottages.
Facilities Dining/living room with fireplace, piano; library. 25 acres for hiking,
fishing. 1 m to swimming, trout fishing. 8 m to downhill skiing.
Location 5 m from town. From Gatlinburg, take Hwy. 321 N 5 m; turn left at
Buckhorn Rd. Go 1 m and turn right on Tudor Mt. Rd. to inn.
Restrictions Smoking "permitted without enthusiasm" in guest rooms only. Chil-
dren welcome in cottages; no children under 10 at dinner.
Credit cards None accepted.
Rates B&B, $95–103 cottage, $65–83 double, $59–77 single. Extra person in room,
$12. 2-night weekend minimum. Prix fixe dinner, $18.
Extras 2 rooms wheelchair accessible.

KNOXVILLE   Map 5

Once an outpost of the western frontier, Knoxville is today a manufacturing center and home of the University of Tennessee. Its location in eastern Tennessee, about 50 miles northwest of Gatlinburg, makes it a common starting point for visits to the Smokies.

Also recommended: The Middleton (800 West Hill, 37902; 615–524–8100) was student housing, late in 1981, until a major renovation of the interior, and replacement of the wiring and plumbing. Rooms are individually decorated with original art and antiques; some have canopied beds and Jacuzzi tubs.

The Graustein Inn   *Tel:* (615) 690–7007
8300 Nubbin Ridge Road 37923

As its name implies, the Graustein, a new inn owned by Darlene and Jim Lara, is made of gray stone. The interior features a cathedral-ceilinged great room, and guest rooms are highlighted with 18th- and 19th-century antiques. The three-course breakfast includes a hearty entrée, homemade granola with Austrian-style cottage cheese, fresh fruit, and home-baked rolls and pastries. Dinner selections change frequently, but a recent meal included mushrooms stuffed with walnuts and cheese; roast beef tenderloin with peppers and onions and a brandy Dijon sauce, accompanied by vegetables and salad; and poached pears glazed with chocolate set on raspberry sauce.

"The many extras include a robe and magazines in your room, homemade candy on the nightstand, fresh flowers, and the smell of baking bread in the early morning. Guests have the run of the house, from the television room on the lower level, to the chess set in the lovely sitting room on the upper level." *(Mr. & Mrs. David House)*

"First, the setting is beautiful—secluded, lovely woods and paths, quiet and very natural. Second, nothing was spared in the decoration of the inn. The quality of the furnishings, wall coverings, bed linens, and pillows was excellent. The bathroom that I shared was well appointed with not only the necessities, but the luxuries of special soaps, shampoos, and fluffy towels." *(Sydney Summers)*

"You immediately sense the peace and quiet of the countryside on driving up the lane. The stone patios and decking outside the inn make for a relaxed area to enjoy the out-of-doors or an informal breakfast. A hike on the nature trails was a welcome change. Inside, the great room is equipped with a large variety of music and reading materials, and the fire was set for our enjoyment. The freestanding stairway that reaches three floors is a work of art that shouldn't be missed.

"Retiring to our room, we found our fire blazing and easy chairs ready for some quiet reading. Breakfast in the morning was another highlight and included fresh fruit and juice, the inn's own granola, omelets, freshly baked muffins and coffee that Jim & Darlene blend for use at the inn." *(Joseph & Wanda Krause)*

Open All year. Restaurant closed Sun.
Rooms 2 suites, 3 doubles—3 with private bath and/or shower, 2 with maximum of 4 people sharing 1 bath. All with telephone, radio, air-conditioning, fan. 2 with desk, 3 with balcony, 1 with fireplace.
Facilities Great room with fireplace, library, games, stereo; breakfast porch; dining rooms; bar. 20 acres with patio, gardens, nature trail, forest, basketball court. Golf nearby.
Location 20 min. W of downtown Knoxville. From I-40, take Cedar Bluff exit, go S .5 m to Kingston Pike. Turn left on Kingston Pike; go .3 m and go right on Peters Rd. (at Hawkeye's Restaurant). Go 1.6 m, through stop sign, over railroad tracks. Take 1st left after tracks onto Westland Dr. Go 1.5 m; turn right on Sanford Day Rd. Go .3 m to T-intersection. Go straight and take right-hand driveway to inn.
Restrictions No smoking. No children.
Credit cards Amex, MC, Visa.
Rates B&B, $84–98 suite, $55–80 double, $49–69 single. 2-3 night minimum for special event weekends. Lunch, dinner by advance request; prix fixe lunch, $9–14; prix fixe dinner, $22–29. Alc dinner, $33.
Extras Airport/station pickups for fee. Some Spanish spoken.

MEMPHIS 38105   Map 5

We'd like to see more listings for west Tennessee's major city. The city's best known hotel is the **Peabody** (149 Union Avenue 38103; 800–PEA-BODY), an American classic. Although attractively restored, at 450 rooms, it's too big for this guide, especially when jam-packed with convention-eers. In any case, do stop by at either 11 A.M. or 5 P.M. to see the famous duck march through the lobby.

The Lowenstein-Long House   *Tel:* (901) 527–7174
217 North Waldran

The Lowenstein-Long House was built by department-store owner Abraham Lowenstein at the turn of the century and is listed on the National Register of Historic Places.

"Charles and Martha Long restored this B&B about five years ago, after it had been deserted and derelict for several years. (Vagrants lived in it and sold off much of the original furniture and fixtures in yard sales.) The exterior is a Victorian stick-style castle, executed in gray stone blocks. You enter through an impressive etched glass front door into an entrance hall with a handsome fireplace. One of the downstairs sitting rooms is done all in blue, while the other has lovely gilded decorative moldings. Guest rooms are immaculate and decorated in soft, harmonious color schemes, with a good deal of warmth and charm—quilts, attractive patterns, fireplaces. The location is central; the neighborhood is not wonderful but not bad either—convenient for sightseeing and to major hotels and restaurants." *(Ann Delugach)* "We were greeted warmly, and shown to our room; soon after, they brought up a tray of tea and cookies for us." *(Sharon Clymore)*

"We stayed in the Mauve Room, which was spacious and decorated with a comfortable couch, tables with magazines, and a writing desk. After dinner, we watched a show in the TV room, sipping wine that the hostess had chilled for us. The breakfast buffet consisted of fruits, cereal, juice, coffee, and sweet rolls, served in the large dining room with stunning crown moldings. Southern hospitality at its best. The only negative is the neighborhood in which the house is located." *(Vicki Turner, also Guy Page)*

Open All year.
Rooms 4 doubles—all with full private bath, desk, air-conditioning, fan.
Facilities Dining room, sitting rooms, TV room. Patio, large backyard with garden. Secure off-street parking.
Location SW TN. Center city; residential/light commercial area. 5 min. from downtown Memphis, Mud Island, Victorian Village, Overton Square.
Restrictions No smoking in common rooms.
Credit cards Amex, MC, Visa.
Rates B&B, $50 double. Extra person in room, $10. Senior discount.
Extras French, German spoken.

NASHVILLE   Map 5

Nashville is both the capital and commercial center of Tennessee, and, as everyone knows, it's the country music capital of the world. It's also home to seventeen colleges and universities and to tourist attractions ranging from the sublime to the ridiculous, starting and ending, of course, with Opryland.

Also recommended: Although too big at 300 rooms for the focus of this guide, *Louis Papalos* wrote to recommend **The Maxwell House** for its comfortable rooms, friendly courteous staff, and convenient location (2025 MetroCenter Boulevard 37228; 615–259–4343 or 800–CLARION).

The Hermitage Hotel   *Tel:* (615) 244–3121
231 Sixth Avenue North   In TN: (800) 342–1816
                                              Outside TN: (800) 251–1908

Built in 1910 at a cost of $1,000,000, the Hermitage boasted the most luxurious rooms of its day, with such amenities as hot and cold distilled running water, private baths, telephones, electric fans, and a device to show the arrival of mail. The Beaux Arts-style decor included velvet upholstered furniture, Persian carpets, and palm trees. Public rooms were lavishly ornamented with marble from Greece, Italy and Tennessee, while the dining room was paneled in Circassian walnut from Russia. The hotel was the focal point for many political and social gatherings, and scores of famous people dined and stayed here over the years. In 1986 the hotel was restored to its early elegance, after years of decay. Its original 250 rooms were redone as 112 suites. Rates include turndown service, luxury soaps, and the morning paper. The hotel restaurant offers continental cuisine in an elegant atmosphere.

"Our suite was comfortable and quiet, with modern Oriental-style furnishings. The bathroom had a sink in the dressing area, with tub and toilet separate, and a powerful massaging shower. Although the high-ceilinged marble lobby is handsome, it felt cold to me. The Oak Dining room is in the basement, with arched beams and plaster ceilings. Some find it pretty; I felt like I was in a cave. Breakfasts were OK, and very reasonable in price." *(SHW, also Robin Cranton)*

Open All year.
Rooms 112 suites—all with full private bath, telephone, radio, TV, desk, air-conditioning, wet bar.

Facilities Lobby with etched glass skylight, dining rooms, bar/lounge with entertainment. Concierge service. Parking garage next door.
Location Downtown. 1 block from capitol. At corner of Union St.
Restrictions No smoking in some guest rooms.
Credit cards All major credit cards accepted.
Rates Room only, $88–98 suite. Extra person in room, $10. Children under 12 free in parents' room. 10% senior discount. Weekend rates. "Suite Romance," Opryland packages.
Extras Some rooms equipped for the disabled. Pets permitted by prior arrangement.

ROGERSVILLE 37857   Map 5

Hale Springs Inn   *Tel:* (615) 272–5171
110 West Main Street, Town Square

Rogersville is one of Tennessee's oldest towns, founded in 1786, when this area was still the western frontier. The Hale Springs Inn was built in 1824 and is the oldest continuously running inn or hotel in Tennessee. Presidents Jackson, Polk, and (Andrew) Johnson all stayed here. Originally called McKinney's Tavern, the inn was used as Union headquarters during the Civil War. Confederate headquarters were located across the street, in Kyle House. In 1982, Capt. Carl Netherland-Brown purchased the inn and began its restoration. Many of the original furnishings are still intact, including several Victorian settees and side chairs, original claw-foot bathtubs, and working fireplaces. The decor also includes comfortable velvet covered wing chairs, handsome brass chandeliers, canopied four-poster beds, Oriental carpets, and handmade quilts. The Captain says that "we cater to nice people who like places in the style of Savannah, Charleston, and Williamsburg, yet we are small and off the beaten track." He also reports a recent improvement: "The movie theater which had been next door to the inn has been torn down, and the formal gardens which had occupied the site for the preceding 116 years have been restored." Now that's progress!

"One of the finest restoration projects we have ever visited. Staff members Julia Fain and Bryan Shaw went out of their way to make us feel welcome. The atmosphere can only be described as true Southern." *(John Hogin)*

Open All year. Restaurant closed Sun. evening, Mon.
Rooms 2 suites, 8 doubles—all with private shower and/or bath, TV, air-conditioning. Some with desk, fireplace.
Facilities Restaurant, library with fireplace, sitting room with fireplace, lobby, balcony. Formal garden with gazebo. Swimming, boating, fishing, tennis, golf nearby.
Location Upper E TN. 65 m E of Knoxville; 30 m W of Kingsport. 16 m NW of I-81 on Rte 11W. In center of town.
Restrictions Light sleepers should request back rooms; inn is on a main street. Dry county; "brown bagging" permitted. No children under 7.
Credit cards Amex, MC, Visa.
Rates B&B, $55–60 suite, $35–55 double. Extra person in room, $15. Alc lunch, $7.50; alc dinner, $16.
Extras Pets permitted by prior arrangement.

Texas

Prince Solms Inn, New Braunfels

Texas really is big—the size of Austria, Belgium, Britain, Denmark, Switzerland, and West Germany combined. The distance from Houston, in the east, to El Paso, in the west, is 742 miles—just a little less than the distance between New York and Chicago. Although those who've never been here think of the state as being endless flat plains interspersed with flashy modern cities, there's a tremendous variety in the terrain, from the jungle-like tropical vegetation of Big Thicket National Park in East Texas, to the historic towns of Hill Country, to the jagged landscape of Big Bend National Park along the Mexican border to the west.

All Texas travelers should be absolutely sure to get a free copy of the *Texas State Travel Guide,* published by the state tourist office (see appendix for address). Its 200-plus pages cover the state's sites of historic and scenic interest, town by town, including some historic inns.

Reader tip: One of our best respondents noted that although they're not suitable for individual listings in the guide, the **La Quinta** chain of motels, found throughout Texas, represents a very good value and "is a cut above the other chains." She went on to point out that in some of the state's historic inns, air-conditioning is not always among the items added during updating. Although the owners may feel that a fan is all that's needed when they have high ceilings, "I can guarantee you that in the summer, even we Texans want more than that, let alone some poor Yankee!" She also cautions the uninitiated about the individual open gas heaters used to warm a few of these older homes in winter—they can present a fire hazard

576

to the careless. *(MAA)* We'd recommend inquiring about both of the above when making reservations.

Information please: There's a large white space on our map of the Texas panhandle, and a newly restored old hotel may help to fill the gap. The **Hotel Turkey** in where else but Turkey, Texas, was bought by Scott and Jane Johnson in 1988. Located 80 miles northeast of Lubbock, and about the same distance southeast of Amarillo, the 60-year-old building offers down-home cooking, country music on Saturday nights, and rooms decorated in period (Third and Alexander Streets, P.O. Box 37, Turkey 79261; 806–423–1151). It's probably worth visiting just to send a postcard back to your old boss! Another area possibility 16 miles south of Amarillo is **Hudspeth House**, a turn-of-the-century Victorian home close to West Texas State University now restored as a B&B (1905 Fourth Avenue, Canyon 79015; 806–655–9800).

In East Texas, about 120 miles southeast of Dallas and about the same distance northeast of Houston, is "the oldest town in Texas," Nacogdoches. Lots of Texas "firsts" and "oldests" were recorded here: first oil well, oldest public street, oldest college in the Republic, oldest union church, and more. It's also home to the **Haden Edwards Inn** (106 North Lanana, Nacogdoches 75961; 409–564–9999), named for one of the fore-runners of Texan independence. This historic home was built in 1860, remodeled in 1890, and restored with all modern conveniences in recent years; its four guest rooms are furnished with antiques and the work of local artists. Rates range from $65–90 and include a continental breakfast.

Rates do not include 6% state lodging tax, plus local taxes where applicable.

AUSTIN 78701   Map 11

Information please: The **Southard House** is a turn-of-the-century B&B located in downtown Austin, offering reasonable rates for its charming rooms, decorated in period (908 Blanco 78703; 512–474–4731). Reports, please.

For a meal as big as Texas, mosey on over to Threadgill's Restaurant (6416 N. Lamar; 512–451–5440). Favorite dishes include chicken-fried steak, mashed potatoes and gravy, and rich southern-style vegetables cooked with lots of cheese or butter.

The Driskill   *Tel:* (512) 474–5911
604 Brazos Street at Sixth   (800) 252–9367

Built over 100 years ago, the Driskill was the first hotel south and west of St. Louis to have electricity and was known as the finest hotel in the Southwest. Room rates in those days ranged from $2.50 to $5.

"The Driskill has been refurbished with reproduction furnishings which I prefer in many ways to the real thing. The beds aren't skimpy and the drawers don't stick, but the ambience still fits the high ceilings and transomed doorways. The lobby gives you an instant feeling of 'old elegance,' and it must do the same for the personnel because we found them to be accommodating without acting like the 'well-trained monkeys' found in many chain hotels. The hotel is in the heart of old Austin; with all the restoration that's taken place, there are lots of eating places within walking distance. It has very attractive weekend rates as well. The drawbacks are minimal: valet parking (it takes time to retrieve one's car) and the lack of a swimming pool." *(MAA)* More comments, please.

Open All year.
Rooms 180 suites and doubles, all with full private bath, telephone, TV; most with desk.
Facilities Restaurant, bar/lounge with entertainment, meeting rooms, health club.
Location Downtown, 1 block S of Capitol, 2 blocks E of I-35.
Credit cards Most major credit cards accepted.
Rates Room only, $160–800 suite, $89–125 double, $70–100 single.

BANDERA 78003   Map 11

Information please: Another dude ranch in the "Cowboy Capital of the World" is the **Silver Spur**, owned by the Winchell family, with lots of riding and comfortable accommodation in stone cottages (P.O. Box 1657; 512–796–3639).

Mayan Dude Ranch   *Tel:* (512) 796–3312
P.O. Box 577

The Mayan Dude Ranch is the biggest family-owned dude ranch in Texas, and it is owned by what may well be one of the biggest families—Don and Judy Hicks and their 10 children. Not surprisingly, the Mayan caters to families, with special activities planned for kids ages 2 to 18. Rates include all meals and all activities, including two horseback rides daily. Although breakfast is served daily in the dining room, many guests prefer to ride by horse or wagon to the outdoor cowboy breakfast, cooked over the open fire. "Meat and potatoes" are available in the dining room at lunch, while a salad buffet is offered at poolside. Dinners tend to follow themes: one night may bring barbecue by the riverside, another an Italian feast, and a Mexican fiesta another evening. *(Mrs. Arnold Miller)* More comments, please.

Open All year.
Rooms 30 motel units, 30 cottages, all with full private bath, TV, radio, desk, air-conditioning. Some with fireplaces.
Facilities Dining room, lounge, living room, deck, game room, TV room, coin-operated laundry, gift shop. 400 acres with Olympic-size swimming pool, 2 tennis courts, weight room, playground, volleyball, basketball, hayrides, horseback riding, hiking trails; on Medina River for fishing, tubing, swimming. 9-hole golf course nearby.
Location Central TX, Hill Country. 45 m NW of San Antonio. From San Antonio, take Rte. 16NW to Bandera. Turn right at the stop light, go 3 blocks and turn left at Pecana St.; 1½ m to ranch.
Credit cards Amex, CB, DC, Discover, MC, Visa.
Rates Full board per person, $75 double, $80 single, plus 10% service. 12 and under, $40; 13–17, $50. Weekly discounts. 2-night minimum stay.

Extras Wheelchair accessible. Airport/station pickups. Cribs, babysitting, play equipment available. Spanish, German spoken.

BELLVILLE 77418   Map 11

High Cotton Inn   *Tel:* (409) 865–9796
214 South Live Oak

This Victorian gingerbread house was built in 1906 by the Hellmuth family of Bellville. Today's owners, the Hortons, restored the house's original cypress siding and have decorated the rooms with period wallpaper and furniture. "Our guests are usually looking for a quiet weekend away from their busy lives, without TV and telephones; although available, they are seldom used. Things around here stay pretty much the same—laid back."

"Innkeepers Anna and George Horton treat guests warmly, like family, and are full of information on what to do in the area. They'll pack a large lunch for those who want to explore Round Top, New Braunfels, and the other Texas-German communities within a 30- to 45-minute drive. A delicious plantation breakfast is served every morning, with smoked sausage, eggs, bacon, grits, biscuits, and homemade preserves!" *(Irene Rawlings)*
More comments, please.

Open All year.
Rooms 5 doubles sharing 2½ baths, all with desk, air-conditioning, ceiling fan.
Facilities Parlor with piano, games; dining room, upstairs sitting room with TV. Wraparound porch and balcony with swings, play equipment. 1 acre with swimming pool, herb garden. Tennis, golf nearby.
Location 65 m W of Houston, 100 m E of Austin. On Hwy. 36, 2 blocks from only stop light in town. 4 blocks from town square.
Restrictions No smoking. Traffic noise might disturb light sleepers in front rooms.
Credit cards None accepted.
Rates B&B, $50 double, $40 single. Extra person in room, $5. Discount for extended stays. Prix fixe weekend lunch and dinner by advance reservation, $8–12.
Extras Crib available.

BIG SANDY 75755   Map 11

Annie's B&B   *Tel:* (214) 636–4355
Highway 155 North, P.O. Box 928F   (214) 636–4303

Innkeepers Les and Martha Lane invite guests to partake of the varied attractions Annie's offers, from the delicious food served at breakfast, lunch, dinner, and tea in Annie's tea room, to the craft and needlework shops, and the Victorian-style bedrooms.

"Annie's is a delightful B&B in the sleepy East Texas town of Big Sandy. We especially like the Balcony Room on the second floor and the third-floor room with a loft and large balcony. The decor is Victorian, and each room is open for inspection until occupied for the evening. Saturday morning breakfast is waiting in your room refrigerator (disguised as an old safe) and is a delicious arrangement of fresh fruit and muffins (the innkeepers maintain the Sabbath from sundown Friday to sundown Saturday, thus the in-room breakfast). We enjoyed ours on the balcony of our room. Sunday breakfast, served across the street in Annie's tea room, is very elegant and special. The grounds are lovely with fountains and flowers and Annie's needlework shop is great fun to visit." *(Marilyn Bolling)* **More comments, please.**

Open All year. Restaurant closed Saturday.
Rooms 4 suites, 9 doubles—8 with private bath and/or shower, 5 with shared bath. All with refrigerator. Some with balconies, lofts, ceiling fans.
Facilities Restaurant, parlor with books, games, TV; gift shop, needlecraft gallery, bakery, porch. Landscaped grounds with fountain.
Location Central E TX, between Dallas and Shreveport, LA; 2-hour drive from either. At intersection of Hwys. 155 and 80.
Restrictions No smoking.
Credit cards Amex, MC, Visa.
Rates B&B, $68–115 suite, $38–88 double. Weekend rates. Sunday brunch, $13.

CASTROVILLE 78009   Map 11

Landmark Inn   *Tel:* (512) 538–2133
Florence at Highway 90

Henri Castro, a nineteenth-century French entrepreneur, agreed to provide settlers for the new Republic of Texas in exchange for a huge land grant. He advertised throughout Europe, and had the best response from the provinces of Alsace and Lorraine. A settlement of nearly 1,000—both families and single men—was established by 1850 and was named Castroville. After early years of tremendous hardship the town finally prospered, without losing its strong Alsatian cultural identity and customs. Much of its Alsatian-style architecture has been preserved; the area has been recognized as a historic district on the state and national level.

The Landmark Inn dates back to 1849 when it was originally a general store. The second floor was added in 1853 and rooms were rented to travelers on the busy road between San Antonio and El Paso. Later, a stone grist mill and dam were constructed along the river. In 1925 the inn and mill were bought by the Lawler family, who renamed it the Landmark. Ruth Lawler developed the inn's reputation as a peaceful oasis and donated it to the Texas Parks and Wildlife Department as a state historic site.

"What a contrast to San Antonio, jut 20 miles away! A night in this peaceful setting brought us back to another century. Our room had antique furnishings and a handmade quilt; on the wall was an Alsatian inn motto translated as: 'He who values his own tranquility knows to respect that of others.' Since we visited in the early spring, the lack of air-conditioning was no problem." *(MW)* **More comments, please.**

Open All year.
Rooms 8 doubles—4 with private shower, 4 with a maximum of 4 people sharing a bath. All with ceiling fan. 2 rooms in annex.
Facilities Lobby. 4 acres with walks. River nearby.
Location In town. ½ block from Highway 90.
Restrictions No smoking in public areas.

Credit cards None accepted.
Rates Room only, $30 double, $25 single. Extra adult in room $5; extra child (6-12) $2. Children under 6 free. No tipping.
Extras 1 room with handicapped facilities. Spanish spoken.

CHAPPELL HILL 77426   Map 11

Chappell Hill is a slow-paced rural town, founded in 1848, and once known as the "Athens of Texas" for its early prominence in literature and culture. It's located in east central Texas, 60 miles west of Houston, 100 miles east of Austin. Take Route 290 to Brenham, then Route 36 south to Chappell Hill.

For a scenic drive, take the F. M. 1155 road northeast to Washington-on-the-Brazos State Park, which commemorates Texas's becoming an independent state. This area is especially lovely in spring when the bluebonnets are in bloom. A half-dozen festivals celebrate the season. For more information about the area, contact the Washington Country Chamber of Commerce, 314 South Austin, Brenham, Texas 77833.

The Browning Plantation   *Tel:* (409) 836–6144
Route 1, Box 8

Col. W. W. Browning, a prominent community leader, began construction of this beautiful three-story Greek Revival plantation home in 1857, using slave labor and cedar trees grown on the property. It's now listed on the National Register of Historic Places. Owners Mr. and Mrs. R. P. Ganchan took 31 months to restore the house, opening it up for B&B in 1983. Mr. Ganchan reports that "We are the only operating plantation B&B in Texas, and we have the largest model train layout in the state. Our guests particularly enjoy the restful atmosphere and antique decor."

Framed by gracious verandas, the guest rooms are painted in pastel colors characteristic of Browning's day and are furnished with nineteenth-century antiques, including plantation and tester beds. Although you're unlikely to see any ships coming in, climb to the rooftop widow's walk anyway for a panoramic view of the plantation. Rates include a tour and a full country breakfast, served in the formal dining room.

"The Browning is a step back into history. The Ganchans are knowledgeable and delightful hosts. The food is outstanding, a rare treat." *(Patricia & Donald Pranke)*

Open All year.
Rooms 6 doubles—2 with full private bath, 4 with maximum of 4 people sharing bath. All with radio, air-conditioning, fan.
Facilities Dining room, library, parlor, porch. 11 acres with gardens, swimming pool, lakes for fishing. Golf nearby.
Location From US Rte. 290, go S on F.M. 1155, at blinking traffic light 2 blocks. Turn left to driveway for inn on right.
Restrictions No smoking. No children under 12.
Credit cards None accepted.
Rates B&B, $75–110 double. Extra person in room, $20.
Extras Station pickups.

The Mulberry House
P.O. Box 5

Tel: (409) 830–1311
(713) 589–1340

The only surviving example of Queen Anne–style architecture in the area, the Mulberry House is listed on the National Register of Historic Places. Built in 1874 by a prosperous cotton farmer and rancher, the house has been restored by Myrv and Katie Cron. It's decorated in period with some original furnishings. Rates include a full breakfast.

"The Mulberry House, while not on the grand style of the Browning Plantation, is equally delightful, as are its hosts. Delicious food." *(Patricia & Donald Pranke)*

Open All year.
Rooms 1 suite, 2 doubles, all with full private bath, air-conditioning.
Facilities Dining room, parlor, porch.
Location .2 m E of intersection of Main (FM 1155) and Chestnut (FM 2447) Sts.
Credit cards None accepted.
Restrictions No smoking.
Rates B&B, $75 suite, $55 double.

Stagecoach Inn
Main Street at Chestnut, P.O. Box E

Tel: (409) 836-9515

In 1846, when Austin became the state capital of Texas, decent places to stay on the dusty stagecoach route to Houston were hard to find. By 1850 construction of the Stagecoach Inn had begun, and travelers soon found comfortable accommodation at this Greek Revival–style inn, which featured such nineteenth-century luxuries as a water pitcher and basin in each room. The exterior of the house still boasts such unusual details as a Greek key frieze along the cornice surrounding the building and downspouts highlighted with the lone star of Texas and the year, 1851.

Today, Harvin and Elizabeth Moore, owners of the Stagecoach since 1976, have restored the house, adding the up-to-date amenities noted below. They have furnished the house with a mixture of European, New England, and Texan antiques, rugs both Oriental and braided, and American primitive paintings and quilts. The Moores also own Lottie's B&B, located in a historic building just across the street; doubles cost approximately $55. *(Dr. & Mrs. Donald Pranke)*

Open All year.
Rooms 1 cottage, 2 suites, 2 doubles, 1 single—3 with full private bath, 3 with maximum of 5 sharing bath. All with telephone, radio, TV, desk, air-conditioning.
Facilities Dining room, living room, library. 4 acres with terraces, flower and vegetable gardens, wildflowers, antique shop.
Location In center of town, at main intersection.
Restrictions No smoking. No children under 10.
Credit cards None accepted.
Rates B&B, $85–98 suite, $55–85 double. No tipping.

DALLAS
Map 11

Located in northeastern Texas, Dallas displays the character of both a southern and a western town, along with the cosmopolitan style of a northern city. A center of banking and insurance in the Southwest and a popular convention city, downtown Dallas features commercial highrises that tower over the surrounding prairies. Because the city's growth was swift and unexpected, Dallas is a confusing city to get around in—one-way streets intersect with numerous highways, and streets often change their names but not their directions.

Dallas is a sister city to Fort Worth; the two cities share one of the country's largest airports. Dallas is 245 miles northwest of Houston and 270 miles northeast of San Antonio.

Ambassador Plaza Hotel
1312 South Ervay Street 75215

Tel: (214) 565–9003

We are delighted to add a more affordable entry to our Dallas listings. Standard rates at the Ambassador are generally under $100, but numerous specials apply in spring and summer, on weekends. Business travelers and government employees, be sure to inquire when booking to see which one applies to you.

When the Ambassador opened in 1905 as the Majestic Hotel it was Dallas' finest, boasting the very first elevator west of the Mississippi. It hosted such dignitaries and celebrities as Presidents William Taft, Teddy Roosevelt and Woodrow Wilson, plus Sarah Bernhardt and John Philip Sousa. The hotel was modernized in 1932, the original red brick covered with white stucco, and a red tile roof was added. After a period of decline the hotel was restored in 1983 and was returned to its original elegance. Amenities include free shuttle service within a five-mile radius, morning newspaper, and turndown service.

"The lobby of this restored historic hotel is very elegant and the rooms are nice, although not luxurious. The staff is congenial and very helpful." *(Kathleen Hardy)*

Open All year.
Rooms 8 suites, 106 doubles—all with private shower and/or bath, telephone, radio, TV, desk, air-conditioning, fan. Some with wet bars.
Facilities Restaurant, bar/lounge, lobby, gardens with outside sitting area. Free valet parking. Across from Old City park.
Location From I-30 E take Ervay exit to St. Paul South. From I-30 W take Griffin St. exit to Cadiz East to St. Paul South.
Restrictions Smoking in designated areas only.
Credit cards Amex, CB, DC, MC, Visa.
Rates Room only, $75–175 suite, $60–95 double, $50–85 single. Extra person in room $10. Children and family discounts. 50% senior discount. Weekend, corporate, government rates, $45–60. Prix fixe lunch $5–9; prix fixe dinner $9–15. Alc lunch $8; alc dinner $20.
Extras Handicap facilities. Airport/station pickups. Courtesy van to downtown. Spanish spoken.

Hotel Crescent Court
400 Crescent Court 75201

Tel: (214) 871–3200
(800) 654–6541

Under the same ownership and management as the Mansion on Turtle Creek (see below), this new hotel was designed by Philip Johnson to bring the mood of Versailles to this boomtown on the prairie. The hotel is the cornerstone of a complex of office buildings and exclusive shops, and is elegantly decorated with traditional furnishings in neutral and soft pastel tones; the interior designer, Kalef Alaton, also designed the widely acclaimed Bel-Air in Los Angeles. Rooms are equipped with all the luxuries one would expect from a Rosewood Hotel, with rates to match. The spacious lobby has gleaming travertine floors, with Louis XV–style furniture and tapestries and parlor palm trees. Its restaurant, the Beau Nash, has an excellent reputation developed under the creative touch of Dean Fearing; southwestern flavors are combined with classic recipes in innovative combinations: lobster tacos with jicama salad, duck paté with pickled okra, and veal chops with onion pudding. *(MAA, also KJ)*

Open All year.
Rooms 28 suites, 190 doubles, all with full private bath, telephone, radio, TV, desk, air-conditioning. Some suites with fireplaces.
Facilities Restaurants, bar/lounge, spa program, shops, courtyard, swimming pool. Free weekday downtown trolley service.
Location Northwest downtown, between Cedar Springs and McKinney.
Credit cards Amex, CB, DC, JCB, MC, Visa.
Rates Room only, $350–980, 1- and 2-bedroom suites, $205–295 double, $175–265 single. Weekend packages. 2-night weekend minimum. Alc lunch, $25; alc dinner, $80.
Extras Wheelchair accessible; 3 rooms equipped for disabled. Airport pickups; free downtown trolley service. Small pets allowed. Cribs, babysitting available. Spanish, German, French spoken. Member, Rosewood Hotels, Inc.

The Mansion on Turtle Creek

2821 Turtle Creek Boulevard 75219

Tel: (214) 559–2100
In TX: (800) 442–3408
Outside TX: (800) 527–5432

The Mansion on Turtle Creek was Caroline Hunt Schoellkopf's first entry into the hotel business in 1980. Since then her corporation, Rosewood Hotels, has built or bought several more of the country's finest hotels. Although their rates are on a par with their top reputation, we've had excellent reports on nearly all of Rosewood's properties. Luxury is their cachet, so it's not surprising that the weekly flower bill alone at the Mansion exceeds $3,000.

This hotel/restaurant is comprised of two parts, the Spanish-style Sheppard King Mansion, completed in 1925, and the new hotel, built to coordinate with the original mansion. The restaurant, one of Dallas's most exclusive and expensive, is housed in the original mansion. Some of its unusual architectural features include a freestanding stairway, a nineteenth-century Spanish cathedral door, a sixteenth-century stone mantel, stained-glass windows, and a dining room ceiling composed of 2,400 pieces of inlaid wood. The cuisine includes international, American, and southwestern food.

The hotel rooms are equipped with every luxury one would expect to find in a hotel of this caliber and are furnished with traditional, comfortable furniture, highlighted with antiques, original art, and fresh flowers and plants.

"Wonderful hotel, superb food, fully deserving of its top reputation. Another dining alternative two blocks away is the Routh St. Restaurant, set in a former private home, offering good food, attractively presented. The decor is spare, the atmosphere elegant, the wine list computerized." *(Truman Talley, also MAA)*

"Imaginative Southwestern cuisine, incredibly varied and creative. Although the terrace suites are lavish, with views of downtown Dallas, we prefer the regular guest rooms. They're spacious yet intimate, with marble baths and all the amenities you could want." *(Paul Lasley & Elizabeth Harryman)*

Open All year.
Rooms 14 suites, 129 doubles, all with full private bath, telephone, TV, radio, desk, air-conditioning, living area. Some with fireplaces, balconies, wet bars, powder rooms, pantries.
Facilities Restaurant, breakfast/tea room, bar with piano music nightly. Valet parking. Swimming pool, heated in winter. Jogging trails, parks nearby. Complimentary limo to downtown.
Location 5 min. from business district, 30 min. from DFW Airport. Adjacent to Highland and University Parks. At the corner of Gillespie St., Cedar Spring, and Turtle Creek Blvd.
Credit cards Amex, CB, DC, MC, Visa.
Rates Room only, $575–1,060 suite, $205–280 double, $175–250 single. Extra person in room, $30. Alc lunch, $25–50; alc dinner, $50–75.
Extras Wheelchair accessible; 1 room equipped for disabled. Airport/station pickups. Pets allowed. Cribs, babysitting available. German, French, Spanish spoken. A Rosewood Hotel; Member, Leading Hotels of the World, Preferred Hotels Worldwide.

EL PASO 79901   Map 11

We're trying hard to track down some El Paso inns or small hotels more typical to this guide than the hotel listed below, but sure could use your help with suggestions!

Westin Paso del Norte   *Tel:* (915) 534–3000
101 South El Paso Street   (800) 228–3000

"What a treat! A refurbished old hotel (listed on the National Register of Historic Places) with a new section built on in front. The result is a top notch hotel. Huge bathrooms and wonderful rooms done with nice wood, real brass, harmonious drapes. Room service was the best we've ever had, although we weren't brave enough to try the 'old Paso Del Norte Peanut Butter Sandwich, consisting of whole wheat bread with peanut butter, avocado slices, and pimientos . . . an original recipe served since 1930.' One highlight of the hotel was the bar located in the old hotel's lobby. Overhead is an enormous stained-glass dome made by Tiffany." *(SC)* More comments please.

Open All year.
Rooms 375 suites and doubles, all with full private bath, telephone, TV; most with desk.
Facilities 2 restaurants, lobby/lounge, courtyard, health club. Swimming pool, underground parking garage.

Location W TX. Downtown, 1 block from Civic Center, 10 min. from airport. Walking distance to Mexican border.
Credit cards All major credit cards.
Rates Room only, $210–950 suite, $108–210 double, $93–210 single. Extra person in room, $15. No charge for children under 18 in parents' room. Reduced weekend rates.
Extras Wheelchair accessible; some guest rooms specially equipped for disabled.

FORT DAVIS 79734 Map 11

Information please: Another Fort Davis possibility is the **Limpia Hotel**, a 20-room restored turn-of-the-century hotel on the town square; rates are very reasonable and rooms presumably live up to the hotel's name and more (P.O. Box 822; 915–426–3237).

Indian Lodge
State Highway 118, Box 786

Tel: (915) 426–3254

The original part of the Indian Lodge was built in the 1930s by the Civilian Conservation Corps; many walls in this part of the adobe structure are more than 18 inches thick. The workers also constructed much of the lodge's furniture. In 1967, 24 additional rooms were added and the entire structure was renovated.

Located in the Davis Mountains State Park at an elevation of about 5,000 feet, this area stays relatively cool even in summer and is somewhat greener than the surrounding region.

"The Trans-Pecos region of Texas is filled with rugged scenery, historical sites, and a fascinating variety of birds and wildlife, but it has few places to stay that match the surroundings. The Indian Lodge is a notable exception. The road to the park winds next to a river, with cottonwoods overhead and rocky crags on either side, leading to the white adobe lodge stretching across the green hillside. Inside, the rooms are clean and attractive, with magnificent furniture, including some of the most comfortable beds we've ever found on the road. Our reception was matter-of-fact rather than warm, but everyone responded quickly to any request we made, and the waitresses were friendly and fast. The food is plain, down-home American, and the menu is limited. But what they do, they do well—good biscuits and rolls, tender liver and onions, and wonderful homemade pies—pecan and buttermilk one night, apple and coconut the next—just like Mom used to make. The restored cavalry outpost at Fort Davis, the McDonald Observatory, the spring-fed swimming pool at Balmorhea State Recreational Area, and Big Bend National Park are all within driving distance. Indian Lodge is also a great place to watch birds, hike, read, or just to gaze down the canyon from the veranda." *(Theresa Ryan)*

Open All year. Closed 2 weeks in mid-Jan.
Rooms 1 suite, 38 doubles, all with full private bath, telephone, TV, air-conditioning.
Facilities Restaurant, lobby, veranda. Heated swimming pool. Hiking nearby.
Location W TX. Trans-Pecos Country, Davis Mts. Approx. 4 m NW of Rtes. 17 and 118 in Fort Davis.
Credit cards None accepted.
Rates Room only, $45 suite, $35–40 double, $30 single. Extra adult in room, $5; extra child 6–12, $2; under 6, free. $2 daily park entrance fee additional.

FORT WORTH 76106   Map 11

Stockyards Hotel   *Tel:* (817) 625–6427
109 East Exchange Avenue, P.O. Box 4558   (800) 423–8471

Adjoining Dallas to the west, Forth Worth lacks the flash of the "Big D" but has retained more of its frontier traditions. The Stockyards Hotel is located in the heart of the Stockyards Historic District, where cattle are still penned and auctioned. Along with assorted cattle barons and oil magnates, Bonnie and Clyde are said to have stayed at this hotel in 1933. The hotel has been beautifully restored and refurnished, and rooms are decorated in one of four themes: Indian, cowboy, mountain, or Victorian; public rooms are done in what the hotel calls "Cattle Baron Baroque." *(Keith Jurgens, also CI)*

Open All year.
Rooms 6 suites, 46 doubles, all with telephone, radio, TV, air-conditioning. Some with desk, fireplace, Jacuzzi, wet bar.
Facilities Restaurant, saloon, 3 atrium lobbies.
Location N TX. Historic District, on Riverwalk. From I-35W, take NE 28 St. W exit for 1½ m to N. Main, turn left (S) on Main, left on Exchange.
Credit cards Amex, CB, DC, MC, Visa.
Rates Room only, $175–350 suite, $105–145 double, $95–135 single. Extra person in room, $15. 20% AARP discount. Weekend packages. Alc breakfast, $4.50–6.50; alc lunch, $6; alc dinner, $20–25.
Extras Wheelchair accessible; some guest rooms specially equipped for the disabled. Cribs available. Spanish spoken.

FREDERICKSBURG   Map 11

One of Texas' most attractive towns, Fredericksburg was settled by German farmers in 1846. A strong sense of its original heritage has been retained, and some families still speak German. Traditional German food is widely available, from delicious baked goods to sausages and Wienerschnitzel. Bed and breakfast accommodation is available in dozens of homes, many of them tiny Sunday Houses, built to accommodate farmers when they came to town for Saturday market and Sunday church. Most of these Sunday houses can be booked through one of the following reservation services: Bed & Breakfast of Fredericksburg (102 South Cherry Street; 512–997–4712); Gastehaus Schmidt (501 West Main Street; 512–997–5612); Varney's Chemist Loft (310 East Main Street; 512–997–8615 or 800–284–0526).

Fredericksburg is in Hill Country, 78 miles west of Austin, and 69 miles northwest of San Antonio.

Baron's Creek Inn   *Tel:* (512) 997–9398
110 East Creek Street

One of Fredericksburg's larger B&Bs, the Baron's Creek Inn is a stone block building with gingerbread woodwork on its two-story porches. Built in 1911, several gables and indoor plumbing were added in later renovations.

The backyard has a grape arbor and a Sunday House. Also on the grounds is a circular tank house that was used originally for storing meat and water, and for making wine. In 1983 it was bought by Sandra and Spencer Switzer, who restored it as a B&B. Soft colors and rattan furnishings highlight Texas antiques; rates include a continental breakfast. *(Keith Jurgens)*

Open All year.
Rooms 1 Sunday House, 4 suites with private bath, TV, air-conditioning, ceiling fans, kitchenette.
Facilities Porch, gardens.
Location 1 block E and 2 blocks S of Courthouse. At corner of E. Creek St. and Llano St.
Restrictions No smoking. Children under 13 in Sunday House only.
Credit cards None accepted.
Rates B&B, $75–85 double. Extra person in room, $15.

GALVESTON 77550   Map 11

Texas's oldest city of prominence, Galveston has a restored historic area of note that is home to several historic hotels and B&Bs

Information please: Two B&Bs we'd like reports on are **Dickens Loft,** occupying a restored commercial building, with spacious rooms done in contemporary and antique furnishings (2021 Strand; 409–762–1653), and the **Gilded Thistle,** one of Galveston's first B&Bs, in a century-old home furnished in period (1805 Broadway; 409–763–0194).

Start your Galveston visit at the Visitors Center, at #2016 on the historic Strand, to learn how the "Queen of the Gulf" developed, decayed, and was restored.

Since Galveston is very much a weekend escape for Houstonians, rates tend to be much higher on weekends.

The Tremont House   *Tel:* (409) 763–0300
2300 Ships Mechanic Row   (800) 874–2300

The history of the Tremont House goes back to 1839, when the fashionable hotel hosted such legendary folks as Sam Houston, Ulysses S. Grant, Clara Barton, Anna Pavlova, and Buffalo Bill. Destroyed by fire, the hotel was rebuilt in 1872 and maintained its prominence well past the turn-of-the-century, before it closed. Under the ownership of George and Cynthia Marshall, the Tremont reopened in 1984 on a new site, in a nineteenth-century building once home to a dry goods emporium. The handsome French mansard exterior now has a totally rebuilt interior, with a white-stuccoed atrium and guest rooms combining Victorian design elements with twentieth-century comforts. Most of the rooms have 14-foot ceilings and 11-foot windows, and are done in a dramatic color scheme of black and white, highlighted by brass beds. The hotel is home to two of Galveston's best restaurants, the Merchant Prince and the more elegant Wentletrap. *(TL)* More comments, please.

Open All year.
Rooms 8 suites, 103 doubles, all with full private bath, telephone.

Facilities Restaurant, bar/lobby.
Location 50 m S of Houston. Downtown, in historic Strand area. On Mechanic St., between 23rd and 24th Sts.
Credit cards All major cards.
Rates Room only, $115–140 suite, $100–115 double,$70–85 single. Extra person in room, $15; child under 14, free.
Extras Wheelchair accessible. Spanish, Chinese spoken.

Virginia Point Inn   *Tel:* (409) 763–2450
2327 Avenue K

Eleanor Catlow restored her turn-of-the-century neo-Mediterranean home as a B&B in 1985. Rates include a full breakfast of fresh fruit and juice, eggs, sausage, muffins, and coffee cake, plus afternoon wine and cheese.

"Gracious hospitality, beautiful home, and complete friendliness. Galveston's history, culture, and traditions are fascinating; one can really see the ongoing efforts at restoration and rehabilitation." *(GR)*

"Eleanor Catlow is a down-to-earth person who enjoys welcoming you into her home and making you comfortable. Renovated fairly recently, the inn is decorated with family antiques." *(Laurie Zampini)* More comments, please.

Open All year.
Rooms 4 doubles with private screened porches, 1 single—1 with full private bath, 4 with maximum of 4 people sharing bath. All with air conditioning.
Facilities Dining room, living room. 2/3 acre with flower gardens, croquet, badminton, bicycles. Off-street parking. Sailing on 40-ft. sloop offered to guests staying 2 or more nights. 9 blocks to Gulf of Mexico for swimming, fishing charters.
Location E TX. 45 m SE of Houston, on the Gulf of Mexico. Silk Stocking District, 7 blocks from both Strand and beach. Going S on Seawall Blvd., go right on Broadway, left on 24th to inn at corner of 24th and K Sts.
Restrictions No smoking in bedrooms. No children under 12.
Credit cards Amex, MC, Visa.
Rates B&B, $85–125 double, $60 single. 2-night minimum stay on holiday weekends. Corporate rates.
Extras Spanish spoken.

White Horse Inn   *Tel:* (409) 762–2632
2217 Broadway   (800) 762–2632

The White Horse Inn was built in 1884 by J.F. Smith, and remained in the Smith family until 1978. The finest materials available were used in its construction—mahogany, cypress, and yellow pine. The ceilings are nearly 15 feet high, and the massive 12-foot doors were painted to look like fancy burl woods. The elegant slate mantels have Eastlake mirrored overmantels, and stained glass windows are in good supply. The Smith family were prominent local hardware and ships' merchants, and operated a three-story store on the Strand, now home of La King's Confectionery.

The residence was converted into an inn in 1985, and was purchased by Robert Clark in 1987. Rooms are furnished with period antiques and reproductions, including half-tester beds. The floors are original, and the wall coverings are hand-printed reproductions of Victorian designs. The brass chandelier in the front parlor is original to the house, and was still gas-operated as late as 1984. Rates include a continental breakfast.

"This B&B is housed in a gracious and spacious Victorian home built in 1885. Owner Robert Clark has filled it with objets d'art gathered by him from every corner of the earth, all displayed with elegance and taste. The rooms are spacious, each with a private bath. Drinking an afternoon glass of wine on the porch with Mr. Clark is a rewarding experience." *(Michael Leviton)*

Open All year.
Rooms 6 doubles—all with private bath and/or shower, air-conditioning. 2 rooms in main house with balcony, 4 rooms in carriage house.
Facilities Dining room, parlor, porch, patio, garden. Limited off-street parking.
Location Close to downtown. Some traffic noise in front rooms.
Credit cards MC, Visa.
Rates B&B, $80–100 double. Corporate, weekly rates; senior discounts.

HILLSBORO 76645   Map 11

Tarlton House of 1895   *Tel:* (817) 582–7216
211 North Pleasant Street   (214) 349–0266

In 1985 native Texans Jean and Charles Rhoads opened the Tarlton House as an inn, after extensive renovation and redecorating. Built in 1895, this three-story Queen Anne Victorian features a front entrance with 123 pieces of beveled glass, seven carved oak mantels with tiled fireplaces, and period furnishings.

"The inn is a very large Victorian that carries a national and Texas commemorative marker. The family lives on the first floor, and the guest rooms are on the second and third levels. The house is beautiful and is furnished with antiques. We had a delicious breakfast of pancakes, locally made sausage, fruit, and coffee. It was a wonderful escape from Dallas, and we are eager to return." *(Timothy Ladd)* More comments, please.

Open All year.
Rooms 2 suites, 7 doubles—7 with private shower and/or bath, 2 with maximum of 4 sharing bath. Some with desk, radio, fan, TV; all with air-conditioning.
Facilities 2 dining rooms, parlor, library, porch, flower garden. Tennis, golf nearby. 18 m to lake for swimming, fishing.
Location N TX, 60 m S of Dallas. Take I-35E from Dallas, I-35W from Fort Worth to Hillsboro. Take Hwy. 22 to Courthouse Sq. Turn E onto Franklin St., go 2 blocks to Pleasant St.
Restrictions No smoking. No children under 12.
Credit cards MC, Visa.
Rates B&B, $172–211 suite, $68–86 double. Extra person in room, $15. 2-night holiday minimum. Alc lunch $8, alc dinner $15.
Extras Airport/station pickups, $5 local, $30 Dallas.

HOUSTON   Map 11

Houston is the largest and most cosmopolitan city in Texas. It's home to a major convention and sports complex—the Astrodome—three prominent universities, and NASA's Lyndon B. Johnson Space Center, the center of the U.S. space program (yes, you can see "Mission Control").

Information please: The **Remington on Post Oak Park**, a 248-room Rosewood Hotel listed in earlier editions, recently underwent a change of name and ownership. As of January, 1989, it became the **Ritz-Carlton, Houston** (1919 Briar Oaks Lane, 77027; 713–840–7600 or 800–241–3333). Since both Rosewood and Ritz-Carlton have equally good names in the ranks of luxury hoteliers, we expect the same high standards to prevail, but would appreciate your reports.

La Colombe d'Or   *Tel:* (713) 524–7999
3410 Montrose Boulevard 77006

In 1980 Stephen Zimmerman purchased this elegant mansion, built in 1923, and transformed it into a jewel of a hotel and restaurant. Each suite has its own dining room, furnished with original art, antiques, and quality reproductions. Rates include a continental breakfast plus evening wine and fruit. Guests may dine in their suite or in the restaurant. Although the menus change seasonally, a recent dinner included grilled marinated duck with salad and julienned vegetables with Creole mustard dressing, Gulf snapper topped with crabmeat and lemon-butter sauce, and white chocolate mousse with mocha cream for dessert.

"The restaurant is perfectly divine! If you arrive after it's closed, cold food, fruit, and wine (chilling in a bucket) await you. Rooms are stunning." *(Irene Rawlings)* "The public rooms are lavishly done and our leisurely meal was cooked to perfection." *(CI)*

And another viewpoint: "My suite could have used better lighting and soundproofing—I was disturbed by the rather animated conversation of my neighbors." *(MA)*

Open All year. Closed Christmas Day, New Year's.
Rooms 6 suites, all with full private bath, telephone, radio, TV, desk, air-conditioning, dining room.
Facilities Restaurant, bar, living room, library, hot tub.
Location 5 min. SW of downtown, near University of St. Thomas, Museum of Fine Arts, Rice University, and Menil Art Foundation. Take Rte. 59 or Main St. SW from downtown, N on Montrose.
Credit cards Amex, DC, MC, Visa.
Rates B&B, $150–400 suite. Alc lunch, $14–18; alc dinner, $40–50.
Extras French, Spanish spoken. Member, Relais et Chateaux.

The Lancaster Hotel   *Tel:* (713) 228–9500
701 Texas Avenue at Louisiana 77002   (800) 231–0336

The Lancaster is a small luxury hotel offering every possible service and amenity, from terry robes and mineral water, to a daily newspaper and personal umbrella. Designed to give the feeling of an exclusive English club, rooms are decorated with marble, brass, English fabrics, and 19th-century landscapes and furniture. The Lancaster Grille carries out the same theme with dark woods and hunting prints. The cuisine (fortunately) is not British and favors fresh Gulf seafood. *(Keith Jurgens)* More comments, please.

Open All year.
Rooms 9 suites, 85 doubles—all with full private bath, telephone, radio, TV, desk, air-conditioning.
Facilities Restaurant, bar, lobby. Health club adjacent; jogging trails nearby. Concierge service. 24-hr. room service. Valet parking.
Location Downtown. Across the street from Texas Commerce Tower, Johnes Hall, Alley Theater. Short walk to Pennzoil Plaza, Shell Plaza, Republic Bank Center, Convention Center.
Credit cards All major credit cards.
Rates Room only, $275–700 suite, $150–185 double, $130–160 single, not including 14% tax. Extra person in room, $25. Alc breakfast, $5–12; alc lunch, $25; alc dinner, $35. Weekend rate, $99; theater package.
Extras Wheelchair accessible; 11 guest rooms equipped for disabled. Free downtown limo service. Small pets allowed, deposit required. Cribs, babysitting available. Spanish spoken.

Sara's Bed & Breakfast Inn
941 Heights Boulevard 77008

Tel: (713) 868–1130

We are delighted to add this reasonably priced B&B to our list of elegant but mostly expensive hotel entries in Houston. Sara's B&B was built at the turn-of-the-century as a one-story Victorian cottage. Expanded many times over the years, the most recent addition—a second floor with a turret and widow's walk—was not constructed until 1980. In 1983, Donna and Tillman Arledge bought the building and restored it as a B&B. Rates include a breakfast of bread or muffins, fresh fruit and juice, and coffee. "One of the cleanest, most elegant B&Bs I've ever visited." *(Kerstin Block)* The inn is in Houston Heights, in a historic area with over 90 structures listed on the National Register.

Open All year.
Rooms 1 2-bedroom suite with 2 baths, kitchen; 11 doubles—1 with private bath, 10 with shared bath.
Facilities Parlor, balcony, widow's walk, deck with hot tub.
Location Houston Heights. 4 m to downtown.
Restrictions Smoked restricted.
Credit cards Amex, MC, Visa.
Rates B&B, $96 suite, $50–60 double.

JEFFERSON 75657   Map 11

Jefferson was a boom town in the late 1800s, a major inland port where goods from the East were unloaded and cargoes of cotton and timber were onloaded for the return trip to New Orleans. Today many of its historic antebellum homes and buildings have been restored and are open to visitors. You can tour the area by surrey, on a bayou cruise, or by steam train. The town offers a wide selection of restaurants, antique shops, and B&B inns. Jefferson lies between two lakes, Caddo (the only natural lake in Texas) and Lake O' The Pines, for swimming, fishing, and boating.

Jefferson is located in the piney woods of northeast Texas, 15 miles north of Marshall, 50 miles south of Texarkana, and 50 miles west of Shreveport, Louisiana. From I-30 or I-20, take Highway 59 to Jefferson; exit at Highway 49E.

Information please: Current reports on the **Hotel Jefferson** (124 West Austin; 214–665–2631) are requested. Erected in 1851 for use as a cotton warehouse, it was later used as a livery stable, skating rink, concert hall, and saloon, and has had almost as many names as functions. Rates for its 22 rooms are reasonable; meals are not served but several restaurants offering a full breakfast are located within walking distance.

Excelsior House
211 West Austin

Tel: (214) 665–2513

The Excelsior House is a small hotel that has been in continuous operation since the late 1850s and has been owned and run by the Jessie Allen Wise Garden Club for the past 27 years. The hotel is built of brick and timber and has a lacy ironwork gallery. Rooms are furnished with authentic antiques of fine rosewood, cherry, and mahogany.

"The hotel staff is proud of the Excelsior, and their pride is apparent in the relaxed and friendly way in which they greet guests. The rooms are charming, and many have a historical background; a number of famous guests have shared in the hotel's history, including Ulysses S. Grant and Oscar Wilde. The famous plantation breakfast is itself worth a trip to Jefferson." *(Bill Mays)*

Open All year. Closed first weekend in May.
Rooms 2 suites, 12 doubles, all with private shower and/or bath, TV, air-conditioning, ceiling fan. 5 with desk.
Facilities Drawing room, dining room, sun porch, enclosed courtyard with fountains, flowers.
Location Historic downtown district. At intersection of Hwys. 59 and 49, go E on 49 (Broadway) and bear to right at Polk. Turn right at second light (Austin).
Restrictions No smoking in lobby. No children under 4.
Credit cards None accepted.
Rates Room only, $60 suite, $40–$50 double. Extra person in room, $5. Full breakfast, $4.50 adult; $2.25 child.
Extras Limited wheelchair access.

McKay House
306 East Delta Street

Tel: (214) 655–7322
(214) 348–1929

Tom and Peggy Taylor, owners of the historic McKay House since 1985, provide their guests with Victorian-style nightgowns and sleep shirts to put them in the mood of 1851, when their Greek Revival cottage was built by the founder of Jefferson. Rooms are completely furnished in antiques and have 14-foot ceilings and heart-of-pine floors. Guests are called in for breakfast to the melodies of the Taylors' antique music box and can relax on the porch swing with a cold glass of lemonade.

"From the minute you step inside the front door until the innkeepers bid you farewell, you feel pampered. The Taylors are knowledgeable about the history of the McKay House and of the town of Jefferson. They have made it a point to know the 'must do and see' places in Jefferson, and are always ready to make recommendations. They can suggest a restaurant to please both taste and pocketbook, and will gladly make reservations as well. The charm of the McKay House is evident in the meticulous care taken in decorating each room with period furnishings. The Taylors carry out the period theme to the last detail, dressing in period clothing to serve an ample, delicious, and nutritious breakfast. Breakfast in bed is served on special occasions." *(Nina Cox)*

"McKay House is beautifully and authentically restored. It is on a quiet side street within easy walking distance of downtown tourist attractions, restaurants, and museums. Tom and Peggy make you feel right at home. The house is always immaculately clean, and beds have excellent mattresses and pillows; bathrooms have all the extras—Crabtree & Evelyn soaps, shampoos, and hand lotion." *(Eric Johansen)*

Open All year.
Rooms 1 2-bedroom suite, 4 doubles—all with private bath and/or shower (suite with 1 bath). All with desk, air-conditioning, fan, fireplace. 2 rooms in annex.
Facilities Morning room, common room with organ, music box. Veranda with porch swing, gardens.
Location 6 blocks from center, near intersection of Hwys. 59 and 49.
Restrictions No smoking. Children welcome by prior arrangement.
Credit cards MC, Visa.
Rates B&B, $120 suite, $55–80. Extra person in room, $15. 2-night minimum for special events/holidays.

Pride House   *Tel:* (214) 665–2675
409 East Broadway

This turn of the century Victorian is owned by Ruthmary Jordon, a former restaurateur and an initiator of Texas's bed & breakfast boom. Six guest rooms are in the main house; an additional four are in the "Dependency"—a saltbox cabin in the side yard that was the original servants' quarters.

"Ruthmary immediately makes you feel at home and treats you like a special friend." *(Roberta C. Selvidge)* "The bath, heating, cleanliness, plumbing, etc., were all fine. The food was served elegantly in charming dishes, and the smell of breakfast cooking woke me—what a nice way to be awakened." *(Dan & Linda West)*

"The house is comfortable and quiet, and each room has its own distinctive personality. The breakfast was very good sausage, croissants, and poached pears with crème fraiche. Best of all were the stained-glass windows in the rooms." *(NN, David W. Palmlund, Leslie Finer)*

"The Pride House is very large, with a beautiful staircase leading to the bedrooms. In the hallway is a 'food receiver' on which Ruthmary places your breakfast each morning. The house is located right at the edge of town, convenient to everything. I especially liked the old-fashioned bathtubs with the curtain that encircles them for the shower." *(Darlyne Stewart)*

An area for improvement: One respondent would have preferred the breakfast coffee to be served both hotter and weaker, most writers very much enjoyed their stay at the Pride House.

Open All year.
Rooms 1 suite, 9 doubles, all with private bath and/or shower, radio, desk, air-conditioning, ceiling fan. Some with balcony. 4 bedrooms in annex.
Facilities Dining room, common room with games, front porch.

Location In downtown historic district.
Restrictions Some traffic noise in front rooms. Children allowed in March only.
Credit cards MC, Visa.
Rates B&B, $65–75 suite, $55–65 double, $49 single. Extra person in room, $10.
2-night weekend minimum.
Extras Airport/station pickups.

Stillwater Inn
203 East Broadway

Tel: (214) 665–8415

Sharon and Bill Stewart opened their 1890s-era Eastlake Victorian home as a restaurant in 1984; more recently they restored and insulated the upstairs for bed & breakfast guests. Rooms are furnished with antiques and contemporary country decor, and the queen-size beds are supplied with all-cotton sheets and down pillows. Bill is the chef in their French-accented restaurant; a recent dinner included a salad of lettuce, poached garlic, walnuts, and bacon with vinaigrette; grilled duck breast with wild rice and green peppercorn sauce; and Grand Marnier flan for dessert.

"The inn sits in a lovely tree-shaded lot near the center of town. One can easily walk to the many antique and specialty stores, local restaurants, and historic attractions. We stayed in a small guest cottage adjacent to the inn. A large raised four-poster bed occupied the main room, which had a raised ceiling and hand-hewn beams. There were many interesting accessories and decorations and the color scheme was beautifully chosen. A small front porch with comfortable antique rocking chairs and a flower basket added to its charm. Meals were served in the main building, appointed with period decor. Mr. Stewart is a superb chef; the wine list is impressive and the service excellent. Mrs. Stewart is a fabulous hostess." *(Mr. & Mrs. W.N. Cooke)*

"The breakfast room is cheerfully furnished with comfortable white wicker chairs and original antique Singer sewing-machine tables with white marble tops. Bill is an excellent chef; the service was very good, friendly and polite." *(Arie & Anna Ter Poorten)* "Breakfast consisted of freshly squeezed orange juice, coffee or tea, pastry, eggs, bacon, grits, and sourdough rolls. The guest rooms were immaculately clean, and everything was in good working order. The spacious modern bath held a supply of Crabtree & Evelyn toiletries." *(Paula & Terry Decker)* "Guest rooms are appointed with four-poster beds with antique quilts. A commitment to the use of fresh ingredients and beautiful presentation helps make the food taste even better." *(Moira Kuchla)*

Open All year. Restaurant closed Mon., Tues.
Rooms 1 cottage, 3 doubles—all with private bath and/or shower, TV, desk, air-conditioning. Radio, ceiling fan, refrigerator, coffeemaker in cottage.
Facilities Restaurant, breakfast room, living room, upstairs common areas with library, games, porch, garden.
Location 2 min. drive from center. 1 block from Hwy. 59.
Restrictions No smoking in guest rooms.
Credit cards MC, Visa.
Rates B&B, $80 cottage, $65–75 double. Extra person in room, $10. No tipping. Alc dinner, $25.
Extras Airport/station pickups.

KERRVILLE 78028 Map 11

Y. O. Ranch Hilton
2033 Sidney Baker, P.O. Box 1529

Tel: (512) 257–4440
In TX: (800) 531–2800

In 1880 Charles Schreiner founded the Y. O. Ranch, which now encompasses 50,000 acres (80 square miles). More recently the Schreiner family built the Y. O. Hilton, a luxury resort hotel constructed of native stone and timbers. The striking lobby is decorated with a seven-foot-high bronze sculpture, chandeliers made from Chisolm Trail branding irons, locally found arrowheads, and trophy mounts. Room furnishings are what you would expect to find in any first-class hotel but are highlighted by distinctively Texan rugs and wall decorations. The hotel restaurant offers continental cuisine, ranch-style cooking, and wild game from the Y. O. Ranch.

The original Y. O. Ranch is 30 miles away from the hotel. Still in the hands of the Schreiner family, this massive spread is a working ranch, with more than 1,000 registered Longhorns and other breeds of cattle, sheep, and goats, plus champion quarter horses. The ranch is also home to the nation's largest collection of free-roaming exotic animals—from antelope to giraffes to zebra. Ranch visits are by reservation only, so be sure to inquire in advance. Accommodations in rustic cabins are available on the ranch; call or write for details.

"We are native Texans and feel very strongly about our state not looking like the show *Dallas* in the eyes of the world. We believe the Kerrville area best represents our state's warm hospitality, friendly open people, and distinctive food and crafts.

"We stayed in the Y. O. Hilton, and although their brochure is too slick for my taste, the hotel and its staff are not. They have combined the old and the new Texas with an eye to the artistic and the convenient. If you want anything special, we found an interesting and intelligent fellow named Vic Jones; he stands by the front desk and is only too happy to answer questions about the ranch and hotel and to accommodate your special requests. During our stay, we ate at a wonderful French restaurant on the Ingram Road, called the Hunter's Lodge; readers should ask the hotel staff for details." *(Yvonne & Arnold Miller, also Keith Jurgens)*

"We stopped by for breakfast and enjoyed a wonderful meal with excellent service. Can't wait to return for an overnight stay." *(Carol Moritz)*

Open All year.
Rooms 12 suites, 188 doubles in 7 separate buildings. All with full private bath, telephone, radio, TV, air-conditioning. Some with wet bar, fireplace.
Facilities Restaurant, saloon with live entertainment, bar, video game room, meeting rooms. Tennis, hot tub, heated swimming pool, golf course. Canoeing, tubing, fishing, swimming, sailing, waterskiing at nearby Guadalupe River and Ingram Lake.
Location Central TX Hill Country. 1 hr. NW of San Antonio, 2 hrs. W of Austin, 15 min. from Kerrville. Hotel is near intersection of Rtes. 534 and 16. 1½ m from town.
Credit cards Amex, CB, DC, Discover, MC, Visa.
Rates Room only, $150–230 suite, $85–105 double, $75 single. No charge for children of any age in parents' room. Extra person in room, $10. Senior discount. Alc breakfast, $3–9; alc lunch, $5–12; alc dinner, $10–20.

Extras Wheelchair accessible; 10 rooms equipped for disabled. Airport pickups, $30. Pets permitted. Cribs, babysitting available. Spanish spoken.

LAJITAS ON THE RIO GRANDE 79852 Map 11

Information please: Another possibility within the boundaries of Big Bend Park itself is the **Chisos Mountains Lodge,** with a handsome setting at 5400 feet. Both motel rooms and cottages are available at very reasonable rates, but reservations must be made well in advance (National Park Concessions, Big Bend National Park 79834-9999; 915–477–2291).

Badlands Hotel　　　　　　　　　　　*Tel:* (915) 424–3471
Mailing address: Star Route 70,　　　　　　　(800) 527–4078
Box 400, Terlingua 79852

Bordering the Rio Grande, right at the western edge of Big Bend National Park, Lajitas is a restored frontier town, with an old trading post, saloon, and the historic Badlands hotel, completely restored with four-poster beds and period decor. More contemporary facilities were also added during the reconstruction—air-conditioning, a swimming pool, and tennis courts, as well as the Lajitas Museum and Desert Garden displaying the history of the area and the flowers and plants native to the Big Bend. *(KJ)* More comments, please.

Open All year.
Rooms 19 condominiums, 81 doubles, all with full private bath, telephone, TV, desk, air-conditioning.
Facilities Restaurant, saloon with live entertainment, meeting rooms, art gallery. Tennis courts, heated swimming pool, horseback riding, float trips, golf. Near the Rio Grande for rafting, fishing.
Location SW TX. Near NW entrance of Big Bend National Park.
Credit cards Amex, MC, Visa.
Rates Room only, $60 double, $55 single. Extra person in room, $2. Tipping "not expected."
Extras Wheelchair accessible. Airport/station pickups. Pets permitted. Play equipment available. Spanish spoken.

MARATHON 79842 Map 11

The Gage Hotel　　　　　　　　　　　*Tel:* (915) 386–4205
West Highway 90, P.O. Box 46

In the 1920s Alfred Gage, an ex-Vermonter and prosperous Texas banker, businessman, and rancher, decided he needed a suitable place to stay while checking on his 500,000-acre ranch. Marathon was then the major area railhead for shipping cattle east, so he hired the region's finest architects and builders. In 1927 the hotel opened, and it quickly became popular with the cattlemen and ranchers of West Texas. After years of neglect, the hotel was purchased in 1978 by J. P. Bryan of Houston and has been completely restored to its original atmosphere. Rooms are decorated with Texan and

Mexican antiques and artifacts of the Tarahumara Indians. The restaurant specializes in West Texas border cuisine, from the traditional chicken steak to enchiladas.

"The Gage Hotel caught my interest one evening while traveling on U.S. 90 through Marathon. I stopped in and found a small, reasonably priced restaurant inside the hotel, with delicious mesquite-smoked fajitas and blueberry cobbler for dessert. Many points of interest are within an hour or two drive, including Big Bend National Park, float trips on the Rio Grande, and the McDonald Observatory." *(John E. Austin, also MM)*

Open All year.
Rooms 13 doubles, 7 singles—7 with private shower, 13 with maximum of 5 people sharing bath. All with air-conditioning, fan.
Facilities Lobby, bar/lounge, restaurant, ¼ acre. Fishing, swimming, horseback riding, hiking, bicycling nearby.
Location SW TX, at intersection of Hwys. 90 and 385. 50 m N of Big Bend National Park, 150 m SW of Midland, 58 m S of I-10 at Fort Stockton. In center of town.
Restrictions No smoking in restaurant.
Credit cards MC, Visa.
Rates Room only, $35–55 double. Extra person in room, $5. Children under 13 free in parents' room. Full breakfast, $4–6; alc lunch, $6–10, alc dinner, $17.
Extras Airport/station pickups, fee. Pets permitted. Cribs available. Spanish spoken.

MARSHALL 75670   Map 11

Marshall was settled in 1838, and when Texas seceded from the Union, it was one of the state's largest and richest towns. Today, three square blocks surrounding the Ginocchio have been declared a National Historic District.

Information please: In addition to the listing below, another B&B possibility is **La Maison Malfacon**, an 1881 Greek Revival home with five antique-filled guest rooms and hand-crafted woodwork. Children are welcome (there's a bedroom with toys just for them); bicycles and a swimming pool are available for guest enjoyment. The $45–60 rates include a full breakfast (700 East Rusk Street; 214–935–6039).

Ginocchio Hotel   *Tel:* (214) 935–7635
707 North Washington

In its heyday, 26 trains passed through Marshall daily, each stopping in at the Ginocchio Hotel for food, water, and accommodation. For 25 years the hotel was known as the finest lodging and dining establishment between New Orleans and Denver. Three U.S. Presidents—Harding, Taft and Wilson—slept here. Shortly after the hotel opened in 1896 a representative from Thomas Edison convinced owner Charles Ginocchio to install two Edison arches, some newfangled lights that operated off wet cell batteries, recharged with a wind generator. He agreed, and the hotel had the first electric lights in the southwestern U.S.—a major tourist attraction in those days. Equally unusual is the woodwork in the hotel's lobby, a kind of curly pine found only in a small Louisiana forest. Ginocchio bought the entire stand of trees, and no similar wood has ever been found since.

After dining cars were added to the trains in 1921, the hotel began a slow decline, and was on the verge of demolition when the O'Tysons rescued it in 1987. They bought and restored its structural integrity, then went on to return the hotel to its turn-of-the-century style and elegance. The Edison arches are still in place, as are the original pressed tin ceilings, chandeliers, and woodwork. Rates include coffee and the newspaper brought to your door at 7:30, followed by a breakfast of orange juice, fresh grapefruit or melon, pecan French toast and Canadian bacon; entrées change daily. Dinner portions are hearty with favorites ranging from chicken-fried steak to seafood pasta.

"An old hotel beautifully restored. All of the guest rooms are lovely, and the food, both in the casual lunch room and the formal dining room, is wonderful. The hotel even has a ghost." *(Gail Brown)*

Open All year. No lunch served Sat.; dinner served Thurs.–Sat.
Rooms 5 suites, 7 doubles with private bath and/or shower, air-conditioning.
Facilities Restaurant, lobby.
Location E TX, 150 m E of Dallas, 30 m W of Shreveport, Louisiana, 15 m S of Jefferson. Center of Historic District.
Restrictions Train noise in some rooms.
Credit cards MC, Visa.
Rates B&B, $85–125 suite, $50–75 double. Alc dinner, $15.

NEW BRAUNFELS 78130   Map 11

New Braunfels was founded in 1845 by Prince Carl of Solms, who left Germany with several hundred of his countrymen and purchased 1,000 acres in the new state of Texas. The town's heritage is preserved in a number of historic buildings; visitors also enjoy its many antique shops and Landa Park, with a small lake, two swimming pools, and a golf course. Two rivers, the Comal and the Guadalupe, flow through the city; the Comal—billed as "America's shortest river"—is everyone's favorite for tubing, and both are fun for swimming, canoeing, rafting, and fishing. Canyon Lake is 13 miles away for boating and waterskiing.

New Braunfels is in Hill Country, 32 miles northeast of San Antonio and 47 miles southwest of Austin in central Texas.

The Faust   *Tel:* (512) 625–7791
240 South Sequin

The Faust Hotel, built in 1928 and listed on the National Register of Historic Places, is elegantly decorated with period antiques. It underwent a major renovation in 1983. The hotel restaurant offers such American staples as blackened chicken, baby back ribs, and stuffed rainbow trout. *(Jan Walpole, also KC)* More comments, please.

Open All year.
Rooms 61 suites and doubles, all with private bath and/or shower, telephone, TV, desk, ceiling fans, air-conditioning.
Facilities Restaurant, bar/lounge.
Location Downtown. From I-35, turn N onto Seguin and follow Seguin to inn.
Credit cards Amex, DC, Discover, MC, Visa.

Rates Room only, $97–110 suite, $35–60 double, $32–55 single. Children stay free in parents' room. 10% senior discount.
Extras Cribs available. Spanish spoken.

Prince Solms Inn
Tel: (512) 625–9169
295 East San Antonio Street

One of Texas's best-known historic inns, the Prince Solms has been in continuous operation since it was built, by German craftsmen, in 1898. Constructed to last, the inn is set on 36-inch footings, with 13- and 14-foot ceilings and exterior walls 30 inches thick in the cellar and 18 inches thick on the first and second floors, designed to keep out the Texas heat. The inn is furnished entirely with antiques and has Victorian reproduction wallpapers throughout. The innkeepers note (with refreshing candor) that the furnishings, decor, fixtures, air-conditioning, and plumbing of the inn are constantly being upgraded, but that "the thin [interior] walls are original, so don't slam your doors. If you plan to laugh loudly, pull the covers up over your head."

"The food was good, and the atmosphere charming, with a good piano player; the inn is most appealing." *(Bob Brosewell, also YM)* More comments, please.

Open All year. Restaurant closed Mon., Christmas Eve, New Year's Day.
Rooms 2 suites, 8 doubles—8 with full private bath, 2 with private shower. All with air-conditioning.
Facilities Restaurant, bar/lounge with piano player, parlor with TV, games; patio, balcony, courtyard. Swimming, fishing, tubing, rafting, tennis, golf, biking nearby.
Location 1 block from main plaza. 1 block east of traffic circle.
Restrictions Considerable traffic noise; thin interior walls. No children.
Credit cards MC, Visa.
Rates B&B, $95–110 suite, $50–80 double. Extra person in room, $10. Tipping discouraged. 2-night weekend minimum May–Sept. Alc lunch, $5–8; alc dinner, $20.
Extras Station/airport pickups with 48 hours' notice.

SALADO 76571
Map 11

Founded in the 1850s, Salado prospered through the end of the century, with the swift current of Salado Creek powering eight local textile and gristmills. When the railroads bypassed the town, the population dropped, and little changed in Salado. Today the town has been revitalized, with travelers enjoying the fine food at the famous Stagecoach Inn (see below), the haute couture at Grace Jones's boutique, the unusually large number of historic homes (many now home to antique and craft shops), and the Central Texas Museum, founded to relate the history of Central Texas.

Salado is 45 miles north of Austin via I-35.

Inn on the Creek
Tel: (817) 947–5554
Center Circle, P.O. Box 261

The oldest section of the Inn on the Creek was built in 1892 and was moved to its current location when the inn was started in 1985. Although a modern wing was added at the same time, most of the guest rooms and common rooms are in the older portion and feature the original wood detailing, trim, and doors. Innkeepers Lynn and Suzi Epps have furnished the inn with Victorian pieces and rugs, including brass, walnut, and canopy beds, plus old family photographs. Rates include a full country breakfast; a fixed menu four-course dinner is served on weekends by advance reservation. *(Marlene Fisher)* More comments, please.

Open All year. Restaurant open Fri., Sat. evenings only.
Rooms 1 suite, 6 rooms, all with full private bath, telephone, TV.
Facilities Dining room, living room, porch. On creek. Golf nearby.
Location From I-35, take Robertson Rd. exit and go E to Main St. Go right on Main St., then left on Royal. After two blocks, go N on Center Circle to inn on left.
Restrictions No smoking. "Small children welcome but must be supervised at all times."
Credit cards Amex, MC, Visa.
Rates B&B, $105 suite, $65–75 double.

Stagecoach Inn   *Tel:* (817) 947–5111
Old Chisholm Trail, Box 97

Dating back to the 1850s, the Stagecoach was built to accommodate travelers following the Chisolm Trail. It was restored by the Van Bibber family over 40 years ago. The inn's restaurant is famous for its country Texas cooking and has long been a popular stop for those driving between Austin and Dallas. Fixed-price lunches and dinners include prime rib and plate-size steaks, fried chicken, baked ham, and lamb, accompanied by salads, fresh vegetables, and the "tastiest hush puppies in Texas." Homemade pies and ice creams and hot fruit cobblers head up the dessert list. The guest rooms are all located in an adjacent motel wing, with spacious rooms and the decor you'd expect in a quality motel.

"Delicious food and very comfortable rooms. The waitresses quote the menu, which always consists of several delicious courses. The inn is set on the banks of a creek where one sees children inner-tubing and swimming." *(Marlene Fisher)*

Open All year.
Rooms 80 suites and doubles, all with full private bath, TV, air conditioning. Some with private balcony, patio.
Facilities Restaurant, meeting rooms, coffee shop. Swimming pool, mineral therapy pool, lighted tennis courts, shuffleboard, horsehoes, Ping-Pong, badminton, volleyball, play equipment. Fishing, tubing, jogging, hiking, bicycling, golf nearby.
Location 48 m N of Austin, 16 m S of Temple. Just off on I-35.
Credit cards Amex, DC, MC, Visa.
Rates Room only, $67 suite, $43–54 double, $37–48 single. Extra person in room, $3; children under 12 stay free in parents' room.
Extras Cribs, babysitting available.

SAN ANTONIO   Map 11

San Antonio, in South Texas, combines over 250 years of Spanish, Mexican, German, and Texan cultures with the attractions of the contemporary downtown area and its handsome Riverwalk. Although most Americans know of the city because of the Alamo, its Spanish heritage can best be seen in the missions of San Antonio and the Spanish Governor's Palace.

Information please: San Antonio has a number of historic hotels, most dating back to the turn of the century, which have recently been totally restored. **The Crockett Hotel** borders the Alamo and is listed on the National Register of Historic Places. Its 202 rooms have been completely restored in very contemporary decor (320 Bonham 78205; 512–225–6500 or 800–531–5537). Several other San Antonio hotels—the Menger, the Gunter, and the Mansion del Rio—combine nineteenth-century history and twentieth-century amenities but have over 300 rooms. A B&B possibility is **Terrell Castle** (950 East Grayson Street 78208; 512–271–9145), a 25-room mansion built a century ago. Reports on all are requested.

Another B&B possibility in San Antonio is the **Norton Brackenridge House** (230 Madison, 78204; 512–271–3442), located six blocks from downtown in the King William Historic District. Its five guest rooms feature original pine floors, double-hung windows, high ceilings, antique decor, and king- and queen-sized beds; rates range from $65–85 daily.

If you need a rest from San Antonio's big-city pace, drive about 20 miles (and 100 years) west along Route 90 to Castroville, home of the **Landmark Inn** (see entry). Near Castroville is the town of La Coste, home to the **Swan and Railway Inn**, a rather unusual five guest room B&B with swimming pool, sauna, Jacuzzi, and daily exercise classes. Rates include three light vegetarian meals per day (North Front Street & FM 471, P.O. Box 446, La Coste, 78039; 512–762–3742).

The Fairmount Hotel
401 South Alamo

Tel: (512) 224–8800
(800) 642–3363

Built in 1906, the Fairmount is a brick Italianate Victorian structure with limestone trim. In 1985 it was noted in the *Guinness Book of World Records* as the largest building ever moved in one piece, and the heaviest object ever transported over city streets. The restoration process which followed its move resulted in rooms luxuriously decorated in soft colors with canopy beds and overstuffed chairs, along with first-rate contemporary art. The hotel restaurant enjoys a good reputation, combining southwestern and nouvelle cuisine. *(MW)* More comments, please.

Open All year. Restaurant closed Sun.
Rooms 17 suites, 20 doubles—all with private bath and/or shower, telephone, radio, TV, desk, air-conditioning, fan. Some with balcony. Suites with VCR, stereo.
Facilities Lobby, restaurant, breakfast room, bar with entertainment; living room/parlor on each floor. Courtyard. Concierge service, valet parking, 24-hr. room service.
Location Downtown historic district. At corner of S. Alamo and Nueva Sts. 1 block to Riverwalk, 2 blocks to Alamo, across street from convention center.
Restrictions Light sleepers should request rooms away from street side.
Credit cards Amex, CB, DC, MC, Visa.
Rates Room only, $275–375 suite, $145–200 double, not including 13% tax. Corporate, package rates. Weekend B&B rate, $195 suite, $125 double. Alc lunch, $10–12; alc dinner, $40–50.
Extras Some rooms equipped for disabled. Cribs, babysitting available. Spanish spoken. Member, Small Luxury Hotels & Resorts.

Plaza San Antonio
555 South Alamo 78205

"The Plaza is San Antonio's quintessential hostelry—a garden hotel with all sorts of colorful game birds wandering the grounds by day and perching high in the trees at night. Small enough to pay personal attention to each guest, but not so small as to lack such luxuries as tennis courts, exercise room, swimming pool, and private dining rooms in small landmark restored buildings with fireplaces. The Anaqua Dining Room is noted for being one of the best in Texas. Scene of famous wine-tasting dinners and headquarters for both 'Kings of Fiesta' in April." *(Logan Stewart)*

Another reader had a very different experience: "Although we had no complaints about the physical appearance of the hotel, we thought the hotel was cold, pretentious, unfriendly and overpriced. The desk clerk and concierge gave us the impression that they had better things to do than helping us." More comments, please.

Open All year.
Rooms 10 suites, 240 doubles, all with full private bath, telephone, radio, TV, air-conditioning, hair dryers. Some with desk, balcony.
Facilities Restaurant, bar/lounge with entertainment. 6 acres with gardens, 2 lighted tennis courts, heated swimming pool with whirlpool, health club with sauna, bicycles, croquet. Hunting, golf, riding, water sports nearby. Valet parking.
Location Downtown historic district. 3 blocks from Alamo, across street from convention center, 1 block to Riverwalk.
Restrictions No smoking in some guest rooms.
Credit cards All major cards accepted.
Rates Room only, $260–370 suite, $125–165 double, $105–145 single. Extra person in room, $20. No charge for children under 18 in parents' room. Package rates $79–89. Alc breakfast, $6–10; alc lunch, $15; alc dinner, $35.
Extras Wheelchair accessible; 2 rooms equipped for disabled. Airport/station pickups. Free limo to business district. Small pets on leash permitted. Cribs, babysitting, play equipment available. French, Spanish, German spoken.

SAN MARCOS 78666   **Map 11**

Crystal River Inn
326 West Hopkins Street

Tel: (512) 396–3739

The gateway to Hill Country, some people may know San Marcos only for the caves of Wonder World and for Aquarena Springs, a popular commercial attraction whose highlight may well be Ralph the Swimming Pig. Others appreciate the town on a more intellectual level as the home of Southwest Texas State University. But perhaps the best of San Marcos can be found at the Crystal River Inn, owned by Cathy and Mike Dillon since its founding in 1984. The inn was built in 1883 by Judge William Wood, a successful banker and rancher and a founder of the local university. Three additional rooms, well-equipped for business travelers, are found across the street from the inn in an equally historic home. Rooms are named after Texas rivers, and shades of blue figure prominently in the color scheme. As you might expect, the Dillons love canoeing and tubing in the area rivers, and can tell you about all the best places to go for water sports and to see San Marcos' historic sites. Breakfast is available at the guests' convenience, and consists of expanded continental fare on weekdays, with a full brunch on weekends.

"A comfortable old-style home with beautifully decorated bedrooms, and excellent breakfasts. I particularly enjoyed sitting in a rocking chair on the second-floor porch. Mike and Cathy are very cordial hosts, who make their guests feel relaxed and at home. The location is both quiet and convenient."*(Jack Marshall)*

Open All year.
Rooms 1 suite, 7 doubles—6 with full private bath, 2 with a maximum of 4 people sharing a bath. All with telephone, radio, air-conditioning, fan. 3 with TV, desk, fireplace. 3 rooms in annex.
Facilities Dining room, library, veranda, covered courtyard with pool. Shuttle to nearby river for swimming, fishing, rafting, tubing.
Location SE TX. 30 m NE of San Antonio. 25 m SW of Austin.
Restrictions No smoking. Children over 10 preferred. Noise may disturb light sleepers in 3 rooms.
Credit cards Amex, MC, Visa.
Rates B&B, $90 suite, $50–70 double, $40–60 single. Extra person in room $7.50. 10% senior discount weeknights. 2-night minimum busy weekends.
Extras Station pickups. Spanish, Italian spoken. Cribs, babysitting, play equipment, games available.

TYLER 75702   Map 11

Rosevine Inn   *Tel:* (214) 592–2221
415 South Vine

The Rosevine is a new structure, built as an inn on the site of an older home that burned to the ground about 20 years ago. Bert and Rebecca Powell have furnished their B&B with antiques and collectibles, some of which are for sale, and describe the Rosevine as "one of the friendliest inns around." Becca also notes that "our historic area is undergoing a resurgence, with many restored homes opening as art and craft galleries and antique shops." Tyler is a city of flowers, with annual events celebrating the blossoming of its dogwoods, azaleas, and roses. Rates include wine and cheese on arrival and a full breakfast of muffins, breads, and coffee cakes, with a hot entrée.

"Tyler is a good place for an overnight between Dallas and Shreveport. It is gorgeous when the azaleas are blooming. The town is 'dry' though, so if you're planning to stay at a B&B, you'd best bring your own." *(MAA)*
"Becca's home-cooked breakfasts are excellent, the beds comfortable. Best of all was sitting by the light of the fire on the patio, sipping wine and nibbling on cheese. Bert has never met a stranger. He makes you feel right at home the minute you drive up." *(CS, also VC)*

Open All year.
Rooms 5 doubles, all with private shower, radio, air-conditioning.
Facilities Dining room, living room with fireplace, TV, piano; large entry hall with TV, games. ½ acre with courtyard, fountain, hot tub, horseshoes, croquet. 2 lakes, state parks within 15 m.

Location NE TX, 100 m from both Dallas and Shreveport, LA. 6 m from center of town. Take I-20 to exit 69S to Loop 323 and turn right. Go left on Hwy. 31 (Front St.), right on Vine. Inn is 1st house on right.
Restrictions Light sleepers should request rooms on south side. No smoking.
Credit cards MC, Visa.
Rates B&B, $65 double, $55 single. Extra person in room, $10. No tipping. Discounts for midweek stays, stays of 3 or more nights.
Extras Airport/station pickups. French spoken.

UTOPIA 78884   Map 11

Utopia on the River   *Tel:* (512) 966–2444
Highway 187, P.O. Box 14

Although the accommodations may be recent, the history of this property goes back to the dinosaurs, whose tracks can clearly be seen below the surface of the Sabinal River, which flows right by the German-style lodge. Owned by Polly and Aubrey Smith, Utopia is located on a working ranch originally settled (and named) by French immigrants who returned home after their visionary leader died. Rates include a full country breakfast.

"Utopia is a tiny town of 350 souls, one café, a gas station, two general stores, plenty of churches, and a store-front library. Go into the library where the town's volunteer ladies will show you around. The setting is peaceful, restful, and bucolic—truly utopian—although you're stuck with the town cafe for lunch and supper—try the chicken-fried steak.

"Polly and Aubrey have created a little utopia within the bigger one on the Sabinal River. Set among tall trees up the bank from the crystal clear stream, their facility is motel-modern with the feeling of a lodge. They have created a 'great hall' where hearty breakfasts are served. Good conversation is conducted either on the front porch or before the huge fireplace. (Ask Polly how the fireplace forecasts the weather.) In a corral near the entrance are goats, horses, and an amorous zebra.

"Aubrey is sheriff of Uvalde County, and he cuts a fine figure in his western suit and ten-gallon hat. He is anxious to tell any interested guest about the adventures of the Uvalde Sheriff's office." *(Michael Leviton, also KJ)*

Open All year.
Rooms 12 doubles, all with full private bath, air-conditioning.
Facilities Dining room, "great hall" with fireplace, meeting rooms, gift shop, porch. Swimming pool, hot tub, sauna, hunting, fishing, hiking, jogging, tubing, barbecue and picnic areas.
Location Central TX. 350 m SW of Dallas, 80 m NW of San Antonio. 2½ m from town. From San Antonio, take US 90 W 61 m to Sabinal, then RR 187 20 m N to lodge.
Credit cards Amex, MC, Visa.
Rates B&B, $69 double, $59 single. Extra person in room, $10. Children under 6 free.

Utah

Washington School Inn, Park City

Most Americans are quick to associate Utah with Mormons. In fact, there's probably not another state in all 50 that is so dominated by one religious group. Although not everyone in Utah is a member of the Church of Jesus Christ of Latter-Day Saints, most people are, and as a result cities here have a somewhat old-fashioned air and their citizens have a shared sense of purpose.

People are also quick to connect Utah with skiing. Within an hour's drive of Salt Lake City are several of the country's finest ski resorts, each blessed with an average annual snowfall of 300 to 500 inches of light, fluffy powder. Park City has fine skiing, yet it retains some of its old-time mining town ambience amidst the condos and lodges. We list a wide range of choices for Park City, but we still have received no recommendations for lodges in Alta or Snowbird; more comments would be appreciated!

Utah makes its most lasting impression by the startling diversity and grandeur of its five national parks (Arches, Bryce Canyon, Canyonlands, Capitol Reef, and Zion), six national monuments, and 48 state parks. Since you can't see them all in a single trip, here are our recommendations: In southeastern Utah: Hovenweep National Monument with its ancient Pueblo Indian ruins and Natural Bridges National Monument, where the largest of three bridges is 268 feet long and 31 feet wide. Further north, see how eroding sandstone has formed over 500 arches in Arches National Park.

Just been to the Grand Canyon? Enter Utah on scenic Route 89, past colorful Vermilion Cliffs, then travel to Bryce Canyon where thousands of fairyland spires show off their delicate pastel shapes. For contrast, see Zion National Park's narrow canyon and towering cliffs (Route 9 from the east offers the prettiest entry).

606

Dinosaur fan? Watch the bones being excavated at Dinosaur National Monument, north of Jensen, or at Cleveland-Lloyd Dinosaur quarry south of Price, where over 12,000 bones have been uncovered. Staying in Salt Lake City? Get tickets to see one of three highly rated dance companies, including Ballet West which is considered one of the finest in the country.

Information please: If you're traveling on Route 89 between the Grand Canyon and the national parks of southwestern Utah, we have a new B&B for you to try: **Miss Sophie's B&B** is right in the center of Kanab, about a mile from the Arizona border. Owners Ron and Aprile Barden have years of experience in the hospitality business, and offer three air-conditioned guest rooms with private bath in their century-old, antique-filled home (30 North 200 West, Kanab 84741; 801–644–5952). Much further north on Route 89 is Mt. Pleasant, about 35 miles south of Provo. One of the town's most attractive homes is the **Mansion House**, built in the 1890s with hand-painted ceiling, scrolled oak staircase and stained glass windows. Rooms have private baths and the B&B rates are very reasonable (298 South State Street, Mt. Pleasant 84647; 801–462–3031). A similar distance from Provo, but via I-15 is the **Whitmore Mansion Inn**, a turreted Queen Anne-style home listed on the National Register of Historic Places. Built in the Eastlake style, the six guest rooms have private baths, and rates include a full breakfast; fresh apple muffins and German pancakes are favorites, and dinners are available by advance reservations (110 South Main Street, Nephi 84648; 801–623–2047).

Note: Due to Mormon prohibitions against drinking alcohol, liquor sales are tightly controlled by the state. You may buy wine and liquor from state stores or purchase minibottles from shops in many hotels and motels. You then bring your own bottle into a restaurant and order the "setups." Private clubs have also been set up to circumvent these regulations, and short-term memberships are offered (at the door) to out-of-state visitors.

Rates do not include state taxes of 6%.

BRYCE CANYON   Map 12

Bryce Canyon Lodge & Cabins   *Tel:* (801) 834–5322
Route 63   For reservations: (801) 586–7686
Mailing address: P.O. Box 400, Cedar City UT 84720

Early Mormon settler Ebenezer Bryce, for whom the canyon is named, is said to have described the area as a "hell of a place to lose a cow!" Fortunately, today's visitors are seeking beauty, not bovines. They come to see the stark grandeur of the area's time-sculpted rocks, its eroded limestone tinted to delicate shades of red, orange, brown, yellow, and purple by iron and manganese oxides. The lodge and cabins are set on the canyon's rim, with numerous hiking trails descending from the 8000-foot-high plateau to the Paria River below.

"It was well worth booking six months ahead to reserve a cabin on the canyon's rim. Ours had a spectacular view and was very clean. Newly renovated, it offered every comfort and convenience, without losing its rustic charm. The only place to eat is the lodge dining room; there's no coffee shop. If you want a lighter meal, the only option is to pick up a snack at the general store." *(AF)*

Open May 1–Oct. 16
Rooms 110 motel units, 40 cabins with gas fireplace. All with private shower and/or bath, some with radio, telephone.
Facilities Restaurant, bar, gift shop, general store. Hiking, bus tours, horseback riding.
Location SW UT. Take U.S. 89 to Rte. 12 E. Go 14 m E on Rte. 12 to Rte. 63 S into park.
Credit cards Amex, CB, Discover, MC, Visa.
Rates Room only, $69 double in cabin, $58 double in motel. Children under 12 free, extra adult $5.

CEDAR CITY 84720   Map 12

Information please: A B&B right in Cedar City is the **Woodbury Guest House**, a turn-of-the-century home with spacious rose-lined lawns and five guest rooms with private baths; the Shakespeare Festival is just a three-minute walk away (237 South 300 West; 801–586–6696). On Highway 14 in Duck Creek, 30 miles east of Cedar City, near Cedar Breaks National Monument, is the **Meadeau View Lodge**, with nine rooms available for B&B (P.O. 356, Cedar City 84720; 801–682–2495).

Zion National Park Lodge   *Tel:* (801) 772–3212
P.O. Box 400   For reservations: (801) 586–7686

The 229 square miles of Zion National Park include some of America's most spectacular scenery, with Zion Canyon as its focal point; its rock formations rise to nearly 8,000 feet, changing in color with the time of day and the season. Readers are very pleased with accommodations in the lodge, but we'd like to request reports from anyone who has recently overnighted in the cabins.

"This national park lodge is fairly new and is located deep on the valley floor, in the middle of Zion National Park. There was a herd of deer grazing on the lawn when we arrived in the early evening, and they sauntered away leisurely. From our balcony we could see massive cliffs looming on both sides. The main portion of the lodge is about 20 years old and contains a gift shop, meeting rooms, and the dining room (where the food is ordinary family fare). Our rooms were in one of the motel-style wings, which are constructed in lovely dark-brown wood and stone, and are definitely a step above an ordinary motel in quality; the sylvan surroundings and spectacular scenery make it special. There are several motels on the main highway in the little town outside of Zion, but nothing could equal the morning views we had here of the waterfall cascading down the mountains." *(Susan W. Schwemm)*

"We stayed in the motel; our room was satisfactory in every way—good view, well appointed, comfortable, and clean. Food in the dining room is adequate and reasonably priced; the coffee shop is very convenient for lighter meals." *(AF)*

Open March through Nov.
Rooms 121 suites, doubles, cabins all with private bath and/or shower, telephone. Some with private balcony or porch.
Facilities Restaurant, cafeteria, gift shop. Guided walks, information sessions, slide presentations. Horse and mule trailriding, bus tours available.

Location In Zion Natl. Park. From I-15, take Rte. 9 to park.
Credit cards Amex, MC, Visa.
Rates Room only, $65–75 cabin (sleeps 4), $95–105 suite, $57–74 double. Children under 12 free in parents' room. Alc lunch, $7; alc dinner, $17.

MANTI 84642   Map 12

Manti House Inn   *Tel:* (801) 835–0161
401 North Main Street (Hwy. 89)   (800) 288–1893

Built in 1880 of native stone and completely restored in 1985, this historic inn once housed the workers who built the Manti Temple. A full breakfast is served every morning, while weekend dinners might feature fresh vegetable soups, fruit salad with sorbet, prime rib, and apple pie with ice cream.

"A delightful house, well furnished to create a turn-of-the-century mood. The owners made us feel most welcome and meals were beautifully served in a lovely dining room." *(Bernice Bradley)* "A delicious dinner of homemade rolls, onion soup, shrimp cocktail, corn and broccoli, and tender prime rib, topped off by a sinful chocolate dessert. Although we were still full from dinner, we managed to find room at breakfast for the tasty omelets and blueberry muffins." *(DN)* "Creative and original food, many family recipes. The atmosphere is one of warmth, caring, and love." *(Margene Moore)* "Our room was cozy and clean; we loved the interior design." *(Jack Sloan)*

A few minor drawbacks: "The adjacent building is unattractive, but the far view of the Temple is beautiful. We wish Manti had more to offer—that's being worked on, but progress is slow."

Open All year. Restaurant open weekends only. Ice cream parlor open April –Sept.
Rooms 2 suites, 4 doubles—all with private bath and/or shower. All with air-conditioning; TV available on request. 1 suite with double Jacuzzi, balcony.
Facilities Dining room, front parlor with games, ice cream parlor, indoor hot tub. Fishing, hunting, hiking, bicycling, golf nearby. Bike, fishing gear rentals. Horse and carriage rides, $25–40; available by reservation.
Location Central UT, 2 hrs. S of Salt Lake City, 1 hr. S of Provo. In center of town, near Manti Temple, on U.S. Rte. 89.
Restrictions No smoking. Traffic noise in some rooms.
Credit cards Amex, MC, Visa.
Rates B&B, $65–85 suite, $37–60 double, $30–48 single. Extra person in room, $7. Alc lunch, $5; alc dinner, $23.
Extras Airport pickups. Cribs available.

MIDWAY 84049   Map 12

The Homestead   *Tel:* (801) 654–1102
700 North Homestead Drive, Box 99   (800) 327–7220

It's not easy to grow alfalfa when the warm springs on your property keep getting it soggy, so homesteader Simon Schneitter soon realized that it was a lot easier to accommodate the neighbors who kept dropping in to soak in the hot springs. He built a pool, and his wife kept busy cooking and serving meals to their guests. About 100 years later, Carole and Jerry

Sanders, owners of The Lodge at Cloudcroft in New Mexico (see entry), took over the Homestead, investing nearly $2 million in upgrading and expanding all its rooms and facilities. Most recently, they have added seven guest cottages with three to six rooms each, added swimming pools and tennis courts, stables and a riding area, and an 18-hole golf course, making the Homestead a full-scale resort. Maintaining a long tradition, most rooms have been redone with Victorian antiques and reproductions, while meals, served in the main house, offer everything from famous fried chicken to other American classics—prime rib, mountain trout, and rack of lamb.

"The whole family kept busy with the Homestead's full range of activities—it was hard to get them away to explore the other sights of the mountain-ringed Heber Valley, including the historic train, the 'Heber Creeper.'

"Charming and elegant; each of the guest rooms has its own flavor, and all are furnished with antiques. Food is outstanding." *(Debby Joost)* "Exceptionally gracious and accommodating staff, without a trace of snobbery. Homey ambience with a real family feeling. Fantastic range of activities. The manager even lent me a fishing pole, then had the chef cook the trout I'd caught." *(Dr. & Mrs. Ren Halverson)*

Open All year.
Rooms 1 suite, 30 doubles, 12 singles—all with private bath and/or shower, telephone, radio, air-conditioning . Most with TV. 2 with whirlpool tub. Accommodations in 7 cottages.
Facilities Restaurant with entertainment, lobby, sitting room, game room, porch. 60 acres with heated indoor and outdoor swimming pools, hot tub, sauna, trout fishing, tennis court, golf, children's programs, horseback riding, sleigh and hay rides, hiking, lawn games, ballooning, water sports, cross-country skiing, rentals, instruction.
Location N central UT, Heber Valley. 45 m SE of Salt Lake City, 13 m to Park City. 2 m from Midway. Take US 40 to Midway exit then follow signs to Wasatch Mountain State Park. Inn is adjacent.
Credit cards Amex, MC, Visa.
Rates Room only, $150–165 suite, $59–79 double, $49 single. Extra person in room, $7.50. Senior discount. Minimum stay requirement during holidays. Alc lunch, $6; alc dinner, $23.
Extras Free shuttle to Park City, Sundance. Cribs, $5; babysitting, play equipment available. Spanish, German spoken.

MOAB 84532 **Map 12**

Pack Creek Ranch *Tel:* (801) 259–5505
P.O. Box 1270

Ken Sleight really knows the rivers and canyons of Utah—he's been running rivers professionally for 35 years now. In 1986 he and his wife Jane realized a long-held dream when they bought the Pack Creek Ranch, "a place where guests can come and enjoy a home base while visiting the canyons." Set at an elevation of 6,000 feet in the foothills of the LaSal Mountains, the ranch offers accommodation in a variety of log cabins; meals are available at reasonable cost in the ranch restaurant, and meal-plan packages are available. Trail rides (not included in the rates) cover everything from a morning ride through Arches National Park, to evening sunset rides, to four-night river and pack trips.

"Wonderful food, lovely decor with dried flowers everywhere. Real wood paneling. Husband very involved in environmental issues." *(Bonnie Jacobs)* "Nestled amid spectacular desert and mountain scenery, a stone's throw from the Arches and Canyonlands National Parks. Comfortable cabins, hospitable staff." *(Gary Weiss)*

"Lived up to your description and then some. Best of all are the wonderful owners and staff." *(Johanna Moran)*

Open All year. Restaurant closed Nov. through April.
Rooms 9 1–4-bedroom log cabins with private full bath and/or shower, fan, dining area, kitchen. Most with living room, 5 with fireplace, 1 with patio.
Facilities Restaurant with weekend entertainment, fireplace; library, swimming pool, canyon-country bookstore. 230 acres with unheated swimming pool, trail rides, pack trips. River rafting, mountain biking, scenic flights nearby.
Location SE UT. 250 m SE of Salt Lake City.
Restriction No smoking in lodge.
Credit cards Amex, MC, Visa.
Rates B&B, $60–90 double, $45–65 single. Extra person in cabin, $15. Rates include continental breakfast. Alc dinner, $15–21.
Extras Cribs, babysitting available.

MONUMENT VALLEY 84536   Map 12

Goulding's Trading Post & Lodge   *Tel:* (801) 727–3231
U.S. 163, P.O. Box 1

Located just east of Lake Powell on the Arizona border, Goulding's Trading Post and Lodge rests in the shadow of a large red rock mesa. Harry Goulding and his wife Mike established their trading post in 1923, and over the years expanded the accommodations to their present size. The original trading post is still in operation, specializing in Navaho rugs, crafts, and jewelry. In the late 1930s, Harry convinced film director John Ford that Monument Valley would be an ideal local for western films. "Stagecoach" was filmed here in 1939 and the Stagecoach Dining Room was built for the set of "She Wore a Yellow Ribbon," starring John Wayne. It serves an American menu with Southwestern, Mexican, and Navajo specialties. Each room in the motel building has a private balcony with a view of the stone sentinels in Monument Valley.

"Make reservations well in advance. The view from our stone patio brought a whole new meaning to those TV Westerns we've been seeing for years. Awe-inspiring natural beauty." *(Jack & Sue Lane)*

Open All year.
Rooms 62 doubles, all with full private bath, TV, air-conditioning.
Facilities Restaurant, laundry facilities, food shop, gift shop, gas station, campground, air strip, indoor pool, valley tours.
Location SE UT. 2 m W of town.
Credit cards Amex, MC, Visa.

Rates Room only, $75 double, $65 single. Extra person in room, $6. Admission to Navajo land, $1.
Extras Pets permitted. Guided tours of Monument Valley.

PARK CITY 84060 Map 12

Originally founded as a silver mining camp in 1869, Park City is now best known as an outstanding downhill ski area, home to Park City Ski Area (Treasure Mountain), Park West, and Deer Valley, all connected by a free shuttle bus. Other snow-season activities include cross-country skiing, ice skating, helicopter skiing, and sleigh rides. Although the area is less popular in summer, there's still plenty to do; attractions include golf, tennis, hiking, fishing, horseback riding, and hot-air ballooning. Summer rates are 40 to 60% lower than winter rates and often include other specials as well.

Park City is located 45 minutes east of Salt Lake City. From Salt Lake City, take Interstate 80 east to Park City South exit. Take Utah Highway 224 approximately six miles to Park City, where it changes its name to Park Avenue. For information on Park City, call (800) 453–1360 (outside Utah).

Information please: The Imperial Hotel was built as a miner's boarding house in 1904, and was restored as an inn in 1985, complete with antique decor and hot tub (221 Main Street, P.O. Box 1628; 801–649–1904). The **Snowed Inn** (get it?) is a Victorian mansion at the entrance to town, furnished with European antiques; rates include continental breakfast and a restaurant is on the premises (3770 North Highway 224, P.O. Box 1846; 801–649–5713).

Blue Church Lodge and Townhouses
424 Park Avenue
Tel: (801) 649–8009

Listed on the National Register of Historic Places, the Blue Church was constructed in 1897 as Park City's first Mormon church but was destroyed a year later during the great fire of 1898. It was reconstructed in 1900 and served as the town's Mormon church until 1962. In 1975 the building was purchased by Robert Lewis, who converted it to apartments. In 1982 the building was again destroyed by fire. This time Mr. Lewis rebuilt it as a five-level cluster of condominiums, with additional townhouses across the street. The units are furnished in a country look, with lots of pine and oak and a few antique reproductions; the lodge is managed by Nancy Schmidt. Rates include a continental breakfast buffet of coffee, tea, hot chocolate, and an assortment of doughnuts, rolls, muffins, and Danish pastries.

"Charming, historic, warm, and friendly, and an architectural surprise! We enjoyed the beautiful lobby with its massive fireplace, cathedral ceiling, arched window, steeple roof, and the completely renovated interior with first-class accommodation.

"We had doughnuts and coffee every morning and relaxed in the enormous hot tub every evening. There is a game room and laundry facilities, but the most important thing is the location. It's a short walk to the town ski lift to buy lift tickets and get right to the slopes. Coming home we skied all the way to the door. At night we walked across the street and went

shopping in all the quaint shops off Main Street." *(Thomas & Nannette King)*
"Helpful, attentive staff, facility well kept and clean." *(M.L. McGreaty)*
"Exceptional previsit communications and readily available managers."
(RM) "The attractive and very livable units have well-equipped kitchens
and good laundry facilities." *(Ralph & Nancy Timmerman)*

One guest, who has made reservations for a return trip, did mention that
the heating system in his unit was rather loud, making "noises like a huge
percolator."

Open Nov. 1–April 30.
Rooms 12 1–4-bedroom townhouses, all with full private bath, telephone, radio,
TV, kitchen, washer, dryer, fireplace.
Facilities Lounge, game room, Jacuzzi spa, Ping-Pong, ski lockers, laundry room. 3
blocks to downhill, 1 m to cross-country skiing.
Location "Old Town," 75 ft. from Main St. From Park Ave., go left on Heber,
immediately right on Main.
Restrictions Some street noise in a few units.
Credit cards MC, Visa.
Rates B&B, $120–350 suites (1 to 4 bedrooms, sleep 4 to 10), $70–135 double.
3-night minimum stay.
Extras Cribs available. Spanish spoken.

Old Miners' Lodge
615 Woodside Avenue, P.O. Box 2639

Tel: (801) 645–8068

"The Old Miners' Lodge is a restored lodge originally opened in 1893 to
house miners seeking their fortune in the area. The rooms are decorated
with antiques and mementos of the late 1800s, and each room is named
after a famous person of the silver rush era." *(Vicki & Dick Slade)*

"The two couples who own and operate this wonderful place have
designed it to suit their guests' every need. You can walk to the ski lifts,
great shops, and restaurants, so a car isn't necessary. Rooms are comfortable and immaculate, with down comforters and mattress heaters." *(Pat
Hardy)*

"A warm, cozy, friendly spot, run by people who actually care about
how your day went. Hugh, Susan, and Jeff (who run the lodge and really
make it into a home for their guests) were terrific. Great home-style breakfasts are served in the main room (a combination living/dining room)
around a large oak table covered with a homespun cloth. It also has a huge
fireplace where a fire is always roaring, plus large overstuffed couches and
a wonderful rocking chair by the fireplace. Everyone gathers in this room
after skiing to sip drinks, chat, relax, and swap stories. The location is great,
only a block or so from the free shuttle that connects the three local ski
areas, and 100 yards to the 'town lift.' In fact, you can actually ski into the
backyard at the day's end if you're skiing Park City Ski Area; just be
careful not to run into the hot tub! After a full day of skiing, once you get
into the hot tub, you may forget about going out to dinner—it's so relaxing,
especially as you look up into the black sky dotted with millions of stars."
(KFR)

"Hugh and Susan are superb hosts. The lodge is excellent for all ages,
and certainly was ideal for my vintage (58 years). The atmosphere takes
me back to a time when life was simpler and more honest." *(Kenneth Allen)*

Open All year.
Rooms 3 suites, 7 doubles—all with private bath and/or shower, 4 with desk. Suites with refrigerator.
Facilities Dining room; parlor with library, games, organ, fireplace; porch with swing. Horseshoes, croquet, hot tub. 100 yds. to chair lift for downhill skiing. Cross country skiing, hiking, golf, tennis, water sports nearby.
Location National Historic District, 1 block from center. From Park Ave. proceed to where town lift crosses over Park Ave. and turn right on 8th St. Go up 1 block to Woodside Ave. and turn left. Lodge is on right approx. 200 yards up the street.
Restrictions Smoking in parlor only. "Children welcome, but young ones find us boring."
Credit cards Amex, Discover, MC, Visa.
Rates B&B, $65–165 suite, $40–105 double. Extra person in room, $5–20. Reduced rates for children under 12. Minimum stay during holiday periods. Prix fixe lunch, $7–15; prix fixe dinner, $12–25; for groups by prior arrangement only.
Extras Crib available by prior arrangement.

Washington School Inn
543 Park Avenue, P.O. Box 536

Tel: (801) 649–3800
(800) 824–1672

The Washington School was constructed of limestone in 1889, and is listed on both the National and the Utah Historic Registers. Although it was heralded as one of the best schools in the state at the time, by the 1950s it lay abandoned. In 1984 the building was restored as an inn by Frank and Donna O'Bryan at a cost of $1.4 million; it's managed by Richard Scott. Many of the distinctive features of the schoolhouse were combined with a country elegant decor. Rates include a full breakfast and après-ski wine and hors d'oeuvres.

"Warm and friendly spot. Great breakfasts. Large rooms kept cozy with down comforters." *(Pat Carroll)* "Charming, elegant and attractive. Competent, friendly staff keep things clean and comfortable." *(Pauline & Bell)* "Facilities, staff, and food all excellent. Summer rates an excellent value." *(Samuel Northcote)*

Open All year.
Rooms 3 suites, 15 doubles—all with private bath and/or shower, telephone. Suites with radio, TV, desk. Some suites with fireplace.
Facilities Dining room, living room, mezzanine with TV, games, library. Spa with Jacuzzi, sauna, steam showers, ski lockers. 1 m to downhill skiing.
Location National Historic District. Go up Main St. and turn R on Park Ave.
Restrictions Smoking in mezzanine area only. No children under 12.
Credit cards Amex, MC, Visa.
Rates B&B, $100–225 suite, $75–170 double.

PROVO 84601   **Map 12**

The Pullman Inn
415 South University Avenue

Tel: (801) 374–8141

An imposing yellow-brick Romanesque Revival Victorian built in 1898, the Pullman Inn was restored by the Morganson family in 1985. Interior highlights include a circular staircase that winds through a two-story turret, stained-glass windows, hand-carved woodwork, and crystal chandeliers; each guest room has a brass or hand-carved wooden bed. A typical dinner might be pork roasted in cranberry-ginger sauce with apple garnish; Cornish game hen with orange/grapefruit glaze and pecan stuffing; or halibut baked in sour cream and Parmesan sauce. During dessert, the three Morganson brothers—Tim, Kelly, and Dennis, along with singer/waitress Shelly Eves—come out to entertain guests with a half-hour musical show of unexpected quality and professionalism. During the summer, dinner moves out to the garden patio, where the Pullman Country Picnic includes a buffet of barbecue spare ribs, fresh salads, baked beans, hot bran muffins and homemade peach cobbler; of course, the accompanying music is country and western.

"This railroad executive's home has been lovingly and beautifully restored. It has three floors, each with a small comfortable sitting area. Each room has floral wallpaper, some antique furniture, and beautiful quilts handmade by the owners' mother. The rooms are a little small but each has some interesting architectural detail. We love the beautiful woodwork and plaster moldings. Dinner may be had by reservation on Friday and Saturday nights. The menu is set but is always excellent and generous. Dinner ends with a delicate chocolate mint and a rose for each woman present." *(Virginia & Dale Wright)*

Open All year. Restaurant open weekends only.
Rooms 6 doubles—4 with full private bath, 2 with a maximum of 4 people sharing 1 bath. All with radio, air-conditioning.
Facilities 2 dining rooms with entertainment Fri. & Sat., parlor on 1st floor; sitting room with TV on other 2 floors. 1/3 acre with flower garden, patio, off-street parking. Fishing, sailing, waterskiing, swimming, skiing nearby.
Location Central UT. 40 m S of Salt Lake City. 4 blocks from town square. ¾ m off University Ave. exit off I-15.
Restrictions No smoking.
Credit cards Amex, MC, Visa.
Rates B&B, $36–50 double. 10% discount for 3-night stay or 2-room rental; 15% discount for 5-night stay. Alc dinner $11–17.

ST. GEORGE 84770   Map 12

St. George was settled by pioneers sent south in 1850 by Brigham Young. They struggled against extremely adverse conditions for years, trying to grow crops of fruit and cotton. Eventually Young decided that first a Mormon tabernacle and, later, a temple would be the key to stabilizing the community. To keep an eye on the temple's construction, Young established a winter home in St. George. Today St. George's Pioneer Museum has preserved many objects of interest from those difficult early days.

Information please: St. George is extremely hot in the summer but enjoys very mild winters, perfect for golf, tennis, or visits to Zion National Park.

We'd like to have reports on the **Greene Gate Village Inn,** a collection of seven restored historic pioneer homes dating back to 1862, along with such up-to-date pleasures as tennis courts, a swimming pool, and Jacuzzi. B&B rates are a reasonable $35 double, $65 suite (76 West Tabernacle;

801–628–6999). Another possibility, about 18 miles northeast of St. George and about 20 miles south of Zion National Park, is the **Pah Tempe Hot Springs B&B**, set in a grove of hundreds of trees on an ancient Piaute Indian healing ground in the Virgin River Canyon. The very reasonable rates include use of the hot springs and mineral pools and a full breakfast; other meals are served at their vegetarian restaurant (34-4 Hurricane 84737; 801–635–2879). Reports, please.

Seven Wives Inn
217 North 100 West

Tel: (801) 628–3737

The Seven Wives Inn was built about 1873 by a local judge, who sheltered polygamous men being hunted by federal marshals. When innkeepers Donna and Jay Curtis renovated the home, they discovered a secret door that had been used to let the men in and out of the attic, once the coast was clear.

The inn is named in honor of Donna's polygamous great-grandfather, Benjamin Johnson, who probably hid in the attic more than once. Seven of the inn's guest rooms are named after his wives. Rooms are furnished primarily with Victorian antiques, highlighted with pine woodwork hand-grained to look like birds-eye maple or oak. Rates include a full breakfast—perhaps homemade granola, juice and fruit, sausage en croute, scrambled eggs, and coffee or tea.

"Donna has spent much time adding personal touches and handwork to all the rooms. The inn is located near the heart of St. George and across the street from the winter home of Brigham Young." *(Pamela Rush)*

"The inn is only one block off the main street, yet it is always quiet and peaceful. The innkeepers are very friendly and see to it that all your needs are met. Each room is decorated in a different manner, but all are delightful, comfortable, and clean. We always look forward to breakfast, as the home-cooked meals are always delicious and filling." *(James Neal)*

Open All year.
Rooms 12 doubles, 1 single—all with private bath and/or shower, TV, air-conditioning; some with fireplace or woodstove, desk, fan, porch. 1 with whirlpool tub. 4 rooms in annex.
Facilities Dining room with fireplace, parlor with pump organ, game table. Garden, heated swimming pool, hot tub, on-site parking. Hiking, golf, tennis, fishing, boating nearby.
Location SE UT. 125 m NE of Las Vegas, NV; 300 m S of Salt Lake City. Approx. 40 m SW of Zion National Park. 1 block N of St. George Blvd., diagonally across from Brigham Young winter home.
Restrictions No smoking.
Credit cards Amex, MC, Visa.
Rates B&B, $35–65 double, $25–65 single. Extra person in room, $7. Picnic lunch by prior arrangement.
Extras Airport/station pickups. Pets permitted. Crib available.

SALT LAKE CITY   Map 12

The valley between the mountains to which Brigham Young led his followers in 1847 is now the large and prosperous city of Salt Lake. At its heart is Temple Square, home to the Temple, the Tabernacle—with its famous choir and 11,000-pipe organ—the Genealogical Library, and Assembly Hall. The city experienced secular growth in the nineteenth century, with the coming of the railroads and the discovery of Utah's mineral wealth.

Seven first-rate ski resorts, including Alta, Park City, and Snowbird, are within an hour's drive of the city. Many skiers make Salt Lake their base, visiting a different area every day, and a number of hotels offer special skier's packages.

Salt Lake City is located in northwestern Utah, set between the Wasatch and Oquirrh mountains, with the Great Salt Lake to the northwest. It's 534 miles west of Denver and 750 miles east of San Francisco. Streets in Salt Lake are numbered based on their distance from Temple Square.

Information please: A short drive from downtown is the **National Historic B&B**, built a century ago and newly renovated by Mike and Kate Bartholome. The decor is eclectic, with four guest rooms each done in Colonial, Victorian, Art Deco, and 1950s styling (936 East 1700 South 84105; 801–485–3535). Another possibility is the **Mountain Hollow B&B** at the base of Little Cottonwood Canyon, about 20 miles south of Salt Lake via I-15 or Rte. 89. This contemporary home has a secluded wooded setting and a ten-person hot tub amid the mountain scrub oak, with beautiful mountain views. The cathedral-ceilinged common room features a two-story native stone fireplace and a restored 1942 Wurlitzer jukebox. The reasonable rates include a full breakfast; the nine guest rooms are decorated with original Western art and both contemporary and antique furnishings (10209 Dimple Dell Road, P.O. Box 1841, Sandy 84092; 801–942–3428).

Brigham Street Inn
1135 East South Temple 84102
(formerly Brigham Street)

Tel: (801) 364–4461

Built in 1896 by a prosperous wool merchant, this red-brick Victorian's history follows the pattern of many others of a similar vintage—many years as a private home, a number more as a boardinghouse, and some time serving unappealing functions, with a final renovation and resurrection as a B&B inn.

What is unusual about the Brigham Street Inn are the circumstances under which Nancy and John Pace purchased this home in 1981. Nancy was looking for a house that could be used as a designer showcase to raise money for the Utah Heritage Foundation; when she found this one, she realized that converting it to an inn would be a way to cover the substantial renovation expenses.

Each of 12 different designers selected a room to decorate, and the results are striking. While the common rooms reflect something of the house's Victorian background, the guest rooms are a beautiful balance of traditional and contemporary looks. Equal attention was paid to the behind-the-scenes work—each bedroom received a completely new bathroom, with sprinklers and smoke detectors added throughout. Rates include a continental breakfast buffet of juice, fresh fruit, croissants or muffins, and coffee, tea, or hot chocolate.

"Combines all the conveniences of a business hotel with many of the best qualities of a B&B—beauty, comfort, and class. Lovingly restored architectural details. The location is in an area of many beautiful old stately homes not far from the center of the city." *(VW)* "Terrific place. Mrs. Pace checks in daily to see that all runs smoothly and indeed it does." *(Dorothy Helfat)*

Open All year.
Rooms 1 suite, 7 doubles, 1 single, all with private bath and/or shower, telephone, radio, TV, desk, air-conditioning.
Facilities Living room with piano, parlor, dining room. On-site parking.
Location 11 blocks E of Temple Square, 2 min. by car from downtown.
Credit cards Amex, MC, Visa.
Rates B&B, $140 suite, $85–95 double, $65 single. Tipping "not encouraged." Extra person in room, $10.
Extras Cribs available.

Carlton House

140 East South Temple Street 84111

Tel: (801) 355–3418
(800) 633–3500

The Carlton was built in 1935 and was recently remodeled. Manager Bob Baird notes that "we cater to genealogists doing research here, and our limo service provides transportation to seven different ski resorts."

"The owners are constantly remodeling, redecorating, and upgrading the rooms, the halls, and the lobby. The hotel is quiet, clean and well kept. The location is convenient to the main part of town, yet shielded from traffic noise. The management is friendly, cheerful, and readily available to assist guests, without being overly 'chummy.' " *(Mary Ann Seymour)*

"The lobby is comfortable, homey, and immaculate. A small flower shop off the lounge is owned by an artist whose work enhances the decor with beautiful bouquets and seasonal decorations. My room looked out on maple trees, filling my windows with greenery. The lawn in front is tidy and planted with flowers." *(J.M. Wilke)*

One area for improvement: "Higher wattage in the light bulbs would be an aid to elderly eyes." (And younger ones, too!)

Open All year.
Rooms 5 suites, 38 doubles—29 with private bath and/or shower, 14 with maximum of 3 people sharing bath. All with telephone, TV/VCR, desk, air-conditioning, refrigerator.
Facilities Restaurant, meeting room, exercise room with sauna, hot tub. Free parking. Health club access.
Location In center. 1½ blocks E of Temple Sq.
Restrictions No smoking in some guest rooms.
Credit cards Amex, DC, Discover, MC, Visa.
Rates B&B (for rooms with private bath), $59–69 suite, $44–49 double, $34–39 single. Extra person in room, $5. No charge for children under 16 in parents room. 10% senior discount. Ski packages. Weekly, group rates.
Extras Limited wheelchair accessibility. Free airport/station pickups. Cribs available. Some German, Spanish spoken.

Vermont

Strong House Inn, Vergennes

Vermont is full of lovely inns; we've had more glowing recommendations for this state than for almost any other in the East. In fact, only California has more entries—and it's seventeen times bigger than little Vermont! Winters and summers are beautiful in Vermont, although lodges are most crowded during the first half of October. In general, peak-season rates apply during winter and during fall foliage season. Summer is still considered off-season in many ski towns, and rates are often extremely reasonable. Many lodges offer lower "ski-week" rates from Sunday through Friday nights, except during Christmas and February vacation periods. A number of lodges and restaurants close or scale back their activities in the spring and fall "mud seasons," when the state is not at its best.

The state lodging tax of 6% will be added to all rates quoted.

Reader tip: Bicycle tours are extremely popular in Vermont, and a number of companies arrange delightful ones from inn to inn. However, "if you are traveling independently, looking for peace and quiet, don't hesitate to ask if a tour will be staying overnight during your visit. The innkeeper will provide this information *only* on request." *(Ed Okie)*

ARLINGTON 05250   Map 1

A quiet village set along Route 7A, Arlington is in southwestern Vermont, 3½ hours north of New York City and about the same distance northwest of Boston. It's 15 miles north of Bennington and 8 miles south of Manchester. Of particular interest is the Norman Rockwell Exhibition, housed in an 1875 church. More than 1,000 magazine covers and illustrations are on display, many of them pictures of local residents who modeled for Rockwell during the fourteen years he lived here. Arlington is intersected by the Battenkill River, one of Vermont's best trout-fishing streams.

Also recommended: The **Arlington Inn** (Route 7A at Route 313; 802–375–6532) is a Greek Revival mansion built in 1848, and unusual in snowy Vermont, with a flat roof and oversize windows. Food is a highlight here (rates include a continental breakfast) and menus change seasonally; one recent entrée included Vermont pheasant with green peppercorns and red currants with cranberry chutney. Enthusiastically recommended too late for a full entry is the **Keelan House** (Route 313, RD 1, Box 1272; 802–375–9029), "a spacious Federal home built in 1820 and delightfully restored by Don and Verrall Keelan. Their three–guest-room B&B is decorated with exceptional antiques and beautiful colors, highlighted by the original wide-plank flooring. There's a table and chairs for picnicking out back, and a path leading down to the Battenkill River. The Keelans are charming and serve a delicious full country breakfast." *(Betty Norman)*

Information please: Some places we'd like to hear more about are **The Inn at Sunderland,** a Victorian B&B decorated with antiques (Route 7A, RR 2, Box 2440; 802–362–4213); **Roaring Branch**, a collection of rustic log cabins set in a pine forest just the other side of a covered bridge (Sunderland Road; 802–375–6401); and the **Hill Farm Inn**, a casual family inn with reasonable rates and modest but comfortable rooms (RR 2, Box 2015; 802–375–2269).

West Mountain Inn
Route 313 and River Road

Tel: (802) 375–6516

Mary Ann and Wes Carlson are relaxed and friendly innkeepers who have welcomed guests to the West Mountain Inn since 1978. The inn is casually decorated with some antiques and offers beautiful views from almost every room. A specialty is the African violets found in each guest room—meant to be taken home by the occupants as a souvenir. Good food is a priority here, and breakfast might include granola with yogurt, blueberry pancakes or cheese omelets, sausage or bacon, and even pie à la mode. Dinner might start with brie en croûte served in the library, followed by a candlelit meal of French cream of mushroom soup, poached red snapper with asparagus and hollandaise sauce or roast duck with ginger sauce, served with salad, sorbet, and home-baked bread, and walnut-raisin carrot cake for dessert. An added plus is the Carlsons' international menagerie—llamas, African pygmy goats, flop-eared rabbits, and Japanese goldfish.

"Service attentive yet relaxed. The food makes the visit— delicious hors d'oeuvres fireside at 6 P.M., followed by a five-course meal, unusual yet tasty." *(Wende Cleary)*

"A gorgeous inn with big comfortable rooms. Wes, Mary Ann, and their staff are some of the nicest people I've ever met. Evenings are social, with guests gathering at the bar for appetizers before dinner. The grounds are wonderful—you can hike in the woods, visit their animals, or fish in the Battenkill River at the bottom of the hill." *(Joanne Friedrick)*

Reader suggestions: "Although some guest rooms are beautiful, others are a bit drab, yet they're priced all the same." Also: "Rooms pleasant but unremarkable. Food inconsistent—some dishes very good, others indifferent."

Open All year.
Rooms 3 suites, 10 doubles—all with private bath and/or shower. Some with desk.
Facilities Dining room, living room, game room, enclosed porches, library, bar. 150 acres with gardens, pond with exotic goldfish, 50 evergreen species, animals—llamas, goats, rabbits. Battenkill River borders property for trout fishing, swimming, canoeing, tubing. Tennis, golf nearby. Cross-country skiing on property; 4 m to Bromley; 21 m to Stratton.
Location ½ m to town. Take exit 3 off Rte. 7; go W on Rte. 313 to Rte. 7A; go N on 7A, W again on 313 for ½ m. Turn left on River Road, cross river, and stay left up hill to inn.
Restrictions No smoking in guest rooms, dining room.
Credit cards Amex, MC, Visa.
Rates MAP, $180 suite, $155 double, $90 single, including service. Extra adult in room, $55; children age 5–12, $30; under age 5, free cot/crib fee. 2-night weekend minimum. 5 nights for price of 4, Sun.–Mon. in winter, spring. Prix fixe dinner, $21.
Extras Wheelchair accessible; 1 guest room/bath equipped for disabled. Station pickups. Cribs, babysitting, play equipment available.

BENNINGTON 05201   Map 1

South Shire Inn   *Tel:* (802) 447–3839
124 Elm Street

Bill and Judy Raffaele are the new innkeepers at the South Shire Inn, and are working hard to make a lovely inn both bigger and better. Originally built as the Graves Estate in 1895, this mansion was created by many of the same craftsmen who built the Victorian "cottages" of Newport; examples of their work include the raised plaster moldings, the leaded-glass pocket doors, and mahogany paneling.

"The inn is one of three surviving 'sister' houses (there were five originally) built by the Graves family. Every room was spotlessly clean. The Victorian decor is consistent, with mostly antique furniture; what new pieces were in evidence were very nice reproductions. The modern baths (for me, 'antique' stops at plumbing) feature dainty lace-trimmed towels and great water pressure and temperature. The library is paneled in richly hued Honduran mahogany that was originally polished daily; from the looks of it, it still is. The Victorian theme fortunately stops short of stiffly uncomfortable Chippendale sofas; instead, two brightly upholstered traditional sofas flank the fireplace. The dining room is finely detailed with molded plaster decorating all surfaces but the floor and a crystal chandelier in the center of the ceiling. The light color of the walls and the large windows keep it from feeling overdone despite the ornate decor. Breakfast consisted of fresh grapefruit, juice, and huge waffles with strawberries and whipped cream all served on fine china accompanied by freshly ironed linens." *(Judi Lamberti)*

Open All year.
Rooms 9 doubles—all with private bath and/or shower, desk. 7 with fireplace.
Facilities Parlor with piano, dining room, library with fireplace, porch. ½ acre with

gardens. Near many rivers and lakes for fishing, swimming. Downhill and cross-country skiing, 20–35 min. away. Golf nearby.

Location W central VT. 130 m NW of Boston. From Rte. 9, take Rte. 7 S. Turn right onto Elm St. Inn is on left.

Restrictions No smoking. No children under 14.

Credit cards Amex, MC, Visa.

Rates B&B, $75–125 double. Extra person in room, $10. 4% service. 2-night minimum, foliage and holiday weekends. Weekly, corporate rates

Extras Limited wheelchair access. Bus station pickups.

BRANDON 05733   Map 1

Brandon is located in west-central Vermont, on Route 7, halfway between Middlebury and Rutland, 50 miles south of Burlington.

Information please: Current feedback on the **Brandon Inn** (20 Park Street at Route 7; 802–247–5766) would be most appreciated. Really more of a hotel than an inn, it enjoys a good reputation—especially for its food—but after some frequent ownership changes we need to hear more from you.

Beauchamp Place   *Tel:* (802) 247–3905
31 Franklin Street (U.S. Route 7)

"A Victorian jewel" is the phrase Georgia and Roy Beauchamp (pronounced Beacham) use to describe the inn they've owned since 1985. Dating back to 1860 and listed on the National Register of Historic Places, the inn has a Second Empire French mansard roof; rooms are furnished with reproduction Victorian wallpapers, Victorian and Empire pieces (acquired at Vermont auctions), along with comfortable mattresses and down comforters. Rates include a full breakfast of juice and fruit, cereal, hot breads, eggs, and coffee (served on bone china and in a silver coffeepot), and afternoon wine and cheese.

An exquisitely furnished Victorian restored to its original beauty by the Beauchamps, who lived in England for fifteen years. Breakfast is elegantly served, and Mrs. B's granola is delicious. *(Ina Gartenberg, also SM)*

Open All year.

Rooms 8 doubles, all with shared bath, desk, ceiling fan.

Facilities Living room, study, dining room. 1 acre with flower garden, hammock, croquet, badminton. 5 m to Lake Dunmore for swimming, fishing, boating. Skiing, golf nearby.

Location 15 m N of Rutland. In center of village.

Restrictions No smoking. No children under 13.

Credit cards Amex, MC, Optima, Visa.

Rates B&B, $70–90 double, $55–80 single. Some minimum stay requirements.

CHESTER 05143   Map 1

Incorporated in 1764, Chester is home to two National Historic Districts, including the Stone Village, a group of nineteenth-century buildings faced in gleaming mica schist. Six downhill ski areas are within a 25-minute drive. This quiet town is located in southeastern Vermont, about 30 miles north of Brattleboro, and is best reached by taking I-91 to exit 6, Rockingham; take Route 103 northwest 10 miles to Chester. Where 103 takes a sharp right in the village, continue straight on Route 11 (Main Street) to the village green.

Also recommended: The Hugging Bear Inn (Main Street, Box 32; 802–875–2412) has a special appeal for families; it is home to a thousand cuddly bears waiting to be hugged. This comfortable 140-year-old Victorian home is far more casual than the many inns where breakfast assumes nearly ceremonial status; here, Monty, the puppet bear, greets guests as they arrive at the table.

Although there wasn't time for a full write-up, *Ed Okie* was delighted with **Rowell's Inn** in the tiny hamlet of Simonsville, seven miles west of Chester. Sturdily built of brick in 1820 as a stagecoach stop, it has white-painted porches perfect for sitting and rocking on, while its cozy tavern and fireplace invite you with a welcoming drink. Owners Lee and Beth Davis have furnished the rooms with lovely antiques, and a home-cooked dinner is available by advance request to overnight guests only (Route 11, RR #1, Box 269, Chester 05143; 802–875–3658). Reports please.

Inn at Long Last
Route 11, P.O. Box 589

Tel: (802) 875-2444

Starting a new career as an innkeeper is not unusual for people who've had it with the high-pressure life of the big corporations, but innkeeper John Coleman, owner of the Inn at Long Last (previously the Chester Inn), brings new meaning to the concept. Coleman, a former president of Haverford College, came into the public eye when he wrote about his experiences living as a homeless man through a frigid New York City winter. Something of a George Plimpton of the nether world, he also spent time as a prison inmate, on a southern chain gang, and on a New Mexico oil rig. Another change of direction came in 1985, when he bought and totally renovated this inn, naming each of its rooms after a place or person of significance to him. The inn is well worth a visit for the food alone; chef Michael Williams presents a new menu daily. A recent dinner offered a choice of such entrées as roasted lamb sauced with leeks and merlot; duck with roasted shallots and tangerine-port wine sauce; lobster and crab ravioli with pistachio butter. The inn gladly shares many of its recipes with guests. "Lovely inn, delicious food, fascinating innkeeper." *(Barbara & Jim Kelly, also RB)*

Open Open May through March.
Rooms 3 suites, 27 doubles, all with full private bath, fan. 15 rooms with desk.
Facilities Dining room, lobby with fireplace, library/bar with fireplace, porch. Tennis courts, fishing. Golf, skiing nearby.
Location Center of town, on village green.
Restrictions Smoking in library only.
Credit cards Amex, MC, Visa.
Rates MAP, $120–140 suite or double, $60–80 single, plus 15% service. B&B, $90–110 double, $45–65 single. ½ price for children 3–15; children under 3, free. 10% senior discount on request. 2-night holiday weekend minimum. Alc dinner $37.
Extras Airport pickups. Some French spoken.

CHITTENDEN 05737 Map 1

Also recommended: The **Mountain Top Inn** (Mountain Top Road; 802–483–2311, 800–445–2100) is an all-inclusive family resort, beautifully situated on a lake high in the mountains and offering a full range of summer and winter sports.

Tulip Tree Inn *Tel:* (802) 483–6213
Chittenden Dam Road

Too often, readers are disappointed because the quiet country inn they'd dreamed about is, in fact, alongside a busy highway—which is why we're glad to assure you that this is *not* the case with the Tulip Tree Inn. Chittenden itself is well off the beaten path, and the inn is a half mile from the center of this tiny town. Originally this was the rambling summer home of William S. Barstow. Innkeepers Rosemary and Ed McDowell have decorated their inn with Victorian antiques, Oriental carpets, and soft plush couches.

Rosemary's ample breakfasts include pancakes or French toast, cereal, fruit and yogurt, and homebaked sweet breads. Dinners are served by candlelight, with background music playing, and Ed personally seats each guest at the tables for eight, creating a dinner party atmosphere, so that "our guests can get to know each other and we can get to know them. We do more than feed our guests nightly—we have a dinner party."

"Rosemary and Ed are wonderful innkeepers; she is a gourmet cook and her pumpkin cheesecake with maple syrup is a standout. Menus vary from filet mignon to veal *française.* Ed's knowledge of fine wine enhances every meal. The rooms are spotless, as is the entire inn. A short walk away is the Chittenden Reservoir where one can boat, fish, or swim. Their English sheepdog Guiness is a part of the family and a highlight of the cocktail hour." *(Sandra & Matthew Keysers)*

Open Mid-May through March.
Rooms 8 doubles—7 with full private bath, 1 with private shower. All with fan; some with Jacuzzi.
Facilities Dining room, library pub, living room and den with fireplace, porch, hot tub. 5 acres with trout stream. Canoeing, swimming, skiing, golf, tennis, horseback riding nearby.
Location 7 m N of Rutland. From Rutland, take Rte. 7 to fork in road. At fork, bear right on Chittenden Road 6 m. At fire station, go straight ½ m to inn.
Restrictions Smoking in sitting room only. No children.
Credit cards MC, Visa.
Rates B&B, $100–140 double. MAP, $120–200 double. 15% service additional. 2-3 night minimum holiday weekends; midweek discounts.

DORSET 05251 Map 1

Dorset is located in southwestern Vermont, 1½ hours northeast of Albany, 4 hours north of New York City, and 3½ hours northwest of Boston. It's

6 miles north of Manchester Center on Route 30, and 12 miles to downhill skiing at Bromley, 22 to Stratton.

A picture-postcard New England country village, Dorset is listed on the National Register of Historic Places. Activities include the country's oldest nine-hole golf course, tennis, hiking, quarry swimming, and cross-country skiing. The Battenkill River and Lake St. Catherine are nearby for fishing and boating. In summer there is theater as well as concerts and art exhibits at the Southern Vermont Arts Center.

Also recommended: The Little Lodge at Dorset (Route 30, Box 673; 802–867–4040), an 1820 colonial, is set back from the road on a quiet hillside overlooking a small pond. It's furnished with antiques, and features much of the original wide-board flooring. Rates include afternoon tea or hot chocolate and Vermont cheese and crackers.

Information please: Built in 1796, the **Dorset Inn** is one of the state's oldest hostelries, and has recently been renovated to combine eighteenth-century charm with twentieth-century comfort. Chef/owner Sissy Hicks blends New England tradition with contemporary flair in the inn's kitchen (Church & Main Streets; 802–867–5500).

Barrows House
Route 30

Tel: (802) 867–4455

Tim and Sally Brown, transplanted New Yorkers, bought Barrows House in 1986. Barrows House is an attractive and comfortable country inn, with added features such as a swimming pool and a tennis court, and a reputation for excellent food. The menu is changed nightly and emphasizes fresh vegetables and homemade bread and pastries. A typical dinner might begin with mushroom sin puff pastry with garlic cream, followed by salmon with saffron leeks, accompanied by dilled carrots and wild rice pilaf, and concluded with a fresh fruit tart or chocolate cake.

"The Barrows House is a marvelous complex, consisting of the main inn and outbuildings, designed to accommodate a single traveler or a family of fifteen. The innkeepers, Tim and Sally Brown, go out of their way to match the rooms to the needs, wishes, and comfort of their guests. The menus for both breakfast and dinner are extensive—'Yankee gourmet' someone called it. The rooms were clean and comfortable—definitely not professionally decorated, but with a collection of patterns and colors and pieces from earlier periods that somehow worked together quite well. The librarylike pub was my favorite room—warm and intimate, with backgammon boards on some tables." *(Ann Brown)*

"Our small cottage easily accommodated a king-size bed and sectional sofa; there was also a writing-and-TV room. The dinner competed with most we enjoy in New York City and was presented with smooth, courteous service. We had our own parking area and didn't have to contend with others' comings and goings." *(Michael Treiber)*

"There is cross-country skiing from your door, easy access to Stratton and Bromley, and the discount emporiums of nearby Manchester village." *(Stephen Lash, also Mr. & Mrs. James Finseth)*

Open All year. Restaurant closed early Nov.
Rooms 5 suites; 28 doubles, 3 singles—30 with private bath and/or shower; 2 singles

share 1 bath. All suites with air-conditioning. All rooms with fan; some with TV, desk. 21 rooms in 7 separate buildings.

Facilities Restaurant, tavern with TV, piano, live entertainment; game room, library, sitting room with fireplace. 6 acres with lawn games, gazebo, heated swimming pool, sauna, 2 tennis courts, badminton court. Bicycles, cross-country skiing and rentals; downhill skiing nearby.

Location Walking distance to town. 6 m N of Manchester Center on Rte. 30.

Credit cards Amex, MC, Visa in restaurant only.

Rates B&B, $150 suite, $115–130 double, $60–80 single; extra person in room, $35. MAP, $190 suite, $155–170 double, $80–105 single; extra person in room, $55; 15% service. Reduced rates for children. 2-3 night minimum stay, some weekends and holidays. Prix fixe or alc dinner, $15–25, alc lunch, $5–10. Midweek non-holiday discounts, Jan.–June.

Extras Ground-floor guest rooms, dining rooms wheelchair accessible. Station pick-ups. Pets permitted with prior approval only. Cribs, babysitting available. French spoken.

EAST MIDDLEBURY 05740   Map 1

The Waybury Inn   *Tel:* (802) 388–4015
Highway 125

If you are struck by a feeling of déjà vu upon arrival at the Waybury, it's not your imagination—you really have seen the inn before. The Waybury is featured on TV on the *Bob Newhart Show*; its front side appears on the show's exterior shots at the beginning and end of each show.

The Waybury dates back to 1810 and was originally built to house women workers from a nearby glass factory. Listed on the National Register of Historic Places, it was purchased by Pete Varty in 1986, but has been managed for over twenty years by Sandra Wimmett. The inn restaurant offers a full selection of fish and meat dishes, including fresh Vermont lamb.

"A charming, friendly inn close to Middlebury College. Our room was decorated with lovely antiques and a king-size four-poster bed. The private bath was large and well supplied with towels. We enjoyed a full breakfast with fresh eggs and biscuits, served by the warm and helpful staff." *(Cindy Lindemeyer)*

"Everything as you described it, except they forgot to replace our bath towels and our morning coffee wasn't steaming hot." *(MW)*

Open All year. Restaurant closed Christmas Eve.

Rooms 14 doubles—all with private shower and/or bath, desk. 2 with air-conditioning.

Facilities Restaurant, library, pub with fireplace; lobby with TV, fireplace. 3 acres with tennis. Swimming, fishing in river gorge 1 block away. Golf, downhill, cross-country skiing nearby.

Location E central VT. 4 m S of Middlebury. On Rte. 125 1 m E of Rte. 7.

Restrictions Smoking on first floor only. No children under 5.

Credit cards Amex, MC, Visa.

Rates B&B, $100–115 double, $80–95 single. Extra person in room, $20. Alc dinner, $30; Sunday brunch, $12. Meals ½ price for children under 12. 2–3 day weekend minimum holidays/special events.

Extras Restaurant wheelchair accessible.

GRAFTON 05146   Map 1

Information please: If there's no room at the Old Tavern, some other local possibilities include the **Inn at Woodchuck Hill** (Middletown Road; 802–843–2398), a 200-year-old house surrounded by meadows and woods, complete with swimming pond and antique shop; the **Wayfarer**, right in town with working fireplaces in several bedrooms (Main Street, P.O, Box 147; 802–843–2332); and the **Woodshed**, with reasonably priced rooms in a converted nineteenth-century barn (Route 121 East; 802–843–2365).

The Old Tavern at Grafton   *Tel:* (802) 843–2231
Main St./Route 121

Longtime manager Richard Ernst notes that "with its hand-hewn beams, wide pine flooring, pewter and brass, the Old Tavern looks very much the way it did in the old days, when it accommodated Daniel Webster, Oliver Wendall Holmes, Ulysses S. Grant, Nathaniel Hawthorne, Ralph Waldo Emerson, and Henry David Thoreau." The Windham Foundation operates the Old Tavern, as well as seven separate restored colonial houses that can be rented by the day or week. "This inn is so typically New England that I would really like to see it in the fall or in the snow. It's colonial inside and out. The drawing rooms are filled with antiques, and excellent food is served in the attractive dining rooms. The rooms are lovely, and the baths are modern and clean." *(Mrs. John Schmunk)* "We had a short but delightful stay. The rooms were charming! The atmosphere was quiet but friendly." *(Mrs. George Kobulnicky, also Susan Kiviat).* "Most desirable for its location and the character of its surroundings; facilities are adequate but comfortable." *(Samuel C. Cantor, also David Tripple)* More comments, please.

Open All year, except Christmas and month of April.
Rooms 42 doubles, 1 cottage—all with private bath and/or shower; some with desk. 28 rooms in annex. Accommodation also in 6 separate guest houses.
Facilities Restaurant, tavern, 2 TV rooms, library, living rooms, game room. Swimming pond, 2 tennis courts, platform tennis, shuffleboard, billiards, Ping-Pong, horseback riding, 18 m of cross-country ski trails, fishing, canoeing, kayaking. 30–40-min. drive to 4 major downhill ski areas.
Location SE Vermont. 2½ hrs to Boston, 5 hrs to NYC. 12 m E of I-91 in center of town.
Restrictions Children under 8 and pets restricted to accommodation in specific areas.
Credit cards Amex, MC, Visa.
Rates Room only, double $50–120. Extra person in room, $20. 2–3 night minimum stay, weekends, foliage, some holidays. Alc breakfast, $2–5; alc lunch, $10; alc dinner, $35; children's menu available.
Extras Wheelchair access to rooms in main tavern. Horses boarded. German, Dutch, French spoken.

LOWER WATERFORD 05848   Map 1

Rabbit Hill Inn   *Tel:* (802) 748–5168
Pucker Street, Route 18

In the 1830s, a very active trade route developed between Portland, on the Maine coast, and interior New England and Montreal. To accommodate the dozens of passing wagon teams—carrying produce, Fairbanks scales from St. Johnsbury, and maple syrup (going east) and spices, molasses, textiles, and general merchandise (going west)—the home built by Jonathan Cummings in 1825 was converted into an inn in the 1830s. Not a great deal has changed in Lower Waterford since then. John and Maggie Magee, who bought the Rabbit Hill Inn in 1987, report that "ours is a classic country inn offering gentility, period decor, and a romantic atmosphere. Our setting is classic too, with a restored 150-year-old village—no traffic lights or shops. Everything is white clapboards and dark green shutters. We light over 70 candles every night to help transport guests back to another era. Our 15 acres include hiking trails that lead over a country bridge spanning the stream that feeds our swimming pond, continuing by a meadow where cows graze and ending up at a beaver colony. Our most recent addition is a green house where we can cultivate herbs and flowers (both edible and decorative) year-round."

"We were graciously greeted with a cup of hot orange-spice tea to sip by the fireplace and an assortment of homemade cakes and cookies. The parlor decor is charming and the lounge comfortable with books, maps, game tables, and corner bar. Our rooms were in the wing attached to the inn, decorated in country colonial style, as were the rooms in the big white inn itself and in the adjacent tavern building. Beautiful quilts complemented the color scheme and bright flower arrangements, along with antique pieces, stuffed ducks, dolls, toys, and, of course, rabbits of all descriptions. A personal note awaited us and announced the dinner hour. The candlelit dining room was lovely, and our napkins rested in pewter rabbit rings. It was difficult to choose among the entrées and appetizers of the evening as we sampled the warm loaf of just-baked natural grain bread. Shrimp cocktail, fresh cream of mushroom soup, green salad, fresh swordfish with a vegetable medley and rice were all a treat. Hot Vermont apple pie with cheese or ice cream and chocolate pecan pie were delicious desserts. Upon returning to our rooms, we found a lighted candle, soft music playing, and a tiny heart pillow gift on the turned-down beds. The morning breakfast buffet included fresh-squeezed orange juice and steaming coffee, homemade granola, hot apple compote, an egg casserole, assorted fruits, muffins and jam, with crisp bacon brought to each table. The handwritten personal note we received at checkout time made us even more eager to return." *(Gladys & Bob Dunn, also DM)*

Open May through Oct., Nov. 15 through March.
Rooms 2 suites, 13 doubles, 3 singles, all with full private bath and/or shower, fan, radio. 4 with desk, some with fireplace. 14 rooms in main inn, 4 rooms in separate building.
Facilities Dining room with guitarist or flutist; parlor with fireplace; pub with fireplace; lounge with wood stove, TV/VCR, games; library; covered porches. 15 acres with herb and flower gardens, gazebo, greenhouse, lawn games, pond for swimming, fishing, cross-country skiing. Canoes for use on nearby CT River. Golf, downhill skiing, hiking nearby.
Location NE VT, Northeast Kingdom, 10 m from St. Johnsbury and Littleton, NH. From I-93, exit onto Rte. 18. Follow Rte. 18 2 m to inn across from church.
Restrictions No smoking. No children under 11.
Credit cards MC, Visa.

Rates MAP, $180–190 suite, $130–170 double, $85–105 single. 15% service. Extra person in room, $55. Prix fixe dinner, $25.
Extras French spoken.

LUDLOW 05149   Map 1

Ludlow is in south-central Vermont, 4½ hours north of New York City and 2½ hours northwest of Boston. From I-91, take exit 6 to Rte. 103 west to Ludlow. It's 22 miles southeast of Rutland and about 20 miles from I-91. Okemo is 1 mile from the center of Ludlow, and Killington is 16 miles north. Eight golf courses lie within 30 miles of Ludlow.

Also recommended: The **Black River Inn** (100 Main Street; 802–228–5585), built in 1835 in the Federal style, is intended to be a romantic getaway for couples. A full breakfast can be brought to your room at the time requested, so that you enjoy breakfast in bed, or you may choose to go to the dining room. Rates also include a five-course, single entreé dinner.
The Combes Family Inn (RFD 1, Box 275; 802–228–8799) is a century-old farmhouse with an attached motel section of more recent vintage. Children (and other family members) are welcome to share their hugs and affection with the dogs, cats and goats which reside on the farm. Rooms decorated in "country comfortable" make families feel even more at home.

The Governor's Inn   *Tel:* (802) 228–8830
86 Main Street

In 1982, Deedy and Charlie Marble purchased Vermont governor William Wallace Stickney's former summer home, a Victorian mansion built in the 1890s. They've restored and renovated the rooms to a state of lovely Victorian elegance, leavened with a sense of humor. The key elements at the Governor's are the cuisine and the Marbles themselves.

MAP rates include four-course breakfasts prepared by Charlie, complementary afternoon tea at 3 P.M., hot appetizers at 6 P.M., and a 6-course dinner served at 7. Deedy does all the cooking for dinner, and uses only fresh ingredients. For an additional charge, she will also prepare gourmet picnic hampers.

We received absolute rave reports on this inn; space limitations don't allow us to quote all of them—our apologies. Advance reservations are essential.

"Without doubt the inn-of-inns. It is the standard by which all other inns can be judged—what Elizabeth Taylor is to Hollywood (but not husbands)—what Rolls-Royce is to cars. All that it lacks is a remote, secluded location. Otherwise, it's as close to perfection as one could ask, if attention to detail, warmth, personality, and true gourmet food are the criteria. It's so far above the rest in overall quality, consistency, romance, and intimacy that I'd be inclined not to assign any other inn a second-spot rating— starting at third position would be more appropriate. Meals are selected by the innkeepers, not chosen from a guest menu. The teenage dining staff provides a level of professional dining service and appearance that is remarkable. It's a tribute to their training by the innkeepers and an indication of attention to detail throughout. Though it's not necessarily a suit-and-tie place, neither is it a place to flop down on the floor and read a magazine, or put your feet up on the coffee table. Innkeepers don't come much better than Deedy and Charlie Marble." *(Ed Okie)*

"Even though it is rather expensive, this inn should be included on the itinerary of all persons looking for a top-notch country inn in New England or, for that matter, the U.S. The Marbles and their staff are on top of things at all times and make their guests feel genuinely welcome. The inn is beautifully restored, rooms are cheerful and comfortable, and extra touches are everywhere. Most noteworthy were the outstanding meals—the food and service at both breakfast and dinner were excellent." *(James & Janice Utt)*

Open May through Oct., Dec. through March. Restaurant closed Tues. evening.
Rooms 8 doubles with private bath and/or shower. All with fan; some with air-conditioning.
Facilities Dining room, lounge, 3 common rooms with fireplaces, heirloom antiques, books, and board games. Tea garden. Black River flows through backyard. Surrounded by 5 lakes for swimming and fishing. Cross-country and downhill skiing nearby.
Location On the village green, at the intersection of Rtes. 100 and 103.
Restrictions Some traffic noise at peak travel times. Smoking "very limited." No children under 16.
Credit cards Visa for dining room and securing reservation; cash, check, or traveler's check necessary for payment.
Rates All rates per person. MAP, $170–180 double, $140–150 single. 15% service additional. Picnic lunch $48. Prix fixe dinner $40. Weekend, holiday minimum stay requirements.
Extras Free airport/station pickups. Special meals with advance notice.

MANCHESTER 05254   Map 1

Manchester is located in southwestern Vermont, 1½ hours northeast of Albany, 3 hours northwest of Boston, and 4½ hours north of New York City. The town is about 25 miles north of Bennington and 30 miles south of Rutland via Route 7 or 7A. It's a 10- to 25-minute drive to Bromley, Stratton, and Magic Mountain for downhill skiing, and there are four cross-country ski centers within a 20-minute drive. Summer activities cover Vermont's full range of hiking, bicycling, antiquing, golf and tennis, lake and quarry swimming, trout fishing in the Battenkill River, and summer theater. Shopping is a favorite year-round activity, with a supply of discount stores to rival those in North Conway or Freeport. For a change of pace, visit the American Museum of Fly Fishing, or Hildene, the summer home of Abraham Lincoln's son.

Also recommended: The **Equinox Sky Line Inn** (Box 325; 802–362–1113), built in 1950, is one of Vermont's few remaining mountaintop hotels. (Time, the weather, and inaccessibility during the ski season have taken their toll on most of the others.) Located atop Mt. Equinox, at an altitude of 3,835 feet, the inn affords unforgettable views in all directions of the surrounding mountains and valleys below. Three meals are served daily to overnight and daytime visitors. The **Reluctant Panther Inn** (West

Road, Box 678; 802–362–2568), built in the 1850s, is under the new owner-ship of Robert Bachofen, originally from Switzerland and formerly with the Plaza Hotel in New York City. The updated menu features French country cuisine with a Vermont accent; and the new decor focuses on soft-toned Pierre Deux fabrics and wall coverings. The **Village Country Inn** (Route 7A, P.O. Box 408; 802–362–1792), built a century ago as the summer home of the Kellogg family, was converted into an inn in the 1920s. Renovated in 1985 and decorated with a country French atmo-sphere, the inn's size gives it the feel of a small hotel but with the charm and personal attention that makes it a welcome place to stay. The **Wilbur-ton Inn** (River Road, Box 468; 802–362–2500, 800–648–4944) dates back to the turn of the century, when many wealthy families built summer "cottages" in which to escape the city heat. This mountaintop brick man-sion is furnished with period antiques, some original to the house, and Oriental rugs; rates include full breakfast in season, continental in off-season. The warmth and friendliness of this private home make it very highly recommended by several of our readers.

Information please: The **Equinox,** a 200-year-old Vermont classic, was restored in 1985 at a cost of $20 million; it has 154 rooms and full resort facilities (Route 7A, P.O. Box 46; 802–362–4700). On a far smaller scale is the **Birch Hill Inn,** set off the main highway yet convenient to area attrac-tions; five guest rooms are available in this 200-year-old farmhouse (West Road, Box 346; 802–362–2761).

1811 House
Route 7A, Box 39

Tel: (802) 362–1811

The 1811 House offers elegance, quiet, and relaxation in a beautiful setting. Though the rooms are elegantly decorated, the inn is still casual enough that you are free to wander into the kitchen to make yourself a cup of tea. Built in the late 1700s, the house has been operated as an inn since 1811, except for a brief period when it was a private residence of Mary Lincoln Isham, Lincoln's granddaughter. It has been owned by Jack and Mary Hirst and Jeremy and Pat David since 1982.

"Spectacularly renovated home. It looks as though it's been prepared for an article in *Architectural Digest* and is filled with good-quality family an-tiques, excellent reproductions, antique silver and crystal in each room. Our room had a four-poster bed and beautifully appointed bath. The hosts are gracious and friendly. In the morning a fine full English breakfast is served in the formal dining room, and each evening the bar is filled with guests and locals." *(MJF, also MB)*

Open All year. Closed Christmas week.
Rooms 1 suite, 13 doubles, all with full private bath, air-conditioning; most with desk. 3 rooms with fireplace.
Facilities Pub, dining room, living room, library, game room with pool table. TV room. 8 acres with flower gardens, pond. Trout fishing, golf, swimming, skiing nearby.
Location 1.1 m S of blinking light at main intersection in town.
Restrictions No cigar or pipe smoking. No children.
Credit cards Amex, MC, Visa.

Rates B&B, $100–160 all rooms. 15% gratuity additional. 2-night minimum weekends, holidays, foliage. Midweek discounts.

MENDON 05701   Map 1

Red Clover Inn at Woodward Farm   *Tel:* (802) 775–2290
Woodward Road

Well known for its comfortable rooms, excellent food, and attractive rural surroundings, the Red Clover was sold late in 1988 and is now under the management of Ed and Judy Rup. The inn's restaurant has a good reputation locally; five to seven entrées are offered nightly, and a recent dinner included a strudel of lemon chicken, mushrooms, and Vermont cheddar; scallops and crab meat in sherried cream sauce; salad with maple Dijon dressing; and French apple cobbler for dessert.

The main house, built in 1840, holds the dining rooms, library/living room and ten antique-filled bedrooms. "The large family-style lounge has an extensive selection of books and games and a warming fieldstone fireplace. It's comfortable for relaxing—complimentary raw vegetables, crackers, and local Vermont cheddar are served at cocktail time." *(Hilary Huebsch Cohen)* The Plum Tree House next door has more modern furnishings, with suites appropriate for families.

"Ed and Judy Rup are delightful, making you feel like instant family. The staff is helpful, warm, and friendly, and every room was always fresh, no matter what time of day you walked through. The grounds are well kept and the out-of-the-way yet convenient location is terrific." *(Karen & Willie James)*

"Peaceful, quiet, and very relaxing. After a day of skiing, having a drink by the fire was exactly what we needed. The food was the highlight of our stay. The preparation, presentation and quality was excellent. I'm an early riser, and the breakfast staff made sure we were sent on our way well fed." *(J. Hardy LeGwin)* "We came here for Christmas weekend and found the atmosphere festive but quiet. The inn is spotless and service was available when we needed it and invisible when we did not. Loved the banana bread." *(Gayle & Rich Metzger)*

Open All year. Closed 2 weeks in April.
Rooms 1 suite, 14 doubles—11 with full private bath, 4 with shared bath. All with fan; some with TV, desk. 5 rooms in annex.
Facilities Dining room, living room/library with books, games, TV/VCR; billiard room; bar. 7 acres with lawn games, swimming pool, ice skating, sleigh rides, cross-country skiing. Tennis, hiking, fishing, boating, downhill and cross-country skiing nearby.
Location Central VT; 5 m to Rutland, 3 m to Pico Peak, 9 m to Killington. Go S off Rte. 4 on Woodward Rd., 5 m E of intersection of Rte. 4 and 7.
Restrictions Smoking limited to certain areas.
Credit cards Amex, DC, MC, Visa.
Rates B&B, $85–125 double. MAP, $124–155 double, $95–125 single. Extra person in room, $40. 15% service. 2- to 3-night weekend minimum in season. 3-, 5-, and 7-day packages available.
Extras Airport/bus station pickups.

MIDDLEBURY 05753   Map 1

Swift House Inn   *Tel:* (802) 388–9925
25 Stewart Lane

Swift House was built in 1815 and was expanded in 1890. Along with her father, the governor, Jessica Swift moved to the house at the age of 5 and lived there until she died in 1981 at the age of 110. John and Andrea Nelson bought Swift House in 1985 and restored it as an inn. Andrea notes that the Swift House is "a very warm, friendly, elegant house that is a perfect romantic getaway, but everyone seems to feel comfortable, and families are welcome." Rooms are decorated with Queen Anne and Chippendale antiques, Oriental rugs, four-poster beds, and handmade quilts. The full breakfast includes granola, eggs Benedict, mushroom omelets, and homemade popovers, along with Vermont maple syrup and bacon or sausage. Dinner is formal, served by candlelight on white linen; Vermont products are used whenever possible.

Middlebury is, of course, home to Middlebury College, and also makes a good base for touring this area of Vermont; area attractions include the Sheldon Museum, the Morgan Horse Farm, and the State Craft Center at Frog Hollow.

"Quaint, charming town. The inn is exquisitely decorated with a fine attention to detail. The food was superb—especially the popovers baked each morning. Impeccable service." *(Wende Cleary)*

"Charming, warm, sophisticated inn with gracious, informative and friendly owners. Impeccably clean. Andrea is the chef and does an outstanding job." *(Joyce & Julian Jackson)*

Open All year. Restaurant close Tues., Wed.
Rooms 14 doubles—all with private bath and/or shower, telephone, radio, desk, fan. Some with air-conditioning, fireplace, whirlpool bath. 5 in separate gatehouse.
Facilities Dining room, bar, living room, TV room, library, family room; most with fireplaces. Screened and open porches. 3 acres with formal garden. Swimming, fishing, hiking, golf nearby. Downhill, cross-country skiing 10–45 min. away.
Location E central VT. 45 min. S of Burlington on Rte. 7. 2 blocks N of village green, at corner of Stewart Lane and Rte. 7.
Credit cards Amex, Discover, MC, Visa.
Rates B&B, $60–115 double, $60–110 single. Extra person in room, $15. Alc dinner, $28–40.
Extras Cribs, babysitting, play equipment, games available.

PROCTORSVILLE 05153   Map 1

Proctorsville is located in southeastern Vermont, 20 miles southwest of Woodstock, 30 miles southeast of Rutland, and 3½ miles south of Ludlow. It's both 5 miles to Okemo for downhill skiing, and to Fox Run for cross-country skiing. Five other major ski areas are within an easy drive. From I-91, take the Rockingham Exit, and go northwest approximately 16 miles via Route 103 to Proctorsville.

Also recommended: The **Castle Inn** (Routes 131 and 103, Box 157; 802–226–7222) does not fit the typical image of a Vermont country inn; this imposing mansion was constructed in 1904 of 18-inch-thick gneiss quarried on the property. Rates include a welcome basket of cheese and fruit and a full country breakfast. The **Okemo Lantern Lodge** (Main Street, P.O. Box 247; 802–226–7770) was built in the early 1800s, and has been an inn since 1943. Owners Pete and Dody Button note: "We want people to be comfortable. We don't stand on ceremony and we try not to be pretentious. We hope to attract people who feel the same way." The inn is furnished with comfortable chairs and couches in the common areas; guest rooms are decorated with antiques, wicker, and, in some rooms, canopied beds.

The Golden Stage Inn
Depot Street, P.O. Box 218

Tel: (802) 226–7744

In 1985, innkeepers Kirsten Murphy and Marcel Perret left New York City careers as flavor experts. They are now devoting their tastebuds and culinary skills to preparing the delicious full breakfasts and Swiss-style dinners served at their inn. Kirsten's particular responsibility is to make sure the living room cookie jar is always full. Although there's no choice in the menu, guests are usually delighted with the house's selections; a recent dinner included a pasta roll stuffed with spinach and smoked ham, topped with basil tomato sauce; green salad with mustard dressing; filet of sole in tarragon cream sauce, with parsley potatoes and fresh garden vegetables; and a dense chocolate soufflé wrapped around vanilla whipped cream.

The Golden Stage Inn is over 200 years old; it served as a stop on the Underground Railroad during the Civil War. Kirsten and Marcel have renovated the house by adding private baths, stripping and polishing the wide-board floors, and decorating with country wallpapers, handmade quilts, and antiques.

"We arrived in the late afternoon and Kirsten showed us to a gloriously sunny corner room—clean, spacious, and inviting—complete with two double beds, a bookcase filled with books, and a private bath with full-length mirror. The large swimming pool in full sun was surrounded by a profusion of flowers. Though we were among the last to shower, there was ample hot water to meet our needs and unusually luxurious towels." *(Roger & Elaine Bermas, also Louis Van Leeuwen)*

"We loved the informal pre-dinner gatherings in the living room, filled with plants and books. We had cocktails there by a cozy fire, with soothing music and interesting conversation. Appetizers and Kirsten's ever-present homemade cookies were divine. Dinner is a relaxing, unhurried five-course affair served at tables seating four to six people—fresh, homemade, and perfectly prepared. Breakfast is served in the sun room, overlooking the landscaped grounds. We could order anything we wanted, and all was outstanding, especially the homemade granola. Our room was light, airy, and sparkling clean. The wooden plank floors gleamed, the wallpaper was old-fashioned, and the antique dresser was topped with a basket of chocolate candies. The bed was firm, and although the room next door was occupied, we never heard a sound. From the front porch you can see the

Black River Valley and Okemo Mountain, and we could just imagine the old stage coach pulling up in front." *(Bob & Anne Emigh)*

Open Dec. through March, May through Oct.
Rooms 10 doubles—6 with private shower, 4 with maximum of 4 people sharing bath.
Facilities Dining room, living room with fireplace, library with games; sun room, wraparound porches. 4 acres with swimming pool & flower, herb, vegetable gardens. Tennis, bicycling, hiking, fishing, hunting nearby. 3 m to golf, cross-country/down-hill skiing.
Location ¼ m to town. Depot St. connects Rtes. 103 & 131.
Restrictions Smoking in first floor public rooms only. No children under 9.
Credit cards MC, Visa.
Rates MAP, $140–150 double, $90–100 single. Extra person in room, $50. 15% service additional. 10% senior discount. 2-night weekend minimum. Prix fixe dinner, $25.
Extras Station pickups. German, French, Swiss-German spoken.

SOUTH NEWFANE 05351 Map 1

The Inn at South Newfane
Dover Road

Tel: (802) 348–7191

Connie and Herb Borst left a home in Westchester County and jobs in New York City to start new careers as innkeepers. They converted this manor house, built as a private home at the turn of the century, to an inn in the summer of 1984. Their daughter Lisa, a Culinary Institute of America graduate who has won many cooking awards in the past three years, is the inn's chef. South Newfane is located near Mt. Snow for winter skiing, and is a short drive to Marlboro for the summer music festival. In just a few years, the inn has developed an excellent reputation for its French cuisine. Everything is made from scratch daily. Menus change seasonally, with daily specials; a typical dinner might include herbed tomato mousse, boneless duck breast with ginger sauce, and one of Herb's freshly baked chocolate cakes.

"The inn is located right on the main road through a tiny Vermont town, but has about 100 acres that extend behind it." *(Marcia & Davis Spencer)* "The very warm welcome we received from the Borsts and the clean, comfortable, attractively decorated rooms, coupled with the personal service and exquisite food, made our stay outstanding. The inn is set among manicured gardens, with a lovely pond for swimming and the Green Mountains in the background." *(Marion Bock)* "Hanging potted plants highlight a veranda lined with rocking chairs, and splashes of color are provided by the small gardens of annuals planted nearby." *(Joni & Paul Meisel)*

"The small breakfast room is a cozy area where you can enjoy home-baked breads with jam, fruit, and delicious fresh farm eggs. Chef de Cuisine Lisa Borst outdoes herself daily. Everything was delicious, from the fresh salad with edible flowers to the pumpkin soup served in a small pumpkin to the braised rabbit to cakes galore. Our waiter was extremely competent, and Herb suggests and serves the wines." *(Eileen & Jack Ingrassia, also Soren Noring)*

"Even though we arrived late, Connie offered us a beverage before retiring and fresh fruit awaited us in our room. No towel was ever used twice; shampoos, soaps, talc, and bath oil were all provided. Sherry and four different kinds of homemade cookies greeted us in the living room when we returned from a day of antiquing." *(Sheryl Bernhard)*

"Without requesting it, we were given an extra quilt for the cool nights. The shower water was always hot, and the toilet worked on cue. Our breakfast choices were accompanied by the inn's standard assortment of fresh muffins, homemade bread for tasting, cereals, juices, coffee, and tea. Herb's breads, served with each delicious meal, were absolutely delectable." *(Joanne & Joseph Zipfel)*

"Our lovely room had a brass queen-size bed with a firm mattress, comfortable upholstered furniture, an antique chest of drawers with matching mirror, wall-to-wall carpeting, and a table full of information on area activities." *(Mr. & Mrs. Joe Vogel)* "Bedside lights perfect for reading; no need to bring your traveling light." *(Dr. & Mrs. Eugene Katz)*

And recently, a less favorable reaction: "After the rave reviews in your guide, we were disappointed. Although the dining room is exceptionally handsome, we thought the food was good but not great—excellent in presentation, but lacking in taste. We felt the Borsts were suffering from a case of innkeeper's burnout, and that the prices were among the highest we encountered on our Vermont trip."

Open May through Oct.; Dec. through March.
Rooms 6 doubles, with private bath and/or shower, fan. Some with desk.
Facilities Restaurant; living room with fireplace, TV, games, books; family room; bar/lounge; library; porch. 103 acres, spring-fed swimming pond, lawn games. Lakes, streams, 10 min. Downhill, cross-country skiing, golf, 15–20 min.
Location SE VT, Windham County. 20 min. NW of Brattleboro. Village center. From Brattleboro, go N on Rte. 30 for 9 m. Turn left (W) at sign for inn, and go 2 m thru Williamsville, then 1¼ m past covered bridge to the inn.
Restrictions No smoking in dining room. No children under 12. Limited traffic noise in front rooms.
Credit cards None accepted.
Rates MAP, $160–198 double, $115–135 single, plus 15% service. Extra person in room, $60. Alc dinner, $25–30. 10–20% midweek discounts. Minimum stay requirements.
Extras Some French, Norwegian spoken. Airport/station pickups.

SOUTH WOODSTOCK 05071   Map 1

Kedron Valley Inn   *Tel:* (802) 457–1473
Route 106

The Kedron Valley Inn dates back to 1822. Over the years, many changes and additions have been made, including a six-unit log addition built in 1968. In 1985 the inn was bought by Max and Merrily Comins. Max worked on Wall Street for eight years for the sole purpose of accumulating enough capital to buy a country inn. Merrily is particularly proud of her 40-piece heirloom quilt collection, many annotated with stories and photos of the women who made them. The menu features French cuisine, with entrées ranging from duck glazed with maple, cranberry and Madeira to Vermon rack of lamb with rosemary and Cabernet sauce to poached salmon with seafood mousse wrapped in puff pastry.

"Our room was just recently refinished and was truly beautiful. The wallpaper of the bedroom and bath was coordinated with the canopy bed and antique furniture, along with the lovely old handmade quilt at the foot of the bed. The living room was inviting, with a large fireplace and oak bar; we spent several evenings there, enjoying a glass of wine and the conversation of the other guests. The dining room was similar, with antique furnishings and a large fireplace, but the key feature here was the fine food served at breakfast and dinner. The inn's most impressive feature is its innkeepers—Max and Merrily Comins are outgoing, warm, and friendly." *(Gary & Diane Orlando, also Paul & Judy Doyle)*

"The atmosphere here is like being at home, but with waiters and maids to do all the work. The staff is friendly, accommodating, and efficient. The inn is clean and well kept. Lighting, plumbing, and parking are all adequate. The food is exquisite—the prime rib melts in your mouth, and the pheasant is prepared and seasoned to perfection." *(Armand J. LeVasseur)*

"Our room had a queen-size canopy bed with an heirloom quilt, his and hers rocking chairs, and a large clean bath. A big plus is the swimming pond with sandy beach and lawn chairs." *(Susan Prizio)*

"Unlike some over-glitzed inns, Kedron retains a sense of history and reality. We have three small children, which has never presented any problem or kept us from enjoying the ambience. The nearby Kedron Stable is wonderful, and the trail riding superb." *(David Tripple)* "Our favorite room is #26, which was lovely before but is even better now with its colonial-style fireplace and plush carpet." *(Mr. & Mrs. John Potter)*

Open May through March.
Rooms 7 suites, 21 doubles with private bath and/or shower. Some with TV, desk, fireplace, fan, air-conditioning, deck. 13 rooms in annex.
Facilities Restaurant, living room/bar, sitting room, library. 15 acres; swimming lake with beach, 7 m to downhill, 3 m to cross-country skiing. Bicycling, horseback riding, tennis, hiking, golf nearby.
Location S central VT, 5 m S of Woodstock. From I-91, take Exit 8 to Hwy. 131. Go N onto Rte. 106. 14 m to inn.
Credit cards Amex, MC, Visa.
Rates Room only, $90–136 suite, $50–88 double, $50–80 single; extra person in room, $15. B&B, $100–146 suite, $60–98 double, $55–85 single; extra person in room, $20. MAP, $140–186 suite, $100–138 double, $75–105 single; extra person in room, $40. 15% service additional. 2-night weekend minimum. Alc dinner, $36.
Extras Wheelchair accessible. Cribs, babysitting available. Pets permitted. French, Spanish spoken.

STOWE 05672   **Map 1**

Stowe, one of Vermont's best-known towns, calls itself the "Ski Capital of the East" and offers superb downhill skiing at Mt. Mansfield and Spruce Peak. Stowe also has four cross-country ski touring centers; the Trapp Family Lodge is the best run and most well known. Summer and fall are equally lovely, with many special activities in addition to the usual summer mountain pleasures. A 5-mile paved recreation path has recently been completed, offering cross-country skiers, walkers, and joggers a delightful car-free experience. Stowe is located in north central Vermont, 35 miles from Burlington. It's about 6½ hours north of New York City, 4 hours northwest of Boston, and 2½ hours south of Montreal.

Also recommended: The **Andersen Lodge: An Austrian Inn** (RR 1, Box 1450; 802–253–7336) is a contemporary-style lodge with a large and airy dining room and several common rooms. Well prepared meals, a cozy and inviting atmosphere for socializing, and an up-to-date game room make this inn very welcoming for families. **The Gables Inn** (Mountain Road, Rte. 108, RR 1, Box 570; 802–253–7730, 800–GABLES 1), an old farmhouse converted into an inn, is known in Stowe as *the* place for breakfast. Families will especially enjoy the spacious basement-level game room, complete with fireplace and lots of comfortable seating, a TV, and a big supply of games. The guest room decor is country comfortable, with both antiques and reproductions, and lots of canopy beds. The **Green Mountain Inn** (Main Street, P.O. Box 220; 802–253–7301, 800–445–6629) was a country inn long before country inns became fashionable—it opened in 1833. Renovated in 1983, the inn's central location is a key advantage—a health spa, tennis courts, and many of Stowe's charming shops are within an easy walk.

Ten Acres Lodge

Tel: (802) 253–7638

Corner of Luce Hill and Barrows Road, P.O. Box 3220   (800) 327–7357

Dave and Libby Helprin have owned the Ten Acres since 1983 and continue to maintain this inn's long-standing reputation for excellence. Locals as well as guests feel that their restaurant is particularly outstanding. Although menus change daily, the "creative American cuisine" might include such entrées as lamb steak with cracked peppercorns and black currants, roast loin of pork with blood oranges, and red snapper with sea scallops, baked in parchment with squash, peppers, and onions. Rates include continental breakfast and afternoon refreshments.

"The breakfast buffet includes muesli, assorted breads, juices, yogurt, ham, cheese, fresh fruit, tea, and coffee." *(Diane & Lawrence Garber)*

"Dave and Libby are often on hand to greet and converse with guests and their warmth is spread throughout the staff. Rooms are eclectically decorated with warm quilts and cheerful small-print wallpapers. The intimate parlors with fireplaces are conducive to reading, conversing, or a game. Classical music playing softly in the background adds to the soothing ambience."*(Judi Lamberti, also Leslie Ellis)*

"Gets my vote for the best inn in Stowe. Perfect location, convenient yet generally off the beaten path. Bucolic views over cow-studded fields to the mountains beyond. Many of the rooms in the main inn have been completely redone in the past year, but even the least expensive ones are perfectly acceptable, with adequate reading lights (even three-way bulbs that work!), and the larger ones all have comfortable seating areas. The cabins are particularly casual in decor, ideal for families. Best for a romantic escape are the rooms in the Hill House, combining all modern amenities with charming country decor and a light, airy mood. From your room it's

STOWE

just a few steps to the second-floor hot tub with great views of the fields and mountains beyond. The bathrooms don't have a lot of fancy toiletries but, more important, are well supplied with large thick towels and double sinks where space permits." *(SWS)*

Open Mid-June through Oct.; mid-Dec. through March; also Thanksgiving weekend.
Rooms 8 suites, 10 doubles—16 with private bath and/or shower, 2 with maximum of 4 people sharing bath. All with telephone, radio; some with desk, air-conditioning. 8 suites in Hill House annex with fireplace, sitting area, TV, air-conditioning, deck, or terrace. 2 cottages (sleep 4–6 persons) with fireplace, TV, kitchen, outdoor grill.
Facilities Restaurant, living room with fireplace, lounge, library with fireplace, games, puzzles. 6½ acres with garden, swimming pool, hot tub, tennis court. Golf nearby.
Location Follow signs from Mt. Road. 1 m to Trapp Family Lodge. 2½ m to village.
Restrictions No smoking in dining rooms. Children discouraged in main lodge.
Credit cards Amex, MC, Visa.
Rates B&B, $180–250 cottages, $110–150 suites (Hill House), $50–120 double (lodge). Extra person in room, $20. 10% service on lodging. Alc dinner, $40. 10% discount on 3-day stay, 20% discount on 7-day stay, excluding foliage season (mid-Sept. through early Oct.). Ski packages.
Extras Pets allowed in cottages only. French spoken. Cribs available.

Timberholm Inn   *Tel:* (802) 253–7603
Cottage Club Road, RR 1, Box 810

Built in the sixties as a ski lodge, the Timberholm was bought by Susan and Wes Jensen in 1988. Guests gravitate to the living room's huge fieldstone fireplace to relax after a hard day on the ski slopes, and to enjoy the beautiful mountain views from the inn's large picture windows and deck. Rooms at the Timberholm are clean and comfortable, and have been recently redecorated with new wallpaper and some antiques. Susan's full breakfasts include a substantial buffet for early risers, and French toast with Vermont maple syrup or eggs Florentine for all.

"Ideal location. Unlike many of Stowe's inns, the Timberholm is a short way off the Mountain Road, away from the traffic. The inn sits on a lovely hillside, with a deck overlooking the valley and mountains. The common room is very spacious and airy, with breakfast tables and lots of comfy couches. The downstairs rec room is ideal for kids. The guest rooms are very simply decorated, and the 'standard' rooms are quite small; the 'deluxe' rooms cost only a little more and are bigger, with country wallpapers and antique beds." *(SWS)*

"The main part of the inn is paneled in wood, with a huge fireplace, wood floors, area rugs, and large windows with beautiful valley vistas. Susan goes out of her way to be accommodating. The buffet-style breakfast includes various types of cereal, granola, French toast, maple syrup, bacon, coffee, milk, and juices. In the evening, cheese, crackers, and wine are set out by the fireplace—a lovely way to meet other guests and relax."
(Leslie Ellis)

Open All year.
Rooms 2 2-bedroom suites, 8 doubles—all with private shower and/or bath, fan.
Facilities Living room and library with fireplaces, books, TV/VCR, piano, and

639

stereo; game room. 4 acres with deck and flower gardens in summer. Cross-country and downhill skiing, swimming, tennis, golf, boating, fishing nearby.

Location 2½ m from Stowe village. From village, take Rte. 108 N to Cottage Club Rd. Turn right (E) on road, ½ m to inn on right.

Restrictions Smoking allowed in game room and guest rooms only.

Credit cards MC, Visa.

Rates B&B, $85–100 suite, $55–90 double. Extra person in room, $15. 10–15% service. 10% senior discount. Children's discount during ski season.

Extras Cribs, babysitting available.

VERGENNES 05491 Map 1

Strong House Inn
West Main Street (Route 22A), RD 1, Box 9

Tel: (802) 877–3337

Strong House is an 1824 Federal-style house, with Greek Revival influences, listed on the National Register of Historic Places. It was built by Samuel Paddock Strong, a local businessman who served as the president of the Bank of Vergennes and director of the Rutland and Burlington Railroad. Vergennes is the third oldest city in the U.S., and with only 2,500 residents, one of the smallest. Nearby sights of interest include the Shelburne Museum, the Champlain Shakespeare Festival, Shelburne Farms, and the Vermont Wildflower Farm, as well as Middlebury's Sheldon Museum. The area is very flat (for Vermont), and excellent for bicycling.

Michelle and Ron Bring have owned the inn since 1987, and have furnished it with antiques and country crafts. All guest rooms were redecorated in 1989 with an eye to enhanced guest comfort. Landscaping has also been upgraded to complement the beautiful view of the Adirondacks, to the west.

"The house is elegant, with wide hallways, high ceilings, stunning proportions. Our room had rich yellow and blue wallpaper, an old sleigh bed and a working fireplace. We travelled with our 16-month-old baby and Ron and Michelle even let us feed her at their kitchen counter. Breakfast was sumptuous—omelets, homemade granola, muffins, juice and fruit. The Brings run this inn with a marvelous combination of informality and elegance." *(Angela & David Silver)* "The room we stayed in (#7) was fabulous—large and spacious with a beautiful working fireplace." *(Carol Beachley)* "The area is very quiet at night, even though the inn is not fifty yards from the road leading into the lovely little town of Vergennes." *(Harry & Sandra Swayne)*

Open All year.

Rooms 1 suite, 5 doubles—2 with full private bath, 2 with private shower only, 2 with maximum of 4 people sharing bath. 1 with fireplace; some with fans.

Facilities Dining room, living room with fireplace, piano, games, books. 2 acres with courtyard, garden, volleyball, croquet, lawn games. Swimming pool, tennis, golf, Lake Champlain for swimming, fishing, boating nearby. 45 min. to cross-country/downhill skiing at Sugarbush, Mad River. Canoeing, bicycling, hiking.

Location W central VT, Champlain Valley. 5½ hrs. N of NYC, 4½ hrs. NW of Boston. Near juncture of rtes. 22A and 7, 30 min. S of Burlington, 15 min. N of Middlebury, 7 m E of Lake Champlain. On Rte. 22A, ¾ m S of traffic light in town.

Restrictions No smoking.

Credit cards MC, Visa.
Rates B&B, $85 suite, $55–70 double, $35–75 single. Extra person in room, $10. Children under 6 free in parents' room. Prix fixe dinner, only by prior arrangement, $20. 2-night weekend minimum, summer and fall. Special packages.
Extras Airport/station pickups.

WAITSFIELD 05673   Map 1

Waitsfield is located in north central Vermont, close to excellent downhill and cross-country skiing at Sugarbush, Sugarbush North, and Mad River. Summer and fall attractions include hiking, bicycling, gliding, canoeing, golf, tennis, horseback riding, and swimming, plus exploring Vermont's antique and craft shops and auctions. Don't miss the nearby Bundy Gallery of art and outdoor sculpture, with evening concerts on the grass on summer Sundays. Waitsfield is 4 hours northeast of Boston, 6 hours north of New York City, and 35 miles southeast of the Burlington airport.

Also recommended: The **Mountain View Inn** (Route 17, RFD Box 69; 802-496-2426), a 150-year-old farmhouse, is furnished with handmade quilts and braided rugs, and meals are served family-style around an antique harvest table. The hearty breakfasts may include bacon and eggs, pancakes, waffles, or French toast. The **Valley Inn** (Route 100, Box 8; 802-496-3450) was built in 1949 as one of the Mad River Valley's first ski lodges. It's been expanded and redecorated many times since then, but retains its character as a comfortable family lodge. Most of the lodge is paneled in pine, and guest rooms are furnished with quilts and country antiques. **The Waitsfield Inn** (Route 100, Box 969; 802-496-3979) was constructed in true Vermont fashion, with many additions made over the years since its origin in 1825. What was once the attached barn and woodshed (built in 1835) now houses the inn's lounges, complete with the original wood-planked floors, walls, and ceilings. The owners take pride in their restaurant, which features a changing menu of American cuisine, with a particularly good selection of veal and seafood dishes.

Inn at the Round Barn Farm   *Tel:* (802) 496–2276
East Warren Road, RR 1, Box 247

This round (actually 12-sided) barn has been a Waitsfield landmark since it was built in 1910, and is one of only 12 such structures still standing in the state of Vermont. In the ownership of the Joslin family for over a century, the farm was bought by Doreen, Jack and Annemarie Simko in 1986. After extensive renovation of the farmhouse (built in 1810) and the barn, the Simkos opened their elegant country inn, furnished with antiques from country auctions and such luxurious extras as canopied king- and queen-size beds and Jacuzzi tubs. Fluffy cottage cheese pancakes with raspberry-maple sauce are a breakfast favorite, often accompanied by baked apple and blueberry muffins. The restored barn is now used as a theater/conference center and craft center.

"The inn sits on a hill outside the village, and is reached by driving up a country road and over an old covered bridge. Windows in the breakfast room overlook ponds and fields, and the view is idyllic. The guest rooms are lavish, with beautiful window treatments and coordinating bedspreads, and good reading lamps on both sides of the bed." *(SWS)*

"Doreen, Jack and Annemarie Simko have an extraordinary gift for making guests feel they've joined the family. Eating one of Annemarie's legendary breakfasts in the sun room often turns into an all morning event. In the evening, the living room with its book-lined walls, ever-ready fireplace, and fine music is a frequent gathering place." *(Susan Pentecost)*

"The restoration work is impeccable. Moldings fit snugly, paint is where it should be, the wallpaper matches, and the furniture is all period antique. Fresh towels, clean sheets, and flowers create the perfect lodging. Even lighting could be regulated for mood!" *(Sam & Gay Gray)*

"The bed was firm, the comforter cozy, and each room has its own thermostat. Not a speck of dirt in guest or common rooms. Outstanding breakfasts—giant waffles with whipped cream one day, French apple pancakes the next." *(Tom Frazee, also Stephen Fischer)*

Open All year.
Rooms 1 suite, 6 doubles—all with private bath and/or shower, desk, fan. 2 with Jacuzzis.
Facilities Breakfast room, library with fireplace, game room with TV/VCR, workout room, theater-conference center, art gallery. 85 acres with pool, pond, river for fishing, canoeing, cross-country skiing. 8 m to downhill skiing.
Location 1½ m to town. From Rte. 100 in Waitsfield drive through covered bridge, up East Warren Rd. to inn on left.
Restrictions No smoking. No children under 14.
Credit cards Amex, MC, Visa.
Rates B&B, $125 suite, $85–105 double, $75–95 single. 2-night weekend minimum. 10% discount on 5-day midweek stays.
Extras Airport/station pickups, $35–50. Hungarian spoken.

WARREN 05674   Map 1

Warren is a tiny village located 3 miles south of Waitsfield on Route 100. It doesn't contain much more than the Warren Store, which once sold little more than bologna and white bread, but has developed into almost a Zabar's North (gourmet deli) over the last 20 years. About a mile north of the village, the Sugarbush access road extends east from Route 100 to Sugarbush village and the ski area; many inns and restaurants are located along here. Area activities include the usual Vermont outdoor pleasures, including a rather difficult Robert Trent Jones golf course, as well as gliding, polo, and, in late July and early August, the Sugarbush Grand Prix Horse Show.

"The village of Warren is on Old Route 100, and looks like one of the places time forgot. Don't let its looks fool you, though—the people of Warren are transplanted fifties and sixties political activists, artists, and writers. They are interesting, creative, politically aware (the *New York Times* is the biggest selling Sunday paper in town), and contentious. We loved them and the little community." *(Dave & Cheri Kendall)*

Warren is 200 miles northwest of Boston, 300 miles north of New York City, and 1 hour from the Burlington airport, in north-central Vermont.

Beaver Pond Farm Inn *Tel:* (802) 583–2861
Golf Course Road, RD Box 306

A small restored Vermont farmhouse, Beaver Pond Farm Inn is surrounded by cross-country ski trails in winter; in the summer, golfers are challenged by the adjacent eighteen-hole Robert Trent Jones course. Of course, downhillers will head straight for Sugarbush, just a mile away. A prix fixe dinner, including wine, is served three nights weekly. A recent meal included tomato bisque, salad with celery seed dressing, rack of lamb garni, poppy seed bread, and frozen orange-lemon soufflé.

"The old farmhouse is warm and charming, with spectacular views of Sugarbush and the surrounding mountains. The owners, Betty and Bob Hansen, are an ideal combination—they're gracious, relaxed, and have a grand sense of humor. Betty's country-style breakfasts were outstanding!" *(Jean Lamphear)*

"My favorite approach to the inn is up a quiet back road, lined with sugar maples. The inn welcomes me with inviting candles in each window and the rooms are cozy and romantic. The breakfasts are a gourmet delight and can easily seduce you into a half-day ski ticket." *(Virginia Huber, also SWS)* "The Hansens greet returning skiers with hot apple cider and freshly baked cookies." *(Michelle & John Perkoff)*

Open June to April.
Rooms 5 double rooms—3 with full private bath, 2 with maximum of 4 people sharing bath. All with radio.
Facilities Living room with fireplace, TV room, BYOB bar, deck. Flower and vegetable gardens, pond. Adjacent to Sugarbush golf course and cross-country skiing. Fishing and swimming nearby; trout fishing guide service. 1 m to Sugarbush, 5 m to Mad River Glen.
Location 1 m from Warren village. From I-89, take Exit 9 to Rte. 100. Go S on Rte. 100 to Sugarbush Access Rd. Turn left at Sugarbush Ski Area Parking Lot onto Inferno Rd. Go 1.3 m, then left at mailboxes onto Golf Course Rd. Inn is on right.
Restrictions Smoking in living room only. No children under 7.
Credit cards Amex, MC, Visa.
Rates B&B, $64–90 double, $44–65 single, plus 15% gratuity. Extra person in room, $25. 20% discount for 2-night midweek stays. 2-night weekend minimum. 3–5-day ski packages. Prix fixe dinner, $18–20.
Extras French spoken. Airport/station pickups.

WEST DOVER 05356 Map 1

West Dover is in south central Vermont, about 20 miles west of Brattleboro and east of Bennington, and 5 miles north of Wilmington, at Route 9. It is about a 4-hour drive north of New York City, and about 3 hours northwest of Boston. To get there, take I-91 or Route 7 to Route 100, then go north on 100 to West Dover.

West Dover is the closest town to Mt. Snow, the largest ski area in southern Vermont, with both downhill and cross-country skiing available. Stratton, Bromley, and Magic Mountain are a 45-minute drive to the north. Summer activities include golf and tennis at Mt. Snow, with lakes and streams for swimming, fishing, and boating, as well as the summer music festival at Marlboro.

Also recommended: The **Snow Den Inn** (Route 100, P.O. Box 625; 802–464–9355, 802–464–5852), built in 1885 and listed on the National Register of Historic Places, the Snow Den Inn was converted in 1952 to become the first guest house in the Mt. Snow area. The innkeepers, Marjorie and Andrew Trautwein, pride themselves on being very attentive to their guests in the homey and comfortable surroundings of the inn.

The Inn at Sawmill Farm
Route 100, Mt. Snow Valley

Tel: (802) 464–8131

Arguably Vermont's best-known country inn, The Inn at Saw Mill Farm was built and decorated by innkeepers Rodney and Ione Williams, who started with an old Vermont barn twenty years ago, and have come a very long way since then. Brill Williams, their son and the chef, is also part owner; he oversees the dining room and 20,000-bottle wine cellar, and the cuisine here consistently wins raves from top food critics.

"Now we know why this inn is ranked as one of the best in New England. It would be hard to fault it in any way. Service was great. The location is very quiet and picturesque. We had a beautiful room with fireplace." *(Jo Carol Wood)* "Expensive, but the food is the most fabulous we've ever tasted anywhere!" *(Marjorie Berg)*

"Comfortable yet elegant. It's a basic country inn but the food and wine make it exceptional. We've sampled rabbit, delicious veal, fish, all served beautifully, and they have an amazing wine selection. This is not a place to take the kids; Saw Mill Farm is the spot to go for an 'I'd like to get to know you again' weekend with your spouse. There's a pool and golf in summer, and cross-country and downhill skiing in winter. But who needs to go outside?" *(Patti Barrett, also Samuel Cantor)*

After twenty years in this exceptionally demanding business, Rod Williams notes that "you can't be all things to all people. You must set your goals and hope a small percentage of guests enjoy them. For us, the goals are quietude in a relaxing atmosphere, unpretentious but curiously sophisticated." In other words, it's not an inn for everyone. If you can afford it, the fireplace suites are probably the most attractive; one reader felt the decor in her room needed some updating, especially at over $200 a day. Another thought the candlelit dining room too dark and formal for a country inn, and would have preferred a more isolated location. Comments?

Open All year.
Rooms 10 suites with fireplace, 11 doubles—all with private bath, radio, desk, air-conditioning. 10 rooms in main inn, 11 in cottages.
Facilities 6 public rooms include library, lounge, game room with TV. Lounge features piano player 5 nights a week. 21 acres. Tennis, swimming pool, trout ponds, cross-country skiing on grounds. ½ m to golf and downhill skiing. Restaurant for guests only.
Location In village. Take first left past village church.
Restrictions No smoking in guest rooms. No children under 10. Men are requested to wear jackets after 6:00 P.M.
Credit cards None accepted.
Rates MAP, $220–240 suite or double, $175–195 single. Cottage (MAP), $240–270

double, $195–225 single. Extra person in room, $75–85. 15% service additional.
2-night weekend minimum. Alc dinner, $55.
Extras French, German spoken. Member, Relais & Chateaux.

WEST TOWNSHEND 05359   Map 1

Windham Hill Inn   *Tel:* (802) 874–4080
RR 1   874–4976

From the moment you open the invitation-style brochure for the Windham Hill Inn, you know that its owners have a personal vision of the ideal country inn. Unfolding the envelope, you realize that it is a beautifully designed die-cut of the owners' barn, containing a postcard-style montage of pictures of the inn, bearing the handwritten message: "Wish you were here!"

Though the inn dates back to 1825, the location is great, on a quiet country road distant from traffic noise. Set into the mountainside, the inn provides lovely views of the valley and the surrounding mountains. The decor complements the quiet mood perfectly, with restored country antiques (many found by the Busteeds when they bought the inn in 1981), and rooms are done in soft colors, many in ivory and taupe with deep blue highlights, creating a very restful atmosphere. The bathrooms have antique touches as well, along with herb- and spice-scented soaps.

"Outstanding. If one likes peace, quiet, and solitude in a mountainside location with sensuous vistas, consider this paradise. A touch of elegance combined with informality—spacious, and very well decorated and maintained. It's the type of place one tries to describe to friends back home but words seem inadequate. Exceptional dining. Breakfasts are marvelous and hardy. Music is a specialty at the inn—with tape recorded music in the dining room and occasional chamber music concerts in the converted barn. Horse-drawn carriage rides to a deluxe picnic in the surrounding scenic countryside can be arranged for those wanting to be completely seduced. A superb combination of low-key innkeepers and informal excellence. Reasonable in cost for value received." *(Ed Okie)* And after a return visit a year later: "Improving on near perfection is a noteworthy achievement, but the Busteeds have succeeded." *(Ed Okie)*

"Gourmet meals, concerned friendly innkeepers, and beautiful location with mountain views. We stayed in the main house where we had a clean, comfortable room with a queen-size bed with pastel linens, and a welcoming decanter of sherry. Our room had a private bath, the air perfumed with cinnamon soap. The common rooms were decorated with antiques, except for the glassed-in porch, done in white wicker. We chose to join the other guests at dinner, and arrived to find place cards on the table. Dinner included salmon paté; curried carrot vichyssoise; sourdough rye bread and salad; a palate cleanser of raspberry sorbet; individual beef Wellington with fresh green beans and tiny tomatoes. Dessert was a delicious strawberry and whipped cream concoction. Sunday breakfast brought juice, homemade banana bread, eggs Mornay and good coffee. Since it was a very hot day, Ken suggested a walk in the woods to their crystalline spring-fed waterfall. Refreshing and delightful." *(Amy Peritsky)*

Open May through March.
Rooms 15 doubles—all with private bath and/or shower, desk. 4 with balconies. 5 rooms in restored barn.
Facilities Dining room; 3 common rooms with fireplace, Franklin stoves; library; mini-bar. 150 acres with flower gardens, pond, lighted ice-skating, hiking trails, cross-country skiing trails, including rentals and instruction. Horsedrawn carriage rides/picnics. Tennis, golf, swimming, fishing, downhill skiing nearby.
Location SE VT. From I-91, take Exit 2 to Rte. 30 W for 21 m. Go right at the red country store in W. Townshend and go 1½ m up hill to inn.
Restrictions Smoking in common rooms only. No children under 12.
Credit cards Amex, MC, Visa.
Rates MAP, $150–170 suite and double, $100–115 single, plus 15% service. Extra person in room, $60. 2-night weekend/foliage-season minimum.
Extras Station pickups with prior arrangement. Limited wheelchair access.

WILMINGTON 05363 — Map 1

Wilmington is located in south central Vermont, 17 miles west of Brattleboro, on Route 9, a major east-west route. It is approximately 4 hours north of New York City, and 2½ hours northwest of Boston. West Dover and Mount Snow lie about 5 miles north of Wilmington, up Route 100. Four downhill ski areas are within a 15-minute drive; four cross-country areas are 10 minutes away. Summer pleasures include golf at Haystack or Mt. Snow; hiking in the surrounding mountains; swimming, boating and canoeing in Lake Whitingham; and theater and music in Wilmington and Marlboro.

Also recommended: The **Hermitage Inn** (Coldbrook Road, P.O. Box 457; 802–464–3511), under the direction of innkeeper Jim McGovern, provides and displays a range of services and enterprises most unusual in a country inn—early-spring maple sugaring and summertime jam and jelly making, maintaining a stocked trout pond, raising dozens of species of game birds, breeding English setters, and keeping current a 30,000-bottle wine cellar. House specialties, served in the inn's lovely dining rooms, include pheasant, duckling, and trout (all raised on the property). Rooms vary in size, but all are attractive and furnished with antiques. **The Red Shutter Inn** (Route 9, P.O. Box 636; 802–464–3768), built in 1894, is a colonial-style building, set back from the road and framed by maples, pin oaks, and evergreens. Rates include a full breakfast, and home-cooked dinner is served both to guests and the public. **The White House of Wilmington** (Route 9; 802–464–2135) sits high on a hill overlooking the Vermont countryside, a symmetrical mansion with some Greek Revival elements in its balanced design. No expense was spared in its construction in 1915; it features two-storied balconies, hand-crafted French doors, beautiful woodwork, and imported French wallpaper. The living room has a real country house feel to it, with lots of comfortable couches and wing chairs, while the guest rooms are decorated with antique and reproduction furnishings. Rates include both a full country breakfast and an elegant dinner of continental classics.

Nutmeg Inn   *Tel:* (802) 464-3351
Route 9 West (Molly Stark Trail), Box 818

The Nutmeg is an early 1800s Vermont farmhouse, with connecting carriage house, which was converted to a country inn in 1957. It was bought by Neal and Rachel Jordan in 1988.

"The Nutmeg is everything a country inn should be—charming, quaint, warm, and cozy. It is clean, with very comfortable rooms that combine modern conveniences with beautiful quilts, wallpapers, and country accents." *(Dr. & Mrs. Joseph Sozio)*

"The inn has a beautiful country decor. Our suite had a private entrance and living room with cable TV and working fireplace. The bedroom had a queen-size bed and loads of closet space, a private bath, and a sliding glass door to the outside. The Jordans were very friendly, helping us with suggestions for shopping, horseback riding, restaurants, and more. Breakfast was cooked to order very morning, with a choice of eggs, bacon, French toast, pancakes, cereal, and more. At night they were happy to fix us a cup of hot cocoa or tea." *(Johanna & Anthony Valente)*

"The living room was rustic with a lovely old stone fireplace, a game section on one side and television on the other, a bar with ice, refrigerator, and glasses always available, and plenty of comfortable chairs for reading." *(Alice McCarthy)*

"The inn, although located on a major southern Vermont route, is nestled off the road on a large piece of property that gives you a real country feeling. Although full when we were there, it was quiet, with plentiful, well-lit parking conveniently close to the inn." *(Kathleen & Jack DiMaggio)*

Open All year.
Rooms 3 suites, 10 doubles—3 with full private bath, 10 with private shower. Some with TV, desk, air-conditioning.
Facilities Dining room; living room with fireplace, game corner, TV, library, bar. 3 acres with lawn games, brook. Golf, tennis, hiking, cross-country and downhill skiing, lake for swimming, fishing, boating nearby.
Location On Rte. 9, 1 m W of Wilmington.
Restrictions Light sleepers should request quiet rooms. Children over 8 preferred. Smoking in living room only.
Credit cards MC, Visa.
Rates B&B, $95–150 suite, $60–95 double, plus 15% service. Extra person in room, $25. Midweek, ski-week discounts. Prix fixe dinner, $19 (Sat. nights only). 2-3 night minimum stay, weekends and holidays.

WINDSOR 05089   **Map 1**

Juniper Hill Inn   *Tel:* (802) 674-5273
Juniper Hill Road, RR 1, Box 79

Juniper Hill was built at the turn of the century by Maxwell Evarts of Windsor as his private residence. It's not hard to imagine the gatherings of prominent railroad and shipping magnates of the day who were entertained in the inn's large first-floor rooms—the oak-paneled entry parlor measures 30 by 40 feet! Evarts was also a friend of President Teddy Roosevelt, who stayed at Juniper Hill when touring the northeast. The building remained in the Evarts family until 1944, when it was converted into an inn, and, later, a center for Catholic retreats. Jim and Krisha Pennino bought Juniper Hill in 1984 and began the ongoing process of restoring it to its original grandeur; the inn is now listed on the National Register of Historic Places.

"The inn's hilltop location offers a breathtaking view of Mt. Ascutney, the Connecticut River, and the surrounding countryside, and is best enjoyed on their gracious portico or next to the brand-new swimming pool." *(Michelle & Robert Bullard)*

"Casual elegance would be an apt description of this place. Lots of space, wonderful fireplaces. But the innkeepers are the ones who tie it together with warmth and personality, and who make one want to keep coming back. Evening dining ranks with some of the best inns, yet without the least bit of stuffiness." *(Ed Okie)*

"This magnificent Georgian-style colonial mansion is built on a grand scale. The old master bedroom, where we stayed, is a real charmer, with a great view of the surrounding countryside. Other choice bedrooms are off the library; most are furnished in period antiques. Dinner was served at the original dining table—it's about 25 feet long and required extra support in the floor joists to bear its 1,000-pound mass." *(Patrick E. Kelley)*

Open May through Oct.; Dec. 15 through mid-Mar.
Rooms 15 doubles—all with private bath and/or shower, fan. 9 rooms with working fireplace; some with desk.
Facilities Dining room, library with games, bar, 2 large parlors, TV room. 14 acres with heated pool, nature trails, croquet, snowshoeing. 1 m from CT River for canoeing. 3 m to golf, tennis, swimming. 7 m to downhill skiing, 3 cross-country ski areas within 15 m.
Location SE VT, Upper CT River Valley. 2½ hrs. N of Hartford and NW of Boston. 2 m from town. Exit 9 off I-91, 3 m S on Rte. 5, right on Juniper Hill Road for ¼ m. Left at fork for another ¼ m to driveway on right with sign.
Restrictions No smoking in guest rooms or dining room. No children under 12.
Credit cards Amex, MC, Visa.
Rates B&B, $65–100 double, $60–90 single, plus 15% service. Extra person in room, $15. Prix fixe dinner, $16–18. 2-night minimum, holidays and fall foliage. Bicycling, canoeing packages.
Extras Station pickups.

WOODSTOCK 05091   Map 1

An archetypal New England town, Woodstock offers a picture-perfect village green, surrounded by beautifully restored historic homes and an ample supply of tasteful shops—even a covered bridge. Skiers stay here in winter (it's 4 miles to Suicide Six and 12 miles to Killington and Pico, plus cross-country skiing at the Woodstock Country Club), while summer offers hiking, fishing, golf, and tennis. A visit to the Billings Farm Museum will take you back to the farm life of a century ago.

Also recommended: The **Jackson House** (Route 4 West; 802–457–2065, 800–448–1890), an 1890s inn, is one of the most luxurious in the Woodstock area. Rooms are beautifully furnished in French, American, and

English antiques. Lavish breakfasts vary daily; evening libations and an hors d'oeuvres buffet include an open wine and champagne bar, caviar, pâté, imported cheese, lobster and shrimp, quiche, and more. Rates also include turndown service with Godiva chocolates and late-night liqueurs.

The Woodstock Inn and Resort (On the Green; 802–457–1100), an imposing white building centrally located near Woodstock's green, offers access to nearly every conceivable sports activity, from racquetball to sleigh riding. Rooms are decorated with reproduction furnishings and handmade quilts, while the food is hearty and tasty; the luncheon buffet is an especially good value.

Woodstock is set on Route 4 in east-central Vermont, about 10 miles west of the intersection of I-91 and I-89 at White River Junction. Boston is 153 miles southeast, while New York is 280 miles southwest.

The Charleston House
21 Pleasant Street

Tel: (802) 457–3843

Located in the beautiful village of Woodstock, The Charleston is a restored 1835 Greek Revival town house, listed on the National Register of Historic Places. It's attractively and comfortably furnished with a mixture of antiques, reproductions, and contemporary pieces, plus a varied collection of art and Oriental rugs. Rates include a full breakfast, and owners Bill and Barbara Hough will be glad to point out Woodstock's many interesting features.

"Everything is amazingly clean. All the rooms are decorated in beautiful prints and soothing colors of peach, mint, and mauve. Hand-done needlepoint pillows and family antiques add a personal touch. Breakfast is served family-style on nice china with good silver and linens. The parking lot has a light that turns on automatically when you walk outside or drive in." *(DDR, also Mary Danley)* "Relaxed atmosphere, accommodating hosts." *(Christine Mickles)*

Open All year.
Rooms 7 doubles, all with full private bath. 1 with TV, 2 with desks, all with air-conditioning.
Facilities Dining room, living room with TV, fireplace, books, and games, patio. Bicycles available to guests. Swimming, tennis, fishing, and golf available nearby. Cross-country and 5 major downhill ski areas nearby.
Location Central VT, 150 m from Boston. 2 blocks from center of village.
Restrictions Smoking restricted. Noise in 1 room might bother light sleepers. No children under 9.
Credit cards MC, Visa.
Rates B&B $100–125 double. Extra person in room, $20. 2–3 night weekend/holiday minimum.
Extras Airport/station pickups.

Virginia

Fassifern Bed & Breakfast, Lexington

Few states equal Virginia's importance in the birth of this country. The first permanent English settlement in America was at Jamestown, in 1619. Eight U.S. presidents were born in Virginia; of the founding fathers of the U.S., Washington, Jefferson, Madison, Marshall, Monroe, and Henry were all Virginians. More Civil War battles were fought in Virginia than in any other state; Civil War buffs will want to visit all the battle sites. There is much of historical interest for all to explore in the state. The Virginia Division of Tourism has helpful brochures specifically dealing with many facets of Virginia history; ask for details when you call or write.

Northern Virginia is noted for its historic towns and is known as horse country. Tidewater is home to Jamestown, Williamsburg, and Yorktown, plus Virginia Beach. The Eastern Shore is an isolated finger reaching out into the Chesapeake Bay from Maryland—Assateague National Seashore is perhaps its best-known feature. The central and southern portions of the state are rich in history, particularly of the Civil War. The Shenandoah Valley and Mountains are where Washingtonians go to cool off, literally and figuratively; the scenery is breathtaking in all four seasons.

Virginia's spa country is located in the Allegheny Mountain Valley towns of Warm Springs, Hot Springs, and White Sulphur Springs, along the West Virginia border. You can soak in medicinal waters, or enjoy the equally recuperative effects of the peaceful mountain air.

Rates do not include the 6% state sales tax on lodging, and the 4% tax on meals. Rates do not change seasonally in most locations, but tend to be highest on weekends and lower midweek. If you plan to stay at an inn for three or four nights during the week, be sure to ask if any midweek discounts apply.

ALEXANDRIA 22314   Map 4

Morrison House   *Tel:* (703) 838–8000
116 South Alfred Street   In VA: (800) 533–1808
                                         In US: (800) 367–0800

At first sight, you might assume that the elegant Federal-style Morrison House was built in 1785, not two centuries later when it was actually constructed by Robert Morrison. A European-style small luxury hotel, it is furnished with high-quality period reproduction furnishings, brass and crystal lighting, elaborately swagged curtains in tones of soft yellow, green, and peach; modern amenities such as televisions are of course discreetly tucked away in custom-made armoires. The hotel is home to two restaurants, Le Chardon d'Or, for elegant French dining, and the more casual Grill; both are served by the same kitchen, and both have been well received by local critics.

"The perfect combination—period charm combined with every modern amenity. The bathrooms have imported marble vanities, with Lancôme soaps and lotions, with lighting designed for putting on makeup—no fluorescents. Owner Robert Morrison is very pleasant and cordial. He was very much involved in every detail of the design of his inn; to avoid the blank wall usually found at the end of a hotel corridor, he had a window added to provide sun. The inn is on a quiet residential street in the heart of Old Town Alexandria, two to three blocks from the main thoroughfare." *(Frank & Dotty Scarfone)* "The food is outstanding and afternoon tea, delightful." *(Carolyn Myles, also Peter Keim)*

Open All year.
Rooms 3 suites, 42 doubles—all with full private bath, telephone, radio, TV, airconditioning. Some with fireplace. Concierge service.
Facilities Parlor with fireplace, library, two restaurants, bar/lounge with fireplace, piano. Health club, pool, sailing nearby. Indoor valet parking.
Location Historic Old Town. Two blocks W of S. Washington St., between King and Prince Sts.
Credit cards Amex, CB, DC, MC, Visa.
Rates Room only, $230 suite, $135–190 double. Extra person in room, $20. Weekend B&B rates, $180 suite, $100–130 double. Children under 12, free. Full breakfast $9. Alc lunch $12, alc dinner $35–55.
Extras Wheelchair accessible. Pets permitted by prior arrangement. Cribs, babysitting available. French, Spanish, German, Russian, Japanese, Arabic spoken.

BEDFORD 24523   Map 4

With a newly restored downtown and a population of fewer than 6,000 people, Bedford makes a lovely place to overnight when you're traveling the Blue Ridge Parkway along Virginia's western border. It's about 30 miles west of Lynchburg, 100 miles southwest of Charlottesville, and 225 miles southwest of Washington, DC.

The Longwood Inn
517 Longwood Avenue (Route 221)

Tel: (703) 586–2282

This turn-of-the-century Victorian is encircled with porches; the interior features the original oak and pine floors and tiled fireplaces, along with collections of antique lace and glass and an eclectic mixture of nostalgic and contemporary furnishings. Owner Lou Wright particularly enjoys preparing uncomplicated yet tasty breakfasts and dinners.

"The front porch is most inviting, with ample current reading material and newspapers, a beautifully manicured lawn, and gentle woodwind music floating from a hidden speaker." *(Eric Bivens)* "A mixture of traditional and modern decor, with a blend of calm colors and soft fabrics. Great food." *(Wink & Becky Glover)* "The inn's fresh, light interior, with plants in the windows, gives it a homey feel, and the collection of framed handkerchiefs are a source of interest as well as a charming touch. All my needs were met—plenty of towels, artistic writing materials, and a delicious, simple breakfast. The inn is surrounded by a well-tended garden—plants are marked with their common names. The inn occupies the highest elevation in town, in a neighborhood of stately old homes." *(Kristen Bedford)* "The inn is within easy walking distance of the newly restored quaint downtown area. Our room was large and most pleasant, done in beiges and white, with a hardwood floor, reading materials, fresh flowers, full-length mirror, good lighting, and handsome window treatments. Our room was very quiet—we couldn't hear a sound from the other rooms—and our bath was new, with good plumbing. The inn is immaculately clean throughout." *(Mrs. Jack Hammond)* "The beds are big and comfortable; chocolate-chip cookies are there for the eating and sherry is available for a nightcap. Daily newspapers are found in front of the fireplace, where a cheery fire crackles." *(Charles Perry)*

Open Jan. 10 to Dec. 15

Rooms 8 doubles—5 with private bath and/or shower, 2 with maximum of 4 sharing bath. All with radio, desk, air-conditioning. 1 with TV. 3 rooms in annex.

Facilities Dining room, parlor, common area with guest refrigerator, porch with swing, glider. 1 acre with herb, vegetable, and flower gardens. Tennis and lake for fishing and swimming nearby. 10 m to cross-country skiing.

Location 9 m to Blue Ridge Parkway, 9 m to Peaks of Otter. 4 blocks to center of town.

Restrictions No smoking.

Credit cards MC, Visa.

Rates B&B, $50–80 double, $40–70 single. Extra person in room, $10.

Extras Handicap accessible. Cribs, babysitting, swings, games available.

CHARLOTTESVILLE
Map 4

Charlottesville is best known as the home of Thomas Jefferson's Monticello and the University of Virginia. Other sights of interest include Castle Hill, Ashlawn, Michie Tavern, Court Square, and the nearby Skyline Drive. The best place for information on all these sights is the Thomas Jefferson Visitors' Bureau, located at the intersection of I-64 and Rte. 20

South. The area also offers lakes for boating and swimming; it's a 40-minute drive to downhill and cross-country skiing. Albemarle County is horse country, with many fox hunts and steeplechase events; there's no shortage of golf courses and tennis courts, either.

Also recommended: The Boar's Head Inn & Sports Club (P.O. Box 5185 (Ednam Forest), 22905; 804–296–2181), built 25 years ago as a small country inn, has grown into a large resort hotel and sports complex. Although it's much larger than most of our listings, it is well recommended by quite a few respondents. The **Clifton** (Route 9, Box 412, 22901; 804–971–1800), set on a cliff overlooking the Rivanna River, was built in 1799 on land originally part of the Jefferson family estate, Shadwell; Monticello can be seen on a neighboring hill when the trees are bare. Guest rooms have the original pine floors, wall paneling, and working fireplaces, with period decor and quality linens. Rates include a multicourse breakfast, and dinners are also available. The **200 South Street Inn** (200 South Street, 22901; 804–979–0200) is a combination of two buildings built in the 1850s and restored in 1986. Rooms are comfortably but elegantly decorated with English and Belgian antiques; the inn is filled with classic English art, works of contemporary Virginian artists, and historical photographs.

Charlottesville is 125 miles southwest of Washington, DC, and 75 miles northwest of Richmond.

Silver Thatch Inn
3001 Hollymead Drive 22901

Tel: (804) 978–4686

Built by captured Hessian soldiers during the Revolutionary War, the Silver Thatch has been added onto many times during the past 200 years. New owners Mickey and Joe Geller bought the inn late in 1988, and have added top-quality sheets, plenty of thick towels, and down comforters to the antique decor. Rates include a breakfast of juice, melon, cereal, granola, muffins and coffee, and picnic lunches are available on request. The Gellers note that "we are working with Virginia growers and producers and have two wonderful chefs creating modern country cuisine; our wine list features three local Virginia vineyards, and our homemade desserts and breads are fabulous." The menu changes monthly with daily specials always available.

"Mickey and Joe Geller have created a warm and friendly atmosphere. The three dining rooms are very romantic with candle lit tables, crisp white linens, and soft background music. The staff attended to all my needs, and the food was fabulous. I had Santa Fe chicken, a spicy dish served with corn sticks and a hot black bean salsa. Dessert was a white chocolate mousse filled with raspberry purée." *(Elizabeth Bright)*

"Although under new ownership, we were told by Lisa Workman (a most delightful staff member who was of great help to us) that very few changes have been made. Because dinner was not being served the night we stayed, we were referred to the Galerie, where we enjoyed superb French cuisine. Breakfast was very good and the decor has a pleasant country motif. We stayed in the James Monroe Room with a canopied

653

queen-size bed. Drinks on the patio overlooking the garden was most enjoyable." *(Barbara Hornbach)*

Open All year. Closed Dec. 23-25, 1st 2 weeks Jan. Restaurant closed Sun., Mon.
Rooms 7 doubles—all with private shower and/or bath, air-conditioning. 4 with fireplace.
Facilities Restaurant, common room, library, bar/lounge with TV, fireplace. 1½ acres with swimming pool, tennis court. Fishing nearby.
Location 5 m to town, on Rte. 1520, ½ m E of Rte. 29N.
Restrictions No smoking.
Credit cards MC, Visa. Personal checks not accepted.
Rates B&B, $95–125 double, $75–105 single. Extra person in room, $20. Corporate rates. 2-night minimum weekends, holidays. Alc lunch $25–30 alc dinner, $45–50.
Extras Airport pickups.

FREDERICKSBURG 22401   Map 4

Fredericksburg dates back to the early eighteenth century; it served as an important river port city in the colonial period, and was a central meeting point for George Washington, Thomas Jefferson, Patrick Henry, James Monroe, and John Paul Jones. Sights of interest include Mary Washington's home, James Monroe's law office, the Rising Sun Tavern, and the Kenmore plantation house, as well as the town's many craft and antique shops. Surrounding Fredericksburg are a number of major Civil War battlefields, including Chancellorsville, Wilderness, and Spotsylvania.

Fredericksburg is located in northern Virginia, 50 miles south of Washington, DC, and 55 miles north of Richmond, just a short distance off the Route 3 East exit of I-95.

Richard Johnston Inn   *Tel:* (703) 899–7606
711 Caroline Street

The Richard Johnston was built in the Federal style in the 1780s. It has been owned and operated by Dennis and Libby Gowin since 1985. In several guest rooms, the exposed bricks and hand-hewn beams contrast handsomely with the plain white walls. Rates include a continental breakfast of home-baked breads, biscuits, fresh fruits, and coffee.

"Fredericksburg is a quaint, history-packed town, located between Washington and Richmond—a nice place to go for a romantic extended weekend away from the city. The inn is decorated in a very charming manner; each room is styled differently. The atmosphere is warm and conducive to meeting new people." *(Susan P. Hartman)*

"Spotless, completely renovated row house in the heart of town. Antique furnishings, beautiful quilts, and rag rugs on wood floors in all rooms. Selection of accommodation to suit your budget. The innkeeper could easily be your aunt. A great place to stay in a great town to visit." *(Mrs. Peter Payne)*

"Particularly enjoyed suite #10, tastefully furnished with a working fireplace. Access to room from back patio very convenient. Nice family-style breakfast." *(H. Richard Hoepfner)*

Open All year.

Rooms 2 suites, 9 doubles—7 with full private bath, 4 with maximum of 4 sharing bath. All with radio, air-conditioning. Some rooms with TV and working fireplaces.

Facilities Living room, dining room, library, courtyard with tables, chairs. Rappahannock River in backyard; fishing, hiking nearby.

Location Historic district, across from Visitors' Center. Take I-95 to Rte. 3 E (Williams St.). Turn right on Caroline St. 3 blocks from Amtrak station.

Restrictions Smoking discouraged. No children under 12.

Credit cards Amex, MC, Visa.

Rates B&B, $120 suite, $75–85 double, $55 single. Extra person in room, $10. Senior discount. Corporate rates.

HOT SPRINGS 24445   Map 4

The Carriage Court   *Tel:* (703) 839–2345
Route 220, Route 2, Box 620 (mail)

Carriage Court is a group of old farm buildings that have been remodeled and converted into a country inn and restaurant, set halfway between Warm Springs and Hot Springs. It's been owned by the Aborn family since 1985, and rates include a continental breakfast. Much replanting has been done in 1989 to enhance the inn's flower gardens.

"A charming, comfortable treasure, appealingly decorated with period furniture, pictures, and pottery. It is perfectly situated for taking the waters at Warm Springs and tea at the Homestead, and for walking the roads and trails in the countryside. The management is attentive, with a casual homeyness. Parking is at the door, and everything works as it should. It is quiet, convenient, warm, and friendly." *(Melva Chanslor)*

"We enjoyed our early-morning coffee on our private deck overlooking beautiful rolling hills and woods that contain many hiking trails. We were asked frequently if there was anything we needed. We also appreciated personal touches such as the handmade needlework pictures and ample supply of paperbacks." *(Jane Goldsberry & Judy Abshire)*

"Very good Italian-style food for dinner, and service from people who care about you. A golfer's paradise." *(Elizabeth Matarese)* "Although the owners were hardly ever around, we loved everything else about the inn. Our room was wonderful, clean, quaint, and quiet, with our very own herd of cows out back." *(AMC)*

Open All year.

Rooms 3 suites, 3 doubles in 2 adjacent buildings. All with full private bath, telephone, TV. Some with desk, deck, porch, kitchenette.

Facilities Breakfast room, restaurant, deck. 2 acres with flower gardens. Lakes, rivers, golf, fishing, downhill skiing, ice-skating nearby.

Location Western VA, Allegheny Mts. Bath County, "Spa Country." 200 m SW of Washington, DC, 150 m W of Richmond. On Rte. 220, 1 m from the Homestead and Hot Springs.

Credit cards MC, Visa.

Rates B&B, $59–120 suite, $48–59 double. Extra person in room, $12. Group golf packages.

Extras Pets permitted. Airport pickup by arrangement. Wheelchair accessible. Cribs available. Babysitting by arrangement.

LEXINGTON 24450   Map 4

Lexington is a nineteenth-century town with a handsome historic district and the homes of both Robert E. Lee and Stonewall Jackson; Washington and Lee University and Virginia Military Institute are also located here. Nearby attractions include Natural Bridge and the Blue Ridge Parkway.

Lexington is in the Shenandoah Valley, in the western part of Virginia, 54 miles northeast of Roanoke, and 69 miles southwest of Charlottesville.

Also recommended: The **Llewellyn Lodge** (603 South Main Street, Route 11 South; 703–463–3235) was opened as a B&B in an eclectically furnished 1930s-era home in 1985. Rates include a breakfast of fruit, omelets, bacon, sausage, and muffins.

Fassifern B&B   *Tel:* (703) 463–1013
Virginia Route 39, RR 5, Box 87

After 26 years of traveling the world with the military, Jim and Pat Tichenor decided to open a B&B, furnishing it with antiques and other treasures collected over the years. Fassifern dates back to 1867, although it was built on the foundations of a much older building. The Tichenors note that "many of our guests enjoy wandering about the grounds or sitting on the dock watching the wildlife on and in the pond."

"Although the house is over 120 years old and filled with antiques, it was like walking into a brand-new home because everything was fully restored and in mint condition. The stairway, which rises to the third floor, is a showpiece. Thick, thick towels, lace-edged sheets, beautiful four-poster twin beds in our room. Elegant breakfast on china dishes, heavy solid gleaming silver. Owners Pat and Jim said that as long as they had the good stuff they might as well use it. We were pleased that the Tichenors took time to sit and visit with us during breakfast. Very friendly, interesting people who have created a truly outstanding B&B." *(Mary Wabeke, also John & Patricia Keilty)*

"Instant quiet, instant beauty. Weeping willows swaying gently in the breeze, a small pond and much greenery. Pat graciously heated up the pizza we had brought from Due's in Chicago, and we immediately felt at home. The Tichenors had recently been to Scotland, and told us what they had learned about the original Fassifern homestead there." *(Diane Haen)*

"All the rooms are decorated differently, some with Victorian antiques, but all are delightful and clean. The location in the country by a pond is within minutes of downtown Lexington." *(John W. Roberts, Jr.)*

"Stunning dark woodwork, great layout. Our third-floor room had a little sitting room with interesting magazines and wonderful nooks and crannies, perfect for curling up with a book. Be sure to read the history book on Fassifern in the living room." *(BLK)*

Open All year.
Rooms 6 doubles—4 with private shower and/or bath, 2 with maximum of 4 people sharing bath. All with clock/radio, air-conditioning, 1 with deck. 2 rooms in outbuildings.
Facilities Parlor, dining room, conservatory, sitting areas. 3½ acres with gardens, pond, pasture. Swimming, fishing nearby.

Location 2 m from center. From I-64, take Exit 13 to Rte. 11 N. Go 50 yds., and turn W (left) on Rte. 39 toward Goshen. Inn is ¾ m on left.
Restrictions No children under 16. No smoking.
Credit cards Amex, MC, Visa.
Rates B&B, $95 suite, $45–73 double, $40–68 single. Extra person in room, $15. No tipping. 2-night minimum some weekends.
Extras Station pickups.

LURAY 22835   Map 4

Shenandoah Countryside   *Tel:* (703) 743–6434
Route 2, Box 370

A custom-designed farmhouse, this small B&B has been owned by Phel and Bob Jacobsen since 1980, who note that "guests are treated as personal friends and members of the family. Our home is located in the shadow of the Blue Ridge Mountains and Shenandoah National Park."

"As you drive up the winding driveway, you have a feeling of relaxation and comfort. Phel and Bob Jacobsen greeted us, and gave us a tour of their lovely new brick home. There are three porches overlooking the Shenandoah Valley; the views are breathtaking. Our upstairs room had walnut twin beds, an overhead fan, and fresh flowers. They even provided us with attractive robes and slippers, since our private bath was across the hall. The bathroom was roomy, had a nice old clawfoot tub, with decorative country touches. Phel has a way of coordinating her colors perfectly. Breakfast was served in the lovely dining room, with outstanding valley views. Table settings were so attractive. We were served a waffle topped with sliced banana, fresh peaches, a scoop of cottage cheese, and a sprig of freshly cut mint. We had our second and third waffles plain, topped with Vermont maple syrup. Freshly squeezed orange juice was combined with cranberry and raspberry juices—this ideal combination is Bob's speciality. A perfect B&B." *(Arlene & Colette Craighead)*

Open All year.
Rooms 3 doubles—1 with private bath, 2 rooms sharing 2 baths. 1 room with desk.
Facilities Living room, dining room, keeping room, screened porches, deck, recreation room, Finnish sauna. 45 acres with gardens, hammocks, swings, Christmas tree farm, walking trails, bicycles. River and reservoir nearby for water sports.
Location 4 m SE of Luray.
Restrictions No children under 10.
Credit cards None accepted.
Rates B&B, $60 double. Extra person in room $15. No tipping. 2-night minimum holiday weekends, foliage season.
Extras Airport pickups.

MIDDLEBURG 22117   Map 4

The Red Fox Inn and Tavern   *Tel:* (703) 687–6301
2 East Washington Street, P.O. 385   Outside VA: (800) 223–1728

In 1728, Joseph Chinn built this tavern, known then as Chinn's Ordinary. In 1812, the tavern was enlarged and its name changed to the Beveridge

House. During the Civil War, the tavern also served as a hospital; the pine bar in the Tap Room was made from an operating table. The name was changed to the Red Fox in 1937, and in 1976, Turner Reuter, Jr., took over the inn and began a major renovation effort. The nearby Stray Fox Inn and McConnell House date back to the nineteenth century and are decorated with period reproductions; guests preferring a quieter atmosphere should request rooms in either one. Rates include continental breakfast.

"We had a lovely room with a working fireplace, pleasantly furnished with reproduction pieces. There was a *Washington Post* outside our door each morning and a dish of chocolate truffles and fresh fruit slices left by the bedside each night. We ate dinner downstairs at a table next to the fireplace, which gave the room a wonderful atmosphere. Our meal was very good and the service friendly. The town of Middleburg is charming, and the surrounding countryside lovely, with rolling hills and thoroughbred horse farms, and very convenient to DC." *(Barbara Hornbach)*

One otherwise satisfied guest, who much enjoyed his luxurious well-equipped room at the Stray Fox, was unhappy with the fact that he had to get dressed and walk over to the Red Fox to get his breakfast. He felt that at $200 a night for a suite the option of having breakfast in bed should be offered. More reports, please.

Open All year.
Rooms 5 suites, 12 doubles—all with private bath and/or shower, telephone, TV, desk, air-conditioning, canopy bed. 13 of the rooms are in the nearby Stray Fox Inn & McConnell House. 8 with fireplace.
Facilities Restaurant, bar, pub, terraces. Riding lessons, ballooning trips, equestrian events and activities nearby.
Location NE VA, Loudoun County (horse country). 50 min. W of Washington, DC, 30 min. W of Dulles Int'l. Airport, 35 min. E of Winchester. Center of town.
Credit cards Amex, MC, Visa.
Rates B&B, $125–200 suite, $115–140 double. Extra person in room, $25. Crib, $10. Alc dinner, $30–40; child's portions under 12.
Extras Cribs available.

MOUNT CRAWFORD 22841   Map 4

Mount Crawford is located in the Shenandoah Valley of western Virginia, between Harrisonburg and Staunton, about 130 miles west of Washington, D.C. It's a good base for visiting one of the four area colleges—James Madison University, Bridgewater College, Eastern Mennonite College, and Mary Baldwin College, and makes a good center for touring other area attractions in Staunton, Charlottesville, and Luray. Local attractions include horseback riding, canoeing on the Shenandoah River, hiking, and downhill and cross-country skiing.

The Pumpkin House Inn   *Tel:* (703) 434–6963
U.S. Route 11, RR 2, Box 155

John Craun built this brick home on part of a 120-acre land grant, and it stayed in the hands of his descendants until it was sold at auction in 1941. In 1947, it was bought by the parents of the present innkeepers, brother and sister Tom Kidd and Liz Umstott, and was renovated as an inn in 1986. It's named after the pumpkin patch behind the inn, where pumpkins had been grown for the past 35 years. The inn has wide-board heart-pine floors, carved woodwork, and hand-stenciled walls, and rooms are furnished with antiques (some of which are family heirlooms, while others are for sale). Rates include a continental breakfast, with pumpkin bread a featured favorite.

"An absolutely charming inn in an 1847 restored home located in scenic farm country. Each bedroom has its own beautiful decor—ours was the Quilt Room. Mr. Kidd suggested a nice family restaurant nearby." *(Arlyne & Colette Craighead, also Esther Bittinger)*

Open All year.
Rooms 7 doubles—3 with private shower, 4 with maximum of 4 sharing bath. 6 with air-conditioning. 4 with fireplace.
Facilities Dining room; lounge with TV, fireplace; library. 3 acres.
Location 4 m S of Harrisonburg, VA. ½ m S of Mt. Crawford on W side of U.S. Rte. 11, between exits 60 and 61 on I-81.
Credit cards Amex, MC, Visa.
Rates B&B, $40–70 double, $35–65 single. Extra person in room, $5.

ORANGE 22960   Map 4

Orange is in north-central Virginia, 60 miles southwest of Washington, D.C., 30 miles northwest of Charlottesville, and 5 miles from Montpelier. From Washington, D.C., take I-495 to I-66 west to Route 29 south. Take the Orange exit of Route 29 to Route 15 to Orange.

"This area is rich in history. Montepelier, home of James and Dolley Madison, is ten minutes away and is now open to the public. Ash Lawn, (President James Monroe's home) is about 30 minutes away." *(Carolyn & Bill Myles)*

Also recommended: The **Mayhurst Inn** (Route 15, P.O. Box 707; 703–672-5597) is an impressive Italianate Victorian mansion, noted for its fine architecture, most particularly the oval spiral staircase ascending four floors. A southern-style dinner is served on Saturday nights only. The **Willow Grove Inn** (Route 15 North; 703–672-5982) shows strong influence of Thomas Jefferson's preference for classic Greek architecture, with its imposing center pediment and four supporting Doric columns. The house dates back to the 1770s, and the house and grounds have been fully restored to their original beauty, with antique furnishings inside, and rolling lawns, formal gardens, magnolias, and willow trees outside.

The Hidden Inn   *Tel:* (703) 672–3625
249 Caroline Street

Ray and Barbara Lonick bought the Hidden Inn in 1986, and describe it as being a particular favorite with "young and middle-aged couples from the Washington, D.C., area who are looking for a romantic getaway. Our inn is quiet, cozy, and a little elegant—there are wicker pieces on the verandas; Oriental rugs in the public rooms; silver, and lace tablecloths in the dining room. Our color scheme is rose, white, and light blue, with lots of fresh flowers."

The decor is largely Victorian, and rooms have brass or canopy beds. Rates include a full breakfast and afternoon tea. A typical breakfast might include granola, corn muffins with strawberry jam, grits, eggs, fried apples, ham, and toast, while the single-entrée dinner offering might be pâté, cream of broccoli soup, salad, beef chasseur with wild rice and asparagus, and Oreo cookie cheesecake for dessert. Although breakfast and dinner are available only to house guests, light lunches are served to the public.

"Friendly new owners Roy and Barbara really try to offer a touch of old-fashioned elegance. We slept in brass twin beds; they placed a chocolate on our pillow; breakfast was served in the pretty dining room. Great service—quiet and peaceful atmosphere." *(Arlyne & Colette Craighead)*

Open All year.
Rooms 3 suites, 6 doubles—all with private bath and/or shower, air-conditioning, fan, desk. Some with radio, TV. 2 2-bedroom cottages adjacent to inn, with private verandas or living room.
Facilities Dining room, living room with fireplace and TV, wraparound verandas. 6 acres with vegetable gardens, croquet, and badminton. 5 m to lake for fishing and boating.
Location N central VA. 30 m N of Charlottesville, 5 m from Montpelier. 3 blocks from center. From Washington, DC, take I-495 to I-66 W to Rte. 29 S. Take Orange exit off Rte. 29 S to Rte. 15 to Orange.
Restrictions Morning train might disturb light sleepers. No smoking.
Credit cards MC, Visa.
Rates B&B, $109–119 suite, $79–89 double, $59–69 single. Extra person in room, $15. 2-night minimum on holiday weekends. Alc lunch, $10, alc dinner $30, plus 15% service.
Extras Cribs available. Spanish spoken.

RICHMOND 23223　　　　　　　　　　　　　　　　　Map 4

Richmond has had a dramatic history, including such high points as Patrick Henry's famous "Give me liberty or give me death" speech in 1775, the attack by the British not long after, and its tenure as the capital of the Confederacy from 1861 to 1865. The city is still home to several churches of significant historic interest, and a number of historic James River plantations lie within an easy drive, as does the Richmond National Battlefield Park. Also of interest are the Museum and White House of the Confederacy, the Edgar Allan Poe Museum, and other museums devoted to science and fine art. If you're visiting Richmond on a weekend, take the Cultural Link Trolley, connecting most hotels with the city's major attractions; ride all day for only $2.

Also recommended: The **Carrington Row Inn** (2309 East Broad Street, 23223; 804–344–7005) is one of three attached houses in the now historic Church Hill district. Very sophisticated for their era in 1818, the houses have separate entrances in front, with a shared veranda overlooking a garden in the back. The inn has been furnished with antiques and period reproductions. Rates include a continental breakfast and evening sherry. The **Hanover Hosts in the Fan** (P.O. Box 4503, 23220; 804–355–5855) is a B&B in a turn-of-the-century Federal townhouse, with high ceilings, period decor, and huge old-fashioned bathrooms well supplied with towels.

Information please: Some places we'd like to hear more about are the **Jefferson Sheraton Hotel**, an elaborate Beaux-Arts structure built in 1895, meticulously restored in 1986 at a cost of $35 million and listed on the National Register of Historic Places. Even if you can't stay overnight, stop by to see the Tiffany stained-glass dome in the Palm Court lobby, and the magnificent marbled two-story Rotunda. At 276 rooms, it's no small hotel, so we'd appreciate your comments (Franklin & Adams streets 23220; 804–788–8000 or 800–325–3535). An equally luxurious option on a smaller scale is the **Commonwealth Park**, an all-suite hotel with 49 units overlooking the State Capitol. Rooms are elegantly furnished with eighteenth-century mahogany reproductions, highlighted by brass chandeliers, and weekend rates are available (9th and Bank streets 23230; 804–343–7300 or 800–343–7302). Another B&B possibility is the recently opened **Abbie Hill**, two adjacent turn-of-the-century Colonial Revival homes in the historic Fan District (P.O. Box 4503, Monument Avenue 23220; 804–355–5855). Reports please.

Reader tip: "Several B&Bs are located in the Church Hill district, a charming enclave surrounded by very poor inner-city neighborhoods. Although the area is only 12 blocks from downtown, night-time strolls are definitely *not* recommended."

Richmond is in the eastern part of the state, 106 miles south of Washington, D.C., and 50 miles west of Williamsburg.

The Catlin-Abbott House
2304 East Broad Street 23223

Tel: (804) 780–3746

When Jim and Frances Abbott bought The Catlin House in 1980, it had been vacant for eight years and was condemned. Back in 1845, William Catlin had the house built by his slave, William Mitchell, now recognized as Richmond's finest brick mason and the father of Maggie Walker, the first woman to found a bank in America. The Abbotts managed to salvage the beautiful wide-board floors and the fireplaces, but nearly everything else had to be rebuilt in the renovation process. They've decorated the rooms with period antiques, crystal chandeliers, and Chinese rugs; rates include a full breakfast, served on fine china with sterling flatware in the formal dining room or, upon request, in your room.

"A pleasant B&B, with the feel of an inn, not a private home (a plus to us). We were pleased with the suite we had on the first (below the parlor) floor, though it was a bit dark during the day. It had a working fireplace, and diverting magazines. Breakfast was fine—scrambled eggs, bacon, biscuits, decent coffee. Parking was easy on the street in front. " *(Rachel Gorlin)* Another reader alerted us to the fact that a change of ownership may be in the works: "We understand that the Abbotts have put the inn up for sale since they've reached the age where they'd like to take it easier." More comments, please.

Open All year.
Rooms 2 2-bedroom suites (1 with kitchen), 3 doubles—all with private bath and/or shower, telephone, TV, desk, air-conditioning, fireplace.

Facilities Living room, dining room with fireplaces.
Location Church Hill District. 12 blocks from center. From I-95 S, take Exit 11, 3rd St. Ramp, to 5th traffic light (Broad St.). Turn left and go E to 2300 block. From I-95 N, take Exit 10, E. Broad St. ramp, to 1st traffic light. Turn left on Broad St.
Restrictions No children.
Credit cards Amex, MC, Visa.
Rates B&B, $120–140 suite, $78–93 double, $73–83 single including tax and service. Extra person in room, $15.
Extras Station pickups. Airport delivery.

SCOTTSVILLE 24590 Map 4

Also recommended: The **Chester B&B** (State Route 726, Route 4, Box 57; 804–286–3960) is a Greek Revival mansion, built in 1847 and surrounded by equally venerable plantings. The inn was renovated carefully with period furniture and lovely antiques to maintain ambience without sacrificing amenities or comfort. In addition to a full breakfast of fresh fruit and juice, eggs, pancakes and Virginia sausage, guests may enjoy complimentary wine, beer, soft drinks, tea or coffee at any time.

High Meadows Inn *Tel:* (804) 286–2218
RR 4, Box 6; Route 20 South/Constitution Highway

Peter and Mary Jae Sushka restored High Meadows, doing much of the work themselves, and decorated the rooms with period antiques. The inn is composed of two buildings, one dating from 1832 and the other from 1882, connected by a covered hallway; both are listed on the National Register of Historic Places. The Sushkas describe the inn as being "especially attractive to people interested in history, yet looking for all the modern conveniences. It's the perfect place for people who love to travel but hate to leave home." Dinners are served on weekends, and include a choice of French, Italian, and game dishes along with Virginia wines; weeknights the Sushkas offer guests a supper picnic basket. Local attractions include the area's numerous historic sights and antique shops, as well as canoeing, tubing, and fishing on the James River, plus winery tours and hiking.

"High Meadows Inn is a unique blend of Federal and Victorian architecture made even more distinctive by Peter and Jae. This Renaissance couple's sense of history is reflected in the meticulous attention to detail they have shown in restoring and furnishing each of the theme bedrooms with authentic antiques. (We slept in an original Jenny Lind bed.) A friendly and gracious atmosphere prevailed in the intimate dining room, where we were served a tantalizing breakfast of fresh fruits, family-recipe muffins, eggs, and a special blend of coffee. Conversing with our hosts, while their son played classical guitar music, made these meals a highlight of our weekend. We walked the grounds, admiring the flowers, azaleas, and dogwood while en route to the gazebo, pond, and vineyard. Closeness to other historical points of interest—including Ashlawn, Monticello, and the University of Virginia—added to the pleasures of our stay." *(Ann & John Glenson, also Marcella Burris)*

"We were greeted on arrival with Virginia wine, cheese, and friendly conversation. Our room had a fascinating photo album showing its step-by-step restoration and explaining the origin of its furnishings. Breakfasts and dinners are delightful, with new recipes introduced constantly." *(Becky & Les Crenshaw)* "From the flowers in the rooms to the mints on the pillow to assistance with tours of local wineries and Monticello to a gourmet breakfast, you will truly be spoiled by the Sushkas." *(Mr. & Mrs. James L. Bailey and others)*

And another opinion: "It seemed to us that the outside of the inn could use some work."

Open All year except 2 weeks in Mar. & Aug.
Rooms 1 suite, 6 doubles—all with private bath and/or shower, desk.
Facilities Dining/breakfast rooms, bar/lounge, library, music room, porches. 23 acres with formal gardens, ponds, vineyards. On the James River for tubing, canoeing, rafting, fishing. Hiking nearby. 40 min. to downhill skiing.
Location Central VA, Albermarle County. 20 m S of Charlottesville, in Monticello wine region. 1 m N of Scottsville, on Rte. 20.
Restrictions Smoking discouraged. No children under 8.
Credit cards None accepted.
Rates B&B, $130 suite, $85 double, $65 single. Extra person in room, $15. 10% senior discount. 2-night weekend minimum spring and fall. Weekend prix fixe dinner with wine $25. Weeknight picnic supper basket with wine, $35 for two.
Extras French spoken. Pets occasionally permitted with prior notice.

SMITHFIELD 23430 Map 4

Isle of Wight Inn
1607 South Church Street

Tel: (804) 357–3176

Smithfield is an old river town, best known as the home of famous Smithfield ham—salty and always very thinly sliced. It's not too far from Williamsburg; you cross the James River by ferry between Jamestown and Surry (a lovely ride), and take Route 10 south to Smithfield. Built in 1984, the Isle of Wight is owned by Bob Hart, Marcella Hoffman, and Sam Earl, and furnished with traditional and reproduction furniture. While not exactly a traditional inn, it's clearly a reader favorite.

"Beautifully furnished rooms, continental breakfast in an intimate, elegant dining room." *(Carol King)*

"A real favorite. We were welcomed with great friendliness to this luxurious small motel/inn with an attractive antique shop. Our very large and pleasant room had its own external door, fireplace, small but well-equipped bathroom with large shower and excellent queen-size bed. Breakfast, served in the room, was Smithfield ham rolls (only one each) and good coffee. Be sure to visit Joyner's ham shop, more or less opposite the inn." *(David Felce)* "Exactly as you described it in last year's edition. Extremely helpful and friendly service. Would make an excellent base for visiting Williamsburg. The Smithfield Inn in the center of town provided an excellent Sunday evening buffet supper." *(Michael Crick)*

Open All year.
Rooms 4 suites, 6 doubles—all with full private bath, telephone, cable TV, desk, air-conditioning. Several suites with fireplace, 1 with Jacuzzi.
Facilities Living/family room, with player piano; dining room, kitchen, antique shop. Fishing, tennis, jogging trail, golf nearby.
Location Southeast VA, Tidewater, Isle of Wight County. 12 m W of Newport News, 27 m W of Norfolk. Approx. 22 m S of Williamsburg. 2 m from town, on Rte. 10 near James River Bridge.
Restrictions No smoking in public rooms.
Credit cards Amex, MC, Visa.
Rates B&B, $59–69 suite, $49 double, includes service. Extra person in room, $8. Senior discounts.
Extras Crib available.

STANLEY 22851	Map 4

Jordan Hollow Farm Inn　　　　　　　　　　　　　*Tel:* (703) 778–2209
Virginia Route 626, Route 2, Box 375　　　　　　　　　　　 778–2285

Jordan Hollow is a horse-breeding farm, where plenty of horses are available for riding or "just looking." The dining rooms, where breakfast and dinner are served, are in the 200-year-old farmhouse. Guest rooms are located in a separate lodge built in 1983 to complement the other farm buildings. Marley and Jetze Beers have owned and run the farm since it became an inn.

"We arrived at Jordan Hollow in the pitch dark, bedraggled after a long day of traveling. Imagine our thrill the next morning when we awoke to the country quiet, stepped out onto the balcony, and saw stretching before us verdant hills and glens, green meadows sparkling with wildflowers, fine-looking horses grazing with their foals skittering about. We wandered in the barns, roamed the pastures, enjoyed excellent food in the pretty dining rooms, and sipped drinks in the friendly bar/recreation room. We took trail rides through the lovely countryside on their well-trained mounts, hiked in the adjacent Shenandoah National Park, and relaxed on the inn lawns, reading and playing with the resident kittens—and never had to dress up once!" *(SG)*

"The Beers are bright, talented, interesting people who gather you into their home as friends. The service was perfect—delivered by friendly, helpful local residents. The sleeping lodge was new, clean, and comfortable. This is not a fancy, formal facility! It is, in our opinion, a true country inn with all the hoped-for ambience." *(Nancy & Fritz Thompson)*

"This is a real working farm; three horses, which had foaled recently, were out in paddocks where the guests could watch them for hours. Our room was spotlessly clean and very homey, with special touches like a bottle of wine and nice, colored towels, instead of the standard motel white. The old farmhouse's three small dining rooms are decorated nicely in country calico, other odd antiques, and African artifacts. The food was excellent—everything from soup to desserts was cooked to perfection." *(Mike & Doris Donch)*

"After dinner each night we all went to the pub, where there is something for all ages. My five-year-old son loved the pool table, games, and dart board, while we enjoyed conversations with the other guests. The horseback riding is well organized, with riders separated by ability." *(Piper Starr)* More comments, please.

Open All year.
Rooms 1 suite, 16 doubles—all with private bath and/or shower, telephone, desk, air-conditioning.
Facilities Restaurant, bar/lounge/pub, game room, library, meeting rooms. Weekend entertainment in pub. 45 acres with trails, horseback riding. Shenandoah River nearby for canoeing, fishing, swimming. Golf, tennis nearby. Cross-country, downhill skiing 15–30 min.
Location N VA, Shenandoah Valley. 2 hrs. W of Washington, DC, NW of Richmond, VA. 6 m S of Luray. From Luray, take Rte. 340 S 6 m. Go left on Rte. 624, left again on Rte. 689, right on Rte. 626 and follow signs.
Restrictions No smoking in barn.
Credit cards DC, MC, Visa.
Rates Room only, $75–85 suite, $65–75 double, $55–65 single. Extra person in room, $10. Under age 16, free. Riding packages. Alc lunch $5, alc dinner, $20.
Extras Guest room and bath equipped for disabled. German, Dutch, some French spoken. Cribs, babysitting available. Pets permitted by special arrangement.

STAUNTON 24401   **Map 4**

In easy reach of many area sights, Staunton is a popular base for touring the Shenandoah Mountains. Staunton itself has undergone considerable renovation of its historic downtown. In addition to the birthplace of Woodrow Wilson, the Museum of American Frontier Culture has opened recently.

Also recommended: The **Belle Grae Inn** (515 West Frederick Street; 703–886–5151), restored in 1983, is a rambling brick Victorian mansion with white gingerbread trim, and is Staunton's oldest B&B. In addition to accommodation in two adjacent homes, the Belle Grae offers formal and casual dining in its restaurant and bistro. The **Thornrose House** (531 Thornrose Avenue; 703–885–7026), a gracious Georgian-style brick home, has been a B&B since 1985. Rooms are decorated with period antiques, and rates include a full breakfast of birchermuesli—a delicious Swiss cereal—followed by eggs, bacon or sausage, and toast.

Frederick House   *Tel:* (703) 885–4220
18 East Frederick Street, P.O. Box 1387   Outside VA: (800) 334–5575

Frederick House is composed of three connected town houses, built between 1810 and 1910. It's located right across the street from Mary Baldwin College, and near to Woodrow Wilson's birthplace, Stuart Hall, and many shops and restaurants. Joe and Evy Harman restored the inn in 1984, and have decorated it with antiques and reproduction pieces. For dinner, the Harmans recommend McCormick's, a restaurant located next door to the inn.

"The rooms were spotless, and innkeeper Evy Harman is a gracious hostess. Our room had a charming antique baby cradle." *(Mrs. Peter Payne, also Patricia DeMonte)*

Open All year.
Rooms 5 suites, 6 doubles—all with private bath and/ or shower, telephone, cable TV, desk, air-conditioning, fan.
Facilities Dining room, parlor. Small vegetable, herb gardens. Free pass (for 2) to Staunton Athletic Club indoor swimming pool, hot tub (next door). Tennis, golf nearby. 45 min. to downhill skiing, hiking, canoeing, Skyline Drive, Blue Ridge Parkway.
Restrictions No smoking.
Location NW VA. 150 m SW of Washington, DC, 40 m W of Charlottesville, 100 m NW of Richmond. Exit 57, I-81, then Rte. 250 W. Center of town, across from Mary Baldwin College.
Credit cards Amex, DC, Discover, MC, Visa.
Rates Room only, $55–60 suite, $30–35 double or single; extra person in room, $10–15. B&B, $65–70 suite, $40–45 double, $35–40 single; extra person in room, $15–20. Senior discounts.
Extras Cribs, babysitting available.

WARM SPRINGS 24484   Map 4

A historic town nestled at the base of Little Mountain in the Alleghenies, Warm Springs offers pleasant streets lined with beautiful old buildings, and makes a good base for exploring the area's natural beauty—and of course, for taking the baths here or at nearby Hot Springs or Bolar Springs.

The Inn at Gristmill Square   *Tel:* (703) 839–2231
Route 645, Box 359

Located right at the center of Warm Springs, Gristmill Square comprises a cluster of five restored nineteenth-century buildings including the inn's guest rooms, a restaurant, an antique gallery, and a country store. The inn was created in 1972 and has been owned by the McWilliams family since 1981. Rooms are decorated in a variety of styles, from antique to country-comfortable to more modern furnishings. The inn's restaurant, the Waterwheel, is housed in a mill dating back to 1900; both continental and American dishes are offered, but native brook trout is a particular specialty—you can have it smoked, broiled, or pan fried with black walnuts. Rates include a continental breakfast of juice or fruit and homemade breads.

"We stayed in the Silo Room, which included a round living area with a couch and fireplace, and plenty of interesting reading materials, adjoined by comfortably sized bedroom and bath. The furnishings were lovely and well kept. There were plenty of huge, fluffy towels and a basket of toiletries in the bath. The restaurant was very good, and we enjoyed selecting our own bottle of wine from the cellar. The surrounding countryside is picturesque and peaceful. We took some pleasant walks on the country back roads and also enjoyed poking around the nearby town of Hot Springs." *(Linda & Phillip Burcham)*

"A comfortable place, especially the better rooms. It is quiet, intimate, and comfortable." *(Samuel Cantor)* "Exceptional restaurant, excellent service." *(Margaret Katzenberg)*

Open All year.
Rooms 6 suites, 8 doubles—all with private shower and/or bath, TV, fan, telephone. Most with desk, fireplace, refrigerator; some with kitchens. Rooms in 3 buildings.
Facilities Restaurant, bar. 1 acre with sauna, swimming pool, 3 tennis courts, Jackson River for fishing. Golf, horseback riding nearby. 4 m to skiing.
Location From Staunton, follow Rte. 250 to Rte. 254 to Buffalo Gap. Then take Rte. 42 to Millboro Spring, Rte. 39 to Warm Springs. Inn is on Rte. 645.
Credit cards MC, Visa.
Rates B&B, $65–95 suite, $65–75 double, $55–60 single. No charge for children under 10. Extra person in room, $10. Alc lunch $7, alc dinner $25.
Extras Airport/station pickups. Well-attended pets permitted. Wheelchair accessible. Cribs, babysitting available.

WILLIAMSBURG 23187   Map 4

Williamsburg was selected as the new colonial capital of Virginia when it became clear that the original capital at Jamestown was disease-ridden and undefensible. It was planned and built starting in 1700 by Governor Francis Nicholson, and grew rapidly. In 1780, the capital was moved again, this time to Richmond. Williamsburg continued as the county seat and as the home of William and Mary College and the Public Hospital for the Insane. Fortunately, a large number of eighteenth-century houses survived, and, in 1926, the Reverend W.A.R. Goodwin persuaded John D. Rockefeller, Jr., to finance the city's restoration. Today, the historic area is operated by the nonprofit Colonial Williamsburg Foundation. All visits to Colonial Williamsburg should begin at the Visitor's Center, for full information on what to see and do.

More than one million visitors come to Williamsburg every year. Remember that Williamsburg is very hot and crowded in the summer; late fall or early spring are probably the best times to visit. Although the weather can be quite chilly and damp, special programs and reduced-rate packages are available from January to early March.

Williamsburg is located 155 miles south of Washington, D.C., and 50 miles southeast of Richmond.

Information please: About 18 miles west of Williamsburg is the historic town of Charles City, on the James River. The **Edgewood Plantation** is a restored Victorian mansion, dating back to 1849. It played an important role during the Civil War, and was restored to its original elegance in 1978. The six guest rooms are graciously furnished in period, highlighted by the owner's collection of vintage clothing (Route 2, Box 490; Charles Ctiy 23030; 804–829–2962).

Also recommended: A locally owned and operated motel recommended by a Williamsburg reader *(DFV)* is the **Quarterpath Inn**, located within walking distance of the restored area. "The staff is very friendly and helpful, proud of the very clean rooms and ample parking," and the motel has a swimming pool and adjacent tennis court. Double rates range from $35–70, depending on season, and there's no charge for children under 18 (620 York Street, Route 60 East 23185; 804–220–0960 or 800–446–9222). We'd love more Williamsburg-area suggestions, please!

For an additional area entry, see **Smithfield.**

Williamsburg Inn
Francis Street, P.O. Box B

Tel: (804) 229–1000
(800) HISTORY

The Colonial Williamsburg Foundation owns and operates 1,000 rooms spread over seven different lodging establishments, including the Williamsburg Inn, the Williamsburg Lodge, the Motor House, the Colonial Houses, Providence Hall, the Cascades, and the Governor's Inn (call the toll-free phone number above for information on all of them). Here's a sample of the excellent reader feedback received:

The Inn: The Williamsburg Inn is a very well known full-service hotel, with a five-star Mobil rating, high standards, and corresponding rates. "Truly the epitome of elegance and good taste. Rooms are furnished in the Regency manner, with muted Schumacher fabrics, original paintings and prints, and brass candlestick lamps. The Regency Dining Room is the most elegant restaurant in town; a harpsichordist plays during dinner." *(Michael Spring, also Jane Hill)*

The Colonial Houses: "Although expensive, they are truly outstanding and worth the splurge. The house where we stayed, 3008 Francis St., was a real dollhouse, beautifully furnished with reproductions. The bathroom was adorable, with its steeply pitched ceiling, fresh flowers, thick towels. Our beds even had real feather pillows." *(Mary Wabeke)* "We rented the second floor of a small house on Duke of Gloucester Street in the heart of Colonial Williamsburg. The guest room and bath were large and appropriately decorated, but the best part came in the evening, when we could step out the door of our little home and walk throughout the town, looking into the shops and buildings and pretending to be an actual part of this marvelous eighteenth-century town." *(Jack & Sue Lane)*

The Motor House: "Delightfully clean. Easy walking distance to local transportation to all events and meals. A wonderful place to be off-season." *(Robert Rieger)*

Open All year.
Rooms 25 suites, 210 doubles—all with full private bath, telephone, radio, TV, air-conditioning. Many with desk.
Facilities Restaurant, 4 lobbies, 2 cocktail lounges. Music nightly, dancing weekends. 200 acres. Swimming pool, tennis courts, golf.
Location Center of town.
Credit cards Amex, MC, Visa.
Rates Room only, $350 suite, $165–210 double. Extra person in room, $15. Alc lunch, $14; alc dinner, $35. Special packages.
Extras Station pickups. Portable ramp for wheelchair access to first-floor rooms. French, German, Spanish, Italian spoken. Cribs, babysitting, games available.

WOODSTOCK 22664   Map 4

Also recommended: The Candlewick Inn (127 North Church Street; 703–459–8008) is a turn-of-the-century Victorian with the old-fashioned charm of random-width pine flooring and a parlor window seat with a view of the Massanutten Mountains. Rooms are decorated simply with antiques, period pieces, and country touches, with a light and airy look.

The Inn at Narrow Passage
U.S. 11 South, P.O. Box 608

Long before Shenandoah Valley travelers rolled down Interstate 81, stage-coaches bumped their way along the Wilderness Road, past what is now known as The Inn at Narrow Passage, site of Indian raids and in 1862 the headquarters of Stonewall Jackson. Portions of the inn date back to 1740, although some of the guest rooms are housed in a recent addition. The inn was restored by Ellen and Ed Markel in 1984, who exposed the original log construction and pine floors. They've furnished the inn with colonial reproductions and queen-size canopy beds. Ellen notes that "the guests we most enjoy having are married couples who appreciate the history and beauty of this area and like the warm, family hospitality we try to provide."

"Located on the banks of the Shenandoah River, the inn is graced with the constant and soothing melody of running water. It is both rustic and delightfully charming, with an almost eerie historical presence. We stayed in the bedroom that Stonewall Jackson used during the Civil War." *(Paul Embroski)* "Our comfortable room had a four poster bed and working fireplace. The inn is easily accessible from the highway but is far enough away that traffic noise is not bothersome. Best of all is Ed's genuine friendliness and his easy, unobtrusive manner." *(Richard Merritt)*

"The Markels' greeting is as warm as the slow burning fire in the living room and the hot herbal tea they served on a chilly evening. Breakfasts are delicious, the bacon outstanding." *(Mr. & Mrs. Robert Ward)* "Relax in the sitting room reading or playing checkers, then stretch your legs by paying a visit to the inn's pet rabbit or strolling along the Shenandoah River." *(Fred & Martha Sisk)*

Open All year.
Rooms 12 doubles—8 with private bath and/or shower, 4 with a maximum of 4 people sharing bath. All with radio, air-conditioning. Some with desk, fireplace. Four rooms in annex.
Facilities Living room with fireplace, dining room with fireplace, porch. 5 acres on Shenandoah River. Fishing, water sports nearby. 30 min. to downhill skiing at Bryce Mt.
Location N VA, Shenandoah Valley. 90 m W of Washington, DC. From Washington, take I-66 W to I-81. Take I-81 S to Woodstock (Exit 72, Rte. 11). 2 m S of Woodstock on Rte. 11.
Restrictions Smoking in living room only. Light sleepers should request rooms away from street. No smoking in guest rooms. "We prefer infants or children over 4 because of stairs and fireplaces."
Credit cards MC, Visa.
Rates B&B, $55–80 double, $45–75 single. Extra person in room, $8. "We appreciate a tip for our housekeepers." 2-night minimum holiday and October weekends.
Extras Cribs, babysitting available.

Washington

The Saratoga Inn, Langley

About the only things eastern and western Washington have in common are a governor and a shared border, the Cascade mountain range. Western Washington, dominated by water and mountains, includes most of the state's population and scenic highlights: the Olympic Peninsula, Puget Sound, the San Juan Islands, and the Cascade Mountains and volcanoes.

The Olympic Peninsula   The large central core of this peninsula is a vast wilderness incorporating the world's only temperate rain forest and the glaciers, peaks, and rugged terrain of the Olympic Mountains. Going west, toward the Pacific Ocean, a national wildlife refuge, four Indian reservations, and delicate archaeological digs make public access to the ocean difficult. The north side of the peninsula faces the Strait of Juan de Fuca and is known for Victorian Port Townsend, the Manis Mastodon Site, and six-mile Dungeness Sandspit, home to over 250 species of birds. Hood Canal and its nearby parks form the eastern edge of this varied peninsula. Access to the Pacific is found southeast of the peninsula between Ilwaco and Pacific Beach. Here you can walk the 28-mile Long Beach, dig for clams, go deep-sea fishing, or fly kites. Virtually the only road on the peninsula is Route 101, often referred to as the Olympic Loop.

Puget Sound   Puget Sound extends like a giant thumb into the center of western Washington. Most of the state's population lives along its eastern shore, from Olympia north to Seattle and Everett. In Tacoma visit 698-acre Point Defiance Park to survey its extensive flower gardens, forest roads, and outstanding views. From Seattle take a round trip on one of the ferries linking urban Washington to nearby commuter islands.

Or board the Mukilteo-Clinton ferry to Whidbey Island and there drive north through rolling farmlands, past sandy beaches, to impressive Deception Pass. In the spring be sure to see the acres of blooming daffodils and tulips in Skagit Valley north of Everett. Scuba divers can don their gear to visit the extensive network of underwater parks. If you're heading up to British Columbia, get off the freeway at Burlington and take scenic Route 11, which hugs the coast and provides gorgeous views of the San Juan Islands.

San Juan Islands   If you can visit only one part of this state, choose the San Juans. Depending on the tide, between 175 and 300 rock-cliffed islands dot the area between Puget Sound and Canada. Here you will find secluded bays and densely forested ridges inhabited by eagles. From Anacortes on the mainland, ferries travel to Victoria, Canada, stopping at four of the more populous islands. The largest is Orcas, where you can climb Mt. Constitution for spectacular views of the other islands, Canada, and the Olympic and Cascade mountain ranges. Lopez is perfect for cyclists; on San Juan visit the site of the infamous "Pig War" between the U.S. and England; and Shaw is known for the nuns who operate its ferry dock. One warning: If you're traveling in the summer, advance reservations for accommodations and ferry passage are *essential.*

The Cascades and Volcanoes   Every bit the equal of the Colorado Rockies, the rugged, snowcapped Northern Cascade Mountains (Route 20 from Marblemount to Winthrop) are at their best during the fall, when the leaves change color. In the central Cascades you can ski, hike, fish, and visit the 268-foot high Snoqualmie Falls. To the south the Cascades are interrupted by 14,410-foot Mt. Rainier, offering rock and glacier climbing, cross-country skiing, spring wildflower bonanzas, and summer hiking. Also plan to visit Mt. St. Helen's National Volcanic Monument to witness the devastation that occurred there on May 18, 1980.

Eastern Washington   Although it includes two-thirds of the state, eastern Washington offers little to tourists. The exceptions are the Yakima Valley, center of Washington's wine country; Spokane, a lively city centered around a refurbished riverfront park; and the Palouse country of rolling hills and lush vegetation south of Spokane along Route 195 between Spokane and Colfax. In between these points, visitors will find miles of apple orchards, wheat farms, and desert. Worth stopping to see are the waterfalls in Palouse Falls State Park located south of Washtucna; 55-mile-long Lake Chelan; Okanogan Valley ghost towns; the Ginkgo Petrified Forest east of Ellensburg; and, near Coulee City, the unusual Dry Falls that, in prehistoric times, was the site of a 3½-mile-wide, 400-foot waterfall. More recommendations for this area would be especially welcome.

Note: Summer is very much peak season in western Washington, especially in the San Juans; make reservations two to three months ahead to avoid disappointment.

Washington has an exceptionally active state association of B&Bs, called the Washington State Bed and Breakfast Guild (WBBG). The membership criteria includes such reasonable requirements as a resident owner or manager, at least one common room for guest use, and a reasonable level of professionalism. We think it's worth watching for their logo.

Rates do not include 7.8% sales tax and additional local taxes where applicable.

ANACORTES 98221   Map 13

The Channel House   *Tel:* (206) 293–9382
2902 Oakes Avenue

This Victorian home was originally designed and built for an Italian count in 1902. The house is set on the Guemes Channel, and rooms are decorated with many antiques. In the morning guests are served a full breakfast, from scones to French toast stuffed with cheese and fruit; in the evening they particularly enjoy soaking in the outdoor hot tub, while watching the boats and the sunset over Puget Sound. The Channel House was purchased by Dennis and Pat McIntyre in 1986.

"Dennis and Pat are warm, friendly, helpful people who made our stay with them like staying with old friends. The house was spotlessly clean." *(Mrs. Penny Pulliam)* "Delicious bedtime snack of coffee and oatmeal cookies. Very clean bathroom, well supplied with towels, soaps, and shampoos. Owners very knowledgeable about the area." *(Julie Thompson)*

"All the ferries to the San Juan Islands leave from Anacortes. During the busy summer months that often means it's best to put your car in line for the morning ferry and spend the night in Anacortes. The best place to do that is at the Channel House, located only a few minutes from the ferry dock. Here you can anticipate the slower-paced island life while soaking in the hot tub or surveying the islands from your cozy room." *(Michele Blanchard)*

Open All year.
Rooms 6 doubles—4 with private bath and/or shower, 2 with a maximum of 6 sharing bath. 2 doubles in cottage have fireplace, Jacuzzi; 1 with deck.
Facilities Living room, library, dining room, all with fireplace. Hot tub, croquet. Bicycles available by prior arrangement. Boating, fishing, hiking, golf, swimming beaches nearby.
Location NW WA. Fidalgo Island. 2 hrs. S of Vancouver, BC, 1½ hrs. N of Seattle via I-5 and Hwy. 20. 2 m from International Ferry Landing, serving San Juan Islands and Vancouver Island. From I-5 take Exit 230 to Anacortes and San Juan Ferry. Enter Anacortes, continue right on Commerical Ave. to 12th St. (Chevron station on corner). Turn left and inn is 1½ m on the right.
Restrictions Light sleepers may be disturbed by early ferry traffic. No smoking. No children under 12.
Credit cards MC, Visa.
Rates B&B, $65–85 double. Extra person in room, $10. Off-season rates.
Extras Local airport/station pickups.

BELLINGHAM 98225   Map 13

Snuggled along the northwest shore of Puget Sound, Bellingham is definitely worth a stop on the way from Seattle to Vancouver. Getting to this midsize town with a Victorian flavor and a smattering of counterculture shops and eateries is half the fun: Route 11 between Burlington and Bellingham winds prettily along the wooded shore, providing outstanding views of the San Juan Islands. The town is home to Western Washington State University, and recommended stops include a stroll among the contemporary sculptures scattered about the campus, a self-guided tour of its Victorian homes (call 206–733–2900 for a brochure), and a browse through the Old Town antique shops.

Reader tip: On a recent visit, it seemed that the town was in a bit of a slump, with a number of vacant storefronts—perhaps a major local employer had just closed up? Further comments?

Also recommended: The **DeCann House** (2610 Eldridge Avenue; 206–734–9172), built at the turn of the century, overlooks Bellingham Bay and the San Juan Islands. Owners Van and Barbara Hudson, lifelong Northwest residents, are teachers whose talents extend to the restoring of old homes and working in stained glass. The **North Garden Inn** (1014 North Garden Street; 206–671–7828; 800–922–6414), a handsome 1897 Queen Anne Victorian home with superb views of Bellingham Bay, provides a musical opportunity for interested guests—the chance to either listen to, sing along with, or play one of the two grand pianos in the house or in the teaching studio of host Frank DeFreytas. His wife, Barbara, orchestrates events in the kitchen, and even grinds her own flour to use in such treats as lemon curd and scones, muffins, and speciality breads.

Bellingham is located in the northwest corner of Washington, 40 miles south of Vancouver, BC, and 90 miles north of Seattle, easily accessible via Interstate 95.

The Castle B&B

Tel: (206) 676–0974

1103 15th Street & Knox Avenue

High on a hill overlooking historic Fairhaven and Bellingham Bay sits the Castle, built in 1889. Newly listed on the National Register of Historic Places, it is described by owners Larry and Gloria Harriman, with pride (and alliteration), as a "majestic mauve mansion." Many years in the antiques business have resulted in enough art objects and antique furnishings to fill the castle's 21 rooms; the elaborately hand-carved European pieces range in age from 200 to 400 years old. The Harrimans also own a fully equipped beachside cottage, called Seagoat, which is ideal for families.

"Well, it's not exactly a castle, and the mauve exterior is a bit startling at first, but this is an intriguing place to stay. As antique collectors, we felt as if someone had given us a key to our own private playpen. The Harrimans are very knowledgeable and love to share the history and provenance of items in their superb collection. Everything is authentic, even the wallpapers on the walls and ceilings. But there's more—wonderful views of Bellingham Bay, comfortable beds, and an enormous breakfast." *(Sue Monroe)*

"The hostess was cordial, friendly, and knowledgeable about the house and its history, giving us a delightful and complete tour. The house is baronial in atmosphere and reflects the owners' personalities and eclectic tastes. Breakfast of coffee, juice, toasted crumpets and jam, cold meats, cheese, fresh fruit, and yogurt with granola was quite satisfying." *(Mr. & Mrs. Earl Thurston)*

Open All year.
Rooms 1 3-bedroom cottage, 1 suite with private bath, 2 doubles sharing 1 bath. Cottage has living room, kitchen, bath, fireplace. 1 with telephone, radio.
Facilities Living room, dining room, library, veranda. 5 city lots with off-street parking. Cottage on beach.
Location 2 m to center, 4 blocks above Fairhaven. To inn, take exit 250 off I-5, go W on Old Fairhaven Parkway. Turn N (right) on 14th St. Go 5 blocks and turn right on Knox to inn on far right corner at 15th. Seagoat Cottage is located on beach 12 m NW of Bellingham. Get key and directions from inn.
Restrictions No smoking. No children under 12 in Castle; OK in cottage.
Credit cards MC, Visa.
Rates B&B, $75 suite, $65 double, $35–45 single. Extra person in room, $12. Cottage, $75 double, $100 quad. 10% discount for weekly stays.
Extras Airport/station pickups.

COUPEVILLE 98239
WHIDBEY ISLAND
Map 13

Also recommended: Although time constraints precluded a full writeup, *Susan Schwemm* suggests the **Colonel Crockett Farm** (1012 South Fort Casey Road; 206–678–3711), a 1855 farmhouse listed on the National Register of Historic Places. This B&B's cozy rooms are done in Victorian antiques, and the ample grounds offer views of Puget Sound and walks by the neighboring salt marshes.

The Captain Whidbey Inn
2072 West Captain Whidbey Inn Road

Tel: (206) 678–4097

Overlooking Penn Cove, the Captain Whidbey offers rooms with antique charm (and shared baths) in the original inn, along with more modern rooms overlooking the lagoon. Although you can no longer arrive directly by steamer from Seattle at the inn's private dock, as did visitors 80 years ago, the atmosphere here has changed very little under the longtime ownership of Captain John Stone. The inn's restaurant uses herbs from the kitchen garden to season such favorite lunch specials as mussels in white wine or duck salad with apples and walnuts, and such dinner entrées as grilled salmon with seafood sauce, halibut with ginger loganberry sauce, pecan chicken, and roast beef with Yorkshire pudding.

"This old place, built in the early 1900s of madrona logs, is a delight and a real find. It sits in a forest surrounding picturesque Penn Cove. The rooms are rustic and quaint, with lots of old furniture; those with a view of the cove are best. The main lobby is a cozy room with a fireplace and lots of comfortable sitting space. There are plenty of outdoor activities around the inn, but this is a place to take a good book or a special person and get away from it all." *(Pam Phillips)*

Open All year.
Rooms 2 suites, 7 cabins with fireplace, 24 doubles in two separate buildings—19

with full private bath, 14 with shared bath. All with desk, some with telephone, veranda.

Facilities Dining room, lounge with fireplace, library, deck, gazebo. 7 acres with beach, walking trails, boat rentals. Sailing charters. Fishing nearby.

Location Penn Cove, Ebey's Landing National Historical Reserve, Whidbey Island. 28 m N of Columbia Beach. 2 hrs. N of Seattle, S of Vancouver. From S, take Rte. 525 S to inn. From N, take Rte. 20 S to inn.

Restrictions Smoking permitted in some rooms.

Credit cards All major credit cards.

Rates B&B, $85–95 suite; $65–85 double. Extra person in room, $10. 2- to 3-night weekend/holiday minimum. Full breakfast, $5. Alc lunch, $10; alc dinner, $25.

Extras Airport/station pickups. French, German, Spanish spoken. Babysitting, play equipment, games available. Pets permitted in cottages.

EASTSOUND 98245   Map 13
ORCAS ISLAND

Eastsound is a little town on Orcas Island, in the San Juan Islands of northwestern Washington. By ferry it's three hours north of Seattle and the same distance south of Vancouver and east of Victoria. The ferry from Anacortes takes about an hour.

Also recommended: The **Rosario Island Resort and Spa** (206–376–2222; in WA, 800–562–8820), set on the shores of Cascade Bay, combines elegant dining, music, and dancing in the historic Mediterranean-style Moran Mansion (listed on the National Register of Historic Places) with modern guest rooms in separate buildings close by, plus full spa and sports facilities.

Turtleback Farm Inn   *Tel:* (206) 376–4914
Crow Valley Road
Route 1, Box 650

"The Turtleback Farm Inn is certainly a place to experience the three R's—rest, relaxation, and romance, not necessarily in that order. The atmosphere is peaceful and calm, yet invigorating. The inn is situated on 80 acres of forest and farmland near Turtleback Mountain.

"Our favorite room has an expansive view with a private deck, queen-size bed, and antique furnishings. The main living room with its terrific fireplace is a perfect place to relax.

"During the spring and summer, breakfast is served on the deck overlooking the valley; during the winter and fall, it's presented in the dining room (which has light hardwood floors and walls), on bone china, with white linen and table flowers. Starting off with fresh fruit and juice and the 'world's best' homemade granola, a hearty country breakfast follows; the meals are always fresh, healthful, varied, and quite filling.

"The proprietors, Susan and Bill Fletcher, are charming, caring, and informative. They do whatever they can to make your stay more wonderful—from restaurant reservations to sightseeing suggestions." *(Rikki Rothenberg-Klein)*

Open All year.

Rooms 7 doubles, all with private bath and/or shower.

Facilities Dining room with wet bar, refrigerator. Living room with fireplace, game table. 80 acres with 6 ponds, 1 stocked with trout. All fresh- and saltwater activities, plus hiking, bicycling, golf nearby.

Location 2.4 m from West Sound Marina, 4 m from Eastsound, 6 m from ferry landing. From ferry, take Horseshoe Hwy.; take first left, then right onto Crow Valley Rd.; inn is on right.

Restrictions No smoking. Children "by special arrangement only."

Credit cards MC, Visa.

Rates B&B, $65–130 double, $55–120 single. Extra person in room, $25. Tipping "not expected." 2-night holiday minimum.

Extras Airport/ferry pickups.

FRIDAY HARBOR 98250   Map 13
SAN JUAN ISLAND

Although Friday Harbor is the county seat of the San Juan Islands, it is still a sleepy small town with some new shops and galleries, a busy waterfront, the Whale Museum, and a newly opened performing arts center. From Friday Harbor, take a drive around the craggy western end of the island for superb views, or better yet, follow the popular bike route. Continue on to the site of the "Pig War," which started when an American farmer killed a British pig as part of a general dispute about the western boundary of the U.S. While here, watch out for the hundreds of wild rabbits that live in this area! Be sure to stop at Lime Kiln Park on the west side of the island, the only whale-watching park in the continental U.S.

Also recommended: The **Moon & Sixpence** (3021 Beaverton Valley Road; 206–378–4138), a B&B located in the heart of San Juan Island, has several guest rooms in the main farmhouse with two others in a cozy cabin and in a restored water tower. An accomplished weaver, Evelyn Tuller welcomes guests to her studio, where traditional fabrics are woven from island fleece and locally gathered dyes. The **Tucker House** (260 B Street; 206–378–2783), a remodeled turn-of-the-century house, is located across from City Park. Manager Mitzi Stack notes that "families with small children feel particularly welcome here. Everything in town is within walking distance, which is good for 'walk-on' ferry passengers." The **Wharfside Bed & Breakfast** (P.O. Box 1212; 206–378–5661) is a 60-foot gaff-rigged motor-sailer ketch called the *Jacquelyn,* with such luxuries as a tiled bathtub and Victorian antiques. Two guest rooms are available—one with one double bed and two seaman-size bunks, ideal for families, and another with a queen-size bed and settee. Owners Bette and Clyde Rice say that their B&B is for those who have "an adventurous spirit and a certain flexibility of mind and body."

Friday Harbor is located on the eastern side of San Juan Island and is the stop for the ferry connecting Anacortes, Washington, and Sidney, Vancouver Island. Travel time from Seattle is about four hours: two driving, two on the ferry.

Olympic Lights   *Tel:* (206) 378–3186
4531A Cattle Point Road

"A carefully restored and sensitively updated 1890s Victorian farmhouse on five acres of gently sloping meadowland, open to the southwest with views of the Olympic Mountains and the San Juan Channel, across which the evening lights of Victoria, B.C., twinkle in the clear air. The inn is simply furnished, with a comfy wood-burning stove providing a welcome gathering place in the sitting room and lots of books to curl up with. The guest rooms all have queen- or king-size beds and down comforters, with light-toned carpets and fresh flowers. Breakfasts are served in the large kitchen/dining room, and include juice, fresh fruit, eggs from the family chicken coop, granola and heart-shaped biscuits or other home-baked bread. They furnish ample fuel for a walk through the meadows and woods or along the nearby rocky beach." *(Clyde & Lois Coughlin)*

"Absolutely spotless room with comfortable bed and gorgeous view of mountains and water. Clean and spacious bath with large thick towels and massage showerhead. Quiet, peaceful atmosphere with tons of light and space; sunny kitchen without a speck of dirt. Owners Christian and Lea Andrade provide island maps and a list of the best places to see/ shop/eat." *(Randi & Jeff Petersen)*

Open All year.
Rooms 5 doubles—1 with full private bath, 4 with maximum of 4 people sharing a bath.
Facilities Dining room/kitchen, living room, parlor, porch. 5 acres with croquet, horseshoes. Fishing, boating, scuba diving nearby. Walking distance to American Camp National Park.
Location 5 m S of town. From ferry landing, follow Argyle Rd. S to Cattle Point Rd. to inn.
Restrictions No smoking. Children by prior arrangement. No shoes upstairs.
Credit cards None accepted.
Rates B&B, $55–80 double, $50–75 single. Extra person in room, $15. No tipping. 2 night minimum holiday weekends.
Extras Spanish spoken. Member, WBBG.

LANGLEY 98260   Map 13
WHIDBEY ISLAND

A tiny town suspended in the 19th century, Langley has a charming (and short) main street lined with antique shops and friendly restaurants. From First Street, you can look across Saratoga Passage to the mainland, the Northern Cascade Range, and volcanic Mt. Baker. "Langley is one of those beautiful, small hamlets on Puget Sound and is a charming place to visit. Lots of great little shops and galleries to knock around in and while away the time." *(Pam Phillips)*

Also recommended: The **Country Cottage of Langley** (215 Sixth Street, P.O. Box 459; 206–221–8709), a fully renovated 1920s-era farmhouse, has a recently constructed second building that is a smaller copy of the original; the new rooms have sitting rooms and dressing areas, oversize showers, and private porches overlooking the water. The **Lone Lake Cottage and Breakfast** (5206 South Bayview Road; 206–321–5325), surrounded by farm estates and forested hillsides, has lakeside cottages with almost every conceivable convenience, including free use of a 200-tape VCR library. You'll enjoy their assortment of boats and canoes, and Lone Lake is excellent for trout fishing. **The Whidbey Inn** (106 First Street, P.O. Box 156; 206–221–

7115), a cliffside building where every room has a breathtaking vista—from the Camano Peninsula to the snowcapped peaks of volcanic Mt. Baker—appeals primarily to couples looking for a romantic escape. The front door opens right onto the main street of Langley for leisurely strolls to its antique shops and restaurants; a full breakfast is brought to your door each morning at 9:00 A.M..

Langley is on the east side of South Whidbey Island, about 50 miles from Seattle. To reach the island, take Interstate 5 or 405 north from Seattle approximately 25 miles to the Mukilteo exit 182. Take State Highway 525 west to Mukilteo. Take ferry to Clinton, then follow 525 about 5 miles north to Langley.

Log Castle B&B
3273 East Saratoga Road

Tel: (206) 321–5483

This is the house that Jack built. No ordinary house, mind you, but a stunning log home designed by Norma Metcalfe and built by her husband, state senator Jack Metcalfe. In fact, Jack continues to improve and expand on the house whenever he's home from Olympia. Highlights include the cathedral-ceilinged common room with fieldstone fireplace, leaded glass windows, a wormwood stairway, and the third-story turret bedroom with five picture windows overlooking the water, beach, mountains, and pasture.

"Right on the beach for great views, especially in the Turret Room. The atmosphere in this secluded spot is one of relaxation and quiet, and the Metcalfs are gracious hosts. In the morning Norma brings coffee, tea, or juice to your room before breakfast. Later, she prepares a fabulous breakfast of homemade cinnamon rolls, eggs, sausage, old-fashioned oatmeal and very special cottage cheese hot pancakes. In the evening Norma serves hot cider and cookies in the living room, with plenty of light and room to read, play cards or do jigsaw puzzles." *(Karen Martin, also SHW)*

Open All year.
Rooms 1 suite, 3 doubles, all with private shower and/or bath.
Facilities Common room with fireplace. 2½ acres with 500 ft. of waterfront on Saratoga Passage. Rowboat for fishing. Walking trails.
Location 1½ m to village. From Langley, follow Saratoga Rd. to inn on right.
Restrictions No smoking. No children under 10.
Credit cards MC, Visa.
Rates B&B, $80 suite, $60–80 double. Extra person in room, $12.50. 2-night minimum holiday weekends.

The Saratoga Inn
4850 South Coles Road

Tel: (206) 221–7526

Debbie and Ted Jones built the Saratoga Inn in 1982. The exterior is clad in unstained shingles, highlighted by sunburst gables, while the interior combines the advantages of a new house with an antique-accented decor, Oriental rugs and hardwood floors. One guest thought the Willow Room the prettiest but said that the best view was from the Queen Anne's Lace Room. Although guests are unanimous in their praise of this "perfect" inn, one small cloud has appeared on the horizon: we understand that the inn may be for sale at this writing. Check for details when you call for reservations.

"An inngoer's dream. The gardens, grounds and meadows are bursting with gorgeous colorful flowers, and numerous walking paths lead to resting spots—a treehouse, a hammock, a church pew on the inn's grounds. In winter, the inn is filled with fresh holly, fir and juniper swags and the smell of gingerbread and cider. The Christmas tree was splendid and at night, candles illuminated the house and entryway. Rooms have reading lights by every bed and ample closet space. Bathrooms are supplied with English soaps, hairdryers, toothbrushes, cotton balls, razors, sewing kits, bubble bath, sea sponges and more. The buffet-style breakfasts are terrific, with wild blackberries and raspberries, pastries, and preserves—all served on lovely dishes with linen napkins and family silver. The ambience is a wonderful amalgam of Nantucket propriety and California exuberance—urbane and outdoorsy at the same time. Debbie is very low key but was there to help us when we needed it. She puts the focus on comfort and ease and lets guests enjoy their time together." *(Alexa & Johnathan Ferguson, also Susan Waller Schwemm)*

Open Jan. through Nov.
Rooms 5 doubles—all with full private bath, desk.
Facilities Dining room, living room with fireplace, decks. 25 acres with treehouse, lawn swing, English country gardens, bicycles, croquet. Hiking, boating, fishing, golf, tennis nearby.
Location 5 min. to Langley.
Restrictions No smoking. No children.
Credit cards None accepted.
Rates B&B, $75–90. Extra person in room, $15. 2-night weekend minimum for 3 rooms.

ORCAS 98280   Map 13
SAN JUAN ISLANDS

Orcas Hotel   *Tel:* (206) 376–4300
P.O. Box 155 (at the ferry landing)   376–4306

Listed on the National Register of Historic Places, the Orcas Hotel is a turn-of-the-century Victorian resort hotel, extensively restored in 1985 by Barbara and John Jamieson. Located right next to the ferry landing, the hotel overlooks Harney Channel, Wasp Passage, Shaw Island, and Blind Bay. Rooms are furnished with Victorian antiques, reproduction wallpapers, handmade quilts, modern queen-size beds, and the works of many Orcas Island artists.

Rates include a continental breakfast of a croissant, juice, and coffee, or a $2 credit toward a full breakfast from the two-page menu. Lunches include a full range of deli or croissant-style sandwiches; dinner selections emphasize fresh local seafood, along with a good choice of chicken, beef, and vegetarian dishes.

"Set on a bluff overlooking the little harbor, the Orcas Hotel is made special by its innkeeper, Barbara Jamieson. She is a delight, and we thoroughly enjoyed talking with her throughout our stay. She is a warm and friendly person, who runs a solid business and works hard to follow through on the details. Barbara sets the tone, and as a result, the inn is very friendly; it's fun to talk with the other guests about where they're going and where they've been.

"The inn has a charming parlor off the main entryway that is a great place to write postcards or chat with the other guests. There is also a cocktail lounge with a big veranda for drinks. Guest rooms are sizable, comfortable, and furnished in antiques; some have views of the ferry landing. We enjoyed the tiny balcony on the second-floor landing; we would sit on the two antique rockers early in the morning and late at night to have coffee and watch the goings-on in the harbor.

"Breakfasts are very hearty and delicious, and the corn fritters are out of this world. Live music is scheduled from time to time, and a very pleasant trio was there during our stay." *(Pam Phillips)*

"If you don't mind sharing a bath, this place is a class act, with excellent innkeepers, a great breakfast, and an atmosphere that is bustling but not frantic." *(Amy & Ernie Fleishman)*

Open All year.

Rooms 2 suites, 10 doubles—2 with private bath, 3 with private toilets and sinks; 6 bathrooms with showers available to all guests. 8 rooms with desk; all with fan.

Facilities Restaurant, lounge with stained glass, TV; parlor with games, fireplace; sitting room, veranda. Music, dancing Saturday nights in season, holidays year round. 2 acres with Victorian English landscaping. Free moorage. Swimming in Cascade Lake; bicycling, hiking, golf, canoeing, kayaking, ocean and lake fishing nearby.

Location NW WA, San Juan Islands. S end of Orcas Island, 9 m to Eastsound village. Turn left at top of ferry ramp. Drive around picket fence and park at inn.

Restrictions No smoking in parlor, dining room. Children "may be more comfortable at other hotels." Noise from ferry dock twice a day.

Credit cards Amex, MC, Visa.

Rates B&B, $125 suite, $62–75 double, $38–65 single. Extra person in room, $15. 2 nights for price of 1 midweek, off-season. 2-night minimum holiday weekends. Full breakfast, $2–6; alc lunch, $8; alc dinner, $25. Children's menu.

Extras 2 rooms, dining room, and lounge wheelchair accessible. Airport pickups. Cribs, highchairs, baby-sitting available. French, Spanish, German spoken. Member, WBBG.

PORT ANGELES 98362   Map 13

Port Angeles is located in northwestern Washington, midway up the northern end of the Olympic Peninsula, along the Strait of Juan de Fuca. It's a popular place to overnight for those traveling the Olympic Loop Highway (Rte. 101) and for those taking the ferry to or from Victoria, on Vancouver Island, British Columbia.

Nearby attractions include Hurricane Ridge, just 17 miles from town. At 5,000 feet, it offers a beautiful view of the surrounding valleys, mountains, and sea. Other area attractions include Lake Crescent, the Dungeness Spit Wildlife Refuge, the Sole Duc Hot Springs, charter fishing and boating in the straits or the Pacific, hiking and backpacking, and cross-country skiing in the winter.

Also recommended: The **Tudor Inn** (1108 South Oak; 206–452–3138 or 452–4860), a half-timbered house built in 1910, is an English-style B&B furnished with English antiques and collectibles; rooms have brass and canopy queen- and king-size beds.

Lake Crescent Lodge
Star Route 1, Box 11

Tel: (206) 928–3211

"Located 20 miles west of Port Angeles, the lodge is spread out on the south bank of Lake Crescent, at the base of Storm King Mountain, and set between the rain forest to the south and the Strait of Juan de Fuca to the north. Although it's not luxurious, it is a wonderful place to bring the kids and to wear comfortable clothes. The buildings include the early 1900s-era wooden main lodge, with its huge wraparound porch and fireplace; 17 cabins (including 13 built in 1985); and two motel-type buildings to the east. The best rooms are in the four large cabins with fireplaces—book early, everybody wants them. The rooms in the lodge on the north side are worth the view over the lake, even with shared baths.

"Although the food is not gourmet, the fish is fresh and well presented, the vegetables are nicely prepared, and the breakfasts are good.

"In any case, you don't come here to stay indoors. You come to play on the beach, paddle about in rowboats, fish, play badminton, and walk on the nearby Marymere Falls trail. The dining room serves large portions of simple food, with friendly college students waiting on tables. There are evening nature programs and many impromptu card games; bring your Frisbee, kites, and other outdoor games." *(Suzanne Carmichael, also Mrs. Arnold Miller)*

Open April 28–Oct. 28.
Rooms 35 doubles, 17 cabins—47 with full private bath, 5 with maximum of 10 people sharing bath. Most with desk.
Facilities Lobby/lounge, sun porch, dining room, gift shop, covered porches. 35 acres with lakefront dock, walking trails. Downhill skiing nearby.
Location NW WA, Olympic National Park. On Hwy. 101, 20 m W of Port Angeles. ¼ m from park entrance.
Credit cards Amex, CB, DC, MC, Visa.
Rates Room only, $50–95 double, $45–95 single. Extra person in room, $8. Alc breakfast, $3–8; alc lunch, $8–12; alc dinner, $19.50–27.50.
Extras Pets permitted. Cribs available.

PORT TOWNSEND 98368   Map 13

Port Townsend has been designated a National Historic District and is considered to be the best example of a Victorian seacoast town north of San Francisco. Nearly 70 Victorian buildings can be seen, along with the town's many appealing craft shops, art galleries, and restaurants. Good salmon fishing is available, along with beaches for crabbing, clamming, and oystering. The town offers public golf courses and tennis courts and is within a short drive of the Olympic National Park. Because of the protection of the Olympic Mountains, the climate is fairly mild, with more than 200 sunny days a year and about 20 inches of rainfall (less than half of Seattle's).

Also recommended: The **Heritage House** (305 Pierce Street; 206–385–6800), a restored 1870s home, is furnished in authentic Victoriana, from the Eastlake parlor grouping to the fold-away tin-and-oak claw-foot tub; period wallpapers and window treatments complete the effect. Firm mattresses and updated plumbing add a welcome non-Victorian touch; rates include a full breakfast. The **James House** (1238 Washington Street; 206–385–1238), built in 1891, claims to be the Northwest's first B&B, and is set on a bluff with sweeping views of Port Townsend, the Olympic and Cascade ranges, and Puget Sound. The **Ravenscroft Inn** (533 Quincy Street; 206–385–2784), set on a bluff overlooking Admiralty Inlet, is a colonial recreation of an early American seaport inn—a dramatic change in architecture from the Victorian buildings prevalent in Port Townsend. Guest rooms have beamed ceilings, French doors opening to the balconies, floral comforters, and period furniture. The **Starrett House Inn** (744 Clay Street; 206–385–3205) is one of the most frequently photographed buildings in the Pacific Northwest. The interior is heavily ornamented and features an elaborate free-hung circular stairway; many rooms offer sweeping water and mountain views.

Recommended too late for a full write-up is the **Arcadia Inn** (1891 South Jacob Miller Road; 206–385–6800), built in 1908, and now a B&B owned by the famous Flying Karamazov Brothers juggling/theatrical team. The seven guest rooms are furnished with antiques, and the inn is "set on many acres of peaceful farmland. It used to be a speakeasy, and has a very interesting history. There's a hot tub in the yard, woods to explore, and a big barn theater that the K's use for practice." *(Pat Spaeth)*

Port Townsend is located on northwest Washington's Olympic Peninsula, on Puget Sound. It's less than 60 miles from both Seattle and Victoria and is 13 miles north, via Route 20, off the scenic Olympic Loop, Highway 101.

Lizzie's *Tel:* (206) 385–4168
731 Pierce

Built by Lizzie Grant in 1887, this Victorian has been beautifully restored and furnished in period; it's owned by Patti and Bill Wickline. Although each room has its charms, guests are particularly fond of Sarah's Room, because of its beautiful view and lovely furnishings, and Lizzie's Room, which has an ingenious canopy, a faux marble fireplace, and a super bath. Three claw-foot tubs are available to guests for long hot soaks; Lizzie's own brand of bubble bath and lotion is provided. The ample continental breakfast includes fresh fruit, eggs, dried fruit compote, yogurt, scones or muffins, juice, and coffee or tea; coffee, tea, fruit, and ice are available throughout the day.

"We stayed in Jessie's Room, which we liked since it had a private half-basin bath, a large sitting area, and, best of all, we could look out the bathroom window at the most beautiful 'egg plum' tree brought over from the Orient almost a century ago. The living room is decorated with an unusual antique wallpaper made in Paris with gold leaf. Be sure to ask Bill to show you the seven-foot wood sheet-music cabinet with its secret locking device. Before breakfast you can sit on the back porch with a fresh cup of coffee or tea. Breakfast was so good and filling that we forgot to even think about lunch!" *(Suzanne Carmichael)*

"The Wicklines are very personable hosts, and you soon feel comfortable and relaxed. The rooms are yet very inviting and comfortable. The area is quiet and you can walk everywhere. At night we sat in front of the roaring parlor fire, chatting with the other guests, and in the morning shared a delicious breakfast in the warm country kitchen." *(Mary & John Marsh, also Jeffrey McKelvy, Alicia Comstock-Litwin)*

"Recently expanded in very good taste. The backyard has a playhouse replica of the big house. Come in August to get big yellow plums off the tree in the side yard." *(Pat Spaeth)*

Open All year.
Rooms 7 doubles—3 with private bath and/or shower, 4 with shared bath. 1 with fireplace.
Facilities 2 sitting rooms with fireplaces, library, piano. Garden. Beach for walking, swimming, charter fishing nearby.
Location 10 min. walk to historic downtown. From Hwy. 20, turn left at 1st stop light, right on Lawrence, left on Pierce.
Restrictions No children under 10.
Credit cards MC, Visa.
Rates B&B, $45–85 double, $39–79 single. Extra person in room, $6. 2-night holiday weekend minimum.
Extras Free ferry/local airport pickups. Member, WBBG.

QUINAULT 98575   Map 13

Lake Quinault Lodge   *Tel:* (206) 288–2571
South Shore Road, Box 7

Olympic National Park, with an average annual rainfall of almost 150 inches, offers many sights of interest. One of the most popular, the Koh Rain Forest, is filled with massive Douglas firs that are covered with shaggy green moss. The area was set aside as a forest reserve in 1898 by Grover Cleveland and was declared a National Monument by Teddy Roosevelt in 1909. In 1938 it was toured by Franklin Roosevelt (he stayed at the Lake Quinault Lodge), who declared it a national park.

The lodge was built in 1926, in only 10 weeks, at the then-considerable cost of $90,000. All building materials and furnishings had to be hauled over 50 miles of dirt road. Many area artisans were used, and their work can be seen in the stenciled designs on the lobby's beamed ceiling. Much of the wicker lobby furniture is original to the building. The lodge had been owned for 16 years by Marge and Larry Lesley but was sold in January of 1988 to ARA Leisure Services of Philadelphia.

Rooms are decorated with handsome brass beds and oak night tables as well as inexpensive reproduction lamps and out-of-period wall-to-wall carpeting. Rooms in the adjacent Lakeside Inn are furnished in typical motel fashion. The dinner menu offers a full range of choices but highlights northwestern seafood—both smoked and fresh trout and salmon, plus oysters and prawns.

"The experience of staying in the middle of the world's only temperate rain forest, in a historic building with a sumptuous lawn that sweeps down to lovely Lake Quinault, is not to be missed. Request a room in the old portion of the lodge with windows facing the lake. The rooms are quite nice and the view spectacular. Expect the lodge to be somewhat crowded in the summer. The lobby is inviting and old-fashioned—just close your eyes to the kitsch for sale nearby in the gift shop. You'll eat well if you stick to fish and simple dishes." *(Anne Michaels)*

"Great location, with an incredible feeling of serenity to it. Even the children spoke in hushed tones. Come here for the experience, not for the food." *(Amy & Ernie Fleishman)*

Unfortunately, readers have also written to say that a few rooms are way below par, especially in the summer, when heavy demand far exceeds the supply. One couple complained that they were once given a room without a window, while another respondent had a room in the annex, which was well supplied with windows but had a ghastly green carpet, gaudy floral spreads, and dreadfully uncomfortable brass beds. Their door had a large window, covered by a shade patched with medical tape. Complaints to the desk clerk produced no satisfaction. We'd suggest that when making reservations, you ask for a confirmed reservation in either the main lodge or the motel section—not the annex; if there's a problem and the front desk staff is unresponsive, ask to speak to the manager. Reports, please.

Open All year.
Rooms 16 suites, 38 doubles—26 with full private bath, 12 with tub only, 8 with shower only. 8 rooms with sink in room and maximum of 8 people sharing bath. 8 rooms in annex. Some with fireplace.
Facilities Dining room, lounge, lobby with fireplace, game room, gift shop. Pianist or singer in lounge summer weekends. 5 acres on lake, with lawns, gazebo, heated indoor swimming pool with hot tub. Fishing, canoeing, hunting, hiking nearby.
Location NW WA, Olympic Peninsula. In Olympic National Forest, 38 m N of Aberdeen/Hoquiam, via Hwy. 101N. Exit 101 at South Shore Rd.; 2 m to Quinault.
Credit cards Amex, MC, Visa.
Rates Room only, $70–90 double in lodge, $70–74 double in annex. Extra person in room, $10. Children under 5 free. 2- to 3-day minimum summer and holiday weekends. Alc breakfast, $3–6; alc lunch, $5–8; alc dinner, $18–26. Off-season midweek packages.
Extras Pets permitted in annex ($8 fee). Cribs, babysitting available.

SEATTLE   Map 13

Snuggled on six steep hills between Puget Sound and Lake Washington, Seattle is both sophisticated and friendly. It's known as a "city of neighborhoods." Visitors can sample the unusual restaurants and shops in the International District, home to Seattle's Asian population, or stroll through Ballard, the Scandinavian enclave.

On the southern end of downtown Seattle, Pioneer Square Historic District boasts unusual boutiques, the Seattle Children's Museum, and sidewalk cafés. Pike Place Market, in the middle of the business district overlooking Elliot Bay, opened as a farmer's market in 1907. Here you will find fishmongers and fresh produce stands, street musicians and handcrafts, ethnic markets and superb eateries. A few blocks north is Seattle Center, the site of the 1962 World's Fair. Take a ride up the center's 605-foot Space Needle for wonderful views, and take your kids to the excellent exhibits at the Pacific Science Center. Stop by the Center House for a variety of ethnic fast-food choices.

Tour the waterfront by boarding one of the vintage 1927 Australian trolley cars. Be sure to visit the Seattle Aquarium, where an underwater viewing area provides fish-eye views of Puget Sound's sea life. For something really different, take the underground Seattle tour to see nineteenth-century sidewalks and storefronts left underground when the streets were raised to avoid the spring mud. In the evening visit jazz clubs in the University District or the lively restaurants and nightclubs on Capital Hill.

Seattle has outstanding public art collections, starting with the 18 works displayed at the airport. (Get a guidebook from the Seattle Arts Commission, 305 Harrison Street, 98109.) Excellent theater can be found at Seattle Repertory Theater, A Contemporary Theater, or The Empty Space. Also worth attending are the Pacific Northwest Ballet and the Seattle Opera's Wagner Festival.

The best of Seattle's various festivals include the Seafair Festival in late July, the Bumbershoot street art festival around Labor Day, and the Christmas cruise in December.

Also recommended: The **Chelsea Station** (4915 Linden Avenue North, 98103; 206–547–6077), a 1920 red-brick Federal colonial home, is located near the south entrance to the Woodland Park Zoo. Rooms are decorated with traditional furniture and English antiques; rates include a full breakfast, hot beverages and a bottomless cookie jar. The **Gaslight Inn** (1727 15th Avenue, 98122; 206–325–3654), constructed in 1906 as a private home, offers quiet and solitude in a location only ten blocks from the center of Seattle. Carefully restored and decorated, most common rooms have their original oak paneling; the stairway landing has a superb stained glass window. **Roberta's B&B** (1147 16th Avenue East, 98112; 206–329–3326), a classic turn-of-the-century home decorated with antiques, is in a nice old neighborhood convenient to downtown Seattle. Rates include a breakfast that is hot, hearty, and homemade. The **Salisbury House** (750 16th Ave. East, 98112; 206–328–8682), a 1900s home with wraparound porch looking out at the distant Olympic mountains, is just a short stroll away from Volunteer Park. The sunny guest rooms are individually furnished, but all have down comforters.

Although it's clearly not a "little" hotel at 450 rooms, two readers highly commended the **Four Seasons Olympic** for its "beautifully furnished large rooms, excellent service and staff, and a top location." *(Jack & Sue Lane, also LS)* Contact the hotel at 411 University Street, 98101; (206) 621–1700 or (800) 332–3442.

Two B&Bs recommended too late for a full writeup are the **Lake Union B&B** (2217 North 36th Street, 98103; 206–547–9965) and the **Queen Anne Hill B&B** (1835 West Seventh Street, 98119; 206 284-9779). The Lake Union offers two very spacious suites with excellent views overlooking Puget Sound from its setting at the crest of a hill in the Queen Anne district. The owner has a restaurant nearby, and dinners can be brought on request. The Queen Anne is owned by Chuck and Mary McGrew, with a deck offering handsome views of the city and sound. "The deck and gardens are lovely, and the home is a collector's paradise (though not for those with more spartan tastes). The setting is very quiet and the views outstanding. Mr. McGrew is in the communications business, and offers business travelers complimentary cellular phones for the car; you pay only for calls made." *(SHW)*

Rates do not include state tax of 7.8% in B&Bs, 12.9% in hotels.

Alexis Hotel Seattle
Tel: (206) 624–4844
1007 First Avenue at Madison 98104   Outside WA: (800) 426–7033

Originally an office building designed in 1901, the Alexis underwent a total renovation, resulting in an award-winning European-style luxury hotel. Listed on the National Register of Historic Places, the Alexis offers rooms decorated in soothing, muted tones, highlighted with flowers and antiques, with complimentary sherry. Those planning a longer stay in Seattle may wish to inquire about rates at the adjacent Arlington Suites, under the same ownership.

The Café Alexis has seasonally changing American cuisine, featuring fresh, locally grown ingredients. "We had a delicious meal in a quiet, elegant atmosphere at a very reasonable price." *(SHW)* "While at the Alexis, stop by the Legacy, one of the best shops in Seattle selling Northwest Coast Indian masks, sculpture, jewelry, and prints." *(SC)*

"Accommodations are exquisite, with not a detail left unnoticed. Fabrics and furnishings are high quality and very well done. Bathrooms are large, feature whirlpools, romantic lights, and any other extra you could possibly think of. Especially comfortable beds and pillows, with 100% cotton sheets. The restaurant is exceptional both in service and quality of ingredients. The atmosphere is rather subdued and very peaceful, making for a romantic, restful stay. Parking is a bit of a problem in Seattle, but they seem to handle it fine." *(Pam Phillips)*

Open All year.
Rooms 25 suites, 29 doubles, all with full private bath, telephone, TV, desk, air-conditioning. Some with fireplace, balcony, whirlpool tub, wet bar.
Facilities Restaurant, bar with piano music weekdays, lobby, interior courtyard, banquet facilities. Concierge, 24-hr. room service. Valet parking. Steam room, spa with whirlpool, guest membership at nearby athletic club.
Location Downtown, 1 block from waterfront. At corner of First Ave. and Madison.
Credit cards Amex, CB, DC, Discover, Visa.
Rates B&B, $180–275 suite, $140–155 double, $120–150 single. No tipping. Extra person in room, $15. Weekend, corporate rates.
Extras Wheelchair accessible; 3 rooms equipped for disabled. Pets permitted. Cribs available. Spanish, French, Japanese, Thai spoken. Member, Alexis Distinctive Hotels.

Chambered Nautilus
Tel: (206) 522–2536
5005 22nd Avenue Northeast 98105

Perched on a hill in the University District, this handsome Georgian colonial mansion was built in 1915 by one of the early faculty members at the

University of Washington, and was bought in July of 1988 by Connecticut transplants Bunny and Bill Hagemeyer. A typical breakfast might include cereals, fruits and juices, apple quiche, French toast with homemade syrup, pumpkin-blueberry muffins, and fresh-ground regular and decaf coffee. The Hagemeyers have newly landscaped the inn's gardens, planting them extensively with flowers. The inn offers lovely views of the gardens and of the Cascade Mountains in the distance.

"The atmosphere is comfortable and relaxing. The seashell theme predominates—each room is a different shell. The rooms are large and private and are decorated with English and American antiques, comforters, and pillows. Each is provided with mineral water, a Japanese bathrobe, and a guide to 'Seattle's Best.' A large living room serves as a common space where hot tea is served; there's a fireplace for cold nights, and lots of books and magazines. The living room opens onto a sun porch and a green Seattle garden.

"Our favorite room is the Rose Chamber, which has beautiful windows, a big old bed, and lots of books. Perhaps the most elegant room is the one on the third floor, painted in peach tones, with gabled windows." (Carol Jung) "The Hagemeyers are exceptionally warm, welcoming hosts." (Mark Lane)

Open All year.
Rooms 6 doubles—2 with full private bath, 4 with maximum of 4 people sharing bath. All with radio, desk, fan. 4 with porch.
Facilities Living room with fireplace, piano; dining room with fireplace, sun porch, open porches. ½ acres with landscaped gardens, sitting areas. Burke-Gilman Trail, Green Lake, Ravenna Park nearby for jogging, walking.
Location University District. 10 min. from downtown Seattle, walking distance to U. of WA. Take exit 169 off I-5N. Go right (E) on NE 50th St. to stop sign at 20th Ave. NE and turn left. Go 4 blocks to NE 54th St. Turn right and go 2 blocks to 22nd Ave. NE and turn right to inn at #5005.
Restrictions On-street parking only. No alcohol on premises. No smoking. Children under 12 "by prior arrangement only."
Credit cards Amex, MC, Visa.
Rates B&B, $60–89 double. $55–80 single. Extra person in room, $10. Corporate rates. No tipping. 2-3 night minimum holiday weekends.
Extras German spoken. Member, WBBG.

Inn at the Market
86 Pine Street 98101

Tel: (206) 443–3600
(800) 446–4484

Since its opening in June 1985, this small luxury hotel has quickly gained a top reputation. Some have told us that once you've stayed here, you won't stay anywhere else in Seattle (if you can afford it), although others prefer the more peaceful atmosphere of our other hotel listings.

"Romantic and charming. Accommodations are superb, especially the rooms with a view of Puget Sound. The location is one of the best any-where—right in the heart of the Pike Place Market area. You can walk right out the door for fresh coffee, bakeries, street vendors, and more. The decor is very sophisticated and restful, and the bathrooms are way above aver-age—very large and well designed, with lots of extra goodies. The cleanli-ness of the whole facility is above average; rooms are spacious, with ample closet space. The best deals are the two-story townhouse suites, which feature a bedroom upstairs, living room/ kitchen downstairs with the option of an additional bedroom if desired.

"The staff is helpful and accommodating and will assist in making suggestions and reservations. Limited parking is available underground, but you have to check in early to get a space; otherwise you have to park in the lot across the street, which is slightly inconvenient.

"The lobby is inviting, decorated with a country French theme, and usually there's a big fire in the fireplace. The staff also sets up coffee and tea service each morning in the lobby, which is nice if you're meeting someone there to start the day." *(Pam Phillips, also RL)*

"We felt as though we were in a country inn in a big city. From the roof garden we had a great view of the market, the ferries, and the sunset. The atmosphere is uncommercial—the staff doesn't wear uniforms and everyone helps out. The market is authentic, not at all posh, with real market smells and wonderful places to buy coffee." *(Amy & Ernie Fleishman)*

Two small drawbacks to this otherwise luxurious establishment—room service is very limited both in terms of the hours it's available and the menu offered. "The room service breakfast is prepared by an organic-vegetarian restaurant, which may not be everyone's cup of tofu." Also: "The bar is *very* popular. We stopped by for an after-dinner drink and had no chance of getting served."

Open All year.
Rooms 7 suites, 58 doubles—61 with full private bath, 4 with shower only. All with telephone, radio, TV, desk, refrigerator, coffee makers.
Facilities Restaurants, lobby, sun deck, inner courtyard, off-street parking. Room service. Health club nearby. Complimentary downtown limo service.
Location Downtown, in Pike Place Market. On 1st Ave. between Pine and Stewart. From I-5N, take Seneca St. exit on left and continue to 1st Ave. Go right to 1st Ave. and go 4 blocks N to Pine. Go left to inn on right.
Restrictions No smoking in some guest rooms. Heavy street traffic occasionally disturbs light sleepers on the city-side rooms.
Credit cards Amex, DC, Discover, JCB, MC, Visa.
Rates Room only, $165–200 suite, $90–160 double, $80–140 single. Extra person in room, $15. No charge for children under 16 in parents' room. Senior and weekend discounts. Alc breakfast, $4–9.
Extras Wheelchair accessible; some rooms specially equipped for disabled. Non-smoking rooms available. Airport/station pickups. Cribs, babysitting available. French, Spanish, German, Dutch spoken.

The Sorrento Hotel
900 Madison Street 98104

Tel: (206) 622–6400
(800) 426–1265

The Sorrento derives its name from its grand façade, designed by Pacific Northwest architect Harland Thomas in the tradition of the houses of Sorrento, Italy, with terra cotta trim and an Italian fountain. The lobby area is paneled in Honduran mahogany, and the fireplace mantel features a handpainted tile landscape. Guest rooms provide all the luxuries one expects in a hotel of this type—antiques, fresh flowers, goose-down pillows, bathrobes and oversized towels, turndown service, and bedwarmers for chilly nights. The hotel restaurant, the Hunt Club, prepares innovative northwestern cuisine as well as traditional American.

"Come to the Sorrento for an appreciation of the past. Sitting in the lobby listening to the grand piano as the flickering firelight is reflected in the polished paneling can make everyday cares fade away. Built in 1909 and still operating with one elevator (which will teach any guest a lesson in patience), the Sorrento is home to the Hunt Club, one of Seattle's finest establishments. It's a long walk to the center of the city, which may be an advantage when you consider the construction going on downtown. If you want a view of the city or bay, be sure to request a room above the third floor." *(Laura Scott)* "Great room service; the best rooms are the lovely corner suites." *(SC)* "Exceptionally helpful, courteous staff." *(SHW)*

"Beautiful. Elegant. Service generally good, although we hit a new desk clerk on day one and had a bit of a mix-up, which was soon straightened out with many apologies from the management. Afternoon tea is lovely and can be taken out on the terrace. Service is slow, but the food is good and the servings generous. While waiting for dinner, the house special drink (peach schnapps and champagne) is a treat. And chef Barbara Figueroa does marvels in the kitchen. This is the Northwest, so of course the salmon is spectacular. But her rabbit is, simply, to die for. The wine list is extensive, with many interesting Washington and Oregon wines, and the wine steward is ready to advise. Try to save room for desserts." *(Hilary Huebsch Cohen)*

Open All year.
Rooms 42 suites, 36 doubles—all with private bath and/or shower. All with telephone, radio, cable TV, desk, air-conditioning, refrigerator, bar.
Facilities Restaurant, lounge with piano/jazz entertainment, lobby with fireplace. Valet parking.
Location Downtown; 4 blocks E of downtown business district on First Hill. From I-5, take exit 165, marked James/Madison St. Continue to Madison, and go right 2 blocks to corner of Madison and Terry.
Credit cards Amex, DC, MC, Visa.
Rates Room only, $160–300 suite, $130–150 double, service included. Extra person in room, $15. Children under 18 free in parents' room. B&B weekend rates, $90–110. Alc breakfast, $6–12; alc lunch, $15–20; alc dinner, $40–50.
Extras Wheelchair accessible. Airport/station pickups. Cribs, babysitting available. Spanish, Chinese spoken. Complimentary downtown limo service.

Williams House   *Tel:* (206) 285–0810
1505 Fourth Avenue North 98109

"A beautiful turn-of-the-century house, with a magnificent view of the city lights at night and the Space Needle. It is immaculately clean, and Susan's breakfast, with fresh-ground coffee, juice, fruit, homemade breads, muffins, and granola, is great.

"The house is a beauty: bright with windows on Seattle's landscape, mellow with dark wood, warm with traditional prints and furnishings. We've stayed in the Brass and Satin Room with a big brass bed and view of the city and Puget Sound and also in the large front bedroom with a queen-size bed under a delicate lace awning, offering a special view through three windows to the east. The sunrises here are worth an early awakening. The delicious breakfasts range from plum cake to whole-wheat waffles to French toast, in addition to fresh fruit or homemade applesauce every morning. Sue and Doug were quick with a welcoming smile and a reviving cup of tea, a laugh, or a sympathetic story. The house is immaculate, with ample light for reading, and inviting public rooms. The location makes access to downtown Seattle a matter of minutes, and the house is attractively situated on a corner surrounded by flower and vegetable gardens in this classic Queen Anne neighborhood." *(Sarah Ellison, also Susan Schwemm)*

Open All year.
Rooms 5 doubles—1 with private bath, 1 with ½ bath, 4 rooms sharing 2 baths.
Facilities Parlor, sun porch, dining room, TV room. Swimming pool, tennis courts nearby.
Location Queen Anne district, 1 m from downtown. From I-5, take Mercer St./Seattle Center exit, and follow signs to Seattle Center. Turn right at sign to Opera House and Space Needle, right onto 5th Ave. Go left on Highland, right on 3rd Ave., right on Galer St. Inn is at corner of Galer and 4th Ave.
Restrictions Smoking on sun porch only.
Credit cards Amex, DC, MC, Visa.
Rates B&B, $65–90 double, $60–$85 single. Extra person in room, $15. Discount for 5-night stay Oct.–April. 2 night holiday minimum.
Extras Crib, babysitting available. Member, WBBG.

SEAVIEW 98644   Map 13

Shelburne Inn   *Tel:* (206) 642–2442
103 at 45th St., P.O. Box 250, Pacific Hwy.

Listed on the National Register of Historic Places, the Shelburne was built as a hotel in 1896—perhaps the oldest continuously run hotel in the state. After years of neglect, the inn was purchased in 1977 by Laurie Anderson and David Campiche, who have been fixing it up ever since. Recent improvements include a new kitchen and dining-room area, highlighted by Art Nouveau stained-glass windows from a church in England, and five new bedrooms. Care was taken to see that these additions blend in with the character and style of the inn.

The inn is also home to the Shoalwater Restaurant, owned by Ann and Tony Kischner. Its innovative menu features local seafood and changes with the seasons. A recent dinner might have included sautéed calimari with onions and mushrooms in pesto cream sauce; or grilled fillet of sturgeon marinated with ginger, scallions, black beans, sherry, and lemon juice; served with fresh vegetables, salad, and homemade bread, and a choice of Ann Kischner's pastries for dessert.

"The Shelburne provides a bit of authentic charm in the midst of an otherwise non-descript seaside town. The beach here is miles and miles of flat sand (no shells, no driftwood, pretty during spectacular sunsets). The inn itself is a tasteful dark green on the outside, with warm woods inside. The bedrooms on the whole are cozy with many nice touches—I'd recommend them all except our room, #11, at least in summer. It was small and dark, with a nice little sitting porch. Unfortunately, the door to this porch provided the only light and air. Since it was hot, we kept the door open, but the bugs decided they were included in the cost of the room. Rooms on the second floor are charming, with antiques and well-coordinated decor—one in pink, another in shades of blue, some with delicate cro-cheted coverlets. My favorite was the front suite, which had a large bed-room area, a small sitting area with wicker chairs, and an enormous bath. Almost every room on the second floor had a private small porch. The three attic rooms are done in green, with slanted dormer walls and a shared bath. I suspect these would be warm in summer. All rooms had high-quality soaps, shampoo, and even a French mint toothpaste, as well as a saucer with two chocolate candies and some chocolate pebbles.

"You get a choice of four entrées at breakfast, all filling and well pre-pared. We had a creole omelet with big chunks of ham and tomato, four cheeses, and creole sauce, and another omelet with herbs and smoked salmon. Other choices included special French toast and pancakes. All were accompanied by six different kinds of fresh fruit, perfectly cooked potatoes, and homemade fruit bread. Even the decaf was special—the coffee was scented with pecans.

"Dinner was quite good, if a bit uneven. Appetizers were a standout—grilled Oregon duck sausage with blueberry mustard and light sauerkraut, and pâté with cranberry chutney. My duck entrée sounded better than it tasted, but my husband's pasta with marinated prawns, tomatoes, garlic and pine nuts was very tasty." (SC, also Paul Lasley & Elizabeth Harryman)

Open All year. Restaurant closed Wed. from Oct.–May.
Rooms 2 suites, 14 doubles—13 with private bath and/or shower, 3 with maximum of 6 people sharing bath. 3 with desk. Some with deck or porch.
Facilities Restaurant, pub, lounge, lobby with fireplace. Antique shop. ½ acre with herb and flower gardens. Charter boat fishing (for salmon), bird-watching nearby. 3 blocks to beach.
Location SW WA, near OR border. 2 hrs. N of Portland, 3 hrs. S of Seattle. Follow Hwy. 101 to Seaview, gateway to the Long Beach Peninsula. In Seaview go N on State Hwy. 103 to inn on left at 45th St.
Restrictions Light sleepers might be disturbed by thin walls in the older rooms and close-to-road location. Smoking permitted in special area in restaurant, lounge. "Well-behaved, quiet children welcome."
Credit cards Amex, MC, Visa.
Rates B&B, $129–135 suite, $85–97 double, service included. Extra person in room, $10. Reduced rates for children. 2-night summer minimum. Alc lunch, $8.50; alc dinner, $40–50.
Extras 1 room wheelchair accessible. Airport/station pickups. Crib available. Span-ish, German, Dutch spoken.

West Virginia

The Thomas Shepherd Inn, Shepherdstown

West Virginia is a rural, mountainous state, with areas of great beauty. Most of our listings are in the Eastern Panhandle, a region of historic interest and natural attractions. Because this area is only a 60- to 90-minute drive from Washington, D.C., and Baltimore, MD, it is particularly popular on weekends. Rates are most often highest Friday and Saturday nights, and can be substantially lower midweek. Rates don't usually vary much with the seasons, although October is generally the most popular period.

Rates do not include 5% state sales tax, plus additional local taxes of 3-4%.

BERKELEY SPRINGS 25411   Map 4

"We this day called at Ye Famed Warm Springs," says the March 18, 1748, journal entry of 16-year-old George Washington, who was traveling with a Virginia surveying group. He was referring to the warm mineral waters of what is now called Berkeley Springs, the nation's oldest spa, which nowadays offers a full range of mineral baths and massage, as well as a regular swimming pool. Other sights of interest include nearby Prospect Peak, with a three-state view; Cacapon State Park, with a lake for swimming and boating, and an eighteen-hole Robert Trent Jones golf course; hiking and riding on Cacapon Mountain; Berkeley Castle; and the historic Chesapeake and Ohio Canal Tunnel in Paw Paw, completed in 1850.

Berkeley Springs is located in the Eastern Panhandle region of West

Virginia, 100 miles west of Washington, D.C., and Baltimore, MD, and 165 miles southwest of Philadelphia, PA.

Highlawn Inn
304 Market Street

The Highlawn is a turn-of-the-century Victorian home, owned by Sandy Kauffman and Timothy Miller. Rooms are decorated with period antiques and feature designer linens, English soaps, and other bath amenities. Rates include a country breakfast buffet of local apple butter, country bacon or sausage, Swiss cheese and egg casserole, plus fresh fruit and juice, and home-baked biscuits and pastries. Guests enjoy relaxing on the Highlawn's porch rockers, with a lovely view overlooking the town.

"Everything is so fresh—the wonderful West Virginia air, the beautiful bedrooms with special linens and appointments, and the magnificent country-style breakfast." *(Virginia Schatken)* "Sandy Kaufman is warm and cordial, and runs an exquisite rest haven. We stayed in the downstairs suite and were delighted with the combination of privacy and accessibility to the living and dining areas of the inn." *(Timaree Bierle & Richard Re)*

"Sandy and Tim are full of information on local sights and happenings. We relaxed in front of a glowing fire, and visited with the other guests. Our room was spacious with comfortable beds and lovely antiques. The fresh baked pastries will put Jane Fonda's Workout tape right out of mind." *(Jean Morrissett)*

Open All year.
Rooms 1 suite, 5 doubles, all with private bath and/or shower, TV, air-conditioning.
Facilities Sitting room with fireplace, games, books, puzzles. ¾ acre with picnic table, wraparound veranda with porch swings, rockers. Antique/craft shop. 9 m to Cacapon State Park for golf, tennis, hiking, swimming.
Location 3 blocks from center, 3 blocks to Berkeley Springs Mineral Baths. From I-70, I-81, take Rte. 522 to Market St. At the top of the hill on the left is the inn.
Restrictions No children.
Credit cards MC, Visa.
Rates B&B, $90 suite, $70–85 double.

CHARLES TOWN 25414   Map 4

Charles Town is home to the Charles Town Races and the Old Opera House. Harper's Ferry National Historic Park and Antietam Battlefield are both nearby. Charles Town is located on the Eastern Panhandle, 70 miles west of both Washington, D.C., and Baltimore, MD.

Also recommended: Built in 1858 and restored in 1985, **The Carriage Inn** (417 East Washington Street; 304–728–8003) offers country-style furnishings, a full breakfast, and an evening glass of wine. Set on a hilltop, the **Hillbrook Inn** (Route 13, RR 2, Box 152; 304–725-4223) is a rambling structure with many chimneys, gables and leaded glass windows. Rooms come with Oriental rugs, original paintings, antique beds and goose down comforters. Rates include a full breakfast.

For an additional Charles Town–area entry, see listing under Middleway.

The Cottonwood Inn
Route 2, Box 61-S

Tel: (304) 725–3371

Eleanor and Colin Simpson have turned their Federalist-era (1800) farm-house into an inviting B&B, decorated with antiques and period reproductions. Rates include a full breakfast, with pecan griddle cakes and sausage links, southern-style French toast and bacon, and huevos rancheros among the favorite choices.

"A charming, quiet B&B in the country, a short but beautiful drive through rolling farmland. Our room was comfortable and clean, the owners warm and friendly, the breakfast wonderful." *(Janet Payne)*

"Excellent location, with well-kept grounds, comfortable furnishings, and service beyond reproach. The Simpsons are both enjoyable and professional hosts." *(Vickie & Rhea McGee)* "The living room is a quiet, warm place to sit and read." *(Elizabeth Ingles)* "Very sophisticated decor, porch swing a delight." *(Nancy Riker)*

Open All year.
Rooms 6 doubles, all with private bath and/or shower, TV, air-conditioning. 3 with desk, 1 with fireplace.
Facilities Living room with library, fireplace; dining room with fireplace; porch with swing. 6 acres with stocked trout stream. Fishing, swimming, boating on Shenandoah & Potomac rivers nearby.
Location 6 m S of Charles Town. From Charles Town, take Rte. 9 S. Go 2.6 m to Kabletown Rd. and turn right. Go 3.2 m to silos at fork in road. Take right fork to inn.
Credit cards MC, Visa.
Rates B&B, $75–85 double. Extra person in room, $10. 2-night minimum holiday/craft festival weekends.
Extras Station pickups.

LEWISBURG 24901
Map 4

The General Lewis Inn
301 East Washington Street

Tel: (304) 645–2600

Listed on the National Register of Historic Places, Lewisburg is associated with both the Revolutionary and Civil wars. The inn is composed of a home built in 1834 housing the inn's restaurant and lobby and the main section of the inn, which dates to 1929.

"Wonderful hospitality. We enjoyed afternoon tea with strawberries, short biscuits, and cream on a beautiful veranda. Dinner was excellent—a pleasure to find a chef who knows how to cook salt-cured country ham properly!" *(Mr. & Mrs. A.D. Moscrip)*

"The exterior of the inn is a long, lovely white-pillared affair. The public rooms are extremely pleasant and comfortable." *(MFD)* "Antique-filled guest rooms with comfortable beds. Attentive owner and innkeeper, delicious home-cooked meals, and very reasonable rates." *(Joyce Willington)* More comments, please.

Open All year.
Rooms 2 2-bedroom suites, 26 doubles, all with full private bath, telephone, TV, air-conditioning. Some with desk.

Facilities Living room, restaurant, porch with rocking chairs. Pioneer items & stage-coach on display. 1 acre with gardens. Fishing, swimming, white-water rafting, hiking, golf, tennis nearby.

Location SE WV. 103 m E of Charleston, WV, 72 m W of Lexington, VA. Historic district. 2 blocks to center. From I-64 Lewisburg Exit, go S on Rte. 219 to 1st traffic light (Washington St.), then left 2 blocks.

Credit cards Amex, MC, Visa.

Rates Room only, $70–90 suite, $45–70 double, $45–55 single. Extra person in room, $5. No charge for children under 10. Alc breakfast, $3–6; alc lunch, $6; alc dinner, $22. Picnic baskets.

Extras Pets permitted. Cribs, babysitting available.

MARTINSBURG 25401   Map 4

Boydville: The Inn at Martinsburg   *Tel:* (304) 263–1448
601 South Queen Street

Built in 1812 by Elisha Boyd, a general in the War of 1812, the estate was almost burned down by the Union Army during the Civil War. Only a last minute personal telegram from President Lincoln averted the disaster. After the war, the house served as a family home for U.S. senators and ambassadors, changing hands only twice in its 175-year history.

Innkeepers Owen Sullivan and Ripley Hotch purchased the property in 1987, and after months of work, they re-opened Boydville as an inn. The original woodwork and nineteenth-century wallpaper have been restored, complemented by the owners' lifelong collection of art and antiques. Breakfasts include such specialties as puffed apple pancakes, frittatas, and homemade breads and muffins, and guests note with pleasure that repeats are rare.

"We received the grand tour, and were shown the original wallpaper shipped from France, the moldings of crafted pineapples, and the beautiful mural in a paneled bedroom (a similar one by the same artist is in the White House). We wandered all over the house, but the family room with a huge fireplace was our favorite. You can sip a glass of sherry, socialize, or just sit and read." *(Paula Abramson)*

"The spacious rooms are brimming over with antiques. On each visit a guest can discover some curio not noticed before. The inn holds a wonderful art collection of paintings, glass, and porcelain. The library contains volumes to keep one busy for hours." *(Philip Wilson)* "Rip and Owen are always there when you need them, yet are unobtrusive hosts. The house is clean and well-maintained, the atmosphere relaxed, and the location convenient. We shopped in the factory outlet stores two blocks away, and visited Harper's Ferry National Park nearby." *(Steven Golob, also Renée Buck)*

Open All year.

Rooms 7 doubles, 5 with private bath and/or shower, 2 with a maximum of 5 sharing a bath. All with desk, air-conditioning, fan.

Facilities Dining room, living room with fireplace, stereo; music room, game room with TV, library, porch. 11 acres with plantation out buildings. Lake and river nearby for fishing, rafting, canoeing, swimming. Cross-country skiing nearby.

Location WV panhandle. 75 m NW of Washington D.C., 75 m W of Baltimore. From

I-81 take Exit 13. Go E on West King St. Turn right on South Queen St. Go 3½ blocks. Inn on right.
Restrictions No smoking. No children under 12.
Credit cards Amex, MC, Visa
Rates B&B, $110 double. Extra person in room $20. 2-night minimum holiday weekends.
Extras Station pickups. French, German spoken.

MIDDLEWAY 25430   Map 4

The Gilbert House   *Tel:* (304) 725–0637
Mailing address: P.O. Box 1104, Charles Town, WV 25414

Middleway, a village dating back to the 1700s, is one of West Virginia's oldest settlements. The Gilbert House was built of stone around 1760, and is listed on the National Register of Historic Places; the oldest flagstone sidewalk in the state is in front of the inn. Jean and Bernie Heiler have owned this B&B since 1984, and have decorated it with antiques, tapestries, original paintings, and Oriental rugs. Jean says, "We specialize in romance and celebrations. Refreshments such as tea, wine, crackers and cheese, cake, cookies, etc., are available at any time. Breakfast includes fresh-squeezed juice, fruit, homemade breads and muffins, omelets, plus a meat or fish dish. Historical documents and records of the area are available in our guest rooms."

"The Gilbert House is a quiet, refined bed & breakfast somewhat off the major tourist trails. Our room was furnished with a comfortable bed with down pillows, quaint rugs, and country accents. The bath was large, with fresh towels provided twice daily." *(Donald Staley)*

"One of the nicest examples of Georgian-colonial hospitality I have ever had the pleasure to encounter. The inn, parts of which were built in the 1760s, is wonderfully restored, with the added convenience of modern plumbing." *(Kathleen Barry)*

"Bernie and Jean are very warm, enthusiastic people. Jean just loves sitting down and getting to know her guests. She likes to regale them with the legends of the era, and loves to feed everyone. After a day of sightseeing, we were greeted with a fire, hot mulled cider, and stollen. Our room had a fireplace, a sitting area, and a huge bathroom with modern plumbing, along with fresh flowers, candies, and champagne. Many of the antiques throughout the house are for sale. Walking in the back of the property we discovered old cemeteries and a waterwheel. Breakfasts were delicious and unusual—bratwurst and mushroom scrambled eggs, fresh spinach, chocolate croissants, all delicious." *(Rebecca & Jeff Ward, also Brian & Cynthia Unwin)*

"Jean is very active in the historic preservation efforts in Middleway and takes guests on an informative walking tour of the historic district. Special touches include calligraphic place cards made by Jean, fruit, candy and beverages in your room, and the special feeling that you are truly a guest in their home. We used Gilbert House as a base to explore the area, and particularly enjoyed visits to the Skyline Drive, the castle in Berkeley Springs, Antietam Battlefield, Harpers Ferry, antique shops and malls, and factory-outlet centers." *(Andy & Karen Menzyk)*

Open All year.
Rooms 2 suites, 1 double, with full private bath, radio, air-conditioning. Telephone, TV on request. Some rooms with desk, fireplace.
Facilities Living/family room with piano, games; library/parlor; dining room; kitchen. Canoeing, rafting, hiking, golf nearby.
Location E WV, Eastern Panhandle. Near Harper's Ferry, 5 miles from Charles Town. In historic district, at juncture of rtes. 1 and 51, halfway between I-81 and Charles Town.
Restrictions No smoking in public rooms. No children.
Credit cards MC, Visa; plus 5% service charge.
Rates B&B, $110–135 suite, $75–95 double. Extra person in room, $20. Weekly discounts. 2-night minimum.
Extras German, Spanish spoken.

SHEPHERDSTOWN 25443   Map 4

Shepherdstown, West Virginia's oldest community, was founded in 1730. Area attractions include the Old Opera House in Charles Town, Harper's Ferry, Antietam Battlefield, and the races at Charles Town and Summit Point, plus golf, tennis, horseback riding, white-water rafting and canoeing, and jogging and walking on the old C&O Towpath across the Potomac River.

Shepherdstown is in the upper Shenandoah Valley of the Eastern Panhandle, at the Maryland border. It's 8 miles from Harper's Ferry and 4 from Antietam Battlefield. Washington, D.C., and Baltimore, MD, are an hour and a half away by car. From Washington, take I-270 to the Frederick bypass, then onto I-70 to Exit 49. Turn left at Route 34 in Boonsboro to Sheperdstown.

Also recommended: The **Bavarian Inn and Lodge** (Route 1, Box 30; 304–876–2551) includes a handsome stone colonial residence and four chalet-style structures—all perched over the Potomac River. Guest rooms feature oak furniture, canopied beds, tiled fireplaces, and balconies. The inn has received four diamond/star ratings from Mobil and AAA.

The Thomas Shepherd Inn   *Tel:* (304) 876–3715
Corner of German and Duke streets, P.O. Box 1162

The Thomas Shepherd Inn was built as a parsonage in 1868, and was restored in 1984 by Ed and Carol Ringoot. Extra touches include Belgian chocolates at bedside, thick fluffy towels, and special soaps. The full breakfasts include such favorites as Belgian waffles, puffed Dutch apple pancakes, and ham and cheese soufflés.

"The Thomas Shepherd is a brick Victorian, with a wide central hall, a real double parlor, and a formal dining room. The rooms are big, with nice Victorian pieces; the inn is made up of two houses, connected at the back. The Ringoots served us coffee and cookies at bedtime. Ed Ringoot is originally from Belgium and is a terrific host. We enjoyed a good dinner at the nearby Yellow Brick Bank." *(David Vogel, also Nancy Harrison & Nelson Ormsby)*

"We enjoyed the living room for a pre-dinner glass of wine with the hosts and other guests, the library to find a couple of good books to read at night, and the summer porch when we were too tired to tour any more but still wanted to enjoy the beautiful spring day. Our hosts were gracious and accommodating—Carol took time to walk with us through the inn and tell us of its restoration. She made dinner reservations for us and was helpful in giving us ideas for touring the town. The inn is bright and airy, decorated with antiques and a lovely collection of rugs both on the floors and exhibited on the walls. Delicious coffee and the *Washington Post* are my favorite way to wake up, and both of these awaited me in the living room before breakfast." *(Carol Knight)*

"The full breakfast was beautifully served in the lovely dining room, with linen napkins and elegant china. The food was fresh and delicious. The inn was so clean—the bath, bedroom, and sitting room all were spotless. There was off-street parking, and even though the inn is located in town, it was very quiet." *(Mrs. Jerrold D. Snow)*

"We had a delicious breakfast of Belgian apple pancakes and homemade sausage." *(Mr. & Mrs. Jim Gatewood)*

Open All year.
Rooms 6 doubles—4 with private bath, 2 with maximum of 4 people sharing bath. All with air-conditioning, 1 with desk.
Facilities 2 dining rooms; living room with fireplace; library with writing desk, books and magazines, chess set, TV, porch. Garden, bicycles. Golf, fishing, white-water rafting, canoeing, hiking, bicycling nearby.
Location Historic district. In center of town.
Restrictions Smoking on porches only. No children under 12; no 3rd person allowed in rooms.
Credit cards MC, Visa; plus 5% service charge.
Rates B&B, $70–85 double, $60–75 single. Senior discount. Picnic lunch with advance notice.
Extras French, Flemish spoken. Station pickups.

We Want to Hear from You!

As you know, this book is only effective with your help. We really need to know about your experiences and discoveries.

If you stayed at an inn or hotel listed here, we want to know how it was. Did it live up to our description? Exceed it? Was it what you expected? Did you like it? Were you disappointed? Delighted?

Have you discovered new establishments that we should add to the next edition?

Tear out one of the report forms at the back of this book (or use your own stationery if you prefer) and write today. Even if you write only "Fully endorse existing entry" you will have been most helpful.
Thank You!

Wisconsin

Old Rittenhouse Inn, Bayfield

Wisconsin is a big state, with abundant agricultural and natural resources. From Milwaukee in the southeast corner of the state to our northernmost listing in Bayfield, on Lake Superior, it's 380 miles. Most of our listings are found in Door County (noted under "Location" heading), an attractive and accessible resort area, with several more in the Madison area.

Information please: Recommendations for hotels in Milwaukee would be greatly appreciated. Especially welcome would be any feedback on the **Astor Hotel**, listed on the National Register of Historic Places (800–558–0020), and the **Pfister Hotel** (800–558–8222). Rates quoted do not include Wisconsin sales tax of 5%.

Door County Located in northeastern Wisconsin, 150 miles north of Milwaukee, Door County is a peninsula that extends like a pinkie finger from the town of Green Bay 80 miles out into Lake Michigan. Its extensive shoreline provides plenty of opportunities for fishing, boating, and swimming; its many trails and country roads are perfect for walking and bicycling. There are wildflowers in spring and summer, foliage in autumn, and cross-country skiing in winter; the county is home to five state parks. Door County is also well supplied with attractive shops, art and craft galleries, summer theaters, and 400 apple and cherry orchards, as well as a major Great Lakes shipbuilding center in Sturgeon Bay.

The area is famous for its fish boils, started 100 years ago by the Scandinavian settlers of the peninsula. Here's how the White Gull Inn describes it:

"Fresh Lake Michigan whitefish is cut in chunks and cooked (in boiling water with small red potatoes) in a cauldron over an open fire. Salt is the only spice used. Fish oils rise to the surface of the boiling water, and when the fish is perfectly done, the 'master boiler' tosses a small amount of kerosene on the flames underneath the pot. The great burst of flames causes a boilover, spilling the fish oils over the sides of the pot and leaving the fish steaming hot and ready to serve." The fish and potatoes are then served indoors with homemade breads and coleslaw.

Information please: About three hours north of Milwaukee is the **Rosenberry Inn**, on a quiet residential street of Wausau, convenient to downtown and to skiing at nearby Rib Mountain. Built in 1908 in the Prairie Style, the inn was bought by the Artz family in 1986. Rooms are furnished with Victorian or primitive antiques, and the very reasonable rates include a continental breakfast (511 Franklin Street, Wausau 54401; 715–842–5733).

BAILEYS HARBOR 54202 Map 7

Baileys Harbor Yacht Club & Resort   *Tel:* (414) 839–2336
Ridges Road

A weatherbeaten replica of the U.S. Coast Guard watchtower that once stood on this site dominates the club's architecture. Originally a restaurant with a few summer cottages, Baileys has recently expanded, adding more luxurious villas and one building with rooms open year-round. The restaurant serves American cuisine, specializing in fresh fish and vegetables, along with home-baked breads and desserts.

"Yellow ladyslippers adorn the roadsides in June on the way to Baileys Harbor. This resort's peaceful setting, next to Lake Michigan, has a marina of pleasure and fishing boats. Whitefish are caught every day for Chef Willy to prepare. The Friday night buffet is excellently served and includes shrimp, clams, whitefish, scrod, and fillet of sole with lobster sauce." *(Helen Magnusson)* More comments please.

Open All year.
Rooms 12 1- or 2-bedroom villas, 6 1- to 3-bedroom housekeeping cottages, 4 suites, and 14 doubles, all with full private bath. Most with TV, refrigerator, patio or balcony. 3 cottages have fireplaces. 56-boat marina with full service hook-ups.
Facilities Restaurant, bar/lounge with entertainment, dancing; laundry room, gift shop, heated swimming pool, tennis courts, bicycle rental, fishing, marina, hiking trails, golf, cross-country skiing.
Location Door County. 1 m from town.
Credit cards Amex, MC, Visa.
Rates Room only, $55–110 villa, $425–1,150 (weekly) cottage, $100–110 suite, $70–105 double. Extra person in room, $10 for villa, suite, double. 2-3 night weekend/holiday minimum in villa.
Extras Cribs available, $5 per day.

BARABOO 53913 Map 7

The Barrister's House   *Tel:* (608) 356–3344
226 9th Avenue

Mary and Glen Schulz invite guests to share their colonial-style home built in the 1930s. Baraboo is home to the Circus World Museum, and is close to Devil's Lake State Park and the Wisconsin Dells.

"Beautifully decorated; very clean; quiet neighborhood. We were served wine, cheese, and crackers on the screened porch before dinner, then returned later to sit and visit with Mary Schulz on the patio. Breakfast, served formally in the dining room, consisted of fresh fruit compote and two kinds of freshly baked muffins, accompanied by more good conversation." *(Geri & Jim Becknell)* More comments, please.

Open May through Oct.; weekends Nov. through April.
Rooms 4 doubles, all with private bath and/or shower, air-conditioning.
Facilities Dining room with fireplace; living room with piano, game table, fireplace; library with fireplace; screened porch; veranda; terrace. Downhill, cross-country skiing nearby.
Location S central WI. 40 m N of Madison, 12 m S of Wisconsin Dells. 5 blocks from center. From I-90, take Hwy. 33 (Ringling Blvd.) to Baraboo. Go 1 block past blinking light and go right onto Birch St. Go 1 block to inn at corner of 9th Ave. From Hwy. 12, turn E onto Hwy. 33; go left onto Birch St. 1 block to inn.
Restrictions No smoking. No children under 6.
Credit cards None accepted.
Rates B&B, $45–55. Extra person in room, $5.
Extras Station pickups.

BAYFIELD 54814   Map 7

Old Rittenhouse Inn   *Tel:* (715) 779–5111
301 Rittenhouse Avenue, P.O. Box 584

The Old Rittenhouse Inn is a beautiful Victorian mansion built in 1890. It has 26 antique-filled rooms and twelve working fireplaces, and is located in Bayfield's historic district, only a few blocks from the shores of Lake Superior. Jerry and Mary Phillips renovated the inn in 1976, and have recently acquired two other nearby historic homes, **Le Chateau Boutin**, a handsome yellow Queen Anne Victorian, and the **Grey Oak Guest House**, a less elaborate turn-of-the-century home, which also offer B&B accommodation to guests. Guests at these two houses take a short walk to the Rittenhouse in the morning for a buffet-style continental breakfast. The dinner menu changes daily, but always features fresh fish, fruits and vegetables, homemade breads, and tempting desserts; favorite entrées include trout in champagne, roast lamb, and scallops Provençal.

"Bayfield is a New England–type town, its economy once based on commercial fishing and logging. Today it is a vacation village, located at the northernmost tip of Wisconsin, at the gateway to the Apostle Islands National Seashore.

"Jerry and Mary Phillips are so friendly you can't help but feel as though they are good friends right from the first visit. Mary's cooking is gloriously delicious, presented by Jerry and the staff in a mouth-watering oral menu style that make you want to holler 'Uncle.' Our favorite room is Number 7, with a view of the lake, a wonderful king-size bed, private bath and fireplace with wood just waiting to be lit." *(Carol Thacher & Steve Ross)*

Open Mid-Jan. through Dec. Midweek Nov.–April by reservation only.
Rooms 1 suite, 10 doubles—all with shower and/or bath, desk. 7 other rooms in Le Chateau Boutin, 4 in Grey Oak Guest House 4 blocks away. Suite with whirlpool bath, library. All but 1 room with fireplace.

Facilities Guest lounge with books, games. Indoor community pool, whirlpool, racquetball, tennis, cross-country skiing, sailing, fishing, boating nearby.
Location In historic district. 80 m E of Duluth, MN; 370 m N of Milwaukee. Short walk to shops, galleries.
Restrictions No smoking in public rooms.
Credit cards MC, Visa.
Rates B&B, $139 suite, $69–119 double. 15% service. Extra person in room, $15. Child in parents' room, $10. 2-night weekend minimum at Rittenhouse. Continental breakfast included, $3.50 extra for full. Sunday brunch, $13. Prix fixe dinner, $30 plus 15% service. Off-season midweek packages.
Extras Children's portions, cribs, babysitting during dinner available. Vegetarian entrées with advance notice. One guest room and dining rooms accessible to disabled.

BRANTWOOD 54513 Map 7

Palmquist's "The Farm" *Tel:* (715) 564–2558
River Road, Route 1, Box 134

"The Farm" is a logging, dairy, and beef cattle operation sprawling over 800 acres that has been in the Palmquist family for nearly 100 years. Rustic, family-style accommodation has been available for the last thirty. The atmosphere is friendly, relaxed, and unpretentious: Helen Palmquist notes that "breakfast is not served in bed unless someone is ill."

"The day we arrived, one of the Holsteins presented the herd with its newest heifer, and our children watched and clucked encouragement as the baby struggled to his feet for the first time. Later, the kids commandeered some bales of hay at the front of the barn and played hide and seek with the tiny kittens. They picked green apples to feed to the horses; watched a swallow sitting on her eggs in the horse barn; trekked off to round up 'Houdini,' a spirited heifer who managed to escape any confinement; supervised the four o'clock milking; and explored fields and buildings until they finally collapsed in the swing before dinner.

"And what a dinner! Roast chicken, Finnish meat loaf, wild rice with wheat berries, fresh vegetables from the garden, homemade bread, and peach shortcake. Helen serves guests and family together around a big table in the country kitchen. The conversation is as good as the food!

"After dinner, Jim and Art harnessed the Percherons to a flatbed wagon and we set off on a hayride through fields, pine woods trails, and groves of sugar maples. On our final turn through a clover field, a doe emerged from the woods and leapt across the field into the sunset. That night, we heard coyotes howl.

"During the winter, cross-country skiing and sleigh rides are the main activities. The farm is open during the holidays, and traditional Finnish dishes are served. The Palmquists maintain over 20 miles of groomed trails and a ski shop where you can rent equipment. Summertime activities include hiking, swimming, wandering country roads, and picnicking.

"The rustic charm of the farmhouse and guest cottages (simple, but comfortable—no TV) and incomparable hospitality of the Palmquist family make this a marvelous place to really get away." *(Maria & Carl Schmidt)* More comments, please.

Open All year.
Rooms 4 cabins sleep 4 to 12, all with bath and/or shower, woodstove.
Facilities Country kitchen; living room; lodge with large fireplace, games; sauna. 800 acres with farm buildings. Hiking, biking, hay rides, pond, 20 m cross-country ski trails, sleigh rides. 20 min. to lake for swimming, fishing, boating.
Location N central WI. 20 m W of Tomahawk, 12 m E of Prentice. "Farm" is ¾ m N of U.S. Hwy. 8, 2½ m E of Brantwood.
Restrictions No smoking.
Credit cards MC, Visa.
Rates FAP, $46 per person; $23 for children under 12. 2-night minimum. Weekend packages. Ski trail fee, $3 per day, per person.
Extras Airport/station pickups. Pets by prior arrangement. Cribs, babysitting, play equipment available. Finnish spoken. Ski rentals.

CEDARBURG 53012   Map 7

Less than half an hour away from Milwaukee, Cedarburg offers a relaxing escape back to a slower time. With its many restored nineteenth-century buildings, the little town offers plenty of attractions—a visit to the Cedar Creek Settlement, a collection of antique and specialty shops, restaurants, and a winery, housed in an old woolen mill; the Ozaukee Art Center; and Pioneer Village. Other more vigorous pastimes include swimming, hiking, golf, tennis, horseback riding, and canoeing. In winter, there's cross-country skiing and ice-skating on Cedar Creek. Wisconsin's last original covered bridge is just a few miles outside of town.

Cedarburg is located in southeast Wisconsin, in Ozaukee County, 20 miles north of Milwaukee. From Milwaukee, take I-43 or Route 57 north to Cedarburg, where it becomes Washington Avenue.

Stagecoach Inn   *Tel:* (414) 375–0208
W61 N520 Washington Avenue

The Stagecoach Inn, which dates back to 1853, was built to accommodate both passengers (upstairs) and drivers (in the basement) traveling by stagecoach. Brook and Liz Brown, who have owned the inn since 1985, describe the Stagecoach as "a cozy and comfortable place. We have authentically restored the inn, using period furniture and fixtures. We used pictures from the late 1800s to help us." In addition to the guest rooms, the inn houses a candy shop, a bookstore, and the Stagecoach Pub, where guests can enjoy evening games of Trivial Pursuit and cards. The pub functioned as a bar for over 100 years, and the Browns spent many long hours scrubbing off decades of tobacco smoke to expose the original stamped tin ceiling.

"Liz and Brook Brown are the most congenial of hosts. The rooms are always well kept and project a feeling of early American warmth, due in part to the antique decor. The Stagecoach Pub is an ideal setting for a pleasant breakfast of cereal, hot croissants, coffee, and juice. A wide selection of beers, wine, and special summer and winter drinks are also available. Pretzels with mustard-honey dip complement the drinks. There are activities in the town of Cedarburg 28 out of 52 weekends a year, along with appealing shops and restaurants." *(Jack & Sharyl Dobson)* "Our room was lovely, and the continental breakfast of hot chocolate (or coffee or tea), juice, and warm croissants was delicious." *(Laura & William Hitt)* More comments, please.

Open All year.
Rooms 5 suites, 7 doubles, all with private bath, air-conditioning, and TV. Suites with whirlpool tubs.
Facilities Tavern with games; gathering room; gift and chocolate shops. Boating, canoeing, bicycling, hiking, ice-skating, cross-country skiing nearby.
Location SE WI; 25 m N of Milwaukee. In center of town historic district.
Restrictions No smoking.
Credit cards Amex, MC, Visa.
Rates B&B, $85 suite, $55 double, $45 single. Additional person in room, $10.
Extras Cribs available.

The Washington House Inn
W62 N573 Washington Avenue

Tel: (414) 375–3550

The Washington House Inn, a Victorian cream-city brick building, was built as a hotel a century ago. Rooms are decorated either with a Victorian look, including period antiques, lace, Laura Ashley prints and papers; or in a country decor, with pencil-post canopy beds, planked floors, patch-work quilts, and exposed beamed ceilings. The inn was restored in 1983 by Jim and Sandy Pape, developers of the Cedar Creek Settlement; Judith Drefahl is the innkeeper. A new wing opened in 1988 with nine country-style suites with two fireplaces and large whirlpool tubs. Rates include a continental breakfast of muffins, breads, cereals, fresh fruit, and juices, plus an afternoon social hour with local wines and Wisconsin cheeses.

"Friendly helpful staff, enjoyable atmosphere in both gathering room and in guest rooms." *(Marsha Jones)*

Open All year.
Rooms 11 suites, 18 doubles, all with full private bath, telephone, radio, TV, desk, air-conditioning. 26 rooms with whirlpool baths, oversize tubs. 9 rooms with fire-place.
Facilities Gathering room with fireplace; sauna.
Location Historic district.
Restrictions No smoking in public rooms.
Credit cards Amex, DC, Discover, Enroute, MC, Visa.
Rates B&B, $129 suite, $59–129 double. Extra person in room, $10. 10% senior discount.
Extras Wheelchair accessible; elevator; 2 rooms equipped for disabled. Cribs, baby-sitting available.

EGG HARBOR 54209
Map 7

The Alpine Resort
7715 Alpine Road

Tel: (414) 868–3000
868–3236

The Alpine is a comfortable family resort, founded by the Bertschinger family 68 years ago and staffed by college students. Activities are offered for all ages, and many families return year after year at the same time. Food is hearty, and rooms are simply furnished with motel-style furniture. Manager Bill Bertschinger says that The Alpine has the most scenic golf hole in Wisconsin, set high on a bluff—the green is 130 feet lower than the tee.

"The Alpine Resort is run by lovely people. Every year they make improvements, adding new attractions. Home-cooked meals, beautiful, clear water, golf courses, music for dancing, and much more brought us back every year. The area offers over 8 miles of lovely parks, with Green Bay on one side and Lake Michigan on the other. There are islands to visit, charming little towns, lighthouses, nice shops, and boat rides." *(Mrs. Merrit Gates)*

"Homey welcoming atmosphere, accommodating owners, and clean neat accommodations. The food is excellent, especially the homebaked pastries. The grounds are well maintained, including the golf course." *(Edward Decancq)*

Open Mid-May to mid-Oct. Dinner served mid-June through early Sept.
Rooms 60 doubles, 40 cottages, all with private bath and/or shower, TV, desk.
Facilities Dining room, game room, sitting rooms; evening activities in July, Aug. 300 acres with ½ mile lake frontage, 27-hole golf course, heated swimming pool, 3 tennis courts, bicycle rentals, hiking. Swimming, fishing, boating, dockage in Green Bay.
Location Door County. 60 m NE of Green Bay. ¾ m SW of village, on Hwy. G.
Credit cards Amex, MC, Visa.
Rates Room only, $47–75 double. MAP, $80–107 double. Extra person in room, room only, $8; MAP, $25. Tipping encouraged. Prix fixe dinner, $14. Inquire for cottage, housekeeping home rates; accommodates 4–9 people.
Extras German spoken. Station pickups. Cribs, babysitting available. Pets permitted in housekeeping cottages.

ELLISON BAY 54210   Map 7

Also recommended: Received too late for a full writeup was a report on the "charming and friendly" **Nelson Farm**, a 25-acre rural escape, home to horses, ducks, and plenty of raspberry bushes. Its two guest rooms are reasonably priced and rates include a full breakfast (1526 Ranch Lane; 414–854–5224). *(KJ)*

The Griffin Inn   *Tel:* (414) 854–4306
11976 Mink River Road

Antique beds and hand-pieced quilts will soon put you in the mood for a relaxing stay at the Griffin Inn. Built in 1910 with a New England look, a gambrel roof and ample porches, the inn has been owned by Jim and Laurie Roberts since 1986. A recent breakfast included juice and fresh fruit, an egg-apple-bacon-cheese bake, scones and muffins; cottage guests receive a continental breakfast tray. Laurie cooks a five-course dinner on Saturday nights.

"Jim and Laurie Roberts are great hosts. The inn is restored and decorated beautifully. Breakfast is homemade everything—even the syrup. You won't be hungry for five hours if you eat it all. We had no problems with the shared baths. Lively conversation fueled by popcorn by the living room fireplace in the evening. Excellent restaurants within two blocks." *(M. Voigt)*

Open All year.
Rooms 4 cottages with private bath, 10 doubles sharing 2½ baths.
Facilities Living room with fireplace, dining room with wood stove. 5 acres with sports court, gazebo, cross-country skiing.
Location Door County. 10 m N of Fish Creek via Rte. 42 N. After descending the Ellison Bay hill, turn right onto Mink River Road, at Trinity Chruch. Continue about 2 blocks to inn on left.
Restrictions No smoking. No children under 6 in main house.
Credit cards None accepted.
Rates B&B, $66–72 cottage, $63 double, $59 single. Extra person in room, $6. 2-3 night weekend/holiday minimum.

EPHRAIM 54211   Map 7

Eagle Harbor Inn & Cottages   *Tel:* (414) 854–2121

Regardless of whether you're traveling with kids and want a relaxed family vacation, or whether you're looking for an elegant adult atmosphere, Eagle Harbor may be the right place for you. The white clapboard inn is furnished with antiques, hand-pegged wooden floors, period wall coverings, and coordinated fabrics. Rates include a breakfast of juice and fresh fruit, coffee cake, muffins, and croissants. The nearby cottages with casual furnishings, TVs, play equipment, and barbecue grills are ideal for families. Both the inn and cottages have been owned by Ronald and Barbara Schultz since 1986. *(MW)* More comments, please.

Open All year.
Rooms 9 doubles, 12 cabins—all rooms with private bath, fan; all cottages with 1 bath each, TV, fan.
Facilities Dining room, living room with fireplace, TV; library. 5 acres. Golf, cross-country skiing, lake for swimming, fishing, boating nearby.
Location WI peninsula. 65 m NE of Green Bay. Center of town.
Restrictions No children under 15 in main house.
Credit cards MC, Visa.
Rates B&B, $50–85 cottage, $60–90 double. 2-3 night minimum weekends, holidays.
Extras Airport/station pickups.

FISH CREEK 54212   Map 7

Fish Creek is a pleasant resort village with many specialty shops. It offers swimming at a clear, sand-bottomed beach, a full range of water sports and tennis, and a summer theater company and music festival. The village is adjacent to Peninsula State Park, with thousands of acres of forest, miles of beaches, and bicycling, hiking, and cross-country ski trails. Three golf courses are within an easy drive.

The Whistling Swan   *Tel:* (414) 868–3442
P.O. Box 193

Although built in 1887, The Whistling Swan has been at its present location since the winter of 1896, when Dr. Herman Welcker suddenly decided to get into the resort business. To save construction time, he bought a number of whole buildings in Marinette, and used teams of horses and giant sleds to move them across the frozen waters of Green Bay. What is now The Whistling Swan was called Dr. Welcker's Casino; it had gaming tables for gentlemen guests and fourteen small bedrooms. Jan and Andy Coulson, longtime owners of the White Gull (see below), renovated it in 1985, rebuilding the interior to provide the comforts expected by modern tastes. Rooms are furnished with original and newly acquired antiques and period pieces, and summer and fall rates include a continental breakfast served on the porch.

"A Gatsby kind of house, with large rooms and a wide side veranda. We've been there twice since it opened in the summer of 1986 and we love it. On the ground floor is a sitting room with sofa and books and a baby grand piano. There is also a lovely shop that carries children's clothes, quality linens, Crabtree & Evelyn products, and thick sweaters. Our favorite suite is done in bright yellow and blue; the sitting and sleeping areas are separated by curtained French doors. The bathroom is old, with new, convenient fixtures, special soaps, and a view of the street below. No welcoming detail is forgotten, and the staff is friendly. Jan Coulson is nearly part of every day, and is a wonderful person, truly a professional innkeeper." *(Kathleen Novak)*

Open Daily May through Oct., Christmas week, weekends rest of year.
Rooms 3 suites, 4 doubles, all with full private bath, air-conditioning.
Facilities Enclosed porch, lobby with fireplace, foyer with piano, TV. 2 blocks from lake.
Location Take Hwy. 42 to Fish Creek. Turn left at stop sign and watch for inn.
Restrictions No smoking.
Credit cards Amex, MC, Visa.
Rates B&B, $104–124 suite; $80–119 double. Extra person in room, $10. 2-3 night holiday/weekend minimum. 10% discount on weekly stays.
Extras Airport/station pickups. Crib available.

White Gull Inn
Tel: (414) 868–3517
4225 Main Street, P.O. Box 159

What is now the White Gull was originally part of Dr. Welcker's resort (see The Whistling Swan, above). Guests would arrive from Chicago and Milwaukee by steamship for long relaxing visits. Many of the original furnishings—iron and brass beds, wicker chairs, and walnut and oak dressers—are still in use at the inn today. The White Gull has been owned and operated by Andy and Jan Coulson since 1972.

The White Gull's restaurant is open to the public, serving three home-made meals a day. The fish boil steals the spotlight several nights a week (see chapter introduction), although other entrées are also available.

"Although the lodging is pleasant, what we recommend most are the fish boils. We have savored a few of Door County's fish boils and feel that the White Gull does the best job. The food is wonderful, especially the nut breads, and the 'show' is great. The fish boilmaster is Russ, who has been there over twenty years and entertains the guests with an old-fashioned concertina while he cooks." *(Terri & Jeff Patwell)* More comments, please.

Open All year, except Thanksgiving, Dec. 25.
Rooms 11 doubles, 1 single—9 with private bath, 3 with maximum of 5 sharing bath; 4 cottages of 2, 3, and 4 bedrooms, all with fireplace, TV. 4 rooms have TV, fireplace.
Facilities Lobby with fireplace, TV. Cedar-edged patio. 3 blocks to beach. ½ m to cross-country skiing. Golf, tennis nearby. Children's games, swings, sandbox.
Location Take Hwy. 42 to Fish Creek. Turn left at bottom of hill to inn. 3 blocks from only stop sign in town.
Credit cards Amex, MC, Visa.
Rates Room only, $52–96 double, $40 single. $115–175 cottage (sleeps 2-8 people). Extra person in room, $10. No charge for infants in cribs. 2-3 night minimum holiday and summer weekends; 3-night minimum in cottages July, Aug. 10% discount on weekly stays. Midweek packages Nov. 1–Dec. 23, Jan. 2–May 11. Lunch, $5–8; alc dinner, $37.
Extras Airport (private aircraft)/bus station pickup. Cribs available.

GREEN LAKE 54941   Map 7

Oakwood Lodge   *Tel:* (414) 294–6580
365 Lake Street

The first resort built west of Niagara, the Oakwood Lodge overlooks the entire seven-mile-length of Green Lake. The inn's large lakefront provides guests with a full range of water sports; its old-fashioned rooms are furnished with antiques, white wicker, and flowered wallpapers. Owned by Marcy and Wayne Klepinger since 1985, the inn is a popular place for breakfast for guests and visitors alike. Buttermilk pancakes, omelets, and homemade coffee cake and sweet rolls are even more delicious when eaten on the deck overlooking the lake. *(GR)* More comments, please.

Open April through Oct., Dec. through Feb.
Rooms 11 doubles—6 with private bath and/or shower, 5 with a maximum of 6 people sharing a bath. All with fan.
Facilities Dining room with fireplace, family room with TV, piano. On lake for fishing, swimming boating. Cross-country skiing nearby.
Location 60 m NE of Madison. ½ m from center.
Credit cards None accepted.
Rates B&B, $45–70 double, $40–65 single. Extra adult in room, $10; extra child $5. 2-3 night minimum weekends, holidays.
Extras Cribs, babysitting available.

HAZEL GREEN 53811   Map 7

We'd also like to have more comments about **The Parson's Inn** (Rock School Road, Glen Haven 53810; 608–794–2491), roughly 40 miles upriver from Hazel Green and about 25 miles south of Prairie du Chien. Owner Julie Cull specializes in providing a homey atmosphere and lavish breakfasts; rates are very reasonable. Glen Haven is a peaceful village, nestled between the bluffs along the Mississippi River.

Wisconsin House Inn
2105 East Main Street

Tel: (608) 854–2233

Wisconsin House is an 1846 stagecoach inn, sturdily built of native white oak in post-and-beam construction. From 1853 to 1958 the house was owned by the Crawford family of Crawford & Mills Mining Company; Ulysses S. Grant was a close friend of Jefferson Crawford and a frequent visitor. When John and Betha Mueller bought the inn in 1985, it had been converted into apartments; the Muellers did a total renovation, installing new wiring, heating, and plumbing, and decorating the inn with their exceptional collection of country antiques and collectibles, including a beautiful display of cast-iron toys in the breakfast room. John's creative wall stenciling is found throughout the house. Rates include a full breakfast, served family-style at a 15-foot ash table. A set menu dinner is served on weekends and includes wine, dessert, and ethnic entertainment (John's family is from Switzerland, Betha's from Norway). Guests enjoy antiquing in Galena's shops and visiting its historic buildings; nearby Platteville is home to the Chicago Bear's Training Camp in summer.

"Each room of the inn is furnished in early American antiques and fine collectibles. What catches one's eye upon entering each room are the hand-painted stencil borders, which differ from room to room. All the guest rooms are ample in size and are named after notable people from Hazel Green's past. This inn is quiet and comfortable at all hours. Betha's breakfasts are scrumptious; a typical one might be French toast with fresh strawberry sauce or applesauce/pecan pancakes with fresh country sausage. A special blend of coffee complements the food. Most notable are the innkeepers, who have a very special way of making one feel at home. They delight in giving their guests a complete tour of their home upon arrival. In the morning Betha moves from room to room, knocking on guests' doors to give them personal wakeups, eliminating traffic jams in the shared baths. Country-style dinners are served on weekends by reservation only. Lucky diners congregate around the table to share an abundance of hearty food, wine, and good conversation." *(Susan Laugal)*

"John is an adept tinsmith. His lanterns throughout the house are handsome indeed. Betha's applesauce pancakes or her chili sauce with scrambled eggs are delicious. Weekend dinners (for up to 24 people) are equally superb. John and Betha do all the preparation themselves; Yankee pot roast and stuffed pork loin with chestnut dressing are favorites. The lovely gazebo in the side yard is a pleasure in good weather. Hazel Green is a quiet town, not far from Galena, an antique lover's haven." *(Dorothy Timm)*

"We enjoy John's wry humor, his yodeling and Betha's accordion playing after dinner. Relaxing in the kitchen, drinking coffee and visiting with Betha and John while they're baking sweet-smelling pies is a favorite memory." *(Frank & Bonnie Malone)*

Open All year.
Rooms 1 cottage, 9 doubles—5 with private bath and/or shower, 4 with maximum of 4 people sharing bath. All with air-conditioning.
Facilities Dining room, living/TV room with bar, porch, balconies. Antique/gift shop, flower garden, gazebo. Cross-country skiing; Mississippi River nearby for fishing, boating, swimming.

Location SW WI. 9 m N of Galena IL, 13 m E of Dubuque IA, 14 m S of Platteville WI. In center of village, 1 block E of intersection of hwys. 11 & 80 on County Trunk W.
Restrictions No smoking.
Credit cards None accepted.
Rates B&B, $40–65 double, $35–60 single. Prix fixe lunch $6–8, prix fixe dinner $15–17. Winter specials Jan.–Mar.
Extras Airport/station pickups.

KOHLER 53044   Map 7

The American Club   *Tel:* (414) 457–8000
Highland Drive   In WI: (800) 472–8414
            In Midwest: (800) 458–2562

Now a magnificent resort and conference center, the American Club began modestly in 1918 as a temporary home for Kohler Company's European immigrant workers, and served as their classroom and meeting place. The building was enlarged in 1924, and remodeled in 1941. In 1978 it was listed on the National Register of Historic Places, and in the early 1980s it was completely renovated and redecorated as a luxury resort and conference center. The club has received the AAA's five diamond award annually since 1986. The rooms combine elegance and comfort in a traditional mood, with hand-crafted oak paneling, stained glass, crystal chandeliers, Oriental rugs, and some antiques. Since Kohler is a famous manufacturer of just about everything you find in a bathroom, it's not surprising that the bathrooms here are both modern and luxurious. A variety of dining experiences are offered, ranging from the elegant atmosphere of the Immigrant restaurant (reflecting Wisconsin's varied cultural heritage) to the wine-cellar atmosphere of the Winery to the Greenhouse, built entirely of stained glass.

"Rooms are heavenly, with skylights to let in the morning sun, bathrooms fit for a king, down comforters, and more. When the hotel is booked to capacity, it is still very quiet. As for housekeeping: The day I witnessed one of the cleaning people on his hands and knees with a toothbrush, cleaning the corners of a corridor, is one I'll never forget." *(Therese Lukaszewski)*

"Expensive by Wisconsin standards, but it's an outstanding facility in the state. The staff is particularly accommodating." *(Charles Krause)*

"Food is excellent. The only problem with this place is that it's hard to get a reservation." *(Jim Wilkes)*

Open All year.
Rooms 160 doubles, all with whirlpool bath, telephone, radio, TV, desk, air-conditioning. 52 rooms in annex, some with hot tub on enclosed terrace.
Facilities Sitting rooms, library, 4 restaurants with entertainment, patio, room service, separate conference center, underground parking. Health & fitness center on private lake, with beach, 12 tennis courts, heated swimming pool, hot tub, fitness classes, massage, jogging trail, Nautilus, racquetball. 27 holes of golf; formal gardens; 600-acre wilderness preserve with hunting, fishing, hiking, canoeing, skeet shooting, dining lodge; 20 m of marked cross-country ski trails.
Location SE WI. Near Lake Michigan, 55 m N of Milwaukee. From Milwaukee, take

I-43 N to Exit 53B to Hwy. 23B, go 1 m W to County Trunk Y–Kohler and go S on County Trunk Y to Club.
Restrictions No smoking in some areas.
Credit cards Amex, CB, DC, MC, Visa.
Rates Room only, $105–273 double, $83–238 single. Extra person in room, $12. Children under 10 free. Alc lunch, $10; alc dinner, $30. Holiday, hunting, winter packages.
Extras Wheelchair accessible; some rooms specially equipped for disabled. Airport/station pickups, for fee. Cribs, babysitting available. Spanish, French, German, Japanese, Italian, Welsh spoken.

LAKE MILLS 53551   Map 7

Fargo Mansion Inn   *Tel:* (414) 648–3654
406 Mulberry Street

Not quite halfway between Milwaukee and Madison is the little town of Lake Mills, named for Rock Lake and the sawmills which were the town's most distinguishing features at its founding around 1840. It's hardly the sort of place you'd expect to find an imposing stone and yellow brick Queen Anne mansion listed on the National Register of Historic Places. Much less would you expect to find an antique-filled inn, its winding staircase leading to suites complete with fireplaces and Jacuzzi baths. But that's just what Tom Boycks and Barry Luce have created since they bought the Fargo Mansion in 1985. Built at the turn of the century by Enoch Fargo, a descendant of the Wells Fargo family, guest rooms are named for persons who had a unique relationship with the town's most famous and somewhat eccentric family—ask the innkeepers for details. A favorite room is the E.J. Fargo Suite, with a bath that's more private than most: it's hidden behind a bookcase that swings out when a certain volume is moved.

"The inn is set on a quiet street, and the people of Lake Mills are warm and friendly; you feel like you've gone back in time. Tom Boycks and Barry Luce are delightful and so accommodating. Classical music fills the house and the house's architecture and decor is fascinating—we loved the sunken tubs and marble treatments. Breakfast is served at a huge old-fashioned dining table, and the freshly baked fruit muffins with an egg and vegetable casserole were delicious. Guests visit and compare notes on their explorations, and Barry's young children help to serve the breakfast. Afterwards, we saw a tape of the mansion as it looked before the restoration—the transformation is unbelievable." *(Kathy & Rod Kadet, also Kathy & Jeff Shaffer)*

Open All year.
Rooms 9 suites with full private bath, radio, air-conditioning, fan. 8 with Jacuzzi; 2 with fireplace.
Facilities Dining room, music room, library, entertainment lounge, sitting rooms. 1½ acres with picnic area, tandem bicycle. Bike trails nearby.
Location 30 m E of Madison. 50 m W of Milwaukee. 2 blocks from town square.
Restrictions No smoking.
Credit cards MC, Visa.
Rates B&B, $65–135 suite. Extra person in room $10.

Extras Airport/station pickups. Play equipment available. Babysitting by prior arrangement.

LEWIS 54851   Map 7

Seven Pines Lodge   *Tel:* (715) 653–2323
Route 35, Box 104

These days, the environment is on everyone's list of priorities, but in the early 1900s only a few realized that our supply of natural resources was finite. Charles Lewis, a prominent grain broker from Minneapolis, decided that one of the area's last natural stands of white pine, along with a wonderful natural trout stream, were worth saving from the lumber mills. He bought 1,500 acres in the late 1800s and built a trout hatchery (still in operation) to ensure a goodly supply of fish. In 1903, he built Seven Pines to provide comfortable wilderness accommodation for himself and his cronies, including President Calvin Coolidge. Now listed on the National Register of Historic Places, Seven Pines was bought in 1975 by Joan and David Simpson, who restored many of the lodge's original furnishings, adding a minimum of modern amenities—there are no phones or TVs. The lodge is still a favorite with trout fishermen, offering year-round trout fishing for the purist, with a private stream teeming with wild brookies. Not surprisingly, trout is the house dinner specialty. Joan notes that "we feature a warm, rustic atmosphere. Love, laughter, and friends are always welcome." *(MW)* More comments, please.

Open All year.
Rooms 2 cabins with half-bath (closed in winter), 2 suites, 5 doubles—2 with private bath and/or shower, 5 with maximum of 7 sharing bath.
Facilities Dining room, living room, screened porch. 57 acres with trout fishing, hiking. Fly fishing schools. Canoeing, bicycling, horseback riding, cross-country/downhill skiing, sleigh rides nearby.
Location NW WI. 1½ hrs. NW of Minneapolis. From Minneapolis, take I-35 N to Exit 132, Forest Lake. Go E on Rte. 8, then N on Rte. 35 to Lewis.
Restrictions No smoking.
Credit cards Visa.
Rates B&B, $79 suite, $59–75 double. $55–95 cabin depending on occupancy of 2 to 6 persons. Extra person in room, $15. 15–20% service additional. Children under 10, ½-price meals. 2-3 night minimum high season or holiday weekends. Alc dinner, $19.50. Ski packages.
Extras Airport pickups.

MADISON 53703   Map 7

Set between two lakes, Madison, the capital of Wisconsin, is best known as the home of the main campus of the University of Wisconsin. Take in the view from the top of the domed State Capitol, attend one of the many concerts, plays, and sport competitions on campus (but park elsewhere), and take a self-guided tour of Frank Lloyd Wright's architecture.

Madison is in south-central Wisconsin, 77 miles west of Milwaukee, and 150 miles northwest of Chicago.

The Collins House
704 East Gorham Street

In the early 1900s, Frank Lloyd Wright started the Prairie School of Architecture, then considered a fresh and innovative architectural form typifying the spirit of the Midwest. In 1911, lumber executive William Collins commissioned local architects to build his home in the Prairie style. It's now listed on the National Register of Historic Places. Barb and Mike Pratzel opened The Collins House for B&B in 1986. The living room highlights the original mahogany-beamed ceiling, leaded-glass windows, and wall stencils; while not contemporary in style, it has a distinctive post-Victorian appeal. The spacious guest rooms are furnished with antiques and homemade quilts, and rates include a weekday continental breakfast of fruit, cheeses, juice, and homebaked cranberry streusel muffins or cinnamon buns. A full breakfast is served on weekends, with such specialties as Swedish oatmeal pancakes or soufflés. Homemade chocolate truffles, a house specialty, always greet guests on arrival. *(JK)*

Open All year.
Rooms 2 suites, 2 doubles, all with full private bath, telephone, radio, desk, air-conditioning.
Facilities Breakfast rooms, dining room, sitting room, library, living room. On lake, with pier, beach nearby. Off-street parking.
Location On Lake Mendota, 6 blocks from Capitol, at corner of E. Gorham & N. Blount.
Restrictions No smoking in guest rooms. Street noise in some rooms in summer.
Credit cards MC, Visa.
Rates B&B, $85 suite, $65–75 double. Extra person in room, $10. 2 night minimum some weekends.

Mansion Hill Inn
424 North Pinckney Street

The Mansion Hill Inn, listed on the National Register of Historic Places, opened in 1985; it is one of the new, luxury-type B&B inns, whose goal is to provide everything for business as well as vacation travelers.

"The Mansion Hill Inn is an intimate facility that includes every amenity a guest could desire. The mansion was constructed in 1858 by the architect who built the second state capitol in Wisconsin, using many of the same materials—thick limestone for the exterior, Carrara marble, Venetian glass on the inside. Built as a private residence, the mansion was last used as student apartments. A $1 million renovation began in the summer of 1985, and the inn has evolved into an exceptional lodging experience. Each room is decorated in a different theme, but all are appropriate to the Victorian era. Bathrooms are spacious and lavish, with marble walls and whirlpool baths. The rooms have floor-to-ceiling windows, complete stereo systems, and sophisticated telephone systems.

"The inn serves a continental breakfast and an elegant afternoon tea; they will even shine shoes left outside the door at night. The attention to detail is apparent in everything the staff does. The inn is beautifully located, and there's a marvelous view from the fourth-floor cupola up on top of the inn—Lake Mendota, with spectacular sunsets, to the west, and the white-domed capitol to the east." *(Mrs. Ward Remington)*

"The staff was happy to give us a tour of the unoccupied rooms, but I liked ours—the McDonnell Room—the best. It had a fireplace, whirlpool tub, and a romantic ten-foot-tall draped tester bed. Double French-doors lead outside to a veranda overlooking a garden, where we enjoyed breakfast the next morning." *(Kathleen Mahoney)* "Courteous, friendly, and personable staff; I felt like a millionaire." *(Scott Barbeau)*

Open All year.
Rooms 2 suites, 9 doubles, all with private bath and/or shower, telephone, radio, TV, stereo, desk, air-conditioning, mini-bar. Many also with whirlpool tub, fireplace, veranda or balcony.
Facilities Parlor, conference room. Victorian garden with fountain, lawn furniture. 1 block to Lake Mendota, swimming beach. Valet parking.
Location Downtown, 4 blocks to State Capitol, 1 block to U. of Wisc. At the corner of E. Gilman and N. Pinckney sts.
Restrictions No children under 12.
Credit cards Amex, MC, Visa.
Rates B&B, $100–250 suite, double, $80–230 single. Extra person in room, $20. Tipping appreciated. Frequent traveler discounts.

MARINETTE 54143   Map 7

Lauerman Guest House   *Tel:* (715) 732–4407
1975 Riverside Avenue

The Lauerman Guest House is a turn-of-the-century Victorian, built in the Colonial Revival style by Joseph Lauerman, a local department store tycoon. In 1985, the inn was bought by the Spaude and Home families, who have combined historical accuracy and modern comforts in their restoration.

"This elegantly restored mansion is located near the Menominee River. The main floor is beautifully decorated in period. Our room, located in an addition built onto the back of the house, was simply decorated with few furnishings, and even fewer antiques, and lacked character, although the rooms in the original part of the house were nicely decorated. In the morning, we were served a delicious full breakfast. The inn also has a gourmet restaurant, and although they weren't serving the night we stayed, the menu looked fantastic." *(Jeff & Lauri Patwell)* More comments, please.

Open All year. Restaurant closed Thanksgiving, Dec. 25.
Rooms 2 suites, 5 doubles, all with full private bath, TV, air-conditioning. Some with desk; 2 with whirlpool baths, 1 with fireplace.
Facilities Dining room, parlor. 2 blocks to marina for fishing. Golf nearby.
Location E central WI. 1½ blocks from Hwy. 41; 2 blocks from downtown.
Restrictions No children under 12.
Credit cards MC, Visa.
Rates B&B, $55-65 double. Extra person in room, $10.
Extras Airport/station pickups.

OSCEOLA 54020   Map 7

St. Croix River Inn   *Tel:* (715) 294–4248

If your idea of the perfect escape is to days of vigorous outdoor exercise—
canoeing and hiking in summer, cross-country or downhill skiing in winter—with evenings spent in the lap of luxury, then this inn may be just
for you. Built in the early 1900's of stone from a nearby quarry, the house
remained in the same family until Robert Marshall bought it in 1985. In
the renovation process, all rooms were provided with Jacuzzi tubs and
stereos, and all but one have a river view. Furnishings are antique reproductions, and rates include a continental breakfast of fruit and muffins
brought to your room. Vickie Farnham is the resident manager. *(WS)* More
comments please.

Open All year. Closed Christmas.
Rooms 7 suites—all with Jacuzzi bath with shower, radio, air-conditioning, stereo.
Some with fireplace, TV/VCR.
Facilities Sitting room, game room. Near state parks with canoe rentals, swimming,
hiking. Golf.
Location W WI. 50 m NE of Minneapolis, MN. In town. From Rte. 95 N, take Rte.
97 to Osceola. Turn left at stop sign. Go N to 3rd Ave. Go left. Pass hospital, church.
Inn on left.
Restrictions No smoking in guest rooms. No children.
Credit cards Amex, MC, Visa.
Rates B&B, $85–150 suite. Extra person in room $5.

STURGEON BAY 54235   Map 7

Sturgeon Bay, in mid–Door County (see chapter introduction for more on
Door County), marks a historic portage point between Sturgeon Bay and
Lake Michigan, now connected by a canal. Potawatomi State Park, along
the bay, is nearby for waterskiing, fishing, boating, and canoeing, with
trails for hiking in summer and cross-country skiing in winter; several
other state parks are close as well.

Scofield House   *Tel:* (414) 743–7727
908 Michigan Street, P.O. Box 761

Hidden for decades under layers of gray paint, Scofield House has been
returned to its original glory—both inside and out—by Bill and Fran Cecil,
owners since 1987. This beautifully restored Queen Anne mansion, built
in 1901, boasts a five-color paint job, authentic to the period; the interior
combines Victorian furnishings with floral fabrics and white lace. Especially fine is the original woodwork with oak paneling and inlaid borders
on the hardwood floors. Rates include a full breakfast, with a menu that
varies daily, afternoon tea and home-baked cookies.

"The atmosphere is warm, comfortable and charming—the antiques are
usable, the furnishings comfortable, and the rooms spotless. The inn is
located in a safe quiet residential area, conducive to long walks in the early

morning or late evening. The front porch is a wonderful gathering spot with a swing and chairs for guests to sip coffee early in the morning or relax later in the day with homemade cookies and hot cider. A full breakfast is served every morning—perhaps hot apple cinnamon compote, homemade mini muffins, then either an omelet, a bacon-egg-cheese casserole or eggs Benedict. Fran and Bill's genuine hospitality is exceptional. " *(Kathy & Michael Quast)*

"Bill and Fran are warm, gracious, entertaining, and fun. Bill's breakfasts are a gourmet delight and Fran bakes the best cookies and brownies in town." *(Darlene Roberts)*

Open All year.
Rooms 1 suite, 3 doubles—all with private bath and/or shower, air-conditioning, fan. 1 with telephone, 2 with radio, whirlpool bath.
Facilities Parlor with piano, board games; dining room. Gazebo. Golf, beaches, boating, fishing, skiing nearby.
Location WI peninsula. 40 m NE of Green Bay. 5 blocks from center.
Restrictions No smoking. No children under 14.
Credit cards None accepted.
Rates B&B, $65–110 double, $60–105 single. 2-3 night minimum weekends, holidays.
Extras Airport pickups.

White Lace Inn
16 North 5th Avenue

Tel: (414) 743–1105

The White Lace Inn was built in 1903; the adjacent Garden House was built in the 1880s, and moved to its present location in July of 1983. Innkeepers Bonnie and Dennis Statz opened the main inn in 1982, and opened the Garden House, after a year of renovation work, in 1984. Their most recent addition is the Washburn House, across the backyard from the inn, with four luxurious and inviting rooms.

"This renovated Victorian inn is beautifully decorated with period antiques, lace curtains, decorator towels, crocheted bedspreads, and live plants. Continental breakfast includes muffins, juice, coffee, and tea. The bran muffins alone are worth a return trip, and over twenty kinds of tea are available. A downstairs closet is loaded with games for guests to play in the parlor or in their rooms. The grounds are beautifully landscaped, with lovely rock gardens. We have been there several times, and Bonnie and Dennis go out of their way to make us feel remembered." *(Terri & Jeff Patwell)*

"Bonnie and Dennis Statz are two of the most personable people we have ever met. They spent much time visiting with us and sharing favorite sights and restaurants." *(Celeste Burnett Ruebe, also Richard & Iris Miller)*

Open All year.
Rooms 1 suite, 14 doubles, all with private bath and/or shower, radio, air-conditioning. 5 rooms in Main House, 4 rooms in Washburn House with fireplace, double whirlpool tub, stereo, TV; 6 rooms in Garden House with fireplace. Some rooms with desk.
Facilities Dining room, parlor with fireplace, sitting room with game tables, TV, stereo. 1 acre with gardens. Beaches, hiking, cross-country skiing nearby.
Location 2 blocks to downtown; 5 blocks to bay. Take Business Rte. 42/57 into

Sturgeon Bay; cross the bridge into downtown and follow road to 5th Ave. Turn left (N) onto 5th Ave. The inn is on the right.
Restrictions 7 no-smoking rooms. No children under 11.
Credit cards MC, Visa.
Rates B&B, $110–135 suite, $60–95 double. 2- to 3-night weekend and holiday minimum stay. 3- to 5-night winter, spring packages.
Extras 1 guest room equipped with ramp. Airport/station pickups.

We Want to Hear from You!

As you know, this book is only effective with your help. We really need to know about your experiences and discoveries.

If you stayed at an inn or hotel listed here, we want to know how it was. Did it live up to our description? Exceed it? Was it what you expected? Did you like it? Were you disappointed? Delighted?

Have you discovered new establishments that we should add to the next edition?

Tear out one of the report forms at the back of this book (or use your own stationery if you prefer) and write today. Even if you write only "Fully endorse existing entry" you will have been most helpful.

Thank You!

Key to Abbreviations

For complete information and explanations, please see the Introduction.

Rates: Range from least expensive room in low season to most expensive room in peak season.
Room only: No meals included; sometimes referred to as European Plan (EP).
B&B: Bed and breakfast; includes breakfast, sometimes afternoon/evening refreshment.
MAP: Modified American Plan; includes breakfast and dinner.
Full board: Three meals daily.
Alc lunch: À la carte lunch; average price of entrée plus nonalcoholic drink, tax, tip.
Alc dinner: Average price of three-course dinner, including half bottle of house wine, tax, tip.
Prix fixe dinner: Three- to five-course set dinner, excluding wine, tax, tip unless otherwise noted.
Extras: Noted if available. Always confirm in advance. Pets are not permitted unless specified.
Zip codes: If only one zip code applies, it is listed with the town name. If there is more than one, it is noted as part of the address.

Wyoming

Spahn's Big Horn Mountain Bed & Breakfast, Big Horn

Even though Wyoming naturally conjures up images of cowboys and wide open spaces, it's worth noting that this rugged western state was the first to give women the vote (in 1869) and the first to elect a woman governor. But don't get confused—Wyoming is still dominated by the macho aura associated with ranching, oil-drilling, and a rugged backcountry.

Most people come here to see Yellowstone, our nation's first national park. Unfortunately, it's difficult to experience the peace and beauty of this superb park elbow-to-elbow with summer mobs. To avoid crowds, traffic jams, and frayed nerves, either get out of your car and start hiking, or come during off-season (October is perfect). The awesome peaks, glaciers, and sizable lakes of the Grand Tetons can also be enjoyed most between the floods of summer visitors and winter skiers.

Somewhat less famous (and less crowded) but still worth seeing are: Flaming Gorge National Recreation area, which offers all types of water-related activities; Fossil Butte National Monument, where you can see 50-million-year-old freshwater fish fossils (three gold stars if you can say the last four words fast); and bizarre Hell's Half Acre, where Mother Nature left a trail of extravagant colors and fantastic shapes.

Wyoming's cities are friendly, overgrown cow towns with no pretension of sophistication. In Cody, don't miss the Buffalo Bill Historical Center, where four museums introduce visitors to every aspect of the American West, from ancient Indian culture to Remington paintings. In Cheyenne, the Wyoming State Art Gallery (part of the State Museum) is recommended. In the east, along the Oregon Trail, a stop at Fort Laramie is recommended; a nearby overnight possibility is the **Guernsey Hotel** (15 South Wyoming Avenue, Guernsey 82214; (307) 836–2414).

Although they're really too big to be within the scope of this guide, we should mention the famous Yellowstone hotels—the **Mammoth Hot Springs Hotel and Cottages** and the **Old Faithful Inn.** TW Services handles reservations for these facilities, as well as all other accommodations within the park; call or write them for details: Yellowstone National Park 82190; 307–344–7311 or 344–7901.

Information please: We'd love to have more listings for all parts of Wyoming. Guest ranches, historic hotels, or bed & breakfast inns—all recommendations will be most appreciated. One possibility is **The Ranch at Ucross**, about 30 miles southeast of Sheridan via Route 14. Bunk down in the old ranchhouse or in well-equipped cabins, dine on gourmet cuisine, and spend your days riding, fishing, swimming, playing tennis or cross-country skiing; hunting and fishing packages are also available (2836 Highway 14/16 East, Clearmont 82835; 307–737–2281).

Rates listed do not include 5% Wyoming sales tax.

BIG HORN 82833   Map 10

Spahn's Big Horn Mountain Bed & Breakfast   *Tel:* (307) 674-8150
70 Upper Hideaway

The 100-mile view from Spahn's porch overlooks mountain meadows and pine-filled valleys—a million acres of the Big Horn National Forest. Deer, moose, turkey, and an occasional mountain lion pass the site. In the spirit of the pioneers who first settled the area, Ron and Bobbie Spahn, and their children Heather and Eric, built their own log home. But don't expect a one-room cabin. The Spahn's three-story house is complete with a hot tub for relaxing after a day of cross-country skiing, hiking or fishing. The lodge is furnished with both Victorian antiques and rustic log furniture. They generate electricity with solar energy. Rates include a hearty-all-you-can-eat breakfast. Ron is a geologist and former Yellowstone Park Ranger; Bobbie is a nurse. Their location makes a convenient stopover if you're traveling on I-90/Rte. 14 or I-25 to Yellowstone.

"The Spahn's home is warm and cozy. Ron and Bobbie have that special ability to make strangers feel like family." *(Jim & Mary Horan)* More comments, please.

Open All year.
Rooms 2 doubles in main house with private shower. Cabin with 2 doubles, shower, wood stove, kitchen, porch. All rooms with desk.
Facilities Living room with fireplace, piano, library; breakfast room, decks, hot tub. 40 acres with walking trails, cross-country skiing. Hunting, fishing nearby. Adjacent to 1 million acres public forest.
Location N central WY. 15 min. from I-90, 15 m SW of Sheridan. From I-90 take Exit 25 at Sheridan. Follow signs to Big Horn via Rtes. 87 and 335. Go 9 m past Big Horn on 335 to end of pavement, then ½ m on gravel to Spahn's sign.
Restrictions No smoking.
Credit cards MC, Visa.
Rates Room only, $45-75 cabin (up to 4 people). B&B, $45 double, $35 single. Extra adult in room, $15; extra child, $10.

Extras Airport pickups $25. Cribs, babysitting, play equipment, games available. Pets by prior arrangement.

BUFFALO 82834   Map 10

Paradise Guest Ranch   *Tel:* (307) 684–7876
P.O. Box 790

Paradise Ranch dates back to the 1890s, when it was founded by N. H. Meldrum. Paying guests first arrived in 1907, making Paradise one of the West's oldest guest ranches. In 1981 the ranch was purchased by the Minneapolis-based Apache Corporation. Since then over $1 million has been invested in upgrading and modernizing the cabins and facilities.

Guests stay in rustic but attractive log cabins, gathering for meals three times a day in the dining hall. The food is hearty ranch-style cooking, with pancakes, eggs, sausage, hash browns, and fresh-caught trout for breakfast, soup and sandwiches for lunch, and steaks, fried chicken, and fresh fruit pies at dinner. Rates include two trail rides a day, fishing in the ranch's streams, and relaxing by the pool or in the hot tub. Riding lessons are offered, and guests are assigned one horse for the length of their stay. A special activity program is available for children six and over; it culminates in a ranch rodeo on Saturday afternoon. Wilderness pack trips are arranged for avid fishermen and hunters, as are visits to nearby cattle ranches, golf courses, tennis courts, and shopping trips to Buffalo and Sheridan.

Managers Jim and Leah Anderson describe the favorite activities at Paradise as "horseback riding, #1; fishing, #2; and eating, #3!"

"Paradise Guest Ranch truly lives up to its name because of the scenic beauty of the area, the accommodations, and the hospitable atmosphere. The Andersons and all their help go out of their way to make sure everyone has a good time. The accommodations are very comfortable, with such extra touches as wood laid in the fireplaces and turned-down beds at night. The riding is geared to all abilities, so everyone can enjoy a ride and see the beauty of the mountains, woods, and wildlife. After dinner each night there's an entertainment program with guest participation for those interested. Food is ample in quantity, average in quality. We have made many friends here and tend to meet annually, since families keep returning." *(P. A. Anderson, also Dorothy Jordon, Marjorie Cohen)*

Open June 1–Oct. 15.
Rooms 35 1-, 2-, and 3-bedroom cabins, each with full private bath, kitchen, fireplace.
Facilities Dining room, recreation building, bar/lounge, laundry room. Nightly entertainment. 160 acres with heated swimming pool, hot tub; horseback riding; pond, stream trout fishing; games, play equipment. Golf, tennis nearby. Children's activity/riding program for 6 and over; basic activity program for under 6.
Location N central WY, bordering Big Horn National Forest. 16 m W of Buffalo, which is at intersection of I-90 and I-25. From Buffalo, take Hwy. 16W 13 m, turn right at Hunter Creek Rd. to ranch road.
Credit cards None accepted.
Rates Full board, including all activities, $100–115 daily per adult; about $80 daily for children 6–12; from $50 daily 3–5. Under 3 free. Minimum 7-day, Sunday-to-

Sunday stay required. 10–15% service recommended. Early and late season discounts.
Extras Cabins wheelchair accessible. Free airport pickups. Cribs, babysitting available.

CODY 82414 Map 10

Cody's "don't miss" attraction is the Buffalo Bill Historical Center, home to four museums—the Buffalo Bill Museum, the Plains Indian Museum, the Whitney Museum of Western Art, and the Winchester Arms Museum. Plan to spend a day at this celebration of the western spirit on your way to or from Yellowstone, 50 miles farther west. Also of interest is Old Trail Town, a collection of historic buildings and memorabilia depicting the Wyoming frontier. A white-water rafting trip on the Shoshone River and a visit to the Cody Rodeo, held nightly in the summer, will round out your visit. July and August are the peak periods here, during which reservations are essential.

Irma Hotel
1192 Sheridan Avenue

Tel: (307) 587–4221

When Buffalo Bill built the Irma Hotel in 1902, it immediately became the social hub of the town. The hotel remains so to this day. Rooms in the original part of the hotel combine the atmosphere of the old West—Victorian decor and western art—with modern amenities. The Irma was bought by Doug Greenway in 1988; reports on any changes resulting from new management would be appreciated.

"The Hotel Irma was built by Buffalo Bill Cody for his daughter Irma, and it looks like the kind of hotel you'd see in a cowboy movie. The large high-ceilinged dining room houses a long, elaborately carved cherrywood back bar sent over as a gift from Queen Victoria—a modest $100,000 gift. I expected the sheriff to burst through the door at any moment as I sipped my iced tea (should have been a sasparilla, I guess); they serve the kind of prime rib you'd expect to get in cattle country—big and juicy. My old-fashioned room was very large and comfortable, although it looked out on an alley, not the main street." *(Deborah Joost)*

Open All year.
Rooms 15 suites, 25 doubles, all with private bath and/or shower, telephone, TV, air-conditioning. Some with desk. 25 rooms in motel annex.
Facilities Restaurant, lounge, bar. Swimming pool 1½ blocks away.
Location Center of town.
Credit cards Amex, CB, DC, MC, Visa.
Rates Room only, $56–120 suite, $56–96 double, $28–48 single. Alc breakfast, $4–10; alc lunch, $5–8; alc dinner, $20. Hunting packages, Sept.–Dec. 15.
Extras Cribs available.

Lockhart Inn
109 West Yellowstone Avenue

Tel: (307) 587–6074

Caroline Lockhart was an extraordinary woman by the standards of any era. Born in the Midwest, she made a name for herself during her many daring exploits as Boston's first woman reporter—she believed she needed to experience a way of life to write about it. In 1904 she interviewed Bill Cody and decided to move to his hometown. She became well known for her stories and novels about the West and went on to publish Cody's weekly paper and to run her own ranch, in between her worldwide travels; she died here in 1962 at the age of 92.

Mark and Cindy Baldwin have owned the Lockhart since 1984 and have decorated the rooms with antiques. Rates include an all-you-can-eat breakfast of homemade breads, preserves, biscuits and gravy, pancakes, French toast, quiche, and eggs.

"Mark and Cindy are most cordial owners and have done a fine job of furnishing the rooms in period. Breakfast is homemade and delightful. Motel-type rooms at the back are where families with children stay—walls in the main house are too thin for the noise of children's voices. It's located near the rodeo and close to town." *(Peter Bridges)*

Open All year.
Rooms 1 cabin with kitchen, private bath. 12 doubles—all with private shower and/or bath, telephone, TV, air-conditioning. 6 rooms in inn, 6 in motel units.
Facilities Dining room, parlor with piano, games, library. 2 acres with river frontage. Swimming, tennis, golf, fishing, rafting nearby.
Location 2 m W of center. On US Rte. 14-16-20.
Restrictions Smoking in parlor only. No children under 5.
Credit cards Amex, CB, DC, Discovery, MC, Visa.
Rates B&B, $50–70 double. Extra person in room, $10. Picnic lunch, $5. Fall hunting, winter sports packages.
Extras Airport pickups.

Rimrock Dude Ranch   *Tel:* (307) 587–3970
2728 North Fork Route

Nestled in the pines along the banks of Canyon Creek, Rimrock has been a dude ranch since 1927 and has been owned by the Fales family since 1958. With some expert guidance, you'll pick a horse from the 70-horse herd and can head into the 10,000-foot-high passes of the Absaroka range in the Shoshone National Forest. Wranglers lead the rides in the morning and afternoon; full-day and overnight trips are also available. The log cabins are rustically fitted out with western furnishings; rates include everything from room, board, and riding to breakfast rides, float trips, rodeo tickets, square dancing, and a tour of Yellowstone.

"About as western as you can get, down a mile-long dirt road with a stream running through this cabin colony. Our cabin, called Long Horn, had a gigantic stone fireplace. With a maximum of only 35 guests, the atmosphere is very personal, and many families return annually. Food is served home-style. Horses are matched to your ability; my Daisy was duly docile. Children and adults go out on trail rides together. There were families of all ages, from all parts of the U.S.—an interesting mix. The breakfast ride was especially wonderful. A truly relaxing getaway." *(D. Slavitt)*

Open June through Aug.
Rooms 9 cabins with full private bath, desk, air-conditioning. Several with living room, fireplace.

Facilities Lodge with dining room, bar, living room with piano and fireplace, game room with billiards, Ping-Pong, shuffleboard. Evening entertainment, square dances, laundry room, horseshoes. Fish pond, trail rides, pack trips. Fishing, swimming, rafting nearby. Trips to Yellowstone Park available.
Location 26 miles E of Yellowstone, 26 miles W of Cody. 1 m off Rte. 14-16-20.
Restrictions Children 6 over preferred.
Credit cards None accepted.
Rates Full board, weekly rates, $1,120 double, $735 single. Children under 4 free if a non-rider. Children's, group rates. Hunting, pack trip packages. 15% service suggested.
Extras Airport/station pickups in Cody.

Seven D Ranch *Tel:* (307) 587–3997
P.O. Box 100 Winter: (307) 587–9885

The Seven D has been owned by the Dominick family since 1958. Marshall and Jane Dominick invite you to relax in the cool mountain air of the Sunlight Basin, at an elevation of 6,800 feet. Marshall notes that "our ranch is an ideal place to learn horsemanship, observe the flora and fauna of the Rockies, improve your fly fishing skills, explore the wilderness with seasoned guides, or just plain relax, rest, and unwind."

"I'll never forget the ride to the Seven D. The road that winds through the Sunlight Basin (and I do mean winds—it takes about an hour once you reach the dirt road that leads to the ranch) is dramatic and colorful; then you arrive in the shady green spot where the ranch is set. What a peaceful place. The lodge is rustic and dinner is served family-style. You really feel as though you've gotten away from it all." *(Deborah Joost)*

Open June 5–Sept. 10.
Rooms 11 1- to 4-bedroom cabins with private bath.
Facilities Lodge with living room, library, dining room. Rec hall with pool table, Ping-Pong, piano. Children's program. Trail rides, trap shooting, square dancing, hiking, trout fishing, softball. Pack trips, fishing trips, hunting.
Location 50 m NW of Cody. From Cody, take Rte. 120 N to Rte. 296 N through Dead Indian Pass. Turn left (W) off Rte. 296 to ranch, approx. 1½ hour trip.
Credit cards None accepted.
Rates Full board, weekly, $1350–1550 suite, $1,200–1,500 double, $715–825 single. 15% children's discount. 15% service suggested. Group rates. Hunting packages.
Extras Airport pickups, for fee. Day care provided. Spanish spoken.

DOUGLAS 82633 **Map 10**

Akers Ranch B&B *Tel:* (307) 358–3741
81 Inez Road

At George and Lucy Akers' working cattle ranch there are no "dude activities," but you can play in the hayfield in summer, feed calves in winter, brand them in the fall, and mend fences, feed horses, and bake bread year round.

"We arrived in the late evening, were offered coffee, and then were shown to the 'bunkhouse,' a three-bedroom house, complete in every detail, including toiletries and laundry supplies. We soon put the washer and dryer to use, then we snacked on homemade cookies and a lovely platter of meat and cheese with crackers. Our beds were comfortable and breakfast was a feast, enhanced by homemade chokecherry syrup for the pancakes. Lucy's steak dinner was fit for kings. Best of all was the personal touch of the owners. As we chatted with Lucy in the kitchen or wandered the ranch with George, we learned about life on a western cattle ranch—irrigation, beef prices, auction sales, and more. Cleanliness and service were superb, parking more than sufficient. It is extremely quiet, and plumbing and lighting are fine. " *(Betsy Booth)*

Open All year.
Rooms 1 cabin with living room, private bath, refrigerator; 1 3-bedroom bunkhouse with 1 full bath, living room, cable TV, kitchen, laundry. Both with radio, air-conditioning.
Facilities Dining room, kitchen, laundry, gift shop. 1,500-acre ranch with cattle, horses, wildlife. Swimming, tennis, golf 12 m away. 40 m to skiing in Casper, WY.
Location E central WY. 35 m E of Casper, 12 m W of Douglas. Take I-25 to exit 150 and turn right. When pavement ends and road forks, bear left. Look for ranch with red barn with green roof, about 1 m from I-25.
Restrictions "We are smokers."
Credit cards MC, Visa.
Rates B&B, $42–63 cabin, $42–47 double, $36–42 single, including tax, service. $20 for children 6–12; no charge under 6. 10% senior discount. Prix fixe lunch, $5–7; prix fixe dinner, $10–16.
Extras Airport pickups. Crib available.

GLENROCK 82637   Map 10

Hotel Higgins   *Tel:* (307) 436–9212
416 West Birch, Box 11

Over 80 years old, the Hotel Higgins is listed on the National Register of Historic Places and is decorated with period antiques, some original to the hotel. Longtime owners Jack and Margaret Doll are especially proud of the hotel's restaurant, The Paisley Shawl. The prix fixe dinner there includes an appetizer, soup, salad, entrée, dessert, and tea or coffee, with a choice of three entrées. On a recent evening, the entrées offered were veal parmigiana with risotta alla Milanese; curried chicken; and shrimp pesto. Margaret's family settled in Glenrock 100 years ago, and the restaurant is named after her grandmother's prized possession, a paisley shawl, which is now on display in the dining room.

"The Dolls are so friendly, so willing to please—nothing, but nothing, is too much trouble. The accommodations are 'old timey'—it's very clean, with comfortable beds, plenty of hot water and towels. The food is excellent. My favorite dessert is the chocolate mousse. The breakfast is very full, not just croissants and coffee. The hotel has an interesting history; ask Mrs. Doll to relate it to you." *(Mrs. Putnam Reno)*

"A very quiet, restful, out-of-the-way spot with excellent food and service. With just a little more work on the guest rooms, it will be a truly wonderful stopping place in the wilds of Wyoming." *(James Malin)*

Open All year. Restaurant closed Jan.
Rooms 1 suite, 7 doubles—5 with full private bath, 3 with maximum of 4 people sharing bath. All with desk. Telephone by request.

Facilities Breakfast room, TV room, bar/lounge with evening entertainment occasionally, dining room. Fishing nearby.
Location E central WY. 18 m E of Casper. Town is just off I-25, halfway between Casper and Douglas. Hotel is in center of town.
Credit cards Amex, MC, Visa.
Rates Room only, $39 suite, $35 double, $26 single. B&B, $55 suite, $51 double, $36 single. Extra person in room, $7–15. Alc lunch, $4–8; prix fixe dinner, $12–21.
Extras "Very small pets permitted by prior arrangement." Crib available.

JACKSON 83001   Map 10

Set just south of Grand Teton National Park, Jackson is a real cowboy town and gateway to the Jackson Hole area, which offers opportunities for spectacular outdoor activities in all seasons. (Confused Easterners should note that other than the ski area, there is no actual town of Jackson Hole; the "Hole" in question here refers to the 60- by 20-mile valley ringed by the mountains. Its name supposedly derived from the fact that early trappers holed up here through the long winters.) Jackson Hole Ski Resort offers first-class downhill skiing, with some exceptionally challenging runs, along with cross-country skiing, while summer pleasures include the usual western favorites—hiking, riding, white-water and scenic float trips on the Snake River. Summer in-town activities include the rodeo, music and art festivals, and western theater and melodramas; you won't be able to miss the Town Square with its elk antler arches (although some might prefer to try).

Jackson is 10 miles south of Grand Teton National Park and 60 miles south of Yellowstone.

Information please: If the bustle of Jackson is too much for you, try **A Teton Tree House** eight miles to the west. Set on a quiet mountainside, the five rustic guest rooms have valley views, and rates include a breakfast of fruit, granola and yogurt, whole-grain breads, oatmeal and huckleberry pancakes. Owners Chris and Denny Becker are former wilderness guides who can direct you to the best places for hiking and fishing (6175 Heck of a Hill Road, P.O. Box 550, Wilson 83014; 307–733–3233).

Big Mountain Inn   *Tel:* (307) 733–1981
Highway 390, P.O. Box 7453

Built in the early 1900s the Big Mountain Inn was hauled 85 miles from Idaho Falls over the Teton Pass to its present location in an aspen grove. In 1988 the inn was purchased by Penny Foster. Rates include a breakfast of yogurt, cereals, waffles, pancakes, muffins, eggs, and fruit.

"Big Mountain Inn is a delightful New England–type home set among the aspens and framed by the mountains. It's a birder's paradise. The location is perfect, not far from Jackson and near Teton Village. The rooms are large, the decor is antique, the beds are excellent, the plumbing new, and the floors comfortably covered with thick carpeting." *(Deborah Nimmick)*

"Penny is a warm and welcoming hostess. Her home is small but comfortable, old-fashioned in feeling and very clean. The house is tucked into the woods, so birdsong is the only sound you hear. Breakfast includes fruit, juice, cereal, eggs or pancakes, and good hot coffee." *(Sylvia & Jason Kirshen)*

Open May–Sept., Dec.–March.
Rooms 1 suite, 4 doubles—all with private shower and/or bath, telephone, TV, desk. 2 with Japanese soaking tubs.
Facilities Dining/living room with fireplace. 3.5 acres with aspens. 4 m from Jackson Hole Ski Resort. ¼ m to golf, tennis, swimming, fishing outfitters. Horseback riding nearby.
Location 9 m from Grand Teton National Park, 9 m from town. From Jackson, take Hwy. 22 toward Wilson, turn right on Hwy. 390 and go 3 m to inn on left. ¼ m past the Aspens, heading toward Teton Village.
Restrictions No smoking in guest rooms. Children over 10 preferred.
Credit cards MC, Visa.
Rates B&B, $95–135 suite, $65–100 double. Extra person in room, $15. Weekly rates. AARP discounts. 2-night minimum.
Extras Airport pickups, $11 round-trip. Spanish spoken.

Sundance Inn
135 West Broadway

Tel: (307) 733–3444

Originally a 1950s era Art Moderne–style motel, the Sundance has been remodeled as an inn by Amy and Casey Morton, a pair of well-traveled and experienced innkeepers. The Mortons have worked at inns from Stowe, Vermont to Martha's Vineyard, Massachusetts to Zermatt, Switzerland, so they had a pretty good idea of what they wanted to achieve when it came time to buying a place of their own. Affordability was one criteria, and an inn where families could feel comfortable was another. Fortunately, they succeeded on both counts. The reasonable rates include a continental breakfast plus afternoon lemonade or tea and cookies.

"Centrally located, within walking distance of shops, art galleries, and restaurants, yet quiet and restful at night. The exterior is basic, but our room was newly painted, decorated, and draped. Matching lamps, bedspreads and paintings complete a very pleasant decor. Attention to detail was everywhere—lined drawers, bath salts, cleaning rags for skis and cars." *(Frank & Delia Ellsworth)* "Amy and Casey introduced themselves to us, helped us out with activities and restaurants, and followed up to learn how we enjoyed ourselves." *(Lauren Tomasian)*

"A delicious breakfast of fresh fruit and juice, home-baked muffins and coffee cake is served in the lobby. Our hosts were gracious and outstandingly helpful with information and directions. In this B&B guests are the most important consideration." *(A.C. & Helen Hinkle)* "Amy's home-baked cookies and brownies were a welcome refreshment in the early evening, along with coffee, tea and lemonade. She follows this up in the morning with great muffins and fresh orange juice. The rooms are neat and clean with plenty of linens and herbal soaps."*(Roger & Wanda Acton, and others)*

Open Mid-Dec.–Nov. 1
Rooms 1 suite, 26 doubles, 1 cabin—all with private bath and/or shower, telephone, TV, desk, fan. Some with air-conditioning.
Facilities Breakfast room, lobby with games, hot tub. On-site parking. ½ m to skiing.
Location Center of town. 5 m from Grand Teton National Park. 1½ blocks W of Antler Arch.
Restrictions "Light sleepers should request a 'quiet' room." No smoking in some guest rooms.
Credit cards Amex, Discover, MC, Visa.

Rates B&B, $45–95 suite or cabin, $44–75 double, $38–65 single. Extra person in room, $4. Children's rates. Senior citizen discount.
Extras Limited wheelchair accessibility. Some pets permitted by prior arrangement. Station pickups. Cribs, babysitting available.

Wort Hotel
Broadway and Glenwood, P.O. Box 69

Tel: (307) 733–2190
(800) 322–2727

Whether you're staying here or not, don't miss taking a look at the famous Silver Dollar Bar, inlaid with 2,032 silver dollars, a vivid reminder of the hotel's gambling heyday. Although gambling is no longer permitted (it was allowed until the 1950s), the bar remains a favorite hangout. Built in 1941 by the Wort brothers, the hotel was intended to have the look of a Swiss chalet; unfortunately, a devastating fire in 1980 destroyed everything but the exterior stone walls. The rebuilt hotel is surprisingly elegant given its cowboy heritage; rooms are decorated in traditional furnishings, with muted colors and quality reproductions. Its western heritage still comes through in the massive rock fireplace and animal heads mounted in the lobby.

"Luxurious room, fun bar, decent food, pleasant staff, convenient shuttle to the slopes." *(MW)* More comments, please.

Open All year.
Rooms 3 suites, 57 doubles—all with full private bath, telephone, radio, TV, air-conditioning. Some with desk.
Facilities Restaurant, café, bar/lounge with entertainment, conference rooms. 1 block to lighted parking lot. Full swimming, tennis, Jacuzzi, work-out room privileges at Spring Creek Ranch.
Location Center of town.
Restrictions No smoking in some rooms. Traffic noise could disturb light sleepers on Broadway side.
Credit cards Amex, DC, Discovery, MC, Visa.
Rates Room only, $150–215 suite, $70–100 double. Extra person in room, $15. Senior discounts. Summer, golf, ski packages. Alc breakfast, $3–6; alc lunch, $5; alc dinner, $6–18 in café, $20–30 in Goldpiece Room.
Extras Wheelchair accessible; 1 room equipped for disabled. Free shuttle to ski areas, Spring Creek Ranch; airport/station pickups. Crib, babysitting available. Spanish spoken. Member, Somerset Hotels.

KELLY 83011   Map 10

Red Rock Ranch
P.O. Box 38

Tel: (307) 733–6288
Winter: (307) 733–2225

Established as a cattle ranch in 1890, the Red Rock opened its doors to guests in 1976 under the ownership of David and Deborah MacKenzie. Set in a secluded valley of the Gros Ventre Mountains, the ranch is surrounded by the Teton National Forest. Longtime managers Ken and Garey Neal combine the activities of a guest ranch with the hard work of running cattle. The ranch is very much geared to families, with an active children's program; kids generally eat dinner together, then head to the rec room, leaving their parents to enjoy a bit of peace and quiet. The once-a-week campout for the kids is a don't-miss experience. Accommodations are in rustic log cabins, with comfortable but basic furnishings.

"Now I know what 'Big Sky Country' really means. This ranch is way up in the high hills, with rolling meadows, a roaring river nearby, and a huge expanse of sky. The individual cabins are clean and plain, the ranch-style food hearty. I especially liked the grilled steaks at the cookout. The crew is very friendly and so patient with children. There are also nifty trail rides which lead through the hills, and you can even find some unusual mementos. I found a cattle skull, a friend found a mountain goat skull, and the children found some pretty crystals in a nearby cave." *(Don Carmichael)*

Open June 10–Oct. 10
Rooms 9 1-2 bedroom cabins with living room with fireplace or wood stove, private bath, sun porch.
Facilities Lodge with dining room, living room, children's game room, adult game room with billiard table; laundry room. 640 acres with horses, cattle, hiking. Supervised children's program, heated swimming pool, hot tub, pickleball court, volleyball, fishing pond. On Crystal Creek for catch-and-release fly fishing. Pack trips, fishing float trips, whitewater float trips.
Location 30 m N of Jackson, 9 m SE of Grand Teton National Park. From Jackson, take Hwy. 26 N 6 m. Turn right on Airport Rd. to Kelly. In Kelly, turn left, go N 1 m to Gros Ventre Rd. Turn right and go 16 m to ranch.
Restrictions No smoking in barn. No children under 6.
Credit cards None accepted.
Rates Full board, $700–735 weekly per person, plus 15% service. 10% discount after Sept. 1. 10% discount for stays longer than 7 nights (cannot be combined with off-season discount). Pack trips, $120 per person per day (not charged ranch rates during trip).
Extras Airport pickups, $20 per car.

MOOSE 83012   Map 10

Triangle X Ranch   *Tel:* (307) 733–2183
Hwy 187-26-89

The Triangle X Ranch is a working dude ranch owned and operated by the Turner family for over sixty years, offering a full range of activities year-round and a variety of float trips on the Snake River. A special feature of the Triangle X is the summer "Little Wranglers" activities program for children under the age of twelve; children also have their own dining room in the lodge. An old-fashioned swimming hole in a side channel of the Snake River gives parents an opportunity to demonstrate (and experience possibly for the first time) what swimming was like in the 'good old days.' Guests stay in rustic log cabins, with simple but comfortable furnishings, while meals are served in the sun porch dining room of the main lodge. Evening activities include cookouts and moonlight rides, sing-a-longs and square dances, and trips to town to the rodeo and melodrama theater.

The variety of float trips provides an opportunity to see the wide range of wildlife that abounds in Grand Teton National Park; every day there is either an early sunrise float, a day float or possibly an evening supper float with a cookout on the banks of the river. Hiking and photography trips provide another way of experiencing the beauty of the valley, set at an elevation of 6,800 feet. Adventurous families enjoy four-day pack trips into the high country wilderness. *(CM)* More comments, please.

Open All year.
Rooms 20 1-3 bedroom cabins with private bath and/or shower.
Facilities Main lodge with dining rooms, lounge with games. Laundry room, gift/snack shop. Evening entertainment, swimming hole, river fishing, hiking, horseback riding, float trips, cross-country skiing. High country pack trips, fall hunting trips.
Location SE border of Grand Teton National Park. 15 m N of Jackson Hole airport, 25 m N of Jackson (town), 35 m S of Yellowstone.
Credit cards None accepted.
Rates Full board, per week, $1,080–1,230 double, $565–760 single. Children too young to ride, ½ daily rate. Pack trips, $340 per day, double. 10-15% suggested gratuity. Separate charges for float trips, pack trips, excursions.
Extras Airport pickups, $20.

MORAN 83013   **Map 10**

Information please: A guest ranch we'd like to hear more about is the **Heart Six Dude Ranch,** with a cluster of cabins surrounded by mountains and a full complement of family-oriented ranch activities—trail rides, fishing, swimming, and a children's program. It's one of the few ranches without a weekly minimum stay, which is helpful for those with limited vacation time (P.O. Box 70; 307–543–2477).

Jenny Lake Lodge   *Tel:* (307) 733–4647
Jackson Lake Lodge
Grand Teton National Park, P.O. Box 240

Almost a half-century ago John D. Rockefeller was so impressed by the natural beauty of Jackson Hole that he purchased 33,000 acres and presented it to the federal government as the nucleus of Grand Teton National Park. The principle concessionaire in the park is the Grand Teton Lodge Company, which operates a range of accommodations from luxury cabins at Jenny Lake, to the motor lodge at Jackson Lake Lodge, to the log cabins, tent cabins, and RV park at Colter Bay Village. Guests staying at one facility are welcome to use the amenities of the others.

The cabins at Jenny Lake Lodge are the most appropriate for a listing in this guide. Geared more to adults, they are rustic but relatively luxurious, and rates include two meals a day at the Jenny Lake Lodge. Known for its superior food, the lodge offers continental cuisine that is well prepared and well served. If you're not staying at Jenny Lake Lodge, it's a good idea to make your dinner reservations well in advance.

"Although the cabins combine rustic comfort with modern amenities, the dining is world-class, with innovative dishes based on local fresh produce." *(Paul Lasley & Elizabeth Harryman)*

"For a family vacation, Jackson Lake Lodge is ideal. It's well run for such a big place and offers a wide range of activities for kids to enjoy—both the horseback riding and the float trips were safe and well supervised. The early-morning breakfast rides and the float trips do fill up quickly in July and August, so we'd recommend making reservations for these events when you reserve your room. Coming from the East, we'd recommend taking the early-morning breakfast ride on your first or second morning there, when the time change makes it easier to be ready for the 8 A.M. ride. Our kids managed to find something they liked on the menus, both in the main dining room and the snack bar. The main dining room has a gorgeous view of the Tetons; in the evening, the curtains are opened just as the setting sun is turning the mountains deep shades of pink, purple, and blue, and everyone applauds!" *(Pam Koob)*

Open Early June–late Sept.

Rooms Jenny Lake Lodge: 30 1- and 2-room log cabins with private bath, five with fireplaces. Jackson Lake Lodge: 42 doubles in main lodge, 343 doubles in motor lodge; some suites available; all with full private bath.

Facilities Jenny Lake: Dining room with entertainment, lounge with fireplace; ranger-naturalist presentation weekly; musical entertainment several nights a week. Jackson Lake: Dining room, lounge, coffee shop; gift shops, card room, heated swimming pool, horseshoe pit. Trail rides, white-water and scenic float trips, swimming, bicycling, hiking, trout fishing. 30 m to golf, tennis.

Location NW WY, in Grand Teton National Park. 36 m N of Jackson, 20 m S of Yellowstone. Accessible by Rtes. 26, 89, 187, 287.

Restrictions No-smoking rooms available at Jackson Lake Lodge. "Children under 8 not encouraged at Jenny Lake Lodge."

Credit cards Amex, MC, Visa.

Rates Jenny Lake Lodge: MAP, $355 for 2-room cabin with fireplace, $245 for 1-bedroom cabin, $205 single, plus 15% service. Extra person in room, $80. Alc lunch, $8. Prix fixe dinner for nonresident guests, $30. Jackson Lake Lodge: Room only, $160–216 suite, $73–108 double. No charge for children under 12 in parents' room. $7.50 rollaway.

Extras Leashed pets permitted at Jackson Lake Lodge. Cribs, limited babysitting available. Managed by Rockresorts, Inc.

We Want to Hear from You!

As you know, this book is only effective with your help. We really need to know about your experiences and discoveries.

If you stayed at an inn or hotel listed here, we want to know how it was. Did it live up to our description? Exceed it? Was it what you expected? Did you like it? Were you disappointed? Delighted?

Have you discovered new establishments that we should add to the next edition?

Tear out one of the report forms at the back of this book (or use your own stationery if you prefer) and write today. Even if you write only "Fully endorse existing entry" you will have been most helpful.

Thank You!

Puerto Rico

The Horned Dorset Primavera, Rincon

Although Puerto Rico does not have the cachet of many of the other Caribbean islands, it offers beautiful beaches, attractive and reasonably priced accommodations, and frequent, inexpensive air connections from major U.S. cities, particularly New York and Miami. Peak season in Puerto Rico runs from December 15 to April 15–30; off-season from April 15–May 1 to December 14. Rates do not include 6% room tax, and a $2 to $3 energy surcharge for air-conditioning. If you're staying outside of San Juan, a rental car is essential for sightseeing and exploring.

We are especially anxious to hear more from readers who have visited any of the *paradores puertorriqueños*—country inns modeled after Spain's successful network of *paradores*. The program, established in 1973 by the Puerto Rico Tourism Company, requires high standards of service and cleanliness, and each independently owned inn "must be situated in a historic place or site of exceptional beauty, and must meet demanding criteria." The program currently includes 14 inns, found mostly along the coast, with a few in the mountains inland. Initial reader feedback indicates more than a little leeway in the application of these allegedly demanding criteria—some are indeed quite special, and are described in this chapter, while others appear bastions of ersatz modernity, with green plastic roofed courtyards, plastic plants, and near plastic food.

For more information and reservations for all the paradores, contact the Puerto Rico Tourism Company, 575 Fifth Avenue, New York, NY 10107 or P.O. Box 4435 Old San Juan Station, San Juan 00905; 212–599–6262, 800–223–6530, or 800–443–0266.

We were also concerned by a few reports during the past year of crime problems in San Juan and elsewhere—primarily muggings and robberies. But a reader reported the opposite experience: "We drove around the island for a week and had only lovely experiences. We never felt the least threatened or endangered, even in remote areas. Old San Juan felt quite safe to walk at night, although we weren't out after 10:30 P.M.."

We'd love to have your comments, please!

Information please: The independently owned and run **Le Petit Chalet Mountain Inn of Lucy Mongual** at the edge of the Caribbean National Forest (El Yunque) is very rustic, a favorite of students and scientists alike; it's a 40-minute-drive south of San Juan (P.O. Box 182, Rio Grande 00745; 809–887–5802 or 5807). To the southeast is the relatively unspoiled island of Vieques, known for its beautiful beaches; one possibility is the **Casa del Frances** (809–741–3751), a turn-of-the-century plantation home, although a number of more modest guest houses may also be acceptable. Moving clockwise around the island, another possibility in the southwest is **Mary Lee's by the Sea**, a group of seven brightly furnished accommodations, ranging from a studio apartment to a five-bedroom house (P.O. Box 394, Guanica PR 00653; 809–821–3600). Feedback would be especially appreciated on these and any other finds.

Reader tip: "The Río Camuy Caves, the island's 'newest' tourist attraction, is worth visiting. We were advised to go on a weekday, to avoid the crowds. A trolley takes you down through a tropical ravine to the caves, where a 45-minute guided walk leads though enormous underground rooms and passages. It's about a 90-minute drive from San Juan." *(CM)*

JAYUYA

Parador Hacienda Gripinas   *Tel:* (809) 828–9750
P.O. Box 387   (800) 443–0266

Puerto Rico's parador system is modeled after the one in Spain, only here they've used coffee plantations, not castles. The Parador Hacienda Gripinas is a restored 200-year-old plantation home, painted white with green trim, surrounded by lush gardens. Taino Indian petroglyphs were the inspiration for the blue-stenciled white bedspreads. The restaurant specializes in Puerto Rican food, although reports on its quality are mixed. "One of the best paradors." *(Renée Gold)*

Open All year.
Rooms 19 doubles with full private bath. Most with ceiling fans.
Facilities Restaurant, swimming pool, garden.
Location Center of island.
Credit cards MC, Visa.
Rates Room only, $50 double, $40 single. MAP, $18 additional per person. Extra person in room, $7. No charge for children under 12 in parents' room.

PATILLAS 00723

Caribe Playa   *Tel:* (809) 839–6339
HC 764-Buzon 8490, Rd. 3, Km. 112   (212) 988–1801

In 1970, Esther and Dan Geller left Long Island, NY, to build the three breezeway-styled, two-story concrete buildings that make up the Caribe Playa. Its location, between the Caribbean Sea and the Guardarraya Mountains, maximizes breezes and keeps annoying insects at a minimum. Guests do much of their own cooking; it's a short drive to the village markets at Patillas and Arroyo. The inn serves three meals a day, and many seafood restaurants are nearby. Rooms are simple and pleasantly decorated with motel-style decor, and the setting is idyllic: a crescent-shaped beach, reef-protected swimming area, and a beach ringed with coconut palms. According to the Gellers, guests comment very favorably on the warmth and hospitality of the staff, and the high standards of cleanliness and maintenance.

"If you're looking for a friendly, homey atmosphere, this is certainly the place to come. We have met people from all over the world. We do our own cooking most of the time, and the accommodations are adequate and clean. Rooms have two firm and comfortable double beds, one table light and two ceiling lights, and plenty of hangers and shelf space. There are several large windows with screens and louvers; a ceiling fan kept the room very comfortable even when the temperature was in the high 80s. Palm trees line the shore and provide shade and a picturesque setting for each unit. The owners are extremely friendly and accommodating." *(Mr. & Mrs. Stanley Sirenek)*

"This extraordinary combination of sea and mountains in a tropical environment provides Puerto Rico's best year-round climate for enjoyable vacationing. Caribe Playa attracts friendly, venturesome guests from all walks of life for relaxed fun, featuring sea swimming and snorkeling, plus horseshoe pitching and nature walks. The Gellers started this business from scratch and have trained their personnel to be just as friendly, hospitable, and efficient as you could wish." *(Michael Kalba)* More comments, please.

Open All year.
Rooms 32 studios—all with private shower, radio, ceiling fan, fully equipped kitchenettes, patio or balcony. Can accommodate up to 4.
Facilities Lounge with TV, radio, library, games, honor bar; outdoor dining terrace. 75 feet to water's edge for swimming, shell collecting, snorkeling in coral reefs, spearfishing, surf casting. 45 acres with coconut farm, barbecue, beach chairs, lounges, tables, hammocks, volleyball, badminton, horseshoes. Golf, tennis nearby.
Location SE coast on Caribbean Sea; 1½–2 hrs. S of San Juan. 15 min. to Patillas. Take Rd. 3 E from Patillas
Credit cards Amex, DC, MC, Visa.
Rates Room only, $59–65, plus 5% service. Children under 10 free in parents' room (maximum 2 children). Extra person in room, $12. 10% senior discount. 2-night minimum. Reduced rates for 10-day stay. Alc breakfast, $3–5; alc lunch $3.50–7; alc dinner, $12–15; advance notice required for dinner only.

Extras Airport pickups $60. Pets permitted. Spanish, English spoken. Cribs, babysitting, play equipment available.

RINCON 00743

The Horned Dorset Primavera   *Tel:* (809) 823–4030
Rd. 429, P.O. Box 1132   (809) 823–4050

Puerto Rico and *elegant* are words rarely used in the same sentence, but in the case of this new jewel of a resort, an exception must be made. The owners of The Horned Dorset in Leonardsville, New York (see entry in New York chapter), decided to try their hands at a tropical (ad)venture in 1987. The reports are extremely positive. This Horned Dorset is done in white stucco with classical Spanish arches, red tiled roofs, and black and white tiled floors. Rooms are decorated with mahogany four-poster beds, marble bathrooms, and European antiques. The six-course dinners carry on The Horned Dorset's reputation for fine French cuisine.

"A gem of a resort. The site and layout of rooms were very well thought out, and the rooms are furnished beautifully. The landscaping is also to be complimented. One of the chefs from the Horned Dorset in Leonardsville prepared the expected exquisite cuisine. Our stay pleased all the senses completely." *(Renee Gold, also MW)*

"Indisputably the most elegant inn in Puerto Rico. Superb service. Only the beach falls short of perfection, and the management can't be faulted for that." *(MA)*

Open All year.
Rooms 24 villa-style suites, all with full private bath, desk, air-conditioning, ceiling fan, balcony.
Facilities Dining room, library, bar, veranda. 5 acres with gardens, swimming pool, beach, snorkeling, surfing. Golf, casino, boat rentals, scuba diving, deep-sea fishing, whale watching nearby.
Location W coast on Mona Passage. 8 m from Mayaguez. 2½ hrs. from San Juan airport. From Mayaguez take Rte. 2 N to Anasco intersection, turn left at Rte. 115 (toward Rincon). Go approx. 4 m and make a sharp left just past El Coche Restaurant onto Rte. 429. Go approx. 1 m; hotel is on left, at distance marker Km .3.
Restrictions No children under 12.
Credit cards Amex, MC, Visa.
Rates Room only, $130–210 double, $80–165 single. Extra person in room, $55.
Extras 1 suite equipped for disabled. English, Spanish, French spoken.

SAN GERMAN 00753

Parador Oasis   *Tel:* (809) 892–1175

Set in the Spanish colonial town of San German, the Parador Oasis is set in a 200-year-old mansion. *Renée Gold* was delighted with her stay here, while another reader arrived possibly somewhat later to disappointment: "Another historic dwelling K-Marted with plastic covering the interior patio, plastic plants, and plastic furniture." Reports please!

Open All year.
Rooms 34 doubles with full private bath, TV, air-conditioning.
Facilities Restaurant, living room.
Location SW PR. Approx. 30 m N of Caribbean; near Rte. 2.
Credit cards MC, Visa.
Rates Room only, $60 double, $50 single.

SAN JUAN 00911

Information please: We'd really like to add the **Hotel El Convento** (100 Cristo Street, P.O. Box 1048; 809–7234–9020 or 800–468–2779) to our list of full entries. Built in 1651 as a convent, it was converted into a hotel while preserving its beamed ceilings, handmade tiles, and mahogany doors. Sounds ideal, but less appealing was the reader report noting that the "plastic roof over the center patio can be avoided only by booking a room on the top floor. Our room was a bit seedy, and the pleasant dining room offered excellent service but undistinguished, expensive food." Another guest was delighted with his room: "Large and immaculate, with hand carved doors and ample storage space." The potential is there, the location in Old San Juan very appealing; reports please.

There are two other possibilities we'd like to hear more about. The **Galeria San Juan**, a magnificently restored building in Old San Juan dating back to 1750, is owned by artist Jan D'Esopo. The Galeria houses an art gallery, working artists' studios, and six handsomely furnished guest rooms (Boulevard del Valle 204-206, 00901; 809–722–1808). The **El Canario Inn,** just a block from Condado beach, is a modestly priced B&B inn, with 25 comfortable units surrounding a tropical patio (1317 Ashford Avenue 00907; 809–722–3861).

Wind Chimes Guest House
53 Calle Taft

Tel: (809) 727–4153

The Wind Chimes is a restored Spanish-style villa; guest rooms are furnished in basic "motel modern," but are clean and comfortable. Wayne Berry and Nolan Hacking have owned and operated the inn since 1984.

"The location is perfect—the beach, casinos, and lots of restaurants are all within five blocks." *(Pamela Burdick)*

"The special thing about it was the relaxing atmosphere in the flower-filled patio. We started our day enjoying the hot coffee, fruit, and pastries they offered us. The owners were friendly and accommodating; it was obvious they wanted to make our stay very pleasant. Drinks and tasty light meals were served in the bar area near the patio; you could usually go there to chat with the other guests or with Wayne Berry." *(Val & Janice Bess)* More comments, please.

Open All year.
Rooms 7 suites, 5 doubles, all with private bath and/or shower, radio, desk, air-conditioning, ceiling fans. Some with TV.
Facilities Library with balcony; bar with TV lounge; patio. Sun deck with lounges; garden patio with tropical plants, orchids. 1 block to Condado Beach.
Location NE coast. Walking distance to Condado, 15-min. bus ride to Old San Juan.

Restrictions Children over 10 preferred. Some street noise on Friday nights.
Credit cards Amex, MC, Visa.
Rates B&B, $65–110 suite, $45–70 double, $35–70 single, plus 10% service. Extra person in room, $10.
Extras Pets with prior approval. Spanish, English, some German spoken.

We Want to Hear from You!

As you know, this book is only effective with your help. We really need to know about your experiences and discoveries.

If you stayed at an inn or hotel listed here, we want to know how it was. Did it live up to our description? Exceed it? Was it what you expected? Did you like it? Were you disappointed? Delighted?

Have you discovered new establishments that we should add to the next edition?

Tear out one of the report forms at the back of this book (or use your own stationery if you prefer) and write today. Even if you write only "Fully endorse existing entry" you will have been most helpful.
Thank You!

Key to Abbreviations

For complete information and explanations, please see the Introduction.

Rates: Range from least expensive room in low season to most expensive room in peak season.
Room only: No meals included; sometimes referred to as European Plan (EP).
B&B: Bed and breakfast; includes breakfast, sometimes afternoon/evening refreshment.
MAP: Modified American Plan; includes breakfast and dinner.
Full board: Three meals daily.
Alc lunch: À la carte lunch; average price of entrée plus nonalcoholic drink, tax, tip.
Alc dinner: Average price of three-course dinner, including half bottle of house wine, tax, tip.
Prix fixe dinner: Three- to five-course set dinner, excluding wine, tax, tip unless otherwise noted.
Extras: Noted if available. Always confirm in advance. Pets are not permitted unless specified.
Zip codes: If only one zip code applies, it is listed with the town name. If there is more than one, it is noted as part of the address.

Canada

Yellowpoint Lodge, Ladysmith, British Columbia

Canada is a huge and beautiful country with a number of wonderful places to visit, from the exciting, cosmopolitan cities to the peaceful countryside. Our correspondents have discovered some very wonderful hotels and inns from Nova Scotia to British Columbia, but we would love to have more suggestions.

A few notes for first-time visitors to Canada: Radar detectors are illegal and seat belts are mandatory. When consulting maps and speed limits remember that Canada is metric. Ask your auto insurance company for a free "Canadian Non-Resident Inter-Provincial Motor Vehicle Liability Insurance Card"—it will immeasurably speed up any procedures if you are involved in an accident. Finally, it is often advantageous to purchase Canadian funds in the U.S.—so make some comparison calls first (the rate varies from bank to bank).

Rates quoted in this section are noted in Canadian, not U.S., dollars. *US $1 = Canadian $.86;* exchange rates are subject to constant fluctuation.

Alberta

Alberta is home to the Canadian Rockies; Banff, Jasper, and Lake Louise are the major resorts where most visitors go for hiking and fishing in summer and skiing in winter. This province's key cities are Edmonton and Calgary. Though Edmonton is the capital, its major claim to fame seems to be the West Edmonton Mall, a mile-long indoor shopping and recreation complex containing about every imaginable shop and recreation facility, even a 360-room hotel, the Fantasyland, with a selection of theme rooms devoted to different countries and periods (403–444–3000). Calgary is a center for agriculture and oil production. Its most famous event is the annual Stampede, a combination rodeo and state fair; it is also home to a fine collection of museums devoted to telecommunications and energy, along with more traditional subjects of art and history.

All rates quoted in Canadian dollars, and do not include 5% room tax.

BANFF T0L 0C0   Map 17

Although we didn't receive enough information for a full entry, **Emerald Lake Lodge** in Yoho National Park is recommended for its fabulous fishing and handsome lodging. Built in 1902 of hand-hewn logs, the lodge was totally renovated in 1986. With hot tub and sauna, and in-room fireplaces, it's considerably more posh than **Lake O'Hara Lodge** (listed below), and is quite a bit larger, with 85 units accommodating 200 people. Room only rates range from $95 to $360 per night. (Canadian Rocky Mt. Resorts, P.O. Box 1598, Banff AB T0L 0C0; 800–661–1367). *(DB)*

Lake O'Hara Lodge   *Tel:* (403) 762–2118
Yoho National Park, P.O. Box 1677   (604) 343–6418

Deciding where to place this entry was a bit tricky—Lake O'Hara is in Yoho National Park in British Columbia, not Alberta. It's on the opposite side of Victoria Glacier from Lake Louise. But since the lodge's mailing address is in Banff, and because a visit here is likely to be combined with this area's other Alberta attractions, we've put it here. (Life is full of big decisions.) More important, the two-story wooden lodge was built by the Canadian Pacific Railroad in 1926. At 6,700 feet, it is the highest resort in the Canadian Rockies. It's been owned and managed by Michael and Marsha Laub and Tim and Leslee Wake since 1976. Rooms are simply decorated, but comfortable. The French cuisine is excellent (enhanced perhaps by the hearty appetites generated by lots of exercise in the clean mountain air) and quite sophisticated. A typical set dinner might consist of coquilles St. Jacques, consommé, roast duck with raspberry sauce, wild rice, red cabbage with chestnuts, and sabayon. In addition to three squares a day, rates include afternoon tea and cookies or gluhwein. The setting is blissful—the blue waters of Lake O'Hara ringed by dark evergreens and golden larches, with the snowcapped 11,000-foot peaks piercing the bright blue sky. Access is limited, and it's hard to believe that bustling Lake Louise lies just on the other side of the mountains. Lake O'Hara regulars know a good thing when they find it; many key weekends are fully booked a year ahead.

"Exactly as described in their brochure. The innkeepers were very congenial and pleasant. The hiking and fishing are excellent; guests return year after year. The foliage is pretty, but to this dyed-in-the-wool Yankee it does not compare with that of New England." *(DB)*

Open Mid-June–Oct.1; Dec. 25–mid-April. Cabins closed in winter.
Rooms 15 1- to 2-room cabins, all with private bath and/or shower. Lodge with 7 doubles, 1 single sharing 2 baths. All with desk.
Facilities Dining room, lounge. Sat. night entertainment in summer. 5 acres. 50 m of hiking trails, fishing, mountain climbing, cross-country skiing.
Location W AB, in Yoho National Park, Canadian Rockies. 120 m W of Calgary, 8 m W of Lake Louise. From Lake Louise, take Trans-Canada Hwy. W to Rte. 1A. Turn left and park in O'Hara gate parking lot. In summer, bus makes 3 round trips to lodge daily; in winter, access on skis only.
Restrictions No smoking.
Credit cards None accepted.
Rates Full board, $330 cabin, $210–296 double, $145–210 single. Extra adult (over age 15) in cabin, $105. Child in cabin with parents—under 2 free; age 2–6, $18; age 6–15, $40. Central tip pool for all staff, no individual tipping. 2-night minimum. 5% weekly discount.
Extras Station pickups.

LAKE LOUISE T0L 1E0   Map 17

Post Hotel   *Tel:* (403) 522–3989
Box 69   (800) 661–1586

The Post Hotel is comprised of a 50-year-old log building, which houses the hotel's restaurant, and a brand-new addition, handsomely built of wood and stone that is home to the hotel's luxurious guest rooms. The redevelopment cost nearly $6 million. The hotel had been owned since 1978 by the Schwarz family, but in 1986 Husky Oil Operations acquired a 50% interest in it. Today Andre, Barbara, and George Schwarz continue to operate the hotel and restaurant. The dinner menu of the hotel's well-known restaurant has a Swiss accent but offers a full range of continental specialties. A typical dinner might include salmon and halibut marinated with dill, rack of lamb with Dijon mustard and herbs, and homemade cheesecake for dessert.

"The Schwarzes wisely retained their chef during renovation to feed the construction crew, so that the dining room is as outstanding as ever—we had the best meal of our Alberta trip. Everything in the renovation was top-notch in quality." *(Dev Barker)*

Open All year.
Rooms 14 suites, 79 doubles, all with full private bath, telephone, TV, desk, balcony. Some with fireplaces, whirlpool tubs, kitchenettes. 2 cabins, 1 with 4 bedrooms and conference facilities.
Facilities Dining/breakfast rooms, bar/lounge with fireplace, pub with TV, conference rooms. Jacuzzi, heated indoor pool, exercise and steam room. Tennis, fishing, trail rides, canoeing, bicycling, downhill and cross-country skiing nearby.
Location SW AB, Banff National Park. 120 m W of Calgary. In Lake Louise village, on Pipestone River.
Credit cards Amex, MC, Visa.
Rates Room only, $175–250 suite, $110–180 double. 4-night minimum stay Dec. 24–Dec. 29. Alc breakfast, $5–9; lunch, $8–20; alc dinner, $30–50. Ski package rates.
Extras Wheelchair accessible. Free station pickups. Cribs available. French, Swiss, German, Italian spoken.

British Columbia

Bordering Washington, Idaho, and part of Montana, British Columbia stretches north to the Yukon and Northwest Territories and west to the Pacific. Although British Columbia is 50% larger than Texas, more than 75% of its population (of only 2,744,000) lives near the two principal cities, Vancouver and Victoria. Since British Columbia is something of a mouthful to say, just about everyone in Canada and the northwestern U.S. refers to the province as "BC," which is just what we're going to do here.

Summer is very much peak season in BC; we'd strongly recommend making your reservations two to three months ahead.

Vancouver Island is located 40 miles away from the city of Vancouver on the mainland. To get here, take a ferry from Anacortes, Washington, through the beautiful San Juan Islands; from Port Angeles, on Washington's Olympic Peninsula; or from the city of Vancouver. Victoria, the very British capital of BC, sits at the southern tip of Vancouver Island and is the starting point for island explorations. Near Victoria, gathered like jewels off the southeastern coast, are the 100 Gulf Islands (see entry for **Ganges**), for bucolic getaways.

Be sure to travel beyond Victoria when visiting Vancouver Island. There are no continuous roads on the west shore of the island, so you must take Route 1 up the east coast. Turn inland near Parksville, then either stop in Port Alberni to board the MV *Lady Rose* for a romantic cruise to Bamfield or visit Pacific Rim National Park, between Tofino and Ucluelet, for beach-combing and scuba diving. For more adventure, take Route 1 to Campbell River, Route 28 to Gold River, and board the MV *Uchuck III,* which sails the remote fjords of the northwest part of the island.

Mainland BC Plan to spend several days in the city of Vancouver and the surrounding area. For one good side trip, take Route 99 north past a long inlet, then into the Coast Range Mountains, ending at Whistler, an excellent ski area near Garibali Provincial Park. For another, follow picturesque Route 101 up the "Sunshine Coast" from Vancouver to Powell River. This route includes crossings on tiny ferries at both Horseshoe Bay and Earls Cove.

Routes 1 and 3, east of Vancouver, lead you to the most interesting interior spots in the province. On Route 7, stop first at historic Harrison Hot Springs (worth a look but not an overnight), then drop south at Agassiz to Route 1 and the multilayered Bridal Veil Falls. From here you begin seeing the sharply sculptured, snowcapped Cascade Mountains rising directly behind the Fraser River Valley. At Hope you have a choice. Route 3 winds through the mountains and past the apple orchards of the Okanagan Valley to Penticton and Lake Okanagan, a popular but overcrowded resort area. Alternatively, Route 1 follows the Fraser River Canyon past dramatic Hell's Gate (take the tram across the narrow canyon) into the dry, high plains near Kamloops. From there you enter remote forested back country until you reach the spectacular Mt. Revelstroke and Glacier National Parks, with their massive sharp peaks, rolling alpine meadows, and hundreds of glaciers. For accommodations in Yoho National Park, on the BC/Alberta border, see the entry for **Banff, Alberta.** To the north, the remaining two-thirds of interior BC is sparsely populated; with extreme distances between towns and rustic accommodations in the towns, it's not high on our must-see list.

Rates do not include 6 to 8% provincial and local sales taxes. *All rates are quoted in Canadian dollars.*

GANGES V0S 1E0   **Map 17**
SALT SPRING ISLAND

Hastings House   *Tel:* (604) 537–2362
Box 1110, 160 Upper Ganges   (800) 661–9255

Hastings House is an elegant seaside farm estate, composed of five restored buildings—the Manor House, the Farmhouse, Cliffside, the Post, and the Barn. The Tudor-style Manor House contains the inn's dining and common rooms, while the guest rooms and suites are spread out among the inn's other facilities.

Meals are a highlight at Hastings House. Each evening a five-course gourmet dinner is served. A recent meal included wild mushroom and potato bisque, paupiette of crab-stuffed sole with caper sauce, salad, breast of duckling, wild rice, fresh broccoli, sautéed red cabbage, and wild blackberry and brandy mousse.

"The Gulf Islands are blessed with wonderful weather, scenery, and people! We stayed in the Farmhouse. With eiderdown quilts, plenty of towels and bath extras, a refrigerator, bar sink, fireplace, and porch, we felt most comfortable. Each morning a continental breakfast was delivered to our door so quietly that we didn't even hear it being done. The food and the attitudes of the people there were wonderful. It is very clean, quiet, and lovely. You can fly from Seattle right to the harbor. You really don't need a car—the walking will be just what you need after eating all that good food! Although there is no choice of entrée at dinner, we told our hosts that we don't eat red meat, and it was no problem." *(Laura Scott)*

"Close to total perfection. It is very expensive and yet the service and atmosphere are so special that you feel you have a bargain. Everything is superb, from the personal nameplate on your door, table, and menu to the thermos of coffee and hot bran muffins that are left outside your door in the early morning, to the fact that when you order cocktails in the beautiful Tudor living room before dinner, the servers will remember and ask you if you want the same the next night. The refreshening of your room while you are at dinner (absolutely wonderful food) and the little gift that is always left with the chocolates on your pillow are both nice touches too." *(Judith Brannen)*

Open Early March–late Nov.
Rooms 6 1- to 2-bedroom suites, 4 doubles, all with private bath, telephone, radio, desk, fireplace; TV on request. All with wet bar or kitchen. Guest rooms in several separate buildings.
Facilities Dining room, library, living room, conference room. 30 acres with lawns, herb and vegetable gardens, croquet, bicycles; 1,000 ft. of waterfront for fishing, boat moorage. Hiking, bicycling, golf, tennis nearby.

Location SW BC. Gulf Islands, 20 m N of Victoria. At N end of Salt Spring Island, at head of Ganges Harbour; 2 m N of town. Take ferry from Victoria or Vancouver or float plane from Vancouver or Seattle.
Restrictions Smoking in living room only. No children.
Credit cards Amex, MC, Visa.
Rates B&B, $225–345 suite, $170–215 double. Extra person in room, $25. 2-night minimum July, August. 3-night holiday weekend minimum. Prix fixe dinner, $32–40. Alc lunch, $8–12. Cooking courses in fall, spring.
Extras Free ferry pickups. Ramps for wheelchair access. Member, Relais et Chateaux.

LADYSMITH V0R 2E0 Map 17

Yellow Point Lodge *Tel:* (604) 245–7422
3700 Yellow Point Road, RR3

Yellowpoint Lodge is a country resort that has been owned by the Hill family for over 50 years. Guests eat their meals together at common tables and stay in a wide variety of accommodations, from comfortable lodge rooms and cottages to rustic beach cabins. Rebuilt after a 1985 fire, the main lodge is where guests come for meals and to socialize; it's built of massive logs, with natural wood siding and a large stone fireplace.

"Yellow Point is an experience everyone should try at least once, if not more often. The setting is breathtaking and the fresh air, the peacefulness, and the wonderful friendly people—both guests and staff—make this resort a delightful retreat. You can relax and read a book in front of a huge fireplace, ease your aches and pains in the hot tub overlooking the ocean, or swim, windsurf, play tennis or Ping-Pong. When you feel like being alone, take a long walk along the beach or deep into the forest." *(Gayle P. Hawton)*

"The view is terrific, the mood one of sublime self-indulgence. In the lodge, Room 5 is best (it has its own balcony), but the cabins are nice too, and very private. The guests are very congenial, with interesting lives and stories to tell." *(Suzanne Carmichael)*

"Three outstanding meals and delicious snacks are served, so you never have to argue about what restaurant to go to. At breakfast, you can order whatever you like, in any combination and quantity—eggs, bacon, sausages, oatmeal, pancakes, hash browns, and more. The seating at tables for 10 allow you to meet new people, yet there is ample opportunity for privacy when desired. Although the lounge area is huge, with a beautiful view, there are little living room groupings scattered around, and all kinds of games. We especially like the White Beach cottages. Ours had lovely furniture, including a very high bed, from which we could enjoy the view out our window." *(PE)*

"The sea lions gathered in great numbers to feed off the herring runs. After their feeding they lolled about, appearing to wave their flippers at us onlookers!" *(Chriss & Ross Ball)*

Although readers were unanimous in their praise of Yellow Point, with all planning to return, they did suggest a few minor improvements: "Beds do tend to be noisy, and this could be corrected with more cross supports."

Also: "A non-smoking environment would further enhance the delightful atmosphere here." And: "The food is wonderful in taste and presentation, but sometimes the service is a tiny bit rushed at dinner."

Open All year.
Rooms 9 doubles in main lodge, 42 rooms in a variety of cabins and cottages. 21 rooms with private bath and/or shower, 7 rooms with a maximum of 6 sharing bath. Also 24 beach and field cabins with no running water and sharing communal-style washrooms.
Facilities Large living room with dance floor, fireplace; game room; dining room with ocean view, guest refrigerator. 180 acres with 1 m waterfront; walking/jogging trails; outdoor saltwater swimming pool, hot tub, sauna, 2 tennis courts, badminton, volleyball, mountain bikes; beach swimming, canoeing, boating, windsurfing. Golf nearby. Midweek cruises off the Gulf Islands.
Location SE BC. On SE coast of Vancouver Island, 70 m N of Victoria. 15 m S of Nanaimo. From Nanaimo, take Rte. 1 S 3 m to Cedar Rd. Go left on Cedar 5 m to Yellow Pt. Rd. Turn left and go 7 m to lodge. From Ladysmith, go N 3 m to Cedar Rd. Turn right on Cedar; go 2 m, and turn right on Yellow Pt. Rd. 4 m to lodge.
Restrictions Smoking "strongly discouraged." No children under 16.
Credit cards MC, Visa.
Rates Full board, $80–155 double, $45–100 single. Extra person in room, $47. 2-3 night minimum weekends, holidays; 1-week reservations preferred in July, Aug. 20% off-season midweek discount.
Extras Wheelchair accessible; 1 room specially equipped. Free ferry, station, airport pickups.

MAYNE ISLAND V0N 2J0   Map 17

Mayne Island is in the Gulf Islands of southwestern British Columbia and is approximately 30 miles from both Victoria and Vancouver. It can be reached by ferry from either Tsawwassen (just south of Vancouver) or from Vancouver Island. Heavily wooded, with rolling hills and a tiny village center, Mayne offers a variety of beaches from pebbled ones to small sandy coves surrounded by soft sandstone ledges which jut out into the Strait and have been so scoured by other stones that they resemble lace.

Also recommended: The **Fernhill Lodge** (Box 140; 604–539–2544) was started by Brian and Mary Crumblehulme as an herb farm (with over 200 varieties), then expanded to a B&B in 1983. Theme dinners are a specialty here, with menus dating from the first through the seventeenth centuries, in addition to more contemporary "farm dinners."

Gingerbread House   *Tel:* (604) 539–3133
Campbell Bay Road

Although the Gingerbread House dates back to the turn of the century, it has been at its present location only since 1980, when it was maneuvered down steep streets to an awaiting barge at Granville Island and floated 30 miles across the Strait of Georgia.

"The Gingerbread House is a 1900 carpenter Gothic Victorian set high above Campbell Bay with beautiful views of the Gulf Islands and the Strait of Georgia. This little-known island has great beaches and many trails and roads for hiking and bicycling. The inn is beautifully decorated with antiques and lots of fresh flowers. The owners, Ken and Karen Somerville, are warm and gracious hosts. Karen cooks and Ken serves an enormous breakfast; we've also enjoyed full gourmet dinners featuring fresh produce from their garden. All rooms are bright and pleasant and well maintained. A highlight of our stay was seeing the bald eagles fishing in the bay!" *(Eileen Cassidy & Arthur Faro)* More comments, please.

Open All year.
Rooms 4 doubles–2 with private shower and/or bath, 2 with maximum of 4 people sharing bath. All with desk.
Facilities Dining room, sun room, library. 3 acres on bay with dock, tennis court. Outboard, sailboat rentals. Beach for swimming, fishing nearby.
Location NE Mayne Island 1½ m to center. From ferry landing, take Village Bay Rd. to Fernhill Rd. Go right on Fernhill, then left on Campbell Bay Rd.
Restrictions Smoking on sun porch only. No children under 12.
Credit cards MC, Visa.
Rates $59–90 double, $55–85 single. Extra person in room, $20. Prix fixe dinner by prior arrangement, $24. 10% senior discount midweek. 2-night holiday weekend minimum.
Extras Free ferry/seaplane pickups. Moorings available.

SOOKE V0S 1N0 Map 17

Sooke Harbour House   *Tel:* (604) 642–4944
1528 Whiffen Spit Road, RR 4   642–3421

Sooke Harbour House, a small white clapboard farmhouse, sits on a bluff overlooking Whiffen Spit. Originally built in the 1930s, the inn was recently expanded; 10 new guest rooms were added to the original five. Rates include breakfast *and* lunch.

Frederica and Sinclair Philip, owners of this inn, describe it as being located on the "edge of the wilderness, with whales, otters, seals, bears, cougars, and bald eagles nearby. Honeymooners love the romantic location, while adventurous diners can try the sea urchins, sea cucumber, pickled kelp, lavender ice cream, edible flower salads, and more."

Sooke Harbour House is known as one of Vancouver Island's best restaurants. Menus change daily but feature the freshest possible local foods, creatively prepared. Their garden is home to more than 100 kinds of edible flowers and 200 varieties of herbs, along with dozens of summer salad greens and vegetables and orchards to supply fresh fruits and berries. Although the choice was a hard one to make, a recent dinner included stuffed breast of rabbit with endive and radicchio and hazelnut dressing, trout and salmon mousse with tarragon butter, and blueberry mousse for dessert.

"The breakfast consisted of fresh orange and plum juice, lots of hot coffee or tea, fresh-baked blueberry muffins, fruit, granola with milk, pancakes, and eggs cooked to your choice. The restaurant looks out on the harbor and there are windows all around to view the mountains, sea, and sky. The tables are set with teapots filled with fresh flowers." *(GR)*

"Although the location is gorgeous, the main point of a visit is the food. Either fast for several days before staying here or come for a final binge before a diet. You will eat fish caught only a few hours before being served, fresh eggs, fruits, and meats from local farmers, plus vegetables from the inn's extensive gardens. Expect the unexpected here when these local items are combined in unusual ways. We liked some of the dishes that included kelp and their suckling kid with herbs." *(Anne Michaels)*

"Sinclair and Frederica Philips are wonderful hosts and cooks, and their inn is set in one of the most beautiful harbors I've ever seen—I don't believe I will ever see the sky such a beautiful shade of violet again. Their sense of style is straight out of *Metropolitan Home*; Room 8, with its tiled bath, fireplace, and whirlpool is a special favorite." *(Anne Blumenstein)*

Open All year.
Rooms 4 suites, 9 doubles, all with private bath, radio, desk, fireplace, balcony, or terrace. Some with Jacuzzi, wet bar, hot tub.
Facilities Dining/breakfast rooms with fireplace, lounge, library, living room. 2 acres with herb, flower, vegetable gardens; orchard, beach. Swimming, fishing, hiking nearby.
Location SW BC. At SW end of Vancouver Island, 23 m SW of Victoria. Take Hwy. 1 to Hwy. 14 to Sooke. ³⁄₅ m after Otter Point Rd. (at Gulf station), turn onto Whiffen Spit Rd.
Restrictions No smoking in some rooms.
Credit cards Amex, CB, DC, MC, Visa.
Rates B&B plus lunch, $85–230 double, plus 15% service; rates include breakfast and lunch. Extra person in room, $10–25. Tipping only for meals. Alc dinner, $40.
Extras Common rooms, one guest room wheelchair accessible. Pets permitted for small fee. Cribs available. French, German, Tongan, Mandarin, Cantonese spoken.

VANCOUVER   Map 17

Dramatically situated on a peninsula where towering mountains sweep down to the sea, Vancouver is Canada's loveliest city. At once cosmopolitan and amiable, Vancouver offers exciting cultural, shopping, and recreational opportunities. The compact heart of the city is located on a tiny peninsula, one-half of which is Stanley Park, known for its gardens, zoo, golf course, bathing beach, and jogging trails. Downtown Vancouver is a wonderful amalgam of apartment houses, hotels, sidewalk cafés, smart shops, galleries, and office buildings. It is lively, clean, and safe, and bubbles with people late into the night.

Vancouver's rich ethnic mix adds to its charm and makes for diverse shopping and dining adventures. Chinatown and nearby Japantown are a jumble of exotic markets, shops, and restaurants. In south Vancouver (near Main and 49th) is a thriving East Indian community where you can buy beautiful silk saris and outrageously colored sweets. The Greeks and Italians have also left their mark on this wonderful city.

Originally a tidal flat known as Mud Island, Granville Island had developed by 1930 into an industrial park. In the late 1970s the island was the focus of a major waterfront redevelopment project, and it is now home to a variety of commercial and artistic endeavors: a public market, selling everything from mussels to bagels; a kids' market and water-play park; a brewery; two theaters; and a variety of trendy cafés and boutiques, restaurants, and art galleries. Although fun for families and shoppers alike, one

745

reader, warned that "parking is impossible, so take the False Creek ferry if you do go." She goes on to note that another restored area is Gastown, "a well-conceived redevelopment area with charming restored buildings and an interesting steam clock. The shops, unfortunately, are pure tourist kitsch."

Do *not* miss a trip to the Museum of Anthropology on the campus of the University of British Columbia. In a dramatic building designed by Arthur Erickson, you will see 40-foot totem poles, ancient canoes, and other items emphasizing the artistic diversity of the Northwest Coast Indians.

For a wonderful view of southeastern British Columbia, go up to the top of 3,900-foot Grouse Mountain where you can see the city of Vancouver, Vancouver and the Gulf islands, the Fraser River, the Strait of Georgia, and, on a clear day, the Olympic Mountains in Washington State. In winter you can ski here in the morning, then lunch in town. Visit Andusen Botanical Gardens for vibrant displays of flowers during the spring and summer.

Vancouver is located in the southwest corner of the mainland of British Columbia.

Blue Willow B&B   *Tel:* (604) 984–9028
506 West 19th Street
North Vancouver V7M 1X9

Arlene and John England spent several years living in Europe. Their travel experience is reflected in the charm of their B&B, and in the enthusiastic manner in which they welcome their guests. The house is decorated in the style of an English country cottage, highlighted by their collection of blue and white china. Rates include a full English-style breakfast with fresh-baked blueberry muffins, cinnamon buns, or scones, fresh fruit with cream, and coffee or tea.

"This B&B is located in a private home in a residential area of Vancouver. My husband, two young children, and I slept in a cozy room with an adjoining bath. It was equipped with a remote-control TV, clock radio, and lots of literature about Vancouver. Breakfast included wonderful home-made breads, jam, cheese, eggs, tea or coffee, and juice. The Englands have a lovely backyard with a magnificent vegetable garden. They are very warm people and extremely loving and accommodating to children." *(Martha I. Pollack)*

"Arlene's taste is exquisite. Her breakfast table looks like a scene out of *House and Garden,* and the scrumptious breakfast was all carefully prepared with homemade everything; we lingered over coffee, chatting with these two lovely people, who never encroached upon our privacy. They made restaurant reservations, suggested lovely walks, and more." *(Peggy King)*

Open All year.
Rooms 1 suite, 2 doubles—all with private bath and/or shower. All with telephone, radio, TV. 1 with fireplace.
Facilities Dining room, living room, patio/breakfast area, laundry privileges. Garden with fruit trees, flowering shrubs. Beaches, tennis, hiking, bicycling, sailing, kayaking, fishing, downhill and cross-country skiing nearby.
Location 15 min. N of downtown. 20 min. by Seabus across harbor. ½ block from main bus route. Go N on Lions Gate Bridge; stay in N. Vancouver lane at end of

bridge onto Marine Drive. Take 1st left onto Capilano Rd. After 3 blocks, go right on Hwy. 1E, right again on Westview. Go 6 blocks S, and go left on W. 19th St. to #506.

Restrictions Some traffic noise in one room. No smoking.
Credit cards None accepted.
Rates B&B, $55 suite, $45 double, $35 single. Extra person in room, $15. Tipping "not expected." Family rates.
Extras Small pets permitted. French, German spoken.

Ming Court Hotel
1160 Davie Street
Vancouver V6E 1N1

Tel: (604) 685–1311
(800) 663–1525

"When you're in Vancouver you will want to stay right in the downtown area, near all the enticing little shops, but most of the hotels are outrageously expensive, tacky, run down, or just boring. The Ming Court is the wonderful exception. It's located on one of the major east/west streets, only several blocks from the center of downtown. The lobby is small, pretty, and efficient. The rooms are attractively decorated with very comfortable sitting areas and lots of closet space. The staff is very pleasant and eager to provide you with extra hangers, restaurant suggestions, or anything else you need. Request a room facing west, and from your porch you will be able to see much of West Vancouver, ships coming in to dock, the Coast Mountains to the north, and, on a clear day, the Olympic Mountains to the south. The restaurant provides large breakfasts served by cheery waitresses, but for dinner try one of Vancouver's wonderful ethnic restaurants." *(SC)* More comments please.

Open All year.
Rooms 2 suites, 190 doubles, all with full private bath, telephone, TV. Most with balconies, kitchens.
Facilities Restaurant, coffee shop, lounge with live entertainment. Heated swimming pool, sauna. Indoor parking. Room service. Beaches, park nearby.
Location Downtown, near corner of Thurlow.
Credit cards All major credit cards.
Rates Room only, $250 suite, $120–155 double, $110–135 single. Extra person in room, $15. No charge for child under 14 in parents' room. 10% senior discount. Alc breakfast, $6–8; alc lunch, $9; alc dinner, $35.
Extras Airport pickups, $6.50. Cribs, babysitting available. Japanese, Chinese, German, French spoken.

Park Royal Hotel
540 Clyde Avenue
West Vancouver V7T 2J7

Tel: (604) 926–5511

A stay here offers the opportunity to be in the city yet outside of its hubbub. An ivy-covered Tudor-style building, the Park Royal offers a lovely setting on extensive grounds amid beautiful flower gardens. Managed by partner Mario Corsi, this hotel is what this guide is all about—it's a true hotel, not a B&B, yet its service is extremely personal, as its many repeat customers will fervently attest. It's well worth a visit just for the food—a combination of French and West Coast cuisines, with an emphasis on local seafood, meat, and produce. Lunch is popular on the terrace in summer, while dinner might include such treats as salmon and Camembert pâté with celery root salad, breast of pheasant with currants and brandy, and cheesecake for dessert.

"The Park Royal's restaurant is a favorite with Vancouverites. Breakfasts are wonderful. The people who run this place are very pleasant, although the focus is on the restaurant. The rooms are comfortable and well maintained; those looking out over the Capilano River evoke the mood of the best English country house hotels. It is this setting that really makes this place so special.

"The hotel is isolated on a little backwater, set on a park-like strip of land at the edge of the river that flows into the sound by the bridge. Totally quiet, the back rooms and the restaurant look out over lovely gardens onto the tree-lined river banks. The traffic consists of dog walkers and joggers. Truly restful." *(Stephen Holman)*

"The staff was extremely helpful and friendly. The outside dining area is a delightful setting for lunch." *(Michael Crick)*

One otherwise pleased guest noted: "My room was very small and the fan in the bathroom was extremely noisy."

Open All year.
Rooms 1 suite, 29 doubles–all with full private bath, telephone, radio, TV, desk. 6 with fan.
Facilities Restaurant, pub, piano bar, patio, gardens. 5-min. walk to ocean for swimming, fishing.
Location W. Vancouver. 10 min. drive from downtown, 25 min. from airport. 1 block N of Marine Dr.; 1 block E of Taylor Way.
Credit cards Amex, CB, DC, ER, EC, MC, Visa.
Rates Room only, $130–214 suite, $70–93 double, $60–86 single. Extra person in room, $8. Alc breakfast, $5–15; alc lunch, $15–20; alc dinner, $30–50. Children's portions available.
Extras Cribs, babysitting available. French, Italian, Spanish, German, Hindi, Portuguese, Chinese spoken.

VICTORIA   Map 17

Set at the southeastern tip of Vancouver Island, Victoria is known for its British ambience, combined with a distinctly un-British mild and sunny climate. Among the city's many beautiful gardens and parks, Butchart Gardens is the most famous of all and is well worth the trip 14 miles north of town. On summer evenings the gardens are illuminated until 11 P.M. Other attractions include the Houses of Parliament, a grand edifice built in 1893; and the Provincial Museum, with an excellent Northwest Coast Indian Collection, along with exhibits on natural history and 19th-century development. The city is small, so be sure to wander through Beacon Hill Park, the Old Town area, the now-compact Chinatown, and explore the shops—those specializing in Indian and Eskimo art and handicrafts as well as those offering the best of British imports. Although there are many excellent restaurants, the Indian and Chinese ones offer the most interesting dining at the most reasonable prices.

Also recommended: The Beaconsfield Inn (998 Humboldt Street, V8V 2Z8; 604–384–4044), under the same ownership as Abigail's Hotel, is a beautifully restored Edwardian mansion furnished with period antiques and special touches such as steam-heated towel racks. Located on a quiet street only a few blocks from shops and museums, rates include a full breakfast and afternoon social hour. The **Laurel Point Inn** (680 Montreal Street, V8V 1Z8; 604–386–8721; 800–663–7667), a contemporary building in a parklike setting, offers an unusual combination–a convenient in-town location with resort facilities and atmosphere. Ideally suited for families, you can park your car and walk to all attractions. The **Oak Bay Beach Hotel** (1175 Beach Drive, V8S 2N2; 604–598–4556) is a 50-year-old, Tudor-style hotel overlooking the Haro Straits and Mt. Baker. Rooms are individually furnished, some with English-style chintzes, antiques and reproductions; "standard" rooms have more of a basic motel look. The **Olde England Inn** (429 Lampson Street, V9A 5Y9; 604–388–4353), built in l910 in the Tudor half-timbered style, has become, under the ownership of Sam and Rosina Lane, an English village with replicas of Shakespeare's birthplace, Anne Hathaway's Cottage, and other landmarks. Each guest room has an appropriate historical theme and the staff is dressed in period clothing to further enhance the atmosphere.

Abigail's Hotel

906 McClure Street V8V 3E7

Tel: (604) 388–5363

An English Tudor, Abigail's is owned by Bill McKechnie, who also owns the **Beaconsfield Inn**. Renovated in 1986, Abigail's now features an elegant country-style decor, with lots of soft colors and flowers, and goose-down comforters on the beds.

"This small hotel was bright, clean, and charming, with antique furniture throughout. We enjoyed going downstairs each morning, to be greeted by an open fire and wonderful smells coming from the kitchen. The innkeeper and her staff were all very pleasant and helpful. The hotel is situated in a quiet residential area and the grounds are beautifully landscaped. It's only a few blocks into town for sightseeing, shopping, and dining." *(Mr. & Mrs. Albert Betzel)*

"Our room had a canopy bed, a chaise lounge, wingback chairs in front of the working fireplace, a Jacuzzi tub, and a wonderful nighttime view of the illuminated BC Parliament. The full breakfast was served at long tables 'inn style' and was absolutely gourmet. The staff was helpful with advice on what to see and do and where to eat." *(Judith Brannon)* "We looked at several rooms and would recommend the ones at the front if available." *(Frank & Pat Harvey)* "The hotel is spotless and beautifully cared for. Guests were friendly and at ease with each other. The off-street parking is ample." *(Ken & Diane Gignac)*

Open All year.
Rooms 16 doubles, all with private bath and/or shower. Some with radio, desk, fireplaces, Jacuzzi.
Facilities Breakfast room with fireplace, library with fireplace. Formal gardens.
Location 3 blocks to center. On McClure St., between Quadra and Vancouver Sts.
Restrictions Smoking discouraged.
Credit cards MC, Visa.
Rates B&B, $90–175. Extra person in room, $22.50. Children under 5 free in parents' room.
Extras Cribs available.

Holland House Inn   *Tel:* (604) 384–6644
595 Michigan St. V8V 1S7

Don't come to the Holland House Inn for more of Victoria's "Olde En-
glande Quainte Looke." Instead, come to Lance Olsen and Robin Birsner's
bright and airy small hotel to enjoy their fine collection of paintings,
sculpture, and drawings by Victoria's leading artists. Aware that one cannot live on aesthetics alone, the owners have complemented their art with
antique and traditionally styled furniture, good lighting, comfortable beds,
lots of flowers inside and out, and a varying full breakfast—baked eggs
with ham and brie or German apple pancakes with spiced apples and maple
yogurt were two recent options.

"What a breath of fresh air! Although we liked our visit to Victoria, we
got sick of the ersatz Britannia that envelops everything except the superb
Provincial Museum and this great place. We were delighted by our quiet
room, complete with fireplace and good-sized bath. Our balcony proved
a nice retreat before we braved the tourists at dinnertime, and the owners
even served us our breakfast out there the next day. We were quite taken
by some of the modern art which punctuates the rooms in the inn and were
surprised to learn that much of it is done by Lance Olsen. In fact, the
highlight of our stay was a lively art discussion over breakfast the next
day." *(SC)*

Open All year.
Rooms 10 doubles, all with full private bath, telephone, TV. 9 with balcony, 2 with
fireplace.
Facilities Lounge/breakfast room with art gallery. Room service. Entryway gardens.
2 blocks to harbor, Seattle/Port Angeles ferries, Beacon Hill Park.
Location 2 blocks to Inner Harbor. Take Government St. S to Michigan St. Turn
right on Michigan.
Restrictions No smoking. Light sleepers should request "extra quiet rooms."
Credit cards DC, MC, Visa.
Rates B&B, $100–165 double, $90–155 single. Extra person in room, $25. Children
under 10 free in parents' room. Winter packages from Seattle via *Victoria Clipper*.
Extras Some rooms equipped for disabled. Crib available. French spoken.

New Brunswick

New Brunswick is on Atlantic Standard Time; don't forget to set your
watches forward 1 hour when crossing the border! The season generally
runs from about mid-May to mid-October; very few inns are open year-
round. Rates do not include 11% sales tax.

CAMPOBELLO ISLAND E0G 3H0   **Map 9**

Owen House   *Tel:* (506) 752–2977
Welshpool

The Owen House was built in 1829 by Admiral William Fitzwilliam Owen,
son of the British captain who was granted the island in 1769. The Owen

family ran Campobello Island as a private fiefdom for nearly a century. In the late 1800s a number of wealthy American families, including the Roosevelts, established summer homes here.

Rooms are eclectically furnished with many nineteenth-century antiques, some contemporary pieces, and colorful wallpapers; all have water views. Rooms on the second floor have private baths, while those on the third have shared baths, but better views. Longtime owner Joyce Morrell notes that the inn is "especially popular with artists, writers, and bird- and whale-watchers. People talk to each other and relax during long conversations around the fireplace. We have no streetlights, no sidewalks; our night life consists of late-night walks on the moonlit beach." Owen House is close to the 34-room Roosevelt Cottage and the International Park; the Deer Island ferry is within walking distance.

"Owen House is quiet and peaceful, with a glorious view and spacious grounds. The proprietor is a charming, caring person, very proud of her delightful house. She keeps it in immaculate condition." *(Margaret Guar)* "Old mansion, comfortable accommodations, large rooms. Extraordinary location on Passamaquoddy Bay." *(Helen & Kent Coes)*

"A feeling of gentle beauty pervades; there's pride in being part of a world that is still clean, fragrant, quiet, unhurried. A fire glows in the fireplace every evening; guests start to read but a lively conversation soon ensues. The owner and many guests are artists, and a portion of the inn is a gallery filled with excellent work. The floors may creak, the water needs to be conserved, but it all fits together with the handmade quilts and distant fog horns." *(Carol & George Schoenhard)*

Open May through early Oct.
Rooms 1 suite, 7 doubles, 1 single—5 with private bath, 4 with maximum of 6 people sharing bath.
Facilities Dining room; living room; TV room; library with fireplaces; sun-room; porches. 10 acres with beach, woods. Golf, fishing, whale-watching nearby.
Location SE NB, at U.S. border. 150 m N of Bangor, ME. Take bridge from Lubec, ME. In Campobello, follow Rte. 1 waterside. Stay left, then turn left at flashing light. West side of island, overlooking Passamaquoddy Bay.
Restrictions Smoking in sun-room only.
Credit cards Visa.
Rates B&B, $65–75 suite, $50–60 double, $45 single. Extra person in room, $5–15.
Extras One ground-floor room wheelchair accessible.

GRAND MANAN ISLAND   Map 9

Six miles off the coast of far northeastern Maine in the Bay of Fundy, Grand Manan is about 5 miles wide and 15 miles long. Settled in the late 1700s, it was once the world's largest producer of smoked herring; you can still buy plenty today, along with dulse—dried seaweed.

The east side of the island offers protected harbors and small fishing villages; the west is mainly rocky cliffs facing the Bay of Fundy. Hiking trails crisscross the interior. With 240 species in residence, Grand Manan is ideal for year-round bird-watching, although June and July are nesting season for puffins, razorbills, and terns; James Audubon did many of his sketches here. August and September are whale-watching season; wildflowers are beautiful all season.

The island is about 50 miles southwest of St. John, and a 2-hour ferry ride from Blacks Harbour (near St. George) to North Head on the northeast side of the island. (Take something against seasickness if you're susceptible; the trip can be bumpy if the ship is running against the area's famous tides.) Call (800) 561–0123 for ferry information.

Also recommended: Compass Rose is a simple but cheery little inn right on the harbor with ten shared bathrooms, reasonable rates, and delicious seafood dinners (Bowden & L'Aventure; 506–662–8570). "Cecilia Bowden was very pleasant and full of good ideas on touring the island. Our small room overlooked the harbor, and appeared fresh and pretty in whites and blues." *(Mrs. James Todd)*

Shorecrest Lodge *Tel:* (506) 662–3216
North Head E0G 2M0

New owners Cindy and Andy Normandeau welcome all visitors, but feel that their inn is the center for nature lovers on Grand Manan. "We are able to give up-to-date information on what can be found and where, advise on the best locales for birding and photography, arrange boat tours, and set people out on the most scenic hiking trails."

"A white clapboard with green trim and a long veranda stretching across the front and along one side. Shorecrest is surrounded by lush vegetation—lilacs, mock orange, and fields of lupines of every hue. I had a charming double-bedded room overlooking the beach and the harbor of North Head. Like most of the other rooms, it was ten steps away from an old-fashioned country-size bathroom outfitted with thick towels, a mammoth tub, and lots of hot water." *(Ann Sinclair)*

"The Shorecrest sits on a hill overlooking the Bay of Fundy and North Head harbor. It is a two-story renovated old farmhouse, with a couple of units especially for families with children. There is a large lounge with fireplace and TV plus a great selection of literature on birds, plants, and wildlife. The service is friendly and unassuming, making you feel right at home." *(Mrs. E. Nicolaidis)*

"Service, cleanliness, nourishing home-cooked food, plumbing, lighting, parking, homey ambience—all are tops. The lodge is located by a fairly busy road, yet is still relatively quiet." *(Beryl Thompson)* More comments, please.

Open May 15 through Oct. 15.
Rooms 2 suites, 13 doubles, 2 singles—8 with full private bath, 9 with maximum of 3 people sharing bath. All with desk. 3 rooms in annex.
Facilities Dining room; lounge with fireplace, TV, natural history library; game room with pool table, dart board; meeting/lecture room. 2½ acres with veranda, garden. Overlooking ocean for whale watching. Hiking, nature, and bird sanctuary tours nearby.
Location From ferry wharf, turn left on main road and proceed a few hundred yards.
Credit cards MC, Visa.
Rates B&B, $100 suite, $55 double, $45 single. Prix fixe dinner, $15.
Extras Some French spoken. Cribs available. Ferry pickups.

SACKVILLE E01 3C0   Map 9

Marshlands Inn   *Tel:* (506) 536–0170
73 Bridge Street, Box 1440

A gracious Victorian inn dating back to the 1850s, the Marshlands has been owned by Mary and John Blakely since 1984.

"Relaxing and charming. All the rooms are different and all are furnished with antiques (the genuine kind, not just old furniture). We looked in as many rooms as possible and all were pretty; several have private baths of the old-fashioned, huge variety. This is a full-service inn with a very big, very attractive dining room offering an extensive selection—nice for those of us who don't like the bother of looking for restaurants, particularly in a place like Sackville. The food is above average country fare, with everything homemade, including breads and jams. You can get delicious oatmeal porridge and stewed foxberries for breakfast.

"The owners are very gracious and take a good deal of pride in the fact that Queen Elizabeth stayed there (or at least 'freshened up' there) in 1984. Sackville is a pretty little town that centers around Mount Allison University; you see many students and faculty in the dining room. The exterior of the building and the grounds were impeccably kept, even in February." *(Judith Brannon)*

Open Early Feb. through Nov.
Rooms 1 suite, 22 doubles, 2 singles—15 with private bath and/or shower, 10 with maximum of 4 sharing bath. All with telephone, radio, desk. 3 with air-conditioning. 9 rooms in main inn, 4 in Hanson House, 12 in Stone Haven.
Facilities Restaurant, living room with fireplace, library. 7½ acres. Golf, bird sanctuary nearby.
Location SE NB. 35 m SE of Moncton. Near center of town.
Credit cards Amex, Enroute, MC, Visa.
Rates Room only, $50–65 double, $45–60 single. Extra person in room, $10. Tipping encouraged. Alc breakfast, $2–7; alc dinner, $30–35.
Extras Small pets permitted with prior approval. French spoken. Cribs, babysitting available.

ST. ANDREWS E0G 2X0   Map 9

A resort town with a New England atmosphere, St. Andrews was founded in 1783 by English Loyalists. Many buildings from this period have been preserved. Those with more contemporary interests will enjoy the Huntsman Marine Aquarium, explaining the marine life of the Bay of Fundy. Golf, tennis, sailing, hiking, swimming, bicycling, salt-water fishing, and whale-watching cruises are all recreational favorites; a supply of quaint boutiques will keep shoppers happy.

St. Andrews is located in southeast New Brunswick at the tip of a small peninsula pointing into Passamaquoddy Bay. It's 50 miles southwest of St. John, 75 miles south of Fredericton, and 100 miles north of Bangor, ME.

Rossmount Inn   *Tel:* (506) 529–3351
Route 127, RR 2

Robert and Lynda Estes, owners of the Rossmount since 1985, have decorated their inn with many unusual antiques, including a piano originally built for Kaiser Wilhelm and a coronation chair used by the King of Belgium at Queen Elizabeth's coronation. Lynda is the chef, and prepares meals with a French flair.

"The Rossmount Inn, built in 1783, is a three-story manor house converted to a sixteen-room inn, situated on an 87-acre estate at the foot of Chamcook Mountain, the highest point in the Passamaquoddy Bay area. Each of the rooms is furnished with different antiques, and the dining room, with its fine old fireplace and an alcove of three stained glass windows taken from an eighteenth-century English chapel, is decorated in Victorian style. Fresh fish selections from Passamaquoddy Bay head the menu, and each table features a different place setting of china. The innkeepers, Robert and Lynda Estes, make every effort to see that you are comfortable. The owners are Anglophiles, and museum-quality antiques accent the lobby." *(Vicki Turner)*

"The bedrooms are airy, comfortable, and spotless, with modern baths. The dining is exceptionally attractive with large windows looking out at the bay or at the lawns and pool. Our food was well-above average and was very nicely presented and served." *(Judith Brannen)*

"Elegant entry hall, wonderful woodwork and antiques, large pleasant guest room with king-sized bed, good breakfast, accommodating hosts." *(Mrs. James Todd)*

Open May 1 to Oct. 15.
Rooms 16 doubles, all with private bath and/or shower, desk, fan.
Facilities Dining room with fireplace, living room with piano, lounge with TV, bar, porch. 87 acres with swimming pool, nature preserve, hiking trails, heated swimming pool. Beaches, fishing, whale watching, aquarium, golf nearby.
Location 3 m NE of town on Rte. 127.
Restrictions Smoking in designated areas only. No children under 12.
Credit cards MC, Visa.
Rates Room only, $70–90 double, $60–80 single. Extra person in room, $10. Reduced rates for families. Weekly rates. Alc breakfast, $5–10. Prix fixe dinner, $17–25.
Extras Cribs, babysitting available.

Northwest Territories

Some folks like to get away from it all, and others *really* like to get away from it all. A visit to the Northwest Territories will suit the latter group. Imagine an area equivalent in size to India, with a population of only 50,000! Over half the area of the Northwest Territories is above the Arctic Circle, so it's not surprising that the region enjoys over 20 hours of sunlight daily during June. The Northwest Territories are home to the Dene, Inuit, and Metis peoples as well as more recent arrivals from the south.

There are no room or sales taxes in the Northwest Territories (aaah!).
All rates are quoted in Canadian dollars.

RESOLUTE BAY X0A 0V0   Map 16

High Arctic International Tourist Home   *Tel:* (819) 252–3875
Box 200

Owners Terry and Bezal Jesudason welcome those visiting Resolute but are primarily involved in organizing a variety of snowmobile/sledge expeditions in the High Arctic. They write: "We can show visitors some of the interesting cultural and historical sites of this Eskimo village. It's a scenic snow-covered area for almost 10 months of the year, but during the short Arctic summer, flowers bloom and birds come back to breed. It is possible to experience some of the old Eskimo culture and live in the modern world too. The best months to visit are in May, when there are 24 hours of sunshine and beautiful ice and snow formations, or in July, when the snow is gone and the Arctic summer is at its height. If guests want to try northern specialties, we can prepare local foods such as caribou, musk-ox, Arctic char, or seal. We get salad makings and fruit from Yellowknife so we offer a pretty balanced diet. "

"Try to imagine comfort and convenience in the bleak, awesome, and austere setting of the Canadian High Arctic, where summer as we know it never comes and where there are only a few miles of roads in a tiny Inuit (Eskimo) village. There are two flights from Montreal and two from Edmonton every week. The nearest highway system is 1,000 miles away.

"This place is the best there is between here and the North Pole. The home is spotlessly clean, and there is the ultimate Arctic luxury of flush toilets and hot showers. It is comfortably furnished and even has satellite TV and a VCR for those interested. There is a fine library of Arctic lore and a paperback collection for escape reading. The living and dining area are spacious and light, and the bedrooms, while simply furnished, are very comfortable and afford privacy and coziness.

"The bottom line in this austere and trying environment, aside from companionship, is good food. Both are here in abundance. Considering that all food is flown in by jet from Yellowknife, 1,000 miles away, the quantities of fresh fruits and vegetables, homemade baked goodies, fresh meats, and fresh milk are remarkable. Breakfasts are as small or as hearty as requested, lunches are simple but plentiful, and dinners are often gourmet if not haute cuisine. All food is prepared with care and imagination.

"Terry and Bezal Jesudason make people feel welcome and at home, and have a knowledge and love of the environment that they successfully impart to those who stay with them. Everyone has the run of the house, but somehow everyone's privacy is respected." *(Arthur & Victoria Spang)*

Open Feb. 15–Dec. 15.
Rooms 5 doubles share 2 baths. All with desk.
Facilities Living room with TV/VCR, library of Arctic books and videos; dining room; common room with desk. ¼ m from Northwest Passage.
Location 1000 m N of Yellowknife and Frobisher Bay, NWT. 4 m from Resolute Bay airport.
Restrictions No smoking in guest rooms.
Credit cards None accepted.

Rates Full board, $90 per person. 5- to 11-day Arctic expeditions to Resolute Bay, Northern Ellesmere Island, Beechey Island, and the Magnetic North Pole.
Extras Free airport pickups. Eskimo, German, minimal French spoken.

Nova Scotia

Nova Scotia is on Atlantic Standard Time; don't forget to set your watches forward 1 hour when crossing the border. The season generally runs from about mid-May to mid-October; very few inns are open year-round.

Dining suggestions would also be in order: "We found the food in Nova Scotia to be generally uninspired. It's worth some checking around to find the few decent restaurants."

Reader tip: "Nova Scotia is bigger than I realized. From Yarmouth, where the ferry lands, to Baddeck is about 450 miles; give yourself plenty of time if you want to relax and enjoy the beautiful scenery and winding coastal roads."

All rates quoted in Canadian dollars, and do not include 10% sales tax.

DIGBY B0V 1AO   **Map 9**

Pines Resort Hotel   *Tel:* (902) 245–2511
Shore Road, P.O. Box 70   (800) 341–6096

Whenever you see a truly grand resort in Canada, odds are good that it was built in the late 1920s by the Canadian Pacific Railway. The Pines, an imposing four-story Norman chateau, certainly maintains that tradition. Set high on a wooded hillside, and surrounded by acres of lawns and woods, the hotel overlooks the Annapolis Basin and the town of Digby. The provincial government bought the hotel from the CPR in 1965, and by all accounts has done a good job of maintaining standards. Old-fashioned charm has been preserved with the tradition of afternoon tea on the veranda and a dress code at dinner. Rooms are well-kept, the guest room furnishings are standard hotel issue.

"Our family had a homey cabin, very clean and comfortable, with a good bathroom and firm beds. A trail led through the woods to the pool and we had a view past the highway to the ocean. We enjoyed the many activities, from croquet on the lawn to the swimming and tennis, and our kids loved the chance to explore on their own. The all-you-can-eat buffet breakfasts were a great hit, but the slow service at dinner was torture for our active, hungry children. We tried a couple places in town, but were disappointed with the quality." *(PMN)*

Open Late May to mid-Oct.
Rooms 90 doubles, 30 multi-bedroom cottages—all with private bath, telephone, radio, TV, desk. Fan on request. Cottages with living room, fireplace.
Facilities Dining room, bar/lounge, library, living room, meeting rooms, 300 acres with 18-hole golf course, tennis, heated pool, shuffle board, croquet, hiking trails, inland and deep-sea fishing, boating.
Location 110 m E of Halifax. From Highway 101 take Exit 26; follow signs to St. John NB ferry terminal on Shore Rd.

Restrictions Non-smoking rooms and dining room areas.
Credit cards Amex, CB, DC, Enroute, MC, Visa.
Rates Room only, $151–217 suite, $101–126 double, $88–113 single. Extra person in room $18–30. MAP, $229–295 suite, $179–204 double, $127–152 single. Extra person in room $57–69. Children under 3 free. Children 4–12 half price in parents' room. Full breakfast $8. Alc lunch $13, alc dinner $34. Golf, honeymoon packages.
Extras Airport/station pickups. Handicap equipped. French spoken. Cribs, babysitting, play equipment, games available.

MAHONE BAY B0J 2E0   Map 9

Sou'wester Inn   *Tel:* (902) 624–9296
788 Main Street (Route 3), Box 146

The Sou'wester is a turn-of-the-century Victorian, built by one of Nova Scotia's many yacht builders. Innkeepers Mabel and Ron Redden have owned the Sou'wester for many years, and have furnished it comfortably with Victorian and more recent pieces. The Reddens also make Victorian and castle dollhouses for collectors of fine miniatures. Mahone Bay is known for its craft and antique shops and art galleries.

"When we arrived Ron came out to park our car and assist my mother and me with our bags. This beautiful old home has a peacefulness and quiet charm, and the owners share those qualities. The 'creature comforts' are excellent—good beds, everything beautifully clean, but always a feeling of being in an older, more relaxed time period. The Reddens' evening tea (included in the rates) surprised us—it wasn't just a pot of coffee or tea set out for guests' convenience; we all sat around in the living room, got to know each other, and felt relaxed, comfortable, and at home. During tea, the Reddens told us about nearby Lunenberg and its Fishermen's Museum, which turned out to be one of the highlights of our trip." *(Louise D. Smith)*

Open May through Oct.
Rooms 4 doubles—1 with private shower, 3 rooms sharing 1½ baths.
Facilities Dining room; living room; den with library, TV; verandas. 1 acre with picnic table, fish pond, bicycles. On water; canoe, dory available. Charter fishing, sailing, 7 m.
Location SE Nova Scotia. 60 m SW of Halifax. ¾ m to town; on Rte. 3 toward Lunenberg.
Restrictions Smoking in living room only.
Credit cards MC, Visa.
Rates B&B, $43–48 double, $33–38 single. Extra person in room, $9. No tipping. Children under 5 free in parents' room. Honeymoon packages.
Extras Small pets accommodated. Bus stops in front of inn.

PORT DUFFERIN B0J 2RO   Map 9

Marquis of Dufferin Inn   *Tel:* (902) 654–2696
Highway 7, Marine Drive, RR 1   In NS: (800) 565–7105

The Marquis of Dufferin, now the home and restaurant of Michael and Eve Concannon, combines the comfort of an eight-unit motel with the historic feel of an inn built in 1859. Both the guest rooms and the dining room overlook Balcom Bay, and seafood is always featured on the menu. A recent dinner included smoked salmon, poached halibut with fresh vegetables, and a sherry trifle with real whipped cream for dessert.

"The inn is owned by a very friendly English couple. They're always around during dinner to pour the coffee and chat. The food was very good and the motel units most comfortable." *(Polly Bryan)*

Open Late May to mid-Oct.
Rooms 8 doubles—all with full private bath, radio, TV, balconies.
Facilities Dining room, lounge, gift shop, deck. 4½ acres with lawn games, boating, fishing, dock. Hiking trails, beaches nearby.
Location 85 m E of Halifax. Just off Highway 7. On oceanfront.
Restrictions Smoking in lounge, and guest bedrooms only. "Not suitable for small children."
Credit cards MC, Visa.
Rates B&B, $58–65 double, $55–58 single. Extra person in room $10. MAP, available on request. Children under 2 free. Senior discounts. Alc dinner $30.

SMITH'S COVE B0X 1S0   Map 9

Information please: The Harbourview Inn (P.O. Box 35; 902–245–5686) offers nine comfortable guest rooms with private bath, a swimming pool and tennis court, play equipment for the kids, a family restaurant specializing in seafood, and very reasonable rates. All we need is your report!

Mt. Gap Resort   *Tel:* (902) 245-2277
P.O. Box 40, Route 1

The Mt. Gap Resort makes an ideal family base in Nova Scotia. *Linda Phillipps* reports that its motel-style rooms and cottages are "comfortable and clean, and the atmosphere is friendly, relaxed, and casual. The grounds are nicely landscaped, and a giant-size outdoor chess set was a big hit with our kids, as were the bingo games and evening bonfire."

Open June 1 to Oct. 10.
Rooms 8 cottages, 5 multi-unit lodges, 88 motel units—all with full private bath, TV. Some with kitchen, veranda.
Facilities Restaurant, bar/lounge with entertainment, lobby, sitting room. 45 acres with heated swimming pool, tennis court, outdoor chess set, volleyball, playground, gift shop, flower gardens, bicycles, boating, nightly bonfires. Golf nearby.
Location 4 m E of Digby. Exit 25, Hwy. 101.
Credit cards Amex, DC, MC, Visa.
Rates Room only, $80–125 suites & cottages, $70–75 double, $55–60 single. Extra adult in room, $10; no charge for children under 16 in parents' room. Packages available.

Ontario

Ontario offers much to travelers—the cosmopolitan city of Toronto; the country's capital in Ottawa; and, of course, Niagara Falls. Major festivals include the Shakespeare Festival in Stratford, and the Shaw Festival at Niagara-on-the-Lake. Several provincial parks offer outstanding facilities for outdoor recreation.

Information please: Recommendations for Stratford would be especially welcomed. Some possibilities include the **Hazen House**, a well furnished B&B (129 Brunswick Street N5A 3L9; 519–271–5644); the **Stone Maiden House**, decorated primarily with Victorian furnishings (123 Church Street, N5A 2R3; 519–271–7129); and, about 20 minutes away, the **Westover Inn**, a country inn and restaurant with spacious grounds and a swimming pool (300 Thomas Street, Box 280, St. Marys N0M 2V0; 519–284–2977).

Rates do not include 5% provincial sales tax on room, 7% on meals. *All rates quoted in Canadian dollars.*

ALGONQUIN PARK POA 1K0   Map 9

Information please: Also in Algonquin Park is **Arowhon Pines**, a group of rustic but comfortable cabins and lodges, set on a private lake with a full complement of water sports and miles of hiking trails; it's also known for fine cuisine (Huntsville P.O., Huntsville P0A 1K0; 705–633–5661 or 416–483–4393).

Killarney Lodge   *Tel:* (705) 633–5551
Route 60

Algonquin is Ontario's oldest provincial park, founded in 1893. Killarney Lodge, built in 1935, allows one to combine modern comfort with wilderness exploration.

"Beautifully situated on a peninsula jutting into the Lake of Two Rivers. The lodge is located on the only road through the southern section of Algonquin Provincial Park, a wildlife sanctuary with beautiful rugged scenery and a real sense of wilderness. It is best explored by canoe and on foot, and includes picnic grounds and nature trails.

"The main building contains the reception and dining room. Accommodation is in well-built, comfortable log cabins dispersed under trees along the lakeside. The food was among the best we have found anywhere— fresh vegetables and homemade dishes, with great care and attention to detail. Breakfast included delicious pancakes and maple syrup, jams and marmalade, and homemade rolls. At dinner we were delighted with the local specialties and a variety of fruit pies." *(Harry Robinson)*

"Each cabin is from Algonquin's native white pine, decorated in rustic chic decor. Each has a view of the lake and its own canoe. The central lodge has a classic Canadian atmosphere including the requisite stone fireplace. The food is robust and satisfying. The owners, Linda and Eric Miglin, circulate throughout the dining area chatting with each table in their friendly and hospitable manner. Housekeeping is prompt, efficient, and friendly. One of the lodge's best features is the landscaping, with hundreds of annuals planted around the brightly painted cabins. Killarney provides civilized accommodations in a Canadian wilderness with full access to the park's activities and scenery." *(Barry Crouse & Kelli Carroll)* "Immaculate accommodation, firm beds, good food. But best of all is the magnificent scenery." *(Frank Laslow)*

"Immaculate housekeeping, modern plumbing, and more than adequate lighting. The lodge is located on a spit of land jutting into the Lake of Two Rivers. Each cabin comes with its own canoe. There's a nice sandy beach with deck chairs and tables. There are nature trails everywhere and we spotted moose, loons, herons, beavers, and otters." *(Ann & Terry Brunstrom)*

Open Mid-May through mid-Oct.
Rooms 26 1- and 2-bedroom cabins, all with private bath and/or shower, electric heat, deck, private canoe.
Facilities Restaurant, reception area. 12 acres, lake with sandy swimming beach. Hiking, canoeing, fishing, shuffleboard, play equipment, nature talks, rental boats.
Location SE ONT, on Rte. 60. 48 m East of Huntsville, 188 m N of Toronto. Lodge at 22-mile post, about midway between east and west gates of park.
Restrictions No smoking or alcohol in dining room.
Credit cards MC, Visa.
Rates Full board, $170–290 double. Lower rate for third adult in cottage. Children's rates $18–53, depending on age. Picnic lunches on day's notice. Prix fixe lunch, $14; dinner, $30.
Extras Cribs available.

ALTON L0N 1AO   Map 9

The Millcroft Inn   *Tel:* (519) 941–8111
John Street, P.O. Box 89   (416) 791–4422

The Millcroft is set in an 1881 knitting mill, built of hand-cut stones. Its 22 guest rooms combine both antique and contemporary decor, and an additional 20 condo-style units are located in the Crofts, just across the bridge. The Millcroft is known for its fine food; you can eat in the timbered dining room or in the glass "pod" overlooking the old mill falls. *(WVE)* More comments, please.

Open All year.
Rooms 42 doubles, all with full private bath, telephone, radio, desk, air-conditioning. Some with fireplace, patio.
Facilities Restaurant, bar/lounge, sitting/TV rooms, game room, patio. 100 acres with heated swimming pool, 2 hot tubs, tennis court, hiking. Golf, downhill, cross-country skiing nearby.
Location 50 m NW of Toronto. Take Hwy. 10 N to Caledon. Go W on Hwy. 24 5 km. to Rte. 136. Turn right and go N 5 km. to Alton. Go left at stop sign. Go 1 km. to 2nd stop sign. Bear right on John St. to inn.
Credit cards Amex, DC, Enroute, MC, Visa.
Rates Room only, $138–150 double. 15% service. 2-night weekend/holiday minimum. Alc breakfast, $5–10; alc lunch, $25; alc dinner, $50. Weekend packages.

ANCASTER L9G 3K9   Map 9

Philip Shaver House   *Tel:* (416) 648–5225
1034 Highway 53 West, RR 1

The Shaver family was one of the first to settle in this area in the late 1700s; Philip Shaver, one of thirteen Shaver children, built this Georgian house in 1835. The house remained in the same family until 1982, when it was converted into an inn. Many of the original furnishings have survived, including a spinning wheel.

"George Moran and Marcy Gardner are wonderful innkeepers, happy to tell you the history of their inn. Located on the outskirts of Hamilton, Caster was one of Ontario's three earliest towns and was the stopping-off point for travelers going between Toronto and Niagara. There are two large and spotless guest rooms, each beautifully decorated with antiques. The restaurant gets rave reviews from all. Meals are carefully prepared—the pork with spinach-ricotta stuffing is unbelievable. The three-course breakfasts are George's department and he is careful to find out your favorites." *(Wendi Van Exan)*

Open All year. Closed Mon.
Rooms 2 doubles with private bath.
Facilities Restaurant, bar with fireplace, sun-room. Hiking trails, cross-country skiing.
Location S ONT. 10 min. SW of Hamilton, 1 hr. to either Toronto or Niagara-on-the-Lake. S. of Hwy. 2 & Hwy. 403, E of Duff's Corners on Hwy. 53 W and Shaver Rd.
Credit cards None accepted.
Rates B&B, $90–100 double. MAP, $135–145 double.

BAYFIELD N0M 1G0 Map 9

The Little Inn of Bayfield *Tel:* (519) 565–2611
Main Street, P.O. Box 100

An old coaching inn dating back to the 1830s, this once little inn is now actually a small hotel, where antique furnishings and decor are combined with some very modern amenities and a reputation for excellent food.

"Bayfield lies on the shore of Lake Huron, about 1 hour, along good country roads, from Stratford. The village was built in the expectation of the railway, which went to Goderich instead, leaving a Victorian ghost town of large houses set on spacious, shady lots, beside a small estuary. This is a comfortable adaptation of an earlier tavern where good food is served and a cheerful and welcoming atmosphere prevails." *(Dugal Campbell)* "We had a lovely lunch here, and would definitely return for an overnight stay. Bayfield has some interesting shops with unusual items." *(Karen Hughes)*

Open All year.
Rooms 31 suites and doubles, all with full private bath. Some suites with whirlpool tub; fireplace in adjacent guest cottage.
Facilities Restaurant, meeting rooms, porches. Spa with sauna, whirlpool. Beach swimming, bicycling, golf, tennis, fishing, sailing, boating, hiking, cross-country skiing, snowshoeing nearby.
Location SW Ontario on Lake Huron. 50 m N of London, 135 NE of Detroit, 13 m S of Goderich. From Goderich, take Rte. 21 S to Bayfield.
Credit cards Amex, Enroute, MC, Visa.
Rates Room only, $150–170 suite, $90–115 double, $75 single. 2-night packages including breakfast, dinner—from $380 suite, $300 double. Alc lunch, $7–12; alc dinner, $12–18.

FERGUS   Map 9

Breadalbane Inn   *Tel:* (519) 843–4770
487 St. Andrew Street West

One of the finest examples of Scottish limestone architecture in this area,
the Breadalbane Inn was built in 1860 by the cofounder of Fergus, and
stayed in the Ferguson family for over sixty years. A picturesque little
town on the Grand River, Fergus is home to 200 similarly built stone
structures, including the Farmer's Market, where local produce and arts
and crafts are sold each weekend.

"Phil Cardinal and his wife escaped Toronto in 1975, bought this lovely
old Victorian home on the main street of Fergus, and made a B&B and
restaurant out of it. He is a jovial host and excellent cook (steaks, scallops,
ribs, and rack of lamb are specialties) and she does wonderful things with
breakfast. The rooms are large and clean, and if you share one of the many
baths (some with saunas), cozy bathrobes are provided. The dinner was
exceptional, and if weather permits you can eat or drink on the attached
patio in the delightful garden. Fergus and nearby Flora make for a great day
of exploring, with lots of shops and antiquing." *(Wendi Van Exan)*

Open All year. Restaurants closed Mon.
Rooms 8 doubles, 1 with private bath, 7 with a maximum of 4 people sharing a bath.
All with radio, air-conditioning; 4 with TV. 1 in annex with kitchenette.
Facilities Restaurant, living room, library, patio, sauna. Tennis, canoeing, fishing,
sailing, hiking nearby.
Location S ONT. Approx 65 m W of Toronto. 12 m N of Guelph on Hwy. 6. Turn
left at traffic light on St. Andrew St. to inn in center of town.
Credit cards MC, Visa.
Rates B&B, $65 suite, $55 double. Extra person in room $4. Tipping appreciated. Full
breakfast $3 extra. Alc lunch, $10; alc dinner, $25. Children's portions.
Extras French spoken. Cribs, babysitting, play equipment available.

JACKSON'S POINT LOE 1L0   Map 9

Briars Inn   *Tel:* (416) 722–3271
Hedge Road, Box 100   In Toronto: (416) 364–5937

This resort dates back to 1839, and has been owned by the Sibald family
for nearly a century. It's been taking summer visitors since the 1900s, and
became a full-scale year-round facility in 1977. A full program of activities
for both children and adults is offered and included in the rates, with the
exception of greens fees for golf.

"This family-run inn and resort is elegant, yet relaxed and informal. The
rooms are clean and the public rooms attractive. It's especially appealing
to families and older couples. The kitchen produces excellent meals using
local produce. Accommodations include modern motel units, summer cottages, and antique-furnished rooms in the main house. The owners take
an active interest in the needs and desires of their guests. The golf course

is excellent and is used for cross-country skiing in winter." *(Mr. & Mrs. V. Raymond)* More comments please.

Open All year.
Rooms 4 suites, 76 doubles, 11 cottages— all with full private bath, telephone, TV, air-conditioning. Some with radio, desk, fireplace, balcony, kitchenette.
Facilities Dining room, bar/lounge, living rooms with fireplaces, library, game room with billiards, exercise room, sauna, hot tub. 200 acres with children's program, indoor and outdoor swimming pools, lakeside beaches, canoeing, boating, windsurfing, sailing, tennis, shuffleboard, walking trails, fishing, 18-hole golf course, cross-country skiing, skating, tobogganing, snowshoeing.
Location Central ONT, 45 m N of Toronto. On Lake Simcoe, ½ m E of Jackson's Point. From Toronto, take Hwy. 48 and bear left into Sutton; go right on Dalton Rd. to Lake Dr. E at light. Go right on Lake, right again on Hedge to resort.
Restrictions No pipe or cigar smoking in dining room.
Credit cards MC, Visa.
Rates Rates per person. MAP, $125–141 suite, $124 double, $149–159 single. Full board, $131–141 suite, $119–129 double, $154–164 single. 15% service. Reduced rates for children. Weekend, weekly rates. Prix fixe lunch $14, prix fix dinner $30.
Extras Cribs, babysitting available. Wheelchair accessible. Station pickups. French, German spoken.

KINGSTON K7L 3G9   Map 9

The Hochelaga Inn
24 Sydenham Street South

Tel: (613) 549–5534
(800) 267–0525

The Hochelaga Inn was constructed as a private house in the 1880s by John McIntyre. After his death the Bank of Montreal used it as a residence for the bank's managers. It was eventually divided up into small apartments, until its 1984 restoration by "Someplace(s) Different," a company focusing on the renovation and restoration of historic properties. Rooms are decorated with period antiques and reproduction furnishings. Rates include a continental breakfast of fruit and juice, cereal, croissants, muffins, coffee, and tea. The managers are Carol and Guy Lefort. *(Douglas M. Slack, also DC, D. Brickman)*

Someplace(s) Different Ltd. also owns four other recently restored Ontario properties: The Glenerin Inn, Mississauga; the Idlewyld Inn, London (see below); and the Isaiah Tubbs Inn—a brick farmhouse built in 1820— and Merrill Inn—an 1870s gothic villa—in Picton. Call the toll-free number listed above for details.

Open All year.
Rooms 5 suites and 18 doubles, all with private bath and/or shower, telephone, radio, TV, desk, air-conditioning. 8 rooms in annex. Most with queen-size mattresses; many with fireplaces, ceiling fans.
Facilities Living room, breakfast room, guest kitchen, patio, conference room.
Location SE ONT, SE end of Lake Ontario. 200 m E of Toronto, 250 m S of Ottawa. Downtown, historic area.
Credit cards Amex, Enroute, MC, Visa.
Rates B&B, $99–129 suite, $89–119 double, $79–89 single, service charge included. Extra person in room, $10. No charge for children under 3. Senior discount in off season.
Extras Some French spoken. Crib, playpen available.

LONDON N6C 1K8 Map 9

Idelwyld Inn   *Tel:* (519) 433–2891
36 Grand Avenue   (800) 267–0525

A Victorian mansion built in 1878, the Idlewyld was restored by Some-place(s) Different Ltd. in 1985, and is managed by Dave and Nancy Jarrett. The downstairs features intricately carved woodwork and a massive stair-case, while the bedrooms combine modern comfort and period decor.

"Charming inn, decorated through an interior designer showcase, when different designers did each room according to their particular vision. Located in the heart of a lovely old residential district, just minutes from Highway 401. I've also heard very good reports from travelers who've visited other inns owned by Someplace(s) Different Ltd."*(Helen Nisbet)*

Open All year.
Rooms 1 suite, 24 doubles, all with full private bath, telephone, radio, TV, desk, air-conditioning. Some with whirlpool, fireplace.
Facilities Dining room with fireplace; living room with fireplace; breakfast room; whirlpool; sauna. Patio, garden.
Location SW ONT. 6 blocks from center. Take Exit 186 from Hwy. 401. Go N on Wellington 3 blocks; turn left at Grand to inn between Carfrae and Ridout sts.
Credit cards All major cards.
Rates B&B, $130 suite, $105 double, $80 single. Senior discount.
Extras Wheelchair accessible; elevator. Small pets permitted. Crib available. Member, Someplace(s) Different Ltd.

NEW HAMBURG N0B 2G0 Map 9

New Hamburg is a small town, set halfway between Kitchener and Strat-ford (12 miles each way) in southeastern Ontario. Many travelers combine a stay in New Hamburg with visits to the Shakespeare Festival in nearby Stratford. We'd like to ask for more feedback on the **Black Walnut Inn**, a pleasant place to stay or dine (230 Peel Street; 519–662–2245).

The Waterlot Inn   *Tel:* (519) 662–2020
17 Huron Street

Since The Waterlot opened in the fall of 1974, travelers have been detour-ing to enjoy an outstanding meal at this historic inn, built in 1846 and now owned by W. Gordon Elkeer. The restaurant specializes in French cuisine. Whenever possible, only fresh local produce is used, along with skim milk, yogurt, and whole-grain flours, to produce dishes that are both healthy and rich in taste. A recent dinner included an appetizer of tomatoes stuffed with mussels, followed by tenderloin of lamb baked in phyllo with fresh local goat cheese in Madeira wine sauce, and concluded with fresh fruit and champagne. The guest rooms, far less well known than the restaurant, are tucked upstairs under the eaves, allowing guests to sample The Waterlot's excellent list of Canadian wines untroubled by worries about driving home. *(Dugal Campbell)*

Open All year. Closed Christmas, Good Friday. Restaurant closed Mon.
Rooms 1 air-conditioned suite with private bath, 2 doubles sharing 1 bath. Both doubles with fan.
Facilities Restaurant, gift shop. 1 acre on river for boating, fishing. Tennis, golf, downhill skiing nearby.
Location In center. From Hwy. ⅞, turn onto Peel St., then go left at Huron.
Restrictions No smoking in guest rooms. No children.
Credit cards Amex, Enroute, MC, Visa.
Rates B&B, $75–100 suite, $60 double. Alc lunch, $12–15; alc dinner, $25–35; half-price meals for children under 10.
Extras Wheelchair accessible restaurant. German spoken.

NIAGARA-ON-THE-LAKE L0S 1J0   Map 9

Set on Lake Ontario, at the mouth of the Niagara River, Niagara-on-the-Lake, with its many restored nineteenth-century homes, is one of Ontario's prettiest towns. From May to September, its main attraction is the Shaw Festival, with plays presented at three local theaters. For a break from all that culture, the town is amply supplied with tennis courts, golf courses, and bicycle trails, plus cross-country skiing in winter.

Information please: Three places we'd like to hear more about are the **Prince of Wales Hotel**, a beautifully restored Victorian hotel dating back to 1865, with two modern wings bringing the room count to 104 (6 Picton Street; 416–468–3246); the **Kiely House Heritage Inn**, a gracious inn originally built as a private home in 1832 and expanded in 1900 to its present size, with twelve guest rooms (209 Queen Street, P.O. Box 1642; 416–468–4588); and the **Old Bank House**, built in 1817 as a financial institution and now dispensing filling Irish breakfasts and warm Irish hospitality instead of debit slips (10 Front Street, P.O. Box 1708; 416–468–7136).

Oban Inn   *Tel:* (416) 468–7811
160 Front Street, Box 94

Built in 1824 by Duncan Milloy, a lake captain from Oban, Scotland, the Oban Inn has been owned by the Burroughs family since 1963. The grounds have a lovely English feeling, with lots of flowers everywhere, and the rooms are decorated with traditional furnishings and flowered wallpapers. The menu is also an Anglophile's delight, with such traditional favorites as steak and kidney pie for lunch, or prime rib with Yorkshire pudding for dinner.

"Our first choice of accommodation here. Just off the hustle and bustle of the main street, towards the lake where it is peaceful and lovely. Most of the rooms are not large, but all are decorated beautifully. The hotel has a great piano bar. The dining room has the best food in town and overlooks the lake and golf course. They have a great front porch where you can have light lunches or drinks. " *(Wendi Van Exan)*

"We stayed in the Garden Room in the Oban House next door, and were

765

delighted with our accommodation and in every aspect of the inn. The food was outstanding, especially the poached salmon." *(Carol & Nick Mumford)*

Open All year.
Rooms 1 suite, 22 doubles, all with private bath and/or shower, radio, TV, desk, air-conditioning. 3 rooms in cottage.
Facilities Dining room with fireplace; lounge/bar with fireplace, weekend piano music; meeting room. 2 acres with gardens. Lake Ontario for fishing; boating; theater, golf, orchards, wineries nearby.
Location S ONT, on Lake Ontario. Center of town. 12 m N of Niagara Falls, Ontario, 75 m S of Toronto, 60 m N of Buffalo, NY. Take Niagara Pkwy. (Rte. 55) and exit at Gate St. in Niagara-on-the-Lake. Turn N on Gate and go N 2 blocks to inn on corner of Gate and Front sts.
Restrictions Smoking in public rooms only.
Credit cards Amex, MC, Visa.
Rates Room only, $115–150 suite, $95–115 double, $70 single. Extra person in room, $10. Off-season package rates. Alc lunch, $12; alc dinner, $35–43.
Extras Airport/station pickups. French, Portuguese, Italian spoken.

The Pillar and Post Inn

Tel: (416) 468–2123

King and John streets, P.O. Box 1011 In Toronto: (416) 361–1931

Built in the 1890s as a fruit canning factory, and converted into a basket factory in 1957, the building started a new life in 1970 as a restaurant and craft center. Shortly thereafter, The Pillar and Post expanded to add rooms for overnight visitors. Guest rooms are furnished in colonial-style hand-crafted pine with patchwork quilts; there is a shop featuring the work of over 200 Canadian artists and craftspeople. The continental menu offers such specialties as red snapper stuffed with spinach and topped with oyster sauce; beef tenderloin with wild mushrooms, cracked pepper, and white wine; or fettuccine with shrimp, prosciutto, and peppers; during the Shaw Festival, the prix fixe dinner is a very good value. *(NA)* More comments please.

Open All year.
Rooms 90 suites and doubles, all with private bath, telephone, radio, TV, desk, air-conditioning. Most with fireplace.
Facilities Dining room; living room; lounge/bar with fireplace, piano; meeting rooms; craft shop. Heated swimming pool, saunas, whirlpool, tandem bicycle rental. Golf, tennis, theater nearby.
Location S Ontario, on Lake Ontario. 4 blocks from town center. 75 m S of Toronto, 60 m N of Buffalo, NY. From Niagara Parkway (Rte. 55), exit at King St. and go S to inn at corner of King and John sts.
Credit cards Amex, MC, Visa.
Rates Room only, $180–190 suite, $125–130 double. Extra adult in room, $10; extra child, $5. Off-season packages. Alc breakfast, $3–12; alc lunch, $13; alc dinner, $43; prix fixe dinner, $25.
Extras One room equipped for disabled. Cribs, babysitting available. French spoken.

Victoria Cottage

Tel: (416) 468–2570

178 Victoria Street, Box 445

The Victoria Cottage is a two-story apartment adjoining the 150-year-old restored Victorian home of Angie and Hartley Strauss. It's decorated with Victorian antiques, Tiffany-style lamps, and period china, in a color scheme of rose, cream, and forest green. Angie Strauss is a very talented watercolorist, quite well known in Canada, and her studio is worth a visit. *(Flora Blumenthal)* More comments, please.

Open All year.
Rooms 1 carriage house with bed/sitting room, with twin beds and sofa bed, kitchen, full bath, radio, TV, desk, air-conditioning, fan.
Facilities Art studio, private courtyard and rose garden. 1 block from Lake Ontario for sailing, picnicking; theater, shopping, wineries, golf nearby.
Location SE ONT. Approx. 25 m N of Buffalo. In Old Town district, just off Queen St.
Restrictions No smoking. No children under 12.
Credit cards None accepted.
Rates Room only, $120. Extra person in room, $10. No tipping. Weekly rates.

OTTAWA   Map 9

A visit to Ottowa, the capital of Canada, should start with Parliament Hill, which offers a good view of this small and livable city with a population of only 300,000. Try and make it by 10 A.M. on a summer morning, to enjoy the Canadian version of the Changing of the Guard. If you're traveling with kids, another favorite is the nearby Royal Canadian Mint, to see money in the making. The city has a wonderful collection of museums to suit all interests, from the Museum of Science and Technology to the dramatic new National Gallery. The newest star in this galaxy is the Museum of Civilization, across the river in Hull, with outstanding galleries devoted to Canadian Indians and Inuits. Parks and recreational opportunities are plentiful; in warm weather, the city's miles of bicycle trails are a pleasure, and in winter, there's the Rideau Canal, which has been described as the world's longest skating rink. Call the Convention and Visitors Bureau for details; 613–237–5158 or 800–267–0450.

Cartier House Inn   *Tel:* (613) 236–4667
46 Cartier Street K2P 1J3

This turn-of-the-century brick Victorian mansion was built for Supreme Court Justice Thibodeau Rinfret. Although bordered by high-rise apartment buildings, the Cartier House was mercifully saved from the wrecker's ball, and was renovated in 1986 at cost of over $1 million. The eclectic but elegant decor combines handsome fabrics—both period florals and contemporary abstracts—with new brass fixtures and Victorian, Georgian, and other antiques. Rates include a breakfast of fresh fruit and juice, cereals, whole-grain breads, and other home-baked goodies, served in the dining room or brought to your room with the morning paper. Evening turndown service, with bedtime chocolates, is among the other amenities.

"We were welcomed with refreshing raspberry soda by the attentive innkeeper. Our room was beautiful, the breakfasts relaxed, and the staff accommodating. When we asked about cross-country skiing, the innkeeper provided information on several nearby areas, as well as restaurants and things to do. We had delightful discussions with him about poetry (his own and that of other Canadian poets), about Canadian culture and society, and about Ottawa." *(William Blauvelt & Lisa Barsky)*

Open All year.
Rooms 3 suites, 8 doubles, all with full private bath, telephone, radio, TV, desk, fan. Suites have Jacuzzis.
Facilities Large breakfast room, lounge with library, fireplace; veranda, off-street parking. Rideau Canal for walking, jogging, bicycling nearby. 12 m to Gatineau Hills for downhill and cross-country skiing.
Location NE Ont. Downtown. From Queensway (Hwy. 417), exit at Metcalfe St. and go N to Somerset St. West. Turn right on Somerset and go 2 blocks to inn at corner of Somerset and Cartier sts. Walking distance to Parliament Hill, Rideau Centre.
Restrictions No smoking. Some traffic noise in corner room might disturb light sleepers. Children discouraged.
Credit cards Amex, DC, MC, Visa.
Rates B&B, $119–129 suite, $99–119 double, $89–109 single. Extra person in room $10. 10% senior discount. Packages, corporate, weekly rates Nov.–April.
Extras French spoken.

McGee's Inn   *Tel:* (613) 237–6089
185 Daly Avenue K1N 6E8

Once home to many of Canada's prime ministers and leaders, the fine houses of Daly Avenue declined lamentably as the twentieth century proceeded. In 1984, when Anne Schutte decided to restore the dilapidated 1886 home of John McGee—Canada's first clerk of the Privy Council—as a B&B, she received an exceptionally quick approval from local authorities. A major political convention would soon be in full swing, and beds were in short supply. Within a matter of a few months, the house received a new roof, eight bathrooms, and innumerable coats of paper and wallpaper. Its exterior stone-trimmed brick was chemically cleaned to show out its fine Victorian detailing. Inside, Anne, working with her mother, Mary Unger, decorated in soft tones of ivory, rose, and taupe, with English antiques, beautiful flowered fabrics. Rates include a full breakfast, with blueberry pancakes with Canadian maple syrup among the favorites. *(MA)* More comments, please.

Open All year.
Rooms 2 suites, 12 doubles—10 with private shower and/or bath, 4 with maximum of 4 people sharing bath. All with telephone, radio, TV, desk, air-conditioning. Some with fireplace.
Facilities Breakfast room with fireplace, parlor with piano. Near Rideau Canal for boating, skating.
Location Downtown, Sandy Hill area. At corner of Daly and King Edward Sts. Walking distance to Rideau Centre, Congress Centre, Ottawa University. From the Queensway (417), exit at Nicholas Ave. Turn right onto Laurier Ave. E, then left on Nelson St.
Restrictions No smoking in common areas. No children under 5.
Credit cards MC, Visa.
Rates B&B, $98–108 suite, $58–88 double, $52–82 single. Extra person in room, $15. Tipping encouraged. 2-night holiday weekend minimum.
Extras French, Spanish spoken.

Gasthaus Switzerland *Tel:* (613) 237–0335
89 Daly Avenue K1N 6E6

In 1984, Josef and Svetlana Sauter, newly emigrated from Switzerland, arrived in Ottawa and converted this sturdy brick and stone building into a little piece of Switzerland. Each cheery guest room has a queen-size futon mattress, kept cozy with a duvet; the duvet covers and curtains are all a bright red and white plaid, handmade by Svetlana.

"The Sauters are a charming couple who like to meet people and are available to help with any problem. They serve an extraordinary Swiss breakfast, featuring Birchermuesli, made with homemade yogurt with fresh fruits and raw oats, followed by hard-boiled eggs, Swiss cheese, home-made bread, and jam. The rooms are ample in size, well equipped, perfectly heated and clean; hot water is always in good supply."*(Ursula Lehmkuhl)*

Open All year.
Rooms 23 doubles—6 with private shower and/or bath, 11 with maximum of 6 sharing bath. All with telephone, TV, desk, fan.
Facilities Breakfast room, laundry facilities, garden, off-street parking. Near Ottawa River for fishing, swimming. 15 min. to downhill, cross-country skiing.
Location Downtown. From Queensway (Hwy. 417), take Nicholas Exit, turn right on Laurier Ave.; go left on Cumberland to inn at corner of Daly & Cumberland. From Hwy. 16, take Bronson N, Laurier E until Cumberland, turn left.
Restrictions No smoking in guest rooms.
Credit cards MC, Visa.
Rates B&B, $44–62 double, $34–52 single. Extra person in room, $20 discount for weekly stays.
Extras Serbo-Croatian, German, Rumanian, Russian, French, Swiss-German spoken. Airport/station pickups; small fee.

PORT STANLEY N0L 2A0 **Map 9**

Kettle Creek Inn *Tel:* (519) 782–3388
Main Street

Squire Samuel Price built a sturdy two-story summer home for his family in 1849; in 1918 it was converted into an inn, and in 1983 the Kettle Creek Inn reopened, after extensive renovations, under the ownership of Gary and Jean Vedova. The guest rooms are highlighted by fluffy white duvets, and terry robes to wear en route to the shared baths. The inn's dining room has a good reputation; the fare has an Oriental slant, with such dinner entrées as Szechuan beef, pork Polynesian, and stir-fried chicken with pineapple, peppers, mushrooms, and onions.

In the early 1900s, Port Stanley was known as the "Coney Island of Canada," attracting thousands of summer visitors who arrived by rail and steamer; recent years have seen a revival of the town's appeal as a summer resort.

"Wonderful atmosphere in this refurbished inn located in an attractive Lake Erie fishing village. Several good fish restaurants, specializing in perch dinners, are nearby, along with a great beach and harbor. Excellent host-ess/owner, charming bar and residents' lounge. Beautiful gardens with gazebo and water garden." *(Helen Nisbet)*

"A delight escape from the urban hubbub. Rooms are small and spartan, yet surprisingly comfortable. Loved the large, elegant shared bath with sauna. Spent hours reading in library, garden, and gazebo. Good food! Owners and staff delightful." *(Jack Johnstone)*

Open All year.
Rooms 10 doubles with shared men's and women's bathrooms.
Facilities Dining room, pub, living room with fireplace, library, sauna, patio, gazebo. Fishing, sailing, swimming, bicycling, ice fishing and ice-skating, cross-country skiing nearby.
Location SW ONT. 30 min. S of London, 141 m SW of Toronto, 125 m NE of Detroit, MI.
Credit cards Amex, MC, Visa.
Rates B&B, $60–78 double, $50–58 single. No charge for children in parents' room. Senior discount midweek. Midweek, off-season MAP specials. Alc lunch, $5–10; alc dinner, $50.
Extras Crib, babysitting available. French, German spoken.

ST. JACOBS N0B 2N0   Map 9

Jakobstettel Guest House   *Tel:* (519) 664–2208
16 Isabella Street

The Jakobstettel Guest House is a handsome, ninety-year-old brick mansion, originally built for the owner of the village mill (which now houses crafts shops). It was converted to an inn in 1982, and is managed by Ella Brubacher. Rooms are attractively fitted out with reproduction furniture, although to some tastes, the rooms may seem overly "decorated" with matching everything.

"The Jakobstettel House is an ideal place to stay for rest and relaxation. The bedrooms are large—all differently furnished. Comfortable armchairs, large windows with quiet vistas help to make one feel at once at home and relaxed. The appointments and bathrooms are spotlessly clean. An informal continental breakfast of home-cooked muffins, fruit, and cheese is provided; you help yourself from the kitchen. St. Jacobs is a small Mennonite town with much farming and local crafts." *(Geoffrey Steel)*

"Quiet little village with nice shops, restaurants, churches. Staff is extremely accommodating and friendly." *(Robert Boian)*

"Great aromas come from the kitchen at breakfast and when late-night snacks are being prepared. We had the Blue Room and found it spacious and comfortable. The innkeepers were friendly and informative about local points of interest. Even on a rainy day the canal walk nearby is a good reason for a morning stroll." *(Janis Feron)*

Open All year.
Rooms 11 doubles, 1 single, all with private bath and/or shower, telephone, radio, desk, air-conditioning, fan.
Facilities Living room/lounge, library, meeting room, kitchen, deck, patio. Games, books, snacks. 5 acres with badminton, swimming pool, horseshoe pits, bicycles, rose garden, tennis court, hiking, cross-country skiing. Fishing nearby.
Location S ONT, Waterloo County. 75 m W of Toronto. From Hwy. 401, take Hwy. 8 W to Kitchener; take Conestoga Pkwy., follow Hwy. 86 N signs to St. Jacobs exit Regional Rd. 17. In St. Jacobs, turn right at mill and proceed to Isabella St.

Restrictions No children under 6.
Credit cards Amex, MC, Visa.
Rates B&B, $85–120 double, $60–105 single. Extra person in room, $10. No tipping. Lunches, dinners for groups of 12 or more. Prix fixe lunch, $9; prix fixe dinner, $17.
Extras Pennsylvania German spoken.

TORONTO   Map 9

With a population of 3 million, Toronto is Canada's largest city, offering visitors the advantages of a major metropolitan center with few of the usual accompanying urban problems. Set on Lake Ontario, less than 100 miles north of Buffalo, Toronto offers first-rate theaters, major league sports, and a variety of shops (especially at Eaton Centre) and ethnic restaurants. Top sightseeing attractions include the Art Gallery of Ontario, the Royal Ontario Museum, and the Ontario Science Center; when you're ready for some greenery, take the ferry to Toronto Island for strolling, swimming, and picnicking, along with a beautiful view of the city.

Also recommended: With 379 rooms, the **Four Seasons** is too big for this guide, but is recommended by many as tops in the luxury hotel category (21 Avenue Road M5R 2G1; 416–964–0411). Another possibility in the "grand luxe" class is the **King Edward Hotel** (416–863–9700 or 800–225–5843; 37 King Street East M5C 1E9), a 315-room historic landmark hotel, recently restored to its turn-of-the-century elegance. The public rooms boast inlaid marble floors, a columned rotunda, and elaborately carved ceilings, while the well-appointed guest rooms have been redone in traditional decor; reader reports have generally been most positive.

Information please: The **Hotel Victoria** is a comfortable 48-room hotel in the heart of Toronto's business and financial districts. Rates range from $90 to 110, and rooms are equipped with the expected amenities (56 Yonge Street M5E 1G5; 416–363–1666).

Weekend rates at most Toronto hotels offer substantial savings; be sure to request details when making reservations.

The Bradgate Arms
54 Foxbar Road (Avenue Road at St. Clair) M4V 2G6

Tel: (416) 968–1331
(800) 268–7171

The Bradgate was created by Herman Grad a number of years ago from several turn-of-the-century apartment buildings and three rambling old houses. The result is a luxury hotel containing a six-story covered atrium with trees, plants, and a fountain; a piano lounge; and 109 traditionally furnished guest rooms. The hotel's simple but elegantly appointed restaurant has been well reviewed and has an extremely good reputation.

"Clean room, exceptional service, good kitchen. I suggest Hilton, Hyatt, and Marriott send their management to The Bradgate to learn how it should be done." *(A.P. Pastonna)*

"This is a delightful, friendly, beautifully decorated hotel. Rooms are spacious; beds are large and comfortable. Plumbing is modern and the valet parking is free and efficient. The food is excellent; dinners are expensive but the food is gourmet French cuisine." *(Dr. & Mrs. Mordecai Treblow)*

"Our room was large, with a fireplace (electric log), comfortable king-size bed, beautiful mahogany furniture. The balcony overlooked a small park with beautiful flowers. There's a relaxing courtyard in the center of the hotel." *(John C. Newton)*

"Staying at The Bradgate puts one in walking distance of restaurants and Toronto's efficient public transportation system. The hotel evokes a European feeling with its small but bright lobby. Our room had a comfortable king-size bed, wet bar, and sitting area, and we enjoyed the hotel's many appointments and amenities. Breakfast was not included with the room, so we headed down the street to Fran's, a Toronto institution, where hearty Canadian breakfasts are served at reasonable prices." *(Carolyn & Bill Myles)*

Although all reports were very positive, two minor complaints expressed the need for an extra mirror and for better lights for reading in bed.

Open All year.
Rooms 5 suites, 104 doubles, all with full private bath, telephone, radio, TV, desk, wet bar/refrigerator. Some with fireplace, balcony.
Facilities Restaurant, library, whirlpool, bar, piano lounge, atrium, free valet parking.
Location Midtown Toronto, residential district of Forest Hill.
Restrictions Light sleepers should request rooms on the Foxbar Rd. side of the hotel, not on Avenue Rd. side.
Credit cards Amex, DC, Enroute, MC, Visa.
Rates Room only, $225–595 suite, $145–165 double, $135–145 single. Weekend rates, off-season packages. $15 for extra bed in room. Alc lunch, $15; alc dinner, $35–45.
Extras Wheelchair accessible; emergency bells; handrails. Cribs available. French, Arabic, Italian, Spanish spoken.

Windsor Arms Hotel
22 Saint Thomas Street M5S 2B9

Tel: (416) 979–2341

The Windsor is a small European-style luxury hotel, with an ivy-covered Tudor exterior and a variety of guest rooms individually decorated with European and Canadian antiques. The hotel is home to several small restaurants, each with a distinctive decor and cuisine.

Under the same ownership is the Millcroft Inn, a restored woolen mill, now a luxurious resort and conference center forty miles northwest of Toronto (see listing under Alton).

"The Windsor's rooms are larger than those of most modern hotels, have decent solid reproduction antique furniture, and sometimes the genuine article. Bathrooms tend to be old-fashioned in their fittings and lack a few niceties, like enough room to put toiletries, and adequate lighting for makeup. Service is discreet, friendly, and quick. There are three small restaurants in the basement, as well as the large, cheerful Gateway Café by the lobby, a coffee house. All Torontonians I spoke to agreed that this hotel was the most agreeable hotel in the city, much patronized by visiting literary celebrities." *(Hilary Rubinstein)*

"The lobby and sitting room are quite charming (afternoon tea is served), and certainly intimate. Another plus is that the hotel contains two of Toronto's best known restaurants—the Courtyard Café and Three Small Rooms. The former is a wonderful place for the voyeur at lunch—there are always people you know or feel you should know at a nearby table, all very well dressed and looking vaguely theatrical. The food and service are both exceptional." *(Judith Brannon)*

"We enjoyed the lively location—it was fun just to walk along the street and watch the people. The sidewalk cafés are open until one A.M., and there are an amazing number of people around on weekends—it's fun and safe. Everyone we met just raves about this hotel—its location, charm, and food." *(Robert Preston)* "Fully endorse existing entry; afternoon tea is excellent." *(Robert Crick)*

Other respondents pointed out a few areas for improvement here: "The rooms are well done but to us they felt 'old.' Our mattress was too soft and the hallways are dark." And, about one of the restaurants: "We only tried the most expensive of the trio of eating places downstairs, called The Restaurant, serving French cuisine. Sadly, we found it deplorably pretentious—the descriptions of the dishes were a parody of menu-speak; the prices were steep, far beyond the merits of the cooking; and the muzak was intrusive."

Open All year.
Rooms 11 suites, 70 doubles, all with private bath and/or shower, telephone, radio, TV, desk. Some suites with kitchens.
Facilities Restaurant, courtyard café, piano lounge.
Location Midtown, Bloor St. shopping district, near Yorkville area. 2 blocks to subway.
Credit cards Amex, CB, DC, Enroute, MC, Visa.
Rates Room only, $225–335 suite, $120–185 double. Weekend rates lower in winter. No charge for children in parents' room. Alc breakfast, $5–9; alc lunch, $17; alc dinner, $42.
Extras Member, Relais et Chateaux. Well-trained pets permitted. Wheelchair accessible. French, German, Italian, Spanish, Greek spoken. Cribs, babysitting available.

WIARTON N0H 2T0   **Map 9**

Glenbellart House   *Tel:* (519) 534–2422
285 Mary Street

The Bruce Peninsula was still very much a wilderness when James Patterson and his family arrived here in the 1860s—he was the first white male child to settle here, and his mother, a midwife, the only medically trained person in the area for years. Patterson grew up to be a prosperous pharmacist, and built Glenbellart House in 1886, complete with stained-glass windows, ceiling medallions, and hand-carved mantelpieces. The design motif throughout the house is Eastlake, the British interpretation of Oriental design very popular after the clipper ships opened up the trade routes with China and Japan.

From September through June, when the pace slows a bit, owners Sally and John Wright serve five-course (no choice) dinners; a recent meal included mushroom soup, cantaloupe with peach schnapps and fresh mint, chicken with brandy and apples, served with snow peas, acorn squash, and potatoes, and "Positively Sinful Chocolate" for dessert.

"We were on our way south from Mackinac and Sault Sainte Marie, and decided to take the Lake Huron ferry to the Bruce Peninsula, which sticks out into the lake like a giant thumb. The ferry ride is terrific—the ship is very large and you really understand that Huron is an inland sea when you see the size of the swells, and completely lose sight of shore.

"Wiarton was a convenient stopover, and Glenbellart House an ideal place to stay. It's a beautiful Victorian; the rooms are just delightful, although not all pieces are authentic antiques. We shared a bath, but it was very luxurious—complete with pine paneling and stained-glass windows. The breakfast was delicious and more than ample, with eggs any way you want, bacon, homemade bread, scones, and jam. We had a chance to walk into town the next morning, and took the time to explore some of the trails and caves that line the shore." *(Maria & Carl Schmidt)* More comments please.

Open Closed Dec. 24–Dec. 26. Restaurant closed July, Aug.
Rooms 4 doubles share 2 bathrooms.
Facilities Dining room, library, parlor, veranda. Beaches, swimming pool, fishing, cross-country skiing, ice fishing, snowmobiling nearby.
Location W ONT, Bruce Peninsula, between Lake Huron & Georgian Bay. 3 hrs. N of Toronto. In town. 1 block N of Wiarton Gates. Turn left on Mary St., go 1 block to inn.
Restrictions No children under 12.
Credit cards None accepted.
Rates B&B, $40 double. Extra person in room, $15. Prix fixe dinner, $25–30. 2-night weekend minimum. Getaway weekend package for two, $140 (includes 2 nights, 2 breakfasts, 1 dinner).
Extras Airport pickups, $5. Some French, German spoken.

Prince Edward Island

Prince Edward Island, or P.E.I. as it is usually called, is Canada's smallest and most densely populated province. The island is peaceful and agricultural (potatoes are a major crop), with hundreds of miles of sandy beaches to explore, excellent opportunities for inland and deep-sea fishing, golf courses with beautiful ocean views, and varied terrain for bicycling. Traditional island crafts have made a comeback in recent years, with many craftspersons working in pottery, wood carving, weaving, quilting, and knitting. The Charlottetown Festival offers original musical theater throughout the summer, and, of course, no one who's ever read *Anne of Green Gables* would miss a visit to the Green Gables House in Cavendish. More P.E.I. recommendations would be most welcome.

Rates do not include 10% provincial sales tax.

All rates quoted in Canadian dollars.

SUMMERSIDE C1N 2Z3   **Map 9**

Silver Fox Inn   *Tel:* (902) 436–4033
61 Granville Street

William Critchlow Harris, a well-known architect of the period, built the Silver Fox as a private residence in 1892. Innkeeper Julie Simmons chose the inn's new name to commemorate an interesting period in the island's history: In the 1880s two poor trappers began breeding foxes, hoping to cultivate the rare silver-black fox, which in nature occurs only once in a thousand litters. Their success generated an extraordinary, if short-lived, boom; in 1911 a single pelt sold for $20,000, and by 1913 there were 277 fox ranches on Prince Edward Island. Shortly thereafter, fox fur went out of fashion, regaining a portion of its earlier popularity only recently.

"Julie Simmons is a very pleasant, caring lady who makes her guests feel as if they are relatives or friends come to visit. The rooms are spotlessly clean, elegant, and very well decorated with a mixture of modern and antique furniture. The beds are antique, and comfortable too.

"The inn is located in a quiet residential area surrounded by older, well-kept homes. It is within walking distance of stores, restaurants, and the main part of town. In summer one can easily travel to beaches, tourist sites, plays, lobster suppers, etc." *(Marge & Bob Cochrane)*

"All the nice things said about Julie in last year's entry are true. We thoroughly enjoyed our visit, and Julie gave us a walking tour brochure which lead us to the old homes and buildings of Summerside." *(Mrs. James Todd)*

Open All year.
Rooms 6 doubles with private bath and/or shower, radio. 1 with fireplace, 2 with desk.
Facilities Living room with TV, fireplace; sun-room; balcony. ½ acre. 1 m to bay swimming; 8 m to ocean swimming; 3 m to cross-country skiing. Tennis nearby.
Location 36 m from Charlottetown. 3 blocks from downtown. From Borden Ferry, take Hwy. 1A W to Rte. 11 W to Summerside. Turn right onto Granville St. Go 3 blocks to inn.
Restrictions No children under 10.
Credit cards Amex, MC, Visa.
Rates B&B, $43–53 double, $38–48 single. Additional person in room, $5. Weekly rates.
Extras Station pickups.

Quebec

Quebec is an enormous province, stretching from Montreal in the south to the far northern reaches of Hudson Bay. French is the language of the province, although most people involved with the travel industry speak English as well. If you're willing to attempt a few phrases of high school French, your efforts are sure to be appreciated.

Most visitors to Quebec head for Montreal and Quebec City, places of considerable historic and cultural interest. The old walled city of Quebec gives the feeling of a town in France, yet is within driving distance of much of the northeastern United States. To get a feeling for the countryside, explore the Laurentian Mountains, about an hour's drive northwest of Montreal, or travel to the Eastern Townships, just north of Vermont. For those who really want to get away, we'd suggest traveling up either the north or south sides of the St. Lawrence River, where it widens to over 15 miles.

All rates are quoted in Canadian dollars, and do not include 10% sales tax.

MONTREAL   Map 9

Montreal is often called Canada's most cosmopolitan city. In the summer, the city moves outside—to outdoor cafés and parks. In winter, much of the action moves inside and underground, into the extended complex of shops, restaurants, and movie theaters found underneath major office buildings. Montrealers do emerge, properly booted and bundled, to enjoy skiing and skating on Mount Royal. Montreal is known for its many restaurants, most of them specializing (as you might expect) in French cuisine.

Information please: We've heard good things about the following, but would like to find out more from you: **Hôtel Shangrila** (3407 rue Peel H3A 1W7; 514–288–4141 or 800–361–7791), a sleek new 162-room hotel with Oriental touches in both decor and cuisine; **Hôtel de la Montagne** (1430 rue de la Montagne H3G 1Z5; 514–288–5656), a 130-room rococo-style hotel and restaurant; the **Citadel**, a 180-room "European-style" hotel (410 Sherbrooke Street West H3A 1B3; 514–844–8851 or 800–263–8967) with contemporary decor in soft pastels and an indoor rooftop swimming pool; the **Manoir le Moyne**, an all-suite hotel with a welcoming atmosphere, indoor swimming pool, terrace garden, and casual restaurant; its 262 units are well equipped with balconies, kitchens, and living/dining areas (2100 boulevard de Maisonneuve West H3H 1K6; 514–931–8861 or 800–361–7191); and finally the **Four Seasons**, known here as Les Quatre Saisons, a luxury hotel with the services and amenities one expects and usually gets from this quality chain (1050 Sherbrooke Street West H4A 1R6; 800–268–6282).

Be sure to ask for weekend rates and packages when making reservations at any Montreal hotel, for savings of 25–50%.

Château Versailles Hotel and Tower   *Tel:* (514) 933–3611
1659 Sherbrooke Street West H3H 1E3   U.S.: (800) 361–3664
                                                   Canada: (800) 361–7199

Andre and Marie Louise Villeneuve began fulfilling their dream of having their own hotel nearly thirty years ago. They started with the Château Versailles's first town house, built in 1911, and eventually expanded to four adjacent buildings. In the renovation process, they were able to keep much of the handsome interior wood- and plasterwork, and also maintained the original exterior appearance of the town houses. Rooms are individually furnished with traditional pieces, highlighted by a number of modern sculptures. Full or continental breakfast can be ordered in the dining room; the latter can be delivered to your room as well. In 1988, the Villeneuves took over a modern high-rise apartment building across the street, increasing their room total by 112. Rooms here are more modern, and are geared to business travelers with fax machines, secretarial staff and even free laptop computers.

"The Château Versailles is perfectly located on Sherbrooke Street, an address comparable to New York City's Madison Avenue. Old-fashioned, traditional service awaits the visitor. Boutiques, night life, and the subway are all close by; the Museum of Fine Arts is four blocks away." *(Joy Bloom)*

"This fashionably located European-style hotel has spacious, well-decorated rooms. A lovely alternative to other big-city hotels." *(Vicki Turner)*

"Perfect honeymoon setting. The staff was friendly, competent, and knowledgeable about the surrounding area and the city as a whole. Great location." *(Bob & Julie Gerchen)*

Another reader was less impressed: "My basement room was dingy and furnished with Fifties furniture, although the bed was very comfortable. I'd suggest booking a suite in the hotel's annex, a highrise across the street."

Open All year.
Rooms 22 suites, 160 doubles in four connecting town houses, all with full private bath, telephone, radio, TV, desk, air-conditioning.
Facilities Restaurant, breakfast room, lobby, library, meeting room. Room service. Garden with reflecting pool, sculpture. Free outdoor parking.
Location Downtown, Sherbrooke Ouest. 1-min. walk to Métro. From Champlain Bridge, take Hwy. 15 to Atwater exit. Take Atwater to Sherbrooke, turn right. Hotel on left.
Credit cards Amex, Enroute, MC, Visa.
Rates Room only, $180–212, $94–136 double, $86–124 single. Additional person in room, $8. No charge for children under 14 in parents' room. Winter weekend rates. Continental breakfast, $4.75; full, $6.25.
Extras French, Spanish, English spoken. Cribs available.

NORTH HATLEY J0B 2C0 Map 9

North Hatley is a quiet resort town in the Eastern Townships of southeastern Quebec, set at the north end of Lake Massawippi and surrounded by steep hills. The town's southern exposure and protected geography give it a climate considerably milder than that of surrounding towns. North Hatley was settled by United Empire Loyalists who left the U.S. after the Declaration of Independence in 1776; its development was further influenced by wealthy American southerners who refused to vacation in Yankee New England after the Civil War. They built many hotels and private mansions, a number of which have been renovated as inns today. The small town offers plenty of art galleries and craft and antique shops to explore, as well as Quebec's only English-speaking summer stock theater. Warm-weather activities include all water sports on the lake, plus golf, tennis, and hiking; winter brings cross-country and downhill skiing and ice-skating.

North Hatley is 90 miles east of Montreal, and about 25 miles north of the Vermont border. From Montreal, take Highway 10 east to Exit 121. Turn onto Route 55 in Magog and go south to Exit 29 in North Hatley. From Vermont, take I-91 to the border at Derby Line where I-91 becomes Route 55; follow directions above to North Hatley.

Also recommended: The **Auberge Hatley** (P.O. Box 330; 819–842–2451, 800–668–8106) is an old-fashioned country inn, combining antique-filled rooms done in flowered wallpapers, handmade traditional quilts, and braided rugs, with rather new-fashioned French and Quebeçois cooking emphasizing nouvelle cuisine. The atmosphere is quite formal, both in the dining room and in the inn. The **Cedar Gables B&B** (4080 Magog Road,

Box 355; 819–842–4120), a turn-of-the-century lakeside home, offers recently redecorated rooms highlighted by antique Oriental carpets. Of particular interest is the fly fishing right from the inn's own dock, and the quality beer—Don Fleischer, the owner, opened Quebec's first microbrewery in 1986.

Hovey Manor

Tel: (819) 842–2421

Hovey Road, P.O. Box 60

If you could afford to travel in the late 1800s you certainly didn't travel light. When Henry Atkinson of Atlanta summered in North Hatley, he always showed up with two private railway cars, ten horses, several carriages, and eighteen servants. At the turn of the century he built himself this impressive mansion, with broad verandas and white columns, inspired by George Washington's Mount Vernon.

Hovey Manor has been owned by Stephen Stafford since 1980, who has combined its appeal as a traditional country inn, furnished with antiques and quality reproductions, with all the facilities of a resort. Belgian chef Marc de Canck has earned the inn a top reputation for fine nouvelle cuisine using the freshest Quebec produce.

"Our room was beautifully furnished with antiques, the bath typical of the 'afterthought' facilities found in many old inns. The Staffords and their staff were gracious and helpful, the atmosphere casual and warm. Food is excellent, nouvelle in presentation, yet thankfully ample in quantity." *(MA)* More comments, please.

Open All year.
Rooms 27 doubles, 8 cabins—all with private bath, telephone, desk. Some with Jacuzzi, fireplace, ceiling fan, balcony.
Facilities Dining room with fireplace, solarium, chamber music on weekends; parlor/library with fireplace; 2 bars with fireplace; game room; ski/waxing room. 25 acres with formal gardens, 1000 ft. of waterfront with 2 beaches on Lake Massawippi, lighted clay tennis court, canoes, paddleboats, sailboards, rowboats. Cross-country skiing on property. 15 min. to downhill skiing at Mont Orford.
Location S QUE, 90 m SE of Montreal. 1 m from town. Take Hwy. 10 E from Montreal to Rte. 55 S. Go to Rte. 108 and turn E to North Hadley.
Restrictions Children discouraged.
Credit cards Amex, DC, MC, Visa.
Rates MAP, $160–280 double, $120–160 single, tax and service included. Extra person in room, $80. Children ½ price when sharing parents' room. 2- to 7-day package rates. Prix fixe lunch, $13; dinner, $31. Alc lunch, $12; dinner, $50.
Extras Crib, babysitting available by prior arrangement. French, English spoken.

QUEBEC CITY   Map 9

People go to Quebec for a taste of Europe, closer to home. The language and people are predominantly French, and the walled Upper Town is almost medieval in feeling. Many buildings dating back to the 18th century in both the upper and lower towns have been restored, and several are open to the public.

Rates in Quebec City are highest during the Winter Carnival in February; a minimum stay is frequently required during this period as well.

Also recommended: The **Château de Pierre** (17 Avenue Ste. Genevieve, G1R 4A8; 418–694–0429), an English colonial mansion, is now a small hotel eclectically decorated with Victorian antiques and colonial reproductions. Although no breakfast is served, Lily Couturier, the longtime owner, notes that many restaurants are nearby. The **Hôtel Cap Diamant** (39 Avenue de Ste. Genevieve, G1R 4B3; 418–694–0313), built in 1826, is a charming small hotel, furnished with many antiques and highlighted by the marble fireplaces in many rooms. Florence Guillot, owner since 1979, provides guests with a warm welcome to Quebec. Rooms have a view of the Parc Cavalier du Moulin and the rooftops of the old city. The **Au Manoir Ste. Genevieve** (13 avenue Ste. Genevieve, G1R 4A7; 418–694–1666) was built 150 years ago by a commander of the garrison of the Citadel for his family. It is located in the heart of Old Quebec, just behind the Château Frontenac, in front of the Jardin des Gouverneurs' Park, with a nice view of the St. Lawrence River.

Château de Lery
8 rue Laporte G1R 4M9

Tel: (418) 692–2692

The Château de Lery, built as a private house in the late 1800s, has a beautiful view of the Governor's Park and the St. Lawrence River, and is close to the Old City walls and the Citadel. Although no meals are served in the hotel, a number of good restaurants are close by.

"For a very reasonable price we had a clean and sunny double room with private bath at the back of the hotel. Other rooms have a lovely view of the park and water. The location, right behind the Château Frontenac and next to the Plains of Abraham, is very central. There are a number of other hotels in this area that looked equally nice." *(Deborah Gray, also Joyce Engelson)*

Open All year, except Dec. 25.
Rooms 1 suite, 17 doubles, 1 single—all with private bath and/or shower, TV, desk; 1 with kitchen.
Facilities Breakfast room. Public parking nearby.
Location Old City, near Château Frontenac. Take St-Louis from Old Walls at St. Louis Gate to Haldimand, turn right. Go 1 block to Laporte.
Credit cards Amex, MC, Visa.
Rates Room only, $85 suite, $55 double, single. Additional adult in room, $9. Continental breakfast, $3.
Extras French, English spoken.

Le Manoir D'Auteuil
49 rue D'Auteuil G1R 4C2

Tel: (418) 694–1173

This old manor house dates back to 1835, although it was extensively rebuilt after a fire in 1853. In 1933 the interior was completely redone in the Art Deco style, still seen in the swirling metal bands of the staircase, the Egyptian-style columns of the dining room, the smooth marble surface of the fireplace, and the repeating mahogany diamond patterns of the floors, door, and walls of the dining room. Georges Couturier, owner since

1982, reports that the hotel underwent major renovations in 1989 to improve and upgrade the rooms.

"Located just inside the Old City walls on a fairly quiet street. Our room on the top (fourth) floor was small but very cozy and clean, combining old-world charm and new plumbing. The hotel staff, including the college students who worked at the desk at night, were incredibly polite and helpful. In the front it overlooks the city park where the famous 'snow man' who hosts the winter carnival stands. To the back, it overlooks the rest of the Old City, with its jumble of buildings and crooked streets. Park your car and walk everywhere in the historic district. Within a few blocks you'll find the Citadel, Frontenac, rue du Trésor, ramparts, city hall, dozens of little shops, and many fantastic restaurants." *(Katherine Hutt)*

"We felt as though we were in Europe in our newly redecorated and immaculately clean room. The friendly staff even volunteered to carry our overstuffed bags up four flights of stairs. We loved being just inside the city walls, with a view of both horse drawn carriages and modern Quebec City." *(Kathleen Owen)*

Open All year.
Rooms 16 doubles, all with private bath and/or shower, telephone, TV, desk.
Facilities Living room with fireplace, parlor with fireplace, breakfast room. Public parking nearby.
Location Old City. At gate St. Louis d'Auteuil, make 1st left after gate.
Restrictions No smoking in some rooms. Traffic noises in 3 front rooms might disturb light sleepers. No children under 12.
Credit cards Amex, Enroute, MC, Visa.
Rates Room only (breakfast served Nov. to April), $55–115 double, $50–75 single. Extra person in room, $10. Continental breakfast, $4.
Extras 6 nonsmoking rooms. French, English, Spanish spoken.

SAINT-MARC-SUR-RICHELIEU J0L 2EO Map 9

Information please: Another possibility even closer to Montreal than the listing below is the **Hostellerie River Gauche**, also on the Richelieu River, just 20 minutes from the city. Although a modern structure, its 22 balconied rooms are decorated traditionally, with Victorian-style lamps. Its restaurant occupies a plant-filled solarium, and a swimming pool and two tennis courts round out the facilties (1810 Richelieu Boulevard, Beloeil J3G 4S4; 514–467–4650).

Hostellerie Les Trois Tilleuls
290 rue Richelieu

Tel: (514) 584–2231

Whether your visit to Montreal allows for just a brief sortie into the countryside, or a longer, more restorative visit, the consensus is that a trip down the Richelieu River valley is always in order. Though just one half-hour's drive from Montreal, this inn, owned by transplanted Frenchmen Michel Aubriot and Bernard Môme since 1974, is firmly planted in the countryside. Les Trois Tilleuls began life as a riverside farmhouse a century ago. Guests can sip aperitifs on the shaded patios, then move inside for classic French cuisine. A modern addition houses the luxurious guest rooms that are decorated in soft colors with hand-crafted Canadian furniture and original art by Canadian artists. *(MA)* More comments please.

Open All year.
Rooms 2 suites, 22 doubles—all with full private bath, telephone, radio, TV, desk, air-conditioning, balcony. Some with Jacuzzi tubs.
Facilities Dining room, bar/lounge, living room/library with TV. Heated swimming pool, 2 tennis courts, gazebo, putting green. Along river for swimming, boating, fishing.
Location 15 m E of Montreal on Highway 20.
Credit cards Amex, CB, DC, Enroute, MC, Visa.
Rates Room only, $200–375 suite, $85–145 double, $71–87 single. Extra person in room, $20. Full board, $315–493 suite, $210–283 double, $135–285 single. Reduced rates for children. Prix fixe lunch $15. Alc lunch $27, alc dinner $70.
Extras French, English, Dutch, German, Spanish, Danish, Hungarian, Slavic languages spoken. Cribs, babysitting available. Member, Relais & Chateaux.

We Want to Hear from You!

As you know, this book is only effective with your help. We really need to know about your experiences and discoveries.

If you stayed at an inn or hotel listed here, we want to know how it was. Did it live up to our description? Exceed it? Was it what you expected? Did you like it? Were you disappointed? Delighted?

Have you discovered new establishments that we should add to the next edition?

Tear out one of the report forms at the back of this book (or use your own stationery if you prefer) and write today. Even if you write only "Fully endorse existing entry" you will have been most helpful.

Thank You!

Appendix

STATE AND PROVINCIAL TOURIST OFFICES

Listed here are the addresses and telephone numbers for the tourist offices of all the United States and the Canadian Provinces. When you write or call one of these offices, be sure to request a map of the state and a calendar of events. If you will be visiting a particular city or region, or if you have any special interests, be sure to specify this as well.

Alabama Bureau of Tourism and Travel
532 South Perry Street
Montgomery, Alabama 36104
(205) 261–4169 or (800) 252–2262 (out of state) or (800) 392–8096 (within Alabama)

Alaska Division of Tourism
P.O. Box E
Juneau, Alaska 99811
(907) 465–2010

Arizona Office of Tourism
1100 West Washington Street
Phoenix, Arizona 85007
(602) 542–8687

Arkansas Department of Parks and Tourism
1 Capitol Mall
Little Rock, Arkansas 72201
(501) 682–7777 or (800) 643–8383 (out of state) or (800) 482–8999 (within Arkansas)

California Office of Tourism
P.O. Box 189
Sacramento, California 95812–0189
(916) 322–1396 or (916) 322–1397 or (800) 862–2543

Colorado Department of Tourism
1625 Broadway
Suite 1700
Denver, Colorado 80202
(303) 592–5410 or (800) 255–5550

Connecticut Department of Economic Development—Vacations
865 Brook Street
Rocky Hill, Connecticut 06067–3405
(203) 258–4290 or (800) 243–1685 (out of state) or (800) 842–7492 (within Connecticut)

Delaware Tourism Office
99 Kings Highway
P.O. Box 1401
Dover, Delaware 19903
(302) 736–4271 or (800) 441–8846 (out of state) or (800) 282–8667 (in Delaware)

Washington, D.C., Convention and Visitors' Assoc.
Suite 600 1212 New York Avenue, N.W. 1575 I Street, N.W.
Washington, D.C. 20005
(202) 789–7000

Florida Division of Tourism
Welcome Center, Plaza Level
New State Capitol Building
Mailing address: 126 West Van Buren Street, Tallahassee, Florida 32399–2000
(904) 487–1462

Georgia Tourist Division
Box 1776
Atlanta, Georgia 30301
(404) 656–3590 or (800) 847–4842

Hawaii Visitors Bureau
Waikiki Business Plaza, Suite 801
2270 Kalakaua Avenue
Honolulu, Hawaii 96815
(808) 923–1811
New York Office
441 Lexington Avenue, Room 1003
New York, N.Y. 10017
(212) 986–9203

Idaho Travel Council
Hall of Mirrors, 2nd Floor
700 West State Street
Boise, Idaho 83720
(208) 334–2470 or (800) 635–7820

Illinois Office of Tourism
310 South Michigan Avenue
Suite 108
Chicago, Illinois 60604
(312) 793–2094 or (800) 359–9299
    (within Illinois) or (800) 223–0121
    (out of state)

Indiana Tourism Development Division
1 North Capitol, Suite 700
Indianapolis, Indiana 46204–2288
(317) 232–8860 or (800) 289–6646

Iowa Tourism Office
200 East Grand Avenue
Des Moines, Iowa 50309–2882
(515) 281–3679 or (800) 345–4692

Kansas Department of Economic
    Development—Travel and Tourism
    Division
400 West 8th Street, Suite 500
Topeka, Kansas 66603
(913) 296–2009 or (800) 252–6727
    (within Kansas)

Kentucky Department of Travel
    Development
Capitol Plaza Tower, 22nd Floor
Frankfort, Kentucky 40601
(502) 564–4930 or (800) 225–8747 (out
    of state)

Louisiana Office of Tourism
P.O. Box 94291
Baton Rouge, Louisiana 70804–9291
(504) 342–8119 or (800) 334–8626 (out
    of state)

Maine Publicity Bureau
97 Winthrop Street
Hallowell, Maine 04347
(207) 289–2423 or (800) 533–9595

Maryland Office of Tourist
    Development
217 E. Redwood Avenue
Baltimore, Maryland 21202
(301) 333–6611 or (800) 543–1036

Massachusetts Division of Tourism
Department of Commerce and
    Development
100 Cambridge Street, 13th Floor
Boston, Massachusetts 02202
(617) 727–3201 or (800) 447–MASS
    (out of state)

Michigan Travel Bureau
Department of Commerce
P.O. Box 30226
Lansing, Michigan 48909
(517) 373–1195 or (800) 543–2 YES

Minnesota Tourist Information
    Center
375 Jackson Street
Farm Credit Service Building
St. Paul, Minnesota 55101
(612) 296–5029 or (800) 657–3700 (out
    of state) or (800) 652–9747 (in
    Minnesota)

Mississippi Division of Tourism
P.O. Box 22825
Jackson, Mississippi 39205
(601) 359–3297 or (800) 647–2290

Missouri Division of Tourism
P.O. Box 1055
Jefferson City, Missouri 65102
(314) 751–4133

Montana Promotion Division
1424 9th Avenue
Helena, Montana 59620
(406) 444–2645 or (800) 541–1447

Nebraska Division of Travel and
    Tourism
P.O. Box 94666
Lincoln, Nebraska 68509
(402) 471–3796 or (800) 228–4307 (out
    of state) or (800) 742–7595 (within
    Nebraska)

Nevada Commission on Tourism
Capitol Complex
5151 South Carson Street
Carson City, Nevada 89710
(702) 687–4322 or (800) NEVADA–8

New Hampshire Office of Vacation
    Travel
P.O. Box 856
Concord, New Hampshire 03301
(603) 271–2343 or (603) 271–2666 or
    (800) 224–2525 (in the Northeast
    outside of New Hampshire)

New Jersey Division of Travel and
    Tourism
C.N. 826
Trenton, New Jersey 08635
(609) 292–2470 or (800) 537–7397

New Mexico Travel Division
Joseph Montoya Building
1100 St. Francis Drive

Santa Fe, New Mexico 87503
(505) 827–0291 or (800) 545–2040 (out of state)

New York State Division of Tourism
1 Commerce Plaza
Albany, New York 12245
(518) 474–4116 or (800) 225–5697 (in the Northeast except Maine)

North Carolina Travel and Tourism Division
430 North Salisbury Street
Raleigh, North Carolina 27611
(919) 733–4171 or (800) VISIT NC (out of state)

North Dakota Tourism Promotion
Liberty Memorial Building
State Capitol Grounds
Bismarck, North Dakota 58505
(701) 224–2525 or (800) 472–2100 (within North Dakota) or (800) 437–2077 (out of state)

Ohio Office of Tourism
P.O. Box 1001
Columbus, Ohio 43266–0101
(800) 848–1300, extension 8844 or (800) 282–5393

Oklahoma Division of Tourism
500 Will Rodgers Building
Oklahoma City, Oklahoma 73105
(405) 521–2409 or (800) 652–6552 (in neighboring states) or (800) 522–8565 (within Oklahoma)

Oregon Economic Development Tourism Division
595 Cottage Street, N.E.
Salem, Oregon 97310
(503) 378–3451 or (800) 547–7842 (out of state) or (800) 543–8838 (within Oregon)

Pennsylvania Bureau of Travel Development
Department of Commerce
453 Forum Building
Harrisburg, Pennsylvania 17120
(717) 787–5453 or (800) 847–4872

Puerto Rico Tourism Company
23rd Floor
575 Fifth Avenue
New York, NY 10107
(212) 599–6262 or (800) 223–6530 or (800) 443–0266

Rhode Island Department of Economic Development

Tourism and Promotion Division
7 Jackson Walkway
Providence, Rhode Island 02903
(401) 277–2601 or (800) 556–2484 (East Coast from Maine to Virginia, also West Virginia and Ohio)

South Carolina Division of Tourism
1205 Pendleton Street
Columbia, South Carolina 29201
(803) 734–0122

South Dakota Division of Tourism
Capitol Lake Plaza
711 Wells Avenue
Pierre, South Dakota 57501
(605) 773–3301 or (800) 952–2217 (within South Dakota) or (800) 843–1930 (out of state)

Tennessee Tourist Development
P.O. Box 23170
Nashville, Tennessee 37202
(615) 741–2158

Texas Tourist Development
P.O. Box 12008
Capitol Station
Austin, Texas 78711
(512) 462–9191 or (800) 888–8839

Utah Travel Council
Council Hall
Capitol Hill
Salt Lake City, Utah 84114
(801) 538–1030

Vermont Travel Division
134 State Street
Montpelier, Vermont 05602
(802) 828–3236

Virginia Division of Tourism
202 North 9th Street
Suite 500
Richmond, Virginia 23219
(804) 786–4484 or (800) 847–4882

Washington Department of Trade and Economic Development
Tourism Division
101 General Administration Building
Olympia, Washington 98504
(206) 586–2088 or 586–2102 or (800) 544–1800 (out of state)

Travel West Virginia
West Virginia Department of Commerce
State Capitol
Charleston, West Virginia 25305
(304) 348–2286 or (800) CALL WVA

Wisconsin Division of Tourism
P.O. Box 7970-B
123 W. Washington
Madison, Wisconsin 53707
(608) 266–2161 or (800) 372–2737
(within Wisconsin and neighboring
states) or (800) 432–8747 (out of
state)

Wyoming Travel Commission
I–25 and College Drive
Cheyenne, Wyoming 82002
(307) 777–7777 or (800) 225–5996 (out
of state)

Travel Alberta
15th Floor
10025 Jasper Avenue
Edmonton, Alberta, Canada T5J 3Z3
(403) 427–4321 (from Edmonton area)
or (800) 222–6501 (from Alberta) or
(800) 661–8888 (from United States
and Canada)

Tourism British Columbia
1117 Wharf Street
Victoria, British Columbia, Canada
V8W 2Z2
(604) 387–1642

Travel Manitoba
Dept. 6020
155 Carlton Street, 7th Floor
Winnipeg, Manitoba, Canada R3C 3H8
(204) 945–4345 or (800) 665–0040 (from
mainland United States and Canada)

Tourism New Brunswick
P.O. Box 12345
Fredericton, New Brunswick, Canada
E3B 5C3
(506) 453–8745 or (800) 561–0123 (from
mainland United States and Canada)

Newfoundland/Labrador Tourism
Branch
Department of Development
P.O. Box 8700
St. John's, Newfoundland, Canada A1B
4J6
(709) 576–2830 (from St. John's area) or
(800) 563–6353 (from mainland
United States and Canada)

Travel Arctic
Government of Northwest Territories
Yellowknife
Northwest Territories, Canada X1A 2L9
(403) 873–7200

Nova Scotia Tourism
P.O. Box 130
Halifax, Nova Scotia, Canada B3J 2M7
(902) 424–4247 or
136 Commercial Street
Portland, Maine 04101, U.S.A.
(800) 341–6096 (from mainland United
States except Maine) or (800)
492–0643 (from Maine)

Ontario Ministry of Tourism and
Recreation
Customer Sales and Services
Queens Park
Toronto, Ontario, Canada M7A 2E5
(410) 965–4008 (within Canada) or
(800) 268–3735 (from mainland
United States and Canada—except
Yukon and the Northwest
Territories)

Department of Finance and Tourism
Visitor Services Division
P.O. Box 940
Charlottetown, Prince Edward Island,
Canada C1A 7N5
(902) 368–4444 or (800) 565–7421 (from
New Brunswick and Nova
Scotia—May 15 to October 31) or
(800) 565–9060

Tourisme Québec
C.P. 20 000
Québec (Québec), Canada G1K 7X2
(800) 443–7000 (from 26 eastern States)
or (514) 873–2015 (collect from all
other United States locations)

Tourism Saskatchewan
1919 Saskatchewan Drive
Regina, Saskatchewan, Canada S4P 3V7
(306) 787–2300 or (800) 667–7191 (from
Canada and mainland United States
except Alaska) or (800) 667–7538 (in
Saskatchewan)

Tourism Yukon
P.O. Box 2703
Whitehorse, Yukon, Canada Y1A 2C6
(403) 667–5340

_____MAPS

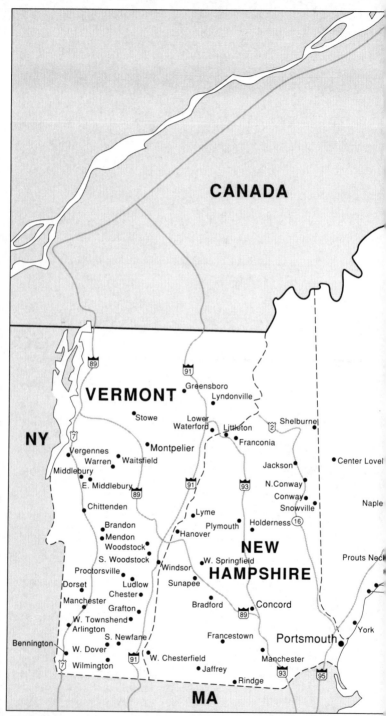

Map #1

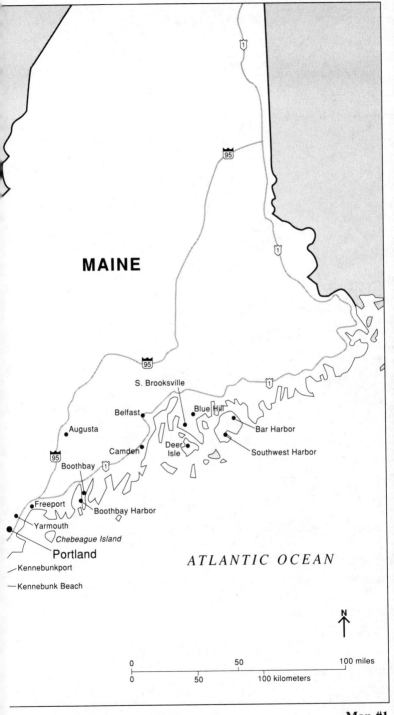

Map #1

Map #2

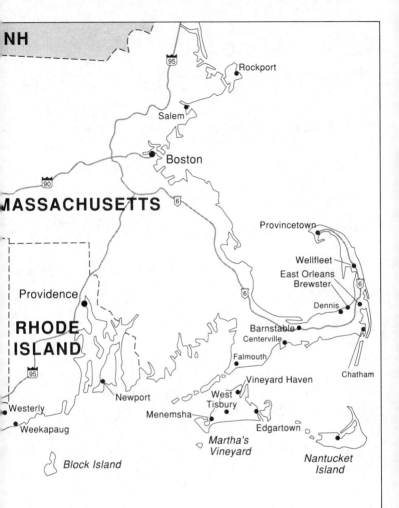

NH

Rockport

Salem

Boston

MASSACHUSETTS

Provincetown

Wellfleet

East Orleans
Brewster

Dennis

Providence

RHODE
ISLAND

Barnstable

Centerville

Falmouth

Vineyard Haven

Chatham

Newport

West
Tisbury

Westerly

Menemsha

Edgartown

Weekapaug

Martha's
Vineyard

Nantucket
Island

Block Island

ATLANTIC OCEAN

Map #2

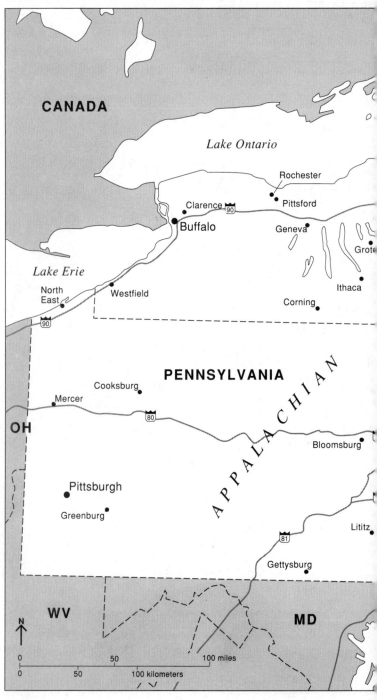

Map #3

Map #3

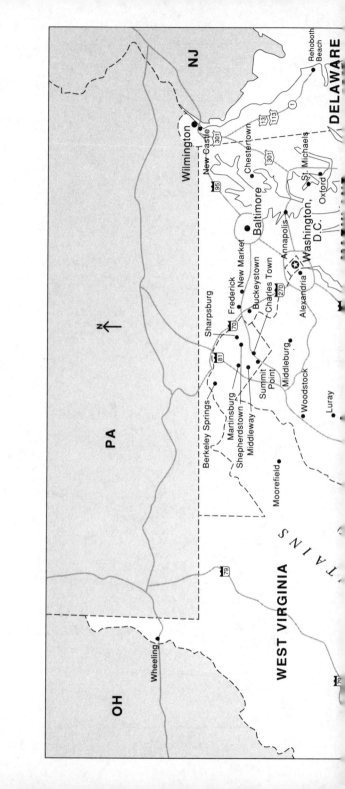

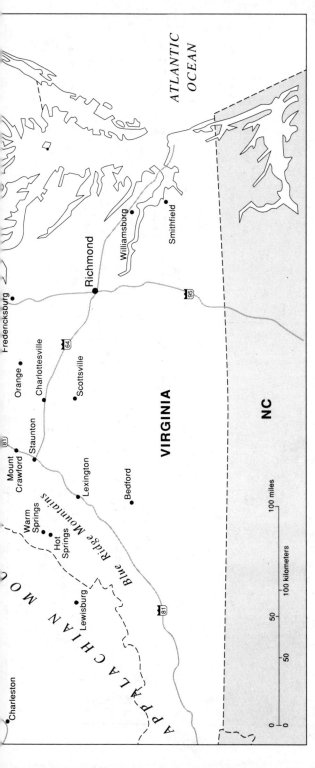

Map #4

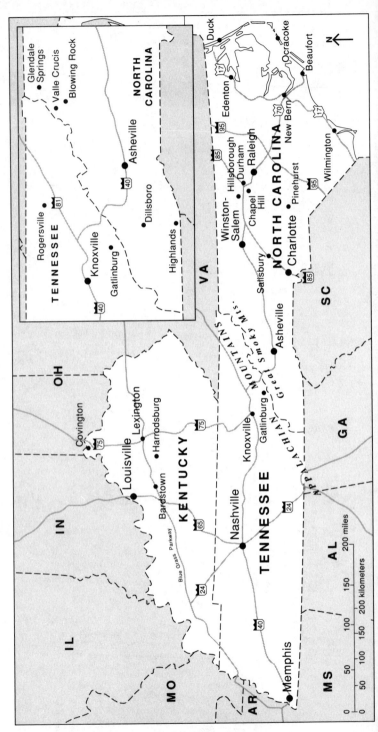

Map #5

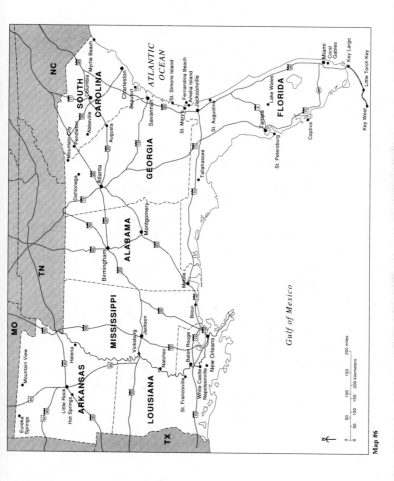

Map #6

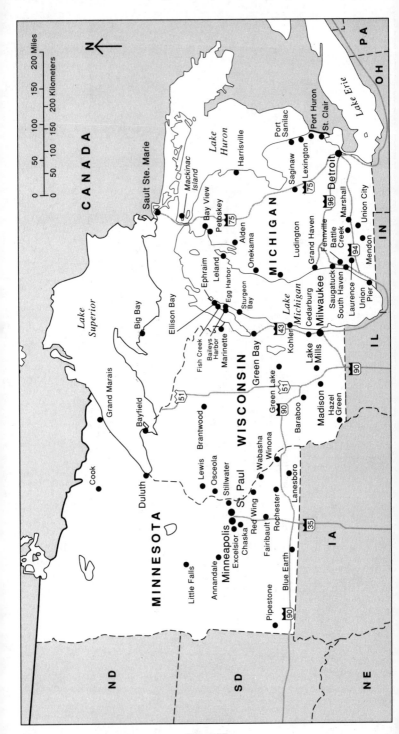

Map #7

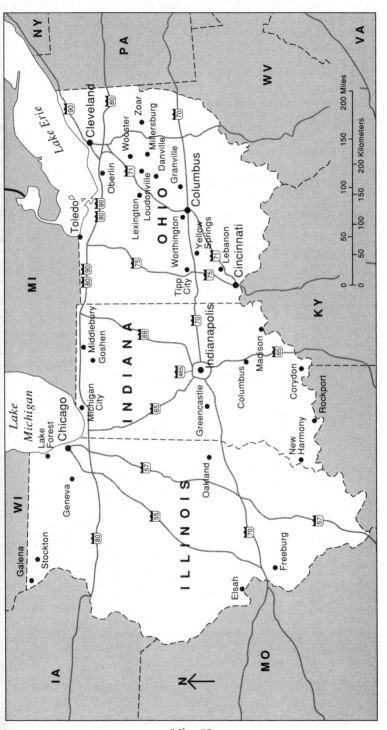

Map #8

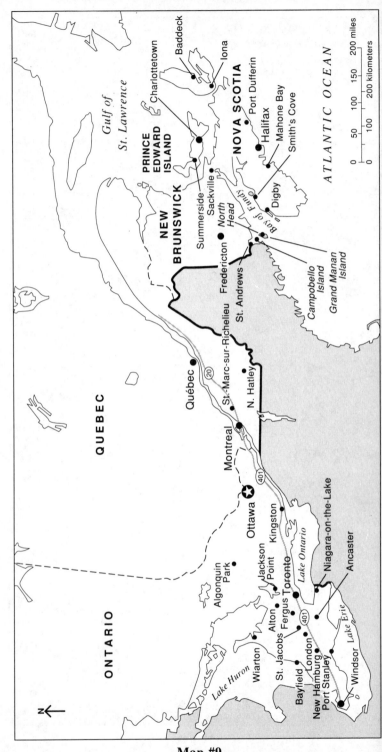

Map #9

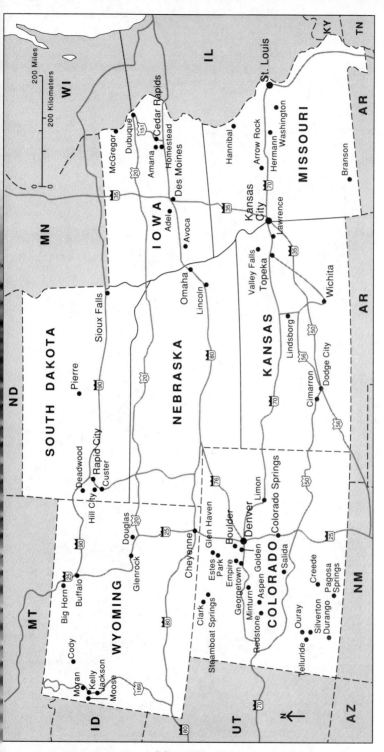

Map #10

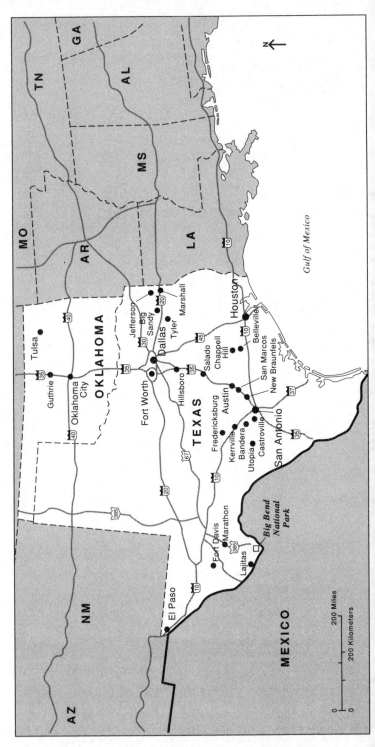

Map #11

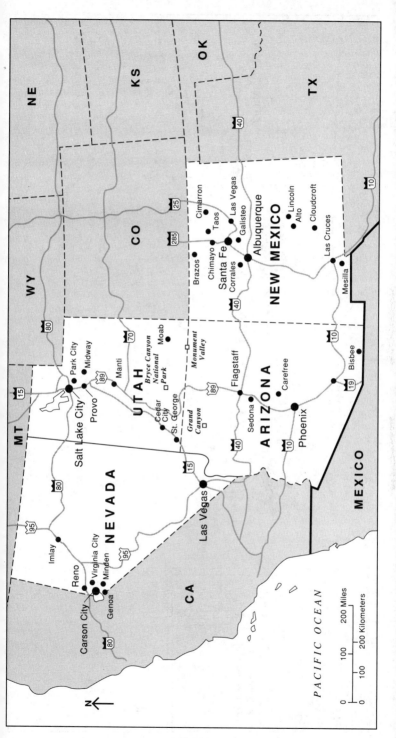

Map #12

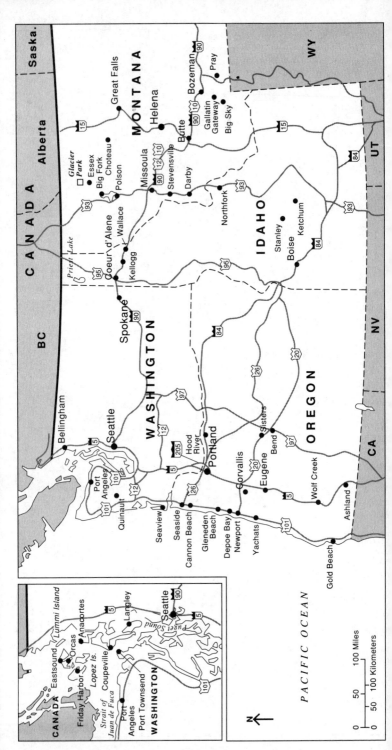

Map #13

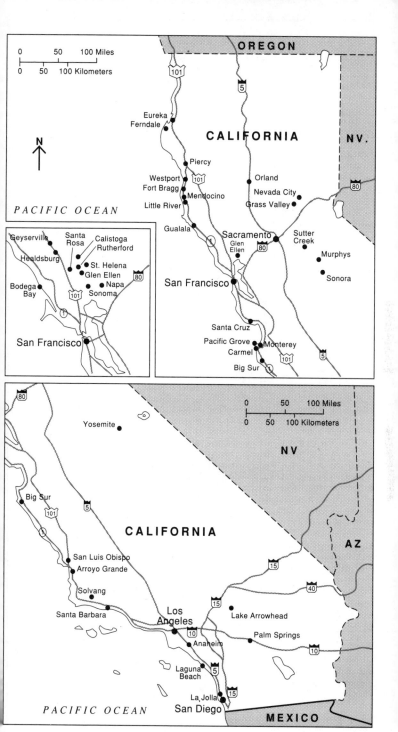

Map #14

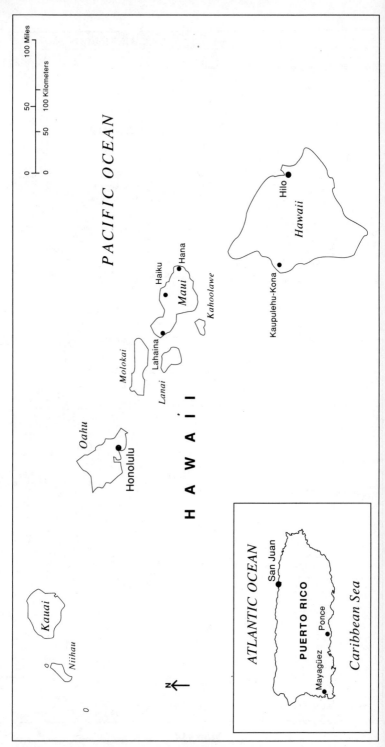

Map #15

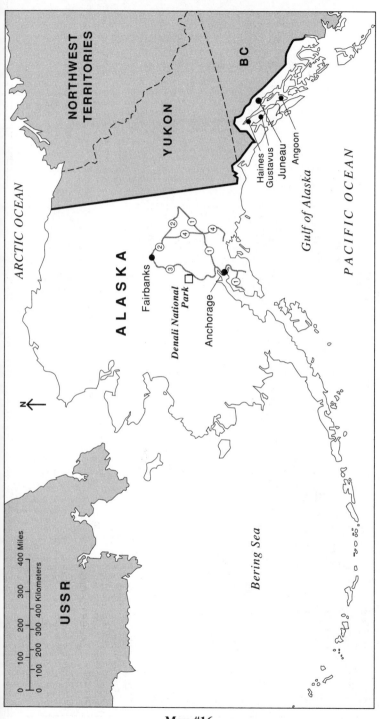

Map #16

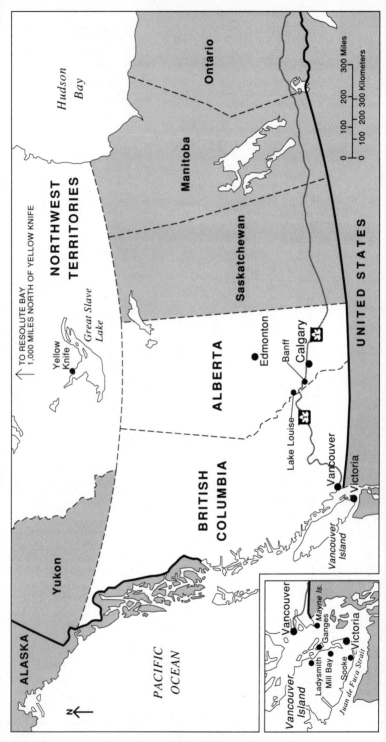

Map #17

Index of Accommodations

Congratulations!

We are delighted to announce that we have mailed over 500 copies of the *America's Wonderful Little Hotels & Inns* guides to our most helpful respondents. These were people who sent us particularly insightful or useful reports, either positive or negative, on two or more establishments.

Hotel/Inn Report Forms

The report forms on the following pages may be used to endorse or critique an existing entry or to nominate a hotel or inn that you feel deserves inclusion in next year's edition. Whichever you wish to do, don't feel you have to use our forms, or, if you do use them, don't feel you must restrict yourself to the space available. All nominations (each on a separate piece of paper, if possible) should include your name and address, the name and location of the hotel or inn, when you have stayed there, and for how long. A copy of the establishment's brochure is also helpful. Please report only on establishments you have visited in the last eighteen months, unless you are sure that standards have not dropped since your stay. Please be as specific as possible, and critical where appropriate, about the character of the building, the public rooms, the accommodations, the meals, the service, the nightlife, the grounds, and the general atmosphere of the inn and the attitude of its owners. Any comments you have about area restaurants and sights would also be most appreciated.

Don't feel you need to write at length. A report that merely verifies the accuracy of existing listings is extremely helpful, i.e., "Visited XYZ Inn and found it just as described."

On the other hand, don't apologize for writing a long report. Although space does not permit us to quote them in toto, the small details provided about furnishings, atmosphere, and cuisine can really make a description come alive, illuminating the special flavor of a particular inn or hotel. Remember that we will again be awarding free copies to our most helpful respondents.

There is no need to bother with prices or with routine information about the number of rooms and facilities. We obtain such details directly from the hotels selected. What we are eager to get from readers is information that is not accessible elsewhere.

Please note that we print only the names of respondents, never addresses. Those making negative observations are never identified by name. Although we must always have your full name and address, we will be happy to print your initials, or a pseudonym, if you prefer.

These report forms may also be used, if you wish, to recommend good hotels in Europe to our equivalent publication, *Europe's Wonderful Little Hotels & Inns* (published in Europe as *The Good Hotel Guide*). Reports should be sent to *Europe's Wonderful Little Hotels & Inns,* St. Martin's Press, 175 Fifth Avenue, New York, NY 10010; to P.O. Box 150, Riverside, CT 06878; or directly to *The Good Hotel Guide,* 61 Clarendon Road, London W11. Readers in the UK can send their letters postage-free to *The Good Hotel Guide,* Freepost, London W11 4 BR.

To: *America's Wonderful Little Hotels & Inns,*
P.O. Box 150, Riverside, CT 06878.

Name of hotel _____

Address _____

Telephone _____

Date of most recent visit _____ Duration of visit _____

☐ New recommendation ☐ Comment on existing entry

Please be as specific as possible about furnishings, atmosphere, service, and cuisine. If reporting on an existing entry, please tell us whether you thought it accurate, and whether you would return.

Unless you tell us not to, we shall assume that we may publish your name in the next edition. Thank you very much for writing.

Report (use your own stationery if you wish):

I am not connected directly or indirectly with the management or owners.

Signed _____

Name _____
(Please print)

Address _____
(Please print)

_____

To: *America's Wonderful Little Hotels & Inns,*
   P.O. Box 150, Riverside, CT 06878.

Name of hotel—————————————————————————

Address—————————————————————————————

Telephone————————————————————————————

Date of most recent visit————— Duration of visit—————

☐ New recommendation ☐ Comment on existing entry

Please be as specific as possible about furnishings, atmosphere, service, and cuisine. If reporting on an existing entry, please tell us whether you thought it accurate, and whether you would return.

Unless you tell us not to, we shall assume that we may publish your name in the next edition. Thank you very much for writing.

Report (use your own stationery if you wish):

I am not connected directly or indirectly with the management or owners.

Signed————————————————————————————————

Name————————————————————————————————
                        (Please print)

Address—————————————————————————————
                        (Please print)

To: *America's Wonderful Little Hotels & Inns,*
    P.O. Box 150, Riverside, CT 06878.

Name of hotel_____

Address_____

Telephone_____

Date of most recent visit_____ Duration of visit_____

☐ New recommendation   ☐ Comment on existing entry

Please be as specific as possible about furnishings, atmosphere, service, and cuisine. If reporting on an existing entry, please tell us whether you thought it accurate, and whether you would return.

Unless you tell us not to, we shall assume that we may publish your name in the next edition. Thank you very much for writing.

Report (use your own stationery if you wish):

I am not connected directly or indirectly with the management or owners.

Signed_____

Name_____
                        (Please print)

Address_____
                        (Please print)

To: *America's Wonderful Little Hotels & Inns,*
    P.O. Box 150, Riverside, CT 06878.

Name of hotel_____

Address_____

Telephone_____

Date of most recent visit_____ Duration of visit_____

☐ New recommendation   ☐ Comment on existing entry

Please be as specific as possible about furnishings, atmosphere, service, and cuisine. If reporting on an existing entry, please tell us whether you thought it accurate, and whether you would return.

Unless you tell us not to, we shall assume that we may publish your name in the next edition. Thank you very much for writing.

Report (use your own stationery if you wish):

I am not connected directly or indirectly with the management or owners.

Signed_____

Name_____
                          (Please print)

Address_____
                          (Please print)

_____

To: *America's Wonderful Little Hotels & Inns,*
    P.O. Box 150, Riverside, CT 06878.

Name of hotel _____

Address _____

Telephone _____

Date of most recent visit _____ Duration of visit _____

☐ New recommendation   ☐ Comment on existing entry

Please be as specific as possible about furnishings, atmosphere, service, and cuisine. If reporting on an existing entry, please tell us whether you thought it accurate, and whether you would return.

Unless you tell us not to, we shall assume that we may publish your name in the next edition. Thank you very much for writing.

Report (use your own stationery if you wish):

I am not connected directly or indirectly with the management or owners.

Signed _____

Name _____
                        (Please print)

Address _____
                        (Please print)

_____

To: *America's Wonderful Little Hotels & Inns,*
    P.O. Box 150, Riverside, CT 06878.

Name of hotel_____

Address_____

Telephone_____

Date of most recent visit_____ Duration of visit_____

☐ New recommendation   ☐ Comment on existing entry

Please be as specific as possible about furnishings, atmosphere, service, and cuisine. If reporting on an existing entry, please tell us whether you thought it accurate, and whether you would return.

Unless you tell us not to, we shall assume that we may publish your name in the next edition. Thank you very much for writing.

Report (use your own stationery if you wish):

I am not connected directly or indirectly with the management or owners.

Signed_____

Name_____
                        (Please print)

Address_____
                        (Please print)

To: *America's Wonderful Little Hotels & Inns,*
    P.O. Box 150, Riverside, CT 06878.

Name of hotel_____

Address_____

Telephone_____

Date of most recent visit_____ Duration of visit_____

☐ New recommendation   ☐ Comment on existing entry

Please be as specific as possible about furnishings, atmosphere, service, and cuisine. If reporting on an existing entry, please tell us whether you thought it accurate, and whether you would return.

Unless you tell us not to, we shall assume that we may publish your name in the next edition. Thank you very much for writing.

Report (use your own stationery if you wish):

I am not connected directly or indirectly with the management or owners.

Signed_____

Name_____
                        (Please print)

Address_____
                        (Please print)

_____

To: *America's Wonderful Little Hotels & Inns,*
P.O. Box 150, Riverside, CT 06878.

Name of hotel _____

Address _____

Telephone _____

Date of most recent visit _____ Duration of visit _____

☐ New recommendation   ☐ Comment on existing entry

Please be as specific as possible about furnishings, atmosphere, service, and cuisine. If reporting on an existing entry, please tell us whether you thought it accurate, and whether you would return.

Unless you tell us not to, we shall assume that we may publish your name in the next edition. Thank you very much for writing.

Report (use your own stationery if you wish):

I am not connected directly or indirectly with the management or owners.

Signed _____

Name _____
(Please print)

Address _____
(Please print)

_____

THE INNGOER'S

Europe's Wonderful Little Hotels and Inns, 1990, *Great Britain and Ireland* ◄

Europe's Wonderful Little Hotels and Inns, 1990, *The Continent* ►

America's Wonderful Little Hotels and Inns, 1990, *U.S.A. and Canada* ◄

America's Wonderful Little Hotels and Inns, 1990, *New England* ►

America's Wonderful Little Hotels and Inns, 1990, *The Middle Atlantic* ◄

America's Wonderful Little Hotels and Inns, 1990, *The South* ►

America's Wonderful Little Hotels and Inns, 1990, *The West Coast* ◄